W9-BHZ-394

Text Features
Engage and Enlighten

CHAPTER OPENING CASES

Each chapter begins with a case scenario about an actual company, product, or situation that illustrates key concepts discussed in the chapter.

MARKET

For every   show how
consumer   such basic
marketing   n, positioning,
market res

EMPHAS   OMMERCE

Througho   of cross-cultural
and Intern   he text emphasize
the text's p

CURREN   E

In additio   ychological
(micro) ar   behavior, the text
provides t   eral *novel chapters*
that often   r Behavior,"
"Knowing   r Behavior and
Marketin

2ND EDITION

CONSUMER BEHAVIOR

Wayne D. Hoyer
University of Texas at Austin

Deborah J. MacInnis
University of Southern California

HOUGHTON MIFFLIN COMPANY BOSTON NEW YORK

DEDICATION

To my wonderful family, Shirley, David, Stephanie, and Lindsey, and to my parents, Louis and Doris, for their tremendous support and love. To all of you I dedicate this book.

Wayne D. Hoyer
Austin, Texas

To my loving family—my life-spring of energy and my center of gravity.

Debbie MacInnis
Los Angeles, California

Executive Editor: George Hoffman
Associate Sponsoring Editor: Joanne Dauksewicz
Senior Project Editor: Tamela Ambush
Senior Production/Design Coordinator: Sarah Ambrose
Senior Manufacturing Coordinator: Marie Barnes
Marketing Manager: Melissa Russell

Cover Design: Sarah Melhado Bishins
Cover Image: ©2000 James Steinberg c/o theispot

Printed in the U.S.A.

Library of Congress Catalog Card Number: 00-133901

Student Book ISBN: 0-618-01326-1

123456789-CRK-04 03 02 01 00

ABOUT THE AUTHORS

WAYNE D. HOYER

Wayne Hoyer is the Tom E. Nelson, Jr. Regents Professor in Business and chairman of the Department of Marketing at the University of Texas at Austin. He received his Ph.D. in Consumer Psychology from Purdue University in 1980. Wayne has published over 60 articles in various publications including the *Journal of Consumer Research*, *Journal of Marketing*, *Journal of Marketing Research*, *Journal of Advertising Research*, and *Journal of Retailing*. In addition to *Consumer Behavior*, he has co-authored two books on the topic of advertising miscomprehension. Dr. Hoyer's research interests include consumer information processing and decision making (especially low involvement decision making) and advertising effects (particularly miscomprehension and the impact of humor). He is currently an associate editor for the *Journal of Consumer Research* and serves on the editorial review boards of the *Journal of Marketing*, *Journal of Advertising*, and the *Journal of Public Policy and Marketing*, and he is an active reviewer for the *Journal of Marketing Research*. Dr. Hoyer is a member of the American Psychological Association, the Association for Consumer Research, and the American Marketing Association. His major areas of teaching include consumer behavior, human information processing, and marketing communications.

DEBORAH J. MacINNIS

Debbie MacInnis is an Associate Professor at the University of Southern California. She received her Ph.D. in marketing from the University of Pittsburgh in 1986. She also holds a B.S. degree in psychology from Smith College. Before joining USC in 1994, she worked as Associate Professor of Marketing at the University of Arizona. Debbie has published papers in the *Journal of Consumer Research*, *Journal of Marketing Research*, *Journal of Marketing*, *Journal of Advertising*, *Journal of Advertising Research*, and *Journal of Personality and Social Psychology* in the areas of marketing communications, information processing, imagery, emotions, and brand images. She has served as a member of the editorial review boards of the *Journal of Marketing Research*, *Journal of Consumer Research*, *Journal of Marketing*, and *Journal of Market Focused Management* and served as a reviewer for the *Journal of Advertising* and the *Journal of Consumer Psychology*. She is a past recipient of the Alpha Kappa Psi award, an honor awarded to the best paper published in the *Journal of Marketing*. She has also worked as a consultant to several major advertisers and advertising agencies, and served as co-chairperson for the 1996 Association for Consumer Research Conference. Her major areas of teaching include consumer behavior, marketing communications, and marketing management.

BRIEF CONTENTS

CONTENTS

PART TWO

THE PSYCHOLOGICAL CORE

3 MOTIVATION, ABILITY, AND OPPORTUNITY

4 EXPOSURE, ATTENTION, AND PERCEPTION

5 KNOWLEDGE AND UNDERSTANDING

6 ATTITUDES BASED ON HIGH CONSUMER EFFORT

7   ATTITUDES BASED ON LOW CONSUMER EFFORT

8   MEMORY AND RETRIEVAL

ix

CONTENTS

CONTENTS

11 JUDGMENT AND DECISION MAKING BASED ON LOW CONSUMER EFFORT

12 POST-DECISION PROCESSES

x

PART FOUR

THE CONSUMER'S CULTURE

13 REGIONAL, ETHNIC, AND RELIGIOUS INFLUENCES ON CONSUMER BEHAVIOR

14 SOCIAL CLASS INFLUENCES ON CONSUMER BEHAVIOR

15 AGE, GENDER, AND HOUSEHOLD INFLUENCES ON CONSUMER BEHAVIOR

16 SOCIAL INFLUENCE

17 PSYCHOGRAPHICS: VALUES, PERSONALITY, AND LIFESTYLES

PREFACE

W̲e engage in some form of consumer behavior at just about every moment of our lives. When we watch an ad on TV, talk to friends about a movie we just saw, brush our teeth, go to a ball game, buy a new CD, or even throw away an old pair of shoes, we are behaving as a consumer. In fact, being a consumer reaches just about every part of our lives.

Given its omnipresence, the study of consumer behavior has critical implications for areas such as marketing, public policy, and ethics. It also helps us learn about ourselves—why we buy certain things, why we use them in a certain way, and how we get rid of them.

In this book we explore the fascinating world of consumer behavior, looking at a number of interesting and exciting topics. Some of these are quickly identified with our typical image of consumer behavior. Others may be surprising. We hope you will see why we became stimulated and drawn to this topic from the very moment we had our first consumer behavior course as students. We hope you will also appreciate why we choose to make this field our life's work, and why we developed and remain committed to the writing of this textbook.

WHY THE NEW EDITION OF THIS BOOK?

There are a number of consumer behavior books on the market. An important question concerns what this book has to offer and what distinguishes it from other texts. As active researchers in the field of consumer behavior, our overriding goal was to provide a treatment of the field that is up-to-date and cutting-edge. There has been an explosion of research on a variety of consumer behavior topics over the last twenty-five years. Our primary aim was to provide a useful summary of this material for students of marketing. However, in drawing on cutting edge research, we wanted to be careful to not become too "academic." Instead, our objective is to present cutting edge topics in a manner that is accessible and easy for students to understand.

TEXTBOOK FEATURES

As award-winning teachers, we have tried to translate our instructional abilities and experience into the writing of this text. The following features have been a natural outgrowth of these experiences.

Conceptual Model. First, we believe that students can learn best when they see the big picture—when they understand what concepts mean, how they are used in business practice, and how they relate to one another. In our opinion consumer behavior is too often presented as a set of discrete topics with little or no relationship to one another. We have therefore developed an overall conceptual model that helps students grasp the big picture and see how the chapters and topics are themselves interrelated. Each chapter is linked to other chapters by a specific model that fits within the larger model. Further, the overall model guides the organization of the book. This organizing scheme makes the chapters far more *integrative* than most other books.

Practical Orientation, with an Emphasis on Globalization and E-commerce. Another common complaint of some treatments of consumer behavior is that they reflect general psychological or sociological principles and theories, but provide very little indication of how these principles and theories relate to business practice. Given our notion that students enjoy seeing how the concepts in consumer behavior can apply to business practice, a second objective of the book was to provide a very practical orientation. We include a wealth of contemporary real-world examples to illustrate key topics. We also try to broaden students' horizons by providing a number of international examples (often more than twenty per chapter), and these are highlighted by global icons in the margins throughout the text. Given the importance of consumer behavior to electronic commerce, we also provide a number of examples of consumer behavior in an e-commerce context. Computer icons in the margins of the text highlight these e-commerce examples. The abundance of global and e-commerce examples makes our book *more* global and *e-commerce based* than other texts on the market.

Current and Cutting-Edge Coverage. Third, we provide coverage of the field of consumer behavior that is as current and up-to-date as possible (including many of the recent research advances). This includes several *novel chapters* that often do not appear in other textbooks: "Symbolic Consumer Behavior," "Knowing and Understanding," and "The Dark Side of Consumer Behavior and Marketing." These topics are at the cutting edge of consumer behavior research and are likely to be of considerable interest to students.

Balanced Treatment of Micro and Macro Topics. Fourth, our book tries to provide a balanced perspective on the field of consumer behavior. Specifically we give treatment to both psychological (micro) consumer behavior topics (e.g., attitudes, decision making) and sociological (macro) consumer behavior topics (e.g., subculture, gender, social class influences). Also, although we typically teach consumer behavior by starting with the more micro topics and then moving up to more macro topics, we realize that some instructors prefer the reverse sequence. The Instructor's Resource Manual therefore provides a revised table of contents and model that shows how the book can be taught for those who prefer a macro first, micro second approach.

Broad Conceptualization of the Subject. Fifth, we present a broad conceptualization of the topic of consumer behavior. While many books focus on what products or services consumers *buy*, consumer behavior scholars have recognized that the topic of consumer behavior is actually much broader. Specifically, rather than studying buying per se, we recognize that consumer behavior includes a *set* of decisions (what, whether, when, where, why, how, how often, how much, how long) about *acquisition* (including, but not limited to buying), *usage*, and *disposition* decisions. Focusing on more than what products or services consumers buy provides a rich set of theoretical and practical implications for both our understanding of consumer behavior and the practice of marketing.

Finally, we consider the relevance of consumer behavior to *many constituents*, not just marketers. Chapter 1 indicates that CB is important to marketers, public policy makers, ethicists and consumer advocacy groups, and consumers themselves (including students' own lives). Some chapters focus exclusively on the implications of consumer behavior for public policy makers, ethicists, and consumer advocacy groups. Other chapters consider these issues as well, though in less detail.

CONTENT AND ORGANIZATION OF THE BOOK

One can currently identify two main approaches to the study of consumer behavior: a "micro" orientation, which focuses on the individual psychological processes that consumers use to make acquisition, consumption, and disposition decisions, and a "macro" orientation, which focuses on group behaviors and the symbolic nature of consumer behavior. This latter orientation draws heavily from such fields as sociology and anthropology. The current book and overall model have been structured around a "micro to macro" organization based on the way we teach this course and the feedback that we have received from reviewers. (As mentioned previously, for those who prefer a "macro to micro" structure, we provide in the *Instructor's Resource Manual* an alternative Table of Contents that reflects how the book could be easily adapted to this perspective.)

Chapter 1 presents an introduction to consumer behavior and provides students with an understanding of the breadth of the field and its importance to marketers, advocacy groups, public policy makers, and consumers themselves. It also presents the overall model that guides the organization of the text. Chapter 2 is new to the second edition. It focuses on the groups that conduct research on consumers and how that research is both collected and used by different constituents.

Part I, "The Psychological Core" focuses on the inner psychological processes that affect consumer behavior. We see that consumers' acquisition, usage, and disposition behaviors and decisions are greatly affected by the amount of effort they put into engaging in behaviors and making decisions. Chapter 3 describes three critical factors that affect effort: the (1) *motivation* or desire, (2) *ability* (knowledge and information), and (3) *opportunity* to engage in behaviors and to make decisions. In Chapter 4, we then examine how information in consumers' environment (i.e., ads, prices, product features, word of mouth communications, and so on) is internally processed by consumers—how they come in contact with these stimuli (*exposure*), notice them (*attention*), and *perceive* them. Chapter 5 continues by discussing how we compare new stimuli to our knowledge of existing stimuli, a process called *categorization*, and how we attempt to understand or *comprehend* them on a deeper level. In Chapters 6 and 7, we see how attitudes are formed and changed depending on whether the amount of effort consumers devote to forming an attitude is high or low. Finally, because consumers often must recall the information they have previously stored in order to make decisions, Chapter 8 looks at the important topic of consumer *memory*.

Whereas Part I examines some of the internal factors that influence consumers' decisions, a critical domain of consumer behavior involves understanding how consumers make acquisition, consumption, and disposition decisions. Thus, in Part II we examine the sequential steps of the consumer decision-making process. In Chapter 9, we examine the initial steps of this process—*problem recognition* and *information search*. Similar to the attitude change processes described earlier, we next examine the consumer decision-making process, both when *effort is high* (Chapter 10) and when it is *low* (Chapter 11). Finally, the process does not end after a decision has been made. In Chapter 12 we see how consumers determine whether they are *satisfied* or *dissatisfied* with their decisions and how they *learn* from choosing and consuming products/services.

Part III reflects a "macro" view of consumer behavior that examines how various aspects of *culture* affect consumer behavior. First, we see how *regional* and *ethnic* groups (Chapter 13) can affect consumer behavior. Chapter 14 then examines how *social class* is determined in various cultures and how it affects acquisition, usage, and disposition behaviors—such as how we strive to improve our standing, to impress others, and to distribute our wealth to our progeny. Chapter 15 examines how *age*, *gender*, and *household* influences affect consumer behavior. Chapter 16 considers how, when, and why the specific *reference groups* (friends, work group, clubs) to which we belong can influence acquisition, usage, and disposition decisions and behaviors. Combined, these external influences can influence our *personality*, *life style*, and *values*, the topics covered in Chapter 17.

Part IV, "Consumer Behavior Outcomes," examines the effects of the numerous influences and decision processes discussed in the previous three sections. Because products and services often reflect deep-felt and significant meanings (e.g., our favorite song or restaurant), Chapter 18 focuses on the interesting topic of *symbolic consumer behavior*. Chapter 19 builds on the topics of internal decision-making and group behavior by examining how consumers adopt new offerings and how their *adoption* decisions affect the spread or *diffusion* of an offering through a market.

Part V, "Consumer Welfare," covers two topics that have been of great interest to consumer researchers in recent years. Chapter 20 directs our attention to *consumerism and public policy* issues. Chapter 21 examines the "*dark side of consumer behavior*" and focuses on some negative outcomes of consumer-related behaviors (compulsive buying and gambling, prostitution, etc.) as well as marketing practices that have been the focus of social commentary in recent years.

PEDAGOGICAL ADVANTAGES

Based on our extensive teaching experience, we have incorporated a number of features that should help students learn about consumer behavior.

Chapter Opening Cases. Each chapter begins with a case scenario about an actual company or situation that illustrates key concepts discussed in the chapter and their importance to marketers. This will help students grasp the "big picture" and understand the relevance of the topics from the start of the chapter.

Chapter Opening Model. Each chapter also begins with a conceptual model that shows the organization of the chapter, the topics discussed, and how they relate to both one another and to other chapters. Each model reflects an expanded picture of one or more of the elements presented in the overall conceptual model for the book (described in Chapter 1).

Marketing Implication Sections. Numerous *Marketing Implications* sections are interspersed throughout each chapter. These sections illustrate how various consumer behavior concepts can be applied to the practice of marketing, including such basic marketing functions as market segmentation, target market selection, positioning, market research, promotion, price, product, and place decisions. An abundance of marketing examples (from both the US and abroad) provide concrete applications and implementations of the concepts to marketing practice.

Marginal Glossary. Every chapter contains a set of key terms that are both highlighted in the text and defined in margin notes. These terms and their definitions should help students identify and remember the central concepts described in the chapter.

Global Icons. Cross-cultural examples abound in every chapter and are highlighted by global icons that appear in the margins of the accompanying text. These examples illustrate the applicability of the concepts to other cultures. In certain cases, they also illustrate how application of the concepts differs across cultures.

Internet Icons. Given the importance of electronic commerce to both consumers and marketers, we provide examples in every chapter of the use or implications of consumer behavior concepts for electronic commerce contexts. Indeed, many of our opening vignettes reflect e-commerce examples. We also include a number of experiential exercises that allow students to delve into consumer behavior phenomena through their use of the Internet.

Abundant Use of Full-Color Exhibits. Each chapter contains a number of illustrated examples, including photos, advertisements, charts, and graphs. These illustrations help to make important topics personally relevant and engaging, help students remember the material, and make the book more accessible and aesthetically pleasing, thereby increasing students' motivation to learn. All diagrams and charts employ full color, which serves to both highlight key points and add to the aesthetic appeal of the text. Each model, graph, ad, and photo also has an accompanying caption that provides a simple description and explanation of how the exhibit relates to the topic it is designed to illustrate.

End of Chapter Summaries. The end of each chapter provides students with a simple and concise summary of topics. These summaries are a good review tool to use with the conceptual model to help students to get the big picture.

End of Chapter Exercises. Each chapter comes with a set of exercises designed to involve students on a more experiential and interactive level. Included are experiential exercises (e.g., watching and analyzing consumers and ads), mini-research projects, or thought-provoking questions.

COMPLETE TEACHING PACKAGE

A variety of ancillary materials have been designed to help the instructor in the classroom. All of these supplements have been carefully coordinated to support the text and to provide an integrated set of materials for the instructor.

Instructor's Resource Manual. The *Instructor's Resource Manual,* prepared by Professor Deborah Brown McCabe, has been completely revised and updated to provide a thorough review of material in the text as well as supplementary materials that can be used to expand upon the text and to enhance classroom presentations. An alternate table of contents and consumer behavior model for presenting the text in a "macro to micro" approach has been provided as well as different sample syllabi. Included for each chapter are a chapter summary; learning objectives; a comprehensive chapter outline; a list of useful Web sites, with descriptions of how they might assist the instructor in preparing for or teaching a class session; and several suggested classroom activities. Classroom activities include questions for each chapter that stimulate group discussion, suggestions for bringing additional examples (videos, readings, etc.) into the classroom, and special experiential activities created by Professor Sheri Bridges, with detailed guidelines for facilitation.

Expanded Set of Color Transparencies. A set of 50 color transparencies includes illustrations not found in the text. The transparencies consist of print ads that may be used to illustrate various concepts discussed in the chapters. Teaching notes are provided to facilitate integrating the transparencies with lectures.

Test Bank/Computerized Test Bank. An extensive test bank prepared by Professor David Ackerman is available to assist the instructor in assessing student performance. The test bank contains approximately 2,100 questions, including a mix of both conceptual and applied questions for each chapter. All test bank questions note the page in the book from which the relevant item came. An electronic version of the printed test bank is available for Windows. This computerized test bank allows instructors to edit and easily generate multiple forms of tests.

PowerPoint Presentation Package. A package of professionally developed PowerPoint slides is available for use by adopters of this textbook. Slides include some text illustrations as well as additional presentations that highlight chapter concepts. Instructors who have access to PowerPoint can edit slides to customize them for their classrooms. A PowerPoint viewer is also provided for instructors who do not have the program. Slides can also be printed for lecture notes and class distribution.

Videos. A completely new video package has been provided to supplement and enliven class lectures and discussion. Videos include many real-world scenarios that illustrate certain concepts in a given chapter. The clips are intended to be interesting, to ground the concepts in real life for students, and to provide an impetus for stimulating student input and involvement.

NEW! STUDENT AND INSTRUCTOR WEB SITES

Specially designed Web pages enhance the book content and provide additional information, guidance, and activities.

The **student site** includes chapter previews, chapter outlines, learning objectives, Internet exercises with hyperlinks, interactive quizzes that help students assess their progress, chapter links to key companies mentioned in the opening cases and chapter examples, a resource center, providing links to consumer behavior research sites, and term paper help.

The **instructor site** provides lecture notes, PowerPoint slides, suggested answers to the Internet exercises, additional teaching tips, sample syllabi, and various classroom enhancement materials, such as additional experiential exercises and project ideas.

ACKNOWLEDGMENTS

We have been extremely fortunate to work with a wonderful team of dedicated professionals from Houghton Mifflin. We are very grateful to Joanne Dauksewicz, Kathy Hunter, Susan Kahn, Tamela Ambush, and Naomi Kornhauser whose enormous energy and enthusiasm spurred our progress on this second Edition. We also appreciate the efforts of Sheri Bridges at Wake Forest University for her work on the Experiential Exercises, Deborah McCabe at Arizona State University for her work on the Instructor's Resource Manual, and David Ackerman from Cal State Northridge for his work on the Test Bank.

The quality of this book and its ancillary package has been helped immensely by the insightful and rich comments of a set of researchers and instructors who served as reviewers. Their thoughtful and helpful comments had real impact in shaping the final product. In particular, we wish to thank:

Larry Anderson
Long Island University

Sharon Beatty
University of Alabama

Russell Belk
University of Utah

Joseph Bonnice
Manhattan College

Margaret L. Burk
Muskingum College

Carol Calder
Loyola Marymount University

Dennis Clayson
University of Northern Iowa

Joel Cohen
University of Florida

Sally Dibb
University of Warwick

Richard W. Easley
Baylor University

Richard Elliott
Lancaster University

Abdi Eshghi
Bentley College

Frank W. Fisher
Stonehill College

Ronald Fullerton
Providence College

Philip Garton
Leicester Business School

Peter L. Gillett
University of Central Florida

Debbora Heflin
Cal Poly–Pomona

Elizabeth Hirschman
Rutgers University

Raj G. Javalgi
Cleveland State University

Harold Kassarjian
UCLA

Patricia Kennedy
University of Nebraska–Lincoln

Robert E. Kleine
Arizona State University

Scott Koslow
University of Waikato

Phillip Lewis
Rowan College of New Jersey

Kenneth R. Lord
SUNY–Buffalo

Bart Macchiette
Plymouth State College

Lawrence Marks
Kent State University

David Marshall
University of Edinburgh

Anil Mathur
Hofstra University

Martin Meyers
University of Wisconsin–Stevens Point

Vince Mitchell
UMIST

Lois Mohr
Georgia State University

James R. Ogden
Kutztown University

Thomas O'Guinn
University of Illinois

Michael Reilly
Montana State University

Gregory M. Rose
The University of Mississippi

Mary Mercurio Scheip
Eckerd College

Marilyn Scrizzi
New Hampshire Technical College

John Shaw
Providence College

C. David Shepherd
University of Tennessee–Chattanooga

Robert E. Smith
Indiana University

Eric R. Spangenberg
Washington State University

Bruce Stern
Portland State University

Phil Titus
Bowling Green State University

Stuart Van Auken
Cal State University–Chico

Janet Wagner
University of Maryland

Tommy E. Whittler
University of Kentucky

THE CONSUMER'S CULTURE

Age, Gender, and
Household Influences
(Ch. 15)

Social Class Influences
(Ch. 14)

Social Influences
(Ch. 16)

Regional, Ethnic and
Religious Influences
(Ch. 13)

THE PSYCHOLOGICAL CORE

- Motivation, Ability and
  Opportunity (Ch. 3)
- Exposure, Attention and
  Perception (Ch. 4)
- Knowing and
  Understanding (Ch. 5)
- Attitude Formation
  (Chs. 6 & 7)
- Memory and
  Retrieval (Ch. 8)

Psychographics:
Values, Personality
and Lifestyles
(Ch. 17)

THE PROCESS OF MAKING DECISIONS

- Problem Recognition and Information Search (Ch. 9)
- Judgment and Decision Making (Chs. 10-11)
- Post-Decision Processes (Ch. 12)

CONSUMER BEHAVIOR OUTCOMES

- Symbolic Consumer Behavior (Ch. 18)
- Adoption of, Resistance to, and Diffusion of
  Innovations (Ch. 19)

PART ONE

An Introduction to Consumer Behavior

Part One introduces the subject of consumer behavior and provides an understanding of the breadth of the field. You will learn that consumer behavior involves more than the purchasing of products. It also involves consumers' use of services, activities, and ideas. You will come to understand that marketers are interested in the decision making inherent in all consumer behavior.

Chapter 1 defines consumer behavior and discusses its importance to marketers, advocacy groups, public policy makers, and consumers themselves. It also presents and explains the overall model (shown here on the opposite page) that guides the organization of this text. You will learn that consumer behavior encompasses four basic domains: (1) the psychological core (the internal processes that consumers use to make decisions), (2) the consumer's culture (the external factors that influence consumers' decisions), (3) the process of making decisions, and (4) the outcomes of consumer behavior.

Chapter 2 focuses on the critical importance of consumer behavior research and it special implications for marketers. Various research methods are explored and types of data discussed. The chapter sets the stage for understanding how consumer research helps marketers develop strategies and tactics for reaching customers. It also explores various ethical issues relating to consumer research.

UNDERSTANDING CONSUMER BEHAVIOR

INTRODUCTION

In 1994, Peter Schniedermeier recognized that customers were not completely satisfied with the way they purchased tickets for concerts, sporting events, and theater—and with how much they paid. So he and his partners set out to offer a more customer-focused approach to ticket acquisition. Their idea grew into a viable competitor to Ticketmaster, known as ETM.

Using ETM, customers buy tickets over the phone, either by talking to a live operator or by using an automated, interactive voice response system, which can handle up to 10,000 calls at a time. A menu enables customers to obtain concert information, find desirable seating, select a payment method, and purchase tickets—all in an average of 4 minutes.

ETM also lets customers buy tickets from its visually attractive and easy-to-use Web site (see Exhibit 1.1). Visitors to the site can buy concert merchandise, listen to music, watch videos, and enter special contests or promotions.

Most recently, ETM has introduced self-serve ticketing kiosks in supermarkets. Each kiosk has a 27-inch monitor and a 360-degree sound system. A combination of kiosks and phone sales helped sell out a September 1998 Pearl Jam concert in 2 hours. In addition to the range of products and services it offers, ETM also accepts various payment methods. Customers can pay by check, cash, credit card, or debit card. And they can buy tickets at any time—24 hours a day.[1]

EXHIBIT 1.1

ETM's Web site

ETM's Web site lets customers buy tickets on-line. Its Web site is also interesting and attracts and holds consumers' attention.

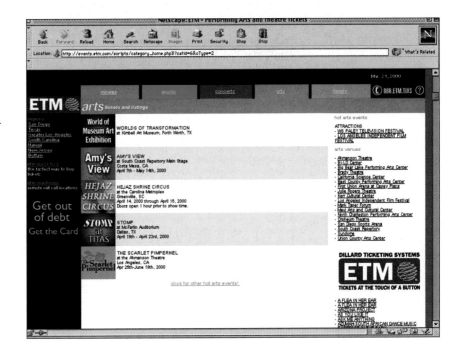

ETM's success is largely due to its understanding of consumer behavior. First, ETM developed a system that meets customers' needs for convenience—giving them more choices about where, when, and how they purchase tickets. Second, its Web site and kiosks are attention getting and give customers easy-to-process links so they can search effortlessly, and without pressure, for the seating arrangements and prices they want. Furthermore, courteous operators strive to create favorable attitudes toward the ETM service among phone-in customers, and customers who use the Web and kiosk have the opportunity to think about their choices without feeling pressured to buy. By offering a variety of payment options, ETM also demonstrates its understanding of customers' economic constraints and preferences for how and when they wish to pay for goods and services. Providing the option of buying concert merchandise further demonstrates ETM's recognition of consumers' desire for products with symbolic meaning. Wearing a T-shirt from a Pearl Jam concert can both help consumers remember the concert experience and communicate to others something about who they are and what they like.

Many customers are highly satisfied with the ETM experience. No doubt they have spread positive information about the service to friends and family. Understanding consumer behavior can therefore be critical to the success of a new product or service—using this type of knowledge is the way that businesses such as ETM can truly thrive.

In this chapter we provide a general overview of (1) what consumer behavior is, (2) what factors affect it, and (3) why you should study it. Because you are a consumer yourself, you probably have at least a vague idea about these three issues. However, we think you will be surprised at how broad the domain of consumer behavior is, how many factors help explain consumer behavior, and how important the field of consumer behavior is to a number of different disciplines.

consumer behavior The totality of consumers' decisions with respect to the acquisition, consumption, and disposition of goods, services, time, and ideas by (human) decision-making units [over time].

If you were asked to define **consumer behavior**, you would probably say it refers quite simply to the study of how a person buys products. Although the study of how a person buys products *is* of interest to marketers, consumer behavior really involves quite a bit more. A complete definition of consumer behavior follows.

> Consumer behavior reflects the totality of consumers' decisions with respect to the acquisition, consumption, and disposition of goods, services, time, and ideas by (human) decision making units [over time].[2]

This definition has some very important elements, summarized in Exhibit 1.2. Let us look at each more closely.

Consumer Behavior Involves Products, Services, Activities, and Ideas

Consumer behavior means more than just how a person buys products such as laundry detergent, breakfast cereal, personal computers, and automobiles. It also includes consumers' use of services, activities, and ideas (see Exhibit 1.2). Going to the dentist, signing up for aerobics classes, taking a trip, celebrating Thanksgiving, getting children immunized, saying no to drugs, and donating to the Boys and Girls Clubs of America are all examples of consumer behavior.

Marketing efforts therefore also focus on our consumption of services, activities, and ideas, such as the activities shown in Exhibit 1.3. Because consumer be-

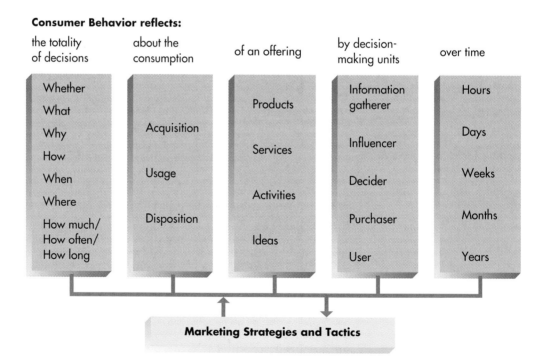

Consumer Behavior reflects:

the totality of decisions	about the consumption	of an offering	by decision-making units	over time
Whether			Information gatherer	Hours
What	Acquisition	Products		Days
Why		Services	Influencer	
How	Usage		Decider	Weeks
When		Activities		
Where	Disposition		Purchaser	Months
How much/ How often/ How long		Ideas	User	Years

Marketing Strategies and Tactics

EXHIBIT 1.2
What Is Consumer Behavior?

This exhibit shows that consumer behavior reflects more than simply how a product is acquired by a single person at any one point in time. Think of some marketing strategies and tactics that try to influence one or more of the dimensions of consumer behavior shown in the exhibit.

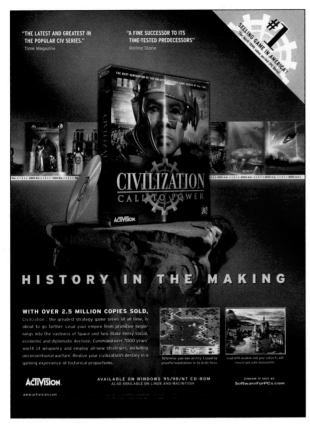

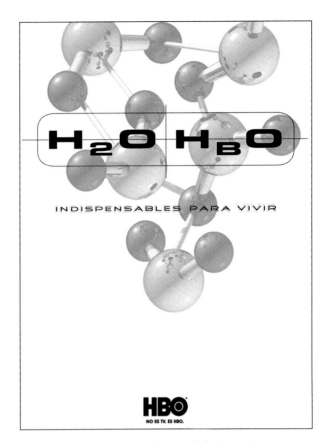

EXHIBIT 1.3
Affecting Consumers'
Decisions About Activities

Consumer behavior includes consumers' decisions about how they spend their time. Sports teams, travel agencies, software companies, and television entertainment networks are only some of the organizations that develop marketing efforts designed to include consumers' decisions about what activities they will pursue.

Sources: left: Courtesy of Activision; *right:* Courtesy of HBO.

offering   A product, service, activity, or idea offered by a marketing organization to consumers.

havior can reflect such diverse entities as products, services, activities, or ideas, we sometimes use the term **offering** to refer to the entity around which marketing efforts revolve.

Consumer Behavior Involves More Than Buying

Consumer behavior describes more than just buying (or purchasing). Although the manner in which consumers buy is extremely important to marketers, it is not the only activity of interest.

acquisition   The process by which a consumer comes to own an offering.

Acquiring   Buying represents one type of **acquisition** behavior. (See Exhibit 1.4 for some interesting information on how most of us spend our money.) As you will see in greater detail later in the chapter, acquisition includes other ways of obtaining products and services, such as leasing, trading, or borrowing.

usage   The process by which a consumer uses an offering.

Using   After a product or service has been acquired, it will typically be used in some manner. Although much consumer research has studied acquisition, **usage** is at the very core of consumer behavior.[3] First, usage has important symbolic

EXHIBIT 1.4
It All Adds Up: What do we buy?

We buy lots of different things from a host of product categories. A few of the more common categories of consumption are shown here.

Source: U.S. Bureau of Labor Statistics. Used with permission.

AVERAGE ANNUAL CONSUMER-UNIT EXPENDITURES BY CATEGORY, 1995

AVERAGE AFTER-TAX INCOME		$33,893
AVERAGE EXPENDITURES		$32,277
HOUSING		$10,465
OWNED DWELLINGS*	$3,754	
UTILITIES, FUELS, AND PUBLIC SERVICES	$2,193	
ELECTRICITY	$ 870	
TELEPHONE SERVICES	$ 708	
RENTED DWELLINGS	$1,786	
HOUSEHOLD FURNISHINGS AND EQUIPMENT	$1,403	
HOUSEHOLD OPERATIONS	$ 508	
HOUSEKEEPING SUPPLIES	$ 430	
TRANSPORTATION		$6,016
VEHICLE PURCHASES	$2,639	
GASOLINE AND MOTOR OIL	$1,006	
VEHICLE INSURANCE	$ 713	
MAINTENANCE AND REPAIRS	$ 653	
FOOD		$4,505
PERSONAL INSURANCE AND PENSIONS		$2,967
PENSIONS AND SOCIAL SECURITY	$2,593	
LIFE AND OTHER PERSONAL INSURANCE	$ 374	
HEALTH CARE		$1,732
APPAREL AND SERVICES		$1,704
ENTERTAINMENT		$1,612
CASH CONTRIBUTIONS		$ 925
MISCELLANEOUS**		$ 766
EDUCATION		$ 471
PERSONAL-CARE PRODUCTS AND SERVICES		$ 403
ALCOHOLIC BEVERAGES		$ 277
TOBACCO PRODUCTS AND SMOKING SUPPLIES		$ 269
READING		$ 163

*Excludes payment on mortgage principal

**Includes legal and accounting fees, funeral expenses, finance charges other than home/vehicle

implications for the consumer. The products we use at Thanksgiving (pumpkin pie, whether made from scratch or store bought) may symbolize the importance of the event, how much we have worked to make a nice dinner, and how important our guests are to us. The music to which we listen (BoyZn the Hood or Tony Bennett) and the jewelry we wear (diamond rings or belly button rings) can also symbolize who we are and how we feel. As you will see in later chapters, understanding consumers' usage of products and services can guide marketing strategy and tactics.

Second, usage can also influence other behaviors. Dissatisfied and angry consumers may communicate negative experiences to others, sometimes with devastating results.[4] For example, negative word-of-mouth can kill a Hollywood film within a few weeks of its release. Dissatisfied consumers can also complain—sometimes to the offending company and sometimes to agencies like the Federal Trade Commission (FTC) or the Federal Communications Commission (FCC). The FCC gets roughly 1,500 complaints a week from customers about cable TV rates and programming.[5]

Disposing Finally, consumer behavior examines **disposition**—that is, how consumers get rid of an offering they have previously acquired. Disposition behavior can have extremely important implications for marketers.[6] A sizable segment of the market is concerned about the environment and will pay extra for products that do not pollute when disposed of.[7] Some companies make considerable money buying trash and recycling it.[8]

Consumer Behavior Is a Dynamic Process

Consumer behavior suggests that acquisition, consumption, and disposition can occur over time in a dynamic sequence. As Exhibit 1.2 indicates, the time period that describes this sequence could occur over a matter of hours, days, weeks, months, or even years.

To illustrate the sequence, a family can use a new car after acquiring it. Usage of the car provides the family with information—such as that it drives well, is reliable, impresses others, and does minimal harm to the environment—that affects when, whether, how, and why the family will dispose of the car by selling, trading, or junking it. Because a family always needs transportation, disposition of the car is likely to affect when, whether, how, and why its members acquire another car in the future.

Entire markets are designed around linking one consumer's disposition decision to other consumers' acquisition decisions. For example, when consumers buy used cars, they are buying cars that others have disposed of. Organizations like Goodwill Industries, antique stores, electronic auctions, and used clothing and used CD stores are all examples of businesses that link one consumer's disposition behavior with another's acquisition behavior.

Consumer Behavior Can Involve Many People

Consumer behavior does not necessarily reflect the action of a single individual. Planning a birthday party, deciding where to have dinner, or going to Disneyland could be done by a group of friends, a few coworkers, or a family. Moreover, the individuals engaging in consumer behavior can take on one or more consumer roles. In the purchase of an automobile, for example, one or more family members might take on the role of information gatherer by collecting information about potential models. They or others might take the role of influencer and try to affect the outcome of a decision. One or more members may take the role of purchaser by actually paying for the car, and some or all may be users. Finally, several family members may be involved in the disposal of the product.

Consumer Behavior Involves Many Decisions

Consumer behavior involves understanding whether, why, when, where, how, how much, how often, and how long consumers will buy, use, or dispose of an offering (see Exhibit 1.2).

Whether to Acquire/Use/Dispose Of an Offering Consumers must decide whether to acquire, use, or dispose of an offering. They may need to decide whether to spend or save their money when they get a raise. They may need to decide whether to eat dessert or not, clean out their bulging closets, or go to a movie. In some cases decisions about whether to acquire, use, or dispose of an offering are related to safety concerns. For example, some consumers are concerned about whether they should buy and use cellular phones because the phones have been found to adversely affect pacemakers. Concern about the risks associated with cell phones is also fueled by a recent study which suggested that a 50 percent increase in brain tumors among Western Australian consumers may be related to cell phone use. A comprehensive eight-country study investigating the link between cell phones and tumor development is under way by the World Health Organization.[9] Concerns about economic risk, social risk, and psychological risk may also motivate consumer decisions.

What to Acquire/Use/Dispose Of an Offering Consumers in each household in the United States spend $90 per day on goods and services. Clearly, we make decisions every day about what to buy.[10] In some cases we make choices among product or service *categories*. Exhibit 1.4 summarizes the major categories of things we buy. In other cases we choose between *brands*. Should you buy a Mariah Carey CD or a Jewel CD?

Why Acquire/Use/Dispose Of an Offering Consumption can occur for a number of reasons. Among the most important, as you will see later, are the ways in which an offering meets someone's needs, values, or goals. For example, some consumers have various body parts pierced because they believe that this process is a form of self-expression. Others do it to fit into a group. Still others believe body piercing is a form of beauty, whereas for some piercing is done to enhance sexual pleasure.[11] Some consumers buy and use products because they want a fantasy experience. In Phnom Penh, Cambodia, tourists can fantasize that they are in a war, firing grenades or shooting from Uzis or AK47s from a specially designed shooting range.[12]

Sometimes our reasons for using a product or service are filled with conflict. Teenagers may smoke despite knowing it is harmful because they think smoking will help them gain acceptance. Low-fat margarine is probably better for us than regular margarine is, but we avoid it because its taste has been described as similar to "melted plastic."[13] These conflicts can lead to some difficult consumption decisions.

Sometimes consumers simply cannot stop acquiring, using, or disposing of products. People may be physically addicted to a product such as cigarettes, drugs, or alcohol; or they may have a compulsion to eat, purge, gamble, or buy.

Finally, sometimes consumers want to consume but cannot. In Hungary, for example, many consumers are desperate for new housing, but so few new apartments and houses are available that people must either stay in dingy and deteriorating places or invest in extensive repairs and redecorating.[14]

Why Not to Acquire/Use/Dispose Of an Offering Marketers also want to know why consumers do *not* acquire, use, or dispose of an offering. Consumers may be averse to the idea of buying a DVD player because they do not think they can handle the technology or they do not believe it will offer them anything special. They may believe that technology is changing so fast, whatever they buy will soon be outdated. They may even believe that DVD suppliers will go out of business and hence not be around to provide after-sale support or service.

How to Acquire/Use/Dispose Of an Offering   Marketers gain a lot of insight from understanding how consumers acquire, consume, and dispose of an offering.

Ways of Acquiring an Offering   How do consumers decide whether to pay for an item with cash, check, debit card, or credit card? In China, where bank notes are in short supply and the use of counterfeit money is widespread, the government is trying to increase consumers' use of debit cards.[15]

- *Buying.*   Although we typically understand how consumers buy products and services as a form of purchasing behavior, they can acquire products and services in other ways.
- *Trading.*   Consumers could receive a product or service as part of a trade. For example, some music stores allow consumers to trade in old CDs, albums, or tapes for new CDs, new tapes, or cash.
- *Renting or Leasing.*   Goods like videotape players, tuxedos, carpet cleaners, furniture, vacation homes, and computers can be rented or leased. Leasing is now a very popular way of acquiring automobiles.
- *Bartering.*   Thousands of businesses and consumers engage in the practice of bartering. Hotels, for example, barter free rooms for plumbing services, electrical work, and carpet cleaning. In 1994 more than $2 billion worth of travel products and services were bartered.[16]
- *Gift Giving.*   Consumers can also acquire products as gifts. Gift giving is common throughout the world, and most societies have many gift-giving occasions. Each society also has formal and informal rules that dictate how gifts should be given, what is appropriate as a gift, and what is an appropriate response to gift giving. Marketing efforts are sometimes designed to induce gift giving. Have you noticed that on Mother's Day items ranging from lingerie to irons to computers are touted as appropriate gifts for Mom?
- *Finding.*   In some instances consumers simply find goods that someone else has lost (books left on the bus, shampoo left at the gym, umbrellas left in class) or thrown away.
- *Theft.*   Goods can also be acquired through theft. Interestingly, new products are sometimes developed to deter this mode of acquisition. A huge number of antitheft devices like The Club, Lo-Jack, and car alarms attempt to reduce the likelihood of car theft.
- *Borrowing.*   Products can also be acquired by borrowing. Interestingly, we typically think of borrowing as a willing and conscious exchange between borrower and lender. However, some types of "borrowing" are illegal and border on theft. It is not uncommon, for example, for consumers to pay for new clothes, wear them, and then return them for a full refund. This situation happens frequently with formal wear, and the trend increases during hard economic times.[17] Illegal borrowing is also hurting publishing companies, movie studios, software producers, and music producers who produce copyrighted material. Companies whose products are in a digital format are particularly vulnerable to this form of "bootlegging," since their products can be copied via computer with a simple click of a mouse.[18]

Ways of Using an Offering   In addition to understanding how consumers acquire products and services, marketers are also interested in how consumers use an offering.[19] For example, marketers have found that consumers are using their cars and vans as mini-homes, complete with phones, faxes, radios, stereos, TVs, VCRs,

EXHIBIT 1.5

Affecting How a Product Is Used

Consumers' decisions about how an offering is used can affect how satisfied they are with it. As such, marketing communications like this ad sometimes need to communicate these uses.

Source: Used by permission of De Longhi America, Inc.

refrigerators, and automatic alarms, and that this usage is reducing demand for traditional automotive features such as stick shifts.[20] An ad designed to influence consumer usage of a convection toaster oven is shown in Exhibit 1.5 at the left.

For obvious reasons, marketers want to ensure that their offering is used correctly. For example, marketers of the female condom have found that their biggest challenge is not in getting consumers to buy the condom but rather in educating them about how to use it correctly.[21] Improper usage of some products or services, such as oven cleaner or cough medicine, can create health and safety problems for a consumer.[22] Because of these hazards, potentially dangerous products must have warning labels, but unfortunately, many consumers ignore them. Therefore, to make these labels more effective, marketers must understand how consumers process them.

Ways of Disposing of an Offering   Finally, consumers can decide how to dispose of products. In making this decision, they generally have several options:[23]

- *Finding a New Use for It.*   Using an old toothbrush to clean rust from tools or making shorts out of an old pair of jeans are some of the ways in which consumers deal with an original item without actually disposing of it.

- *Getting Rid of It Temporarily.*   Renting or lending an item is one way of getting rid of it temporarily.

- *Getting Rid of It Permanently.*   Throwing an item away probably represents the most common option for permanently getting rid of it; but there are also the options of trading it, giving it away, or selling it.

Some consumers refuse to throw away things they regard as special, even if the items no longer serve a functional purpose. Other consumers are interested in collecting, not disposing of items.[24] Consumers collect many things, from stamps, CDs, dolls, and teddy bears to string, coffee beans, and flip-top lids. Some consumers are "pack rats" who can alienate neighbors and create health risks by failing to throw out anything (see Exhibit 1.6).

When to Acquire/Use/Dispose Of an Offering   Our tendency to rent videos, hire plumbers, call a tow truck company, or shop for clothes is greatly enhanced in cold weather. These same weather conditions reduce our tendency to eat ice cream, shop for a car, or look for a new home.[25] Dentists have found that the demand for teeth bleaching increases dramatically among politicians and lobbyists in the pre-election season.[26] Time of day also influences consumption decisions. Few of us are likely to want wine and lobster for breakfast, although we may happily anticipate the same items in the evening.

Our need for variety can affect when we acquire, use, or dispose of an offering. We may decide not to eat yogurt for lunch today if we have had it every day this week. Transitions such as graduation, birth, retirement, and death also affect when we acquire, use, and dispose of offerings. For instance, we buy products like wedding rings, wedding dresses, and wedding cakes only when we get married.

EXHIBIT 1.6
Problems in Disposition

Some consumers create public health problems by failing to throw anything away, even things that have lost their functional value.

Source: Ricardo DeAratanha/Los Angeles Times.

When we consume can also be affected by traditions imposed by our families, our culture, and the area in which we live. Every spring, St. George, South Carolina, hosts the World Grits Festival. In addition to providing grits in considerable quantities, the festival allows consumers to have fun in unusual ways. Some participate in a rollin' in the grits contest, which awards prizes to the person who gets the most grits stuck to himself or herself after rolling in a huge vat filled with cooled grits.[27]

Our decisions about when to use an offering are also affected by knowing when others might or might not be using it. Thus we might be motivated to travel by air, eat dinner, go on vacation, work out, or get a haircut when we know that others will *not* be doing so. We may also wait to purchase goods and services until we know they are likely to be on sale.

Where to Acquire/Use/Dispose Of an Offering Recent advances in information technology allow us to buy goods and services through the mail, over the telephone, from TV, and over the Internet.

Consider that consumers who have traditionally gone to places like Las Vegas and Reno to gamble now can do so in cyberspace casinos on the Internet.[28] On-line shopping has dramatically changed where we acquire goods. Consider the fact that during the 1999 holiday season, 8.6 million households will do at least some of their holiday shopping on-line, and they will buy an estimated $6 billion in merchandise. The rush of on-line shopping during the 1999 holiday season came at such a fast pace that many "e-tailing" sites had trouble keeping up with demand and servicing customers adequately. Convenience drives many consumers to acquire goods on-line, but so too does the fact that sites are offering services that blur the distinction between traditional and on-line shopping. At Williams-Sonoma, for example, brides-to-be can log on to the gift registry and view up to the moment data on who has bought them what. At Sears, Roebuck and Co. on-line consumers can obtain store credit cards instantly. Circuit City and Penney's even lets customers return merchandise purchased on-line at local stores.[29] The Internet has also changed where we acquire services. For example, some banks allow consumers to get a loan through automated loan machines set up at supermarkets.[30]

Consumers sometimes choose to buy products that have been used. Indeed, buying secondhand goods has become almost chic. Some consumers even believe that some secondhand merchandise can make wonderful gifts.[31]

In addition to acquisition decisions, consumers also make decisions about where they wish to consume various products. For example, the need for privacy motivates consumers to seek the privacy of their own homes to get drunk or to use products that determine whether they are ovulating, pregnant, or diabetic. Advances in technology allow consumers to check e-mail while on the road, to engage in on-line banking, and to "watch" the news from one's computer. Finally, consumers make decisions regarding where to dispose of goods. Should an old magazine be put in the trash or the recycling bin? Should an old photo album be packaged and put in the attic or given away to one's family?

Clearly, marketers and retailers try to influence consumers' decisions about where to acquire products. Insurance companies are currently developing Web sites to try to encourage prospective customers to buy policies over the Web.[32] Marketers can affect consumers' decisions about where to use an offering. For example, many restaurants give consumers the option of eating meals in or taking them out.

Some marketers can influence where consumers dispose of goods. Hewlett-Packard will pay shipping charges if consumers return empty printer toner cartridges to the company. Reusing these plastic cartridges is good for the environment, and the company can also refill them more cheaply than making new ones, allowing it to sell the recycled cartridges to consumers at a lower price.

EXHIBIT 1.7
Affecting How Often a Product Is Used

Marketers can often stimulate sales not by getting more consumers to buy the offering but by making existing consumers acquire, consume, or dispose of it more often.

Source: Courtesy of CIBA Vision

How Much, How Often, and How Long to Acquire/Use/Dispose Of an Offering Consumers also make decisions about how much of a good or service they need; how often they need it; and how long they will spend in acquisition, usage, and disposition.[33] Usage decisions can vary widely from person to person and from culture to culture. For example, Chinese consumers drink far less coffee than U.S. consumers do. Instead, Chinese consumers drink an average of 1,500 cups of tea per year.[34]

Sales of a product can be increased when the consumer (1) uses larger amounts of the product, (2) uses the product more frequently, or (3) uses it for longer periods of time. The ad in Exhibit 1.7, for example, shows that marketers of disposable contact lenses wish consumers would change their lenses every day. Bonus packs are ways of motivating consumers to buy more of a product, just as frequent-flyer programs encourage them to fly more often.[35]

Some consumers have problems because they engage in too much consumption. Some people have a compulsion to engage in more acquisition, usage, or disposition than they would like. These compulsions can occur in spending, gambling, smoking, exercising, drug abuse (including legal drugs), and eating. In the United States, for example, roughly 35 percent of all adults are overweight; see Exhibit 1.8.[36] Excessive consumption can cause many kinds of problems. For instance, doctors are blaming a rise in drug-resistant strains of bacteria on consumers' excessive use of antibiotics.[37]

In summary, consumer behavior reflects the multitude of factors revealed in Exhibit 1.2. You now can see that consumer behavior involves much more than understanding which products a consumer buys.

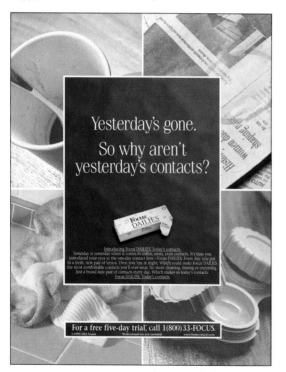

EXHIBIT 1.8
Growing Larger

Are we getting fat? Do we consume too much? From the data, it appears that the number of people who are overweight has been increasing over time.

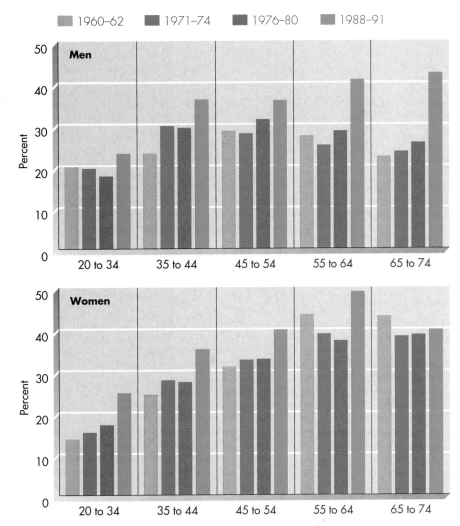

Note: Percent of U.S. adults aged 20 to 74 who are overweight, by sex and age, 1960–62, 1971–74, 1976–80, 1988–91.

WHAT AFFECTS CONSUMER BEHAVIOR?

What affects consumers as they make their acquisition, usage, and disposition decisions? The many factors are shown in the model in Exhibit 1.9, which also serves as an organizing framework for this book.

As shown in Exhibit 1.9, consumer behavior encompasses four domains: (1) the psychological core, (2) the process of making decisions, (3) the consumer's culture, and (4) consumer behavior outcomes. Although the four domains are presented in separate sections of this book, each domain is related to all the others. For example, to make decisions that affect outcomes like buying new products or using products for symbolic reasons, consumers must first engage in processes described in the psychological core. They need to be motivated, able, and have the opportunity to be exposed to, perceive, and attend to information. They need to think about this information, form attitudes about it, and form memories.

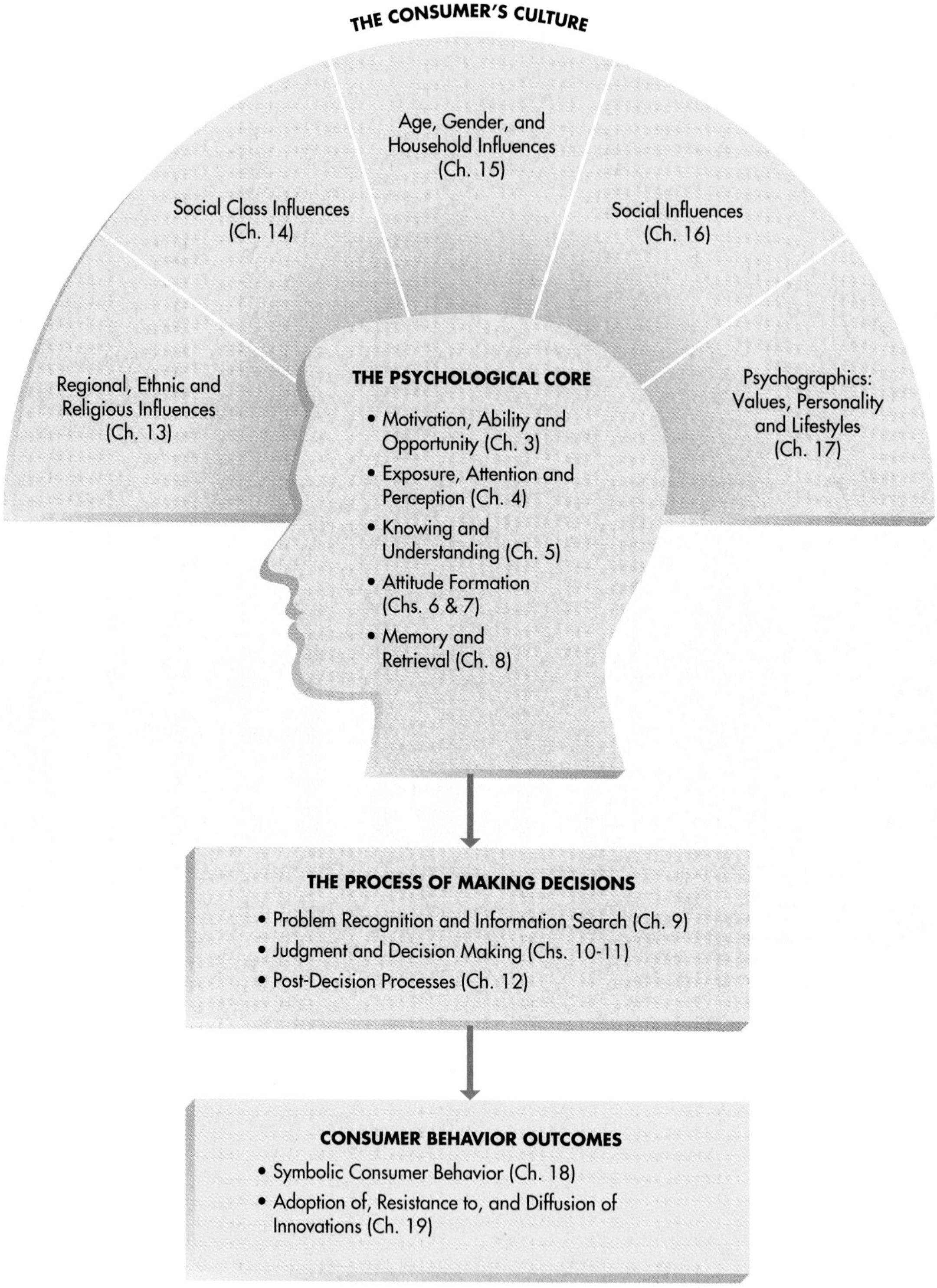

THE CONSUMER'S CULTURE

Age, Gender, and
Household Influences
(Ch. 15)

Social Class Influences
(Ch. 14)

Social Influences
(Ch. 16)

Regional, Ethnic and
Religious Influences
(Ch. 13)

Psychographics:
Values, Personality
and Lifestyles
(Ch. 17)

THE PSYCHOLOGICAL CORE

- Motivation, Ability and
  Opportunity (Ch. 3)
- Exposure, Attention and
  Perception (Ch. 4)
- Knowing and
  Understanding (Ch. 5)
- Attitude Formation
  (Chs. 6 & 7)
- Memory and
  Retrieval (Ch. 8)

THE PROCESS OF MAKING DECISIONS

- Problem Recognition and Information Search (Ch. 9)
- Judgment and Decision Making (Chs. 10-11)
- Post-Decision Processes (Ch. 12)

CONSUMER BEHAVIOR OUTCOMES

- Symbolic Consumer Behavior (Ch. 18)
- Adoption of, Resistance to, and Diffusion of
  Innovations (Ch. 19)

EXHIBIT 1.9
A Model of Consumer Behavior

Consumer behavior encompasses four domains: (1) the psychological core, (2) the process of making decisions, (3) the consumer's culture, and (4) consumer behavior outcomes. As the exhibit shows, Chapters 3–19 of this book relate to the four parts of this overall model.

The cultural environment also affects what motivates consumers, how they process information, and the kinds of decisions they make. Age, gender, social class, ethnicity, families, friends, and other groups affect values and lifestyles and hence influence the decisions consumers make and how and why they are made.

Let us consider each domain separately and illustrate the interrelationships among the domains with an example. We use the example of a vacation decision to illustrate these concepts and domains. However, to reinforce the point that decisions are affected by lifestyles and values, which are in turn affected by factors such as age, gender, social class, ethnicity, families and friends, consider the types of vacations in Exhibit 1.12, on page 19, and the characteristics of consumers who are likely to enjoy them.

The Psychological Core: Internal Consumer Processes

Before consumers can make decisions, they must have some source of knowledge or information upon which their decisions can be based. This source is the psychological core.

Having Motivation, Ability, and Opportunity   Consider the case of a hypothetical consumer named Jessica who is deciding on a ski vacation. In Jessica's mind a vacation decision is very risky—her vacation consumes lots of money and time, and she does not want to make a bad choice. In light of this risk, Jessica is very motivated to learn as much as she can about various vacation options, think about them, and fantasize about what they will be like. She has put other activities aside to give herself the opportunity to learn and think about this vacation. Finally, because Jessica already knows how to ski, she has the ability to determine what types of ski vacations she would find enjoyable.

Exposure, Attention, and Perception   Because Jessica is greatly motivated to decide where to go on vacation and she has the ability and opportunity to do so, she will make sure she is exposed to, perceives, and attends to any information she thinks is relevant to her decision. She might look at travel ads, read travel-related newspaper and magazine articles, and engage in discussions with friends and travel agents. Note, though, that Jessica's attention is selective. She will probably not attend to *all* vacation information; she is likely to be exposed to information she will never perceive or pay attention to.

Categorizing and Comprehending Information   Jessica will use the information that she does perceive and attempt to categorize and comprehend it. For example, she might categorize the vacation in Exhibit 1.10 as a honeymoon vacation. Because she does not want this type of vacation, she will not consider it further. She might infer that Kitzbühel, Austria, is a reasonably priced vacation destination because the brochures show images consistent with this interpretation.

Forming and Changing Attitudes   Jessica is likely to form attitudes toward the vacations she has categorized and comprehended. She may have a favorable attitude toward Kitzbühel because one of the brochures describes it as affordable, educational, and fun. However, her attitudes might undergo considerable change as she encounters new information.

Attitudes do not always predict our behavior. For example, many of us probably have a positive attitude toward working out. Nevertheless, our positive attitude and our good intentions do not always culminate in a trip to the gym. For this reason, attitudes and choices are considered as separate topics.

Room 1210.

Never want

to see

another caterer,

photographer,

or tailor for

as long as they

both shall live.

The formalities are over. Let the honeymoon begin with
Marriott Offshore Resorts' Honeymoon Packages that include:
deluxe accommodations, complimentary bottle of champagne, daily breakfast for two, and more.
For a memorable honeymoon, contact your travel professional or 1-800-223-6388.

Rates starting from $115.*

Aruba Marriott Resort & Stellaris Casino   Marriott's Castle Harbour Resort, Bermuda
Marriott CasaMagna Cancún Resort   Costa Rica Marriott Hotel
Nassau Marriott Resort & Crystal Palace & Casino   Marriott CasaMagna Puerto Vallarta Resort

Marriott
HOTELS·RESORTS·SUITES
when you're comfortable you can do anything.®
www.marriott.com

*Rate is per room, per night, and varies per resort. Subject to availability. Restrictions apply. All package rates are for 1999

EXHIBIT 1.10
Categorizing a Vacation

Whether we decide to search for more information about an offering (e.g., a vacation destination) depends on how we categorize it (e.g., as a honeymoon vacation). If we categorize it as something different from what we want, we will not consider it further.

Source: Marriott International, Inc.

Forming and Retrieving Memories   One reason that our attitudes may not predict our behavior is that we may or may not remember the information we used to form our attitudes when we later make a decision. Thus Jessica may have formed memories based on certain information, but her choices will be based only on the information she retrieves from memory.

The Process of Making Decisions

The processes that are part of the psychological core are intimately tied to the process of making decisions. Four generally recognized stages characterize the process of making consumer decisions: problem recognition, information search, decision making, and postpurchase evaluation.

Problem Recognition and the Search for Information   Problem recognition occurs when we realize we have an unfulfilled need. Jessica realized she needed a vacation, for example. Her subsequent search for information gave her insight into where she might go, how much it might cost, and when the best travel times might be. She also examined her financial situation. Elements of the psychological core are invoked in problem recognition and search because once Jessica realizes that she needs a vacation and begins her information search, she exposes herself to information, attends to and perceives it, categorizes and comprehends it, and forms attitudes and memories.

Making Judgments and Decisions   Jessica's decision is characterized as a *high-effort decision*, meaning that she is willing to exert a lot of time and mental and emotional energy in making it. She identifies several decision criteria that she thinks will be important in making her choices. First, she wants the trip to be educational. She also wants it to be fun and exciting. Third, she does not want to spend a lot of money. Finally, she wants to make sure the place she selects is safe.

Not all decisions involve a lot of effort. For Jessica some low-effort decisions include deciding on what brand of toothpaste to take on the trip, whether to use traveler's checks, or whether to take along a camera. Again, the psychological core is invoked in making judgments and decisions. With a high-effort decision, Jessica will be motivated to expose herself to lots of information; she will think about it deeply, analyze it critically, and form attitudes about it. She may have lasting memories about the information she sees because she has thought about it so much. In a low-effort decision, such as a decision about what brand to toothpaste to buy, one would not expect considerable information search, deep processing of information, and enduring attitudes and memories for that information.

Making Post-Decision Evaluations   Evaluating the decision is the final step of the decision-making process. This step allows the consumer to judge whether the decision was the correct one and whether the product or service is one that will be purchased again. When she returns from her vacation, Jessica will probably evaluate how good her decisions were. If her expectations were met and the vacation is everything she thought it would be, she will feel satisfied. If the vacation exceeds her expectations, she will be delighted. If it falls short, she is likely to be dissatisfied. Once again, aspects of the psychological core are invoked in making post-decision evaluations. Jessica may expose herself to information that validates her experiences, she may update her attitudes, and may selectively remember aspects of her trip that were extremely positive or extremely negative.

The Consumer's Culture: External Processes

Why did Jessica decide to go on a skiing trip in the first place? In large part our consumption decisions are affected by the culture of which we are members. **Culture** refers to the typical or expected behaviors, norms, and ideas that characterize a group of people. It can be a powerful influence on all aspects of human behavior. Jessica had certain feelings, perceptions, and attitudes because of the unique combination of groups to which she belongs. Culture can clearly affect the decisions we make as well as how we process and communicate information.

culture The typical or expected behaviors, norms, and ideas that characterize a group of people.

Regional and Ethnic Influences   Jessica is a member of many groups that directly or indirectly affect the decisions she makes. For example, her decision to ski at a place far from home is fairly typical for a working woman from North America; it is doubtful that a consumer from the Third World or a single woman from a Hindu culture would have made the same set of vacation choices.

Age, Gender, and Household Influences   Jessica's social class, as well as her age, gender, and household circumstances, might have affected her impressions of what constitutes a good vacation. The fact that she is woman in her 20s and a college graduate who has moved in with her parents might have affected her decision to go skiing abroad, as opposed to staying at home, for instance.

Reference Groups   When Jessica sees groups of others she perceives as similar to herself, she regards them as **reference groups,** or people whose values she shares and whose opinion she values. She might also see people whom she admires, even though she does not know them, as people whose behavior she would like to emulate. Thus well-known athletes, musicians, artists, politicians, or movie stars may serve also as reference groups.

reference groups A group of people we compare ourselves to for information regarding behavior, attitudes, or values.

Reference groups can exert influence by conveying information. As such, they can influence the psychological core and the process of making decisions by affecting who we get information from and how we evaluate it. Reference groups can also make us feel as if we should behave in a certain way. Thus Jessica may feel some pressure to go to Kitzbühel because her friends think that doing so is cool.

Jessica's personality is also likely to affect her decisions. Because she is an extrovert and a moderate risk taker, she wants a vacation that is exciting and affords opportunities to meet people.

Consumer Behavior Outcomes

As Exhibit 1.9 on page 14 indicates, the psychological core, decision-making processes, and the consumer's culture affect consumer behavior outcomes such as the symbolic use of products and the diffusion of ideas, products, or services through a market.

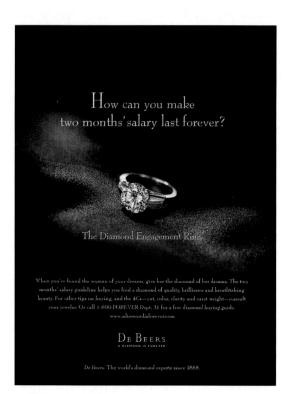

How can you make
two months' salary last forever?

The Diamond Engagement Ring.

When you've found the woman of your dreams, give her the diamond of her dreams. The two months' salary guideline helps you find a diamond of quality, brilliance and breathtaking beauty. For other tips on buying, and the 4Cs—cut, color, clarity and carat weight—consult your jeweler. Or call 1-800-FOREVER Dept. 31 for a free diamond buying guide.
www.adiamondisforever.com

DE BEERS
A DIAMOND IS FOREVER

De Beers. The world's diamond experts since 1888.

symbols External signs that we use to express our identity.

EXHIBIT 1.11
Consumption Symbols

Products like diamond engagement rings and wedding bands can symbolize meaning. Some brands and companies also have symbolic meaning. Think about the symbolic meaning of different products, brands, and companies. Is the meaning specific to a certain culture or group?

Source: Reprinted by permission.

Consumer Behaviors Can Symbolize Who We Are The groups we belong to and our own sense of self can affect the **symbols** or external signs we use, consciously or unconsciously, to express our identity. For example, while she is on vacation, Jessica may use clothing and brand-name merchandise such as her Nike sneakers to communicate her status as a young female from the United States. She might also take home objects that symbolize her vacation, such as postcards and T-shirts.

In our culture, jewelry such as engagement rings and wedding bands have obvious symbolic meaning. The ad in Exhibit 1.11 illustrates the cultural meaning of the engagement ring and attempts to convey the notion that the symbol is definitely worth the price.

Consumer Behaviors Can Diffuse Through a Market After she makes her vacation decision, Jessica may tell others about her prospective trip. Her choice of Kitzbühel as a vacation destination therefore becomes known to other consumers and may influence their vacation decisions as well. Hence the idea of going to Kitzbühel on vacation may diffuse, or spread, to others. Had Jessica resisted the idea of going to Kitzbühel (perhaps because she thought it was too expensive or unsafe), she might have communicated information that made others less likely to go there on vacation. Thus the diffusion of information can have both negative and positive effects for marketers.

In the following chapters we expand on the ideas expressed in Exhibit 1.9. We first consider the psychological core (Part 1) and then delve into decision-making processes (Part 2). We next consider how the consumer's culture affects consumer behavior (Part 3) and how individual and cultural factors affect consumer behavior outcomes (Part 4). In the final two chapters, we conclude by examining consumer welfare issues (Part 5).

Clearly, every consumer is unique and is affected by a unique set of background factors. Consider the vacation choices shown in Exhibit 1.12 and try to imagine the background factors that predispose consumers to choose these as vacation options.

WHO BENEFITS FROM THE STUDY OF CONSUMER BEHAVIOR?

The final question we address in this chapter is, Why should we study consumer behavior? The reasons are as varied as the four different groups who use consumer research: marketing managers, ethicists, public policy makers and regulators, and consumers.

EXHIBIT 1.12
Vacation

The word *vacation* means different things to different people. Your idea of a "relaxing get away" may be quite different from someone else's idea. Can you see how factors like social class, ethnic status, economic conditions, group affiliations, and gender affect the kinds of vacations we are likely to find attractive? These examples show us that some marketers are successful precisely because they understand their customers and what they value.

Sources: Kevin Helliker, "Guests Pay Better Than Cattle for Many Ranchers," *Wall Street Journal,* August 1, 1997, pp. B1, B7; Linda K. Nathan, "Spas Ask: May I Check Your Heart Rate?," *Wall Street Journal,* January 19, 1996, p. B7; Timothy Aeppel, "For Great Adventure, What Could Match a Prairie-Dog Safari?," *Wall Street Journal,* August 1, 1995, pp. A1, A5; Jim Carlton, "Japanese Skip Waikiki, Head for Kmart," *Wall Street Journal,* June 29, 1995, p. B1; Timothy Aeppel, "At One with Indians, Tribes of Foreigners Visit Reservations," *Wall Street Journal,* August 6, 1996, pp. A1, A6; Josh Greenberg, "Some Lawnmowers Stay Home: Others Like Life in the Fast Lane," *Wall Street Journal,* March 27, 1997, p. B1.

ON VACATION, WOULD YOU LIKE TO...?

BE A RANCHER? You can visit one of the more than 100 ranches in Wyoming and Montana, and at some pay upwards of $150.00 per day. At all, you can help herd cattle, and ride horses on beautiful terrain. Some have you stay in luxurious accommodations. At others, you can sleep in a cabin and use the local outhouse.

VISIT YOUR DOCTOR? At some vacation spas you can have your blood tested, metabolism checked, have a cardiogram and get a mammogram. Of course, the spas also have the standard fare as well: mineral soaks, facials, massages, exercise and diet classes, outdoor activities, and a tranquil environment.

SHOOT PRAIRIE DOGS? At various places in the Great Plains (from Texas to Montana), vacationers can buy or rent hunting clothes, high-powered rifles with scopes, and buy maps indicating prairie dog sites and go with a trail guide on a prairie-dog safari. Hunters argue that shooting prairie dogs is good for the environment as the animals carry disease and eat grass intended for sheep and cattle. Others, however, have a different point of view.

FLY TO KMART? In the mid 1990s, the Waikiki Hawaii Waikele Factory Mall, which includes such discount warehouse shops as Kmart, Home Depot, and Eagle Hardware, became one of the hottest Japanese tourist destinations, attracting roughly half a million Japanese consumers per year. Coming with empty suitcases and bags, these tourists would hunt up bargains in categories which included bulk spaghetti and crates of dog-food.

BECOME AN INDIAN? You can sleep on a grass floor of a teepee, ladle water onto heated rocks in a sweat lodge, visit a medicine man, pick organic vegetables, make jewelry decorated with porcupine quills, clear grass from the powwow ring, and observe sacred ceremonies on Native American Indian reservations. These vacations are particularly popular among European travelers. Approximately 60,000 Germans belong to clubs that focus on Indian culture.

RACE IN A RIDING LAWNMOWER COMPETITION? On or around Labor Day, finalists—members of the U.S. Lawnmower Racing Association, will compete for the national championship of the national riding lawnmower competition. Races, held on specially prepared tracks, last for about 20 minutes at speeds of up to 55 miles per hour. In addition to paying for travel to the competition site in Rockford, Ill., contestants spend upwards of $3,000 souping up their machines for the race.

Marketing Managers

The study of consumer behavior provides critical information to marketing managers for developing marketing strategies and tactics. We can emphasize this point by examining a classic definition of **marketing**:

> Marketing is a social and managerial process by which individuals and groups obtain what they need and want through creating and exchanging products and value with others.[38]

According to this definition, to effectively market a product or service, marketing managers must first clearly understand consumers' needs and wants. The study of consumer behavior provides this information and suggests how marketing programs should be designed to bring about the exchange process. In Chapter 2 we expand on the role of marketing research and the strategic and tactical decisions it supports.

marketing A social and managerial process by which individuals and groups obtain what they need and want through creating and exchanging products and value with others.

Ethicists and Advocacy Groups

Marketers' actions sometimes raise important ethical questions. For example, the Transportation Department is investigating the airline industry for what the department calls deceptive fare promotions. Some airlines have set such unusually high ticket prices for two-for-one specials that they exceed the price of two seats at the regular price.[39] R.J. Reynolds Tobacco International has provided the city of Bucharest, Romania, with a year's supply of yellow traffic lightbulbs bearing the Camel cigarette logo.[40] A case can be made that such a seeming "gift" might influence Romanians' decisions to smoke.

Consumers concerned about the ethical practices of marketers sometimes form advocacy groups to create public awareness of inappropriate marketing practices and may even engage in consumer-resistance strategies like boycotts. One advocacy group publicly criticizes Time Warner for its production of rap music. According to the advocacy leader, the company is making money from music that "celebrates the rape, torture, and murder of women."[41]

Sometimes consumers band together to form cooperatives—institutions in which consumers minimize costs and control marketing practices by acting as both owners and consumers of a business or service. Food co-ops are common in the United States. In Canada and Europe, an increasing number of funeral co-ops have been formed to help consumers avoid skyrocketing funeral costs.[42]

Some consumer groups are also concerned about the proliferation of interactive video games in which the protagonist engages in practices like murder, physical violence, and rape. The characterization of women in these video games is also under fire. Not only are women beaten and brutalized, they are often scantily clad and depicted in stereotypical ways.[43] We explore ethical issues throughout the book—particularly in Chapter 21, "The Dark Side of Consumer Behavior and Marketing."

Public Policy Makers and Regulators

Lawmakers and public policy groups strive to protect consumers from unfair, unsafe, or inappropriate marketing practices. In the 1960s, President Kennedy declared that consumers have four basic rights: the right to safety, to information, to choice, and to be heard. The right to a clean environment and protection for minorities and the poor were added later.

In protecting consumers' right to be safe, the Food and Drug Administration (FDA) has recently instituted a seafood regulation plan to minimize the risk of food poisoning. Approximately 15 to 20 percent of all food poisoning cases are linked to seafood, and some types of seafood poisoning are deadly. The plan requires that seafood processors identify and offer solutions for potential health hazards associated with the use of their products.[44]

In protecting the right to be informed, consumer researchers have investigated deceptive and misleading advertising. Therefore, understanding how consumers comprehend and categorize information is important to recognizing and guarding against misleading advertising. Researchers want to know what impressions an ad creates and whether these impressions are true.

For example, a new nutritional product is targeted toward consumers who are HIV positive. A person depicted in the ad states that since he found out he is HIV positive, he has tried to do everything he can to "maintain my energy, strength, and quality of life." Doctors are concerned that the ad suggests that the product will help every patient who has AIDS or tests HIV positive, when this outcome is not the case.[45]

Consumer researchers also investigate advertising to children. Research has shown that children under the age of 6 do not have the cognitive abilities to understand that advertisements are trying to persuade them. Consequently, many people believe that young consumers need to be protected against messages that may depict products in overly glamorous or extraordinarily attractive ways.

Camel cigarettes came under fire for the Joe Camel campaign when research indicated that young consumers recognized the Joe Camel character more readily than they recognized Mickey Mouse. Partly in response to this research, the FTC brought a case against R.J. Reynolds, charging that its Joe Camel character attempts to attract children to cigarettes.[46]

Clearly, public policy decisions about consumer behavior affect marketers. Recent laws have stated that food products must conform to certain definitions before they can be labeled "low fat" or "lite." Moreover, companies need to tell consumers what these terms mean and do so on the product's packaging.[47] We have much more to say about these issues in Chapter 20, titled "Consumer Behavior and Public Policy." For now, the important point is that consumer behavior can be quite useful to regulators and government agencies in developing laws and policies designed to protect consumers.

Consumers

An understanding of consumer behavior can help make a better environment for consumers. For example, consumer behavior research has shown that we better understand how brands on the market differ when we can view a chart, matrix, or grid that compares various brands and their attributes.[48] Matrices such as those now presented in *Consumer Reports* are likely to help many consumers make effective decisions.

Product and service developments designed to protect certain segments of consumers have also grown out of the way consumers behave. For example, many parents worry that their children may inadvertently put themselves in danger by using the Internet. Methods for protecting children are currently being used, and more methods are being studied. Several laws to implement these protective measures are in effect.[49]

Finally, consumer research on disposition behavior has the potential to affect programs that conserve natural resources. In Exhibit 1.13 we see an ad that attempts to educate consumers about the benefits of recycling.

SUMMARY

The goal of this chapter has been to introduce the topic of consumer behavior. Specifically, we defined consumer behavior, examined the factors that affect consumer behavior, and identified why consumer behavior is an important topic to study.

The term *consumer behavior* is often conceived rather narrowly as the study of the products a person buys. Consumer behavior actually means several things: understanding the set of decisions (what, whether, why, when, how, where, how much, how often) made about the acquisition, use, or disposition of products, services, ideas, or activities by one or more decision-making entities over time.

A consumer's motivation, ability, and opportunity affect his or her decisions. These factors influence what a consumer is exposed to, what he or she pays attention to, and what he or she perceives.

They also affect how a consumer categorizes or interprets information, how he or she forms and changes attitudes, and how he or she forms and retrieves memories. Each aspect of the psychological core has a bearing on consumer decision making. In the decision-making process, the consumer first engages in problem recognition and information search. The consumer then makes judgments based on criteria that he or she has determined are important. Afterward the consumer usually evaluates whether or not he or she is satisfied with the decision that was made. Consumer decisions are affected by the consumer's culture. *Culture* is broadly defined as the myriad groups and social systems to which an individual belongs. These groups share the values and beliefs the individual holds as well as the symbols used to communicate group membership. Consumer behavior can be symbolic and express an individual's identity. Consumer behavior is also indicative of how forcefully or quickly an offering can spread throughout a market.

Knowledge of consumer behavior can provide useful input to marketing strategies such as market segmentation, target market selection, and positioning. This type of knowledge can also guide marketing tactics like product, pricing, distribution, and promotion decisions. In addition, consumer behavior is of interest to ethicists and advocacy groups. Consumer behavior information can be helpful in designing laws and regulations that protect consumers. Finally, the study of consumer behavior can improve consumers' own lives as marketers learn to make products more user-friendly and to show concern for the environment.

EXERCISES

1. Pick a product or service category in which you have some interest. Answer the following questions:

    a. How can this product or service be acquired? (Try to think of more than one way.) What are the implications for marketing strategy?

    b. How is the product or service consumed? How can this information be used to develop marketing strategy?

    c. How can the product or service be disposed of? How might this factor influence the next acquisition?

2. Based on the definition of consumer behavior presented in the first part of the chapter, identify the consumer behavior activities you have engaged in today.

3. How might a study of the way children process advertisements be useful to public policy makers? What kinds of industries might be affected by the study of children? Why?

2

DEVELOPING AND USING INFORMATION ABOUT CONSUMER BEHAVIOR

INTRODUCTION

The automotive industry is a pioneer in the use of consumer research. In large part the industry strives to be customer focused—strengthening customer ties, helping customers make better decisions, and preventing them from switching to different models in the future. Nowhere is the use of research for this purpose more evident than in the marketing of the Mazda Protegé.

Working with a research company called Yankelovich Partners and also undertaking research on its own, Mazda conducted surveys and observational studies of its customers, examining who they were, where they shopped, how they spent their time, and how they drove their cars. The research revealed some critical insights that helped Mazda develop its marketing strategy and tactics for the Protegé (see Exhibit 2.1).

Surveys and observational studies helped Mazda understand the demographics and lifestyles of its current customers. Typical customers were men and women in their 20s who liked to use the Internet. This information was instrumental in helping Mazda develop advertising and sales promotions for the Protegé. In the fall of 1998, for example, Mazda developed a Web site that featured an on-line launch party. Partygoers could take a virtual road trip and make stops along the way to learn more about the car. They could also request product information and

EXHIBIT 2.1
The Protegé

Mazda's consumer research led to a number of decisions about Protegé's features, promotion and price.

Source: Courtesy 1999 Mazda North American Operations. Used by permission.

brochures. By tracking hit rates, or the number of times Internet users visited the site, Mazda learned that its site was very popular, particularly among its target consumers.

An additional survey revealed that 84 percent of consumers in the Protegé's target market described themselves as "risk takers," and 61 percent described themselves as "out of the box" (people who think independently and creatively). This information helped identify a celebrity endorser for the car whose image was consistent with the image of target customers. The celebrity was Jane Krakowski, a 29-year-old actress who stars as an independent and out-of-the-box secretary on the TV show *Ally McBeal.*

Consumer behavior research also helped Mazda develop its product ideas. For example, by watching target customers use their cars, Mazda found that most listen to CDs while driving. Hence Mazda made the CD player standard in the Protegé.

Research also helped Mazda managers make price decisions. Knowing the income and spending habits of its target customers helped Mazda price the Protegé at $12,420 for the DX model and $13,580 for the LX model.[1]

As this example shows, marketing managers often need to collect information about current and prospective consumers. Consumer research is, in fact, fundamental to insights about the marketplace, such as how markets are segmented, what demographic and psychographic characteristics describe consumers within a segment, and whether customers are satisfied with existing offerings. It also guides decisions about the four elements that constitute the *marketing mix:* product, promotion (marketing communications), price, and place (distribution).

Furthermore, consumer research can uncover information relevant to the consumer behavior issues described in Chapter 1. Understanding these issues is essential to developing effective marketing strategies such as target market selection, positioning, and marketing mix tactics. Some consumer research explores consumers' motivation, ability, and opportunity to process information from marketing communications and the media. Other research attempts to uncover whether customers are exposed to, perceive, and pay attention to stimuli in their environment, including ads, TV programs, and products on store shelves. Consumer research may also focus on a firm's image in the minds of consumers or on understanding whether consumers comprehend the marketing communications targeted to them. Marketers often spend considerable time determining whether consumers' attitudes toward a particular offering are positive or negative or how well consumers like and remember a company's advertising. Research that assesses how and where consumers search for information about products and how they make their decisions is also common. Finally, marketers often conduct research to learn whether consumers feel satisfied after they have purchased and used an offering.

Companies also undertake marketing research to learn about the external influences that affect consumers' behavior. As you will see, marketers often conduct research on consumer demographics (age, gender, ethnic background, and so on), lifestyles, reference groups, and the types of symbols consumers use to communicate who they are to others. This information can be very critical to making effective product, marketing communications, pricing, and distribution decisions. Marketers also collect information about consumers' reactions to new products; this information enables marketers to improve the ways in which they introduce future offerings and increase their chances of success.

This chapter is organized as follows. First, we describe the tools marketers use to collect information about consumers. Second, we provide a general overview of the players in the marketing research industry. Third, we show that research about consumers has several purposes: application, protection, and general knowledge. We emphasize application, showing how research helps marketers segment their markets, select a target market, develop a positioning strategy, and develop their marketing mix. Finally, we look into some ethical issues in the conduct of consumer research.

CONSUMER BEHAVIOR RESEARCH METHODS

A number of tools are available in the consumer researcher's "tool kit." Some are based on what consumers say, others on what they do. Some collect data from relatively few people; others compile data from huge samples of consumers. These tools are valuable precisely because they are so different. Each can provide unique insights that, when combined, reveal very different perspectives on the complex world of consumer behavior.

Surveys

survey A written instrument that asks consumers to respond to a predetermined set of research questions.

One research tool with which we are all familiar is the **survey**, a written instrument that asks consumers to respond to a predetermined set of research questions. Some responses may be open-ended, with the consumer filling in the blanks; others may ask consumers to use a rating scale. Surveys can be conducted in person, through the mail, or over the phone. Researchers are increasingly using the Web to collect survey data; this method allows data to be collected very quickly and with minimal expense.[2]

While companies often undertake specialized surveys to better understand a specific customer segment, some research organizations carry out broad-based surveys that are made available to marketers. The U.S. Bureau of the Census is a source of demographic information widely used by marketers. The Census of Population and Housing, taken in 1990 and 2000, asks consumers a range of questions regarding their age, marital status, gender, household size, education, income, child care arrangements, and home ownership. Marketers often find this database quite valuable for learning about population shifts that might affect their offering or the industry in which they operate. The survey itself and the data collected from it is available on-line (www.census.gov), in libraries, or on CD-ROM.

Survey data can also tell marketers something about media usage and product purchase. One company called Simmons Market Research Bureau (SMRB) conducts yearly surveys of consumers' media habits, demographics, and purchase of more than 3,000 products. The survey is also useful because it tells marketers which media their customers use. Exhibit 2.2 shows some of the data found in one of SMRB's summary volumes.[3] This page characterizes the media habits of consumers who are "heavy users" of shopping malls—meaning they have shopped at malls five or more times in the last 4 weeks. The column labeled "B" or "% down" shows which media these consumers use. For example, the % down column for the magazine *Better Homes and Gardens* is 14 percent. This means that among people who very often visit shopping malls, 14 percent read *Better Homes and Gardens*. This data is useful to marketers trying to target mall shoppers, as it tells them that they will reach a comparatively large sample of mall shoppers by advertising in this magazine compared to many others. This particular set of data from Simmons shows retail store patronage. However, Simmons data includes media habits of people who purchase a variety of products and services, such as computers, frozen pizza, and checking accounts, as well as the habits of those who use specific brands, such as Tony's Pizza.

EXHIBIT 2.2

Simmons Data: Media Usage of Consumers Who Are "Heavy Users" of Shopping Malls[1]

Every year, Simmons surveys thousands of people, obtaining purchase information on purchase and media habits.

Source: From Simmons Data: Media Usage of Consumers Who Are "Heavy Users" of Shopping Malls, from Simmons Media Research Bureau 1994. Reprinted with permission.

		A '000	B[2] % DOWN	C % ACROSS	D INDEX
MAGAZINES	American Baby	281	1.3	11.8	102
	American Health	419	2.0	15.8	138
	Architectural Digest	340	1.6	11.6	102
	Audubon	*85	0.4	6.3	55
	Barron's	*228	1.1	15.8	138
	Better Homes and Gardens	2987	14.0	13.6	119
	Bon Appetit	514	2.4	12.2	107
	Bridal Guide	*198	0.9	16.8	147
TV PROGRAMS	Diagnosis Murder	1404	6.6	10.2	90
	Dr. Quinn Medicine Woman	1983	9.3	10.1	88
	Eye to Eye/Connie Chung	1477	6.9	11.7	102
	Family Matters	1530	7.1	11.0	96
	Frasier	2601	12.1	11.8	104
	Fresh Prince of Bel Air	1949	9.1	13.5	118
	48 Hours	1643	7.7	11.8	104
	Full House	1295	6.0	10.4	91
	Grace Under Fire	2442	11.4	13.5	119
	Home Improvement	3119	14.6	12.5	109

[1] A Heavy User is defined as someone who has shopped at shopping malls more than five times over the last four weeks.
[2] Represents the percentage of consumers who are heavy users of shopping malls who are reached using this particular medium.
* These estimates may not be reliable because the sample size is so small.

Focus Groups

focus group A form of in-
depth interview involving 8 to
12 people; a moderator leads
the group and asks participants
to discuss a product, concept,
or other marketing stimulus.

Surveys are often based on input from hundreds of people, who respond to the questionnaire individually. A very different research tool is the focus group. A **focus group** is a marketing research tool in which a group of 6 to 12 consumers are asked to gather to discuss an issue or an offering. Led by a trained moderator, the people in the focus group express their opinions about a given product or topic. Often the researcher does not have prior insights about how the group might feel. Instead, the views held by the group become known only as the discussion unfolds. Unlike surveys, focus groups are often designed to provide qualitative, as opposed to quantitative (numerical), insights into how consumers feel. Focus groups are particularly useful for testing new product ideas.

Although most focus groups are conducted in person, marketers are finding that for some groups of consumers, such as teens, telephone focus groups can yield useful data, particularly when the topic is sensitive or embarrassing. For example, boys who participate in telephone focus groups sometimes admit that they watch educational TV and avoid violent video games. Telephone focus groups also give teens more opportunity to disagree with the group—something that is less likely to happen in a traditional focus group.[4]

Another new trend is the use of computer-based focus groups. Consumers go to a computer lab site where their individual comments are displayed anonymously on a large screen for viewing by the group. Like telephone focus groups, this new method may be very useful for gathering information on sensitive topics. Unfortunately, however, anonymity also prevents researchers from obtaining other information, such as facial expressions and body language, that is relevant and available in a more traditional focus group context.

New market research companies have recently sprung up to conduct focus groups on the Web. In one project for PBS, focus group participants were asked to watch documentaries on PBS and then discuss them on-line. Although these types of focus groups are very economical and relatively easy to conduct, researchers worry that they may not have much control over the size of the group as Web users join or leave the discussion without penalty. Also, stimulating interaction of group members, called "group dynamics," which is so central to traditional focus groups, may be difficult to establish on-line.[5]

Interviews

Like focus groups, interviews involve direct contact with consumers. Interviews are often more appropriate than focus groups when the topic under study is sensitive, embarrassing, confidential, or emotionally charged. They are more appropriate than surveys when the researcher wants to "pick consumers' brains." A researcher who wants to really understand the symbolic significance of a brand to consumers, for example, may ask respondents open-ended questions about their usage of the product; its meaning; their purchase and usage history; and the people, activities, and events they associate with it.

In some interviews customers are asked to report on the process they use to make a purchase decision. One marketing research company provides tape recorders to professional interviewers and has them record consumers' thoughts while they shop for groceries. The data helps marketers understand the factors in the shopping environment that motivate or hinder a purchase. Knowing, for example, that a consumer didn't buy a particular cereal because it was placed too close to the laundry detergent is informative.[6]

Traditional interviews require a trained interviewer who attempts to establish rapport with consumers. Interviewers are often trained to look for nonverbal behaviors like twitches, fidgeting, eye shifting, voice pitch changes, and folded arms and legs as clues to whether the respondent is open to the discussion or whether certain questions are more sensitive than others. Interviews are often recorded and later transcribed so that the answers can be studied through qualitative or quantitative analysis. Sometimes videotapes help capture the nonverbal responses that cannot be captured in the transcription process. Interviews with 30 people may yield more than a thousand pages of transcriptions. Trained researchers then cull through the interviews, attempting to identify patterns or themes. As you can probably see, interviews involve trained people and reams of data. Hence interviewing can be a very expensive data collection method.

Storytelling

storytelling A research method that asks consumers to tell stories about product acquisition, usage, or disposition experiences. These stories help marketers gain insights into consumer needs and identify the product attributes that meet these needs.

A new and fairly provocative tool for conducting consumer research is **storytelling** in which consumers tell researchers stories about their experiences with a product. At Patagonia researchers collect stories from consumers about their backpacking, river rafting, and other outdoor experiences. These stories are used to develop Patagonia's catalogs. In some cases the catalog shows real consumers wearing the clothing they wore on their adventures. The stories not only provide information relevant to the marketing of the product but also convey the impression that Patagonia is in touch with its customers and values what they have to say.[7]

Although the methods mentioned here use real stories of real consumers, sometimes marketers ask consumers to write stories about hypothetical situations that the marketer has depicted in a picture or scenario. The idea is that a consumer's needs, feelings, and perceptions will be revealed by the way he or she interprets what is going on in the picture or scenario. For example, a consumer may be shown a picture of a woman standing in line at a Costco store. Above her head is a bubble. Consumers are asked to write inside the bubble what they think the customer is thinking. These kinds of stories can provide very interesting information about what consumers think of a given store, purchase situation, person, and so on. You will learn more about the use of these techniques in Chapter 3.

Use of Photography and Pictures

One research technique is to show consumers pictures of experiences they have had. This approach helps consumers remember their experiences and hence report on them more completely to the researcher.[8] Another approach asks consumers to draw or collect pictures, either their own photographs or clippings from magazines, that they think best represent their thoughts and feelings about the topic at hand (i.e., What does Ivory soap mean to me?). Still another practice is to ask consumers to put their pictures together in a collage that reflects their lifestyles. Researchers then ask questions about the pictures and the meaning behind them. Having the consumer write an essay can help pull together the images and thoughts suggested by the pictures.[9]

One manufacturer of stockings used this method to try to better understand women's experiences with nylon stockings. Although traditional research methods revealed that women hated wearing stockings, consumers' pictures, coupled with interview results, revealed that stockings made them feel sexy, sensual, and attractive to men. Consequently, new ads have been developed that depict a less "executive" and a more "sexy" view of women in stockings[10] (see Exhibit 2.3).

Seeing Inside The Mind Of Your Customer

To measure customers' true feelings about pantyhose, Du Pont asked women to assemble magazine clips that evoked their emotions about the product. The composite of clips at right, produced at the Harvard business school, was used to improve marketing tactics.

Shopping for stockings can be confusing. This photo suggests the experience should be as easy as picking out fruit from an outdoor stand.

The spilled ice cream symbolizes the disappointment involved in buying an expensive pair of hose, only to have them run again after only two or three wearings.

These secretaries, hunched over their spartan desks, evoke the discomfort and frustration of having to wear stockings at work.

Joan Crawford represents glamour and sensuality. Her choice suggests that women really do like hose because they feel sexy.

EXHIBIT 2.3
Pictures as a Research Tool

Pictures were used to uncover women's attitudes toward stockings. The stories and pictures revealed that women associated stockings with feeling sexy. Other associations are also revealed by these pictures.

Sources: Picture from Seeing the Voice of the Customer Lab, Gerald Zaltman, Olson Zaltman Associates. Article by Ronald B. Lieber, "Storytelling: A New Way to Get Close to Your Customers," *Fortune,* February 3, 1997, pp. 102–110.

Research using pictures can also help marketers understand how consumers think about other consumers and the products they use. For example, consumers may be asked to sort pictures into categories that reflect different types of product users, such as a Mercedes user, a Volvo user, and so on.

Diaries

Sometimes asking consumers to keep diaries provides important insights into their behavior. Marketers have, for example, asked preteens and teenagers to keep diaries of their everyday lives. These documents often reveal how friends and family affect a young person's decisions about clothes, music, fast foods, videos, concerts, and so on.[11] Diaries have also been used to track the shows consumers watch on TV and the products they purchase.

One company called National Purchase Diary (NPD) asks approximately 14,500 consumers to use diaries to track their purchases in about 50 product categories. Companies that buy this data from NPD can use it to learn whether consumers are brand loyal or brand switchers and whether they are heavy or light users of the product category. By linking this data with demographic data, marketers can also learn more about who these consumers are.

Experiments

Consumer researchers also conduct experiments to determine whether some marketing phenomenon affects consumer behavior. For example, an experiment can be designed to find out whether consumers' attitudes toward a brand are affected by the brand name, as opposed to other factors such as product features, package, color, logo, room temperature, or the consumer's mood.

With experiments, consumers are randomly assigned to receive different "treatments" and the effect of these treatments is observed. For example, consumers might be assigned to groups that are shown different brand names. Participants' attitudes toward the name are then collected and compared across groups. In a taste-test experiment, consumers might be randomly assigned to groups, one of which is asked to taste one product while another is asked to taste a different one. An important aspect of experiments like this is that groups are designed to be identical in all respects except the treatment, called the **variable**. Thus, in a taste-test experiment, only the taste of the food or beverage is varied. Everything else is the same across groups—consumers eat or drink the same amount of the product, at the same temperature, from the same kind of container, in the same room, in the presence of the same experimenter, and so on. After consumers taste and rate the product, researchers can compare the groups' responses to see which taste is preferred.

Experiments can also be useful in determining what catches consumers' attention and affects their purchase decisions. One researcher has designed a virtual shopping environment in which consumers use a computer to "walk down" store aisles, "pick up" products, and "put" them in their shopping baskets (or not). Consumers can be assigned to different groups for which package colors, space arrangements, layouts, and product features are varied. By comparing how attention and behavior differ across different store conditions, the experimenters can determine what makes a retail environment most effective.[12]

Experiments are sometimes used in advertising to determine whether ads are effective. Consumers might, for example, be exposed to different test ads. By measuring emotional arousal, salivation levels, and eye movements of participants, marketers may determine which ads are most arousing and attention getting.

Field Experiments

Although experiments are often conducted in controlled laboratory situations, sometimes marketers are interested in conducting experiments in the real world. These experiments are called "field experiments." One common type of field experiment is a **market test**. This kind of experiment provides marketers with information about whether a product is likely to sell in a market and which potential marketing-mix elements will enhance its sales. As an example, let's say a new product is being introduced and marketers are interested in how much advertising support they should give it. One way to answer this question is to conduct a market test. Two test markets, similar to each other in factors like size and demographic composition, are selected. One market receives one level of ad spending while the other receives a different level. By observing sales of the product across the two markets over a certain time period, researchers can identify which level of advertising expenditure is most effective at enhancing sales.

Observations

Researchers sometimes observe consumers to gain insight into potentially effective product, promotion, price, and distribution decisions. At the Fisher-Price

variable The entity that is studied or that varies in a research project. In a study on how humor in ads influences attitudes toward a brand, one variable might be the level of humor in the ads.

market test A study in which the effectiveness of one or more elements of the marketing mix are examined by evaluating sales of the product in an actual market (e.g., a specific city).

EXHIBIT 2.4
Hello Kids

At the Fisher-Price Playlab, researchers observe children's reactions to determine whether they
like Fisher-Price toys.

Source: Nicolas Reynard/Liaison

Playlab (see Exhibit 2.4), researchers observe children's reactions to toys. At the
Gerber lab, scientists observe babies' reactions to Gerber food. After observing
babies' reactions, Gerber has made such product changes as taking oregano out of
its Italian Spaghetti baby food product and changing the texture of its beef stew.
Gerber also conducts research worldwide, observing how mothers feed their babies. This knowledge helps the company understand what products might appeal
to foreign customers. Observing Japanese consumers' feeding practices, for example, led to the development of freeze-dried Sardines and Rice baby food.[13]

Intuit, the maker of the financial software package Quicken, goes into consumers' homes and watches them use Quicken. By observing the problems they
are having, Quicken learns how it can develop a better product. Intuit also studies
non-Quicken users in their homes, noting how they track and manage their finances. These observations also help in the development of new product features
that might convert nonusers to users.[14]

Purchase Panels

Although the research we've described so far studies individual consumers, sometimes research is conducted electronically on the behaviors of large numbers of respondents. This kind of research simply records whether a behavior occurred; for
instance, did a consumer buy Heinz or not? Sometimes this behavioral data is collected from special panel members, consumers chosen to be representative of the
general population or the marketer's target market. Every time these panel members
go shopping, their purchases are recorded at the cash register. By merging this data
with demographic data about the panel members, marketers can tell who is purchasing a product, whether those consumers are also buying competitors' products, and
whether the purchase was motivated by the use of a coupon. Marketers can also use
this data to determine whether the shelf space allocated to the product, or the existence of added advertising in the test area, affected sales of the product among panel
members. Companies like BehaviorScan and IRI collect data of this sort.

Database Marketing

Recently, marketers have attempted to combine different forms of consumer research into a common database. For example, a common database might contain

information collected from target consumers about their demographics and lifestyles. That data may be combined with information about their purchases in various product categories over time, their media habits, and their usage of coupons and other promotional devices.

Harrah's Entertainment has been developing one of the gambling industry's more comprehensive consumer databases. Information compiled from banking reports, credit card records, and data about casino usage is collected into a database, which then provides information such as the meals consumers ate at Harrah's restaurants, the items consumers purchased at Harrah's gift stores, how much consumers spent on gambling, whether they gambled at competitor locations, the size of their mortgages, and how much they are likely to spend on gambling the next time they visit one of Harrah's casinos. Harrah's uses this information to target customers with communications and packaged vacation offers that are specifically geared to their lifestyles and spending patterns.[15] Although one might question whether the collection of such data invades consumers' privacy and perpetuates a consumer behavior that has potentially dysfunctional consequences (issues we discuss in Chapter 21, titled "The Dark Side of Consumer Behavior and Marketing"), Harrah's use of databases clearly illustrates the database marketing concept.

A recent move is the development of marketing databases geared to electronic retailing. The development of these databases may allow marketers to send consumers e-mail messages and electronic pictures of products they might find appealing.[16]

TYPES OF CONSUMER RESEARCHERS

Many types of entities that study consumer behavior utilize market research tools. Indeed, Exhibit 2.5 shows the many types of organizations that collect consumer research and the different motivations they have for conducting consumer research.

EXHIBIT 2.5
Who Conducts Consumer Research?

www.

A number of different organizations conduct research on consumers, though they differ in their objectives. Some do research for application, some for consumer protection, others to obtain general knowledge about consumers.

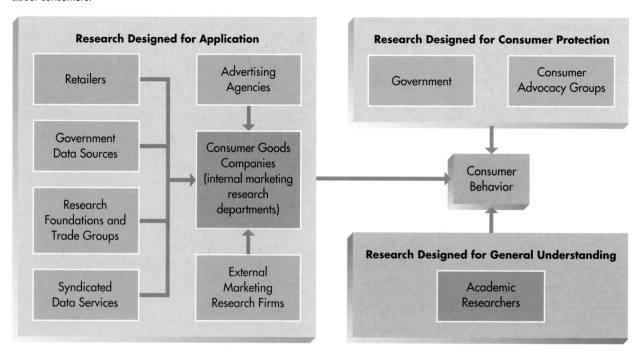

Research Designed for Application

Retailers

Government Data Sources

Research Foundations and Trade Groups

Syndicated Data Services

Advertising Agencies

Consumer Goods Companies (internal marketing research departments)

External Marketing Research Firms

Research Designed for Consumer Protection

Government

Consumer Advocacy Groups

Consumer Behavior

Research Designed for General Understanding

Academic Researchers

On the one hand, some organizations, such as consumer goods and service companies, ad agencies, and marketing research firms, conduct research for application purposes. They use this information to make decisions about the marketing of a specific product or service. On the other hand, government organizations and academics conduct research so as to protect consumers or simply to understand why and how consumers behave as they do.

In-house Marketing Research Departments

Research for market application can be conducted through a company's own internal marketing research department. The benefits of conducting "in-house" research are that the information collected can be kept within the company and that opportunities for information to leak to competitors are minimized. However, internal departments are sometimes viewed as less objective than outside research firms since they may have a vested interest in how the research comes out. For example, people within the company may be motivated to show that the company is making good decisions, and this motivation may unwittingly bias the nature of their research or the outcomes they report. Consequently, some companies decide to use outside research companies to gather their consumer research.

External Marketing Research Firms

External research firms often help design a specific research project before it begins. They develop measuring instruments to measure consumer responses, collect data from consumers, analyze the data, and develop reports for their clients.

Some marketing research firms are "full service" organizations that perform a variety of marketing research services. Others specialize in one or more types of research. Some develop their own "products," which gives them a differential advantage in the market. For example, one company named Roper Starch Worldwide has (among other products) a product called STARCH scores. Panels of approximately 200 readers of a specific magazine go through a magazine issue with a trained interviewer who asks them whether they have seen each ad in the issue. The respondents are also asked whether they saw the picture in the ad, read the headline, read all or some of the body copy, and saw the slogan for the ad. The percentage of respondents who have seen each part of each ad is compiled into a report. An advertiser can buy the report to find out whether its ad is seen more and read more than other ads in the issue or other ads in the product category. Ads that receive low STARCH scores may be viewed as ineffective and be redesigned. An example of an ad for which STARCH scores have been tabulated is shown in Exhibit 2.6.

Advertising Agencies

Some advertising agencies have their own in-house research departments. As part of the service they provide to their clients, these agencies may conduct research to test concepts for advertising. They may also conduct advertising pretesting, using drawings of ads or finished ads, to make sure that an ad is fulfilling its objectives *before* it is placed in the media. Ad agencies also conduct tracking studies, monitoring the effectiveness of advertising over time. For example, tracking studies can determine whether the percentage of target market consumers who are aware of a brand has changed as a function of the amount, duration, and timing of its advertising.

EXHIBIT 2.6
A "Starched" Ad

Companies like Starch collect data on what consumers remembered, if anything, from an ad. The percentages noted on the stickers placed at the top of the ad indicate the percentage of respondents sampled who remembered having seen or read various parts of the ad.

Source: Reprinted courtesy of Seiko Corporation of America and Roper Starch Worldwide, Inc.

Syndicated Data Services

Syndicated data services are companies that collect and then sell the information they collect, usually to firms that market products and services to consumers. For example, one company called Yankelovich Partners collects data on consumer lifestyles and social trends in 2$\frac{1}{2}$-hour interviews at the homes of approximately 2,500 adults. Its reports describe current and projected lifestyle trends. Advertising agencies may buy these reports and use them to develop creative content for advertising.

Nielsen is a syndicated data service that tracks TV viewing. Approximately 1,200 households are equipped with an electronic device called an audimeter that sits on their TV and records which TV shows are seen and for how long. The data from the audimeter can be supplemented with diaries that consumers fill in to show who within the household is watching each show. Nielsen provides a rating that indicates the number and percentage of all households watching a particular TV program. By combining demographic and TV viewing behavior, Nielsen can also examine who is watching which shows. Networks, cable stations, and independent channels use this information to determine whether TV shows should be renewed and how much the stations can charge for advertising time on a particular show. The more popular the show (the higher its rating), the higher the advertising fee. Advertisers who buy Nielsen data can assess which TV shows they should advertise in, based on the match between the demographic characteristics of viewers and the demographic characteristics of the sponsor's target market.

Retailers

Large retail chains often conduct consumer research. By using electronic scanners to track sales of a brand or product category, they can determine which are their best- and worst-selling items. This data can also be used to examine the relationship between sales of an item and the item's location in the store. Retailers can also use this data to see how responsive consumers are to different types of promotions such as coupons or discounts. Because retail salespeople often interact directly with customers, studies sometimes assess customer satisfaction and identify areas in which service quality can be improved.

Research Foundations/Trade Groups

research foundation A nonprofit organization that sponsors research on topics relevant to the foundation's goals.

Research foundations and trade groups also collect consumer research. A **research foundation** is a nonprofit organization that sponsors research on topics relevant to the foundation's goals. As an example, the Advertising Research Foundation is a nonprofit association designed to improve the practice of advertising, marketing, and media research. The organization sponsors conferences related to the conduct of research in these areas and publishes reports on current research issues and trends. It also publishes the *Journal of Advertising Research*, which reports advertising research findings from academics and practitioners.[17] The Marketing Science Institute is another nonprofit organization that sponsors consumer and marketing research projects conducted by academics, that have relevance to marketing researchers in companies.

Specialized trade groups may also collect consumer research to better understand the needs of consumers in their own industries. A **trade group** is an organization formed by people who work in the same industry, such as the Recording Industry Association of America whose members all have something to do with the recorded music industry. The association membership includes retailers who sell recorded music, marketers from the record labels who develop artists and sign contracts, and distributors who sell recorded music from the label to the retailer. This organization has sponsored a host of research projects, including those that attempt to understand how American music tastes have changed over the past 20 years.

Although many of the organizations noted here collect consumer research for the purposes of marketing an offering, we show below that other organizations conduct consumer research for a different purpose.

trade group A professional organization made up of marketers in the same industry.

Government

Government research such as the census is often used by marketers to estimate the size of various demographic markets. But other government data gathering is designed for another purpose—to protect consumers. The Federal Trade Commission (FTC), for example, conducts research on the potentially deceptive, misleading, or fraudulent nature of certain brands' advertising.

Several years ago the FTC filed a case against Kraft, arguing that consumers might have been misled by ads claiming that one slice of its cheese was made from 5 ounces of milk. The FTC worried that consumers might infer that the cheese had as much calcium as 5 ounces of milk (which it did not) or that Kraft cheese was superior to its competitors in terms of calcium content (which it was not). The FTC conducted research with consumers to assess the existence and severity of these inferences.[18]

The Consumer Products Safety Commission is a federal regulatory agency that protects consumers against injury and death associated with consumer products. It has jurisdiction over some 15,000 consumer products. The Department of Transportation protects consumers from problems with cars, trucks, and motorcycles. The Food and Drug Administration protects consumers from impurities and contamination in foods, drugs, and cosmetics. Each organization conducts research on product features and can set standards related to the safety of products or recall them. A few products recalled by the Consumer Product Safety Commission are listed in Exhibit 2.7. Each organization also plays a role in educating consumers about product safety problems.

Consumer Organizations

Independent consumer organizations also conduct research, often for the purpose of protecting or informing consumers. Consumers Union is an independent, nonprofit testing and information organization designed to serve consumers. This organization publishes the well-known *Consumer Reports* magazine. Many of the products described in *Consumer Reports* are tested in Consumers Union's

EXHIBIT 2.7
Product Recalls

Research on products and how consumers use them can sometimes reveal safety hazards. The Consumer Product Safety Commission conducts research on product safety and has the authority to recall products deemed unsafe. This list includes some of the products recalled during 1998.

Source: Neal Lorenzi, "Consumer Product Safety Commission Product Recalls," *Professional Safety,* 43 (November), p. 12 and (September), p. 9.

COMPANY	PRODUCT	POSSIBLE PROBLEM	NUMBER RECALLED
Ohio Art Little Tykes Today's Kids Fisher-Price	Nets on toy basketball sets	Children could strangle on loops or openings in nets to come unhooked from rim	10.1 million
Brass Eagle Inc.	Paint-ball masks	Existing lens on mask can crack when struck by paint ball, posing an eye injury hazard	42,300
Pyramid Accessories	Children's backpacks and rolling luggage auxiliary units	Both products contain high levels of lead	3,700 backpacks 1,800 luggage units
Tara Toy Corp	Flying Warrior dolls	Wings can break off, causing eye and other injury	670,000
First Choice Products Inc.	Power strip surge protectors	Undersized, cracked, or corroded wiring and misaligned plugs which present fire, shock, and electrocution hazards	194,200
Payless ShoeSource Inc.	Children's sneakers	Metal clasps on zippers can break off easily, causing a choking hazard	80,000
Ekco Housewares	Cooking skillets	Handles can break or bend easily, causing hot contents to spill	16,800
Rite Aid Corp.	Butane lighters	Defective on/off switches can ignite in the off position and stay lit	225,000

independent product-testing lab. You can learn more about the research conducted by Consumers Union and the books and monographs it publishes by visiting its Web site (http://www.consumersunion.org).

Academics and Academic Research Centers

Finally, consumer research is conducted by academics. Although academic research involving consumers can be used for application purposes and may have implications for public policy, it is often designed simply to enhance our general understanding of why consumers behave as they do. Indeed, much of the research we report in this book describes state-of-the-art research conducted by academics on the behavior of consumers.

Academics sometimes develop research centers that focus on a specific area of consumer behavior. Georgia State University, for example, has a center for the study of mature consumers. SUNY Albany has a center for the study of social and demographic analysis, and the University of Michigan has a center for the study of consumer satisfaction. The University of Texas at Austin has a center called the Center for Consumer Insight.

PRIMARY VERSUS SECONDARY DATA

primary data Data originating from a researcher and collected to provide information relevant to a specific research project.

The research groups we have described vary in the extent to which they use primary or secondary data. Data that one entity collects for its own purpose is called **primary data**. When marketers use surveys, focus groups, experiments, and the like to collect consumer research for developing their own marketing strategies and tactics, they are collecting primary data. When the government conducts research to determine whether consumers are inferring things from ads that are not true of the advertised product, the government is engaging in primary research.

secondary data Data collected for some other purpose that is subsequently used in a research project.

Data collected by one entity for one purpose and subsequently used by another entity for a different purpose is called **secondary data**. When marketers use census data gathered by the government for, say, tax purposes, in order to estimate the size of various markets in their own industry, they are using secondary data. The government is a big provider of secondary data. Likewise, when companies use research reports of syndicated data services or reports developed by trade associations or research centers to develop marketing ideas, they are using secondary data.

MARKETING IMPLICATIONS OF CONSUMER BEHAVIOR

Because this textbook focuses primarily on providing a useful summary of consumer behavior information for students of marketing, the following section highlights the marketing implications of consumer behavior. Throughout the text, starting with Chapter 3, you will find numerous sections titled "Marketing Implications," which illustrate how various consumer behavior concepts are applied to the practice of marketing.

Consumer research helps marketers develop product-specific plans as well as broader marketing strategies. These broader strategies determine, for instance, how the firm might approach its market segmentation, targeting, and positioning decision, as well as how it can make decisions about product, promotion (marketing communications), price, and place (distribution)—traditionally known as the four P's.

Developing a Customer-Oriented Strategy

Early in the 20th century, marketing efforts revolved around a production-oriented philosophy, with activities focused on the efficient production of the product. Later, emphasis shifted to selling and to developing tactics that would move the most units of the product. The prevailing view today, in contrast to both these earlier eras, is that marketing activities are designed *to fulfill consumer needs*. This consumer-oriented, market-driven approach automatically makes consumer research pivotal within the company. In other words, if a firm is to develop offerings that accurately meet customers' needs, its marketers must do considerable

Road Warriors:
Generally higher-income, middle-aged men who drive 25,000-50,000 miles a year... buy premium gas with a credit card...purchase sandwiches and drinks from the convenience store...will sometimes wash their cars at the carwash.

Price Shoppers:
Generally aren't loyal to either a brand or a particular station, and rarely buy the premium line of gas...frequently on tight budgets...efforts to woo them have been the basis of marketing strategies for years.

True Blues:
Usually men and women with moderate to high incomes who are loyal to a brand and sometimes to a particular station ...frequently buy premium gasoline and pay in cash.

Generation F3 (for fuel, food and fast):
Upwardly mobile men and women — half under 25 years of age — who are constantly on the go...drive a lot and snack heavily from the convenience store.

Homebodies:
Usually housewives who shuttle their children around during the day and use whatever gasoline station is based in town or along their route of travel.

16% 16% 27% 20% 21%

EXHIBIT 2.8
Mobil's Segmentation Study

By understanding consumer behavior, marketers may discover different segments with different needs. Mobil found that the needs of the Road Warrior, True Blue, and Generation F3 segments were not being met. Their marketing activities therefore focused on capturing those segments.

Source: Data from Allanna Sullivan, "Mobil Bets Drivers Pick Cappuccino over Low Prices," *Wall Street Journal,* January 30, 1995, pp. B1, B4.

research to describe the various segments or groups of consumers in its market, all of which may have different needs. This consumer orientation guides research practices in each of the strategic and tactical decisions described below.

How Is the Market Segmented?   All consumers in a market are unlikely to have the same needs and wants. For example, Mobil Oil found that patrons of gas stations belong to one of the five segments noted in Exhibit 2.8. By understanding what these segments are and finding out how well existing companies tapped the needs of each, Mobil identified the segments it would find most profitable. One study has attempted to identify segments of customers around the world. This research concluded that four types of consumers could be identified: deal makers, price seekers, brand loyalists, and luxury innovators.[19]

How Profitable Is Each Segment?   Knowing the size of a market segment can be important, because marketers can profit substantially by concentrating on large segments that competitors have not similarly targeted For example, marketers have found that the biggest users of the prepaid calling card are immigrants and consumers who do not have residential phone service.[20]

Consumer research can also help marketers identify underserved segments—consumers who have clearly identifiable needs that are not being met. For example, demographic research has shown that more than 80 percent of consumers are over age 45. To appeal to younger and underserved segments, marketers of classical music are adding popular performers to its lineup, while others are offering free passes to college students.[21] Marketing research also helped identify consumers' needs for hybrid cars—cars that combine sport-utility pickups and light-duty pickups with four carlike doors.[22] As another example, gay men and women are being targeted by more and more marketers who have traditionally ignored them.[23]

What Are the Characteristics of Consumers in Each Segment?   After determining how the market is segmented and whether it is potentially profitable, marketers often wish to learn about the characteristics of consumers in each segment. This information is critical to future marketing decision making because it helps marketers project whether the segment is likely to grow or to shrink over time. For example, condominium marketers project large increases in sales in 10 to 20 years as baby boomers enter retirement. Understanding each segment's demographics, values, and lifestyles, how they are influenced, and how they make their decisions also provides valuable information about how consumers in each segment can be reached and persuaded. The Mobil study revealed that consumers in the Homebody segment were women with small children. The lifestyle of these women, who place a high value on their kids, is characterized by considerable shuttling of kids to school and afterschool events. The women's decisions about where to buy gas are largely driven by whether the station is along their route and whether it offers full service. You can understand how this information helps the firm reach and persuade customers in this segment.

Are Customers Satisfied with Existing Offerings?   Marketers often do considerable research to determine whether consumers are currently satisfied with the company's offering. Based on its market segmentation study and its understanding of customers in each segment, Mobil concluded that Road Warriors and True Blues wanted better snacks from the convenience stores, fast and personal service, and special treatment. Generation F3s wanted *food* and *fuel*, and they wanted it *fast* (hence the term *F3*).[24] Reebok International has identified a unique way of conducting "research" on customers' satisfaction with their running shoes: It sponsors a 100-mile running race in Colorado to test its products. Entrants are given free Reebok shoes and are asked to participate in a 30-hour run designed to uncover design glitches in the shoes. This intensive usage allows marketers to find problems that would otherwise not be evident until months after consumers had purchased the brand.[25]

Selecting the Target Market

Understanding consumer behavior also helps marketers determine who might represent the most viable targets for marketing tactics. In China, for example, numerous marketers are targeting children. The reason is that the government's "one child per family" regulation means that parents, grandparents, and aunts, and uncles have fewer children to indulge. Consequently, China's children, known as "Little Emperors," are being doted on.[26]

Knowledge of consumer behavior also helps marketers identify the individuals most likely to be involved in acquisition, usage, and disposition decisions. To illustrate, condom marketers currently see tremendous growth in the purchase of condoms by women. Although women do not actually use (wear) traditional condoms, they often buy them. Moreover, women are very influential in men's use of condoms. Recognizing these gender effects, more marketers are explicitly targeting women.[27] Automobile marketers are also recognizing the influence of women (and children) in the car-buying process. Although auto companies have traditionally ignored women, these marketers now acknowledge that women play key roles in searching for information, influencing the decision, financing the car, using it, and disposing of it.[28]

Positioning

An important strategic choice determines how an offering should be positioned in consumers' minds. In other words, marketers need to decide on their offering's desired image. Ideally this image both reflects what the product is and indicates how it is different from the competition. Slogans like BMW's "The Ultimate Driving Machine," United's "Fly the Friendly Skies," and UPS's "Moving at the Speed of Business" reflect the image these companies would like consumers to have of their products and services.

How Are Competitive Offerings Positioned?   Consumer research can often provide very valuable insight to marketers about how consumers perceive and categorize different brands in the marketplace. In turn, this information gives marketers some interesting perspectives on how their offering should be positioned. Indeed marketers sometimes conduct research to see how consumers view other companies' brands in comparison with their own. This information can be plotted into a graph called a "perceptual map." The map in Exhibit 2.9 shows how consumers perceive various music retailers. Those in the same quadrant of the map are perceived to offer similar benefits to consumers. Hence the closer various companies are to one another, the more likely they are to be competitors.

How Should Our Offerings Be Positioned?   Consumer research is also useful in helping a company understand what image a new offering should have in the eyes of consumers. In the early 1980s, Darden Restaurants conducted field research and focus groups and identified statistics on consumer lifestyle and demographic trends. Focus groups were also used to determine what consumers thought of Italian restaurants. The purpose of this research was to investigate the possibility of a national chain of Italian restaurants and to determine what kind of image would be most successful in the minds of customers. Through this analysis, the company realized that consumers wanted a "warm and homey place that served lots of food in a casual environment." Darden subsequently introduced a new restaurant—now known as the Olive Garden—with this positioning in mind.[29]

reposition To give a brand or company a new and/or different image from the image it had before.

Should Our Offerings Be Repositioned?   Consumer research also helps marketers **reposition** existing products (i.e., change their image). In Germany, 4711 eau de cologne had been a staple item among Germany's older consumers. The brand, developed 200 years ago as a remedy for headaches and irregular heartbeats, rose during the 1900s to become a venerated eau de cologne. However, its consumer base had given it the image of an old, low-value brand designed for German grannies. When consumers were asked what product they thought was evocative of 4711, many mentioned holy water.

When Wella purchased the company that made 4711, the new owners tried to reposition the product—changing its image to that of a fresh brand for young

EXHIBIT 2.9

Consumer Perceptions of Brands in a Market

A perceptual map plots consumers' perception of how various brands stand in relation to one another. These perceptual maps plot consumers' perceptions of how various music stores compare with one another. The top map compares the stores on variety and service. The bottom compares them on family friendliness and environment.

Source: Class project for Professor Debbie MacInnis, University of Southern California, by Alexander Moreno, Robert Frahm, Daniel McGill, and Jillian Weinstein, April 1998. Reprinted with permission.

(a) Perceptual Map Comparing Variety and Service

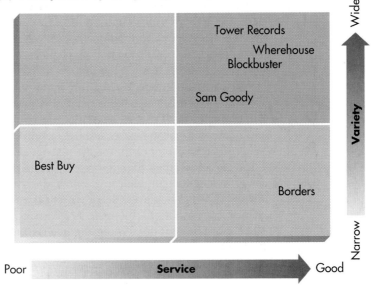

(b) Perceptual Map Comparing Environment and Family-Friendliness

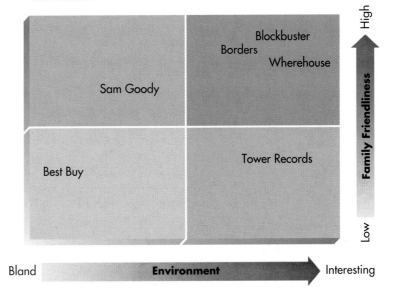

people. To achieve this positioning, Wella used what it described as "loud, pungent, and aggressive" advertising. Ads appearing in such publications as *Rolling Stone*, *Sport*, and *US* showed a person using 4711 and claiming, "It feels Unreal."[30]

Developing Products or Services

Developing products and services that satisfy consumers' wants and needs is a critical marketing activity. Consumer research can provide useful information about several product decisions.

What Ideas Do Consumers Have for New Products? First, marketers need to design an offering that contains the benefits target consumers desire. One company, using focus groups, uncovered a new product idea from mothers who complained that their children didn't want to use soap. The product was a bar of soap with a plastic toy inside. The more children wash, the more they can see the toy.[31]

What Attributes Can Be Added to or Changed in an Existing Offering?

Consumer research also helps marketers know when products must be modified or tailored to meet the needs of new or existing groups of consumers. For example, consumer research revealed that Japanese consumers prefer less lather in skin care products, prompting Amway to produce a low-lather product. Research that asked kids about their ideas for new bikes helped a major bicycle manufacturer develop new color combinations and redesign frames for boys and girls. It also helped the manufacturer identify new bike accessories.[32] In response to its segmentation research, Mobil made its facilities cleaner and encouraged its attendants to be more helpful in meeting the needs of the Road Warriors, True Blues, and Generation F3 consumers. One station even had attendants run to the station's convenience store to buy drinks for motorists.[33]

What Should Our Offering Be Called? Goodyear used considerable research from consumers to name its tires. The name Eagle Aquatech EMT (for extended mobility technology) was chosen for a tire that when flat can go for 50 miles at 55mph on wet surfaces.[34] Brand names like Obsession and Jolly Green Giant are used because consumer research suggested that these names would be liked, easy to remember, and suggestive of the brand's benefits.

What Should Our Package and Logo Look Like? Consumers are likely to think that food (including cookies) is good for them if it comes in green packaging.[35] This information is valuable in the design of packages with a "healthy" positioning.

The development of logos can also benefit from consumer research, which was essential to the development of the Oppenheimer Funds symbol shown in Exhibit 2.10. The four interconnected hands conveyed images of strength, unity, security, and responsible management—associations that were directly consistent with the desired image of the company.[36]

What About Guarantees? In response to consumer research, the cable industry is now using guarantees to enhance its image and reduce consumer complaints. The guarantees give consumers a free month of service if service calls and installations are not performed when they are scheduled.[37]

Making Promotion (Marketing Communications) Decisions

Marketing decisions are also made about a variety of promotional/marketing communications tools, such as advertising, sales promotions (premiums, contests, sweepstakes, free samples, coupons, and rebates), personal selling, and public relations.

What Are Our Advertising Objectives? Consumer research can be very useful in determining what objectives should guide the development of advertising. It may reveal, for example, that very few people have heard of a new brand, suggesting that the primary advertising objective should be to enhance brand-

EXHIBIT 2.10
Helping Hands

Research helped determine that the associations linked to the Oppenheimer Funds, symbol were consistent with the image the company wanted to convey about itself. What associations do you link with Oppenheimer Funds based on this symbol?

Source: Courtesy of Oppenheimer-Funds, September 1999.

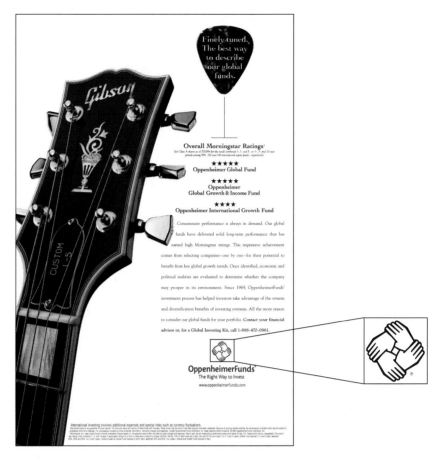

name awareness. Other research may suggest that consumers have heard of the brand but don't know anything about it. In this case the advertising objective should be to enhance brand knowledge. If research reveals that consumers know the brand name but don't really know the characteristics of the brand that make it desirable, the objectives for advertising should be to enhance brand knowledge and brand attitudes.

What Should Our Advertising Look Like?   If a marketer is interested in establishing brand-name awareness, research by academics on how memory can be enhanced might prove relevant and useful in the design of advertising. For example, a brand name is better remembered when the ad in which it is placed contains interesting and unusual visuals that relate to it. If the visuals are interesting but unrelated, consumers may remember the visuals but forget the name.

Consumer research can also help marketers understand which visuals should accompany ad copy. Recent consumer research has shown not only that a car with "power" is desirable to both men and women but also that the word *power* means different things to different people. Men associate power with excitement, whereas women associate it with being able to maneuver quickly and safely out of tight or dangerous situations.[38] This information suggests the use of clearly distinct visuals and associated copy depending on whether the ad is designed to appeal to men or women. Knowledge of how people understand various words can also be gleaned from research. For example, saying a product is a good "value for the money" does not work in Spain. Instead, marketers use the phrase "price for product."[39]

Where Should Advertising Be Placed?   Demographic and lifestyle data and data from companies like Nielsen and Simmons provides very useful information about the specific media vehicles in which advertising should be placed. Simmons data, for example, provides specific insight into the percentage of a target market that is reached by a particular medium (refer to Exhibit 2.2).

When Should We Advertise?   Research may reveal seasonal variations in purchases due to weather-related needs, variations in the amount of discretionary money consumers have (which changes, for instance, before and after Christmas), holiday buying patterns, and the like. These variations bear directly on the timing of advertising.

Has Our Advertising Been Effective?   Finally, advertisers can conduct studies to determine whether advertising has been effective. This research can be conducted at various times in the advertising development process. Sometimes marketers or ad agencies conduct research called advertising *copy testing* or *pretesting*, which tests ads for their effectiveness before they are placed in the media. If the advertising objective is brand-name awareness and a new ad does not enhance awareness, the ad may be thrown out and a new one developed.

Effectiveness research can also be conducted after the ads have been placed in the media. The STARCH scores described earlier in the chapter are one way of assessing the effectiveness of ads with brand-name awareness objectives. Advertisers sometimes conduct tracking studies to examine changes in the achievement of advertising objectives over time.

What About Sales Promotion Objectives and Tactics?   Research to develop advertising objectives can also point to sales promotion objectives and help identify various tactics that might achieve them. A racetrack outside Los Angeles is using a database to develop its sales promotion objectives and tactics. By tracking attendance, the database revealed that the company needed to focus on getting customers to come to the racetrack more often. To achieve this objective, the track created a Thoroughbred Club and issued members a card that entitled them to reduced admission. Furthermore, every time these customers came to the track, their admission price became lower.[40]

When Should Sales Promotions Happen?   Consumer research can also help in the timing of sales promotions. The racetrack managers, for example, can use their marketing database to determine when sales have been slowest and hence when sales promotions tactics might be most important in drawing in customers.

Have Our Sales Promotions Been Effective?   Consumer research can answer this question. Seeing how many consumers use the Thoroughbred Club card and evaluating how much they receive in discounts helps marketers know whether the card is effective in enhancing attendance.

How Many Salespeople Are Needed to Serve Customers?   By tracking store patronage at different times of the day or different days of the week, retailers can determine the appropriate number of store personnel needed to best serve customers.

How Can Salespeople Best Serve Customers?   Finally, research can be quite informative in helping managers in selecting salespeople and affecting how they serve customers. For example, although there is some debate about it, one general finding suggests that the more similar the salesperson is to the customer, the more effective he or she will be.[41] Research has shown that salespeople can better serve customers when the salespeople are in a good mood.[42] This information implies that managers should devise tactics to enhance the moods of their sales personnel.

Making Pricing Decisions

The price of a product or service can have a critical influence on consumers' acquisition decisions. It is therefore very important for marketers to understand how consumers react to price and to use this information in their pricing decisions.

What Price Should Be Charged?   Have you ever wondered why prices often end in 99? Consumer research has shown that people perceive $.99 or $9.99 or $99.99 to be cheaper than $1.00, $10.00, or $100.00. Perhaps this is one reason why so many prices end in the number 9.[43]

Although simple economic theory would suggest that a decrease in price will increase the likelihood of purchase, consumer research shows this theory isn't always so. A price that is too low may make consumers' suspicious of the product's quality, since higher price generally means higher quality.[44] Consumer research has also shown other ways in which consumers' reactions to price are complicated. For example, if a company gives catalog customers the chance to save $8 on shipping charges, they will spend $15 or more on catalog purchases. This finding has caused some catalog marketers to absorb shipping fees.[45]

How Sensitive Are Consumers to Price and Price Changes?   Consumer research also shows variations on the importance consumers place on price. In some cases consumers are very price sensitive, meaning that a small change in price will cause a large effect on consumers' willingness to purchase the product. In other cases consumers are price insensitive. They are likely to buy the offering no matter what the price is. Research helps to determine which consumers are likely to be price sensitive and when. For fashion or prestige goods in particular, a high price symbolizes status. Thus some consumers, particularly those seeking status, may be less sensitive to the price of a product and pay more than $50 for a simple T-shirt that carries a prestigious manufacturer's label.

When Should Certain Price Tactics Be Used?   Research on consumer behavior also helps us understand when consumers are likely to be most responsive to various pricing tactics. Historical data, for example, shows that consumers are very responsive to price cuts on linens and sheets during January. These "white sales" are effective because consumers have come to anticipate them and are unlikely to buy these products after Christmas without a financial incentive to do so.

Making Distribution Decisions

Another important marketing decision involves the manner in which products or services are distributed.

Where Are Target Consumers Likely to Shop?   Marketers who understand the value consumers place on time and convenience have developed distribution channels that allow consumers to acquire or use goods and services whenever it is most convenient for them. The advent of 24-hour grocery stores and health clubs and catalog ordering systems are examples of marketers' attempts to develop distribution channels that give consumers flexibility in the timing of their acquisition, usage, and disposition decisions. Another is the multitude of places that consumers can shop for cars. We can now acquire cars through the Internet, auto brokers, warehouse clubs, giant auto malls, used-car superstores, and traditional auto dealers.

How Should Stores Be Designed?   Supermarkets are often designed so that similar or complementary items are stocked near one another because consumer research shows that customers think about items in terms of categories based on similar characteristics or use. Thus diapers are found near toilet paper because they have some similar physical similarities. Peanut butter is found near jelly because they are often used together.

Consumer research can also help marketers develop other aspects of their retail environments. Research has shown that bright colors and loud, up-tempo music make consumers move quickly through the store. Softer, subdued colors and gentler music have the opposite effect.[46] Stores can also be designed in such a way that truly conveys the image marketers wish them to have. As Exhibit 2.11 indicates, Restoration Hardware's store design and atmospherics go a long way toward conveying its upscale image.

ETHICAL ISSUES IN CONSUMER RESEARCH

Consumer research is a huge field, essential to the development of successful goods and services. Our discussion would not be complete without a consideration of some ethical issues involved in the conduct of this research.

The Positive Aspects of Consumer Research

Many positive benefits result from consumer research. Consumers generally have better consumption experiences. The potential for marketers to build stronger relationships with their customers is also fostered by consumer research.

EXHIBIT 2.11
Atmosphere Creates a Mood

Colors, textures, and lighting all have an important psychological impact on consumer behavior. What mood and image do you associate with the Restoration Hardware store depicted here?

Source: Lisa Quinones/Black Star.

Better Consumption Experiences   Because consumer research is designed to make marketers more customer focused, one benefit is that consumers get better designed products, better customer service, clearer usage instructions, more information that helps them make good decisions, and more satisfying postpurchase experiences. Consumer research should also protect consumers from unscrupulous marketers.

Potential for Building Customer Relationships   Consumer research also has the potential to build and enhance relationships between marketers and their customers. Consumers who believe that marketers truly understand them and are interested in serving consumer needs will be motivated to develop a relationship with marketers and return to them when future needs for the product or service arise. From a marketer's perspective, consumer research may be vital to the development of a loyal customer base.

The Negative Aspects of Consumer Research

Consumer research is a very complex process. Conducting research in foreign countries can be complicated, and understanding diverse cultures is not easy. Consumer research can also be expensive to conduct and may lead to greater costs to the consumer. Many believe that consumer research can promote the invasion of privacy. Consumer research can also provide opportunities for deceptive practices.

Tracking Consumer Behavior in Different Countries   Consumer research can pose special challenges for marketers when conducted in other countries. Data may be difficult to gather or may require different approaches from what is customary in the United States. Focus groups that include husbands and wives may be desirable in the United States for exploring attitudes toward products like appliances or cars. However, in countries like Saudi Arabia women are unlikely to speak freely and are highly unlikely to disagree with their husbands. Focus groups may also be different in Japan where cultural pressures dictate against disagreeing with the views of a group. Telephone interviewing, common in the United States, is far less prevalent in Third World countries. The use of surveys also varies with literacy rates of the country of interest. Questionnaires may need to be carefully worded, translated into the language of the country of interest, and then translated back into English to make sure the specific meaning generated by the question is being conveyed.[47]

Information from secondary sources may also differ from that gathered in the United States, making comparisons difficult. Government census data may be gathered during different years or at different intervals. Countries may also use various categorization schemes for describing demographics like social class and education level. Different or fewer syndicated data sources may also be available in other countries, limiting the extent of information available to marketers.

Potentially Higher Marketing Costs   Some consumers worry that information gathered about them leads to higher marketing costs, which in turn translate into higher prices for products. Some marketers, however, argue that they can market to their customers more efficiently if they know more about them. For example, product development, advertising, sales promotion costs, and distribution costs are all lowered if marketers know exactly what consumers want in a product and how they can be reached.

Invasion of Consumer Privacy   A potentially more serious and widespread concern is that marketers' conduct and use of marketing research may invade consumers' privacy. This issue is nowhere more apparent than in the area of database marketing. Consumers are worried that marketers know too much about them and that they will sell private information about them, their financial situation, and their purchasing behaviors to companies without their knowledge or permission. They also worry that information about them might be used for purposes of which they disapprove. We discuss these issues in detail in Chapter 21, "The Dark Side of Marketing and Consumer Behavior."

Deceptive Research Practices   Finally, unscrupulous marketers may engage in deceptive practices, one of which is to lie about the sponsor of the research (e.g., saying it is being conducted by a nonprofit organization when in reality it is being conducted by a for-profit company). Another deceptive practice is to promise that respondents' answers will remain anonymous, when in fact identifying information is being tied to their answers and can later be used to market a product to them. Telling consumers they will receive compensation for their responses and then failing to deliver on this promise is also regarded as deceptive.[48]

SUMMARY

Consumer research is a valuable tool that helps marketers design better marketing programs, aids in the development of laws and public policy decisions regarding product safety, and promotes our general understanding of how and why we behave as consumers. Toward this end researchers from profit and nonprofit organizations utilize various research tools to understand consumption practices. These tools include techniques that collect data on what consumers say (surveys, interviews, storytelling, and focus groups) and techniques that collect data on what consumers do (observations). These tools may involve data collection on relatively few individuals (focus groups) or many individuals (surveys) and may study consumers at a single point in time (experiments) or track their behavior across time (database marketing, tracking studies).

Many types of organizations collect consumer research. Some firms have internal marketing research departments; others use external research firms to conduct research activities. Advertising agencies and syndicated data services, for example, are two types of outside agencies that collect consumer research information. Large retail chains often conduct consumer research through the use of electronic scanners to track sales of a brand or product category. Research foundations and trade groups, as well as the government and consumer organizations, also collect consumer information. Many academics and academic research centers conduct consumer research simply to enhance our general understanding of consumer behavior, although this research may have application purposes as well.

Marketers utilize consumer research information to understand how markets are segmented and to determine the characteristics of consumers in each segment. Consumer research information is also helpful in selecting a target market and deciding how an offering should be positioned. Research is essential to product, promotion, price, and distribution marketing-mix decisions.

Consumer research raises some ethical issues. The positive aspect of consumer research is that it is conducted by companies and organizations that adhere to a consumer-oriented view of marketing and hope to provide better consumption experiences and build better customer relationships. However, some critics point out that the collection of this information may invade consumers' privacy and lead to higher marketing costs. In addition, unscrupulous marketers can easily misuse consumer information.

EXERCISES

1. Look up some of the following sites on the Web and try to understand (a) whether they provide primary or secondary data, (b) which research tools they use, and (c) whether they design research for a specific industry or many industries.

   www.claritas.com
   www.ars1.com
   www.acnielsen.com
   www.npd.com
   www.maritz.com/mmri
   www.colapublib.org/fyi/city/demo/index.html

2. Ask a friend to identify a favorite possession. Interview your friend to find out as much as you can about the possession. Ask your friend to find photographs from magazines that best symbolize why that item is meaningful. Then ask him or her to keep a diary for a few days that indicates whether and how he or she used the possession. Finally, conduct a focus group with a few of your friends about their special possessions. What do these combined tools reveal to you about these possessions?

THE CONSUMER'S CULTURE

Age, Gender, and
Household Influences
(Ch. 15)

Social Class Influences
(Ch. 14)

Social Influences
(Ch. 16)

Regional, Ethnic and
Religious Influences
(Ch. 13)

Psychographics:
Values, Personality
and Lifestyles
(Ch. 17)

THE PSYCHOLOGICAL CORE

- Motivation, Ability and
  Opportunity (Ch. 3)
- Exposure, Attention and
  Perception (Ch. 4)
- Knowing and
  Understanding (Ch. 5)
- Attitude Formation
  (Chs. 6 & 7)
- Memory and
  Retrieval (Ch. 8)

THE PROCESS OF MAKING DECISIONS

- Problem Recognition and Information Search (Ch. 9)
- Judgment and Decision Making (Chs. 10-11)
- Post-Decision Processes (Ch. 12)

CONSUMER BEHAVIOR OUTCOMES

- Symbolic Consumer Behavior (Ch. 18)
- Adoption of, Resistance to, and Diffusion of
  Innovations (Ch. 19)

PART TWO

The Psychological Core

Consumer behavior is greatly affected by the amount of effort consumers put into their consumption behaviors and into their decisions about consumption. Chapter 3 describes three critical factors that affect effort: the (1) motivation, (2) ability, and (3) opportunity consumers have to engage in behaviors and make decisions.

Chapter 4 discusses how consumers come into contact with marketing stimuli (*exposure*), notice them (*attention*), and *perceive* them. Chapter 5 continues the topic by discussing how consumers compare new stimuli to their existing knowledge, a process called *categorization*, as well as attempt to understand or *comprehend* it on a deeper level.

Chapter 6 describes how attitudes are formed and changed when consumers spend a great deal of effort forming attitudes. Chapter 7 discusses how attitudes can be influenced when consumer effort is low.

Finally, because consumers are not always exposed to marketing information when they actually need it, Chapter 8 focuses on the important topic of consumer memory.

CHAPTER

3

MOTIVATION, ABILITY, AND OPPORTUNITY

INTRODUCTION

Women belong to a growing market for companies that perform financial management and financial planning services. Indeed, many TV and magazine ads developed by financial services companies are geared exclusively toward women (see Exhibit 3.1). And it is no wonder. Women are taking to the financial services market in record numbers. Consider that in 1998 more than 1,600 women attended the Money Show in Orlando, Florida. Approximately 2,000 visited the show in Las Vegas in 1996, and more than 1,500 attended the fall show held in San Francisco. Although most attendees were women of preretirement age (55 to 64), 24 percent were between the ages of 45 and 54, and 14 percent were between 35 and 44.[1]

What accounts for this tremendous interest in financial planning by women? In large part it is driven by the fact that women today have greater motivation, ability, and opportunity to engage in investment decisions. They are increasingly motivated to learn about personal finance and plan for their own financial independence. Some of their motivation is driven by the belief that Social Security benefits will not be available by the time they retire. In other cases, a wish to avoid risk enhances their motivation to plan for a secure financial future.

EXHIBIT 3.1
Targeting Women

Financial services marketers are increasingly targeting women given women's motivation, opportunity, and ability to use financial management services.

Source: Black Rocket and Discover Brokerage.

Women also have greater opportunities to take advantage of investment options than ever before. Compared to their mothers and grandmothers, today's women are more financially independent and are more likely to earn extra income and run a household on their own. Financial advisors, workshops, money management shows, financial management newsletters, and seminars are also giving women knowledge about investment opportunities and how to evaluate them. Companies like Merrill Lynch, the Bank of America, Prudential, and Smith Barney have developed financial initiative programs geared toward women. The information they provide enhances women's ability to process information about investment opportunities and make sound investment decisions.

Motivation, ability, and opportunity to make acqusition, usage or disposition decisions are key factors that affect whether consumers will pay attention to and perceive information, what information they notice, how they form attitudes, and what they remember. These factors also affect how much effort consumers put into searching for information, how they make choices, and how they judge whether their experience is satisfactory.

Women who are motivated to achieve financial independence are likely to search for information that will educate them about stocks, bonds, and mutual funds. These consumers are likely to pay attention to ads for companies that offer investment services. They carefully read about investment opportunities, attend seminars and workshops, read investment-related articles, examine their investment performance continuously, and consider how well they have done in the past. These women are likely to develop strong attitudes toward investments that have performed either extremely well or extremely poorly and tend to be very satisfied with high-performance investments.

In this chapter we focus exclusively on motivation, ability, and opportunity, noting the factors that affect these consumer influences and the implications they have for marketers. Exhibit 3.2, which offers an overview of the chapter, shows that motivated individuals may invest a great deal of thought in and take active steps to reach their goals. The exhibit shows that motivation is enhanced when we regard something as (1) personally relevant; (2) consistent with our needs, values, and goals; (3) risky; and/or (4) moderately inconsistent with our prior attitudes.

Whether motivated consumers actually achieve a goal depends on whether they have the ability to achieve it. The exhibit shows that ability depends on (1) knowledge and experience; (2) cognitive style; (3) intelligence, education, and age; and (4) money.

Achievement of goals also depends on whether consumers have the opportunity to attain them. Exhibit 3.2 shows that the opportunity to achieve goals is determined by (1) time, (2) distractions, (3) the amount of information we are exposed to, (4) the complexity of that information, and (5) the extent to which it is repeated.

CONSUMER MOTIVATION AND ITS EFFECTS

motivation An inner state of arousal that denotes energy to achieve a goal.

Motivation is defined as "an inner state of arousal," with aroused energy directed to achieving a goal.[2] The motivated consumer is energized, ready, and willing to engage in a goal-relevant activity. For example, if you learn that your favorite music group is playing at a nearby concert venue, you may be motivated to go. If you find out that throwing away motor oil is bad for the environment, you might be motivated to recycle it. Consumers can be motivated to engage in behaviors, make decisions, or process information, and this motivation can be seen in the context of acquiring, using, or disposing of an offering. Let's look first at the effects of motivation, as shown in the middle of Exhibit 3.2.

Goal-Relevant Behavior

One outcome of motivation is goal-relevant behavior. When our motivation is high, we are willing to engage in behaviors relevant to our goal. For example, if we are motivated to buy a good car, we are willing to visit dealerships, take test drives, ask friends for advice, and so on. Likewise, if we are motivated to lose weight, we are willing to buy low-calorie foods, measure food portions, and exercise. Motivation not only drives behaviors consistent with a goal but also creates a willingness to expend time and energy engaging in these behaviors. Thus a consumer motivated to attend a concert may earn extra money for tickets, endure many long hours waiting in line to buy them, and drive through adverse weather conditions to get there.

High-Effort Information Processing and Decision Making

Motivation also affects the how we process information and make decisions.[3] When motivation to achieve a goal is high, consumers are more likely to pay careful attention to the goal, think about it, attempt to understand or comprehend information presented about it, evaluate it critically, and try to remember the infor-

EXHIBIT 3.2

Chapter Overview: Motivation, Ability, and Opportunity

Motivation, ability, and opportunity (MAO) to engage in various consumer behaviors is affected by many factors. Outcomes of high MAO include (1) goal-relevant behavior, (2) high-effort information processing and decision making, and (3) felt involvement.

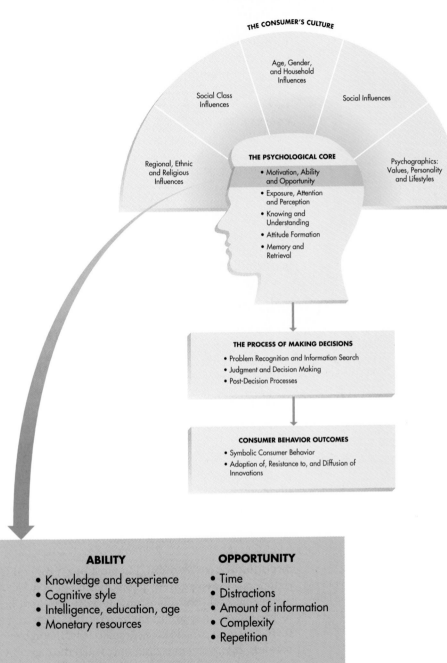

THE CONSUMER'S CULTURE

Age, Gender, and Household Influences

Social Class Influences

Social Influences

Regional, Ethnic and Religious Influences

THE PSYCHOLOGICAL CORE
- Motivation, Ability and Opportunity
- Exposure, Attention and Perception
- Knowing and Understanding
- Attitude Formation
- Memory and Retrieval

Psychographics: Values, Personality and Lifestyles

THE PROCESS OF MAKING DECISIONS
- Problem Recognition and Information Search
- Judgment and Decision Making
- Post-Decision Processes

CONSUMER BEHAVIOR OUTCOMES
- Symbolic Consumer Behavior
- Adoption of, Resistance to, and Diffusion of Innovations

MOTIVATION
- Personal relevance
- Consistency with values, goals, and needs
- Perceived risk
- Moderate inconsistency with attitudes

ABILITY
- Knowledge and experience
- Cognitive style
- Intelligence, education, age
- Monetary resources

OPPORTUNITY
- Time
- Distractions
- Amount of information
- Complexity
- Repetition

- Goal-related behavior
- Information processing and decision making
- Felt involvement

mation so that it can be used later. Doing all this takes a lot of effort. For example, if you are motivated to go to a sold-out U2 concert, you might scour the classifieds hoping to find someone who is selling extra tickets. You might think about other ways to get these tickets, and if someone tells you the name of somebody who has some, you might actively try to remember this person's name and phone number.

When motivation is low, however, consumers devote little effort to processing information and making decisions. For example, our motivation to purchase the best pad of paper on the market is likely to be low. We are unlikely to devote much attention to learning about the characteristics of paper pads. Nor are we likely to think about what it would be like to own and use various types of pads. We are unlikely to devote much attention to advertisements for various brands of paper, and once in the store we will not spend a lot of time comparing brands. We may even engage in various decision-making shortcuts, such as deciding to buy the cheapest brand or the same brand we bought last time.[4] The purchase of most common grocery products falls into the same category.

As you can see then, the level of motivation affects how much effort consumers devote to obtaining and processing information, how they form attitudes, and how they make decisions.

Felt Involvement

A final outcome of motivation is that it evokes a psychological state in consumers called *involvement*. Specifically, researchers have introduced the term **felt involvement** to refer to the psychological experience of the motivated consumer.[5] As Exhibit 3.2 shows, four kinds of felt involvement have been identified: (1) enduring (2) situational, (3) cognitive, and (4) affective.[6]

Enduring Involvement   **Enduring involvement** exists when we show interest in an offering or activity over a long period of time.[7] Car enthusiasts are intrinsically interested in cars and exhibit enduring involvement in them. Enthusiasts engage in activities that reveal this interest (e.g., going to car shows, reading car magazines, visiting dealerships). A consumer might express enduring involvement in any object or activity—searching for stereo equipment, adding CDs to a personal collection, or working out. For most consumers, enduring involvement occurs for relatively few offerings or activities.

Situational Involvement   In most instances consumers experience **situational** (temporary) **involvement** in an offering or activity. For example, consumers who exhibit no enduring involvement with cars may be involved in the car-buying process when they are in the market for a new car. After they buy the car, their involvement in cars declines dramatically. Involvement with gift giving is often situational. Involvement is high only when the consumer is trying to achieve the goal of deciding on a gift.

Cognitive Involvement   A distinction has also been made between cognitive and affective involvement.[8] **Cognitive involvement** means that the consumer is interested in *thinking about* and processing information related to his or her goal. The goal therefore includes *learning* about the offering. A sports enthusiast who is interested in learning all he can about basketball player Dennis Rodman or a car enthusiast interested in learning all she can about a new-model sports car would be exhibiting cognitive involvement.

---

felt involvement   The psychological experience of the motivated consumer. Includes psychological states such as interest, excitement, anxiety, passion, and engagement.

enduring involvement Interest in an offering or activity over an extended period of time.

situational involvement Temporary interest in an offering or activity, often caused by situational circumstances.

cognitive involvement Interest in thinking about and processing information related to one's goal.

affective involvement Interest in expending emotional energy and heightened feelings regarding an offering or activity.

Affective Involvement   **Affective involvement** means that the consumer is willing to *expend emotional energy* or has heightened *feelings* about an offering or activity. The consumer who listens to music to experience intense emotions is exhibiting affective involvement. If we watch a tender scene in a movie and begin to cry, we are displaying high affective involvement in the movie.

Objects of Involvement

We can also identify the various objects with which consumers may be involved.

Involvement with Product Categories   As many of the preceding examples indicate, consumers may exhibit cognitive and/or affective involvement in a certain product category, such as cars, computers, or clothes.[9] Involvement may also involve a pastime or activity. For example, in the United States increasing numbers of consumers are showing high involvement in soccer, an international sport that was once barely noticed in this country.[10]

Involvement with Brands   Consumers can also exhibit cognitive and/or affective involvement with a brand. This phenomenon is commonly called brand loyalty. As you will see in later chapters, brand-loyal consumers are consistent purchasers of the brand, hold strong beliefs about its quality, feel considerable devotion toward it, and often resist competitors' efforts to attract them. Some product collections represent brands toward which people are loyal. The Beanie Baby craze, for example, has made some consumers eager to own Beanie Babies. Recognizing the brand loyalty of these consumers, companies like McDonald's and some banks have offered Teenie Beanie Babies as sales promotion incentives. Kids in the United States and Japan are currently crazy about buying, collecting, and trading Pokemon cards.

Involvement with Ads   Consumers can also be involved with ads. This involvement may be revealed by consumers' motivation to attend to and process information contained in the ad. Typically, involvement in an ad is high if consumers view the advertised message as relevant to them.[11] Consumers may also be involved in the ad simply because they find it interesting. Ads for shaving cream that present sports questions and ask readers to "make the call" usually elicit involvement among sports fans. In Japan ads that emphasize interpersonal relationships, social circumstances, and nonverbal expressions generate more involvement than do ads with clearly articulated and spoken messages.[12] Advertisers use many techniques to increase consumers' involvement in an ad and hence increase their motivation to process the ad's contents. To illustrate, the ad in Exhibit 3.3 may be involving for many consumers because of its focus on sexuality. We consider other methods for stimulating involvement in ads and motivation to process them later in the chapter.

Involvement with a Medium   Consumers can also be involved in the medium in which an ad is placed. Television, for example, is generally viewed as a relatively low-involvement medium because viewers are typically passive and do not have to think much to process what they see. Print media such as magazines and newspapers, on the other hand, are considered to generate higher levels of involvement because the reader must interact with these media.

Consumers can also be involved in a specific television or radio program or a particular magazine or newspaper.[13] Thus advertisers sometimes want to advertise

57

CHAPTER 3 Motivation, Ability, and Opportunity

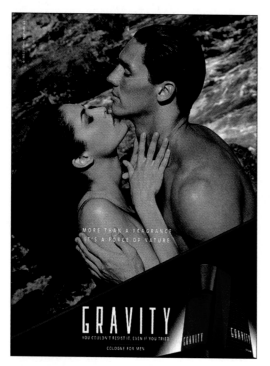

EXHIBIT 3.3
Creating Involvement in the Ad

Marketers might use a variety of tactics—like the sex appeal used in this ad—to stimulate consumers' involvement in an ad.

Source: Coty, Inc.

response involvement
Interest in certain *decisions* and *behaviors.*

personal relevance Something that has a direct bearing on the self and has potentially significant consequences or implications for our lives.

self-concept Our view of who we are.

their brands on popular television shows. On the other hand, research has also found that higher levels of program involvement can sometimes lower consumers' ad involvement. The reason is that an interesting program can temporarily distract us and suspend our processing of an ad.

Involvement with Decisions   Finally, consumers can be involved in certain decisions and behaviors.[14] This type of involvement is commonly called **response involvement**. For example, consumers may be highly involved in the process of making a decision between brands. A consumer who loves shopping may do a lot of browsing and not buy anything at all. Consumers can also find the act of using certain products or services involving. For example, consumers generally enjoy reading books, watching movies, playing video games, or attending sporting events because these activities are highly involving.

Specifying the Object of Involvement   Because consumers can be involved with so many different entities, *we need to specify the object of involvement when we use the term involvement*. For example, brand-loyal consumers are highly involved in the *brand*, but because they believe their brand is the best, they are unlikely to be involved in making a *decision* about which brand to buy. Likewise, consumers can be very involved in an *ad* because it is funny, interesting, or novel but show little involvement in the *brand* depicted in the ad because they are loyal to other brands.

WHAT AFFECTS MOTIVATION?

Motivation is influenced by the extent to which the ad, brand, product category, or other characteristic is personally relevant to consumers. Things are seen as personally relevant and important when they are (1) consistent with consumers' values, goals, and needs; (2) risky; and/or (3) moderately inconsistent with their prior attitudes.

Personal Relevance

A key factor affecting motivation is the extent to which something is **personally relevant**—that is, the extent to which it has a direct bearing with significant consequences or implications on your life.[15] For example, if you own a particular car model and you learn it is being recalled because its gas tank explodes on impact, chances are you will find this issue to be personally relevant. It has a direct bearing on you, and its consequences are very important. Careers, college activities, boyfriend or girlfriend or spouse, car, apartment or home, clothes, and hobbies are likely to be personally relevant because the consequences they have on you are significant.

Things are also personally relevant to the extent that they bear on our **self-concept,** or our view of ourselves, and the way we think others view us. Our self-concept helps us define who we are, and it frequently guides our behavior. When we buy clothing, we are often making a statement about who we are—a professional, a student, or a member of a sports team. Some consumers find brands like Jeep Wrangler and vehicles like vans relevant to their self-concept. Thus owning such products is important to their self-definition and, of course, is personally relevant.

When we think things are personally relevant, we will be motivated to behave, process information, or engage in effortful *decision making* about these things. And we will experience considerable involvement when buying, using, or disposing of them. Think about all the behaviors you engaged in, for example, when you were deciding where to go to college—writing away for applications and information packets, talking with friends, calling alumni, and so on. You are also likely to have devoted considerable time and effort to processing the information about each school and making a decision about where to go. Chances are, you found the task of making the decision personally involving. You may have found that it even preoccupied you and that reading material about various schools generated interest, enthusiasm, and perhaps a bit of anxiety.

MARKETING IMPLICATIONS Marketers can enhance consumers' motivation to process promotional materials by trying to make the information as personally relevant as possible. Salespeople can explore consumers' underlying reasons for a purchase and tailor sales pitches to those reasons.

Similarly, ads can be geared toward consumers' special concerns. Volvo once ran a campaign that attempted to make Volvo seem more personally relevant to consumers. The campaign, called This Car Saved My Life, showed real-life accident victims who had been saved from serious injury by riding in a Volvo. Demonstrating how the Volvo could prevent disastrous consequences made the ad personally relevant.

Exhibit 3.4 is a good example of an issue that some men might find personally relevant and that might generate motivation and its effects. Hair loss can be an emotionally charged problem for some men. Thus these men are likely to be motivated to read this information carefully and will likely devote considerable attention and information-processing resources to understanding and remembering its contents. ■

EXHIBIT 3.4
Appealing to Personal Relevance

Marketers can enhance consumers' motivation to process their message by making sure it is personally relevant to them. Some men might be motivated to process this message because it deals with an issue that they may find personally relevant.

Source: Courtesy of Merck.

Introducing the first and only pill clinically proven to treat hair loss in men.

If you think losing more hair is inevitable, think again.

PROPECIA
(finasteride)
Helping make hair loss history

Values, Goals, and Needs

As Exhibit 3.2 indicated, one reason things are personally relevant is that they are consistent with our values, goals, and needs.

values Culturally held beliefs about what is good or appropriate.

Values Consumers are more motivated to attend to and process information when they find it relevant to their values. **Values** are beliefs that guide what we regard as important or good. Thus, if we see education as extremely important, we are likely to be motivated to engage in behaviors that are consistent with this value, such as pursuing a degree.

goals Objectives that we would like to achieve.

Goals Another factor affecting personal relevance and motivation is goals.[16] **Goals** are objectives that we would like to achieve. They are specific to a given behavior or action and are often determined by the situation at hand. If we are tired, one of our goals for the evening might be to go to bed early. If we have been repeatedly late for class, one of our goals might be to arrive at class on time. When goals have been set, we are likely to be very motivated to engage in behaviors that are relevant to them. Thus when we are tired, we might engage in behaviors to ensure a restful night's sleep—taking a hot bath, avoiding work, eating a satisfying dinner.

needs An internal state of tension caused by disequilibrium from an ideal/desired physical or psychological state.

Needs A third and very powerful factor affecting personal relevance and motivation is **needs**. Each need has an equilibrium level at which it is in a state of satisfaction. Any departure from this equilibrium produces tension. Thus the activation of the need (tension) produces arousal in the individual and motivates him or her to find some way of fulfilling the need. For example, at certain times of the day, your stomach begins to feel uncomfortable and you realize it is time to get something to eat. Motivation directs your behavior toward certain outcomes (e.g., going to the refrigerator, going to a certain restaurant, ordering takeout food). After you eat, your need is satisfied, and the tension (in this case, hunger) is removed.

Just as needs can lead us toward a product or service, they can also keep us away. For example, have you ever put off going to the dentist? If so, you were probably motivated by a need to avoid pain.

A variety of needs can operate in a given situation. But what needs do consumers experience? One well-known theory of needs is based on the research of psychologist Abraham Maslow.[17] Maslow grouped needs into the five categories or levels shown in Exhibit 3.5: (1) physiological (the need for food, water, and sleep), (2) safety (the need for shelter, protection, and security), (3) social (the need for affection, friendship, and acceptance), (4) egoistic (the need for prestige, success, accomplishment, and self-esteem), and (5) self-actualization (the need for self-fulfillment and enriching experiences). These needs are arranged in a hierarchy in which lower-level needs must be satisfied before higher-level needs become activated. Thus before we can worry about prestige and success, our lower-level needs for food, water, and shelter must be met.

Although Maslow's hierarchy is useful in providing some organization to the complex issue of needs, some critics say the hierarchy is too simplistic. Specifically, needs are not always ordered in the exact manner specified here. For example, some consumers place a higher priority on buying lottery tickets than on acquiring necessities such as food and clothing. The hierarchy also ignores the intensity of needs. It is not simply the existence of needs but also their intensity that affects motivation. Finally, the ordering of needs may not be consistent across cultures. Some societies, particularly Asian cultures, for example, place a higher value on social needs and belonging and less on egoistic needs and self-actualization.

EXHIBIT 3.5
Maslow's Hierarchy of Needs

Maslow proposes that our needs can be categorized into a basic hierarchy. Fulfillment of lower-order needs (e.g., physiological needs for food, water, sleep) is necessary before higher-order needs can be fulfilled.

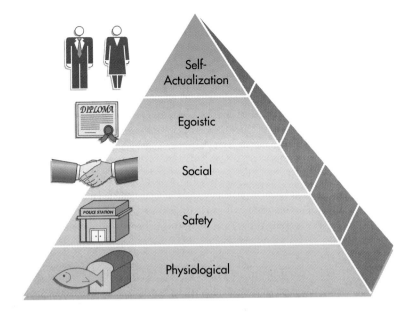

Types of Needs   Another way to categorize needs is as (1) social and nonsocial needs or (2) functional, symbolic, and hedonic needs (see Exhibit 3.6).

Social Needs   Social needs are externally directed and relate to other individuals. Fulfilling these needs thus requires the presence or actions of other people. For example, the need for esteem drives our desire to have others hold us in high regard. In our need for support, we desire others to relieve us of our burdens; and the need for modeling reflects a wish to have others show us how to behave. We may be motivated to buy products and use services like Hallmark cards and AT&T long-distance

EXHIBIT 3.6
Types of Needs

One scheme categorizes needs according to whether they are (1) social or nonsocial and (2) functional, symbolic, or hedonic in nature. This provides marketers with a fairly simple scheme for thinking about consumers' needs.

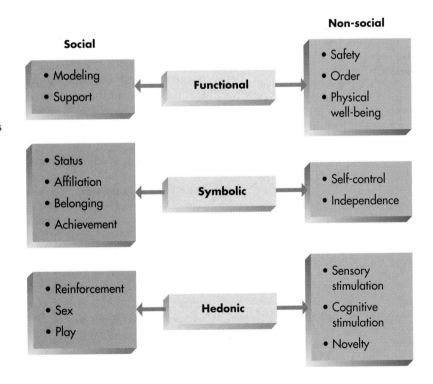

dialing because they help us achieve our need for affiliation. Other products may be valued because they are consistent with our need for status or to be unique.[18] Still other products are consumed in a social setting and may be relevant to social needs. For example, Gallo positions its wine as an integral part of family festivities.

We also have antisocial needs—needs for space and psychological distance from other people. If plane seats, theater seats, restroom stalls, or park benches are too close together, our needs for space are violated and we experience an urge to escape the constraining environment.

Nonsocial Needs   Nonsocial needs are those in which achievement is not based on other people. For example, our needs for sleep, novelty, control, and understanding involve only ourselves. Again, however, activation of these needs affects the usage of certain products and services. We might purchase the same brand time and again to maintain consistency in our world. Alternatively, we might buy something totally different to fulfill a need for variety.

Functional Needs   As mentioned above, needs can also be classified as functional, symbolic, or hedonic.[19] **Functional needs** motivate the search for products that solve consumption-related problems. Functional needs can also be social or nonsocial. For example, consumers might consider buying certain products like a Volvo wagon with side airbags because they appeal to our safety needs (a functional, nonsocial need). California Closet Co. solves our needs for order (a functional, nonsocial need). Hiring a nanny would solve the need for a baby sitter (a functional, social need).

functional needs   Needs that motivate the search for products to solve consumption-related problems.

Symbolic Needs   **Symbolic needs** affect how we perceive ourselves and how we are perceived by others. Our needs for achievement, independence, and self-control are symbolic needs because they are connected with our sense of self. The need to avoid rejection and the need for self-esteem, status, affiliation, and belonging are symbolic needs because they reflect our position or role within a social group. For example, some consumers wear Tommy Hilfiger clothing because it communicates something about the age and social group to which they belong.

symbolic needs   Needs that relate to how we perceive ourselves, how we are perceived by others, how we relate to others, and the esteem in which we are held by others.

Hedonic Needs   **Hedonic needs** reflect our inherent desires for sensory pleasure. We attend concerts and sporting events and purchase CDs, perfume, and art for the sensory pleasures they can bring. For the same reason, certain products (e.g., food products made with fake fat or without sugar) have failed because they have not met hedonic needs. As shown in Exhibit 3.6, the needs for sensory stimulation, cognitive stimulation, and novelty are nonsocial hedonic needs, whereas the needs for reinforcement, sex, and play are social hedonic needs.

hedonic needs   Needs that relate to sensory pleasure.

Needs for Cognition and Stimulation   Certain personality characteristics are also relevant to needs. Consumers with a high need for cognition[20] (what we might also call a need for mental stimulation) tend to be highly involved in activities like reading, solving puzzles, and playing games that are mentally taxing. They are also more likely to actively process information during decision making. People with a low need for cognition may be more involved in activities that require less thought, such as watching TV or going to escapist movies, and they are less likely to actively process information during decision making.

We also have needs for other kinds of stimulation. Individuals with a high optimum stimulation level (OSL) enjoy high levels of sensory stimulation. They tend to be involved in shopping and seeking information about brands.[21] They also show a heightened involvement in ads. Some consumers have thrill-seeking tendencies. They live for activities like skydiving, bungee jumping, mountaineering, and whitewater rafting.

Consumers sometimes find themselves overstimulated and want to get away from people, noise, and demands. This desire is revealed in the increasing popularity of vacations in monasteries or other such sanctuaries.[22]

Characteristics of Needs   Each need described above has several characteristics.

Needs Are Dynamic   Needs are never fully satisfied; satisfaction is only temporary. Clearly, eating once will not satisfy our hunger forever. Also, as soon as one need is satisfied, new needs emerge. After we have eaten a meal or purchased a new CD, we might next have the need to be with others (the need for affiliation) or the need to study (a need for achievement). Thus we might think of our daily lives as a constant process of need fulfillment. For this reason, we say that needs are dynamic.

Needs Exist in a Hierarchy   Although several needs may be activated at any one time, some assume higher importance than others. To illustrate, you may experience a need to eat during an exam, but your need for achievement may assume a higher priority—so you stay to finish the test. The fact that needs exist in a hierarchy does not suggest that only one need affects a given decision. Because many needs may be activated simultaneously, multiple needs may affect our acquisition, usage, and disposition behaviors. Thus your decision to go out for dinner on Saturday night with friends may be driven by a combination of needs for stimulation, food, and companionship.

Needs Can Be Internally or Externally Aroused   Although many needs are internally activated, some needs can be externally cued. Smelling pizza cooking in the apartment next door may, for example, affect your perceived need for food.

Needs Can Conflict   A given behavior or outcome can be seen as both desirable and undesirable if it satisfies some needs but fails to satisfy others. The result is called an **approach-avoidance conflict** in which we both want to engage in the behavior and want to avoid it. You might experience an approach-avoidance conflict if you are invited to a great party the night before an important exam. The act of going to the party will satisfy some needs, such as for fun and affiliation and thus will enhance your desire to attend the party. But going to the party will fail to satisfy other needs, such as the needs for achievement and self-control, which would be met by staying home to study.

Similarly, teenagers may experience an approach-avoidance conflict in deciding whether to smoke cigarettes. They may believe that others will think they are cool for smoking (smoking is consistent with needs for self-esteem). However, they may also know that smoking is bad for them (it is incompatible with needs for safety). Approach-avoidance conflicts also explain the strong desire we have to eat foods that are high in calories and fat because they taste good and our simultaneous desire to avoid these foods because we know they are bad for us.

An **approach-approach conflict** occurs when the individual faces the task of choosing among two or more equally desirable options that fulfill different needs. A consumer who is invited to an important career-night function might experience an approach-approach conflict if he is also asked to attend an important neighborhood watch meeting for the same evening. One activity is consistent with his needs for achievement, the other with his needs for safety. As long as the two options are viewed as equally desirable, conflict will result.

approach-avoidance conflict
A conflict that occurs when a given behavior or outcome is seen as both desirable and undesirable because it satisfies some needs but fails to satisfy others.

approach-approach conflict
A conflict that occurs when a consumer must choose between two or more equally desirable options that fulfill different needs.

avoidance-avoidance conflict
A conflict that occurs when the consumer must choose between two equally undesirable options.

An **avoidance-avoidance conflict** occurs when the consumer faces the task of choosing between two equally undesirable options. A consumer who experiences airline delays while trying to get home might have to decide between waiting for an 11:00 P.M. departure or staying overnight and taking the first flight out the next morning. She may want to avoid the first choice because she will be extremely tired by the time she arrives home. She may want to avoid the second choice because she will arrive home after her family has left for the day (need for affiliation). Because neither option is desirable, conflict will result.

Identifying Needs Because needs influence motivation and its effects, marketers are keenly interested in identifying and hence measuring them. However, consumers are often unaware of their needs and have trouble explaining them to researchers. Inferring consumers' needs based only on behaviors is also difficult because a given need might not be linked to a specific behavior. In other words, the same need (affiliation) can be exhibited in various and diverse behaviors (going to bars, visiting friends, going to the gym), and the same behavior (going to the gym) can reflect various needs (affiliation, achievement).

Inferring needs in a cross-cultural context is particularly difficult. For example, some research has shown that use of toothpaste among U.S. consumers is primarily based on its cavity-reducing capabilities (a functional need). In contrast, in England and some French-speaking areas of Canada, usage is primarily derived from the ability of toothpaste to freshen breath (a hedonic need). French women drink mineral water so they will look better (a symbolic need), whereas German consumers drink it for its curative and health powers (a functional need).[23]

Given these difficulties, marketers sometimes use indirect techniques to uncover consumers' needs.[24] Essentially, these techniques ask consumers to interpret a set of relatively ambiguous stimuli such as cartoons, word associations, incomplete sentences, and incomplete stories. For example, using Exhibit 3.7, one consumer might reveal needs for esteem by interpreting the man in the cartoon as saying, "My friends will think I'm really cool for riding in this car!" Another might reveal needs for affiliation by filling in the cartoon with "I could take all my friends for rides with me." Still another might reveal needs for novelty by saying, "This car will be so different and so much more exciting than the one I have now." Consumers needs might also be revealed by asking them to tell a story about what is happening with the gift being unwrapped in Exhibit 3.7.

One study asked cigarette smokers to indicate why they smoked. Most indicated they enjoyed smoking and believed that smoking in moderation was fine. However, when they were given incomplete sentences like "People who never smoke are _____," respondents filled in the blanks with words like *happier* and *wiser*. And when given sentences like "Teenagers who smoke are _____," respondents answered with words like *crazy* and *foolish*. Thus smokers were more concerned about smoking than their explicit answers indicated.[25]

Projective techniques can also be put to other uses, such as identifying consumers' images of brands and their users. In one study consumers were provided with two nearly identical shopping lists; the only difference was that one list contained the name of one deodorant (brand A) and the other contained the name of a different deodorant (brand B). Consumers were then asked to describe the personality and characteristics of the consumer based on the shopping list. The consumer whose list included brand A was described as less clean, less intelligent, and less popular than the consumer whose list contained brand B.[26]

EXHIBIT 3.7
Projective Techniques

Marketers sometimes uncover needs by using ambiguous stimuli like cartoon drawings, sentence completion tasks, and tell-a-story tasks. Consumers' needs, wishes, and fantasies are presumably projected onto these ambiguous stimuli.

Source: B and C adapted from Mary Ann McGrath, John F. Sherry, Jr., and Sidney J. Levy, "Giving Voice to the Gift: The Use of Projective Techniques to Recover Lost Meanings," *Journal of Consumer Psychology,* 2 (1993), pp. 171–191.

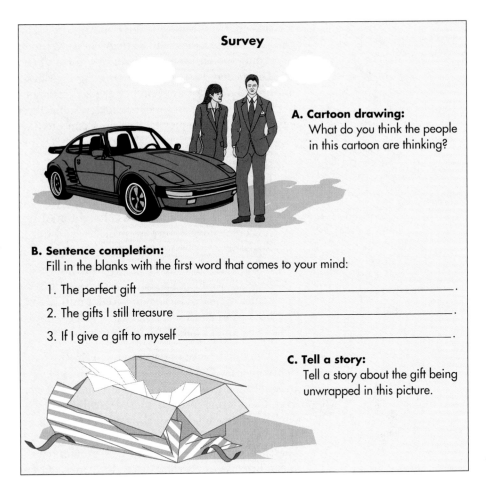

Survey

A. Cartoon drawing:
What do you think the people in this cartoon are thinking?

B. Sentence completion:
Fill in the blanks with the first word that comes to your mind:

1. The perfect gift _____.
2. The gifts I still treasure _____.
3. If I give a gift to myself _____.

C. Tell a story:
Tell a story about the gift being unwrapped in this picture.

MARKETING IMPLICATIONS

Consumers' needs, values, and goals have some important implications for marketers.

Segmenting Markets Based on Needs. First, needs can be used to segment markets. Diet and caffeine-free soft drinks resulted from the recognition of different needs in different consumer segments. The ultrafast speed offered by the Concorde jet meets the needs of consumers in the "thrill seeking" segment, whereas low fares offered by other airlines meet the needs of the financially constrained segment. Financial services companies often segment markets based on consumers' needs and then develop specific products relevant to each segment (e.g., those who need retirement planning versus those looking for growth opportunities; those interested in buying securities over the Internet versus those preferring more traditional exchange media).[27]

Creating New Needs. Sometimes marketers can attempt to create new needs. For example, riding on the wave of the very popular sports trading cards, a number of companies introduced other kinds of trading cards. Elvis Presley and soap opera stars and Pokemon cards have been introduced. These companies tried to create the need for a new type of entertainment. In another area, sales of audio books are rapidly on the rise.[28] This product was originally developed for blind consumers, but marketers have also successfully created a need for this entertainment product among the sighted. Given the amount of time consumers typically spend in their cars and the limited time they have to devote to reading, books on tape offer a new form of entertainment-on-the-go.

Developing Need-Satisfying Offerings.   Marketers can also identify currently unfulfilled needs or develop better need-satisfying alternatives. Indeed, this type of research is often essential to the development of new products—a topic we discuss in detail in Chapter 19. For now, consider the following examples:

- Sales of alternative newspapers have been on the rise, particularly among 20-somethings. These papers fulfill consumers' needs for information delivered in a hip and irreverent format.

- Research indicating that kids are often bored (and hence need stimulation) has prompted publishers such as Houghton Mifflin Co. to use more photo essays, full-color covers, how-to projects, and fun facts in their school and college textbooks.[29]

- Some companies have profited by addressing consumers' needs for safety. Sales of products like gates, fences, walls, security systems, video-surveillance cameras, guard dogs, gated communities, car alarms, and mace have all benefited from consumers' needs for safety coupled with their perception that the environment outside their home is unsafe.

The importance of developing need-satisfying offerings clearly operates cross culturally as well. Over the years McDonald's has experienced tremendous success in fulfilling international consumers' desires for fast food. In some instances, however, the offering must be altered to fulfill specific cultural needs. In Germany the McRib sandwich is one of the top sellers because Germans eat a lot of pork. Beer is also offered at McDonald's in Germany and wine in France.[30] Likewise, theme parks, such as Disneyland, and U.S. movies have been tremendously successful in Japan because of a strong desire for American-style entertainment.[31] Some consumers in Budapest, Hungary, are willing to wait in line for up to 4 hours to purchase Adidas running shoes.

Managing Conflict.   Finally, new product ideas or novel communications might be developed to resolve need conflicts. The marketers of new scooters have a challenge in enhancing consumers' desires for a fun, efficient, and affordable means of transportation while also reducing their perception that the product might make them look goofy.[32] The marketers of Propecia, a prescription tablet for treating male baldness, must promote the benefits of the drug and counter the perception that it will reduce sexual desire (which it can).[33]

Enhancing Communication Effectiveness.   By suggesting that the product or service fulfills a need, value, or goal, marketers can increase the likelihood that consumers will process the message and engage in desired behaviors. The makers of Head and Shoulders shampoo, for example, recognize that consumers have a strong need to be accepted by others. The shampoo manufacturer appeals to this need by suggesting that having dandruff will lead to social rejection. Thus needs can serve as an effective way of positioning a product or service.[34] This principle is also directly applicable to personal selling. Salespeople are trained to identify a consumer's needs and then offer the product or service as a need-satisfying alternative.

Marketing communications should also be developed so that the offering appears relevant to consumers' needs, values, and goals. The ad in Exhibit 3.8 is designed to appeal to both functional and hedonic needs. ■

EXHIBIT 3.8
Appealing to Functional and Hedonic Needs

Consumers' motivation to engage in a behavior (e.g., process information in an ad) is enhanced when the stimulus (e.g., the ad) is relevant to their needs, values, and goals. This ad for Ford is designed to appeal to consumers' functional and hedonic needs.

Source: Courtesy Ford Motor Company.

Perceived Risk

Perceived risk is another factor affecting personal relevance and hence motivation.[35] Because perceived risk can increase consumers' motivation to process information, consumers are more likely to pay attention to and carefully process marketing communications when perceived risk is high. In addition, as perceived risk increases, consumers tend to collect more information and evaluate it carefully.

perceived risk The extent to which the consumer is uncertain about the consequences of an action (e.g., buying, using, or disposing of an offering).

Perceived risk reflects the extent to which the consumer is uncertain about the consequences of buying, using, or disposing of an offering. If negative outcomes are likely or positive outcomes are unlikely, perceived risk is high. Perceived risk can be associated with any product or service but tends to be higher under the following conditions:

- Little information is available about the offering.
- The offering is new.
- The offering has a high price.
- The offering is technologically complex.
- Fairly substantial quality differences exist between brands, so the consumer might make an inferior choice.
- The consumer has little confidence or experience in evaluating the offering.
- The opinions of others are important, and the consumer is likely to be judged by the acquisition, usage, or disposition decision.[36]

Perceptions of risk have also been found to vary across cultural groups. In particular, high levels of risk tend to be associated with many more products in less developed countries, perhaps because the products in these countries are generally of poorer quality.[37] Also, perceived risk is typically higher when travelers purchase goods in a foreign country.[38] Risk perceptions also vary within a culture.[39]

For example, Western men take more risks on the stock market than women take, and younger consumers take more risks than older ones take.

Types of Perceived Risk Researchers have identified six types of risk.[40]

Performance risk reflects uncertainty about whether the product or service will perform as expected. If a consumer is buying a new car and is uncertain whether the car will be reliable, perceived performance risk is high. Many U.S. consumers are still reluctant to purchase an Audi because of problems with the accelerator and brake pedals back in the late 1970s, although these problems have been corrected and Audi is a top-selling car in Europe.

Financial risk is higher if a product or service costs more. A home or a major investment in the stock market is an expensive purchase, and the level of risk associated with making this kind of monetary investment is high.

Physical (or safety) risk refers to the potential harm a product or service might pose to one's safety. Many consumer decisions are driven by a motivation to avoid physical risk. For example, some consumers in markets underserved by a traditional police force have taken to hiring private security guards to ward off break-ins, shootings, and drug dealing.[41] Many parents are increasingly attuned to the risks involved in having their children use the Internet. Children may inadvertently put themselves at risk by giving out their address and phone number to unknown people on-line. Some research has reported considerable differences across consumers in various states based on their average concern over health and safety risks. Consumers in some states (e.g., Hawaii) are very attuned to health and safety risks and take considerable health and safety precautions. Exhibit 3.9 summarizes how various states stand on these risk-avoiding tendencies.[42]

Social risk is the potential harm to one's social standing that may arise from buying, using, or disposing of an offering. For example, although you may secretly adore Barbra Streisand, you may know that others in your group do not. Therefore, you may find that going to a Barbra Streisand concert or buying one of her CDs entails social risk. Your friends might make fun of you if they learn of these activities. Likewise, you may not wear a sweater given to you by your great aunt because it is terribly out of style and wearing it would entail considerable social risk.

Psychological risk reflects consumers' concern about the extent to which product or service fits with the way they perceive themselves. For example, if you view yourself as an environmentalist, buying disposable diapers and using products made of nonrecyclable materials may be psychologically risky.

Time risk reflects uncertainties over the length of time that must be invested in buying, using, or disposing of the product or service. If the offering involves considerable time commitment, learning to use it requires significant time, or it commits the individual to a specified length of usage (such as a health club that requires a 3-year contract), time risk may be high.

Risk and Involvement We noted earlier that products can be described as high- versus low-involvement products. Some researchers have classified high- versus low-involvement products in terms of the amount of risk they pose to consumers. Thus consumers are likely to experience more involvement in purchasing products such as homes, computers, cars, and clothing than in purchasing crackers, picture frames, or coffee because the former generate higher levels of economic, performance, safety, social, psychological, or time risk and hence have more extreme personal consequences for the consumer.

---

performance risk Uncertainty about whether the offering will perform as expected.

financial risk Risk associated with monetary investment in an offering.

physical (or safety) risk The potential harm that an offering might pose to one's safety.

social risk Potential harm to one's social standing that may arise from buying, using, or disposing of an offering.

psychological risk Risk associated with the extent to which the offering fits with the way consumers perceive themselves.

time risk Uncertainties over the length of time consumers must invest in buying, using, or disposing of the offering.

EXHIBIT 3.9

How Risky are People in Your State?

In some states, more consumers engage in risky behaviors like not using a seat belt or drinking and driving. What accounts for these differences between states?

Source: Reprinted from *American Demographics* magazine, August, 1997, Copyright 1997. Courtesy of Intertec Publishing Corp., Stamford, Connecticut. All rights reserved.

	HAVE FAIR/POOR HEALTH	CURRENT SMOKER	DONT ALWAYS USE SEATBELT	BINGE DRINKING PAST MONTH	EVER DRINK AND DRIVE	OVERWEIGHT MEASURED BY BMI*	NO PHYSICAL LEISURE ACTIVITY PAST MONTH	DON'T GET 5 FRUITS/ VEGGIES DAILY
Alabama	18.3%	24.5%	16.3%	13.6%	2.6%	31.8%	45.8%	75.0%
Alaska	8.2	25.0	17.9	19.2	1.3	31.4	22.8	81.2
Arizona	13.4	22.9	12.7	13.5	2.7	24.5	33.5	75.7
Arkansas	18.6	25.2	17.5	8.8	1.5	30.1	35.1	74.7
California	14.3	15.5	5.5	15.3	1.9	26.4	22.7	71.0
Colorado	10.7	21.8	17.5	16.3	3.1	21.9	17.2	78.4
Connecticut	10.9	20.8	17.9	14.4	2.5	24.7	21.9	66.5
Delaware	13.4	25.5	17.7	8.6	1.4	29.5	36.4	83.3
Florida	14.3	23.1	12.1	13.1	2.6	29.8	27.9	74.6
Georgia	12.3	20.5	17.2	12.0	2.2	28.2	32.9	73.6
Hawaii	11.6	17.8	4.5	12.4	2.1	21.8	20.7	80.3
Idaho	11.2	19.8	19.6	12.9	2.0	27.2	21.8	78.3
Illinois	14.0	23.1	18.8	13.6	1.8	30.1	32.4	77.8
Indiana	14.7	27.2	24.2	12.8	2.6	34.7	29.6	80.3
Iowa	11.3	23.2	16.2	18.0	3.3	31.6	33.3	82.1
Kansas	12.2	22.0	24.5	13.9	3.2	27.8	28.2	79.1
Kentucky	21.1	27.8	17.6	9.7	0.6	28.8	45.9	82.7
Louisiana	17.2	25.2	18.9	14.0	2.8	30.7	33.4	80.7
Maine	12.9	25.0	37.8	11.5	0.9	26.9	40.7	79.0
Maryland	10.4	21.2	11.4	8.2	1.1	29.1	30.2	79.6
Massachusetts	12.3	21.7	25.8	17.8	3.5	21.9	24.0	69.7
Michigan	14.7	25.7	13.5	18.3	3.3	31.6	23.0	69.4
Minnesota	9.7	20.5	19.4	18.0	4.9	28.4	21.7	80.5
Mississippi	21.4	24.0	25.4	8.7	1.1	31.6	38.4	86.1
Missouri	12.7	24.3	18.9	14.1	2.1	32.9	31.8	79.0
Montana	11.3	21.1	22.6	14.3	3.4	24.9	21.0	78.8
Nebraska	10.6	21.9	24.6	15.8	2.8	29.2	24.2	80.2
Nevada	14.1	26.3	14.7	19.0	3.7	26.9	21.6	79.1
New Hampshire	10.2	21.5	32.5	16.6	1.6	25.9	25.6	73.1
New Jersey	10.9	19.2	20.3	14.0	2.0	24.4	30.2	70.3
New Mexico	17.2	21.2	6.7	14.1	3.3	23.8	19.4	76.7
New York	11.6	21.5	15.1	12.4	0.9	27.8	37.1	80.1
North Carolina	18.6	25.8	5.7	5.8	1.1	28.9	42.8	81.1
North Dakota	13.5	22.7	33.0	17.0	4.2	30.7	32.0	82.3
Ohio	14.2	26.0	18.4	9.9	1.6	31.5	38.0	78.4
Oklahoma	13.1	21.7	22.6	6.7	1.2	24.1	40.6	81.6
Oregon	11.3	21.8	5.6	13.9	1.8	28.8	20.8	78.8
Pennsylvania	13.2	24.2	21.1	19.4	3.6	30.1	26.3	75.3

(continued)

*BMI means Body Mass Index.

	HAVE FAIR/POOR HEALTH	CURRENT SMOKER	DONT ALWAYS USE SEATBELT	BINGE DRINKING PAST MONTH	EVER DRINK AND DRIVE	OVERWEIGHT MEASURED BY BMI*	NO PHYSICAL LEISURE ACTIVITY PAST MONTH	DON'T GET 5 FRUITS/ VEGGIES DAILY
Rhode Island	14.2%	24.7%	33.6%	18.7%	3.7%	24.9%	—%	—%
South Carolina	15.5	23.7	11.7	9.2	1.4	28.7	36.1	75.9
South Dakota	12.7	21.8	29.3	14.4	5.2	28.7	38.2	79.1
Tennessee	17.7	26.5	21.4	5.2	1.0	31.0	39.7	74.3
Texas	17.2	23.7	10.4	15.3	3.7	28.6	27.8	76.9
Utah	11.8	13.2	17.7	9.9	1.2	25.0	20.9	77.9
Vermont	11.5	22.1	13.3	16.0	2.4	25.4	23.2	71.7
Virginia	11.5	22.0	13.2	14.5	2.5	29.2	27.0	70.2
Washington	10.8	20.2	9.1	13.4	2.1	25.4	18.2	78.6
West Virginia	22.6	25.7	14.8	5.9	0.9	31.9	45.3	77.3
Wisconsin	10.1	21.8	21.2	22.9	4.5	30.2	25.9	78.8
Wyoming	11.0	22.0	23.7	15.6	3.2	27.3	23.6	76.5
U.S. average	13.9%	22.2%	15.3%	13.7%	2.3%	28.5%	29.8%	76.1%

EXHIBIT 3.9
How Risky are People in Your State? (continued)

High risk is generally uncomfortable. As a result, consumers are usually motivated to engage in any number of behaviors and information-processing activities that reduce or resolve risk in some way. For example, to reduce the uncertainty component of risk, they can collect additional information by reading news articles, engaging in comparative shopping, talking to friends or sales specialists, or consulting an expert. Being brand loyal (buying the same brand as last time) can also reduce uncertainty because it ensures that the product will be at least as satisfactory as the last purchase.

Other strategies attempt to reduce the consequence component of perceived risk. In this case consumers may employ a simple decision rule that results in a safer choice. For example, consumers might buy the most expensive offering or a nationally advertised brand because of the general belief that these brands are of higher quality than other brands on the market.

MARKETING IMPLICATIONS

Perceived risk has a number of marketing implications.

Reducing Risk Perceptions. When perceived risk is high, marketers can either reduce uncertainty or reduce the perceived consequences of failure. The ad for Discover Brokerage, shown in Exhibit 3.1 on page 53, does both. It shows how the company can minimize consumers' uncertainties over making investment decisions by using Discover Brokerage. Consumers are told that the service is easy to use, that they can use it on a trial basis, that they can receive help in setting up investment options, and that they can receive information and planing worksheets to help them make sound decisions. The ad copy also attempts to reduce the perceived consequences of using the service and making bad investment choices. Consumers are told that they can see how their money is doing every second and that they can make investment decision 24 hours a day, every day of the year. They can get quotes customized to their portfolio, they can get access to thousands of funds, and they are charged extremely low commissions.

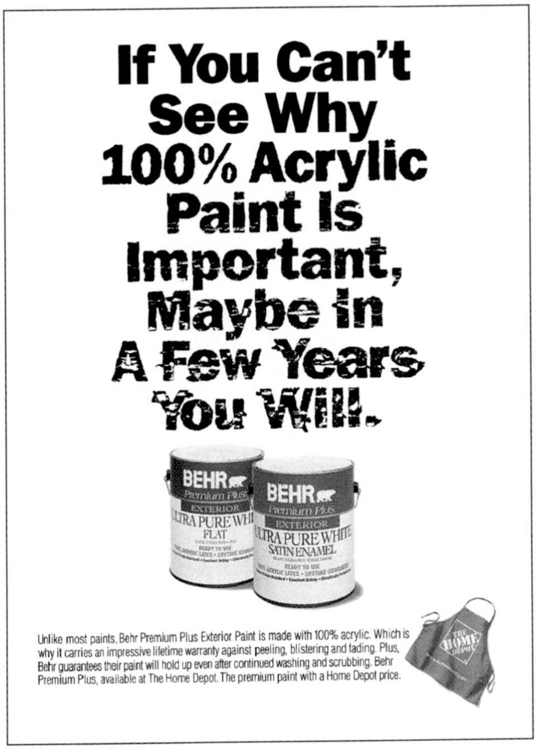
If You Can't See Why 100% Acrylic Paint Is Important, Maybe In A Few Years You Will.
BEHR Premium Plus EXTERIOR ULTRA PURE WHITE FLAT
BEHR Premium Plus EXTERIOR ULTRA PURE WHITE SATIN ENAMEL
READY TO USE
Unlike most paints, Behr Premium Plus Exterior Paint is made with 100% acrylic. Which is why it carries an impressive lifetime warranty against peeling, blistering and fading. Plus, Behr guarantees their paint will hold up even after continued washing and scrubbing. Behr Premium Plus, available at The Home Depot. The premium paint with a Home Depot price.
THE HOME DEPOT

EXHIBIT 3.10

Enhancing Perceived Risk of Not Using Products

Sometimes marketers develop communications to make consumers see that *not* using their offering could be very risky. If consumers see that not using an offering (e.g., a certain brand of paint) is very risky, they may be motivated to use it.

Source: Agency: The Richards Group. Creative Director: Gary Gibson.

Enhancing Risk Perceptions. When risk is low, however, consumers are less motivated to think about the brand and its potential consequences. Marketers sometimes need to enhance risk perceptions to make their promotional appeals more compelling. For example, the ad in Exhibit 3.10 is clearly enhancing the perception of risk for paint buyers who do not buy the Behr brand.

Interestingly, in some cases consumers do not see a particular action as risky, when in fact it is. Poor condom sales and consumers' failure to be persuaded by safe-sex ads, for example, have been blamed on the fact that consumers do not think negative outcomes from unprotected sex are likely to happen to them.[43] Condom advertisements attempt to enhance our risk perceptions and position the product as a solution to this risky outcome.[44] Marketers can also enhance consumers' understanding of how their own behavior can create risky negative outcomes. Researchers know that consumers are more likely to adhere to the advice of ads designed to reduce the risk of AIDS when those consumers think about how their own behavior could cause AIDS.[45] Public service announcements regarding drinking and driving similarly point out the risks of alcohol and drug consumption and indicate appropriate behaviors that reduce risky outcomes. ■

Inconsistency with Attitudes

A final factor affecting motivation is the extent to which new information is consistent with previously acquired knowledge or attitudes. We tend to be motivated to process messages that are moderately inconsistent with our existing knowledge or attitudes because they are perceived as moderately threatening or uncomfortable. Therefore, we try to remove or at least understand this inconsistency.[46] For example, if a consumer sees an advertisement for a car that brings forth slightly negative information about the brand she currently owns (perhaps it gets slightly lower gas mileage than the competitor), she will want to process the information in order to understand and perhaps resolve the uncomfortable feeling.

Consumers are less motivated to process information that is highly inconsistent with their prior attitudes. Thus a consumer who is brand loyal to Heinz ketchup would not be motivated to process information from a comparative ad that says that Heinz is bad or that other brands are better. Other brands would simply be rejected and not considered as viable options.

CONSUMER ABILITY: RESOURCES TO ACT

ability The extent to which consumers have the resources (knowledge, intelligence, and money) necessary to make an outcome happen.

Motivation may not result in action without the ability to process information, make decisions, or engage in behaviors. **Ability** is generally defined as the extent to which consumers have the necessary resources (generally knowledge, intelligence, and money) to make the outcome happen.[47] If our ability to process information is high, we may engage in active decision making. As shown in Exhibit 3.2, knowledge, experience, cognitive style, intelligence, education, age, and money are factors that affect ability.

Product Knowledge and Experience

Consumers vary greatly in their knowledge about an offering.[48] Knowledge can come from product or service experiences such as ad exposures, interactions with salespeople, information from friends or the media, previous decision making or product usage, or memory.

A number of studies have compared the information-processing activities of consumers who have a lot of product knowledge or expertise with consumers who do not.[49] One key finding is that knowledgeable consumers, or "experts," are better able to think deeply about information than equally motivated but less knowledgeable consumers, or "novices." A good example of a situation in which consumers' knowledge may be lacking occurs when drug companies advertise to consumers. The federal government strictly regulates these ads, and they must provide detailed technical information (as shown in Exhibit 3.11). Although consumers who have expertise in pharmaceuticals could process this information, most of us have a difficult time doing so. Similarly, in the car-leasing industry consumers rarely understand the concept of a car's capitalized costs, which is the number used to determine lease payments. Most consumers don't understand these costs and how they are determined. Nor do they understand that unless they are negotiated down, the dealer will get a big profit on the deal.[50]

One study found that novices and experts process similar amounts of information but differ in how they do so.[51] Experts were able to process information when it was stated in terms of its attributes (what the product has—such as a Pentium chip), whereas novices could do so only when the information was stated in terms of its benefits (what the product can do for the consumer—such as help you be efficient). Novices may also be able to process information when they are

EXHIBIT 3.11
Ability to Process Information from Marketing Communications

Consumers may lack sufficient background knowledge or expertise to understand the technical information that the federal government requires drug companies to provide. The technical information to the right of this ad appeared on the reverse side of the original ad.

Source: Copyright Westwood-Squibb Pharmaceuticals. Illustration used with their permission.

given an analogy that helps them understand it. For example, the product shown in Exhibit 3.12 may be unfamiliar to consumers, who may not be able to relate it to their prior knowledge. However, an analogy between the new product and the expert skier makes the attributes of the product more understandable.[52]

Cognitive Style

Consumers can also differ in **cognitive style**, or their preferences for how information should be best presented. Some consumers are adept at processing information visually, whereas others prefer to process information verbally. For example, when in need of directions, some consumers prefer to see a map and others prefer to read directions.

One important aspect of cognitive style is called **cognitive complexity**.[53] A cognitively complex individual is more likely to engage in complicated processing of information from marketing communications, accepting new and/or contradictory information, making finer distinctions when processing information, and considering a greater diversity of information when making a decision.

Intelligence, Education, and Age

Intelligence, education, and age have also been related to the ability to process information. Specifically, higher levels of intelligence and education will enhance the consumer's ability to process more complex information and make decisions.

Age is also associated with differences in information-processing ability. For example, older children seem to be sensitive to the fact that the benefits of searching for information sometimes outweigh the costs. Younger children don't seem to have this same ability.[54] Old age has been associated with a decline in certain cognitive skills and thus reduced ability to process information. One study found that, compared to younger consumers, older consumers took more time to process nutrition information and made decisions that were less accurate.[55]

Money

Obviously, the lack of money also constrains consumers who might otherwise have the motivation to engage in a behavior. Although lack of money does not reduce information processing or decision making by motivated consumers, it does constrain whether they will engage in a monetary exchange with marketers.

MARKETING IMPLICATIONS Factors affecting ability suggest several implications for marketers.

Understand Consumers' Knowledge and Processing Styles. First, marketers should be sure that target consumers have sufficient prior knowledge to process marketing communications. To the extent that consumers do not have this knowledge, marketing communications may need to educate consumers.

EXHIBIT 3.12
Learning by Analogy

Sometimes when we are unfamiliar with something, we can understand what it is only in terms of how it is similar to something else. In this ad, advertisers are trying to show how a new digital camera is similar to an expert skier.

Source: JVC Company of America.

Extreme performance.

The JVC GR-DVL9500 Digital CyberCam.
Taking digital video technology to the edge...and beyond.

You're about being the best. In everything you do. In everything you own. And now, JVC proudly presents your camcorder — the GR-DVL9500. With an unprecedented array of features that delivers the most incredible digital image you've ever seen, this digital camcorder simply blows away anything else in its class.

These features are just the tip of the iceberg:
- Crisp 500-line resolution with Progressive Scan CCD
- An amazing 200x digital zoom
- Integrated snapshot mode with built-in auto flash for superb digital photographs
- A bright, clear 3.8-inch flip-out LCD monitor
- High-speed recording with ProSlow for high-density slow motion playback
- PC connectivity, including RS232 cable and 5-piece software package — everything you need is in the box (software value $180.00)
- Digital Interface, including DV in/out terminal (IEEE/1394) and Digital Still Picture Output (RS232)
- Built-in digital effects, editing capabilities and more

And it's all packed into a sleek, yet rugged compact unit that's extremely user-friendly. So if you've ever imagined being limited only by your imagination, the JVC GR-DVL9500 is the camcorder for you.

JVC
When Performance Matters. Mini DV
www.jvc.com

Match Communications with Knowledge and Processing Styles. Marketers also need to be sensitive to the potentially different processing styles, education levels, and ages of target consumers. For example, highly motivated but visually oriented parents may not be able to assemble toys for their children if the written instructions are too complex and, thus, incompatible with their processing style. Putting instructions in both words and pictures covers both processing styles.

Facilitate Ability. Finally, because a lack of money constrains behaviors, marketers can facilitate first-time and repeat buying by providing monetary aid. Allowing consumers to buy cars with 0 percent down or with low financing rates, deferring payment for several months, and allowing payment on an installment basis are ways of enhancing purchasing ability. Marketers can also provide education and information that facilitates consumers' abilities to process information, make decisions, and engage in consumption behaviors. For example, many companies provide product information at Web sites that explain product features and how they differ from the features of competitors' products.[56]

CONSUMER OPPORTUNITY

The final factor affecting whether motivation results in action is consumers' opportunity to process it. For example, a consumer may be highly motivated to work out and have sufficient money to join a club (ability); however, her time may be so constrained that she has little opportunity to actually go. Thus even when motivation and ability are high, other factors including lack of time; distractions; and the amount, complexity, and repetition of relevant information can prevent our taking action. Physical limitations also affect the opportunity to use products. For example, some observers predict that on-line magazines will never replace traditional media because consumers can't use them in places where they traditionally read (such as in bed or the bathtub).[57]

Time

Time can affect the opportunity to process information, make decisions, and perform certain behaviors. Some research has found that consumers are more likely to buy things for themselves during the Christmas season. The reason is that this season is one of the few occasions when time-pressed consumers actually go shopping.[58]

Consumers under time pressure to make a decision will engage in limited information processing. For example, a consumer who has to buy 30 items in a 15-minute grocery shopping trip will not have the time to process a lot of information relevant to each decision. Research has shown that time-pressured consumers not only process less information but also put more weight on negative information; they are quicker to reject brands because of negative features.[59]

In an advertising context, the opportunity to process information is also limited when the message is presented in a short amount of time; when consumers cannot control the pace of message presentation, as is the case with television and radio ads; or when consumers zip (fast-forward) through the ads.[60]

Distraction

Distraction refers to any aspect of the processing situation that can divert consumers' attention away from the message. For example, if someone is talking while the consumer is viewing an ad or making a decision, the consumer's ability to process the information is inhibited. Likewise, parents whose children are crying or misbehaving in a store cannot easily listen to salespeople. Certain background factors in an ad such as music or attractive models can also distract consumers from an advertised message.[61] Finally, consumers may be distracted from ads if the program in which the ad is embedded is very involving.[62]

Amount of Information

The amount of information present can also affect processing opportunity. For example, processing information related to the ad in Exhibit 3.13 would be very hard even if you had the ability and the desire to do so because there is so little of it.

Complexity of Information

As information becomes more complex, our opportunity to process it decreases. What makes information complex? Research has shown that technical or quantitative information is more difficult for consumers to handle than is nontechnical and qualitative data[63] and, therefore, inhibits processing. Complex information is common for many technological and pharmaceutical products (as shown in Exhibit 3.11). Research has also indicated that messages containing only pictures without words tend to be ambiguous and therefore hard to process.[64] Information may also be complex if the individual needs to sort through a huge volume of it.

Repetition of Information

Whereas the three previous factors limit consumers' opportunity to process information, one factor—repetition—actually enhances it.[65] If consumers are repeatedly exposed to information, processing is made easier because they have more chances to think about, scrutinize, and remember the information.

EXHIBIT 3.13
Amount of Information and Opportunity

This ad contains so little information, consumers may not have much opportunity to process it.

Source: David Young-Wolff/ PhotoEdit.

MARKETING IMPLICATIONS

Often marketers can do little to enhance consumers' opportunities to process information, make careful decisions, or engage in purchase, usage, or disposition behaviors. For example, advertisers cannot make living rooms less distracting during TV commercials or give consumers more time to engage in shopping activities. However, marketers can play some role in enhancing opportunity, as shown below.

Repeat Marketing Communications and Make Them Easy to Process. Repeating marketing communications (up to a point) increases the likelihood that consumers will attend to and eventually process them. Presenting messages at a time of day when consumers are least likely to be distracted and pressed for time is another way of enhancing the likelihood that the messages can be processed. Likewise, communications should be stated slowly and in simple terms so consumers understand them. Note, though, that although repetition increases the opportunity to process information, repetition can also reduce consumers' motivation to process it!

Reduce Time-Pressured Decision Making. Marketers can also reduce some of the situational constraints that make decisions difficult for consumers. For example, retailers may have extended hours so consumers can take advantage of the store, product, or service at times that are least distracting and least time pressured. Many catalog and all on-line shopping companies allow consumers to place orders 24 hours a day. Marketers can also offer ancillary services that remove time constraints. For example, some health clubs offer extended hours (opening at 5:00 A.M. and closing at midnight) and baby-sitting services for consumers who would otherwise be unable to attend.

Reduce Purchase/Usage Time. Marketers can also reduce the amount of time needed to buy or use a product. The increasing user-friendliness of computers is a direct response to the learning costs consumers associate with them. Clear signs and directories in stores help consumers to locate goods and increase the likelihood that consumers will actually buy goods they are motivated to purchase.

 Provide Information. Finally, sometimes the simple availability of information enhances consumers' abilities to process information, make decisions, and engage in consumer behaviors. In Zimbabwe, consumers are increasingly becoming overweight, given the influx of fast food and processed food. Some of these consumers are being helped by joining Weight Watchers. The availability of information about the high fat and calorie content of foods enables consumers to learn ways to modify their diet to achieve a healthier body.[66] ■

SUMMARY

Motivation reflects an inner state of arousal that directs the consumer to engage in goal-relevant behaviors, effortful information processing, and detailed decision making. We are motivated to attend to, approach, and think about things that are important and personally relevant.

Motivated consumers often experience affective or cognitive involvement. In some cases, this involvement may be enduring; in other cases, it may be situational, lasting only until the goal has been achieved. Consumers can also be involved in many different kinds of objects: product categories, brands, ads, the media, and consumption behaviors. Motivation tends to be greater when consumers see a goal or object as personally relevant—meaning that it relates to their needs, values, and goals; entails considerable risk; or is inconsistent with their prior attitude.

Even when motivation is high, consumers may not achieve the goal of their motivation if their ability and/or opportunity to do so is low. If consumers lack the knowledge, experience, intelligence, education, or money to engage in a behavior, process information, or make a decision, they cannot achieve a goal. Goal achievement may also be blocked if consumers are attending to information that is incompatible with their processing styles or if the information is presented in too complex a fashion.

Highly motivated consumers may also fail to achieve goals if lack of time, distractions, or insufficient or overly complex information limit the opportunity to do so.

EXERCISES

1. Randomly select ten advertisements from a magazine. Develop questions that attempt to assess the consumer's involvement in the ad (both cognitive and affective) and motivation to process information from the ad. Show the ads and ask the questions to a sample of 20 to 30 consumers. Which types of ads tend to be higher in involvement? Which types of ads tend to be lower in involvement? How do these ads tend to differ in terms of (a) recognition of consumers' needs, (b) structure and content, and (c) assumption of consumer knowledge or expertise?

2. Develop your own projective test, depicting some purchase or usage situation for a product or service of your choice. What kinds of needs are revealed by your test?

3. Watch TV and the associated ads for half an hour. At the end of your viewing, write down the ads you remember. Use the concepts of motivation, ability, and opportunity to describe why you processed and remembered these commercials. What was it about the ad, your prior knowledge or use of these products, or the environment in which you viewed the ads that made them memorable?

CHAPTER 4

EXPOSURE, ATTENTION, AND PERCEPTION

INTRODUCTION

Sales of Reese's Pieces jumped after the candies were featured as a favorite treat of the character E.T. in Steven Spielberg's movie. Since then, there has been increasing emphasis on featuring brand-name consumer products in films and on TV. Some advertisers report incredible success with these product placement strategies. BMW's Z3 (see Exhibit 4.1) and the Omega watch were featured in the 1995 James Bond film *Golden Eye*. After the film was released, BMW had orders for the Z3 up to one year in advance, and Omega reported a 40 percent increase in its watch sales. Products as props are not restricted to the movies; consumer items are routinely shown in TV shows and even in computer and virtual-reality games.[1] Rosie O'Donnell gave Drake's Cakes a sales boost by eating them on air,[2] and episodes of *Ellen* and *Seinfeld* showing cast members wearing milk moustaches gave a boost to the Drink Milk campaign developed by the Milk Processor Board.[3]

Products are not always shown in the best light on TV and in movies. For example, actress Joanna Lumley's character is shown in the British comedy *Absolutely Fabulous* carrying Stolichnaya vodka in her purse and drinking it right from the bottle. In some cases the presence of products on TV shows causes a public outcry. For example, the public was upset over the prominent display of the Sony logo

EXHIBIT 4.1
Brand Exposure Through TV and Movies

When BMW's Z3 was featured in the James Bond film *Golden Eye*, BMW had orders for the Z3 up to one year in advance.

Source: Photofest

on a computer monitor at the televised O. J. Simpson trial. Sony had to replace the logo with a less obtrusive one. And Philip Morris was asked to remove or relocate billboards in sports arenas so consumers would not be exposed to its cigarette ads when watching sports on TV.[4]

Product placement raises some interesting questions. First, are these product appearances dangerous because they blur the lines between programming and advertising? Second, are people less resistant to potential messages about these products because they appear in programs? Third, do the products force exposure to advertising messages? (Although consumers can avoid advertising messages in regular commercials by changing channels, they are less likely to do so when the same products appear in TV shows or on film.) The complex answers to these questions are examined this chapter.

First, if consumers are to be affected by a communication, they must be exposed to it. Marketers are clearly aware of the importance of exposure, and they have been relying on many nontraditional forms of advertising such as product placement to increase consumers' exposure to products. Interestingly, however, marketers cannot completely control the exposure of their product when it is shown on TV programs or in films. Advertisers do not pay the TV or film studios directly for products placed in film and TV. Instead, advertisers pay product-placement firms who work with set decorators. The set decorators use the product in the way they believe will enhance the realism of the film or TV show.[5]

Second, if consumers are to register any message being made about the brand, they must pay attention to the product. Whether they do so depends on a host of factors, such as whether the product is relevant to them, prominent, or surprising in its context.

Third, whether consumers' are affected by exposure to the products in these media depends on whether the consumers can perceive the product in the show or film. For example, the brand name might be out of focus, too much of the package might be obscured, or the camera might pan past the brand so quickly that consumers cannot even see it.

This chapter examines exposure, attention, and perception in detail, along with the resulting marketing implications. As Exhibit 4.2 indicates, exposure, attention,

EXHIBIT 4.2
Chapter Overview: Exposure, Attention, and Perception

Consumers do some processing of a stimulus (e.g., an ad, brand) once they have been exposed to it, pay attention to it, and perceive its characteristics. Once it is perceived, consumers may attend to it some more. The exhibit also indicates the topics that will be covered for each concept.

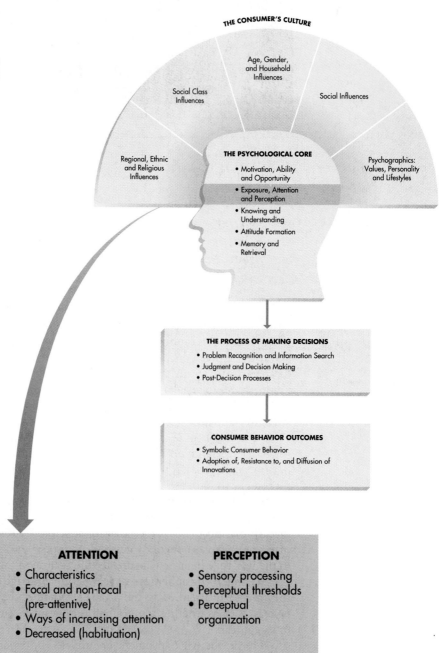

THE CONSUMER'S CULTURE

Age, Gender, and Household Influences

Social Class Influences

Social Influences

Regional, Ethnic and Religious Influences

THE PSYCHOLOGICAL CORE
- Motivation, Ability and Opportunity
- Exposure, Attention and Perception
- Knowing and Understanding
- Attitude Formation
- Memory and Retrieval

Psychographics: Values, Personality and Lifestyles

THE PROCESS OF MAKING DECISIONS
- Problem Recognition and Information Search
- Judgment and Decision Making
- Post-Decision Processes

CONSUMER BEHAVIOR OUTCOMES
- Symbolic Consumer Behavior
- Adoption of, Resistance to, and Diffusion of Innovations

EXPOSURE
- Ways of gaining exposure
- Selective
- Measuring exposure

ATTENTION
- Characteristics
- Focal and non-focal (pre-attentive)
- Ways of increasing attention
- Decreased (habituation)

PERCEPTION
- Sensory processing
- Perceptual thresholds
- Perceptual organization

and perception are important because they affect what consumers comprehend, the attitudes they have, and what they remember. This information, in turn, affects the decisions consumers make.

EXPOSURE

exposure The process by which the consumer comes in physical contact with a stimulus.

marketing stimuli Information about products or brands communicated by either the marketer (via ads, salespeople, brand symbols, packages, signs, prices, and so on) or nonmarketing sources (e.g., the media, word of mouth).

Before any type of marketing stimulus can affect consumers, they must be exposed to it. **Exposure** simply reflects the process by which the consumer comes into physical contact with a stimulus. We use the term **marketing stimuli** to mean information about products or brands communicated by either the marketer (via ads, salespeople, brand symbols, packages, signs, prices, and so on) or nonmarketing sources (e.g., the media, word of mouth). Consumers can be exposed to marketing stimuli at the buying, using, or disposing stages of consumption. Because exposure is critical to consumers' subsequent processing of any stimulus, marketers need to make sure that consumers are exposed to marketing stimuli.

MARKETING IMPLICATIONS In marketing, gaining exposure typically begins with the selection of media, such as radio and the Internet, and the development of sales promotions that target consumers can use. For example, many beer drinkers enjoy watching sports. Therefore, advertising beer during a football or basketball game, sponsoring an athletic event, and selling advertising specialties like T-shirts or mugs with the beer's name on it at sports events represent ways to increase exposure to beer brands. Nike paid approximately $120 million to sponsor the U.S. Soccer Federation, giving the brand tremendous exposure to soccer fans all over the United States.[6] ■

Factors Influencing Exposure

The *position of an ad within a medium* can affect exposure. Exposure to commercials is greatest when they are placed at the beginning or end of a commercial break because consumers are still involved in the program or are waiting for the program to come back on. Exposure to magazine ads is greatest when they appear on the back cover because the ad is in view whenever the magazine is placed facedown. Also, consumers are most likely to be exposed to ads placed next to articles or within TV programs that interest them.[7]

Finally, *product distribution and shelf placement* affect exposure. The more widespread the brand's distribution (the more stores in which it is available), the greater the likelihood that consumers will encounter it. Likewise, the location or the amount of shelf space allocated to the product can increase consumers' exposure to a product. Consumers are most likely to be exposed to products that are featured in an end-of-aisle display or that take up a lot of space on the shelf. Products placed from waist to eye level also get more exposure than those placed higher or lower. Finally, exposure increases if products are placed at points in the store where all consumers must go and spend time. For example, supermarkets, hardware stores, automotive stores, and restaurants find that point-of-purchase displays at the checkout counter can enhance the sales of some products.[8]

MARKETING IMPLICATIONS In addition to the traditional ways of reaching consumers, such as strategic placement of television commercials or effective product displays and shelf placement, marketers have been experimenting with other communications that gain exposure for marketing stimuli. Buick has handed out tens of thousands of packs of peanuts and cookies wrapped in plastic covers with the Buick and Regal emblems on some Northwest Airlines and United Airlines flights.[9] Shell has installed TV sets at some of its pumps to advertise products sold at its gas station convenience stores.[10] Advertising in media such as airlines' in-flight entertainment programs, luggage carousels, home video rentals, shopping carts, school news programs, hot air balloons, and turnstiles at sports arenas are other ways of increasing exposure. In some American towns and cities, cash-strapped governments are allowing companies to place ads on public buses, garbage trucks, and police cars.[11] In Egypt some advertisers use feluccas (boats that sail along the Nile River) to advertise brands.[12] Using "human directionals"—people who stand on street corners wearing crazy outfits, waving their hands, and shouting information—is one way that retailers and home developers affect consumers' exposure to the store or development (see Exhibit 4.3). ∎

Selective Exposure

While marketers can work very hard to affect consumers' exposure to certain products and brands, ultimately consumers control whether exposure occurs or not. In other words, consumers can actively seek certain stimuli and avoid others. Readers of *Vogue* magazine selectively expose themselves to its fashion-oriented ads, whereas readers of *Car and Driver* choose to look at different kinds of ads. Some readers may ignore the ads altogether.

Consumers' avoidance of marketing stimuli is a big problem for marketers.[13] While watching TV, consumers can simply leave the room or do something else when commercials air. Zipping and zapping—the "dreaded zs"—are two common avoidance practices. **Zipping** occurs when consumers tape television shows on their VCR and fast-forward through the commercials. Zipping is a serious problem for advertisers because 50 to 60 percent of the ads in recorded programs are fast-forwarded. When **zapping**, consumers avoid exposure by using remote controls to switch to other channels during the commercial break. Approximately 20 percent of consumers zap at any one time, and more than two-thirds of households with cable TV zap also on a regular basis. Men zap significantly more than

zipping Fast-forwarding through the commercials recorded on a VCR.

zapping Use of a remote control to switch channels during commercial breaks.

EXHIBIT 4.3
Human Directionals

Marketers sometimes use human directionals like the person shown here to increase the likelihood that they will be exposed to marketing messages.

Source: Spencer Weiner/ Los Angeles Times.

women do. Zapping of commercials at the half-hour or hour mark is also more likely than during the program itself.[14]

Why do consumers want to avoid ads? In part, it is because they are exposed to so many. No one can possibly process them all. *Bride's* magazine now has more than 1,000 pages, many of which are ads. Readers of *Harper's Bazaar*, *Mademoiselle*, and *Elle* must sometimes flip through more than 125 pages of ads before they find the first feature article.[15] Consumers also avoid ads for product categories that they don't use and are therefore irrelevant to them. Consumers also tend to avoid ads that they have seen before because they know what these ads will say.

Measuring Exposure

In January 1999 advertisers paid upwards of $1.6 million for a single 30-second spot on the Super Bowl. Why did they spend such exorbitant sums of money? In part, because of projections of exposure rates based on 1998 data. That data in 1998 showed that nearly one of every two people in the United States watched the Super Bowl.[16] Determining which media will generate exposure to marketing stimuli, and then determining whether the desired exposure rates have actually been reached, is therefore an important activity for marketers.

As we discussed in Chapter 2, one research tool that is extremely valuable in assessing potential exposure is Simmons data. Simmons Market Research Bureau surveys thousands of consumers annually, asking each about the products they consume and the TV programs, magazines, and types of radio formats they watch, read, and listen to. The company publishes a multivolume compendium that tells advertisers which vehicles might best reach target consumers.

Several syndicated research services help advertisers determine whether their ads actually reach target consumers. The Neilsen Television Index has a panel of approximately 2,000 consumers who agree to have their TV viewing monitored. These consumers place an electronic device called a "people meter" on their TV. The people meter monitors which channel is viewed when the TV is on. Monitoring takes place every 30 seconds. Each viewer has a special switch or light to turn on when he or she (as opposed to someone else in the household) is watching TV. In this way Neilsen can monitor not only which commercials and programs are being watched but also who in the household is watching. An-other company, called Arbitron, uses diaries to collect information about which radio stations consumers are listening to (see www.arbitron.com). Traffic counters are sometimes used to count the number of cars that drive by billboards every day. Unfortunately, counters tabulate only car traffic (not pedestrians) and cannot tell how many consumers are in each car or whether they actually see the particular billboard.

An issue of considerable concern in the advertising industry is how to measure exposure to Internet advertising. This issue is significant for several reasons. First, advertisers do not know how much consumers look at ads on the Internet. Second, different methods of counting ad exposures often yield very different numbers. For example, independent research firms such as Media Metrix (www.mediametrix.com) rely on random samples of Internet users and track their on-line viewing behavior. From this information researchers make projections about exposure levels. However, the research firms' exposure figures often differ from those of Web sites that keep traffic logs of site visits. Currently, the advertising industry is working hard to develop a standard system of measuring Internet exposure levels.[17]

attention The process by which an individual allocates part of his or her mental activity to a stimulus.

Attention is the process by which we devote mental activity to a stimulus. Notice that Exhibit 4.2 shows a double line connecting attention and perception. This double line indicates that a certain amount of attention is necessary for information to be perceived—for it to activate our senses. However, after information has been perceived, additional levels of attention may be paid to the information. This additional attention allows us to perform the higher-order processing activities discussed in the next few chapters. Given this relationship between attention and perception, understanding the characteristics of attention and how marketers can enhance consumers' attention to marketing stimuli is very important.

Characteristics of Attention

Key characteristics of attention are that it is selective, it is capable of being divided, and it is limited.

Attention Is Selective   One key aspect of attention is that it is selective. *Selectivity* means that we decide which of possibly hundreds of things we want to focus on at any one time. The number of stimuli to which we are exposed at any given time is potentially overwhelming. For example, although you are currently paying attention to the information in this book, you are simultaneously being exposed to a number of other stimuli. Stop a moment and think about it. Sounds of traffic might be coming in through an open window. Someone else may be in the room talking on the phone or humming a tune. Perhaps unanswered mail sits in view, or a fragrant meal is simmering on the stove. In the same way, we are exposed to hundreds of marketing stimuli. Consider a shopper who goes to the grocery store to buy snacks and soft drinks. She is exposed to numerous products, brands, ads, displays, signs, prices, logos, and packages. Most people are not able to examine all these stimuli simultaneously. Instead, we must somehow determine which are worthy of processing. The fact that attention is selective means that we can control what we focus on.

Attention Can Be Divided   A second aspect of attention is that it is capable of being divided. Thus we can parcel our mental resources into units and allocate some to one task and some to another. For example, we can drive a car and talk at the same time. We can allocate attention flexibly to meet the demands of things in our environment, but we also have the potential to become distracted; that is, one stimulus can pull our attention away from another. We would be distracted from our conversation while driving, for example, if a dog ran in front of the car. Likewise, if we are distracted from a product or ad, the amount of attention we devote to it will be greatly reduced.[18]

Attention Is Limited   A third and critical aspect of attention is that it is limited. Although we may be able to divide our attention, we can attend to multiple things only if processing them is relatively automatic, well practiced, and effortless.[19] Consider the fact that although you can sometimes drive and talk at the same time, if traffic becomes heavy or driving conditions worsen, you need to stop talking and devote all your attention to driving. Likewise, although you can sometimes watch an ad on TV and listen to your friends talk, if the conversation gets too serious, you need to turn down the TV. The fact that attention is limited explains why consumers in an unfamiliar store are less likely to notice new products than when those same consumers are shopping in a familiar store. Because they are trying to attend to many unfamiliar things, some of those products will be missed.

Focal and Nonfocal Attention

Because attention is selective and capable of being divided, there is a question of whether we can attend to something in our peripheral vision even if we are already focusing on something else. For example, when we read an article in a magazine, can we process information presented in an adjacent ad—even if our eyes are directed squarely at the article and we are not aware of the presence of the ad? When we drive down the highway, can we process any information from a billboard placed by the side of the road even if we are focusing only on the road?

Preattentive Processing   To the extent that we can process information from our peripheral vision even if we are not aware that we are attending to it, we are engaged in **preattentive processing**. With preattentive processing most of our attentional resources are devoted to one thing, leaving very limited resources for attending to something else. We devote just enough attention to an object in peripheral vision to process *something* about the object. But because the amount of attention is so limited, we are not aware of the fact that we are attending to and processing it.

Hemispheric Lateralization   Our ability to process information preattentively depends on (1) whether the stimulus in peripheral vision is a picture or a word and (2) whether it is placed in the right or left visual field (to the right side or the left side of the object on which we are focused). The reason these factors are influential has to do with the way the two halves of the brain process information (see Exhibit 4.4). The human brain is divided into two hemispheres. The right hemisphere is best at processing music, grasping visual and spatial information, forming inferences, and drawing conclusions. The left hemisphere, in contrast, is best at processing units that can be combined. Tasks such as counting, processing unfamiliar words, and forming sentences are performed in the left hemisphere.[20]

Interestingly, stimuli placed in the right visual field (ads on the right side of the focal article or billboards on the right side of the road) tend to be processed by the left hemisphere; those in the left visual field tend to be processed by the right hemisphere. Stimuli on which we directly focus are processed by both hemispheres. These findings suggest that stimuli such as pictures in ads are most likely to be preattentively processed if they are placed to the left of a magazine article because they will be processed in the right hemisphere—the hemisphere that is best at processing visual stimuli. Likewise, stimuli such as brand names or ad claims are most likely to be preattentively processed if they are placed in the right visual field because they will be processed by the left hemisphere. Several studies have indeed found that consumers' ability to preattentively process pictures, brand names, or claims in ads depends on whether the ad is placed in the right or left visual field.[21]

Preattentive Processing, Brand-name Liking, and Choice   Although we may be able to attend to and devote some minimal level of processing to stimuli placed in peripheral vision, an important question is whether such preattentively processed stimuli affect our liking for an ad or brand or, more important, our decisions to buy a particular brand. Some research suggests that they do. Some evidence suggests that consumers will like the same brand name more if they have processed it preattentively than if they have not been exposed to it all.[22] One

preattentive processing
The nonconscious processing of stimuli in peripheral vision.

EXHIBIT 4.4
Hemispheric Lateralization

The two hemispheres of our brain are best at processing different types of information. When a stimulus is in *focal* vision, it is processed by *both hemispheres*. When it is in *peripheral* vision (i.e., it is not being focused on), it is processed by the *opposite hemisphere*. Information presented in the left visual field is therefore processed by the right hemisphere.

Source: Adapted from Chris Janiszewski, "The Influence of Nonattended Material on the Processing of Advertising Claims," *Journal of Marketing Research,* August 1990, p. 265. Reprinted with permission of the American Marketing Association.

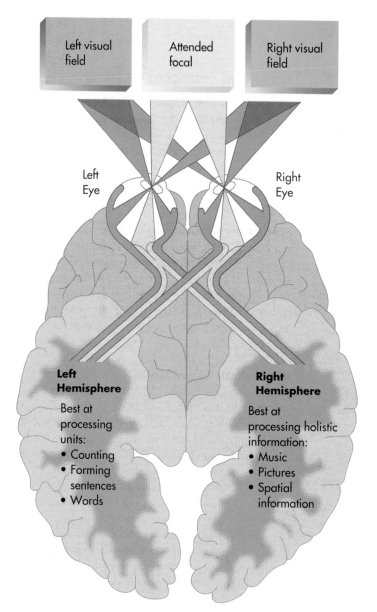

explanation for this finding is that preattentive processing makes a brand name familiar, and we tend to like things that are familiar.[23]

Other evidence suggests that stimuli processed preattentively can affect consumer choices. One study found that consumers were more likely to consider choosing a product if they had previously been preattentively exposed to an ad that contained that product than if they had not been exposed to the ad. In this case preattentive processing of the ad affected consumers' consideration of the product, even though they had no memory of having seen the ad.[24]

MARKETING IMPLICATIONS Although consumers can process information preattentively, information will clearly affect consumers more when they devote full attention to it. Unfortunately, a marketing stimulus competes with many other types of stimuli (including other marketing stimuli) for consumers' attention. Moreover, consumers may have limited motivation and opportunity to attend to marketing stimuli in the first

EVER HAVE A 12 LB.

FROZEN TURKEY

FALL ON YOUR FOOT?

I used to have a fridge with the freezer on top. And every time I opened the door there would be this avalanche of frozen food. I finally had to put a FALLING ROCKS sign on the door. But look at this, the folks at Amana put the freezer on the bottom so the stuff you need all the time—like fresh fruit and vegetables—is right on top. Easy to see and easy to reach. In fact, it's even called the Easy Reach. Now is that smart or what! It sure makes more sense than dropping a 12 lb. turkey on your foot. I mean, try explaining that to your HMO.

Amana
BUILT BETTER THAN IT HAS TO BE

www.amana.com   ©1999 Amana Company, L.P.

EXHIBIT 4.5
Rhetorical Questions Capture Attention

Rhetorical questions can be relevant to the self and can attract attention when they include the word *you.*

Source: Photo courtesy of Amana Appliances.

www.

place. Consequently, marketers often try to attract consumers' attention. Exhibit 4.2 on page 80 outlines the four major ways of capturing attention: making the stimulus (1) personally relevant, (2) pleasant, (3) surprising, and (4) easy to process.

Making Stimuli Personally Relevant. Messages tend to be personally relevant when they (1) appeal to your needs, values, and goals; (2) show sources similar to the target audience; (3) use dramas; and (4) use rhetorical questions.

One of the most powerful ways for a stimulus to be perceived as personally relevant is for it to appeal to your needs, values, or goals.[25] If you are hungry, you are more likely to pay attention to food ads and packages relevant to that need. You may pay attention to ads that show young people skateboarding or roller-blading if these activities are consistent with your goals of having fun and your values regarding exercise.

You are also more likely to notice individuals whom you perceive as similar to yourself.[26] Many advertisers use "typical consumers," hoping that consumers will relate to these individuals and thereby attend to the ad.

Ads that resemble dramas—mini-stories that depict the experiences of actors or relate someone's experiences through a narrative—can enhance consumers' attention. With dramas the viewer in essence eavesdrops on the scene depicted in the ad. Some dramas unfold through a series of ads, whereas other ads convey an entire story in 30 seconds. Dramas draw the consumer into the action and make the action in the ad relevant to the consumer.

Another way to capture consumers' attention is to ask rhetorical questions—those asked merely for effect.[27] No one really expects an answer to a rhetorical question because its answer is so obvious. Examples include "What are you, a wise guy?" and "How would you like to win a million dollars?" These questions appeal to the consumer by including the word *you* and by asking the consumer (if only for effect) to consider answering the question. They also represent an attempt to draw the consumer into the advertisement. The ad in Exhibit 4.5 attracts the consumer's attention by asking, "Ever have a 12 lb. frozen turkey fall on your foot?"

Making Stimuli Pleasant. People tend to approach things that are inherently pleasant. Marketers can use this principle to increase consumers' attention to marketing stimuli.

- *Using Attractive Models.* Advertisements containing attractive models have a higher probability of being noticed than those that do not because the models arouse positive feelings or a basic sexual attraction.[28] Ads featuring popular and/or attractive individuals such as Michael Jordan, Cindy Crawford, Mel Gibson, and Christie Brinkley have been quite effective in generating attention. Victoria's Secret created tremendous attention for its 1999 on-line fashion show when a preview aired during the Super Bowl. That one commercial brought more than 1 million viewers to the company's Web site within an hour after the broadcast.[29] The presence of highly attractive models in the commercial and fashion show was surely the reason for this huge response. Clearly, individual differences influence people's opinions on what is attractive. For example, although some people enjoy the sight of naked bodies in advertisements, other viewers find this type of display offensive. Clear cross-cultural differences also account for what is considered attractive. Ultrathin models represent a Western standard of beauty; elsewhere in the world, such models would be perceived as poor, undernourished, and unattractive.

- *Using Music.* Familiar songs and popular entertainers have considerable ability to attract us in pleasant ways.[30] For example, Reba McEntire is paid to appear in snack-food commercials because of her attention-getting powers. Music relating to a pleasant and nostalgic past is also used to attract attention. Commercials for Budweiser use the song "Ants," and commercials for Burger King play the song "That's the Way I Like It." Music can draw attention to an ad and enhance the attention we pay to the ad's message—provided that the music is coordinated with the ad's theme.

- *Using Humor.* Humor can also be an effective attention-getting device.[31] Pepsi used humor in a recent ad showing a sweet little girl dining with her grandfather. When the girl is told that the restaurant serves only Coke, her voice changes into something straight out of *The Exorcist.* The frightened waiter runs away, only to return moments later with a Pepsi.[32] The girl returns to her sweet normal self after the Pepsi is delivered. Daewoo, the Korean-based car manufacturer, used humor in Britain in launching two of its new car models. The ads attracted consumers' attention with the humorous slogan "Daewho? The biggest car company you've never heard of."[33] The ad in Exhibit 4.6 also illustrates the use of humor.

Making Stimuli Surprising. Consumers are also likely to process a stimulus when it is surprising. Two characteristics make a stimulus surprising: novelty and unexpectedness.

- *Using Novelty.* We are more likely to notice any stimulus that is new or unique—because it stands out relative to other stimuli around us. Products, packages, and brand names that are unusual or novel command attention. A perfume company is attracting attention with novel perfume fragrances—one labeled Dirt smells like potting soil; another labeled Carrot smells like the vegetable.[34] Fragrance marketers are also developing novel packages to attract attention to their brands. For example, Catalyst for Men is packaged in test tubes and laboratory flasks. Because the packaging looks like a chemistry set, the product stands out from other brands on the shelf. As shown in Exhibit 4.7, the makers of King Tut's Party Mix developed a novel package so the brand would stand out. Unusual looks work even for cars; for example, the Lamborghini Countach is very different in shape from most cars on the road. Marketers sometimes change their products or packages so the otherwise familiar will appear more interesting. Heinz held a major contest a few years ago to get suggestions from consumers about a new trademark to replace its stodgy old one.[35]

Advertising formats can be novel, too.[36] Neiman Marcus is attempting to make its catalog stand out from the clutter by mailing some of its customers a

EXHIBIT 4.6
Humor in Ads

This ad uses both an unexpected image (a baby hanging from a ceiling fan) and humor to attract attention to the ad and get across the point that wallpaper can be captivating.

Source: Wallpaper Council Incorporated.

Nothing gets your attention like wallpaper.
For simple ways to make your home more striking, see a local wallpaper dealer. © 1999 Wallpaper Council.

EXHIBIT 4.7
Novel Packaging

Consumers pay more attention to things that are novel or different. This package for King Tut's Party Mix is very different from most party mix packages. Can you think of some brand names, packages, ads, promotions, stores, etc. that attract attention by being novel or different?

Source: Designed by Debora Michel.

180-page "book" that features interviews with fashion designers, recipes, and fashion tips in addition to the store's merchandise.[37]

Novel ads also command attention. To communicate that British Airways flies more people each year than the number that live in Manhattan, the carrier ran a now-famous campaign that showed the island of Manhattan flying overhead. Some advertisers have attracted consumers' attention by surprising them with Internet ads with sounds. One AT&T ad opens to the sound of someone knocking. The AT&T logo appears on a door, and a little girl is heard saying, "Hey, let me in!"[38]

Although novel stimuli attract our attention, we do not always like them better. For example, we often dislike food that tastes different from what we usually eat, new clothing styles that deviate from the current trend, or new and unusual music. Thus the factors that make a stimulus novel may not be the same factors that make it likable.

- *Using Unexpectedness.* A second aspect of surprise is unexpectedness. Unexpected stimuli are not necessarily new, but their placement is different from what we are used to. Because they are different, they arouse our curiosity and cause us to analyze them further to make sense of them.[39] The ad for Evian in Exhibit 4.8 uses an unexpected picture of a bartender mixing water to call attention to its ad. 3M Company, the makers of Post-it Notes, created attention with ads that featured chickens with fluorescent notes with words like *Rush* and *Copy* stuck to their bodies.[40] The placement of Post-it Notes on chickens was unexpected and hence attention getting.

Making Stimuli Easy to Process. Although personal relevance, pleasantness, and surprise attract consumers' attention by enhancing their motivation to attend to stimuli, marketers can also enhance attention by boosting our *ability* to process stimuli. Four things make a stimulus easy to process: (1) its prominence, (2) its concreteness, (3) the extent to which it contrasts with the things that surround it, and (4) the extent to which it competes with other information.

EXHIBIT 4.8
Using Unexpectedness to Attract Attention

Few people expect to see a bartender mixing water. The image therefore attracts consumers' attention to the ad.

Source: Photographer: Guzman. Agency: MVBMS/EURO RSCG.

prominence The intensity of stimuli that causes them to stand out relative to the environment.

concreteness The extent to which a stimulus is capable of being imagined.

- *Prominent Stimuli.* Prominent stimuli stand out relative to the environment because of their intensity. The size or length of the stimulus can affect its **prominence.** For example, consumers are more likely to notice larger or longer ads than to notice smaller or shorter ones.[41] Thus a full-page ad has a greater chance of attracting attention than a half- or quarter-page ad. Yellow Pages advertisers have reported that doubling an ad's size increases sales fivefold, whereas quadrupling the size increases sales by a factor of 15.[42] Making words prominent by the use of boldfaced text also enhances consumers' attention.[43] The principle of prominence also explains manufacturers' use of huge end caps or displays in retail stores. Sales of Barnum's animal crackers rose more than 15 percent in 1998, in part because consumers entering stores were confronted with a 76-inch-high, gorilla-shaped cardboard tower filled with cookie boxes.[44] Similarly, retailers sometimes try to attract attention to their stores by affixing huge inflatable characters to the store's roofs.

  Things that are moving also tend to be prominent. Attention to commercials tends to be enhanced when the ad uses dynamic, fast-paced action.[45] Moving billboards and moving displays in grocery stores are other examples.

  Loud sounds can also enhance prominence. Television and radio stations sometimes turn up the volume for commercials so they will stand out relative to the program. Loud rock or dramatic classical music can serve the same purpose.

- *Concrete Stimuli.* Stimuli are also easy to process if they are concrete as opposed to abstract.[46] **Concreteness** is defined as the extent to which we can imagine a stimulus. Notice how easily you can develop images of the concrete words listed in the left column of Exhibit 4.9 compared to the abstract words listed in the right column. A good example of concreteness is illustrated by the brand names of some well-known dish-washing liquids. The name Sunlight is much more concrete than the names Dawn, Joy, or Palmolive and may therefore have an advantage over the others in attention-getting ability.

- *Contrasting Stimuli.* A third factor that makes stimuli easier to process is contrast. Notice in Exhibit 4.10 that the Palmolive bottle in the left photo stands out from the other bottles much better than in the photo on the right, thanks to color contrast. Consider other examples in which contrast operates. A color advertisement in a newspaper is more likely to capture attention because everything around it is black and white. A black-and-white ad on color TV is likely to stand out for a similar reason. Wine makers have found that packaging their wine in blue bottles instead of the traditional green or amber profoundly affects sales because the blue bottles stand out on the shelf.[47] Sounds have even been used to make one product stand out from another. As an example, Nokia launched a model of cell phones that offered a huge menu of distinctive rings that could be downloaded from the Internet. Cell phone rings that sound like Tarzan's yodel or a polka would clearly distinguish one person's cell phone ring from another's.[48]

- *The Amount of Competing Information.* Finally, stimuli are easier to process when few things surround them to compete for your attention.[49] You are more likely to notice a billboard when traveling down a deserted rural highway than in the middle of a congested, sign-filled city. You are also more likely to notice a brand name in a visually simple ad than in one that is visually cluttered. ■

EXHIBIT 4.9
Concreteness and Abstractness

We may pay more attention to things that are concrete and capable of generating images than to things that are abstract and difficult to represent visually.

Source: Allan Paivio, John C. Yuille, and Stephen A. Madigan, "Concreteness, Imagery, and Meaningfulness Values for 925 Nouns," *Journal of Experimental Psychology, Monograph Supplement,* January 1968, pp. 1–25. Copyright © 1968 by the American Psychological Association. Adapted with permission.

CONCRETE WORDS	ABSTRACT WORDS
Apple	Aptitude
Bowl	Betrayal
Cat	Chance
Cottage	Criterion
Diamond	Democracy
Engine	Essence
Flower	Fantasy
Garden	Glory
Hammer	Hatred
Infant	Ignorance
Lemon	Loyalty
Meadow	Mercy
Mountain	Necessity
Ocean	Obedience

Customer Segments Defined by Attention

One set of researchers asked the following question: If we do pay attention to things that are relevant, pleasant, surprising, and easy to process, can we identify groups or segments of consumers who are more affected by relevance, pleasantness, surprise, and ease of processing? To answer this question, the researchers hooked up consumers to eye-tracking devices that monitored the focus of their visual attention in a print ad. The ads were divided into basic parts like picture, package shot, and headline and categorized as big or small, in color or black and white. The researchers identified three groups of consumers by how they attended to the ad.

One group paid minimal attention to the ad because the elements in the ad were not relevant to them. A second group spent a longer time looking at the ad and seemed to focus on things that were visually pleasant such as the picture. The last group spent the longest time looking at the ad. These consumers were affected by the size of the ad, but they devoted equal amounts of time to the picture, package, headline, and body text. The researchers concluded that this group may have attended to each element because the product was personally relevant and its purchase potentially risky. Hence sustained attention was necessary to properly evaluate the information in the ad.[50]

Habituation

habituation The process in which a stimulus loses its attention-getting abilities by virtue of its familiarity.

When a stimulus becomes familiar, it can lose its attention-getting ability. This result is called **habituation**. Think about the last time you purchased something new for your apartment or room (such as a plant or picture). For the first few days,

EXHIBIT 4.10
Contrast and Attention

The Palmolive bottle stands out and attracts attention only when its color contrasts with (is different from) the bottles that surround it. What implications does contrast have for merchandising products?

Source: Lawrence L. Garber, Jr., Appalachian State University. "The Role of Package Appearance in Consumer Choice," dissertation, University of North Carolina at Chapel Hill.

you probably noticed the object every time you entered the room. As time passed, however, you probably noticed the item less and less to the point where you probably do not notice it at all now. You have become habituated to it.

MARKETING IMPLICATIONS Habituation poses a problem for marketers because consumers readily become habituated to ads, packages, and other marketing stimuli. The most straightforward solution is to alter the stimulus every so often. Advertisers sometimes develop multiple ads that all communicate the same basic message but in different ways. Habituation is also the reason that marketers sometimes change the packaging of the product. A new and fresh package or label often attracts consumers' attention anew. ■

PERCEPTION

perception The process by which incoming stimuli activate our sensory receptors (eyes, ears, taste buds, skin, and so on).

After we have been exposed to a stimulus and have devoted at least some attention to it, we are in a position to perceive it. **Perception** occurs when stimuli are registered by one of our five senses: vision, hearing, taste, smell, and touch.

Perceiving Through Vision

What arouses our visual perception?

Color Color is an extremely important factor in visual perception. Research suggests, in fact, that color determines whether we see stimuli.[51]

Color Dimensions A given color can be described according to three dimensions: hue, saturation, and lightness. *Hue* refers to the pigment contained in the color. Researchers have tended to classify colors into two broad categories or color hues: warm colors, such as red, orange, and yellow, and cool colors, such as green, blue, and violet. *Saturation* (also called "chroma") refers to the richness of the color. For example, we can think about a pale pink or a deep, rich pink. *Lightness* refers to the depth of tone in the color. A saturated pink could have a lot of lightness (a fluorescent pink) or a lot of darkness (a mauve).

Effects of Color on Physiological Responses and Moods In addition to affecting whether we perceive stimuli, color can also influence our physiological responses and moods. Color psychologists have discovered that warm colors generally encourage activity and excitement, whereas cool colors are more soothing and relaxing. Thus the restful and calming cool colors are more appropriate in places such as spas or doctors' offices, where it is desirable for consumers to feel calm or spend time making decisions.[52] In contrast, the high-energy warm colors are more appropriate in environments such as health clubs and fast-food restaurants, where high levels of activity are generally desirable.[53] One study found that deeper and richer colors (greater saturation) and darker colors evoked more excitement than did less deep and lighter colors.[54]

Color and Liking Colors can have a great effect on consumers' liking for a product. For example, some consumers like Ivory soap because the blue-and-white packaging looks pleasing.

MARKETING IMPLICATIONS Because colors can have a great effect on consumers' liking for a product, marketers rely on the advice of "color forecasters" when deciding which colors to use in products and on packages. For example, the Color Association of the United States provides information to manufacturers and designers about the colors consumers are likely to prefer 2 to 3 years into the future. These forecasts are very important—the right color can make consumers believe they are buying products that are very now and current. The wrong color can produce disastrous sales results. Researchers have also found differences among social classes in color preferences. Hot, bright colors have historically appealed to lower-end markets, whereas deep, rich colors have historically appealed to higher-end markets.[55] Some research has identified other color segments described in Exhibit 4.11.[56] ■

Perceiving Through Hearing

Sound represents another form of sensory input. A major principle determining whether a sound will be perceived is its auditory intensity.[57] Thus loud music or voices and stark noises can increase the probability that the stimulus will be perceived. In magazines, advertisers have used a technique in which ads "sing out" with a phrase or jingle. To illustrate, during one holiday season, the producers of Absolut vodka created a talking magazine ad by embedding a computer chip into the magazine page.

MARKETING IMPLICATIONS Fast music, like that played at aerobics classes, tends to energize; in contrast, slow music can be soothing. The type of music being played in a retail outlet can have an interesting effect on shopping behavior.[58] Specifically, a fast tempo creates a more rapid traffic flow, whereas a slower tempo has the opposite effect. A slow tempo can increase sales as much as 38 percent because it encourages leisurely shopping. Consumers tend to be completely unaware of this influence on their behavior. Alternatively, a fast tempo is more desirable in restaurants because consumers will eat faster, thereby allowing greater turnover and higher sales.[59]

EXHIBIT 4.11
Color Segments

One set of researchers found that consumers could be classified as falling into one of three color segments. Where do you fall? Can you think of people who fall into the other two segments?

Source: Reprinted with permission from *Marketing News,* published by the American Marketing Association, Tim Triplett, August 28, 1995. Vol. 30, pp. 1, 39.

SEGMENT NAME	COLOR PREFERENCES	CHARACTERISTICS
The Color Forward Segment	First to try a new color. Willing to spend more for a product in a fashionable color	Women under 30 or over 50. Men under 30. City dwellers. Impulse buyers. People who make < $35,000/year
The Color Prudent Segment	Buy a new color only after seeing friends buy it. Put quality ahead of color in purchase decisions	Men and women aged 30–50. Suburban. People who make > $50,000/year
The Color Loyal Segment	Replace a product with another of the same color. Prefer safe colors such as blue and gray as opposed to fashionable colors	Men over 60. Suburban or rural. People who dislike shopping

Music can also affect moods.[60] Likable and familiar music can induce good moods, whereas discordant sounds and music in a disliked style can induce bad moods. This effect is important because, as you will see in later chapters, bad moods may affect how we feel about products and consumption experiences.[61] ■

Perceiving Through Taste

Taste perceptions must be stressed in marketing efforts for foods and beverages. For example, the major challenge for marketers of light or low-calorie products is to provide healthier foods that still taste good. Yet what tastes good to one person may not taste good to another. Moreover, clear cross-cultural differences in taste preferences have important marketing implications.

MARKETING IMPLICATIONS Marketers often try to monitor consumers' tastes through taste tests. Many food and beverage products are thoroughly taste tested before they are placed on the market. Sometimes, however, these taste tests can backfire, as happened when Coca-Cola introduced new Coke. Because Coca-Cola's market share among younger consumers had been shrinking relative to Pepsi's, Coca-Cola designed a cola that tasted more like Pepsi. This decision was bolstered by blind taste tests that showed that consumers preferred the newer formula to the old one. What Coca-Cola executives failed to realize, however, was the power of the brand name. Long-time Coca-Cola drinkers were firm in their strong preference for the original formula. Thus when the old and new formulas were identified by name, consumers strongly preferred the original formula. Some consumers even signed petitions and formed special-interest groups in an attempt to alter the company's decision. As a result, Coca-Cola was forced to reintroduce the old formula as "Coca-Cola Classic." ■

Perceiving Through Smell

If you were blindfolded and asked to smell an item, you would probably have a hard time identifying it.[62] In addition, individual differences characterize consumers' abilities to label odors. Compared with younger consumers, the elderly have a harder time identifying smells,[63] and men in general are worse at the task than are women.[64]

Effects of Smells on Physiological Responses and Moods   Like the other senses, smell produces physiological and emotional outcomes. For example, the smell of peppermint makes us more aroused, and the smell of lily of the valley makes us feel relaxed.[65] In fact, some studies report that people can feel tense or relaxed depending on whether a scent is in the room and what the scent is.[66] This theory has been key to the development of aromatherapy. Some of our most basic emotions are also linked to smell. For example, children hate having their security blankets washed, in part because washing removes the smells that comfort the child. In addition, the smell of the ocean or of freshly baked cookies can revive very emotional and basic childhood memories.[67]

Smells and Product Trial   The sense of smell has been used to gain exposure to stimuli. Scratch-and-sniff advertisements expose consumers to fragrances and other types of products that involve the use of smell. Also, some perfume and cologne ads are doused with the product to increase sensory processing. Notably though, this technique can backfire. Some consumers are offended by ads that include scents. Some even have allergic reactions to the smells!

Smell and Liking Retailers also realize that smells can attract consumers. Kmart Corp. has recently reconfigured its Super Kmart stores so that the bakery kiosk (with its smell of freshly baked breads, pretzels, cinnamon rolls, and muffins) is the first food area customers encounter in the store. The smell also draws consumers to other food attractions.[68]

Smell and Buying Research has found that providing a pleasant-smelling environment can have a positive effect on shopping behavior. In one study shoppers in a room smelling of flowers evaluated Nike shoes more positively than did consumers in an odor-free room. Perhaps this factor explains why retailers like Federated Department Stores, The Limited, and Thomasville Furniture are trying to determine the feasibility of using scent in their retail environments.[69]

MARKETING IMPLICATIONS Obviously, we like some products, for example, perfumes and scented candles, for the smell they produce. However, other products, such as mouthwashes and deodorants, are liked because they mask aromas. One company has introduced a new spritzer that hides cigarette smells on hair and clothing.[70] Several other companies have introduced perfumes for dogs. Les Pooches, for example, is a dog perfume sold in chic department stores. The product, which sells for $18 for 1.7 ounces, is packaged in a bottle with gold tassels.[71]

Smell can also work to marketers' disadvantage. For example, many consumers dislike the smell of plastic containers that are used to pack prepared deli salads.[72] The smell of gasoline, paint, fertilizer, greasy food, and bleach is offensive to many and even harmful to some. One problem with using scent in the ambient retail environment is that consumers might dislike the scents or find them irritating. As such, some products are valued because they are devoid of smell. Thus some consumers prefer unscented deodorants, fabric softeners, carpet cleaners, and laundry detergents.

 Finally, substantial cross-cultural differences account for consumers' preferences for smells. Spices that are normal in one culture can literally make consumers ill in another. Only one smell (cola) is universally regarded as pleasant. The wide acceptance of the cola smell is good news for companies such as Coke and Pepsi that are trying to secure global acceptance of their brands.[73] ■

Perceiving Through Touch

Although we know far less about the sense of touch than of smell, we do know that touch (both what we touch with our fingers and how things feel to us as they come in contact with our skin) is a very important element for many products and services.

Effects of Touch on Physiological Responses and Moods Like the other senses, touch has important physiological and emotional effects. Depending on how we are touched, we can feel stimulated or relaxed. And research has shown that consumers who are touched by a salesperson are more likely to have positive feelings and are more likely to evaluate both the store and salesperson positively. In addition, customers who are touched by the salesperson are more likely to comply with the salesperson's requests.[74] Notably, however, clear cross-cultural differences are evident in the effectiveness of touching in the sales context. Compared with U.S. consumers, those in Latin America are more comfortable with touching and embracing. In Asia, however, touching between relative strangers is seen as an inappropriate gesture.[75]

Touch and Liking   Clearly, some products are liked because of the way they feel. Skin creams and baby products are purchased for the soothing effect they have on the skin, and massage therapists are sought for the tactile sensation and relaxation they provide. In making a purchase, consumers often want to touch before they buy. The way shoes, clothes, jewelry, and dentures feel on our bodies is a critical factor in our purchasing decision. Some marketers are even incorporating touch in novel ways into their products. A company named Immersion has developed the Feelit Mouse—a mouse that allows the computer user to feel a slight bump when something dragged across the screen reaches a software icon (for instance, when a file dragged to the trash can actually reaches the trash can). The user can determine whether the bumped-into item should feel hard, rough, smooth, or rubbery.[76]

When Do We Perceive Stimuli?

At any given time, our senses are exposed to numerous inputs. To perceive each one would be overwhelming and extremely difficult. Fortunately, our sensory processing is simplified by the fact that many stimuli do not enter conscious awareness. For us to perceive something, it must be sufficiently intense.

Stimulus intensity is measured in units. In the area of smell, intensity can be measured by the concentration of the stimulus in a substance or in the air. Stimulus intensity of sounds can be measured in decibels and frequencies, and stimulus intensity of colors can be measured by properties like lightness, saturation, and hue. In the area of touch, stimulus intensity can be measured in terms of pounds or ounces of pressure.

absolute threshold   The minimal level of stimulus intensity needed to detect a stimulus.

Absolute Thresholds   The **absolute threshold** is the minimal level of stimulus intensity needed for a stimulus to be perceived. Put another way, the absolute threshold is the amount of intensity needed to detect a difference between something and nothing. Think about the hearing tests you had as a child. In this context the absolute threshold means how loud the tone needs to be before you can hear it. To illustrate with a marketing example, suppose we are driving on the highway and a billboard is in the distance. The absolute threshold is that point at which we can first see the billboard. Before that point, it is below the absolute threshold and not sufficiently intense to be seen.

MARKETING IMPLICATIONS   The obvious implication is that for a marketing stimulus to be perceived, it must be sufficiently high in intensity to be above the absolute threshold. Thus if images or words in a commercial are too small or the sound level is too low, consumers' sensory receptors will not be activated and the stimulus will not be perceived. ■

differential threshold/just noticeable difference (j.n.d.)   The intensity difference needed between two stimuli before they are perceived to be different.

Differential Thresholds   Whereas the absolute threshold deals with whether a stimulus can be perceived, the **differential threshold** refers to the intensity difference needed between two stimuli before people can perceive that the stimuli are different. Thus the differential threshold is a relative concept; it is often called the **just noticeable difference** (or **j.n.d.**). For example, when we get our eyes checked, the eye doctor often shows us a row of letters through different sets of lenses. If we can detect a difference between the two lenses, the new lens is sufficiently different to have crossed the differential threshold.

The basic properties of the differential threshold were first outlined in the 19th century by the psycho-physiologist Ernst Weber. **Weber's law** states that the stronger the initial stimulus, the greater the additional intensity needed for the second stimulus to be perceived as different. This relationship is outlined in the following formula:

$$\frac{\Delta s}{S} = K$$

where S is the initial stimulus value, Δs is the smallest change in a stimulus capable of being detected, and K is a constant of proportionality. A practical example will clarify this principle.

Suppose consumer testing found that 1 ounce would need to be added to a 10-ounce package before consumers could notice that the two packages weighed different amounts. Suppose we now have a 50-ounce box and want to know how much we must add before consumers could detect a difference. According to Weber's law, K would be = 1/10 or 0.1. Thus to determine how much would need to be added, we would solve for Δs as follows:

$$\frac{\Delta s}{50} = .10$$

The answer is .10 of the package weight, or 5 ounces.

MARKETING IMPLICATIONS The differential threshold has several important marketing implications.

When Marketers Do Not Want a Differential Threshold to Be Crossed. For one thing, sometimes marketers *do not* want consumers to notice a difference between two stimuli. For example, marketers might not want consumers to notice that the size of the product has decreased or that the price has increased. In the early 1980s candy bars in vending machines got smaller and smaller until finally the differential threshold was passed. Consumers became angry, and companies were pressured to return to larger sizes. A similar phenomenon occurred when consumers noticed that Long John Silver's was serving smaller portions of food at the original price. In the airline industry, a j.n.d. was reached when consumers noticed that the seats in airplanes were getting pushed closer together (leaving less and less leg room).

Although these practices raise some interesting ethical issues, marketers also use the differential threshold concept in more positive ways. Marketers of nonalcoholic beers, for example, have hoped that consumers would not be able to tell the difference between the taste of real and nonalcoholic beers.[77]

When Marketers Do Want a Differential Threshold to Be Crossed. In other instances marketers *do* want consumers to perceive a difference between two stimuli. For example, McDonald's once increased the size of its regular hamburger patty by 25 percent but left the price the same, hoping that consumers would notice the change.[78] Likewise, if marketers decided to lower the price of a brand or service to stimulate sales, the sale price would need to be perceived as different from the regular price. If a product is improved in some way, the changes must be above the differential threshold for the consumer to notice. To illustrate, one brand of sunscreens differentiates itself on the basis of length of wear. Whereas other sunscreens last only 80 minutes, this brand lasts 6 hours—a difference that consumers

Weber's law The stronger the initial stimulus, the greater the additional intensity needed for the second stimulus to be perceived as different.

will surely notice. Similarly, the ad in Exhibit 4.12 suggests that customers will not be able to tell the difference between brewed coffee and coffee singles. As another example, the success of DVDs depends at least in part on their ability to look and sound perceptibly better than movies recorded on tape.

Many marketers hope that consumers can tell the difference between an old and an improved product. However, sometimes consumers cannot make the distinction because the differential thresholds for different senses vary. For example, our sense of smell is not well developed, and we often fail to differentiate the smell of two versions of the same object. ■

subliminal perception The activation of sensory receptors by stimuli presented below the perceptual threshold.

EXHIBIT 4.12
Surpassing Perceptual Thresholds

If consumers are able to tell the difference between brewed coffee and coffee singles, the new singles have passed a perceptual threshold.

Source: © The Procter & Gamble Company. Used by permission.

Freshly brewed coffee for ten.

For one.

Folgers Coffee Singles

Aroma-fresh pouch.

Contains ground roast coffee in its own filter.

Folgers Coffee Singles
THE ULTIMATE ONE CUP COFFEE MACHINE.

Subliminal Perception The concept of the perceptual threshold is important for another phenomenon—**subliminal perception**. Suppose we are sitting at a movie and are exposed to messages like "Eat Popcorn" and "Drink Coke." However, each message is shown on the screen for only a fraction of a second, so short a time that we are not consciously aware of them. Stimuli like these, presented below the threshold level of our awareness, are called subliminal messages, and our perception of them is called *subliminal perception*.

Subliminal perception is different from preattentive processing. With preattentive processing our attention is directed at something other than the stimulus, for instance, at a magazine article instead of an ad in our peripheral vision. With subliminal perception our attention is directed squarely at the stimulus. Also, with preattentive processing the stimulus is fully present—if we shift our attention and look directly at the ad or billboard, we can easily see it. In contrast, subliminal stimuli are presented so quickly or are so degraded that the very act of perceiving them is difficult.

MARKETING IMPLICATIONS The question of whether stimuli presented subliminally affect consumers' responses has generated considerable controversy in the marketing field. A widely known but fraudulent study in the advertising industry claimed that consumers at a movie theater were subliminally exposed to messages on the movie screen that read "Eat Popcorn" and "Drink Coke." Reportedly, subliminal exposure to these messages influenced viewers' purchase of Coke and popcorn.[79] Since that time, considerable public concern has arisen over the use of subliminal messages in advertising. Although advertising agencies deny using these stimuli, some people have claimed that marketers are brainwashing consumers and attempting to manipulate them. These people also believe that ads containing these stimuli are effective.[80] This perception is perhaps fostered by the availability of self-help tapes with subliminal messages that claim to help consumers stop smoking, lose weight, and feel more relaxed. ■

Does Subliminal Perception Affect Consumer Behavior?
Despite public concern, research suggests that subliminal perception has limited effects on consumers.[81] Such stimuli have not been found to arouse motives like hunger. Nor do subliminally presented sexual stimuli affect consumers' attitudes or preferences. Research has also failed to show that subliminal stimuli affect consumers' memory for ads or brands. Based on these null findings, the advertising community tends to dismiss subliminal perception research.

Interestingly, however, there is some evidence that stimuli presented below the threshold of conscious perception can reach our sensory registers. Researchers have found that if consumers are subliminally exposed to a word (e.g., *razor*), that word is recognized faster than words they have not been exposed to subliminally.[82] Moreover, some preliminary evidence suggests that stimuli perceived subliminally affect consumers' feelings. Consumers in one study were found to have stronger responses to ads with sexual subliminal implants than to those without.[83] Thus stimuli perceived subliminally are somehow analyzed for their meaning, and they can elicit primitive feeling responses. Notably, though, these effects are likely to be so small or so unimportant that they make the use of subliminal stimuli ineffective from an advertising perspective. In other words, these effects do not appear to be sufficiently strong to alter consumers' preferences or to make an ad or brand more memorable. Exposing consumers to the message at or above the threshold level of awareness should have just as much, if not more, impact, making the use of subliminal stimuli unnecessary.[84]

How Do Consumers Perceive a Stimulus?

Some research has focused on how individuals organize or combine the visual information they perceive. Consumers tend not to perceive a single stimulus in isolation; rather, they organize and integrate it in the context of the other things around it. Also, many stimuli are really a complex combination of a number of simple stimuli, and these stimuli must be organized into a unified whole. The organizing process is called **perceptual organization**. This process represents a somewhat higher, more meaningful level of processing than simply having stimuli register on our sensory receptors. Marketers have borrowed some basic principles from Gestalt psychology to understand this phenomenon. These include the principles of figure and ground, closure, and grouping.

perceptual organization
The process by which stimuli are organized into meaningful units.

Figure and Ground The principle of **figure and ground** suggests that people interpret incoming stimuli in contrast to a background. The figure is well defined and in the forefront, and the ground is indefinite, hazy, and in the background. In other words, the figure is the focal point of attention and perception, and the ground is everything else around it. The key point is that individuals tend to organize their perceptions into figure-and-ground relationships, and the manner in which this process occurs will determine how the stimulus is interpreted.

figure and ground According to this principle, people interpret stimuli in the context of a background.

This principle suggests that important brand information should be the figure, not the background. Moreover, the background should not detract from the figure. This principle is often violated when sexy or attractive models are used in advertising. Often the attractive model will be the figure and the focal point, and the product or brand name will go unnoticed.

Closure Closure refers to the fact that individuals have a need to organize perceptions so that they form a meaningful whole. Even if a stimulus is incomplete, our need for closure will lead us to see it as complete. We therefore try to complete the stimulus. The key to using the need for closure, then, is to provide consumers with an incomplete stimulus.

closure According to this principle, individuals have a need to organize perceptions so that they form a meaningful whole.

For example, putting a well-known television ad on the radio is effective in getting consumers to think about a message. The radio version of the ad is an incomplete stimulus, and our need for closure leads us to picture the visual parts of the ad. Likewise, severely cropping objects in ads so that they appear ambiguous may be one way of getting consumers to think about what the object is and to gain

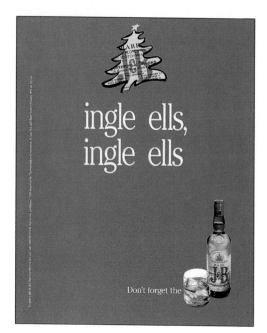

ingle ells,
ingle ells

Don't forget the

EXHIBIT 4.13
Closure

Because of our need for closure (our need to organize perceptions so they form a meaningful whole), we try to complete incomplete stimuli. Here we obtain closure by adding a *J* to *ingle* and a *B* to *ells*. Closure here is clever because J&B is the name of the brand.

Source: Courtesy of the Paddington Corporation.

closure.[85] The ad in Exhibit 4.13 cleverly uses the closure principle to get consumers to provide the letters *J* and *B* of the brand name J&B.

Grouping Grouping refers to the fact that we often group stimuli to form a unified picture or impression, making it easier to process them. We view similar or nearby objects as belonging together. Marketers can often influence the image or perception of a product or service by grouping it with other stimuli. For example, in the right photo of Exhibit 4.10, the green bottles are grouped together, and they are seen as different from the bluish green bottle. In merchandising, marketers often create a unified impression by displaying related items as a group. Consumers may perceive a table setting as elegant when the napkins, napkin holders, wine goblets, silverware, dishes, and serving bowls are cleverly grouped.

grouping A tendency to group stimuli to form a unified picture or impression.

SUMMARY

For a marketing stimulus to have an impact, consumers must be exposed to it, allocate some attention to it, and perceive it. Attention and perception are mutually reinforcing processes. A basic level of attention is needed for a stimulus to be perceived. After it is perceived, further mental resources can be used to process the stimulus at higher levels.

Exposure occurs when the consumer is presented with a marketing stimulus. Marketers are using a variety of traditional and nontraditional tactics (such as product placement) to increase stimulus exposure, particularly because consumers' exposure to marketing stimuli is selective. Consumers engage in processes like zipping and zapping to avoid exposure to unwanted ads.

Attention occurs when the consumer allocates processing capacity to the stimulus. Attention is selective, divided, and limited. Hence even tactics such as product placement in TV programs and movies do not guarantee that consumers will directly attend to marketing stimuli—though consumers may attend to the stimuli preattentively. Our ability to process stimuli preattentively raises concerns about whether tactics such as product placement blur the lines between programming and commercial content. Marketers believe that because the marketing environment is so cluttered they must attract consumers' attention to particular offerings. Making a stimulus personally relevant, pleasant, surprising, or easy to process enhances its attention-getting properties. A number of factors influence these outcomes.

After a stimulus has received some attention, it may be perceived through one of the five senses. The processing of visual stimuli is influenced by color. Intensity and music are important aspects of aural stimuli. Taste perceptions are critical for some products; however, marketers should be aware that taste perceptions vary across cultures. Finally, the use of both smell and touch can be an effective marketing strategy for some products. Perceptual thresholds determine the point at which stimuli are perceived. The absolute threshold is the lowest point at which an individual can experience a sensation. The differential threshold is the minimal difference in stimulus intensity needed to detect that two stimuli are different. For a marketing stimulus to be perceived, it must be above the absolute threshold. The differential threshold is important both when marketers do not want consumers to notice a difference between two stimuli (like a price increase) and when they do (such as in the case of product improvements). Consumers appear to have some abilities to perceive things that are outside their conscious level of awareness, a phenomenon called subliminal perception. However, the perception of these stimuli seems to have limited impact on consumers' motives or behaviors. Finally, perceptual organization occurs when consumers organize a set of stimuli into a coherent whole. The Gestalt principles of figure and ground, closure, and grouping affect this process. These principles raise some interesting implications for how consumers perceive items in ads and in merchandise displays.

EXERCISES

1. Select a product or service that would typically be considered high in involvement and one that would be considered low in involvement. Design an advertisement to ensure proper perception and attention. After doing so, examine and discuss how these two situations are similar and different.

2. Select a copy of one of your favorite magazines. Find three ads that you think are most effective for generating exposure, attention, and perception. Also find three ads that are ineffective for each process. What makes the good ones effective? What do you think is wrong with the others, and how could they be improved?

3. Watch TV for 1 hour (record on a VCR if possible). During this period, describe the ads that got your attention. Why were they successful in attracting you? For which ads did you want to engage in zipping or zapping and why?

4. Identify as many examples as you can in which marketers *want* consumers to perceive a just noticeable difference between their product and a competitor's, or between an old product and a new one. Also find examples in which marketers *do not want* consumers to perceive such a difference. Consider not only visual aspects of the product or service, such as how big or small it is, but other perceptual differences as well (how it tastes, feels, smells, sounds).

5. Take a trip to a local shopping mall and examine the interiors of several stores. Describe the physiological and psychological responses different stores try to create. How do they do so through the use of color, brightness, and contrast?

5

KNOWLEDGE AND UNDERSTANDING

INTRODUCTION

Although beer and distilled spirits are both alcohol products, beer has developed an image as a relatively benign drink. This perception dates back to the early part of the 20th century, when beer actually acquired a reputation as a healthy product. Some consumers perceived beer as "liquid bread" because it used yeast in the production process. During Prohibition, it was hard liquor—not beer—whose image was the more tarnished, as the liquor industry became the clear target of critics. The relative lack of social criticism of beer and beer advertising continued during the 1930s and 1940s, when beer advertisers needed little advertising compared to manufacturers of hard liquor. A positive image of beer carried into the 1960s and 1970s, when beer ads linked beer with traditional U.S. values: sports, hard work, and male bonding.

Today many consumers view beer as the beverage of baseball and picnics, the beverage of moderation, and a product that can be part of a healthy lifestyle. Many consumers are also quite knowledgeable about different brands of beer and their images. The situation is vastly different elsewhere. In China, for example, Budweiser is attempting to craft an image for itself. The problem is that consumers in China don't even know what Budweiser is (a beer? motor oil? orange juice?), let alone what image they should have of it.

Although the image of beer has generally been positive in the United States, beer companies have devoted considerable effort to developing unique images of various brands, hence differentiating the brands from one another. Some beer producers use brand symbols, such as Spuds MacKenzie, and animal symbols like croaking frogs, penguins, and lizards. Others, such as Rolling Rock, avoid traditional sports and male-bonding themes. The industry has also witnessed a rash of specialty beers. Some consumers prefer these beers, believing that they are made in tiny breweries by master beer makers. However, many are actually made by large, relatively unknown breweries that make the beer and then sell it to small beer companies.

Consumers' perceptions about beer are also of concern to public policy makers and consumer advocates. One issue that concerns them is the misperception that beer is not a potent form of alcohol. In reality, a 12-ounce can of beer is equivalent to a 5-ounce glass of wine or one mixed drink made with $1\frac{1}{2}$ ounces of hard liquor. Furthermore, although consumers may perceive beer as the drink of moderation, moderation means different things to different people. To many adults, moderation means two to three drinks per occasion. To many college students, moderation means five drinks per occasion.[1] Exhibit 5.1 is an ad sponsored by Anheuser-Busch that encourages parents to talk to teenagers about drinking.

This example illustrates many concepts relevant to this chapter. First, consumers in our culture have a number of favorable associations linked with the product category of beer. Different brands of beer have different images, allowing customers to view brands as different from one another. Consumers perceive different brands as having different personalities—Budweiser is young and fun, whereas Heineken is older and more upscale.

Beer is also seen as part of the broader category of alcohol. Product categories such as wine, hard liquor, and beer are basic-level categories under this general category. Within the basic category of beer, we can identify various categories of beer: malt beer, ale, regular beer, and lite beer. Consumers have prior knowledge that allows them to categorize new brands into these varieties and to see beer as different from hard liquor and wine. Consumers' knowledge also serves as a basis for interpreting information from advertising. Unfortunately, what consumers subjectively comprehend from beer ads may not be in line with beer's actual characteristics. Consumers inappropriately infer that beer sold by small companies is made by these companies, and some consumers misinterpret the meaning of the term *moderation*.

In the preceding chapter, we looked at how consumers attend to and perceive things. This chapter goes a step further, asking how consumers understand the world around them. To answer this question we need to know how consumers relate what they perceive and attend to with what they already know—their prior knowledge. As Exhibit 5.2 shows, this chapter describes two broad domains of knowledge—knowledge content (stored information) and knowledge structure. The chapter also describes how prior knowledge is used for understanding. Two levels of understanding are categorization and comprehension.

Knowledge content reflects the information we have already learned—brands, companies, product categories, stores, ads, people, how to shop, how to use products, and so on. Marketers sometimes engage in efforts to develop, add to, or change knowledge content. **Knowledge structure** refers to the way knowledge is organized. Knowledge is often organized into categories, with similar things stored in the same category. For example, certain brands of toothpaste, such as Gleem and Pearl Drops, may be stored in a category called whitening toothpastes. These brands along with others, for example, Crest and Close-Up, may be stored in a more general category called toothpaste. All these brands and other products like dental floss and mouthwashes might be stored in a category called dental hygiene products.

Prior knowledge is essential for two levels of consumer understanding—categorization and comprehension. **Categorization** is the process of labeling or identifying an object that we perceive in our external environment based on its similarity to what we already know. Thus we might label Trident dental gum as a dental hygiene product and relate it to our knowledge of other dental hygiene products. **Comprehension** is the process of using prior knowledge to understand more about what we have categorized. For example, we might relate a picture, headline, and ad copy in an ad for Trident dental gum and understand that "Trident dental gum is good for teeth and can achieve some of the same benefits as brushing."

KNOWLEDGE

We say that we "know" something when we have encountered it before and have somehow come to understand what it means and what it is like. Knowing therefore has to do with our prior knowledge—both what we have encountered and how it relates to other knowledge. Accordingly, we describe two aspects of knowledge: knowledge content and knowledge structure.

KNOWLEDGE CONTENT

The content of our knowledge reflects the set of things we have learned in the past. Our prior knowledge may consist of many facts. For example, we may know that a banana has 100 calories, that Utah is the Beehive State, and that we need to get our car serviced after 800 miles. These facts are not random facts; rather, they are generally linked to or associated with a concept. The set of associations linked to a concept is called a **schema**.[2] A schema for the concept banana has many associations—for example, has 100 calories, is yellow, bruises easily, and can be very slippery if stepped on. The associations that some consumers link to the brand concepts Gucci and Prada are noted in Exhibit 5.3 on page 106. A schema is elaborated when we have many associations linked to the concept.

knowledge content Information we already have in memory.

knowledge structure The way in which knowledge is organized.

categorization The process of labeling or identifying an object. Involves relating what we perceive in our external environment to what we already know.

comprehension The process of deepening understanding. Involves using prior knowledge to understand more about what we have categorized.

schema The set of associations linked to a concept.

EXHIBIT 5.2
**Chapter Overview: Knowl-
edge and Understanding**

We categorize information that
we perceive by comparing it with
what we already know. Prior
knowledge includes two basic
domains: content and structure.
Once something is categorized,
we use prior knowledge to comprehend more about it.

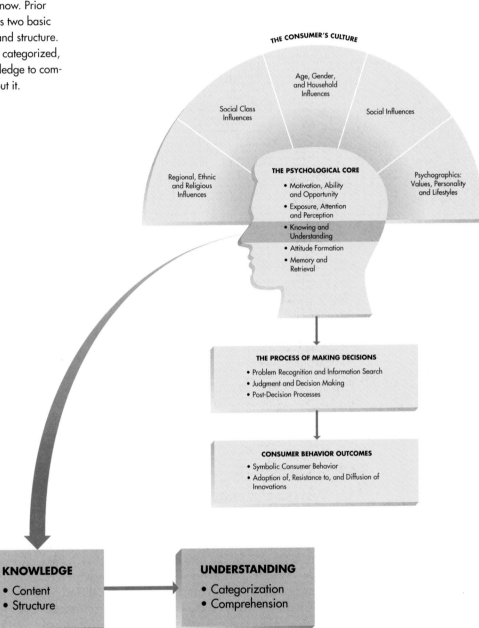

THE CONSUMER'S CULTURE

Age, Gender,
and Household
Influences

Social Class
Influences

Social Influences

THE PSYCHOLOGICAL CORE
- Motivation, Ability
  and Opportunity
- Exposure, Attention
  and Perception
- Knowing and
  Understanding
- Attitude Formation
- Memory and
  Retrieval

Regional, Ethnic
and Religious
Influences

Psychographics:
Values, Personality
and Lifestyles

THE PROCESS OF MAKING DECISIONS
- Problem Recognition and Information Search
- Judgment and Decision Making
- Post-Decision Processes

CONSUMER BEHAVIOR OUTCOMES
- Symbolic Consumer Behavior
- Adoption of, Resistance to, and Diffusion of
  Innovations

KNOWLEDGE
- Content
- Structure

UNDERSTANDING
- Categorization
- Comprehension

GUCCI	PRADA
Los Angeles	New York
Goldie Hawn	Uma Thurman
Brad Pitt	Willem Dafoe
Bamboo/calf bag	Black nylon backpack
Swingers	Intellectuals
Hip-huggers	Flat-front pants
Skin-tight	Boxy
Frivolous	Utilitarian
High tart	High concept
Boisterous	Ethereal
Stiletto	Clunky square toe
Strapless	Patchwork
Edgy	Minimal
Caviar	Truffles
Single-malt scotch	Vodka on rocks
Bikini wax	Eyebrow wax

EXHIBIT 5.3
Associations Linked to Gucci and Prada

Different brand names evoke different associations. Here are a set of associations that some consumers link to the names Gucci and Prada.

Source: Republished with permission of the *Wall Street Journal* from "Houses of Style" from "How to tell two hot fashion names apart," January 27, 1999; permission conveyed through Copyright Clearance Center, Inc.

Schemas and Associations

The associations in schemas can be described along several dimensions.[3]

- *Types of Associations.* We have many types of associations. Our schema for banana might include associations that reflect (1) the attributes of a banana (it is yellow, long, soft, has a lot of potassium), (2) its benefits (nutritious, low in fat), (3) people who use it (athletes who lose a lot of potassium through sweating), (4) times when it is used (as a snack, for breakfast), (5) places it is used (at home, at school), (6) ways it is used (peeled, sliced), (7) places it is purchased (at a grocery store), (8) places it is grown (in South America), and so on.

- *Favorability.* Associations can be described in terms of their *favorability*. The notion that Coke tastes great might be evaluated as favorable. The fact that South Africa has been associated with apartheid might not.

- *Uniqueness.* Associations vary in their *uniqueness*—that is, the extent to which they are also related to other concepts. "Greasiness" is not unique to McDonald's, but the Golden Arches and Ronald McDonald are.

- *Salience.* Associations vary in their *salience*, or the ease with which they come to mind when the concept is activated. For example, we might always retrieve the association of Golden Arches when we hear the McDonald's name. Less salient associations may be retrieved only in certain contexts. Thus the association that McDonald's works to make its packaging environmentally friendly may be less salient, and we may think about it only if someone starts talking about the environment.

Try to apply these ideas to the brand concepts in Exhibit 5.3 or to other brand concepts such as Disney, Pillsbury, or Mercedes-Benz. What associations do you link with these concepts? Which are attributes, which are benefits, which are favorable, and which are unique? Are the associations equally salient?

Types of Schemas

We have schemas for many entities. The banana example is an illustration of a *product category* schema; however, we also have schemas for *brands*. Russian consumers' schema for Aeroflot, the state airline of the former Soviet Union, includes associations such as stale air, cramped seats, and dilapidated interiors. We also have schemas for *people* like our mothers, Michael Jordan, African Americans, working-class people, and so on. We have schemas for *services* and for *stores*. The associations linked to Nordstrom may be quite different from the associations linked to Kmart. We have schemas for *salespeople* (cosmetics salesperson, used car salesperson), *ads* (Coke, Benetton ads), *companies* (McDonald's, IBM), *places* (Lake Tahoe, Vail), *countries* (South Africa, Somalia, Switzerland), and *animals* (lynx, cougar, moose). We even have a schema for ourselves, called a *self-schema*.

Images

brand image A subset of salient and feeling-related associations stored in a brand schema.

An image is a subset of associations that reflect what a brand stands for and how favorably it is viewed.[4] Thus our **brand image** of McDonald's may be favorable, and it may include such associations as a family friendly place and fast food. An

brand personality The set of associations that reflect the personification of the brand.

107

image does not represent *all* the associations linked to a schema—only those that are most salient. Thus although we may know that McDonald's serves some high-fat products, this knowledge need not be used to form our brand image. We also have images for other marketing entities like stores, companies, places, and countries. The Gap and Victoria's Secret have very strong images in the United States.[5] In Japan, images of companies such as Sony, Takashimaya, and Matsushita Electric are very strong.[6]

Our schemas can also include associations that reflect the **brand's personality**—that is, how we would describe the brand as if it were a person.[7] Consumers from one study described the Whirlpool brand as gentle, sensitive, quiet, good-natured, flexible, modern, cheerful, and creative. Researchers found that these associations, if linked to a person, would suggest a modern and family-oriented suburban woman who is neighborly, successful, attractive, and action oriented. Whirlpool's personality was quite different from KitchenAid's, whose name personified a smart, aggressive, glamorous, wealthy, elegant, and fashionable career woman.[8]

Stores, places, and salespeople may also have personalities. Home Depot's personality is that of a down-home, honest, thrifty, helpful, working-class neighbor. New York City has a personality that is sophisticated, wealthy, elite, and cosmopolitan. Sometimes brand personalities are embodied in brand characters like Spuds MacKenzie, Charlie the Tuna, Tony the Tiger, Aunt Jemima, and the Maytag repairman. Think about the personality exemplified by each of these characters and how the character's personality says something about the personality of the brand. One study found that many brands could be described according to their position on five brand personality dimensions. Exhibit 5.4 identifies these. Can you think of brands whose personalities exemplify each of these dimensions?

MARKETING IMPLICATIONS Schemas, images, and personalities are important to marketers for a number of reasons. One is that marketers are sometimes in the position of creating them. In other cases, marketers must build or elaborate on these elements. Finally, in some cases schemas, images, or personalities need to be changed.

Creating New Schemas, Images, and Personalities. When marketing offerings are new, marketers must create schemas, images, and/or personalities to help consumers

EXHIBIT 5.4
A Brand Personality Framework

One researcher found that many brands can be described according to one or more of the five personality types described below. Which dimensions best describe Pepsi's brand personality? Which describe the personalities of Starbucks? Saturn? Dell?

Source: Reprinted with permission from *Journal of Marketing Research,* published by the American Marketing Association, Jennifer L. Aaker, August 1997, Vol. 34, pp. 347–356.

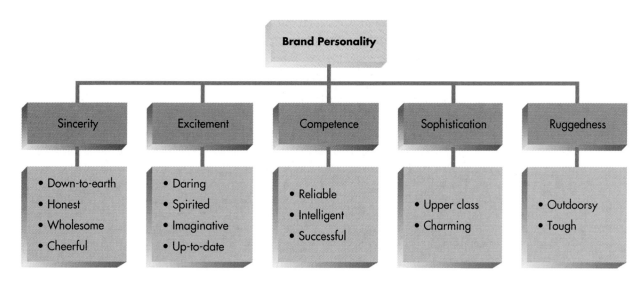

understand the offering, what it can do for them, and how it is different from other offerings on the market. Creating schemas is especially important for new products because consumers may not yet understand what these new products are or what they have to offer. Creating schemas and images for companies is also important so that consumers understand the general types of products produced by the firm. ITT Industries, which makes sewage pumps, electronic connectors, and military hardware, is trying to create an image for itself because very few people know what the firm does. To highlight its products and the benefits they offer, ITT's recent TV spot shows fish, crabs, seals, and turtles performing an underwater version of Handel's *Hallelujah Chorus*. The ad's tag line is "engineered for life."

Schemas, images, and personalities can sometimes be created by means of brand extensions, licensing agreements, and brand alliances.

brand extension A marketing strategy in which a firm that markets a product with a well-developed image uses the same brand name but in a different product category.

licensing A marketing strategy in which a firm sells the rights to the brand name to another company who will use the name on its product.

brand alliance A marketing strategy in which a two companies' brand names are presented together on a single product.

- A **brand extension** occurs when a firm that markets a product with a well-developed image, like Jell-O gelatin, uses the same brand name but in a different product category, such as Jell-O pudding pops. Other examples of brand extensions include Victoria's Secret cosmetics, Avon clothing, and Skippy peanut butter cookies.

- **Licensing** occurs when a firm sells the rights to the brand name to another company that will use the name on its product. For example, Betty Crocker licensed its name to a bread machine company, and Arm and Hammer licenses its name to the manufacturers of Odor Eaters deodorizing shoe insoles.

- A **brand alliance** occurs when a two companies' brand names appear together on a single product. Examples include Intel chips in Compaq computers, Breyer's ice cream with Reeses Pieces in it, and the Northwest Airlines Visa card.

One consequence of brand extensions, license agreements, and alliances is that consumers develop an image for the new brand by transferring to it associations and positive feelings from the original brand's schema.[9] If consumers think Skippy peanut butter is rich and smooth, they may infer that Skippy peanut butter cookies will also be rich and smooth. Unfortunately, these strategies can also sometimes hurt the image of the core brand. For example, if a consumer has a bad experience with Skippy peanut butter cookies, the negative feelings generated may affect the image of Skippy peanut butter. Furthermore, if the Skippy name appears on too many different products—Skippy cookies, bread, rice, frozen dinners—consumers may be confused about what Skippy actually stands for. Given these potential problems, marketers need to be concerned about how effective these strategies might be in the long run.[10]

At a more fundamental level, creating a set of associations linked to an offering helps to position it so that consumers understand what the offering is and what it competes against. For example, Clinique's clinical and scientific positioning is different from Maybelline's fresh and natural positioning. Delta is trying to position itself as a global, urbane airline that pampers every customer. This positioning approach is drastically different from Southwest's price-oriented position.

Developing Existing Schemas, Images, and Personalities. Although marketers must sometimes create new schemas, in other cases they must develop or elaborate a schema—that is, add information to an existing schema so that consumers understand more about it.[11] Xerox is currently elaborating its image so that consumers see it as more than simply a document company, and much more than a company that makes copy machines. By introducing products that allow consumers to share and print documents from the Web and digital copiers that allow consumers to scan and print documents, Xerox is creating an image for itself as a digital document company.[12] Best Western also is trying to elaborate its image. Although most consumers know the Best Western name, few know it as the world's largest hotel chain. The company is now advertising the fact that it has more than 3,400 hotels in 68 countries.[13]

One way to develop schemas is with multiple brand extensions. Although the name Arm & Hammer was once associated only with baking soda, the extension of the name to such categories as kitty litter, carpet deodorizer, and refrigerator deodorizer has reinforced its deodorizing image.

Changing Schemas, Images, and Personalities. Sometimes consumers' schemas, images, and brand personalities contain associations that require change. When a brand image becomes stale or outdated or when negative associations develop, marketers need to engage in activities that add new and positive associations.

In Europe, Häagen-Dazs ran into this problem. The brand had no consistent marketing messages, and consumers saw it as an expensive treat that wasn't necessarily any better tasting than Ben and Jerry's. Marketers have recently changed the image of Häagen-Dazs, positioning it as an affordable luxury with interesting and delicious flavors. A big advertising campaign will accompany the launch of new sorbets and ice-cream bars.[14] As another example, Sailor Jack, the brand symbol for Cracker Jack, was recently revised to give him a newer, friendlier, and healthier look. Exhibit 5.5 shows how Jack has changed over the years.[15]

Although these examples focus on changes in *brand* images and personalities, sometimes the images of media vehicles require change. For example, *Rolling Stone* magazine has had trouble getting marketers of mainstream products as advertisers. The reason is that many marketers have an image of the *Rolling Stone* reader as being a granola-eating, antimilitary, marijuana-smoking hippie. In response, *Rolling Stone* launched an ad campaign targeted to these marketers. The ads visually depicted the marketers' image of the typical reader and then countered it with visuals describing actual readers.

Changing images of places is also important to economic developers and tourism marketers. For example, the city of Los Angeles is trying to change the image of Hollywood Boulevard. Although many people assume that this street is glamorous, it is actually quite seedy. To change its image, the seedier parts are being replaced by new stores, museums, and restaurants.[16]

Retail and services images may also require change. Denny's restaurant has suffered from customer suits alleging racial discrimination by employees, and new management has worked hard hard to improve the chain's damaged reputation.[17] Sometimes entire industries need to brush up on their image. The steel industry has recently launched a massive advertising and public relations effort designed to make people feel good about using steel in their homes, cars, and other products. The associations consumers currently link with steel are technologically backward and old. Steel marketers hope to change these associations to strong and durable.[18] A similar phenomenon is happening in the gun industry, as gun makers and retailers are working to portray guns as sporting equipment, not as deadly weapons used in crime.[19] ■

EXHIBIT 5.5
Sailor Jack, Mascot of Cracker Jack

Over the years, Sailor Jack has undergone several updates from the original design, a characterization of the younger grandson of Cracker Jack inventor F.W. Rueckheim. Today's Jack looks more like a kid of today, a consumer that the company wants to target.

Source: Frito-Lay.

Scripts

script A special type of schema that represents knowledge of a sequence of events.

Schemas represent our knowledge about objects or things.[20] A **script** is a special type of schema that represents knowledge of a sequence of events. For example, we may have a script for how to arrange roses bought from the store. We open the cel-

EXHIBIT 5.6

A Script for Product Usage

A script is a set of associations linked with how we do something. Radio Shack's Gift express service may be relevant to consumers because it performs all the activities that are part of a consumer's script for "giving a gift to someone who is far away."

Source: Ad reprinted with permission.

taxonomic category An orderly classification of objects, with similar objects in the same category.

lophane wrapping, get scissors, fill a vase with water, run the roses under water, cut them, and then arrange them in the vase. This knowledge helps us do things quickly and easily. In contrast, when we are doing something for the first time, such as assembling a piece of Ikea furniture, having no prior script may prolong the task.

MARKETING IMPLICATIONS Scripts help marketers understand how consumers buy and use an offering. In turn, marketers use this knowledge to make marketing decisions that improve products or services. Marketers may also perform tasks that are part of consumers' scripts. As the ad in Exhibit 5.6 indicates, Radio Shack facilitates gift buying by performing the packaging and shopping tasks that are normally part of consumers' gift-buying scripts. Likewise, marketers of kosher products perform scripted activities for consumers by "making clean" or blessing food.

In other cases marketers may want consumers to consider using a particular brand as part of a scripted activity—incorporating the use of cellular phones as part of their driving-to-work or waiting-in-line script, for example. New technologies like interactive shopping and interactive advertising are changing the way consumers perform scripted activities such as buying products and processing ads. ■

KNOWLEDGE STRUCTURE

Although schemas and scripts reflect the content of what we know, our lives would be utter chaos if we did not have some way of organizing or structuring our knowledge. Fortunately, as we discuss in the next sections, we are quite adept at organizing our knowledge and can sort it into categories with relative ease.

Categories and Their Structure

Objects can be organized into **taxonomic categories**.[21] A taxonomic category is simply an orderly classification of objects with similar objects in the same category. For example, although we have schemas for Coke, Pepsi, Diet Coke, and so on, these schemas might be clustered in a category called soft drinks. Moreover, subcategories may cluster specific brands and separate them from others. Thus we might have one subcategory for diet soft drinks and a different subcategory for nondiet soft drinks. Soft drinks may in turn be part of a larger category, beverages, that also includes coffees, teas, juices, and bottled water. Exhibit 5.7 on page 111 illustrates this idea.

Graded Structure and Prototypicality Things that are in the same taxonomic category share similar features, and the features they share are different from the features that characterize objects in other categories. Another way of saying this is that a category member like Diet Coke shares many associations with members of its own category of diet colas and few with members of other categories like herbal teas. Note that in Exhibit 5.7 Diet Coke has associations a-d, and Diet Pepsi has many but not all the same associations (a-c and e). In contrast, Lipton tea has associations a and f-h. It thus has few associations in common with Diet Coke.

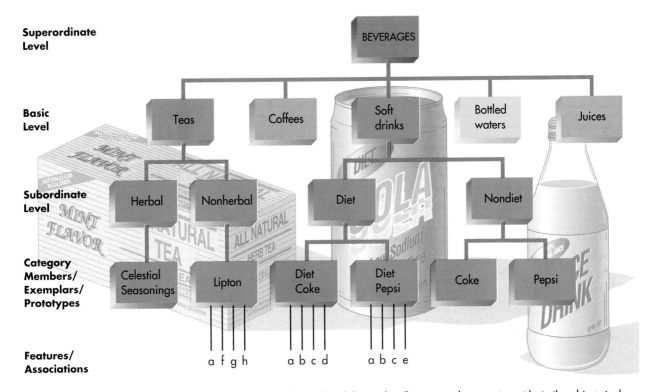

Superordinate Level — BEVERAGES

Basic Level — Teas | Coffees | Soft drinks | Bottled waters | Juices

Subordinate Level — Herbal | Nonherbal | Diet | Nondiet

Category Members/ Exemplars/ Prototypes — Celestial Seasonings | Lipton | Diet Coke | Diet Pepsi | Coke | Pepsi

Features/ Associations — a f g h | a b c d | a b c e

EXHIBIT 5.7
Taxonomic Category Structure

Objects can be organized in ordered, hierarchically structured categories, with similar objects in the same category. For example, herbal and nonherbal teas are subordinate to the basic-level category of teas. Teas, coffees, and soft drinks are members of the superordinate category, beverages.

Even though a category includes members that share similar features, not every member is perceived to be an equally good category member. For example, we perceive a robin to be a better example of the category bird than a flamingo is. Likewise, we are likely to view Coke as a better example of a soft drink than Shasta is. The fact that category members vary in how well they are perceived to represent a category illustrates the principle of **graded structure**.[22]

Specifically, within a category, category members can be ranked according to how well we believe they represent the category. The category **prototype** is that category member that we perceive to be best example of the category. Thus a robin is a prototypical bird, and Coke is a prototypical soft drink. Exhibit 5.8 identifies brands generally regarded as prototypes in their product categories.

graded structure The fact that category members vary in how well they represent a category.

prototype The best example of the category.

What Affects Prototypicality? Several factors affect whether something is regarded as a prototypical category member.[23] The first is shared associations. Specifically, a prototype shares the most associations with other members of its own category and shares the fewest with members from different categories. Potato chips are a prototypical snack food because they have associations common to many snack foods (taste good, finger food, come in many varieties, high in calories) and few associations in common with other categories such as dinner foods. A second feature that affects prototypicality is the frequency with which an object is encountered as a category member. Amazon.com is regarded as a prototypical place to buy books on the Internet because we are likely to have encountered its name many times when we are on the Internet or searching for places to buy books on-line. The first or "pioneer" brand in a category may also be a prototype because it sets a standard against which brands introduced subsequently are compared. Amazon.com is a prototypical brand in this regard as well.

PRODUCT CATEGORY	PROTOTYPICAL BRANDS
Children's entertainment	Disney
Laundry detergent	Tide
Film	Kodak
Toothpaste	Crest
Electronics	Sony
Peanut butter	Skippy
Tuna fish	Starkist
Soup	Campbell's
Bologna	Oscar Mayer
Ketchup	Heinz
Bleach	Clorox
Greeting cards	Hallmark
Jeans	Levi's
Tires	Goodyear
Grape jelly	Welch's
Copiers	Xerox
Mustard	French's
Gelatin	Jell-O
Hamburgers	McDonald's
Men's underwear	Fruit of the Loom
Baby lotion	Johnson & Johnson
Tools	Black & Decker
Cereal	Kellogg's
Tissue	Kleenex
Acetaminophen	Tylenol

MARKETING IMPLICATIONS Prototypes have important implications for marketers. First, they represent the main point of comparison that consumers use to categorize a new brand, which could develop its identity by being positioned as either close to or different from the prototype.

Positioning Close to the Prototype. Positioning a brand as close to the category prototype would be appropriate when the goal is to appeal to a broad segment of consumers. Because the prototype best defines the category and is well liked, a new brand positioned as similar to it may appeal to a large segment of consumers.

Comparative advertising may be a useful tool for making a brand seem similar to a prototype. If a challenger brand such as Barnesandnoble.com comes into the market and directly compares itself to Amazon.com, the challenger may be seen as similar to the prototype.[24] Positioning close to the prototype is also a strategy used by knockoff brands. A product called the Fitness Strider sold through infomercials was a knockoff of the Fitness Flyer, also sold through infomercials. Touting the same benefits and design, the Strider was able to leverage the hard work the Flyer had already done in making consumers aware of the general product type.[25]

Positioning away from the Prototype. An alternative strategy is to position the new brand away from the prototype. An excellent example is Nabisco SnackWell's cookies, positioned as a health cookie (the prototypical cookie is not considered healthy). Häagen-Dazs successfully promoted its decadent, ultrarich ice cream when consumers were fixated on bran and low cholesterol.[26]

Positioning a brand as different from the prototype is a good strategy when the brand is different from others (particularly from the prototype) and the point of difference represents a credible reason for buying. In the airline industry, United Airlines is trying to position itself as different from other airlines by having great food. The airline even hired culinary expert Sheila Lukins to help create good tasting meals.[27] Positioning the brand as different from the prototype is also appropriate when the goal is to appeal to consumers with specific needs. For example, whereas most rental car companies offer basically the same service, Enterprise differentiated itself by providing vehicle delivery and customer pickup service.[28] ■

Correlated Associations While graded structure reflects one way knowledge is structured, another way depends on whether the associations linked to category members are correlated, or go together. For example, in the category of automobiles, car size is positively correlated with safety (larger cars are generally safer), and engine size is negatively correlated with miles per gallon (the bigger the engine, the fewer miles per gallon). In addition, if consumers believe that car size and safety are generally correlated, they may infer that a new car with a large engine is also safe. Thus **correlated associations** can have important effects on the inferences consumers make about a new brand that is seen to be a member of a category.

correlated associations The extent to which two or more associations linked to a schema go together.

superordinate level The broadest level of category organization containing different objects that share few associations but are still members of the category.

basic level A level of categorization below the superordinate category that contains objects in more refined categories.

subordinate level A level of categorization below the basic level that contains objects in very finely differentiated categories.

Hierarchical Structure A final way in which taxonomic categories are structured is in terms of their hierarchical structure. As Exhibit 5.7 indicates, taxonomic categories can be hierarchically organized into basic, subordinate, and superordinate levels. The broadest level of categorization is the **superordinate level**. Objects at this level share a few associations but also have many different ones. Diet Coke and Arrowhead bottled water are both members of the beverages category. Although they have some common associations, they also have many that are different.

Finer discriminations among these objects are made at the **basic level**. Thus beverages might be more finely represented by categories such as teas, coffees, and soft drinks. The objects in the teas category have more in common with each other than they do with objects in the coffee category. The finest level of differentiation exists at the **subordinate level**. For example, soft drinks might be subdivided into categories of diet and nondiet soft drinks. Again, members of the diet soft drink category have more associations in common with each other than they do with members of the nondiet category. In some cases we may have many levels of subcategorization. Consumers may think about whether soft drinks are diet or nondiet, colas or not colas, have caffeine or are decaffeinated.

In sum, more associations are used to describe the objects as we move from the superordinate to the basic to the subordinate levels. The associations "drinkable" and "used throughout the day" are common to members of the beverages category. Other associations—carbonated, served cold, and sold in six-packs—are added to describe members of the soft drink category. Finally, the associations no calories and contains artificial sweeteners are added at the subordinate level.

MARKETING IMPLICATIONS Understanding consumers' hierarchical category structure helps marketers identify their competitors. Although consumers often make choices among brands at the basic or subordinate level, in some cases they choose from brands that belong to a common superordinate category. For example, if you are deciding whether to buy a CD player for your home or a new car stereo, you are making a decision among products that belong to different basic categories within a common superordinate-level category (music entertainment products). The brands in both categories might be compared based on higher-order attributes that link the brands to the same superordinate-level category (how much entertainment they provide, how much they cost). Moreover, although marketers of CDs might not normally think about themselves as competing with brands of car stereos, in this case, stereos are competing with CDs. Thus superordinate-level categories can help the firm identify a broader view of its potential competitors.

In line with this thinking, Nestle is trying to get consumers to think about its Nescafe coffee as being a beverage, not just a coffee product. Positioning it more widely may make consumers think about Nescafe coffee whenever they want any kind of beverage.[29]

Establishing a Competitive Position. Marketers can glean a broad view of their competition from an understanding of consumers' superordinate-category structure and can often rely on their understanding of that structure to establish a competitive position. Creating subordinate categories also helps marketers determine which attributes to emphasize to ensure that the brand or service is categorized correctly. For example, the fact that nonalcoholic beer has been positioned as a subordinate category of beer suggests that advertising should not only stress features central to beer (great beer taste) but also clarify its subordinate-category membership by promoting associations (without the alcohol).

Designing Retail Channels and Web Sites.   Basic, subordinate, and superordinate category levels, also have implications for consumer search and the design of retail environments and Web sites. Generally, grocery stores are designed so that objects in taxonomically similar categories are shelved together, as are items in the same basic- and subordinate-level categories. For example, most grocery stores have a dairy (superordinate level) section. Within the dairy section are sections for milk, yogurt, cheese, eggs, and so on (basic level). Within each of these sections in turn are subordinate categories of items such as low-fat, nonfat, and whole milk. Placing items in ways that are consistent with the structure of consumers' knowledge helps consumers find products efficiently.

Similarly, Web sites are likely to be easier to use if they first take consumers to superordinate categories, say, toys, then to more basic-level categories such as toys for boys, and then to subordinate categories such as toys for boys ages 7 to 8. Sites such as www.etoys.com and www.clinique.com do a great job of matching a typical consumer's hierarchical category structure for these categories.

Goal-Derived Categories

goal-derived category
Things that are viewed as belonging in the same category because they serve the same goals.

Taxonomic categories reflect one way in which we organize or structure our prior knowledge. Our knowledge may also be organized according to **goal-derived categories**. A goal-derived category contains things we view as relevant to the goal. Sometimes we assign things to the same category because they serve the same goals—even though they belong to different taxonomic categories.[30] For example, when traveling on an airplane, we might see novels, blankets, and peanuts in the same category because all are part of the goal-derived category "things that make air travel more pleasant". Because we have many goals, we can have many goal-derived categories. For example, if you are on a diet, you might form a category for foods to eat on a diet. Likewise, you might have goal-derived categories like things to do on Friday nights or interesting sites on the Web.

Some goals are encountered frequently and are well established in prior knowledge. For example, if you give a lot of parties, the goal-derived category of "things to buy for a party" probably comprises a fairly stable and constant set of products. However, less frequently encountered goals, and the category members that are relevant to their achievement, may be based on the situation.

The same object can be part of a goal-derived and a taxonomic category. Thus, Diet Coke might be part of the taxonomic categories diet colas, soft drinks, and beverages. It might also be a member of the following goal-derived categories: things to eat on a diet, things to take on a picnic, and things to drink at a ball game. Category structure is therefore quite flexible.

Like taxonomic categories, goal-derived categories also exhibit graded structure. Some members are regarded as better examples of the category because they best achieve the goals of the category. Thus compared to baked crackers, lettuce is a better example of foods to eat on a diet because it is lower in fat and calories. Because goal-derived categories exhibit graded structure, prototypes of goal-derived categories can also be identified. As with taxonomic categories, the frequency with which an item is encountered as a category member affects its prototypicality. We tend to classify lettuce as a prototype for things to eat on diet and would probably rate it as more prototypical than a food that is equally appropriate but encountered less frequently, like kohlrabi.

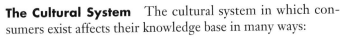

MARKETING IMPLICATIONS

Positioning a product or service as relevant to a goal can be an important marketing objective. To illustrate, Special K is positioned as consistent with the goal-derived category things to keep you thin. In Germany and France, countries where women do not shave their legs on a regular basis, shaving products are positioned as members of the goal-derived category things to use on a special occasion. The ad in Exhibit 5.9 uses pure and simple images like honey and flowers to convey the notion that Back to Basics shampoo and conditioner are part of the goal-derived category of things that are pure and simple.

Grocery store design is also consistent with goal-derived category structures. Bottles, diapers, baby food, and juice are displayed in the same aisle, although they are in different taxonomic categories. Note that diapers are probably similar to tissue, baby juice to juice for older kids, and baby food to other food sold in the store. However, because these products are part of a goal-derived category—things you need to take care of a baby—they are shelved together. This arrangement helps parents find the items and decide which brands to buy. Similarly, Web sites can be designed with consumers' goal-derived categories in mind. Web sites for travel services, for example, should be designed so that segments of consumers with different goals can search efficiently for options. Links to family-friendly vacations, budget vacations, and luxury vacations allow different segments of consumers to research their different travel goals. ■

Why Consumers Differ in Their Knowledge

Several background factors affect our knowledge structure and content. The cultural system in which consumers exist affects their knowledge base. Also, consumers vary in their expertise or in the extent of their prior knowledge.

The Cultural System   The cultural system in which consumers exist affects their knowledge base in many ways:

- *Different Associations Linked to a Concept.*   First, the nature and strength of associations linked to a concept may vary considerably across cultural systems.[31] In the United States, for example, Visa is associated with Tiger Woods and golf. These associations are unlikely to be as meaningful in countries where Tiger Woods is less well known and golf is less popular. This information would clearly have implications for Visa's ability to use Tiger Woods as a global endorser.

- *Different Category Members.*   Second, although consumers may have similar goal-derived categories such as "things to have for breakfast," cultural groups vary considerably in what they regard as relevant category members. In the United States, category members might include cereal, donuts, fruit, and eggs; in Japan, fish, rice, and pickled vegetables.

- *Different Category Prototypes.*   Third, category prototypes and members may vary across cultures, and this factor may require a different positioning strategy. In the Netherlands, Heineken beer is like Budweiser in the United States—frequently encontered and prototypical. In the

EXHIBIT 5.9
Pure and Simple Things

To convey the notion that Back To Basics hair care products are pure and simple, pictures of pure and simple things were included in the ad.

Source: Courtesy of Graham Webb International.

United States, however, Heineken has associations linked with an imported, expensive, status beer; hence Heineken resides in a subordinate category. Because the beers have different competitors in the two markets, the same positioning strategy is unlikely to work equally well in both countries.

- *Different Correlated Associations.* Fourth, culture may affect whether associations are correlated and the direction of their correlation. For example, in the United States mega-stores like Price Club and Wal-Mart tend to have lower prices than small stores do because the large stores are often discounters. In India and Sri Lanka, large stores tend to have higher prices than small stores do because the former have higher overhead costs.

- *Different Goal Derived Categories.* Finally, different cultures may not only have different entities in goal-derived categories but, in fact, have different goal-derived categories. For example, the goal to have clothing that looks sexy is not likely to apply in cultures with strict religious values.

Level of Expertise   Consumers vary in their ability to process information based on the extent of their prior knowledge. *Experts* are people whose prior knowledge is well developed, in part because they have had a lot of experience, knowledge, and familiarity with an object or a task. The content and structure of experts' prior knowledge differs from that of novices in several ways.[32] For one thing, experts' overall category structure is more developed than the category structure of nonexperts. They have more categories, more associations with concepts in a category, and a better understanding of whether associations in a category are correlated. Experts also have more subordinate-level categories and can therefore make finer distinctions among brands. For example, car experts would have many subordinate categories of cars such as vintage cars and roadsters. Experts and nonexperts thus tend to search for information and make decisions in different ways.

USING KNOWLEDGE TO UNDERSTAND

Simply attending to and perceiving stimuli is not sufficient to influence consumers' decisions. Consumers must also interpret or give meaning to the objects they perceive in light of their prior knowledge.

Categorization

A first step in this process occurs when consumers categorize an object. Categorization occurs when consumers use their prior knowledge to label, identify, and classify something new. Thus consumers might categorize IMAC as a type of computer, eBay as a new place to buy secondhand merchandise, and Behind the Music as a place to get the scoop on the past lives of music stars. Once we have categorized an object, we know what it is, what it is like, and what it is similar to. How we categorize an offering has many implications for marketers, since categorization affects how favorably we evaluate the offering, the expectations we have for it, whether we will choose it, and how satisfied we may be with it.

 Incorrect Categorizations   We do not always categorize things correctly. For example, Japanese women initially and incorrectly categorized *Good Housekeeping* magazine as a magazine for housemaids.[33] Lever Brothers once distributed samples of Sunlight dish-washing liquid to households across the United States. Based on the product's yellow package and the lemon displayed on the label, some consumers categorized the product as lemon juice—and added it to their iced tea![34] Once consumers have categorized an offering, they may not be able to categorize it differently. To illustrate, consumers who perceive Kmart as a discount store may not be able to recategorize it as a place to buy fashion-oriented clothing.

MARKETING IMPLICATIONS Categorization is a basic psychological process that has far-reaching implications for marketers, including the following:

- *Inferences.* If we categorize a product as a member of a category, we may infer that the product has features or attributes that are typical of that category. For example, we may infer that because the IMAC is a computer, it comes with a color monitor, is Y2K compliant, and includes a zip drive. In many cases our inferences are correct, but sometimes they may not be.

- *Elaboration.* Categorization influences how much we think about something. We tend to be more motivated to think about or process information that we have trouble categorizing. We are more motivated to watch ads that are different from the typical ad, and we are more motivated to think about products that look different from others in the category.[35] Seeing a Honda Accord with a spoiler and racing stripes might prompt elaboration because these features suggest a mixture of the sports car and compact car categories.

- *Evaluation.* Categorization also influences how we feel about an object, also known as our "affect" toward it. Once we categorize something as a member of a category, we may simply retrieve the feelings or affect stored about the category and use it to evaluate the object.[36] For example, if we hate lawyers and see an ad for a lawyer on TV, we may use the category-based affect and decide that we hate this one, too. Likewise, if our category for chocolate bars contains favorable affect, we may retrieve and use this affect to evaluate a new brand in the category.

- *Consideration and Choice.* Whether and how we label a product or service affects whether we will consider buying it. For example, if a new phone/fax/printer is categorized as a phone machine, we will consider it if we are in the market for phones. If it is categorized as a printer, we will consider it if we are in the market for a printer. If consumers categorize Clorets as a medicinal product, it will compete with Scope. Categorized as a chewing gum, however, Clorets will be considered along with Trident.

- *Satisfaction.* Finally, categorization has important implications for consumer expectations and satisfaction.[37] If we categorize something as a word processor, we will expect it to meet all the performance characteristics of a word processor. If a product's performance falls short of category expectations, we are likely to be dissatisfied with that product. ■

Comprehension

While categorization reflects the process of identifying an entity, comprehension is the process of extracting higher-order meaning from it.

Marketers are concerned with the two aspects of comprehension. The first is objective comprehension—the meaning that consumers extract from a message consistent with what the message actually stated. The second is subjective comprehension—the different or additional meaning consumers attached to the message, whether or not these meanings were intended.[38]

objective comprehension The extent to which the receiver accurately understands the message a sender intended to communicate.

subjective comprehension Reflects what we think we know, whether or not it is accurate.

Objective and Subjective Comprehension Objective comprehension reflects whether we accurately understand the message a receiver intended to communicate. Interestingly, many people miscomprehend marketing messages. Miscomprehension may be caused by the way the information is presented (its language), differences between the sender's and the receiver's prior knowledge, or both. **Subjective comprehension** reflects what we think we know, whether or not it is accurate. Elements of the marketing mix such as price, pictures in ads, and store atmosphere can play a powerful role in affecting what we think we know. To illustrate, we may infer that Trident dental gum is as powerful as whitening toothpastes are in getting teeth white because the package uses white sparkles, the model in the ad has very white teeth, and the package uses terms like *whitening agent*. Notably, though, the product may not actually be such a powerful whitening agent. The inferences that we make and the reasons certain communications cause us to make them raise some important public policy implications.

Objective Comprehension—and Miscomprehension Objective comprehension reflects the extent to which consumers accurately understand or have learned what is stated in a communication. One way to measure objective comprehension is to ask consumers whether an idea was conveyed in a communication. Because marketing communications, including ads and packaging, are often fairly simple, you might assume that achieving objective comprehension is not much of a challenge for marketers. Research has indicated that it is.

miscomprehension Inaccurate understanding of a message.

Miscomprehension occurs when consumers inaccurately receive the meaning contained in a message. Several studies have found a surprisingly high amount of miscomprehension of TV and magazine ads. The estimated rate of comprehension was only about 70 percent for TV ads and 65 percent for print ads. Furthermore, the rates of miscomprehension for directly asserted information and implied information were fairly equal. Miscomprehension rates for programming, editorial material, and advertising were also roughly equal.[39] Furthermore, miscomprehension also occurred across all demographic segments.

Miscomprehension occurs not just for advertising. Consumers sometimes fail to understand how to use a product. This tendency has led to some rather bizarre warning signs on products, as Exhibit 5.10 illustrates. Miscomprehension can even occur for gestures as the same gesture can have different meanings in different cultures. Forming a circle with the thumb and forefinger means "okay" in the United States, means "money" in Japan, and is a rude comment in Brazil.[40]

Effect of MAO Miscomprehension is clearly affected by consumers' motivation, ability, and opportunity (MAO) to process messages. Consumers are probably most likely to miscomprehend something when their motivation to process it is low.[41] Even when motivation is high, however, comprehension may not be accurate. One study found that although consumers want to see nutritional information on packaging (implying high motivation to process it), most do not comprehend it once they have acquired it.[42] Comprehension may improve with expertise and ability. Thus young children are less able than older consumers to comprehend some of the finer points of a message.[43] Finally, consumers are more likely to miscomprehend messages when the opportunity to process them is limited. Miscomprehension is generally greater when messages are complex, shown for only a few seconds, and viewed only once or twice.

Effect of the Cultural System The cultural system can also affect comprehension and miscomprehension. Low-context cultures such as those in North America and northern Europe generally separate the words and meanings of a com-

On a hair dryer:	Do not use while sleeping
On a bag of corn chips:	You could be a winner! No purchase necessary! Details inside.
On a bar of soap:	Directions: Use like regular soap
On frozen dinners:	Serving suggestion: defrost
On a hotel provided shower cap:	Fits one head
Printed on *the bottom* of a Tiramisu dessert:	Do not turn upside down
On bread pudding product:	Product will be hot after heating
On packaging for an iron:	Do not iron clothes on body
On sleep aid:	Warning: may cause drowsiness
On jar of peanuts:	Warning: contains nuts
On packet of nuts:	Instructions: open packet, eat nuts
On a child Superman costume:	Wearing of this garment does not enable you to fly

In some cases, manufacturers developing labels for products used in other countries do not always convey precisely the intended meaning.

On a string of Christmas Lights:	For indoor or outdoor use only
On a Korean kitchen knife:	Warning: keep out of children
On a Japanese food processor:	Not to be used for the other use.

EXHIBIT 5.10

Comprehension and Product Warnings

Consumers don't always understand how to use products, and may use them in inappropriate ways. Perhaps because they are concerned about liability issues, manufacturers have come up with some very odd instructions on packages.

munication from the context in which it appears. Consumers in these parts of the world place greater emphasis on what is said than on the surrounding visuals or the environmental context in which the message is stated. In contrast, in high-context cultures much of what is meant in a communication is implied indirectly and communicated visually rather than through words. Characteristics of the message sender such as social class, values, and age play an important role in the interpretation of a message.[44]

Because cultures differ in the level of attention they pay to the content and context of the message, we might expect differences in consumers' comprehension of the same message across cultures. Miscomprehension can also occur because marketers' translation of a message has a different meaning from what consumers interpret (see the bottom half of Exhibit 5.9 for several examples). Language differences further raise the possibility of miscomprehension. For example, Volkswagen tried to use the German concept of *fahrvergnugen*, or driving pleasure, in the U.S. market.[45] Unfortunately, U.S. consumers did not understand what this term meant, and most could not pronounce it.

 Culture also affects the meanings attached to words.[46] For example, in the United Kingdom, a *billion* is "a million million," whereas in the United States a *billion* means "a thousand million." Likewise, in the United Kingdom a movie that is a *bomb* is a "success;" in the United States, a *bomb* means a "failure." One U.S. airline promoted its "rendezvous lounges" in Brazil—however, among the Brazilians the phrase implied "a room for lovemaking."

Different cultures may also be interpret slang and idioms in different ways. One U.S. firm described its dealings with a Japanese company as "a whole new ball game." The Japanese executives thought their U.S. counterparts, who described the potential contract as a game, were not serious about the deal and, therefore, canceled it.

Improving Objective Comprehension Fortunately, consumer researchers have provided some guidelines for improving objective comprehension.[47] One obvious method is to keep the message simple. Another is to repeat the message—

stating it multiple times within the same communication and repeating it on multiple occasions. Finally, comprehension can be improved by presenting the message in different forms. For example, information on TV can be presented both visually and verbally.

Subjective Comprehension

Subjective comprehension describes the meanings consumers generate from a communication, whether or not these meanings were intended by the sender.[48] Public policy makers are often concerned that what consumers take away from an ad may be different from what the ad objectively states. The Federal Trade Commission recently went after R.J. Reynolds, claiming that consumers would infer that a new brand of cigarettes advertised as having no additives would be safer than other cigarettes. In this case, the claim refers to the brand's flavor, not its taste.[49]

Levels of Subjective Comprehension   Some researchers use a series of levels to describe the interpretations consumers make when they process a message. In this scheme each level indicates more thinking or elaboration.[50] For example, suppose a consumer sees an ad for a car CD player that says, "If you have an FM radio in your car, you can play CDs." The ad also states that the advertised CD player comes with a six-disc magazine. The consumer exposed to this ad might think, "I guess if you only have an AM radio, you can't install a CD player in your car." At a higher level of elaboration, the consumer might make logical inferences derived directly from what is said in the ad. For example, she might logically infer that CD players and FM radios involve similar electronic interconnections because the radio is necessary for this CD player to work. At even higher levels of elaboration, the consumer might make inferences based on her general knowledge. For example, she may infer that because the CD player has a six-disc magazine, it might also have programmable functions. At the highest level, the consumer might think about or imagine future interactions with the stereo. For example, she might think that such a system would be attractive to thieves and therefore might wonder whether getting one also requires getting a car security system.

MARKETING IMPLICATIONS   Like categorization, subjective comprehension involves some interaction between what is in a message and what consumers know. Marketers can thus have a large influence on what consumers subjectively perceive from a communication by designing or structuring their communications in a way that is consistent with prior knowledge. Sometimes, when consumers do not know much about a new product, marketers may be best able to develop a message that is informative by drawing an analogy between the product and something that has similar benefits. For example, they may try to communicate the idea that a particular brand of boots is waterproof, soft, and lightweight by using the analogy of a duck.[51] The Mercedes-Benz ad in Exhibit 5.11 draws an analogy between its Vito F. Geht minivan and a Swiss army knife—emphasizing the vehicle's versatility.

In many cases designing an ad so that consumers form the "correct" inferences about the offering is a key to success. However, marketers may also (wittingly or unwittingly) create inferences that do not accurately characterize a product or service and result in miscomprehension.[52] Some important ethical implications are therefore raised when marketers deliberately create false inferences about an offering. ■

EXHIBIT 5.11
Analogies

Sometimes marketers can communicate information about their brands by drawing analogies to other things.

Source: Reprinted by permission of DaimlerChrysler Vertriebsorganisation Deutschland.

Alles über den multifunktionalen Vito F unter 0180/5 101 102*

Vito F. Geht nicht gibt's nicht.

Mercedes-Benz

Consumer Inferences

Specific elements of the marketing mix can work with consumers' prior knowledge to affect the correct or incorrect inferences they make about an offering. The following sections describe how brand names and symbols, product features and packaging, price, distribution, and promotion can affect the inferences consumers make about products.

Brand Names and Brand Symbols   Subjective comprehension of a marketing communication can be based on the inferences consumers make from a brand symbol. The Pillsbury Dough Boy has slimmed down over the years because the company's marketers are afraid that consumers will infer that he is fat from eating Pillsbury products.

Brand names can also create subjective comprehension and inferences. For example, alphanumeric brand names like Mazda's RX7 tend to be associated with technological sophistication and complexity. Thus consumers may infer that brands with these names have these characteristics. Foreign brand names may also create inferences based on cultural categories and stereotypes. Thus Häagen-Dazs, a German-sounding name, may evoke favorable associations when applied to ice cream even though it is manufactured in the Bronx. French and Italian names like Armani, Vuarnet, Paco Rabanne, and Pierre Cardin imply high fashion. Descriptive names can also create inferences. For example, consumers may infer that Country Hearth bread is wholesome, earthy, home baked, and warm. Brand names such as Obsession for perfume, Speedo for bathing suits, Gleem for toothpaste, Ray Ban for sunglasses, and Sure View for contact lenses may create inferences about the particular brand's benefits.[53]

Inferences Based on Misleading Names and Labels   Although some brand names may accurately characterize a product's attributes and benefits, others have been called misleading because they suggest false inferences about the product's benefits. For example, consumers may infer that lite olive oil has fewer calories when it is really only light in terms of its color.[54] Exhibit 5.12 reveals the confusion consumers feel over the meaning of terms used in brand names. This confusion has prompted the development of labeling laws designed to make names and product ingredients accurately describe the offering. The U.S. Department of Agriculture has enacted regulations that standardize the meaning of the term *organic.* The term is restricted to crops untouched by herbicides, pesticides, or fertilizers for at least 3 years or to livestock raised without antibiotics or hormones. Advertisers cannot use the word organic to describe a product's taste.[55]

Inferences Based on Inappropriate or Similar Names

Some brand names lead to inappropriate inferences about the product. One gas company came up with the new name Enteron, but later learned that *enteron* is a real word that means "the alimentary canal."[56] Others names fail because they do not create unique associations or inferences that help their brand stand out from others. As of 1996 the word *web* had been included in more than 1,000 trademarks.[57] You can imagine how difficult it is now for Web marketers to find a name that says what they do but also helps them stand out from other companies.

Sometimes brand or company names are too similar. Consumers may inadvertently infer that the brands are similar or that they are made by the same company. Typically these situations create legal battles, with companies fighting over who can use the original brand name. This situation happened when *Polo* magazine began to reposition itself from a magazine devoted to the sport of polo to an upscale magazine—a magazine with an image similar to that of Polo Ralph Lauren.[58]

Product Features and Packaging

Consumers can also subjectively comprehend aspects of an offering based on inferences they make from the product and the way it is packaged.

Inferences Based on Product Attributes

Inferences about attributes that are naturally correlated in a product category may lead consumers to infer that the presence of one attribute in a brand implies the other. Thus consumers may infer that a product with a low repair record also has a long warranty.[59] Consumers may make inferences about products based on package size. A consumer who encounters a large, multipack item may use prior knowledge about the correlation between price and package size to infer that the large-sized brand is also a good buy.[60]

Inferences Based on Country of Origin

Knowledge about a product's country of origin may also affect how consumers think about it.[61] Just as we stereotype people based on where they were born, we also stereotype products based on where they are made. Products labeled "Made in France" are likely to create inferences about elegance and style.[62] Unfortunately, country of origin inferences can also work to a product's disadvantage. German companies and products evoke very negative associations from some Jews who will always associate Germany, and hence German-made products, with the Holocaust.[63]

Inferences Based on Package Design

Package characteristics can also create inferences. In one study consumers inferred that potato chips packaged in polyvinyl bags were crisper and better tasting than chips packaged in wax-coated bags, even though the bags contained the exact same chips.[64] Consumers may

EXHIBIT 5.12
Confusing Brand Names

Brand names may create inferences about attributes or benefits of the product. People may not agree on what these attributes or benefits are, and these inferences may not be correct.

Source: Adapted by permission from Bonnie B. Reece and Robert H. Ducoffe, "Deception in Brand Names," *Journal of Public Policy and Marketing,* 6, 1987, pp. 93–103.

EXAMPLE NAMES*
"Salad's" Lo-Cal Italian Dressing
"Oatman's" Natural Cereal
"Lean" meals
"Lisson" Trim Beef Cup-a-Soup
"Fruitobia" Low-Sugar Grape Spread
"Just Desserts" Plus Chocolate Cake Mix

	INFERENCES	PERCENTAGE WHO AGREE THAT THIS IS WHAT THE NAME IMPLIES
LO-CAL	1/3 fewer calories than regular dressing	49[†]
	1/3 fewer calories than regular Salad's	59[†]
	Not fattening	30
	Made with no oil	11
NATURAL	Nothing artificial added	81[†]
	No preservatives	75[†]
	Fewer calories than most cereals	8
	No sugar added	20
LEAN	1/3 fewer calories than regular	56
	1/2 less fat than regular	34
	Smaller portions than regular	45
	Healthier than regular	30
TRIM	1/3 fewer calories than regular	52[†]
	10 calories per serving	35[†]
	All fat removed	21[†]
	Less flavor	21
LO-SUGAR	1/2 sugar of regular	62[†]
	Artificial sweetener	54
	10 calories per serving	19
	1/3 fewer calories than regular	47[†]
PLUS	Richer taste than regular	64
	Nuts or chocolate bits added	36
	More calories than regular	28
	Pudding added for moistness	61[†]

* Consumers in this study were presented with the names of actual brands. These brand names have been replaced with hypothetical brand names.
† Indicates what the name actually means.

also make inferences about a brand if its package, name, or design looks like that of other brands in the category. For example, the packaging for Organza shown in Exhibit 5.13 is shaped like the organza dress worn by the model. The silhouette of the female form creates inferences about the elegance and sexiness of the product.

EXHIBIT 5.13
Inferences Based on Packaging

Organza perfume uses packaging shaped like a long organza gown, conveying the notion that the brand is elegant and sexy.

Source: Courtesy of Givenchy.

Sometimes packages are designed to look like the packages of well-known brands. Walgreen's Impressions fragrances are designed to look like major designer brands, such as Drakkar Noir and Polo. Sometimes packaging similarity spurs legal battles. Kendall-Jackson sued Gallo, alleging that Gallo's Turning Leaf Chardonnay copied Kendall-Jackson's colored leaf logo, its tapered neck, the design of its label, and its leaf-stamped cork. Kendall-Jackson charges that the packaging similarity will make consumers believe that it is a Kendall-Jackson brand when it really is not.[65]

Inferences Based on Color   Finally, consumers can make inferences about an offering based on its color or the color of its package. We have color categories stored in prior knowledge. The category of things that are green includes grass, trees, leaves, and mint as members. These members have associations like refreshing, new, organic, peaceful, and springlike. Because of this category-based knowledge, consumers can make inferences about a stimulus based on its color. They may infer that a brand of green toothpaste that comes in a green package is refreshing, minty, and healthy. A bag of "M&M's®" contains a disproportionate number of brown "M&M's®" compared with the other colors, perhaps because marketers have found that the brown color makes consumers think that "M&M's®" taste more "chocolate-y."

Because colors can affect consumers' inferences, some companies have taken legal steps to protect the color of their brand. Owens-Corning gained trademark protection for its pink home-insulation products, and Keds gained trademark protection for the blue rectangular label on the heels of Keds shoes. Such protection prohibits other firms from using these colors on their products—and thus reduces the possibility that consumers will either categorize the product incorrectly or draw false inferences about it.[66]

Because category content varies with culture, the meaning associated with colors and hence inferences based on color will also vary.[67] For example, white is usually associated with purity and cleanliness in Western societies, but in Asian countries it signifies death. Green is a popular color in Muslim countries but is negatively perceived in Southwest Asia. Black has negative overtones in Japan, India, and Europe but is perceived positively in the Middle East. Thus marketers must be careful to account for these cultural differences when marketing and designing communications in other countries.

Price   Consumers may also make inferences about a product or service based on its price. For example, category-based knowledge suggests that price and quality are correlated. Thus a consumer may infer that a high-priced product is also high in quality.[68] This inference is often made when consumers are not knowledgeable about brands and are simply using price as a shortcut to infer quality or when they have no other basis for discriminating among brands.

Retail Atmospherics   Category-based knowledge about aspects of the distribution mix, such as retail design, layout, merchandising, and service, can also affect consumers' inferences. For example, the inferences you might make when you walk into a warehouse-type store like Price Club are likely to be different from the inferences you might make when going to a more upscale, service-oriented store like Macy's. Atmospherics are, in fact, a major tool used by retailers to develop, elaborate, and change their images. The British retail chain Comet Group PLC has developed a large no-frills, warehouse concept store that will undoubtedly affect consumers' inferences about the quality and price of the store's merchandise.[69]

Advertising and Selling   Advertising and selling efforts certainly affect the inferences consumers make about an offering. In personal selling and advertising, inferences can be based on body language. An advertisement that shows a woman touching a man's hand for longer than a second could lead us to believe that they are romantically involved. Consumers might infer that a salesperson whose handshake is weak is not interested in taking their business. The nonverbal aspects of communication are particularly important in Asian cultures.[70] In Japan, for example, a verbal *yes* often means "no"; the speaker's body language communicates the true intent.[71]

Physical space, or the distance between people, may also be interpreted differently in different cultures. Asians tend to leave much more distance between people than Westerners do and prefer limited physical contact. A U.S. salesperson who is accustomed to less space and more contact may give Asian consumers the impression of being pushy and unacceptably physical. However, compared with people in the United States, consumers in Latin America are comfortable with a much smaller distance between people. Thus a U.S. salesperson may create an impression of being standoffish among Latin American consumers.[72]

EXHIBIT 5.14
Stimulating Inferences with Pictures

Lubriderm effectively uses an alligator and the slogan, "See you later alligator" to convey the idea that Lubriderm helps heal rough, dry skin.

Source: Courtesy of Warner-Lambert Company.

Pictures   Advertisers frequently use pictures to stimulate inferences. To illustrate, our schema for alligator includes the associations rough and scaly. Lubriderm effectively uses an alligator and the slogan "See you later alligator" to convey the idea that Lubriderm removes these offensive skin conditions (see Exhibit 5.14).

Language   Just as specific words like brand names or adjectives can clearly affect inferences, the way in which words are structured into sentences can also affect subjective comprehension.[73] The word structure of the hypothetical ad in Exhibit 5.15 can lead to the following (potentially incorrect) inferences:

- *Juxtaposed Imperatives.*   The headline contains two sentences placed next to one another (juxtaposed). Consumers might interpret the headline as saying, "The Starfire AD7 gives you luxury and sportiness at its finest." However, the ad does not actually make this statement.

- *Implied Superiority.*   Another set of inferences commonly made from advertising is implied superiority. The statement "nobody gives you more," as in the exhibit, could be technically true if all brands on the market were equal in their performance benefits. However, consumers may interpret such statements as implying superiority—that is, "This brand is the best." Likewise, the

EXHIBIT 5.15

A Hypothetical Car Ad

The way that a message is worded can affect our inferences. What do you think this ad is saying? Is it really saying what you think? How does its wording affect what you comprehend?

Headline: **Experience luxury and sportiness at its finest. It's the AD7 from Starfire.**

Body copy: Automotive World's toughest tests found that no other brand gives you more than Starfire's AD7. It performs better than the Porsche in interior comfort, has better braking ability than the RX7, has a smoother ride than the Corvette, and it's less expensive.

Tag: **Starfire's AD7. Nobody gives you more.**

---

statement provides an incomplete comparison. Nobody gives you more of what? Consumers are likely to fill in a comparison object, rightly or wrongly.

- *Incomplete comparisons.* Ads will sometimes provide a comparison but leave the object of comparison either incomplete or ambiguous.[74] The statement "it's less expensive" in Exhibit 5.15, for example, does not indicate what the Starfire AD7 is less expensive than. Is it less expensive than the other brands listed in the ad? than last year's model? than the most expensive car on the market?

- *Multiple Comparisons.* Ads might also make comparisons to multiple brands. For example, the ad in Exhibit 5.15 states that the Starfire AD7 performs better than a Porsche in interior comfort, better than an RX7 in braking ability, and better than a Corvette in smoothness of ride. However, consumers may infer that the AD7 is better than all these brands on all these attributes. Readers may also infer that the Porsche is the best brand in the market in interior comfort because it is being used as the standard for comparison. However, the ads could still technically be true if the Porsche were less comfortable than an RX7 and a Corvette but still marginally less comfortable than the AD7.

Language can also lead to misleading inferences drawn from comparative ads, as Exhibit 5.16 shows. This exhibit shows three versions of the same ad for a hypothetical brand of toothpaste called Dazzle. The first ad is a noncomparative ad—it simply describes the brand's benefits, but does not compare its benefits to a competitor. The second is a partial comparative ad. It compares Dazzle to Crest, but only on one benefit, cleaning ability. The third is a direct comparative ad that compares the product to Crest on all benefits. Partial comparative ads can be misleading because consumers are likely to infer that the advertised brand is better than the compared brand on all benefits, not just the stated one.[75]

Ethical Issues

These inferences raise a number of interesting ethical and public policy questions. On the one hand, marketers are apparently able to develop elements of their marketing mix (brand name, visuals, price, store atmosphere, ad copy) that not only make their brand look favorable but also mislead consumers. On the other hand, one might argue that consumers allow themselves to be misled by marketers and that marketers cannot be held accountable for the inaccurate inferences and miscomprehension of ads. What do you think?

NEW DAZZLE TOOTHPASTE IS *THE BRAND FOR YOU.* **HERE ARE 4 REASONS WHY.**

REASON #1: EFFECTIVE CLEANING ABILITY

Independent clinical tests conducted at Stanford, Harvard, and Northwestern dental schools have documented Dazzle's cleaning ability — Dazzle removes plaque!

REASON #2: POWERFUL WHITENERS

Other clinical tests have shown that Dazzle is effective in removing stains from your teeth.

REASON #3: A REFRESHING TASTE

Recent tests conducted by Consumer Reports have shown that 9 out of 10 consumers tested liked the refreshing taste of Dazzle.

REASON #4: AN ALL-NATURAL FORMULA

Dazzle is all natural — it contains <u>no</u> artificial colors or preservatives.

NEW
DAZZLE *FLUORIDE TOOTHPASTE*

Try New Dazzle Toothpaste! A Complete Toothpaste for Today's Consumer!

NEW DAZZLE TOOTHPASTE IS *THE BRAND FOR YOU.* **HERE ARE 4 REASONS WHY.**

REASON #1: MORE EFFECTIVE CLEANING ABILITY

Independent clinical tests conducted at Stanford, Harvard, and Northwestern dental schools have documented Dazzle's cleaning ability — Dazzle removes twice the amount of plaque than Crest!

REASON #2: POWERFUL WHITENERS

Other clinical tests have shown that Dazzle is effective in removing stains from your teeth.

REASON #3: A REFRESHING TASTE

Recent tests conducted by Consumer Reports have shown that 9 out of 10 consumers tested liked the refreshing taste of Dazzle.

REASON #4: AN ALL-NATURAL FORMULA

Dazzle is all natural — it contains <u>no</u> artificial colors or preservatives.

NEW
DAZZLE *FLUORIDE TOOTHPASTE*

Try New Dazzle Toothpaste! A Complete Toothpaste for Today's Consumer!

NEW DAZZLE TOOTHPASTE IS *THE BRAND FOR YOU.* **HERE ARE 4 REASONS WHY.**

REASON #1: MORE EFFECTIVE CLEANING ABILITY

Independent clinical tests conducted at Stanford, Harvard, and Northwestern dental schools have documented Dazzle's cleaning ability — Dazzle removes twice the amount of plaque than Crest!

REASON #2: MORE POWERFUL WHITENERS

Other clinical tests have shown that Dazzle is effective in removing stains from your teeth. In fact, Dazzle has been proven to get teeth over 60% whiter than Crest.

REASON #3: A MORE REFRESHING TASTE

Recent tests conducted by Consumer Reports have shown that 9 out of 10 consumers tested preferred the refreshing taste of Dazzle over the taste of Crest.

REASON #4: AN ALL-NATURAL FORMULA

Unlike Crest, Dazzle is all natural — it contains <u>no</u> artificial colors or preservatives.

NEW
DAZZLE *FLUORIDE TOOTHPASTE*

Try New Dazzle Toothpaste! A Complete Toothpaste for Today's Consumer!

EXHIBIT 5.16
Ad Stimuli Used in One Study

Consumers may inappropriately conclude that the second version of this ad (the partial comparative ad) says that the brand is superior to the compared brand on all attributes. Really, the ad says that the brand is really superior on the first attribute only.

Source: Reprinted with permission from *Journal of Marketng Research,* published by the American Marketing Association, Michael Barone and Paul W. Miniard, February 1999, Vol. 36, p. 63.

SUMMARY

We understand something in our environment by relating it to what we already know—our prior knowledge. Knowledge content is represented by a set of associations about an object or an activity linked in schemas and scripts. Understanding the content of consumers' knowledge is important because marketers are often in the position of creating new knowledge—that is, developing brand images or brand personalities, creating brand extensions, positioning a brand—developing existing knowledge, or changing knowledge through repositioning.

Our knowledge is also organized or structured into categories. Objects within a category are similar to objects in the same category and different from objects in other categories. Objects within a category exhibit graded structure, meaning that some are better examples of the category than are others. The best example of the category is the prototype. Knowledge may be hierarchically organized, with similar objects organized in basic, subordinate, or superordinate levels of categorization. Furthermore, within a category, objects may have associations that are correlated. Categories may also be organized around things that serve similar goals. The topic of how knowledge is organized has important marketing implications for product positioning, product development, and retail design. Consumers obviously differ in their knowledge. One reason is that consumers live within different cultural systems. Another reason is that their levels of expertise differ, with some consumers having more knowledge than others.

Prior knowledge combined with information from the external environment also affects how we categorize something and what we comprehend. How we categorize something has far-reaching implications for what we think about it, how we feel about it, what we expect from it, and whether we choose and will be satisfied with it. One way of thinking about comprehension is to ask whether consumers accurately understand what was stated in a message. We call this concept objective comprehension. Consumers often fail to accurately acquire the meaning advertisers or marketers directly state in marketing communications. Motivation, ability, and opportunity affect miscomprehension. Consumers may fail to accurately understand what is explicitly stated in a communication because they form inferences based on elements of the marketing mix such as price, brand names, brand symbols, packaging characteristics, product features, and advertising communications. Subjective comprehension, or what consumers think they know or have understood from a message, may not always match what a message states. Unscrupulous marketers can take advantage of these inferences and deliberately mislead consumers.

EXERCISES

1. Identify a brand whose image you believe is negative.
   a. Indicate your schema for that brand.
   b. How is that brand currently being positioned? How might it be better positioned?
   c. Should the brand be positioned close to or away from the category prototype?
   d. Describe some brand symbols, visuals, packaging decisions, and advertising strategies that might be used to develop a new image for the brand.

2. Take a well-known brand and describe its associations. Based on these associations, indicate what its brand personality might be. Then indicate how this knowledge would facilitate your brand name, packaging, pricing, advertising, and product decisions.

3. Go to the supermarket and to a large department store and find as many examples of brand extensions as you can. For each indicate the following:
   a. Whether you think they are good brand extensions or not, and why.
   b. Whether any negative effects might be associated with these brand extensions.

   Then take a new product for which no brand extensions exist. Indicate new product categories this brand might successfully extend to.

4. Go to a Web site where you can buy products (e.g., Amazon.com, ebay.com, travelocity.com). Think about how the Web experience alters the basic "shopping-for-products" script that consumers would enact in a typical store. Does this site enable you to perform activities that you would normally perform if you were actually shopping for products in a store? How could the site be improved to enable you to perform scripted activities more easily?

5. Find a brand that is positioned close to the category prototype and another that is positioned away from the category prototype. Why do you think marketers chose to position these brands in this way?

6. Illustrate the principles of basic-, subordinate-, and superordinate-level categories for a product category of your choosing. In one case, assume that consumers' subordinate-category structure is complex; in the other case, assume it is simple. Now assume that one of the manufacturers is planning to introduce a new brand. Indicate in which case the new brand will compete with the brands the firm already makes.

7. Find an advertisement that contains juxtaposed imperatives, implied superiority, multiple comparison inferences, or incomplete comparisons.

   a. Let half the class work for the Division of Advertising Practices at the Federal Trade Commission. The commission is charging the company with creating misleading advertising. Argue that the ad is misleading and explain why the advertiser is at fault. Indicate how the ad should be rewritten, or use added or different visuals to create inferences that are more likely to be correct about the product.

   b. The other half of the class works for the legal division of the company. The company is arguing that the ad is not misleading and that advertisers should not be held accountable for the incorrect inferences consumers may make about the brand.

CHAPTER 6

ATTITUDES BASED ON HIGH CONSUMER EFFORT

INTRODUCTION

For years many high-tech companies have focused their advertising on the technological features and benefits of their products. As one example, Unisys used to promote itself as the "information management company." The problem with this approach is that in the highly competitive and cluttered world of high-tech advertising, this message might seem old, dull, and undifferentiated.

When Lawrence Weinbach was brought into resuscitate the sluggish Unisys, he decided he wanted a new message that would portray youthfulness and stand out in the midst of the many high-tech ads. In response the company's advertising agency, Bozell Worldwide, has produced an offbeat, almost surreal, $20 million ad campaign that is clearly designed to change how consumers think about Unisys. In these ads hip, young models (who are supposed to be Unisys employees) are golfing, dancing, and skiing. However, instead of having heads, computer monitors sit on top of their shoulders! (See Exhibit 6.1.) The key point is that Unisys employees are supposedly thinking 24 hours a day about how to solve real-life problems for customers. Executives hope that this campaign will improve the company's image and increase sales. This campaign has been shown in 25 markets including Australia, South America, China, Korea, South Africa, and Europe.[1]

attitude A relatively global and enduring *evaluation* of an object, issue, person, or action.

cognitive function How attitudes influence our thoughts.

affective function How attitudes influence our feelings.

connative function How attitudes influence our behavior.

favorability The degree to which we like or dislike something.

attitude accessibility How easily an attitude can be remembered.

attitude confidence How strongly we hold an attitude.

EXHIBIT 6.1
Changing High Effort Attitudes

Source: Reprinted with permission by Unisys.

It's not that we can't stop working on a client's problem.
It's just that we hate to quit when we're on a roll.

UNISYS We eat, sleep and drink this stuff.

This campaign illustrates a number of important points that stem directly from the concepts covered in the previous chapter. First, consumers probably had certain beliefs about Unisys based on the mental associations they had linked to the brand (old and dull versus youthful). Second, these beliefs likely affected consumers' attitudes toward Unisys (whether they liked the brand or not). Third, these attitudes might also affect consumers' buying behavior (consumers may be more likely to buy a computer from a company that cares about their problems and is youthful). Thus just as Unisys needed to change its brand image, it also needed to change consumers' attitudes. Fourth, attitudes can be based either on the functional features of the offering or on emotional or pleasure-seeking aspects. Therefore, in trying to change consumers' attitudes, Unisys could have chosen to provide information on product features or to elicit emotions related to the use of the offering, thereby creating new beliefs and associations. These observations reflect the central ideas that are addressed in this chapter.

WHAT ARE ATTITUDES?

An **attitude** is an overall evaluation that expresses how much we like or dislike an object, issue, person, or action.[2] Attitudes are learned, and they tend to persist over time. Our attitudes also reflect our overall evaluation of something based on the set of associations linked to it. Thus we have attitudes toward brands, product categories, ads, people, types of stores, activities, and so forth.

The Importance of Attitudes

Attitudes are important because they serve several functions. They (1) guide our thoughts (the **cognitive function**), (2) influence our feelings (the **affective function**), and (3) affect our behavior (the **connative function**). Therefore, we might decide which ads to read, whom to talk to, where to shop, and where to eat based on our attitudes. Likewise, attitudes influence the acquisition, consumption, and disposition of an offering—our buying behavior.

The Characteristics of Attitudes

Attitudes can be described in terms of five main characteristics. Attitudes can be described in terms of their **favorability**—how much we like or dislike an attitude object. Another characteristic is **attitude accessibility**.[3] An accessible attitude can be easily and readily retrieved from memory. If you went to a movie last night, chances are you can remember with relative ease what your attitude toward it was. Likewise, you might be able to remember your attitude toward an important object, event, or activity with relative ease (e.g., your attitude toward your first car). Attitudes can also be described in terms of their **attitude confidence**, or strength, as well. In some cases we hold our attitudes very strongly and with a great

attitude persistence How long our attitude lasts.

attitude resistance How difficult it is to change an attitude.

deal of confidence, whereas in other cases we feel a lot less certain about them. Attitudes may also vary in their **persistence**, or endurance. Some attitudes, particularly the ones we hold with confidence, might last for an extremely long time. Others may last for a shorter time. Finally, attitudes can be described in terms of their **resistance** to subsequent change. Attitude change may be relatively easy when consumers are not loyal to a particular brand or do not know much about a product. However, when consumers are brand loyal or think they are experts in the product category, attitude change is likely to be more difficult.

FORMING AND CHANGING ATTITUDES

An understanding of how attitudes are formed makes us better able to create or affect consumers' attitudes toward new offerings or novel behaviors. Knowing how attitudes are formed also provides useful information about how attitudes about existing offerings or established consumer behaviors might be changed. Exhibit 6.2 illustrates the ways in which attitude formation and change processes have been conceptualized. This framework provides a useful overview of the topics discussed in this and the next chapter.

The Foundation of Attitudes

Attitude formation and change has to do with what lies at the basis of those attitudes, or the kind of information consumers use to form their attitudes. As Exhibit 6.2 shows, two foundations of attitudes can be identified. Some views hold that attitudes are based on *cognitions (thoughts)* or beliefs.[4] Hence attitudes can be based on thoughts we have about the information we receive from an external source (e.g., advertising, salesperson, magazines, or a trusted friend) or information we recall from memory. Attitudes can also be based on *emotions*. Sometimes we have a

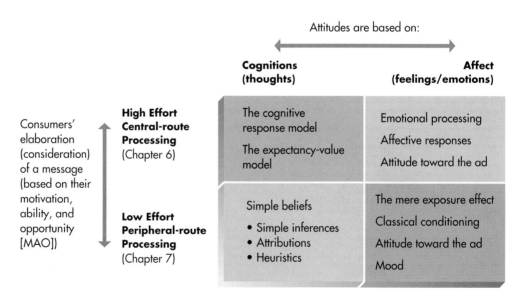

EXHIBIT 6.2
General Approaches to Attitude Formation and Change

As discussed in Chapter 3, consumers' processing differs when elaboration is high versus low. Processing can also be either cognitive or affective. This leads to four basic ways in which consumers can form attitudes. The focus of this chapter is on the ways in which attitudes can be formed and changed when consumer effort is high.

favorable attitude toward an offering (e.g., music, clothes, movies, furniture) simply because it feels good or seems right. Likewise, we can acquire attitudes because we observe and vicariously experience the emotions of others who are using an offering. For example, if we see that people riding a roller coaster are having fun, we may believe that we will too.

A second set of issues affecting attitude formation and change has to do with how much extensive thinking or *elaboration* consumers put forth in forming and changing their attitudes. As Exhibit 6.2 on page 132 shows, attitude formation and change processes can also be described as involving an extensive amount of or very little effort.

The Role of Effort in Attitude Formation and Change

When do consumers make a conscious effort to form or change an attitude? In Chapter 3 we discussed that in some cases consumers' motivation, ability, and opportunity (MAO) to process information and make decisions is high. When MAO is high, consumers are more likely to devote a lot of effort and to experience considerable personal involvement in the act of forming or changing attitudes and making decisions. Some researchers have used the term **central-route processing** to describe attitude formation and change processes when thinking about a message is likely to involve effort.[5] Processing is central because consumers' attitudes are based on a careful and effortful analysis of the true merits or central issues contained within the message. As a result of this extensive and effortful processing, consumers are likely to form strong, accessible, and confidently held attitudes that are persistent and resistant to change.

When MAO is low, however, consumers' attitudes are based on a more tangential or superficial analysis of the message, not on an effortful analysis of its true merits. Because these attitudes tend to be based on peripheral or superficial cues contained within the message, the term **peripheral-route processing** has been used to describe attitude formation and change that involves limited effort (or low elaboration) on the part of the consumer.

This chapter focuses on several ways in which attitudes can be formed and changed when effort (i.e., MAO) is high. The next chapter focuses on attitude formation and change when effort is low. Because attitudes tend to be more accessible, persistent, resistant to change, and held with confidence when consumers' MAO to process information is high, much of the chapter focuses on what affects the favorability of consumers' attitudes.

Exhibit 6.3 on the following page serves as a framework for the ideas discussed in this chapter. It shows that when consumers are likely to devote a lot of effort to processing information, marketers can influence their attitudes either (1) *cognitively*—influencing their thoughts or the beliefs they have about the offering, or (2) *affectively*—influencing the emotional experiences associated with the offering. Furthermore, marketers can try to influence consumers' attitudes through characteristics of the source used in a persuasive communication, the type of message used, or some combination of both. Finally, after they are formed, attitudes may play a powerful role in influencing consumers' intentions and their actual behavior.

THE COGNITIVE FOUNDATIONS OF ATTITUDES

Various theories have been proposed to explain how thoughts are related to attitudes when consumers are likely to devote a lot of effort to processing information and making decisions. This chapter focuses on the cognitive response model and expectancy-value models (see Exhibit 6.3).

central-route processing
The attitude formation and change process when effort is high.

peripheral-route processing
The attitude formation and change process when effort is low.

EXHIBIT 6.3

Chapter Overview: Attitude Formation and Change: High Consumer Effort

Following the first two stages (exposure, attention, and perception; and categorization and comprehension), consumers can either form or change their *attitudes*. This chapter examines how consumers form high-effort attitudes based on both cognition and affect. It also examines how marketers can influence attitudes through *source factors* (credibility, company reputation, and similarity) and *message factors* (argument quality, emotional appeals, etc.).

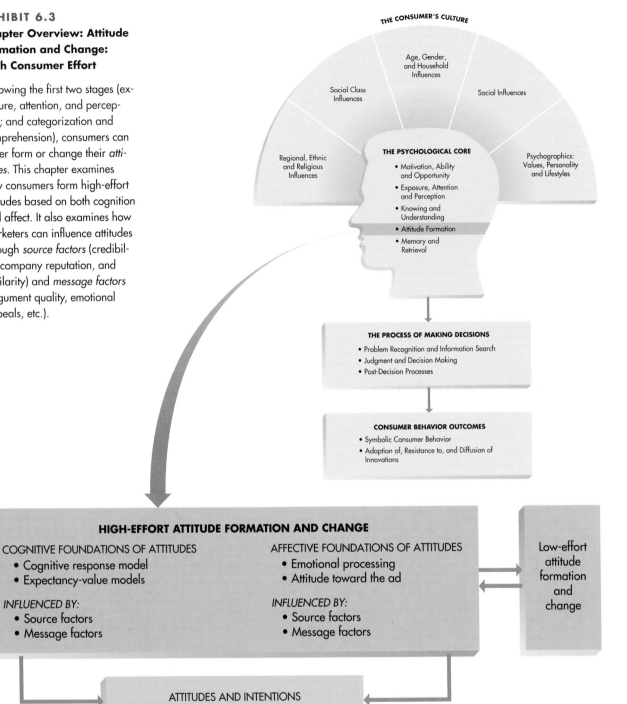

THE CONSUMER'S CULTURE

Age, Gender, and Household Influences

Social Class Influences

Social Influences

Regional, Ethnic and Religious Influences

THE PSYCHOLOGICAL CORE
- Motivation, Ability and Opportunity
- Exposure, Attention and Perception
- Knowing and Understanding
- Attitude Formation
- Memory and Retrieval

Psychographics: Values, Personality and Lifestyles

THE PROCESS OF MAKING DECISIONS
- Problem Recognition and Information Search
- Judgment and Decision Making
- Post-Decision Processes

CONSUMER BEHAVIOR OUTCOMES
- Symbolic Consumer Behavior
- Adoption of, Resistance to, and Diffusion of Innovations

HIGH-EFFORT ATTITUDE FORMATION AND CHANGE

COGNITIVE FOUNDATIONS OF ATTITUDES
- Cognitive response model
- Expectancy-value models

INFLUENCED BY:
- Source factors
- Message factors

AFFECTIVE FOUNDATIONS OF ATTITUDES
- Emotional processing
- Attitude toward the ad

INFLUENCED BY:
- Source factors
- Message factors

Low-effort attitude formation and change

ATTITUDES AND INTENTIONS

The Cognitive Response Model

cognitive responses
Thoughts we have in response to a communication.

The basic idea behind the cognitive response model is that consumers' thought reactions to a message affect their attitudes. **Cognitive responses** are simply the thoughts that we have when we are exposed to a communication. These thoughts can take the form of recognitions, evaluations, associations, images, or ideas.[6] Suppose a balding man sees an ad for Rogaine, a product that claims to restore lost hair. In response to this ad, he could think, "I really need a product like this," "This product will never work," or "The guy in the ad was paid to say this." The cognitive response model predicts that these spontaneously generated responses will determine his attitude toward Rogaine.[7]

Researchers have developed three categories to describe the types of cognitive responses consumers have to communications:

counterarguments (CAs)
Thoughts that disagree with the message.

- **Counterarguments (CAs)** are thoughts that express disagreement with the message (from the preceding example: "It will never work" or "It will not help hair grow back").

support arguments (SAs)
Thoughts that agree with the message.

- **Support arguments (SAs)** are thoughts that express agreement with the message ("This sounds great" or "I really need something like this").

source derogations (SDs)
Thoughts that discount or attack the source of the message.

- **Source derogations (SDs)** are thoughts that discount or attack the source of the message ("The guy is lying" or "He was paid to say this").

According to the cognitive response model, these responses affect consumers' attitudes. Specifically, counterarguments and source derogations result in a less favorable initial attitude or resistance to attitude change. Returning to the Rogaine example, having the thoughts "It will never work" or "The guy was paid to say this" are likely to lead to a negative attitude toward Rogaine. Thus consumers do not always blindly accept and follow suggestions made in persuasive messages; rather, they can use their knowledge about marketers' goals or tactics to effectively cope with or resist these messages.[8] The presence of support arguments, on the other hand, results in positive attitudes. Thus having the thoughts "This sounds great" or "I really need something like this" are likely to create a more positive attitude toward the offering. According to the cognitive response model, consumers exert a lot of effort in responding to the message—at least enough effort to generate counterarguments, support arguments, and source derogations.

MARKETING IMPLICATIONS

Marketers want consumers to be exposed to and comprehend the marketing message. However, marketers also want consumers' responses to the message to be positive, not negative. To the extent that consumers generate counterarguments and source derogations, their attitude toward the offering will be weakened or even negative. Marketers can combat this problem by testing marketing communications for cognitive responses before placing ads in the media. This process involves asking consumers to think aloud while they view the ad or to write down their thoughts immediately after they see it. Marketers can then classify the responses and identify problem areas in order to strengthen the message.

belief discrepancy When a message is different from what consumers believe.

Consumers tend to generate more counterarguments and fewer support arguments when messages say something different from what consumers already believe. Thus a message supporting handgun control will generate a lot of counterarguing among National Rifle Association members. This **belief discrepancy** creates more counterarguments because consumers want to maintain their existing belief structures and do so by arguing against the message.[9] We also see more counterarguments and fewer support arguments when the message presents weak versus strong arguments. For example, saying that Bic disposable razors come in many colors is not a strong and compelling reason to buy them. Consumers are therefore more likely to derogate the source (Bic) or generate counterarguments to the message ("Why would I care about what color it is?").[10]

In contrast, we see more support arguments and fewer counterarguments when consumers are involved with the program in which the message appears. This outcome occurs because the program distracts consumers from counterarguing, thereby enhancing the persuasive impact of the message.[11] Finally, we also see more-favorable reactions to communications when consumers are in a positive mood. Because consumers often want to preserve their positive mood, they resist counterarguing.[12] ◼

Expectancy-Value Models

Expectancy-value models have been widely applied in the consumer behavior field to explain how attitudes form and change. According to these models, attitudes are based on (1) the beliefs or knowledge consumers have about an object or action and (2) their evaluation of these particular beliefs.[13] Thus we might like a Toyota because we believe it is reliable, modestly priced, and stylish; and we think it is good for a car to have these traits.

A variety of expectancy-value models have been proposed in psychology and marketing. These models differ in terms of the components of attitude and how these components should be measured. They also vary as to whether they examine consumers' evaluation of a product attribute or its importance.

The **Theory of Reasoned Action (TORA)** has been one of the more successful models for understanding attitudes. Exhibit 6.4 explains the components of the TORA model. This model is also useful because it provides an expanded picture of how, when, and why attitudes predict behavior. It also improves on previous models in several important ways.

First, the TORA model incorporates the principle of **attitude specificity**; that is, the more specific the attitude is to the behavior of interest, the more likely the attitude will be related to the behavior. In a marketing context, this principle means that if we are trying to understand consumers' acquisition, usage, and disposition behaviors, we will be more successful if we examine attitudes toward engaging in these behaviors as opposed to attitudes toward offerings in general. Thus knowing a consumer's attitude toward *buying* a Toyota should predict car-purchase behavior better than the attitude toward the *object itself* (the Toyota).

Second, in its attempts to predict behavior, the TORA model includes not only consumers' attitudes and how they are formed or changed but also how other people in the social environment influence consumer behavior. In some situations **normative influences** from others can play a powerful role in how people behave. For example, even though you might have a positive attitude toward signing an organ donation card, you may not do so because you know that your parents would be horrified if you did. Normative influences could also make you behave a certain way even though you have a negative attitude toward doing so. You may have a negative attitude toward eating fast food but do so anyway because of pressure from your friends.

Third, rather than trying to explain behavior per se, the TORA model tries to predict one's intentions (tendency) to act. Thus rather than trying to predict whether we will actually buy a Toyota, the TORA model tries to predict whether we will *intend* to buy one. Trying to predict behavioral intentions from attitudes is

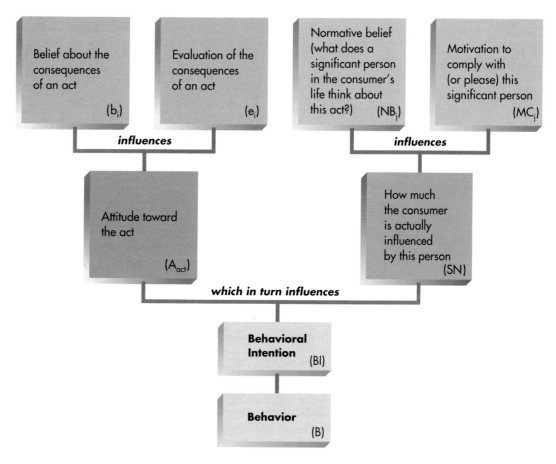

| Belief about the consequences of an act (b_i) | Evaluation of the consequences of an act (e_i) | | Normative belief (what does a significant person in the consumer's life think about this act?) (NB_i) | Motivation to comply with (or please) this significant person (MC_i) |

influences   *influences*

| Attitude toward the act (A_{act}) | | How much the consumer is actually influenced by this person (SN) |

which in turn influences

Behavioral Intention (BI)

Behavior (B)

EXHIBIT 6.4

The Theory of Reasoned Action

According to TORA, behavior is a function of one's *intent to behave* (BI), which is determined by one's *attitude toward performing that behavior* (A_{act}) as well as the influence of *others' opinions* (SN). To form A_{act}, the beliefs one has about the consequences of performing the behavior (b_i) are multiplied by an evaluation of the consequences (e_i) and summed. Similarly, SN is a function of beliefs about what important people think (NB_i) and the motivation to comply with these people (MC_i). The exhibit on page 139 provides an example of these concepts.

much easier than trying to predict actual behaviors because many situational factors could cause us not to engage in an intended behavior.[14] For example, we may intend to buy a Toyota but do not because we are short of money.

MARKETING IMPLICATIONS The TORA model helps marketers understand not only what attitudes consumers have but also why consumers have the attitudes they do and how their attitudes can be changed.

Diagnosing Existing Attitudes. The TORA model helps marketers understand why consumers like or dislike an offering and whether they want to engage in or resist performing a behavior. In particular, the TORA model can help identify the perceived strengths of a brand, its weaknesses, and other influential people who might also be targeted (what are their beliefs and how much does the consumer listen to them). An analysis of these factors can be useful in diagnosing why an offering may or may not be doing well in the marketplace.

Devising Strategies for Attitude Change. The TORA model also provides very useful guidance on how to change attitudes, intentions, and (marketers hope) behavior. Specifically, it suggests four major strategies:

- *Change Beliefs.* One possible strategy would be to change the strength of the beliefs that consumers associate with the consequences of acquiring an offering. Specifically, marketers could try to (1) strengthen beliefs that the offering

Components of the TORA Model

behavior (B) What we do.

behavioral intention (BI) What we intend to do.

attitude toward the act (A$_{act}$) How we feel about doing something.

subjective norms (SN) How others feel about us doing something.

The most basic proposition of the model is that **behavior (B)** is a function of the person's **behavioral intention (BI)**, which in turn is determined by (1) the person's **attitude toward the act (A$_{act}$)** and (2) the **subjective norms (SN)** that operate in the situation. The model then specifies what affects these two components. Consistent with most expectancy-value models, A$_{act}$ is determined by the consumer's *beliefs* (b$_i$) about the consequences of engaging in the behavior and the consumer's *evaluation* (e$_i$) of these consequences. Subjective norms are determined by the consumer's *normative beliefs* (NB$_i$)—or what the consumer thinks someone else wants him or her to do—and the consumer's *motivation to comply* (MC$_i$) with this person. Although this model might seem complex, it can be illustrated fairly easily with an example.

We begin by identifying the consumer's most important beliefs about the consequences of engaging in the behavior. For example, suppose a consumer named David would like to go take skydiving lessons and his beliefs about the consequences are that it will be fun, educational, dangerous, and probably cost a lot of money. Thus we have determined what beliefs (b$_i$) David has about skydiving lessons, and we have determined that he has four of them (i = 4). These beliefs can vary in terms of how *strongly* they are held, and this can be assessed using a subjective probability scale ranging from (-3) very unlikely to ($+3$) very likely (see the exhibit on the opposite page). In our example we can see that David thinks it is very likely that skydiving lessons will be fun (b$_1$ = +3), somewhat likely it will be educational (b$_2$ = +2) and dangerous (b$_3$ = +2), and slightly likely that it will cost a lot of money (b$_4$ = +1). Each consequence can now be evaluated in terms of how desirable (how bad [-3] to good [$+3$]) it is. The exhibit on the next page shows that David rates the consequences of potential danger and cost as negative (e$_3$ = -3 and e$_4$ = -1) but rates the fun and educational aspects positively (e$_1$ = +3 and e$_2$ = +2). To determine David's attitude toward taking skydiving lessons (A$_{act}$), we multiply each belief strength rating (b$_i$) times its associated evaluation rating (e$_i$) and add these multiplied totals (as specified by the model). From these computations, we can see that David has a positive attitude toward taking skydiving lessons (A$_{act}$= +5).

To predict behavioral intentions, however, we must also examine David's subjective perceptions of the normative influences, also known as subjective norms. There are likely to be people whose opinions and beliefs will affect what David does. We see in the exhibit that there are four people (j = 4) whose opinions matter to David. He can estimate whether each person believes he should or should not take the lessons. This is the normative belief (NB$_i$) component. We see in the exhibit that David's father is somewhat negative about it (NB$_1$ = -1) and his mother is very negative (NB$_2$ = -3), but his two friends think he should take the lessons (NB$_3$ = +1 and NB$_4$ = +3). David can also think about how motivated he is to comply with the beliefs of each person mentioned (the MC$_i$ component). As shown in the exhibit, these components are also measured on a seven-point subjective probability scale. In this case David is motivated to comply with each person, particularly his girlfriend (MC$_3$ = +3). To determine the subjective norm (SN), we multiply each NB by its associated MC and then add these multiplied totals. In this case, the SN is positive but near zero. Thus David is likely to feel some ambivalence about taking lessons because the opinions of these other people are contradictory.

Finally, the model predicts that behavioral intentions (BI) are determined by the combination of the person's attitudes (A$_{act}$) and the normative influences that operate in the situation (SN). In this case David is likely to take the lessons because his attitudes are positive and, overall, others have slightly positive feelings about him doing so. Note that A$_{act}$ and SN do not always have an equal impact on BI. In some cases, consumers' behavioral intentions are guided more by what they think (A$_{act}$); in other cases, they are guided more by the opinions of others (SN).

Applying the Theory of Reasoned Action

Here TORA is used to determine David's intention of taking skydiving lessons. His attitude toward the act (A_{act}) is a function of his beliefs about the consequences (e.g., it will be fun, educational, etc.) as well as his evaluation of these consequences. The strength of his beliefs are rated on a likelihood scale from -3 to $+3$ (how likely will skydiving be fun, educational, etc.). His evaluations about these beliefs are rated on a scale of very bad (-3) to very good ($+3$). For example, it is very good that skydiving is fun; it is very bad that skydiving is dangerous. These numbers are multiplied and added to get a $+5$ (a positive attitude toward the act of taking skydiving lessons). Another aspect of the model SN is based on the opinions of important people in David's life as well as how much he values these opinions. These are also multiplied and summed to get a score of $+1$. Thus, David is likely to feel some ambivalence about taking lessons because the opinions of significant persons in his life are contradictory.

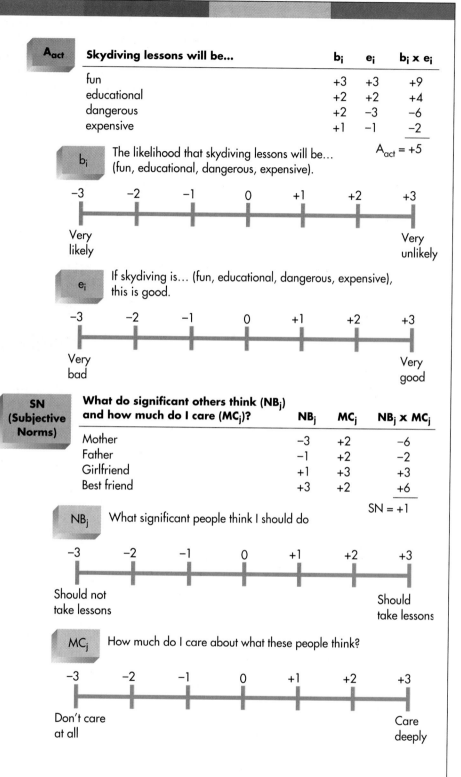

A_{act}

Skydiving lessons will be...	b_i	e_i	$b_i \times e_i$
fun	+3	+3	+9
educational	+2	+2	+4
dangerous	+2	−3	−6
expensive	+1	−1	−2

$A_{act} = +5$

b_i The likelihood that skydiving lessons will be... (fun, educational, dangerous, expensive).

| −3 | −2 | −1 | 0 | +1 | +2 | +3 |

Very likely ... Very unlikely

e_i If skydiving is... (fun, educational, dangerous, expensive), this is good.

| −3 | −2 | −1 | 0 | +1 | +2 | +3 |

Very bad ... Very good

SN (Subjective Norms)

What do significant others think (NB_j) and how much do I care (MC_j)?	NB_j	MC_j	$NB_j \times MC_j$
Mother	−3	+2	−6
Father	−1	+2	−2
Girlfriend	+1	+3	+3
Best friend	+3	+2	+6

$SN = +1$

NB_j What significant people think I should do

| −3 | −2 | −1 | 0 | +1 | +2 | +3 |

Should not take lessons ... Should take lessons

MC_j How much do I care about what these people think?

| −3 | −2 | −1 | 0 | +1 | +2 | +3 |

Don't care at all ... Care deeply

possesses positive, important consequences or (2) lessen the belief that there are negative consequences. To illustrate, Hallmark spent $10 million to convince consumers that its cards aren't expensive, and SnackWell's has been trying to persuade consumers that its brand tastes good (in addition to being low in fat).[15] Likewise, the banking industry developed a high-profile campaign to convince consumers that banks aren't just for checking accounts anymore.[16]

Because many consumers believed that foreign companies were contributing to the economic decline in Asia, McDonald's developed a patriotic image campaign to persuade consumers in Thailand that the fast-food chain was actually helping the economy.[17] Similarly, the Italian government developed a $25 million ad campaign to convince U.S. consumers that Italian fashion designers and craftspeople are the world's finest, and Korean car manufacturers have undertaken an aggressive campaign to change consumers' beliefs that Korean cars are of very poor quality.[18]

Although this type of attitude-change strategy is commonly employed when consumers are more likely to consider the message, changing consumers' beliefs can be difficult when they already have strong prior beliefs. For example, if you strongly believe that bungee jumping is dangerous, someone would probably have a hard time convincing you otherwise. In trying to

market products to post-Soviet Central Asia, some major companies have had to work hard in their marketing efforts to change old consumer myths or beliefs.[19] For example, many Central Asian consumers believed that if you put a tooth in a cup of Coke, the tooth would disappear by morning. Likewise, consumers perceived Barbie to be an American brand and thought the product was a fake if stamped "Made in Hong Kong." Many U.S. and European brands carry shorter "sell by" dates to ensure product freshness, but Central Asian consumers thought this notation meant inferior Russian brands with longer dates were superior.

- *Change Evaluations.* Another strategy for changing attitudes is to change consumers' evaluations about how good or bad a consequence is. By making this belief more positive or less negative, attitudes can become more positive. For example, to counter health concerns about the fat substitute Olestra, Procter & Gamble ads stressed that the product is made of natural ingredients (soybeans).[20] A number of American companies, including Levi's, Goodyear, Jim Beam, and Tiffany, have attempted to increase the value of "made in America" as a sign of quality in selling to European countries.[21] As a result of the sluggish Asian economy, the Thai electric company extolled the virtues of energy-efficient light bulbs.[22]

- *Add a New Belief.* A third strategy is to add a new belief altogether. In other words, adding another set of positive beliefs would make the attitude more positive. This strategy is most effective when the brand has inferior existing features, lower perceived quality, or a higher price compared to its competitors.[23] For example, the Cross Pad introduced the new attribute of "a notepad that uploads right to your computer."[24] In redesigning the Jeep Cherokee, Chrysler added the new features of roominess ("room enough for eight golf bags") and a high-tech navigational tool ("a trip computer in five languages").[25]

- *Target Normative Beliefs.* Finally, the model provides information on how normative beliefs influence behavior. If these beliefs are particularly strong, we can develop communications that target them specifically. Exhibit 6.5 is a

credibility Extent to which the source is trustworthy, expert, or has status.

EXHIBIT 6.5
Normative Influence

This ad from Germany uses normative influence to attack the problem of drinking and driving by stating, "You don't have to search for bottles on our motorcycles. We enjoyed our beer with intelligence." Social or normative acceptance of this view is communicated through the picture of a group of typical motorcyclists. Can you think of other products or situations in which these types of normative influences would play an important role in influencing your behavior?

Source: Courtesy German Brewers' Association.

good illustration of this strategy. This message from German brewers says, "(You) don't have to search for bottles on our motorcycles. We enjoy our beer with intelligence." This ad is trying to emphasize social acceptance by making a statement about drinking and driving. On the other hand, condom ads have been unsuccessful in increasing sales because they have *not* stressed normative beliefs (what others will think of you if you *don't* use them).[26] Note that the importance of normative beliefs varies across cultures. In countries that stress group values over the individual (such as Japan and other Asian nations), appeals to normative beliefs take on greater significance.[27] ■

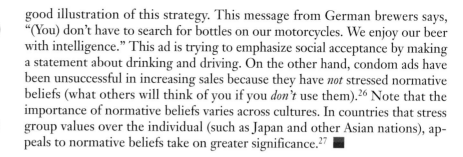

HOW COGNITIVELY BASED ATTITUDES ARE INFLUENCED

The previous sections explained how cognitive responses and beliefs can affect consumers' attitudes. This section examines how marketing communications can affect consumers' cognitively based attitudes when the processing effort is extensive. As Exhibit 6.2 shows, characteristics of the source and the message can affect how favorable an attitude will be.

Communication Source

When information processing is extensive, consumers whose attitudes are based on cognitions are likely to be influenced by believable information. Thus the most important goal for marketers is to provide such information. If the message is to generate support arguments, restrict counterarguments and source derogations, and increase belief strength, the message must be credible. Several factors, including spokesperson credibility and company reputation, enhance the credibility of a message.

Spokesperson Credibility In many marketing messages, information is presented by a spokesperson, usually a celebrity, an actor, a company representative, or a real consumer. In any sales encounter the salesperson is a spokesperson for the retailer and the offering. The **credibility** of these sources influence consumers' attitudes.[28]

In general, credible sources are thought to have one or more of the following major characteristics: trustworthiness, expertise, and status. First, someone who is perceived as trustworthy is more likely to be believed than someone who is not. Second, we are more likely to accept a message from someone who is perceived as knowledgeable *or an expert* about the topic than from someone who knows little. Thus a salesperson who demonstrates a high level of product knowledge will generate higher credibility than an uninformed one.

Third, someone who has a high position *or status* in society (i.e., status) can also be perceived as credible. That is why many companies feature their CEOs in ads and why Microsoft Chief Technology Officer, Nathan Myhrvold, endorsed a Gulfstream private jet.[29] In Latin America, having products endorsed by famous people who are respected is an effective technique, particularly in Venezuela and Mexico.[30]

Research has shown that credible sources have considerable impact on consumers' acceptance of the message when consumers' prior attitudes are negative, when the message deviates greatly from their prior beliefs, when the message is complex or difficult to understand, and when there is a good "match" between the product and endorser.[31] On the other hand, credible sources have less impact when consumers hold their existing attitude with confidence (even a credible source will not convince them otherwise) and when they have a high degree of ability to generate their own conclusions from the message (they have a lot of product-relevant knowledge, particularly if based on direct experience).[32] Also, consumers are less likely to believe that a source is credible when the source (e.g., a celebrity) endorses multiple products.[33]

MARKETING IMPLICATIONS Bill Cosby, Alan Alda, and Candice Bergen have been successful endorsers because consumers perceive these stars as honest and straightforward. Likewise, consumers might perceive a salesperson who has an "honest face" as a credible source of information. Interestingly, a simple two-word ad in the *Wall Street Journal* that stated "Honest Stockbroker" was successful in generating a number of clients.[34] Ordinary people can also be perceived as credible endorsers. Companies such as MCI and Subway Sandwiches feature their employees as spokespersons because they are similar to the target market and they are often seen as trustworthy.[35] Latin American consumers tend to give positive evaluations to ads that feature real people.[36]

Because of their expertise, sports figures Michael Jordan and Andre Agassi have been successful expert sources for athletic shoes. American sports figures have been very popular lately in Japan in the selling of sports-related products such as T-shirts and sportswear. The fact that the average Japanese consumer does not know who most of the stars are does not seem to matter; anything American tends to be "hip."[37] Expert sources can also be popular, another factor that can contribute to an effective ad. Interestingly, one survey indicated that women endorsers are often seen as more popular and credible than are male endorsers.[38]

A low-credibility source *can* be effective in some circumstances. In particular, if a low-credibility source argues against his or her own self-interest, positive attitude change can result.[39] Political ads, for example, often feature a member of the opposing party who endorses a rival candidate. In addition, the impact of a low-credibility source can actually increase over time (assuming a powerful message). This **sleeper effect** occurs because the memory of the source can decay more rapidly than the memory of the message.[40] Thus consumers may remember the message but not the source. ■

sleeper effect Consumers forget the source of a message more quickly than they forget the message.

Company Reputation Many marketing communications do not feature an actual person. In these instances consumers' judgments of credibility stem from the reputation of the company that is delivering the message.[41] Thus messages from companies that have a reputation for producing quality products, for dealing fairly with consumers, or for being trustworthy are more likely to be believed than those with a lesser image and hence are capable of changing attitudes.

MARKETING IMPLICATIONS Having a strong company reputation is one reason that many companies devote time and money (billions of dollars per year) to developing a positive image through corporate advertising. The accounting firm Coopers & Lybrand tried to overcome negative publicity from several lawsuits by engaging in heavy advertising, including two spots during the 1993 Super Bowl, thereby breaking the tradition of not advertising in its industry.[42] ■

The Message

Just as consumers evaluate whether the source is credible when their processing effort is high, so too do they evaluate whether the message is credible. Three factors enhance the credibility of a message: the argument quality of the message, whether it is a one-sided versus two-sided message, and whether it is a comparative message.

Argument Quality

One of the most critical factors affecting whether a message is credible concerns whether it uses strong arguments.[43] **Strong arguments** present the best features or central merits of an offering in a convincing manner. Master Lock has convincingly demonstrated its product's toughness by showing that its lock does not break when you shoot a hole through it. To demonstrate its timeliness, Fidelity Investments offered a series of ads featuring up-to-the-minute news headlines with the message: "To most people this is news. To Fidelity, it's history."[44] Messages can also present supporting endorsements or (see Exhibit 6.6) research, such as the Good Housekeeping Seal, the *Consumer Digest*'s Best Buy designation (see Exhibit 6.6). *PC Magazine*'s infomercials (commercials that are typically 30 minutes long) have the advantage of being able to present a convincing argument for the offering and have been successfully used to sell health and beauty aids, exercise equipment, and financial advice. This form of advertising has also become quite popular with Asian consumers.[45] Finally, Internet advertising enables companies to supplement complicated messages with convincing information and to have a positive impact on consumers.[46]

MARKETING IMPLICATIONS If messages are weak and not very compelling, consumers are not likely to think they offer credible reasons for buying. Saying that you should buy a particular brand of mattress because it comes in decorator fabrics is not very convincing. Nevertheless, messages do not always have to focus on substantive features of the product or service. When brands are similar and many competitors emphasize the same important attributes, less important features can actually play a key role in influencing attitudes.[47] Also, a message should match the amount of effort consumers want to use to process it. A message that is either too simple or too complicated is unlikely to be persuasive.[48] ■

One- Versus Two-Sided Messages

Most marketing messages present only positive information. These are called **one-sided messages**. In some instances, however, a **two-sided message**, containing both positive and negative information about an offering, can be effective. In a series of ads featuring comedians Louie Anderson, Brett Butler, and Gilbert Gottfried, 7-Eleven poked fun at past problems such as high prices, cramped stores, and stale food. Jaguar has also apologized for past mechanical problems.

---

strong argument A presentation that features the best or central merits of an offering in a convincing manner.

one-sided message A marketing message that presents only positive information.

two-sided message A marketing message that presents both positive and negative information.

EXHIBIT 6.6
Argument Quality

When a company announces that its products or services have won awards or endorsements, the company's advertising can become more credible and convincing to consumers.

Source: Courtesy Ford Motor Company.

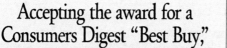

Accepting the award for a Consumers Digest "Best Buy,"

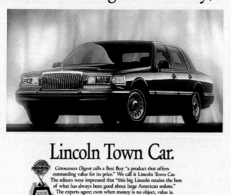

Lincoln Town Car.

Consumers Digest calls a Best Buy "a product that offers outstanding value for its price." We call it Lincoln Town Car. The editors were impressed that "this big Lincoln retains the best of what has always been good about large American sedans." The experts agree: even when money is no object, value is.

Three Ways To Lease

$499/$1,999	$589/$0	$12,596
per month / down	per month down	One-Time Lease Payment
24-Month Red Carpet Lease	24-Month Red Carpet Lease	
First Month's Payment.......$499	First Month's Payment.......$589	AFP Payment (Net of RCL Cash)..$12,596
Down Payment (Net of RCL Cash)..$1,999	Down Payment (Net of RCL Cash)......$0	Refundable Security Deposit......$125
Refundable Security Deposit......$500	Refundable Security Deposit......$600	Cash Due At Signing.......$13,121
Cash Due At Signing.......$2,998	Cash Due At Signing.......$1,189	Cash Outlay Over 24 Months**..$12,596
30,000-Mile Lease	30,000-Mile Lease	30,000-Mile Lease

To learn more, call 1 800 446-8888 or, for information via the Internet, enter http://www.Lincolnvehicles.com

LINCOLN
What A Luxury Car Should Be

EXHIBIT 6.7
Comparative Advertising

Sometimes ads will mention a competitor by name and point out how a product or service is different from the competitors. In this ad, Barnesandnoble.com is comparing its inventory and title selection with Amazon.com.

Source: barnesandnoble.com.

comparative messages
Messages that make direct comparisons to competitors.

Like strong message arguments, two-sided messages may affect attitudes by making the message more credible (that is, they increase belief strength) and reducing counter-arguments. When consumers see negative information in an ad, they are likely to draw the inference that the company must be honest. Consumers are then given reasons to still be interested in the offering despite these problems (i.e., consumers add a new belief).

MARKETING IMPLICATIONS Two-sided messages seem to be particularly effective when (1) consumers are initially opposed to the offering (they already have negative beliefs) or (2) they will be exposed to strong countermessages from competitors.[49] Two-sided messages are also well received by more-intelligent consumers who prefer messages that are more balanced and less biased. However, the use of two-sided advertising is not always in the marketer's best interest. The positive effects of two-sided messages on brand attitudes occur only if the negative message is about an attribute that is not extremely important. ■

Comparative Messages **Comparative messages** show how much better the offering is than a competitor's. Two types of comparative messages have been identified.[50] The most common type is the *indirect comparative message* in which the offering is compared with unnamed competitors (e.g., "other leading brands" or "Brand X"). For example, IBM indirectly attacked Sun Microsystems's bold and distinctive headline advertising (all-white background with very large capital letters) by introducing a series of similar ads.[51] Levi's introduced a series of billboards with simple messages: "Calvin Wore Them," "Tommy Wore Them," and "Ralph Wore Them" (referring to famous designers who have worn Levi jeans).[52] This strategy can improve consumers' perceptions of a moderate-share brand relative to other moderate-share brands (but not the market leader).[53]

With *direct comparative advertising*, advertisers explicitly name a competitor or set of competitors and attack them on the basis of an attribute or benefit. This approach is usually used when the offering has a feature that purportedly makes it better than a competitor's offering. American Express and Visa credit cards have been exchanging attacks for several years. In the ad in Exhibit 6.7, Barnesandnoble.com is comparing its title-selection database and inventory with that of Amazon.com—indicating that the former offers more titles than its competitor offers. Companies such as Pepsi, Levi's, IBM, Dell, AT&T, MCI, Sprint, and Qwest have made heavy use of direct comparative advertising.[54] Salespeople in a personal-selling situation frequently use this technique to convince consumers of the advantages of their brand over the competition.

In general, research has found that direct comparative messages are effective in generating attention and brand awareness and positively increasing message processing, attitudes, intentions, and behavior.[55] They do not, however, have higher credibility. These messages are particularly effective for new brands or for those with a low market share that are attempting to take sales away from more popular brands.[56] Essentially, the new or low-share brand can enhance attitudes by highlighting how it is different from or better than other brands—which gives consumers a credible reason for purchasing the brand. These messages are especially effective when they contain other elements that make them believable, such as a credible source or objective and verifiable claims (a strong argument),[57] and when the featured attribute or benefit is important within the product category.[58]

MARKETING IMPLICATIONS   Direct comparative messages are best used when consumers' MAO to process the message is high. When MAO is high, consumers exert more effort in processing the message and are hence less likely to confuse the advertised brand with its competition.[59] Marketers must also be careful that all information contained in the message is factual and verifiable; otherwise, competitors may consider taking legal action. Finally, the use of direct comparative advertising is restricted in some areas. Although it is widely used in the United States and Latin America, this form of advertising is illegal in many other countries. And some consumers do not like comparative advertising. The Japanese, for example, respond better to a softer sell than they do to comparative ads.[60] ∎

THE AFFECTIVE (EMOTIONAL) FOUNDATIONS OF ATTITUDES

Most of the consumer research on attitudes when MAO and processing effort are high has focused on the cognitive models of attitude formation. Now, however, researchers are recognizing that consumers might exert a lot of mental energy in processing a message on an emotional basis. Emotional reactions, in turn, may serve as a powerful way of creating attitudes that are favorable, enduring, and resistant to change. Thus this section examines when and how attitudes can be changed through consumers' feelings when MAO and processing effort are high.

affective involvement The emotional response to a message that consumers experience.

When **affective involvement** with an object or decision is high, consumers can experience fairly strong emotional reactions to a stimulus. These feelings can, in turn, influence attitudes. In this case the consumer's *feelings* act as a source of information, and consumers will rely on these feelings to evaluate the stimulus.[61] Feelings are more likely to play a key role in attitude change when they fit with or are viewed as relevant to the product or service being offered.[62] For example, someone who is in love might have a *more positive attitude* toward an expensive perfume or a nice restaurant than someone who is not experiencing this emotion. Feelings can also be a factor when consumers see others experiencing strong emotion while using an offering or when situational factors hamper the consumer's effort to develop a cognitive attitude.[63] For example, if a consumer is under severe time pressure, he or she could simply recall a previous emotional experience rather than develop a cognitive attitude.

In marketing situations, certain factors can activate experiences or episodes from memory that may be associated with strong emotions.[64] For example, you might experience positive emotions such as joy and excitement if you suddenly see an ad for the car you have just bought. If you are a dog lover, you might experience affective involvement toward an ad that shows a cute dog.

Unfortunately, we do not yet have a solid understanding of the emotional bases of attitudes. Nevertheless, it is possible to make some generalizations. We know that when consumers are emotionally involved in a message, they tend to process it on a general level rather than analytically.[65] This process involves the generation of images or feelings, called **affective responses** (or ARs),[66] rather than cognitive responses. Affective responses are particularly important when the ad builds toward a "peak emotional experience."[67] Consumers can also either

affective responses When consumers generate feelings and images in response to a message.

recall an emotional experience from memory or vicariously place themselves in the situation and experience the emotions associated with it.[68] These feelings will then influence attitudes. For example, in the Logitech ad (Exhibit 6.8) marketers hope that the happy nuns will create positive affective responses (recalling happy experiences or imagining a similar situation) that might then transfer to the product (the MouseMan).

emotional appeals
Messages that elicit an emotional response.

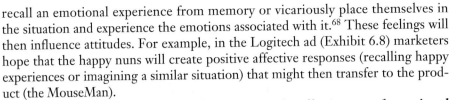

Cross-cultural differences can also influence the effectiveness of **emotional appeals**. One study found that messages that evoked ego-focused responses (such as pride or happiness) led to more favorable attitudes in group-oriented cultures, whereas empathetic messages led to more positive attitudes in individualist cultures.[69] The reason for this apparent reversal is that the novelty or uniqueness of these appeals increases the motivation to process and consider the message.

Finally, negative emotions can sometimes have a positive effect on attitude change. In one study the exposure to a public service announcement for child abuse initially created negative emotions (sadness, anger, fear) but then led to a feeling of empathy, and this response led to a decision to help.[70] In addition, consumers can actively try to avoid decisions associated with strong negative emotions by making choices to minimize these emotions.[71]

Note that cognition can still influence whether experienced feelings will influence our attitudes. For feelings to have a direct impact on attitudes, consumers must cognitively link them to the offering.[72] To illustrate, if you saw a bank ad showing a tender scene of a father holding his baby, you might experience an immediate emotional response (warmth and joy). However, this feeling will only affect your attitude toward the bank if you consciously make a connection between the feeling and the bank ("This bank makes me feel good" or "I like this bank because it cares about people").

MARKETING IMPLICATIONS The key implication of the preceding section is that marketers can try to influence emotions in order to affect consumer attitudes. In particular, marketers can try to ensure that the emotions experienced in a particular situation will be

EXHIBIT 6.8
An Emotional Appeal

This ad uses feelings and emotions to sell a high-technology product. Rather than focusing on its technological specifications (a more cognitive approach), the ad simply stresses how good this mouse will make you *feel*. Can you think of other products or services that could be sold in a similar manner?

Source: © 1991 Logitech Inc. All rights reserved. Used by permission.

Feels Good.

Feels Better.

EXHIBIT 6.9
Eliciting Positive Emotions

Marketers often use emotional appeals to influence consumer attitudes. In this ad, the Howard Miller marketing team employs a situation with high affective involvement—giving a loved one a nice gift—to elicit positive emotions in consumers. The team hopes that consumers will transfer the positive emotions to the brand and purchase Howard Miller clocks.

Source: © Howard Miller Company.

attractiveness A source characteristic that evokes favorable attitudes if a source is physically attractive, likable, familiar, or similar to ourselves.

match-up hypothesis The idea that the source must be appropriate for the product/service.

positive. Car salespeople, for example, often try to do everything possible to make customers happy so that they will develop positive attitudes toward the dealer and the car. The importance of creating positive emotions also explains why many service providers, such as airlines, restaurants, and financial institutions place a high value on being friendly.

Consumers can potentially experience emotions in response to marketing communications, although the ability to do so is typically quite limited—ads are better at creating low-level moods than they are at creating intense emotions. Nevertheless, in situations where affective involvement in the product or service is often high, marketers may be able to generate the images and feelings necessary to change attitudes. This outcome most often occurs in product and service categories in which a strong pleasure-seeking or symbolic motivation is present—when feelings or symbolic meanings are critical. Mercedes has changed its informational advertising approach to a more emotional appeal. One ad depicts a tender scene between a father and a son who are standing in a showroom, thus communicating that the car is durable enough to hand down from father to son. In Exhibit 6.9, Howard Miller uses an emotional situation (giving a loved one a nice gift) to create positive feelings toward the brand. ■

HOW AFFECTIVELY BASED ATTITUDES ARE INFLUENCED

When MAO and effort are high and attitudes are affectively (emotionally) based, several strategies shown in Exhibit 6.2 can be employed to change attitudes. As with cognitively based attitudes, marketers can use characteristics of the source and the message to change consumers' attitudes by affecting their emotions.

The Source

Perceived **attractiveness** is an important source characteristic affecting high-effort emotionally based attitudes. Research on source attractiveness has suggested that when consumers' MAO and effort are high, attractive sources tend to evoke favorable attitudes if the sources are appropriate for the offering category (e.g., a luxury automobile, fashion, cosmetics, and beauty treatments).[73] This effect has been called the **match-up hypothesis** (the source should match the offering). The relevant attractive source probably enhances attitudes, either by making the ad informative and hence likable or by affecting consumers' beliefs that the product must be good. A source that is attractive but not relevant can distract the consumer from the ideas of the message.[74] When golfer Tiger Woods agreed to endorse American Express, some observers wondered whether he could sell financial services.[75] Others believed, however, that his image of success, hard work, and integrity fit well with the company.

The relationship between attractiveness and attitude change applies to selling encounters as well. Consumers perceive physically attractive salespeople as having more favorable selling skills and are more likely to yield to their requests.[76] Customers also tend to be attracted to and buy from salespeople that they (the customers) perceive as similar to themselves.[77]

MARKETING IMPLICATIONS Marketers need to remember that although attractiveness is most often thought of in terms of physical features, sources can also be attractive if they are perceived as similar, likable, or familiar (in terms of physical appearance or opinions).[78] For example, when middle-aged tennis player Jimmy Connors advanced through the U.S. Open in the early 1990s, he stirred the hearts of middle-aged weekend warriors across the United States. Because Connors was a highly familiar figure to whom these individuals could relate, his ad campaign for Nuprin increased sales by 20 percent.[79] In honor of India's 50th anniversary of independence, Cadbury Schweppes enlisted India's most popular singer, Lata Mangeshkar, to serve as spokesperson for its Freedom Salvo promotion.[80] In marketing to China, Nike abandoned its popular Western athletes in favor of popular Chinese athletic heroes (a better match for the Chinese consumer).[81] ∎

The Message

Just as characteristics of the source are useful in understanding affective processing, so too are characteristics of the message.

Emotional Appeals Marketers can sometimes attempt to influence consumers' attitudes by using appeals that elicit emotions such as love, wanting, joy, hope, excitement, daring, fear, anger, shame, or rejection. In this case the positive emotions are used to attract consumers to the offering, whereas the negatives are used to create anxiety among consumers about what might happen if they do not use the offering. Messages can also present situations that express positive emotions with the hope that consumers will vicariously experience these emotions. In these situations marketers can induce consumers to imagine how good the product will make them feel or look. An ad for the impotency drug Viagra shows a happy, dancing couple.[82] Realizing that travelers experience glee in accumulating airline miles, an ad for the Citibank Aadvantage credit card shows a dozen roses and states "Was he sorry? Or was it the miles?"[83]

Emotional appeals may limit the amount of product-related information consumers can process.[84] For example, the ad in Exhibit 6.8 might inhibit cognition about the Logitech MouseMan because consumers may be thinking more about feeling good than about the product's features. Thus emotional appeals are more likely to be effective when the arousal of emotions is in some way related to the consumption or use of the product, which is common when hedonic or symbolic motivations are important. For example, several manufacturers of expensive sunglasses (Ray Ban, Serengeti) directed their advertising appeals away from functional features, such as sun filters and protection, and toward a focus on fashion appeal and sexiness.[85] Also, Volvo switched the focus of some of its campaigns away from safety and toward "driving pleasure and excitement" because it had developed such a strong image of being safe and stodgy.[86]

MARKETING IMPLICATIONS Typically, marketers can attempt to arouse emotions by using techniques such as music, emotional scenes, visuals, sex, and attractive sources. To illustrate, Mercedes presented images of a rubber duckie and child, and Medicare tried to adopt cartoon mascots and cute names, both in an effort to generate positive feelings.[87] The German army is using action-packed adventure and tense music to attract 16 to 25 year olds into the service.[88] In trying to create a distinctive image in

EXHIBIT 6.10

Fear Appeal

This ad stresses the unfortunate consequences of not protecting children against chickenpox.

Source: Courtesy of Merck.

fear appeals Messages that stress negative consequences.

Japan, Saturn departed from the traditional information ads to cast itself as the "cozy" company with friendly employees.[89] Note, however, that generating emotions is a challenge unless the message has personal relevance.[90] ■

Fear Appeals **Fear appeals** attempt to elicit a specific kind of emotion of fear or anxiety by stressing the negative consequences of either engaging or not engaging in a particular behavior. By arousing this fear, marketers hope consumers will be motivated to think about the message and behave in the desired manner.[91] The ad in Exhibit 6.10, for example, stresses the consequences of not protecting children against chickenpox. Correctol used fear in a comparative ad, stating that some laxatives such as Ex-Lax (the major competitor) could cause cancer.[92] Similarly, Allstate Insurance Co. and First Alert showed pictures of burned-out houses to motivate the purchase and maintenance of smoke detectors.[93]

Research examining the effectiveness of fear appeals in changing attitudes and behavior has been mixed. Early studies found that fear appeals were ineffective because consumers' perceptual defense helped them block out and ignore the message (due to its threatening nature).[94] This research provides one explanation for why the surgeon general's warning on cigarette packages and ads has been largely ineffective.

MARKETING IMPLICATIONS Under certain conditions, fear appeals can also be effective.[95] First, the appeal must suggest an immediate action that will reduce the fear. In the ad in Exhibit 6.10, the fear can be easily reduced by talking to a doctor, who might recommend vaccination. Second, the level of fear must be generally moderate.[96] If the fear induced is too intense (as it was in early studies), the consumers' perceptual defense will take over and the message will not have an impact. Third, at higher levels of involvement, lower levels of fear can be employed because the consumer has a higher motivation to process the information.[97] Factors such as personality, product usage, and socioeconomic status also have an impact on the effectiveness of fear appeals.[98] Finally, the source providing the information must be credible; otherwise, the consumer can easily discount the message by generating counterarguments and source derogations. ■

●TTITUDE TOWARD THE AD

attitude toward the ad (A_{ad}) Whether the consumer likes or dislikes an ad.

Although most attitude research has focused on consumers' attitude toward the brand, some evidence suggests that the overall **attitude toward the ad (A_{ad})** in which the brand is advertised will influence brand attitudes and behavior.[99] In other words, if we see an advertisement and like it, our liking for the ad may rub off on the brand and thereby make our brand attitude more positive.

Most of the research on A_{ad} has been done in the context of low MAO processing. However, researchers are finding that A_{ad} can also have an impact

utilitarian (functional) dimension An ad that is informative.

hedonic dimension An ad that creates positive or negative feelings.

when consumers devote considerable effort to processing the message. Thus far, research has identified three major sources that can lead to a positive A$_{ad}$ in this context.[100]

First, ads that are more *informative* tend to be better liked and generate positive responses.[101] These reactions to the ad will, in turn, have a positive influence on brand attitudes. This factor is called the **utilitarian** (or **functional**) **dimension**. For example, ads on the Internet are often liked because they are seen as more informative than ads in other media.[102] On the other hand, if ads are not informative, negative attitudes can result. A good example is the rising negativity toward political ads that are increasingly viewed as "mudslinging" and as providing very little useful information about the candidates.[103]

Second, consumers can like an ad if it creates positive feelings or emotions (the **hedonic dimension**).[104] We tend to like ads that either make us feel good or elicit positive experiences from memory. This positive attitude can transfer to the brand and make beliefs about the brand (b$_i$) more positive as well.[105] Thus people might like the ad for the Howard Miller clock (Exhibit 6.9) because it shows affection and cheerful humor, and the positive feelings created might make the consumer's attitudes toward the company more positive. Advertisers are also using a wide variety of techniques to make ads on the Internet look "cool," "hip," and fun."[106]

Third, consumers can like an ad because it is interesting—that is, it arouses curiosity and gets attention. When consumers exert a lot of effort and thoughtfully elaborate on a message, it can be viewed as interesting and generate a positive A$_{ad}$.

WHEN DO ATTITUDES PREDICT BEHAVIOR?

Marketers are interested not only in how attitudes are formed and can be changed but also in knowing whether, when, and why attitudes will predict behavior. The TORA model comes closest to providing this information by predicting which factors affect consumers' behavioral intentions. However, as was previously noted, what we intend to do does not always predict what we actually will do. Therefore, it is also useful to consider which factors affect the attitude-behavior relationship. Considerable research has tried to examine this issue with the general conclusion that many factors, including the following, affect whether one's attitudes will affect one's behavior.

- *Level of Involvement/Elaboration.* Attitudes are more likely to predict behavior when cognitive involvement is high and consumers elaborate or think extensively about the information that gives rise to their attitudes.[107] Attitudes also tend to be strong and enduring and therefore more predictive of a consumer's behavior when affective involvement is high. Thus attitudes toward emotionally charged issues such as owning handguns or getting an abortion tend to be strongly held and related to behavior.

- *Knowledge and Experience.* Attitudes are more likely to be strongly held and predictive of behavior when the consumer is knowledgeable about or experienced with the object of the attitude.[108] Thus when making a computer decision, for example, an expert is more likely to form an attitude that is based on more detailed and integrated information than is a novice. This attitude would then be more strongly held and more strongly related to behavior.

- *Accessibility of Attitudes.* Attitudes are more strongly related to behavior when they are accessible or "top of mind."[109] Conversely, if an attitude cannot be easily remembered, it will have little effect on behavior. Direct experience (product usage) generally increases attitude accessibility for attributes that must be experienced (e.g., tasted, touched), whereas advertising can produce accessible attitudes for search attributes (e.g., price, ingredients), especially when the level of repetition is high.[110]

- *Attitude Confidence.* As we noted earlier, sometimes we are more certain about our evaluations than at other times. Thus a fourth factor affecting the attitude-behavior relationship is attitude confidence. Confidence tends to be stronger when the attitude is based on either a greater amount of information or more trustworthy information. And when we are confident, our attitudes are more likely to predict our behaviors.[111]

- *Specificity of Attitudes.* Attitudes tend to be good predictors of behavior when we are very *specific* about the behavior that they are trying to predict.[112] Thus if we wanted to predict whether a person will take skydiving lessons, measuring his or her attitude toward skydiving in general will be less likely to predict behavior than measuring his or her attitude toward taking skydiving lessons specifically.

- *Situational Factors.* Intervening situational factors can also prevent a behavior from being performed and can thus weaken the attitude-behavior relationship.[113] You might have a very positive attitude toward a Porsche, but you might not buy one because you do not have the money. Your attitude might also not have culminated in your buying because the dealer was out of stock when you went to buy one. In other circumstances, the usage situation may alter the attitude. Your attitudes toward different wines might depend on whether you are buying wine for yourself or a friend.

- *Normative Factors.* As the TORA model indicated, normative factors are also likely to affect the attitude-behavior relationship. You may like going to the ballet, but you do not do so because you think your friends will make fun of you. Thus the normative beliefs and motivation to comply will also affect the attitude-behavior relationship.

- *Personality Variables.* Finally, certain personality types are more likely to exhibit stronger attitude-behavior relationships than are others. Individuals who really like to think about things will evidence stronger attitude-behavior relationships because their attitudes will be based on high elaboration thinking.[114] Also, people who are guided more by their own internal dispositions (called low self-monitors) are more likely to exhibit similar behavior patterns across situations and therefore more consistent attitude-behavior relationships.[115] People who are guided by the views and behaviors of others (called high self-monitors), on the other hand, try to change their behavior to adapt to every unique situation. Thus a high self-monitor's choice of beer might depend on the situation; a low self-monitor would choose the same beer regardless of the circumstances.

SUMMARY

This chapter examined how consumers' attitudes are formed and changed when their MAO to engage in a behavior or process a message is high. In these instances, consumers tend to expend a lot of effort in forming their attitudes. An attitude is a relatively global and enduring evaluation about an offering, issue, activity, person or event.

Attitudes can be described in terms of their favorability, accessibility, confidence, persistence, and resistance. When MAO is high, consumers devote considerable effort to processing a message. Their thoughts and feelings in response to this situation can affect their attitudes, either through a cognitive or an affective route to persuasion.

From a cognitive perspective, attitudes can be based on cognitive responses, which are defined as the thoughts that individuals have in response to a stimulus. Three major types of cognitive responses are counterarguments, support arguments, and source derogations. Many counterarguments and source derogations would suggest that consumers' attitudes toward an offering are negative. A second cognitively based perspective on attitudes is the expectancy-value approach. The theory of reasoned action (TORA) is an extension of this model, which is designed to predict not only attitudes but also behavioral intentions. This model predicts that intentions are affected by consumers' attitudes toward the act and normative factors. The model also identifies how attitudes and intentions can be influenced by four major strategies: (1) change beliefs, (2) change evaluations, (3) add a new belief, and (4) target normative beliefs.

Also, under elaborative processing, messages can be effective if they (1) have a credible source, (2) have a strong argument, (3) present positive and negative information (under certain circumstances), or (4) involve direct comparisons (if not the market leader). Attitudes are also formed from feelings or emotions such as joy and fear. In essence, consumers can experience emotions by being affectively involved with a communication or when the message involves an emotional appeal. In either case the consumer holistically processes the communication, and the feelings that result (either positive or negative) can determine attitudes.

When attitudes are affectively based, sources that are likable or attractive can have a positive impact on affective attitude change. Emotional appeals can affect communication processing if they are relevant to the offering (the match-up hypothesis). Fear appeals are a specific type of emotion-eliciting message. A consumer's attitude toward the ad (A_{ad}) can play a role in the attitude change process if the ad is informative or associated with positive feelings. The A_{ad} can then rub off on brand beliefs and attitudes.

Finally, attitudes will better predict a consumer's behavior when (1) involvement is high, (2) knowledge is high, (3) attitudes are accessible, (4) attitudes are held with confidence, (5) attitudes are specific, (6) no situational factors are present, (7) normative factors are not in operation, and (8) we are dealing with certain personality types.

EXERCISES

1. Collect three advertisements (either from magazines or TV) that you think would generate elaborative processing. Engage in a detailed analysis of these ads in terms of the following:

   a. What type of cognitive responses might consumers have when seeing/reading these ads? (Be sure to identify counterarguments, support arguments, and source derogations.) Based on these responses, how effective do you think the ad will be in changing attitudes?

   b. In terms of the TORA model, what types of attitude-change strategies are these ads using?

   c. What kinds of affective responses (feelings or emotions) might occur? How would these responses affect the attitude change process?

2. Find three ads that you think will generate a fair amount of cognitive responses from consumers. Show these ads to a sample of 15 consumers and ask them to think aloud as they read the ad. In other words, ask them to speak out every thought they have while reading the ad. Record these responses either on tape or by hand. Then classify the responses into the categories of counterarguments, source derogations, support arguments, and affective responses. Use this information to answer the following questions:

   a. What are the major strengths of each ad?

   b. What are the major weaknesses of each ad?

   c. How could each ad be improved?

3. Find ten magazine ads that you think will elicit elaborative processing. Analyze these ads for the types of source and message factors discussed in the chapter. Based on this analysis, answer the following questions:

   a. Which types of source and message factors are most frequently used?

   b. Which ads do you think are most effective and why?

   c. Which ads do you think are least effective and why?

4. Identify and interview three individuals who engage in personal selling for a business. Develop a short questionnaire that will identify the types of strategies they use to persuade consumers to buy particular products. First ask some open-ended questions about how the salespeople try to influence consumers. Then ask some specific questions regarding the source and message factors discussed in the chapter. Be sure to ask how often the salespeople use each technique and how effective they think the techniques are. Summarize this information and answer the following questions:

   a. Which type of persuasion techniques are most likely to be used in a personal selling situation?

   b. Which message factors are most effective and why?

   c. Which message factors are least effective and why?

CHAPTER 7

ATTITUDES BASED ON LOW CONSUMER EFFORT

INTRODUCTION

One of the most successful advertising campaigns in recent years stars a Chihuahua named Dinky on a never-ending quest for Taco Bell. Dinky makes the now famous statements: "*Yo quiero* Taco Bell" ("I want Taco Bell") and "Drop the chalupa." These ads have become enormously popular for a number of reasons. First, consumers have a positive feeling toward the dog because he is cute (see Exhibit 7.1). Second, most people find it funny that the dog is presumed to be able to talk. Third, the primary target market, teenage guys, can relate to the character, which is "perceived as a 19-year-old guy in a dog's body who thinks about food and girls."[1] Finally, the ads' punch lines are becoming part of the U.S. vernacular along with classic lines like "Where's the beef?" and "I've fallen and I can't get up." All these factors lead to positive consumer feelings that can transfer to the brand. The campaign has even led to an increase in demand for Chihuahuas as pets.

EXHIBIT 7.1
**Dinky the Taco Bell
Chihuahua**

Dinky the chihuahua has been a
popular character in Taco Bell
ads in recent years.

Source: Courtesy of Taco Bell Corp.

The Taco Bell campaign illustrates how marketers can influence our attitudes even when we devote little effort to processing a message. Because
consumers in this situation do not actively process message arguments or
become emotionally involved in the message, marketers must employ other techniques to create positive evaluations of the brand. In this chapter we discuss techniques such as the use of humor, attractive sources, and emotion to influence
consumer attitudes when the effort made to process the message is low.

HIGH-EFFORT VERSUS LOW-EFFORT ROUTES TO PERSUASION

When consumers are either not willing or not able to exert a lot of effort or devote a lot of emotional resources to processing the central idea behind an ad communication, we characterize it as a low-effort situation. Here consumers are
unlikely to think about what the product means to them, relate empathetically to
the characters in the ad, or generate arguments against or in support of the specific message about the brand. As a result, when processing effort is low, consumers usually do not form strong beliefs or accessible, persistent, resistant, or
confident attitudes.

You saw in Chapter 3 that low-effort situations are likely to be those in which
consumers do not have the motivation, ability, or opportunity (MAO) to process
the information provided. Rather, they tend to be passive recipients of the message. Low-effort situations thus require a new marketing strategy that takes into
account this lower level of processing.

In other words, instead of using the central route, which focuses on the key
message arguments, the communication takes the **peripheral route to persuasion**.[2] Processing is called *peripheral* when consumers' attitudes are based not on a
detailed consideration of the message or their ability to relate to the brand empathetically but on other easily processed aspects of the message, such as the source
or visuals, called **peripheral cues**. In particular, if peripheral cues such as visuals
are related to the product or service, consumer attitudes can persist over time.[3]

Just as there are both cognitive and affective routes to persuasion when processing effort is high, so also can consumers form low-effort attitudes in both a

**peripheral route to persua-
sion** Aspects other than key
message arguments that are
used to influence attitudes.

peripheral cues Easily
processed aspects of a message
such as music, an attractive
source or picture, or humor.

cognitive and affective manner. Marketers can try to design their ads to enhance the likelihood that consumers' thoughts (the cognitive base), feelings (the affective base), or both will be favorable. Exhibit 7.2 provides a framework for thinking about the peripheral bases of consumer behavior.

Understanding how consumers form attitudes with low effort is important to marketers because, in most cases, consumers will have limited MAO to process marketing communications. Think about the countless marketing messages you receive every day. How many of them actually attract your attention and stimulate you to think about the ad and how you feel about the offering? Consider how you normally watch TV. Chances are you have limited exposure to ads because you are channel surfing. You may comprehend very little about the messages because you are watching them in a distracting environment, or you may even tune them out because they are advertising products you do not care about. For marketers, these behaviors are challenges to overcome.

COGNITIVE BASES OF ATTITUDES WHEN CONSUMER EFFORT IS LOW

In Chapter 6 you learned that beliefs form an important cognitive basis for attitudes. When processing effort is low, attitudes may be based on a few simple and not very strong beliefs, because consumers have not processed the message deeply. Interestingly, because these beliefs are not very strong, marketers may actually be *more* successful in changing them than when processing effort is high. The attitudes of low-effort consumers may be less resistant to attack than those of high-effort consumers because the former may "let their guard down" and not resist the message or develop counterarguments.

PART TWO The Psychological Core

156

simple inferences Beliefs based on peripheral cues.

When processing effort is low, consumers may acquire simple beliefs by forming **simple inferences**. For example, consumers may infer that a brand of champagne is elegant because it is shown with other elegant things, for example, a richly decorated room or a woman in a black dress and pearls. Likewise, if an ad is perceived to be similar to the prototypical ad for a product or service category, consumers may believe that the offering is just like the prototypical brand and develop similar attitudes toward both.[4] You saw in Chapter 5 that inferred beliefs about the brand may also come from consumers' superficial analysis of its brand name, country of origin, price, or color.

Consumers can also form simple beliefs based on attributions or explanations for an endorsement.[5] If consumers attribute an endorsement to the endorser's desire to earn a lot of money, they will not find the message believable. If, on the other hand, they perceive that the endorser truly cares about the offering, the ad may be more credible.

heuristics Simple rules of thumb used to aid judgments or decisions.

frequency heuristic Beliefs based simply on the number of supporting arguments or amount of repetition.

Finally, consumers can form **heuristics**, or simple rules of thumb, that are easy to invoke and require little thought.[6] For example, consumers could use the heuristic "If it is a well-known brand, it must be good" to infer that brands with more frequent ads are also higher in quality.[7] A special type of heuristic is the **frequency heuristic** with which consumers simply form a belief based on the number of supporting arguments.[8] They may think, "It must be good because there are ten reasons why I should like it." Research has also indicated that consumers are actually likely to have stronger beliefs when they hear the same message repeatedly.[9] Rather than having to think about and evaluate the information, consumers find it easier to use their familiarity with the message as a way of judging its accuracy ("This 'rings a bell' so it must be true").

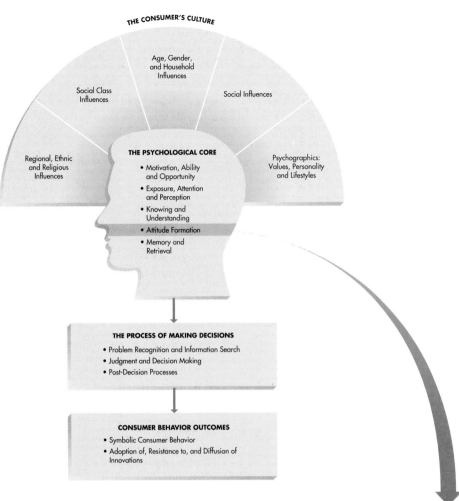

THE CONSUMER'S CULTURE

Age, Gender, and Household Influences

Social Class Influences

Social Influences

Regional, Ethnic and Religious Influences

THE PSYCHOLOGICAL CORE
- Motivation, Ability and Opportunity
- Exposure, Attention and Perception
- Knowing and Understanding
- Attitude Formation
- Memory and Retrieval

Psychographics: Values, Personality and Lifestyles

THE PROCESS OF MAKING DECISIONS
- Problem Recognition and Information Search
- Judgment and Decision Making
- Post-Decision Processes

CONSUMER BEHAVIOR OUTCOMES
- Symbolic Consumer Behavior
- Adoption of, Resistance to, and Diffusion of Innovations

EXHIBIT 7.2

Chapter Overview: Attitude Formation and Change: Low Consumer Effort

This chapter examines attitude formation and change when processing effort is low. Just as in high-effort cases, attitudes can be formed cognitively and affectively; however, the specific processes are different. Low-effort cognition involves simple beliefs, and affect involves classical conditioning, mere exposure, attitude toward the ad, and mood. Attitudes also can be influenced (both cognitively and affectively) by source, message, and context factors.

CHAPTER 7 Attitudes Based on Low Consumer Effort

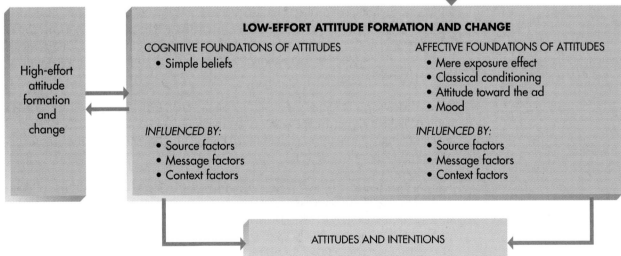

LOW-EFFORT ATTITUDE FORMATION AND CHANGE

High-effort attitude formation and change

COGNITIVE FOUNDATIONS OF ATTITUDES
- Simple beliefs

AFFECTIVE FOUNDATIONS OF ATTITUDES
- Mere exposure effect
- Classical conditioning
- Attitude toward the ad
- Mood

INFLUENCED BY:
- Source factors
- Message factors
- Context factors

INFLUENCED BY:
- Source factors
- Message factors
- Context factors

ATTITUDES AND INTENTIONS

Marketers need to consider several factors when trying to influence cognitive attitudes. One is the strength and importance of consumers' beliefs. The second is the likelihood that consumers will form favorable beliefs based on the inferences, attributions, and heuristics they use in processing the message. In their effort to design communications that overcome these hurdles, marketers must consider three major characteristics of a communication: (1) the source, (2) the message, and (3) the context in which the message is delivered.

Communication Source

Characteristics of the source play an important role in influencing consumers' beliefs when processing effort is low. Credible sources can serve as peripheral cues for making a simplified judgment, such as "Statements from experts can be trusted" or "Products endorsed by an expert must be good."[10] Note that source expertise is used here as a simple cue in making a judgment about the credibility of the message, and, unlike the case in high-effort situations, little cognitive effort is required. Marketers may also enhance the likelihood that consumers believe the endorser by making sure the endorser does not advertise many other products.

The Message

There are a number of ways the message itself influence our attitudes when processing effort is low.

Category- and Schema-Consistent Information   Many elements of a communication affect the inferences that consumers form from a message. For example, consumers may infer a brand has certain characteristics based on its name, for example, "Healthy Choice cereal must be good for me." We may make inferences about quality based on price, as discussed earlier, or about attributes based on color, such as when blue suggests coolness. Thus in designing ads for low-effort consumers, marketers place close attention to the immediate associations consumers have for easily processed visual and verbal information. These associations are likely to be consistent with category and **schema** information stored in the consumer's memory.

Many Message Arguments   The frequency heuristic can also affect consumers' beliefs about the message. Consumers do not actually process all the information but simply form a belief based on the number of supporting arguments as a simplifying rule.

Simple Messages   In low-processing situations a simple message is more likely to be effective because consumers will not process a lot of information. Marketers often want to get across basic information and make consumers understand why a particular brand is superior, especially when it has a point of differentiation that distinguishes it from the competition. However, rather than attempting to provide a lot of detailed information about the brand that will overload low-processing consumers, marketers should provide a simple message that communicates one or two key points. For example, increasing competition from Burger King led McDonald's to engage in a barrage of advertising to defend its fries with the simple slogan: "America's favorite fries—go get 'em!"[11]

schema   A knowledge structure stored in memory.

self-referencing Relating a message to one's own experience or self-image.

mystery ad An ad in which the brand is not identified until the end of the message.

incidental learning Learning that occurs from repetition rather than from conscious processing.

EXHIBIT 7.3
Increasing Active Processing

This ad tries to draw consumers into the message by challenging them to look at the image in different ways.

Source: Courtesy Ernst & Young LLP.

What do you see?
It might be your future.

Do you think there are many ways to look at a problem? As well as an opportunity? We want people who look at the future and are excited by the possibilities. See for yourself. www.ey.com

CONSULTING · TAX · ASSURANCE

≡ ERNST & YOUNG
FROM THOUGHT TO FINISH.™

Involving Messages Marketers will sometimes want to *increase* consumers' involvement with the message as a way of ensuring that the information is received. One common strategy is to increase the extent to which consumers engage in **self-referencing**, or relating the message to their own experience or self-image.

Studies have shown that a self-referencing strategy can be effective in developing positive attitudes and intentions, especially if moderate levels are used and involvement isn't too low.[12] Similarly, remembering and using the consumer's name in a personal selling context will increase purchase.[13]

Marketers can increase self-referencing by (1) directly instructing consumers to use self-reference (Think of the last time you had a good meal.), (2) using the word *you* in the ad, (3) asking rhetorical questions (Wouldn't you like your clothes to look this clean?),[14] or (4) showing visuals of situations to which consumers can easily relate.

Marketers can employ various other techniques to increase situational involvement and processing effort. One type of involving message is the **mystery ad** (also called the "wait and bait" ad), in which the brand is not identified until the end, thereby arousing the consumer's curiosity and involvement. To introduce its new DCC tape player, Philips developed a 3-minute ad with a series of arresting images.[15] A clear sound comes down from the sky and government officials try to decipher it, a Russian coffeehouse waitress boogies to it, a circus clown is moved by it, and a monsignor receives inspiration from it. Only at the end can the consumer figure out that the ad is for Philips. Research has suggested that this strategy is particularly effective in generating category-based processing and storing brand associations in memory.[16]

Scratch-and-sniff ads have been effective in increasing consumer processing because most consumers cannot resist the excitement of trying something new. In Exhibit 7.3, Ernst & Young draw consumers into the message by challenging them to look at the illustration in different ways. Miller beer introduced an ad with an interactive football game; consumers in more than 1,000 bars could "make the call" during a live broadcast.[17] ■

Message Context and Repetition

Although source and message factors can influence consumers' attitudes, the context in which the message is delivered can affect other aspects of beliefs—the strength of those beliefs and the prominence (or salience) of those beliefs to the consumer. The strength and salience of consumers' beliefs can be enhanced through message *repetition*, which helps consumers acquire basic knowledge about important features or benefits. Consumers do not try to actively process this information; rather, the constant repetition increases recall through effortless or **"incidental" learning**. For example, you may have prominent beliefs that Pepsi is a drink for younger consumers or that Allstate is a reputable company, simply because you have been exposed to messages from these companies many times.

Second, repetition may enhance brand awareness, make a brand name more familiar,[18] make it easier to recognize in the store, increase the likelihood that consumers will remember it when making a decision,[19] and increase confidence in the brand.[20] To illustrate, a series of ads for California avocados increased sales by 16 percent.[21] On the other hand, Vlassic pickles experienced a significant decline in sales when insufficient advertising resulted in lower brand awareness.[22] Third, as you have seen, repetition can make claims more believable (the truth effect). These repetition effects are even stronger when ads are spaced out over time.[23]

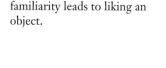

AFFECTIVE BASES OF ATTITUDES WHEN CONSUMER EFFORT IS LOW

The establishment of low-level beliefs based on peripheral cues is not the only way that consumers can form attitudes about brands with little effort. Attitudes can also be based on consumers' affective or emotional reactions to these easily processed peripheral cues. We divide the study of low-effort affective processes into four major areas: (1) the mere exposure effect, (2) classical conditioning, (3) attitude toward the ad, and (4) mood.

The Mere Exposure Effect

mere exposure effect   When familiarity leads to liking an object.

According to the **mere exposure effect**, we tend to prefer familiar objects to unfamiliar ones. Thus our attitudes toward an offering such as a new style of clothing should change as we become more and more familiar with it, regardless of whether we perform any deep cognitive analysis of it. The mere exposure effect may explain why many of the top 30 brands in the 1930s are still in the top 30 today. It is also the reason why the music industry likes to have recordings featured on the radio or music videos on TV. These repeated exposures build familiarity with the music, which in turn enhances consumers' liking of it.

Most demonstrations of the mere exposure effect have occurred in tightly controlled laboratory studies, and some experts question whether it will generalize to the real world.[24] It is also possible that repeated exposure reduces uncertainty about the stimulus or increases consumers' opportunity to process it[25] and that these factors (rather than mere familiarity) are what affect consumers' attitudes.

MARKETING IMPLICATIONS   If the mere exposure effect is valid, marketers may be able to enhance consumers' liking for a new product or service by repeatedly exposing consumers to the offering or messages about it. Research suggests that when consumers' MAO is low, marketers need to devise creative tactics for increasing exposure to products and messages, perhaps by using the right medium, the right placement within medium, optimal shelf placement, and sampling.

Consistent with the mere exposure effect, the advertising industry certainly recognizes the importance of developing and maintaining brand-name familiarity. According to advertising authority Leo Bogart, repetition is used to impress "the advertised name upon the consumers' consciousness and make them feel comfortable with the brand."[26] In the optometry industry, Bausch & Lomb contact lenses are by far the most requested brand, even though they are not the only quality lenses. Consumers prefer the Bausch & Lomb product in part because it is the best-known brand. Likewise, Burger King faced a very tough battle when it entered the Japanese market because McDonald's is so well known and is strongly preferred there.[27]

Note that repeated exposures build familiarity and liking only up to a point.[28] After this, consumers typically experience "**wearout**," which means they become bored with the stimulus, and brand attitudes can actually become negative.[29] However, this problem can be overcome by developing different executions for the same message or variants on the same offering. Wearout is the reason that many advertisers develop an entire campaign of ads rather than a single execution.[30] The goal is to get the same message across in many different ways. Absolut vodka has been very successful with its campaign featuring artistic variations on a beautiful bottle, and the familiar "milk moustache" series of ads has been used to promote one of the world's most boring products: milk. ∎

Classical Conditioning

One way of influencing consumers' attitudes without invoking much processing effort is **classical conditioning**. Classical conditioning became well-known from work in the early part of this century by a Russian scientist named Ivan Pavlov. Normally, hungry dogs will salivate automatically when they see food. Pavlov discovered that he was able to condition hungry dogs to also salivate at the sound of a bell. How did this happen?

According to Pavlov, the food was an *unconditioned stimulus* (*UCS*), and the salivation response to the food was an *unconditioned response* (*UCR*) (see Exhibit 7.4). A stimulus is called unconditioned because it automatically elicits an involuntary response. In other words, the dogs could not help but salivate when they saw the meat powder. In contrast, a *conditioned stimulus* (*CS*) is something that does not automatically elicit an involuntary response by itself. Thus until Pavlov paired the food with the bell, the bell alone was not capable of making the dogs salivate. Repeatedly pairing the conditioned stimulus (the bell) with the unconditioned stimulus (the meat powder) automatically elicited the involuntary unconditioned response (salivation). However, salivation eventually became conditioned on the sounding of the bell. In other words, the dogs had come to associate the food and the bell so closely that eventually they salivated in the presence of the bell alone. Because the response could now be evoked in the presence of the conditioned

EXHIBIT 7.4
Classical Conditioning

These diagrams illustrate the basic process of classical conditioning. An unconditioned stimulus, or UCS (e.g., food or pleasant scenes), will automatically produce an unconditioned response, or UCR (e.g., salivation or positive affect). By repeatedly pairing the UCS with a conditioned stimulus, or CS (e.g., a bell or soft drink), the CS can be conditioned to produce the same response, a conditioned response, or CR (e.g., salivation or positive affect). Can you think of any other examples of when this process occurs?

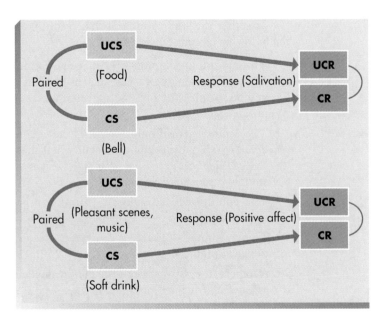

stimulus alone, the response was said to be a *conditioned response* (*CR*). As another illustration of this phenomenon, many cat owners may have noticed how their kitties will usually come running when they hear the can opener. This behavior occurs because the noise of the can opener has been repeatedly paired with feeding.

MARKETING IMPLICATIONS You may be wondering what possible significance salivating dogs have for consumer behavior, but in fact classical conditioning theory is sometimes used to explain the effectiveness of marketing communications. Here, however, the unconditioned response is not a physiological one like salivating but rather a psychological one like an emotion. As Exhibit 7.3 shows, certain unconditioned stimuli such as a happy scene or a catchy jingle automatically elicit an unconditioned emotional response such as joy or warmth. By repeatedly pairing one of these unconditioned stimuli with a conditioned stimulus, such as the brand name, we may be able to evoke the same emotional response, now the conditioned response, to the conditioned stimulus, the brand name itself. Similarly, consumers might be conditioned to have a negative emotional response to an offering, say, cigarettes, if ads by health advocacy groups repeatedly show the product with stimuli that automatically elicit a negative emotional response, for example, pictures of stained teeth.

In one of the first consumer studies to demonstrate classical conditioning, subjects viewed a slide of a blue or beige pen that was matched with a 1-minute segment of either pleasant or unpleasant music. Subjects who heard pleasant music selected the advertised pen, the one played with that music, 79 percent of the time, whereas only 30 percent of those who heard the unpleasant music selected it.[31] Although these findings were subject to alternative interpretations (subjects may simply have done what they thought the experimenter wanted them to do or the music may have put the consumers in a more positive mood),[32] more recent and more tightly controlled studies have found support for the classical conditioning phenomenon. For example, by using unconditioned stimuli such as *Star Wars* music and pleasing pictures, experimenters have affected consumers' attitudes toward such conditioned stimuli as geometric figures, colas, and toothpaste.[33] It has also been found that attitudes created by classical conditioning can be fairly enduring over time.[34]

Together the studies suggest that conditioning is most likely to occur when the following circumstances exist:

- The conditioned stimuli–unconditioned stimuli link is relatively novel or unknown. Thus unique visuals, such as pictures of beautiful scenery, exciting situations, or pleasing objects, are often used as unconditioned stimuli to create positive feelings.

- The conditioned stimulus precedes the unconditioned stimulus (*forward conditioning*). Conditioning is weaker when the unconditioned stimulus is presented first (*backward conditioning*) or at the same time as the conditioned stimulus (*concurrent conditioning*).

- The conditioned stimulus is paired consistently with the unconditioned stimulus.

- The consumer is aware of the link between the conditioned and unconditioned stimuli.

- A logical fit exists between the conditioned and unconditioned stimuli, such as between Michael Jordan and Nike.[35]

Interestingly, the first condition can cause problems for marketers because unconditioned stimuli are often well-known celebrities, music, or visuals for which consumers possess many associations. This situation might suggest that highly visible celebrities are not as effective in creating a classical conditioning effect. However, other research suggests that this problem can be overcome by using highly familiar stimuli such as popular songs and personalities because they elicit very strong feelings in many situations. ■

Attitude Toward the Ad

attitude toward the ad (A_{ad})
Whether the consumer likes or dislikes an ad.

dual-mediation hypothesis
Explains how attitudes toward the ad influence brand attitudes.

EXHIBIT 7.5
The Dual-Mediation Hypothesis

This hypothesis explains how attitudes toward the ad (A_{ad}) can influence attitudes toward the brand (A_b) and intentions (I_b). When you read an ad you can have responses (C_{ad}), that are both cognitive (this ad has information about a brand) and affective (positive feelings from finding the ad). These responses may then cause you to like the ad (A_{ad}), which can then (1) make you either more accepting of brand beliefs (C_b), leading to a more positive brand attitude (A_b), or (2) give you positive feelings that simply transfer over to the brand (I like the ad so I like the brand). Both processes then lead to an increase in intention to purchase.

Another concept that has been useful in understanding the affective bases of attitudes in low-effort situations is the consumer's **attitude toward the ad (A_{ad})**. Sometimes consumers may really like an ad so much that they transfer their positive feelings from the ad to the brand.[36] Thus you may decide that you really like Benetton because you find the ads so interesting, or Monster.com because its ads are so humorous.

One study found that beliefs or knowledge about the brand did not fully account for brand attitudes and that A_{ad} provided a significant additional explanation—brands with liked ads were evaluated more favorably.[37] Furthermore, a study done in India, Greece, Denmark, New Zealand, and the United States found that the A_{ad} principle was globally applicable.[38] In fact, an Advertising Research Foundation project suggests that attitudes toward ads may be the best indicator of advertising effectiveness.[39]

The **dual-mediation hypothesis** is a somewhat more complex explanation of the relationship between consumers' liking for an ad and brand attitude (see Exhibit 7.5).[40] According to this hypothesis, consumers can have a favorable attitude toward an ad either because they find it believable or because they feel good about it. Thus the dual-mediation hypothesis proposes that A_{ad} can affect brand attitudes (A_b) either through believability or liking. These responses, in turn, may positively affect consumers' intentions to purchase (I_b). Thus consumers who like the ad in Exhibit 7.6 on the following page might be more likely to (1) accept the claim that the Nikon F100 is more balanced, agile, and lightweight (C_b) or (2) like Nikon more because they like the ad.

MARKETING IMPLICATIONS The clear implication of the attitude-toward-the-ad theory is that by providing ads that are pleasing, marketers may be able to make consumers' brand attitudes more positive as well. Thus by using techniques such as humor, music,

Cognitive or affective responses to ad (C_{ad})	Attitude toward the ad (A_{ad})	
Brand beliefs (C_b)	Attitude toward the brand (A_b)	Intention to purchase (I_b)

The new F100. 785 grams. Eager to please.

Nikon

F100

Introducing the newest addition to Nikon's Total Pro Imaging System, the F100.™ Balanced and agile, it packs heavy duty technology inside its lightweight magnesium alloy frame. You like speed? Try the world's fastest Dynamic Autofocus. Crisp, sharp exposures? Say hello to 3D Matrix Metering. Even tricky flash situations are a non-issue with its Automatic Balanced Fill flash system. Now, if it only knew how to fetch. See the F100 at your authorized Nikon dealer.

Photo: Geof Kern ©1999 Nikon Inc.

EXHIBIT 7.6
Affectively Pleasing Ad

This ad is likely to create positive feelings because it is humorous and appealing. Consistent with the dual-mediation hypothesis, a positive A_{ad} may make consumers (1) more likely to accept the claim that the Nikon F100 is more balanced and agile, or (2) like Nikon more because of the ad.

Source: Nikon Inc.

pleasant pictures, and sex (all of which will be discussed in more detail shortly), marketers can develop positive attitudes toward the ad. Hence Procter & Gamble has finally abandoned its long tradition of information ads in favor of ads with drama or emotion to "prevent people from hitting the channel changer."[41]

Also note that the effect of ad attitudes on brand attitudes may depend on whether consumers already have a strong attitude toward the brand. In other words, when brands are well known and attitudes about them have been formed, consumers may not like the brand more just because they like the ad. However, when brands are new or not well known, consumers' liking for the ad can play a more significant role in their liking for the brand.[42] Studies also suggest that the effect of attitude toward the ad on attitude toward the brand dissipates over time.[43] In other words, as memory of the ad fades, liking for the ad and the brand also becomes weaker. ∎

Mood

Another somewhat different explanation for affective attitudes is that they are influenced by the consumer's mood. A stimulus can create a positive or a negative mood, and this mood can, in turn, affect consumers' reactions to any other stimulus that they happen to evaluate. Thus we are more likely to say that we like something if we are in a good mood and that we dislike something when we are in a bad mood. Mood can therefore bias attitudes in a *mood-congruent direction*. Note that mood is different from classical conditioning because mood (1) does not require a repeated association between two stimuli and (2) can affect consumers' evaluations of any object, not just the stimulus.

Researchers have also examined the impact of lighting on mood. In general, brighter in-store lighting increases the extent to which shoppers examine and handle merchandise.[44] Brighter lighting does not, however, lead to an increase in the amount of time spent shopping or the number of purchases. Color can also have a major impact on mood. Warm colors such as red, orange, and yellow tend to be more stimulating and exciting, whereas cool colors such as blue, green, and violet tend to be more soothing.[45]

Brands may be liked better when the ads or the programs in which they appear put consumers in a good mood. Consumer research has focused on the kinds of emotions or moods that ads invoke and the variety of ways these factors might affect consumers' ad and brand attitudes.[46] One study identified three major categories of affective responses: *SEVA* (surgency, elation, vigor, and activation), which is present when the communication puts the consumer in an upbeat or happy mood; *deactivation feelings*, which include soothing, relaxing, quiet, or pleasant responses; and *social affection*, which encompasses feelings of warmth, tenderness, and caring.[47] For example, Heublein's ad for Blossom Hill wine associates the brand with the romantic notion of giving flowers, in the hope that the ad will generate positive feelings.[48]

Another study found that ad-induced feelings of warmth and humor could have a direct and positive impact on brand attitudes.[49] Thus the ad for the Nikon in Exhibit 7.6 might also generate humor and warm feelings in consumers that could transfer to the brand.

If mood effects do operate, retailers have considerable incentive to use physical surroundings and the behavior of store employees to put consumers in a good mood. Warm colors are more likely to draw customers to an outlet but can also create tension. Cool colors, on the other hand, are more relaxing but do not attract customers.[50] Thus when the goal is to stimulate quick purchases or activity, warm colors are more appropriate. Discount stores such as Target and Kmart often use a red-based color scheme. Kmart recently switched from light blue to red to remove a disadvantage in this area. Warm colors would also fit health clubs, sports stadiums, and fast-food restaurants where a high level of activity and energy is desirable. The predominant color at McDonald's, for example, is orange.

On the other hand, cool colors would be more appropriate when the goal is to have consumers feel calm or spend time deliberating. Stores that sell expensive consumer durables are a good example. The same is true of doctors' offices, hotel rooms, spas, banks, resorts, and upscale restaurants. ■

HOW AFFECTIVE ATTITUDES ARE INFLUENCED

When processing effort is low and attitudes are formed on the basis of feelings, the same three factors that influence cognitive reasoning affect consumers' affective attitudes: the source, the message, and the context. However, this time these factors are based on low-effort processes such as classical conditioning, mere exposure, mood, and attitude toward the ad.

Communication Source

The source of the message can have an important impact on the way consumers process a message. Under conditions of low effort, two factors play a major role in determining whether or not the source evokes favorable affective reactions: its physical attractiveness and its likability. These two factors also explain why marketers like to feature celebrities in ads.

Attractive Sources   We do not have to look far to find an ad featuring an attractive model, spokesperson, or celebrity. In fact, unattractive people rarely appear in ads. Obviously, marketers have accepted the long-held belief that beauty sells. One example is the "hair-color war" between superstars Cindy Crawford (Revlon) and Heather Locklear (L'Oréal).[51]

Research studies generally support the notion that beauty sells. When consumers' motivation to process an advertised message is low, attractive sources will enhance the favorability of consumers' brand attitudes regardless of whether the message arguments are strong or weak.[52] Consumers also rate ads with physically attractive models as more appealing, attractive, eye-catching, impressive, and interesting than ads with unattractive models. These ratings may affect consumers' attitudes toward the products these models sponsor.[53] Attractiveness can also have beneficial effects on advertiser believability and actual purchase.[54] These effects can occur for both male and female models (consumers are most strongly attracted to models of the opposite sex) and have been found to operate for direct-mail responses, point-of-purchase displays, and personal-selling interactions as well.[55]

Likable Sources   The likability of the source can also influence affective attitudes.[56] For example, Wendy's chairman Dave Thomas has been a success spokesperson because of the homey, warm image he projects. Likable sources may serve as unconditioned stimuli, create a positive mood that affects consumers' evaluations of the ad or brand, and make consumers feel more positive about the endorsed products. Although physically attractive sources can also be likable, sometimes the source can be physically unattractive but have features or a personality that the consumer likes. For example, Rodney Dangerfield, Jay Leno, Tony Randall, and Wilfred Brimley are well liked, but are generally not considered to be extremely attractive.

We also tend to like people of average looks because they are more similar to ourselves and we are better able to relate them. One popular spokesperson is Chris Dollard, a slightly nerdy actor with loose curls who has appeared in ads for Tostidos, J.C. Penney, and MCI.[57] An ad showing a man going overboard to be a doting dad was very popular in Japan (where men are usually depicted as remote corporate warriors).[58] Disabled people are becoming increasingly attractive endorsers for companies such as GM, AT&T, IBM, and Sears because of a desire to represent human diversity and because consumers admire courageous individuals.[59]

Celebrity Sources   Physical attractiveness and likability explain why celebrities are among the most widely used sources, sometimes accounting for as much as a third of all television advertising. In particular, celebrity sources can be effective when they are related to the product or service (the match-up hypothesis).[60] Companies are often willing to pay huge sums—sometimes as high as $2 to $3 million—to get a celebrity to endorse their products. Basketball star Michael Jordan has been one of the most popular endorsers, earning more than $36 million a year. Rising Olympic stars such as U.S. hockey player Cammi Granato and skier Picabo Street are also attractive to companies.[61] Stars from popular TV shows such as *Melrose Place*, *Friends*, and *Beverly Hills 90210* have appeared in ads (Polaroid, Diet Coke, and Pepe Jeans, respectively). Noted drag queen RuPaul was an endorser for Bailey's Irish Cream. Even deceased celebrities such as James Dean, Buddy Holly, Marilyn Monroe, the Marx Brothers, Laurel and Hardy, and Babe Ruth have strong marketing appeal. Some celebrities even place their names on products (Jimmy Dean's sausage and Paul Newman's salad dressing).[62] TV stars Jay Leno and Jerry Seinfeld were featured on boxes of Kellogg's cereal. And some celebrities do commercial voice-overs without actually appearing in the ad.

Other celebrity sources include company executives like Dave Thomas of Wendy's, Victor Kiam of Remington, and Frank Perdue of Perdue Farms, and even cartoon characters. When the Butterfinger candy bar used Bart Simpson as an endorser, sales increased by 26 percent.[63] Time Warner has used some of its own icons such as Batman and Bugs Bunny for its corporate image campaign.

The Taco Bell Chihuahua, Charlie the Tuna (Starkist), and the AT&T Lucky Dog (a bulldog) have also been popular.[64] Joe Camel, although now banned in the United States, is alive and well in Argentina.[65] Secret agent James Bond has been licensed to sell everything from credit cards to cars to cell phones to watches.[66] Finally, Exhibit 7.7 shows the Peanuts character Woodstock presenting information about financial strategies.

The Message

Just as the source can influence consumers' feelings and moods, so too can characteristics associated with the message. These message characteristics include pleasant pictures, music, humor, sex, and emotional content.

HATCHING NEW FINANCIAL STRATEGIES.

Times have changed. Some things you used to count on have suddenly become problems you have to solve on your own. Like rethinking your family insurance or savings plans. Or your retirement plan.

This calls for some new financial strategies. If you don't know where to start,

we're here to help you make sense of it all. We'll work with you to plan your insurance coverage, and help with your investing and retirement needs as well.

For starters, phone 1-800-MetLife, and ask for our new brochure, *To Help You Decide.*

GET MET. IT PAYS.
1/800-MetLife

SCHULZ

EXHIBIT 7.7
Celebrity Sources

Sometimes cartoon characters can be the source or endorser in a message. Here we see how the Woodstock character from the cartoon Peanuts is used to present information about MetLife's financial strategies brochure. This character may generate a positive effect that may transfer to the company.

Source: Peanuts © United Feature Syndicate, Inc.

Pleasant Pictures   One of the most frequently employed ways to influence message processing is to use pleasant pictures. Visual stimuli can serve as a conditioned stimulus, affect consumers' mood, or make an ad likable by making it interesting. Research has generally supported the view that pleasant pictures can affect ad and brand attitudes when they are processed peripherally, beyond the effect they have on beliefs about the product.[67] A picture of a sunset, for instance, can influence the choice of a soft drink.[68]

As another example, an ad for 3M's Post-it Flags shows an unusual scene of a 'star' chicken covered with very colorful Post-it Flags, being admired by a group of the chickens.[69] Numerous advertisers employ high-powered special effects rivaling those used in the movies. In one ad a Budweiser truck turns into a racing car; in another a speeding car turns into the Exxon tiger (through a process called *morphing*).

Internet advertising often uses pleasing pictures and visuals to catch consumers' attention and generate positive attitudes as well. A key goal of these ads is to look cool, thereby creating positive feelings about the ad.[70] However, advertisers need to figure out a way to speed up the processing time for these ads because they often take a long time to download and consumers do not like to wait.[71]

Music   Music is frequently used as a communications tool by many companies including Chevrolet ("Like a Rock") and Pepsi. Further, the use of music is progressing beyond the traditional use of the "jingle." ITT used crabs, fish, and seals singing the *Hallelujah Chorus* as part of an image campaign.[72] A British firm hired more than 60 popular artists including Smokey Robinson, the B-52s, Arrested Development, and Barry White to create original ad music.[73] Sometimes the music ads can become popular and drive album sales, as was the case with (then) obscure groups such as the Crystal Method and Republica.[74] To promote the movie

Lethal Weapon 4 in Hong Kong, Warner Brothers used a song by the widely popular local group Beyond, even though not a single note of the song is in the film.[75] This type of promotion is considered crucial for success in marketing films in Asia. Interestingly, McDonald's has even piped music by Bach into its restaurants to scare away troublemakers.[76]

The popularity of music as a marketing device should not be surprising, given that music has been shown to stimulate a variety of positive effects.[77] First, music can be an effective conditioned stimulus for a classical conditioning strategy. Second, music can put the consumer in a positive mood and lead to the development of positive attitudes. Third, music can be effective in generating positive feelings such as happiness, serenity, excitement, and sentimentality. Finally, music can

MUSICAL ELEMENT	EMOTIONAL EXPRESSION								
	SERIOUS	SAD	SENTIMENTAL	SERENE	HUMOROUS	HAPPY	EXCITING	MAJESTIC	FRIGHTENING
MODE	Major	Minor	Minor	Major	Major	Major	Major	Major	Minor
TEMPO	Slow	Slow	Slow	Slow	Fast	Fast	Fast	Medium	Slow
PITCH	Low	Low	Medium	Medium	High	High	Medium	Medium	Low
RHYTHM	Firm	Firm	Flowing	Flowing	Flowing	Flowing	Uneven	Firm	Uneven
HARMONY	Consonant	Dissonant	Consonant	Consonant	Consonant	Consonant	Dissonant	Dissonant	Dissonant
VOLUME	Medium	Soft	Soft	Soft	Medium	Medium	Loud	Loud	Varied

EXHIBIT 7.8

Musical Characteristics for Producing Various Emotional Expressions

As you have probably experienced in your life, music has the strong ability to affect people's emotions. Research has pinpointed the specific effect that various aspects of music can have on feelings. As shown here, the mode, tempo, pitch, rhythm, harmony, and volume of music can influence whether individuals feel serious, sad, sentimental, serene, humorous, happy, excited, majestic or frightened.

Source: Gordon C. Bruner, "Music, Mood, and Marketing," *Journal of Marketing,* October 1990, p. 100. Reprinted by permission.

stimulate emotional memories. If a song in an ad reminds you of your high school days or of an old boyfriend or girlfriend, the emotions associated with these memories may transfer to an ad, brand, store, or other attitude object. Several studies have found that music can have a positive impact on purchase intentions.[78]

Whether music evokes a positive affective response depends on the music's structure. Exhibit 7.8 shows several musical characteristics and the emotional responses they may elicit. The style of music used and the product meanings it conveys can vary considerably across different cultures.[79] Marketers must be careful to employ the kind of music that best produces the desired affective responses.

Humor Anywhere from 24 to 42 percent of all television ads contain some form of humor.[80] An ad can use humor in many different ways, including puns, understatements, jokes, ludicrous situations, satire, and irony. Although humor is not as widespread in other media as in television, it is nevertheless extensive, particularly in radio.[81] The popularity of humor as a message device is not surprising because it increases liking of both the ad and the brand.[82]

Consumers often rate humorous ad campaigns very positively. Many advertisers of low-involvement products have used humor, including Little Caesar's, Subway, and Snicker's. An ad for Alliance Capital mutual funds poked fun at people's blase or negative attitudes about retirement by showing an adoring grandfather being ordered out of the house by the mother. He protests: "I want to spend time with the baby." She responds: "The movers won't be here till four."[83] Most U.S. products fare very poorly in Japan, but Joy dish detergent was able to capture 20 percent of the market largely by featuring comedian Junji Takada in a series of offbeat ads.[84] Sometimes ads can even parody competitors' ads. For example, in response to Nissan's popular ad where a macho male doll impresses an attractive girl doll with his sports car, Acura developed an ad where the couple is run over by an Acura.[85]

Humor appears to be more appropriate for low-involvement offerings in which generating positive feelings about the ad is critical.[86] Humor is also most effective when it is tied or related to the offering. Otherwise, consumers will only pay attention to the humor and ignore the brand.[87] For example, the "M&M's"®

ad in Exhibit 7.9 does a good job of tying the humor to the key selling point—"M&M's"® are deliciously irresistible.

MARKETING IMPLICATIONS Humor tends to work best on TV and radio because these media allow for greater expressiveness.[88] Even traditionally hard-sell infomercials are turning to humor. An infomercial for Atlantic Bell featured a situation comedy starring a family called the Ringers.[89] Interestingly, the use of humor has also been extended to sales promotions. A company called Communications Diversified creates customized comedy videotapes that can be used as a premium item or sales incentive.[90]

Humor tends to work better for certain audiences than for others. In particular, younger males with higher education tend to respond most positively—apparently because aggressive and sexual types of humor appear more frequently than other types of humor and men enjoy this more than women do.[91] Also, humor appears to be more effective for consumers who have either a lower need for cognition or a positive attitude toward the advertised brand.[92] Finally, humor can be used effectively for consumers throughout the world. One study examined humorous ads from Germany, Thailand, South Korea, and the United States for similarities and found that most humorous ads in all four countries contained the same basic structure—contrasts between expected/possible and unexpected/impossible events.[93] However, ads in Korea and Thailand tended to emphasize humor related to group behavior and unequal status relationships, whereas the other two countries focused the humor on individuals with equal status. In all four countries, humor was more likely to be used for pleasure-oriented products. Not all countries appear to employ humor more for low-involvement products than high-involvement ones. In Germany and Thailand, for example, humor is used equally in both cases. Finally, humorous ads tend to be more heavily employed in the United Kingdom than in the United States.[94] ■

EXHIBIT 7.9
The Use of Humor

This ad uses humor to illustrate the key copy point that "The feeding frenzy has begun." In other words, guess which of these two individuals will be lunch.

Source: © Mars, Incorporated.

WHAT ARE YOU STARING AT?

INTRODUCING NEW CRISPY m·m's

m·m's

m&m's CRISPY

Crispy center, milk chocolate, colorful candy shell.
The feeding frenzy has begun.™
www.m-ms.com

Sex Sex as a communication technique appears in two major forms: sexual suggestiveness and nudity. Sexual suggestiveness involves situations that either portray or imply sexual themes or romance. For example, an ad for Uncle Ben's rice shows a couple flirting with each other in the kitchen.[95] An unusual campaign for "M&M's"® suggested that green "M&M's"® might have aphrodisiac powers.[96] Another good example of sexual suggestiveness is the ad for Dark Vanilla perfume in Exhibit 7.10. Close-Up has been using "kissy face" ads to sell toothpaste for years.

Another use of sex is through nudity or partial nudity, often used by brands in the fragrance industry.[97] Exhibit 7.11 shows a billboard ad that also employs this technique. Females are more likely to be shown nude or partially nude than are men. Compared with men, females react more positively to suggestiveness and negatively to nudity.[98]

You might be surprised to learn that the percentage of ads that have sexual overtones has not changed over the years. However, the type of sex appeal has. From 1964 to 1984, the use of sex in the United States became more overt and blatant.[99] However, as the country became more conservative in the late 1980s, the trend moved toward ads that were lighter, more playful, and more subtle, suggestive

EXHIBIT 7.10
Romantic Message

Sometimes messages have romantic or sexual themes or implications. This ad suggests that romance (and perhaps sex) will be the result of wearing Dark Vanilla perfume.

Source: Courtesy of Coty.

rather than open.[100] In the 1990s, ads are became more blatant again. In addition to the usual product categories in which sex is used (such as jeans and perfume), such diverse categories as cars, gloves, Scotch, and watches are adopting sexual themes.[101] An ad for Timex states, "Make your husband really shine in bed." Interestingly, women are now being pictured more often as sexual aggressors or equal partners rather than just sex objects. In a Sansabelt campaign women were featured discussing men's pants in a sexually suggestive way.[102]

MARKETING IMPLICATIONS Research on sexual themes in messages suggests that they can be effective in several ways. Sexual messages attract the consumer's attention,[103] and they also have the ability to evoke emotional responses, such as arousal, excitement, or even lust, which can affect consumers' moods and their ad and brand attitudes.[104] However, this effect is not guaranteed. For some consumers, sexual messages can create negative feelings such as embarrassment, disgust, or uneasiness, any of which would have a negative effect. In particular, research has found that women are more likely to react negatively to ads with sexy female models.[105]

 An ad for Sony's MiniDisc player was considered offensive because the line "If you play it, they will come" implied that women were objects to be ordered with push-button ease.[106] Similarly, a beer campaign in Hong Kong was called sexist

EXHIBIT 7.11
Nudity in Advertising

Sometime ads contain naked or scantily clad models to attract attention and emotion toward a product. Here we see a Benetton billboard that shows a group of naked males and females. Its aim is to entice people to purchase Benetton products, as well as, perhaps, to generate some controversy.

Source: Barbara Alper/Stock Boston.

because in it men describe what they like best about women's legs.[107] Finally, an ad from Italy's Benetton showing 56 close-ups of male and female genitalia (including children's) created a furor in usually more liberal Europe.[108]

One survey indicated that 84 percent of females and 72 percent of males believe that TV ads place too much emphasis on sex.[109] In another survey 49 percent said they have been embarrassed in front of friends or family by sexy TV ads, and 47 percent indicated they would not buy a product if they found an ad offensive.[110] Thus the moral is that sexual themes should be used very carefully and should not be demeaning, sexist, or offensive.

Whether a positive or negative reaction to a sexual ad will occur often depends on the appropriateness of the sexual content to the product/service. One study found that using a seductive model to sell body oil was very appealing, but having a nude model endorse a ratchet set was not.[111] Thus sexual themes would be relevant for products such as perfume, cologne, suntan lotion, and lingerie but inappropriate for industrial equipment, tools, computers, and household cleaners. Toothpaste brands that sell a "sexier" smile, such as Plus White and Rembrandt, have been successful, capturing a large share of the U.S. market.[112]

 Finally, the use of sexual messages varies widely from culture to culture. In some societies, such as in Europe, sexual attitudes are fairly open and the use of sex in advertising is more widespread than in other countries. For example, the Benetton campaign mentioned earlier was shown only in Europe. Another campaign for Swissair showed a carefree nude man flying through the skies, each successive ad showing more of his body.[113] Shown only in Europe and North Africa, the ads increased sales by 30 percent. In other countries (such as Muslim and Asian countries), attitudes are more conservative, and the use of sex is much more restricted. Showing intimacy and kissing, as is done in many ads in the United States, would be totally inappropriate and even offensive in many Asian countries.[114] ■

Emotional Content   Communications can accommodate or enhance consumers' existing MAO and processing effort in the presence of cognitive attitudes. The same holds true for affective attitudes, which is where emotionally involving messages come into play.

transformational ads   Ads that try to increase emotional involvement with the product or service.

One special type of emotional message is called **transformational advertising**.[115] The goal of a transformational ad is to associate the experience of using the product with a unique set of psychological characteristics. In other words, these ads try to increase emotional involvement by making the use of the product or service a warmer, more exciting, more pleasing, and richer experience (compare this type of ad with informational ads that present factual information). An ad for Reebok, for example, tried to provide deeper meaning and commitment to an individual's sneakers than would normally be the case by stating, "Nicolette Lyons: Over the last ten years she switched coasts, she switched hairdressers, she switched political parties. But she hasn't switched her sneakers." Diet Coke has tried to present itself as the "ultimate in cool" with the slogan "You are what you drink."[116]

dramas   Ads with characters, a plot and a story.

Dramas can also increase emotional involvement in a message. A drama message has characters, a plot, and a story about the use of the product or service.[117] It tends to appeal more to feelings to get the consumer to empathize with the characters and become involved emotionally. For example, over the years Tasters' Choice ran an involving, romantic ad miniseries about a couple who meet over a cup of coffee at a friend's house. Consumers eagerly anticipate each installment of the story.

Message Context The program or editorial context in which a message appears also affects the way it is evaluated. First, ads embedded in a happy TV program may be evaluated more positively than those in sad programs, especially if the ads are emotional.[118] Similarly, how well we like the program can affect our feeling about the ad and the brand.[119] One explanation is that the programs influence us to process information in a manner consistent with our mood. Or, according to the *excitation transfer hypothesis*, we feel the way we do about the ad because we mistakenly attribute to it our feelings about the TV program.[120]

One note of caution: A TV program can become too arousing and thus become distracting. In an interesting study that compared consumers' reactions to ads during the Super Bowl, ad responses in the winning city were inhibited in contrast to those in the losing and neutral cities.[121] Another study shows that placing ads in violent programs can inhibit processing and ad recall.[122]

SUMMARY

This chapter looked at the processes by which marketers can change consumers' attitudes when motivation, ability, and opportunity (MAO) are low and hence the effort consumers use to process information, make decisions, or engage in behavior is also low. The first part examined cognitive bases of attitudes and how marketing communications can be designed to enhance consumers' attitudes. When attitudes of low MAO consumers are based on cognitive processing, the message should affect their beliefs, which may be formed by simple inferences, attributions, or heuristics.

Marketers can also affect the salience, strength, or favorability of consumers' beliefs on which attitudes are based. Credibility of the source, information consistent with the offering category, a large number of message arguments, simple arguments, and the extent of repetition can influence one or more dimensions of beliefs.

According to the mere exposure effect, when effort (MAO) is low, consumers' attitudes toward an offering become more favorable as they become more familiar with it. Classical conditioning predicts that consumers' attitudes toward an offering (the conditioned stimulus) are enhanced when it is repeatedly paired with a stimulus (the unconditioned stimulus) that evokes a positive emotional response (the unconditioned response). This effect is most likely to occur when the unconditioned stimulus is novel, when the consumer is aware of the link, when the conditioned and unconditioned stimuli fit together, and when the conditioned stimulus precedes the conditioned one. Furthermore, if consumers like a particular ad (attitudes about the ad are called A_{ad}), these feelings may be transferred over to the brand (attitudes about the brand are called A_b). Consumers' moods and their tendency to evaluate the offering in accordance with their moods can also affect attitudes toward an offering.

Finally, attitudes based on affective processes can be made more favorable when consumers' motivation, ability, opportunity, and effort are low. Characteristics of the source (attractiveness, likability); the message (attractive pictures, pleasant music, humor, sex, emotionally involving messages); and the context (repetition, program or editorial context) can influence affective attitudes.

EXERCISES

1. Watch at least 4 hours of commercial television. Prepare a chart that lists all the techniques discussed in this chapter across the top as columns (attractive source, likable source, visuals, music, humor, sex, repetition, and so on). For

PART TWO The Psychological Core

172

each ad, tally which techniques are used. Also make a brief assessment of the effectiveness of each ad in terms of creating positive A_{ad} and A_b, attitudes about the ad and the brand. After collecting this information for all ads during the 4 hours, answer the following questions:

a. Which techniques are used most frequently?

b. In your judgment, which ads tend to be the most effective in influencing attitudes toward the ad and the brand? Why?

c. In your judgment, which ads tend to be the least effective? Why?

2. Collect examples of five types of magazines that are directed at different target audiences. Prepare a chart that lists all the techniques discussed in this chapter across the top as columns (attractive source, likable source, music, humor, sex, emotion, simple message, repetition, and so on). Down the side of this chart, generate a running list of different product and service categories that appear in each ad. For each ad in each magazine, make a tally of the type of product advertised and the type(s) of techniques used. Then answer the following questions:

a. Which techniques are used most frequently?

b. Do certain types of techniques tend to be used more often for certain product or service categories?

c. Do the magazines in general use certain techniques more often for certain target audiences?

CHAPTER 8

MEMORY AND RETRIEVAL

INTRODUCTION

These days, many marketers are trying to create positive attitudes for products by bringing back old brands, ads, logos, and songs. In fact, marketers have coined a term to describe such marketing efforts—"nostalgia marketing."

Old brands like the VW Bug, NECCO Wafers, Burma Shave, and Cracker Jack have recently been revitalized. Ads like the one in Exhibit 8.1 encourage baby boomers to remember when the VW Beetle was their car of choice—and to think about it as being even better now. Even old programs have come back, as illustrated by the success of the Nickelodeon channel. Old logos and brand symbols like Star-Kist's Charlie the Tuna and KFC's Colonel Saunders are reappearing on packaging. Old jingles like Diet Coke's "Just for the Taste of It" and Ace Hardware's "Ace Is the Place" are also making a comeback. And popular old songs are being used to market new products. Consider, for example, Levi's use of the Partridge family's "I Think I Love You" song, Senokot laxative's use of James Brown's song, "I Feel Good," and AT&T's use of Elton John's song "Rocket Man."[1] What's driving the popularity of nostalgia marketing? Some of the factors are related to concepts we discuss in this chapter.

EXHIBIT 8.1
Nostalgia Marketing

Many marketers today are bringing back products of our youth
that stimulate memories of a
more pleasant time.

Source: Courtesy of Volkswagen
of America and Arnold
Communications.

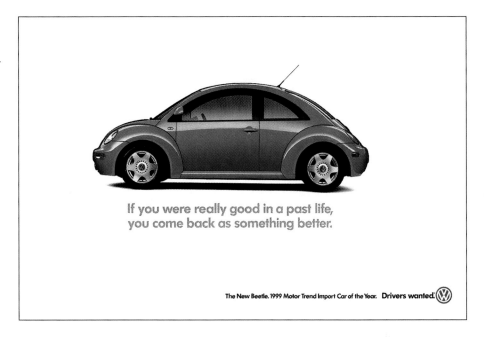

If you were really good in a past life,
you come back as something better.

The New Beetle. 1999 Motor Trend Import Car of the Year. **Drivers wanted.** VW

First, consumers in today's fast-paced, information-intensive age are feeling overwhelmed by the new and unfamiliar, which leaves them more receptive to familiar products, songs, and images. Reminders of familiar offerings can also enhance brand awareness and brand knowledge because consumers already have a rich storehouse of personal experiences associated with these offerings in memory. Many of these memories reflect a quieter, more peaceful time. Hearing the name of an old product or seeing an old ad or hearing an old jingle reminds consumers of their positive feelings about this earlier time and makes them feel good.

WHAT IS MEMORY?

consumer memory A personal storehouse of knowledge
about products and services,
shopping, and consumption
experiences.

retrieval The process of
remembering.

Consumer memory is a vast personal storehouse of knowledge about products, services, shopping excursions, and consumption experiences. In essence, memory reflects our prior knowledge. **Retrieval** is the process of remembering, or access-ing, what we have stored in memory.

We can store and remember information such as what brands or services we have used in the past; features of these products or services; how, where, when, and why we bought them; their price; how, where, when, and why we used them; and whether or not we liked them. We can store and remember information about old products we have disposed of, such as a favorite car we sold. We also have memo-ries of special experiences, for example, a sporting event we attended with friends. The information we store and can retrieve is learned from many sources—mar-keters, the media, word of mouth, and personal experience.

Our memory and ability to retrieve information depends at least in part on our motivation, ability, and opportunity to process the information to which we have been exposed. Our ability to carry out day-to-day activities clearly depends on our being able to put new information into our memory and retrieve old information

EXHIBIT 8.2
The Value of Memory

We value our memory so highly, we may be willing to take vitamins or supplements that claim to improve our memory.

Source: Courtesy of Natural Balance.

when we need it. Indeed, because we place a high value on the ability to remember, products like ginko biloba and the product depicted in Exhibit 8.2, as well as services like memory improvement seminars, are very popular.

Knowledge, Attitudes, and Memory

We began to discuss certain aspects of memory and retrieval in the previous three chapters. Chapter 5 noted that information stored in memory affects whether and how we interpret and categorize objects. Chapters 6 and 7 indicated that attitudes are part of our memory—they represent stored summary evaluations of objects. Moreover, attitudes can be and often are recalled when we make decisions. Thus, as shown in Exhibit 8.3, memory and retrieval are affected by attention, categorization, and comprehension and by attitude formation processes.

Memory, Retrieval, and Decision Making

How do memory and retrieval influence the way we act and the decisions we make? If you need toothpaste, you might simply remember the brand you bought last time and buy it again the next time you go shopping. You may decide to buy season tickets to a sporting event because you can vividly remember what a good time you had when you went with your friends. You may decide not to go to a certain restaurant because you remember the bad service from your last visit.

We often receive information about an offering at one time and use that information to make purchase, usage, or disposition decisions at another time. Memory and retrieval are the factors that make this two-stage process possible.

WHAT ARE THE TYPES OF MEMORY?

Memory represents more than the prior knowledge we discussed in Chapter 5. Exhibit 8.3 shows three types of memory: sensory memory (iconic and echoic memory), short-term memory (imagery and discursive processing), and long-term memory (autobiographical and semantic memory). Let us look at how we use each of these.

Sensory Memory

Assume for a minute that you are talking to someone at a party. You happen to overhear something being said a few tables away about a new movie you want to see. You do not want to appear rude, so you try to pay full attention to your dinner partner, but you really want to hear what the other people are saying about the movie. Even though you cannot listen to both conversations simultaneously, you can store, for a relatively short duration, bits and pieces of the other conversation. For example, you might be listening to your dinner partner but switch your attention to the other conversation once you hear the word *fabulous*. As another example, assume that you are doing your homework in front of the TV. Your roommate

EXHIBIT 8.3
Chapter Overview:
Memory and Retrieval

We can identify three types of memory: sensory memory, short-term memory (STM), and long-term memory (LTM). Once information is in memory, it can then be retrieved (recognized or recalled). This chapter shows (1) what influences the transfer of information from STM to LTM and (2) what affects the likelihood that information will be retrieved from memory.

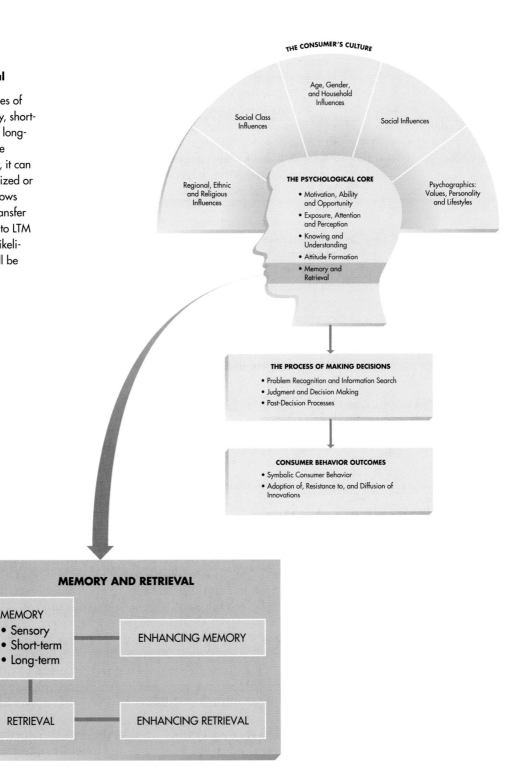

comes in and says, "That's a great commercial." Even though you have not been listening, right after your roommate makes this statement, you realize that you heard the words *Diet Coke*. You realize it is a Diet Coke commercial, and you say, "Yeah, I really like that one."

The ability to store sensory experiences temporarily as they are produced is called **sensory memory,** and it uses a short-term storage area called the sensory store. Sensory memory operates automatically, and if we quickly switch our attention to our sensory store, we may be able to interpret what is in it. If we do not analyze this information right away, however, it disappears from the sensory store, and we cannot determine its meaning.

sensory memory Sensory experiences stored temporarily in memory.

Echoic and Iconic Memory   The sensory store can house information from any of the senses, but **echoic memory**—memory of things we hear—and **iconic memory**—sensory memory of things we see—are the most commonly studied.[2] The preceding example illustrates echoic memory. Here is another example. You may have found that when someone asks you a question and you are not really listening, you can say, "What did you say?" and actually "play back" what the person said. Iconic memory is at work when we drive by a sign and see it quickly, only to realize after we pass that it was a sign for McDonald's.

echoic memory Very brief memory for things we hear.

iconic memory Very brief memory for things we see.

Characteristics of Sensory Memory   Information in sensory memory is stored in its actual sensory form. In other words, we store *fabulous* as it sounds, and we store it exactly, not as a synonym. Information in sensory memory is also short-lived, generally lasting from a quarter of a second to several seconds.[3] If it is relevant, we will be motivated to process it further, and it may enter what is called short-term memory. If we do not analyze that information, it is lost.

Short-Term Memory

Short-term memory (STM) is the portion of memory where we encode or interpret incoming information in light of existing knowledge.[4] The processes of knowing and understanding discussed in Chapter 5 occur in short-term memory. As you read this book, you are using your short-term memory to comprehend what you read. You also use short-term memory when you watch an ad on TV or make a decision in a store. Thus short-term memory is very important because it is where most of our information processing takes place.

short-term memory (STM) The portion of memory where incoming information is encoded or interpreted in light of existing knowledge.

Imagery and Discursive Processing   The information in short-term memory can take one of several forms. When we think about an object, for example, an apple, we might use **discursive processing** and represent it by the word *apple*. Alternatively, we could represent it visually, as a picture of an apple, or in terms of its smell, its feel, what it sounds like when we bite into it, or what it tastes like. Representing the visual, auditory, tactile, gustatory, and/or olfactory properties of an apple uses **imagery processing.**[5] Unlike the case of discursive processing, an object in imagery processing bears a close resemblance to the thing being represented.[6] Thus if you were asked to describe an apple and a car, imagery processing would ensure that you preserve their relative sizes.

discursive processing The processing of information as words.

imagery processing The processing of information in sensory form.

For both imagery and discursive processing, information in short-term memory also varies in how much we elaborate on it.[7] When motivation, ability, and opportunity are low, short-term memory might consist of a simple reproduction of a stimulus, for example, the word *skier* or a picture of a skier. If motivation, ability, and opportunity are high, however, consumers can use elaborated imagery processing to engage in daydreams, fantasies, and visual problem solving, or elaborated discursive processing to think about upcoming events or work out solutions to current problems. For example, if you are thinking about a skiing vacation, you may develop an elaborate fantasy that involves lounging around the fireplace at a resort hotel; drinking hot mulled cider; and feeling the ache of your tired muscles, the windburn on your face, and the enjoyment of being with your vacation companion. You might also use discursive processing to compare the prices and attributes of various hotels. As you might expect, this information, whether represented as images or words, can serve as an important input for decisions.

Characteristics of Short-Term Memory   Short-term memory also has some interesting characteristics.

Short-Term Memory Is Limited   We can hold only a certain number of things in short-term memory at any one time. For example, suppose you have to go into the store right now and buy two items: chips and hot dogs. Chances are, you can do this task pretty well and will have little trouble remembering what to buy. But suppose you have to buy nine items: chips, hot dogs, coffee, cookies, baking soda, plastic wrap, toothpaste, spaghetti sauce, and dog food. Chances are high that you will forget one or more of these items unless you make a shopping list.

Short-Term Memory Is Short-Lived   The information held in short-term memory is very short-lived unless that information is transferred to long-term memory. Unless we actively try to remember information, it will be lost. This factor explains why we sometimes learn someone's name or the title of a new movie only to forget it 2 minutes later.

MARKETING IMPLICATIONS

Short-term memory and particularly imagery processing has many interesting implications for marketers.

Imagery Can Create Liking for the Product.   First, imagery processing is used often and affects how we behave. We value some of the products we buy (for example, novels or music) because of the imagery they provide.[8] Thus a product's ability to stimulate multisensory imagery might affect how much we like that product. We may, for example, like novels that are so descriptive that we can actually imagine sights, sounds, smells, and gustatory experiences happening to the characters in the book.

Imagery Can Stimulate Memories of Past Experiences.   Second, we value some products or promotional tools because they promote imagery that allows us to vicariously experience a past consumption experience. For example, we might keep a sports program or ticket stub because the imagery it evokes allow us to relive the event.

Imagery Affects Evaluation.   Third, the use of imagery can affect the way we evaluate products. We may be able to process a lot of information about something when using imagery processing simply because more information helps to flesh out the image. You might have a really good idea of whether you would like to stay at a particular hotel, for example, if you can imagine what the room looks like. Adding more information when using discursive processing, however, may lead to information overload.

Imagery Affects Satisfaction.   Finally, imagery may affect how satisfied we are with a product or consumption experience. We may create an elaborate image or fantasy of just what the product or consumption experience will be like (how great we will look in a new car or how relaxing a vacation might be) only to find that it does not materialize as we had imagined. In this case reality disconfirms our expectations, and we may feel dissatisfied. The ad in Exhibit 8.4, for example, may stimulate imagery of the fragrant aroma of tropical flowers. If the product does not live up to the outcomes customers imagine, they may be dissatisfied. ■

Long-Term Memory

Long-term memory (LTM) is that part of memory where information is permanently stored for later use. Research in cognitive psychology has identified two major types of long-term memory: autobiographical and semantic memory.[9]

Autobiographical Memory   Autobiographical or episodic memory represents knowledge we have about ourselves and our past.[10] It includes past experiences as well as emotions and sensations tied to these experiences. These memories also tend to be primarily sensory. Although most involve visual images, they may also include sounds, smells, tastes, and tactile sensations. In a consumer context, we may have autobiographical memories that relate to acquisition, such as buying a specific product or making a specific shopping trip. We may have autobiographical memories regarding consumption or disposition such as attending a particular concert or throwing away a well-worn but loved product. The ad in Exhibit 8.5 shows how autobiographical memory can be used in advertising.

Because each individual has a unique set of experiences, autobiographical memory tends to be very personal and idiosyncratic. If you were asked to remember the road test you took when you got your driver's license, you might have stored in long-term memory the sequence of events that occurred on that day: what car you drove, what your route was, how nervous you were, what your instructor told you to do, what happened after you passed (or failed!).

Semantic Memory   A lot of what we have stored in memory is not related to specific experiences. For example, we have memory for the concept called "dog". We know that dogs have four legs, are furry, wag their tails, and so on. This knowledge

EXHIBIT 8.4
Stimulating Imagery Processing

This ad may help consumers imagine the fragrance of tropical flowers. These images may affect consumers' expectations for the product—they will be satisfied with the product if it smells as fragrant as they imagine.

Source: © The Procter & Gamble Company. Used by permission.

Fresh from the Tropics.

TROPICAL BLOOM
FLORES TROPICALES

Downy Care

Luxuriate in the lush, exotic scent of Tropical Bloom Downy.

INTRODUCING THE GODIVA OF COOKIES.

They make other cookies seem like child's play. Five blissful biscuits. All lavished with chocolate.
Each one irresistible in its own unique way. At Godiva boutiques or finer department stores. Stop in or call 1-800-9-GODIVA for store locations.
Or visit us at www.GODIVA.com. Or Godiva@AOL.

New York   Paris   GODIVA BISCUITS   Tokyo   Brussels

EXHIBIT 8.5
Autobiographical Memory

Although the old-fashioned milk bottle and cookies may remind consumers of childhood—cozy or simpler times—the crystal glass and the lace-edged napkin also allow them to think of milk and Godiva cookies as an adult and elegant snack.

Source: Paul Aresu Photographer.

semantic memory
Knowledge about an entity that is detached from specific episodes.

is true of all dogs and is not tied to any dog in particular. Knowledge about the world that is detached from specific episodes is called **semantic memory.**

MARKETING IMPLICATIONS   Much of the knowledge we have stored in cognitive categories reflects semantic memory. Thus many of the marketing implications we presented about knowledge stored in categories also relate to semantic memory. Autobiographical memory, however, is also important to marketers.

Affecting Decision Making. Each consumer has a large storehouse of consumer-related experiences whose affective associations can influence the way products and services are evaluated. For example, if you ate at a particular restaurant and found a hair in your food, the memory of this experience might prevent you from eating there again. Positive experiences would have the opposite effect. When selecting a restaurant, you might recall a previous episode in which the food was fabulous or the ambiance romantic. These memories would clearly affect your future choices.

Promoting Empathy and Identification. Autobiographical memories can also play a role in creating identification with characters in ads. For example, if advertisements for Hefty trash bags can make consumers think about incidents in which garbage bags they used split open, consumers may be better able to relate to and empathize with an advertisement that shows inferior bags splitting apart while Hefty bags remain strong.

Cueing and Preserving Autobiographical Memories. As the introduction to this chapter suggested, consumers value some products because they promote autobiographical memories by stimulating feelings of nostalgia—a fondness for the past.[11] Consumers often find it important to preserve memories of graduations, weddings, birth of a child, and so on. Entire industries for products such as film, cameras, video cameras and diaries focus on consumers' desires to document these autobiographical memories. For example, consider that the scrapbook industry was a $200 million industry in 1997.[12] Consumers in many cultures want to preserve autobiographical memories.[13] Consumers who have moved to North America from other countries like India often build shrines in their houses to remind them of the culture they left behind. In the Niger Republic, consumers highly value possessions that remind them of their friends, family, and important events in their lives.

Reinterpreting Memories. Some interesting research has shown that advertising can even affect consumers' autobiographical memories. One study had consumers taste various good- and bad-tasting orange juice and then watch ads that described the product's good taste. Those exposed to the ads remembered the juice as being better tasting than it actually was.[14] ■

HOW MEMORY IS ENHANCED

Because attention and memory are always associated, many of the same factors affect them both. Several additional processes, called chunking, rehearsal, recirculation, and elaboration also affect memory.[15] As Exhibit 8.3 shows, these processes are useful for influencing short-term memory or for increasing the likelihood that information will be transferred to long-term memory. Each process has some useful implications for marketers.

Chunking

Traditionally, researchers have believed that the most individuals can process in short-term memory at any one time is three to seven "chunks" of information. More recent research suggests that the number may be closer to three or four.[16] A **chunk** is a group of items that is processed as a unit. For example, phone numbers are typically grouped into three chunks (621-977-4059).

Because we can only process three to four chunks at any one time, marketers can increase the likelihood that consumers will be able to hold information in short-term memory and thus transfer it to long-term memory by providing larger bits of information that chunk smaller bits together. For example, acronyms reduce several pieces of information to one chunk. Brand names like IBM and KFC and the name of the ad agency DMB & B are examples of chunking in a marketing context. Similarly, marketers can facilitate consumers' memory for telephone numbers by providing words rather than individual numbers or digits (1-800-CAL-HOME, 1-800-I-SEE-2020 or 1-800-GO-U-HAUL). Advertisements might draw conclusions that summarize or chunk disparate pieces of information into a single attribute or benefit. For example, an ad that discusses a brand's calorie, fat, sodium, and sugar content might chunk this information into a conclusion about the brand's healthfulness.

Rehearsal

Whereas chunking increases the likelihood that information will not be lost from short-term memory, rehearsal affects the transfer of information to long-term memory. **Rehearsal** simply means that we actively and consciously interact with the material we are trying to remember. We can either silently repeat the material or actively think about the information and its meaning. The process is analogous to studying for an exam.

In marketing contexts, rehearsal is likely to occur only when consumers are motivated to process and remember information. If you are motivated to find the best car on the market, you might study the characteristics of various models so that you do not forget them.

When motivation is low, marketers may use tactics to enhance motivation and perpetuate rehearsal. McDonald's has revived an old campaign that challenged consumers to remember the contents of a Big Mac: "Two all-beef patties, special sauce, lettuce, cheese, pickles, onions on a sesame seed bun." This challenge has been so successful in generating rehearsal that many consumers can still remember the list. Engaging jingles and slogans may be useful means of inducing rehearsal. Sometimes they work too well, as we all know from going through the day singing a commercial's jingle.

Recirculation

Information can also be transferred into long-term memory through the process of **recirculation.** Water is recirculated when it goes through the same pipe again and again. In the same way, information is recirculated through your short-term memory when you encounter it repeatedly. Unlike the case with rehearsal, with recirculation we make no active attempt to remember the information. Rather, if

THERE IS ONLY ONE!

Excedrin® MIGRAINE is now the #1 doctor-recommended brand*
for the relief of migraine pain.

Excedrin MIGRAINE
#1 Doctor Recommended

(use only as directed for mild to
moderate migraine headache pain)
* nonprescription
©1999 Bristol-Myers Squibb Co.

HEADACHE RESOURCE CENTER
1•800•608•8184
www.excedrin.com

EXHIBIT 8.6
Recirculation

This ad illustrates the principle of
recirculation, as the brand name
is repeated mulitple times within
the single ad.

Source: Courtesy of Bristol-Myers
Squibb.

we do remember, it is simply because the information has passed through our brain so many times. For example, you can probably recall the names of the streets adjacent to yours or the name of a market near your house—even if you have never gone down these streets, been to the store, or tried to memorize them. Why do you recall them? Simply because you have probably seen them every day.

Recirculation is an important principle for marketing because it explains why repetition of marketing communications can affect memory, particularly in low-involvement situations.[17] Marketers can strengthen the effect of recirculation by creating different ads that repeat the same basic message. To illustrate, the slogan "Be Young. Have Fun. Drink Pepsi" is likely to be memorable because you have been exposed to it on many occasions, and the ad delivering the message has changed over time. Recirculation may also explain why communications that repeat the brand name frequently, either within an ad or across communications, tend to produce better memory for the brand name. Recirculation may also be at work if we remember the brand name in Exhibit 8.6.

Elaboration

Finally, information can be transferred into long-term memory if it is processed at deeper levels, or elaborated.[18] We can try to remember information through rote memorization or rehearsal; however, this type of processing is not always effective. If you have ever memorized material for an exam, you probably noticed that you have forgotten most of what you learned 2 or 3 days later. More enduring memory is established when we try to relate information to prior knowledge and past experiences. For example, if we see an ad for a new product, we might elaborate on the ad information by trying to think about how to use the product in our day-to-day lives. By elaborating on the message in this way, we may have a better memory for the brand and what was said about it.

Several strategies familiar from previous chapters enhance the likelihood that consumers will elaborate on information. For example, unexpected or novel stimuli can attract attention and induce elaboration.[19] The makers of Glad trash bags used this principle when they developed an ad featuring actor Robert Mitchum. The 77-year-old actor was an unlikely spokesperson for trash bags—and the incongruity between the product and the actor helped raised consumer memory for Glad bags.[20] Elaboration may explain why children and the elderly tend to remember less from marketing communications than do other age groups. The elderly may have less ability to elaborate on information, perhaps because their short-term memory is more limited. Children may elaborate less because they have less knowledge, which in turn makes it more difficult for them to think extensively about a message.[21]

ORGANIZATION OF LONG-TERM MEMORY

What does long-term memory look like? How is the information in it organized? In Chapter 5 we saw that our knowledge is organized into categories and linked to associations. Here, we show how these associations relate to the concepts of memory and retrieval. Memory researchers have also attempted to represent long-term memory, or prior knowledge, in a somewhat different way called a **semantic or associative network**.

Consider the information shown in Exhibit 8.7 and imagine that it represents one consumer's memory or prior knowledge about the category called vacations. In fact, this example depicts the associations the consumer has to Vail ski vacation, a member of the category ski vacations. The ski vacations category, in turn, is part of the higher-order category luxury vacations. A set of links—what we called associations and beliefs in previous chapters—is connected to the concept Vail ski vacation. How did these links get there? They were learned and remembered based on personal experiences or information the consumer heard or read. Some of these links represent autobiographic memories. Others represent semantic memory. This entire network of associations or links connected to the concept of Vail ski vacation is called a semantic (or associative) network. Some researchers think about long-term memory as a series of semantic networks.

Exhibit 8.7 shows something else very important to the concept of long-term memory. Notice that the links in the semantic network vary in strength. Strong links, depicted by the thick lines, are firmly established in memory. Others, depicted by the thin lines, are weakly established in memory. Why are some links strong and others weak? The reason is that some have been rehearsed, recirculated, chunked, and elaborated extensively, making them strong. Others have been

semantic (or associative) network A set of associations in memory that are linked to a concept.

EXHIBIT 8.7
A Semantic (or Associative) Network

A semantic network is a set of concepts connected by links. The links may activate certain concepts when other concepts are activated. Concepts connected by strong links are more likely to activate each other than those connected by weak links.

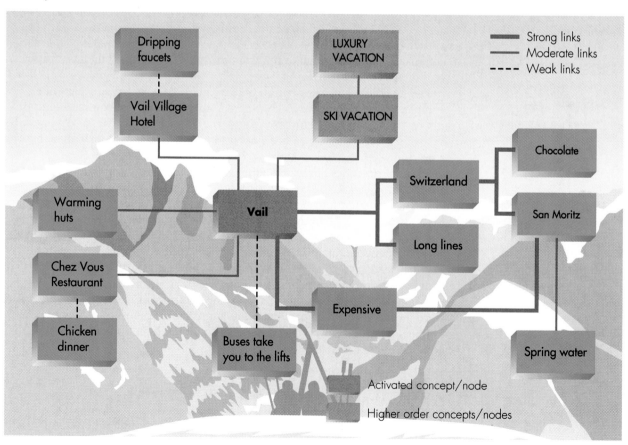

encountered infrequently, have not been accessed in a long time, or have been processed on a very limited basis. Thus their establishment in memory is very weak.

The entire semantic network represents what is available in this consumers' memory about the concept called Vail ski vacation. As you will see in the next section, the semantic network and the strength of the links in memory are very important for the process of retrieval.

WHAT IS RETRIEVAL?

Retrieval is simply the process of remembering. When we retrieve information from memory, we access it from a semantic (or associative) network like the one in Exhibit 8.7.

The Semantic Network

We may have a considerable amount of information available in our memory but be able to retrieve or access only some if it at any given time.[22] We have all been in situations in which we are trying to remember something but cannot. What is it about the semantic network that affects what we remember?[23]

trace strength The extent to which an association (or link) is strongly or weakly linked to a concept in memory.

accessibility The likelihood that an item will be retrieved from long-term memory.

Trace Strength One factor is the strength of the links or associations. Memory researchers call this factor **trace strength.** The stronger the link that connects information to the product, the more **accessible** the information is. You are more likely to remember that BMW is "the ultimate driving machine" if you have a strong association connecting the car with its slogan. Marketers often try to strengthen our memory links. For example, Chrysler found that consumers had a favorable association between the Chrysler name and *trucks.* However, the link between Chrysler and *great cars* was much weaker. As a result, the firm developed a new advertising campaign, "Greater Cars, Great Trucks," designed to strengthen the linkage between Chrysler and great cars.[24] The more marketers can engage in recirculation, or encourage consumers to rehearse or elaborate on information, the greater the likelihood that the link will be strengthened, and the greater the item's accessibility.

Spreading of Activation A second factor explaining what gets retrieved from memory is called spreading of activation. Think of a semantic network as a kind of electric network. Strong links have the potential for generating high-voltage current—weak links the potential for generating low-voltage current. Using the example in Exhibit 8.7, if a concept like Vail is activated in the consumer's semantic network, the strong link between "Vail" and "expensive" will activate or make accessible "expensive." Because the current connecting Vail and expensive is very strong, the electrical potential from this current will spread to adjacent items in the semantic network, particularly along those links that are strong. This spreading of activation will likely lead our consumer also to remember San Moritz. The activation of the concept "Vail" may also activate "Switzerland" and "long lines." Activation from "Switzerland" may, in turn, spread to the concept "chocolate."

Of course, concepts like Switzerland, chocolate, and expensive are linked to many semantic networks, not just to one. Our consumer may think about chocolate when prompted to think about Vail, but chocolate may be linked to other semantic networks that can be cued through spreading of activation. Our consumer may start thinking that last time she bought chocolate she bought it at Godiva, which may, in turn, make her remember that she saw a friend of hers at the store. Spreading of activation can thus explain why we sometimes have what seem to be random thoughts. Activation is spreading from one semantic network to another.

Motivation, ability, and opportunity affect spreading of activation. If motivation and opportunity to process information is high, the number of activated links can also be quite high. On the other hand, when motivation or opportuntiy to process are low, only the closest and strongest links might be activated. Individuals with more knowledge about a concept will have a greater ability to process and a more detailed semantic network, bringing forth any number of associations.[25]

priming Activation of a node in memory, often without conscious awareness.

Because strong links enhance an item's accessibility from memory, they are very important to marketers. Does this mean that weak links are unimportant? Not really. Activation spreads to every link in the semantic network, although the activation may not be sufficient to cause consumers to remember an item. A concept that has been activated but not sufficiently to make it retrievable from memory is said to have been **primed.** It has been given a jump start. Suppose our consumer was trying to remember how she got to the lifts. The link *buses* is very weakly established in memory. Activating Vail might prime the bus concept, but the activation is too weak for the consumer to remember the bus. If the consumer later drives by a school, the activation of school might cue buses, and this activation might be sufficient for her to remember that she got to the ski lift in Vail by taking a bus.

Retrieval Failures

Trace strength and spreading of activation are also useful in explaining forgetting—the failure to retrieve information from memory. Forgetting is a fact of life. We can forget to get our car serviced, forget that we are cooking hard-boiled eggs (until they explode), or forget that we had promised a friend a novel that we have already thrown out. Retrieval failures clearly affect our buying, using, and disposition behaviors.

decay The weakening of nodes or links over time.

Decay Forgetting is partially explained by the trace strength concept. In some cases, we forget things because trace strength fades; that is, memory links **decay** over time, often because they are not used. Thus we tend to forget events from childhood because they happened so long ago. The likelihood of decay is reduced when we are repeatedly exposed to information through recirculation or when we retrieve it often from memory.

Sometimes the details or attributes of the information we have learned decay.[26] For example, we might have heard a lot of detailed information about a new movie, such as what the plot was about, who starred in it, and how film critics described its cinematography. But later we may only remember something general about it ("I've heard it was good").

Forgetting of attributes explains some interesting marketing phenomena. For example, consumers may have equally strong memories for brands about which they have heard either very bad or very good things. They forget the information stated about the brands; all they remember is that they were in the news. Forgetting also explains the sleeper effect, discussed in Chapter 6, in which consumers show more positive attitudes toward a bad ad as time passes. Researchers believe that over time, consumers forget that an ad lacked credibility. Instead, they simply remember what the source said about the brand. In essence, memory for the source decays more rapidly than memory for the message.[27]

interference That which causes us not to remember which features go with which brand or concept due to semantic networks being too closely aligned.

primacy effect The tendency to show greater memory for information that comes first in a sequence.

recency effect The tendency to show greater memory for information that comes last in a sequence.

Interference Spreading of activation and trace strength explain a second cause of forgetting—interference.[28] **Interference** happens when semantic networks are so closely aligned that we cannot remember which features go with which brand or concept. Suppose you are watching a car ad that indicates how safe the car is. If you have a lot of information about similar cars stored in memory, you might confuse which attribute is associated with which car.

Interference also happens when one concept is activated so frequently that we cannot activate a different one. Suppose you are trying to recall all 50 states or the items that you have written down on your grocery list. Chances are you can recall several items very easily and a few more with some difficulty, but the last ones are impossible to remember. The reason is that in trying to remember the missing items, you keep remembering the items you have already recalled, and this act interferes with your ability to activate the missing ones.[29] Because the memory trace for the items you have remembered gets activated repeatedly, activation of the other items is inhibited.

Primacy and Recency Effects Decay and interference can be used to explain **primacy** and **recency effects**—that is, the fact that things we encountered first or last in a sequence are often most easily remembered. As an example of primacy effects, you are likely to remember the first ad you saw during a commercial break because there was no advertising information to interfere with it. That information may also be less likely to decay if we rehearse it. The primacy effect explains why when we study for an exam, we tend to remember best the material we studied first.

As an example of recency effects, you are more likely to remember what you ate for breakfast this morning than what you ate a week ago because (1) this morning's information has not yet decayed, and (2) there is much less information interfering with the retrieval of this information. The primacy and recency effects suggest to advertisers that the best placement for an ad is either first or last in a commercial sequence. Some research supports the importance of being first; evidence in support of being last is not as strong.[30]

Retrieval Errors

The things we do remember are not always accurate or complete; our memory may be subject to distortion or confusion. You might remember that your friend told you about a great new movie, but it was really your neighbor who told you about it. In addition, memory may be selective, meaning that we retrieve only some information, often either very positive or very negative. In anticipating a vacation, we may remember the good things that happened on our last vacation, but not the bad things. Finally, memory may be distorted. If we had a bad experience with a product, we may later remember experiences that were bad but that did not actually happen. For example, we may remember that a waitress who treated us badly at a restaurant clunked our coffee down loudly on the table. While this "memory" is consistent with the "bad waitress" experience, it might not have actually happened.[31]

WHAT ARE THE TYPES OF RETRIEVAL?

Information can be retrieved through two different retrieval systems: explicit and explicit memory.

Explicit Memory

explicit memory Memory for some prior episode achieved by active attempts to remember.

Explicit memory is memory for some prior episode achieved by active attempts to remember it. Explicit memory is revealed when we can consciously remember something that has happened in the past. For example, if we remember something about our last trip to Vail, or the last time we went to McDonald's, we are using explicit memory. We can try to retrieve information from explicit memory by either recalling it or recognizing it.

recognition The process of determining whether a stimulus has or has not been encountered before.

Recognition   Recognition occurs when we can simply identify something we have seen before. Two important types of recognition in marketing are brand recognition (we remember having seen the brand before) and ad recognition (we remember having seen the ad before). Brand recognition is particularly important for in-store decisions because it helps us identify or locate the brands we want to buy. Logos on brands or packages may be particularly important in enhancing brand recognition. For example, we might immediately recognize a product as Green Giant beans by the picture of the giant on the package.

recall The ability to retrieve information from memory.

Recall   In contrast, **recall** involves a more extensive activation of the links in memory. Thus when we see a Coke display, we use recall to retrieve knowledge about Coke that we use as input to our decision-making process.

There are two ways in which we can recall something. *Free recall* exists when we can retrieve something from memory without any help, such as what we had for dinner last night. *Cued recall* exists if we are asked the same question but need a cue: Was it a vegetarian dish?

Implicit Memory

implicit memory Memory for things without any conscious attempt at remembering them.

Sometimes we remember things without conscious awareness. This phenomenon is called **implicit memory.** Suppose you were driving down the highway very fast and you went by a billboard with the word *Caterpillar* (tractors) on it. Later we ask you whether you remember seeing a billboard, and if so, what it was for. You do not remember seeing a billboard, let alone what it was for; thus you have no explicit memory for it. But if we ask you to come up with the first word you can think of that begins with *cat-*, you might answer *caterpillar*. You must have encoded something about the billboard, and hence you must have some information about Caterpillar in prior memory.

How can we have implicit memory of something we cannot explicitly remember? In part, the answer relates to priming, discussed earlier. Your brief exposure to the Caterpillar name activated or primed it in your memory. Even though the activation level was not sufficient for the name to be consciously retrieved, thanks to activation, when you are searching for words that begin with *cat-*, *caterpillar* comes to mind.

MARKETING IMPLICATIONS

www.

Retrieval is vitally important to marketers.

Retrieval as a Communication Objective.   The objective of marketing communications is often to increase retrieval of the brand name, product attribute, or brand benefit.[32] In other cases, the objective of a communication might be to increase consumers' recognition of the brand name, logo or brand symbol, package, advertisement, ad character, brand benefit, and so on. Currently, companies like Lucent Technologies, iVillage.com, and e*trade are working hard to increase consumers' awareness of their brand name in the United States. Acer, Compaq, and Packard Bell are trying to enhance brand name awareness of their products in China. Kraft is trying to boost consumer awareness of the range of products it offers.[33]

Retrieval affects consumer choices. One study found that Japanese consumers' use of a bank declined as their recognition of the name of the bank declined.[34] Getting consumers to recognize or recall specific claims or slogans is also critical. Furthermore, knowing and remembering this information may serve as useful input to consumers' attitudes, and consumers may invoke this information when they are making choices among brands.

Marketers sometimes measure recall of commercials as a way of testing retrieval. Exhibit 8.8 shows a report from a company that assesses consumers' recall of commercials. Consumers were shown a commercial on TV and then queried 24 hours later about what they remembered. This particular page shows cued recall. The percentages in the Exhibit 8.8 show how many people remembered the tested ad.

EXHIBIT 8.8
Recall Results for a 30-Second Commercial

Some marketing research companies test the effectiveness of TV commercials by whether consumers can recall them 24 hours after they are aired. This company measures the percentage of program viewers who can recall the commercial if given the name of the product or brand. Recall by various demographic groups is provided.

Source: Haskings, Jack and Kendrick, Alice, *Successful Advertising Research Methods.* Copyright © 1997 by NTC Business Books. Used with permission.

IN-VIEW

COMMERCIAL	30" GTE CORPORATION, "DESERT CC"	
	PROVED COMMERCIAL REGISTRATION*	
	BASE	PCR%
Total Sample, Men	(142)	46
By income (excl. DK/NA/Ref)		
Under $30,000	(71)	44
Over $30,000	(52)	46
By age (excl. DK/NA/Ref)		
18–34	(98)	46
35–49	(44)	46
Total Sample, Women	(165)	50
By income (excl. DK/NA/Ref)		
Under $30,000	(87)	46
Over $30,000	(57)	56
By age (excl. DK/NA/Ref)		
18–34	(84)	50
35–49	(79)	51

30" PCR NORMS	MEN	WOMEN
All commercials	29	33
All corporate	27	32
18–34	28	33
35–49	26	31

* Proved Commercial Registration (PCR) is defined as the percent of qualified viewers of the program who, given the brand name/product, can recall and accurately describe the commercial on the day following the telecast.

	PITTSBURGH	MINNEAPOLIS	SAN DIEGO
Date	6/18	6/19	6/18
Program	Barnaby Jones	S.W.A.T.	Quincy
Time	8:18	7:14	8:15

The value to marketers of recognition or recall depends, in part, on how consumers typically buy the product. If they typically go through an aisle and look for the brand they usually buy, purchase is based on recognition. Hence recognition of the brand name, package, and logo is important. In other cases, product purchase is based on recall. For example, if you are thinking about where you might go for lunch today, the list of places you will actually consider is likely to depend on which you can recall from memory.

Implicit memory is also important to marketers. Although ad agencies typically measure consumers' explicit memory by what they recall and recognize from an ad, the concept of implicit memory suggests that consumer may have some memory of the information conveyed in advertising even if they do not recognize or cannot recall it. Thus advertisers may try to use measures of implicit memory to gauge whether their ads have affected consumers' memory.

Consumer Segments and Memory.   Unfortunately, although retrieval is an important objective for marketers, not all consumers can remember things equally well. In particular, elderly consumers have been found to have a harder time recognizing and remembering brand names and ad claims. Interestingly, some research has found that elderly consumers' memory for information from advertising can be improved if they form a mental image of things in the ad, like the claims it makes. Imagery apparently makes for a greater number of associations in memory, which, in turn, enhances retrieval.[35] ■

HOW RETRIEVAL IS ENHANCED

Given the importance of retrieval, marketers need to understand how they can enhance the likelihood that consumers will remember something about specific brands. Factors that increase the likelihood that an item will be stored in long-term memory, like chunking and rehearsal, also affect the likelihood that the information will be retrieved because something cannot be recognized or recalled unless it is first stored. However, several additional factors affect retrieval. As shown in Exhibit 8.3, these factors are related to (1) the stimulus itself, (2) what it is linked to, (3) the way it is processed, and (4) the characteristics of consumers. Many of these factors also relate to the concepts of trace strength and spreading of activation.

Characteristics of the Stimulus

Retrieval is affected by the salience (prominence) of the stimulus (the message or message medium). It is also affected by the extent to which the item is a prototypical member of a category, whether it uses redundant cues, and the medium that is used to convey information.

Salience   Something is salient if it stands out from the larger context in which it is placed because it is bright, big, complex, moving, or prominent in its environment.[36] If you saw a really long commercial or a multipage ad, it might be salient relative to the short commercials or single-page ads that surround it. A visually complex figure in an ad will be salient relative to a simple background, and a moving billboard will be salient relative to the traditional stationary ones.

The salience of a stimulus affects retrieval in several ways. For one thing, salient objects tend to attract attention to themselves, drawing attention away from things that are not salient. Because they are prominent, salient stimuli also induce greater elaboration, thereby creating stronger memory traces.[37] This might

EXHIBIT 8.9
Salience

The large type in this ad is visually prominent (salient), and the meaning of the words is also likely to attract attention.

Source: Reprinted with permission from Visa U.S.A. Inc.

retrieval cue Stimulus that facilitates a node's activation in memory.

explain why some research has shown that consumers tend to remember longer commercials better than shorter ones and bigger print ads better than smaller ones. Their length or size makes them salient.[38] The information in Exhibit 8.9 is likely to be salient because the words *Go Naked to the Mall* are set in large type and convey a message that is also likely to attract attention.

Prototypicality We are better able to recognize and recall prototypical or pioneer brands in a product category (see Chapter 5 for a discussion of prototypicality). Because they have been rehearsed and recirculation has been so frequent, the memory trace for brands is strong. These brands are also likely to be linked to many other concepts in memory, making their activation highly likely. The fact that we tend to remember these brands may explain why they have been so successful over time and why so many companies fight to establish themselves as category leaders.[39] Coke, for example, has engaged in intense marketing efforts to establish itself as the market leader in many Eastern European countries.[40]

Redundant Cues Memory is also enhanced when the information items to be learned seem to go together naturally. Thus our memory of brand name, advertising claims, and pictures presented in ads is better when these elements convey the same information, as in Exhibit 8.10 on the following page, where the picture and the copy both convey the notion that drinking a glass of TreeTop juice is like eating two apples. Memory for brands can also be enhanced when two complementary products are advertised together (e.g., Special K with Tropicana orange juice) and the ad tells how they naturally go together.[41]

The Medium in Which the Stimulus Is Processed Advertisers often wonder whether certain media are more effective than others at enhancing consumer memory. Currently, advertisers are trying to determine whether spending money on Internet ads is a good use of advertising dollars. Some research suggests that consumers tend not to look at or remember Internet ads, whereas other studies suggest that these ads can be as or even more effective in generating brand memory than ads shown in traditional media.[42] Unfortunately, our understanding of how the choice of medium affects memory is still rudimentary.

What the Stimulus Is Linked To

Retrieval can also be facilitated by what the stimulus is linked to in memory.

Retrieval Cues The associative network concept explains a related way of facilitating retrieval—providing retrieval cues. A **retrieval cue** is a stimulus that facilitates the activation of memory.[43] For example, if you need to remember to go to a sale at Macy's, you might leave a note on your refrigerator that says, "Macy's." When you see the note later, you remember the sale. The note serves as a retrieval cue.

Where Do Retrieval Cues Come From? Retrieval cues can be generated internally or externally. Internally, a thought can also cue another thought as in, "Today is December 8. Oh my gosh, it's Mom's birthday!" An external stimulus such as a vending machine, an ad, or an in-store display could also serve as a retrieval

Twice as Good

Tree Top puts 2 apples in every glass. And nothing else.

Every delicious glass of Tree Top apple juice is made from the juice of two fresh, Washington state apples. Nothing added (not a single granule of sugar). And nothing taken away. It's simply pure apple juice. Pasteurized. And naturally sweetened by the sun.

EXHIBIT 8.10
Redundant Cues

The picture of two apples in a glass reiterates the claim that Tree Top puts two apples in every glass.

Source: By permission of Tree Top, Inc.

cue—"Oh, there's the new candy bar I've been hearing about." These same retrieval cues can be used to activate images stored in autobiographical memory. Thus if we see an advertisement for our favorite brand of ice cream, this cue might activate both our positive feelings about ice cream and our memory of past experiences with ice cream. Pictures or videos of ourselves engaging in an activity can serve as a powerful retrieval cue to stimulate memories.[44]

The Brand Name as a Retrieval Cue   One of the most important types of retrieval cues is the brand name. If we see brand names such as Porsche, Jif, and Nike, we can retrieve information about these and related brands from memory. Research has found, however, that the impact of brand name as a retrieval cue is not the same for recognition as it is for recall.[45]

If we want consumers to *recognize* the brand on the store shelf, it is important to have high-frequency words or names to which consumers have been heavily exposed, for example, Coast, Glad, or Crest. On the other hand, if we want consumers to *recall* the brand and its associations, it is more important to have brand names that (1) evoke rich imagery (Safari, Passion, or Old El Paso), (2) are novel or unexpected (Screaming Yellow Zonkers, Liquid-Plumr, or Toilet Duck), or (3) suggest the product or service and its benefits (SnackWell's, Minute Rice, or Healthy Request).

Other Retrieval Cues   In addition to brand names, packages can also act as retrieval cues. The picture of the winged bull on the ad and packaging for Taureau Ailé rice is likely to cue consumers to remember the ad and the product depicted in Exhibit 8.11. Category names can also act as retrieval cues. Thus if we encounter the categories car, peanut butter, or athletic shoes, we might recall information about these products from memory. Logos can also be retrieval cues.

Consumer Implications   Retrieval cues have implications for purchasing decisions. Consumers remember very little advertising content when they are actually making a decision in the store.[46] The reason is that advertising is typically seen or heard in a context completely different from the purchase environment. One way to handle this problem is to place a cue from the ad on the brand's package or on an in-store display.[47] This cue will then activate advertising-related links in memory. Thus packages sometimes contain the phrase "as seen on TV" on the label. Another strategy is to place well-known cues from ads on the package, such as the bear on Snuggle fabric softener, "scrubbing bubbles" on Johnson Wax bathroom cleaner, and "Dig 'em" the Smacks frog.

MARKETING IMPLICATIONS   Retrieval cues also have important implications for marketers. First, these cues can affect what we remember from ads.[48] Some research has shown that the most effective retrieval cues match the cues actually used in an ad. Therefore, if an ad uses a picture of an apple in an ad, then a picture of an apple, not the word *apple*, is the most effective retrieval cue. If the ad uses a particular word, then the actual word, not a picture of what it represents, is the most effective retrieval cue.

Other research has shown that music can serve as an effective retrieval cue for ad content, affecting consumers' memories of pictures in an ad.

Interestingly, some marketers have also developed products that generate their own retrieval cues. For example, a new product available on CD-ROM has consumers enter key gift-giving occasions, along with a description of the general likes and dislikes of the person who will receive the gift. Two weeks before the occasion, the program beeps at the consumer, generates a list of potential gifts based on the person's description, and through the Internet, identifies stores with items on sale that might meet the consumer's gift-giving requirements. This program not only acts as a retrieval cue but also facilitates searching and decision-making—issues discussed in the next set of chapters.

dual coding The representation of a stimulus in two modalities (e.g., pictures and words) in memory.

How a Stimulus Is Processed in Short-Term Memory

The way information is processed in short-term memory also affects retrieval. One consistent finding is that messages processed through imagery tend to be better remembered than those processed discursively. The reason may be that things processed in imagery form are processed as pictures *and* as words. This **dual coding** provides extra associative links in memory, which in turn enhance the likelihood that the item will be retrieved.

Information encoded verbally, however, is processed just one way—discursively—and thus it has only one retrieval path. Nevertheless, imagery processing is not necessarily induced by pictures alone. When you read a novel, you can often generate very vivid images about the story and its characters. In this way, verbal information can also possess imagery-generating properties. Inducing imagery via pictures, high-imagery words, or imagery instructions may result in dual coding.[49] Dual coding is one reason that the audio portion of well-known TV ads is often put on the radio. When consumers hear the familiar verbal message, they may provide their own imagery of the visual part, thus promoting dual coding.

Consumer Characteristics Affecting Retrieval

Finally, several characteristics of consumers also affect retrieval.

Mood Mood has some very interesting effects on retrieval.[50] First, being in a positive mood can enhance our recall of stimuli in general. Second, we are more likely to recall information that is consistent with our mood. In other words, if we are in a positive mood, we are more likely to recall positive information. Likewise, if we are in a negative mood, we will recall more negative information. From a marketing perspective, if an advertisement can influence a consumer's mood in a positive direction, the recall of relevant information may be enhanced when the consumer is feeling good.

Several explanations account for these mood effects. One is that feelings we associate with a concept are linked to the concept in memory. Thus our memory of Disneyland may be associated with the feeling of fun. If we are in a fun mood, the fun concept may be activated, and this activation may spread to Disneyland.[51] Researchers have also suggested that we process information in more detail when mood is intense than when it is weak. More detailed processing, in turn, leads to greater elaboration and higher levels of recall.[52]

Expertise   Chapter 5 mentioned that compared to novices, experts have more complex category structures in memory with a greater number of higher- and lower-level categories and more detail within each category. Therefore, experts' associative networks are more interconnected than the networks of novices. The complex linkages and the spreading of activation concept explain why experts can recall more brands, brand attributes, and benefits than novices.[53]

SUMMARY

Memory consists of three memory stores, each with different types of memory. Sensory memory (iconic and echoic) involves a very brief analysis of incoming information. Short-term memory represents active working memory and involves imagery and discursive processing. Long-term memory represents the permanent memory store; it includes autobiographical and semantic memory. Information from the sensory store and from short-term memory can be lost if it does not receive further processing. Long-term memory can be represented as a set of semantic networks with concepts connected by associations or links. Notably, although long-term memory reflects what we have stored, not everything is equally accessible. Thus memory and retrieval are different phenomena.

To enhance the likelihood that information in long-term memory is stored and to reduce the likelihood that information in memory will be lost, marketers can enhance memory by using principles like chunking, recirculation, rehearsal, and elaboration.

Retrieval is the process of remembering information that is stored in memory. Entities are retrieved when concepts are activated in memory and information is made accessible. Concepts may also be activated by the spreading of activation. Even if the activation potential is not sufficient to retrieve an item, the activation may be sufficient to prime the concept in memory, thereby making that concept more easily retrievable when other cues are present. If a concept or a link to it is not activated often, that concept will "decay" in memory. We may fail to retrieve information, or we may retrieve information that is not accurate.

There are two types of retrieval tasks: those that ask whether we can remember things we have previously encountered—called an explicit memory task—and those that *reveal* memory of things for which we have no conscious memory— called an implicit memory task. Recall and recognition are often used as measures of explicit memory.

Finally, marketers place great importance on recognition and recall. They serve as objectives for marketing communications, influence consumer choice, and have important strategic implications. Factors that facilitate recognition and recall include characteristics of the information (its salience, prototypicality, redundancy), what it is linked to (retrieval cues), the way it is processed (particularly in imagery mode), and characteristics of consumers (mood and expertise).

EXERCISES

1. Watch television for 2 hours, also recording the programs on a VCR; page through two magazines; or spend 20 minutes on the Internet and write down the names of the sites you visit. Without taking any notes about the ads, see how many you can remember afterwards and list them. Why do you think you were able to remember these ads? Now go back to the ads and analyze each in terms of its ability to generate (a) rehearsal, (b) elaboration, (c) recirculation, and (d) interference. Also, analyze them in terms of (e) the information's salience, (f) your mood, and (g) your expertise.

2. Given the results of question 1, make recommendations as to how the information in each ad could be made more memorable.

3. Collect a set of autobiographical memories from members of your class about a common consumer behavior experience (what they did on their last vacation, how they spent a holiday). Compile this information and analyze it to determine what implications it might have for marketers (vacation marketers, retailers selling holiday items).

4. Cadillac recently developed a TV commercial using actor Dennis Franz—also known as Detective Andy Sipowicz on ABC's *NYPD Blue*. The commercial shows the actor pulling out a notepad and warning a Mercedes driver that he is going to write him up for driving a luxury car without enough horsepower. The Mercedes driver asks whether he is some kind of cop. The actor winks at the camera and says "Something like that." NBC and CBS refused to run the ad. (*Source:* Sally Goll Beatty, "Networks Nix Ads Featuring Rival TV Stars," *Wall Street Journal*, February 21, 1997, pp. B1, B6.) Using the concepts of spreading of activation, priming, and interference, explain why the networks acted as they did.

5. Collect a set of ads from a magazine. Analyze each ad and determine whether the marketer was trying to establish recall or recognition of information in the ad. Why is recall or recognition an important objective for this marketer? Has it been successful? Why or why not?

THE CONSUMER'S CULTURE

Age, Gender, and
Household Influences
(Ch. 15)

Social Class Influences
(Ch. 14)

Social Influences
(Ch. 16)

Regional, Ethnic and
Religious Influences
(Ch. 13)

THE PSYCHOLOGICAL CORE

- Motivation, Ability and
  Opportunity (Ch. 3)
- Exposure, Attention and
  Perception (Ch. 4)
- Knowing and
  Understanding (Ch. 5)
- Attitude Formation
  (Chs. 6 & 7)
- Memory and
  Retrieval (Ch. 8)

Psychographics:
Values, Personality
and Lifestyles
(Ch. 17)

THE PROCESS OF MAKING DECISIONS

- Problem Recognition and Information Search (Ch. 9)
- Judgment and Decision Making (Chs. 10-11)
- Post-Decision Processes (Ch. 12)

CONSUMER BEHAVIOR OUTCOMES

- Symbolic Consumer Behavior (Ch. 18)
- Adoption of, Resistance to, and Diffusion of
  Innovations (Ch. 19)

PART THREE

The Process of Making Decisions

P art Three examines the sequential steps in the consumer decision-making process. Chapter 9 explores the initial steps of this process—problem recognition and information search. Consumers must first realize they have a problem to solve before they can begin the process of making a decision about it. They must then collect information to help make this decision.

As with attitude change, decision making is affected by the amount of effort consumers expend in making those decisions. Chapter 10 examines the decision-making process when consumer effort is high. The chapter also examines how marketers can influence this extensive decision process. Chapter 11 focuses on decision making when consumer effort is low. The ways in which marketers influence this process are also explored.

Chapter 12 explores the ways in which consumers determine whether they are satisfied or dissatisfied with their decisions and how they learn from choosing and consuming products and services.

PROBLEM RECOGNITION AND INFORMATION SEARCH

INTRODUCTION

One day David, a college student, arrives at his apartment to find an invitation to a birthday party from his good friend, Stephanie. She is known for giving great parties, so he is happy to be invited. However, he realizes that he must now think of something to bring as a gift. He searches his memory to think of things that Stephanie likes and remembers that she is an avid reader of mystery novels. However, not being a fan of mysteries himself, David realizes that he must find some information about good books to buy. Unfortunately, he has three exams and a major project due next week, so he does not have time to go to a bookstore. Suddenly he remembers the well-known Web site for books, Amazon.com (see Exhibit 9.1). When he calls up the Amazon.com home page, he is very pleased to find a box with the main heading Gift Ideas and a subcategory for Mysteries and Thrillers. He clicks on the Mysteries button and is able to view a variety of recommended selections. He selects a new book by Elizabeth George because he remembers that Stephanie likes this author. He orders using his credit card and receives the book in the mail a few days later.

www.

EXHIBIT 9.1

Amazon.com

Source: Amazon.com is a registered trademark or trademark of
Amazon.com, Inc. in the U.S.
and/or other countries. © 2000
Amazon.com. All rights reserved.

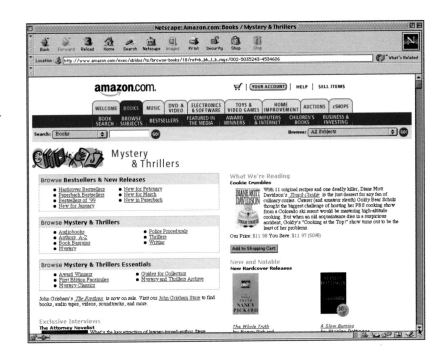

This example illustrates the three central topics of this chapter. Upon realizing he needs to buy a gift, David enters a state of problem recognition
that requires a resolution. He searches his memory to recall that
Stephanie likes mystery novels; this process is called internal search. However, he
does not have enough information about which book to buy. He therefore conducts an external search for information, in this case on the Internet through Ama-
zon.com. This information helped David make his decision.

As Exhibit 9.2 shows, problem recognition, internal search, and external
search represent the early stages of the consumer decision-making process. Although these processes often proceed sequentially, they can also occur simultaneously or in a different order. For example, consumers can be searching for
information and suddenly realize that another problem needs to be solved. Also,
consumers will not necessarily go through every stage in the exact order every
time. However they occur, these three stages are useful in helping us understand
the basic processes that characterize consumer decision making.

PROBLEM RECOGNITION

The consumer decision process generally begins when the consumer identifies a
consumption problem that needs to be solved ("I need a new stereo" or "I'd like
some new clothes"). Formally defined, **problem recognition** is the perceived difference between an ideal and an actual state. This stage is critical because it motivates the consumer to action.

The **ideal state** is the way consumers would like a situation to be (having an excellent stereo or wearing attractive clothing). The **actual state** is the real situation
as we perceive it now ("My stereo is too old" or "My clothing is out of date"). A discrepancy between the actual state and the ideal state activates problem recognition.

problem recognition The
perceived difference between
an actual and an ideal state.

ideal state The way we want
things to be.

actual state The way things
actually are.

EXHIBIT 9.2

Chapter Overview: Problem Recognition and Information Search

Part Two of the book examines the consumer decision-making process. The first step involves *problem recognition* (in which the consumer recognizes a problem that needs to be solved). When this occurs, the next step is to *search for information* to solve the problem either *internally* from memory or *externally* from outside sources (such as experts, magazines, ads). How much consumers search, what they search for, and the process they go through will be discussed.

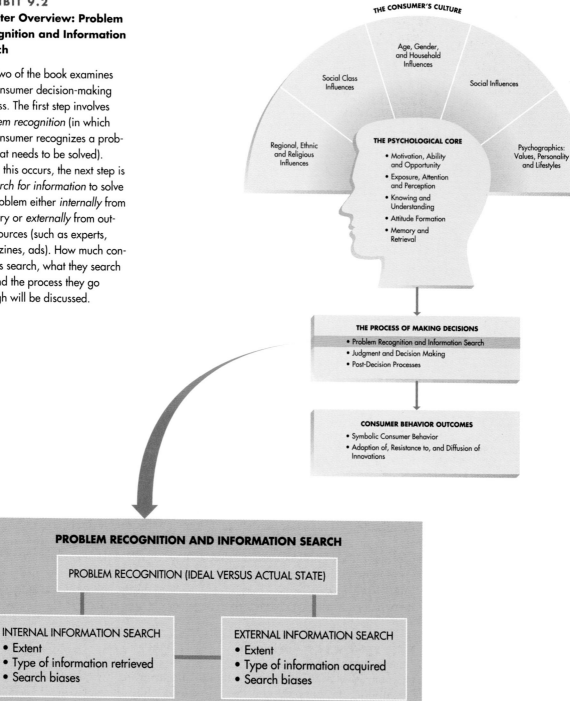

Exhibit 9.3 illustrates the difference between the ideal state and the actual state. The left side of the menu is easy to read, but the right side is blurred. This distinction represents the difference between the ideal state (reading easily) and the possible actual state (not being able to read small print). The greater the discrepancy between the real state and the ideal state and the higher the level of motivation, ability, and opportunity, the more likely the consumer is to act. If consumers do not perceive a problem, their motivation to act will be low.

Problem recognition relates not only to acquisition but also to consumption and disposition. Consumers can recognize problems such as needing to decide what to make for dinner, which item of clothing to wear, what to do with a closet that is too full, or whether to replace an appliance that is old. For example, Procter & Gamble discovered that Japanese consumers were squirting out more dish detergent than they needed, thereby indicating that they needed a more powerful soap (leading to the success of Joy).[1] Because problem recognition stimulates many types of consumer decision making, we need now to examine the factors that contribute to differences between the ideal and the actual state.

EXHIBIT 9.3
Ideal Versus Actual State

This ad is a good illustration of problem recognition and the difference between an actual and ideal state. The ideal state is being able to read easily. However, many people over 40 have trouble seeing both near and far clearly. This ad prompts problem recognition and offers Acuvue Bifocal contacts as a way to solve the problem.

Source: Courtesy of Johnson & Johnson.

The Ideal State: Where We Want to Be

Where do we get our notion of the ideal state? Sometimes we rely on simple expectation, usually based on past experience, about everyday consumption and disposition situations and how products or services fulfill our needs related to them. For example, we consider how we might look in certain clothes, how clean our house should be, how much fun it would be to vacation in a particular location, which old products we should keep, and so on. The ideal state also can be a function of our future goals or aspirations. For example, many consumers might want to drive a car that will provide them with social status (a Porsche, Mercedes, or Lexus) or to join a club that will bring them the admiration or acceptance of others.

 Both expectations and aspirations are often stimulated by our own personal motivations—what we want to be based on our self-image—and by aspects of our particular culture. Some societies are more materialistic than others, and therefore the desire for many goods and services may be higher. For example, consumers in Buddhist cultures such as Thailand tend to be less materialistic than Western consumers. Likewise, social class can exert an influence on the ideal state because many consumers want to be accepted by members of their class or to raise their social standing, aspiring to a higher ideal state. Reference groups also play a critical role, both because we strive to be accepted by others and because reference groups serve as a guide to our behavior.

 Finally, major changes in personal circumstances, such as getting a promotion or having a baby, can instigate new ideal states (see Exhibit 9.4). When you graduate and start a new job, you are likely to develop new ideal states related to where you live, what you wear, what you drive, and so forth. Since the fall of communism, many Eastern European consumers have been desiring Western goods that were formerly unavailable, thereby creating a new ideal state.

NOW MIGHT BE A GOOD TIME TO TALK ABOUT WHERE TO GO AFTER THE PROM.

After the prom, after graduation, what's next?
Now is the time seniors
and their parents look to
the future, a good time to
update your ideas about
the U.S. Armed Forces.
Today's military has
changed to meet the
nation's future needs.
The advantages for
today's ambitious young
people are substantial.
Today's recruits join
one of the most high-
tech organizations in
the world and benefit
from the highest level of
job and career training in
its history. In over 200
career fields, they'll have
an equal opportunity for
advancement and get
more responsibility, faster.
Exciting new careers
have opened to women,
and no one can match
the Armed Forces' array of

advanced education programs.
There are college credit
programs, as well as
state-of-the-art tech-
nical schools within
the military, and
the Montgomery
G.I. Bill helps thou-
sands with cash
for college. In an
age when progress
is constant, the
education and
career advantages of
the military are nonstop
and unbeatable. Think
about it. Talk about it.
Call 1-800-893-LEAD and
find out more. Your son
or daughter needs your
help and advice. After
the prom, they have a
date with the future.

Make It Happen.

U.S. ARMED FORCES
ARMY ※ NAVY ※ AIR FORCE ※
MARINES ※ COAST GUARD ※

EXHIBIT 9.4
An Ideal State

Graduating from high
school represents a
major change in life
situation for many indi-
viduals. Having an excit-
ing and rewarding
career after graduation
is highly desired and
would therefore be a
new ideal state that re-
sults from this transition.
This ad for the U.S.
Armed Forces provides
graduates with one way
of achieving this ideal
state.

Source: Reprinted by permission of the U.S. De-
partment of Defense.

internal search The process
of recalling stored information
from memory.

The Actual State: Where We Are Now

Like your perception of the ideal state, your perception of the actual state can be influenced by a variety of factors. Often these are simple physical factors, such as running out of something, having it malfunction (the stereo breaks down) or grow obsolete (the computer does not have enough memory), or suddenly needing a service (a cavity requires dental work or back pain requires a chiropractor). Needs also play a critical role. If you are hungry or thirsty or if friends make fun of your clothes, your actual state would not be acceptable.

Finally, external stimuli can suddenly change your perceptions of the actual state. If someone tells you that Mother's Day is next Sunday, for example, you might suddenly realize you have not bought a card or present yet. Or opening your closet door may make you realize it is too full.

MARKETING IMPLICATIONS From a marketing standpoint, putting consumers in a state of problem recognition may stimulate the decision process and lead to acquisition, consumption, or disposition of a product or service. Marketing efforts can influence this process. If there is no problem recognition, marketing efforts have a lower chance of success because the consumer may not be motivated to process information.

In general, marketers use two major techniques to try to stimulate problem recognition. First, they can attempt to create a new ideal state. For example, 25 years ago consumers did not think much about the performance of their athletic shoes. However, today we are continually bombarded with newer and better products that will make us run faster and jump higher—a new ideal state. Some consumers are even willing to pay more than $150 for new higher-tech shoes. The portable DVD player is very popular in Asia because consumers want to watch movies "on the go."[2]

Marketers can also try to create dissatisfaction with the actual state. The ad in Exhibit 9.5 is directed toward the stressed-out worker who has to do "the work of two people." Advertisers for new cleaning products, such as Febreze, Banish, and Cool Scent, are trying to convince smokers to use these products to remove a "smoky smell" from their clothing.[3] A new generation of "polite" cigarettes that leave less odor is now popular with young Japanese consumers.[4]

Whether they are creating a new ideal state or dissatisfaction with the actual state, marketers should position their product or service as the solution to the consumer's problem to increase the probability that it will be chosen. Computers have not penetrated the Chinese market in part because the Chinese alphabet has 13,000 characters, requiring a keyboard the size of a kitchen table.[5] Voice recognition, however, is now solving this problem. ■

INTERNAL SEARCH: SEARCHING FOR INFORMATION FROM MEMORY

After problem recognition has been stimulated, the consumer will usually begin the decision process to solve the particular problem. Typically, the next step is **internal search**. As you saw in Chapter 8, almost all decision making involves some

EXHIBIT 9.5

Creating Dissatisfaction with the Actual State

This ad tries to create dissatisfaction with the *actual* state. It shows a very busy worker who has a fax machine that cannot keep up with his workload. If consumers can relate to this worker, they will be dissatisfied with their own fax machine (creating problem recognition) and be motivated to look for a new one (hopefully the Panasonic). Can you think of any current product/service situations that you are unhappy with right now?

Source: Courtesy of Panasonic.

consideration (evoked) set
The subset of brands evaluated when making a choice.

form of memory processing. Each consumer has stored in memory a variety of information, feelings, and past experiences that can be recalled when making a decision. For example, Dave at the beginning of the chapter was able to remember that Stephanie liked mystery novels and that Amazon.com was a good place to look for books.

At this point two factors are important: First, consumers have limitations on their capacity or ability to process information; second, memory traces can decay over time. Thus only a small subset of stored information is likely to be recalled when consumers engage in internal search. As a result, consumer researchers have been very interested in determining (1) the extent of the search; (2) the nature of the search; and (3) the process by which information, feelings, and experiences are recalled and enter into the choice process.

How Much Do We Engage in Internal Search?

The degree of internal search can vary widely from the simple recall of only a brand name to more extensive searches through memory for relevant information, feelings, and experiences. On a general level, we know that the effort consumers devote to internal search depends on their motivation, ability, and opportunity to process information. Thus consumers will attempt to recall more information when felt involvement, perceived risk, or need for cognition are high. Likewise, consumers can engage in active internal search only if information is stored in memory. Thus consumers with a greater degree of knowledge and experience have a greater ability to search internally. Finally, consumers can recall information from memory only if they have the opportunity to do so. Time pressure or distractions will limit internal search.

What Kind of Information Is Retrieved from Internal Search?

Much of the research on the role of internal search in consumer judgment and decision making has focused on what is recalled. Specifically, researchers have examined the recall of four major types of information: (1) brands, (2) attributes, (3) evaluations, and (4) experiences.[6]

Recall of Brands One important aspect of internal search that greatly affects decision making is the set of brands that are recalled from memory whenever problem recognition has been stimulated. Rather than remembering all available brands in any given situation, consumers tend to recall a subset of two to eight brands that we call a **consideration** or **evoked set**.[7] For example, someone buying a soft drink might consider Coke and Pepsi rather than all possible brands.

The consideration set usually consists of those brands that are "top of mind" or easy to remember when making a decision. Many consumers fly rather than take the train even when the train is faster and cheaper simply because they do not consider the possibility of train travel.[8] A small consideration set is usually necessary because our ability to recall information about brands decreases as the size of the set increases. However, even if we do not recall the entire set from memory, stored information aids the recognition process. For example, stored information can help consumers recognize services in the Yellow Pages or identify brands on the shelf.

Research has found that brands that are recalled are more likely to be chosen.[9] Also, consumers' choices can be altered by simple manipulation of which brands they recall, even though there may be no change in their product preferences. Thus if consumers cannot recall brands from memory in order to form a consideration set, the set will tend to be determined by external factors such as availability on the shelf or suggestions of salespeople.[10]

From a marketing standpoint it is critical that a brand be included in the consumer's consideration set; otherwise, it has little chance of being selected. Researchers have therefore been interested in identifying factors that increase the possibility consumers will recall a particular brand during internal search and include that brand in the consideration set.* These factors include the following:

- *Prototypicality.* When consumers engage in internal search, brands that are most typical of a product category—that is, brands that are closest to the prototype or most resemble other members of the category—are recalled more easily and are therefore more likely to be included in the consideration set than brands that are not typical of the category.[11] For example, Armor All created the category of automotive protectant, and its product is the dominant brand not only in the United States but also in Mexico, Canada, Germany, Japan, and Australia.[12] This brand is more likely than other brands to be in the consideration set when problem recognition for the product exists. In Brazil the local food chain Mr. Pizza has tried to increase consumer recall and its inclusion in the consideration set by positioning itself close to the leading import (Pizza Hut).[13]

- *Brand Familiarity.* Well-known brands are more easily recalled during internal search than unfamiliar brands because the memory links associated with these brands tend to be stronger. This factor emphasizes the importance of repeating marketing communications to keep brand name awareness high and associations strong. In Asian cultures ads with high-meaning pictures and words (e.g., Superman fences with a picture of Superman) are very effective in increasing brand name recall.[14] Even in situations of low motivation, ability, and opportunity, where little processing occurs, incidental ad exposure can increase the likelihood of inclusion in the consideration set.[15] Marlboro continues to be one of the strongest selling brands in the world because of its long-repeated global cowboy-image campaign. In fact, many global brands such as Sony, IBM, McDonald's, Mercedes, and Coca-Cola have high familiarity worldwide and are likely to be in many consumers' consideration sets. Familiarity is also the reason makers of drugs such as Rogaine and Propecia (for men's hair loss) advertise so heavily.[16] Brand familiarity helps consumers recognize which of the many available brands in the store should be attended to and reduces misidentification of brands.[17] Japan's Shiseido cosmetics firm is abandoning its 125-year-old name in the United States because it is hard for U.S. consumers to remember.[18]

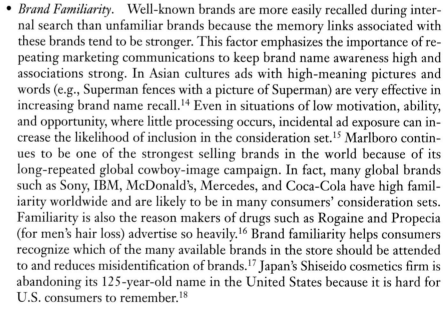

- *Goals and Usage Situations.* As we discussed in Chapter 5, consumers have goal-derived and usage-specific categories in memory, such as drinks to bring to the beach or beer to buy for a party, and the activation of these categories will determine which brands they recall during internal search.[19] Thus mar-

---

*Note that simply being recalled does not guarantee that a brand will be included in the consideration set. Undesirable alternatives could be recalled and subsequently rejected.

keters can attempt to associate products with certain goals and usage situations. For example, the Snickers (candy) bar positions itself as the product for when you are "not going anywhere for a while," and Kodak developed the Fun-Saver 35 for the category of single-use cameras.[20] Finally, Domino's Pizza has tried to make a strong impact in Japan by positioning itself as the "food for delivery."[21]

- *Brand Preference.* Brands for which the consumer has positive attitudes tend to be recalled more easily and be included in the consideration set more often than brands that evoke negative attitudes.[22] This principle points to the importance of developing positive brand attitudes.

- *Retrieval Cues.* By strongly associating the brand with a retrieval cue, marketers can increase the chance that the brand will be included in the consideration set. The Clydesdale horses have helped consumers remember Budweiser for years, and they have been the centerpiece of an aggressive campaign in Japan.[23] In Argentina, Joe Camel is still an effective retrieval cue for Camel cigarettes.[24]

Recall of Attributes For a variety of reasons, only a small portion of the information stored in memory is accessed in internal search. Also, consumers often cannot remember specific facts about a product or service because our memory of details decreases over time. Thus when consumers recall attribute information, it tends to be in summary or simplified form rather than in its original detail. We would be more likely to remember that a car gets good gas mileage or that it is not expensive than to remember the actual miles per gallon or the exact price.

Nevertheless, consumers can often recall *some* details when they engage in internal search, and the recalled attribute information can strongly influence their brand choices.[25] As a result, researchers have been very interested in determining which factors influence the recall of attribute information in the information search and decision-making processes. Some of the major variables they have identified include the following:

accessibility The likelihood that an item will be retrieved from long-term memory.

- *Accessibility or Availability.* Information that is more **accessible** or available—that has the strongest associative links—is the most likely to be recalled and enter into the decision process.[26] Information that is perceived as being easy to recall is also more likely to be accessible.[27] The accessibility of information can be increased by repeatedly drawing attention to it in marketing communications or by making the information more relevant.[28] Macintosh ads repeatedly stress ease of use, hoping that consumers will remember this feature when they buy a computer.

diagnostic information That which helps us discriminate among objects.

- *Diagnosticity of Attributes* **Diagnostic information** helps us distinguish objects from one another. If all brands of computers are the same price, then price is not diagnostic, or useful, in making a decision. On the other hand, if prices vary, a distinction can be made and the information is diagnostic.[29] If information is both accessible and diagnostic, it has a very strong influence in the decision-making process.[30] If accessible information is *not* diagnostic, it is less likely to be recalled.

Interestingly, research has shown that negative information tends to be more diagnostic than positive or neutral information, because the former is more distinctive.[31] In other words, because most brands are associated with positive attributes, negative information makes it easier to categorize the brand as different from other brands. Unfortunately, this factor means negative information tends to be given greater weight in the decision-making process, thereby increasing the chances that the alternative will be rejected. Obviously, some marketers need to avoid associating their products and services with negative information, to plan a two-sided message campaign, or to divert attention away from the negative feature. Thus to overcome increasing criticism of the taste of its food and to be competitive with Burger King and Wendy's, McDonald's considered moving to sell custom-made sandwiches.[32]

In addition, marketers can identify which attributes tend to be most diagnostic for a particular product or service category and try to gain a competitive advantage on one or more of these attributes. In Japan many consumers like strong drinks, so Budweiser actively markets Buddy beer, which has 6 percent alcohol (versus 5 percent for other brands).[33] The quality of many U.S. products has improved in recent years, and some companies, such as Jim Beam, Levi's, and Lands' End, are stressing to European consumers the diagnostic attribute "Made in America."[34]

salient attributes Attributes that are "top of mind" or more important.

attribute determinance Attributes that are both salient and diagnostic.

- *Salience (Prominence)*   Research has clearly shown that very **salient attributes** can be recalled even when the opportunity to process is low.[35] For example, many young women remember Tri-Cyclen because it is the only the birth control pill that prevents acne, a very salient attribute for this group.[36] Exhibit 9.6 summarizes the attributes most likely to be salient for U.S. consumers who are going to purchase a car.[37] It also shows the attributes that are important to Russian consumers in various product categories.[38]

  Consumers do not always have a strong belief about the salience of an attribute.[39] However, by repeatedly calling attention to an attribute in marketing communications, marketers can increase salience and its impact on the decision.[40] For example, in light of recent research wine makers are now promoting the positive health benefits of drinking red wine, such as a lower incidence of heart disease.[41] Because of a slow economy in Japan, many Japanese marketers strongly encouraged local consumers to "buy Japanese" and to vacation in their own country, thereby making the attribute of being Japanese more salient.[42]

  Note, however, that an attribute can be highly salient but not necessarily diagnostic. If you are buying a watch, for example, the attribute "tells time" would be highly salient but not very diagnostic. For information to be recalled and enter into the decision, it must be both salient and diagnostic. In other words, the information must have **attribute determinance**.[43]

- *Vividness.*   Vivid information is presented as concrete words, pictures, or instructions to image (e.g., imagine yourself on a tropical beach) or through word-of-mouth communication. For example, a picture of a hand holding the Canon Elph camera, which is the size of a credit card, is vivid information.[44] Vivid information is easier to recall than less dramatic information but tends to influence judgment and decision making only when consumers have not formed a strong prior evaluation, especially one that is negative.[45] In addition, vividness affects attitudes only when the effort required to process the information matches the amount of effort the consumer is willing to put forth.[46] Otherwise, vivid and nonvivid information affect consumer attitudes in about the same way.

- *Goals.*   The consumer's goals will determine which attribute is recalled from memory. For example, if one of your goals in taking a vacation is to economize, you are likely to recall price. Marketers can identify important goals that guide the choice process and position the product or service in the context of these goals, for example, by offering economy vacation packages. Burger chains such as McDonald's and Wendy's are typically remembered when the goal is fast food with good value.

Recall of Evaluations   Compared with specific attribute information, overall evaluations, that is, our likes and dislikes, are easier to remember because our memory for specific details decays rapidly over time. In addition, evaluations tend

EXHIBIT 9.6
Salient Attributes

This exhibit presents the results of studies that examine which attributes are most salient across a variety of decisions. For American consumers, reliability and durability are the most salient in buying a car. For Russian consumers, quality, availability, and price are the most salient across six different product categories. What attributes are most important to you for these products?

AMERICANS LOOK FOR QUALITY IN THEIR CARS

		AGE		
		16–29	30–49	50+
WHEN BUYING A CAR	Style and looks are most important	21%	15%	14%
	Price is most important	22	27	30
	I have a strong need to have a better way of evaluating the quality and value of the products I buy	21	29	27
STRONG INFLUENCES ON PURCHASE DECISIONS	Reliable, works like it should	68	85	73
	Long lasting, durable	63	78	72
	Easy to fix, maintain	39	49	53
	Low price	40	42	30
	Easy to use	38	40	46
	Easy to purchase	33	31	25
	Known, trusted brand name	26	32	43
	Latest technology, styles	20	13	14
	Many options, features	18	11	13

Source: "Drawing a Bead on Car Buyers for the Nineties," *Brandweek,* September 14, 1992, pp. 17, 20. Reprinted by permission of Yankelovich Partners, Inc.

RUSSIAN CONSUMERS: FACTORS AFFECTING THE PURCHASING DECISION

	FOODSTUFFS (PERCENTAGE)	TOILETRIES/ COSMETICS (PERCENTAGE)	HOUSEHOLD CLEANING ITEMS (PERCENTAGE)	CLOTHES/ SHOES (PERCENTAGE)	ELECTRICAL APPLIANCES (PERCENTAGE)	ELECTRONIC GOODS (PERCENTAGE)
Quality	90%	63%	69%	70%	78%	73%
Price	52	41	33	44	44	48
Availability	52	37	51	26	45	36
Appearance/presentation	38	26	14	64	28	28
Country of origin	8	38	25	40	25	38
Packaging	10	18	23	*	1	*
Variety of designs/ styles/types	9	14	18	13	14	9
Brand name	6	29	19	16	22	27
Advertising support	1	3	5	1	2	3

Source: Leonidas C. Leonidou, "Understanding the Russian Consumer," *Marketing and Research Today,* March 1992, pp. 75–83. Permission for using this material first published in *Marketing and Research Today,* the Journal of the European Society for Opinion and Marketing Research (E.S.O.M.H.R.), J.J. Viottastraat 29, 1071 JP, Amsterdam, The Netherlands.

to form strong associative links with the brand. Again, this principle emphasizes the importance of building positive consumer attitudes.

Evaluations are also more likely to be recalled by consumers who are actively evaluating the brand when they are exposed to the information. For example, if you are ready to buy a new computer and suddenly see an ad for a particular brand, you will probably determine whether you like the brand when you see the ad. This activity is called **on-line processing**.[47] You are subsequently more likely to recall this evaluation rather than the specific information that led to it. Many times, however, consumers do not have a brand-processing goal when they see or hear an ad. In such cases they do not form an evaluation and are therefore better able to recall specific attribute information, assuming that involvement was high and the information was processed.[48]

on-line processing The ability of consumers to process an ad as they are viewing it.

Recall of Experiences Internal search can involve the recall of experiences from autobiographical memory, in the form of specific images and the effect associated with them.[49] Like information in semantic memory, experiences that are more vivid, salient, or frequent are the most likely to be recalled. For example, if you have an experience with a product or service that is either unusually positive or unusually negative, you are likely to recall these vivid experiences later. Furthermore, if you repeatedly have a positive experience with a product or service, it will be easier to recall these experiences. For example, some bowling alleys now offer loud music and flashing lights to appeal to younger bowlers and make the experience more fun and exciting.[50]

MARKETING IMPLICATIONS Obviously, marketers want consumers to recall positive experiences in relationship to a certain product or service. To illustrate, Japanese consumers have developed a desire for new products that look old, such as motorcycles, cars, kimonos, and cameras, because these products remind consumers of simple, happy times.[51] Marketers often deliberately associate their products or services with common positive experiences or images to increase their recall from memory. Prudential Insurance and Sony have filmed ads at the Grand Canyon because it is the "quintessential breathtaking experience," and they hope that consumers will tie this positive memory to the advertisers' brands.[52] ■

Is Internal Search Always Accurate?

In addition to being influenced by factors that affect what we recall, we all have processing biases that alter the nature of internal search. Understanding these search biases is important because they can sometimes lead to the recall of information that results in a less-than-optimal judgment or decision. Three biases have key implications for marketing: confirmation bias, inhibition, and mood.

confirmation bias The greater likelihood of being able to recall things consistent with our beliefs.

Confirmation Bias **Confirmation bias** refers to the fact that we are more likely to recall information that reinforces or confirms our overall beliefs rather than contradicting them, thereby making our judgment or decision more positive than it should be. This phenomenon is related to the concept of selective perception—we see what we want to see—and occurs because we strive to maintain consistency in our views. Thus when we engage in internal search, we are more likely to recall information about brands we like or have chosen in the past than about brands we dislike or have rejected. Furthermore, when the confirmation bias is operating, we are more likely to recall positive rather than negative information about these favored brands. This response can be a problem because, as mentioned earlier, negative information tends to be more diagnostic.

Nevertheless, we sometimes recall contradictory evidence. In fact, we may recall moderately contradictory information because we had consciously thought about it when we first tried to understand it.[53] However, in most instances consumers tend to recall information that reinforces their overall beliefs.

MARKETING IMPLICATIONS From a marketing perspective, confirmation bias presents a real problem when consumers search internally for only positive information about the competition. One way to attack this problem is to draw attention to negative aspects of competitive brands in comparative advertising. Computer companies like Dell and Compaq and telecommunications firms like AT&T and MCI have increasingly used this type of information. If comparative information can be presented in a convincing and credible way, marketers may be able to overcome confirmation bias. ■

Inhibition Another internal search bias is associated with limitations in consumers' processing capacity.[54] In this case all the variables that influence the recall of certain attributes, such as accessibility, vividness, and salience, can actually lead to the **inhibition** of recall for other diagnostic attributes.[55] In buying a house, for example, a consumer might recall information such as the selling price, number of bathrooms, and square footage but not recall other important attributes such as the size of kitchen and the name of the school district. Inhibition can also lead to a biased judgment or decision because important and useful information may be remembered but ignored.

inhibition The recall of one attribute inhibiting the recall of another.

MARKETING IMPLICATIONS From the perspective of internal search, the phenomenon of inhibition is important for two reasons. First, key aspects of a brand may not always enter into the decision process because other more accessible attributes are recalled instead. Particularly if these nonrecalled attributes reflect features that differentiate the brand from others (i.e., if the attributes are diagnostic), it may be desirable to draw strong attention to them in marketing communications. For example, although price advertising is pervasive in the PC market, Dell computers does not want consumers to forget one of its key differentiating features: service. As a result, this attribute (in addition to price) is heavily featured in advertisements.

Second, marketers can sometimes offset the impact of their own disadvantages and/or competitors' advantages by drawing attention to more vivid or more accessible attributes. For example, the ads for SnackWell's cookies emphasize "indulgence" to draw attention away from the fact that they are not as low in fat as other major competitors. In the marketing of Cervana deer meat, ads draw attention to the fact that venison is tasty, tender, and low in fat to deflect attention from the belief that it tastes too gamey.[56] ■

Mood You saw in Chapter 8 that consumers engaged in internal search are most likely to recall information, feelings, and experiences that match their mood.[57] With this in mind, marketing communications that put consumers in a good mood through the use of humor or attractive visuals can enhance the recall of positive attribute information.

EXTERNAL SEARCH: SEARCHING FOR INFORMATION FROM THE ENVIRONMENT

external search The process of collecting information from outside sources (e.g., magazines, dealers, ads).

prepurchase A search that occurs to aid a specific decision.

ongoing search A search that occurs regularly, regardless of whether the consumer is making a choice.

Sometimes a consumer's decision can be based entirely on information recalled from memory. At other times information is missing or some uncertainty surrounds the recalled information. In this case consumers can engage in **external search** of outside sources such as dealers, trusted friends or relatives, published sources (magazines, pamphlets, or books), advertisements, the Internet, or the product package. Consumers can collect additional information about which brands are available, as well as the attributes and benefits associated with brands in the consideration set.

Two basic types of external search are called prepurchase search and ongoing search. **Prepurchase search** occurs in response to the activation of problem recognition. For example, upon deciding to buy a computer, you can visit dealers, search the Internet, talk to friends, or read *Consumer Reports*. **Ongoing search** occurs on a regular and continuous basis, even when problem recognition is not activated.[58] A consumer might consistently read computer magazines, visit interesting Web sites, and go to computer fairs because of a high degree of enduring involvement in computers. Exhibit 9.7 presents an overview of these two types of searches.

Researchers have been very interested in examining five key aspects of the external search process: (1) the source of information (2) the extent of external search, (3) the content of external search, (4) search typologies, and (5) the process or order of the search.

Where Can We Search for Information?

For either prepurchase or ongoing search, consumers can acquire information from various sources. In general, researchers have classified these sources into five major groups:[59]

- *Retailer Search.* Visits or calls to stores or dealers, including the examination of package information or pamphlets about brands.

EXHIBIT 9.7

Types of Information Searches

Consumers can engage in two major types of external search. *Prepurchase search* occurs in response to problem recognition; the goal is to make better purchase decisions. *Ongoing search* results from enduring involvement and occurs on a continuous basis (independent of problem recognition). Here consumers search for information because they find searching enjoyable (they like to browse).

Source: Peter H. Block, Daniel L. Sherrell, and Nancy M. Ridgeway, "Consumer Search: An Extended Framework," *Journal of Consumer Research,* June 1986, p. 120. © 1986 University of Chicago. All rights reserved.

	Prepurchase Search	**Ongoing Search**
Determinants	• Involvement in the purchase • Market environment • Situational factors	• Involvement with the product • Market environment • Situational factors
Motives	To make better purchase decisions	• Build a bank of information for future use • Experience fun and pleasure

Outcomes	• Increased product and market knowledge
	• Better purchase decisions
	• Increased satisfaction with the purchase outcome
		• Increased product and market knowledge leading to
		  – future buying efficiencies
		  – personal influence
		• Increased impulse buying
		• Increased satisfaction from search, and other outcomes

- *Media Search.* Information from advertising, on-line ads, manufacturer-sponsored Web sites, and other types of marketer-produced communications.
- *Interpersonal Search.* Advice from friends, relatives, neighbors, and/or other consumers, including those on chat lines.
- *Independent Search.* Contact with independent sources of information, such as books, the Internet, government pamphlets, or magazines.
- *Experiential Search.* The use of product samples or product/service trials, or experiencing the product on-line.

Traditionally, retailer and media search, followed by experiential search, have been the most frequently used forms of search, and they increase when involvement is higher and knowledge is lower.[60] This finding is significant for marketers because these sources are under their most direct control.

The use of interpersonal sources increases as knowledge decreases. Apparently, when consumers' knowledge is limited, they are motivated to seek out the opinions of others. Furthermore, consumers who believe that their purchase and consumption of certain items (usually hedonic or symbolic products and services such as fashion, music, and furniture) will be judged by others tend to seek out interpersonal sources.[61]

Experiential search is also critical for hedonic products and services. Given the importance of sensory stimulation, consumers want to get a "feel" for the offering. Hence people often want to try on clothing or listen to a stereo before they buy. Finally, independent search tends to increase as available time increases, but this type of search is still generally quite low.

The New Era of the Internet   As illustrated by the example at the beginning of this chapter, the phenomenal growth of the Internet for conducting business, from $3 billion in sales in 1997 to an estimated $1.4 to $3.2 trillion by 2003,[62] has dramatically altered the way consumers shop and search for information. Now without ever having to leave their homes, consumers have access to almost any type of information they need to make their purchase decisions. Computers are excellent tools for rapidly searching through mounds of data to find specific information about anything from a lost friend to a good egg roll. Search engines such as Yahoo!, Infoseek, and Excite allow easy access to information through the use of keywords. In fact, consumers can use the Internet to get information from all five of the sources mentioned above. Sometimes consumers search for specific information; at other times they simply browse.[63] Marketers should keep in mind, however, that information from commercial Web sites is often seen as biased, and consumers will quickly leave a Web site if they do not find it interesting.

Retailers such as Time Warner, Disney, eToys, CDNow, and Amazon.com, to name only a few, have built Internet "superstores."[64] As a result, in 1998 about 19 percent of surveyed consumers said they were shopping less in stores than they had in the past, and 14 percent said they used catalogs less often; industry analysts expect these numbers to keep on growing.[65] The trend toward Internet shopping has been strongest in the United States, but now Europeans consumers are dramatically increasing their use of the Internet. Retailers have already realized that U.S. strategies do not work everywhere, and locally tailored sites have struck a chord with European shoppers.[66]

Information Overload   In fact, consumers have access to so much information that they can actually become overloaded. For example, using common keywords to direct one of the many popular search engines can sometimes produce more than 100,000 references. In response, companies are now producing more efficient search aids that try to identify the most popular or useful information for consumers. As one example, a number of search engines offers programs to prioritize sites according to their popularity or frequency of access by consumers.[67] Alternatively, search agents offer either human or computer-assisted aid for identifying the most important types of information as well as for narrowing the choice set. Finally, shopping robots (like Hotbot and Junglee) search the Internet for bargains. Some retailers, however, try to thwart these because they make it too easy for consumers to compare prices.[68]

Simulations Advances in technology and graphics have also led to dramatic improvements in the Web experience. Web site developers can now simulate the retail experience as well as product trials by creating sites that incorporate a variety of special and interactive effects including audio, video, zoom, and panoramic views.[69] These effects make the user's experience as natural as possible, approximating what it feels like to drive a car or try on clothing styles, for example. In the "virtual grocery store," marketers have been able to re-create the grocery store environment in impressively accurate detail, complete with visuals and music.[70] Shoppers can "fly down" a 3-D aisle and grab what they want. Research has found that these environments are able to simulate consumers' search and purchase behavior in grocery stores fairly accurately.[71] They can also aid consumers in their search. For example, if a consumer is looking for sugarless cereals only, the click of a button eliminates all those brands with sugar, thereby making the consumer's search easier. One downside is that these type of environments have very long downloading times, which has led to limited use. Such problems will be resolved, however, with advances in technology such as IBM's Hot Media, and the future will allow for even more realistic and exciting shopping environments.

The On-line Community The Internet also makes it easier for consumers to talk to each other in an on-line community. People with a common interest or condition related to a product or service can converse with each other via electronic message boards or chat lines.[72] Research indicates that the most common interactions focus on product recommendations and how-to-use-it advice.[73] Often this information is very influential in the decision process because it is not controlled by marketers and is seen as more credible.

Retailers and manufacturers can also track consumer information search and purchase patterns to provide additional assistance. For example, when you examine or buy a book from Amazon.com, you can click on a button that says, "Customers who bought this book also bought _____." After tracking customer purchases, the Web site greets customers with, "Welcome back. We've improved our book recommendations." Consumers are then given a list of recommendations that fit their preferences. Video and CD retailers also provide this type of service.

MARKETING IMPLICATIONS Not all types of products and services are experiencing success on the Internet. The strongest performance has come from areas such as books, music, videos, travel, toys, high technology, software, consumer electronics, and financial services.[74] On the other hand, when quality cannot be judged on-line, as in the case of, say, an oil painting, or when the cost of delivery is high relative to the cost of the items, as in a grocery order, success has not been as high. In some markets consumers will use the Internet to search for information but not to buy, as is the case with homes. The keys to selling on-line are generally super selection, ultra-convenience, and competitive pricing. ∎

How Much Do We Engage in External Search?

Much of the research on external search has concentrated on examining how much information consumers acquire prior to making a judgment or decision. One of the key findings is that the degree of search activity is usually quite limited, even for purchases that are typically considered important.[75] One study found that more than a third of Australian car buyers made two or fewer trips to the dealer before buying.[76] As shown in Exhibit 9.8, consumers typically visit few stores and consult only a few sources across a range of products and services.[77] Note that as more consumers shop on the Internet, search activity may increase because it is now so much easier to do. Nevertheless, it should also be clear from the exhibit that search can vary widely from a simple hunt for one or two pieces of information to a very extensive search relying on many sources. In an attempt to explain

EXHIBIT 9.8
Extent of Search

How much consumers search will vary across individuals, but typically consumers search very little. As shown here, they tend to visit very few stores (most go to only one) and consult only a few sources (usually no more than two). How much search do you typically engage in?

Sources: Data from Geoffrey C. Kiel and Roger A. Layton, "Dimensions of Consumer Information Seeking," *Journal of Marketing Research,* May 1981, pp. 233–39; John O. Claxton, Joseph N. Fry, and Bernard Portis, "A Taxonomy of Prepurchase Information Gathering Patterns," *Journal of Consumer Research,* December 1974, pp. 35–42.

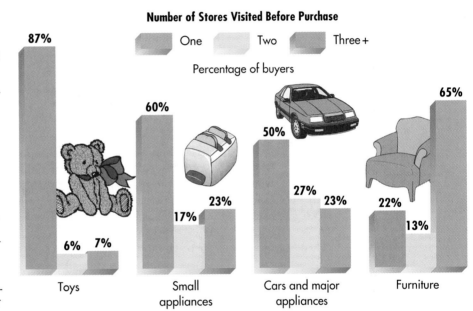

Number of Stores Visited Before Purchase

One Two Three +

Percentage of buyers

Toys: 87%, 6%, 7%
Small appliances: 60%, 17%, 23%
Cars and major appliances: 50%, 27%, 23%
Furniture: 22%, 13%, 65%

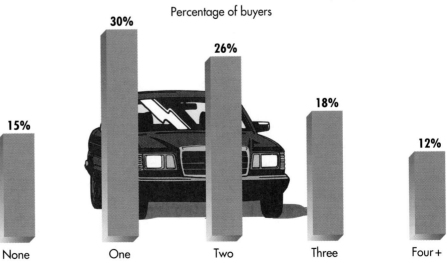

Number of Sources Consulted Before Purchase of a Car or Major Appliance

Percentage of buyers

None: 15%
One: 30%
Two: 26%
Three: 18%
Four +: 12%

this variance, researchers have identified a number of causal factors that relate to our motivation, ability, and opportunity to process information.

Motivation to Process Information   In general, as the motivation to process information increases, external search will be more extensive. Researchers have identified several factors that increase our motivation to do an external search: (1) involvement and perceived risk, (2) the perceived costs and benefits of search, (3) the nature of the consideration set, (4) relative brand uncertainty, (5) attitudes toward the search, and (6) the level of discrepancy of new information.

- *Involvement and Perceived Risk.*   To understand how involvement relates to external search, recall the distinction from Chapter 3 between situational involvement, a response to a particular situation, and enduring involvement, a response that is ongoing over time. Higher situational involvement will generally lead to greater prepurchase search,[78] whereas enduring involvement relates to ongoing search regardless of whether problem recognition exists.[79] Thus consumers with high enduring involvement with computers are more likely to read computer magazines, visit computer fairs, and engage in other efforts to gain knowledge about computers on a regular basis.

    Because perceived risk is a major determinant of involvement, it should not be surprising that the riskier the decision, the greater the external search activity. Remember that one of the key components of perceived risk is uncertainty regarding the consequences of behavior and that external search for information is one way to reduce this uncertainty.[80] Note that we are more likely to search when we are uncertain about which brand to choose than when we are uncertain about a specific attribute. Consumers also search more when they are evaluating services rather than products because services are intangible and hence perceived as more uncertain.[81] Finally, if the various *consequences* are high, such as high financial or social risk, the motivation to search will be higher. This factor explains why searches for higher-priced products or services are often more extensive than searches for lower-priced goods.

- *Perceived Costs and Benefits.*   External search activity is also greater when its perceived benefits are high relative to its costs.[82] The major benefits of search are a reduction in uncertainty and an increased likelihood of making a better decision, obtaining a better value, and enjoying the shopping process. The costs associated with external search are time, effort, inconvenience, and money (including traveling to stores and dealers). All these factors place psychological or physical strain on the consumer (especially if the distance between stores or dealers is great). In general, search tends to continue until the consumer perceives that the costs outweigh the benefits. Note that shopping on the Internet greatly reduces the costs of searching. The desire to reduce searching costs also explains why many supermarkets now offer a variety of nontraditional items like jewelry, electronics, and furniture. These stores want to become places "where people do all their gift shopping."[83]

- *The Consideration Set.*   If the consideration set contains a number of attractive alternatives, consumers will be motivated to engage in external search to decide which alternative to select. On the other hand, a consideration set that contains only one or two brands reduces the need to search for information.

- *Relative Brand Uncertainty.* Sometimes consumers are uncertain as to which brand is the best. In this case consumers are more motivated to engage in external search.[84]

- *Attitude Toward Search.* Some consumers like to search for information and do so extensively.[85] In general, they tend to have positive beliefs about the value and benefits of their search. In particular, extensive search activity appears to be strongly related to the belief that "when important purchases are made quickly, they are regretted."[86] Other consumers simply hate to search and do little.

  Researchers have identified two groups of Internet searchers.[87] Experienced searchers are the most enthusiastic and heaviest users of the Internet, whereas moderate and light users see it as a source of information only, not of entertainment or fun. To appeal to the latter group, some companies have created interesting and engaging games (like "snoop in the dorm room" and the "Simpson") to stimulate consumers to search.[88]

- *Discrepancy of Information.* Whenever consumers encounter something new in their environment, they will try to categorize it by using their stored knowledge. If a stimulus does not fit into an existing category, consumers will try to resolve this incongruity by engaging in information search, especially when incongruity is at a moderate level and the consumer has limited knowledge about the product category.[89] Consumers are likely to reject highly incongruous information.[90]

  Marketers can capitalize on this tendency by introducing moderate discrepancies between their brand and other brands. For example, an ad for Miele vacuum cleaners made the statement: "Lung Damage Control." This feature is not something we normally associate with vacuum cleaners (a moderate discrepancy), and the message may motivate a consumer information search to find out that the brand has filters to control pollution and allergens.[91]

  The same process generalizes to the search for information about new products. If a new product is moderately discrepant or incongruent with existing categories of products, the consumer will be motivated to resolve this discrepancy.[92] In particular, consumers explore the most salient attributes in greater depth, rather than search for a lot of additional attributes. From a marketing perspective, this behavior suggests that positioning new products as moderately different from existing brands may induce consumers to search for more information that might, in turn, affect their decision process. A good example of this phenomenon is the new photo CD technology, which records images on CDs rather than on film, allowing instant viewing and editing. This moderate discrepancy might stimulate consumers to search for additional information about the product that will ultimately affect their decision to buy.

Ability to Process Information External search is also strongly influenced by the consumer's ability to process information. Researchers have examined the impact of three variables on the extent of external information search: (1) consumer knowledge, (2) cognitive abilities, and (3) demographic factors.

- *Consumer Knowledge.* Common sense suggests that expert consumers search less because they already have more complex knowledge stored in memory. However, research results on this subject have been mixed.[93] Part of the problem stems from the way in which knowledge is defined. Some studies have measured *subjective knowledge*, which is a consumer's perception about what he or she knows relative to others. *Objective knowledge* refers to the actual information stored in memory that can be measured with a formal knowledge test. Researchers have linked objective knowledge to information search, although both types of knowledge are somewhat related to each other.

Specifically, several studies have found an inverted-U relationship between knowledge and search.[94] Consumers with moderate levels of knowledge search the most. They tend to have a higher level of motivation and at least some basic knowledge, which helps them to interpret new information. Experts, on the other hand, search less because they have more knowledge stored in memory, and they also know how to target their search to the most relevant or diagnostic information, ignoring that which is irrelevant. An exception to this rule occurs when the search involves new products. The more developed memory structures of experts give them an advantage in learning novel information and can therefore acquire more information about the new product.

- *Cognitive Abilities.* Consumers with higher basic cognitive abilities, such as IQ and the ability to integrate complex information, are not only more likely to acquire more information than consumers with little or no knowledge but also can process this information in more complex ways.[95]

- *Demographics.* Researchers have also been interested in determining whether certain types of consumers search more than others. A few consistent patterns have emerged. Consumers with higher education tend to search more than their less educated counterparts because the former have at least moderate levels of knowledge and have more access to information sources.[96] Searchers on the Internet tend to be male (59%)and well educated (58% college grad and), with a median age of 38.[97]

Opportunity to Process Information Consumers who have the motivation and ability to search for information must still have the opportunity to process that information before extensive search can take place. Situational factors that might affect the search process include the amount of information, information format, and time available.

- *Amount of Information Available* In any decision situation the amount of information available to consumers can vary greatly, depending on the number of brands on the market, the attribute information available about each brand, the number of retail outlets or dealers, and the number of other sources of information, such as magazines or knowledgeable friends. In general, search activity increases as the amount of available information increases. Thus the existence of the Internet can generate greater external search. If information is restricted or not available, however, consumers have a hard time engaging in extensive external search.

- *Information Format.* The format in which information is presented can also have a major impact on the search process. Sometimes information is available from diverse sources or locations, but considerable consumer effort is required to collect it. Good examples include insurance purchases, which require consumers to meet with different agents to collect information about individual policies, or car purchases, which necessitate consumers visiting a number of different car dealers.

  In contrast, presenting information in a manner that reduces consumer effort can enhance information search and usage, particularly when the consumer is in the decision mode.[98] For example, in an effort to increase the use of nutritional information, researchers provided a matrix that makes this information easier for consumers to search, thereby improving opportunity.[99] A related study found that use of nutritional information can be increased by making the rewards of good nutrition more explicit.[100] In addition, consumers will engage in more leisurely exploratory searches if information surrounding an object is made more visually simple and clutter is reduced.[101]

- *Time Availability.* Without time restrictions, opportunity is higher and search can increase. If consumers are under time pressure, however, search activity will be severely restricted.[102] Also consumers will spend less time getting information from different *sources*, the more so as time pressure increases.[103] Note that time pressure is one of the key reasons consumers search and shop on the Internet.

MARKETING IMPLICATIONS The extent to which consumers search for external information has important implications for marketing strategy. For one thing, if a sizable number of consumers tend to search heavily for a particular product or service, marketers need to make information readily available and easily accessible at the lowest cost and with the least effort for the consumer to facilitate the decision process. This realization can help marketers design the package, Web sites, ads, and other promotional materials. The key goal should be to provide information that will alter consumers' attitudes toward the product or service and change their behavior. This goal can be accomplished by providing information about salient and diagnostic attributes, particularly if the brand has a differential advantage. If needed information is not available, consumers might reject the brand from the consideration set.

Marketers should also segment the market for any product or service according to search activity. For example, as shown in Exhibit 9.8, one study found six clusters of searchers in the purchase of a car.[104] Marketers can use this information to determine which types of search activities are most likely to occur for their product or service, to ensure that the information needs of consumers are being met. Low-search consumers, for example, will focus on getting a good deal, whereas high searchers will need a lot of attention and information to offset their low levels of confidence and prior satisfaction. Marketers can be very selective in providing low searchers with information, emphasizing only those attributes that are most salient and diagnostic.

Marketers can also attempt to stimulate external search by providing information in a highly accessible manner. For example, companies like Einstein PC (cell phones) and Chesebrough-Pond's/Bristol-Myers (health and beauty aids) now offer in-store interactive kiosks where consumers can access product information by simply touching a TV screen.[105] The hope is that this additional search will lead low searchers to information that will change their attitudes. Marketers can also provide consumers with incentives to search. In France, Quick Burger has developed an innovative program whereby consumers can collect electronic points through interactive TV for reading ads and then redeem the points for valuable prizes such as clothes, stereos, and vacations.[106] ■

What Kind of Information Is Acquired in External Search?

Consumer researchers have also been interested in determining what types of information are acquired during search because this information has the potential to play a crucial role in influencing the consumer's judgments and decision making.

Brand Name Brand name is the most frequently accessed type of information because it is a central node around which other information can be organized in memory.[107] Thus when we know the brand name, we can immediately activate other relevant nodes. For example, if we know the brand name is Allstate or American Airlines or IBM, we can draw on a wealth of prior knowledge and associations. Many small high-tech firms, after viewing the success of Microsoft, are putting forth great effort in building brand name awareness.

Price   Consumers search for price information not only because it tends to be diagnostic but also because it can be used to infer the values of other attributes such as quality and value.[108] Note, however, that search for price is less important than we might expect, because of the low overall extent of search, and does not improve when price variations increase and costs are higher.[109] Furthermore, the importance of price can depend on the culture. As an example, although the Japanese have not traditionally been fond of discounters, customers in Japan now flock to these retail outlets to search for the best bargains.[110]

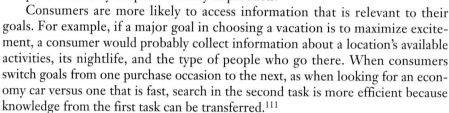

Other Attributes   After brand name and price, any additional information that is sought will depend on which attributes are salient and diagnostic in the product or service category. As Exhibit 9.6 shows, U.S. consumers look for reliability, durability, and low price in selecting a car. Russian consumers search for quality and price when they shop for a variety of products.

Consumers are more likely to access information that is relevant to their goals. For example, if a major goal in choosing a vacation is to maximize excitement, a consumer would probably collect information about a location's available activities, its nightlife, and the type of people who go there. When consumers switch goals from one purchase occasion to the next, as when looking for an economy car versus one that is fast, search in the second task is more efficient because knowledge from the first task can be transferred.[111]

Is External Search Always Accurate?

Consumers can be just as biased in their search for external information as they are during internal search. In particular, consumers tend to exhibit a confirmation bias whereby they search for information that confirms rather than disconfirms their overall beliefs. In one study, consumers with a strong price-quality belief tended to search more for higher-priced brands.[112] Unfortunately, confirmation bias can lead consumers to avoid information that may be important, and this factor can result in a less-than-optimal outcome. Thus if a lower-priced, high-quality brand were available, consumers might never acquire information about it and therefore never select it for purchase.

Knowing which types of information consumers will search for also has important marketing implications. In particular, marketers want to ensure that the specific information consumers seek is easily and readily available. Marketers do so by emphasizing the information in advertising, on a package, in pamphlets, on Web sites, or through the sales force. Consumers are less likely to choose a brand that does not perform well on attributes that are accessed frequently. Thus marketers need to ensure that their offerings are in a strong position on attributes that are heavily accessed. ■

How Do We Engage in External Search?

External search follows a series of sequential steps that can provide further insight into the consumer's decision. These steps include orientation or getting an overview of the product display, evaluation or comparing options on key attributes, and verification or confirming the choice.[113] In particular, researchers have examined the order of information acquisition during evaluation because they assume that information acquired earlier in the decision process plays a more significant role than information acquired later.[114] For example, once a brand emerges

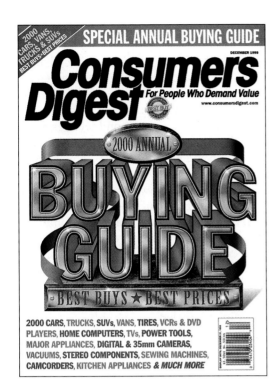

SPECIAL ANNUAL BUYING GUIDE

2000 CARS, VANS, TRUCKS & SUVs BEST BUYS BEST PRICES

DECEMBER 1999

Consumers Digest For People Who Demand Value

www.consumersdigest.com

2000 ANNUAL

BUYING GUIDE

BEST BUYS ★ BEST PRICES

2000 CARS, TRUCKS, SUVs, VANS, TIRES, VCRs & DVD PLAYERS, HOME COMPUTERS, TVs, POWER TOOLS, MAJOR APPLIANCES, DIGITAL & 35mm CAMERAS, VACUUMS, STEREO COMPONENTS, SEWING MACHINES, CAMCORDERS, KITCHEN APPLIANCES & MUCH MORE

EXHIBIT 9.9
Sources of Consumer Information

Consumer Digest publishes a Best Buy list that provides easy-to-understand information about the top brands in many product categories.

Source: © Consumer Digest Inc. Used with permission.

as the leader early in the search process, subsequent information acquisition and evaluation is distorted in favor of that brand.[115]

Search Stages Different sources tend to be accessed at different stages of the search process. Mass media and marketer-related sources tend to be more influential at the early stages of the process, and interpersonal sources are more critical when the actual decision is made.[116] As we would expect, information that is more salient, diagnostic, and related to consumer goals is more likely to be accessed earlier in the search process. However, if consumers can recall salient, diagnostic information from memory, they will have little need to search for this information externally. Thus consumers will search first for information on attributes for which there is greater uncertainty or that are less favorable.[117] Consumers also tend to search first for brands that have a higher perceived attractiveness, again pointing to the importance of developing positive attitudes.

Searching by Brand or Attribute Two major types of processes are (1) **searching by brand**, in which consumers acquire all the needed information on one brand before moving on to the next, and (2) **searching by attribute**, in which brands are compared one attribute at a time.[118] A good example of the latter strategy is price-comparison shopping. Consumers generally prefer to process by attribute because it is simpler and easier.

Consumers are also very sensitive to the manner in which information is stored in memory and the format in which it is presented in the store.[119] If information is organized by brand, as is the case in most stores where all the information is on packages, consumers will process information by brand. In particular, experts will tend to process by brand because they have a larger amount of brand-based knowledge. The fact that consumers are used to processing by brand may bias processing, however, even when information is organized by attribute.[120] Different search strategies affect our decision process differently.[121] Consumers who process by brand remain high in uncertainty until the very end of the search process, whereas those who search by attribute gradually reduce their uncertainty.

Nevertheless, if consumers with less knowledge are given the opportunity to process by attribute, for example, by viewing information in a matrix in *Consumer Reports* or in another format that makes searching easier, they will do so. One study found that presenting lists of nutritional information in the grocery store is popular with consumers. The *Consumers Digest* Best Buy list, which provides information about the top brands in various product categories in a simple format, has become a very popular source of information for consumers (see Exhibit 9.9). Search engines and shopping robots on the Internet also make it easier to process by attribute, especially price.

searching by brand Collecting information on one brand before moving to another.

searching by attribute Comparing brands on attributes, one at a time.

SUMMARY

This chapter examined the three initial stages of the consumer judgment and decision-making process. Problem recognition is the perceived difference between an ideal state and the actual state. When a discrepancy between these two states exists, the consumer may be motivated to resolve it by engaging in decision making.

Internal search is the recall of information, experiences, and feelings from memory. In general, the extent of internal search will increase as motivation (involvement, perceived risk), ability (knowledge and experience), and opportunity (lack of time pressure and distractions) increase. Consumer researchers have been interested in examining which brands, attributes, evaluations, and experiences consumers recall. In general, aspects that are more salient, diagnostic, vivid, and related to goals are the most likely to be recalled. Several biases exist in internal search: confirmation bias, in which information that reinforces our overall beliefs is remembered; inhibition, in which the recall of some information can inhibit the recall of other attributes; and mood, which refers to our tendency to recall mood-congruent information.

 The last part of the chapter focused on external search—how consumers acquire information from outside sources. Methods include prepurchase search and ongoing search. Five major sources of external search were identified. Retailer and media search account for the highest level of search activity, but interpersonal sources increase in importance as consumer knowledge decreases and normative factors increase. The Internet represents a very new and exciting way for consumers to search for information. The extent of search can vary widely, depending on our motivation, ability, and opportunity, but the extent of search is usually rather low. The content of search depends on the salience and diagnosticity of information. Brand name and price are usually the most accessed attributes. Consumers also tend to exhibit a confirmation bias in their external search. Finally, discussion of the search process showed that more salient and diagnostic information tends to be accessed earlier. Also, consumers tend to process either by brand or by attribute. Attribute search is easier and preferred, but often the information is not organized to facilitate this type of processing.

EXERCISES

1. Find 20 magazine, television, or radio advertisements that you think are trying to instigate problem recognition in consumers. Then group these ads into those you think are trying to (a) influence the ideal state and (b) create dissatisfaction with the actual state. Relate each group of ads to the factors discussed in the chapter on influencing the ideal state and the actual state. Which types of ads do you think are effective and why?

2. Interview five consumers on their knowledge about a product or service category for which you think motivation, ability, and opportunity to process are high. Ask consumers to provide

   a. All the brands they would consider

   b. What they know about each brand

   c. Their evaluations of each brand

   d. Any prior experiences they have relative to these brands

After obtaining this information, ask consumers which brand they would choose if they had to decide right now and whether they would want any additional information before deciding. Finally, analyze this information in terms of the principles discussed in this chapter: recall of brands, attributes, evaluations, and experiences. Do your findings support or contradict these notions? If so, why? How does internal search relate to the desire for external search?

3. Interview five consumers about their external search activity regarding a product or service category for which you think motivation, ability, and opportunity to search are high. Be sure to ask them questions about

a. Which brands they would search for information on

b. Which types of information they would look for

c. What sources of information they would use

d. How much time they would take

Analyze the answers in terms of the external search principles discussed in this chapter: the extent, content, and sources of search. Do your findings support or contradict these notions?

CHAPTER 10

JUDGMENT AND DECISION MAKING BASED ON HIGH CONSUMER EFFORT

INTRODUCTION

In Bangkok, Thailand, a Chrysler salesperson races to complete paperwork on a new Jeep Cherokee because the customer has been told by her astrologer that she must drive her new vehicle away at exactly 7:49 A.M.[1] With minutes to spare, the deal is closed and the keys are handed over. Another consumer also chooses a Cherokee over a Land Rover because of its durability, powerful engine, and price (half the cost of a Land Rover).

These examples are typical occurrences in a country that is becoming one of the fastest-growing and hottest car markets in the world (see Exhibit 10.1). In fact, Thais are passionate about their automobiles, listing them as the fifth necessity behind food, lodging, medicine, and clothing. Consequently, many U.S. and Japanese auto companies are engaged in a highly competitive battle in Thailand and other Southeast Asian countries. These manufacturers will succeed, however, only if they learn what consumers want. For example, many consumers have a positive impression of the Jeep Cherokee because it is made in the United States. But only the wealthy can afford it in Thailand, and many of these people do not do their own driving. Yet the Cherokee's back seat is not designed for those who spend the day conducting business over the phone while their drivers navigate potholes.

EXHIBIT 10.1
Traffic in Bangkok

Thai consumers are very passionate about their automobiles despite other means of transportation.

Source: Thierry Falise/Liaison Agency.

This example points out the importance of understanding the consumer's judgment and decision-making process. Marketers must understand the types of judgments consumers make (The car is made in the United States, so it is good) and what types of criteria are important in influencing consumers' decisions (durability, back seat comfort, what others think or say about the purchase, and so on). In addition, marketers must understand the emotions and feelings that influence consumer decisions.

Consumer judgment and decision making when motivation, ability, and opportunity to process are high represent the next stages in our overall model (see Exhibit 10.2) and are the focus of this chapter. By carefully analyzing the factors that enter into judgment and decision making, marketers can acquire valuable insights that help them develop and market product offerings to consumers.

HIGH-EFFORT JUDGMENT PROCESSES

judgments Estimating or evaluating the likelihood of an event.

decision making Making a selection between options or courses of action.

Think about the last time you went to a restaurant. While reviewing the menu, you probably considered some items and thought about how good they would be before making your final choice. In doing so, you were making **judgments**, evaluations or estimates regarding the likelihood of events. Judgments are a critical input into the decision process and represent the next key step of our model.

Judgment and **decision making** are often confused with one another. In a consumer context, *judgments* are evaluations or estimates regarding the likelihood that products and services possess certain features or will perform in a certain manner.[2] Judgments do not require the consumer to make a decision. Thus if we see an ad for a new Mexican restaurant, we can form a judgment as to whether we will like it or not, how similar to or different from other Mexican restaurants it is, or how expensive it is. These judgments can serve as input into our decision on whether or not to eat there, but they do not require an actual choice.

Judgment and decision making can also involve us in different processes. One study found that attributes were searched in a different order in a judgment task as opposed to a decision task.[3] In another study higher levels of brand familiarity made it easier to remember information for a judgment but lowered memory in a decision task.[4] Consumers can also act on different preferences depending on whether the task involves choice or a judgment (especially when the product category is unfamiliar).[5] Given the important role judgment plays in the information processing we do as consumers, researchers are increasingly examining judgment processes, particularly the three we look at here: estimations of likelihood, judgments of goodness or badness, and predictions of the likelihood that two events will occur together.

EXHIBIT 10.2
Chapter Overview: Judgment and Decision Making: High Consumer Effort

After problem recognition and search, consumers can engage in some form of judgment or decision making, which can vary in terms of processing effort (from high to low). This chapter looks at high-effort judgment and decision processes. *Judgments* involve making estimates of how likely something is to occur or how good or bad something is. They serve as inputs into *decision making,* which can be *cognitively* or *affectively* based. The decision-making process can also be influenced by *contextual* factors such as consumer characteristics, task characteristics, and decision framing.

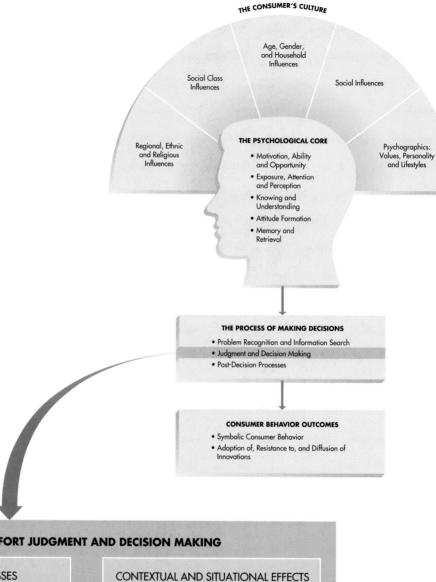

THE CONSUMER'S CULTURE

Age, Gender, and Household Influences

Social Class Influences

Social Influences

Regional, Ethnic and Religious Influences

THE PSYCHOLOGICAL CORE
- Motivation, Ability and Opportunity
- Exposure, Attention and Perception
- Knowing and Understanding
- Attitude Formation
- Memory and Retrieval

Psychographics: Values, Personality and Lifestyles

THE PROCESS OF MAKING DECISIONS
- Problem Recognition and Information Search
- Judgment and Decision Making
- Post-Decision Processes

CONSUMER BEHAVIOR OUTCOMES
- Symbolic Consumer Behavior
- Adoption of, Resistance to, and Diffusion of Innovations

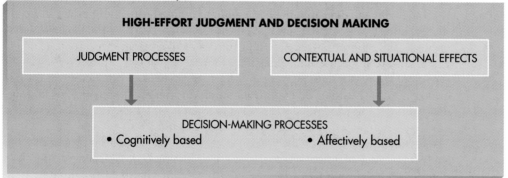

HIGH-EFFORT JUDGMENT AND DECISION MAKING

JUDGMENT PROCESSES

CONTEXTUAL AND SITUATIONAL EFFECTS

DECISION-MAKING PROCESSES
- Cognitively based
- Affectively based

Judgments of Likelihood and Goodness/Badness

estimations of likelihood Judging how likely it is something will occur.

An **estimation of likelihood** is our determination of how probable it is that something will occur. Estimations of likelihood appear in many consumer contexts. For example, when we buy a product or service, we can attempt to estimate its quality and the likelihood that it will satisfy our needs. When we buy clothing, we can estimate the likelihood that others will approve of it. When we view an ad, we can assess the likelihood that it is truthful. The key point is that estimations of likelihood are at the very core of consumer information processing.

judgments of goodness/ badness Evaluating the desirability of something.

Judgments of goodness/badness are the consumer's evaluation of the desirability of product or service features. In other words, in planning a trip we might judge how good or bad it is that Europe is fun and expensive. Most of the research on this kind of judgment has been done in the context of the attitude models covered in Chapter 6. These models suggest that a consumer combines individual judgments into an overall evaluation of goodness or badness in order to form an attitude about the product or service.

anchoring and adjustment process Starting with an initial evaluation and adjusting it with additional information.

Anchoring and Adjustment   In making estimations of likelihood and goodness/badness, consumers tend to employ an **anchoring and adjustment process**.[6] They will first anchor the judgment based on some initial value and then make adjustments or "update" the evaluation as they consider additional information. The initial value can be information or an affective response that is readily available from memory, or it can be attribute information from the external environment that is encountered first.[7] Consumer values and normative influences can also be strong determinants of the initial value.

To illustrate, Starbucks Coffee has a very positive image in Japan. This factor led a local chain to change its name to Seattle Coffee, hoping to form a positive initial anchor that would encourage consumers to see the shops as similar to Starbucks. Additional information from ads or experience may adjust this initial value upward or downward, but the judgment is more likely to be positive given the Starbucks image. If the prior evaluation of Starbucks had been negative, however, the anchor would have most likely resulted in a judgment of quality that was also negative. Thus the same anchor can lead to two different judgments depending on how it is perceived.

Clearly the nature of the initial anchor is extremely important, because it greatly affects the outcome of the judgment. In one study consumers were asked to make judgments about ground-beef samples. One group was told the beef was 75 percent lean, and another that it was 25 percent fat. Even though these two statements contain identical information, the "lean" group produced significantly more positive ratings than the "fat" group.[8] We discuss this process, which is called *framing*, in more detail later in the chapter.

Anchoring and adjustment can occur in two other ways as well. First, when products are *bundled*—that is, when two or more items are offered together—the most important item serves as the anchor, and adjustments are based on evaluations of the remaining items.[9] Second, when low-ability or low-knowledge consumers are evaluating *new* products, they give greater weight to information acquired later in the process, an example of the recency effect.[10]

imagery Imagining an event in order to make a judgment.

Imagery, or visualization, can also play an important role in the judgment process. Consumers can attempt to construct an image of an event, such as how they will look and feel behind the wheel of a new car, to estimate its likelihood or its goodness or badness. Interestingly, visualizing an event can actually make it seem more likely because consumers may form a positive bias when they imagine themselves using the product.[11] Imagery may also lead consumers to overestimate how satisfied they will be with a product or service.[12]

Biases in Judgment Processes   If consumers are susceptible to a confirmation bias and acquire and process only confirming evidence, they become more confident in their judgment than they would be if they acquired negative information. This bias can lead to less-than-optimal choices for future purchases. When consumers are overconfident, they are also not likely to engage in external information search, because they believe that they know almost everything.[13] A study on AIDS found that consumers can have a self-positivity bias ("I am less likely to get AIDS than others") but that this bias can be reduced if important information is made more accessible.[14]

Mood can also have a biasing effect on judgment.[15] Essentially, your mood serves as the initial anchor for your judgment. For example, if you are in a good mood when shopping for a CD, you are more likely to like the new music you hear. One reason for this effect is that consumers want to preserve a good mood and therefore avoid negative information.

MARKETING IMPLICATIONS   Marketers can increase the probability that judgments of their products and services are being anchored by a positive initial value by focusing the consumer's attention on certain attributes. For example, even though most consumers will not be able to afford digital TV for a while, a number of electronics firms are heavily advertising this product because it will define the industry leaders—the initial anchor—for years to come.[16] Our judgment of a product can also be affected by our exposure to other products.[17] Thus placing a picture of a low-priced car like the Nissan Altima alongside a Jaguar could make the Jaguar serve as the judgment anchor.

The country of origin of a product can serve as an anchor and influence subsequent judgments.[18] For example, the Italian government has spent $25 million on ads to convince consumers that Italian fashions are the finest.[19] In China domestic brands are having to market aggressively because consumers now prefer Western versions of the same product.[20]

priming   Creating the anchor in a judgment process.

Priming consumers with positive feelings before giving them information will lead them to evaluate the product or service more positively.[21] The ad in Exhibit 10.3 is a good example of this strategy. The humorous visual of the Dalmatian working at the computer can serve as a positive anchor for the evaluation of Web Easy software. Salespeople also prime consumers by recommending (or raving about) a particular product or service. Companies that publicize their good works, as is the case of Wal-Mart in Exhibit 10.4, can create a positive anchor for judgments of the company. Tobacco companies in Hungary are promoting a more positive image by giving money to schools, hospitals, and the Red Cross.[22] Finally, ads suggesting that consumers engage in imagery—like imagining a delicious pizza—can also produce positive judgments.

brand extensions   Introducing a new brand with an existing brand name.

The judgment process has important implications for the introduction of **brand extensions**. Mercedes's positive image led to tremendous excitement over its new M-class utility vehicle.[23] Likewise, Fruit of the Loom has expanded beyond the U.S. underwear market to offer sweatshirts, turtlenecks, and shorts—and even more stylish merchandise in Europe.[24] When the consumer is exposed to the new extension, the existing brand name and its positive associations will serve as a positive anchor for subsequent judgments related to the new product. ■

EXHIBIT 10.3
Anchoring a Judgement

The light humor created by the picture of the Dalmatian using the computer in this ad attempts to prime consumers with positive feelings. Marketers hope consumers will evaluate the information about Web Easy software positively as well.

Source: Courtesy of Ixla USA.

EXHIBIT 10.4
Publicizing Good Works

Companies often contribute to the good of the community through various service programs and projects. When a company publicizes its good works, consumers may develop positive feelings toward the company and, in turn, may be more apt to purchase its products and services. In this ad Wal-Mart is announcing its program to protect the environment.

Source: Courtesy of Wal-Mart.

Conjunctive Probability Assessment

conjunctive probability assessment Estimating the extent two events will occur together.

Sometimes consumers estimate the likelihood that two events will occur simultaneously or that a relationship exists between attributes. This estimate is called **conjunctive probability assessment**. Prior expectations influence its accuracy.[25] For example, consumers might expect that a rich flavor means high calories or that nationally advertised brands have higher quality than regional ones. Judgment improves when the attributes are diagnostic because then consumers can detect actual relationships between variables. For example, experts are less guided by country-of-origin stereotypes and more by actual attributes when information is unambiguous.[26]

illusory correlation When consumers think two things occur together when they actually do not.

Sometimes, however, consumers are not very adept at making conjunctive probability judgments and think a relationship exists when in fact it does not.[27] Such **illusory correlation** is apt to occur when information is ambiguous. For example, many consumers mistakenly assume that low price means low quality or that all cars made in Asia are high quality despite the well-publicized problems of

Subaru, Suzuki, Isuzu, and Hyundai.[28] Smokers mistakenly thought "clean," smokeless cigarettes were safer.[29] Thus marketers need to point out such fallacies when they occur. For example, Korean electronic products were introduced as budget brands, but now marketers must overcome the expectation of low quality as they try to move these brands to more upscale markets.[30]

HIGH-EFFORT DECISION-MAKING PROCESSES

In many instances, consumers must choose from a set of products, services, brands, or courses of action. In any consumer choice situation, many options are available. Some options, called the **consideration set**, will be evaluated by consumers; some, the **inept set**, will be unacceptable; and some, the **inert set**, will be treated with indifference.[31] Consumers must also decide how and when to dispose of products and services. Thus to engage in most forms of consumer behavior, consumers must make some type of decision even if they decide not to choose, which they may do when a great deal of uncertainty exists.[32]

Much of the extensive research on consumer decision making has tried to understand how we combine the information acquired from internal and external search to make a decision, and various models of the process have been proposed. A basic assumption underlying many models is that consumers behave in a cognitive and rational manner, choosing the brand or service with the best combination of features to satisfy their needs. Thus when buying a new stereo, consumers might investigate a set of brands in terms of reliability, power, warranty, and any other salient attributes before selecting the one that maximizes their utility.

Many times, however, consumers do not operate in such a rational manner. In high-elaboration situations, strong feelings might compel a consumer to buy a new CD or a new pair of shoes, even though he or she already has many. Therefore, consumer researchers have recently become interested in how choices are made when the decision is more hedonic or emotional in nature.

Another key finding is that the decision process can vary according to the situation because consumers are highly adaptive to the task.[33] Each choice situation can vary greatly, not only in terms of the types of brands and information evaluated but also in the consumers' motivation, ability, and opportunity to process information. Thus the process used to select a car is likely to be very different from that used to choose a house, a computer, or any other type of product or service. Furthermore, even the same type of decision context can change over time as new brands are introduced and information becomes outdated.

Finally, decision-making styles can vary across cultures.[34] Some North Americans, for example, tend to be analytical, to rely on factual information, and to search for solutions to problems. In Asian cultures, in contrast, and particularly in Japan, the *kimochi*, or feeling, generally has to be right; logic is sometimes less important. Similarly, many Saudi Arabians are more intuitive in their decision making and avoid persuasion based on empirical reasoning. Russians are said to place more emphasis on values than on facts, and Germans tend to be theoretical and deductive. In North American and European cultures, decisions are usually made by individuals who control their own fate. In Asian cultures the group is of primary importance, and actions arise at random or from other events, rather than being controlled by individuals.

A key point is that consumers do not follow a uniform process every time they make a decision.[35] Instead, consumers construct a strategy depending on the na-

---

consideration set The options consumers evaluate when making a decision.

inept set Options that are unacceptable when making a decision.

inert set Options toward which consumers are indifferent.

ture of the task, and they may employ various decision rules, either alone or in combination. Thus even though a number of choice models have been proposed, each may accurately describe decision making under certain circumstances. With this in mind, the following sections first describe different types of cognitive models and then examine affective decision making.

HIGH-EFFORT THOUGHT-BASED DECISIONS

cognitive models The process by which consumers combine items of information about attributes to reach a decision.

Cognitive models describe the processes by which consumers combine items of information about attributes to reach a decision in a rational, systematic manner. Note that the various models are not intended to describe the same process. Rather, they identify *different* processes that may occur when consumers make a decision. Which model a consumer follows depends on both the consumer and the nature of the situation. Furthermore, the situations that different models fit may lead to entirely different selections by the consumer. Finally, consumers may employ a combination of models rather than just one and may not necessarily be aware of the exact process they are following.

Types of Decision Processes

Cognitive models can be classified along two key dimensions: compensatory versus noncompensatory nature, and brand versus attribute processing.

compensatory model A mental cost-benefit analysis model to make a decision.

Compensatory Versus Noncompensatory Models   In **compensatory models** consumers choose the brand that has the greatest number of positive features relative to negative. These models are essentially a type of mental cost-benefit analysis. A key feature is that a negative evaluation on one attribute can be compensated for (hence the name *compensatory*) by positive features on others. To illustrate, for some U.S. consumers a negative feature of Japanese products is that they are made in another country. However, this shortcoming can be overcome if the products are rated highly on other aspects, such as reliability and price.

noncompensatory model Simple decision model in which negative information leads to rejection of the option.

In contrast, with a **noncompensatory model** negative information leads to the immediate rejection of the brand or service from the consideration set. The knowledge that a product is foreign-made might prevent some consumers from considering it further. Noncompensatory models are easier to implement and require less cognitive effort and strain than compensatory models do.

brand processing Evaluating one brand at a time.

Brand Versus Attribute Models   In making a decision, consumers often evaluate *one brand at a time*. Thus, a consumer making a computer purchase might collect information about an IBM computer and make a judgment about it before moving on to the next brand. This type of **brand processing** occurs frequently, because the environment—in the form of package information, dealerships, and so on—is often organized by brands.

attribute processing Comparing brands, one attribute at a time.

Attribute processing, on the other hand, occurs when consumers compare across brands, *one attribute at a time*. A good example is price-comparison shopping, in which consumers compare each brand on price and select the one with the desired price. Although most consumers prefer attribute processing, because it is easier than brand processing, information is not often available in a manner that facilitates it.

Based on these two distinctions, cognitive models of decision making can be placed into one of the four cells shown in Exhibit 10.5.

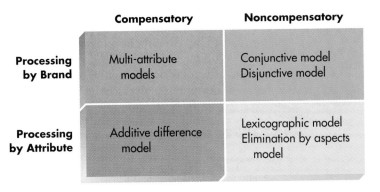

	Compensatory	Noncompensatory
Processing by Brand	Multi-attribute models	Conjunctive model Disjunctive model
Processing by Attribute	Additive difference model	Lexicographic model Elimination by aspects model

EXHIBIT 10.5
Types of Choice Models

Choice models can be characterized along two major dimensions: (a) whether processing occurs one *brand* at a time or one *attribute* at a time, and (b) whether they are *compensatory* (bad attributes can be compensated for by good ones) or *noncompensatory* (a bad attribute eliminates the brand). Each model we discuss can be placed into one of the four cells that result from crossing these two factors.

Compensatory Brand-Processing Models

Much research has focused on brand-based compensatory models, also called **multiattribute models**. We discussed one multiattribute model, the theory of reasoned action (TORA), in Chapter 6. We indicated that consumers' attitudes toward an intended act, coupled with their idea about what important others think is appropriate behavior, predict the consumers' intentions of buying, using, or disposing of a product/service.

Various other models have been proposed,[36] and most of them are computed mathematically. These models differ, however, in which of the following components they include: (1) belief strength, (2) evaluation, and (3) the importance consumers attach to the attribute or outcome. The boxed insert on page 232 discusses a mutliattribute model that uses belief strength and importance as its main components.

MARKETING IMPLICATIONS Because they identify the beliefs consumers have about the outcomes or attributes associated with buying, using, or disposing of a product or about the attributes that characterize the product, brand-based compensatory models are very useful in identifying which alternatives consumers may choose or reject. These models also provide guidance to marketers about which outcomes or attributes associated with the product need to be reinforced or changed.

If consumers do not strongly believe that positive outcomes or attributes are associated with a decision, marketers should stress these outcomes or attributes in their marketing activities so as to strengthen consumers' beliefs. Off-road vehicles such as Toyota's Previa and Mitsubishi's Expo-LRV have become very popular in Japan because the vehicles look rugged and manufacturers have emphasized that children can move around inside when traffic is at a standstill.[37] The Sony Mini-Disc CD player stresses its portability and recording capabilities, attributes not typically associated with CD players.

If a decision analysis reveals certain weaknesses in the product, marketers should address these shortcomings by altering the product and communicating the

multiattribute (expectancy-value) model A type of brand-based compensatory model.

improvements to consumers. For example, because many Germans have negative beliefs about the military, the army has tried to convince young men that it offers many career opportunities and benefits.[38] Ford has a highly trusted name in Europe, so it is now attempting to improve the quality image of Jaguar by acknowledging that it is made by Ford.[39]

Decision models also help identify weaknesses of competitors, which can then be targeted in marketing communications, especially comparative ads. In Japan, Ford attacked VW in ads asking, "Why is the Golf so expensive in Japan?"[40] ■

Compensatory Attribute-Processing Models

additive difference model
Compensatory model in which brands are compared by attribute, two brands at a time.

According to the **additive difference model**, brands are compared by attribute, *two brands at a time*.[41] Consumers evaluate differences between brands on each attribute and then combine them into an overall preference. Note that this process allows trade-offs between attributes—that is, a positive difference on one attribute can offset a negative difference on another.

MARKETING IMPLICATIONS The additive difference model helps marketers determine which attributes or outcomes exhibit the greatest differences among brands, and this information can be used to improve and position the brand. If a brand is performing below a major competitor on a particular attribute, the company needs to enhance consumers' beliefs about its product's superiority. For example, after being vigorously attacked by Dell on the basis of price, Compaq improved its competitive position significantly on this dimension.

On the other hand, if a brand is performing significantly better than competitors on a key attribute, marketers should enhance consumer beliefs by positioning the product or service around this advantage. Chrysler has introduced a small car in Europe which is very inexpensive and gets 50 miles per gallon because it is made of plastic.[42] In South Africa, the fast-food restaurant Africa Hut has become extremely popular because it differs from all other competitors on one key attribute: It serves traditional local dishes such as pap (corn porridge), malamagodu (tripe), morogo (a leafy green vegetable), and skop (sheep's head).[43] ■

Noncompensatory Brand-Processing Models

The compensatory models we have discussed require a significant amount of effort to evaluate each brand on many attributes. Often consumers are not willing to put forth this much effort and instead opt for a simpler noncompensatory process. With noncompensatory brand-processing models, consumers use key attributes to evaluate brands and then eliminate those that are not adequate on any one attribute.[44] These models are called noncompensatory because a negative rating on a key attribute means that the brand is eliminated.

cutoff levels For each attribute, the point at which a brand is rejected with a noncompensatory model.

A common feature of noncompensatory models is that the decision process proceeds in a simple, sequential manner. Consumers set up **cutoff levels** for each attribute and reject a brand if it is below the cutoff. For example, gamblers love to pull the lever on "one-armed bandits" and therefore have rejected electronic slot machines.[45] Cutoffs tend to be chosen to set up the biggest difference between accepted and rejected alternatives. Models differ in terms of the levels of these cutoffs and whether the comparison proceeds by brand or by attribute.

Illustration of Two Compensatory Models

Here's an example of one *multiattribute model* that uses *belief strength* and *importance weights* as its two components. Belief strength represents how strongly consumers hold each belief (some beliefs are held more strongly than others); importance weights represent how important each belief is to a decision (some beliefs are more important than others). The model can be outlined as follows:

$$A_b = \sum(b_i \times I_i)$$
$$i = 1$$

where A_b represents an attitude toward the brand; b_i is the belief strength associated with attribute i, a judgment of likelihood; and I_i is the importance of the attribute. The model can easily be applied to a decision context if we assess A_b for each option in the consideration set. The consumer would choose the option for which he or she has the strongest attitude.

Consider the following example. Suppose Elena wants to go to graduate school in state A, state B, or state C and that the most salient attributes of each school she is considering are cost, distance from home, prestige, and qualifications of the faculty. As shown in the following exhibit, Elena rates b_i and I_i for each option, one at a time. The model then predicts that Elena will select state A because it is rated the most prestigious with the best faculty.

Using the *additive difference model*, Elena first compares state A and state B on the attribute of superior faculty. Using the b_i rating, for example, she finds a difference of +1. She moves on to the prestige attribute, where the difference is +2. Elena continues this process for the other attributes to get a total additive difference of +3, establishing a preference for state A. She repeats the process by comparing state A to state C, also finding that state A is seen as a better choice. (Note that because state A is seen as better than the other two choices, there is no need to compare these two).

Remember that consumers do not formally make these ratings when they make a decision. The numbers are a way of quantifying the mental cost-benefit analysis that consumers might engage in. Nevertheless, compensatory models are useful in helping us identify which factors are most influential in making a decision.

EXHIBIT

How Elena Might Choose a State for College: Compensatory Models*

	DESCRIPTION	OUTCOME OR CONSEQUENCES OF THE DECISION	HOW IMPORTANT IS EACH OUTCOME (1 = not at all; 7 = very important)	HOW STRONG IS ELENA'S BELIEF THAT THE OUTCOME CHARACTERIZES THE ALTERNATIVE (−3 = very weak; +3 = very strong)			ALTERNATIVE CHOSEN AND WHY
				STATE A	STATE B	STATE C	
THE MULTI-ATTRIBUTE MODEL	Decisions are made by brand-based processing. Each alternative's outcome importance weight is multiplied by its belief strength. These totals are then summed across outcomes. The brand with the highest weighted score is chosen.	Has superior faculty	6	+3	+2	+3	State A is chosen because the sum of its importance weights times its outcome rating [6x(+3)]+[4x(+3)]+ [3x(−1)]+[2x(+1)]=29. This value is higher than the summed products of the other alternatives (State B= [6x(+2)]+[4x(+1)]+ [3x(+1)]+[2(−1)]=17, and State C= [6x(+3)]+[4x(−2)]+ [3x(+2)]+[2x(0)]=16).
		Has more prestigious institutions	4	+3	+1	−2	
		Has more expensive tuitions on average	3	−1	+1	+2	
		Will be far from home	2	+1	−1	0	
		Weighted Total (sum of each belief strength × its importance)		29	17	16	

			HOW DO THE BELIEF STRENGTH RATINGS COMPARE ACROSS ALTERNATIVES?			
			STATE A VS. STATE B	STATE A VS. STATE C	STATE B VS. STATE C	
THE ADDITIVE DIFFERENCE MODEL	**DESCRIPTION**	**OUTCOME**				
	Belief strengths about attributes are compared across brands. The brand with the highest total additive difference across the outcomes is chosen.	Has superior faculty	(+3)−(+2)=+1	(+3)−(+3)=0	(+2)−(+3)=−1	State A is chosen because the additive difference of its belief strength ratings compare more favorably to both State B (+3) and State C (+3). State B isn't seen as any better than State C (additive difference = 0).
		Has more prestigious institutions	(+3)−(+1)=+2	(+3)−(−2)=5	(+1)−(−2)=+3	
		Has more expensive tuitions on average	(−1)−(+1)=−2	(−1)−(+2)=−3	(+1)−(+2)=−1	
		Will be far from home	(+1)−(−1)=+2	(+1)−(0)=+1	(−1)−(0)=−1	
		ADDITIVE DIFFERENCE	+3	+3	0	

*Models are compensatory because for any given alternative a high rating on one outcome can compensate for a low rating on another outcome.

conjunctive model A non-compensatory model that sets minimum cutoffs to reject "bad" options.

Conjunctive Model Using a **conjunctive model**, consumers set up *minimum* cutoffs for each attribute that represent the absolute lowest value they are willing to accept.[46] For example, in buying a car a consumer might expect to get at least 15 miles per gallon. She might therefore decide to reject an alternative if she believes it gets fewer miles per gallon. Because the cutoffs represent the bare minimum belief strength levels, the psychology of a conjunctive model is to rule out unsuitable alternatives as soon as possible. The weight is on negative information.

disjunctive model A non-compensatory model that sets acceptable cutoffs to find options that are "good."

Disjunctive Model The **disjunctive model** is similar to the conjunctive model with two important exceptions. First, the consumer sets up *acceptable* levels for the cutoffs—levels that are more desirable. Thus although 15 miles per gallon may be the lowest gas mileage we will accept, 20 miles per gallon may represent a more acceptable level. Second, evaluations are made on *several* of the most important attributes, rather than on all. Thus in a disjunctive model, the weight is on positive information.

MARKETING IMPLICATIONS Identifying consumers' cutoff levels can be very useful for marketers. If a product or service is below any of the cutoffs for many consumers, it will be rejected frequently. Therefore, consumers' beliefs about these attributes must be changed. Until recently many consumers could not afford a cell phone because it was expensive enough to fall below the cutoff on price. But now companies offer no-monthly-fee, prepaid packages, allowing many consumers to get phones.[47] Snapple and PepsiCo have had difficulty in selling iced tea in England because British consumers do not believe iced tea performs well on taste.[48]

In addition, research suggests that marketers can hurt themselves by adding unwanted or unneeded features to products or services because these give the consumer a reason for rejecting the brand.[49] One study found that when two brands offered collector's plate and golf umbrella premiums, the brands were less desirable than when the offer was not made.[50] ■

Noncompensatory Attribute-Processing Models

Noncompensatory models in which processing occurs by attribute include the lexicographic and elimination-by-aspects models.

lexicographic model A non-compensatory model that compares brands by attributes, one at a time.

Lexicographic Model In the **lexicographic model** consumers order attributes in terms of importance and compare the options one attribute at a time, starting with the most important. If one option dominates, it is selected. If a tie develops, the consumer proceeds to the second most important attribute. The process continues until only one option remains. Note that a tie occurs if the difference between two options on any attribute is below the just noticeable difference. Thus two brands that cost $2.77 and $2.79 would likely be seen as tied on price. Another common example of a lexicographic strategy is price-comparison shopping, where the most important attribute is, of course, price.

elimination-by-aspects model Similar to the lexicographic model but adds the notion of acceptable cutoffs.

Elimination-by-Aspects Model The **elimination-by-aspects model** is similar to the lexicographic model but incorporates the notion of an *acceptable cutoff*.[51] This model is not as strict as the lexicographic model, and more attributes are likely to be considered. Attributes are first ordered in terms of importance, and options are then compared on the most important attribute. Those options below the cutoff are eliminated. The process continues until one option remains.

MARKETING IMPLICATIONS Attribute-processing models not only aid in identifying determinant attributes but also provide additional information on the *order* in which attributes are evaluated. Thus if many consumers are employing a lexicographic model and a brand is weak on the most important attribute, the company needs to improve on this feature in order to be selected. For example, performance and reliability tend to be the two most critical attributes in the car market, which is why U.S. car manufacturers have had to emphasize these features so heavily to regain consumer confidence.

Marketers can try to change the order of importance so that the most critical attribute is a major brand advantage. Saturn has been experiencing some success in Japan by convincing consumers that practicality is more important than being distinctive.[52] Brands such as Crystal Pepsi, Ban Clear deodorant, and Ivory clear dish-washing soap tried but failed to increase the importance to consumers of the attribute "clear."[53] ■

Multiple Models That Characterize Decision Making

Consumers often use a combination of decision-making strategies.[54] In particular, when many options are available, consumers can use a noncompensatory strategy (conjunctive model) to reduce the size of the consideration set, getting rid of the bad options, and then use a more thorough model (a compensatory strategy) to evaluate the remaining ones. Or they might use bits and pieces of various strategies in constructing a decision process.[55] As consumers learn more about the alternatives or about the decision task, they may change their strategy to adjust to their new knowledge. They might reorder the importance of attributes or employ a different strategy.[56] Thus consumers tend to be opportunistic and adaptive processors.

MARKETING IMPLICATIONS Given that different models can lead to different choices, marketers may sometimes want to change the process by which consumers make a decision. For example, if most consumers are using a compensatory strategy, switching them to a noncompensatory strategy may be advantageous, particularly if competitors have a major weakness. By convincing consumers not to accept a lower level on an important attribute—that is, not to compensate for the attribute—marketers can sometimes cause consumers to reject competitors from consideration. For example, Adidas and Converse have attacked Nike with low-priced shoes, trying to get consumers to reject Nike on the basis of high price.[57]

When consumers are rejecting a brand with a noncompensatory strategy, marketers can try to switch them to a compensatory strategy—that is, convince them that other attributes compensate for a negative. Chrysler adopted this strategy in the ad in Exhibit 10.6 on the following page. The message is that although the Town & Country is a practical minivan (a negative for some), it can also be considered a luxury car with a spacious, leather-tailored cabin; temperature control; and a ten-speaker, 200-watt CD/cassette stereo. GE has been successful in selling large U.S. refrigerators in Japan by switching consumers from a noncompensatory model (the refrigerators are too big) to a focus on other features and by convincing them to place the fridge in the living room, instead of in the typically small Japanese kitchen.[58]

EXHIBIT 10.6

Changing from a Non-com-pensatory to a Compensatory-Based Decision

This ad attempts to reach consumers who might otherwise reject minivans or luxury cars because they do not meet the consumers' need for either comfort or space. By emphasizing that the Town & Country provides both space and luxury, Chrysler is encouraging consumers to consider both attributes.

Source: The Chrysler Town & Country ad is used with permission from DaimlerChrysler Corp. Michael Ruppert, Hunter Freeman, Photographers.

It blurs the line between needs and wants.

It's the automotive world's most ingenious way of reconciling space with luxury. After all, no other vehicle allows you to seat seven in a cabin tailored with leather and Preferred Suede.' The 1999 Chrysler Town & Country Limited. A vehicle that also features Dual Zone Temperature Control and a fold-down center armrest on the rear bench seat. Add a 10-speaker, 200-watt CD/cassette stereo and it's small wonder that Town & Country won Strategic Vision's 1998 Total Quality Award' for "Best Ownership Experience" in minivans.' Inquiries? Call 1.800.CHRYSLER. Or you can visit www.chryslercars.com.

Trimmed with leather that's perforated to further absorb interior noise, Town & Country boasts Quad Command bucket seats. Also, the front seats have eight-way power, are heated and have two driver's seat memory settings.

ENGINEERED TO BE GREAT CARS   **CHRYSLER** TOWN & COUNTRY

affective decision making Decisions based on feelings and emotions.

HIGH-EFFORT FEELING-BASED DECISIONS

The common feature of cognitive models is that decision making proceeds in a sequential and rational manner. Researchers are now increasingly realizing, however, that consumers also possess another processing mode in which they make decisions in a more holistic manner, on the basis of feelings or emotions.[59] In other words, decisions are sometimes made simply because they *feel* right, rather than because they resulted from a detailed and systematic evaluation. In fact, emotional processing can sometimes overwhelm rational thought and lead consumers to select something that is inconsistent with their rational preferences, making a decision they can sometimes regret later.[60] Although our current knowledge of the role of **affective decision making** is still at a preliminary level, some general findings have emerged.

As you saw in Chapter 6, products and services can be linked with emotions and feelings. Brands can be associated with positive emotions such as love, joy, pride, and elation as well as with negative emotions such as guilt, hate, fear, anxiety, anger, sadness, shame, and greed. These emotions can be recalled to play a central role in the decision process, particularly when they are perceived to be relevant to the product or service.[61] This affective processing is frequently experience based.[62] In other words, consumers select an option based on their recall of past experiences and the feelings associated with them.

In particular, feelings are critical for products and services that have hedonic, symbolic, or aesthetic aspects.[63] In choosing a restaurant, clothing, music, entertainment, furniture, or art, for example, consumers will often base their choice on positive associated feelings. A study of rock music found that emotional, sensory, and imagery responses were the most critical in determining liking and intent to purchase recorded music.[64] Even in a poor economy, Japanese consumers bought more jewelry because it felt good.[65]

Emotions also play a key role in deciding what we consume and for how long.[66] We consume products and services that make us feel good more often and for longer periods than ones that do not.

The line between today's events and tomorrow's dream is balanced on the rim of a teacup.

Sleepytime® Tea & Supplement

At day's end, finding natural relaxation is easier with Sleepytime Tea. Caffeine free with unique herbal calming properties and the gentle flavor of chamomile and spearmint. And try Sleepytime Extra™ natural herbal supplement with valerian. Part of our complete line of herbal supplements and teas, crafted with 30 years of dedication to herbal health. Visit us at www.celestialseasonings.com.

CELESTIAL SEASONINGS
What you do for you.

EXHIBIT 10.7
Stimulating Imagery Through Advertising

Ads sometimes try to induce consumers to imagine themselves in a particular consumption situation. When they do, consumers may experience the feelings and emotions that are associated with consumption. The ad for Celestial Seasonings encourages consumers to imagine the relaxation that comes from drinking Sleepytime tea.

Source: © 1998 Celestial Seasonings, Inc.

Products and services can also serve as a means of removing or reducing negative emotions. Sometimes consumers buy a product, such as new clothing or a new CD, simply to make themselves feel better. In other situations, negative feelings are the direct cause of the choice. Many consumers purchase diet foods and drinks, for example, out of guilt or shame. Negative emotions can also be associated with difficult choices that involve conflict, such as trading off greater safety versus lower price in a car, and consumers will often choose the option that avoids the negative emotion.[67] Brands that require a lot of effort to evaluate may create negative emotions and be selected less frequently than those that require less effort.[68]

Imagery plays a key role in emotional decision making.[69] Consumers can attempt to imagine themselves actually consuming the product or service, and any emotions experienced can then be used as input into the decision. In choosing a vacation, for example, you can imagine the excitement you might experience from each destination. If these images are pleasant (or negative), they will exert a positive (or negative) influence on your decision process. As shown in Exhibit 10.7, ads can also try to get consumers to imagine themselves using a product or service. Note that adding information actually makes imagery processing easier (unlike the case in cognitive processing, in which information overload is a threat) because more information makes it easier to form an accurate image. In addition, imagery tends to encourage brand-based processing because images are organized by brand rather than by attribute.

Consumers can use *both* cognitive and affective processing in making a decision. In fact, they can employ yet another combined strategy in which they first use a compensatory or noncompensatory cognitive model to narrow down a choice set and then use imagery and emotions to make the final decision.[70] In buying a house, for example, consumers often use price, square footage, and number of rooms to narrow down the set and then select the home that "feels right."

MARKETING IMPLICATIONS

Marketers can employ a variety of advertising, sales, and promotion techniques to add to the emotional experience surrounding the product or service. Good service or pleasant ambiance in a restaurant or store, for example, can produce positive feelings and experiences that may influence future choices. In an effort to provide this kind of ambiance, some shopping malls have added entertainment centers, roller coasters, and even a pirate ship.[71] Giving a consumer a free gift with a purchase (as is often done with perfume and cosmetics) can have a positive influence. An ad for American General Insurance shows children strolling through a field with dreamy music in the background to create a positive feeling.[72] ◼

DECISION MAKING WHEN ALTERNATIVES CANNOT BE COMPARED

noncomparable decisions
The process of making decisions from products or services from different categories.

alternative-based strategy
Developing an overall liking or disliking for each option in order to make a noncomparable decision.

attribute-based strategy
Making noncomparable choices by making abstract representations of comparable attributes.

In the decision-making models we have discussed thus far, consumers compare alternatives from the same product or service category on the basis of similar attributes or emotions. However, we often need to make a choice from a set of options that may not be directly comparable on the same specific attributes. For example, you might be trying to select entertainment for next weekend and have a choice of going to the movies, eating at a nice restaurant, renting a video, or attending a party. Each alternative has different attributes, making comparisons more difficult.

In making these **noncomparable decisions**, consumers adopt one of two strategies.[73] Using the **alternative-based strategy** (also called top-down processing), they develop an overall evaluation of each option—perhaps using a compensatory or affective strategy—and base their decision on it. For example, in deciding on entertainment for the weekend, you could evaluate the pros and cons of each option independently and then select the one you like the best.

Using the **attribute-based strategy**, consumers make comparisons easier for themselves by forming abstract representations of comparable attributes. In this type of bottom-up processing, the choice is constructed or built up. To make a more direct comparison for an entertainment decision, for example, you could construct abstract attributes such as fun, likelihood of impressing a date, and ease. Interestingly, because abstractions simplify the decision process, consumers tend to make them even when the options are easy to compare.[74]

Note that both strategies can be employed in different circumstances. When the alternatives are less comparable, consumers tend to use an alternative-based strategy because it is harder to make attribute abstractions.[75] Alternative-based strategies also suit consumers who have well-defined goals because they can simply recall the various options and their results. To illustrate, if the goal is to find fun things to do with a date, the consumer could immediately recall a set of options like going to a movie or going out to eat and an overall evaluation of each one. He or she would then pick the option with the strongest evaluation. On the other hand, when consumers do not have well-defined goals, they are more likely to use attribute-based processing.

One final note on noncomparable choice is that price is often the one attribute on which alternatives can be compared directly. It is typically used to screen alternatives for the consideration set rather than as the main basis of comparison among noncomparable alternatives. Thus in our decision among entertainment alternatives, cost might be used to generate a set of options that are reasonably affordable; then an alternative- or attribute-based strategy might be used to make the final decision.

DOES CONTEXT AFFECT HOW DECISIONS ARE MADE?

contextual effects The influence of the decision situation on the decision-making process.

Consumers use different strategies in different decision contexts, or even for the same decision in different time periods. The best strategy for a specific decision depends both on the consumer and on the nature of the decision.[76] This final section looks at three **contextual effects** on decision making: consumer characteristics, task characteristics, and task definition or framing.

How Consumer Characteristics Can Affect Decision Making

A variety of factors related to consumers affect the nature of the decision process. Consistent with the overall processing model, these factors can be grouped according to consumers' motivation, ability, and opportunity to elaborate on information when making a decision.

Motivation to Process   Although we are more likely to use any of the decision processes described in this chapter when our motivation to process is high, the models still differ in the amount of effort they require. As our incentive to make a correct decision increases, we consider the alternatives more carefully,[77] and the likelihood that we will employ a more active compensatory (versus noncompensatory) model increases. We also use a greater number of attributes to make a decision as our involvement increases.[78] On the other hand, if we perceive the decision to be too risky or if it entails an unpleasant task, we may delay making a decision.[79]

Consumers who are in a good mood are more willing to process information and take more time in making a decision than those who are not in a good mood.[80] Mood can also influence the nature of the evaluation. One study found that consumers in a good mood rated a set of audio speakers more positively than did consumers in a bad mood, when their mood was subconsciously influenced by music (awareness caused the consumers to adjust for mood).[81]

Ability to Process   Consumers are more likely to understand their preferences and decisions when they can relate the evaluation of a product to its features.[82] When consumers have this "consumption vocabulary," they can use more attributes and information in making a decision. Further, expert consumers have more brand-based prior experience and knowledge and, as a result, tend to select brand-based decision strategies.[83] These consumers also know how to identify diagnostic information and ignore irrelevant attributes in their decision making. Finally, the Internet enables consumers to consider a wider variety of information in their decision process than they could without the ready availability of on-line research tools.

Opportunity to Process   As time pressure increases, consumers initially try to process faster.[84] If this technique does not work, they base their decision on fewer attributes and place heavier weight on negative information, eliminating bad alternatives with a noncompensatory strategy, such as a conjunctive model.

Time pressure is also one of the major reasons that consumers fail to make intended purchases. It can reduce the number of impulsive purchases and shopping time.[85] Consumers may also delay decision making if they feel uncertain about how to get product information.[86]

Finally, whether a consumer is present- or future-oriented can lead to different motivations and choices for different products.[87] *Present-oriented* consumers want to improve their current well-being and prefer products that help them do so, such as relaxing vacations and entertaining books. *Future-oriented* consumers want to develop themselves and select life-enriching vacations and books.

How Task Characteristics Can Affect Decision Making

Two task characteristics have been studied in consumer research: the consideration set and information availability.

The Consideration Set   The number and types of alternatives in the consumer's consideration set are key determinants of the decision-making process. As the size of our consideration set increases, we must devote additional cognitive effort to making a decision. As consumers, we typically handle this increased load by adopting a combined strategy—narrowing down the set with a noncompensatory model, followed by a compensatory or affectively based strategy.[88]

The composition of the consideration set is also extremely important because our evaluation of a brand depends on the other brands to which it is compared. In particular, if one brand is clearly more attractive or dominant than others, making a choice does not require much effort.[89] We are more selective in our use of information and process by brand under these conditions. On the other hand, if the brands in the consideration set are similar in attractiveness, we must put forth more effort to make a decision—perhaps using a compensatory or detailed noncompensatory process.[90]

attraction effect The adding of an inferior brand to a consideration, which increases the attractiveness of the dominant brand.

Merely changing the alternatives in the consideration set can have a major impact on the consumer's decision, even without a change in preferences.[91] Adding inferior brands to the set increases decision accuracy and decreases effort. This phenomenon, called the **attraction effect**, occurs because the inferior brands increase the attractiveness of the dominant brand, thus making the decision easier.[92] Interestingly, when product information is presented numerically, such as in the form of graphs or charts, the attraction effect is weakened. However, if we receive the information in words, our greater knowledge now increases the attraction effect.[93] The attraction effect may not occur at all if consumers are more price and less quality conscious.[94]

extremeness aversion Options that are extreme on some attributes are less attractive than those with a moderate level of those attributes.

Consumers also tend to possess an **extremeness aversion**, meaning that they find options that are extreme on some particular attribute less attractive than those that are intermediate. Thus people tend to find moderately priced options more attractive than those that are *either* very expensive or very inexpensive. For example, the mail-order retailer Williams-Sonoma offered two home bread makers; the one introduced first cost $275, and the second one cost 50 percent more. Introducing the second, more expensive unit doubled the sales of the first unit.[95] This result also occurred using Cross pens and microwave ovens.[96]

MARKETING IMPLICATIONS From a marketing perspective, advertisers can sometimes gain an advantage by making comparisons to inferior rather than to equal or superior competitors. This approach maximizes the attraction effect and results in a more positive evaluation of the brand. In one ad, for example, Dell Computers compared itself to Intelligent Electronics, a company that lost $4.3 million in one quarter alone. Although this type of comparison was not the original intent of the ad, Dell benefited from being compared with a seemingly inferior competitor.

Marketers can increase sales of a high-margin item by simply offering a higher priced option.[97] Thus Panasonic could increase the sales of a $179 microwave oven by offering another slightly larger one at $199. The higher-priced brand would not sell well; rather, it would simply make the lower-priced item look like a good deal. Marketers can also sell a new improved model alongside the old model at the same price to make the new one look better. ■

Availability of Information The amount, quality, and format of the information also affect the decision strategy employed. As you might expect, when the amount of information increases, the decision becomes more complex and a more detailed decision strategy must be employed. An increase in the amount of information will lead to a better choice only up to a point; after that the consumer experiences **information overload**.[98]

information overload The negative effect on a decision caused by having too much information.

Good examples of the potential for information overload are ads for pharmaceutical products. The law requires companies to provide detailed prescription information and disclosure of side effects. The sheer amount of information in these ads—usually an entire page of small print—is likely to be overwhelming to most consumers. As another example, one study reports that consumers in both Romania and Turkey have experienced great confusion in judging quality and making choices because "there are so many alternatives now."[99] Information overload is also sometimes a problem in the United States because of the huge number of brands and extensions that are available in many categories.[100] Also, the huge amount of information on the Internet can create overload. Marketers therefore need to be careful not to flood the consumer with too much information and instead to present only key points.

A lack of available information can also hamper decision making, resulting in poorer quality decisions and a lower level of satisfaction. Such a lack of both products and information has been a major problem in the former communist countries.[101]

If the quality of information we acquire from either internal or external search is useful or diagnostic, our processing effort is reduced and we make better decisions.[102] Essentially, we can narrow the consideration set relatively quickly because we need fewer attributes. For example, consumers tend to give good, unique brand features more weight than they give to common features.[103] A focus on quality information further suggests that marketers can benefit from being selective about the information they provide rather than by always focusing on quantity.

On the other hand, if available information is ambiguous, consumers are more likely to stay with their current brand than to risk a new competitive brand, even a superior one.[104] Consumers also can compare numerical attribute information faster and more easily than they can compare verbal information.[105] For example, to help parents select video games, a group of video game manufacturers developed a numerical rating system to indicate the amount of sex and violence in their games.

Finally, the format of the information—that is, the way it is organized in memory or in the external environment—has a major impact on the type of decision strategy employed. For example, a study of VCR purchasers found that consumers are less likely to choose the cheapest brand when products are organized by model (similar offerings by different companies are grouped together) rather than by brand.[106] Thus companies with high-price brands would want the display to be organized by model, and companies offering low-price brands would prefer a brand-based display.

If information is organized by brand, consumers will likely employ a brand-based strategy such as a compensatory, conjunctive, or disjunctive model. On the other hand, if information is organized by attribute or in a matrix, consumers can adopt an attribute-processing strategy, such as the additive difference, lexicographic, or elimination-by-aspects model. Providing information to consumers in a format that requires less effort increases decision effectiveness and accuracy.[107] The easier-to-read nutrition labels introduced by the FDA, for example, are encouraging consumers to be more health conscious in their food choices.[108] The ad promoting the Northwest Airlines and Continental Airlines partnership in Exhibit 10.8 provides a matrix of information that makes comparison easy. One study found that organizing yogurt by flavor instead of by brand encouraged more comparison shopping on the basis of attribute processing.[109] Sometimes

EXHIBIT 10.8
Providing a Matrix of Information

To facilitate comparisons between a particular brand and its competitors, marketers can provide a matrix of information on the most critical attributes for each brand (reducing decision effort and increasing accuracy).

Source: Courtesy of Northwest Airlines, Inc. and Continental Airlines.

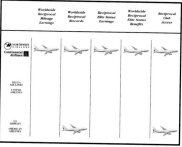

consumers will even restructure information into a more useful format, especially a matrix.[110]

Some researchers expected that the greater availability of information through the Internet would allow consumers to readily apply compensatory models. However, consumers do not appear to be using the Internet in this way because such models are still seen as complex and demanding.[111] (Paradoxically, many consumers do want their decision agents, such as their physician or financial or career advisor, to use these rules in making choices.) The Internet also allows consumers to get information by brand, by attribute, or in a matrix, thereby enabling them to structure the decision the way they want to.

How Decision Framing Can Affect Decision Making

decision framing The initial reference point or anchor in the decision process.

One of the most important contextual influences on the decision process is the manner in which the task is defined or represented, called **decision framing**. The frame is the initial reference point or anchor in the decision process; all subsequent information is processed in light of it. For example, two frames for a car purchase might be: (1) buy an economical car I can afford or (2) buy a car that will impress my friends. Clearly, different models and types of information will be processed under these two frames.

Most of the early work on framing studied people's willingness to take risks in a gamble. Results showed that people are more willing to take risks when a choice is framed as a loss rather than as a gain.[112] For example, one study examined consumer preferences for two different coupons.[113] In one condition consumers were asked to choose between two coupons they could use when buying a jar of Prego spaghetti sauce: With one they would get a can of Campbell's Tomato and Rice Soup free (a 49-cent value), and with another they would buy a can of Campbell's Tomato and Rice Soup and get 49 cents off the total. The first condition was framed as a gain (get something free), and the second was a reduced loss (49 cents off). Even though coupons had the same value, the first choice was much more highly desired.

Framing relates to other common types of consumer decision contexts as well. Specifically, consumers can frame decisions themselves, or the decisions can be framed for them by exposure to external stimuli.

Framing by the Consumer The decision-framing process begins with the consumer's knowledge of the purchase situation.[114] Consumers then activate that portion of memory relating to their goals and the situation. For example, the goals get food that is on my diet and get food that makes me feel good would probably activate different brands and information from memory and result in different decision processes.

The context in which the product will be used can influence the decision process. Thus buying beer for yourself and buying beer for a party are likely to produce different consideration sets, decision criteria, and levels of decision effort. For example, you might spend less on your party because you need a large quantity, but you might be more concerned about image.

One study of mouth-related products (mouthwash, mints, gums and candies, breath sprays, and so on) found that where the product would be used (at home or away from home) and who would use the product (the purchaser or someone else) determined which products were purchased.[115] Another study asked consumers to rate the importance of different attributes for four situations: (1) lunch on a weekday, (2) snack during a shopping trip, (3) evening meal when rushed for time, and

(4) evening meal with the family when not rushed for time.[116] Results indicated that attribute importance depended on the situation. Speed and convenience were the most important attributes for situations 1 and 3, whereas variety of menu and popularity with children were most critical for situation 4.

MARKETING IMPLICATIONS

The decision-framing process has important implications for both the positioning and segmentation of markets. First, marketers can position the product or service in consumers' goal-related or usage categories. That way, when consumers frame the decision, they will be more likely to consider the brand and important related information. For example, a television ad for Compaq computers showed a businesswoman saving the day by firing off a fax from a cab during a traffic jam.[117] Another ad showed a restaurant owner answering the phone, watching a review of her restaurant on TV, and changing the prices on the menu, all on her computer. In both cases the frame is a computer that solves business problems.

Second, marketers can identify large segments of consumers who have similar goal-related or usage-context categories and market directly to these groups. Thus Reebok introduced a shoe with moving air in the sole to appeal to high-performance consumers.[118] AT&T developed the Fax Mailbox, with which faxes can be retrieved from a mailbox anywhere in the world, for business travelers. Likewise, a company in China labels its products as tea for drivers and tea for watching TV so that consumers will link the brand with a specific use.[119] ■

External Framing Decisions can also be framed by the way in which the problem is structured in the external environment. Consumers who were presented with beef that was 75 percent lean (in the study we mentioned earlier in the chapter) rated it significantly higher than those who were told the beef was 25 percent fat.[120] In another study industrial buyers who used low price as an initial reference point were less willing to take risks than those with a medium or high price point.[121] Likewise, consumers react more positively when marketers frame the cost of a product as a series of small payments (pennies a day) instead of as a large one-time expense.[122] Whether a decision is framed positively (How good is this product?) or negatively (How bad is this product?) influences the evaluation differently.[123] Consumers are more likely to choose a brand with negatively framed claims about a competitor when elaboration is low, but higher elaboration may lead them to conclude that unfair tactics are being used.[124]

Priming certain attributes, such as reliability and creativity, can also significantly alter judgments of both comparable alternatives like brands of cameras and noncomparable alternatives like computers *or* cameras.[125] In particular, this priming causes consumers to focus their processing on specific attributes rather than on abstract criteria. Research on charitable contributions found that providing consumers with a high anchor point by asking for $20 increased contributions relative to a low anchor point like a penny.[126] Finally, priming hedonic or symbolic attributes—such as associations—with political concerns (e.g., reduce toxic waste) rather than with functional ones (e.g., no more hassles) can produce a higher willingness to pay for items or social programs.[127]

MARKETING IMPLICATIONS

These findings have important implications because marketers can use communications to influence reference points and the way in which decisions are framed. For example, in marketing the Aurora, General Motors attempted to alter framing by not mentioning that the car is made by Oldsmobile because the latter is perceived as big, clunky, and not hip.[128] In a fight against smoking, new ads frame the message in terms of a new health problem: impotence.[129] Sales promotions generally are more successful when framed as gains rather than as a reduced loss—consumers prefer to get something free than to get money off.

Furthermore, decisions can be framed by the location of products in the store—thereby influencing comparisons. Makers of the Guiltless Gourmet tortilla chip (a low-fat, no-oil snack chip) faced an important decision: whether to place their product in the health food section, where framing would be a health food choice, or in the snack food aisle, where it would be a snack food decision. The company chose the latter strategy because the brand had a distinct competitive advantage over other snack chips. ■

SUMMARY

Judgments simply involve forming evaluations or estimates regarding the likelihood of events, but do not require the consumer to make a formal decision. Two major types of judgments are estimations of likelihood and judgments of goodness or badness, both of which can be made by recalling past judgments from memory using either an anchoring and adjustment process or imagery. Consumers have difficulty making conjunctive probability assessments, which involve determining how two attributes vary together.

Several models help us understand the decision-making process: (1) compensatory brand-processing models, which include the multiattribute or expectancy-value model; (2) compensatory attribute-processing models, which include the additive difference model; (3) noncompensatory brand-processing models, which include the conjunctive and disjunctive models; and (4) noncompensatory attribute-processing models, which include the lexicographic and elimination-by-aspects models. Although it is helpful to describe these models separately, consumers often use a combination of them to make decisions.

Decisions can also be based on emotions or feelings, using a type of holistic processing in which emotions or images play a key role. Consumers can also make decisions when the alternatives are not directly comparable. They can use either an alternative-based strategy, in which overall evaluations are made for each option, or an attribute-based strategy, in which abstract representations of attributes are used to make comparisons.

Finally, contextual or situational factors can exert a strong influence on the decision process. These contextual factors can be grouped according to (1) consumer characteristics, such as their motivation, ability, and opportunity to process; (2) task characteristics, such as the nature of the consideration set and the information available; and (3) decision framing, either by the environment or by the consumer.

EXERCISES

1. This chapter discussed several types of estimations of likelihood that consumers can make (such as estimating quality or likelihood of satisfaction, goodness/badness). What other types of judgments do consumers make? Try to list as many as possible. What do these judgments have in common?

2. Select a product or service category for which you expect the consumers' motivation, ability, and opportunity to process information to be high. Ask five consumers to describe in detail how they would go about making a decision for this product or service category. First ask them which brands they would consider (the consideration set) and then ask them to describe the specific steps they would go through in making a decision. Which brand would they choose? After collecting this information, try to answer the following questions:

   a. How do the descriptions provided by the consumers compare to the decision models discussed in this chapter?

   b. How do these processes vary for different consumers?

   c. Why did one brand tend to be chosen over another?

   d. If these processes were representative of many consumers, how might this information be used to develop a marketing strategy?

3. Pick a product or service category that is likely to generate high-elaboration decision making. Identify the most salient attributes for the decision and collect information about these attributes. Ask ten consumers to rate each attribute in terms of the b_i and I_i ratings from the compensatory model (see the box on page 232) for three major brands in this category. Based on this information, answer the following:

   a. What are the strengths and weaknesses of each brand?

   b. How would each model described in this chapter provide insights into consumers' decision processes in this situation?

   c. How would the information you have collected aid in designing marketing strategy?

CHAPTER

11

JUDGMENT AND DECISION MAKING BASED ON LOW CONSUMER EFFORT

INTRODUCTION

 In Vietnam today brands sold by consumer companies such as Procter & Gamble and Unilever, including locally produced Close-Up toothpaste and Lux soap, are experiencing strong sales. The only problem is that rather than buying them legally in stores, consumers are purchasing goods smuggled in from Thailand and are paying higher prices for them. Vietnamese consumers assume that anything *not* made locally is of superior quality even if it has the exact same brand name as an item made in that country. Ironically, this attitude is putting some Vietnamese out of work because local factories are standing idle.[1]

This interesting situation is the result of several factors that relate to this chapter. First, consumers are making an error in judgment by assuming that the products made in Vietnam are inferior in quality. Second, the brands represent common, repeat-purchase products for which consumers will typically not exert much effort in making a choice. Instead, they employ very simple **heuristics**, or rules of thumb, to make these judgments and decisions.[2] The following heuristics may have been factors in this example:

First, sometimes consumers simply buy the brand that is most familiar. Con-sumers desire the smuggled products because they represent well-known brand

heuristic A simple rule of thumb used to make judgments or decisions.

names. Second, some consumers use price as a heuristic for making decisions. Because these smuggled products are highly priced and consumers perceive a price-quality relationship, they are willing to pay a much higher price for these items.

Third, when consumers are offered a high-quality product, they may form a positive attitude while consuming it, leading to repeat purchases and perhaps brand loyalty. Some Vietnamese consumers have clearly formed positive attitudes toward the foreign-made brands. Fourth, habit is a factor. Consumers may not buy some products from stores because they are in the habit of buying those items on the black market. Finally, consumers can buy brands simply because they feel good about them. In other words, they have positive affect. Clearly, Vietnamese consumers have a positive feeling about foreign-made international brands (see Exhibit 11.1).

The key point is that when consumers have low motivation, ability, and opportunity (MAO) to process information, their judgment and decision processes are different and involve less effort than when MAO is high. This chapter examines the nature of low-effort judgment and decision making—the next stage in our overall model, as shown in Exhibit 11.2. We begin by investigating how judgments can be made in low-effort situations. Next we examine the theory and process of low-effort decision making. This chapter focuses on the cognitive and affective shortcuts or heuristics that consumers use to make judgments and decisions and discusses the marketing implications of this behavior.

EXHIBIT 11.1

Well-known international brands are more popular in Vietnam than locally-produced products.

Source: L. Dematteis/The Image Works.

EXHIBIT 11.2

Chapter Overview: Judgment and Decision Making: Low Consumer Effort

This chapter examines judgment and decision making when processing effort is low. A key aspect of low-effort processing is that consumers tend to use *heuristics* or ways of simplifying the judgment or decision. Both cognitively based heuristics (performance-based tactics, habit, price-related tactics, brand loyalty, and normative influences) and affectively based heuristics (affect-related tactics, variety seeking, and impulse) are used to make decisions.

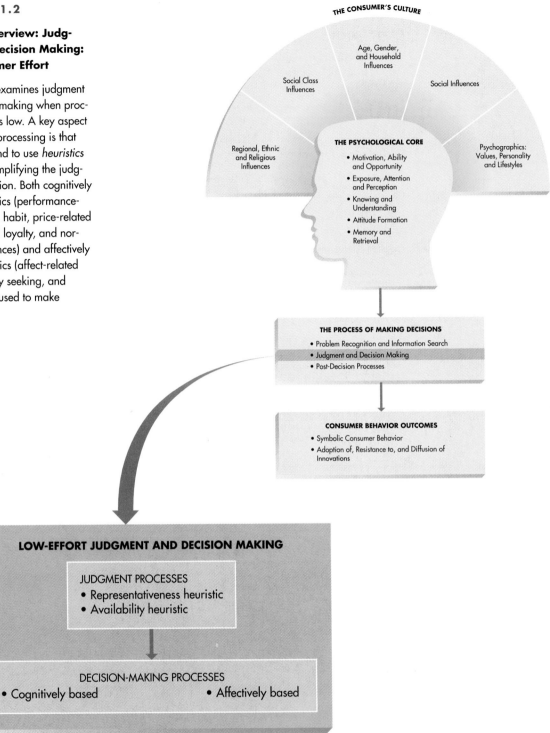

THE CONSUMER'S CULTURE

Age, Gender, and Household Influences

Social Class Influences

Social Influences

Regional, Ethnic and Religious Influences

Psychographics: Values, Personality and Lifestyles

THE PSYCHOLOGICAL CORE
- Motivation, Ability and Opportunity
- Exposure, Attention and Perception
- Knowing and Understanding
- Attitude Formation
- Memory and Retrieval

THE PROCESS OF MAKING DECISIONS
- Problem Recognition and Information Search
- Judgment and Decision Making
- Post-Decision Processes

CONSUMER BEHAVIOR OUTCOMES
- Symbolic Consumer Behavior
- Adoption of, Resistance to, and Diffusion of Innovations

LOW-EFFORT JUDGMENT AND DECISION MAKING

JUDGMENT PROCESSES
- Representativeness heuristic
- Availability heuristic

DECISION-MAKING PROCESSES
- Cognitively based
- Affectively based

Chapter 10 showed that when effort is high, consumers' judgments—such as estimations of likelihood and goodness/badness—can be cognitively complex. In contrast, when MAO is low, individuals are motivated to be cognitive simplifiers and use heuristics to reduce the effort involved in making judgments.[3] Two major types of heuristics are representativeness and availability.

Shortcuts in Making Judgments: The Representativeness Heuristic

representativeness heuristic Making a judgment by simply comparing a stimulus to the category prototype or exemplar.

One way that consumers can make simple estimations or judgments is to make comparisons to the category prototype or exemplar. This categorization process is called the **representativeness heuristic**.[4] For example, if we want to estimate the likelihood that a new toothpaste is of high quality, we can compare it with our prototype for toothpaste, such as Crest.[5] If the new brand is seen as similar to the prototype or exemplar, we will assume that the new brand is also of high quality. This factor explains why the packaging of many store brands is similar to that of the leading brands in various product categories, seeking outward similarity to suggest that the products themselves share many characteristics of quality.

 Like any shortcut, the representativeness heuristic can also lead to biased judgments. The Vietnamese consumers in our example automatically assume anything not made locally is superior in quality (even if the brands are identical), and locally produced brands must work to overcome this bias and convince consumers that local products are of good quality also.[6]

MARKETING IMPLICATIONS The representativeness heuristic is important from a marketing perspective because products or services can be positioned close to a prototype or exemplar that has positive associations in consumers' minds. However, when the shortcut leads to biased judgment, marketers must take steps to overcome it. In the 1960s, radios and electronics that were made in Japan were considered the prototype for poor-quality merchandise. Japanese companies had to spend many years producing high-quality products and heavily marketing them to overcome this bias. ■

Shortcuts in Making Judgments: The Availability Heuristic

availability heuristic Basing judgments on events that are easier to recall.

Judgments can also be influenced by the ease with which instances of an event can be brought to mind, a shortcut called the **availability heuristic**.[7] More accessible or more vivid events are more likely to be recalled and therefore to influence judgments. To illustrate, suppose that years ago you purchased a portable radio that constantly had major mechanical problems. Today you may still recall your anger and disappointment when you see this brand. Your experiences greatly color your estimations of quality for this brand, even though the incidence of breakdowns might actually be very low.

 Word-of-mouth communication is another example of accessible information that leads to the use of the availability heuristic. If a friend tells you about all the problems she had with her radio, this information is likely to affect your estimates of quality, even though her experience might have been an isolated event.

base-rate information How often an event really occurs for all consumers.

law of small numbers The expectation that information obtained from a small number of people represents the larger population.

These judgments are biased because we tend to ignore **base-rate information**—that is, how often the event really occurs—in favor of information that is more vivid or accessible. One study demonstrated this effect in the context of estimating the probability of refrigerators breaking down.[8] One group was given a set of case histories told by consumers, and another was given actual statistics about the incidence of breakdown. As you might expect, people who read the case histories provided breakdown estimates that were 30 percent higher than those of the statistics group. Another study found that consumers can use both base-rate and case information, but their judgment depends on how the information is structured.[9] As case history information becomes more specific, base rates are used less. Another reason we do not use more base-rate information is that it is often not available.

A related bias is the **law of small numbers**, whereby people expect information obtained from a small sample to be typical of the larger population.[10] If friends inform us that a new CD by a particular artist is really good or that the food at a particular restaurant is terrible, we tend to believe that information, even if most people may not feel the same way. In fact, reliance on small numbers is another reason that word-of-mouth communication can be so powerful. In essence, we tend to have confidence that the opinions of friends or relatives are more reflective of the majority than they may actually be.

MARKETING IMPLICATIONS Marketers can attempt to either capitalize on the availability bias or overcome it. To capitalize, they can provide consumers with positive and vivid product-related experiences through the use of marketing communications, or they can ask consumers to imagine such situations. Both strategies will increase consumers' estimates that these events will occur. Or marketers can attempt to stimulate positive word-of-mouth communication. For example, movie studios often show upcoming films in special sneak previews or for free on college campuses. The studios are hoping moviegoers will like the film and talk about it to others, thereby influencing their judgments.

Marketers can attempt to overcome the availability bias by providing consumers with base-rate information about the general population. If this information is vivid and specific, it can help consumers make a less biased judgment. For instance, Bumble Bee ads claim that this brand of tuna is "chosen 2 to1 over competitors" thanks to a new packing technique.[11] Note that the Internet is an excellent vehicle for providing base-rate information. For example, rather than relying on a few reviewers' opinions, some sites provide a large sample of evaluations from "typical" moviegoers. The availability bias is also a common problem in the context of sweepstakes and lotteries. Consumers often overestimate the likelihood of winning, even though their chances are exceedingly small, because they are exposed to highly vivid and available images of winners in the media. Regulators have attempted to overcome this bias by requiring that the odds of winning be clearly posted.

The availability bias is quite common in marketing research that uses focus groups to evaluate marketing programs. Usually groups of 8 to 12 consumers give their opinions on topics ranging from product design to advertising messages. Even though these groups contain a very small number of consumers, marketing managers sometimes mistakenly view the group's responses as mirroring the general consumer population.[12] This problem can be overcome by replicating findings with a quantitative study on a larger and more representative consumer sample. ■

Relative to many aspects of consumers' lives, most low-effort consumer judgment and decision situations are not very important. Clearly, career and family decisions are far more important than deciding which toothpaste or peanut butter to buy. Thus the consumer usually does not want to devote a lot of time and effort to these mundane decisions.[13] In a typical shopping trip, a consumer might purchase 30 to 40 items. Spending even 5 minutes on each decision would stretch the shopping trip to an unlikely 2 or 3 hours. Thus researchers have become interested in examining just how decisions are made in these low-elaboration situations.

How Does Low-Effort Decision Making Differ from High-Effort Decision Making?

Our discussion of high-effort decision making in Chapter 10 outlined the following steps: consumers have certain beliefs about each alternative that are combined to form an attitude that then leads to a behavior or a choice. In other words, the consumer engages in *thinking*, which leads to *feelings*, which results in *behaving*. This progression has been referred to as the **hierarchy of effects**, and it is outlined in Exhibit 11.3.

Herbert Krugman was one of the first researchers to recognize that this traditional hierarchy of effects might not describe all consumer decision-making situations.[14] In studying how television advertising affects consumers, Krugman noticed that, even though viewers could recall ads, the ads appeared to have little impact on viewers' attitudes toward the brand. His finding is inconsistent with the belief-attitude link. To account for this discrepancy, Krugman hypothesized that advertising influences consumers through a process called **passive** or **incidental learning**. He viewed television as a primarily low-involvement medium to which viewers do not pay close attention. Viewers also do not link the advertised product or ad to their previous experiences or beliefs. However, through the constant repetition of ad messages, viewers can pick up and retain messages passively. They can therefore possess low-level beliefs about the product, a kind of basic familiarity, but not form a strong attitude. As a result, purchase decisions can be made in the absence of a strong attitude. If an attitude does develop, it tends to occur *after* purchase when the product is being used.

Thus if a consumer sees an ad for Excedrin, she would probably not pay very close attention to it. However, if she sees the ad repeatedly, she would acquire a basic awareness of the brand and the key claims that it is stronger than aspirin and relieves headache pain fast. If she goes to the store to purchase Excedrin, this low-level knowledge may be enough to influence her choice. But only after taking it will she decide whether she likes or dislikes this brand.

Consistent with Krugman's theory, researchers have proposed an alternative hierarchy of effects for low-effort situations that follows a *thinking-behaving-feeling* sequence.[15] The consumer enters the decision process

hierarchy of effects Sequential steps used in decision making involving thinking, then feeling, then behavior.

passive (incidental learning) Low-level learning that occurs through repetition.

High-Effort Hierarchy	Low-Effort Hierarchy
Beliefs (think)	Beliefs (think)
Attitudes (feel)	Behavior (do)
Behavior (do)	Attitudes (feel)

Learning

EXHIBIT 11.3
Hierarchy of Effects

When effort is high, consumers actively evaluate brands *before* making a decision and purchasing. In low-effort situations, consumers think very little before deciding, and beliefs (often based on basic familiarity) lead directly to choice. Evaluation then occurs after the choice, when the product is being used.

with a set of low-level beliefs that are based on brand familiarity and knowledge obtained from repeated exposures to advertising, in-store exposure, or prior usage. These beliefs then serve as the foundation for the decision or behavior, in the absence of any attitude. After making the decision and while using the product, the consumer evaluates the brand and may or may not form an attitude, depending on how strongly the brand is liked or satisfies needs. For comparison, we present this model next to the traditional hierarchy in Exhibit 11.3.

Some researchers have challenged the belief-behavior link in the low-involvement hierarchy by noting that consumers can sometimes engage in "pure affective choice," making a decision based solely on how they feel rather than on what they think.[16] For example, you might select a flavor of ice cream or a new CD based on positive feelings rather than on any beliefs or knowledge. In these cases the sequence would be feeling, behaving, and then thinking. Obviously, this type of decision making *can* occur, suggesting that consumers can process in both a cognitive and affective manner. With this information in mind, we next discuss the process of low-elaboration decision making in greater detail.

Using Simplifying Strategies when Consumer Effort Is Low

Low-effort purchases represent the most frequent type of decisions that consumers make in everyday life. One study of in-store examination of laundry detergent purchases found that the median amount of time taken to make a choice was only 8.5 seconds.[17] Another study of coffee and tissues found very low levels of decision activity, particularly among consumers who purchased the product frequently and possessed a strong brand preference.[18] Findings were similar for analgesics.[19] Some research has examined consumer decision processes across a number of product categories and has even questioned whether there is any decision process at all.[20]

A decision process probably does occur in low-effort situations, but it is simpler, involves less effort, and is qualitatively different from the processes that occur when MAO is high. Two other factors influence the low-MAO decision process. First, the goal is not necessarily to find the best possible brand, called *optimizing*, as is the case with high-elaboration decisions. To optimize here would require more effort than consumers are typically willing to expend. Instead, consumers are more willing to **satisfice**—that is, to find a brand that simply satisfies their needs. It may not be the best, but it is "good enough." The effort required to find the best may simply not be worth it.

Second, most low-elaboration decisions are made frequently and repeatedly. Thus the consumer may rely on previous information and judgments of satisfaction or dissatisfaction from past consumption. Think of all the times you have purchased toothpaste, breakfast cereal, shampoo, and deodorant. You have acquired information by using these products and from seeing ads, talking to friends, and so forth. Thus you do not need to search for information every time you are in the store. You can simply remember previous decisions and use that information to make your next choice.

In these common, repeat-purchase situations, consumers can develop decision heuristics called **choice tactics** that enable them to make quick and effortless decisions.[21] Rather than making a detailed comparison of the various brands, consumers apply these rules to simplify the decision process.

The study of laundry detergents mentioned earlier supports this view.[22] When consumers were asked how they made their choice, several major categories of tactics emerged, among them *price tactics* (it's the cheapest or it's on sale), *affect tactics*

satisfice Finding a brand that satisfies a need even though the brand may not be the best brand.

choice tactics Simple rules of thumb used to make low-effort decisions.

(I like it), *performance tactics* (it cleans clothes better), and *normative tactics* (my mother bought it). Other studies have identified additional choice tactics: *habit tactics* (I buy the same brand I bought last time), *brand loyalty tactics* (I buy the same brand for which I have a strong preference), and *variety seeking tactics* (I need to try something different). Similar results were produced in a study of shampoo and laundry detergent in Singapore.[23] Finally, related patterns of choice-tactic usage were found in a comparison of consumers in Germany, Thailand, and the United States.[24]

Consumers can develop a choice tactic for each repeat-purchase, low-elaboration decision in the product or service category. If we observe the consumer's decision only once, it will appear very limited. Because all prior purchases serve as input to the current decision, we must look at a whole series of choices and consumption situations to fully understand consumer decision making.

LEARNING CHOICE TACTICS

The key to understanding low-elaboration decision making is knowing the manner in which consumers learn to use their choice tactics. Certain concepts from the behaviorist tradition in psychology are relevant to understanding the way consumers learn. **Operant conditioning** views behavior as a function of previous actions and of the reinforcements or punishments obtained from these actions.[25] For example, while you were growing up, your parents may have given you a present for making good grades or an allowance for mowing the lawn. You learned that these are good behaviors, and you were more likely to do these things again in the future because you were rewarded for them.

operant conditioning The view that behavior is a function of the reinforcements and punishments received in the past.

Reinforcement

For consumer behavior, reinforcement usually comes from a feeling of satisfaction that occurs when we perceive that our needs have been adequately met. This reinforcement then increases the probability that we will purchase the same brand again. For example, if a consumer buys Liquid Tide and is impressed by its ability to clean clothes, his purchase will be reinforced and he will be more likely to buy this brand again. One study found that past experience with a brand was by far the most critical factor in brand choice—over quality, price, and familiarity.[26] Other research has shown that information received from product trials tends to be more powerful and influential than that received from advertising.[27] In particular, the thoughts and emotions experienced during a trial can have a powerful influence on evaluations.[28]

Note that consumers often perceive few differences among brands of many products and services.[29] A positive brand attitude is unlikely to develop when no brand is seen as clearly better than another. However, as long as the consumer is not dissatisfied, the choice tactic he or she used will be reinforced. For example, suppose you buy the cheapest brand of paper towels. If this brand at least minimally satisfies your needs, you are likely to buy the cheapest brand again—and it may be a different brand next time. Thus reinforcement can occur for either the brand or the choice tactic.

Punishment

Alternatively, consumers can have a bad experience with a product or service, form a negative evaluation toward it, and not purchase it again. In operant conditioning terms, this experience is called *punishment*. If you did something bad when you were growing up, your parents may have punished you to make sure you would not behave that way again. In a consumer context, punishment occurs when our needs are not met and we are dissatisfied. Thus we learn that we should not buy the same brand again.

Punishment may also lead the consumer to reevaluate the choice tactic, resulting in the use of a different tactic for the next purchase. Thus if you buy the cheapest brand of trash bags and the bags burst when you take out the trash, you could either employ a new tactic (buying the most expensive brand or the most familiar) or upgrade your tactic (buying the cheapest *national* brand).

Repetition

Learning occurs because the same act is repeatedly reinforced or punished over time, as summarized in Exhibit 11.4. This process occurs whenever we buy a common, repeat-purchase product. Thus we learn and gradually acquire a set of choice tactics that will result in a satisfactory choice in each decision situation. Note that decision-making models have traditionally ignored the key role of consumption in the decision process; most of the attention has focused on processing immediately prior to the decision. But clearly what takes place while the product is being consumed has important implications for future acquisition, usage, and disposition decisions. In other words, whether the consumer forms a positive or negative evaluation of the brand or tactic can be an important input into future decisions.

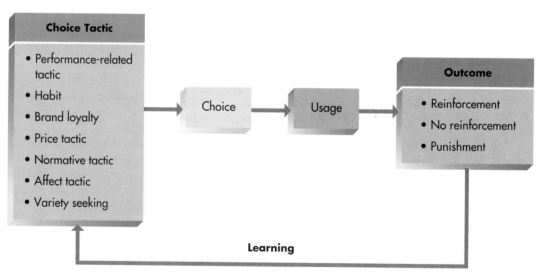

EXHIBIT 11.4
The Learning Process

This diagram shows how the outcome of a decision can help consumers learn which choice tactic to apply in a given situation. After consumers apply one of the seven basic types of tactics to make a choice, they take the brand home and use it. During consumption, they can evaluate the brand, which results in one of three basic outcomes: *reinforcement* (satisfaction leading to positive attitude and repurchase), *no reinforcement* (leading to tactic reinforcement, but no attitude toward the brand), or *punishment* (leading to a negative attitude, no repurchase, and tactic reevaluation).

Choice Tactics Depend on the Product

The choice tactics we use often depend on the product category we are considering.[30] For example, we might be brand loyal to Heinz ketchup but always buy the cheapest trash bags. The tactic we learn for a product category depends on which brands are available and our experiences with them. The amount of advertising, price variations, and the number and similarity of brands influence the type of tactic we employ.[31] Interestingly, the study from Singapore mentioned earlier found that a greater similarity exists in the tactic used for the same product in different cultures (the United States and Singapore) than among products in the same culture.[32] The key point, however, is that our experiences help us learn what works for each product, and we use these tactics to minimize our decision-making effort for future purchases.

LOW-EFFORT THOUGHT-BASED DECISION MAKING

Each tactic consumers learn for making low-elaboration decisions can have important implications for marketers. As in high-elaboration decisions, these strategies can be divided into two broad categories: thought-based and feeling-based decision making. This section examines cognitive-based decision making, which includes performance-related tactics, habit, brand loyalty, price-related tactics, and normative influences.

Performance as a Simplifying Strategy

performance-related tactics
Tactics based on benefits, features, or evaluations of the brand.

When the outcome of the consumption process is positive reinforcement, consumers are likely to use **performance-related tactics** to make their choices. These tactics can represent an overall evaluation (works the best) or a specific attribute or benefit (gets clothes cleaner, tastes better, or has quicker service). The key to development of these tactics is satisfaction. Quite simply, satisfied consumers are likely to develop a positive evaluation of the brand or service and repurchase it based on its features.

MARKETING IMPLICATIONS
A principal objective of marketing strategy should be to increase the likelihood of satisfaction through product or service quality. Only then can a brand consistently achieve repeat purchases and loyal users. Campbell's soup, for example, has provided quality products for years, as evidenced by its 75 percent market share.[33] Despite this obvious point, U.S. business has been frequently criticized for failing to focus enough on product quality. As a result, improving quality became one of the most important concerns in the 1990s and will continue into the future.

Advertising can play a central role in influencing performance evaluations by increasing the consumer's expectation of positive reinforcement and satisfaction and lessening the negative effects of an unfavorable consumption experience.[34] Because we see what we want to see and form our expectations accordingly, marketers should select product features or benefits that are important to consumers, help to differentiate the brand from competitors, and convince consumers they will be satisfied if they buy the product.

To illustrate, an ad for Duncan Hines double-fudge brownies states, "If a brownie this fudgey doesn't satisfy you, maybe you really like vanilla." Other good

EXHIBIT 11.5
Emphasizing Product Quality

When the product has an important feature or benefit which differentiates it from the competition, this feature or benefit is often stressed in ads. Here Hefty stresses its differentiating feature that only one zip is needed to close the bag."

Source: Courtesy of Pactiv Corporation.

examples of increasing expectations are the "Bounty, the quicker picker-upper" and the Campbell's "M'm M'm Good!" campaigns. Gillette introduced the MACH3 razor with three blades to gain differentiation from competitors.[35] Another example is the ad for Hefty in Exhibit 11.5.

Sales promotions, such as free samples, price deals, coupons, or premiums (free gifts or merchandise), are often used as an incentive to get the consumer to try the product or service. Marketers hope that if consumers find the product satisfactory, they will continue to buy it when the incentives are withdrawn. These strategies can be successful, however, only if product performance satisfies and reinforces the consumer. They will not overcome a dissatisfaction that results from poor product quality. For example, Snapple has failed in Japan, despite heavy promotion, because it has features that Japanese consumers loathe: a cloudy appearance and stuff floating in the bottle.[36] ■

Habit as a Simplifying Strategy

habit Doing the same thing every time.

Humans are creatures of **habit**. Once we find a convenient way of doing things, we tend to repeat it without really thinking. For example, you probably engage in the same routine every morning, drive the same way to work or school, and shop at the same stores. You may even have noticed that students tend always to sit in the same general area of the classroom. We do these things because they make life simpler and more manageable.

Sometimes consumers' acquisition, usage, and disposition decisions are based on habit, too. Habit represents one of the simplest and most effortless types of consumer decision making, characterized by (1) little or no information seeking and (2) little or no evaluation of alternatives. Note that habit does not require a strong preference for an offering; rather, it is simply repetitive behavior and regular purchase.[37]

Decision making based on habit also reduces risk.[38] Consumers know the brand will satisfy their needs because they have bought it a number of times in the past.

MARKETING IMPLICATIONS Habit-based decision making has several important implications for marketers who want to develop repeat-purchase behavior and to sell their offering to habitual purchasers of both that brand and competing products.

Developing Repeat-Purchase Behavior. Getting consumers to acquire or use an offering repeatedly is an important marketing objective because repeat purchases lead to profitability. Marketers can use an operant conditioning technique called

EXHIBIT 11.6
Free Samples

Here are three samples of skin products from Thailand. Sampling is a frequently used marketing tool in the Asian country, with many samples given out in shopping centers. What types of product samples do you receive?

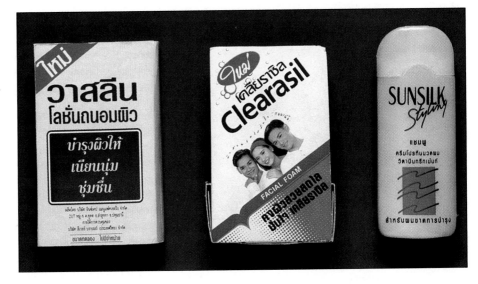

shaping Leading consumers through a series of steps to create a desired response.

shaping that leads consumers through a series of steps to a desired response: purchase.[39] Sales promotion techniques are often employed to shape repeat purchase. First, a free sample might be used to generate a trial of the brand (see Exhibit 11.6 for examples from Thailand). A high-value coupon might be included with the sample to induce the consumer to purchase the product. The next step might be to provide a series of lower-value coupons to promote subsequent repurchase. The hope is that when the incentives are withdrawn, the consumer will continue to purchase by habit.

Marketing to Habitual Purchasers of Other Brands. A variety of marketing opportunities are available for marketers targeting habitual purchasers of a competing brand. The major goal is to break consumers' habits and induce them to switch to another brand. Because the habitual consumer does not have a strong brand preference, this goal is easier to achieve than it is for brand-loyal consumers. For example, Kellogg and General Mills are increasing sales of breakfast cereal in Europe by breaking old eating habits in favor of the U.S. tradition of a "quick bite."[40] By observing consumers' habits in taking over-the-counter medications, Procter & Gamble was able to develop more effective packaging for several of its brands, which led consumers to switch.[41]

Sales promotion techniques to induce brand switching include pricing deals, coupons, free samples, and premiums. These special deals may be enough to capture consumers' attention and get them to try the new brand. For example, an offer of a free cookbook might entice consumers to try a new brand of cake mix. Then, once the old habit is broken, consumers may continue to purchase the new brand either because they like it or because they have developed a new habit.

Habits can also be broken by introducing a new and unique benefit that satisfies needs better than existing brands. This differential advantage then needs to be heavily advertised to get the word out to consumers. Examples include Oral B's toothbrush with an ergonomic rubber handle, Pampers Gentle Touch diapers that are actually good for baby's skin, and Vlasic's 3-inch Hamburger Stacker, a pickle that is big enough to cover an entire burger.[42] Exhibit 11.7 is an example of a product that might induce parents to change their laundry detergent to Tide with Bleach. In the United Kingdom, Brooke Bond introduced a revolutionary pyramid-shaped tea bag that makes better-tasting tea.[43] Shikishima Baking has tried to break the habits of Japanese consumers by introducing self-buttering bread.[44]

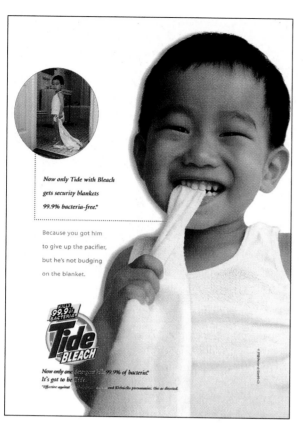

EXHIBIT 11.7
A New and Unique Benefit

In this ad, Tide with Bleach is promoting the fact that it is the only detergent that gets clothes—and security blankets—99.9% bacteria free.
Source: The Procter & Gamble Company. Used by permission.

Finally, distribution policies are very important for habitual purchasing. In general, the greater the amount of shelf space a brand has in the store, the more likely the brand is to get consumers' attention. If a different brand can capture the habitual consumer's attention, the product's location may be enough to plant the idea to buy something else. For example, an end-of-aisle display can sometimes increase a brand's sales by 100 to 400 percent.[45] In one study eye-catching displays increased sales of frozen dinners by 245 percent, laundry detergent by 207 percent, and salty snacks by 172 percent.[46] Thus marketers often try to develop interesting displays, such as the award-winning units shown in Exhibit 11.8. Marketers have also used electronic bulletin boards, shopping-cart ads, and even blinking lights to lure consumers to coupon dispensers.[47]

Marketing to Habitual Purchasers of One's Own Brand. When some of one's own consumers are purchasing by habit, marketers need to make sure that those habits are not broken. Because habitual consumers are susceptible to competitors' deals, marketers need to offer comparable deals to build resistance to switching. For example, in Eastern Europe, Pepsi responded to a Coke sweepstakes by selling 2.25-liter bottles for the same price as a 2-liter bottle of Coke.[48] In the airline industry a fare cut by any one airline is usually matched immediately by all major competitors.

Distribution is also important to prevent habitual consumers from switching to another brand. One major factor that might force a consumer to break a habit is an out-of-stock condition. Without a strong preference, the consumer is more likely to break the habit and buy another brand than to go to another store. Widespread distribution can ensure that the consumer is not forced to buy something else. For Coke, other types of soft drinks, and teas to be successful in Japan, they must be widely available in that country's vast network of vending machines.[49]

Finally, advertising can induce resistance to switching. By occasionally reminding the consumer of a reason for buying the brand and keeping the brand name "top of mind," marketers may be able to keep consumers from switching. ■

Brand Loyalty as a Simplifying Strategy

brand loyalty Buying the same brand repeatedly because of a strong preference.

Brand loyalty occurs when consumers make a conscious evaluation that a brand or service satisfies their needs to a greater extent than others do and buy the same brand repeatedly for that reason.[50] Essentially, brand loyalty results from *very* positive reinforcement of a performance-related choice tactic. Note that the level of

EXHIBIT 11.8
Award-Winning Displays

By designing eye-popping displays, marketers hope to capture consumers' attention and implant the idea to try something else (thereby breaking habit). This can occur because habitual consumers typically do not have a strong preference for their usual brand. Can you think of any displays that have caught your attention recently?

Source: Designed and produced by Henschel-Steinau, Inc., Englewood, N.J. 07631, U.S.A.

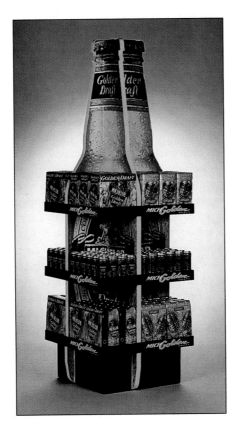

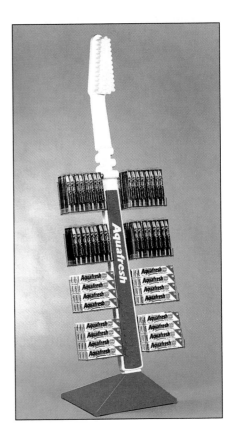

commitment to the brand distinguishes brand loyalty from habit. The stronger this evaluation becomes over time, the higher the degree of brand loyalty. To illustrate, if you purchase Heinz ketchup and decide that it is thicker and tastes better than other brands, you will purchase it again. If this evaluation is reinforced repeatedly, you will develop strong brand loyalty. Consumers can also be **multibrand loyal**,[51] or committed to two or more brands they purchase repeatedly. As an example, if you prefer and purchase only Coke and Sprite, you exhibit multibrand loyalty for soft drinks.

multibrand loyal Buying two or more brands repeatedly because of a strong preference.

Brand loyalty results in low-effort decision making because the consumer does not need to process information when making a decision and simply buys the same brand each time. However, because a strong commitment to the brand or service exists, brand-loyal consumers possess a relatively high level of involvement toward the brand whether their involvement with the product or service category is high or low. Thus even though ketchup might typically be thought of as a low-involvement product, the brand-loyal consumer can exhibit a high level of involvement toward the brand Heinz.

MARKETING IMPLICATIONS Brand-loyal consumers form a solid base from which brand profitability can be built. By identifying the characteristics of these consumers, marketers might be able to discover ways to strengthen loyalty for their brands. Unfortunately, this task is difficult because marketers cannot obtain a general profile of the brand-loyal consumer that applies to all product categories.[52] In other words, the extent to which a consumer is brand loyal depends on the product category; the consumer who is loyal for ketchup may not be loyal for peanut butter. As a result, marketers need to assess brand loyalty for each specific category.

Identifying Brand Loyal Customers. One of the approaches that marketers use to identify brand-loyal consumers focuses on consumer purchase patterns. Consumers who exhibit a particular sequence of purchases (three to four purchases of the same brand in a row) or proportion of purchases (seven or eight out of ten purchases for the same brand) are considered brand loyal.[53] The problem is that because brand loyalty involves both repeat purchases *and* a commitment to the brand, purchase-only measures do not accurately differentiate between habitual and brand-loyal consumers. To truly identify the brand-loyal consumer, marketers must assess both repeat-purchase behavior and a preference for the brand. To illustrate, in one study a measure that looked only at repeat-purchase behavior identified more than 70 percent of the sample of consumers as brand loyal. Adding preference for the brand as a qualifier reduced this percentage to under 50 percent.[54]

Despite these problems, purchase-only measures of brand loyalty are still widely used in marketing. With the availability of scanner data, marketers now have a wealth of information about consumer purchase patterns. An analysis of this information can still provide much relevant information, such as the impact of coupons on consumer purchases or the ways that pricing changes affect consumer buying patterns. Nevertheless, if the goal is to study brand loyalty, an approach that measures both purchase patterns and preference is preferable.

Developing Brand Loyalty. Because brand-loyal consumers have a strong brand commitment, they are more resistant to competitive efforts and switching than other consumers. For example, a brand-loyal user of Heinz ketchup is less likely to be influenced by a coupon or price deal for another brand. Thus a major goal of marketing is to develop brand loyalty. The widespread use of pricing deals in the United States, however, gradually eroded consumer loyalty toward many brands, and more and more consumers are buying on the basis of price. Therefore, marketers are now striving to develop consumer loyalty through product quality or sales promotions. Note that this problem did not developed in European countries, where fewer price promotions are employed and loyalty has remained stable.[55]

Developing Brand Loyalty Through Product Quality. One obvious and critical way to develop brand loyalty is to provide the consumer with a high-quality product that leads to satisfaction. The U.S. pharmaceutical industry is providing high-quality products, accompanied by heavy advertising, which has led to an overall increase in brand loyalty.[56] In Japan "low smoke" cigarettes have been successful because of concern about the effects of secondhand smoke.[57] In China, U.S. com- panies have been successful in inducing consumers to become loyal purchasers of U.S. cigarettes that taste better than local brands (despite criticism that they prey upon unknowing consumers).[58] Also major brands such as Crest toothpaste, Campbell's soup, and Heinz ketchup still have a sizable segment of loyal consumers.

Recent evidence suggests that consumers will become brand loyal to high-quality brands if these products are offered at a fair price. Consequently, many companies have lowered prices on their major brands.[59]

Developing Brand Loyalty Through Sales Promotions. Brand loyalty can also be cultivated through sales promotions. Marketers can use a coupon premium, whereby the consumer saves special coupons, proof-of-purchase seals, or UPC codes to acquire gifts or prizes free or for a small cost. Buying ten pizzas or CDs to get one free is another type of promotion. In Japan consumers lined up for eight hours to trade empty Marlboro packages for free gifts (the more packages, the better the gifts).[60]

EXHIBIT 11.9

Brand-Loyalty Building Program

Many airlines offer frequent-flyer miles as an incentive to fly on the same airline (i.e., by earning free trips or prizes). The Starwood Preferred Guest program offers free nights at selected hotels and free airline miles to stimulate re-peat stays at Starwood Hotels.

Source: Courtesy of Starwood.

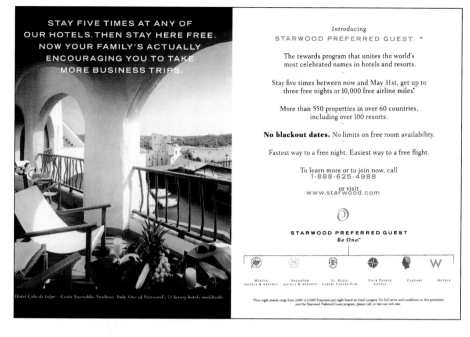

Frequent-flyer programs have been successful in building brand loyalty for various airlines. Consumers repeatedly fly on the same airline to build up mileage points that can be exchanged for free trips. These programs have even been ex-panded so that consumers can earn points by using certain phone companies; stay-ing in certain hotels (see Exhibit 11.9) or charging their purchases on certain credit cards. In France, Quick Burger awards points to consumers every time they eat at the restaurant, and the points can be redeemed for valuable prizes and dis-counts.[61] In addition, the technique of shaping (discussed earlier) can also be em-ployed to develop brand loyalty.

Marketing to Brand-Loyal Consumers of Other Brands. Marketers want to in-duce brand-loyal users of competitive brands to switch to brands. However, be-cause these consumers are strongly committed to other brands, getting them to switch is extremely difficult. As a result, it is usually better to avoid these con-sumers and try to market toward nonloyal or habitual consumers. The one ex-ception is a brand with a strong point of superiority or differentiation over the competitive brands. In this case the superior attribute might be enough to per-suade brand-loyal consumers to switch. For example, to try to convince brand-loyal McDonald's eaters to switch, both Burger King and Wendy's introduced french fries with a coating of potato-starch batter to make them crisper.[62]

Price as a Simplifying Strategy

price-related tactics Tactics based on price or cost.

Price-related tactics, such as buy the cheapest, buy the brand on sale, or use a coupon, are most likely to be used when few perceived differences exist among brands and when involvement with the brands in the consideration set is low. One study found that nine out of ten shoppers entered the store with some strategy for saving money.[63] These strategies are listed in Exhibit 11.10.

Even though price can be a critical factor in many decisions, consumers generally do not remember price information, even for a brand they have just

EXHIBIT 11.10
Pricing Strategies

Consumers can use different types of pricing strategies in their shopping. Which type of shopper are you?

Source: Data from Warwick Baker & Fiore in Laurie Petersen, "The Strategic Shopper," *Adweek's Marketing Week,* March 30, 1992, p. 18.

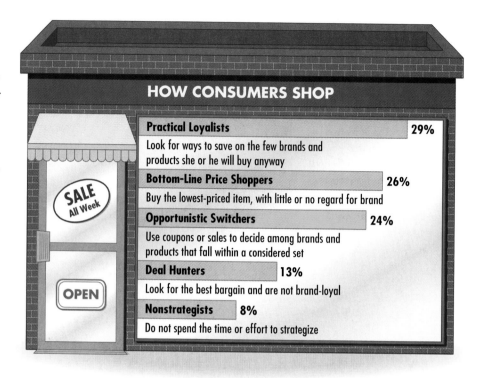

HOW CONSUMERS SHOP

Practical Loyalists — 29%
Look for ways to save on the few brands and products she or he will buy anyway

Bottom-Line Price Shoppers — 26%
Buy the lowest-priced item, with little or no regard for brand

Opportunistic Switchers — 24%
Use coupons or sales to decide among brands and products that fall within a considered set

Deal Hunters — 13%
Look for the best bargain and are not brand-loyal

Nonstrategists — 8%
Do not spend the time or effort to strategize

selected.[64] The reason is that this information is always available in the store, so there is little motivation to remember it.

MARKETING IMPLICATIONS Sometimes marketers make the mistake of assuming that consumers are always looking for the lowest possible price. Although this assumption is certainly true in some instances, a more accurate statement is that consumers have a **zone of acceptance** regarding what constitutes an appropriate range of prices for any particular product or service category.[65] As long as the brand falls within this price range, it can be considered for purchase. Brands falling either above or below the range will be rejected. Those priced too high are eliminated for obvious reasons. As evidence, on occasion food price increases have led many consumers to believe they are getting "ripped off," motivating them to purchase less.[66]

However, products that are priced too low can also be rejected because consumers infer that something is wrong with the product. Buyers would be suspicious if a pair of expensive designer jeans were on sale for $9.99. In addition, consumers will sometimes use price as a heuristic to judge product or service quality (higher price means higher quality).

zone of acceptance The acceptable range of prices for any purchase decision.

Price Perceptions Consumer perceptions also play an important role in the use of price-related tactics. Remember that for consumers to perceive two prices as different, the variation must be at or above the just noticeable difference. Thus consumers might not care if one brand of toothpaste is priced at $1.95 and another at $1.99.

Perceptual processes also play an important role in the consumer's reaction to different price points. Research has consistently indicated that consumers perceive odd prices (that is, those that end with an odd number) as significantly lower than even prices (those that end with an even number); therefore, a CD priced at $11.99 will be perceived as less expensive than one priced at $12.00.[67] Consumers tend to be more responsive to price decreases than they are to price increases.[68] Thus lowering the price of a brand or service will increase sales to a greater degree than increasing price by the same amount will decrease sales.

An interesting study also found that putting restrictions on the deal, such as a purchase limit or time limit, increases the perceptions of the deal's value but only when motivation to process is low.[69] The words used to describe the deal can also have an impact. One study found that comparing the sale price to the "regular price" worked better in the store, whereas comparison to competitors' prices was more effective at home.[70] Sometimes deals can be confusing, as was McDonald's "Campaign 55." Consumers did not understand that they needed to purchase fries and a drink to get 55-cent burgers.[71]

deal-prone consumers
Consumers who are more likely to be influenced by price.

The Deal-Prone Consumer   Marketers are interested in identifying **deal-prone consumers** because they are suitable for more directly targeted price-related strategies. Unfortunately, research findings on this issue have been mixed. One study found that deal-prone consumers are more likely to be older and less educated and to have a lower income than consumers who do not fit into this category, whereas other studies have found that higher-income consumers have better access to price information and are therefore more able to act on it.[72] Part of the problem is that consumers vary in terms of how they react to different types of deals. In other words, some consumers will respond to coupons, and some are more likely to respond to price cuts and to rebates.[73]

MARKETING IMPLICATIONS   Pricing strategy is clearly important to marketers, and they can use a variety of pricing techniques, including coupons, price-offs, rebates, and two-for-ones as long as the savings are at or above the just noticeable difference and within the zone of acceptance. Pepsi's selling 2.25-liter bottles for the same price as a 2-liter bottle of Coke in Eastern Europe is an example of a good pricing strategy.

The importance of deals is evidenced by the deep price cuts made by supermarket chains spurred by the stiff competition from warehouse clubs and discount drugstores. Major consumer products firms have also cut prices in response to competition from store brands. Private-label store brands, which are equal in quality to national brands but sold at a lower price, have experienced strong growth in the United States and in Europe. One study found a 19 percent increase in U.S. shoppers who are buying lower-priced or store brands.[74] In the United Kingdom private-label brands are very profitable and have the choicest spots on supermarket shelves.[75] Price wars have broken out in product and service categories such as cigarettes, drugs, iced tea, breakfast cereals, and airlines.[76] In Japan fast-food restaurants have been engaged in a bitter pricing battle, which McDonald's is winning.[77] The ability to search for lower prices is also the reason many consumers like to shop on the Internet.

In particular, consumers are looking for good value—that is, a high-quality brand at a good price. Fast-food chains such as Burger King, McDonald's, and Taco Bell have experienced great success with their "value meals." Wal-Mart has been very successful in offering better-quality merchandise at low prices.

The Importance of Value.   Note that *value* does not always mean lower price. Consumers will pay a higher price if they believe the product or service provides an important benefit.[78] One way for marketers to avoid lowering prices is to provide a differential benefit and convince consumers that the brand is worth the extra cost.

For example, Colgate bet that consumers would pay more for Total toothpaste, which has a special germ-fighting ingredient.[79] The popularity of Budweiser's "frogs" ads enabled the company to increase the price of its beer in the United States.[80] In Japan, however, where beer drinkers were traditionally willing to pay a higher price for Budweiser because of its trendy image, the firm repositioned the brand toward older, heavy drinkers, and this shift made it difficult to charge a premium price.[81] In Mexico cosmetics are extremely important to a woman's appearance, and many Mexican women will spare no expense in purchasing these products.[82]

Special Pricing. A note of caution is in order. If pricing deals are used too often, the special price can become the regular price, and consumers will not buy unless the brand is on sale, resulting in lost profits. This situation has happened in the past to food chains such as Arby's and Domino's. Too many deals can also damage brand loyalty as consumers become too deal oriented, thereby switching more often. Thus deals tend to work best when they are used intermittently and selectively. Lessened brand loyalty has become a major concern in many product and service categories in the United States and is the reason a number of major brands are starting to move away from deals and toward brand-building strategies such as advertising and sampling.[83]

The use of pricing deals also varies with the country. The trend in the United Kingdom and Italy has been toward quality rather than quantity—that is, fewer coupons but of higher value.[84] A strong economy in Spain has led to a decrease in coupon usage. In many countries coupons are not used for a variety of reasons, including these: the allowed discount is too small (Germany), retailers will not accept them (Holland and Switzerland), and the infrastructure of commerce is insufficient to handle them (Russia and Greece).

Price Consciousness Is Not Static. It may not surprise you that consumers tend to be more price conscious in difficult economic times than in times of prosperity. In the 1990s the slowing of the Japanese economy led to the tremendous popularity of discount stores in a country that once scorned them, and coupon use also increased there.[85] Even the cosmetics industry, known for notoriously high prices, discounted prices as much as 30 percent. Interestingly, when Japanese tourists visited Hawaii, they flocked to the Waikele Factory Stores mall (a collection of warehouse discount stores) because "everything is so cheap." ■

Normative Influences as a Simplifying Strategy

Sometimes consumers' low-elaboration decision making can be influenced by other individuals. A college freshman may buy the brand of laundry detergent his mother uses at home; a sophomore might buy clothing that her friends like. Our use of such **normative choice tactics** can result from (1) *direct influence*, in which others try to manipulate us, (2) *vicarious observation*, in which we observe others to guide our behavior, and (3) *indirect influence*, in which we are concerned about the opinions of others. Normative tactics are particularly common among inexperienced consumers who have little knowledge. Note that chat groups on the Internet can increase the importance of normative influence in decision making because consumers can talk to each other so easily.

normative choice tactics
Low-elaboration decision-making that is based on others' opinions.

MARKETING IMPLICATIONS If normative tactics are particularly evident in a product or service category, these motivations can be emphasized in advertising. A good example of this strategy is an ad for Ritz crackers that shows how pleased party guests will be when you "serve it on a Ritz." Consumers often buy expensive imported products to impress others. Marketers can also attempt to stimulate word-of-mouth communication in ways we describe in a later chapter. ■

LOW-EFFORT FEELING-BASED DECISION MAKING

We now can turn to low-effort strategies based more on feelings than on cognitive processing. These include affective tactics, variety seeking, and impulse purchasing.

Feelings as a Simplifying Strategy

affect Low-level feelings.

Sometimes consumers select a brand or service because they like it, even though they may not necessarily know why. This behavior relies on very basic, low-level feelings that we previously defined as **affect**. Affect differs from cognitive strategies, for example, performance-related attitudes, in that it does not necessarily result from a conscious recognition of need satisfaction and is usually weaker than an attitude.

Affect is most likely to play a role in the decision process when the product or service is hedonic, rather than functional and when other factors, such as performance evaluations, price, habit, and normative influences, are not in operation. If you buy Heinz ketchup because it satisfies your needs the best or if you are motivated to buy the cheapest brand of paper towels, affect is less likely to play a role in your decision. However, these factors are often not in operation in low-effort situations, and affect can then play a central role.

affect-related tactics Tactics based on feelings.

affect referral A simple type of affective tactic where we simply remember our feelings for the product or service.

Affect Referral   **Affect-related tactics** use a form of category-based processing.[86] In other words, we associate brands with global affective evaluations we recall from memory when making a choice, a process called **affect referral** or the "how do I feel about it" heuristic.[87] For instance, when we hear the name *Starbucks*, we might associate it with general feelings of happiness and joy, and we might decide to get coffee there based on these feelings, rather than on a detailed evaluation of Starbucks.

Whenever a consumer encounters a new brand, he or she can also compare it to other brands in the same category. To the extent that the new brand is similar to previously encountered brands, the affect associated with that category can be transferred to the new instance and influence choice.[88] On the other hand, if the new brand is perceived as dissimilar, the consumer is more likely to switch to piecemeal processing, evaluating attributes in the manner described in Chapter 10.[89]

brand familiarity Easy recognition of a well-known brand.

Brand Familiarity   Affect can also be generated from **brand familiarity** (through the mere exposure effect). In one study beer drinkers with well-established brand preferences could not distinguish their preferred brand from others in a blind taste test.[90] However, when the beers were identified, consumers rated the taste of their preferred brand significantly higher than the others. Another study found that "buying the most familiar brand" was a dominant choice tactic for inexperienced purchasers of peanut butter. Even when the quality of the most familiar brand was manipulated to be lower than unfamiliar brands, consumers still greatly preferred the familiar brand.[91] Very young children can be influenced by brand names if they are accompanied with visual cues like the Froot Loops toucan.[92]

These findings were replicated in a study in Singapore, suggesting that the impact of brand familiarity may be a cross-cultural phenomenon.[93] Another study found that brand name was a more important heuristic cue in a low-elaboration situation than in a high-elaboration one.[94] Finally, an interesting study found that

27 brands that were tops in their category in 1930 (and thus were most familiar) are still number one today, including Campbell's soup, Ivory soap, and Gold Medal flour.[95]

Visual Attributes   Affect plays a key role in determining aesthetic responses to marketing stimuli, especially when visual properties are the only basis for judgment. One study found that two key aspects of a product's design produces more positive affective responses to the product.[96] These are *unity*, which means that the visual parts of the design connect in a meaningful way, and *prototypicality*, which means that the object is representative of its category.

MARKETING IMPLICATIONS   Given that feelings can play an important role in the decision process, marketers can attempt to create and maintain brand familiarity, build category-based associations, and generate affect through advertising that creates positive attitudes toward the ad. By creating positive affect toward their brand, marketers can increase the probability that it will be selected (all other things being equal).

The power of brand name familiarity was demonstrated several years ago when Coca-Cola changed its formula. Even though most consumers preferred the taste of New Coke in blind taste tests, a strong preference for the old formula resurfaced when brand names were identified. In fact, the demand for the old brand was so strong that a nationwide consumer movement strongly pressured the company to reintroduce Coca-Cola Classic. As shown in Exhibit 11.11, the Green Giant brand is a highly familiar and positively evaluated brand name for foods. In Romania and Turkey, buying well-known brand names is very important because it increases a consumer's prestige.[97] Most of the status brands, however, are foreign.

U.S. pharmaceutical companies are now permitted to engage in direct-to-consumer advertising. This practice has enabled them to raise the brand familiarity of prescription drugs and increase both requests by patients and sales.[98] Johnson & Johnson placed the name of a well-known nonprofit group on its Arthritis Foundation Pain Reliever in the hope that the associated familiarity and affect will transfer over to the brand. The company is also donating $1 million to the group.[99] Even the Vatican Library is allowing its name to be placed on various products, including watches, jewelry, and greeting cards.[100]

EXHIBIT 11.11
Brand Name Familiarity and Positive Affect

Consumers tend to have more positive feelings toward brands that are more familiar relative to brands that are unfamiliar. The Green Giant brand is a well-known producer of food items and has been in business since 1925.

Source: Courtesy of Pillsbury.

co-branding An arrangement by which two brands form a partnership to benefit from the power of two.

Many companies are now engaging in **co-branding**, an arrangement by which two brands form a partnership to benefit from the power of two.[101] Examples include ConAgra and Kellogg's, Kraft and Boboli, Ocean Spray and Pepsi, and Arby's and ZuZu's. The number of such alliances is growing by 40 percent each year. Liquor companies are using co-branding to get around advertising restrictions by placing their name on food (Jack Daniel's Grill with TGI Friday's and Kahluaccino Drink Mix).[102]

Brands that have positive cross-cultural affect can be marketed internationally. In expanding to Europe and Asia, Nathan's hot dogs hoped that the excitement of New York would create positive category associations and make selling easier.[103] Likewise, U.S. tobacco companies used a positive "Western" association to sell cigarettes in Eastern Europe.[104] The U.S. image has also benefited companies such as Procter & Gamble, Colgate-Palmolive, and Johnson & Johnson in selling toiletries and detergents in China.[105]

Hedonic products or services—those that involve style or taste—rely heavily on affective associations. The marketing philosophy at Frito-Lay is "If you can make people feel better about what they are eating, the propensity to consume more is there."[106] Finally, the familiarity of packaging can play an important role in influencing brand choice, which explains why Coca-Cola introduced plastic versions of its familiar glass bottle. ■

Decision Making Based on Variety-Seeking Needs

Another common consumer-choice tactic in low-effort situations is to try something different. A consumer might normally use baby shampoo on a regular basis but one day suddenly get the urge to use L'Oréal and then return to baby shampoo for later purchases. In marketing and consumer behavior, this phenomenon is called **variety seeking**.

variety seeking Trying something different.

Two major reasons that consumers engage in variety seeking are *satiation* and *boredom*.[107] If you had the same thing for dinner every single night or listened to only one CD over and over, satiation would occur and you would be driven to do something different. Because many consumer decisions occur repeatedly, they can become monotonous. Note that variety seeking is not expressed in every product category. It is most likely to occur when involvement is low, there are few differences among brands, and the product is more hedonic than functional.[108] Marketers can also reduce boredom simply by providing more variety in a product category.[109]

optimal stimulation level (OSL) The ideal level of stimulation in any situation.

sensation seekers Those who actively look for variety.

Consumers are motivated to relieve boredom because their level of arousal falls below the **optimal stimulation level (OSL)**—an internal ideal level of stimulation.[110] Repetitive purchasing causes the internal level of stimulation to fall below the OSL, and buying something different is a way of restoring it. In addition, certain consumers need more stimulation and are less tolerant of boredom than others. These **sensation seekers** are more likely to engage in variety seeking and are often the first to try new and trendy products, making them a good market for new offerings.[111]

vicarious exploration Seeking information simply for stimulation.

Note that purchasing something different is only one way to seek stimulation. Consumers can also express their variety drive by engaging in vicarious exploration and use innovativeness.[112] **Vicarious exploration** occurs when consumers simply collect information about a product, either from reading or talking with others, or put themselves in stimulating shopping environments. For example, many people like to go to a store simply to look around or browse. Many times they have no intention to purchase; the goal is simply to increase stimulation.

use innovativeness Using products in new ways.

Use innovativeness means using products in a new or different way. For example, a consumer could use an aluminum can that held soup or vegetables to organize nails in a workshop or use baking soda to deodorize a kitty litter box. Consumer use innovativeness actually led to the introduction of a new kitty litter deodorizer product by Arm & Hammer. The woman in Exhibit 11.12 is demonstrating another example of use innovativeness.

MARKETING IMPLICATIONS Variety seeking has several important marketing implications. Marketers sometimes need to recognize consumers' need for variety and take steps to combat it. For example, Procter & Gamble introduced lemon-scented Coast soap, recognizing that consumers may experience "burnout" with the original scent. The company hoped consumers would express their need for variety by buying a different scent of Coast rather than switching to another brand. Also, many consumers have tired of the taste of colas, which has led to an increase in sales of flavored brands, such as Dr. Pepper, Mountain Dew, and Mr. Pibb, all of which are owned by either Pepsi or Coca-Cola.[113] Interestingly, the largest increase occurred for single-serve vending machines, which involves less risk than buying a 6- or 12-pack (lending support to the variety notion).

Because the need for variety may induce consumers to switch away from competitive brands, marketers could also induce brand switching by encouraging consumers to "put a little spice into life" and try something different. Note, however, that consumers can be given too much variety. For example, KFC consumers began to cry "No more" in response to the chain's many menu additions.[114] Consumers also became bored with the many new product introductions in the "new age" beverage category (teas and juices).[115]

Buying on Impulse

impulse purchase An unexpected purchase based on a strong feeling.

Another common type of decision process that has a strong affective component is the **impulse purchase**, which occurs when consumers suddenly decide to purchase something they had not planned on buying. Impulse purchases are characterized by (1) an intense or overwhelming feeling of having to buy the product immediately, (2) a disregard of potentially negative purchase consequences, (3) feelings of euphoria and excitement, and (4) a conflict between control and indulgence.[116] They are often instigated by exposure to an external stimulus, such as an in-store display, catalog, or TV ad with phone number. Consumers also often travel based on impulse (the "spur of the moment").[117]

Researchers estimate that anywhere from 27 to 62 percent of consumer purchases can be considered impulse buys.[118] However, an important distinction separates impulse buying and partially planned purchases, or those for which the consumer has an intention to buy the product category but uses the store display to decide which brand to select. When this distinction is made, the proportion of impulse purchases is usually lower.[119] The tendency to engage in impulse purchasing varies; some consumers can be considered highly impulsive buyers, whereas others are not.[120] The tendency to buy on impulse is probably related to other traits such as general acquisitiveness and materialism, sensation seeking, and a liking for recreational shopping.[121] If the costs of impulsiveness are made salient or if normative pressure such as the presence of others with a negative opinion is high, impulse purchasing will be reduced.[122]

MARY MILKOVISCH MADE A HOUSE WITH RECYCLED BEER CANS.

RUFFIES MADE A TRASH BAG WITH RECYCLED MILK JUGS.

Introducing Ruffies® Eco-Choice™ Trash Bags. The first trash bags made with at least 33% recycled plastic bottles (like milk jugs) collected from community recycling centers. Which won't save the planet, of course. But it is something simple you can do to help the environment.

ECO-CHOICE™ TRASH BAGS
Made tough. Made with recycled plastic.
RUFFIES

©2002 Ruffies and Eco-Choice are trademarks of Carlisle Plastics, Inc.

EXHIBIT 11.12
Use Innovativeness

Some consumers think of new and different ways to use products. This consumer made a house with recycled beer cans. Eco-choice is introducing its plastic bags made with at least 33 percent recycled plastic milk bottles. Have you or anyone you know ever demonstrated use innovativeness?

Source: Carlisle Plastics, Inc.

MARKETING IMPLICATIONS Impulse purchases are very important to marketers, and many stores are organized to maximize them. In card shops, for example, typically sought items such as greeting cards are placed in the back of the store so that consumers will have to pass by a number of displays containing higher-margin, impulse items. Eye-level and eye-catching displays that we have mentioned before, including end-of-aisle displays, electronic bulletin boards, blinking lights, and shopping-cart ads, can increase sales dramatically, and much of the increase comes from impulse purchases.[123] Vendors must pay high prices for the best display space in a store.[124] Package design can also increase impulse purchases. For example, in the candy industry, which enjoys a lot of impulse buying, Brach's varieties used to be sold in identical pink bags, but the company redesigned its packages to have a more dramatic and contemporary look, hoping to increase impulse buying.[125] Other marketing innovations, such as credit cards, bank machines, and 24-hour stores, make it easier than ever to make impulse purchases.

 Impulse purchasing tends to decline in difficult economic times. In Japan, for example, consumer buying experienced a slowdown, and many consumers spent money only on things they need, such as clothes and items for children. As a result, marketers had to reposition many products as necessities rather than as impulse items.[126]

SUMMARY

This chapter examined the nature of consumer judgment and decision making when motivation, ability, and opportunity, or MAO—and consequently elaboration—are low. In these situations consumers often use simplified heuristics or decision rules. Consumers use the representativeness and availability heuristics to make judgments; that is, consumers base their judgments on comparisons to a prototype or on accessibility of information, respectively.

Choice tactics used in decision making can be either cognitively based (performance, habit, brand loyalty, price, normative) or based on feelings (affect, variety seeking, impulse). These tactics are learned over repeat purchase occasions through a process called operant conditioning.

Performance-related tactics are more likely to be employed when consumer needs have been satisfied and positive attitudes have been formed, thereby emphasizing the importance of product or service quality. Some consumers purchase by habit or simple repetitive behavior. Marketers want to encourage consumers to continue buying certain brands while attempting to induce users of other brands to switch. Brand loyalty represents the most desirable situation for marketers. Here the consumer possesses a strong commitment to the brand and buys it repeatedly. Marketers can build brand loyalty by offering high-quality products, as well as by providing special incentives to the consumer for repeat purchases. Price-related tactics can be effective when few perceived differences exist among brands or when economic motives are extremely important. As long as the price of the brand or service falls within the zone of acceptance, the purchase will be considered. When the consumer is inexperienced or has little knowledge or when the opinion of others is very important, normative tactics may guide the consumer's decision. In this case marketers can emphasize normative motivations in their ad messages.

Consumers' use of affect-related tactics implies that marketers should attempt to build and maintain brand familiarity and positive attitudes toward their ads. Some consumers will switch brands because of a need for variety. Finally, many purchases are made on impulse and marketers can organize the purchase environment to induce this type of activity.

EXERCISES

1. Interview ten consumers about their decision-making behavior for the following product categories: peanut butter, laundry detergent, canned vegetables, coffee, and ice cream. Ask the consumers to indicate (a) how much time and effort they take in making a decision and (b) how they select the brand they purchase (which choice tactics do they use?). Summarize the responses for each consumer individually and for all consumers; also, answer the following questions:

   a. On average, how much time and effort do consumers spend on these decisions?

   b. What are the major types of tactics employed for each category?

   c. How do the tactics differ for the product categories?

   d. Do consumers use the same or different tactics across product categories?

   e. What are the marketing implications of your findings?

2. Pick two common product categories where low-elaboration decision making is likely to occur. Go to your local store and observe 20 consumers making a choice for these two products. Record the amount of time taken and the number of brands examined. If possible, ask consumers why they chose the brand they did immediately after the choice. (Be sure to get the store's permission first.) Summarize this information and answer the following questions:

   a. How much time and effort did consumers typically devote to these decisions? Are your findings consistent with those reported in the chapter?

   b. What were the most common types of choice tactics employed?

   c. Did the types of choice tactics differ between product categories? If so, why do you think this occurred?

3. Pick ten product or service categories in which low-elaboration decision making is likely to occur. For each category, try to identify the type of choice tactic you would typically use.

a. Does this tactic differ across categories?

b. If so, why?

c. How do you think you learned to use these tactics?

CHAPTER 12

POST-DECISION PROCESSES

INTRODUCTION

Consumers in ever-growing numbers are shopping on the Internet, and at no time is this trend more evident than during the holiday season. Most consumers have had positive experiences making gift purchases in this manner, but some horror stories have emerged. The most common problems were packages that failed to arrive on time (thus no presents to open), credit cards that were charged for items never purchased, and customer service that was inadequate to handle such problems. The end result was that "the whole experience was frustrating and embarrassing."[1] for the few consumers experiencing these problems.

The above mentioned problems are critical for marketers because surveys show that 96 percent of those who received their merchandise on time would consider another on-line purchase, but only 46 percent of those who encountered problems would do so. Thus on-line retailers may need to shift their focus from only acquiring new customers to pleasing existing ones as well (see Exhibit 12.1).

EXHIBIT 12.1

Source: AP/Wide World Photos.

This example illustrates several key topics in Chapter 12. First, it demonstrates how dissatisfaction can occur when consumers believe that a company has not lived up to their expectations. Second, it highlights the importance of customer satisfaction as the foundation of a successful business. Third, it shows how satisfaction can be a function of good performance, creating positive feelings and perceptions of equity (a fair exchange). Finally, it illustrates how consumers can learn about products and services by experiencing them directly, as Internet shoppers have done with this new way of shopping.

All these phenomena occur after the consumer has made a decision. This chapter thus examines the four post-decision processes shown in Exhibit 12.2: dissonance, consumer learning, satisfaction/dissatisfaction, and disposition. Each one has important marketing implications, as you will see.

POST-DECISION DISSONANCE

After you make a decision related to acquisition, consumption, or disposition, you may sometimes feel uncertain whether you made the correct choice. You might wonder whether you should have bought a shirt or dress other than the one you did, or whether you should have worn something else to a party, or kept an old teddy bear instead of throwing it away. **Post-decision dissonance** is most likely to occur when more than one alternative is attractive and the decision is important.[2]

post-decision dissonance A feeling of anxiety over whether the correct decision was made.

Post-decision dissonance can influence consumer behavior because it creates anxiety that the consumer would like to reduce, especially when motivation, ability, and opportunity (MAO) are high. One way of reducing dissonance is to search for additional information from sources such as experts and magazines. This search is very selective and is designed to make the chosen alternative more attractive and the rejected ones less attractive, thereby reducing dissonance.

EXHIBIT 12.2

Chapter Overview:
Post-Decision Processes

The decision does not end after a choice or purchase it made. Consumers can experience dissonance (anxiety over whether the correct decision was made), learn about the product or service by using it, experience satisfaction or dissatisfaction with the product or service, and eventually dispose of it. This chapter examines the theories and implications underlying each of these important processes.

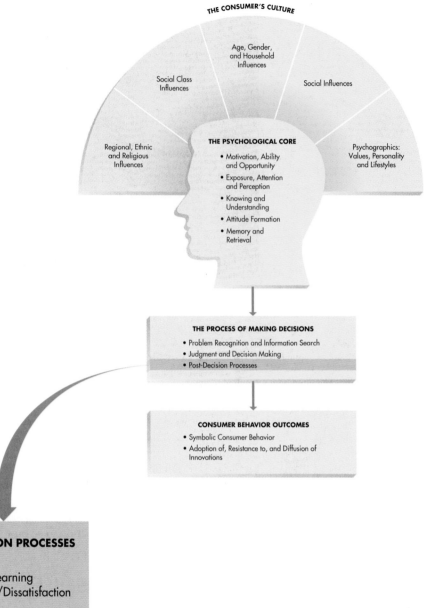

THE CONSUMER'S CULTURE

Age, Gender, and Household Influences

Social Class Influences

Social Influences

Regional, Ethnic and Religious Influences

THE PSYCHOLOGICAL CORE
- Motivation, Ability and Opportunity
- Exposure, Attention and Perception
- Knowing and Understanding
- Attitude Formation
- Memory and Retrieval

Psychographics: Values, Personality and Lifestyles

THE PROCESS OF MAKING DECISIONS
- Problem Recognition and Information Search
- Judgment and Decision Making
- Post-Decision Processes

CONSUMER BEHAVIOR OUTCOMES
- Symbolic Consumer Behavior
- Adoption of, Resistance to, and Diffusion of Innovations

POST-DECISION PROCESSES
- Dissonance
- Consumer learning
- Satisfaction/Dissatisfaction
- Disposition

MARKETING IMPLICATIONS By helping consumers reduce post-decision dissonance, marketers can diminish any negative feelings that might be related to the product or service. They accomplish this reduction by helping consumers obtain supporting information. For example, consumers who purchase a BMW receive a copy of *BMW Magazine*, which is filled with interesting facts and 'feel good' information about the car. One purpose of this information is to reduce dissonance and assist consumers in developing a positive attitude toward the product. Consumers may read supporting information in advertisements after purchase to reduce dissonance as well. ▪

LEARNING FROM CONSUMER EXPERIENCE*

In earlier chapters we discussed how consumers acquire knowledge through processes such as information search, exposure to marketing communications, and observation of others. From a practical perspective, when we think about consumer learning, we most often think about this type of learning because it is usually under the direct control of the marketer, who provides information through marketing communications. However, these efforts are often limited because of their low credibility.[3] Consumers assume that these messages are intended to persuade them to buy the product or service and are therefore generally skeptical about the truthfulness of marketing claims.

Experiences that occur during consumption or disposition, however, can be equally—if not more—important sources of consumer knowledge than those mentioned above for several reasons. First, the consumer tends to be more motivated to learn under these circumstances. Actually experiencing an event is more involving and interesting than being told about it, and the consumer has more control over what happens. Second, information acquired from experience is more vivid and therefore easier to remember than other types of information.[4] Finally, information obtained from experience or product trial can exert a stronger influence on consumers' future behavior than information acquired from advertising or word of mouth for attributes that must be experienced through taste, touch, or smell.[5] For example, an ad can state that a product will taste good, but actually eating it is more likely to result in a strong attitude. On the other hand, ads with repeated exposure can approximate the effect of direct experience when it comes to search or informational attributes such as price or ingredients.[6] If an ad is repeated often enough, it can result in strong beliefs about these characteristics.

A Model of Learning from Consumer Experience

hypothesis testing Testing out expectations through experience.

Consumers can learn from experience by engaging in a process of **hypothesis testing**. On the basis of past experience or another source such as word of mouth or advertising, consumers can form a hypothesis or expectation about a product or service, a consumption experience, or a disposition option and then set out to test it. Such hypotheses are important because without them consumers are less likely to gather the evidence they need to learn. Researchers have proposed that consumers go through four basic stages in testing hypotheses for learning. As outlined

---

*This section draws heavily from an article by Stephen J. Hoch and John Deighton, "Managing What Consumers Learn from Experience," *Journal of Marketing*, April 1989, pp. 1–20.

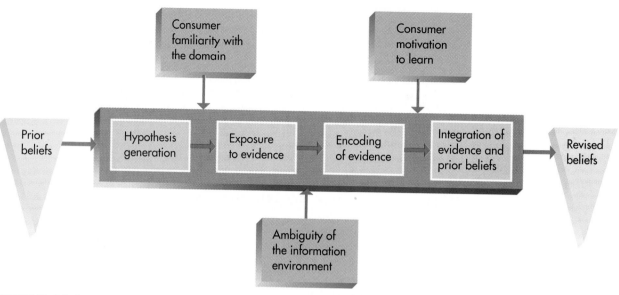

EXHIBIT 12.3
A Model of Learning from Experience

Consumers can acquire a lot of information about product and services by actually experiencing them. This learning process starts with prior beliefs (as one example, "German beers are great"). Upon seeing a new beer from Germany, the consumer can generate hypotheses ("I'll bet this new beer is really good"), get exposure to the evidence (buy the new beer and drink it), encode the evidence (evaluate whether it is good or not), and integrate this evidence with prior beliefs (relate current evaluation with past perceptions). If the beer is not good, the consumer will revise beliefs (not all German beers are good). This entire process is influenced by consumer familiarity, motivation to process, and the ambiguity of the information.

Source: Stephen J. Hoch and John Deighton, "Managing What Consumers Learn from Experience," *Journal of Marketing*, April 1989, pp. 1–20. Reprinted by permission.

in Exhibit 12.3, these are (1) hypothesis generation, (2) exposure to evidence, (3) encoding of evidence, and (4) integration of evidence and prior beliefs. We'll use an example to illustrate these steps.

Suppose a consumer is watching TV and sees an exciting ad for a new Jim Carrey movie. She also remembers some of his previous movies, such as *The Truman Show* or *Ace Ventura*. Based on these sources of information, she **generates a hypothesis** about the quality of the new movie ("It must be great"). Next, she seeks out **exposure to evidence** to either confirm or disprove this hypothesis by going to see the new movie. While watching it, she can assess whether or not it is in fact great; this step is called **encoding the evidence**.

Finally, after watching the movie the consumer can **integrate the evidence** with her existing knowledge or beliefs. Thus if she really likes it, confirming her hypothesis, she may have learned that "you can always count on a Jim Carrey movie to be great." On the other hand, if she does not like it, as was the case for some consumers with *The Cable Guy*, she may form the new belief that "not all Carrey films are great, and I must be careful in the future."

Note that this learning process can occur for any aspect of consumer behavior. In other words, hypotheses can be formed in relation to acquisition (this product/service will fulfill my needs, buying at a flea market will be fun), consumption (sitting in a hot tub will be soothing, listening to the concert will be fun), or disposition (getting rid of this refrigerator will be easy). Learning from experience is also important when a purchasing agent—either a person or a computer-aided

hypothesis generation
Forming expectations about the product or service.

exposure to evidence Actually experiencing the product or service.

encoding of evidence
Processing the information experienced.

integration of evidence
Combining new information with stored knowledge.

program that helps consumers make a decision—is involved. These agents function by using feedback from repeated hypothesis tests to learn what the consumer likes best.[7]

What Affects Learning from Experience?

Four factors affect learning from experience: (1) motivation, (2) prior familiarity or ability, (3) ambiguity of the information environment or lack of opportunity, and (4) processing biases.

Motivation When consumers are motivated to process information, they will generate a number of hypotheses and seek out information to confirm or disprove them. Thus consumers will engage in an active process of learning from experience. On the other hand, when motivation is low, they will generate few or no hypotheses and will be less likely to learn unless the learning process involves the more simple processes classical or operant conditioning (see Chapters 7 and 11). Nevertheless, marketers can still facilitate the learning process when motivation is low, as you will see shortly.

Prior Knowledge or Ability Consumers' prior knowledge or ability affects the extent to which they learn from experience. When knowledge is high, consumers are likely to have well-defined beliefs and expectations and are therefore unlikely to generate new hypotheses. Also, experts are less likely than those with moderate knowledge to search for information.[8] Both these factors inhibit learning. In contrast, low-knowledge consumers lack skills to develop hypotheses to guide the learning process.[9] Without guiding hypotheses, consumers have difficulty collecting evidence and learning. Thus moderately knowledgeable consumers are the most likely to generate hypotheses and learn from experience. Interestingly, experts do have an advantage in learning information about *new* products and services, thanks to their more extensive knowledge base.[10]

Ambiguity of the Information Environment or Lack of Opportunity The situation does not always provide the opportunity for consumers to learn from experience. That is, there may not be enough information to confirm or disprove hypotheses.[11] Such **ambiguity of information** occurs because many products and services are similar in quality and because little information typically comes from the experience.

Ambiguous information can strongly affect consumers' ability to learn from experience. When it is hard to determine product quality (e.g., beer, motor oil), consumers tend to support their hypotheses with information from advertising or word of mouth, mainly because experiencing the product does not disprove this information; the product is seen as consistent with prior expectations.[12] Thus for many years consumers believed that Listerine prevented colds and that STP oil treatment improved engine performance because these claims could not be disproved by usage. Obviously, the marketer in situations such as these has an unfair advantage, which is why deception in advertising is such an important topic (see Chapters 4 and 20).

On the other hand, when evidence is unambiguous and the product is clearly good or bad, perceptions are based on actual experience and learning is high. Unambiguous information tends to be better remembered and to have a greater impact on future decisions.[13] When evidence is ambiguous, evaluations by both experts and novices are strongly influenced by country-of-origin expectations (e.g.,

ambiguity of information
A condition whereby decision options are hard to differentiate.

the knowledge that a product was made in Japan), but when evidence is unambiguous, experts ignore this information and make evaluations based on actual quality.[14]

Processing Biases   Two biases in information processing—the confirmation bias (Chapter 9) and overconfidence (Chapter 10)—can pose major hurdles to the learning process, particularly when evidence is ambiguous.[15] Specifically, these biases inhibit learning by making consumers avoid both negative and highly diagnostic information. For example, a consumer who believes that all Japanese products are of high quality may ignore contrary evidence and not learn anything new about these products.

Negative information is important to the learning process because provides a more balanced picture of the situation and allows us to make a more accurate test of hypotheses; thus such information can be very important to the learning process. Research has also shown the acquisition of disproving evidence has a strong and rapid impact on learning.[16]

MARKETING IMPLICATIONS   One of the major implications of our discussion is that ambiguous information and processing biases often inhibit consumer learning about products and services. From a marketing perspective, these learning principles can have important strategic implications, depending on the market position of the product or service.[17]

Top-Dog Strategies.   A product or service that is the market leader or has a strong share is called a *top dog*. Limitations on learning are advantageous to top dogs because consumers will simply confirm existing beliefs and expectations and display overconfidence, particularly when the motivation to learn is low. Thus consumers are less likely to learn new information that might lead to brand switching.

When motivation to learn is high, however, the consumer will try to acquire information that could be disproving and lead to a switch. In this case marketers can employ three strategies. First, the top dog can reinforce the agenda, that is, state specific claims that justify consumers' evaluation of the brand. For example, in its new global advertising, Heinz ketchup tries to give consumers a reason why "Mine's Gotta Have Heinz."[18] Second, marketers can encourage consumers not to acquire new information, which is called *blocking exposure to evidence*. In other words, marketers can try to get across the theme, Why change if it works? Finally, if evidence about the top dog is unambiguous, the consumer simply needs reinforcement as to why the brand is satisfying, which is called *explaining the experience*, and needs to be encouraged to try it. For example, KFC, the market leader in Shanghai, touts its quality and value compared to that of small local food vendors.[19]

Underdog Strategies.   In contrast to top dogs, *underdogs*, or lower-share brands, have everything to gain by encouraging consumer learning because new information may lead to switching. Motivating the consumer to learn is to the underdog's advantage. When the consumer is not motivated, underdogs face a more difficult task; they must instigate learning by reducing either the product's costs or its perceived risk.

First, the underdog needs to do everything possible to facilitate comparisons with the market leader, such as using comparative ads, setting up side-by-side displays, or providing information on the Internet. Facilitating comparisons is what AeroMexico hopes to accomplish in the ad in Exhibit 12.4. In Japan, Budweiser's Buddy beer touts its alcohol content (6 percent) as higher than that of popular

SORRY,
ALL OUT OF PEANUTS.

INSTEAD YOU WILL BE SERVED
WORLD CLASS DISHES FROM
OUR RENOWNED CHEFS,
MEMBERS OF FRANCE'S
CULINARY ACADEMY. IN FACT,
WE'RE BLESSED WITH MORE
FOOD PER PASSENGER THAN
THAT OTHER AIRLINE YOU FLY.
WHICH IS WHERE
OUR PEANUTS GO. IT'S WHAT
YOU'VE BEEN CRAVING:
WORLD CLASS FOOD.

AEROMEXICO.
Expect it.

EXHIBIT 12.4
Differential Advantage

It is often difficult for consumers to state why one airline is better than another (evidence is ambiguous). Thus the strategy here for AeroMexico is to facilitate comparison with market leaders by pointing out the specific advantages of choosing this airline—the world class dishes prepared by renowned chefs.

Source: Courtesy of AeroMexico Airlines.

competitors.[20] Nevertheless, overconfidence and confirmation biases may stack the odds against these efforts, and they are unlikely to succeed unless the underdog has a strong and distinct advantage.

Second, marketers can disrupt the agenda by employing both advertising to create expectations and promotions such as sampling to provide the actual experience. If the evidence is ambiguous, expectations are unlikely to be disconfirmed. For example, ads created expectations by encouraging consumers to take the "Pepsi challenge" against Coke, for which in-store demonstrations provided the experience. If the evidence is ambiguous, however, consumer expectations are unlikely to be disproved.

 Finally, facilitating product trials is also critical when the motivation to learn is low but evidence is unambiguous, because evidence will lead to a positive learning experience. Two common means of encouraging product trial are sampling and coupons. To develop consumers' taste for cranberry sauce in the United Kingdom, Ocean Spray gave away free samples of the product.[21] The coupon offer in Exhibit 12.5 is another example of this strategy. ■

HOW DO CONSUMERS MAKE SATISFACTION OR DISSATISFACTION JUDGMENTS?

After consumers have made acquisition, consumption, or disposition decisions, they can also evaluate the outcomes of their decisions. If they make positive evaluations—if they feel their needs or goals have been met—**satisfaction** has occurred. Thus you could feel satisfied with the purchase of a new VCR, the choice of a red wine to drink with a home-cooked dinner, or the the cleaning out of a cluttered closet. You might also be pleased with a buying experience, a salesperson, or a retail outlet.[22] Satisfaction can be associated with feelings of acceptance, happiness, relief, excitement, and delight.

Negative evaluation of an outcome results in **dissatisfaction**. Dissatisfaction occurs if you did not enjoy a movie, did not like the taste of a breakfast cereal, were unhappy with a salesperson, or wished you had not thrown out something. Dissatisfaction can be related to feelings of tolerance, distress, sadness, regret, agitation, and outrage.[23]

satisfaction The feeling that results when consumers make a positive evaluation or feel happy with their decision.

dissatisfaction The feeling that results when consumers make a negative evaluation or are unhappy with a decision.

EXHIBIT 12.5
Facilitating Trial

It is hoped that providing a $1.00 off coupon for Arm & Hammer Liquid Laundry Detergent will lower the financial risk and get consumers to try this product. Would this approach affect your behavior?

Source: Reprinted with permission from Church & Dwight Co., Inc.

Most of the research on satisfaction and dissatisfaction has focused on products and services for which the consumer can make an evaluation of both *utilitarian dimensions,* or how well the product or service functions (good or bad), and *hedonic dimensions,* or how it makes someone feel (happy, excited, delighted or sad, regretful, angry).[24] Consumers make a conscious comparison between what they think will happen and actual performance.[25]

Consumers' evaluations and feelings are generally temporary and can change over time. The fact that we are satisfied now does not necessarily mean we will be satisfied the next time. Evaluations also tend to be tied to specific consumption situations—we are satisfied (or not) with the offering as we are using it at the current time. In these ways, satisfaction differs from an attitude, which is relatively enduring and less dependent on the specific situation (see Chapter 5).[26] Note also that a post-decision evaluation can differ from a pre-decision evaluation in that after using the product we may judge different attributes and cutoff levels than we did before.[27] For example, we might like the taste of frozen microwave pizza less after trying it than we thought we would.

Levels of satisfaction vary with our involvement and over time.[28] Specifically, high-involvement consumers tend to express a higher level of satisfaction immediately after purchase, probably due to their more extensive evaluation. However, their satisfaction declines over time. On the other hand, lower-involvement consumers exhibit a lower level of satisfaction initially, but their level of satisfaction tends to increase with greater usage over time.

MARKETING IMPLICATIONS Satisfied customers form the foundation of any successful business. Customer satisfaction is critical: It leads to repeat purchase, brand loyalty, and positive word of mouth.[29] A study of Swedish consumers suggests that satisfaction is especially important for companies that rely on repeat business.[30] Nowhere is this more evident than at Coca-Cola. According to former President Roberto C. Goizueta, consumer satisfaction is Coca-Cola's "most valuable asset. . . [but] the truly successful company creates something beyond simple satisfaction. It creates an emotional bond between its products and consumers."[31] Indeed, Coke is the best-known and most admired consumer brand both in the United States, where it is ranked far ahead of the next most-recognized brand, Campbell's soup, and worldwide, where it is of-ten the most valued brand name. On the Internet, the highly successful retailer Amazon.com attributes 63 percent of its sales to repeat customers.[32]

To further emphasize this point, let's look at satisfied customers in terms of the profit they bring to the firm. A consumer who shops in an upscale supermarket is estimated to spend more than $50,000 in a decade.[33] Likewise, a satisfied customer is expected to provide $150,000 of business over a lifetime for a car dealer, and an appliance dealer will get $3,000 of business over a 20-year period. Even a 5 percent increase in customer retention can raise profits by 25 to 85 percent.[34]

Monitoring Customer Satisfaction. Not surprisingly, many companies now actively monitor customer satisfaction through the use of market surveys. For example, the American Customer Satisfaction Index (ACSI), which monitors satisfaction in a variety of industries, finds fairly high scores in many cases (see Exhibit 12.6).[35] At the company level, Pizza Hut regularly conducts telephone surveys of more than 50,000 customers a week to assess performance of both dine-in and carryout service.[36] Even the U.S. Postal Service conducts surveys to evaluate its performance. The Internet also enables marketers to collect a wealth of information

EXHIBIT 12.6

The American Consumer Satisfaction Index

The ACSI measures customer satisfaction performance across a variety of different industries. Here are a few samples.

Source: The University of Michigan Business School, National Quality Research Center.

Industry

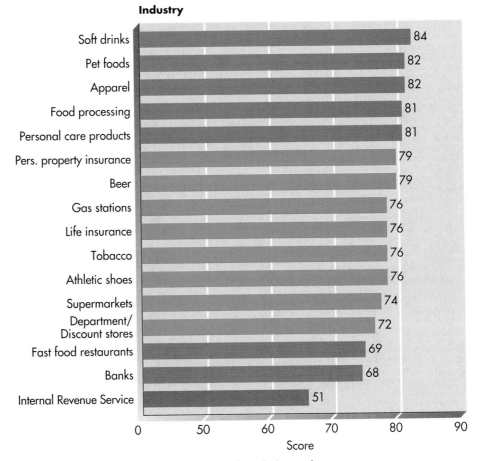

Note: Higher scores indicate higher satisfaction

CHAPTER 12 Post-Decision Processes

about consumers.[37] In conducting this research, marketers need to measure not only satisfaction but also customer wants and expectations.[38]

Interestingly, most consumers find enjoyment and satisfaction in their buying experiences. One study found that more than 90 percent of durable-goods purchases were associated with positive feelings.[39] Satisfaction levels also tend to be similar in most European countries.[40] A study of Swedish consumers even found a slight increase in satisfaction in the early 1990s.[41] Finally, more than 90 percent of Canadian consumers were satisfied with different professional services, with the highest level for pharmacists (99 percent) and the lowest for accountants (still relatively high at 85 percent).[42] The key point is that consumers worldwide are for the most part satisfied. As a result, some companies are going a step further to focus on building customer loyalty as an indicator of success, in the form of willingness to repurchase and to recommend the product or service to others.[43]

The Costs of Dissatisfaction.   Dissatisfaction, on the other hand, can lead to a variety of negative outcomes, including negative word-of-mouth communication, complaints, and reduced purchases with resulting lower profits. If a department store loses 167 customers a month, it would lose $2.4 million in sales (and $280,000 in profit) over the course of just one year.[44] A study of European consumers found that it takes 12 positive experiences to overcome one negative one and that the cost of attracting a new customer is five times the cost of keeping an existing one.[45] Makers of liquid diet products like Slim Fast and Carnation Slender experienced an overall

44 percent decrease in sales (which cost them approximately $35 million) because consumers became dissatisfied with the products' ability to help them lose weight.[46] Dissatisfaction is also on the rise in the service industry. A MasterCard survey found consumers feel good service is so important that 48 percent of respondents said they have the right to demand a new waiter in a restaurant.[47] A number of local phone companies are also experiencing strong dissatisfaction due to poor service.[48]

Finally, even though they have more product choices than ever before, consumers in former communist countries such as Romania have experienced significant levels of dissatisfaction.[49] One reason is that these consumers have had difficulty judging quality, and as a result products do not always live up to expectations. Cheaper products tend to be purchased in open-air markets where there is no guarantee of quality. Finally, dissatisfaction occurs when products are bought but not used. VCRs, for example, are purchased because "everyone is getting one" and then are used little. ■

The Disconfirmation Paradigm

disconfirmation The existence of a descrepancy between expectations and performance.

expectations Beliefs about how a product/service will perform.

The most central idea in the study of satisfaction/dissatisfaction is disconfirmation, diagrammed in Exhibit 12.7. **Disconfirmation** occurs when there is a discrepancy, positive or negative, between our prior expectations and the product's actual performance (see the red arrows in the exhibit).[50] In this case **expectations** are desired product/service outcomes and include "pre-consumption beliefs about overall performance, or . . . the levels or attributes possessed by a product (service)."[51] For example, you might expect a Japanese car to be reliable, economical, and not too expensive. These expectations can be created by advertising, inspec-

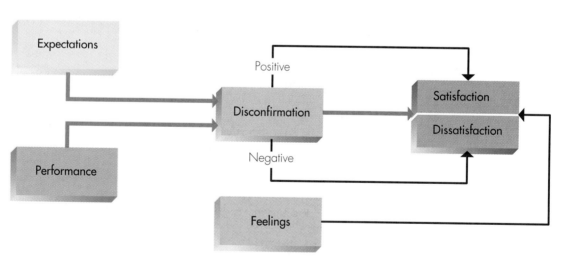

EXHIBIT 12.7
The Disconfirmation Paradigm

Here the disconfirmation paradigm shows how satisfaction or dissatisfaction can occur. Using an example of a new Jim Carrey movie, the consumer enters the situation with expectations (Jim Carrey movies are funny). She can then go see the movie and evaluate it (performance). If she evaluates it as funnier than she expected, positive disconfirmation has occurred and she will be satisfied. If the movie is not funny, a negative disconfirmation and dissatisfaction result. Note that expectations (by increasing the likelihood of seeing the movie as funny), performance (whether the movie actually is good), and feelings (positive or negative emotions experiences during viewing) will also affect satisfaction/dissatisfaction (independent of disconfirmation).

tion of the product, prior experience with similar products or services, and the experiences of other referent consumers.[52]

Satisfaction Based on Expectations **Performance** measures whether these expected outcomes have been achieved. Performance can either be *objective*—based on the actual performance, which is fairly constant across consumers—or *subjective*—based on individual feelings, which can vary across consumers. The objective performance of a car describes how well it runs, how economical its gas mileage is, or how often it needs to be repaired, whereas subjective performance might include an assessment of how stylish it is or "how good it makes me feel." Research suggests that disconfirmation is based more often on subjective than objective performance.[53] If performance is better than expected, a *positive disconfirmation* has occurred and satisfaction results. Note that if performance is as good as expected, a *simple confirmation* has occurred, and this condition will also lead to satisfaction.

If performance is lower than expected, *negative disconfirmation* and dissatisfaction result. As an illustration, AT&T's advertising tries to set up the expectation that it provides the highest quality phone service. However, phone service has gone dead for large blocks of consumers on a number of occasions. Thus performance did not live up to expectations and dissatisfaction resulted. Likewise, in former communist countries, consumers often place too much trust in foreign products, which can lead to dissatisfaction and regret.[54]

The evaluation of services has likewise been found to be susceptible to disconfirmation.[55] In this case expectations pertain to the intangible characteristics of the service provider's facilities and personnel such as reliability, responsiveness, assurance, and empathy, as well as the price in relation to service performance.[56] Ukrops' Super Markets stresses "perfectly packed groceries" (even outlining the packing process on the bag) in response to customer discontent over broken eggs, crushed bread, and soggy ice cream.[57] Finally, a study of Swedish consumers found that average levels of performance and expectations can predict overall levels of service satisfaction.[58]

Other Influences on Satisfaction As Exhibit 12.7 points out, performance, expectations, and feelings can affect satisfaction, *independent* of disconfirmation (as reflected by the blue arrows).[59] Thus to fully understand why satisfaction or dissatisfaction occurs, we must account for all these dimensions together and separately. The simple fact that a product performs well will have a positive influence on satisfaction, independent of expectations.[60] This outcome is particularly true in the case of consumer durables, where risk and involvement are higher. Thus a consumer might not have any expectations about how a new computer may perform and be pleasantly surprised when she sees how may things it can do. Likewise, the poor performance of a product or service alone can lead to dissatisfaction.[61] Thus if you buy a new VCR and it does not work well, dissatisfaction could occur—even without any prior expectations.

Positive expectations about product or service performance can actually increase the likelihood of satisfaction thanks to the process of *selective perception* by which consumers tend to see what they want to see.[62] In blind taste tests several years ago, seven of ten consumers preferred the taste of New Coke (which was similar to Pepsi) over the original formula. However, expectations led many consumers to believe that they liked the old Coke better, and they refused to accept the new product.

In addition, positive and negative **post-decision feelings** can help to explain satisfaction or dissatisfaction judgments independent of disconfirmation.[63]

If consumers feel good (or bad) while using the product or service, they are more likely to be satisfied (or dissatisfied), independent of their expectations and evaluations of performance. Consumers who are happy or content are most likely to be satisfied, followed by those who experience pleasant surprise. Dissatisfaction is most likely to strike consumers who feel angry or upset, followed by those who experience unpleasant surprise.[64] Finally, the consumer's mood can color post-decision evaluations, particularly when the consumption experience itself is not strongly emotional.[65] For example, we might be more likely to like a new CD if we are in a good mood when we hear it.

Note that the disconfirmation paradigm is similar to the learning process we described earlier. The difference is that satisfaction and dissatisfaction are based on a formal evaluation and feelings, whereas the learning process may not be. For example, we can test the hypothesis that rock music is loud or that Mexican food is spicy without making an assessment of like or dislike. Nevertheless, satisfaction or dissatisfaction can still be an important element of the learning process because it provides us with information.

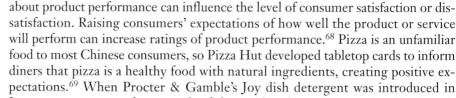

 One implication that follows from the disconfirmation paradigm is that, as we've said before, marketers need to be very demanding about product or service quality and performance. Better performance leads to fulfilled expectations and satisfaction. For example, several airlines have tried to improve and speed up the boarding process in response to customer unhappiness.[66] When Pizza Hut entered the market in China, the company decided to keep consumers satisfied by using a mild cheese that is overwhelmed by the taste of toppings, because the Chinese have little taste for cheese. The company also substituted pineapple for olives because many Chinese love sweets.[67]

 A second important implication is that the expectations created by marketers about product performance can influence the level of consumer satisfaction or dissatisfaction. Raising consumers' expectations of how well the product or service will perform can increase ratings of product performance.[68] Pizza is an unfamiliar food to most Chinese consumers, so Pizza Hut developed tabletop cards to inform diners that pizza is a healthy food with natural ingredients, creating positive expectations.[69] When Procter & Gamble's Joy dish detergent was introduced in Japan, consumers used too much of the product because more familiar brands were weak. With the marketing pitch "A little bit of Joy cleans better . . . ," the proper expectations were created and satisfaction resulted.[70]

 Providing consumers with a good warranty or guarantee can create positive expectations that will lead to satisfaction.[71] Unfortunately, this reassurance has been lacking in many developing countries such as Turkey and Romania where products are often of poor quality and there are no warranties. In addition, consumers often do not understand how to use the products (there are few instructions), and this situation leads to further dissatisfaction.[72]

 If expectations are too high and promises are made that cannot be kept, marketers are setting themselves up for a potential negative disconfirmation and dissatisfaction. In 1997, America Online grew so fast that the system became overloaded and many customers could not get on line for hours at a time, creating strong and very vocal dissatisfaction.[73] Virtual reality games have been a major flop because consumers' expectations were too high and dissatisfaction resulted.[74]

Marketers should also make sure that customers' feelings about buying and using their offerings are as positive as possible. Making customers feel good allows them to bond with the company and develop loyalty, a form of *relationship marketing* whereby long term relationships are built with consumers. Chrysler sponsored

Jeep Jamborees to allow customers to drive their vehicles on rough terrain and "win their hearts."[75] Likewise, salespeople who are cheerful and try to please are more likely to develop consumer satisfaction with the encounter, the retailer, and the purchase. Satisfaction was a major goal of Air Ukraine when it tried to dissociate itself from the old, unfriendly Russian carrier Aeroflot.[76]

Marketers can also use various promotions to increase positive feelings during consumption. Coca-Cola and Coors, for example, both have used a can that "talked" (using a light-activated voice chip upon opening) to inform consumers they had won a prize.[77] In Hong Kong a very popular promotion involved trading in old Marlboro boxes for gifts such as lighters, knapsacks, and lanterns.[78] ▪

Attribution Theory

attribution theory A theory of how individuals find explanations for events.

Another theory that has been useful in determining how and when dissatisfaction occurs is **attribution theory**. This theory was developed in social psychology to explain how individuals find explanations or causes for effects or behavior.[79] In other words, if someone we did not know suddenly gave us a kiss on the cheek, we would be motivated to attribute or find an explanation for this event. The question is, How would we do so?

In a marketing context, when a product or service does not fulfill needs, the consumer will attempt to find an explanation. According to attribution theory, three key factors influence the nature of this explanation:

- *Stability.* Is the cause of the event temporary or permanent?
- *Focus.* Is the problem consumer or marketer related?
- *Controllability.* Is the event under the customer's control?

Dissatisfaction is more likely to result if the cause is perceived to be permanent, marketer related, and not under the customer's control. To illustrate, suppose you find a crack in the windshield of your new car. If you perceive that this problem is only a chance or temporary occurrence, beyond the control of the marketer (maybe a rock hit the window while you were driving), or your own fault, you will probably not be dissatisfied. On the other hand, if you discover that many other consumers are having a similar problem—that is, the cause is more permanent, company related, and under the company's control—you will probably be dissatisfied.

Attribution theory has also found support in research on services, in which consumers were dissatisfied with a travel agent if a problem was permanent and under the control of the firm.[80] Also, in a field study of passengers delayed at an airport, attributions were found to explain the desire to either complain or fly the same airline again. If the delay was seen as permanent and under the control of the airline, consumers were more likely to complain and less likely to fly the airline again.[81]

MARKETING IMPLICATIONS Attribution theory can provide marketers with guidance in how to deal with potential or existing perceptions of consumer dissatisfaction. If the cause of the dissatisfaction actually *is* permanent, marketer related, and under the marketer's control, something must be done to correct the problem or provide the consumer with restitution. For example, TWA added leg room in coach to address customer dissatisfaction with cramped seating.[82] In the banking industry, which counts almost two dissatisfied consumers for every satisfied one, many banks are aggressively adding and marketing services such as financial advice and branches in supermarkets in an attempt to satisfy customers.[83] And U.S. automakers have finally realized that to be successful in Japan, they have to make right-hand-drive cars.[84]

Pepsi is pleased to announce...

...nothing.

As America now knows, those stories about Diet Pepsi were a hoax. Plain and simple, not true. Hundreds of investigators have found no evidence to support a single claim.

As for the many, many thousands of people who work at Pepsi-Cola, we feel great that it's over. And we're ready to get on with making and bringing you what we believe is the best-tasting diet cola in America.

There's not much more we can say. Except that most importantly, we won't let this hoax change our exciting plans for this summer.

We've set up special offers so you can enjoy our great quality products at prices that will save you money all summer long. It all starts on July 4th weekend and we hope you'll stock up with a little extra, just to make up for what you might have missed last week.

That's it. Just one last word of thanks to the millions of you who have stood with us.

Drink All The Diet Pepsi You Want. Uh Huh.

EXHIBIT 12.8
Correcting a Misperception

In response to a situation in which a syringe was found in a Diet Pepsi can, this ad tells consumers that the company and its employees did not cause the event in any way (thereby correcting any incorrect beliefs that consumers might have had).

Source: Courtesy of Pepsi-Cola Company.

As an example of restitution, one of the authors once found a piece of mold at the top of a Coke bottle. The company responded to this problem very quickly by providing a free case of Coke. Another time he noticed an overcharge for dog food at a grocery store and was immediately given the item free with a sincere apology. Both responses reduced his dissatisfaction.

Alternatively, when consumers perceive that the cause of the dissatisfaction is permanent, marketer related, and under the firm's control when in fact it is not, marketers need to correct these misperceptions. Providing consumers with logical explanations for failure, especially if it was not the company's fault, or providing some form of compensation such as a gift or refund can often reduce feelings of dissatisfaction.[85] For example, Pepsi once faced a serious potential consumer dissatisfaction problem when a syringe was found in a can of Diet Pepsi. The company learned that this problem was temporary and consumer related (a consumer had tampered with the can) and not under the control of the manufacturer. Pepsi quickly developed an advertisement to emphasize this point and correct any potential consumer misperceptions, as shown in Exhibit 12.8. The electric utility Con Ed in New York adopted a similar strategy during the 1999 blackout. Con Ed ran ads to explain to consumers that the power outages were not the fault of the company and that it would do everything to reduce the likelihood that they would happen again. ■

Equity Theory

equity theory A theory that focuses on the fairness of exchanges between individuals, which helps in understanding consumer satisfaction and dissatisfaction.

Equity theory is another approach developed in psychology that has been useful in understanding consumer satisfaction and dissatisfaction. Essentially, this theory focuses on the nature of exchanges between individuals and their perceptions of these exchanges. In a marketing context equity theory has been applied to examining the exchange between a buyer and a seller or a more general institution.[86]

According to equity theory, consumers form perceptions of their own inputs and outputs into a particular exchange. They then compare these perceptions to those of the salesperson, dealer, or company. For example, when buying a stereo, consumer inputs might include information search, decision-making effort, psychological anxiety, and money; the output would be a satisfactory sound system. Seller inputs might include a quality product, selling effort, and a financing plan; a fair profit might constitute the output.

fairness of exchange The perception that people's inputs are equal to their outputs in an exchange.

For equity to occur, the buyer must perceive **fairness in the exchange**. Thus the stereo buyer might perceive a fair exchange if he or she purchased a desirable system at a fair price. If the consumer perceives inequity in the exchange—for example, the salesperson did not pay enough attention to the consumer or the deal was not fair—then dissatisfaction results. Note, however, that for equity to occur, a perception of fairness must exist on both sides of the exchange. The consumer must perceive that the seller is also being dealt with fairly in the exchange. Nevertheless, fairness perceptions tend to be self-centered—that is, biased more toward buyer outcomes and seller inputs than to buyer inputs and seller outcomes.[87]

The principles of equity theory complement the disconfirmation paradigm in that equity theory specifies another way dissatisfaction can occur. In other words, both types of processes can be in operation at the same time. However, whereas the disconfirmation paradigm focuses on expectations and performance, equity theory is concerned with more general interpersonal norms governing what is wrong or right and with a consideration of the outcomes of both the seller and buyer, not just the buyer.

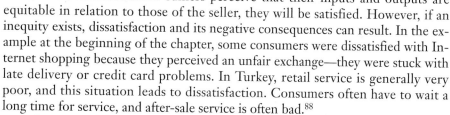

MARKETING IMPLICATIONS Equity theory clearly pinpoints the importance of fairness in marketing exchanges. As long as consumers perceive that their inputs and outputs are equitable in relation to those of the seller, they will be satisfied. However, if an inequity exists, dissatisfaction and its negative consequences can result. In the example at the beginning of the chapter, some consumers were dissatisfied with Internet shopping because they perceived an unfair exchange—they were stuck with late delivery or credit card problems. In Turkey, retail service is generally very poor, and this situation leads to dissatisfaction. Consumers often have to wait a long time for service, and after-sale service is often bad.[88]

The clear implication is that marketers must work toward providing fair exchanges. However, this job is not always easy because consumers' perceptions of fairness tend to be biased toward themselves. One area in which marketers can most directly affect equity perceptions is the salesperson-customer interaction. In these exchanges salespeople must make every effort to ensure that their inputs match customer inputs by listening to consumer needs, answering questions, and attempting to provide a good deal. For example, in the automotive industry Saturn has been successful in offering consumers a "different kind of company"—one that really cares about consumers' needs and does everything to fulfill them. The same principles are now being applied to transactions on the Internet where service is heavily emphasized to create a fair exchange. Similarly, in the ad in Exhibit 12.9, Coldwell Banker states that its success for over 90 years is due to its emphasis on customer service.

Promotions can also increase perceptions of fairness in an exchange. Providing consumers with a lower price or with a free item of merchandise can make consumers feel that they are getting more out of the exchange. Thus many cologne or perfume companies give consumers items like coffee mugs, radios, and sweaters with a purchase. In addition, companies must also ensure that outputs are satisfactory by providing a quality product at a fair price. Wal-Mart, for example, has created strong customer satisfaction by offering "good value every day." ■

RESPONSES TO DISSATISFACTION

Marketers must understand the nature of consumers' responses to dissatisfaction because a variety of mostly negative consequences can result. Specifically,

WHILE OTHERS MAKE LOTS OF NOISE ABOUT SERVICE,

FOR 90 YEARS, IT'S BEEN OUR SOLE FOCUS.

When it comes to consumer service, talk is cheap. That's why for over 90 years, we've focused on doing something about it. From providing the utmost in personal attention, to continually expanding our services, we've never lost sight of your needs. Take our latest development—Coldwell Banker Online."

Now finding the home of your dreams is as easy as accessing the Internet. View thousands of homes from around the country, anytime, day or night, right from the comfort of your home or office, plus find out all the latest information about buying or selling a home. It's just one more reason why more than 9 out of 10 of our customers would recommend us to a friend.

So if you're looking for more than just a lot of talk, call Coldwell Banker. And see for yourself what real service is all about.

SUPPORT
YOU CAN COUNT ON.

COLDWELL BANKER
Expect the best.

http://www.coldwellbanker.com

EXHIBIT 12.9
Creating Equity in an Exchange

Customer service is one of the main reasons why Coldwell Banker has been successful in the real estate market for over 90 years. In this ad the company discusses its new Internet service for customers, "Coldwell Banker Online," which provides prospective home buyers with housing information.

Source: 1996 Coldwell Banker Corporation.

consumer complaints
When consumers voice dissatisfaction with a product or service.

dissatisfied consumers can decide to (1) take no action, (2) discontinue purchasing the product or service, (3) complain to the company or to a third party and perhaps return the item, or (4) engage in negative word-of-mouth communication.[89] In particular, the last two behaviors have been of great interest to consumer researchers.

Complaints

Surprisingly, the majority of dissatisfied consumers do not complain.[90] Nevertheless, even a few **consumer complaints** can indicate marketing-related problems that need attention. When consumers complain, they can voice their dissatisfaction to a manufacturer, the retail outlet, regulatory agencies, or the media. Sometimes consumers can take even more drastic action by seeking formal redress through legal means or from governmental regulatory bodies.

Complaints can be related to a variety of matters, such as the product or service, the retail outlet, and the salespeople. Common complaints about restaurants, for example, include lack of separate checks, too long a wait for a table, specials that are recited instead of being written down, and waiters who are unfamiliar with the menu.[91] Car-rental customers complain about long lines and indecipherable bills.[92] Complaints about the airline industry increased dramatically in the late 1990s (26 percent higher).[93] They include cramped quarters, late flights, poor customer service, and long waits on the tarmac. One newspaper asked readers to indicate their top complaints about area grocery stores and quickly received over 300 gripes. The top ten are listed in Exhibit 12.10.[94] As another example, when Coca-Cola replaced its product with New Coke, consumers were so angry that the company received as many as 12,000 phone calls a day and more than 68,000 letters. Here are two examples:[95]

Dear Sirs: I am disgusted, disenfranchised, dismayed, disillusioned, disputatious, dispirited, disdainful, disheartened, displeased, disserviced, discordant, disputed, and despised with feelings of disloyalty. P.S. I love Diet Coke.

Gentlemen: I would appreciate receiving your signatures on a piece of company stationery. I believe in years to come, the autographs of the two dumbest executives in business history will be very valuable.

When Complaints Are Likely to Occur Complaining is more likely to occur when motivation, ability, and opportunity are high. As you might expect, com-

EXHIBIT 12.10
Grocery Store Complaints

Consumers have a variety of complaints about products and services. Here are the results of a study of the most common consumer complaints about grocery stores. Do these match with your experience in grocery stores? Marketers can respond to these complaints to increase customer satisfaction.

Source: Data from Kitty Crider, "Grocery Store Gripes," *Austin American Statesman,* October 23, 1991, pp. C1, C2.

✓ TOP TEN *COMPLAINTS*

1. No prices on items
2. Scanner prices incorrect
3. Long checkout lines
4. Change in location of items
5. Items out of stock
6. Express-lane abuse
7. Merchandise shelves too high
8. Checkout workers socializing
9. Careless bagging of items
10. Loud music/announcements

plaining is also more likely as the level of dissatisfaction or the severity of the problem becomes greater.[96] In equity theory terms the unfairness of the exchange is higher and the consumer is more motivated to act.[97] However, the severity of the dissatisfaction alone will not explain complaining behavior. In particular, if consumers perceive that complaining will take a lot of time and effort, that their chances of benefiting from it are low, and that the product or service is insignificant, they are less likely to act.[98]

The more the blame or attribution for dissatisfaction is placed on someone else, particularly on the company or society in general, the greater the motivation and likelihood of complaining.[99] Thus complaining is more likely to occur when consumers feel removed from the problem—that is, when the perceived cause is permanent, marketer related, and volitional.[100]

You might expect that consumers who are aggressive and self-confident would be more likely to complain than those who are not[101] or that consumers who have more experience or knowledge ability about *how* to complain might be more likely to do so than their less knowledgeable counterparts. Neither idea has been strongly supported by evidence, although findings suggest experience may influence the likelihood of complaints. Interestingly, consumers are more likely to complain when they have the time and formal channels of communication. Lack of opportunity and knowledge about how to complain has been a major problem in many developing countries.[102] In Turkey only recently have consumers had the means to complain, and this opportunity is now having an increasing impact on the way business is done.

Other studies have examined whether demographic and socioeconomic factors are related to complaining behavior. Although the findings have been somewhat mixed, there are several slight tendencies. Complainers tend to be younger, to have a higher income level, and to be less brand loyal than noncomplainers.[103] Researchers have also found that complaining behavior may vary by ethnic group. For example, Mexican American consumers are more likely to complain about certain aspects of goods and services such as delay or nondelivery than are other consumers.[104] Puerto Ricans are less likely to complain than other U.S. consumers because of cultural norms and values.[105]

Complainer Types Finally, research has suggested that there are different types of complainers.[106] *Passives* are the least likely to complain. *Voicers* are likely to complain directly to the retailer or service provider. *Irates* are angry consumers who are most likely to engage in negative word of mouth, stop patronage, and complain to the provider but not to a third party such as the media or government. *Activists* engage heavily in all types of complaining, including to a third party. Interestingly, some companies feel that listening to the "customer from hell" actually improves their business because these critics often provide good suggestions.[107]

MARKETING IMPLICATIONS Although a large percentage of consumers do not complain, it is still in the marketer's best interests to be responsive when they do. Providing a written response, especially with a coupon or gift, can have a noticeable impact on consumer evaluations.[108] Quick responses, especially ones that involve monetary reimbursement or a fair exchange or refund policy, can lead to greater satisfaction and repeat purchase. In fact, dissatisfied consumers who have been treated fairly can become even more loyal in the future. A study from Singapore found that the length of time taken to respond to a complaint was critical in determining the level of satisfaction—the less time, the higher the satisfaction.[109] Finally, a survey found that 90 percent of managers indicated that satisfying the customer was the primary reason for responding to complaints.[110] Thus companies must have an efficient and responsive mechanism for handling these problems.

Holiday Inn knew from surveys that customers were unhappy with the design of the shower, which was too small and tended to collect dirt. In redesigning its hotel bathrooms, the company paid very close attention to everything from the angle of the shower head to elbow room to grout (which captures dirt).[111]

For Dell Computer—noted for its service and customer satisfaction—responding to customer complaints is a top marketing priority. Every week all employees from top managers to assembly-line workers carefully scrutinize customer complaints during a session called "The Hour of Horror" and determine how best to handle these problems.[112] If problems are not resolved within a week, they are reviewed every Friday until resolved. Dell's motto is that "Customers must be pleased, not just satisfied." European companies tend to be slower in managing complaints because complaints are still viewed as a bad thing.[113] However, many European firms are now adopting the customer-satisfaction concept.

Positive disconfirmation of warranty and service expectations—a response that is better than expected—can result in satisfaction with complaint resolution.[114] For example, a resort hotel in Japan turned a threat of earthquakes on a major holiday weekend to an advantage by offering a free subsequent stay if a large earthquake occurred.[115] Marketers and customers can still experience problems in developing countries, where service is generally poor and warranties are nonexistent.[116]

Sometimes it can be in the company's best interest to encourage complaining because dissatisfied consumers who do not complain are more likely to discontinue purchase.[117] By encouraging complaining when it is justified and actively managing these problems through refunds or compensation, the company can retain its valued consumers.

One note of caution is in order, however. When companies are too responsive to complaints—that is, too eager to please—consumers may actually be more likely to complain, even when a complaint is *not* justified, because they perceive a greater likelihood of success.[118] In particular, consumers are more likely to complain when the cause is ambiguous and the party responsible for the problem is not obvious. Companies should be responsive to complaints when they are justified. ■

Responding by Negative Word of Mouth

negative word-of-mouth communication The act of consumers saying negative things about a product or service to other consumers.

When consumers are unhappy with a product or service, they are often motivated to tell others about it in order to relieve their frustration and to influence others not to purchase a product or not to do business with a particular company. This **negative word-of-mouth communication** is more likely to occur when the problem is severe, consumers are not happy with the company's responsiveness, and the company is perceived to be at fault.[119] Negative word of mouth can be particularly troublesome because it tends to be highly persuasive and very vivid (and therefore easily remembered), and consumers place great emphasis on it when making decisions.[120] Negative word of mouth is more damaging than complaining because consumers communicate word of mouth to other customers who might discontinue (or never begin) doing business with the company. A number of consumers are now airing their complaints by creating scathing sites on the World Wide Web. These sites often have irreverent names such as "Still Searching for the Softer Side of Sears" and "US Worst" (lampooning US West). For companies, these sites present a threat because they are available to consumers world wide and the information is often unfair, nasty, and a "cheap cut."[121]

MARKETING IMPLICATIONS Marketers need to be responsive to negative word of mouth. Most important, they should make an effort to identify the reason for or source of the difficulty so they can take steps to rectify or eliminate the particular problem with restitution or formal marketing communications. The Pepsi ad from Exhibit 12.8 and Jack-in-the Box's effort to dispel any negative word of mouth about tainted hamburger meat are both good examples of this strategy. ■

IS CUSTOMER SATISFACTION ENOUGH?

Despite the fact that customer satisfaction should always be an extremely important goal for any firm, some companies have questioned whether satisfaction alone is enough. As evidence they point out that 65 to 85 percent of customers who defect to competitors' brands say they were either satisfied or very satisfied with the product or service they left.[122] Other studies have found a low correlation between satisfaction and repurchase.[123] Thus customers may need to be "extremely satisfied" or need a stronger reason to stay with a brand or company.[124]

customer retention The practice of keeping customers by building long-term relationships.

A key goal for any marketer should therefore be **customer retention**, the practice of working to satisfy customers with the intention of developing long-term relationships with them. A customer-retention strategy attempts to build customer commitment and loyalty by continually paying close attention to all aspects of customer interaction, especially after-sales service. This approach not only strengthens relationships with customers but also increases profits. Specifically, profits can be increased through repeat sales, reduced costs, and referrals.[125]

How can a company retain its customers? Here are some common principles:[126]

- *Care About Customers.* Two-thirds of consumers defect because they believe that the company doesn't care about them. Thus, a little caring can go a long way.

- *Remember Customers Between Sales.* Companies can contact consumers to make sure they are not having any problems with the product or service or simply contact them on special occasions such as birthdays and anniversaries.

- *Build Trusting Relationships.* Provide consumers with expertise and high-quality products and services.

- *Monitor the Service Delivery Process.* The time consumers need the company most is when they require service or repairs. Every effort should be made to ensure that the company is highly responsive and shows concern in these situations.

- *Provide Extra Effort.* Companies that go above and beyond the call of duty are more likely to build lasting relationships with their consumers than will companies that take the minimalist approach.

ISPOSITION

One more behavior can occur at the post-acquisition stage: disposition.

The Many Ways We Can Dispose of Something

disposition The parting with or getting rid of possessions.

At the most basic level, **disposition** is the simple throwing away of meaningless or used-up items without any thought. Certainly, this process does occur on a regular basis for most consumers. Recent studies, however, suggests that disposition is a much richer and more detailed process than researchers once thought.[127]

Disposition is an action we take toward possessions. Although we tend to think of possessions as physical things, they can be defined much more broadly as anything that reflects an extension of the self and include one's body and body parts, other persons, pets, places, services, time periods, and events. For example, we could end a relationship, give a friend an idea, donate our organs, abandon an unhealthy lifestyle, use up all our leisure time, or discontinue a health club membership. Thus the study of disposition relates to all these types of possessions.

When a consumer decides that a possession is no longer of immediate use, many options are available, as outlined in Exhibit 12.11. Specifically the item can be (1) given away, which can include passing it along or donating it with or without a tax deduction; (2) traded; (3) recycled; (4) sold; (5) used up; (6) thrown away; (7) abandoned, which means discarding it in a socially unacceptable way; or (8) destroyed.[128] Note that disposition can be *temporary* (loaning or renting the item) or *involuntary* (losing or destroying the item).[129] Here we will focus on permanent, voluntary disposition.

Disposition options often have logical and reasonable motives behind them.[130] For example, selling is typically motivated by our wanting to earn an economic return and come out ahead. Donating without a tax deduction and passing an item along are motivated by the desire to help someone, as well as not wanting the product to go to waste.

Situational and product-related factors can also affect disposition options.[131] For example, when time or storage space is limited, a possession is likely to be

EXHIBIT 12.11
Disposition Options

For most of us, disposition often means throwing things away; however, there are many additional ways of disposing of an offering (e.g., give away, trade, recycle). In addition, disposition can involve one person (personal focus), two or more people (interpersonal focus), or society in general (societal focus).

Source: Melissa Martin Young and Melanie Wallendorf, "Ashes to Ashes, Dust to Dust: Conceptualizing Consumer Disposition of Possessions," in *Proceedings, Marketing Educators' Conference,* (Chicago: American Marketing Association, 1989), pp. 33–39. Reprinted by permission.

A TAXONOMY OF VOLUNTARY DISPOSITION

METHODS	PERSONAL FOCUS	INTERPERSONAL FOCUS	SOCIETAL FOCUS
Give away: usually to someone who can use it.	Necessarily requires another person as receiver.	Donate body organs; give clothes to the needy; give a baby up for adoption; give an idea to a friend.	Give land to new settlers; give surplus food to the poor; give military advice to an ally.
Trade or exchange it for something else.	Skin grafts; trade sleep time for work time; trade work time for shopping for bargains.	Trade a car; trade stock; barter; exchange ideas with a colleague; switch boyfriends. Swap meets.	Trade tanks for oil; exchange effluent water for a golf course.
Recycle: convert it to something else.	Convert barn beams to paneling; make a quilt of scraps; turkey sandwiches after Thanksgiving.	Recycle newspapers; recycle aluminum cans; manufacturers recycling of defective parts.	Recycle waste water; convert a slum to a model neighborhood; recycle war ruins as national monuments.
Sell: convert it to money.	Necessarily requires another person as buyer; prostitution; sell one's artwork; sell ideas.	Businesses; sell blood; sell ideals to attain political goals.	Sell wheat; sell weapons; sell land.
Use up: consumption is equivalent to disposal.	Eat food; drive car using up the fuel; shoot ammo; spend one's time; burn wood.	Use employee's time and energy; use someone else's money; use the neighbor's gas.	Use natural fuels or electricity; use a nation's productive capacity; use people as soldiers in wars.
Throw away: discard in a socially acceptable manner.	Put things in the trash; flush the toilet; use a garbage disposal; discard an idea.	Neighborhood cleanup; divorce; end a relationship; resign or retire from a job.	Dump garbage in the oceans; bury nuclear waste.
Abandon: discard in a socially unacceptable manner.	Abandon car on the roadside; abandon morals; abandon an unhealthy, unhappy lifestyle.	Abandon one's child or family; abandon a pet on someone's doorstep; abandon another's trust.	Abandon Vietnam; abandon the Shah of Iran; abandon old satellites in space; abandon the poor.
Destroy: physically damage with intent.	Tear up personal mail; commit suicide; burn house down; shred old pictures.	Raze a building; murder; euthanasia; cremation; abort a child; commit arson.	Conduct war; genocide; execute prisoner; carry out a revolution; burn a flag.

thrown away, given away, or abandoned. A possession of high value is likely to be sold or given to someone who is special, and it is not likely to be thrown away. The frequency of different disposition behaviors depends on the product category.

Research has examined how consumers dispose of unwanted gifts.[132] They can be laterally recycled (swapped, sold, or passed on to someone else), destroyed, or returned. Destruction is a way of getting revenge against the giver but is usually more of a fantasy than a real action. Returning a gift to a store can be a negative emotional experience that retailers need to be sensitive to. Disposition can involve more than one individual, as is the case when we give old clothes to someone, sell a car, or participate in a neighborhood cleanup, or it can consist of activities of a collective or societal nature such as dumping garbage in the ocean or recycling waste water.[133]

By combining the personal, interpersonal, and societal arenas with the eight types of disposition identified in Exhibit 12.11, we can see that disposition encompasses a wide variety of behaviors. Unfortunately, consumer researchers have only begun to explore these options, focusing mostly on personal disposition. Much work is needed before we achieve a more thorough understanding.

Disposing of Meaningful Objects

Although disposition often means simply getting rid of unwanted, meaningless, or used-up possessions, the process is more involved for certain significant items. Possessions can sometimes be important reflections of the self that are infused with significant symbolic meaning.[134] They define who we are, and they catalog our personal history.[135] In these situations, disposition involves two processes: physical detachment and emotional detachment.

physical detachment Physically disposing of an item.

emotional detachment Emotionally disposing of a possession.

We most often think of disposition in terms of **physical detachment**, the process in which the item is physically transferred to another person or location. However, **emotional detachment** is a more detailed, lengthy, and sometimes painful process. Consumers can often still be emotionally attached to possessions, even long after they have become physically detached. For example, it may take a person years to come to grips with selling a valued house or car. Giving up a baby or pet for adoption are examples of difficult emotional detachment; sometimes even grief and mourning can result. In fact, some pack rats have a difficult time disposing of even minimally valued possessions—as evidenced by overflowing basements, closets, and garages.

The disposition process can be particularly important during periods of role transition, such as puberty, graduation, and marriage.[136] In these instances consumers dispose of possessions that are symbols of old roles. Upon getting married, for example, many people dispose of items that signify old relationships, such as pictures, jewelry, and gifts. The disposition of shared possessions is a critical process during divorce. Two types of such disposition have been identified: *disposition to break free*, in which the goal is to free oneself from the former relationship, and *disposition to hold on*, in which the intent is to cling to possessions with the hope that the relationship can be repaired.[137] The more common pattern is breaking free. In some cases the partners attempt to be fair and distribute these other possessions evenly. In other instances one of the partners, most likely the initiator of the divorce, is willing to leave most of the possessions to the other partner to relieve guilt. In still other situations the division of assets can involve a lot of conflict and bitter disagreements. In this case the former partners tend to be motivated by rivalry, punishment, and a desire to cling to power in the relationship.[138]

Consumers also specify how their possessions will be distributed upon death. This process can include giving away valued items to important family members, other individuals, and organizations such as charities and schools, as well as distributing monetary wealth through a will. The subject of intergenerational transfers and inheritance has been of great interest to social scientists.[139]

MARKETING IMPLICATIONS The study of disposition has a number of important implications. First, disposition decisions often influence later acquisition decisions because a consumer who decides to dispose of a particular item often acquires another. Someone who must buy a new refrigerator because the old one stopped working may decide that the old one did not last long enough and eliminate this brand from future consideration. By understanding why consumers dispose of older brands, particularly when a problem has occurred, marketers may be able to improve their offerings for the future.

Second, marketers have become interested in the way that consumers trade, sell, or give away items for secondhand purchases. Used-merchandise retail outlets, flea markets, garage sales, and classified ads are becoming more widespread as consumers increasingly choose to sell or trade old items rather than throw them away. The number of used-merchandise retailers has grown at a rate ten times that of conventional retailers.[140] In the music industry, the market for used CDs has become so large that major record companies have taken legal action against stores that sell used CDs because these sales represent a huge loss of profit for the artists and companies. Similarly, the market for used computers and textbooks is large and growing.

Flea markets are quite popular among consumers, not only because they are a different way of disposing of and acquiring products but also because of the hedonistic experience they provide.[141] Consumers enjoy the process of searching and bargaining for items, the festive atmosphere—almost like a medieval fair—and the social opportunities.

Third, product disposition behaviors can sometimes have a major impact on society in general. For example, if product life can be extended by getting consumers to trade or resell items, waste and resource depletion could be reduced. As another example, the state of Texas was having a tremendous problem with litter on its highways and streets. This situation led to the development of the "Don't Mess with Texas" campaign to influence consumers not to litter. Members of the Dallas Cowboys and popular local musicians, such as Willie Nelson and the Fabulous Thunderbirds, were featured in this ad campaign. Its success is evidenced by a 60 percent reduction in litter.

Fourth, by examining broad disposition patterns, we can gain insights that might not have been otherwise possible. To illustrate, one study examined household garbage to identify group differences in food consumption.[142] Researchers found that region of the country accounted most strongly for differences in consumption patterns, followed by minority status. For instance, more beans are consumed in the southwest United States because of the popularity of Mexican food in that region. The key point is that sometimes this type of *trace analysis* can yield more accurate information than can self-report questionnaires.

Finally, disposition patterns can sometimes serve as economic indicators.[143] In hard economic times consumers are more likely to conduct garage sales and decrease the amount and quality of items given to charities such as Goodwill and the Salvation Army. In particular, consumers are more likely to hold on to major appliances such as stoves, refrigerators, and washing machines for as long as possible. ■

Recycling

We live in an age in which natural resources are rapidly being depleted. Because we can no longer squander resources, the study of disposition behaviors can provide valuable insights for the development of recycling programs.

In light of this fact, a number of researchers have been interested in examining factors that relate to recycling.[144] Unfortunately, variables such as demographics and psychographics are not strong predictors. Attitudes toward recycling in general have also not been helpful, but attitudes toward specific actions such as saving bottles and separating papers have shown more promise.[145] However, what appears to be most useful in understanding consumer recycling is the motivation, ability, and opportunity to recycle.

Motivation to Recycle Consumers are more likely to recycle when the benefits are perceived to outweigh the costs,[146] which include money, time, and effort. Immediate benefits or goals include avoiding filling up landfills, reducing waste, reusing materials, and saving the environment. Higher-order goals are to promote health and avoid sickness, achieve life-sustaining ends, and provide for future generations.[147] Note that these benefits are likely to vary across segments. For example, focusing on environmental effects may have little meaning in low-income neighborhoods where family members are being killed in the streets.[148] Also, consumers who perceive that their efforts will have an impact are more motivated to recycle than consumers who do not.[149]

Ability to Recycle Consumers who know how to recycle are more likely to do so than those who do not.[150] For example, a study of German consumers found that a lack of knowledge led to incorrect disposal and therefore less recycling.[151] Consumers must also possess general knowledge about the positive environmental effects of recycling. Finally, consumers must remember to recycle as part of their daily routine.

Opportunity to Recycle If separating, storing, and removing recyclable materials is difficult or inconvenient, consumers will usually avoid doing so. A program in Germany that offered color-coded, large plastic containers on wheels for recyclable materials was quite popular and successful. In addition, to recycle on a regular basis, consumers must break old waste disposal habits and develop new ones. Providing easy-to-use containers also helps consumers in this regard.

MARKETING IMPLICATIONS Marketers can clearly facilitate recycling by increasing consumers' motivation, ability, and opportunity to recycle. For example, special incentives such as lotteries and contests are effective in increasing motivation. Messages that focus on the negative consequences of not recycling and that are conveyed by personal acquaintances appear to be the most effective means of increasing motivation.[152] For example, sending Boy Scouts to personally deliver messages about the advantages of recycling increased behavior from 11 to 42 percent.[153]

EXHIBIT 12.12

Increasing the Opportunity to Recycle

Companies like Saturn are making it easier for consumers to recycle (increasing opportunity) by offering products that are made of recyclable materials.

Source: Copyright General Motors Corp. Used with permission of GM Media Archives.

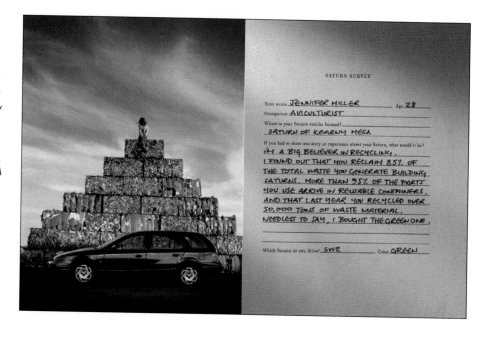

SATURN SURVEY

Your name JENNIFER MILLER   Age 28
Occupation AVICULTURIST
Where is your Saturn retailer located?
SATURN OF KEARNY MESA
If you had to share one story or experience about your Saturn, what would it be?
I'M A BIG BELIEVER IN RECYCLING.
I FOUND OUT THAT YOU RECLAIM 85% OF
THE TOTAL WASTE YOU GENERATE BUILDING
SATURNS. MORE THAN 95% OF THE PARTS
YOU USE ARRIVE IN REUSABLE CONTAINERS,
AND THAT LAST YEAR YOU RECYCLED OVER
50,000 TONS OF WASTE MATERIAL.
NEEDLESS TO SAY, I BOUGHT THE GREEN ONE.

Which Saturn do you drive? SW2   Color GREEN

Neighborhood block leaders can also be effective. The only drawback is that all these techniques must be reintroduced periodically because their effects are usually temporary.

Marketers can increase consumers' ability to recycle by teaching them how to recycle—through personal communications from community or block leaders, flyers, or public service announcements. These messages must be personally relevant and easy to remember. Tags to place on the refrigerator door can remind consumers to recycle.[154]

 Finally, by providing separate containers for recyclable items that can be easily put out and collected along with the trash, recycling programs can increase the *opportunity* to recycle. This type of program has worked well in the United States, Germany, and the Netherlands. Providing easily recyclable products is another way to increase the opportunity to recycle (see Exhibit 12.12). ∎

SUMMARY

Consumers sometimes develop post-decision dissonance—a feeling of anxiety or uncertainty regarding a purchasing decision after it has been made. They are motivated to reduce this dissonance by collecting additional information that is used to upgrade the chosen alternative and downgrade the rejected ones.

Consumers can learn from experience through a process of hypothesis testing in which they attempt to either confirm or disprove expectations by actually engaging in acquisition, consumption, or disposition. This process is influenced by motivation; prior knowledge (familiarity); ambiguity of information; and two types of biases, the confirmation bias and overconfidence. Marketers can use several strategies to influence the learning process, depending on whether the offering is a top dog or an underdog.

Satisfaction is both a subjective feeling and an objective evaluation that a decision has fulfilled a need or goal. Dissatisfaction occurs when consumers have negative feelings and believe that their goals or needs have not been fulfilled. Marketers need to keep consumers satisfied because losing customers can be very costly in the long run.

Three major theories of satisfaction/dissatisfaction are (1) the disconfirmation paradigm, which states that satisfaction occurs when performance disconfirms expectations in a positive way and that dissatisfaction results from negative disconfirmations; (2) attribution theory, which states that dissatisfaction results when the cause of a problem is determined to be permanent, marketer related, and under control; and (3) equity theory, which states that satisfaction results when the buyer perceives fairness in the exchange. Two major ways that consumers can respond to dissatisfaction are by complaining and by engaging in negative word of mouth.

Finally, consumers can dispose of products in a variety of ways. This process has important implications for marketing strategy and an understanding of consumer behavior. Recycling, which is one form of disposition, depends on consumers' motivation, ability, and opportunity to act.

EXERCISES

1. Pick five durable or nondurable product or service categories. Develop a set of questions to (1) ask consumers how satisfied they are with the offerings in each category, (2) recall any instances when they have been dissatisfied in the past, (3) indicate how they dealt with the situation when they were dissatisfied, and (4) identify how they felt about the company or retailer response (if any). Administer this questionnaire to at least 15 consumers. Based on the data, try to answer the following questions:

   a. For what types of products or services are consumers most satisfied? Why do you think this is the case?

   b. For what products or services are consumers most dissatisfied? Why do you think this is the case?

   c. What are the most common types of responses to dissatisfaction?

   d. How well have the companies handled dissatisfaction?

2. Conduct an in-depth interview with two marketing professionals (from different companies) either by phone or in person. Ask them to describe in detail (1) how important satisfaction/dissatisfaction is to their business, (2) how they try to generate satisfaction, and (3) what kinds of experiences they have had with dissatisfied consumers and how they handled these problems. Summarize your findings for each topic.

3. Pick five durable and five nondurable products. Develop a set of questions to determine how consumers disposed of each product the last time they needed to do so. Administer the questionnaire to at least ten consumers. Summarize the responses and answer the following questions:

   a. For each product category, which are the most frequently used methods of disposition?

   b. Which product categories are most alike in terms of disposition patterns? Why?

   c. Which product categories are most dissimilar in terms of disposition patterns? Why?

4. Make an inventory of at least 30 of your possessions. For each, indicate when and how you plan to dispose of it. Also provide detailed reasons for this behavior. Then summarize this information and answer the following:

   a. Which possessions will be the easiest to dispose of and why?

   b. Which possessions will be the hardest to dispose of and why?

   c. What are your most frequent disposition options and why?

THE CONSUMER'S CULTURE

Age, Gender, and Household Influences (Ch. 15)

Social Class Influences (Ch. 14)

Social Influences (Ch. 16)

Regional, Ethnic and Religious Influences (Ch. 13)

Psychographics: Values, Personality and Lifestyles (Ch. 17)

THE PSYCHOLOGICAL CORE

- Motivation, Ability and Opportunity (Ch. 3)
- Exposure, Attention and Perception (Ch. 4)
- Knowing and Understanding (Ch. 5)
- Attitude Formation (Chs. 6 & 7)
- Memory and Retrieval (Ch. 8)

THE PROCESS OF MAKING DECISIONS

- Problem Recognition and Information Search (Ch. 9)
- Judgment and Decision Making (Chs. 10-11)
- Post-Decision Processes (Ch. 12)

CONSUMER BEHAVIOR OUTCOMES

- Symbolic Consumer Behavior (Ch. 18)
- Adoption of, Resistance to, and Diffusion of Innovations (Ch. 19)

PART FOUR

The Consumer's Culture

Part Four reflects a "macro" view of consumer behavior, examining how various aspect of the consumer's culture affect behavior. Chapter 13 focuses on how regional and ethnic groups affect consumer behavior. Chapter 14 examines how social class is determined in various cultures and how it affects consumer decisions and behaviors. Chapter 15 examines how age, gender, and household influences affect consumer behavior and discusses some interesting trends. Chapter 16 considers how, when, and why specific reference groups (such as friends, work groups, clubs) to which we belong can influence consumer decisions and behaviors.

Combined, these external influences can affect our personality, lifestyle, and values, the topics covered in Chapter 17.

Because all of these factors influence consumer behavior, they have many implications for marketing.

CHAPTER 13

REGIONAL, ETHNIC, AND RELIGIOUS INFLUENCES ON CONSUMER BEHAVIOR

INTRODUCTION

Sometimes major TV networks allow advertisers to put *discreet* product placements in programs for a fee. The Hispanic TV station Univision, however, goes further. It invites sponsors to write jingles and skits and prominently display their products on the set of the station's popular show, *Sabado Gigante* (*Gigantic Saturday*).[1] For example, in introducing a segment similar to the *Newlywed Game*, the host announces: "Let's sing to the sponsor who is holding $3,000 for the next contestants," and the audience bursts into the song "*Payless es el amigo de los pies*" ("Payless is the friend of your feet") as the camera pans back and forth from the audience to a display of shoes. The host then states: "Of course you'll feel great at Payless, and a big sale has arrived!" Pointing to a hostess holding a pair of boots, the host announces: "Buy one pair of shoes and take home another at half price. There's great selection for men, women, and children."

Many other products are featured in a similar manner on the show, and more than 80 million Hispanic consumers in 20 countries love it. In the United States, *Sabado Gigante* reaches more than 20 percent of the Hispanic population (particularly in the South and Southwest) and consistently ranks among the top ten Spanish-language programs (see Exhibit 13.1).

EXHIBIT 13.1
Spanish-language Media

Spanish language stations such as Univision are popular among Hispanic cultures.

Source: A. Ramey/PhotoEdit.

The preceding example illustrates several important aspects of culture that are central to this chapter. Most important, the introduction demonstrates how consumer behavior can sometimes vary among subgroups of individuals who have unique patterns of ethnicity, customs, and preferences. It also shows how the region in which consumers reside can influence their behavior. This chapter first discusses how regional influences can have an impact on the consumer. Then it examines subcultures, with a special focus on three major ethnic groups in the United States: Hispanics, African Americans, and Asian Americans. Finally, the chapter explores subcultures based on religion (see Exhibit 13.2).

REGIONAL INFLUENCES

Because people tend to work and live in the same area, residents in one part of the country can develop patterns of behavior that differ from those in another area. For example, a consumer from New England might enjoy lobster and appreciate colonial architecture, whereas someone from Texas may prefer barbecues and rodeos. This section explores how the region in which we live can affect our consumer behavior. We discuss first the various regions that exist within the United States and then we cover various regions in the world.

Regions Within the United States

Although we can speak of an overall U.S. culture, the United States is a vast country in which various regions have developed unique and distinctive identities. These identities result primarily from differing ethnic and cultural histories. For example, California and the Southwest were originally part of Mexico and therefore reflect a Mexican character. California has also been identified as the "land of opportunity," beginning with the 1849 gold rush and continuing with the lure of Hollywood. The Southwest has integrated its Mexican, Native American, and frontier roots. The eastern seaboard from New England to Georgia has a strong colonial flavor (especially in terms of architecture), reflecting the region's roots as

EXHIBIT 13.2
Chapter Overview: Region, Ethnicity, and Religion

This section of the book examines various aspects of consumer behavior that reflect the consumer as a member of a culture. This chapter describes how the region in which one lives, ethnic groups, and religion affect consumer behavior.

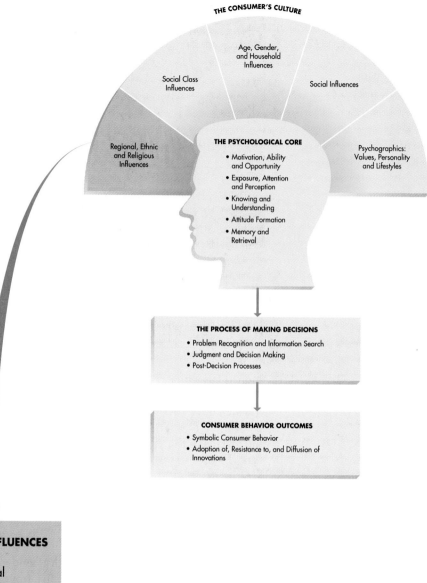

THE CONSUMER'S CULTURE

Age, Gender, and Household Influences

Social Class Influences

Social Influences

Regional, Ethnic and Religious Influences

THE PSYCHOLOGICAL CORE
- Motivation, Ability and Opportunity
- Exposure, Attention and Perception
- Knowing and Understanding
- Attitude Formation
- Memory and Retrieval

Psychographics: Values, Personality and Lifestyles

THE PROCESS OF MAKING DECISIONS
- Problem Recognition and Information Search
- Judgment and Decision Making
- Post-Decision Processes

CONSUMER BEHAVIOR OUTCOMES
- Symbolic Consumer Behavior
- Adoption of, Resistance to, and Diffusion of Innovations

REGIONAL INFLUENCES
- Regional
- Cross-national

ETHNIC INFLUENCES
- In the United States
- Multicultural marketing
- Around the world

RELIGIOUS INFLUENCES

the original 13 British colonies. The wilderness and great expanses of the West and Northwest have greatly determined the more free-spirited personalities of these regions, and the Deep South from Louisiana to Florida owes some of its Dixie, or Southern, character to agriculture, especially the cotton-growing industry, and the rebellion of the Confederacy during the Civil War. Finally, the Midwest is noted for its farms and agriculture.

These statements represent very broad generalizations. Each region also has numerous unique influences and variations that are too numerous to mention. The key point, however, is that these regional differences may affect consumption patterns. To illustrate, due to strong Mexican influence, consumers in the Southwest prefer spicy food and dishes such as tortillas, salsa, and pinto beans. Interestingly, some types of Mexican or more accurately Tex-Mex food such as nachos, chili dogs, and some hot salsas were actually developed in the United States and are only now becoming popular in Mexico.[2] Beef barbecue is particularly popular in Texas due to its large cattle industry, whereas parts of the Deep South lean toward pork barbecue. California has developed a reputation for health consciousness and health foods. Regional differences even show up in the type of stuffing used at Thanksgiving. Cornbread stuffing tends to be more popular in the South, in contrast to oyster stuffing in the North. Asian families on the West Coast, on the other hand, are more likely to substitute rice for stuffing.[3]

Styles of music may also differ in according to region. The Deep South developed a distinct style of southern rock exemplified by the Allman Brothers and Lynyrd Skynyrd. Nashville and Texas have traditionally been strongholds of country music, and Kentucky is known as the home of bluegrass. In the early 1990s, Seattle became recognized as the capital of the "grunge sound," with bands such as Pearl Jam and Soundgarden.

For many years people were moving from rural areas into more heavily populated urban areas. However, tired of high costs, crime, and crowds, recently more and more U.S. city dwellers have been heading for rural areas. Rural areas are especially attractive for retirement and recreation.[4] In addition, the Internet enables individuals in rural areas to be "connected" and work away from the office. Some innovative farmers are even using the Internet to access valuable agricultural information.[5]

Nine Nations of North America Based on a detailed anthropological study of regional differences, journalist Joel Garreau suggested that the North American continent can be divided into the **Nine Nations of North America**, with consumers in each region emphasizing different values and lifestyles (Exhibit 13.3).[6] Self-respect is valued most in the Empty Quarter, followed by the Islands and MexAmerica. Security is more important in Dixie, New England, and the Breadbasket, and warm relationships with others are most emphasized in the Breadbasket, Ecotopia, and MexAmerica.

These conclusions are admittedly very broad. In fact, a test of the Nine Nations theory found that the regions it specified were no better at predicting consumer values than were the regions used by the Census Bureau, such as Middle Atlantic and Mountain Pacific.[7] One reason is that considerable variation exists in values and lifestyles among consumers within a region. To compensate, some researchers have tried to go beyond broad regional differences to describe consumers on the basis of more specific characteristics, a technique called *clustering*.

Identifying Regions Based on Clustering Techniques Clustering techniques are based on the principle that "birds of a feather flock together."[8] This

Nine Nations of North America Nine regions in North America with distinct and identifiable lifestyles and values.

clustering The grouping of consumers according to common characteristics using statistical techniques.

EXHIBIT 13.3
The "Nine Nations" of North America

Author Joel Garreau divided the United States and Canada into nine major areas or nations, each of which he believes shares similar values. This exhibit identifies eight "nations" in North America. (The Canadian province of Quebec is not included.) The regions are identified on the map. The table below shows how values vary according to region. Do you think your region fits these value patterns?

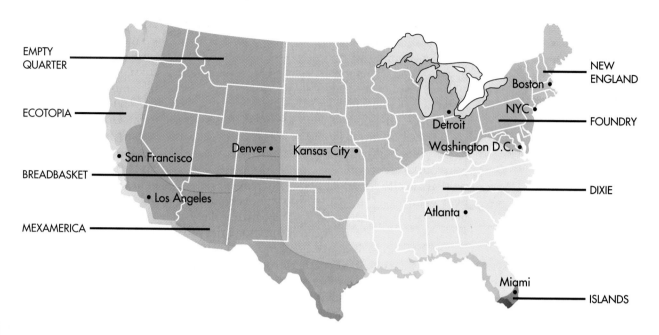

VALUES	NEW ENGLAND	THE FOUNDRY	DIXIE	THE ISLANDS	BREAD-BASKET	MEX-AMERICA	EMPTY QUARTER	ECOTOPIA
Self-respect	22.5%	20.5%	22.5%	25.0%	17.9%	22.7%	35.3%	18.0%
Security	21.7	19.6	23.3	15.6	20.2	17.3	17.6	19.6
Warm relationships with others	14.2	16.7	13.8	9.4	20.5	18.0	5.9	18.5
Sense of accomplishment	14.2	11.7	10.0	9.4	12.4	11.3	8.8	12.2
Self-fulfillment	9.2	9.9	8.4	3.1	7.5	16.0	5.9	12.7
Being well respected	8.3	8.7	11.0	15.6	10.1	2.7	2.9	4.2
Sense of belonging	5.0	8.4	7.5	12.5	7.8	6.7	17.6	7.9
Fun, enjoyment, excitement	5.0	4.5	3.5	9.4	3.6	5.3	5.9	6.9
Total	100.0	100.0	100.0	100.0	100.0	100.0	100.0	100.0

Source: Joel Garreau, *The Nine Nations of North America* (Boston: Houghton Mifflin, 1981), and Lynn R. Kahle, "The Nine Nations of North America and the Value Basis of Geographic Segmentation," *Journal of Marketing*, April 1986, pp. 37–47. Reprinted with permission.

principle suggests that consumers in the same neighborhood tend to buy the same types of cars, homes, appliances, and other products/services. Systems such as ClusterPlus 2000 (developed by Donnelly Marketing) and PRIZM (developed by Claritas, Inc.) group areas and neighborhoods into more precise clusters based on consumers' similarities on demographic and consumption characteristics. Similarity of income, education, age, household type, degree of urbanity, attitudes, and product/service preferences, including the type of car owned and preferred radio format, can all be used to define a cluster. All this information is summarized and grouped by using sophisticated statistical techniques such as multivariate regression.

To illustrate, Exhibit 13.4A presents the 62 major types of neighborhoods derived from PRIZM.[9] This system uses data from automobile registrations, consumer product-usage surveys, magazine subscription lists, and other sources to identify clusters or groups of consumers. The 62 clusters can be grouped into the 15 larger clusters in Exhibit 13.4B based on degree of urbanization and socioeconomic status. Note that because clusters are based on common characteristics, not on geography, consumers from different areas of the country may be grouped in the same cluster. The key point, however, is that these more precise clusters allow marketers to segment and target consumers more effectively than broad regional classifications do.

MARKETING IMPLICATIONS A product, service, or communication can be developed to appeal to different regions of the country. General Foods flavors Maxwell House coffee differently in different regions of the country, and R.J. Reynolds sells different brands of cigarettes in various regions to adjust for local tastes.[10] The Southwest is an attractive market for hot cuisines from Mexico, India, Thailand, and Vietnam, as well as for hotter and spicier picante sauces than those sold in northern regions. Likewise, the southern restaurant chain Cracker Barrel changed its menu when it expanded to northern regions, replacing grits with bratwurst.[11]

Based on the Nine Nations theory, we would expect an ad stressing self-fulfillment ("Set yourself free with Stouffer's") would be more appropriate for western regions than for the South. Similarly, an appeal to security ("Protect your home from break-ins with Electronic Touch Alarm") might work better in the South than in the West. A number of ads in Texas have a distinct western flavor, which reflects the state's cowboy tradition, and ads directed toward the East Coast may take on a more urban theme. Finally, products can be identified with certain regions such as Florida orange juice, Hawaiian macadamia nuts and suntanning lotion, Maine lobsters, and Texas beef.

Clustering systems such as PRIZM and ClusterPlus 2000 can also aid in a variety of marketing tasks, such as finding new customers, developing new products, buying advertising, locating store sites, and targeting direct mail.[12] Marketers can use these systems to learn where their customers are, what they like to do, and what media they are exposed to. When Isuzu launched its new Amigo convertible, it used ClusterPlus 2000 and unexpectedly discovered that Chicago was one of its key target markets. Isuzu also learned that lifestyle magazines were the best way to reach its customers. Buick used PRIZM to determine where to place its billboard ads. With cable TV, marketers can even target specific neighborhoods with TV ads.[13] Finally, in deciding where to place a new store, retailers can determine which neighborhoods are most likely to purchase the type of merchandise offered. ■

EXHIBIT 13.4A
**Sixty-Two Neighborhood
Types Derived from PRIZM**

Rather than identifying regions in terms of geographical boundaries, marketers can classify consumers according to the type of neighborhood they live in. The logic is that consumers are more likely to share similar characteristics and behaviors with others who live in a comparable neighborhood than with those in a broad region. This exhibit shows 62 types of neighborhoods based on the PRIZM system. Which type of neighborhood do you live in?

CLUSTER NO.	CLUSTER DESCRIPTION
S1	**ELITE SUBURBS**
01	Blue-Blood Estates (Elite Super-Rich Families)
02	Winner's Circle (Executive Suburban Families)
03	Executive Suites (Upscale White-Collar Couples)
04	Pools & Patios (Established Empty Nesters)
05	Kids & Cul-de-Sacs (Upscale Suburban Families)
U1	**URBAN UPTOWN**
06	Urban Gold Coast (Elite Urban Singles & Couples)
07	Money & Brains (Sophisticated Townhouse Couples)
08	Young Literati (Upscale Singles & Couples)
09	American Dreams (Established Urban Immigrant Families)
10	Bohemian Mix (Bohemian Singles & Couples)
C1	**2ND CITY SOCIETY**
11	Second City Elite (Upscale Executive Families)
12	Upward Bound (Young Upscale White-Collar Families)
13	Gray Power (Affluent Retirees in Sunbelt Cities)
T1	**LANDED GENTRY**
14	Country Squires (Elite Ex-Urban Families)
15	God's Country (Executive Ex-Urban Families)
16	Big Fish, Small Pond (Small Town Executive Families)
17	Greenbelt Families (Young, Middle-Class Town Families)
S2	**THE AFFLUENTIALS**
18	Young Influentials (Upwardly Mobile Singles & Couples)
19	New Empty Nests (Upscale Suburban Fringe Couples)
20	Boomers & Babies (Young White-Collar Suburban Families)
21	Suburban Sprawl (Young Suburban Townhouse Couples)
22	Blue-Chip Blues (Upscale Blue-Collar Families)
S3	**INNER SUBURBS**
23	Upstarts & Seniors (Middle Income Empty Nesters)
24	New Beginnings (Young Mobile City Singles)
25	Mobility Blues (Young Blue-Collar/Service Families)
26	Gray Collars (Aging Couples in Inner Suburbs)
U2	**URBAN MIDSCALE**
27	Urban Achievers (Midlevel, White-Collar, Urban Couples)
28	Big City Blend (Middle-Income Immigrant Families)
29	Old Yankee Rows (Empty-Nest, Middle-Class Families)
30	Mid-City Mix (African-American Singles & Families)
31	Latino America (Hispanic Middle-Class Families)

CLUSTER NO.	CLUSTER DESCRIPTION
C2	**2ND CITY CENTERS**
32	Middleburg Managers (Midlevel White-Collar Couples)
33	Boomtown Singles (Middle Income Young Singles)
34	Starter Families (Young Middle-Class Families)
35	Sunset City Blues (Empty Nests in Aging Industrial Cities)
36	Towns & Gowns (College Town Singles)
T2	**EX-URBAN BLUES**
37	New Homesteaders (Young Middle-Class Families)
38	Middle America (Midscale Families in Midsize Towns)
39	Red, White, & Blue (Small Town Blue-Collar Families)
40	Military Quarters (GIs & Surrounding Off-Base Families)
R1	**COUNTRY FAMILIES**
41	Big Sky Families (Midscale Couples, Kids, & Farmland)
42	New Eco-topia (Rural White/Blue-Collar/Farm Families)
43	River City, USA (Middle-Class, Rural Families)
44	Shotguns & Pickups (Rural Blue-Collar Workers & Families)
U3	**URBAN CORES**
45	Single City Blues (Ethnically Mixed Urban Singles)
46	Hispanic Mix (Urban Hispanic Singles & Families)
47	Inner Cities (Inner-City, Solo-Parent Families)
C3	**2ND CITY BLUES**
48	Smalltown Downtown (Older Renters & Young Families)
49	Hometown Retired (Low-Income, Older Singles, & Couples)
50	Family Scramble (Low-Income Hispanic Families)
51	Southside City (African-American Service Workers)
T3	**WORKING TOWNS**
52	Golden Ponds (Retirement Town Seniors)
53	Rural Industrial (Low-Income, Blue-Collar Families)
54	Norma Rae-ville (Young Families, Bi-Racial Mill Towns)
55	Mines & Mills (Older Families, Mine & Mill Towns)
R2	**HEARTLANDERS**
56	Agri-Business (Rural Farm-Town & Ranch Families)
57	Grain Belt (Farm Owners & Tenants)
T3	**RUSTIC LIVING**
58	Blue Highways (Moderate Blue-Collar/Farm Families)
59	Rustic Elders (Low-Income, Older, Rural Couples)
60	Back Country Folks (Remote Rural/Town Families)
61	Scrub Plant Flats (Older African-American Farm Families)
62	Hard Scrabble (Older Families in Poor, Isolated Areas)

EXHIBIT 13.4B
PRIZM Clusters

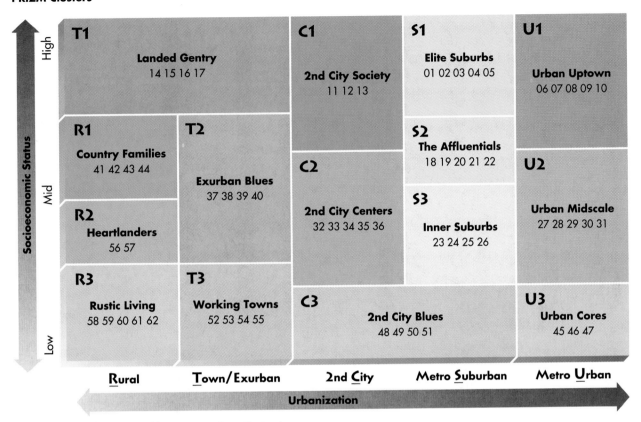

T1
Landed Gentry
14 15 16 17

C1
2nd City Society
11 12 13

S1
Elite Suburbs
01 02 03 04 05

U1
Urban Uptown
06 07 08 09 10

R1
Country Families
41 42 43 44

T2
Exurban Blues
37 38 39 40

C2
2nd City Centers
32 33 34 35 36

S2
The Affluentials
18 19 20 21 22

S3
Inner Suburbs
23 24 25 26

U2
Urban Midscale
27 28 29 30 31

R2
Heartlanders
56 57

R3
Rustic Living
58 59 60 61 62

T3
Working Towns
52 53 54 55

C3
2nd City Blues
48 49 50 51

U3
Urban Cores
45 46 47

Socioeconomic Status — High / Mid / Low

Urbanization — Rural / Town/Exurban / 2nd City / Metro Suburban / Metro Urban

Source: PRIZM Cluster reprinted by permission from Claritas Inc.

Regions Across the World

It should be obvious that the area of the world in which a consumer resides can influence consumption patterns. We've seen through this text that cross-cultural variations exist in just about every aspect of consumer behavior. Here are just a few examples of how regions across the world differ in their consumer behavior.

Consumers in different countries vary dramatically in the way they spend their income. Exhibit 13.5 presents a summary of spending patterns from nine different countries around the world.[14] The proportion spent on food is higher in India (52 percent), Kenya (38 percent), Iran (37 percent), Mexico (35 percent), Thailand (30 percent), and Poland (29 percent) than in the United States (10 percent) and Germany (12 percent). Note that the higher percentages reflect lower incomes rather than lavish eating styles.

Consumers in North America, Western Europe, and Asia are more likely to own radios, TVs, and telephones than are consumers in Latin America, Africa, and the Middle East. Note, however, that most urban Latin households (as compared with rural) have a TV and many have a washing machine, VCR, and phone. Other examples include the fact that many more U.S. consumers own computers (45.3 percent) than do consumers in other parts of the world such as Japan (7.1 percent), Britain (5.2 percent), Germany (4.6 percent), and France (4.2 percent).[15] Six times as many cars pack the roads in Western Europe than in Eastern

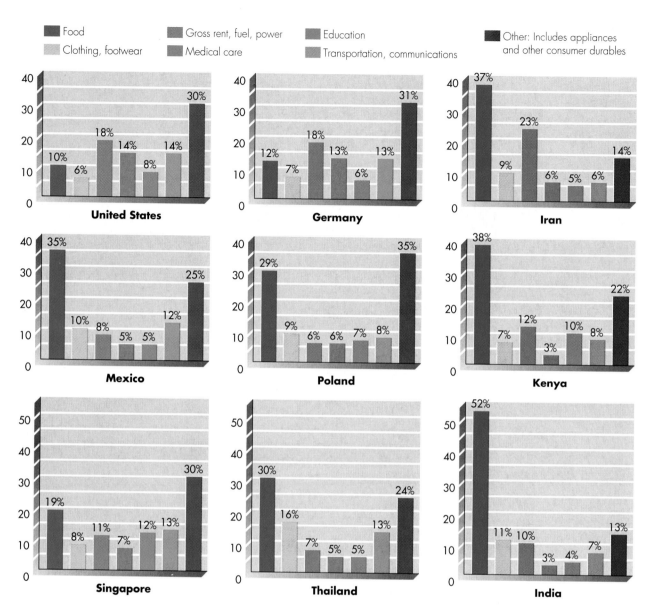

Legend:
- Food
- Clothing, footwear
- Gross rent, fuel, power
- Medical care
- Education
- Transportation, communications
- Other: Includes appliances and other consumer durables

EXHIBIT 13.5
Global Spending Patterns

Consumers in different countries can vary widely in how they spend their money. These graphs present the overall spending pattern of nine countries. Western nations (i.e., the United States and Germany) spend proportionately less on food (10 percent and 12 percent, respectively) than India (52 percent), Kenya (38 percent), Iran (37 percent), Mexico (35 percent), Thailand (30 percent), and Poland (29 percent). This statistic reflects the fact that consumers in these six countries typically have less discretionary income.

Source: Ricardo Sookdeo, "The New Global Consumer," *Fortune*, Autumn/Winter 1993, pp. 68–77. Copyright © 1993 by Time Inc. All rights reserved.

Europe. The most Coca-Cola is consumed in North America, followed by Latin America and the European community; the lowest consumption occurs in Asia, the Middle East, and Africa. The top chocolate markets are Switzerland, Britain, and Germany. Finally, the need for doctors is highest in Asia, including Indonesia, Thailand, Malaysia, India, and Pakistan.

Some nations tend to be strongly associated with certain products, as illustrated in Exhibit 13.6. The consumption of certain types of products is forbidden in cer-

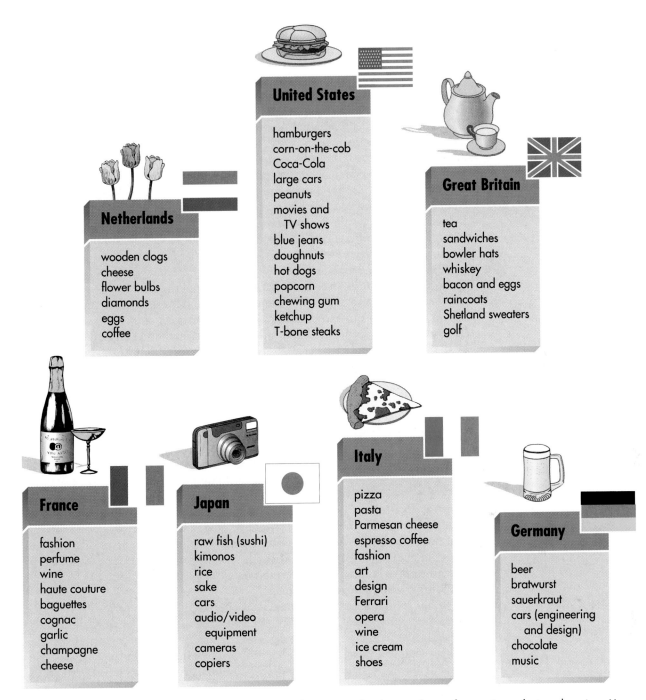

United States

hamburgers
corn-on-the-cob
Coca-Cola
large cars
peanuts
movies and
   TV shows
blue jeans
doughnuts
hot dogs
popcorn
chewing gum
ketchup
T-bone steaks

Great Britain

tea
sandwiches
bowler hats
whiskey
bacon and eggs
raincoats
Shetland sweaters
golf

Netherlands

wooden clogs
cheese
flower bulbs
diamonds
eggs
coffee

France

fashion
perfume
wine
haute couture
baguettes
cognac
garlic
champagne
cheese

Japan

raw fish (sushi)
kimonos
rice
sake
cars
audio/video
   equipment
cameras
copiers

Italy

pizza
pasta
Parmesan cheese
espresso coffee
fashion
art
design
Ferrari
opera
wine
ice cream
shoes

Germany

beer
bratwurst
sauerkraut
cars (engineering
   and design)
chocolate
music

EXHIBIT 13.6
Products and Countries

Many countries tend to be associated with or are known for certain products and services. Here are seven examples. Can you think of any others?

Source: Data from Marieke K. de Mooij and Warren Keegan, *Advertising Worldwide* (Englewood Cliffs, N.J.: Prentice-Hall, 1991).

tain regions of the world. For example, drinking alcohol and smoking are not allowed in Muslim countries, and religious restrictions forbid the consumption of pork in Israel and beef in India. Food preferences in one part of the world can sometimes appear exotic to people in other parts of the world. The Chinese eat fish stomachs and soup made from bird saliva; natives of Thailand like deep fried chicken heads and claws; and the Iraqis snack on dried, salted locusts.[16] A number of Western habits such as eating snails (particularly in France) and using honey or blue cheese dressing appear equally strange to consumers in other parts of the world.

Just as in the United States, regional differences in consumer behavior occur *within* a specific region of the world. To illustrate, consumers in the west of India are generally more affluent and more favorably disposed toward premium products, whereas consumers in the north and east are more price conscious. Those in the south tend to be more conservative and utilitarian consumers. Also, in northern India the staple food and drink are wheat and tea; in the south, rice and coffee. Southern Indians also tend to be more health conscious and to buy more health and beauty aids and cosmetics because of a desire for fair skin. Finally, southern Indians tend to go to the movies more often and to watch more regional TV due to local language differences. Thus advertising tends to be concentrated in the cinema and on regional broadcasts.

In Thailand the food preferences of northern consumers, particularly near the Cambodian and Burmese borders, are different from the preferences of consumers who live in the central plains including Bangkok and those in the southern regions on the seacoast. Catholic consumers in the southern part of Germany, particularly Bavaria, have an identity, heritage, and religious orientation that differs from that of the northern and eastern regions, which are predominantly Prussian and Protestant. Inhabitants of the former East Germany possess a unique worldview as a result of having lived under a police state and command economy for decades.[17] In particular, they focus mainly on home, garden, family, and close friends. Finally, the different provinces of Canada, especially French-speaking Quebec, demonstrate unique cultural characteristics.

MARKETING IMPLICATIONS Global differences in consumer behavior can sometimes lead to alterations in marketing strategy in order to appeal to specific regions and countries. As shown in Exhibit 13.7, certain strategies are more effective in the United States than they are in Latin America.[18] Money-back guarantees give U.S. consumers confidence, but Latin Americans simply do not believe them because they never expect to get their money back. Also, the strategies of using famous endorsers or being the official product of a sporting event are much more effective in Venezuela and Mexico than in the United States.

In the food industry, McDonald's has altered its menu in various parts of the world to appeal to local tastes. Beer and wine are offered in Germany and France, respectively, because these beverages are typically consumed with meals. For strong religious reasons, beef is not consumed by Hindus in India, which led McDonald's to develop a beefless Big Mac.[19] In Brazil, McDonald's has offered northeastern specialties such as *acaraje, bobo de camarao,* and *vatapa,* and Dunkin' Donuts sells both salty chicken and cheese donuts.[20] Finally, Domino's Pizza offers squid and fish toppings to appeal to the Japanese preference for seafood.[21]

In marketing Pampers disposable diapers, Procter & Gamble developed different versions of a TV ad to account for variations in slang and accent in different regions of the German-speaking world. In contrast to the common *hoch Deutsch* (high German, spoken by most actors and announcers), Bavarian, Austrian, and Swiss voice-overs spoke with a heavy accent that reflected the styles of those regions. Exhibit 13.8 on page 314 shows an ad for GM that reflects European regional influences (particularly Switzerland).

Sometimes cultural stereotypes can be used as part of a deliberate communications strategy. For example, U.S. agencies have become enamored with Scot-

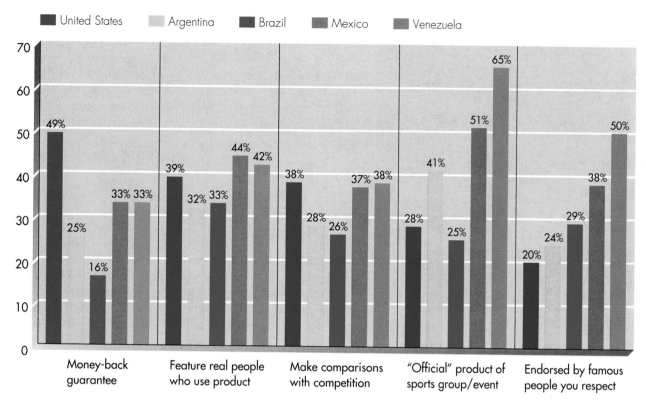

Legend: United States | Argentina | Brazil | Mexico | Venezuela

Money-back guarantee: 49% 25% 16% 33% 33%
Feature real people who use product: 39% 32% 33% 44% 42%
Make comparisons with competition: 38% 28% 26% 37% 38%
"Official" product of sports group/event: 28% 41% 25% 51% 65%
Endorsed by famous people you respect: 20% 24% 29% 38% 50%

EXHIBIT 13.7
Marketing Strategies in Latin America

Some marketing techniques tend to be more believable or effective in Latin American countries than in the United States. For example, being the official product of a sports group/event or being endorsed by famous and respected people appears to be more effective in several Latin American countries than in the United States.

Source: Adapted from Ignacio Galceran and Jon Berry, "A New World of Consumers," *American Demographics,* March 1995, pp. 27–33. *American Demographics* magazine, 1995. Reprinted with permission.

land in a wide number of campaigns featuring kilts, medieval castles, and ancient churches.[22]

If marketers fail to heed these cross-cultural differences, embarrassment and failure can result. U.S. car manufacturers looked ridiculous in the early 1990s when they tried to persuade Japanese consumers to buy American cars. The Japanese drive on the left side of the road, and U.S. manufacturers were not offering right-hand-drive cars at that time.[23] In Germany, Vicks had to change its name to Wicks, because the former term is slang for sexual intercourse. Kentucky Fried Chicken failed in Hong Kong because Asians typically boil or broil rather than fry chicken.[24] In other parts of Asia, therefore, the company altered its chicken recipe to more closely fit local tastes. Finally, the turn of the millennium marketing mania that overtook much of the world was of little interest to Asian consumers because they use a different calendar.[25] ■

ETHNIC INFLUENCES

Ethnicity is another important factor influencing consumer behavior. In discussing this concept, it is important to emphasize that we will be discussing many generalizations about ethnic groups that may or may not apply to individual consumers. Rather these generalizations represent only broad group tendencies.

"Alright, going all out for you."

"Used to be that an American car in Switzerland was something of a rarity. Not anymore. GM sells a lot of cars over here these days—good cars at good value. Which is nice for me—I'm the local dealer."

Fact: GM exports more cars around the world from North America than any other car manufacturer.

1949 Chevrolet Fleetline

GM

Chevrolet · Pontiac · Oldsmobile · Buick · Cadillac · GMC Truck

EXHIBIT 13.8
Regional European Ad

Here is an ad for an American car that tries to appeal to a specific region of Switzerland and other regions in the Alps. The car is in an alpine village with the driver experiencing a problem common to this mountainous, rural region. Consumers in this area will be more likely to relate to this situation and therefore like the ad.

Source: Reprinted with permission of General Motors Corporation.

ethnic groups Subcultures with a similar heritage and values.

acculturation Learning how to adapt to a new culture.

Throughout the history of the United States, individuals from many different cultures have immigrated to form not only a unique U.S. culture but also a number of subcultures or **ethnic groups** within the larger society. Members of these ethnic groups share a common heritage, set of beliefs, religion, and experiences that set them apart from others in society. Larger groups include the Hispanic, African American, Asian, Jewish, Italian, Irish, Scandinavian, and Polish subcultures. Interestingly, the Polish population in Chicago is larger than in most cities in Poland.

A key feature of these groups is that they tend to be bound together by cultural ties that can, in turn, strongly influence their consumer behavior. In addition, through a process called **acculturation**, members of a subculture must learn to adapt to the host culture. In acculturation, consumer knowledge, skills, and behavior can be learned through social interaction, modeling the behavior of others, and reinforcement or receiving rewards for certain behaviors.[26] Thus acculturation is strongly influenced by family, friends, and institutions such as the media, place of worship, and school. Acculturation combines with traditional customs to form a unique consumer culture.

Next, we examine the current ethnic composition of the United States and some major population trends.

Ethnic Groups Within the United States

At present the majority of U.S. consumers (commonly referred to as *Anglos*) can trace their ancestry back to one or more European nations, especially England and Germany. However, immigration and population trends are greatly changing the demographic profile of the country. In particular, as shown in Exhibit 13.9, by the year 2050 more than 180 million non-Anglos will be living in the United States (almost half the projected population). The largest increase will be among Hispanics, who will overtake African Americans as the largest minority group.[27] The Hispanic population is growing nearly eight times faster than the rest of the population and represents 42 percent of the total population growth (due largely to immigration and a high birth rate). The Asian American population is growing at an even faster rate and is expected to increase by more than 400 percent by the year 2050. All these trends suggest that Anglos will not be viewed as much of a majority in the future.

Clearly, these trends will have huge implications for marketers. The Hispanic community, for example, already represents a $240 billion market that will grow

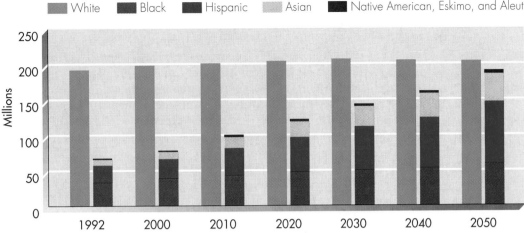

EXHIBIT 13.9
Ethnic Composition of U.S. Consumers

This exhibit shows projected trends in the ethnic composition of U.S. consumers from 1992 to 2050. Hispanic Americans are by far the fastest-growing ethnic group, followed by Asian American. Note also that by 2050, ethnic groups together will represent almost as many consumers as the Anglo population.

Source: Data from U.S. Bureau of the Census, as reported in Jon Berry, "The Population is Taking Off Again; Here's What You Need to Know," *Brandweek,* December 7, 1992, p. 14.

dramatically in the coming years.[28] Emerging subcultures represent attractive markets that can be targeted with specific products, communications, and distribution channels.

Hispanic Americans

Hispanic Americans represent one of the largest-growing ethnic groups in the United States today. This section examines the basic characteristics of the Hispanic subculture and then looks at consumption patterns and marketing implications.

Characteristics The Hispanic American market is both huge and diverse. In fact, some have suggested that there is not a single Hispanic market but rather various submarkets with different origins, values, and behaviors.[29] We can divide the Hispanic population into four major groups: Mexican Americans (62 percent), living primarily in the Southwest and California; Central or Southern Americans (14 percent), Cuban Americans (5 percent), located primarily in southern Florida; and Puerto Ricans (12 percent), centered in New York.[30]

Levels of Acculturation Hispanics can also be divided into several groups based on their level of acculturation to the host culture: (1) the *acculturated*, who speak mostly English and have a high level of assimilation; (2) the *bicultural*, who can function in either English or Spanish; and (3) the *traditional*, who speak mostly Spanish.[31] In California only 25 percent of Hispanics could be classified as acculturated. This percentage is somewhat higher in Texas. The rate of acculturation tends to be slow, usually taking four generations, because 80 percent of all Hispanics marry other Hispanics. Cuban Americans tend to be the least acculturated and Mexican Americans the most. Finally, the proportion of those speaking Spanish at home, more than 70 percent, appears to be on the increase.[32]

Family Orientation and Values   Despite this segment's diversity, certain broad generalizations can be made. Foremost, Hispanics have a distinct identity, set of customs, and language.[33] A defining characteristic is a strong orientation toward the family. The Hispanic extended family is usually a large one that includes aunts, uncles, cousins, grandparents, and even godparents. The family is the center of everything, and all family members participate in holidays and festivals. Dinner is often a social event for the entire extended family. Family elders are given the highest respect because of their experience and knowledge.

In addition, Hispanics place a strong emphasis on responsibility, honesty, independence, self-control, inner harmony, and freedom.[34] They can also be characterized by a strong ethnic pride, work ethic, and religious orientation; more than 70 percent are Roman Catholic. Although Hispanics tend to hold fast to their language, customs, and culture, they *are* willing to participate in the American Dream—that is, increasing the standard of living through hard work. Nevertheless, most Hispanics do not view themselves as materialistic and are not interested in flaunting possessions.[35] Rather, they see themselves as upbeat, colorful, and lively, as reflected by Tejano music, which is very popular among Hispanic consumers.

Demographics   The U.S. Hispanic population is also very young. Almost 30 percent of individuals in this ethnic group are under 14 years of age (as compared with 22.4 percent for the total population), and more than half are under the age of 30 (relative to 44 percent for Anglos).[36] The one exception is Cuban Americans whose median age is around 40. Other important demographics include a lower divorce rate than the general population, reflecting strong family values; larger families with an average of 3.45 people versus 2.6 for the general population; a higher proportion of blue-collar occupations; lower median income; and a lower level of education—52.6 percent have a high school degree or higher, compared with 79.4 percent for the general population. Cuban Americans tend to be the most highly educated, with 20 percent possessing a college degree (compared with 10 percent of Puerto Ricans and 6 percent of Mexican Americans). Note, however, that education and occupational levels have been increasing dramatically in recent years.[37] Politically, Mexicans and Puerto Ricans tend to be Democrats, and Cubans are more likely to be Republican.

Finally, more than 80 percent of Hispanic Americans live in urban and suburban areas—particularly Los Angeles, New York, Miami, and San Antonio. In cities like San Antonio and Los Angeles, Hispanics represent a very sizable proportion of the population. However, 43 percent of Hispanics live in the suburbs and have an income that is 32 percent higher than households in the inner city.[38]

Consumption Patterns   Unique Hispanic customs and language have led to identifiable patterns of acquisition and consumption. One of the strongest and most consistent findings is that Hispanic consumers are brand loyal, likely to buy nationally advertised or prestige brands (particularly those that show an interest in this ethnic group), and less likely to be lured away by a sale than are other consumers.[39] Thus Hispanics tend to place quality and product reputation ahead of price.

In addition, Hispanics spend more on their children and groceries and are less likely to eat away from the home than the general population—all due to the focus on family.[40,41] Because an attractive appearance and good grooming are extremely important, Hispanics spend more on cosmetics and toiletries than the population in general does. They also tend to spend less on insurance than other Americans.

Food-Consumption Patterns Hispanics also exhibit somewhat unique food-consumption patterns. In particular, they prefer fresh meat and produce, hot spices, canned chilies, and salsas.[42] Delicious meals that please the senses are highly desired, and lowering the fat content would lessen the pleasure. A favorite dish is chicken and rice for Puerto Ricans, tacos for Mexican Americans, and pork loin for Cuban Americans. Interestingly, the growth of the Hispanic population is also influencing the rest of the nation's food preferences toward spicier cuisine. As evidence, the sale of salsas has increased dramatically in recent years, whereas ketchup-based cooking is on the decline.[43] The number of Mexican restaurants is rapidly increasing, and fast-food chains such as Taco Bell and Taco Cabana have become very popular.

Influence of Acculturation Important influences on consumption patterns are the consumer's level of acculturation and **intensity of ethnic identification**.[44] Specifically, consumers who strongly identify with their ethnic group and who are less acculturated into the mainstream culture are more likely to exhibit the consumption patterns of the ethnic group. Strong Hispanic identification leads to a higher level of husband-dominant decisions (which we discuss in greater detail in Chapter 15).[45] Furthermore, strong identifiers are more likely to be influenced by radio ads, billboards, family members, and coworkers and less likely than weak identifiers are to use coupons.[46] Weak identifiers are more influenced by magazine ads, brochures, the Yellow Pages, *Consumer Reports*, and product labels than are strong identifiers.

intensity of ethnic affiliation
How strongly people identify with their ethnic group.

The strongest Hispanic identifiers tend to be *both* recent immigrants and younger Hispanics who were born in the United States but have a strong desire to rediscover their Hispanic roots.[47] In addition, ethnic identification is more likely to play a role when it is made salient in a particular situation. In other words, a consumer's ethnicity will stand out and influence behavior more when he or she is in the minority than when surrounded by other members of his or her own ethnic group.[48] One study found that minorities adjust to this situation by reducing perceived dissimilarities rather than by increasing similarities between themselves and the majority group.[49]

Finally, a detailed study of Mexican immigration patterns sheds some light on how acculturation occurs.[50] In addition to the social forces mentioned earlier, immigrants adapt to the new consumer environment through trial-and-error learning, by buying and using products and services. After arrival these items are acquired very quickly, particularly those that are low-cost, highly visible, not language dependent, and symbolic of both the U.S. and Mexican cultures such as food, clothing, and telephones. Most immigrants strive to buy a car, usually used but still a status symbol generally unattainable in Mexico. Sometimes desires for certain products, such as meats, white bread, sugared cereals, and caffeinated drinks, can be even stronger among immigrants than among the majority culture.[51]

Note, however, that some Hispanic Americans resist assimilation and desire to maintain their ethnic identity.[52] As an example, Hispanic Americans strongly dislike frozen and prepackaged foods. These consumers also tend to buy many items from Mexico, such as foods, soaps, laundry detergents, and cassette tapes.

MARKETING IMPLICATIONS With spending power of $356 billion,[53] the Hispanic subculture commands size, growth rate, and characteristics that lead to a wide variety of marketing implications in areas such as product development, media targeting, advertising messages, promotions, and distribution.

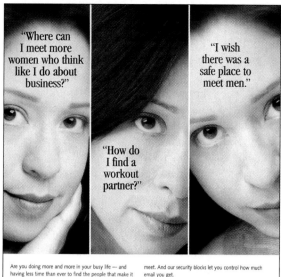

EXHIBIT 13.10

Ad Directed at Hispanic Americans

Hispanics tend to reject image-oriented messages in favor of those that clearly indicate purpose, benefits, or use of the product or service. Although the young woman in the ad is attractive, this ad clearly emphasizes information.

Source: Courtesy of SocialNet.

Product Development. In light of the unique needs and preferences of Hispanic Americans, marketers have begun to develop specific products and services for them. For example, cosmetics firms, such as Revlon, Maybelline, Cover Girl, Estée Lauder, and L'Oréal, have developed cosmetics designed for consumers with darker skin.[54] General Mills recently introduced a new cereal for Hispanic consumers called Bunuelitos, while Kraft launched a fast-melting white cheese called Valle Lindo in Texas.[55]

Media Targeting. Because Hispanic Americans tend to be concentrated in urban areas and share a common language, they can be easily targeted through the use of Spanish-language media, including TV, radio, print, and billboards. Not surprisingly, Hispanic American consumers are heavy users of these media, leading to unprecedented growth in terms of advertising sales.[56] Although radio offers the broadest penetration of Hispanic households, Hispanics, compared to the population as a whole, also spend 26 percent more time watching television. However, they are more easily targeted on Hispanic networks like Univision because they represent only a small proportion of the major network TV audience. Furthermore, even though Hispanic consumers do watch network TV, their tastes vary from the general population's.[57] For example, they are more likely to watch the Fox network than are other groups.

Finally, the number of Spanish-language newspapers is on the rise, and many traditional newspapers, including the *New York Times*, now publish special editions for Hispanic readers.[58] As a result, many advertising research companies, including Nielson, MRI, and Simmons, now closely monitor Hispanic media patterns.[59]

Advertising Messages. At the present time, only a small percentage of corporate advertising is directed toward Hispanic Americans, but this percentage is expected to increase dramatically in coming years.[60] Major companies such as Procter & Gamble, Polaroid, and Chrysler have all increased their budgets for Hispanic campaigns. General Motors is aggressively pitching its Alero model to both Hispanics and blacks.[61] Such advertising is particularly important because Hispanics exhibit a tendency to buy prestige or nationally advertised brands. Corona Beer, which was popular among yuppies in the 1980s, is generating a comeback by advertising to blue-collar Hispanic workers.[62]

The characteristics and consumption patterns of Hispanic Americans can provide guidance when marketers are developing ads. Messages that stress family themes repeatedly win the praise of Hispanic American consumers during ad tests (see Exhibit 13.10).[63] A McDonald's ad showed what looked to most consumers like a birthday party, but the ad had special appeal to Hispanic consumers because they recognized it as a *quinceanera* (a celebration of a girl's coming of age at 15). Ads that portray Hispanics as colorful, upbeat, and lively or that use popular Tejano music also tend to draw a positive response. Finally, advertising can reflect differences between Hispanic segments. In an ad based on the theme, "Coke and your favorite meal," the product was shown with a taco for Mexican Americans, pork loin for Cubans, and chicken and rice for Puerto Ricans.

Hispanics also tend to react positively to ads using ethnic spokespeople, who are perceived as more trustworthy, leading to more positive attitudes toward the brand being advertised.[64] This approach is most effective in environments where ethnicity is more salient (the group is in the minority).[65] Some advertisers try to make ethnic representation in ads proportional to the group's size relative to the general population. This *proportionality criterion* can sometimes be useful in determining how many ethnic members to include in the message.[66]

Hispanics tend to reject image-oriented messages in favor of those that clearly indicate the purpose, benefits, or use of the product or service (see Exhibit 13.10). They also tend to interpret visuals and copy literally. All these points suggest that messages directed toward this group need to be straightforward and clear, especially when communicating with recent immigrants who must be taught how to use products that were not available in their native country.

Creating advertising messages for the Hispanic community does not mean simply translating the message into Spanish. Following are several blunders that have been made in translating advertising messages:[67]

- A Coor's Light campaign, "Turn It Loose Tonight," was translated literally into Spanish but was interpreted as meaning "Have the Runs Tonight" by Hispanics in the Southwest.
- A burrito was accidentally called a *burrada*, which means a big mistake.
- The slogan for Perdue chickens, "It takes a tough man to make a tender chicken," was translated as, "It takes a sexually excited man to make a chick affectionate."
- The word *bichos* means bugs to Mexicans, but it means a man's private parts to Puerto Ricans. Thus an insecticide ad that claimed to kill all *bichos* left Puerto Ricans wondering.

accommodation theory The more effort one puts forth in trying to communicate with an ethnic group, the more positive the reaction.

Accommodation theory can also apply when marketers develop advertising for Hispanics. Essentially, accommodation theory predicts that the more effort a source puts into communicating with a group by, for example, using role models and the native language, the greater the reciprocation by this group and the more positive their feelings. As predicted by accommodation theory, advertising in Spanish increases perceptions of the company's sensitivity toward and solidarity with the Hispanic community, thereby creating positive feelings toward the brand and the company.[68] However, using Spanish messages exclusively can lead to negative ad perceptions. Apparently this practice taps into a language insecurity, implying that Hispanics can speak only Spanish. A number of ads directed toward Hispanic Americans are delivered in English because many viewers are either bilingual or highly acculturated. Thus the best strategy appears to be a combination of English and Spanish messages.

Promotions. The use of sales promotions, such as premiums, sampling, sweepstakes, and pricing deals, is also on the rise. Hispanics are less likely to use coupons, partly because coupons are not available for many ethnic brands, and newer immigrants may not fully understand their purpose (they may be viewed as food stamps and have a negative image).[69] Coupon use tends to increase with acculturation. As evidence, one study found that Hispanics were increasingly buying a brand that used in-store sampling, a cents-off coupon, or a buy-one-get-one-free offer.[70] Another successful promotion featured a Festival Latino that combined coupons with a sweepstakes for cars, trips, and other prizes.[71] Finally, Coor's recently recruited a retired Hispanic baseball star as an endorser to enhance the appeal of a promotion that offered free tickets to the All Star game.[72]

Distribution.   The distribution of products and services is also being tailored to Hispanic American consumers. El Guero and Delray Farms in Chicago, Fiesta Market in Texas, and Varadero supermarkets in southern Florida are full-scale Hispanic markets with a broad selection of Hispanic foods and other products.[73] One popular feature is a bakery where items are made from scratch. A mall in Tucson, Arizona, targets Hispanics by advertising in Spanish-language media and providing live mariachi music on holidays such as Cinco de Mayo (commemorating Mexico's victory over France on May 5, 1862).[74] ▪

African Americans

The African American community represents a large and important segment of the U.S. population. This section examines basic characteristics of this group and its consumption patterns, followed by a discussion of important marketing implications.

Characteristics   More than 31 million African Americans are currently living in the United States, making up about 12 percent of the population, and this number is expected to grow to about 40 million by the year 2008.[75] They represent a very diverse group consisting of many subsegments across different levels of income and education, occupations, and regions. As evidence, the proportion of black families with incomes both over $50,000 and below $5,000 has increased. The percentage of blacks with white-collar occupations is also rapidly on the rising.

Other important aspects of the black subculture include (1) a high proportion of individuals living in urban areas, especially the 15 largest U.S. cities; (2) a younger median age of 28 versus 34 for the population as a whole; (3) a larger number of single-parent families headed by females (more than 58 percent versus 20 percent); (4) a lower median income of $34,000 versus $40,000 for the general population); and (5) less education, although this situation is changing as more blacks are enrolling in college.[76] African Americans like to join and do things as a group rather than individually. Religious organizations, particularly fundamentalist Protestant groups, are very important to everyday life, leading to a high regard for morality and respect. Finally, blacks are more likely to associate with the Democratic party, although the proportion of black Republican voters has increased slightly.

Some have argued that the differences between African American and Anglo consumers are not really that great and can be attributed more to income, social class, and urban influences than to race.[77] Furthermore, many aspects of black culture such as music, arts, and athletics have heavily influenced the mainstream culture, thereby reducing differences between African Americans and other ethnic groups.

However, it can be a big mistake to assume that African American consumers are similar to the majority population in all cases. They can possess differing views on a variety of issues. They are more likely to believe that people should feel free to live, dress, and look the way they want to.[78] Also, blacks do not necessarily aspire to desert their heritage and assimilate with the majority culture.[79] As incomes rise, a strong desire to preserve a cultural identity develops.

Consumption Patterns   A defining element in the consumption patterns of African Americans is the importance of style, self-image, and elegance. "Style—whether captured in an elegant hat, an eloquent phrase, a sophisticated step, or a smooth move—lies at the very heart of the African American culture."[80] Consumption patterns are also related to a strong desire to be recognized. As a result, African Americans tend to be trendsetters in areas such as clothing, music, dance, and language. They have developed their own preferences in fashion and have often been emulated by the majority population, particularly teenagers.[81] The fashion of wearing floppy pants and shorts, for example, began with black youths.

Traditionally, black consumers were thought to be more brand loyal than other minority groups, but evidence calls this belief into question.[82] In fact, one study found black women to be the least brand loyal of all the minority groups studied. Compared to other minorities, blacks are more likely to pay attention to ads, more willing to pay more for prestigious brands, and less likely to cut back on spending during tougher economic times.[83] Furthermore, they respond positively to products and messages targeted toward them and are less likely to trust or buy brands that are not advertised.[84]

African Americans tend to be savvy, investigative, and smart consumers. For example, in the early days of Internet shopping, blacks outspent whites nearly two to one.[85] Blacks enjoy shopping and shop more frequently than other ethnic groups do.[86] In making a purchase, they are more likely to talk to salespeople or to someone knowledgeable about the product or service. They do not exhibit strong store preferences because most retailers have not attempted to appeal to them specifically.

Finally, African American consumers sometimes differ from other groups in terms of the products and services they buy. Blacks tend to spend more on books than on video games.[87] Compared to Anglos, blacks are no more likely as a group to consume alcoholic beverages, but blacks who do drink consume more on average each week. They are also twice as likely to have bought a pager than are other adults.[88]

MARKETING IMPLICATIONS African American consumers have a total income of more than $280 billion, representing more than $60 billion in retail sales, and their buying power is greatly multiplying.[89] Not surprisingly, marketers are now devoting more attention to this segment, as evidenced by an increase of advertising dollars from $400 million to more than $800 million in a 10-year period.

Product Development. Marketers are designing specific product lines for black consumers. Companies such as Revlon, Maybelline, and Estée Lauder have developed cosmetics tailored to blacks, and L'eggs sells panty hose shades for darker skin.[90] An ad for a skin care product, Style Neutra Foam Shampoo is formulated to neutralize and condition African American hair.[91] Clothing manufacturers now realize that black women are different physically from others and are designing more flattering styles for their physique. Colorful styles based on African kente cloth are also gaining in popularity.

In the fast-food area, KFC has added menu items such as red beans and rice and greens to appeal to black consumers.[92] Big-name companies such as Mattel (which makes Barbie), Hasbro, and Tyco have designed dolls for the African American market.[93] One Mattel doll called Shani comes in a choice of three complexions—light, medium, and dark—and has a boyfriend named Jamal. Finally, Hallmark introduced the Mahogany line of greeting cards for African Americans (see Exhibit 13.11), and banks have offered special credit cards that appeal to African American pride.[94]

Media Targeting. A number of companies, including Polaroid, Chrysler, Procter & Gamble, Maybelline, and even Major League Baseball, have been increasing their budgets for campaigns directed at African Americans.[95] In doing so,

EXHIBIT 13.11

An Ad Directed at African Americans

A number of products have been developed to meet the needs of African American consumers. Hallmark's Mahogony line of greeting cards is one such product.

Source: Courtesy of Hallmark Cards, Inc.

the companies noted that 82.3 percent of these consumers seek information from magazines specifically aimed at them.[96] The publications with the highest credibility are *Ebony* and *Essence*. *B.E.T. Weekend* tries to win black readers by distributing its insert inside newspapers.[97] African American TV networks (such as BET) and ethnic programming also represent good vehicles for advertising. Chrysler sponsored an acclaimed documentary called "Hoop Dreams" to appeal to these consumers.[98] Also, African American radio stations have been a cultural lifeline for many years and represent an efficient advertising vehicle.[99] And McDonald's became the first fast-food company to launch a 30-minute infomercial discussing its commitment to the African American community.[100]

Marketers can attempt to reach black consumers through the general media but must be careful to pay close attention to the media habits of blacks. African American consumers represent only 10 to 12 percent of mass-market magazine readership.[101] As a different programs than other groups.

Advertising Messages. African Americans have long been ignored or given only minimal attention in ads, not only in the United States but in Canada and the United Kingdom as well. In one survey more than 50 percent of consumers, 94 percent of whom were Anglo, felt that ads do not include enough blacks.[102] Another survey indicated that more than 60 percent of blacks were alienated by ads because they are "designed for whites."[103] Furthermore, many blacks resent the way they have been portrayed in ads, and this feeling can lead to negative attitudes toward products and services. In the survey mentioned earlier, more than 46 percent of consumers believe that blacks are portrayed inaccurately in ads, often appearing in minor and background roles.[104] However, this situation is now beginning to change.

One major change is that an increasing number of spokespeople and models in ads are African American. In the cosmetic industry more black models are appearing in ads that have traditionally been dominated by blue-eyed, blond models. Federal Express introduced an ad that featured an African American female executive beating out her Anglo male adversaries for a high-stakes deal.[105] Popular African American rap stars have also appeared in ads for malt liquors.[106] However, it is often the case that even when black models, especially women, appear in ads, they tend to have lighter skin as opposed to more African features and darker skin.[107] Thus there is still much room for improvement in the depiction of African American consumers in ads.

Several suggestions have been made for increasing the effectiveness of advertising toward blacks. In particular, marketers should not simply force African American people into an Anglo strategy. Instead, messages should take the unique values and expectations of African Americans into account.[108] It has been recommended that ads for banks and financial institutions "convey a message of respect."[109] Similarly, McDonald's developed a marketing campaign to convince blacks that they are valued customers.[110] Given that blacks are thorough and smart shoppers, ads should provide specific product and service details and depict real-life situations. Businesses can also "personally invite blacks to purchase their products and services and create advertising that blacks see as relevant, realistic, and positive."[111]

In developing ads, marketers should be careful *not* to create the impression that blacks are different. Maybelline found that black women wanted to be treated like all other women and be depicted as strong, contemporary, and self-confident.[112] Cadillac also learned not to create an impression of tokenism in creating ads for blacks.[113] Thus successful advertising toward African Americans does not simply mean using black models. The key is the way the message and the themes are portrayed. In an ad campaign for Calvin Klein underwear, for example, white rap singer Marky Mark appealed to blacks because he stood for "youth and anger."[114] However, black urban teens have been particularly difficult to target because they are very skeptical of advertising and have few role models they trust.[115]

Marketers must also be cautious of the effect that black models have on their target consumers. One study found that Anglo consumers had less favorable attitudes and were less likely to purchase the product when ads featured black rather than Anglo actors.[116] This problem is pronounced when consumers are prejudiced toward minorities. On an encouraging note, research suggests that younger Anglo consumers are more accepting of minority actors, which may reduce the problem over time.[117] Finally, there are some controversial ethical issues related to marketing toward blacks, such as unfair messages and discrimination, which we discuss in Chapter 20.

Promotions.   African American consumers respond positively to a variety of sales promotions, including in-store sampling, cents-off coupons, and buy-one-get-one-free offers.[118] Major League Baseball was concerned that blacks account for only 5 percent of ticket sales and have negative perceptions about the league. In response, the teams sponsored special events, including inner-city baseball leagues, and special promotions, such as free tickets, to appeal to black fans.[119] Quaker Oats hired an African American–owned company to develop promotions targeting African American consumers, especially in inner-city stores that have been largely ignored by competitors.[120] For one promotion Quaker distributed product samples to consumers in more than 7,000 black churches.

Distribution.   Marketers can also adjust distribution strategies to appeal to African American consumers. KFC dressed employees in traditional African garb with kente ties and vests and kufu hats in outlets located in primarily black neighborhoods. Music with up-tempo rhythms was played over the sound system.[121] In Atlanta a shopping mall in a predominantly black neighborhood restyled itself as an "Afrocentric retail center."[122] In areas where blacks represent more than 20 percent of the population, J.C. Penney has developed "Authentic African Boutiques" that offer clothing, handbags, hats, and other accessories imported from Africa.

Finally, because most black consumers do not have a strong store preference, a number of retailers have hired ethnic specialists to develop special merchandise offerings and advertising.[123] As one example, Kmart hired a minority-owned advertising agency to develop its targeted ads. ■

Asian Americans

Asian Americans are the third-largest and fastest-growing minority in the United States. The number of Asian Americans has doubled in the last decade and should reach about 6.6 million by the year 2025—a growth rate much higher than the national growth rate.[124] The largest concentration is in California, especially San Francisco and Los Angeles, and in Hawaii, where more than 65 percent of the population is of Asian decent. Growth has also been high in other areas, such as New Hampshire, where the growth rate was more than 200 percent in the late 1990s.

Characteristics   The Asian American community is even more diverse than the Hispanic American and African American groups because it consists of people from more than 29 countries, from the Indian subcontinent to the Pacific Ocean, each with its own set of principles and customs. The six largest groups include immigrants from the Philippines, China, Japan, Korea, Vietnam, and India.[125] In light of this tremendous diversity, it is risky to rely too much on broad statements about Asian Americans as a whole. Nevertheless, we can make a few generalizations.

Many Asian Americans are young, live much of their lives in multiple-wage-earner households—and thus have greater discretionary income—and are about to enter their prime earning years.[126] More than 34 percent of Asian Americans live in households with incomes greater than $75,000 per year, giving them the highest socioeconomic status of any ethnic minority. They also save money a good deal. These consumers tend to be highly educated, have higher computer literacy, and hold a higher percentage of professional and managerial jobs than the general population. More than half live in integrated suburbs as opposed to ethnic areas such as a Chinatown, and most tend to be highly assimilated by the second and third generations.

One common denominator of most Asian cultures is the strong emphasis they place on the family, tradition, and cooperation.[127] The group is often more important than the individual. Unmarried children, especially in Chinese American families, are expected to live with their parents. Furthermore, traditional customs and language are often stressed, even though Asian American children are generally highly assimilated into the mainstream culture.[128] A very strong work ethic characterizes Confucian subgroups, such as Koreans and Chinese.

Consumption Patterns   Although Asian Americans are quite diverse, they exhibit several similar consumption patterns. For example, Asian Americans like to shop for fun.[129] They want quality and are willing to pay for it, even though they will still react positively to a good bargain. They are often strongly loyal to high-quality established brands and will frequently recommend products and services to friends and relatives.[130] Thus word-of-mouth communication is very important.

Many consumers, especially the Chinese, have a strong desire to get the "eight bigs": a color TV, refrigerator, car, camera, VCR, furniture, telephone, and washing machine.[131] Asian Americans are also more likely than other groups to invest in real estate and jewelry. Relationships are extremely important to Asian Americans. Thus companies must show long-term concern and respect for consumers. Furthermore, Asian Americans prefer to deal with family-owned businesses and with companies that have strong reputations for good service.

MARKETING IMPLICATIONS   Because Asian Americans are a rapidly growing group with considerable economic power—spending about $38 billion a year—this ethnic subculture has important marketing implications.

Product Development.   Marketers are increasingly offering products designed with Asian Americans in mind.[132] Cosmetic shades have been developed to blend better with Asian skin colors, and marketers have been actively involved in teaching consumers proper application techniques. The Pleasant Company has also developed dolls for the Asian American market. One company mistakenly offered golf balls in a four-pack instead of the usual three-pack. Four is an unlucky number because the word *four* sounds similar to the word for death in both Japanese and Chinese.

Media Targeting.   For many years ads were not targeted toward Asian Americans because the group was believed to be too small. However, marketers are now increasingly trying to reach these consumers. For example, TV advertising for the Chinese New Year's parade in both San Francisco and Los Angeles is usually completely sold out by the previous October. Buyers have included McDonald's, Mazda, Bank of America, and AT&T.[133]

One way of reaching this very diverse group is through native-language newspapers. Several banks have used such newspapers to communicate with Chinese Americans.[134] The Asian Yellow Pages is also useful, as evidenced by the 5,500-plus Asian businesses in California that advertise in it. A magazine called *Niko* appeals to affluent and educated Asian American women. Unfortunately, other media may be less promising, since Asian Americans are less likely to watch television, and there are few native-language stations on either radio or TV.[135] The situation may change, however, as this group becomes larger and more economically powerful.

Advertising Messages. The diversity of languages and customs has inhibited advertising to the Asian market. However, some commonalties can be stressed. Asian Americans have been found to respond well to subtle messages that focus on tradition, the family, and cooperation.[136] MCI has been successful by stressing ties to the home. Ads should also present product benefits in a straightforward manner. However, a study found that Asian models tend to be overrepresented in business settings and underrepresented in home and family settings.[137] Emotional messages are generally unacceptable because Asian Americans do not approve of displaying emotions in public.

Asian models may be overrepresented in ads in comparison to their proportion in the population; however, they most typically appear in background roles.[138] Nevertheless, "ethnically correct" endorsers have been well received. Popular spokespeople (liked among Anglos as well) include Olympic figure skater Michelle Kwan and tennis player Michael Chang. The use of Asian models communicates that they are valued customers, which in turn, may enhance consumers' brand loyalty.[139]

Messages can be more effective if they are delivered in the native language, although the diversity of languages used by Asian Americans makes this practice a challenge. Nevertheless, when large segments of consumers are concentrated in an area, the effort can be worthwhile. MCI has attracted Asian consumers by setting up Chinese- and Korean-language operator assistance and 800 numbers.[140] However, simply translating an English message does not always work. Thus many companies now hire ethnic advertising agencies to facilitate the process.[141]

Promotions. Evidence suggests that Asian American consumers will respond positively to a variety of promotions, such as pricing deals, coupons, and sponsorship of events. Remy Martin sponsored a Moon Festival Banquet celebrating an important Chinese holiday for influential leaders of the Chinese community in New York.[142] Sampling might also prove to be a useful technique, especially if it demonstrates the quality of the product.

Distribution. Finally, channels of distribution can be designed to appeal to Asian Americans. The United Savings Bank in San Francisco decorates its branches in popular colors of red and gold.[143] Peterson Bank in Chicago has a special department whose employees speak Korean, and all written materials are available in both English and Korean. A mall near Vancouver (whose customers are 80 percent Chinese Canadians) offers fashions from Hong Kong, a Chinese-language movie theater, a shop with traditional Chinese medicines, and events such as kung fu demonstrations and folk dances.[144] ■

Multicultural Marketing

multicultural marketing
Strategies used to appeal to a variety of cultures at the same time.

Ethnic marketing does not necessarily mean complete segmentation. **Multicultural marketing**, in which strategies appeal to a variety of cultures at the same time, is becoming increasingly popular. This strategy requires both a long-term commitment and consideration of ethnic groups from the outset, rather than as an afterthought.[145]

EXHIBIT 13.12
Multicultural Ad

This ad is a good example of multicultural advertising. Most of the major U.S. ethnic groups are represented in it.

Source: Photographs copyright Dana Gluckstein.

For example, a Schick TV ad showed a variety of different faces, including Asians, Caucasians, African Americans, and Hispanics, dissolving into one another in front of a shaving mirror, thereby recognizing that the "typical" American is multicultural. Another example of multicultural marketing is the Toyota ad in Exhibit 13.12. Pepsi has eliminated its ethnic marketing department altogether with the goal of developing "one image which is powerful for everybody."[146] Finally, Ford created a multicultural ad in Europe but created a stir when African and Indian models had their faces superimposed or replaced with white models for the Eastern European market, where consumers felt such diversity didn't make sense.[147]

Ethnic Groups Around the World

Although few countries are as diverse as the United States, ethnic subcultures do exist in many other nations. It is beyond the scope of this book to discuss each of the numerous ethnic groups from around the world, but a few examples should illustrate their importance.

In Canada the French-speaking subculture has unique motivations and buying habits.[148] French Canadians tend to be lower in income, social class, education, and occupation than the rest of the country; they also have more children and greater family stability. Compared with the rest of the Canadian population, French Canadians use more staples for original or "scratch" cooking; drink more soft drinks, beer, wine, and instant beverages; and consume fewer frozen vegetables, diet drinks, and hard liquor. They also tend to value furniture less than their neighbors. Patriotism and ethnic pride are extremely strong, and this theme has been successfully incorporated into marketing strategies by companies such as Kodak, Inter-Canadian Airlines, McDonald's, and KFC.[149]

The former Soviet Union was also an ethnically diverse country, with more than 100 different ethnic groups speaking more than 50 different languages. The collapse of this large nation permitted many smaller countries with a strong ethnic core to emerge. Examples include the Baltic countries (Lithuania, Estonia, and Latvia), Belorussia, and Ukraine, as well as the larger Russia. In some areas of the world, however, ethnic mixing has been so great that tremendous conflict has arisen. This situation is certainly the case in Bosnia and Kosovo (part of the former Yugoslavia), where the tragic fighting between Serbs and Muslims has captured the world's attention.

In Thailand more than 80 percent of the population is of Thai origin, but several sizable ethnic subcultures are flourishing. The largest, 10 percent of the population, has Chinese roots, and this segment has influenced the Thai culture to a significant degree.[150] Foremost, the Chinese in Thailand exert a powerful economic force because they own many businesses. Their influence is also felt in art, religion, and food. This ethnic group has assimilated very well into the main Thai society, and intermarrying is common. As a result, many in this group consider themselves Thai. Other smaller ethnic groups in Thailand include people of Laotian, Indian, and Burmese origin.

Finally, India has a diverse ethnic population. More than 80 languages and 120 dialects are spoken. Some villagers need only travel 30 miles from home to reach a destination where they are not able to speak the language.

RELIGIOUS INFLUENCES

A final type of subculture is based on religious beliefs. Religion provides individuals with a structured set of beliefs and values that serve as a code of conduct or guide to behavior. It also provides ties that bind people together and make one group different from another. For example, a defining element of Protestantism is the belief that hard work will lead to social mobility. This principle has permeated U.S. culture because most of the original English colonists were Protestant. By stressing strict adherence to its rules and dogmas, the Catholic Church exerts a strong influence on its members and may discourage individualism and innovative thinking. Judaism, on the other hand, stresses individuality and self-education, which can lead to a higher level of innovation, need for achievement, anxiety, and emotionality.[151] Finally, the new religious right of born-again Christians who tend to follow televangelists is "anti-elite, anti-intellectual, anti-big government, [and] socially nostalgic and believes in material blessings for those who love the Lord and live right."[152]

Religious influences can sometimes affect consumer behavior. One study found that Jewish consumers were more likely than non-Jews to be exposed in childhood to information from print media, group memberships, and special training; to seek information from TV, magazines, and other media; to adopt new products; to provide information to others; and to remember more information.[153] A study of weekend leisure activities found that price was the most important factor for Protestants, whereas companionship was more critical for Jews. Catholics were more likely to prefer dancing and much less likely to desire sex as an activity than the other groups.[154] Born-again Christians, on the other hand, are less likely to buy on credit, purchase national brands, or attend rock concerts and movies.[155]

Religion can also prevent consumers from consuming certain products and services. Mormons are prohibited from consuming liquor, tobacco, and caffeine, including cola. Orthodox Jews do not eat pork or seafood, and all meat and poultry must be certified as kosher. Catholic consumers may choose to abstain from eating meat on Fridays during the season of Lent.

Obviously, religious subcultures exist in many parts of the world. In India, for example, most of the population is Hindu, but large groups of Muslims, Christians, and Sikhs exhibit different patterns of consumption. Because Hindus are predominantly vegetarian, Indian manufacturers of food and cosmetics must use vegetable and not animal-based oils and shortening in their products. The Sikh religion forbids the consumption of beef and tobacco, and the sale of such products is low in areas where many Sikhs live. Finally, the color green has significance for Muslims, which has led to its frequent use on product packages that are marketed to this group.

MARKETING IMPLICATIONS Marketers can segment the market by focusing on religious affiliation, delivering targeted messages and promotions, or using certain media. Members of the religious right can be targeted through the Christian Television Network, religious radio stations, and various network religious programs, which have a total audience of more than 15 million. In fact, more than 20 religious cable networks are now engaged in a battle for viewers,[156] and a theme park called Heritage Village, USA is designed as a "blend of religion, broadcasting, shopping, recreation, entertainment, and celebrity."[157] It is third only to Walt Disney World and Disneyland in attendance. Numerous religious magazines can target specific groups effectively. Some Protestant congregations even make money by offering parishioners special tours or excursions.[158]

For years local churches and synagogues have advertised in newspapers to welcome new members and announce services. Now, however, some religions are becoming more active in their marketing activities.[159] The Lutheran Hour Ministries spends $20 million a year on print, TV, and radio campaigns, stressing family themes as opposed to specific religious messages, as well as a toll-free number that offers a free audiocassette on religious values. The Catholic Communication Campaign also advertises heavily, using soft-sell themes such as the power of prayer and antiprejudice. In recent years religious ads have moved away from dry, head-and-shoulders shots of preachers to become well-produced messages with slick soundtracks.[160] To attract young people, Protestant and Catholic churches have been offering Taize, which is a user-friendly type of worship that's "a little bit like disco."[161]

Finally, marketers sometimes use religious themes to sell products. A common example is special products or packages produced during times of religious holidays. To appeal to a broad array of consumers and not alienate certain groups, however, these efforts tend not to use images with overt religious meaning. Snowmen, Santa Claus, and Christmas trees replace religious figures at Christmas time.[162] As a public service the Outdoor Advertising Association ran a series of billboards that were all signed by "God." Sample messages included that "Love Thy Neighbor," "You think it's hot here?" and "Don't make me come down there." ■

SUMMARY

Three major aspects of culture have important effects on consumer behavior: regional, ethnic, and religious differences. First, consumption patterns may differ in various regions of the United States and the world, and marketing strategy can sometimes be tailored specifically to these regions.

Second, the United States has a number of different ethnic groups, and population trends will dramatically alter the demographic profile of the country in the next 50 years. The diverse Hispanic population has a distinct identity and language, strong family and religious orientation, solid work ethic, and youthfulness. These broad characteristics can influence consumption by leading to brand loyalty and the desire for prestige products, and they have important implications for product development, advertising, media targeting, promotions, and distribution.

The African American population is urban, young, social, and religious. Black consumers value prestigious brands and are smart investigative shoppers. The very diverse Asian American subculture is also young, has high socioeconomic status, places a strong value on the family and the group, and is strongly brand loyal. In spite of its diversity, this group can be reached with specific marketing strategies.

Many marketers are now becoming multicultural in their marketing activities by trying to appeal to all subcultures instead of just the majority one. Many important ethnic groups exist in other areas of the world. Finally, religious values and customs can influence consumer behavior.

EXERCISES

1. You have been assigned to develop a marketing strategy for a new fruit drink that provides high energy and is high in nutrients. It is also light and very refreshing, especially on a hot day. How would you market this product in different regions of the world? Develop a detailed marketing plan for two regions that addresses the advertising message, media selection, distribution, and sales promotion.

2. You have been assigned to develop a marketing strategy for a fashion clothing store chain that wants to specialize in providing products for minorities in your area. The stores plan to sell medium- to high-priced clothing for Hispanic, African American, and Asian American women. Develop a questionnaire to collect information about acquisition and consumption patterns among your potential customers. Be sure to ask questions that will provide insight into your decisions about (a) store design, (b) products offered, (3) pricing, and (4) advertising. Administer this questionnaire to at least ten members of one of the three ethnic groups. Summarize the key findings of your research and make a recommendation in each of the areas mentioned.

3. Pick three product/service categories that you think will show consumption differences across different religious subcultures. Design a questionnaire to assess major consumption patterns for each of these products/services and administer it to at least five consumers in each of the major subcultures. Summarize the responses and answer the following questions:

   a. How do these cultures vary in terms of consumption?

   b. How would marketing efforts differ for the groups?

CHAPTER 14

SOCIAL CLASS INFLUENCES ON CONSUMER BEHAVIOR

INTRODUCTION

 In the early 1990s an economic boom, coupled with more liberal government policies, enabled some individuals in China to acquire great wealth.[1] These "new rich" became big spenders and flaunted their wealth by enrolling their children in private schools and buying expensive items such as cars, TVs, and VCRs. Initially, many other Chinese people admired these affluent consumers because they had bucked the system. But when people learned that their neighbors' newfound prosperity had come at the expense of many others whose standard of living had greatly decreased, making them the "new poor," the status of the new rich changed. They are now looked upon with resentment and are often accused of acquiring their wealth illegally. They have reacted by becoming very careful not to be conspicuous or learning not to draw attention to themselves. As a result, over 20 percent of China's nightclubs have closed as expense accounts have dried up, and the rich have become more philanthropic. Lavish spending still occurs, but it is now more private. As evidence, China is the largest market in the world for expensive cognac, at $186 million a year.

This example illustrates how social class can influence acquisition, consumption, and disposition (see Exhibit 14.1). The concept of social class implies that some people have more power, wealth, and opportunity than others do. Some consumers show off their wealth or possessions by engaging in conspicuous consumption, and certain products and services, such as cars and cognac, can serve as status symbols. Finally, this example illustrates how some members of society can raise their social standing, a process called *upward mobility*, whereas others may fall to lower levels through *downward mobility*.

This chapter begins by examining the nature of social class (including its purpose), types of class systems and influences, and ways that social class is measured. Then we discuss some important trends that are influencing and changing social class systems and explain how consumption patterns can vary with social classes. Finally, the chapter examines the marketing implications of social class.

SOCIAL CLASS

social class hierarchy
The grouping of members of society according to status (high to low).

Most societies have a **social class hierarchy** that confers higher status to some classes of people than to others. These social classes consist of identifiable groups of individuals whose behaviors and lifestyles differ from those of members of the other classes. Members of a particular social class tend to share similar values and behavior patterns. Note that social classes are not formal groups with a strong identity, but rather loose collections of individuals with similar life experiences.[2]

Many societies view social class distinctions as important to their existence because they recognize that everyone has a necessary role to play for society to function smoothly. However, some of these roles, such as medical doctor or executive, are more prestigious and more valued than others, such as toll taker or janitor. Nevertheless, the concept of social class is not inherently negative. Even though inequalities are present, social class distinctions can help individuals determine what their role in society is or what they would like it to be (their aspirations). Furthermore, all levels of the social class hierarchy make an important contribution to society.

Types of Social Class Systems

Most societies have three major classes: high, middle, and lower. Often, however, finer distinctions are made. The United States, for example, is typically divided into the six or seven levels presented in Exhibit 14.2 on page 333.[3] Note that the largest number of individuals are concentrated in the middle classes (65 to 70 percent of the population). Thailand has five social classes: (1) an aristocracy (descendants of royalty), (2) an elite (composed of top professionals and political leaders), (3) an upper-middle class (merchants, small businesspeople, and white-collar workers), (4) the lower-middle class (craftspeople and skilled laborers), and (5) the lower class (unskilled laborers and peasants).

Although most societies have some kind of hierarchical structure, the size and composition of the classes depend on the relative prosperity of a particular country (see Exhibit 14.3 on page 334).[4] For example, compared with the United States, Japan and Scandinavia have an even larger and more predominant middle class with much smaller groups above and below. In other words, greater equality exists among people in the two countries than in other societies. The Japanese structure represents a concerted government effort to abolish the social class system and mix people together from all levels of society.[5] Despite this effort, the highly competitive and selective Japanese educational system still restricts entry

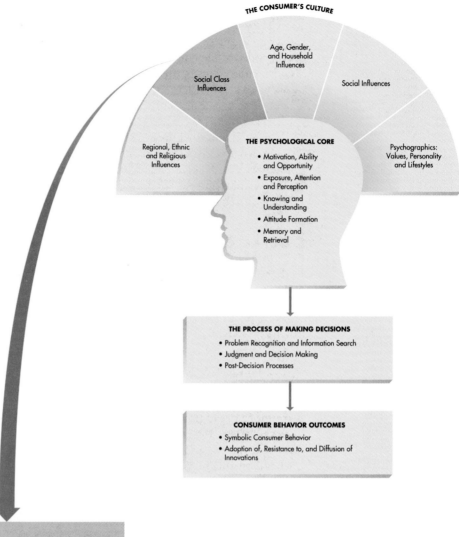

EXHIBIT 14.1

Chapter Overview:
Social Class

Social class is another factor that can influence consumer behavior. This chapter examines what *determines* one's social class (e.g., occupation, education, income), the characteristics of major social classes, and certain social class patterns or *trends* (upward and downward mobility and fragmentation). Finally, it discusses how social class affects specific *outcomes,* such as conspicuous consumption, status symbols, compensatory consumption, and the meaning of money.

THE CONSUMER'S CULTURE

Age, Gender, and Household Influences

Social Class Influences

Social Influences

Regional, Ethnic and Religious Influences

THE PSYCHOLOGICAL CORE
- Motivation, Ability and Opportunity
- Exposure, Attention and Perception
- Knowing and Understanding
- Attitude Formation
- Memory and Retrieval

Psychographics: Values, Personality and Lifestyles

THE PROCESS OF MAKING DECISIONS
- Problem Recognition and Information Search
- Judgment and Decision Making
- Post-Decision Processes

CONSUMER BEHAVIOR OUTCOMES
- Symbolic Consumer Behavior
- Adoption of, Resistance to, and Diffusion of Innovations

SOCIAL CLASS INFLUENCES

- Determinants of social class
- Social class and consumption
- Consumption patterns of different classes
- Social class trends

EXHIBIT 14.2
U.S. Social Classes

Researchers have classified the U.S. social classes in a variety of ways. This exhibit shows a typical classification scheme. Note that the majority of consumers would be considered Middle Americans (70 percent) and that very few are in the top two classes (1.5 percent).

UPPER AMERICANS	*Upper-upper (0.3%):*	The "capital S society" world of inherited wealth, aristocratic names
	Lower-upper (1.2%):	The newer social elite, drawn from current professional, corporate leadership
	Upper-middle (12.5%):	The rest of college graduate managers and professionals; lifestyle centers on private clubs, causes, and the arts
MIDDLE AMERICANS	*Middle class (32%):*	Average pay white-collar workers and their blue-collar friends: live on the "the better side of town," try to "do the proper things"
	Working class (38%):	Average pay blue-collar workers; lead "working class lifestyle" whatever the income, school background, and job
LOWER AMERICANS	*"A lower group of people but not the lowest" (9%):*	Working, not on welfare; living standard is just above poverty; behavior judged "crude," "trashy"
	"Real lower-lower" (7%):	On welfare, visibly poverty stricken, usually out of work (or have the "dirtiest jobs")

Source: Richard P. Coleman, "The Continuing Significance of Social Class to Marketing," *Journal of Consumer Research,* December 1983, p. 267. © 1983 University of Chicago. All rights reserved.

to higher status positions in the executive and prestigious government ranks. In developing areas such as Latin America and India, on the other hand, the largest concentrations are in the lower classes. Most Latin households are truly poor, whereas India displays a more varied lower-middle class of more than 200 million people.

In former communist countries that stressed equality and sameness, the status hierarchy has changed rapidly. Many citizens now have the opportunity to increase their status, which serves as a strong motivation to "get ahead."[6] At the same time, this sudden social climbing can be quite frightening because it brings with it a feeling of venturing into the unknown.

Interestingly, the upper classes in most societies are more similar to each other than they are to other classes within their own countries because the upper classes tend to be more cosmopolitan and international in orientation.[7] The lower classes, on the other hand, are the most likely to be culture bound—unaware of other cultures and therefore little influenced by them. As a result, they tend to be the most different from the other classes in terms of lifestyles, dress, and eating behaviors.

The middle classes are most likely to borrow from other cultures because this practice may represent a means of achieving upward social mobility. Behaving "Western," for example, may serve as a way of achieving status in a Third World country.

Even though the members of a particular class may share similar values, considerable variation exists in the way people maintain these values. For example, the middle class in the United States can be represented by a lower-level manager with a nonworking spouse, a working couple in which both partners have office jobs, an unmarried salesperson, a divorced parent with a college degree supporting two children, or the owner of a bowling alley. All these individuals might strive for a better life—an important middle-class value—but might take different paths to get there.

EXHIBIT 14.3
Class Structure by Culture

The relative sizes and structure of social classes vary by culture. Japan and Scandinavia, for example, are characterized by a large middle class with few people above or below. India and Latin America, on the other hand, have a greater proportion of individuals in the lower classes. The United States by comparison has a large middle class, but also has significant proportions in the upper and lower classes.

Source: Adapted from Edward W. Cundiff and Marye T. Hilger, *Marketing in the International Environment* (Englewoods Cliffs, N.J.: Prentice-Hall, 1988) and Marieke K. de Mooij and Warren Keegan, *Advertising Worldwide* (Englewood Cliffs, N.J.: Prentice-Hall, 1991), p. 96.

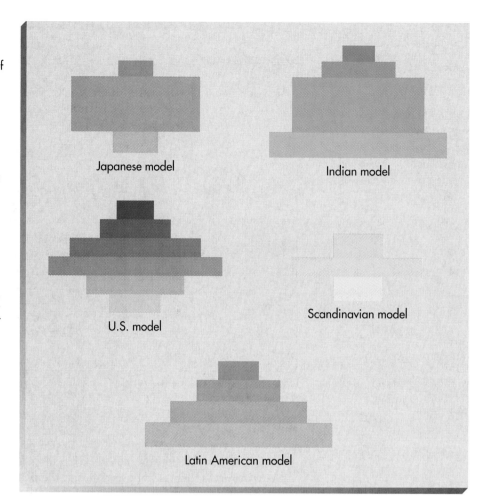

Japanese model

Indian model

U.S. model

Scandinavian model

Latin American model

overprivileged Families with an income higher than the average in their class.

class average Families with an average income in a particular class.

underprivileged Families below the average income in their class.

Finally, different economic substrata can coexist within a particular social class. Specifically, families whose income level is 20 to 30 percent over the median of their class are considered **overprivileged** because they have funds to buy items beyond the basic necessities.[8] **Class average** families are those whose income level is average for their social class. They can therefore afford the type of symbols expected for their status for items such as a house, a car, and clothing. The **underprivileged** have incomes below the median. They have trouble meeting class expectations.

Social Class Influences

Social class structures are important because they strongly affect norms and values and, therefore, behavior. Social class affects behavior because members of a social class interact regularly with each other, both formally and informally. Thus people are more likely to be influenced by individuals in their own social class than by those in other classes. Note that social class influence is not a cultural straitjacket; it merely reflects the fact that people with similar life experiences are likely to exhibit similar lifestyles and behaviors.[9]

It is also possible for the norms and behaviors of consumers in one class to influence consumers in other social classes. A traditional and commonly cited

trickle-down effect Trends that start in the upper classes and then are copied by lower classes.

status float Trends that start in the lower and middle classes and move upward.

theory of class influence is the **trickle-down effect**, whereby lower classes copy trends that begin in the upper classes. A common example is fashion and clothing. Styles that are introduced in the upper class often become popular with other groups. The trickle-down effect occurs because those in lower classes may aspire to raise their social standing by emulating the higher classes. They also accept upper-class influence if they lack the cultural knowledge to make their own judgments of what is and is not acceptable.[10] For example, the middle class often looks to the upper class for guidance on what is "cultural" in music, art, and literature.

More recently, however, the universal validity of the trickle-down theory has been questioned. In some instances, a **status float** can occur, whereby trends start in the lower and middle classes and then spread upward. An excellent example of status float is blue jeans. In the United States this product first gained widespread popularity in the 1950s and 1960s among lower- and middle-class youths, particularly because it symbolized rebellion against the establishment.[11] Eventually this message gained popularity among upper-class youths who wanted to revolt against their rigid parents. In the 1970s and 1980s jeans evolved into a fashion item with the introduction of designer labels such as Vanderbilt, Calvin Klein, and Oscar de la Renta. The phenomenon has spread to other countries as well, where even royalty have been seen wearing jeans. Other fashion statements of the 1990s, such as floppy shorts, a backwards hat, earrings, and tattoos, began in the lower classes and moved into the upper classes. Similarly, some musical styles, particularly blues, rock, and rap music, originated in the lower classes.

How Social Class Is Determined

A key issue in studying social class is determining what social class someone is in. Examining how social class affects consumer behavior requires a way of classifying consumers into different social classes. Unfortunately, this task has not been a very simple, and the exact determinants of social class have been the subject of considerable debate over the years.

Income Versus Social Class   Many people believe that the more money you have, the higher your social standing is. You may be surprised to learn, however, that income is not strongly related to social class for several reasons.[12] First, income levels often overlap social classes, particularly at the middle and lower levels. For example, many U.S. blue-collar workers have higher incomes than some white-collar workers, yet do not have higher social standing. Second, income increases greatly with age, but older workers do not automatically achieve higher social status. Finally, in many countries an increasing number of dual-career families generate a higher than average income but not necessarily higher status. Thus, although income is one factor related to social class, other factors must be examined to obtain an accurate picture.

Some researchers have argued that income can actually be a better predictor of consumer behavior than social class. However, a more common view is that both factors are important in explaining behavior in different situations.[13] Social class tends to be a better predictor of consumption when it reflects lifestyles and values and does not involve high monetary expenditures, such as for clothes, sports equipment, or furniture. For example, middle-class and lower-class consumers favor different styles of furniture, and middle-class consumers tend to spend more money on furnishing their homes even when income levels are roughly similar. Income, on the other hand, is more useful in explaining the consumption of products and services that are not related to class symbols, such boats or recreational vehicles, but that do involve substantial expenditures. *Both* factors are needed to explain behaviors that involve status symbols and at least a moderate expenditure such as buying a house or car.

Although income cannot explain social class, social class can often explain how income is used. As one illustration, upper-class consumers are more likely to invest money, whereas the lower classes are more likely to rely on savings accounts in banks. The key points, however, are that social class aids in the understanding of consumer behavior and that social standing is determined by a variety of factors in addition to income.

Occupation and Education   The greatest determinant of class standing is occupation, particularly in Western cultures. Specifically, some occupations, especially those that require higher levels of education, skill, or training, are viewed as higher in status than others. Furthermore, individuals with the same occupation tend to share similar income, lifestyles, knowledge, and values.

From a research standpoint, occupation is easily measured simply by asking consumers what they do for a living. This response can then be coded and compared with published scales of occupational prestige, such as the widely used socioeconomic index (SEI) or the Nam and Powers scale.[14] Exhibit 14.4 shows rankings from the SEI for a sample of occupations.

Note that the perceived status of an occupation may vary from culture to culture. Compared with the United States, for example, professors have higher status in Germany, Japan, China, Thailand, and Nigeria because of an even stronger emphasis on education in those countries. Engineers typically have higher status in

EXHIBIT 14.4
Status Levels of Various Occupations

A variety of indices have been developed to classify different occupations in terms of their status level. This exhibit presents the status scores of a sample of occupations, using one of these indexes. What major factors do you think cause some occupations to be high in status and others to be low?

Source: Gillian Stevens and Joo Hyun Cho, "Socioeconomic Indexes and the New 1980 Census Occupational Classification Scheme," *Social Science Research,* 14, pp. 142–168. Copyright © 1985 by Academic Press, reproduced by permission of the publisher.

OCCUPATION	SCORE	OCCUPATION	SCORE
Physician	88	Mechanic	31
Lawyer	88	Photographer	30
Marketing professor	83	Bank teller	29
Psychologist	82	Hotel receptionist	29
Architect	80	Mail carrier	27
Civil engineer	77	Plumber	27
High school teacher	75	Shoe salesperson	25
Computer scientist	73	Bartender	24
Airplane pilot	68	Farmer	24
Accountant	65	Carpenter	22
Marketing manager	58	Truck driver	21
Actor	52	Hairdresser	19
Athlete	49	Waiter/waitress	19
Sales representative	48	Machine operator	19
Musician	46	Baker	19
Office supervisor	37	Janitor	18
Police detective	38	Crossing guard	17
Secretary	35	Farmworker	17
Firefighter	33	Maid	16

developing countries than they do in developed countries because of the important role engineering plays in integrating industry and technology into society. Finally, the legal profession enjoys much higher prestige in the United States than it does elsewhere in the world.

Education is also critical because it is one of the key determinants of occupation and therefore social class. In fact, educational attainment is considered the most reliable determinant of consumers' income potential and spending patterns.[15] In particular, a college degree is a crucial factor in gaining entry into higher status occupations. Slightly more than 66 percent of people with bachelor or advanced degrees are in managerial or professional occupations, compared with 22 percent who have only some college education. This gap will only widen as the need for highly skilled and technical training increases in the information age. In addition, marketers know that consumers who are more highly educated tend to read and travel more and to be less averse to trying new things when compared with rest of the population.

Other Indicators of Social Class   Other factors such as area of residence, possessions, family background, and social interactions can also indicate class level. The neighborhood in which we live and the amount and types of possessions we have are visible signs that often communicate class standing. In terms of family background, researchers have made a distinction between **inherited status**, which is adopted from parents at birth, and **earned status**, which is acquired later in life from personal achievements.[16] Inherited status is critical because it serves as the initial anchor point from which values are learned and from which upward or downward mobility can occur. Finally, as mentioned previously, members of a social class often interact with each other, and the company we keep also helps to identify social standing.

The relative importance of these determinants of social class varies from country to country. In former communist countries such as Romania, for example, money and possessions are now the strongest determinants of social standing, as opposed to the former criteria of position in the Communist party.[17] In the Arab world, status is determined primarily by social contacts and family position, both of which are considered far more important than money.[18]

Social Class Indexes   All the factors we've mentioned must be taken into account to determine social class standing, and sociologists have developed a number of indexes to accomplish this task. Over the years the two most widely used tools have been the *Index of Status Characteristics* and the *Index of Social Position*.[19] However, these instruments were developed in the 1940s and 1950s and have recently been criticized as out-of-date. First, the measurement of key variables such as education, occupation, and neighborhood type are based on a society that no longer exists.[20] Second, these indexes fail to account accurately for dual-career households, which generate higher income but not higher status than single-earner households do. Third, the early indexes were based on extensive interviews within a community (called the *reputational method*). These indexes are now difficult to implement because people simply do not know their neighbors as well as they used to.

In light of these problems, more current indexes such as the **Computerized Status Index (CSI)** have been recommended (see Exhibit 14.5). This index assesses consumers' education, occupation, area of residence, and income. In contrast to the reputational method that relies on informants, the CSI is easy for interviewers to administrator and for consumers to answer.

inherited status   Status that derives from parents at birth.

earned status   Status acquired later in life through achievements.

Computerized Status Index (CSI)   A modern index used to determine social class through education, occupation, residence, and income.

Interviewer circles code numbers (for the computer) which in his/her judgment best fit the respondent and family. Interviewer asks for detail on occupation, then makes rating. Interviewer often asks the respondent to describe neighborhood in own words. Interviewer asks respondent to specify income — a card is presented the respondent showing the eight brackets — and records R's response. If interviewer feels this is overstatement or under, a "better-judgment" estimate should be given, along with explanation.

EDUCATION:	Respondent	Respondent's spouse
Grammar school (8 yrs or less)	−1	−1
Some high school (9-11 yrs)	−2 R's age: ___	−2 Spouse's age: ___
Graduated high school (12 yrs)	−3	−3
Some post high school (business, nursing, technical, 1 yr college)	−4	−4
Two, three years of college — possibly Associate of Arts degree	−5	−5
Graduated four-year college (B.A./B.S.)	−7	−7
Master's or five-year professional degree	−8	−8
Ph.D. or six/seven-year professional degree	−9	−9

OCCUPATION PRESTIGE LEVEL OF HOUSEHOLD HEAD:
Interviewer's judgment of how head-of-household rates in occupational status.

(Respondent's description — ask for previous occupation if retired, or if R is widow, ask husband's: _____)

Chronically unemployed — "day" laborers, unskilled; on welfare	−0
Steadily employed but in marginal semi-skilled jobs; custodians, minimum-pay factory help, service workers (gas attendants, etc.)	−1
Average-skill assembly-line workers, bus and truck drivers, police and firefighters, route deliverymen, carpenters, brick masons	−2
Skilled craftsmen (electricians), small contractors, factory foremen, low-pay salesclerks, office workers, postal employees	−3
Owners of very small firms (2-4 employees), technicians, salespeople, office workers, civil servants with average level salaries	−4
Middle management, teachers, social workers, lesser professionals	−5
Lesser corporate officials, owners of middle-sized businesses (10-20 employees), moderate-success professionals (dentists, engineers, etc.)	−7
Top corporate executive, "big business" in the professional world (leading doctors and lawyers), "rich" business owners	−9

AREA OF RESIDENCE:
Interviewer's impressions of the immediate neighborhood in terms of its reputation in the eyes of the community.

Slum area: people on relief, common laborers	−1
Strictly working class: not slummy but some very poor housing	−2
Predominantly blue-collar with some office workers	−3
Predominantly white-collar with some well-paid blue-collar	−4
Better white-collar area: not many executives, but hardly any blue-collar either	−5
Excellent area: professionals and well-paid managers	−7
"Wealthy" or "society" type neighborhood	−9

TOTAL SCORE _____

TOTAL FAMILY INCOME PER YEAR:

Under $5,000	−1	$15,000 to $19,999	−4	$35,000 to $49,999	−7
$5,000 to $9,999	−2	$20,000 to $24,999	−5	$50,000 and over	−8
$10,000 to $14,999	−3	$25,000 to $34,999	−6		

Estimated Status _____

(Inteviewer's estimate: _____ and explanation: _____)

R's MARITAL STATUS: Married _____ Divorced/Separated _____ Widowed _____ Single _____ (CODE _____)

EXHIBIT 14.5
The Computerized Status Index

The CSI attempts to assess consumers' social class by measuring the various key determinants—education, occupation, area of residence, and income—and combining them to form an overall index. The higher the score, the higher the social standing.

Source: Richard P. Coleman, "The Continuing Significance of Social Class to Marketing," *Journal of Consumer Research*, December 1983, p. 277. © 1983 University of Chicago. All rights reserved.

status crystallization When consumers are consistent across indicators of social class (income, education, occupation, etc.).

When consumers are consistent across the various dimensions, social class is easy to determine and **status crystallization** has occurred. Sometimes, however, individuals are low on some determinants but high on others. Thus a new doctor from an inner-city neighborhood might be inconsistent in terms of occupation, income, neighborhood, and family background. In this situation consumers can experience stress and anxiety because they do not know exactly where they stand.[21] It is also difficult for marketers to neatly categorize such consumers into one social class or another.

HOW SOCIAL CLASS CHANGES OVER TIME

Social class structures are not necessarily static, unchanging systems. A number of trends and forces are producing an evolution in social class structures in many countries. We next examine three of these key trends: (1) upward mobility, (2) downward mobility, and (3) social class fragmentation.

Upward Mobility

upward mobility Raising one's status level.

In some cases, individuals can rise to a higher level of status. **Upward mobility** is usually achieved by educational or occupational achievement. In other words, lower- or middle-class individuals can take advantage of educational opportunities, particularly a college education, to facilitate entry into higher status occupations. In the United States, more than one-third of the children of blue-collar workers are now college graduates and have about a 30 percent chance of raising their occupational status.[22] The fact that increasing numbers of consumers have access to education has led to a burgeoning middle class and characterizes the United States as the "land of opportunity."

Excelling in a particular occupation also can lead to rewards and higher status. For example, a mechanic who starts a body shop and is successful or the talented athlete who signs a huge contract may both climb to a higher level of social standing. Statistics indicate that the percentage of business executives from lower-class backgrounds has increased dramatically in the last 40 years.

However, upward mobility is not guaranteed. The lower classes, particularly minorities, are still restricted in terms of economic and cultural resources as well as educational opportunities. They are therefore statistically less likely than the upper classes to have access to higher status occupations.[23] As evidence, individuals from higher status families are twice as likely to maintain their status as members of lower classes are to achieve a higher status. Even when upward mobility is achieved, an individual's behavior can still be heavily influenced by his or her former class level because the behaviors associated with the social class in which we grew up were strongly learned. This factor has been called the "Beverly Hillbillies" phenomenon.[24]

Note that the degree of upward mobility may vary across cultures. Typically, Western nations offer the most opportunities for upward advancement. Even in traditionally rigid class societies such as Great Britain, upward mobility has increased in recent years. However, in less developed countries, upward mobility is also increasing. In former communist countries, old party and state bureaucrats have formed the new upper classes because they have the skills and economic knowledge to thrive in the modern environment.[25] The elimination of state-owned companies created many small, privately owned firms and a growing middle class. In Arab countries the upper and middle class are growing rapidly thanks to the influx of oil money and an increase in Western college education. This change in turn has led to a growing demand for Western goods, including cars, air conditioners, and apparel.[26] Finally, the size of the middle class has been exploding in many developing countries because of increases in international trade, which makes affordable goods more available; global communications, which show consumers what they have been missing; the number of dual-career families, who have greater income; and the need for professionals like managers, accountants, and bankers to support growing economies.[27]

In other nations social class mobility can be quite restricted. In India a person's educational or occupational opportunities—and therefore social class—are primarily determined by inheritance. In Africa continuing economic problems have kept upward mobility low.

Downward Mobility

downward mobility Losing one's social standing.

Downward mobility, or moving to a lower class, is also an increasing trend in many industrialized societies. In the 1970s and 1980s, nearly one-third of the U.S. population suffered a loss in income, and in the 1990s, millions of families slid downward each year.[28] A wide range of individuals, from vice presidents to blue-collar workers, suffered from unemployment associated the cost-cutting measures of many large companies. If these jobs disappear, so does a comfortable middle-class existence. Fortunately, a strong economy in the late 1990s and early 2000s has slowed this trend.

Although inflation slowed in the 1990s, rising inflation has traditionally contributed to downward mobility. When inflation is high, money does not go as far as it once did, and this effect produces pressure to work longer and harder. It can also put pressure on both spouses to work. When both spouses are employed, the additional expense of child care adds another financial burden. These factors can create stress that can threaten the "comfortable life" for many families.[29] In addition, because of increasing material desires, an increasing number of upper-middle and middle-class families have experienced significant difficulty in maintaining a lifestyle characteristic of their status level.

status panic The inability of children to reach their parents' level of social status.

Until recently many parents dreamed of providing their children with a better life and higher status than they had. Some children may now have difficulty reaching their parents' status level. This phenomenon has been labeled **status panic**.[30] In particular, the children of very successful parents, called *savvy skidders*, often have difficulty achieving the same heights as their parents and must settle for more middle-class careers.

The problem of downward mobility is not unique to former communist countries such as East Germany, Czechoslovakia, Hungary, and Poland—the elimination of government-subsidized jobs resulted in a very high level of unemployment. Many factories were closed because their technology was obsolete, and it is cheaper to build new plants than to update old ones. At the same time, prices skyrocketed, resulting in bleak economic conditions. Thus many people now feel worse off than they did before, and workers have faced a loss of class status.

In Japan there has been both upward and downward mobility.[31] On the one hand, a small group of property owners—the *nyuu ritchi* or new rich—have experienced prosperity. A greater number—the *nyuu pua* or new poor—however, have suffered and cannot even afford to buy a home (costing the equivalent of 18 years of wages).

However it occurs, downward mobility creates disappointment and disillusionment. People in this situation face a constant struggle to provide for the family, fight off depression, and maintain a sense of honor. Sometimes acquisition and consumption can serve the purpose of protecting the person's self-worth. For example, someone might buy a new truck or other item to feel good about himself or herself.[32] Alternatively, downward mobility can lead to a loss of possessions, such as a prized car or home, or to a decrease in consumption because people spend less on items that are less important.

Social Class Fragmentation

social class fragmentation
The disappearance of class distinctions.

Interestingly, the old social class distinctions are beginning to disintegrate—a phenomenon called **social class fragmentation**. This fragmentation can be tied to several factors.[33] First, both upward and downward mobility have blurred class divisions. Second, the increased availability of mass media has exposed consumers to the values and norms of other classes and cultures to a greater degree than ever before. In the United States, for example, the TV program *Life Styles of the Rich and Famous* showed the lower classes how the richer segments of society spend their time and money. Shows like the popular *Roseanne* reflected working-class values, and rap and hip-hop music strongly communicates the values and norms of lower-class, inner-city youths to a wide audience in all classes. Thus individuals are now exposed to other classes and can incorporate the idiosyncrasies of these groups into their own behavior.

A third reason for social class fragmentation is that advances in communication technology have increased interaction across social class lines. As one example, the Internet and chat rooms allow strangers to communicate without regard to social class.

These factors have led to the appearance of many social class subsegments with their own distinct patterns of values and behavior. The United States now has dozens of classes ranging from the suburban elite (superrich families) to the hardscrabble (poor, single-parent families). Examples include upwardly mobile young influentials, God's country (former urban executive families), golden ponders (retirement-town senior citizens), downtown Dixie (African American service-worker families), and young suburbanites.[34] Similar trends are occurring in other countries as well. Exhibit 14.6 identifies some of the traditional and emerging classes in Germany.

HOW DOES SOCIAL CLASS AFFECT CONSUMPTION?

Having examined the nature of social class systems, we can now relate social class to consumer behavior. Specifically, social class is often viewed as a cause of or motivation for acquisition, consumption, and disposition. This section examines four major topics: (1) conspicuous consumption, (2) the acquisition of status symbols, (3) compensatory consumption, and (4) the meaning of money.

Conspicuous Consumption

conspicuous consumption
The acquisition and display of goods and services to show off one's status.

Formally defined, **conspicuous consumption** is the acquisition and visible display of luxury goods and services to demonstrate the consumer's ability to afford them.[35] Thus conspicuously consumed items are important to their owner because of what they tell others. The visibility of these goods and services is critical because their message can be communicated only if others can see them, as is illustrated in Exhibit 14.7 on page 343.

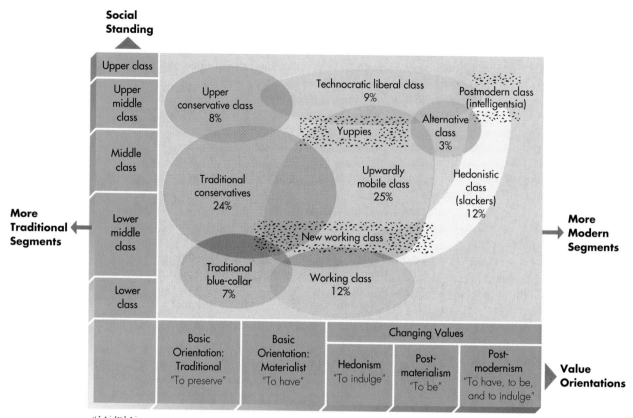

1. Konservatives gehobenes milieu = Upper conservative class
2. Technokratisch-liberales milieu = Technocratic liberal class
3. Alternatives milieu = Alternative class
4. Postmodernes milieu = Postmodern class (Intelligentsia)
5. Aufstiegsorientiertes milieu = Upwardly mobile class
6. Yuppies = Yuppies
7. Kleinbürgerliches milieu = Traditional conservatives
8. Traditionelles arbeitermilieu = Traditional blue-collar
9. Traditionsloses arbeitermilieu = Working class
10. Neue arbeiter = New working class
11. Hedonistisches milieu = Hedonistic class (slackers)

EXHIBIT 14.6
German Social Classes

A detailed depiction of social class structure in German society. The 11 groups are characterized along two dimensions: social standing (low to upper middle class) and value orientations (traditional to very modern values).

Source: Mariele De Mooij and Warren Keegan, *Advertising Worldwide,* Pearson Education (Englewood Cliffs, N.J.: Prentice-Hall, 1991), p. 116. Reprinted by permission of Pearson Education Limited.

Initially, the concept of conspicuous consumption described the behavior of the upper classes who would buy and display very expensive items to communicate their wealth and power. For example, in the 1890s William H. Vanderbilt's private railway car was designed to be more expensive than that of his rival, Leland Stanford, and his third yacht had to be bigger and better than anyone else's. Today, however, conspicuous consumption can be observed in most social classes.[36] In other words, individuals at all levels can "keep up with the Joneses"—acquiring and displaying the trappings that are characteristic of a respected member of their class. For example, a middle-class family might buy a personal

EXHIBIT 14.7
Conspicuous Consumption

Consumers may judge each other by the type of crystal they use when entertaining. This ad recognizes this fact by indicating "Some set a table. Others make a statement." The use of Waterford crystal implies style, sophistication, and affluence.

Source: Ad reprinted with the permission of Waterford Wedgwood USA, Inc.

computer to show the neighbors that the family can afford such a purchase. Or a working-class consumer might buy a new motorboat, stereo, expensive shotgun, or pickup truck to show off to his or her peers. In particular, after emerging from the slow economic times and antimaterialism in the 1970s, baby boomers (born from 1946 to 1964) are expressing a renewed desire to stuff their closets with recognizable status symbols such as designer clothing and expensive jewelry, presumably in a quest for self-gratification.[37]

In the Arab world the newly rich upper classes engage in the conspicuous consumption of items such as cars, planes, and other technologically advanced products. Even in former communist countries, consumers now show consumption competitiveness. The idea is that someone who cannot keep up with others might be the "shame of the village."[38]

conspicuous waste Visibly buying products and services that one never uses.

In addition, consumers can engage in **conspicuous waste**. For example, wealthy individuals may buy houses they never use, pianos that no one plays, and cars that no one drives.[39] The once-struggling singer Engelbert Humperdinck owns a fleet of Rolls-Royces and five mansions in the United States and Europe.

Note, however, that in today's world some consumers may be moving away from conspicuous consumption toward "experience facilators" or items that help consumers pursue pastimes that set them apart from the crowd.[40] Evidence of this trend is an increased rate of purchase for TVs, VCRs, computers, toys, and airline tickets accompanied by a lower rate of purchase for cars, furniture, and restaurant meals.

Status Symbols and Judging Others

status symbols Products or services that tell others about someone's social class standing.

Highly related to conspicuous consumption is the notion that people often judge others on the basis of what they own or possess. In other words, products or services become **status symbols** to indicate their owners place in the social hierarchy.[41] Someone who owns a Rolex watch or a Mercedes will likely be viewed as upper class. In the inner city, drinking premium liquor or wearing gold jewelry is often considered a status symbol.[42] Owning a cellular phone or taking an expensive cruise indicates status in Thailand, and the same is true of having a rock garden or a golf club membership in Japan. In Brazil, eating in fast-food restaurants such as McDonald's and Burger King is a status symbol for lower-middle-class consumers.[43] Similarly, owning a pair of Western jeans, a car, fashion clothing, an apartment, or electronic equipment is a strong indicator of status in former communist countries such as Romania.[44]

Thus consumers' quest to acquire items that reflect not only their current social class but also their class aspirations can explain some acquisitions and consumption behavior. Middle-class consumers, for example, characteristically display a strong desire to own a nice house in a respectable neighborhood so that others will judge them in a positive manner. Furthermore, by acquiring items that are considered above their social standing—that is, items that members of their own social class cannot typically afford—consumers can increase their perception of self-worth.

parody display Status symbols that start in the lower classes and move upward.

fraudulent symbols Symbols that become so widely adopted that they lose their status.

Interestingly, status symbols can sometimes move in a reverse direction, which is called a **parody display**.[45] For example, having a tattoo is now becoming more acceptable in middle and upper classes. In addition, if certain status symbols become widely possessed, they can lose their status connotations and become **fraudulent symbols**. As an example, designer jeans were an important status symbol in the 1980s but lost popularity when they became too popular.

Compensatory Consumption

compensatory consumption The comsumer behavior of buying products or services to offset frustrations or difficulties in life.

The concept of **compensatory consumption** is also related to social class. This behavior is an attempt to offset deficiencies or a lack of esteem by devoting attention to consumption.[46] In other words, a consumer who is experiencing frustration or difficulties in life, particularly in terms of career advancement or status level, can attempt to compensate for this lack of success by purchasing desired status symbols, such as a car, house, or nice clothes. These acquisitions help restore lost self-esteem.

Traditionally, compensatory consumption typified the acquisition patterns of the working classes, who would mortgage their future to obtain a house, car, furniture, and other objects that symbolize status and success. More recently, however, compensatory consumption has been observed in the middle and upper-middle classes, particularly in members of the baby boom generation in the United States. Due to its large size and more difficult economic times during the 1980s when these individuals were at important stages of their careers, many members of this generation did not enjoy the level of career advancement, gratification, and prosperity that their parents did. To offset their disappointment, baby boomers have increasingly turned toward consumption to achieve gratification.[47] Thus the hippies of the 1960s became very materialistic in the 1980s and 1990s, as evidenced by their acquisition of the "right" car, fashion clothing, health club memberships, and foreign travel.

In Japan compensatory consumption has become a major characteristic of middle-class consumers who can no longer afford to buy a home. Not having to spend money on a home gives these consumers more money to buy a variety of status items, such as mink coats, golf memberships, and shiny new foreign cars.[48] Even through recent tough economic times, sales of Tiffany diamond jewelry have shown a strong increase.

The Meaning of Money

An important concept related to social class is money. At the most basic level, economists define money as a medium of exchange or standard of payment. Under this view money fulfills a very functional or utilitarian purpose and facilitates the acquisition of items needed for everyday living. Often, however, the meaning of money goes beyond the utilitarian and comes to symbolize security, power, love, and freedom.

The meaning of money is learned very early in childhood. Parents easily discover that a powerful way of controlling their children is to develop a system of rewards and punishments based on money and buying or not buying things.[49] Children learn that if they behave, get good grades, or do their chores, their parents will buy things for them. This early learning later translates into adult life when money is viewed as a means of acquiring things that will not only bring happiness and life fulfillment but also provide a sense of status and prestige. In some societies this attitude can lead to an almost insatiable desire and quest for making money, which is enhanced by highly visible success stories of those who have "made it" and the belief that "it could happen to anyone, including me." This belief is one reason that state lotteries and get-rich-quick seminars are popular among certain classes.

Understanding money and what it stands for is very important in developing an understanding of consumption patterns. Money allows the acquisition of status objects that are indicators of social class standing. Money is also viewed as a way of rising to a higher level by enabling people to acquire more. Note also that the meaning of money does not have to involve physical cash. The greatly increased use of credit and debit cards means that many transactions do not even involve the physical transfer of cash. In fact, a number of banks are now offering "smart cards," which consumers can purchase in various denominations. These cards are electronic money and can be used to purchase almost anything, eliminating the need to carry cash.[50] Taking this a step further, shoppers can now acquire electronic wallets that allow them to easily make purchases on the Internet.[51]

Of course, consumers vary in terms of how they treat their money. Some people are more likely to spend money to acquire desired items, and others will engage in self-denial in order to save. Interestingly, one study found that spenders tend to be healthier and happier than self-deniers, who tend to have more psychosomatic illnesses and are more unhappy about finances, personal growth, friends, and jobs.[52] However, some individuals who spend more than they have end up in bankruptcy.

Money as Both Good and Evil Money can have both a good and an evil side. On the positive side money can lead to the acquisition of needed items, a higher quality of life, and the ability to help others and society in general. It also can be perceived as the just reward for hard work. On the downside the quest for money can lead to obsession, greed, dishonesty, and a number of potentially harmful practices, such as gambling, prostitution, and drug dealing, as discussed in Chapter 21. The quest for money can also lead to a variety of negative emotions, such as anxiety, depression, anger, and helplessness.[53] This outcome explains why many religions view money as an evil temptation that should be kept in check. Likewise, even though individuals with wealth are generally regarded with esteem, the obsessive desire for money is often viewed with disdain and can lead to alienation from others.[54] Furthermore, individuals who do not share their wealth with others are often looked upon as selfish and greedy.

Money and Happiness Interestingly, money was also viewed as an evil in former communist countries where large differences in income were considered unfair and immoral. Money played almost no role in acquiring what few goods were available because personal connections and bartering were more important than the exchange of cash. As a result, many consumers in these countries still have trouble understanding the concept of spending and accumulating money.

Finally, the popular belief (especially in Western countries) that money can buy happiness is not often true. Examples of very wealthy individuals whose lives were generally unhappy and not fulfilling include J. Paul Getty and Howard Hughes.[55] After some people acquire tremendous wealth, money can become meaningless and no longer highly desired. Furthermore, wealth often enables people to hire others to do many of the things that formerly brought enjoyment, such as gardening and do-it-yourself projects. And, of course, money simply cannot buy many things. Foremost among these are love, health, true friendship, and children. Thus the endless and strong pursuit of money may not end in the fulfilled dreams that many think it will.

THE CONSUMPTION PATTERNS OF SPECIFIC SOCIAL CLASSES

We've seen that social class can influence acquisition and consumption on a general level. In this section we extend our discussion by examining the consumption patterns of specific social classes. Although class distinctions are becoming increasingly blurred, for the sake of simplicity we focus on four major groups: (1) the upper class, (2) the middle class, (3) the working class, and (4) the homeless.

The Upper Class

upper class The aristocracy, new social elite, and the upper-middle class.

The **upper class** of most societies is a varied group of individuals who include the aristocracy, the new social elite (or nouveaux riches), and the upper-middle class (professionals). In the United States the aristocracy consists of traditional old-money families who acquired great wealth and power in the late 19th and early 20th centuries and whose current members live on inherited money. Such families include the DuPonts, Vanderbilts, Rockefellers, and Fords. This group represents less than 1 percent of U.S. society. Thus it is really the middle two groups that are sizable enough to be of major interest to consumer researchers and marketers.

Although small, the upper class is diverse, and its members share a number of common values and lifestyles that relate to consumption behavior. These consumers are more likely to view themselves as intellectual, liberal, political, and socially conscious. That self-image leads to an increase in behaviors such as attending the theater, investing in art, purchasing books, traveling (especially to foreign places), donating time and money to good causes, attending prestige schools, and belonging to private clubs. Self-expression is also important, resulting in the purchase of high-quality, prestige brands in good taste. Interestingly, the desire for prestige goods can be traced back to European (especially French) aristocratic classes in earlier centuries, who were the first to engage in the heavy consumption of fine goods, such as art and furniture, and who were later emulated by the upper classes in other societies.[56]

The nouveaux riches represent those in the upper-class segment who have acquired a great deal of status and wealth in their own lifetimes. These people are often workaholics who feel strongly that they have worked hard for their money. In fact, an analysis of literary media and writings about the affluent identified three themes related to their achievement: entrepreneurialism, celebrity status achieved from consumption, and status achieved from artistry/craftsmanship.[57]

The affluent are concerned about what others think of them, particularly within their class, and as a result often engage in conspicuous consumption to validate their position in society.[58] They are therefore likely to buy items that are known to be high in price and that can be publicly consumed or displayed, like a Rolls-Royce or Mercedes, a Rolex watch, a Mont Blanc pen, or designer clothing. Another nouveau riche characteristic is the tendency to collect items that are symbols of acquired wealth. Examples include furniture, art objects, cars, and jewelry. In each case the expense and image of the item are very important components of its ability to convey power and wealth.

A study of French consumers found identifiable upper-class preferences for food, sports activities, and items related to health and beauty that differed from those of the lower classes.[59] Being rich enables these consumers to "buy beauty" by belonging to upscale gyms; hiring personal trainers; going to famous health spas; and indulging in herbal body wraps, Swedish and shiatsu massage, facials, manicures, and plastic surgery.[60] Even food becomes a conspicuous consumption item. The more exotic the meal, the more status ascribed to it. Furthermore, the nouveaux riches typically stay in hotels that cost from $600 to $1,000 per night and indulge in expensive hobbies such as car racing. Vacations are likely to be taken in the French Riviera (e.g., San Tropez, Cannes), the Virgin Islands, Hawaii, or Aspen. In addition, America's wealthy individuals tend to live in four types of areas: exclusive suburbs, financial centers (like Manhattan), "big money" retirement areas (e.g., Palm Beach, Florida), and (surprisingly) some sparsely populated counties (with oil wells and huge farms).[61]

The preceding description is not intended to imply that the upper classes are spendthrifts. A more accurate picture is that they save and invest money more than members of other classes.[62] When they do purchase items, however, conspicuous consumption is often the goal. Upper-class consumers are also more likely than other classes to engage in careful information search prior to a purchase and are less likely to use price as an indicator of quality; instead they rely on actual product characteristics.

Remember that these observations are only broad generalizations and that behaviors can differ within the upper class. Some consumers, for example, may be highly motivated by conspicuous consumption, and others may be more practical and conservative with their money. Thus we can identify subsegments of consumers with specific and unique consumption patterns. As an example, unlike many other upper-class consumers, upper-class white Anglo-Saxon Protestant (WASP) consumers prefer furnishings that are simple and practical but made with high-quality materials and craftsmanship.[63] Two distinct types of apparel preferences among these consumers are practicality, which means simplicity and comfort, and refinement, which conveys social position.

Most current millionaires do not fit the traditional image of tycoons with stately mansions. In fact, the average millionaire is 57 years old, is married with three children, is self-employed in a practical business, works between 45 and 55 hours a week, has a median income of $130,000, owns a home valued at $320,000, is first-generation affluent, drives an older model car, and has an average net worth of $3.7 million.[64] Millionaires tend to make their money in unremarkable businesses such as funeral homes, bowling alleys, and small manufacturing firms.

The Middle Class

middle class Primarily white-collar workers.

The **middle class** comprises primarily white-collar workers, many of whom have some college but no degree. These consumers want to do the right thing, buy whatever is popular, do whatever is good for the children, and be fashionable.[65] Middle-class consumers also tend to desire a nice home in a nice neighborhood with good schools. As a result, they are likely to spend money on education, shop at somewhat expensive clothing stores with quality brand names, stick with liked brands, be concerned about home furnishings, and buy on credit.

A major feature that distinguishes the middle class is that its members look to the upper class for guidance on certain behaviors such as proper dining etiquette; apparel selections (especially important for those consumers with aspirations of upward mobility); and popular leisure activities such as, golf, tennis, and squash. This tendency also leads to theater attendance, vacations, and adult education classes taken for self-improvement. Furthermore, compared with the lower classes, the middle class spends a greater proportion of its food budget on take-out meals or meals at nice restaurants.

Middle-class values can also determine the types of products and brands middle-class consumers prefer. Exhibit 14.8 presents a sample of product and activity preferences for lower-middle-, middle-, and upper-middle-class U.S. consumers. Not only are there differences between classes, but changes have occurred in the last decade.

Again, remember that these observations are generalizations and that the values and consumption patterns of middle-class consumers vary. Some scholars have suggested, for example, that two distinct subsets of middle-class consumers exist in the United States.[66] The more traditional middle class moved into the suburbs in the 1950s and 1960s when opportunity was abundant and survived recent difficult economic times. These consumers tend to be politically and culturally liberal

EXHIBIT 14.8
Middle-Class Preferences

Social class can lead to preferences for different products and services. These preferences have also changed over time. Here are several preferences for lower-middle-, middle-, and upper-middle-class consumers.

Source: Kenneth Labich, "Class in America," *Fortune,* February 7, 1994, p. 116. © 1994 Time Inc. All rights reserved.

CLASS DISTINCTIONS: YOU ARE WHAT YOU CHOOSE

		LOWER-MIDDLE	MIDDLE	UPPER-MIDDLE
Car	1980s	Hyundai	Chevrolet Celebrity	Mercedes
	1990s	Geo	Chrysler minivan	Range Rover
Business shoe (men)	1980s	Sneakers	Wingtips	Cap toes
	1990s	Boots	Rockports	Loafers
Business shoe (women)	1980s	Spike-heel pumps	Mid-heel pump	High-heel pumps
	1990s	High-heel pumps	Dressy flats	One-inch pumps
Alcoholic beverage	1980s	Domestic beer	White wine spritzer	Dom Perignon
	1990s	Domestic lite beer	California Chardonnay	Cristal
Leisure pursuit	1980s	Watching sports	Going to movies	Golf
	1990s	Playing sports	Renting movies	Playing with computers
Hero	1980s	Roseanne Barr	Ronald Reagan	Michael Milken
	1990s	Kathie Lee Gifford	Janet Reno	Rush Limbaugh

and casual about religion. The other group consists of recent arrivals to the middle class, many of whom are from ethnic groups (particularly African Americans and Asian Americans) or from rising blue-collar groups. Because tough economic times have threatened their jobs, these consumers tend to be rigidly conservative and like to preserve traditional middle-class values. In other words, they have a strong desire to protect hard-won gains.

 Similar middle-class behavior patterns have been found in other countries. For example, the middle class in Mexico has many of the same features as in the United States, spending much of its disposable income on cars, clothing, vacations, and household goods.[67] Among the differences is the fact that members of the Mexican middle class have a lower average income (around $10,000) than their American counterparts. Thus the Mexicans spend more on necessities, rarely use credit, and therefore have little debt repayment. Most children live at home until marriage, providing extra income that is spent on enjoyment.

 Finally, rising prosperity has led to an explosion in the size of the middle class in many poorer developing countries around the world.[68] The greatest change has occurred in parts of East Asia (China, India, Indonesia, and South Korea) followed by some Latin American countries (Mexico, Brazil, and Argentina) and Poland and eastern Germany. Personal consumption has risen, as evidenced by greatly increasing sales of typical middle-class items such as washing machines, TVs, VCRs, and stereo systems. Note that the incomes of middle-class consumers can vary dramatically across countries. In China middle class means $1,000 in household income a year; in Poland it is around $3,000. Furthermore, in Eastern Europe and the Middle East a consumer has to work 40 to 45 days to buy a washing machine, whereas a Western consumer has to work only five. However, the cost of living in these countries is substantially lower than it is in the West, so less is needed for necessities.

The Working Class

working class Primarily blue-collar workers.

The **working class** is mainly represented by blue-collar workers. The traditional stereotype is of a hard-hatted, middle-aged man, but this image is changing as the working class is becoming younger, more ethnically diverse, more female, somewhat more educated, and more alienated from employers.[69] A key bond among the working class is membership in organized labor unions.

Working-class consumers heavily depend on family members for both economic and social support in many areas, including job opportunities, advice—particularly for key purchases and for help during difficult times.[70] As a result, the working class tends to be much more locally oriented socially, psychologically, and geographically than other classes. As an example, working-class men exhibit strong preferences for local athletic teams, news segments, and vacations (typically taken less than 2 hours from home). The working class has also demonstrated the strongest resistance to the foreign car invasion in the United States and to abandoning the macho symbol of a large and powerful automobile.

The working class has in fact remained relatively resistant to change over the years. For example, traditional sex roles have been perpetuated. Women's lives revolve around the home and the children, and their main social contacts are with close relatives, friends, and neighbors—many of whom are lifelong acquaintances. Men's lives focus on their jobs, male camaraderie, and mechanical pursuits like fixing the car and adding on to the home.

Like other classes, the working class exhibits identifiable patterns of consumption. For example, the local/home orientation is exemplified in the purchase of products like Schaeffer (versus Heineken) beer, Ford (versus Toyota) pickup trucks, RCA (versus Sony) TVs, Marlboro cigarettes, *Field and Stream* magazine, Black & Decker tools, and McDonald's fast food.[71] Compared with other classes, this group is more likely to eat at home and live in mobile homes.

The working class is also more likely to spend than save. When saving does occur, savings accounts are preferred over investments. Compared with other consumers, working-class consumers are also more likely to judge product quality on the basis of price (higher price means higher quality), to shop in mass merchandise or discount stores, and to have less product information when purchasing.[72]

The Homeless*

homeless People at the low end of the status hierarchy.

At the low end of the status hierarchy are the **homeless**. Homeless consumers lack shelter and live on the streets or in makeshift structures, cars, or vacant houses.[73] In some countries the homeless represent a very sizable segment of society. In the United States this group has grown in recent years, and its size is currently estimated to be between 600,000 and 3 million. It is made up primarily of drug and alcohol abusers, former mental patients, members of minority female-headed households, and those who have experienced financial setbacks. Major reasons for homelessness include unemployment, release from mental institutions, drug addiction, and lack of low-cost housing.

That the homeless lack basic resources is a sad and troubling problem for many industrialized nations. Along with government relief agencies and volunteers who labor on behalf of these "underclass" citizens, many economists, sociologists, and anthropologists have turned their attention to discovering what persistent homelessness can tell us about our society. The study of consumer behavior can make some contribution to that research.

An overriding characteristic of the homeless is the struggle for survival. Homeless consumers have difficulty acquiring items such as food, medical care, and other goods necessary for everyday living, and they must somehow acquire these goods in the face of little or no income.[74] They are not helpless but rather are a "resourceful, determined, and capable group that proactively deals with its lack of resources in the consumer environment."[75] They also maintain their self-esteem by (1) distancing themselves from more dependent individuals on welfare or in shelters and from institutions like the Salvation Army, (2) accepting their street role identity, or (3) telling fictitious stories about past or future accomplishments.[76] In addition, they have lower expectations about acceptable housing than the middle class.

In light of the size and unique behavior patterns of the homeless population, researchers have become interested in its acquisition, consumption, and disposition patterns. In particular, the consumer behavior of the homeless differs from that of the rest of society in two major ways: (1) how they acquire goods and (2) how they use and dispose of them.

Scavenging, a particularly important survival activity, is the finding of used or partially used goods that other individuals and institutions have discarded. Scavenging is necessary because the homeless are typically denied access to stores and restaurants, given their lack of funds and unkempt appearance. Scavenged items are typically found in garbage cans and dumpsters. The homeless have become fairly adept at not only locating the best places to scavenge but also finding the most useful and important items in a particular location. For example, they often

---

*Much of the discussion in this section is adapted from Ronald Paul Hill and Mark Stamey, "The Homeless in America: An Examination of Possessions and Consumption Behaviors," *Journal of Consumer Research*, December 1990, pp. 303–321.

know which restaurants or grocery stores have the most edible discarded food and sometimes make arrangements with the managers to pick up the discards. They also often vary their scavenging patterns to avoid detection and move within an area wide enough to provide the needed items. They are therefore a mobile or nomadic society.

Many homeless people also have tools to aid in scavenging and recycling activities. These include items such as shopping carts (to transport materials); tire irons (for protection and for entering abandoned buildings); and ice picks, sledgehammers, and screwdrivers (for removal of metal parts). A major problem facing the homeless is how to store and prepare gathered food. Most often it is cooked over an open fire, but some find ways of pirating electricity in order to cook with discarded appliances.

The homeless can rarely acquire everything they need by scavenging. Some form of income-producing activity is therefore required, whether it be begging, recycling glass and plastic bottles and aluminum cans, collecting scrap metal, cleaning windshields at busy intersections, or working as a day laborer. When money is acquired, it is often not spent on everyday goods. Rather, the preference is to splurge or to treat oneself to something special, such as a hot meal, cigarettes, alcohol, or drugs.

Despite their poverty most homeless people do have some valued possessions. Many try to create some form of home, whether it be an abandoned building or car, a makeshift dwelling built out of scavenged materials, or a spot under a bridge or in a tunnel. Homeless people prefer these habitats to either shelters, which are perceived as dirty and inhospitable, or public places such as bus and train stations and shopping centers, which are patrolled by police and security services. These humble homes can often serve as a source of pride, much like those of other classes. A major challenge for those living in colder climates is keeping warm in the winter. Clothing for the homeless population is often shabby, serving primarily as a means of protection from the environment.

Finally, the consumption and disposition behaviors of the homeless differ from the rest of society. In particular, items are consumed to their maximum and are discarded only if they have absolutely no further use. Clothes and shoes are often worn until they disintegrate or fall apart. Food is completely consumed and rarely wasted, even if it is spoiled or rotten. Thus the homeless are secondhand consumers because they consume what others have disposed of.

MARKETING IMPLICATIONS   Social class can have a variety of marketing implications. In particular, it can serve as a way of segmenting the market, thereby influencing product or service development, the advertising message, media exposure, and outlet selection.

Product or Service Development.   Social class motives and values can determine which products or services consumers desire. We know that products and services can be status symbols and motivate acquisition. The upper classes, for example, are willing to pay high prices to satisfy a need for prestige, convenience, and luxury.[77] Therefore, expensive cruises and vacations, foreign automobiles, imported wines, fancy restaurants, and fashion clothing can appeal to this group. For example, British restaurateur Sir Terence Conran has been extremely successful in catering to London's chic set with restaurants that feature exotic meals.[78] High-end restaurants such as Park Avenue Café and Wolfgang Puck's Spago are becoming chains in an effort to reach the growing affluent market outside the restaurants' original locales.[79] Upper-class consumers in Latin America, South America, and the United States are a very attractive market for sellers of computers, electronic equipment, and second cars.[80]

The working class, on the other hand, is more concerned with good quality at a fair price, and many products and services are designed to fulfill this desire. Examples include family-rate motels, cafeterias and fast-food restaurants, economy or used cars, instant coffee, and inexpensive multipurpose clothing. Local brands are also more likely to appeal to this group. As an example, U.S. car manufacturers have found their greatest support among the working class because of strong patriotism.

The very size of the middle class makes it a popular target of products and services. In India, for example, there has been a push to market products to the large upper-middle (100 million) and lower-middle (200 million) classes. The lower-middle class now accounts for 75 percent of sales of soap and radios; 60 percent of laundry detergents; and between 33 and 50 percent of all soft drinks, shampoo, and color TVs.[81]

Sometimes different product lines are developed for various classes. Anheuser-Busch, for example, offers Michelob for the upper-middle class (with a super premium price), Budweiser for the middle class (premium price), and Busch for the working class (low price). Furthermore, Heineken is perceived as an upper-class beer, Coors and Miller as middle class, and Old Style as lower middle.[82] Mercedes is offering smaller and less expensive models to appeal to a broader class of consumers.

Finally, marketers can appeal to the consumer's aspirations for upward mobility by positioning an offering as something that increases one's social standing. To illustrate, a variety of products and services are designed to help consumers become more culturally sophisticated: "best-loved classics" on CD; supermarket encyclopedias; books on topics such as wine and art appreciation; and television programs that are designed to make art, science, and music more accessible.[83] These tools can improve the average person's knowledge of subjects that have been deemed culturally important by the upper classes. Also, bankers are increasingly targeting the middle class with services typically reserved for the upper class, such as banking advice and asset management.[84] Finally, as shown in Exhibit 14.9, products and services can be positioned as evidence that consumers have "made it."

EXHIBIT 14.9
Social Class Aspirations

Sometimes marketers try to appeal to consumers' social class aspirations by positioning a product or service as a symbol of social class standing or achievement. Here we see how Jaguar positions itself as the car for those who have achieved a certain level of wealth and have a high standard of living.

Source: Photo courtesy of Jaguar Cars. All rights reserved.

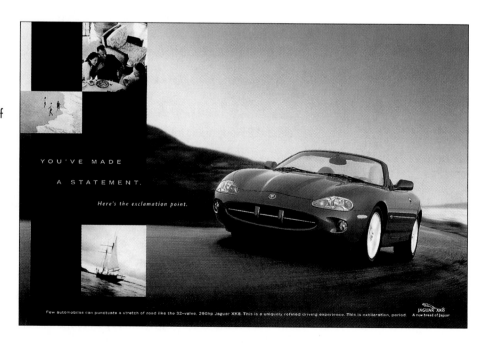

Advertising and Personal Selling Messages. Advertising and personal selling messages can be designed to appeal to various social classes. Messages directed toward the upper classes, for example, might focus on the themes of just reward for hard work, you've made it, or pamper yourself because you deserve it. Interestingly, in South America marketers for Budweiser abandoned the beer's working-class image to position the brand as the "trendy drink for affluent youth."[85] Certain products and services can be positioned as status symbols (e.g., Godiva chocolates). Johnnie Walker Black Label is by far the most popular whiskey in Thailand because of the status message if portrays. Appeals to the Japanese upper classes are made by using English words and Western models.[86] Further, because conspicuous consumption can be an important motivator of consumer behavior, marketing messages can stress the social value or status associated with the product or service. A billboard ad for Rolex, for example, contained the slogan "Get your wrist watched."

Messages successfully directed toward the working class, on the other hand, take on a more localized orientation and focus on home and friends as well as favored activities such as hunting, watching sports events, bowling, and getting together at the local bar. Middle-class messages can focus on important themes such as doing the right thing, being fashionable, and doing what's good for the children (see Exhibit 14.10). In addition, messages can use typical members of a social class as role models. The ad in Exhibit 14.11, for example, represents an appeal to the working class.

Media Exposure. The classes also differ in their exposure to certain media. Advertisers try to reach the upper classes, especially the nouveaux riches, through targeted magazines and newspapers such as the *Robb Report* (whose readers' average income is $755,000 a year), *Town and Country, Veranda,* and *The New York Times.*[87] A new magazine, *The American Benefactor,* can't even be purchased; to qualify for a subscription, a person must have made a large charitable donation. Hence the publication claims that its subscription list is the "purest concentration of wealth that has ever been assembled."[88] The upper classes tend to restrict their TV viewing to public stations and cultural shows. Members of the upper class are also more likely to fit the profile of the Internet shopper, with higher income and education.[89]

The lower classes, on the other hand, are heavy watchers of TV. They are particularly fond of situation comedies, soap operas, and sports programs and, compared with other

In Terms Of Investment, We Think She's Worth Her Weight In Gold.

Stocks, bonds and commodities may be attractive investments for some companies. But at Sallie Mae, we believe that the best investment of all is an investment in people. The people who'll shape the future of America. That's why we put our money into education. In the last twenty-five years, we have funded student loans for nearly twenty million students — thus enabling them to go to college and study to become doctors, teachers, engineers, scientists and programmers to name but a few.

What's more, we help students when they graduate from college, too. For instance, we provide programs that make loan repayment convenient, affordable and less expensive for those who pay on time. As a result, students who use our programs can concentrate on obtaining good grades instead of worrying about how they'll pay for their education when they graduate.

We know that the whole country benefits from a well-educated populace. That's why we believe that our students are worth their weight in gold. And then some. If you would like to learn more about us and how we can help you finance your education, call us at **1-877-881-1009** or visit us on the Web at **www.salliemae.com**.

1-877-881-1009
www.salliemae.com

EXHIBIT 14.10
An Appeal to Middle-Class Values

College is a very expensive endeavor for many middle-class families. However, getting a college education is highly valued by the middle class as a way of getting ahead and improving social standing. This ad for Sallie Mae college loans encouraged students to apply for educational financing as an investment in the future.

Source: Reprinted with permission from SallieMae. Creative by Arnold Communications.

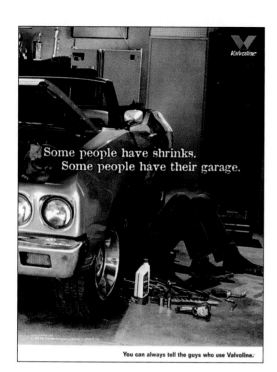

Some people have shrinks.
Some people have their garage.

You can always tell the guys who use Valvoline.

EXHIBIT 14.11
Working-Class Role Model

This ad may appeal to working-class consumers because it acknowledges the simple value of working with one's hands.

Source: Courtesy of the Valvoline Company.

classes, are less likely to read magazines and newspapers. Middle-class consumers, particularly those with only some college, are unique because they tend to be heavy TV watchers *and* magazine readers.

Outlet Selection. Certain outlets are designed to appeal to and pamper upper-class consumers. The merchandise in these stores is generally very expensive, and the service is very personalized.[90] For example, the high-fashion Bijan stores (on Rodeo Drive in Los Angeles and on Fifth Avenue in New York) have sales of $100 million a year from only 15,000 customers, a sales staff of 15, and an average of only 5 customers a day. Bijan sells bulletproof, chinchilla-lined jackets for $27,000; boots for $3,250; men's perfume in Baccarat crystal bottles for $1,500; and a 24-karat gold and leather .38 caliber revolver for $25,000. Other department and specialty stores such as Louis Vuitton, Polo, Tiffany, Sak's Fifth Avenue, Bergdorf Goodman, and Giorgio appeal to the upper class by offering status brands and service. Conspicuous consumption can also be influential because consumers want to acquire items in the "correct" store or outlet, especially if they can be seen doing so (see Exhibit 14.7).[91]

Even mass merchandisers are changing their merchandise mix to offer more snob appeal. Hardware giant Home Depot now offers $7,000 Sub-Zero refrigerators and $39,500 Schonbek chandeliers, and Sears is offering Karastan rugs and Royal Velvet towels in its Great Indoors stores.[92] Even discount merchandisers such as Kmart are Target are selling "cheap chic" apparel and housewares very similar to those offered by pricier retailers.[93]

 Alternatively, to counter sluggish sales, London's traditionally elitist Savile Row area (famous for clothing) has used aggressive marketing tactics to abandon its stuff image and appeal more broadly to other classes.[94] The same is true of Air France and British Airways, both of which are trying to expand the appeal of expensive transatlantic Concorde flights.[95]

On the other hand, mass merchandisers and discount stores have been successful in targeting working-class consumers by offering quality goods at a good price. Wal-Mart has been extremely adept at understanding the needs and desires of these consumers. Garage sales and resale shops are also popular with these consumers. Finally, department and specialty stores, such as The Express, Gap, Sears, Wards, and Mervyn's, appeal to the middle class by offering fashionable clothing, quality merchandise, and good credit terms.

A Note of Caution. Although this chapter has discussed social class differences in consumer behavior, marketers have experienced some difficulty in using social class as a segmentation variable for several reasons. First, as we saw earlier, a variety of factors such as occupation and income can have opposite effects on social class, and this factor makes social class difficult to measure. Second, variations within a class make social class a better predictor of broad behavior patterns, such as conspicuous product-level choice, than of specific behaviors such as brand choice. Finally, because of social class fragmentation, traditional social class distinctions may be becoming too broad to be truly useful.

As a result, greater segmentation is needed. Marketers are responding by developing their ability to target consumers. For example, "marketers can now pinpoint the class status and buying patterns of just about everyone in the U.S. on a neighborhood-by-neighborhood basis,"[96] thanks in part to the increasing ability to communicate with specific consumers more precisely through direct mail, interactive TV, and the Internet. In the future marketers are likely to use detailed social-class profiles of consumers, rather than traditional broad distinctions. As one example, the American Transportation Television Network (ATTN) directly targets working-class truck drivers at truck stops with reports on traffic conditions, weather reports, and summaries of government regulations.[97]

SUMMARY

This chapter discussed the concept of social class—that is, the grouping of individuals in a society into different levels of status (upper, middle, and lower). Class distinctions are significant because members of a particular class share common life experiences and therefore values and behavior patterns. However, many variations occur within groups.

Individuals are most likely to be influenced by members of their own class because of regular social interaction with them, but influence can also cross class lines through either the trickle-down effect (when lower classes copy upper-class values and behavior) or the status float effect (when trends start in the lower classes and spread upward).

A variety of factors determine one's level of social class, the most critical of which are occupation and education. Income, area of residence, possessions, family background, and social interactions are also important. Thus to measure social class, researchers must use a battery of items, such as the Computerized Status Index. Three major trends are producing an evolution in social class structures: (1) upward mobility, (2) downward mobility, and (3) social class fragmentation.

Social class is related to consumption in several major ways. Conspicuous consumption is the acquisition and display of luxury goods and services to demonstrate class status. Also, certain products and services serve as status symbols, and we often judge others on the basis of their possessions. Compensatory consumption occurs when consumers attempt to offset deficiencies in one area by engaging in greater than usual consumption (e.g., buying a new car after losing a job). Finally, the meaning of money can be a key motivator of consumer behavior.

The consumption patterns of four specific social classes were examined. The upper class is hardworking, wealthy, socially conscious, and especially concerned with conspicuous consumption. The middle class wants to buy the right things, live in a nice neighborhood, and has strong aspirations to raise its social standing. The working class is characterized by strong family ties and a local orientation. The homeless engage in a struggle for survival by scavenging, recycling, and collecting items that others have discarded. These class distinctions pose important marketing implications in areas of product and service development, advertising and personal selling messages, media exposure, and outlet selection.

1. Design a battery of questions to measure social class standing. (The CSI on page 338 can be used as a starting point). Make sure to include all the determinants of social class. In addition, pick one product and one service that you think will vary across social class in terms of consumer behavior and develop a series of questions to measure the acquisition and consumption of this product and service (i.e., how much time is spent, what information is collected, where it is purchased, what brands are considered and selected, and so on). Administer this questionnaire to at least 15 consumers who represent the range of social classes and divide the respondents into three major groups (upper, middle, and lower class). Summarize how the three groups vary in terms of consumption behavior for both the product and service.

2. A travel service has hired you to develop a marketing strategy for a vacation package. The company wants to offer different packages to different social classes. Develop a complete package and marketing strategy for each of the following: the upper class, the middle class, and the working class. Be sure to discuss (1) services offered (including destination, accommodations, and so on), (2) pricing, (3) the advertising message, and (4) media targeting. Summarize the key differences among the three marketing strategies.

CHAPTER 15

AGE, GENDER, AND HOUSEHOLD INFLUENCES ON CONSUMER BEHAVIOR

INTRODUCTION

For 20 years the government of mainland China has attempted to curb population growth by limiting urban families to only one child (see Exhibit 15.1). Now the products of these one-child families are growing up and are exhibiting characteristics very different from those of previous generations. Called the "little emperors," these individuals were raised by doting parents and were given everything from the best clothing to the best education money can buy.[1] As a result, members of this generation are supremely self-confident, ambitious, hardworking, less traditional, and much more materialistic than their parents. This generation is also much more fashion conscious and freewheeling than other age groups. Further, females are entering professional careers in much greater numbers than their mothers did. It is expected that this generation will have a huge impact on the economic future of Asia.

EXHIBIT 15.1
The Little Emperor

In one-child families in China, children are treated as "little emperors."

Source: Louise Gugg/The Image Works.

FAMILY PLANNING—A BASIS NATIONAL POLICY OF CHINA

This example illustrates three additional types of influences on consumer behavior, as shown in Exhibit 15.2. First, age can be a factor in acquisition and consumption, and different generations can vary in terms of their behavior. Second, differences in behavior can be based on gender and sex-role changes. Finally, family or household influences can play a very critical role in influencing consumption activity. We discuss these three factors in this chapter.

HOW AGE AFFECTS CONSUMER BEHAVIOR

Marketers often segment consumers by age. The basic logic is that people of the same age are going through similar life experiences and therefore share many common needs, symbols, and memories, which, in turn, may lead to similar consumption patterns.[2] Therefore, in this section we examine the characteristics of four major age groups recognized by marketers: (1) teens, (2) Generation X, (3) baby boomers, and (4) the 50 and older market.

Teens

The transition from childhood to adulthood makes the teen years a time of immense change. During this period, teens strive to develop a distinct identity and self-image, which sometimes results in a rebellion against parents and authority. These years are also marked by a need to gain acceptance from their peers, and teens often do things to be one of the gang. They want to be independent but at the same time dare not deviate too far from the group or face the risk of being rejected.[3] These conflicting forces can create a great deal of pressure and uncertainty. On the other hand, superficially at least, the generation gap between teens and their parents is smaller than in previous generations. Entire families dress in jeans and T-shirts, listen to rock and roll, and watch reruns of old TV shows (like *Bewitched* and *Gilligan's Island*), giving parents and kids a common reference point.[4]

EXHIBIT 15.2

Chapter Overview: Age, Gender, and Household Influences on Consumer Behavior

This chapter shows how factors such as *age, gender,* and *household* affect consumer behavior. It examines different age groups (teens, twentysomethings, baby boomers, and 50 and over), sex roles (masculine versus feminine), and types of households. It also discusses changing trends in household structure and how households influence the decision-making process.

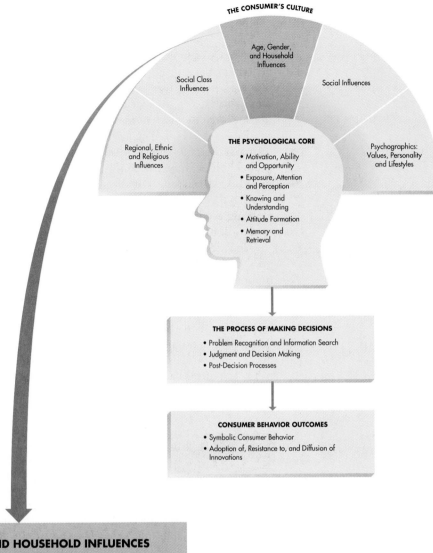

THE CONSUMER'S CULTURE

Age, Gender, and Household Influences

Social Class Influences

Social Influences

Regional, Ethnic and Religious Influences

THE PSYCHOLOGICAL CORE
- Motivation, Ability and Opportunity
- Exposure, Attention and Perception
- Knowing and Understanding
- Attitude Formation
- Memory and Retrieval

Psychographics: Values, Personality and Lifestyles

THE PROCESS OF MAKING DECISIONS
- Problem Recognition and Information Search
- Judgment and Decision Making
- Post-Decision Processes

CONSUMER BEHAVIOR OUTCOMES
- Symbolic Consumer Behavior
- Adoption of, Resistance to, and Diffusion of Innovations

AGE, GENDER, AND HOUSEHOLD INFLUENCES

- Age influences
  - Teens, twenty somethings, baby boomers, 50 and older
- Gender influences
  - Changing roles, differences in behavior
- Household influences
  - Types, structure, roles of members

Today's teens have traveled more than their parents have and are the first computer-literate generation, frequently communicating on the Internet.[5] Far more teenagers earn their own money than ever before, gaining more financial independence than earlier generations did. In Japan teens with money are causing a generational battle as they use their income to try to break free from the strict, traditional world of their parents. At the same time, today's teens are generally more family oriented than previous generations were. Having seen how older generations worked themselves to death, today's teens prefer to go "back to their roots."[6]

Rock and rap music symbolize rebellion and thus are very popular among teens. At the same time, such music allows them to establish an identity and be accepted. Observations at concerts indicate that clothing styles and behavior are remarkably consistent worldwide. In particular, deciding which T-shirt to wear (often with the band's logo) is critical because of its strong symbolism.[7] In fact, clothing establishes an identity and a way of labeling people as jocks, part of the in-crowd, freaks, or dweebs.

Teenagers wield increasing influence in household purchases and have developed fairly sophisticated decision-making skills. In fact, because of the increasing number of working and single parents, today's teens often shop for themselves and are responsible for more decisions than any previous generation was.[8] In these roles they are thrifty and savvy shoppers. They are very particular about how they spend their money and will shop extensively for sales and bargains. Teens tend to do more shopping on weekends, and females shop more than males do.[9] Friends are also a major source of information about products, and socializing is one of the major reasons that teens like to shop. Like adults, teens rely on information from personal sources for high-risk decisions and from mass media for low-risk situations.

MARKETING IMPLICATIONS In the United States teens constitute a very large and fast growing important segment that is expected to reach 30 million by 2006.[10] Their purchasing power is a substantial $95 billion. In particular, female teens spend $37 billion a year on beauty and fashion items and influence the spending of another $74 billion. Furthermore, teens are globally more alike than any other age group.[11] Their universally similar tastes, attitudes, and preferences for music, movies, athletic shoes, jeans, clothing, and video games are partly due to popular entertainment and MTV. Compared with U.S. teens, European teens tend to be closer to their parents, watch less TV, and look more to Eastern Europe for cues on fashion and music.

The fact that initial purchases of many products and services are made in the teen years is also important, since brand loyalties established at this time may carry into adulthood. For example, 50 percent of female teens have developed cosmetic brand loyalties by the age of 15[12] (Exhibit 15.3). Teens can also be trendsetters, particularly in areas such as fashion and music. In fact, today's trends often originate from "cool city teens" rather than fashion designers.[13] This the reason why a number of marketing research firms now monitor what's in and what's out among teens for clients such as Coca-Cola, Pepsi, Levi Strauss, and Microsoft. Companies in Japan have also found that the nation's high school girls have an uncanny ability to predict which products will be hits because a fad that catches on with teenagers usually becomes a big trend among consumers in general.[14]

It should not be surprising, therefore, that a number of products and services are developed to appeal specifically to teens. Often these items are positioned as helping teens deal with the key adolescent pressures of establishing an identity, re-

EXHIBIT 15.3
Teen Loyalities

Teenage consumers are active buyers of a number of products and services and may quickly develop brand loyalty toward their favorite brands. For example, 42 percent of teens buy only one brand of mascara, and 38 percent buy only one brand of eye shadow. Can you think of any brands for which you have been brand loyal since your teen years?

Source: Data from "Those Precocious 13-Year-Olds," *Brandweek,* January 25, 1993, p. 13.

Number of Brands Used in Past Year by 12-15 year-olds

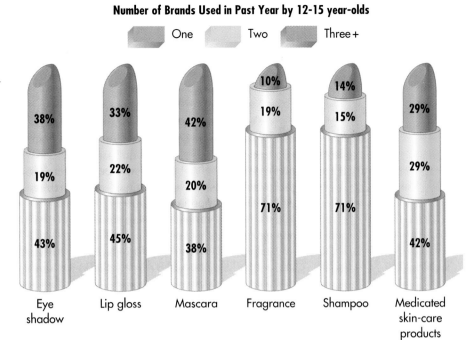

| | One | Two | Three + |

Eye shadow	Lip gloss	Mascara	Fragrance	Shampoo	Medicated skin-care products
38%	33%	42%	10% / 19%	14% / 15%	29%
19%	22%	20%	71%	71%	29%
43%	45%	38%			42%

belling, and being accepted by peers. Carter-Wallace, for example, introduced a line of Teen Image deodorants to compete with Mennen's Teen Spirit line for the $55 million teen deodorant market.[15] Gatorade has successfully marketed to teens by offering products that taste lighter and come in funky flavors such as Riptide Rush (a grape and berry blend).[16] In Asia credit card companies have been targeting the more than 500 million consumers who are under age 16 because they are more likely than their parents to embrace the credit culture.[17] Not all is positive, however. Some upscale malls that target affluent women have been resisting becoming traditional teen hangouts by offering fewer stores that appeal to teens and by playing classical music to drive them away.[18]

Advertising Messages. Advertising messages often incorporate symbols, issues, and language to which teens can relate. In particular, because music and sports tend to be the universal languages of teenagers, popular music and sports figures are frequently featured in ads. The National Football League has been attempting to address declining teen interest in its sport by having pop stars perform at games.[19] Teens are intelligent consumers who are often wary of blatant attempts to influence them.[20] Thus messages need to talk *to* teenagers, not *at* them. Furthermore, because they have grown up with videos and computers, today's teens appear to process information faster than earlier generations do.[21] As a result, teens prefer short, snappy phrases to long-winded explanations. For example, an antismoking ad campaign used the tagline "Tobacco: tumor-causing, teeth-staining, smelly puking habit."[22] Note, however, that using slang can sometimes be dangerous because a phrase may already be out-of-date by the time the ad appears, which can make the product or service look "uncool." Finally, many teenagers do not care about the content of advertising and are more concerned with price.

Teens can be targeted through certain TV networks (MTV), TV programs (*Party of Five* and *The Simpsons*), magazines (*Sassy, Seventeen, Teen People,* and *YM*), and popular-music radio stations.[23] Fashion names such as Gap, Fubu, and Calvin

Klein as well as the discount store Target advertise heavily on MTV to attract teens.[24] One study found that 83 percent of teens read a major magazine at least once every 4 weeks, and most listen to the radio on a regular basis, particularly in their cars.[25] Researchers estimate that about 10 percent of girls aged 12 to 17 are overweight, and new publications such as *Extra Hip* and *Girls* target these plus-size teen girls.[26] Catalogs aimed at teens have greatly increased in number in recent years. Limited Too even targets preteen girls with clothing and fashion tips.[27]

Other Types of Promotion. Some companies communicate with teens in school through electronic communication centers containing calendars of school activities as well as ads.[28] Fast-food chains such as Taco Bell and Pizza Hut now offer menu items in school cafeterias. Special promotions are also employed. For example, promotions run by Channel One advertisers included having students help to write TV commercials (Snapple), design art for vending machines (Pepsi), and save cards for sandwiches (Subway) in order to increase awareness of the brands among teens.

Teens are also frequent Internet users. Therefore, Procter & Gamble is hoping to revitalize its Cover Girl brand by encouraging teens to get a virtual makeover on the company's Web site.[29] Nevertheless teens are fickle users and tend not to be loyal to individual sites. Only if a site appeals to specific interests such as music or popular current movies will it register a lot of visits.[30] ■

Generation X

Individuals born from 1965 to 1976 are often called **Generation X**. A distinguishable feature of this group is a general feeling of alienation and resentment due to difficulties in career placement and advancement, although the strength of this feeling is in debate.[31] In particular, an improved U.S. economy has created greater job opportunities, which has lessened the employment problem for this age group. Nevertheless, some underachievers who are pushing 30 still hang on to their Generation X "angst."[32] Some members of this generation who still believe that they may not be able to match or surpass their parents' level of success continue to feel somewhat disillusioned and are less materialistic than other age groups.

Sometimes feelings of disillusionment are translated into consumption patterns. For example, music that reflects anger such as rap and hard rock tends to be very popular. In fashion, earrings and tattoos make a statement against society in general. Similarly, TV shows like *Southpark* and *Ren and Stimpy* have been popular for a time because of the generally irreverent attitude they portray. However, Xers are a diverse group, and not all identify strongly with these sentiments. In fact, a sizable number resent being stereotyped and claim their negative image is the invention of those who do not understand their generation.[33]

A false stereotype is that Xers are apathetic slackers. On the contrary, they tend to find success and achievement in being at the very cutting edge of technology. Forty-three percent own their own computers, 70 percent use one every day, and the group as a whole makes up the heaviest core of Internet users. Other Xers are finding unique ways to make their fortunes, including a few who have ventured to Vietnam to make investments and start businesses.[34]

A relatively new phenomenon is the so-called *boomerang kids*. These are Xers who live at home, sometimes well into their 30s or until they marry, to save money. Because parents pay for many essentials (just to keep their homes running), boomerang kids have more discretionary income to spend on entertainment and pleasure and are more likely to buy items like a new car, stereo, or television than their counterparts who must pay utility bills and rent or mortgages.

Boomerangers also feel less pressure to settle down than earlier generations and hence often delay marriage.[35] This trend has led to closer relationships with parents, who are often seen as friends or roommates.

MARKETING IMPLICATIONS The Generation X market represents more than $120 billion in spending power. It is a key segment for music, movies, budget travel, beer and alcohol, fast food, clothing, jeans, athletic shoes, and cosmetics (although a recent minimalist trend has flattened sales for this category).[36] Obviously, Xers are also driving the market for PCs, CD-ROMs; on-line services; and video games, products, and services that are therefore often targeted to them.

For example, because Xers spend 24 percent of their discretionary income on eating out, some trendy restaurants have started playing loud techno music, which is popular with this group.[37] Bingo is now popular with Xers in some bars because it is "cheesy."[38] Finally, because only 5 percent of Xers drink scotch, Dewar's targets young sophisticates and Seagram's positions 7 Crown as a "shooter" (popular among this group).[39]

Born and bred on TV, Xers tend to be cynical about obvious marketing techniques.[40] Ads containing exaggerated claims; stereotypes; unpopular products like cigarettes and alcohol; sexually explicit content; and political, religious, or social messages are sometimes objectionable to Xers. However, Xers do react positively to efforts that are seen as clever or in tune with their values and attitudes. In particular, they want to be recognized as their own group and not as mini-baby boomers. Ads should reflect their style, music, fashion, and phrases. For example, Heineken, Zima Gold, and Mountain Dew have used alternative music and fast-paced videos in ads to change their image and attract this generation.[41] Barq's root beer chose "'unglamorous misfits" rather than attractive models for its ad campaign.[42] Ads with the attitude "We know that you know that this is a game" can work well." For example, J & B Scotch ads state: "Drinking J & B cola will make you immortal. Well, OK, it will at least make you fondly remembered by at least some."

To reach Xers, marketers can select media vehicles such as popular or alternative music radio stations. TV shows such as *Friends* and *Dawson's Creek* tend to be popular, although Xers watch less TV than other groups do.[43] Magazines such as *Spin* and music-related publications and messages displayed at concerts, sporting events, and popular vacation spots are also attractive vehicles.

However, the Internet is increasingly becoming the way to reach these consumers, especially because they spend an average of 9.3 hours a week on the Net.[44] Some companies have used small firms composed specifically of Xers to launch promotional sites on the Internet because they develop more cutting-edge sites that appeal to the group.[45] Music and on-line game sites are especially popular among Xers. Makers of alcohol are using these sites heavily to appeal to youthful drinkers.[46] To get Xers to donate to charity, ReliefRock offered an on-line benefit rock music concert rather than send direct-mail letters.[47]

Targeted sales promotions can also be effective. AT&T offers students a free membership in its Student Advantage discount program.[48] During spring break, marketers inundate students with free T-shirts, Frisbees, tank tops, and other items and sponsor events such as "in your face" and wet T-shirt contests. ■

Baby Boomers

baby boomers Individuals born between 1946 and 1964.

The **baby boomers**, who make up the largest demographic group in the United States, were born between 1946 and 1964. Because of their numbers and the fact

EXHIBIT 15.4

Impact of the "Baby Boomlet"

Concern for the safety of the family is a concern for many baby boomers who now have children.

Source: Courtesy of Michelin.

baby boomlet (Generation Y) Mini-population explosion from the children of baby boomers.

that many are in their peak earning years, baby boomers have considerable economic power and are currently the most influential consumer segment. Although boomers are a diverse group, they share many common experiences of the dynamic and fast-changing world of the 1960s and 1970s in which they grew up. Primarily in protest of the Vietnam War, this generation created a revolution in social attitudes, music, fashion, and politics, the effects of which are still with us today. This revolution also led to the rise of individualism in which having the freedom to do what you want, when and where you want, is strongly valued.[49]

Subsegments of consumers exist within this very large and diverse group.[50] One group, called middle-aged, overstressed, semiaffluent suburbanites (MOSS), responds positively to marketing efforts that reduce time and effort in shopping and decision making. This responsiveness makes product quality and strong packaging, availability, and service even more important for marketers.

Some researchers have identified five subgroups of boomers, based on five-year divisions (1946–1951, 1951–1956, and so on). Consumers in these subgroups have in common the life experiences of the same years and may share more attributes with each other than with other segments. If this theory is true, we can expect the oldest and youngest groups to be the most different. Some experts have even suggested the name Gappers for the youngest group (born between 1963 and 1969) because its members really fall in between boomers and Xers in terms of interests and behavior patterns.[51]

MARKETING IMPLICATIONS Because baby boomers are currently the segment with the greatest economic impact, they are the target for many products and services including cars, housing, foreign travel, entertainment, and recreational equipment. Boomers are also heavy consumers of banking and investment services as they try to build equity for the future.[52] They are the heaviest users of frozen dinners and are a growing market for movies, especially highly original ones with adult themes. Repackaged "best of" albums, which remind boomers of the music of their teen and young-adult years, are very popular with this group.[53]

Many boomers delayed child rearing until their late 20s or 30s and created a mini-population explosion called the **baby boomlet** (now called Generation Y). Thus they are often the target of marketing efforts for children's products and services. To illustrate, the purchase of vans has increased dramatically in recent years, and much of the growth can be attributed to boomers who want this kind of family vehicle.[54] The ad in Exhibit 15.4 is also directed at baby boomers who are concerned about car and tire safety for their children. Dial for Kids soap and Baby Dove soap were also introduced for this group.[55] Finally, because many baby boomers are in dual-career families, the need for child care services has been increasing rapidly.

An Aging Population. Because this very large group is getting older, marketers who fail to modify their offerings to the needs of aging consumers will suffer from a shrinking market share. Some products and services are developed specifically for the needs of baby boomers. For example, many boomers grew up wearing jeans and continue to do so. However, as waistlines have expanded, companies have developed lines with larger sizes and different styles to accommodate the middle-aged physique.[56] Automakers are now changing car designs to fit the needs of aging boomers, among other things making cars easier to get into.[57] To appeal to families that are no longer young, Disney now offers golf, tennis, and adult-education classes.[58]

Many boomers are obsessed with aging and are a prime market for products and services that help maintain a youthful appearance, such as health clubs, body-shaping underwear like the Wonderbra, cosmetics, and plastic surgery.[59] Moisturizers, such as Oil of Olay's Hydro-Night Renewal Gel, are specifically positioned as antiaging solutions (a $313 million a year product category), and teeth-whitening toothpastes were designed primarily to help boomers keep their looks.[60] The topic of aging per se is usually not mentioned in marketing communications, however, because boomers are sensitive about this issue.

Advertisers are now starting to treat boomers as grown-ups. For a generation that is so concerned with aging, adulthood can be a tough admission, but advertisers are approaching it playfully with lines like "Oh no, we've become our fathers." An ad for Dewar's shows a bald man with the line: "In an age of miracle hair cures, here's something that will actually grow on you."[61] Vacationing boomers like water parks and water toys at resorts because these activities make them feel young and do not involve strenuous activity.[62] Likewise, in Japan products with a cute cartoon cat, Hello Kitty, have been highly popular among middle-aged consumers who want to show their playful side.[63] Rock music from the 1950s and 1960s can also be used to create a positive and nostalgic feeling.[64] A number of vacation spots including New York and Cleveland are touting rock connections with attractions like the Rock and Roll Hall of Fame and the Hard Rock Café to attract boomer tourism.[65] Exhibit 15.5 is a good example of an ad that appeals to baby boomers' nostalgia.

Special Marketing Communications.   Boomers can be targeted through the use of selective media. The VH-1 network, for example, was created to appeal specifically to boomers' musical interests.[66] Documentaries of old rock stars have also been popular on this channel. Certain cultural TV networks, such as Bravo, the Discovery Channel, and the Arts & Entertainment Network, also tend to attract boomers. Obviously, oldies rock stations target this very large segment as well.

EXHIBIT 15.5
An Appeal Directed at Baby Boomers

Bumper stickers were a popular way to express opinions when baby boomers were growing up.

Source: Schieffelin & Somerset Co., N.Y., N.Y.

Even movie tie-ins, traditionally aimed at children, are now aimed at boomers. For example, McDonald's had a tie-in with the movie *Armageddon* to attract adults.[67] Finally, special-interest videos and direct-mail pieces can be effective ways of reaching boomers.[68] ▪

Fifty and Older

More than 43 percent of the U.S. population is 50 years of age or older (15 percent is over 65), and this percentage will increase dramatically as baby boomers age.[69] Thanks to pension funds, Social Security, Medicare, and the asset boom of the last two decades, this generation is relatively well-off compared with seniors 20 years ago, although this age group is also the most varied in terms of wealth (there are many poor as well as many rich seniors).[70]

young again Individuals age 50 to around 65.

The over-50 market is even more diverse than other age groups.[71] Nevertheless, on a broad level this segment can be divided into two groups that vary significantly in terms of lifestyle and outlook. The **young again** (age 50 to around 65) usually think of themselves as about 15 years younger than they really are in terms of cognitive age.[72] In fact, this group thinks more like older baby boomers than like seniors and leads a very active lifestyle (older boomers are now in this segment). The young again also tend to have considerable discretionary income because they have fewer financial obligations.

gray market Individuals over 65.

The second segment, the **gray market**, consists of the consumers over 65.[73] Better medical care and healthier lifestyles have increased the size and economic clout of this group. Because these consumers lived through the Great Depression, their philosophy is to save rather than to spend. The majority of these individuals—even those 75 and over—are self-sufficient in most activities, including walking, preparing meals, shopping, housework, and bathing. They do not like being referred to as "old." Finally, women outnumber men in this category because women tend to live longer.

In terms of consumer behavior, information-processing skills tend to deteriorate with age. Therefore, older or mature consumers are less likely to search for information and to have more difficulty remembering information and making more complex decisions, especially with large amounts of information.[74] Thus they tend in engage in simpler, more schematic processing.[75] Further, poor recognition memory makes them susceptible to the "truth effect" (believing that often-repeated statements are true—see Chapter 8).[76] As a result, they sometimes need help or consumer education programs when making decisions, as we discuss in Chapter 20.[77] Mature consumers also tend to shop more often at discount stores and buy many of the same items as they did when they were younger.[78] Thus they are price sensitive and fairly resistant to the adoption of new products, especially technology products.

MARKETING IMPLICATIONS Mature consumers will become increasingly important to marketers in coming years. Clearly, this group represents a critical and growing market for health-related and medical products and services and retirement communities (particularly in Florida and the South).[79] Mature consumers already spend more than twice the national average on prescription drugs, accounting for more than 40 percent of total pharmaceutical sales.[80] A new generation of incontinence products is experiencing rapid sales growth.[81] Allergan has also been targeting seniors with information on cataracts and ways to correct the problem.[82] The senior market is very interested in home-based products and services. Comfort House was one of the first companies to recognize the importance of the senior market. Their

Web site comforthouse.com offers a line of products to make seniors' daily lives easier, including those which help with arthritis, incontinence, back pain relief, and home health care. Text telephones and closed captioned television can also benefit this group.

Other types of products are being introduced to appeal to the senior market. Eyewear makers are now introducing chic reading glasses to appeal to the fashion conscious. Johnson & Johnson offers Rx Cream that fights wrinkles.[83] Burma Shave is reviving its well-known road signs (from the 1930s and 1940s), hoping to capitalize on nostalgia for this old brand.[84]

Mature consumers have an active lifestyle and are increasingly the purchasers of leisure-based products and services, such as educational seminars, travel, and sporting goods. Grandparents buy much of the clothing and toys consumed by their grandchildren. After years of being criticized for targeting young consumers, makers of beer and wine are increasingly aiming at the over-50 drinker.[85] Offerings whose value lies in a heavy future orientation, however, are not good prospects for the elderly market.[86] Finally, because mature consumers are more likely to resist new products, new offerings should focus on needs rather than on newness.[87]

Specialized Marketing Communications. Advertisements with positive older role models are perceived as being more credible and believable than those with younger models.[88] Nevertheless, because American society can be considered a youth culture, seniors are more likely to be painted in an unfavorable light than younger consumers and are less likely to appear in ads, although this situation is changing.[89] This negative image is probably why mature consumers tend to have a more negative attitude toward ads than younger consumers have. Thus when advertising to mature consumers, models should be depicted as active, contributing members of society, rather than helpless dependents (see Exhibit 15.6). Mature consumers tend to favor information-oriented messages over imagery, but these messages should be kept simple and focus on a few important attributes.

Although mature consumers favor programs on public television, CNN, and premium pay cable, they may have more difficulty processing TV messages because

EXHIBIT 15.6
Image of Older Consumers

Consumers over the age of 50 take offense at being depicted as old. They prefer messages that show them leading active lifestyles, such as this ad for Kellogg's Mini-Wheats.

Source: KELLOGG'S® MINI-WHEATS® is a registered trademark of Kellogg Company. All rights reserved. Used with permission.

As part of a low fat diet,

Kellogg's Mini-Wheats

can help reduce the

risk of heart disease.

of deteriorating processing skills.[90] Thus marketers need a accommodate for this condition by making messages bigger, louder, or slower. However, mature consumers also tend to be avid readers of both newspapers and magazines, particularly those that focus on news, business, travel, and financial matters. Thus they are more reachable through these media. Specialty magazines that are directed toward mature consumers include *Modern Maturity* and *50 Plus.* The stereotype that reaching mature consumers through the Internet is very difficult is simply not true. More than 36 percent of consumers between 50 and 64 own a computer, and this number is increasing rapidly. Further, these consumers spend more time on the Internet than other groups, partly because they have more leisure time.[91]

Specialized Sales Techniques and Promotions. Retail outlets can be designed to better meet the needs of mature consumers. Features such as easier-to-read labels, comfortable seating throughout the store, well-lighted parking lots, and shelving arranged so customers do not have to bend provide a more age-friendly shopping environment.[92] Point-of-purchase materials can also be helpful in light of the difficulty in remembering information. In addition, convenience, service, feelings of safety, good value, and knowledgeable employees are important.

Companies can also tailor their sales techniques to the needs of mature consumers. CSC Insurance Marketing Systems, for example, developed an integrated program called Selling to Seniors that includes training in the intricacies of this market, generating leads, performing a needs analysis, and managing clients.[93] Note, however, that mature consumers have been more victimized by marketing fraud, especially via telemarketing, than other groups because seniors are too trusting (as we discuss in Chapter 20).[94]

Finally, special promotions such as the senior-citizen discount can be employed. Some mature consumers are heavy users of these discounts and take advantage of them in many product and service categories.[95] Senior discounts are less effective among the young again than among the gray market because the former want to avoid showing their age. Kraft directed a joint promotion for Bran Flakes, Maxwell House decaffeinated coffee, and sugar-free Jell-O at this group.[96] ■

HOW GENDER AFFECTS CONSUMER BEHAVIOR

Clearly males and females can differ in traits, attitudes, and activities that can affect consumer behavior. Because a complete discussion of the many contrasts between men and women is beyond the scope of this text, we discuss just a few that have been the focus of consumer research.

Sex Roles Have Changed

In most cultures men and women are expected to behave according to sex-role norms that are learned very early in childhood. Until recently, males in Western society were expected to be strong, assertive, the primary breadwinner, and emotionless and were guided by **agentic goals** that stress mastery, self-assertiveness, and self-efficacy.[97] Women, on the other hand, have been guided more by **communal goals** of forming affiliations and fostering harmonious relations with others and have been expected to be submissive, emotional, and home oriented. Remember, however, that these are only general tendencies, and considerable individual variation can occur.

On a very general level, men tend to be more competitive, independent, externally motivated, and willing to take risks.[98] In contrast, women tend to be cooperative, interdependent, intrinsically motivated, and risk averse. Men are more

agentic goals Goals that stress mastery, self-assertiveness, self-efficacy, strength, assertiveness, and no emotion.

communal goals Goals that stress affiliation and fostering harmonious relations with others, submissiveness, emotional, and home oriented.

EXHIBIT 15.7

A Modern Woman's Role in Advertising

Over time women have been increasingly rejecting traditional roles related to inhibition and submissiveness in favor of those that stress independence and assertiveness. Here we see an ad that reflects this trend.

Source: Tropicana Products, Inc. 1999

apt to derive pleasure from contact sports, hunting, fishing, and working on mechanical tasks, whereas women are more likely to be patrons of the arts and engage in activities that foster strong social ties.

Over time, however, both female and male roles have been evolving. In particular, many more women are delaying both marriage and starting a family in favor of building a career, and an increased proportion of women are entering occupations that were formerly the domain of men, such as management, engineering, and law. In fact, by the year 2005, women will account for 48 percent of the workforce in the United States.[99] This increase has led to changes in family structure and in women's attitudes in general. Many women, particularly feminists who are younger and better educated, are placing an increasing value on independence and freedom to do what they want.[100] This factor explains why an increasing number of women are taking vacations by themselves. More women are also rejecting traditional roles related to submissiveness, homemaking, and sexual inhibition. As a result, women have made faster gains in their standard of living in the last two decades than in earlier decades.[101] Further, there are relatively few differences between men and women who engage in the same activities (skateboarding, tennis, and so on), illustrating how roles are changing.[102] An ad that reflects this new trend is presented in Exhibit 15.7.

 Changes in traditional sex roles are taking place in many countries, even those that are very conservative and male dominated. For example, in India, where arranged marriages are still the norm, women's attitudes toward careers, marriage, and the family are undergoing radical changes as more women are entering careers and desiring independence.[103] In Japan, where head-to-toe kimonos used to be the rule, working women have been flocking to discos to do "dirty dancing" in G-strings—reflecting a new attitude and challenge to traditional, conservative norms.[104]

Men's sex roles and attitudes have also been changing. In particular, in dual-career families some husbands are assuming greater responsibility for household tasks and child rearing. A significant number still fail to do their share, however. Men are now learning that they can express their emotions, be more sensitive, and be more caring and loving fathers. In light of this trend, a Finnish firm developed a "daddy kit" with everything from a tape measure and diaper-changing mat to books on cooking, child care, and songs.[105] An ad for McDonald's in Japan that showed a man doting over his children was surprisingly popular in a country where fathers are most often portrayed as remote corporate warriors.[106]

Note, however, that sex roles and appropriate behavior are dictated by society and may vary from one culture to another. In the United States, for example, a man will generally feel uncomfortable hugging another man, whereas in European and Latin societies such behavior is widely accepted, and men often hug each other as a greeting. In France men kiss each other on the cheek. In certain Muslim countries the very strict sex roles allow women few rights and demand that they be covered and kept out of view.

Finally, a distinction must made between gender and sexual orientation. **Gender** refers to a biological state (male or female), whereas **sexual orientation** reflects a person's preference toward certain behaviors. *Masculine* individuals (whether male or female) tend to display male-oriented traits, and *feminine* individuals tend toward female characteristics. In addition, some individuals can be *androgynous*, having both male and female traits. These sexual orientations are important because they can influence an individual's preferences and behavior. For example, women who are more masculine tend to prefer ads that depict nontraditional women.[107]

gender Biological state of male or female.

sexual orientation A person's preference toward certain behaviors.

Differences in Acquisition and Consumption Behaviors

Despite sex-role changes, men and women still exhibit a number of differences in their consumption behaviors. In relation to advertising and consumer decision making, females are more likely to engage in a detailed, thorough examination of a message and make extended decisions based on product attributes (similar to high MAO decision making), whereas males are selective information processors, driven more by overall themes and simplifying heuristics (similar to low MAO decision making).[108] Males tend to be more sensitive to personally relevant information (consistent with agentic goals), and women pay attention to both personally relevant information and information relevant to others (consistent with communal goals).[109]

Whereas men are more likely to use specific hemispheres of their brain for certain tasks (the right side of the brain for visual and the left side for verbal), women use both hemispheres of their brain for most tasks. Men also appear to be more sensitive to trends in positive emotions experienced during consumption, such as enthusiastic, interested, active, strong, and proud, whereas women display a tendency for negative emotions, such as scared, upset, distressed, and nervous.[110] Finally, men and women differ in the symbolic meaning they attach to products and services.[111] Women are more likely to have shared brand stereotypes for fashion goods, whereas men are more consistent in their images of automobiles.

Men also tend to have more positive attitudes toward and higher involvement with high-tech products than women do.[112] Men are more likely to base decisions on software, prior experience, and reputation, whereas price is more critical for women. Males are more likely to consult computer magazines and rely on prior knowledge, and females use the shopping experience as the primary means of collecting information.

A general tendency is that females in the United States enjoy shopping more than males do and see it as a pleasurable, stimulating activity and a way of obtaining social interaction. Men, on the other hand, view shopping in functional terms—as a way of acquiring goods—and regard it as a chore, especially if they hold traditional sex-role stereotypes. These differences extend to holiday gift shopping and garage sales, where men are less likely than women are to get involved and participate.[113] These patterns also hold true in other countries such as Turkey and the Netherlands.

Finally, men and women tend to exhibit different eating patterns. In particular, women are more likely to engage in **compensatory eating**—making up for deficiencies such as lack of social contact or depression by eating.[114]

compensatory eating Making up for lack of social contact or depression by eating.

MARKETING
IMPLICATIONS
Obviously, many products such as aftershave, cologne, underwear, clothing, and shoes for men and perfume, pantyhose, clothing, shoes, and feminine hygiene products for women are developed to meet gender-specific needs. In addition, certain products and services appear to be sex-typed or perceived as more appropriate for one gender than the other. A tie, motorcycle, gun, tool kit, and scotch are perceived as more masculine, whereas a food processor, hand lotion, clothes dryer, facial tissue, and wine are seen as more feminine.

Note, however, that products may become less sex-typed as sex roles evolve. For example, Wall Street is increasingly trying to attract female investors.[115] More women have started buying Harley-Davidson motorcycles, a bastion of masculinity for years.[116] Because 41 percent of the primary decision makers for interior design are female, Glidden introduced Dulux paints with more colorful and stylish packaging to attract this market.[117] Likewise companies like Gillette are concentrating their marketing for razors in the female market.[118]

Targeting a Specific Gender. Furthermore, marketers often target a particular gender. Here are only a few of many examples: BMW directly targeted professional women by running ads in *Martha Stewart's Living*, along with a mail-in card for a test drive and a free video, and by sponsoring women's triathlons.[119] In Great Britain, Shell Oil sponsored Women's Workshops to teach women how to perform routine maintenance on their cars. A Diamond Club campaign encourages women to bypass husbands to buy diamonds for themselves.[120]

To appeal to men, Halston introduced a new cologne, Catalyst, with packages in the shape of test tubes and flasks and the slogan "Boys like to experiment."[121]

Interestingly, although the United States is the largest market for men's cologne, men in France, Germany, Britain, Italy, Spain, and Japan all spend more on average for this product.[122] Cosmetic companies have been quite successful in getting Japanese males to be more concerned about personal care even to the point of tweezing eyebrows and pampering their skin.[123]

In line with changing sex roles, ads are now depicting more modern images for both men and women. Men are increasingly shown in emotional and caring roles, whereas women are appearing more frequently in important situations and professional positions. As one example, Volupte perfume featured ads with "openly assertive" women who are surrounded by mystery and romance—the

1990s woman, in contrast to the 1980s woman who often looked to a man for validation.[124] A study of magazine ads found a similar trend in Japan as well.[125]

Orkin Pest Control recently tested an ad featuring a half cyborg, "Terminator-like" Orkin lady because many of its customers and employees are women.[126]

Carlsberg beer abandoned a campaign in Hong Kong in which men were describing what they liked about women's legs because it was considered sexist. These Carlsberg ads are not reflective of today's women who tend to have confidence, a handle on life, and feeling of pragmatic optimism.

Some companies have found that *cause marketing*, which focuses on critical women's issues such as domestic violence, rape, breast cancer, and AIDS, is a particularly effective way to reach women.[127] Sponsors of Lilith Fair music tour (with all female performers) are chosen on the basis of their commitment to women's issues and causes, and the Lifetime channel was a hit among women with its support for and shows about fighting breast cancer.

Media Patterns. Finally, although sex roles are changing, sex differences still exist in media patterns. Men can be reached through certain TV programs, especially sports, and magazines such as *Sports Illustrated*, *GQ*, *Esquire*, and car and motorcycle publications. Women are more likely than men to watch soap operas and home shopping networks.[128] For example, in selling soap, Lever Brothers attempts to reach women during the daytime soap operas, whereas late-night airings are required to reach a more male-oriented audience. Magazines such as *Vogue, Mademoiselle, Ladies Home Journal, House Beautiful, Bon Appetit, Good Housekeeping,* and *Allure* (noted for its hard-nosed reporting about beauty-related issues) target women. The Lifetime channel, considered "television for women," created new television shows to attract young females.[129] To appeal to different types of female fitness enthusiasts, Nike placed ads in *Outside* magazine, for walking and running, and in *Shape* magazine, for aerobics. *Sports* and *Jump* magazines were created for women who like sports.[130] *Mode* magazine was created for full-figured professional women with fashion spreads featuring "real" women in clothes they can actually wear, and *More* magazine is aimed at women over 40 and is billed as "smart talk for smart women."[131]

Finally, men are more frequent Internet shoppers than are women, but retailers are actively designing Web sites with female interests in mind to attract more of these consumers.[132] For example, *HomeArts* provides a large collection of shopping links aimed at women, and Victoria's Secret recently introduced its Web site for shopping.[133] Companies like Procter & Gamble and Unilever are also greatly increasing the number of sites for their brands to attract the 22 million women Web surfers.[134] ■

HOW THE HOUSEHOLD INFLUENCES CONSUMER BEHAVIOR

Some researchers argue that the household is the most important unit of analysis for consumer behavior because many more acquisition, consumption, and disposition decisions are made by households than by individuals. In this section we define families and households and examine the different types of households. We then discuss some of the major trends that are producing changes in household structures and consumer behavior. Finally, we examine how families influence consumer decision making and consumption.

Types of Households

nuclear family Father, mother, and children.

extended family The nuclear family plus relatives such as grandparents, aunts, uncles, and cousins.

A *family* is usually defined as a group of individuals living together who are related by marriage, blood, or adoption. The most typical unit is the **nuclear family**, consisting of a father, mother, and children. The **extended family** consists of the nuclear family plus relatives such as grandparents, aunts, uncles, and cousins. In the United States we most often think of *family* in terms of the nuclear family, whereas in many other countries the extended family is the defining unit.

Although the family is important almost everywhere in the world, some countries exhibit a stronger family orientation than others. In Japan and China, for example, the family is a focal point, and most people feel a very strong sense of obligation to it.[135] The same is true among Latin Americans and U.S. Hispanics.

household A single person living alone or a group of individuals who live together in a common dwelling, regardless of whether they are related.

Household is a broader term that includes a single person living alone or a group of individuals who live together in a common dwelling, regardless of whether they are related. This term includes cohabiting couples (an unmarried male and female living together), gay couples, and singles who are roommates. Because the number of households is on the rise, marketers and researchers are increasingly thinking in terms of households rather than families.

The traditional stereotype of the American family consisted of a husband as the primary wage earner, a wife who was a non-wage earner at home, and two children under the age of 18. Yet only 6 percent of families fit this profile. Trends such as later marriages, cohabitation, divorce, dual careers, boomerang children, greater longevity, and a lower birth rate have greatly increased the proportion of nontraditional families.[136] Note, however, that these trends were strongest from 1970 to 1990. In the 1990s baby boomers settled down, and this trend slowed the decrease in married families with children and leveled off the number of single-parent families.[137] Exhibit 15.8 shows how the types and proportions of households will change over the next 10 years.

	1990 number	1990 percent	2000 number	2000 percent	2010 number	2010 percent	1990–2000 percent change	2000–2010 percent change
All households	93,347	100.0 %	110,140	100.0 %	117,696	100.0 %	18.0 %	6.9 %
Families	66,091	70.8	77,705	70.6	80,193	68.1	17.6	3.2
Married couples	52,317	56.0	60,969	55.4	61,266	52.1	16.5	0.5
with children younger than 18*	24,537	26.3	24,286	22.1	23,433	19.9	−1.0	−3.5
with children 18+ only	6,258	6.7	5,318	4.8	6,884	5.8	−15.0	29.4
with no children	21,522	23.1	31,365	28.5	30,950	26.3	45.7	−1.3
Single fathers	1,153	1.2	1,523	1.4	1,660	1.4	32.1	9.0
Single mothers	6,599	7.1	7,473	6.8	7,779	6.6	13.2	4.1
Other families	6,022	6.5	7,741	7.0	9,488	8.1	28.5	22.6
Nonfamilies	27,257	29.2	32,434	29.4	37,503	31.9	15.6	18.0
Men living alone	9,049	9.7	10,898	9.9	12,577	10.7	20.4	15.4
Women living alone	13,950	14.9	16,278	14.8	18,578	15.8	16.7	14.1
Other nonfamilies	4,258	4.6	5,258	4.8	6,347	5.4	23.5	20.7

* Includes those with children both younger than age 18 and 18 and older.

Note: Numbers in thousands and percent of all households by type, 1990–2010; and percent change 1990–2000 and 2000–2010. Numbers may not add to total due to rounding.

EXHIBIT 15.8
Changes in Household Types

Over the next 15 to 20 years, the profile of the U.S. family will change dramatically. In particular, the proportion of nontraditional families (singles living alone, couple without children, divorced families) is on the rise. As a result, the proportion of families that fit the typical stereotype of husband, wife, two children is diminishing. Here are some specific projections for each type of household.

Source: Adapted from Joe Schwartz, "Family Traditions: Although Radically Changed, the American Family Is as Strong as Ever," *American Demographics*, March 1987, p. 9. *American Demographics*, 1987. Reprinted with permission.

374

family life cycle Different stages of family life depending on the age of the parents and how many children are living at home.

Households can further differ in terms of the **family life cycle**. As shown in Exhibit 15.9 families can be characterized in terms of the age of the parents and how many children are living at home.[138] Thus families progress from the bachelor stage (young and single) through marriage and having children to being an older couple without children at home. There are also unmarried singles, couples without children (younger and older), and older couples who delay having children. Various changes such as death or divorce can alter household structure by, for instance, creating single-parent households. The many arrows in the exhibit illustrate the varied ways that households can change over time.

The point is that the needs of households vary greatly. In general, spending increases as households shift from young singles to young married and then remains high until it falls sharply at the older married or older single stages.[139] However, this pattern depends on what is purchased. New parents tend to spend more on health care, clothing, housing, and food and less on alcohol, transportation, and education. As parents age, they spend more on housing, home maintenance, furnishings, child care, and other household services. Young empty nesters spend more on vehicles, women's clothes, and long-distance telephone services. Older single households and couples increase spending on home-based products, health care, and travel. The affluent gay market is more likely to spend on travel, clothing, and the arts. Finally, households in the midst of a life cycle change are more likely to switch brand preferences and be more receptive to marketing efforts.[140]

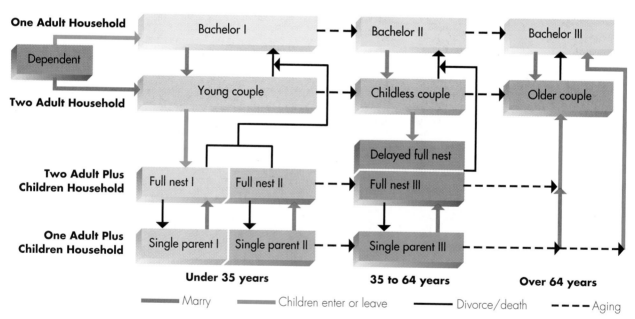

EXHIBIT 15.9
The Family Life Cycle

This chart depicts the varied ways in which families change and mature. Each box represents a stage in the family life cycle, and each line represents a type of change (marriage, divorce, death, children entering or leaving, aging). For example, a typical path might start in bachelorhood and continue through marriage (young couple), having children who then grow up (the three stages of full nest), being an old couple (children living on their own), and being a solitary survivor (one spouse dies). Note that this diagram accounts for other events that can occur (divorce, becoming a single parent, being a childless couple, never marrying). What stage is your family in right now?

Source: Mary C. Glley and Ben M. Enis, "Recycling the Family Lifecycle," in ed. Andrew A. Michell, *Advances in Consumer Research*, Vol. 9 (Ann Arbor, Mich.: Association for Consumer Research, 1982), pp. 271–276. Reprinted by permission.

Note that these stages do not capture all types of households. Notably missing are gay couples and never-married single mothers, both of which are important market segments. Gays, for example, represent anywhere from 5 to 25 million consumers in the United States. They tend to be relatively affluent and highly educated. In addition, more than 4 million women are never-married mothers between 15 and 44 years old.[141] The largest proportion are teenagers at the lower end of the income distribution.

In addition, many households consider their pets to be important family members. In the United States more than 60 percent of families own pets; there are more than 55 million dogs, 63 million cats, 25 million birds, 250 million fish, and 125 million other animals. The economic importance of these household members is evidenced by the fact that consumers spend more than $4 billion a year on pet food and $3.5 billion on veterinary care.[142] Some consumers buy pet mansions, make home-cooked meals, or buy coats for their pets.[143]

Animals are an important source of companionship and can even be social facilitators. In Sweden, for example, 83 percent of owners believe that their animals give them the opportunity to talk to other people. In Germany dogs are held in such high regard that they are allowed to accompany their owners into restaurants. Animals are also often viewed as surrogate siblings or children (owners can experience what it is like to have children in a limited way). Animals can even be incorporated into family rituals. One study found, for example, that 30 percent of owners celebrated their pet's birthday.

Changing Trends in Household Structure

Several factors have altered the basic structure and characteristics of households. These include (1) delayed marriage, (2) cohabitation, (3) dual careers, (4) divorce, and (5) smaller families.

Delayed Marriage   In many Western societies an increasing number of individuals are either delaying or avoiding getting married. As evidence, the proportion of never-married U.S. citizens aged 30 to 34 has risen 9.4 percent for men and 6.2 percent for women since 1970, and the proportion of married couples under age 25 has decreased in the United States by more than one-third since 1980.[144] For many, careers have become more important than marriage. Because it is now more acceptable for a man and a woman to live together before marriage, many do not see an immediate need to enter into a long-term marital commitment. More than 23 million people currently live alone, and the 2000s will see rapid growth in the number of singles and roommates. By 2010 researchers project that single people will account for 27 percent of all households.

This trend is important for marketers because single-person households exhibit unique consumption patterns. For example, single men spend more on alcohol, new cars, restaurant meals, clothes, and education than married men do. Essentially, this group consists of college students and "older men (divorced or never married) living like college students." Compared with married women, single women tend to spend more on new cars, shoes, entertainment, candy, and housing (to live in a safe area).[145] Finally, single men are more likely than married ones to give gifts of jewelry, watches, and clothes, whereas single women are more likely than their married sisters to give housewares and small appliances.

By delaying marriage a few years, couples typically find themselves in a better financial position, with greater discretionary income for designer baby clothes, housekeeping services, and high-quality furniture. Parents over 35 with children under 6 spend more than younger parents do on housing, home maintenance, furnishings, child care, transportation, food, and alcohol. In addition, when couples delay marriage, they also delay having children, which has led to an increase in the use of fertility drugs and the incidence of twins and triplets.[146]

Cohabitation   As a result of changing social norms, more and more consumers are deciding to live with members of the opposite sex outside marriage. About 4.3 million opposite-sex cohabiting couples reside in the United States, and demographers expect a 20 percent rise in that number by 2010.[147] The highest percentage of unmarried couples living together is in Sweden.

A defining aspect of unmarried couples (compared with married couples) is the tendency of the partners to be more self-oriented. They tend to view possessions as personal rather than joint items and leave open the possibility that the relationship may break down.[148] (Identifying possessions as belonging to one or the other protects each person if the relationship ends.) In some cases each partner has his or her own room that contains only that person's items.

Nevertheless, unmarried partners often share expenses, and because both individuals are likely to work, discretionary income can be higher than for married couples of a similar age (with a nonworking spouse). Unmarried couples are therefore more frequent consumers of entertainment, transportation, and vacations than are married couples.

Dual-Career Families   The increasing number of dual-career families has had a dramatic impact on household behavior. In general, two major types of dual-career families can be identified: (1) those in which the woman is concerned about career advancement and personal fulfillment and (2) those in which the woman works out of financial necessity and considers her employment "just a job."[149] The latter group tends to be more like the traditional housewife in terms of outlook and behavior, whereas the former group is more contemporary and progressive.

There are several key implications of dual-career families for consumer behavior. First, having two incomes increases discretionary spending.[150] One study found that dual-career families spend more than other families do on child care, eating out, and services in general. Likewise, dual careers mean that the wife is bringing more financial resources to the family, thereby giving her greater clout in influencing family decisions for expensive or important products and services such as vacations, cars, and housing.

Second, the increased burden of having both career and family, or *role overload*, leaves less time for many activities including cooking, housekeeping, and shopping.[151] Any product or service that saves time is thus particularly valued. Examples are microwavable dinners, instant foods, housekeeping services, child care, and fast food, including food delivery services. Interestingly, full-time employment of married women is a major predictor of microwave oven purchases.[152] Because shopping time is limited for these women, they are more likely to buy the same brands, be brand loyal, buy impulsively, and use catalogs.

Third, more husbands are taking on household responsibilities, including grocery shopping.[153] This trend is reflected in the ads in Exhibit 15.10, which are targeted to men who are sharing responsibility for household cooking. In Asia, however, these ads received a negative response from both men and women because sex roles are viewed more traditionally, even though more men are now doing more housework.

EXHIBIT 15.10
Changing Household Responsibilities

In today's world more men are taking on household responsibilities, such as cooking, cleaning, and shopping. These ads for cheese are designed to appeal to mean who share the household cooking duties.

Source: Courtesy of Dairy Management, Inc.

Divorce Since the turn of the 20th century, the number of marriages that end in divorce has increased dramatically. The trend has recently leveled off, but many divorces still occur each year, and these separations have important implications for consumer behavior. Most important, going through a divorce represents a major transition in which a number of critical tasks must be performed—such as disposing of old possessions, forming a new household, and creating new patterns of consumption.[154] Divorce can lead to a major change in lifestyle, and acquiring products and services can be an integral part of forming a new identity and relieving stress during this transition. For example, a recently divorced consumer might buy a new house, car, furniture, or clothing; get a new hairstyle; or go to singles clubs to assume a new image or to feel better.

Divorce also has important implications for household structure. First, if the couple was childless, the newly divorced often adopt many of the singles' acquisition and consumption patterns discussed earlier. However, these new singles are typically older and have greater discretionary income for housing, transportation, and clothing if they are working.

Second, when children are involved, divorce creates single-parent families. Estimates are that one in three families in the United States now has only one parent, and most of these families have a female head-of-household, although the proportion of single fathers is growing.[155] A major characteristic of these families is a time deficit, because they need to earn income *and* raise children. Thus convenient products or services are a necessity. Compared with their married counterparts, single parents are likely to have lower than average incomes and tend to spend relatively less on most things. Furthermore, they are also more likely to be renters than homeowners.

Finally, divorced individuals with children are remarrying with greater frequency, and when this happens, a stepfamily is created.[156] Demographers estimate that more than one-third of the families in the United States are of this type, and half of all current families will eventually become part of one or more stepfamilies in their lifetime. In nearly two-thirds of stepfamilies, children live with their biological mother, and many such families are lower in income and education and are more youthful than intact families. Due to potential stress and conflicting emotions, about half these families will also end up in divorce. The splintering of families has led some people to predict that members of Generation Y (under 10 years of age) will rely more on friends than on family for emotional stability.[157]

Like other households, stepfamilies can have unique consumption needs. For example, children who travel between families require duplicate supplies of clothes, toothbrushes, and toys.[158] Stepfamilies often plan their vacations around custody considerations.

Smaller Families   In many countries the average household size is getting smaller. In particular, boomer and Xer couples are having fewer children because of dual careers, financial burdens, and concern for overpopulation—some couples believe that having more than two children is socially irresponsible.

Smaller families have important implications for consumer behavior. In particular, they have greater discretionary income, which can be spent on recreational items, vacations, education, toys, and entertainment. Smaller families can also spend more on each child. Smaller families has been a key trend in Japan where parents with fewer children are spending more on education, cultural activities, and colorful clothing.[159] In China one-child families are the rule, as we mentioned at the beginning of the chapter, so parents spare no expense in bringing up baby.[160] China is therefore a very attractive market for makers for baby-care products.

Childless married couples are one of the fastest-growing types of households. The proportion of couples with children under 18 will drop from 47 to 38 percent of all married households between 1990 and 2010.[161] For obvious reasons these households have an even higher level of discretionary income than other households, which they spend on furnishings, vehicles, and liquor. They also spend more on restaurant meals and take-out food than on groceries. This trend does not mean that there will be few births in the future. Rather, the baby boomlet will lead to a slight increase in the number of babies born during the next 10 years. This increase will result in less spending on sports cars, fancy restaurants, and resorts and will be good news for the makers of children's clothing and toys.

MARKETING IMPLICATIONS   Marketers are now recognizing the importance of nontraditional households and are developing offerings that cater to their unique needs. For example, singles require packages that fit the needs of an individual, so many products come in smaller sizes. Products and services that offer convenience can be marketed specifically to dual-career and divorced households. For example, sales of larger American refrigerators are increasing in Japan; more women are working and can't shop for food daily.[162] In the United States, Procter & Gamble has created ads for

Tide that feature adopted children.[163] Some more affluent dual-career couples have begun hiring a personal chef.[164] Because more husbands from dual-career families and men who are divorced or single are doing more grocery and other types of shopping, retailers are increasingly targeting men.[165] Wives in these households have more clout in expensive decisions, so marketers of costly products and services must appeal to both husband and wife. And, in recognition of stepfamilies, Hallmark has developed greeting cards that deal with these relationships ("Happy Birthday to My Stepfather"; "To My Stepmother on Mother's Day"). Finally, American Express and AT&T have been targeting gays with ads featuring homosexual couples.[166] *Poz* magazine and 100 other companies sponsored a trade fair aimed at gay consumers with AIDS.[167] ■

ROLES THAT HOUSEHOLD MEMBERS PLAY

household decision roles
Roles that different members play in a household decision.

A key aspect of households is that more than one individual can become involved in acquisition and consumption. Thus the final section in this chapter discusses various aspects of household consumer behavior, with particular emphasis on **household decision roles** and how household members influence decision processes.

Whenever consumer behavior occurs in the context of a multiperson household, a variety of tasks or roles may be performed in acquiring and consuming a product or service. The household members who perform these tasks or roles are defined as follows:

- *Gatekeeper.* Members of a household who collect and control information important to the decision.
- *Influencer.* Members of the household who try to express their opinions and influence the decision.
- *Decider.* The person or persons who actually determine which product or service will be chosen.
- *Buyer.* The household member who physically acquires the product or service.
- *User.* The members of the household who consume the product.

Each role can be performed by different household members and by a single individual, subset of individuals, or the entire household. For example, in deciding which videotape to rent for entertainment, parents might decide on the movie, but the children may play a role, either directly (by making their preferences known) or indirectly (when parents keep their children's likes in mind). One parent may actually go to the store to get the video, but the entire family may watch (or consume) it.

In fact, parents are often the deciders and purchasers of items consumed by their children such as clothing, toys, food, and videotapes. Pull-Ups disposable training pants (Exhibit 15.11) is an example of such a product. Similarly, more than 70 percent of men's underwear and cologne is purchased by wives and girlfriends. On the other hand, children do influence many household decisions. Exhibit 15.12 on page 381 divides household purchases into nine categories, depending on the decision maker and the user.

instrumental roles Roles that relate to tasks affecting the buying decision.

expressive roles Roles that involve an indication of family norms.

Household decision roles can be **instrumental**, meaning that they relate to tasks affecting the buying decision, such as when and how much to purchase. Roles can also be **expressive**, which means they indicate family norms such as

Presenting Pull-Ups® disposable training pants from Huggies. They look and feel like "big kid" pants, yet offer the protection your child needs. Pull-Ups have super-absorbent padding that soaks up wetness and a moisture proof layer to help protect

Pull-Ups have tear-away sides for easy removal in case of messy accidents.

against leakage. Even overnight. When your child is ready, there's nothing like Pull-Ups.

Go on like underwear. Protect like a diaper.

EXHIBIT 15.11
Marketing to Parents and Children

Although young children are the users or consumers of many products and services, parents are usually the deciders of what to purchase. This ad tries to convince parents who have "bigger kids" that Pull-Ups training pants are a beneficial product. Note also, however, that if children this age saw this ad, they might find it appealing because they would think that "I'm a big kid now."

Source: Used with permission of Kimberly-Clark Corporation.

choice of color or style.[168] Traditionally, the husband fulfilled the instrumental role and the wife the expressive role, but sex-role changes are altering this pattern.

Conflict can often occur in fulfilling different household roles. It might revolve around (1) the reasons for buying, (2) who should make the decision, (3) which option to choose, and (4) who gets to use the product or service.[169] For example, with an increase in computer usage among all members of a family, conflict often arises over who gets to use the computer and for how long.[170]

In general, there are four modes of conflict resolution: problem solving, persuasion, bargaining, and politics. Of the four, persuasion and problem solving appear to be most frequently used.[171] Note, however, that resolution is often not systematic and rational, but rather a "muddling-through" process in which the household makes a series of small decisions to arrive at a solution.[172] Keep in mind, too, that many households avoid conflict rather than confront it.

Note that household decisions are more frequent in some circumstances than in others. Specifically, joint decisions are more likely when the perceived risk associated with the decision is high, the decision is very important, there is ample time to make a decision, and the household is young. In addition, household members can influence each other in terms of brand preferences and loyalties, information search patterns, media reliance, and price sensitivities.[173]

The Roles of Spouses

husband-dominant decision Decision made primarily by the male head-of-household.

wife-dominant decision Decision made primarily by the female head-of-household.

autonomic decision Decision equally likely to be made by the husband or wife, but not by both.

Husbands and wives play different roles in making decisions, and the nature of their influence depends on both the product or service and the couple's relationship. In examining husband-wife influence, a landmark study conducted in Belgium (and replicated in the United States) identified four major categories of decisions:[174]

- A **husband-dominant decision** is made primarily by the male head-of-household (e.g., the purchase of lawn mowers and hardware).

- A **wife-dominant decision** is made primarily by the female head-of-household (e.g., children's clothing, women's clothing, groceries, pots and pans, and toiletries).

- An **autonomic decision** is equally likely to be made by the husband or the wife, but not by both (e.g., men's clothing, luggage, toys and games, sporting equipment, stereos, and cameras).

EXHIBIT 15.12
Buyers and Users

Household purchase decisions can be made by one, some, or all members of the family. Acquired products and services can then be consumed by one, some, or all members. Here is an example of three cells that result from crossing these two factors. Can you think of examples that would fit into the other six cells?

Source: Robert Boutilier, "Pulling the Family's Strings," *American Demographics,* August 1993, pp. 44–48. *American Demographics* © 1993. Reprinted with permission.

A Purchase Decision Maker

		One member	Some members	All members
A Consumer	One member	1	2 Tennis racket	3
	Some members	4 Sugar Pops	5	6
	All members	7	8	9 Refrigerator

For Example:
1. Mom and Dad go to buy a new tennis racket for Mom. Dad advises Mom on her purchase. One member is a decision maker and one member is a consumer: cell 2.
2. Mom goes to the grocery store to buy Sugar Pops cereal for her children. She'll never eat the stuff. One member is a decision maker and some members are consumers: cell 4.
3. Mom, Dad, and the kids go to the department store to buy a refrigerator. All members are decision makers and all are consumers: cell 9.

---

syncratic decision   Decision made jointly by the husband and wife.

- A **syncratic decision** is made jointly by the husband and wife (e.g., vacations, refrigerators, TVs, living room furniture, carpets, financial planning services, and the family car).

Interestingly, as spouses get nearer to a final decision, the process tends to move toward syncratic decision making and away from the other three types, particularly for more important decisions. Note that these role structures are only general trends, and the actual influence exerted depends on many factors. First, a spouse will have greater influence when the financial resources he or she brings to the family are higher and he or she has a high level of involvement in the decision.[175] Second, demographic factors, such as total family income, occupation, and education, are also related to the degree of husband-wife influence.[176] Combined, these factors provide a spouse with a perception of power in the decision-making situation. The higher the degree of perceived power, the more likely the spouse will exert influence. Finally, when the family has a strong traditional sex-role orientation, certain tasks are stereotypically considered either masculine or feminine and more decisions tend to be husband-dominated than in less traditional families.[177] For example, Mexican American families tend to have a strong traditional orientation and are characterized by more husband-dominant decisions.

 General support for the four major patterns of spousal decision roles has been found in a variety of countries, although the United States, France, and the Netherlands exhibited a higher level of joint decision making than Venezuela and Gabon, where autonomous decisions were more prevalent.[178] A recent study of Russian families found that independent decisions occur in less than a quarter of households. The wife makes decisions on toiletries and household cleaning items, and husband dominance occurs only for household durables. Joint decision making is most likely for semidurable goods like small

bargaining A fair exchange of preferences.

concession Giving in on some points to get what one wants in other areas.

appliances and electronics. Furthermore, in many Latin American countries most decisions tend to be husband dominant. Finally, in the United States joint decision making is most common among white families, husband dominance is more likely in Japanese American families, and wife dominance is more prevalent in black families.

Research has examined other aspects of spousal decision making as well. For example, through the processes of **bargaining** (which involves a fair exchange) or **concession** (in which a spouse gives in on some points to get what he or she wants in other areas), couples tend to make equitable decisions that result from compromises.[179] Like household decision making, spousal decisions are often not a formal, systematic process. Instead, couples use a "muddling through" process in which they have limited awareness of each other's knowledge and decision strategy.[180] In fact, husbands and wives are generally not very good estimators of their spouse's influence and preferences for products and services. In making these estimations, consumers tend to start with their own preference and adjust for what they think their spouse will like. Unfortunately, this strategy does not work very well and is accurate only when one spouse has actual knowledge of the other's preferences. Sometimes spouses even disagree on whether certain products have been purchased.

The Roles of Children

Clearly, children can have an important impact on household decision making by attempting to influence their parents' acquisition, usage, and disposition behavior. The most common stereotype is that children nag their parents until they finally give in. Research finds that although children often make these attempts, their success depends on the type of offering, characteristics of the parents, age of the child, and stage of the decision process.[181] Children are more likely to influence parents for child-related products such as cereals, cookies, candy, snacks, ice cream, and frozen pizza, as well as cars, vacations, and new technologies including personal computers. In Europe more families are buying U.S. breakfast cereal, a type of food that has never been part of the traditional European breakfast because kids see ads on TV and ask for it.[182] For clothing and toys, children often use the argument that "everyone else has one," and because parents do not want to be identified as "scrimpers," they will often give in.[183]

Interestingly, children consistently overestimate how much influence they have in most decisions.[184] When parents are more involved in the decision process or are more traditional and conservative, children are less likely to have influence. Working and single parents, on the other hand, are more likely to give in because they face more time pressures.[185] Furthermore, when parents place more restrictions on TV watching, they tend to yield less, but children's attempts to influence parents increase as parents watch more TV with them.

Another important finding is that the older the child, the more influence he or she will exert.[186] Part of the reason is that younger children tend to have lower involvement in the decision process. As evidence, teens believe they have greater influence when the decision is important to them and the family. Older children also generate their own income, giving them more power. Finally, parents are more likely to refuse the requests of younger children.

One study examined the strategies adolescents use in trying to influence parental and family decision making.[187] These strategies include bargaining (making deals), persuasion (trying to influence the decision in their favor), emotional appeals (using emotion to get what they want), and requests (directly asking). Parents, in turn, can use not only the same strategies on their children but also expert (knowledge), legitimate (power), and directive (parental authority) strategies.

The type of household determines the nature of children's influence. Four general categories have been identified in this regard:

- Authoritarian households stress obedience.
- Neglectful households exert little control.
- Democratic households encourage self-expression.
- Permissive households remove constraints.

Children are more likely to have direct decision control in permissive and neglectful families and to influence decisions in democratic and permissive ones.[188] Also, children's influence has been found to vary at different stages of the decision process. Specifically, the greatest impact is at the earliest stages of decision making (problem recognition and information search), and it declines significantly in the evaluation and choice phases.[189] However, because three out of five parents take their children along when grocery shopping, the influence of children may be greater for grocery purchases than it is for other items.

MARKETING IMPLICATIONS Marketers need to recognize that household decision roles exist and may be performed by different household members. Thus appealing only to deciders or purchasers may be a narrow and relatively ineffective strategy. For example, exclusively targeting children for toys and breakfast cereals ignores the fact that parents are usually influencers, deciders, and purchasers of these products. Marketing men's underwear only to males would fail to account for the fact that the majority of decisions and purchases of these items are made by women. Therefore, marketers must acquire a clear understanding of which family members are involved in which acquisition decisions and appeal to all important parties.

For example, to appeal to children, stores now offer play areas and baby-sitting centers.[190] The theory is that if kids have fun at a particular store, they will influence their parents to shop there. Thus McDonald's ensures its success with children by putting toys in Happy Meals, which gets kids to influence their parents to take them to McDonald's again and again. In Belgium a Chiquita Banana Day promotion at a leading amusement park was designed to influence children's purchase and consumption behavior (and to get children to influence their parents).[191] Finally, some Web sites now allow kids to shop on-line without credit cards by setting up special accounts.[192] Before an actual purchase can be made, parents must review and approve it.

Marketers sometimes direct their efforts toward the entire family. Kmart's ads now try to pull the entire family rather than just one shopper into the store.[193] Hilton has been marketing to families by offering check-in folders with information about children's attractions and by stocking a lending desk with toys, games, and books, and Marriott offers home-style suites.[194] Las Vegas has reshaped its image by offering entertainment geared more toward families, such as magic acts, jousting tournaments, and horse shows.[195] Amtrak teamed up with PBS's *Thomas the Tank Engine* to broaden the railroad's family appeal.[196] Finally, in promoting the Voyager, Chrysler sponsored events with a safety theme; attendees received a safety identification kit, played a Twister-like game, and viewed safety features of the vehicle.[197] ■

Household Decision Making Versus Household Consumption Behavior

Most of the research we've described has focused rather narrowly on decision making. More work is needed on how households *consume* products and services. In other words, a variety of events and processes can occur during consumption, which provides us with a deeper understanding of both households and consumer behavior.

To illustrate what consumption patterns can tell us, one study examined how a VCR was used and how it affected family interactions.[198] Soon after the VCR was purchased, it became the center of family togetherness because it was the basis of a family night for watching movies. The family would treat this activity as a major event that was controlled by the dad (holder of the remote control). After several months, however, family members became more fragmented in their interests, and individual members began using the VCR for their own needs. Adolescents watched teen movies as a way of identifying with important social or peer groups; the parents watched old movies to bring back memories or teen movies to help them communicate with their children. The key point, however, is that consumption patterns give us a general feel for how families communicate and interact.

SUMMARY

Age plays an important role in consumer behavior. Teens, who need to establish an identity, are the consumers of tomorrow and have an increasing influence on family decisions. The somewhat disillusioned Generation X consists of smart and cynical young consumers who can easily see through obvious marketing attempts. Baby boomers grew up in a very dynamic and fast-changing world, and this environment has affected their values for individualism and freedom. The 50 and older segment can be divided into two groups—the young again and the gray market. Neither group likes to be thought of as old.

Gender differences also affect consumer behavior. Sex roles are changing; more women are becoming financially independent and working as professionals, and men are learning to become more sensitive and caring. Men and women also differ in terms of consumer traits, information-processing styles, decision-making styles, and consumption patterns.

Households include both families and unrelated people living together, as well as singles. The proportion of nontraditional households has increased because of factors such as (1) later marriages, (2) cohabitation, (3) dual-career families, (4) increased divorce, and (5) smaller families. Households exert an important influence on acquisition and consumption patterns. First, household members can play different roles in the decision process (gatekeeper, influencer, decider, buyer, and user). Second, husbands and wives vary in their influence in the decision process, depending on whether the situation is husband dominant, wife dominant, autonomic, or syncratic. Third, children can influence the decision process by making requests of parents. The nature of this influence partly depends on whether the household is authoritarian, neglectful, democratic, or permissive. However, in general, the older the child, the greater the influence.

EXERCISES

1. Pick a product or service category that individuals of all age groups consume. Conduct a detailed research analysis of the marketing techniques used to attract the four demographic segments discussed in this chapter in the following areas: (a) brands or services offered, (b) package design, (c) advertising content, (d) media selection, (e) sales promotion, and (f) distribution strategy. Collect this information via a library search, a content analysis of advertising messages and media used, in-store visits, and interviews with marketers. Then answer the following questions:

   a. Which similar techniques are used to market to the different age groups?

   b. Which techniques are used to appeal to specific age groups? How do these techniques differ from age group to age group?

2. Conduct a detailed research analysis of the marketing techniques used to appeal to males and females in the following areas: (a) brands or services offered, (b) package design, (c) advertising content, (d) media selection, (e) sales promotion, and (f) distribution strategy. Collect this information in the same manner as described in exercise 1 and then answer the following questions:

   a. Which similar techniques are used to market to both males and females?

   b. Which specific techniques are used to appeal to males? to females?

3. Pick three products and services that households consume. Conduct an interview of individuals from five families and ask them to provide a thorough description of the processes used to acquire, consume, and dispose of these products or services. Summarize this information by answering the following questions:

   a. Which specific roles do household members play in the decision process?

   b. What is the nature of husband-wife interaction in the decision?

   c. Which role do children play in the process?

   d. How do household consumption patterns for these products and services differ from individual consumption patterns?

   e. Who disposes of the products and services and why?

CHAPTER

16

SOCIAL INFLUENCES

INTRODUCTION

Several years ago a rumor spread across the United States about one of the country's most beloved firms—the Walt Disney Company.[1] The rumor held that some of Disney's films, including *Aladdin* and *The Lion King*, contained sexually oriented subliminal messages. It was rumored that in one scene Aladdin murmurs, "All good teenagers take off your clothes," and that in a scene from *The Lion King*, the word *sex* is spelled out in a dust cloud. Although Disney denied the rumors, the company was left with some questions to answer and some decisions to make. Where did these rumors come from? Why did people believe them? And what should the company do about them?

The rumors apparently had traveled a long road. They were reported to the general public by a credible source—the Associated Press—which got the story from a newspaper journalist, who in turn had gotten it from an article in a newsletter published by a religious group. The journalist contacted the group and asked members to show him and a half dozen other reporters the subliminal messages. After seeing the purported evidence, the journalists were skeptical about the story, but they did write a tongue-in-cheek article about it in their paper.

Interestingly, the religious group had not originally discovered the supposed messages either. Its members learned about them from a story in an entertainment review magazine called Movie Guide, whose editors later retracted the story after receiving a letter from Disney telling them that the purportedly offensive line was actually, "Scat, good tiger. Take off and go." However, Movie Guide had not found the subliminal messages either; its article was based on letters from readers. One letter writer heard the story from her daughter, who in turn heard it from her friend, who heard it from her brother.

social influences Information by and pressures from individuals, groups, and the mass media that affect how a person behaves.

T his chapter explores when and why individuals, groups, and the mass media affect consumer behavior. Sometimes information and pressures, which we call **social influences**, are strong because the information source is very credible; at other times they are strong simply because the source can communicate information widely. Social influence is also powerful when individuals within groups are in frequent contact and have many opportunities to communicate information and perspectives. Certain people in groups are sometimes quite influential because their power or expertise makes others want to follow what they believe or say.

We also discuss the kinds of influence individuals have. Individuals can communicate information, as in a rumor, but they can also influence whether, what, when, where, how, how much, and how often consumers think they should acquire, use, and dispose of an offering. Groups can induce not only socially appropriate consumer behaviors but also socially inappropriate and even personally destructive behaviors. For example, excessive consumption of alcohol, use of illicit drugs, and stealing are sometimes affected by group influences. Therefore, marketers need to understand factors such as what kinds of social entities create influence, what kinds of influence they create, and what effects their influence attempts can have. Exhibit 16.1 guides our overall discussion.

GENERAL SOURCES OF INFLUENCE

Consumers in our opening story heard about the Disney rumor from a number of sources. But which had most impact, and why? We can begin to find the answers to these questions in Exhibit 16.2 on page 389.

Marketer-Dominated Versus Non-marketer-Dominated Influence

marketer-dominated source Influence delivered from a marketing agent (e.g., advertising, personal selling).

Sources of influence can be described as **marketer dominated** or **non-marketer dominated**, and as delivered via the mass media or personally.

non-marketer-dominated source Influence delivered from an entity outside a marketing organization (e.g., friends, family, the media).

Marketer-Dominated Sources Delivered via Mass Media Marketer-dominated sources that deliver influence through the mass media (cell 1 in Exhibit 16.2) include advertising, sales promotions, publicity, and special events. You might have learned about the benefits of VISA from TV or Internet ads. Macy's influences your purchase behavior by promoting special sales in your local newspaper.

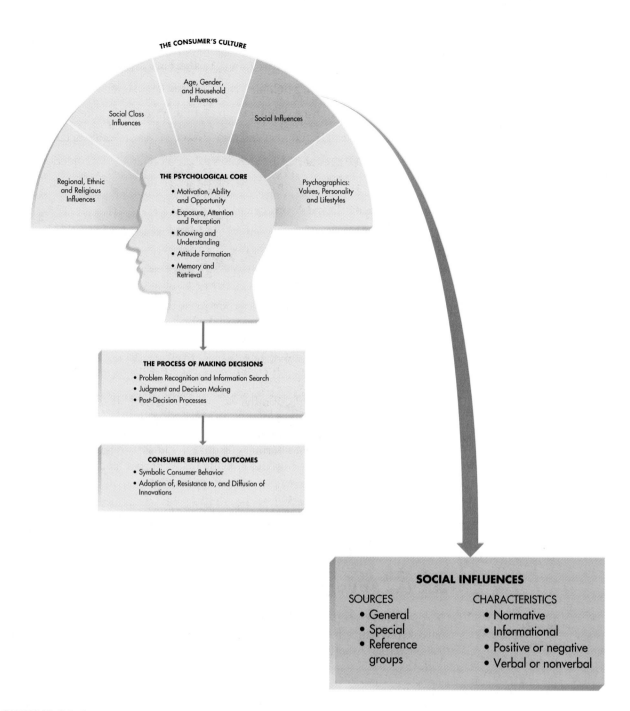

THE CONSUMER'S CULTURE

Age, Gender, and Household Influences

Social Class Influences

Social Influences

Regional, Ethnic and Religious Influences

THE PSYCHOLOGICAL CORE
- Motivation, Ability and Opportunity
- Exposure, Attention and Perception
- Knowing and Understanding
- Attitude Formation
- Memory and Retrieval

Psychographics: Values, Personality and Lifestyles

THE PROCESS OF MAKING DECISIONS
- Problem Recognition and Information Search
- Judgment and Decision Making
- Post-Decision Processes

CONSUMER BEHAVIOR OUTCOMES
- Symbolic Consumer Behavior
- Adoption of, Resistance to, and Diffusion of Innovations

SOCIAL INFLUENCES

SOURCES
- General
- Special
- Reference groups

CHARACTERISTICS
- Normative
- Informational
- Positive or negative
- Verbal or nonverbal

EXHIBIT 16.1

Chapter Overview: Social Influences

This chapter describes various sources of influence (general sources, specific sources and groups) and how they exert influence (by providing normative or informational influence, by providing positive and/or negative information, and by providing information verbally or non-verbally).

EXHIBIT 16.2
Sources of Influence

Social influence can come from marketer- or non-marketer-dominated sources and can be delivered via the mass media or in person. Non-marketer-dominated sources tend to be the more credible of the two sources. Information delivered via the mass media has the benefit of reaching many people but may not allow for a two-way flow of communication.

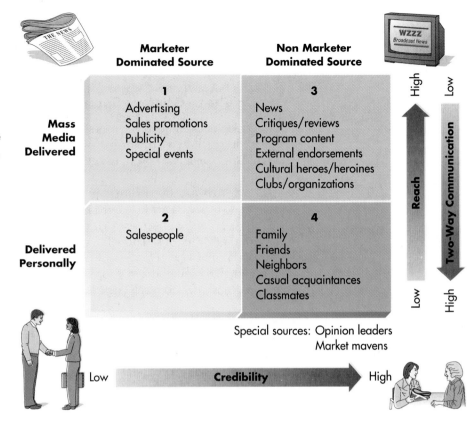

	Marketer Dominated Source	Non Marketer Dominated Source
Mass Media Delivered	**1** Advertising Sales promotions Publicity Special events	**3** News Critiques/reviews Program content External endorsements Cultural heroes/heroines Clubs/organizations
Delivered Personally	**2** Salespeople	**4** Family Friends Neighbors Casual acquaintances Classmates

Reach: High / Low
Two-Way Communication: Low / High

Special sources: Opinion leaders
Market mavens

Credibility: Low → High

Companies often announce a new product or service through publicity, and sports teams announce changes in players or managers by holding press conferences.

Marketer-Dominated Sources Delivered Personally   Marketer-dominated sources can also deliver information personally (cell 2 in Exhibit 16.2). Salespeople, service representatives, and customer service agents are marketer-dominated personal sources of influence, and they deliver information in retail outlets, at consumers' homes or offices, over the phone, or at trade shows.

Non-marketer-Dominated Sources Delivered via Mass Media   Influence can also be wielded by non-marketer-dominated sources and delivered via mass media (cell 3 in Exhibit 16.2). News items about new products, movies, and restaurants; product contamination; accidents involving products; and incidences of product abuse or misuse can all affect consumption practices. Recent media attention to the dangers of breast implants has affected consumers' awareness of this issue. Certain media sources are particularly powerful sources of influence. Many consumers, for instance, will base their moviegoing on recommendations made by film critics; dining decisions on restaurant reviews; acquisition decisions on information provided in *Consumer Reports*; and hotel accommodations based on the American Automobile Association's rating guides. Celebrities and other well-known media figures may also influence consumers' acquisition, usage, and disposition decisions.

Non-marketer-Dominated Sources Delivered Personally   Finally, consumer behavior is influenced by non-marketer-dominated sources that deliver information personally (cell 4 in Exhibit 16.2). Word-of-mouth communication from friends, family, neighbors, casual acquaintances, and even strangers can affect our consumer behavior, as can the behavior we observe from these people. For example, we might hear from friends that a favorite restaurant is opening a new branch, and we may observe from a stranger how to pump gas at a new high-tech gas station.

How Do These General Sources Differ?

The four classes of influence sources shown in Exhibit 16.2 are interesting because they vary in reach, capacity for two-way communication, and credibility. These characteristics can affect how much influence each source can have.

Reach   Mass media sources are important to marketers because they reach large consumer audiences. Part of the reason the Associated Press story about Disney had such a significant effect was that the message it delivered reached many people. With the advent of satellite TV, marketing messages, product news, the behavior of cultural heroes and heroines, and television programs can be seen by increasingly large numbers of people. Access to the Internet also enables marketers and consumers to reach large audiences.

Capacity for Two-Way Communication   Personally delivered sources of influence are important because they provide a two-way flow of information. For example, a car salesperson may have more influence than a car ad because the salesperson can tailor sales information to fit the buyer's information needs, rebut counterarguments, reiterate important and/or complex information, ask questions, and make sure questions are answered.

Personal conversations are often more casual and less purposive than mass-media-delivered information. People are less likely to anticipate what will be said and hence are less likely to take steps to avoid information inconsistent with their own frames of reference. Information received from a real-life source may also seem more vivid than information received from a mass media source simply because the person telling the story somehow makes it more real. This factor in turn may make the information more persuasive.[2]

Credibility   Whereas personal and mass media sources differ in their reach and capacity for two-way communication, marketer- and non-marketer-dominated sources differ in their credibility (see Exhibit 16.2). Information delivered through marketer-dominated sources tends to be perceived as less credible, more biased, and manipulative. Non-marketer-dominated sources appear more credible because they are not perceived as having a personal stake in our decisions to acquire, use, or dispose of an offering. We are more likely to believe a *Consumer Reports* article on cars than information from a car salesperson. And we are more likely to believe another consumer who tells us that the hotel has friendly and accommodating service than to believe a hotel sales agent who provides the same information. Similarly, consumers were likely to believe the Disney rumor because it appeared to come from a credible source (the Associated Press). Because non-marketer-dominated sources are credible, they tend to have more influence on consumer decisions than marketer-dominated sources.[3]

Specific personal and mass media sources vary in their credibility. We are more likely to believe information we hear from people with whom we have strong ties, in part because we are more likely to find them credible.[4] Certain celebrities are also regarded as more credible than others. Denzel Washington has been an extraordinarily successful spokesperson for the Boys and Girls Clubs of America. Magazines also vary in their credibility. We are also more likely to

In 1989, from their home, two guys, three dogs, and a 59¢ biscuit cutter set out to make the world's best dog treats. The result? Five stores, a cooking show and Great Dane-size demand. American Express® Small Business Services was there, extending credit when no one else would. And this year, when they open 80 new stores, our equipment financing program will reduce their cash outlay. All delivered with our usual person-to-person (-to-canine) service. do more

Small Business Services

Call 1-800-SUCCESS or visit www.americanexpress.com.

EXHIBIT 16.3

Using Non-marketer-Dominated Sources to Enhance Credibility

Ads may be more credible when advertisers use non-marketer-dominated sources. Consumers may believe that American Express Small Business Services are effective because these two entrepreneurs have given them a strong endorsement.

Source: Courtesy of American Express.

believe a story that we read in *Time* than one we read in the *National Enquirer.*

MARKETING IMPLICATIONS The notion that marketer- and non-marketer-dominated sources differ in credibility and that personal and nonpersonal sources differ in their reach and capacity for two-way communication have several interesting implications.

Use Non-marketer-Dominated Sources to Enhance Credibility. To the extent possible, it is useful to have non-marketer-dominated sources promote the marketer's offering (see Exhibit 16.3). Testimonials and word-of-mouth referrals may have considerable impact, particularly if they are delivered through personal communication.[5] Likewise, the media have tremendous power to influence consumption trends and behavior. They can make or break new styles and can alter perceptions of what is cool and what is not. As an example, *Teen People* and *Teen Magazine* have worked in partnership with the American Cancer Society to carry stories that deride smoking. As one publisher noted, "We have the power to lead those teens and tell them what brands are hot. . . . We need to leverage that power and make it cool not to smoke."[6]

Sometimes it is difficult for consumers to tell whether information that they see or read in the media is from a marketer- or non-marketer-dominated source. Some ads are disguised to look like the editorial content of a magazine, and magazines often feature articles that mention the names of their advertisers. For example, in one issue of *Home* magazine, a three-page article on the repainting of a cottage mentioned Benjamin Moore paints nine times.[7]

Use Personal Sources to Enhance Two-Way Communication. Marketing efforts may be more effective when personal information sources are used. It is perhaps for these reasons that Smart Talk Network, a Canadian long-distance phone company, put approximately 700 employees to the task of going door-to-door to sell long-distance phone services.[8] Some businesses like day care centers and tutors survive solely on the basis of word of mouth and do not invest in advertising at all.

Use a Mix of Sources to Enhance Impact. Because marketer- and non-marketer-dominated sources differ in their impact, the effect on consumers may be greatest when marketers use complementary sources of influence. One vitamin company, for example, found that although word of mouth had historically sustained the company, competitive pressures forced it to achieve greater reach through advertising. Similarly, given competition from nonbank service providers, banks are finding that word-of-mouth referrals are insufficient to entice consumers to try or stay with a particular bank.[9] Advertisers are finding that mass media ads using superstars are becoming less successful than in the past. Instead, marketing efforts seem to have more impact when these ads are combined with favorable word of mouth.[10] ▪

SPECIAL SOURCES OF INFLUENCE

Some special sources have profound influence. Two such sources—opinion leaders and market mavens—are described here. Both are regarded as non-marketer-dominated sources of influence.

Opinion Leaders

opinion leader An individual who acts as an information broker between the mass media and the opinions and behaviors of an individual or group.

An **opinion leader** is an individual who acts as an information broker between the mass media and the opinions and behaviors of an individual or group. Opinion leaders are people whose position, expertise, or firsthand knowledge renders them particularly important sources of relevant and credible information. Someone is usually an opinion leader in a specific domain. Thus Cindy Crawford is an opinion leader for beauty products, not for computers. Not all opinion leaders are well known. A coworker may be an opinion leader for computers given her extensive experience with various hardware and software products.

Sometimes opinion leaders are friends or acquaintances who possess these characteristics. In other cases they are professional service agents like doctors, dentists, or lawyers who administer advice to their patients and clients. Non-marketer-dominated sources like film critics, restaurant reviewers, and *Consumer Reports* also act as information sources. Harry Knowles, a Hollywood insider publishes Harry Knowles's Web site, Ain't It Cool News (www.aintitcool news.com), an insider's evaluation of new Hollywood movies. Celebrities, models, and leaders of various social groups may also serve as opinion leaders for various products or services. Because they are so credible, opinion leaders can play an important role in other consumers' acceptance of new products and services. Exhibit 16.4 identifies several celebrity opinion leaders and the categories in which they have influence.

gatekeepers Sources that control the flow of information.

Opinion leaders are part of a general category of **gatekeepers**, those who have special influence or power in deciding whether a product or information will be disseminated to a market. For example, the Beijing Telegraph Administration serves as a gatekeeper because it limits the type of information entering China from the Internet. The Chinese government is also a gatekeeper, as it prohibits sexually explicit TV shows and music videos from other countries.[11] Even within the United States, certain people play a very powerful gatekeeping role. For example, the search engine Yahoo! hires people who are Internet "bouncers." Their job is to control admittance of Web sites that might compromise the integrity of the Yahoo! directory. Web sites that don't make the grade are not included in the directory.[12]

What Are the Characteristics of Opinion Leaders?   Because their influence can be profound and because opinion leaders are not always well-known people, researchers have tried to understand who opinion leaders are and how to target them. Several characteristics have been observed.[13] For example, opinion leaders tend to learn a lot about products. They are heavy users of media like newspapers, TV, radio, and magazines, and they tend to buy new products when they are first introduced to the marketplace. Opinion leaders are also self-confident, gregarious, and willing to share product information.

Why Do People Become Opinion Leaders?   People may become opinion leaders because they have an intrinsic interest in and enjoyment of certain products. In other words, they have enduring involvement in a product category.[14] Opinion leaders might also seek their roles because having and sharing information puts them in a position of power. Finally, opinion leaders may communicate information simply because they believe their actions will help others.[15]

Why Do Opinion Leaders Have Influence?   Opinion leaders have influence because they generally have no personal stake in whether consumers actually heed their opinions. Thus their opinions tend to be regarded as unbiased and

WHO ARE THEY?	WHAT ARE THEY KNOWN FOR?	WHO LISTENS TO THEM?
Anna Wintour, editor of *Vogue*	Approving new designers, designs	- Fashion forward consumers
John Doerr, venture capitalist	Funding Silicon Valley start-ups	- Wall Street
George Lundberg, editor of the *Journal of the American Medical Association*	Publishing scientific articles	- Doctors, scientists - Health conscious consumers
Maria Campbell, literary scout	Evaluating how well books will do as movies	- Publishers - Movie producers
Csaba Csere, editor of *Car and Driver* magazine	Providing information to car buffs	- Car dealers - Car manufacturers - Car buffs
Oprah Winfrey, personality, show host, movie star, book club magnate	Popularizing books, people, and ways of dealing with problems	- Book publishers, book buyers - Women
Matt Drudge, Web reporter	Providing news and gossip on the goings on of Washington	- Everyone in Washington
Mark McCarmack, sports agent	Endorsing athletes	- Team owners - Product endorsers - Sports fans
Walter Mossberg, *Wall Street Journal* columnist	Providing straight facts, in easy to digest language, about which software and hardware is worth buying	- Silicon Valley product managers - Consumers contemplating computer hardware or software purchase

EXHIBIT 16.4
Opinion Leaders

Although not all opinion leaders are well-known people, some people are. These well-known opinion leaders have the capacity to influence many people.

Source: Adapted from Rick Martin and Sarah Van Brown, "The Buzz Machine," *Newsweek,* July 27, 1998, pp. 22–26.

credible. In addition, because they have information about and experiences with the product, opinion leaders are often regarded as knowledgeable about acquisition, usage, and disposition options. However, simply because they serve as information brokers does not mean that information always flows from opinion leader to consumers. Indeed, opinion leaders often get information by seeking it from others; they are just as likely to be information seekers as providers.[16]

market maven A consumer who has and communicates considerable marketplace information to others.

Market Mavens

Market mavens are individuals "who have information about *many* products, places to shop, and other facets of the marketplace, and initiate discussions with consumers

INITIAL ITEM POOL FOR THE OPINION LEADERSHIP AND OPINION SEEKING SCALES

The questionnaires below ask consumers questions about rock music. A similar version of the questionnaire asks consumers about fashion and environmentally friendly products. Consumers respond to each question using a scale, where 1 means strongly disagree and 7 means strongly agree. People who have a high score on the first scale are classified as opinion leaders in the area of music. Those who score high on the second are opinion seekers in the area of music.

Opinion Leadership

1. Other people rarely ask me about rock CD's before they choose one for themselves.
2. My opinion on rock [fashion; environmentally friendly products] seems not to count with other people.*
3. My opinions influence what types of recordings other people buy.
4. Other people think that I am a poor source of information on rock music.
5. When they choose a rock music recording [fashionable clothing; "green" products], other people do not turn to me for advice.*
6. Other people [rarely] come to me for advice about choosing CD's and tapes [fashionable clothing; products that are good for the environment].*
7. People that I know pick rock music [clothing; "green" products] based on what I have told them.*
8. People rarely repeat things I have told them about popular rock music to other people.
9. What I say about rock music rarely changes other people's minds.
10. I often persuade other people to buy the rock music [fashions; "green" products] that I like.*
11. I often influence people's opinions about popular rock [clothing; environmentally correct products.]*

Opinion Seeking

1. When I consider buying a CD or tape [clothes; "green" products], I ask other people for advice.*
2. I don't need to talk to others before I buy CD's or tapes [fashionable clothing; products that are good for the environment].*
3. Other people influence my choice of rock music.
4. I would not choose a recording without consulting someone else.
5. I rarely ask other people what music [fashions; environmentally friendly products] to buy.*
6. I like to get others' opinions before I buy a CD or tape [new clothes; "green" products].
7. I feel more comfortable buying a recording [fashion item; product that is good for the environment] when I have gotten other people's opinions on it.*
8. When choosing rock music [fashionable clothing; a "green" product], other people's opinions are not important to me.*

*Items in the final scales.

EXHIBIT 16.5
A Scale Measuring Opinion Leadership

Because opinion leaders can be so important to marketers, it is sometimes important to identify who opinion leaders are. These scales identify which consumers are opinion leaders and opinion seekers in several product categories.

Source: Leisa Reinecke Flynn, Ronald E. Goldsmith, and Jacqueline K. Eastmen, "Opinion Leaders and Opinion Seekers: Two New Measurements Scales," *Journal of the Academy of Marketing Science,* 24(2), p. 146, copyright © 1996 by Sage Publications, Inc. Reprinted by permission of Sage Publications, Inc.

and respond to requests from consumers for market information."[17] The difference between an opinion leader and a market maven is that a market maven tends to know a lot about the marketplace in general. A market maven would know where and when to shop, what is on sale when, and which products are good and bad. Perhaps because of their general interest in the marketplace, market mavens tend to be aware of new products early on, and they are heavy users of a wide range of information sources, both getting and giving marketplace information. Although research about them is limited, market mavens tend to be low-income, female, and non-Caucasian. They are heavy media users and watch more TV and read more magazines than others.

EXHIBIT 16.6
Using Opinion Leaders as Influence Sources

Opinion leaders, people whose expertise or knowledge makes them relevant and credible sources of information, can be influential. Jere Marder's position as champion breeder and handler makes her a credible opinion leader for Pro Plan dog food.

Source: Copyright © 1999 Ralston Purina Company. Photo by Scott Raffe.

MARKETING IMPLICATIONS Marketers use several tactics to influence opinion leaders.

Target Opinion Leaders. Given their potential impact and the fact that they serve as both seekers and providers of marketplace information, one of the most obvious marketing strategies for reaching opinion leaders and market mavens is to target them directly.[18] For example, doctors may be targeted to help consumers learn about health-related products and services. The Ghana government had more success with its inoculation programs when health workers contacted and gained the approval of an opinion leader—in this case, the local healer—before approaching the public.[19] Without the approval of the local healer, the inoculation programs were less successful.

If marketers are to target opinion leaders, it obviously becomes very important to identify them. Exhibit 16.5 illustrates one scale that has been developed to identify opinion leaders.

Use Opinion Leaders in Marketing Communications. Opinion leaders may also be used in advertising (see Exhibit 16.6). Although their influence may be less effective when it is delivered through a marketer-dominated than a non-marketer dominated source, their expertise and association with an offering can still make them effective. An alternative to using an actual opinion leader in ads is to use a simulated opinion leader. For example, although the major television networks forbid the use of medical professionals or actors playing them to endorse a product, a simulated opinion leader may be used. For example, Mentadent toothpaste has used the wives, husbands, and children of actual dentists. Although these individuals are not experts on toothpaste, their affiliation with real experts presumably gives them some credibility.[20]

Refer Consumers to Opinion Leaders. Finally, marketers can target consumers and ask them to refer to a knowledgeable opinion leader. Ads for Zantac (an ulcer medication) tell ulcer and heartburn sufferers to ask an opinion leader, namely, their doctor, about how the advertiser's product can help the consumer. ∎

REFERENCE GROUPS ARE SOURCES OF INFLUENCE

reference group A set of people with whom individuals compare themselves to guide their attitudes, knowledge, and/or behaviors.

We've seen how certain individuals can exert influence. However, how is social influence exerted by specific *groups* of people? A **reference group** is a set of people with whom individuals compare themselves as a guide to developing their own attitudes, knowledge, and/or behaviors.

What Are the Types of Reference Groups?

One way to discuss the concept of reference groups is to identify the types of groups to which a consumer may belong. Three types of reference groups can be described—aspirational, associative, and dissociative.

Aspirational reference groups are groups we admire and *wish* to be like but are not currently a member of. For example, groupies often aspire to be like members of a rock band. A younger brother may want to be like his older brother and other older children. Some Eastern European youths aspire to be like their U.S. counterparts.[21] As another example, in Korea, teachers often reflect aspirational reference groups for students, given the high respect accorded to education.

Associative reference groups are groups that we *do* belong to. For example, you are an accepted member of a clique of friends and an extended family. You might be a member of a particular work group, club, or school group. The gender, ethnic, geographic, and age groups to which you belong are also associative reference groups with whom you identify. Exhibit 16.7 shows the associative reference groups in one high school in Illinois. To what extent do these groups mirror the groups that you belonged to while you were in high school?

Dissociative reference groups are groups whose attitudes, values, and behaviors we disapprove of and hence we do *not* wish to emulate. "Gangsta rap" groups promoting violence are dissociative reference groups for some people. U.S. citizens serve as dissociative reference groups to consumers in some Arab countries, and neo-Nazis serve as dissociative reference groups for many people in Germany and in the United States.

The influence of various types of reference groups has some important implications for marketers.

Associate Products with Aspirational Reference Groups. First, by knowing their target consumers' aspirational reference groups, marketers can associate their product with that group and use spokespeople who represent it. Because celebrities' fame and fortune make them an aspirational reference group for some, many companies implicitly or explicitly use celebrities to endorse their products. Reebok is paying Philadelphia 76ers guard Allen Iverson $5 million per year for 10 years to endorse Reebok shoes. Fila signed basketball

aspirational reference group Groups that we admire and desire to be like.

associative reference group Groups to which we currently belong.

dissociative reference group Groups we do not want to emulate.

EXHIBIT 16.7
Associative Reference Groups

The associative reference groups at one high school in Illinois included these "kid described" groups. Did you have similar groups in your high school? Which one(s) served as associative reference groups for you?

Source: "Beyond Littleton: The Truth about High School," *Newsweek,* May 10, 1999, pp. 56–58.

Jocks rule and nerds still struggle for acceptance just about everywhere. But many schools have their own unique cliques. Take a look at Glenbrook South High in Glenbrook, Illinois: Do any of these groups resemble the groups that existed at your high school? Which ones were associative reference groups for you?

Jocks:	Quintessential athletes.
Nerds:	Superintellectual types.
Trophy case kids:	Named for their hangout under the school awards case. They're punkish in black, hooded sweatshirts.
Wall kids:	Mostly seniors, mostly popular. Lots of preppies and "Abercrombies." Their turf: a wall outside the cafeteria.
Bandies:	Musicians. They stick to themselves outside the rehearsal room. Not especially cool or uncool, just good friends.
Backstage people:	Theatre and arts types (both genders) lounge on couches backstage to talk, do homework, take naps.
Student council kids:	Clean-cut, popular. Lunchtime hangout: the council office.

player Grant Hill to an $80 million contract to be paid over 7 years.[22] Exhibit 16.8 shows that Michael Jordan is the king of celebrity endorsement deals, no doubt because many people aspire to be like him.

Accurately Represent Associative Reference Groups.　Second, marketers need to identify and appropriately represent target consumers in ads by accurately reflecting the clothing, hairstyles, accessories, and general demeanor of their associative reference groups.[23] To sell products like skateboards and mountain climbing equipment, for example, many sports marketers develop promotions that use actual skateboarders and mountain climbers.[24]

Avoid Using Dissociative Reference Groups.　Obviously, dissociative reference groups should be avoided. McDonald's decided to avoid Ronald McDonald in its promotions in the Middle East because it knew that religious Muslims would not consider a zany, brightly colored clown to be an idol.[25] In 1997, allegations of rape by and drug suspensions of several Dallas Cowboys, coupled with poor performance on the football field, threatened sales of the team's licensed merchandise. Some fans were reluctant to wear hats and shirts that linked them with either a losing team or players of questionable character.[26]

How Can We Describe Reference Groups?

Several characteristics describe reference groups.

EXHIBIT 16.8
The King

Michael Jordon was not only king on the basketball court, he is also king of celebrity endorsement deals. The fact that he serves as a hero to so many makes him popular with advertisers.

Source: Adapted from Sam Walker, "Michael Jordan Isn't Retiring from Hot Deals," *Wall Street Journal,* January 15, 1999, pp. B1, B4.

SOME OF THE COMPANIES USING MICHAEL JORDAN	ENDORSEMENT DEAL	CONTRACT DATES
MCI WorldCom	$4 million a year in cash and stock options in return for such activities as providing voice recording saying "Thank you for using WorldCom."	1996–2006
Quaker Oats	$18 million for being pictured in Gatorade ads	1991–2001
Nike	Over $16 million for participating in ads for Nike products	1995–2020
Bijan Fragrances	$1 million annually plus royalties in exchange for ad appearances and Jordan fragrances and shaving products	1996–2006
Rayovac	$2 million annually for appearances in ads	1995–2005
Sara Lee	$2 million annually for appearing biting into Ball Park Franks and appearing in underwear ads with family members	1990–2000
Wilson Sporting Goods	$1 million a year for signature basketballs and Michael Jordan golf equipment	1984–???
Chicagoland Chevrolet Dealers	$1 million plus use of a Corvette for appearances in ads	year to year since 1984

primary reference group
A group with whom we have physical (face-to-face) interaction.

secondary reference group
A group with whom we do not have direct contact.

homophily Similarity among group members.

Degree of Contact   Reference groups vary in their degree of contact. We may have direct and extensive contact with some reference groups like our immediate circle of friends or family and less contact with our former high school classmates. Reference groups with whom we have considerable contact tend to exert the greatest influence.[27] We call a group with whom we have face-to-face interaction a **primary reference group**. Our family, peers, and professors represent primary reference groups. **Secondary reference groups** are those with whom we do not have direct contact but whose behavior may still influence us. We may be members of groups like the American Marketing Association, an Internet chat group, or a musical fan club. Although we interact with the group only through such impersonal communication channels as newsletters, its behavior and values can still influence our behavior.

Formality   Reference groups also vary in formality. Groups like fraternities, athletic teams, clubs, and classes are formally structured, with rules outlining the criteria for group membership and the expected behavior of members. For example, certain requirements must be satisfied before you can enroll in a particular class in college—you must gain admission and fulfill class prerequisites. Once enrolled, you follow specified rules for appropriate conduct by coming to class on time and taking notes.

Other groups are more ad hoc, less organized, and less structured. For example, your immediate group of friends is not formally structured and likely does not have a strict set of rules. Likewise, a neighborhood watch may be formed by an informal neighborhood group. People who serve on the same jury, attend the same party, or vacation on the same cruise also may constitute an informal group.

Homophily: The Similarity Among Group Members   Groups vary in their **homophily**—or the similarity among the members. When groups are homophilous, reference-group influence tends to be strong because similar people tend to see things in the same way, interact frequently, and develop strong social ties.[28] They may have more opportunity to exchange information and are more likely to accept information from one another. Because the sender and receiver are similar, the information they share is also likely to be perceived as credible.

Density   Dense groups are those in which group members all know one another. For example, an extended family that gets together every Sunday operates as a dense social network. In contrast, the network of faculty at a large university is likely to be characterized as less dense because its members have few opportunities to interact, share information, or influence one another. In Korea, network density varies by geographic area. A rural village in Korea may have high density because its families have known each other for generations. By contrast, even though Seoul has a high population density (over 10 million people), many people in the city may not know one another, making network density low.

Degree of Identification   The preceding characteristics describe dimensions along which groups may vary; however, some characteristics of an *individual* within a group are also important. One is the degree of identification a consumer has with a group. Membership in a group does not mean that someone uses it as a reference group. Thus even though you may be Hispanic or Caucasian or a senior citizen, you need not necessarily regard similar individuals as part of your reference group.[29] Instead, what affects how much a group influences our behavior is how much we *identify* with that group.

tie-strength The extent to which a close, intimate relationship connects people.

Tie-Strength Another characteristic describing individuals within a group is **tie-strength.**[30] A strong tie means that two people are connected by a close, intimate relationship. Typically, strong ties are characterized by frequent interpersonal contact. A weak tie means that there is a more distant, nonintimate relationship among two people with limited interpersonal contact.

Exhibit 16.9 illustrates the concepts of strong and weak ties. Suppose that Anne has three very close friends from school: Maria, Kyeung, and Keshia. She also knows Jeff from her health club. Tyrone is Maria's distant cousin. The solid red lines connect individuals who know one another, with the width of the line indicating how strong the tie is. Thus Anne, Maria, Kyeung, and Keshia are strongly tied to one another. Maria has a weak tie with Tyrone, and Anne has a weak tie with Jeff.

MARKETING IMPLICATIONS

The characteristics that describe reference groups have some important marketing implications.

Understanding Information Transmission. Homophily, degree of contact, tie-strength, and network density can have a strong impact on whether, how much, and how quickly information is transmitted among and between consumers within a group. If networks are dense, consumers are in frequent contact with one another and they are connected by strong ties. Thus information about the acquisition, usage, and disposition of an offering is likely to be transmitted very quickly within the group. Members may even transfer information about related offerings. The best way for marketers to disseminate information rapidly in a market is to target individuals in dense networks characterized by strong ties and frequent contact.

Formal Reference Groups as Potential Targets. Second, formal reference groups provide marketers with clear targets for marketing efforts. For example, Mothers Against Drunk Driving can target formal groups like local PTAs, school boards, and so on, and the American Red Cross targets college campuses as part of its blood drives.

Homophilous Consumers as Targets. Third, marketers sometimes use the concept of homophily to market their products. If you log on to Amazon.com and find a book you like, the program points you to more books you might like based on the purchases of others who have bought the book you are considering. The principle is that you might share the reading tastes of people that the Web site considers to be similar to you.

Targeting the Network. A fourth implication is that it sometimes makes sense to target the network itself. For example, an earlier variant of MCI's "Friends and Family" program gave customers discounts when they identified the names and telephone numbers of up to 20 people they frequently called. MCI was thus able

CHAPTER 16 Social Influences

EXHIBIT 16.9
Tie-Strength and Social Influence

Strong ties (denoted by the thick red line) are people with whom we have a close, intimate relationship. As relationships become less close and intimate, tie-strength weakens. If you were a marketer, whom would you target in this network? Why?

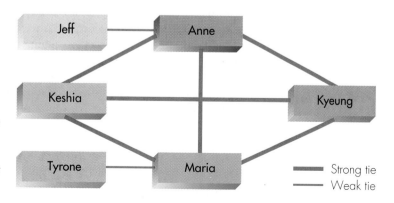

to target an individual who could influence others within his or her own network to become subscribers. Health clubs target networks when they offer consumers a discount if a friend joins. Marketers may also encourage referrals by asking consumers to "tell a friend about us."

Understanding the Strength of Weak Ties. The preceding paragraphs may make you think that weak ties provide little payoff for marketers. But actually the opposite is true. Because weak ties often serve as "bridges" connecting groups, they play a powerful role in propagating information *across* networks. For example, in Exhibit 16.9 Maria serves as a bridge between her four friends and her extended family. Once she gives information to Tyrone, he can communicate it to others with whom he has ties. Weak ties therefore serve a gatekeeping function by transporting information from one group to another.[31]

Marketers can also use weak ties to identify new networks for marketing efforts. For example, direct selling organizations like Avon, Mary Kay cosmetics, and Tupperware and charitable organizations like the American Cancer Society target individual consumers as selling agents and rely on their interpersonal networks for direct selling efforts.[32] Individuals can tap not only consumers with whom they have strong ties but also those with whom ties are weak. Girl Scouts will sell cookies not only to friends and relatives but also to neighbors, parents' coworkers, and people shopping at grocery stores. Perhaps because they have recognized the value of this type of selling practice, more marketers are attempting to sell products through home parties. Today, there are home parties for such diverse products as Bible videos, raspberry salsa, and personal computers.[33]

These types of markets are called **embedded markets** because the social relationships among buyers and sellers change the way the market operates.[34] In other words, the fact that you have a social relationship with the seller may influence the way you react to his or her selling efforts. You are more likely to buy Girl Scout cookies from your neighbor's daughter than from a girl you have never met. Because you want to remain on good terms with your neighbor, your future interactions with her may even depend on whether you buy cookies from her daughter. ■

embedded markets Markets in which the social relationships among buyers and sellers change the way the market operates.

Reference Groups Affect Consumer Socialization

The impact of reference groups can be quite strong. For example, groups can influence whether we buy and use certain products and how we dispose of them.

Reference groups affect our choices in part through socialization. *Socialization* is the process by which individuals acquire the skills, knowledge, values, and attitudes that are relevant for functioning in a given domain. **Consumer socialization** is the process by which we learn to become consumers and come to know the value of money; the appropriateness of saving versus spending; and how, when, and where products should be bought and used.[35]

Consumer socialization can occur in many ways.[36] Parents may, for example, instill values of thriftiness by (1) directly teaching their children the importance of saving money, (2) letting their children observe them being thrifty, or (3) rewarding children for being thrifty. One study found that direct teaching was the most effective means of instilling consumer skills in younger children. For older children, however, observational learning was most effective.

consumer socialization The process by which we learn to become consumers.

People as Socializing Agents It should come as no surprise that reference groups like family and friends play an important role as socializing agents. Parents affect socialization by influencing what types of products, TV programs, and ads their children are exposed to. Some parents are very concerned about children's exposure to violent and sexually explicit programming and products and actively regulate what their children watch and what games they play.[37] Even grandparents can play a powerful socializing role. In fact, the Office of National Drug Control Policy has launched a campaign that attempts to get grandparents to talk to their grandchildren about drugs. In some cases grandparents' more subdued and less emotionally charged relationship with kids may make them better information sources than parents.[38]

The impact of reference groups as socializing agents can change over time. Parents have substantial influence on young children, but it wanes as children grow older and interact more with their peers.[39] Similarly, your high school friends probably had a powerful effect on the values, attitudes, and behaviors you had as a teen, but they likely have much less impact now. Because we associate with many groups throughout our lives, socialization is a lifelong process.

The Media and the Marketplace as Socializing Agents TV programs, movies, music, video games, and ads can also serve as socializing agents. Consider the fact that boys are depicted in ads as more knowledgeable, aggressive, active, and instrumental to actions than girls are. Clearly, these sex role stereotypes can affect children's conceptions of what it is like to be a boy versus a girl.[40] It is also interesting to think about how consumer products are used as socializing agents. Our childhood toys might have influenced who we are and what was expected of us.[41] One study found that parents were likely to give their boys sporting equipment, machines, military toys, and vehicles and to decorate their rooms with animal motifs. In contrast, girls were more likely to receive dolls, dollhouses, and domestic toys, and their rooms were more likely to be decorated in floral motifs, fringes, ruffles, and lace.[42] Not surprisingly, studies have shown children of 20 months have already learned to distinguish "boy" toys from "girl" toys. These effects seem to occur at least in part because parents tend to encourage the use of what they consider sex-appropriate toys and discourage cross-sex interests, especially for boys.[43]

As they grow, children can become more suspicious of media and marketplace socializing agents. Some research has found that teens are particularly skeptical of advertising claims.[44]

SOURCES CAN EXERT NORMATIVE INFLUENCE

Thus far the chapter has identified the various sources of influence—general, special, and groups. Now we will discuss types of influence exerted. Researchers have identified two types of influence—normative and informational (see Exhibit 16.10).

Assume for a minute that you are at a dinner interview with a prospective employer who tells you she is a vegetarian. Although you love beef, you may be reluctant to order it because you want to make a good impression, so you order a vegetarian dish. Your host has just communicated information to you about your expected behavior.

normative influence Social pressure designed to encourage conformity to the expectations of others.

norms Collective decisions about what constitutes appropriate behavior.

Normative influence, which is what you felt in this example, is defined as social pressure designed to encourage conformity to the expectations of others.[45] We spoke of normative influence in Chapter 6 when we described how normative beliefs affect our intentions and consumption decisions. The term normative influence derives from **norms**, which are society's collective decisions about what behavior *should* be. For example, we have norms for which brands and stores are cool, norms that discourage stealing and impulsive shopping,[46] and norms about how much food one should eat at a given meal.

Normative influence implies sanctions or punishments if norms are not followed and likewise implies rewards when expected behaviors are performed. For

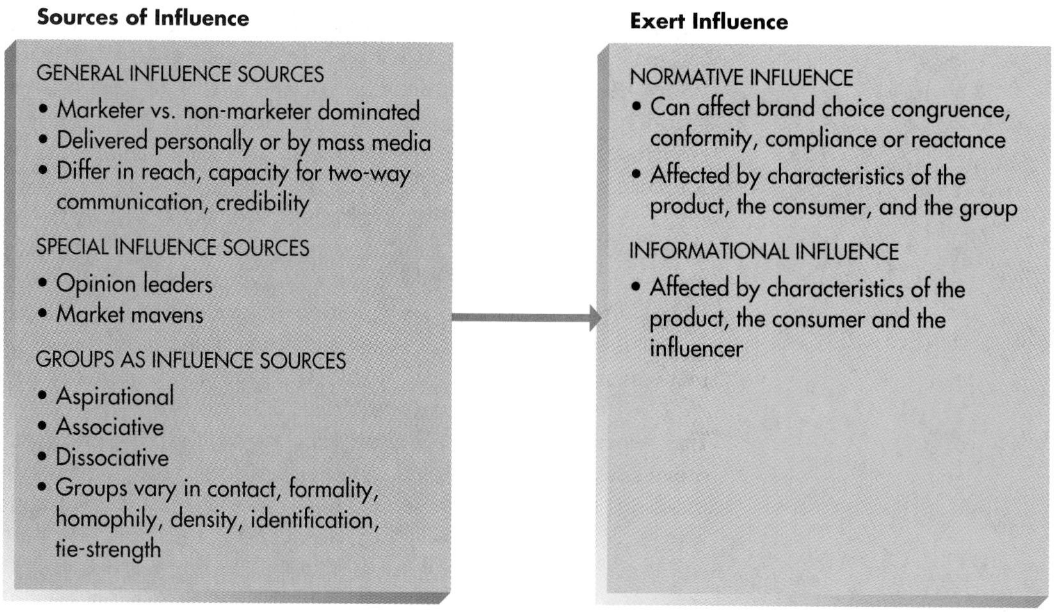

Sources of Influence

GENERAL INFLUENCE SOURCES
- Marketer vs. non-marketer dominated
- Delivered personally or by mass media
- Differ in reach, capacity for two-way communication, credibility

SPECIAL INFLUENCE SOURCES
- Opinion leaders
- Market mavens

GROUPS AS INFLUENCE SOURCES
- Aspirational
- Associative
- Dissociative
- Groups vary in contact, formality, homophily, density, identification, tie-strength

Exert Influence

NORMATIVE INFLUENCE
- Can affect brand choice congruence, conformity, compliance or reactance
- Affected by characteristics of the product, the consumer, and the group

INFORMATIONAL INFLUENCE
- Affected by characteristics of the product, the consumer and the influencer

EXHIBIT 16.10
Sources of Influence and Types of Influence

General sources of influence, special influence sources, and specific groups can affect consumers by exerting normative and/or informational influence.

example, a prospective boss may deny or reward us with a good job, depending on the appropriateness of our interview behavior. College students may impose sanctions on fellow students who do not conform to the dress norm by treating them differently. The London department store Harrods bounces consumers who violate its dress code. Flip-flop shoes or clothing that is dirty and unkempt, exposes hairy armpits, or reveals excess flesh is forbidden. One woman was even bounced for wearing Lycra leggings![47]

What Happens when Consumers Experience Normative Influence?

Normative influence can have several important effects on consumption behaviors.

brand-choice congruence
The likelihood that consumers will buy what others in their group buy.

conformity Doing what others in the group do.

Brand-Choice Congruence and Conformity Normative influence affects **brand-choice congruence**—the likelihood that consumers will buy what others in their group buy. Consider, for example, the types of foods, clothes, music, hairstyles, and cars that you buy and compare them with the selections of your friends. Chances are, you and your friends have made similar choices.[48]

Normative influence can also affect **conformity**—the tendency for an individual to behave as the group behaves. Conformity and brand-choice congruence may be related. For example, you might conform by buying the same products as others in your group,[49] although brand-choice congruence is not the only way for you to conform. You may also conform by performing activities that the group wants you to perform, such as initiation rites, or by just acting the way the group acts. For example, your actions at a party might depend on whether your companions are your parents or your college buddies. In each case you are conforming to a different set of expectations regarding appropriate behavior.

Pressures to conform can be substantial.[50] One study examining group pressure toward underage drinking and drug consumption found that students worried about how others would perceive them if they conformed or refused to conform to the expected behavior of the group. Other studies have found that conformity increases as more people in the group conform. Interestingly, conformity varies by culture. Compared to consumers in the United States, for example, the Japanese tend to be more group oriented and are more likely to go along with group desires.

compliance Doing what the group or social influencer asks.

Compliance Versus Reactance **Compliance**, a somewhat different effect of normative influence, means doing what someone asks us to do. We comply if, when asked, we donate to a political campaign, fill out a marketing research questionnaire, or purchase Tupperware at a home party. Parents comply with children by purchasing foods, buying toys, or allowing activities (such as parties) that kids request.

reactance Doing the opposite of what the individual or group wants us to do.

When we believe our freedom is being threatened, a boomerang effect occurs and we engage in **reactance**—doing the opposite of what the individual or group wants us to do. For example, if a salesperson pressures you too much, you may engage in reactance by saying that you do not want whatever it is he or she is trying to sell.[51] Parents may engage in reactance by staunchly refusing to make a purchase requested by a whining child.

What Makes Normative Influence Strong or Weak?

Several factors—reflecting the product, the consumer, and the group to which the consumer belongs—can all explain whether normative influence is strong or weak.

Product Characteristics Researchers have hypothesized that reference groups can influence two types of decisions: (1) whether we buy a product within a given product category and (2) what brand we buy. However, whether reference groups affect product and brand decisions also depends on whether the product is typically consumed in private or in public and whether it is a necessity or a luxury. As shown in Exhibit 16.11, mattresses and hot-water heaters are considered privately consumed necessities, and camcorders and roller blades might be considered publicly consumed luxuries. Exhibit 16.11 makes predictions, validated in both the United States and Thailand, about when reference groups will affect these decisions.

One prediction is that because we must buy necessity items, reference groups are likely to have little influence on whether we buy such products. However, reference groups might exert some influence on whether we buy a luxury item. For example, your friends will probably not influence whether you buy a hot-water heater or whether you buy shoes, but they might influence whether you get roller blades or a body massager. Part of the reason for this situation is that luxury products communicate status—something that may be valued by group members. Also, luxury items may communicate our special interests and values and thus who we are and with whom we associate. The more the product is regarded as a luxury as opposed to a necessity, the more reference groups affect whether or not the product is purchased.

A second prediction is that products consumed in public give others the opportunity to observe which brand we have purchased. For example, cars are publicly consumed items, making it very easy for individuals to know whether we are driving a Ferrari or a Miata. In contrast, because mattresses are consumed in private, few people see which brand we buy. Because different brand images communicate different things to people, reference groups are likely to have considerable

EXHIBIT 16.11

Reference Group Influences on Publicly and Privately Consumed Luxuries and Necessities

Reference groups tend to influence consumption of a *product category* only when the product is a luxury (not a necessity). Reference groups tend to influence *brand* only when the product is consumed in public (not when it is consumed in private). Give some examples of your own to illustrate the matrix.

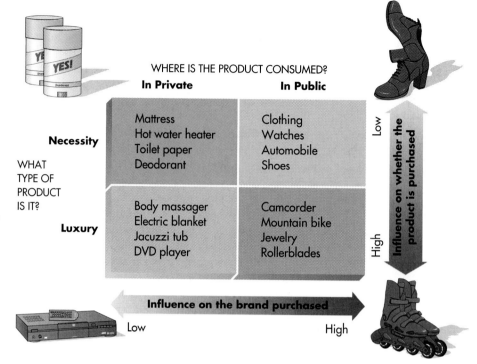

WHERE IS THE PRODUCT CONSUMED?

	In Private	In Public
Necessity	Mattress Hot water heater Toilet paper Deodorant	Clothing Watches Automobile Shoes
Luxury	Body massager Electric blanket Jacuzzi tub DVD player	Camcorder Mountain bike Jewelry Rollerblades

WHAT TYPE OF PRODUCT IS IT?

Influence on whether the product is purchased — Low / High

Influence on the brand purchased — Low / High

influence on the brand we buy when the product is publicly consumed but not when it is privately consumed. Moreover, a publicly consumed product provides opportunities for sanctions. It would be difficult for groups to develop norms and generate sanctions for violating them when the product is consumed privately. The bottom line, then, is that reference groups influence *product category* choice for luxuries but not necessities and influence *brand* choice for products consumed in public but not those consumed in private.[52]

Yet another characteristic of products that affects normative influence is the significance of the product to the group.[53] As we show in Chapter 18, some products designate membership in a certain group. For example, a varsity sports jacket may signify membership on a sports team and may play a significant role in designating in-group and out-group status. The more central a product is to the group, the greater the normative influence the group exerts over its purchase.

Consumer Characteristics Some consumers have personalities that make them readily susceptible to influence by others.[54] Several consumer researchers have developed the scale of "susceptibility to interpersonal influence," which includes the first six items shown in Exhibit 16.12. Consumers who are susceptible to interpersonal influence try to enhance their self-image by acquiring products that they think others will approve of. These consumers are also willing to conform to others' expectations about which products and brands to buy.

A personality characteristic called "attention to social comparison information" (ATSCI) is also related to normative influence. Several items from an ATSCI scale are also shown in Exhibit 16.11. People who are high on this personality trait pay a great deal of attention to what others do and use this information to guide their own behavior.

Tie-strength also affects the degree of normative influence. When ties are strong, individuals presumably want to maintain their relationship with others in

ITEMS INDICATING SUSCEPTIBILITY TO INTERPERSONAL INFLUENCE	1. I rarely purchase the latest fashion styles until I am sure my friends approve of them. 2. If other people can see me using a product, I often purchase the brand they expect me to buy. 3. I often identify with other people by purchasing the same products and brands they purchase. 4. To make sure I buy the right product or brand, I often observe what others are buying and using. 5. If I have little experience with a product, I often ask my friends about the product. 6. I frequently gather information from friends or family about a product before I buy.
ITEMS INDICATING ATTENTION TO SOCIAL COMPARISON INFORMATION	1. It is my feeling that if everyone else in a group is behaving in a certain manner, this must be the proper way to behave. 2. I actively avoid wearing clothes that are not in style. 3. At parties, I usually try to behave in a manner that makes me fit in. 4. When I am uncertain how to act in a social situation, I look to the behavior of others for cues. 5. I tend to pay attention to what others are wearing. 6. The slightest look of disapproval in the eyes of a person with whom I am interacting is enough to make me change my approach.

EXHIBIT 16.12

Measuring Susceptibility and Interpersonal Influence and Attention to Social Comparison Information

Individuals differ in whether they are susceptible to influence from others and whether they pay attention to what others do. What conclusions can you draw about yourself based on your answers to these questions? What implications do these questions have for marketers?

Sources: Susceptibility to Interpersonal Influence Scale from William O. Bearden, Richard G. Netemeyer, and Jesse E. Teel, "Measurement of Consumer Susceptibility to Interpersonal Influence," *Journal of Consumer Research,* March 1989, pp. 473–481; ATSCI Scale from William O. Bearden and Randall L. Rose, "Attention to Social Comparison Information: An Individual Difference Factor Affecting Consumer Conformity," *Journal of Consumer Research,* March 1990, pp. 461–471. © 1989 and 1990 University of Chicago. All rights reserved.

the group and are therefore motivated to succumb to the group's norms and wishes.[55]

A final consumer characteristic affecting normative influence is a consumer's identification with the group.[56] A person may be a member of a group such as a family or a subculture with whose attitudes, behaviors, and values he or she does not identify. In such instances normative reference-group influence is weak.

Group Characteristics   Exhibit 16.10 shows that characteristics of the group also influence the degree of normative influence. One characteristic is the extent to which the group has the capacity to deliver rewards and sanctions, also known as the degree of reward power or **coercive power**.[57] For example, your friends are more likely to influence your clothing styles than your neighbors are because your friends have greater opportunity and more motivation—greater coercive power—to deliver sanctions if they consider your clothing inappropriate.

coercive power   The extent to which the group has the capacity to deliver rewards and sanctions.

Group cohesiveness and group similarity also affect the degree of normative influence.[58] Cohesive groups and groups with similar members may communicate and interact on a regular basis. Thus they have greater opportunity to convey normative influences and deliver rewards and sanctions.

Finally, normative influence tends to be greater when groups are large and when group members are experts.[59] Thus you might be more inclined to buy a bottle of wine recommended by a group of wine experts than one recommended by a casual acquaintance.

MARKETING IMPLICATIONS   Normative influences and the factors that affect how strong they are have several important implications for marketers.

Demonstrate Rewards and Sanctions for Product Use/Nonuse.   First, marketers may be able to create normative influence by using advertising to demonstrate rewards or sanctions that can follow from product use or nonuse. For example, Federal

Express commercials sometimes show social disapproval arising from nonuse of its delivery services. An ad like the one in Exhibit 16.13 may express or imply that others will evaluate us favorably if we use a certain product.

Create Norms for Group Behavior.   Second, marketing organizations may create groups whose norms guide consumers' behavior. Weight Watchers and Alcoholics Anonymous, for example, are groups with behavior norms. Rewards in the form of group praise come to those who adhere to the group's norms by losing weight or avoiding alcohol. Because influence is greater when consumption is public rather than private, another marketing strategy is to make a private behavior public. Group discussions of eating behavior and public confessions of past drinking behavior are ways that Weight Watchers and Alcoholics Anonymous make private information public.

Create Conformity Pressures.   Third, marketers may also attempt to create conformity. For example, they may actively associate a product with a certain group so that their product becomes a badge of group membership. They may simulate conformity by showing actors in an ad behaving similarly with respect to a product. Conformity may also be enhanced by publicizing others' conformity. We see these effects at Tupperware parties or at charity fund-raising events like the Jerry Lewis telethon.

Use Compliance Techniques.   The **foot-in-the-door technique** suggests that compliance is enhanced by getting an individual to agree first to a small favor, then to a larger one, and then to an even larger one. For example, a salesperson may first ask a consumer his or her name and then ask what the person thinks of a given product. After complying with these requests, the consumer may be more inclined to comply with the salesperson's ultimate request to purchase the product.[60] Consumers may comply with large marketing research requests such as filling out a long survey if they have first agreed to smaller requests, for example, answering a few marketing research questions over the phone.[61]

With the **door-in-the-face technique**, the consumer is first asked to comply with a very large and possibly outrageous request, followed by a smaller and more reasonable request. For example, a salesperson might ask a consumer whether she is interested in buying a $500 piece of jewelry. When the consumer says no, the

foot-in-the-door technique
A technique designed to induce compliance by getting an individual to agree first to a small favor, then to a larger one, and then to an even larger one.

door-in-the-face technique
A technique designed to induce compliance by first asking an individual to comply with a very large and possibly outrageous request, followed by a smaller and more reasonable request.

salesperson might then ask the consumer if she is interested in buying a set of earrings on sale for only $25.[62] One reason this technique works is that the consumer may perceive that the requestor has given something up by moving from a large to a small request. In turn, the consumer feels obligated to reciprocate by responding to the requestor's smaller wishes.

A third approach is the **even-a-penny-will-help** technique.[63] Individuals are asked for a very small favor—so small it almost does not qualify as a favor. For example, marketers collecting money for a charity may indicate that even a penny will help those in need. Salespeople making cold calls may tell prospective clients that even 1 minute of their time will be valuable. Because people would look foolish denying these tiny requests, they usually comply and, in fact, often give an amount appropriate for the situation.

Provide Freedom of Choice. Finally, because reactance usually occurs when individuals feel their freedom is being threatened, marketers need to make sure that consumers believe they have freedom of choice. For example, a salesperson might show a variety of styles of a particular dress, discussing the advantages of each. In this way the consumer feels a greater sense of control over whether to buy at all, and if so, which item to buy. ∎

even-a-penny-will-help technique A technique designed to induce compliance by asking individuals to do a very small favor—one that is so small it almost does not qualify as a favor.

SOURCES CAN EXERT INFORMATIONAL INFLUENCE

In addition to normative influence, reference groups and other influence sources can exert **informational influence** by offering information to help make decisions.[64] For example, chat groups on the Internet travel sites provide informational influence by providing travel tips to prospective travelers. Friends provide informational influence by telling you which movie is playing at the local theater, and the media provide informational influence by revealing that certain foods may be hazardous to your health.

informational influence The extent to which sources influence consumers simply by providing information.

What Happens when Consumers Experience Informational Influence?

Informational influence is important because it can affect how much time and effort consumers devote to information search and decision making. Consumers who can get information from others easily may be reluctant to engage in time-intensive information search when making decisions. If, for example, you are looking for a new stereo and a trusted friend tells us that the brand he just bought is the best he has ever had, you might simply buy the same one.

Although informational influence can reduce information search, it is sometimes important for marketers to increase the likelihood that consumers engage in information search. If an offering is new and is superior, few consumers are likely to know about its benefits. Thus campaigns that enhance product awareness and encourage consumers to compare products may be necessary.

What Makes Informational Influence Strong or Weak?

Exhibit 16.10 shows that like normative influence, the extent to which informational influence is strong or weak depends on several factors.

Product Characteristics Consumers tend to be susceptible to informational influence when products are complex. Items like consumer electronics or products whose usage is very difficult to understand are likely targets for informational influence.[65] Susceptibility to informational influence is also high when product purchase or usage is perceived to be risky.[66] Thus consumers may be affected by information they receive about laser hair removal, given its formidable financial and safety risks. Informational influence is also likely to be high when brands are very different from one another. Because distinctiveness among brands may make it more difficult for consumers to determine which brand is best for them, they attach significance to information learned from others.[67]

Consumer and Influencer Characteristics Characteristics of both the consumer and the influencer affect the extent of informational influence. Such influence is likely to be greater when the source or group communicating the information is an expert,[68] especially if the consumer either lacks expertise or has had ambiguous experiences with the product. For example, given their lack of knowledge and confidence about the home-buying process, first-time home buyers are likely to consider carefully the information conveyed by experts such as real estate agents.

Personality traits, such as consumers' susceptibility to reference group influence and attention to social comparison information, should also influence the extent to which consumers look to others for cues on product characteristics.[69]

Like normative influence, informational influence is affected by tie-strength. Individuals with strong ties tend to interact frequently, which in turn provides greater opportunities for consumers to learn about products and others' reactions to them. Notably, informational influence may actually affect the ties between individuals. Bonds of friendship may begin when individuals establish social relationships that involve sharing information.[70]

Finally, culture may influence the impact of informational influence. One study found that U.S. consumers were more likely than Korean consumers to be persuaded by ads with a lot of information. Because the Korean culture often focuses on the group and group compliance, Korean consumers may be more susceptible to normative influence than U.S. consumers are.[71]

Group Characteristics Group cohesiveness also affects informational influence—cohesive groups have both greater opportunity and perhaps greater motivation to share information.

MARKETING IMPLICATIONS Informational influence has several important implications for marketers.

Create Informational Influence by Using Experts. First, because source expertise and credibility affect informational influence, marketers can use sources regarded as expert or credible for a given product category. Using well-known sports figures to advertise sporting goods is an example of this strategy.

Create a Context for Informational Influence. Second, the likelihood that informational influence will occur depends on the situation. Informational influence may therefore be enhanced if marketers can create a context for informational influence to occur. One study found that 80 percent of conversations about drinking a new brand of coffee took place in a situation relevant to food. One way of creating a context for informational influence is to host or sponsor special events related to the product under consideration.

Create Informational and Normative Influence. Finally, marketing efforts may be most successful when *both* normative and informational influence attempts are used. One study found that only 2 percent of consumers donated blood in the absence of any type of influence but between 4 and 8 percent did when either informational or normative influence was present. However, when both forms of influence were used, 22 percent of the consumers donated blood.[72] Also, because source similarity enhances both normative and informational influence, advertisers might enhance influence by using sources that are similar to their target audience. For example, lottery commercials often show sources similar to the target audience winning the lottery. Likewise, testimonials are thought to work at least in part because they use individuals who are like the target audience. ■

HOW CAN "INFORMATION" BE DESCRIBED?

Information can be described by several dimensions—valence and modality.

Valence: Is Information Positive or Negative?

valence Whether information about something is good (positive valence) or bad (negative valence).

Valence describes whether the information is positive or negative. This is very important because researchers have found that negative and positive information have very different effects on consumer behavior.[73] Negative information is more likely than positive information to be communicated. As we discussed in Chapter 12, more than half of dissatisfied consumers engage in negative word of mouth. Moreover, dissatisfied consumers complain to three times more people than the number of people satisfied consumers tell about their pleasure.[74] One study found that consumers who were dissatisfied with their home rental situation were likely to tell eight to ten people about their negative experiences.[75]

It has also been hypothesized that people pay more attention to and give more weight to negative information than they do to positive information. Thus negative information is more influential than positive information is.[76] Because most of the information we hear about products and services is positive, negative information may receive more attention—in general it is surprising, unusual, and different. Negative information may also prompt consumers to attribute problems with an offering to the offering itself, not to the consumer who uses it. Thus if you learn that a friend got sick after eating at a new restaurant, you may attribute the outcome to the food (it must be bad) rather than to your friend (he ate too much). Finally, negative information may be diagnostic—that is, we may attach more significance to it because we believe it tells us something about how offerings differ from one another.

Modality: Does Information Come from Verbal or Nonverbal Channels?

Another dimension describing influence is the modality in which it is delivered—is it communicated verbally or nonverbally? Norms about how one behaves in a group might be explicitly communicated by verbal description. However, consumers can also infer group norms simply by observing others' behavior. Thus you may have a very good idea about what constitutes an appropriate graduation gift because you have observed what others have given in the past. Likewise, informational influence can be delivered verbally or nonverbally. A consumer may learn that a can opener is bad by observing someone struggling with it or by hearing that person relate his or her experiences with it.

The Pervasive and Persuasive Influence of Word of Mouth

word of mouth Information about products or services that is communicated verbally.

Marketers are especially interested in a form of influence called **word of mouth**. Word of mouth refers to information about products or services that is communicated verbally. Consider the number of consumer behaviors that word of mouth is likely to affect. For example, you may go to see the movie *Shakespeare in Love* because your friend told you it was great. You may ask a coworker where she gets her hair cut and then go to the same salon. Your neighbor may recommend an electrician, or you may learn from a stranger at the bank that Nordstrom's semi-annual sale is next week.[77] More than 40 percent of U.S. consumers seek of the advice of family and friends when shopping for doctors, lawyers, or auto mechanics, although men and women differ in how often they seek advice and from whom. Exhibit 16.14 summarizes some of these differences.[78]

Not only is word of mouth pervasive, it is also more persuasive than written information.[79] One study found that word of mouth was the number one source affecting food and household product purchases. It was seven times more effective than print media, twice as effective as broadcast media, and four times more effective than salespeople in affecting brand switching.[80]

Interestingly, on-line forums, chat rooms, bulletin boards, and Web sites have the potential to deepen the impact of word of mouth. Consider the fact that a disgruntled customer can now not only tell other people about good and bad consumption experiences in person—he or she can also tell thousands of people with the click of a mouse. The impact of electronic delivery of word of mouth has some companies worried about how to respond to on-line lamentations. Some companies conduct regular Internet monitoring to see whether and how their company is being lambasted or lauded in these forums.[81]

MARKETING IMPLICATIONS Word of mouth is important to marketers because it can have a dramatic effect on consumers' product perceptions and an offering's marketplace performance. Many small businesses such as hairstylists, piano instructors, and preschools cannot afford to advertise and rely almost exclusively on word of mouth. Others, such as doctors, dentists, and lawyers, have traditionally been reluctant to advertise, fearing that the act of advertising will cheapen their professional image. Thus word-of-mouth referrals are a major factor in building and sustaining some businesses. Moreover, in some industries product success is ultimately tied to favorable word of mouth. For example, the ultimate success of the movie *The Shawshank Redemption* is attributable largely to favorable word of mouth, which stimulated home video rentals after the film had enjoyed only lackluster success at the box office.[82]

Preventing and Responding to Negative Word of Mouth. Given its pervasive impact, marketers need to be particularly concerned about preventing negative word of mouth and then rectifying it once it occurs.[83] Preventing negative word of mouth can best be accomplished by providing quality products and services. To rectify negative word of mouth, firms can try to deal with consumers' dissatisfaction before more negative word of mouth occurs. For example, service providers who empathize with consumers' product problems and interact meaningfully with them may reduce the spread of negative word of mouth. Likewise, companies are far more successful in reducing negative word of mouth by responding to complaint letters with an offer for free goods than by ignoring complaint letters altogether.

Engineering Favorable Word of Mouth. In addition to creating quality products and services,[84] marketers may also try to engineer favorable word of mouth by targeting opinion leaders and using networking opportunities at trade shows, conferences, and public events. Scholastic Inc. used this approach when it decided to turn its popular Babysitters' Club series into a movie. It sent its 50,000 Babysitters Club fans promotional materials tied to the movie and encouraged them to spread the word about the movie.[85] Chevrolet manufactured word of mouth by hosting a Return of the Road driving tour. Twenty new-model Corvette cars were

	FIRST-RANKED	PERCENT CHOOSING	SECOND-RANKED	PERCENT CHOOSING	THIRD-RANKED	PERCENT CHOOSING
PERCENT OF MEN AND WOMEN WHO CHOOSE SELECTED PEOPLE AS SINGLE MOST-TRUSTED SOURCE FOR SELECTED PRODUCTS AND SERVICES, FOR THREE MOST-TRUSTED SOURCES, 1995						
NEW DOCTOR:						
Men	female relative	26	no one	18	male friend	17
Women	female relative	29	female friend	20	no one	14
WHERE TO GET HAIR CUT:						
Men	no one	38	male friend	25	female relative/friend	12
Women	female friend	45	no one	26	female relative	22
WHAT CAR TO BUY:						
Men	no one	31	male friend	26	male relative	22
Women	male relative	46	male friend	20	no one	19
CAR MECHANIC:						
Men	male friend	40	no one	26	male relative	21
Women	male relative	50	male friend	30	no one	10
WHERE TO GET LEGAL ADVICE:						
Men	male relative	26	male friend	23	no one	17
Women	male relative	31	male friend	16	female relative	14
WHERE TO GET PERSONAL LOAN:						
Men	no one	29	male friend	20	male relative	18
Women	male relative	33	no one	21	professional advisor	12
WHAT MOVIES TO SEE:						
Men	male friend	27	no one	22	female friend	18
Women	female friend	40	no one	19	female relative	15
WHERE TO EAT OUT:						
Men	female friend	26	female relative	21	male friend	21
Women	female friend	42	female relative	18	no one/male relative	11

EXHIBIT 16.14
Gender Differences

Men and women differ in how much they ask others' advice and from whom they seek advice. Women are more likely than men to seek word of mouth from others and to use a broader array of sources.

Source: Chip Walker, "Word of Mouth," *American Demographics*, July 1995, pp. 39–45.

showcased in parades, barbecues, and concerts along Route 66 in California. Many people came to the showcase because they had heard about the festivities. The presence of the cars at the showcase also gave consumers the opportunity to talk about how great the Corvettes were.[86]

Dealing with Rumors. Rumors are a special case of negative word of mouth.[87] Many companies, like Disney in our opening story, have been the victims of false rumors. Stories that Corona beer contained urine, that Bubble Yum gum contained spider worms, that Pop Rocks candy caused children to explode, and that Tropical Fantasy soft drink made black men sterile have all been circulated.[88] When rumors surface, the question is how best to deal with them. Several strategies may be used.[89]

- *Do Nothing.* One strategy is to do nothing. Often this strategy is preferred because more consumers may actually learn about a rumor from marketers' attempts to correct it. One study found that 35 percent of consumers learned about the rumor that McDonald's used worms in hamburger meat from McDonald's own anti-rumor campaign.[90] However, this strategy can also backfire. Nike has been accused of condoning low wages and abusive conditions in its Asian factories. Nike did not respond sufficiently to the attacks, and as a result it suffered from some very bad publicity. The firm has subsequently responded to the charges. For example, its Web site has links to labor practices and includes a factory tour. But the initial lack of response has tarnished Nike's image.[91]

- *Do Something Locally.* A second strategy is to do something locally, putting the rumor to rest on a case-by-case basis. Procter & Gamble sent a packet of information about its man-in-the-moon symbol, long rumored to connote devil worship, only to those consumers who called its hotline. In cases handled locally, company personnel who interact with the public need to be informed of the rumor and told how they should respond to it. Management should also try to track down the source of the rumor because it may be tied to a specific source.

- *Do Something Discreetly.* A third option is to do something discreetly. For example, when rumors held that oil companies were contriving oil shortages out of greed, the firms ran a public relations campaign that highlighted all the positive and socially desirable things they did. They did not mention the rumor, but the gist of the campaign clearly ran contrary to the rumor's content.

- *Do Something Big.* A fourth option is to do something big, using all the media resources at one's disposal. Media vehicles such as advertising might be used to directly confront and refute the rumor. GM once launched an all-out advertising campaign designed to squelch rumors that it was going out of business. Included in the marketing effort were print ads that stated, "Oldsmobile sells more vehicles in America than: Mercedes-Benz, Infiniti, Acura, BMW, Volvo and Lexus combined." In smaller type the ad said, "If you've heard rumors that Oldsmobile is thinking about throwing in the towel, don't believe them. Why should a company stop doing business that does this much business?"[92] It is sometimes possible to create news that refutes the rumor. Company spokespeople might also conduct interviews with the media about the rumor and its lack of truth. Credible opinion leaders who are not part of the company may also be hired to help dispel the rumor.

Tracking Word of Mouth. Whether word of mouth is positive, like referrals, or negative, like product dissatisfaction or rumors, it is sometimes useful to track it to see whether a critical word-of-mouth source can be identified. Through a method called network analysis, consumers can be asked where they heard the information. This person, in turn, can be asked how he or she heard the story. By repeating this procedure, marketers can sometimes identify critical information sources.[93]

Marketers can also query consumers as to what specific information they heard from the source. This analysis might track the distortion of information and key sources responsible for perpetuating it.

If critical sources can be identified, one follow-up strategy is to target them directly. For example, if individuals are communicating positive word of mouth and acting as referrals, they can be thanked or more explicitly rewarded for their efforts. Referral-incentive programs can be designed that reward both the referrer and referee.[94]

Finally, institutions may differ in whether they are sources of word-of-mouth information. For example, although U.S. consumers may not find the church to be an important clearinghouse for WOM, Koreans do. ■

SUMMARY

We are influenced by many sources—those that are marketer dominated and those that are non–marketer dominated, and those that are delivered through the mass media versus those that are delivered personally. Non-marketer-dominated sources are regarded as more credible than marketer-dominated sources, and personally delivered information generally has less reach but more capacity for two-way communication than mass media sources.

Opinion leaders and market mavens represent special sources of influence. Opinion leaders are experts in a product category; market mavens are individuals involved in the marketplace in general. Marketers may target these individuals explicitly, given their potential to serve as brokers of information, or simulate opinion leaders in marketing communications.

Reference groups are people with whom individuals compare themselves to guide their values, attitudes, and behaviors. Reference groups are associative, aspirational, and dissociative; they can be described according to their degree of contact, formality, homophily, density, identification, and tie-strength. Reference groups may play a powerful socializing role, influencing consumers' key actions, values, and behaviors.

These influence sources exert normative and informational influence. Normative influence tends to be greater for products that are publicly consumed, considered luxuries, or regarded as a significant aspect of group membership. Normative influence is also strong for individuals who tend to pay attention to social information. Strong ties and identification with the group increase the likelihood that consumers will succumb to normative influences. Finally, normative influence is greater when groups are cohesive, when members are similar, and when the group has the power to deliver rewards and sanctions.

Informational influence operates when individuals affect others by providing information. Consumers are most likely to seek and follow informational influence when products are complex, purchase or use is risky, and brands are distinctive. The more expert the influencer and the more consumers are predisposed to listen to others, the greater the informational influence. Informational influence is also greater when groups are more rather than less cohesive.

Social influence, whether normative or informational, varies in valence and modality. Negative information is communicated to more people and given greater weight in decision making than positive information. Marketers are particularly interested in word-of-mouth information—both positive and negative. Strategies may be designed to identify, target, and reward individuals who serve as positive word-of-mouth referral sources. Sources of negative information, such as rumors, might also be targeted if identified.

EXERCISES

1. Keep a word-of-mouth log for 24 hours. Document (a) what information you heard, (b) whether it was positive or negative, (c) what effect you think it will have on your behavior, and (d) why. Think about what implications the entries in your log have for marketers.

2. Take an entry in your word-of-mouth log (from exercise 1) and try to track down the source of the information. Did the information flow within a relatively dense social network, or did it flow across social networks via weak ties?

Try to diagram the nature of the information flow within and across various groups.

3. Observe a salesperson trying to make a sale. Try to understand which aspects of his or her selling attempts represent informational influence and which represent normative influence. Was the salesperson successful in inducing a sale? Which concepts from this chapter may explain why or why not?

4. As a marketing manager for a new brand of diet hot chocolate, you want to use an opinion leader to stimulate sales of the brand. How might you identify an opinion leader, and what strategies do you have for using an opinion leader in your marketing communications program?

5. You have recently learned that a lot of both positive and negative information is being communicated about the new brand of diet hot chocolate. Should your strategy be to try to bolster the positive information or to stop the negative information? Why?

17

PSYCHOGRAPHICS: VALUES, PERSONALITY, AND LIFESTYLES

INTRODUCTION

Previous chapters pointed out that the Internet is an extremely useful tool for consumers to use in collecting information for buying decisions. In addition, people can access an almost unlimited number of Web sites for information, pictures, sounds, and other materials on an extremely wide variety of topics and areas from cooking and other home-related topics to sports, music, movies, health and fitness, and games. Ten of the 15 topics consumers search for most frequently on the Web are related to sex.[1] Other popular areas are chat rooms, software downloads, games, and the weather. Men like to visit sports-related sites, whereas women prefer those related to the home and family. There are even so-called cyberchondriacs who regularly visit the hundreds of Web sites devoted to health and illnesses.[2]

Some consumers spend a considerable amount of time surfing the Internet as a way of life. Teenagers and college students in particular spend many of their waking hours hunched over their computers linked to fellow users or various Web sites.[3] In fact, some individuals prefer to communicate with others over the Internet rather than face-to-face. An increasing number of people even begin the dating process on-line before meeting in person.

This brief survey of the uses of the Internet illustrates the three topics of this chapter: values, personality, and lifestyles. Values determine which sites people will visit, for example, home- or health-related sites or sexually oriented pages. The fact that introverted individuals may feel more comfortable communicating on the Web rather than in person illustrates the influence of personality. Finally, some consumers just enjoy surfing the Web as an activity in and of itself (a lifestyle).

Together, values, personality, and lifestyles constitute the basic components of **psychographics**, the description of consumers on the basis of their psychological and behavioral characteristics. Traditionally, psychographics measured consumer lifestyles, but more modern applications have broadened the approach to include other concepts such as the psychological makeup of consumers, their values and personality, and the way they behave with respect to specific products (their usage patterns, attitudes, and emotions).

Psychographics provides marketers with a more detailed understanding of consumer behavior than they can get from demographic variables like ethnicity, social class, age, gender, and religion. For example, Generation Xers can be divided into several psychographic groups. So-called Yup & Comers (28 percent of Generation Xers) have the highest levels of income and education and are comfortable about themselves and their future. Bystanders (37 percent) are predominantly practical, hardworking females, with a large percentage of Hispanics and African Americans.[4] Playboys (19 percent) are self-absorbed, fun-loving, impulsive types who live on the edge; and Drifters (16 percent) fit the Xer stereotype of being frustrated, are the least educated members of their generation, and are looking for status.

Exhibit 17.1 diagrams these psychographic variables and the way they relate to group membership. The following sections examine the major components of psychographic research in greater detail, beginning with values.

psychographics A description of consumers on the basis of their psychological and behavioral characteristics.

VALUES

values Enduring beliefs that a given behavior or outcome is desirable or good.

Formally defined, **values** are enduring beliefs that a given behavior or outcome is desirable or good.[5] For example, we may believe that it is good to be healthy, keep our family safe, have self-respect, and be free. As enduring beliefs, our values serve as standards that guide our behavior across situations and over time. For example, the extent to which we value the environment generally determines the extent to which we litter, recycle, use aerosol cans, or buy recyclable products. Values are so ingrained that most people are not consciously aware of them and have difficulty describing them.

value system Our total set of values and their relative importance.

Our total set of values and their relative importance constitute our **value system**. The way we behave in a given situation is often influenced by how important one value is relative to others.[6] For example, deciding whether to spend Sunday afternoon relaxing with our family or exercising will be determined by the relative importance we place on family versus health. Value conflict arises when we do something that is consistent with one value but inconsistent with another equally important value. For example, parents who place equal value on convenience and concern for the environment may experience value conflict if they buy disposable diapers for their babies. Similarly, smoking cigarettes may cause conflict for teenagers if they value health and social acceptance equally.

Because values are among the first things children learn, value systems are often in place by age 10. We learn values through the process of socialization,

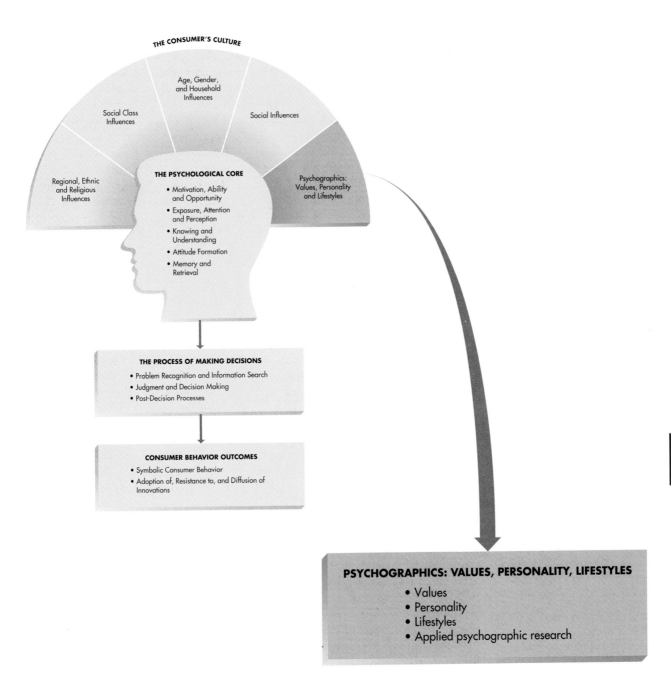

EXHIBIT 17.1

Chapter Overview: Psychographics, Personality, and Lifestyle

Previous chapters demonstrated how membership in certain cultural groups (regional, ethnic, social class, etc.) can affect group behaviors. This chapter examines how these cultural influences can have an impact on an *individual* level—namely, on *values* (deeply held beliefs), *personality* (consumer traits), and *lifestyles* (behavioral patterns that are manifestations of values and personality). Each of these factors is useful in understanding consumer behavior; in addition, they are often combined to measure the overall *psychographic* profile of consumers.

which was discussed in Chapter 16. Socialization results from exposure to reference groups and other sources of influence.[7] We may value education because our parents went to college and because they and our teachers have encouraged this value. Likewise, the value we place on money, technologically sophisticated products, or the environment may come from the exposure to the opinions of our family, friends, or the media. Because values are learned by exposure to people in institutions and cultures, people within the same group often hold similar values.

Finally, acculturation is the process by which individuals learn the values and behaviors of a new culture (see Chapter 13). For example, immigrants arriving in the United States must learn new values to acculturate to American life. Consumers are more likely to take on the values of a new culture if they view that culture as attractive and having values similar to their own. Acculturation is also faster when people in the new culture are cohesive, give a lot of verbal and nonverbal signals about what their values are, and express pride in the values they hold.[8]

How Can Values Be Described?

global values A person's most enduring, strongly held, and abstract values that hold in many situations.

Values can vary in terms of their specificity. At the broadest level are **global values**, which represent the core of an individual's value system. They are highly enduring, strongly held, and abstract and apply in many situations. For example, because much of U.S. political philosophy is based on the idea of freedom, that value permeates many domains of our lives. We believe that we should have the freedom to speak, go where we want, dress as we please, and live where we want.

One of the many ways of characterizing global values is depicted in Exhibit 17.2. This scheme divides global values into seven categories: maturity, security, prosocial behavior (doing nice things for others), restrictive conformity, enjoyment in life, achievement, and self-direction. Note that some categories are similar and are therefore placed close together. Thus achievement and self-direction reflect a similar orientation toward the individual as a person, whereas prosocial behavior and restrictive conformity reflect values that relate to how an individual should deal with others.

terminal values A highly desired end states such as social recognition and pleasure.

instrumental values The values needed to achieve the desired end states such as ambition and cheerfulness.

Within each of the seven domains, we can identify two types of global values: terminal and instrumental. **Terminal values** (shown with an asterisk) are highly desired end states, and **instrumental values** (shown with a plus sign) are those needed to achieve these desired end states. For example, the two terminal values in the prosocial category are equality and salvation. The instrumental values of loving, forgiving, helpfulness, honesty, and belief in God help one achieve these terminal values.[9] Another interesting aspect of Exhibit 17.2 is that values tend to be polarized. In other words, consumers who place a high value on one set of terminal values place less value on the set on the opposite side of the figure. Thus individuals who value security, maturity, and a prosocial orientation might place less value on enjoyment (on the opposite side). Those who emphasize self-direction and achievement would value prosocial behaviors and restrictive conformity less.

domain-specific values Values that may apply to only a particular area of activities.

Global values are different from **domain-specific values**, which are relevant only to particular areas of activity such as religion, family, or consumption. Materialism is a domain-specific value because it relates to the way we view the acquisition of material goods. Global and domain-specific values can be related in that achievement of domain-specific values can be instrumental to the achievement of one or more global values. For example, we may value health because it is seen as one way in which we can achieve global values like inner harmony, pleasure, or self-respect.

Mixed

* Terminal values
+ Instrumental values

MATURITY
* Mature love
* True friendship
* Wisdom
* A world of beauty
+ Courageous

SECURITY
* National security
* Freedom
* Inner harmony
* Family security
* A world at peace

SELF-DIRECTION
* Sense of accomplishment
* Self-respect
+ Imaginative
+ Independent
+ Broadminded
+ Intellectual
+ Logical

PROSOCIAL
* Equality
* Salvation
+ Forgiving
+ Helpful
+ Belief in God
+ Honest
+ Loving

Individual

Collective

ACHIEVEMENT
* Social recognition
* An exciting life
+ Ambitious
+ Capable

RESTRICTIVE
CONFORMITY
+ Obedient
+ Polite
+ Self-controlled
+ Clean
+ Responsible

ENJOYMENT
* Comfortable life
* Pleasure
* Happiness
+ Cheerful

EXHIBIT 17.2
**Global Values and
Value Categories**

One scheme for classifying global values identifies seven major categories. Some values are individual oriented (e.g., self-direction, achievement); others are more collective or group oriented (e.g., prosocial, restrictive conformity). Note that categories close to each other are similar; those farther apart are less so. Terminal values (or highly desired end states) are marked with an asterisk (*); instrumental values have a plus sign (+).

Source: Shalom H. Schwartz and Wolfgang Bilsky, "Toward a Universal Psychological Structure of Human Values," *Journal of Personality and Social Psychology,* 53(3), 1987, pp. 550–562. Copyright © 1987 by the American Psychological Association. Adapted with permission.

Which Values Characterize Western Culture?

Given that values represent an important influence on behavior, it is useful to explore some of the values that characterize consumption in Western societies: materialism, the home, work and play, family and children, health, hedonism, youth, and technology.

materialism Placing importance on money and material goods.

Materialism One value that has become increasingly prevalent in Western cultures is **materialism**.[10] Materialistic individuals place considerable importance on the acquisition of money and material goods. In a materialistic society, satisfaction is judged in terms of what has or has not been acquired in life or what possessions are desired. Individuals high in materialism tend to value items like cars, jewelry, furs, and boats; symbolic items such as mother's wedding gown, family mementos, and photos are more important to those low in materialism.[11] Materialism might lead to the belief that a bigger house, a nicer car, or more expensive clothes will bring happiness. People in a materialistic society are also judged by the quality and quantity of their possessions. Thus a highly paid executive who drives a Mercedes may be looked upon as someone to admire and emulate, whereas a homeless person with few material possessions might be viewed negatively.

Materialism may relate to several of the terminal values noted in Exhibit 17.2. For example, possessions may be instrumental in achieving the higher-order value of social recognition. Or materialism may reflect the fact that a high value is placed on accomplishment, if judgments of self-worth are based on what one has acquired, or on the achievement of a comfortable life.

Clearly, the value placed on materialism may vary. Not all people are unhappy because they have low-paying jobs or little discretionary income. Some individuals, such as members of communes or nuns, priests, and monks, even go so far as to choose a lifestyle that rejects material possessions.[12] In addition, growing numbers of people have reassessed their priorities. They have rejected materialism and decided to "get off the treadmill" and simplify their lives by making and spending less.

Nevertheless, American consumers do have a materialistic bent. More than half the consumers surveyed at the beginning of the 1990s said that having a lot of money is essential to a good life, a share substantially higher than in the previous decade.[13] Studies of Japanese and Chinese consumers also reveal an increasing emphasis on a materialistic lifestyle.[14] To illustrate, although consumers in the People's Republic of China have historically regarded bicycles, sewing machines, and wristwatches as critical consumer goods, by the mid-1980s (after Mao Zedong's death) refrigerators, washing machines, color television sets, cameras, and video recorders were added to the list of "must have" consumer goods. Materialistic tendencies are also regarded as a driving factor in the success of (TV)and catalog

shopping among Japanese consumers. The desire for material goods is particularly acute in former communist countries such as the Czech Republic and Romania, where consumers strive to acquire as many Western goods as possible, especially a car, a TV, and fashionable clothes and shoes.[15]

In a materialistic society consumers will be receptive to marketing tactics that facilitate the acquisition of goods, such as phone-in or on-line orders and credit-card payments, and to messages that associate the acquisition of the good with achievement and status, like ads for a Rolex watch. Special sales, coupons, blue-light specials, two-for-one deals, bonus packs, and warehouse clubs have done exceptionally well in the United States and Japan, perhaps in part because of consumers' materialistic tendencies. These marketing tactics allow consumers to buy some products cheaply, thus saving money to buy other things.[16] Consumers also want to protect their possessions, which creates opportunities for services such as insurance and security companies that protect consumers against loss, theft, or damage.

Home Many consumers place a high value on the home and believe in making it as attractive and as comfortable as possible. Currently, 64 percent of U.S. citizens own their own home, and they spend more time there than in previous eras, a trend called *cocooning*. Because the outside world is becoming more complex, exhausting, and dangerous, the home is often viewed as a haven. Also, more and more families view their home as "command central"—a place where activities are coordinated and resources are pooled before members enter the outside world.

The fact that more and more consumption activities are taking place inside the home reflects this new focus. Take-out and delivery services, video rentals, pay-per-view movie viewing, and shopping from home are increasingly replacing activities such as eating out, going to the movies, and shopping in stores. This trend is reflected by Blockbuster's appeal to families gathered around the TV at home ("Make It a Blockbuster Night").[17] People are even taking more vacations at home.[18] Furthermore, companies such as House of Fabrics, Home Depot, Michael's, and Expressions, which focus on decorating, crafts, remodeling, and home furnishings, are experiencing strong growth.

Work and Play   Consumers in the United States appear to have a rather schizophrenic approach toward work and play. On the one hand, we are working harder and longer than ever before, partly related to the downsizing of many companies and an emphasis on productivity. However, work is increasingly valued for its instrumental function in achieving other values such as a comfortable lifestyle, family security, and self-accomplishment (or accomplishing one's life goals). Thus the Protestant work ethic—the value placed on work itself and on the delay of gratification to the exclusion of leisure and pleasure—is less characteristic of consumers today than it was at the beginning of the 20th century. A similar work-value trend is evident among the Dutch, who see work as a tool to get money as well as security.[19] In contrast, other cultures attach a different meaning to work. In communist countries such as China and North Korea, work is valued because of its contribution to the larger social good.

Perhaps because people are working more, they tend to value leisure time as much as they value money. They will pay for services like housecleaning and errand running in order to spend more of their non-work time on leisure activities. One study even found that two-thirds of U.S. consumers were willing to take a salary cut in order to increase their leisure time.[20] Furthermore, the distinction be-tween work and home life is blurring. Technological advances in computers, fax machines, e-mail, and electronic conferencing now allow many people to work at home. Many people are also spending more time at work doing household errands (e.g., making doctor appointments, calling repairmen, etc.) as well as spending part of their weekend time doing job-related work. A study of working mothers found that a strong concern was "juggling, balancing, and fitting it all in" with the "endless array of competing demands" of work and home.[21]

Thus the value placed on work and play can vary. For example, a study of Dutch youths identified two main groups: the Yups, who value work as a means to achieve something, and the unambitious, who say, "You can work your whole life, so let's have fun now."[22]

Family and Children   Cultures also differ in the values they place on their families and children. Parents in Europe and Asia, for example, tend to place a higher value on educating their young than do U.S. parents. Among Asian middle-class families, educating children is second in priority only to providing food. As evidence, children's books have been the largest sellers among Time Life's offerings in the Asian market, representing a whopping 55 percent of sales.[23]

Nevertheless, American consumers still place a high value on children and are often receptive to child-related products. Consider, for example, the range of cereals, juices, desserts, soft drinks, and other snack products aimed almost exclusively at children. The success of Gymboree, Gap Kids, Warner Brothers stores,

Disney, Discovery Zone indoor playgrounds, and Imaginarium are but a few examples of the high value consumers place on their children. Even status luxury goods like Waterford, Mercedes, and Volvo, designers like Liz Claiborne, and high-tech firms like IBM stress family values in their ad campaigns.[24] The ad in Exhibit 17.3 is a good example of the importance consumers place on children's education.

Health   The value placed on health has been increasing in the United States. In part, these concerns are tied to self-esteem because health is defined as having a lean, trim body. However, health is also related to basic concerns about longevity and survival.

Health values are reflected in the increasing number of products that are low in fat, calories, salt, sugar, or cholesterol. The Lean Cuisine, Healthy Choice, Weight Watchers, Baked Lay's, and SnackWell's brands, for example, have been successful with their snacks and foods because of their low fat content. The ingredient olestra was developed as a fat substitute so products could taste great but have no fat, as in Frito Lay's WOW chips. Just being low fat, however, is not enough. Kellogg and Healthy Meals have unveiled new lines of functional foods called nutraceuticals that claim to lower cholesterol levels, thereby reducing the risk of heart disease.[25] Other new foods such as the Ironman bar and Spiru-tein are "packed with protein" to offer more nutrition.[26] Growing concern over the physical impact of pesticides and other contaminants has enhanced the demand for "natural" foods and supermarkets that sell them, like Whole Foods and Bread & Circus. In Europe, health concerns have led to a deep-seated resistance to genetically modified foods.[27]

The emphasis on health has also paved the way for dieting services like Jenny Craig and Weight Watchers, health clubs, and diet aids. Hospitals now offer aerobics, karate, and aquatics classes in an effort to promote wellness. *Reader's Digest* sent out a health information survey and targeted its readers with pamphlets to help readers deal with specific ailments that they have.[28] Magazines like *Health*, *Shape*, *Fitness*, and *Runners' World* also exemplify health values. In addition, more consumers are turning to health food stores and homeopathic medicine for treating and preventing illnesses.[29] Attacks on both adult and youth smoking, bans on smoking in public places, and tobacco and alcohol warning labels in the United States and increasingly in Europe are also consistent with health concerns.[30] And as the chapter opening mentioned, many consumers like to visit health- and illness-related Web sites.[31]

Values and behavior can differ, however. For example, although many say they want to consume less fat, relatively few consumers drop light or low-fat alternatives into their shopping carts.[32] McDonald's McLean burger was a failure because consumers still had a strong desire for the traditional, high-fat burgers, and Frito Lay's no fat WOW brand hasn't done as well as expected.[33] Even high-fat products like bacon and T-bone steaks are experiencing strong sales, and organic foods are experiencing a decline.[34]

In fact, one in three American consumers is classified as overweight, and the population's average weight is gradually increasing.[35] A variety of specialized offerings such as oversize hangers, romance novels with overweight heroines, and dating services for over weight people have flourished. Some smokers have become even more determined to maintain their lifestyle, and cigarette stores that provide a smoking "oasis" for these consumers are increasingly popular. Cigars have also recently made a comeback.[36]

hedonism The principle of pleasure seeking.

Hedonism Consumers are increasingly operating on the principle of **hedonism**, or pleasure seeking, and they desire products and services that simply make them feel good, such as luxury cars, home entertainment centers, and exciting vacations. Airlines appeal to hedonism by offering more leg room and a video selection on individual screens, and some truck stops now offer massages, movies, and wedding ceremonies to appeal to their customers' pleasures.[37]

Hedonism has led to some interesting eating patterns that contradict health values, witnessed by the booming success of such products as Häagen-Dazs ice cream and President's Choice Decadent Chocolate Chip Cookies on the one hand, and Healthy Choice fat-free chocolate chip cookies and fat-free frozen yogurt on the other.[38] The contradiction is also evident when consumers avoid eating beef at home only to splurge on steaks and potatoes when dining out or when they eat an entire pizza in one sitting while sipping a Diet Coke. Furthermore, despite concerns over health, consumers will not switch to low-fat, low-calorie varieties unless they taste good. Consumers are also demanding larger sizes in the foods they consume, which explains the success of products like Pizza Hut's Big Foot Pizza, Healthy Choice's extra portion dinner, Pillsbury's Grand biscuits, and jumbo serving sizes at fast-food restaurants.[39]

Youth Compared with other cultures, the United States has long placed a high value on youth, as evidenced by the wide range of products and services designed to combat or reduce signs of aging (think of wrinkle creams, desert health spas, skin treatments, hair coloring, and hair transplants). Sales of the acne medicine Retin-A boomed after researchers discovered that it could also eliminate fine lines on the face. Furthermore, plastic surgery is one of the fastest growing medical specialties and appeals to both men and women. Advertising messages also indicate the value we place on youth, as illustrated by Pepsi's "Be Young. Have Fun. Drink Pepsi." campaign. A strong youth orientation is also evident in Latin America, where consumers spend more than $1.6 billion a year on cosmetics.[40]

Technology Consumers in Western cultures are fascinated by technological advances. More consumers than ever before believe that computers, VCRs, ATM machines, answering machines, car phones, and fax machines, not to mention the Internet, improve the quality of their lives. Even low-tech products like fruits and vegetables are improved through the process of genetic engineering.

Nevertheless, technological changes are sometimes so rapid that we have trouble keeping up with them, resulting in a renewed emphasis on simplicity or at least on managing complexity. This trend is reflected in the rise of retail concepts like The Body Shop, which sells natural personal care products, as well as a revived interest in classical music and untreated packaging materials like glass, cartons, and paper. Technology with features that work automatically is increasing in popularity because such features make it easier for the consumer to operate equipment.[41] For example, compared with older software, computer software is now more often designed to make the product do more and be more user-friendly. Thus consumers appear to value technology more for what it can do to make life easier than for the technological advance per se—making technology an instrumental rather than a terminal value.

Why Do Values Change?

Because societies and their institutions are constantly evolving, it should come as no surprise that value systems are also changing. In addition to the key trends already discussed, U.S. values are moving toward casualness in living, more liberal sexual attitudes, greater sophistication in behavior, a change in sex roles, and the wish to be modern.[42] Furthermore, although the United States was different from Western Europe 100 years ago, both cultures, and to a certain extent Japan as well, are becoming more similar in values, even though differences still exist. This increase in value consistency is driven in part by the increase in global communication. For example, some of the consumption patterns of U.S. consumers are regarded as attractive to Western Europeans. Wealthy Japanese consumers are starting to place greater value on personal preferences, a balanced life, and experiences and less value on traditional expectations, work, and possessions.[43]

What Affects Our Values?

How do values differ across groups of consumers? This section explores the ways that culture, ethnicity, social class, and age can influence our values.

Culture and Values   Because people in different countries are exposed to different cultural experiences, it is not surprising that there are cross-cultural differences in values. One study found that the three most important values among Brazilians are true friendship, mature love, and happiness, whereas U.S. consumers named family security, having a world at peace, and freedom.[44] Inner harmony ranked 4th in importance among Brazilians but 13th in the United States. These values all differ from the beliefs of consumers in China, where the most important values are preserving the best that one has attained; being sympathetic to others; having self-control; and integrating enjoyment, action, and contemplation. A study of women in Germany, France, and the United Kingdom found that the value of "having a familiar routine" is most important for German women, but only 10th in importance for the British and 23rd for the French.[45] "Having beautiful things in the home" and "being with people with up-to-date ideas" are more important to Germans, and "having something to do to keep busy" is more critical to the French and British.

A classic study by Hofstede identified four main value dimensions along which cultures can vary:[46]

- *Individualism Versus Collectivism.*   The degree to which a culture focuses on the individuals rather than the group.

- *Uncertainty Avoidance.*   The extent to which a culture prefers structured to unstructured situations.

- *Masculinity Versus Femininity.* The extent to which masculine values (as defined by Hofstede) such as assertiveness, success, and competition are stressed over feminine values such as quality of life, warm personal relationships, and caring.

- *Power Distance.* The degree to which members of a society are equal in terms of status.

All cultures can be classified along these four dimensions. Understanding where a given culture falls may provide insight into cross-cultural differences. For example, one study found that tipping in restaurants is less likely to occur in countries where power distance and uncertainty avoidance are low, feminine values are strong, and individualism is high.[47] Another study found that humorous ad themes are more likely to focus on groups in collectivist societies like Thailand and South Korea and on unequal status relationships in countries with high power distance like the United States and Germany.[48]

Ethnic Identification and Values Ethnic groups within a larger culture can have some values that are different from those of other ethnic subcultures. Remember from Chapter 13 that Hispanics place a strong value on the family and home and are therefore less likely to eat away from home than are Anglos.[49] Furthermore, compared with Anglos, Hispanics place a greater emphasis on equality and inner harmony, and Anglos place a greater emphasis on having a world at peace and true friendships. African and Asian American subcultures place a high value on the extended family.[50] Because Asian American consumers also value tradition and cooperation, they respond well to subtle messages that focus on these values. In addition to family security, African Americans place a higher value on equality, freedom, a sense of accomplishment, and broadmindedness, whereas their Anglo counterparts value world peace to a greater degree.

Differences in ethnic values are present in many countries around the world. For example, Punjabi consumers in northern India place a high value on entrepreneurialism, since many own family businesses. They hold Western values and place great importance on earning a lot of money, becoming upwardly mobile, and showing off products that indicate wealth or status. Getting children into the right schools where they will have the opportunity to achieve is also important. In contrast, Tamils from the southern part of India place higher value on intellectual pursuits. They are idealistic and spend time in intellectual activities like art, literature, and music. Rather than engaging in conspicuous consumption, these consumers are more likely to live a simple and Spartan lifestyle. Tamils and Punjabis are therefore likely to react very differently to status appeals and services designed to help the individual earn money.

Social Class and Values A main characteristic of the different social classes (discussed in Chapter 14) is that each one tends to hold specific values. In the United States working-class consumers have been characterized as valuing family and friendships. Middle-class consumers, in contrast, focus more on individualism, achievement, self-accomplishment, and social recognition. The middle class also values doing the right thing, having a nice home and more possessions, and buying what others buy. Furthermore, as many countries around the world, including those in Eastern Europe, Latin America, and Asia, embrace market economies, the size of the middle class is increasing dramatically, along with middle-class values that include materialism and a desire for less government control over their lives and greater access to information. Upper-upper class consumers value giving back to society, and their prosocial orientation makes them actively involved in philanthropic activities. They are volunteers for social, cultural, and civic causes. Self-expression is prized in the upper-upper class and appears in the design of homes, clothing, cars, artwork, and other forms of consumption.[51]

Age and Values   Members of a generation often share similar values that differ from those of other generations. For example, your grandparents may value security over hedonism, not because they are older but because they grew up during the Great Depression and suffered economic hardship as children. They therefore view hedonic activities as frivolous and unacceptable. Likewise, baby boomers who grew up in the 1960s—a time of political upheaval, self-indulgence, and rebellion—value hedonism, morality, self-direction, and achievement.[52] Note that it is sometimes very difficult to distinguish values we acquire with age from those we learn from our era. Nevertheless, differences by virtue of age or cohort do exist, and they influence the way we behave as consumers.

MARKETING IMPLICATIONS   Consumer values have considerable importance for consumer behavior and marketing, including consumption patterns, market segmentation, new product development, ad development strategy, and ethics.

Consumption Patterns.   Consumers tend to buy, use, and dispose of products in a manner consistent with their values.[53] Thus marketers can know more about what consumers like if they understand their values. For example, those who value warm relationships with others are more likely to buy gifts, send cards, and make long-distance phone calls than those who place less value on relationships.[54] The Body Shop is very popular with some consumers not only because of the value it places on naturalness and health but also because the company goes to great lengths to portray other values such as employing orphan boys in India and buying ingredients from impoverished tribes in Brazil.[55] *Good Housekeeping* was introduced into Japan because many Japanese are questioning their workaholic ways and are anxious to devote more time to home and family.[56] In Taiwan consumption is guided strongly by Confucian values (in contrast to mainland China), and consumers are therefore frugal and sober and have a finely graded system of status symbols for everything from the home to food.[57]

Interestingly, most international marketing blunders stem from a lack of understanding of the values of a particular culture.[58] In essence, marketers sometimes adopt an ethnocentric perspective by assuming that the values of consumers in other cultures are similar to their own. Campbell's soup failed in South America because a woman's behavior as a good mother there is indicated by the amount of time and dedication she devotes to domestic duties. To serve soup from a can is tantamount to saying you do not care enough about your family.

Market Segmentation.   Marketers can identify groups of consumers who have a common set of values different from those of other groups, a process called **value segmentation.** For example, a car company might identify two groups of consumers based on their values—one group that prizes family, convenience, and time and another that values technology, the environment, and health. Marketers could then examine demographic variables that describe these two groups. One group might be middle-aged, working-class consumers, and the other younger and middle class. Different marketing activities could be aimed at these segments. The first group might be attracted to a roomy vehicle like a minivan that has devices to make operation easier. The other might desire high-tech features and pollution controls. In fact, most car manufacturers offer different lines of cars to appeal to different value segments. Japanese companies, for example, introduced

value segmentation   The grouping of consumers by common values.

brands like Lexus and Infiniti to appeal to consumers who value material possessions and achievement. As another example, the People for the Ethical Treatment of Animals (PETA) developed an ad campaign promoting vegetarian values.[59]

Values can also be very useful in understanding just what attributes consumers within a market segment are likely to find important in a product and therefore what may motivate them to buy one brand over another. When buying clothes, individuals who value status might look for attributes like price and luxury, whereas those who value fitting in with the crowd might look for clothing that is particularly trendy.[60] Interestingly, a study of the fragrance market found that women's perfume preferences can be grouped according to value segments such as the Fledgling Career Woman, Working-Class Woman, Frustrated Professional, Traditional Housewife, Successful Professional, and Senior Set Woman. Essentially, women with higher levels of self-confidence tend to prefer more subtle fragrances.[61]

New Product Ideas. Values are also likely to influence consumers' reactions to products that are new and different. For example, consumers who place a high value on change and those who value change less are likely to react very differently to innovations like fax machines or e-mail.[62] The more a new product is consistent with important values, the greater the likelihood of its success. For example, the success of good-tasting, microwavable, low-fat and low-calorie frozen entrees occurred in part because these items are consistent with multiple values like hedonism, time, convenience, health, and technology. New low-fat dog and cat foods are doing well because they match up well with pet owners' regard for the health of their pets.

Ad Development Strategy. An examination of the value profile of a target segment can help marketers design appealing ads.[63] The more compatible the ad copy is with consumers' values, the more likely consumers are to become involved in the advertisement and to find it relevant. The ad in Exhibit 17.4 is likely to appeal to females who value independence and broadmindedness. RC Cola appealed to consumers' value of patriotism with images of red, white, and blue, a Fourth of July parade, and a drive-in movie.[64] McDonald's tried to portray itself as a "Thai Patriot," a firm that was contributing positively to the economy, to counter a perception that the company was contributing to Thailand's economic decline.[65] Connecting product attributes and benefits to consumer values is important because they represent the end state consumers desire to achieve—the driving force behind their consumption of the product. Thus the Avia cross-trainer sneakers in Exhibit 17.4 are meant to help the user who values working out.

Sometimes even good girls want to be bad.

EXHIBIT 17.4
Reflection of Values

Ads often target consumers' values. This ad is likely to appeal to young women who value independence and broadmindedness.

Source: Ed McCabe.

Marketers must also be careful not to conflict with cultural values in their communications. Benetton created a stir with several ads, including one showing a nun kissing a priest, particularly offensive in predominantly Catholic countries like Italy and France, and one showing 56 pictures of genitalia including those of children.[66] A Calvin Klein ad in the United States was viewed negatively because it showed models under 18 in various stages of undress.[67] In Thailand an ad that showed Hitler eating an inferior brand of potato chips and being transformed into a good guy by eating the advertised brand elicited an outcry from a number of groups.[68]

Ethical Considerations. Values also guide consumers' evaluations of the appropriateness of others' behavior, including marketers. For example, those who value morality might look with disfavor on certain products including X-rated videos and cigarettes, on certain consumption practices like prostitution and gambling, and on ads that seem inconsistent with morality, such as in their use of sex. Consumers will also evaluate marketers' behavior for fairness, ethics, and appropriateness.[69] Practices perceived as inconsistent with these values are likely to generate responses like boycotting, protesting, and complaining (which are discussed in Chapter 21). For example, Johnson & Johnson developed a series of image campaigns that stressed preventive health care and caring for consumers to counteract a growing belief that drug manufacturers are "price-gouging medicine men."[70]

How Can Values Be Measured?

To segment the market by values, marketers need some means of identifying consumers' values, their importance, and any changes or trends that affect them. Unfortunately, values are often hard to measure. Part of the reason is that people do not often think about their values and may therefore have a hard time reporting on what is really important to them. Another problem is that people may sometimes feel social pressure to respond to a values questionnaire in a given way to make themselves look better in the eyes of the researcher. Therefore, less obtrusive or more indirect ways of assessing values are sometimes appropriate.

Inferring Values from the Cultural Milieu The least obtrusive way to measure values is to simply make inferences based on a culture's milieu. For example, advertising has often been used as an indicator of values.[71] One researcher examined the values portrayed in print ads in the United States between 1900 and 1980 and found that practicality, the family, modernity, cheapness, wisdom, and uniqueness were among the values that appeared most frequently. Ads are also used to discover cross-cultural differences in values. One study found that because the People's Republic of China, Taiwan, and Hong Kong are at different levels of economic development and have different political ideologies, the countries differed in the types of values reflected in ads.[72] Ads from the People's Republic of China focused on utilitarian themes and promised a better life; Hong Kong ads stressed hedonism and an easier life; and Taiwan ads fell between the other two.

Advertisements are also used to study value trends. For example, a historical analysis of Japanese ads found an increasing number of appeals to status, apparently reflecting a increasing value on status.[73] Given the economic changes currently taking place in China, it is perhaps not surprising to find that these ads are also changing from more utilitarian themes to emphasizing variety in products and product assurances.[74] Advertising, however, is only one domain of material culture that might indicate values. We can also infer values just by looking at the names given to products. Titles indicative of the value of materialism (More), hedonism

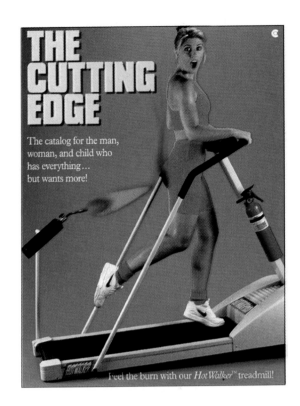

EXHIBIT 17.5

Spoof of Materialism

Materialistic individuals tend to value their possessions highly and this trait can lead to the desire for many items. *The Cutting Edge* catalog is poking fun at *The Sharper Image* catalog and stores, which offer many unusual items for those who have "everything."

Source: © becker & mayer! Kirkland, Washington.

(Obsession), time (Minute Rice), technology (IBM), and convenience (Reddi Whip) are easy to find.

Values are also reflected in the books and magazines we read, the TV programs we watch, and the types of people we regard as heroes or heroines. Spoofs like the one in Exhibit 17.5 reflect an attempt to poke fun at the current value of materialism. Even comic books have been used to indicate consumer values. One study found considerable evidence for materialism as a valued trait in comic books like *Archie*, *The Fox and the Crow*, *Uncle Scrooge*, and *Richie Rich*.[75] Interestingly, this study also found that in some instances materialism was viewed as good, bringing happiness and goodwill, and in other cases it was viewed as bad, abusive, and hurtful. The content of songs can also indicate values. Many people are concerned that violent lyrics in today's song are an indication of a decline in values.

One criticism of cultural milieu as an indicator of values is that researchers never know whether culture *reflects* values or *creates* them. For example, was Madonna's "Material Girl" successful because consumers value materialism, or did the song promote an attitude that other consumers emulate? In light of this problem, other methods have been introduced to measure values.

means-ends chain analysis
A technique that helps us understand how values link to attributes in products and services.

Means-End Chain Analysis Marketers can use the **means-end chain analysis** to gain insight into consumers' values by better understanding which attributes they find important in products. Armed with this information, researchers can work backwards to uncover the values that drive consumer decisions.[76] For example, suppose a consumer likes light beer because it has fewer calories than regular beer. If a researcher asks why it was important to have a beer with fewer calories, the respondent might say, "Because I don't want to gain weight." If the researcher asks why not, the consumer might respond by saying, "I want to be healthy." If asked why again, the consumer might say, "Because I want to feel good about myself." This example is illustrated in the top line of Exhibit 17.6.

Note that the means-end chain has several potential levels. First, the consumer provided an attribute that is considered important, followed by a concrete benefit that the attribute provides. Then the consumer indicated that this benefit was important because it served some instrumental value. This entire process is called a means-end chain because the attribute provides the means to a desired end state or terminal value (in this case, self-esteem).

Several other means-end chains are illustrated in Exhibit 17.6. Combined, they tell us several things. First, the same attribute may be associated with very different values. For example, rather than valuing light beer for its health benefits,

PRODUCT	ATTRIBUTE	BENEFIT	INSTRUMENTAL VALUE (driving force)	TERMINAL VALUE
Light beer (I)	Fewer calories	I won't gain weight	Helps make me healthy	I feel good about myself (self-esteem)
Light beer (II)	Fewer calories Great taste Light taste	Less filling Enjoyable/relaxing Refreshing	Good times/fun Friendship Sharing	Belonging
Rice	Comes in Boiling bag	Convenient No messy pan to clean up	Saves time	I can enjoy more time with my family (belonging)

EXHIBIT 17.6
An Example of Means End Chains

According to the means-end chain analysis, product and service *attributes* (e.g., fewer calories) lead to *benefits* (e.g., I won't gain weight) that reflect *instrumental values* (e.g., Helps make me healthy) and *terminal values* (e.g., I feel good about myself). See whether you can develop a means-end chain for toothpaste or deodorant. This type of analysis helps marketers identify important values and the attributes associated with them.

Sources: Adapted from Jonathan Gutman, "A Means-End Chain Model Based on Consumer Categorization Processes," *Journal of Marketing,* Spring 1982, pp. 60–72; Thomas J. Reynolds and John P. Rochan, "Means-End Based Advertising Research: Copy Testing Is Not Strategy Assessment," *Journal of Business Research,* March 1991, pp. 131–142.

some consumers may like light beer because drinking it occurs in a social context that leads to a greater sense of belonging. Second, the same value may be associated with very different products and attributes. Thus attributes associated with both light beer and rice may appeal equally to the value of belonging. Third, a given attribute may be linked with multiple benefits and/or values. Thus a consumer might like light beer because it helps her feel healthier *and* because it facilitates belonging.

Using the means-end chain analysis, marketers can identify product attributes that will be consistent with these values.[77] As an example, because in the 1990s sports cars were generally expensive and uncomfortable, owning one took on an aspect of "arrogance and irresponsibility." As a result, manufacturers are now offering comfortable cars that are positioned for "people who have friends" in order to be more in line with current values.[78]

The means-end chain model can also be used to develop advertising strategy. By knowing which attributes consumers find important and which values they associate with those attributes, advertisers have a better idea as to the strategy they should pursue in designing ads. Returning to Exhibit 17.4, the smell of the perfume will help young women be "bad," achieve independence, and perhaps obtain pleasure. Note that the ad need not explicitly link a given attribute with a motive. Instead, the linkage could be made much more implicit.

Rokeach Value Survey (RVS)
A survey that measures instrumental and terminal values.

Value Questionnaires Questionnaires can also be employed to directly assess values. One of the best-known instruments is the **Rokeach Value Survey** (**RVS**). This questionnaire asks consumers about the importance they attach to the 18 instrumental values and 18 terminal values identified in Exhibit 17.2. A benefit of this survey is that because the questionnaire is standardized and everyone responds to the same set of items, the researcher can identify which values are most important to a given group of consumers, whether values are changing over time, and whether values differ for various groups of consumers. One of the problems with the RVS is that some values are not relevant to consumer behavior; for example, consider salvation, forgiving, and being obedient. Thus some researchers have recommended the use of a shortened form of the RVS that retains only those values that seem relevant to a consumer context.[79]

List of Values (LOV)
A survey that measures nine principle values in consumer behavior.

Others have advocated the use of the **List of Values (LOV)**; this technique presents consumers with nine primary values and asks them either to identify the two most important or to rank all nine values in terms of their importance. The nine values are (1) self-respect, (2) warm relationships with others, (3) sense of accomplishment, (4) self-fulfillment, (5) fun and enjoyment in life, (6) excitement, (7) sense of belonging, (8) being well respected, and (9) security.[80] The first six are internal values because they derive from the individual; the others are external values. The values can also be described in terms of whether they are fulfilled through interpersonal relationships (warm relationships with others, sense of belonging), personal factors (self-respect, being well respected, self-fulfillment), or nonpersonal things (sense of accomplishment, fun, security, and excitement).

One study found the LOV was able to predict consumers' responses to statements that describe their self-reported consumption characteristics ("I am a spender, not a saver," "TV is my main entertainment"), their actual consumption behaviors (the frequency with which they watch movies or the news, read certain magazines, and engage in activities like playing tennis and going to concerts), and their marketplace beliefs ("I believe the number of companies that satisfy consumer complaints is increasing," "I believe the consumer movement has caused prices to increase"). In addition, compared with the RVS, the LOV is a better predictor of consumer behavior, is shorter, and easier to administer. Finally, the LOV can be useful in identifying segments of consumers with similar value systems. For example, Exhibit 17.7 illustrates the relative importance of the nine LOV values in four U.S. segments.[81]

PERSONALITY

The previous section made the important point that individuals with comparable backgrounds tend to hold similar values. However, even when individuals hold the same values, they do not always act the same way. For example, in listening to a sales pitch, one consumer may state demurely that she finds the product interesting but is not ready to make up her mind right now. Another might act more assertively, interrupting the salesperson midway through his pitch to indicate that she has no interest in the product whatsoever. Thus consumers vary in terms of their personality or the way in which they respond to a particular situation.

personality An internal characteristic that determines how individuals behave in various situations.

Personality consists of the distinctive patterns of behaviors, tendencies, qualities, or personal dispositions that make one individual different from another and lead to a consistent response to environmental stimuli. These patterns are internal characteristics that we are born with or that result from the way we have been raised. The concept of personality helps us understand why people behave differently in different situations.

How Has Personality Been Studied?

The social sciences provide various approaches to studying personality. This section reviews five that are employed in consumer research: psychoanalytic approaches, trait theories, phenomenological approaches, social-psychological theories, and behavioral approaches.

EXHIBIT 17.7
Value Segments

Marketers try to segment consumers in terms of the patterns of values they hold and their relative importance. Here, for example, are four major value segments. Segment A places very high importance on security, and segment D tends to stress warm relationships with others. By identifying value segments, marketers can develop messages that appeal to the specific values of these segments.

Source: Wagner A. Kamakura and Thomas P. Novak, "Value-System Segmentation: Exploring the Meaning of LOV," *Journal of Consumer Research,* June 1992, pp. 112–132. © 1992 University of Chicago. All rights reserved.

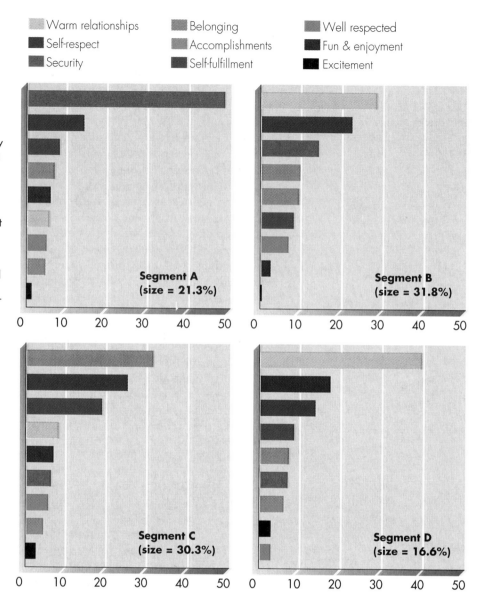

Warm relationships — Belonging — Well respected — Self-respect — Accomplishments — Fun & enjoyment — Security — Self-fulfillment — Excitement

Segment A (size = 21.3%)

Segment B (size = 31.8%)

Segment C (size = 30.3%)

Segment D (size = 16.6%)

Psychoanalytic Approaches Psychoanalytic theories propose that personality arises from a set of dynamic, unconscious internal struggles within the mind.[82] The well-known psychoanalyst Sigmund Freud proposed that we pass through several developmental stages in forming our personalities. At the initial, oral, stage, the infant is entirely dependent on others for need satisfaction, and pleasure is focused on oral gratification derived from sucking, eating, and biting. At the anal stage, the child is confronted with the problem of toilet training. Then in the phallic stage the youth becomes aware of his or her genitals and must deal with desires for the opposite-sex parent (the Oedipal and Electra complexes).

Failure to resolve the conflicts that arise at each stage may influence one's personality. For example, the individual who never received sufficient oral stimulation as an infant may reveal this crisis in adulthood through oral-stimulation activities like gum chewing, smoking, and overeating or through distrust of others' motives (including those of marketers). At the anal stage an individual whose toilet training is too restrictive may become obsessed with control and be overly

EXHIBIT 17.8

**A Trait Conception of
Personality Types**

Consumers can be classified according to whether they have *introverted* or *extroverted* personality traits. These traits can lead to the identification of various personality types (e.g., moody, peaceful, lively, and aggressive). Interestingly, these traits can be grouped into four major groups that correspond to the basic temperaments identified by the ancient Greek physician Hippocrates many centuries ago. How would you classify your personality according to this scheme?

Source: Adapted from Hans Eysenck and S. Rachman, *The Causes and Cures of Neurosis: An Introduction to Modern Behavior Therapy Based on Learning Theory and Principles of Conditioning* (San Diego, Calif.: Knapp, 1965), p. 16.

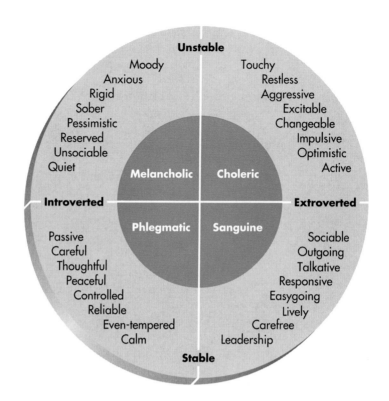

orderly, stubborn, or stingy. Thus neatly organized closets and records, list making, and excessive saving may describe consumers who are fixated at the anal stage. As consumers, they may also engage in extensive information search and deliberation in making decisions relative to others. On the other hand, those whose training was overly lenient may become messy, disorganized adults.

The key point is that these stages give rise to subconscious influences on behavior. Consequently, some advertising agencies conduct research to delve deep into consumers' psyches and uncover subconscious reasons why they buy a particular product.[83] As one example, this type of research led to the discovery of a deep-seated desire for milk that led to the "Got Milk" campaign.

Trait Theories   Trait theorists propose that personality is composed of characteristics that describe and differentiate individuals.[84] For example, people might be described as aggressive, easygoing, quiet, moody, shy, or rigid. One of the most basic trait theory schemes was proposed by psychologist Carl Jung, who believed individuals could be categorized according to their levels of *introversion* and *extroversion*.[85] Introverts are shy, prefer to be alone, and are anxious in the presence of others. Extroverts are outgoing, sociable, and typically conventional. Introverts tend to avoid social channels and therefore may not find out about new products from others. Introverts are also less motivated by social pressure and more likely to do things that please themselves than are extroverts.

More recent work has found that the trait of *stability*, or consistency in behavior, when combined with the introversion/extroversion dimension, can be used as a basis to represent various personality types (see Exhibit 17.8). For example, a person who is reliable tends to be high on both introversion and stability. In contrast, a passive person is introverted, but neither highly stable nor highly unstable. One interesting feature about this scheme is that the personality types identified by these two dimensions match the four temperaments identified by the Greek physician Hippocrates centuries ago—for example, a phlegmatic person is one who is introverted and stable; a melancholic person is one who is introverted and unstable.

Phenomenological Approaches Phenomenological approaches propose that personality is largely shaped by an individual's interpretations of life events.[86] For example, the way a person interprets key events and the nature of that interpretation, rather than internal conflicts or traits, is viewed as a cause of depression.

A key concept of the phenomenological approaches is **locus of control**, or people's interpretations of *why* specific things happen.[87] Some individuals tend to have an internal locus of control, attributing more responsibility to themselves for good or bad outcomes. For example, those who are internally controlled might blame or view themselves as being careless when a product fails. Externally controlled individuals, on the other hand, place responsibility on other people, events, or places, rather than on themselves. Thus they might attribute product failure to faulty manufacturing, poor packaging, or the clumsy delivery person.

Chapter 12 pointed out that locus of control is very important in influencing consumers' perceptions of satisfaction in a consumption experience, as well as in determining which emotions are felt. For example, consumers who attribute product failure to themselves might experience feelings of shame and self-blame. Those who attribute product failure to an external source might feel anger and irritation. In addition, a consumer's life theme or goals (concerns that we address in our everyday lives) can greatly influence the meanings derived from ads.[88] Thus an individual who is more concerned with family might interpret an ad differently than someone who is more concerned with his or her private self.

Social-Psychological Theories Another group of theories focuses on social as opposed to biological explanations of personality. Essentially, these theories propose that individuals act in social situations in order to meet their needs. The researcher Karen Horney, for instance, believed that behavior can be characterized by three major orientations.[89] *Compliant* individuals are dependent on others and can be characterized as humble, trusting, and tied to a group. *Aggressive* individuals have a need for power; move away from others; and are outgoing, assertive, self-confident, and tough-minded. *Detached* individuals are independent and self-sufficient but suspicious and introverted. These three orientations are measured by the CAD scale.[90] One study found that assertiveness and aggressiveness were significantly related to styles of interaction with marketing institutions.[91] In particular, people high on both assertiveness and aggression were likely to perceive complaining as acceptable and to enjoy doing it.

Related to these concepts is the distinction between *state-oriented consumers*, who are more likely to rely on subjective norms to guide their behavior, and *action-oriented consumers*, whose behavior is based more on their own attitudes.[92] Consumers also vary in terms of their attention to information that helps them compare themselves to others (social comparison information). Individuals high on this factor are more sensitive to normative pressure than are those low on this factor.

Behavioral Approaches In contrast to other explanations of personality, behavioral approaches propose that differences in personality are a function of how individuals have been rewarded or punished in the past. In other words, individuals are more likely to have traits or to engage in behaviors for which they have received positive reinforcement. They are less likely to maintain characteristics and behaviors for which they have been punished.[93] Thus an individual might be

locus of control How people interpret why things happen (internal vs. external).

extroverted because outgoing behaviors have been rewarded by parents, caretakers, and other individuals, whereas introverted behaviors have been punished. Likewise, a consumer might prefer colorful clothing if he or she has received positive reinforcement for wearing it in the past. Note that these behavioral approaches to personality involve the principles of operant conditioning discussed in Chapter 11.

Do Personality Characteristics Affect Consumer Behavior?

Much of the consumer-related personality research has followed the trait approach and focused on identifying specific personality traits that explain differences in the purchase, use, and disposition behavior of consumers. A number of studies have attempted to find a relationship between personality and consumer behavior, but reviews of this research generally find that personality does not seem to predict consumer behavior very well.[94] One of the main problems with this approach is that many of the instruments used to measure personality traits were developed in clinical settings and designed to identify personality disorders. Hence these measures may not be appropriate for identifying traits that relate to everyday consumption behaviors.

In addition, consumer researchers have often attempted to use personality traits inappropriately to explain phenomena. One classic study employed the Edwards Personal Preference Schedule (a detailed instrument that measures a variety of personality traits) to examine the difference between Ford and Chevy owners.[95] Results were disappointing. The only significant difference was that Ford owners were more dominant-aggressive (not a very meaningful or useful finding). Thus personality does not appear to be a good predictor of brand choice.

Although personality has not been shown to be strongly related to consumer behavior, some researchers believe that more reliable measures of traits, developed in a consumer context, would reveal a relationship.[96] Indeed, the association between personality and consumer behavior may be stronger for some types of consumer behavior than for others. For example, although personality may not be very useful in understanding brand choice, it may help us understand phenomena such as susceptibility to persuasion, the liking of an ad, or the extent of information processing. The ad in Exhibit 17.9 is likely to appeal to people who are venturesome.

Personality may also be more useful for targeting some product and service categories than others. In particular, our choice of products and services that involve subjective or hedonic features such as looks, style, and aesthetics may be somewhat related to personality. A good example is the selection of a greeting card, which represents a personal message and therefore is an extension of the sender's personality.

Finally, certain types of personality traits may be more related to consumer behavior than others. Following are several examples.

Optimal Stimulation Level Some activities have the potential to provide us with some sort of physiological arousal. For example, we might feel more aroused when we drive extremely fast on the highway, ride a roller coaster, see a scary

EXHIBIT 17.9
Personality and Ad Appeal

Sometimes messages appeal to a particular personality type. Individuals who like thrill-seeking activities are likely to react positively to this ad.

Source: Courtesy of the National Federation of Coffee Growers of Columbia

"Grab life by the beans."

The richest coffee in the world.

optimal stimulation level (or **OSL**) The level of arousal that is most comfortable for an individual.

movie, or go to new and different surroundings. Thus things that are physically stimulating, emotionally energizing, or novel have arousal-inducing potential. Note, however, that highly stimulating activities are not always desirable. In fact, according to the theory of **optimal stimulation level** (or **OSL**), we prefer things that are moderately arousing to things that are either too arousing or not arousing at all.[97] For example, we might prefer eating at a restaurant that offers moderately imaginative food to eating at one that offers the same boring fare we could get at home or one that offers very exotic and unusual food.

Although moderate levels of stimulation are generally preferred, individuals differ in the level of arousal they regard as moderate and hence optimal. Individuals with a low optimal stimulation level tend to prefer activities that are less arousing. They avoid excitement because it can send them over the edge. In contrast, individuals with a high optimal stimulation level are more likely to seek activities that are very exciting, novel, complex, and different. For example, consumers with high needs for stimulation might enjoy activities like skydiving, bungee-jumping, gambling, and river rafting.[98] They are also more likely to be innovative and creative.

Individuals with high and low needs for stimulation also differ in the way they approach the marketplace. Those with high stimulation needs tend to be the first consumers to buy new products, to seek information about them, and to engage in variety seeking (buying something different).[99] They are more curious about the ads they watch but may easily get bored by them. They are more likely to buy products associated with greater risk, enjoy shopping in malls with many stores and products, and prefer products and services that deviate from established consumption practices.

dogmatism A tendency to be resistant to change or new ideas

Dogmatism Consumers can also vary in terms of how open- or close-minded they are. **Dogmatism** refers to an individual's tendency to be more resistant to change and new ideas. We would expect dogmatic or close-minded consumers to be relatively resistant to new marketing offerings, including products, promotions, and advertising. In support, one study found that Nigerian consumers' acceptance of new products depended on how dogmatic the consumers were. The study also found that Muslims were more dogmatic than Christians.[100]

need for cognition (or **NFC**) A trait that describes how much people like to think.

Need for Cognition Individuals may vary in terms of how much pleasure they derive from active thinking and contemplating. Consumers who enjoy thinking extensively about things like products, attributes, and benefits are thought to be high in **need for cognition** (or **NFC**).[101] Those with a low need for cognition do not like to think and prefer to take shortcuts or rely on their feelings.

In consumer behavior, individuals high and low in need for cognition differ in terms of their product interests, information search, and reaction to different ad campaigns. Specifically, those with a high need for cognition enjoy products that carry a serious learning and mastery component such as chess, educational games, and TV shows like *Jeopardy*. They derive satisfaction from searching for and discovering features of new products and react positively to long, technically sophisticated ads describing detailed aspects of products or services. They might also scrutinize messages more carefully than other consumers do, considering the credibility or merits of the message. Low need for cognition consumers, on the other hand, react more positively to short messages that use attractive models, humor, or other cues. These individuals tend to make decisions that involve little thinking.

Susceptibility to Influence Consumers can also vary in terms of their susceptibility to persuasion attempts, especially those that are interpersonal or face-to-face. Some consumers have a greater desire to enhance their image as observed by others and are therefore willing to be influenced or guided by them.[102] Consumers with lower social and information processing confidence tend to be more influenced by ads than are those with higher self-confidence.

Self-Monitoring Behavior Individuals differ in the degree to which they look to others for cues on how to behave. High self-monitors are typically sensitive to the desires and influences of others to guide their own behavior, and low self-monitors are guided more by their own preferences and desires and are less influenced by normative expectations.[103] High and low self-monitors also differ in their responsiveness to advertising appeals. High self-monitors are more responsive to image-oriented ads and more willing to try and pay more for products advertised with an image consistent with high self-monitoring. In contrast, low self-monitors are generally more responsive to ads that make a quality claim and are more willing to try these products and pay extra for them.

National Character Personality traits can sometimes be used to stereotype people of a particular country as having a **national character**. Note that these characterizations typically represent very broad generalizations about a particular country; obviously a great deal of variation exists among individuals. To illustrate, the French and Italians are often thought of as emotional and romantic; the British, as more reserved. German, French, and U.S. citizens have been characterized as more assertive than their British, Russian, or Italian counterparts. German, British, and Russian consumers can be viewed as "tighter" compared with the "looser" French, Italian, and U.S. consumers.[104] The latter are also considered more impulsive, risk oriented, and self-confident than their Canadians neighbors who are stereotyped as more cautious, restrained, and reserved.

national character   The personality of a country.

Countries have also been characterized as different in their needs for achievement, levels of introversion and extroversion, perceptions of human nature as good or evil, and flexibility.[105] We can clearly see potential cross-cultural differences in individual reactions to marketing on the basis of national character. For example, Canadians' aversion to credit cards and borrowing may be tied to their cautious character.[106]

MARKETING IMPLICATIONS   Because some personality traits may be related to consumption behavior, marketers can develop products, services, and communications that appeal to various personality types. For example, ads directed toward compliant or high self-monitoring consumers should focus on the approval of others, whereas appeals to high optimal stimulation level consumers might encourage them to try something different. Cult drinks such as Cheerwine, Big Red, and Moxie appeal to consumers who are "out of the mainstream" or lack the "herd mentality."[107] Newspapers like *The Village Voice*, *XS*, and *New Times* appeal to individuals who are "hip and irreverent."[108] Finally, Nabisco portrayed its SnackWell's cookies and crackers as a way for women in their 30s with low self-esteem to boost their confidence.[109] ■

LIFESTYLES

The concept of lifestyles is highly related to consumers' values and personality. Whereas values and personality represent internal states or characteristics, **lifestyles** are manifestations or actual patterns of behavior. In particular, they are represented by a consumer's **activities, interests, and opinions (AIOs)**—see

lifestyles   People's patterns of behavior.

activities, interests, and opinions (AIOs)   The three components of lifestyles.

EXHIBIT 17.10
Activities, Interests, and Opinions

Lifestyles are represented by consumers' *activities, interests,* and *opinions*. Here are some major examples of each category. Note that these lifestyles provide a more detailed profile of consumers than their demographics do (the last column).

ACTIVITIES	INTERESTS	OPINIONS	DEMOGRAPHICS
Work	Family	Themselves	Age
Hobbies	Home	Social issues	Education
Social events	Job	Politics	Income
Vacations	Community	Business	Occupation
Entertainment	Recreation	Education	Family size
Club membership	Fashion	Economics	Dwelling
Community	Food	Products	Geography
Shopping	Media	Culture	City size
Sports	Achievements	Future	Life-cycle stage

Source: Joseph T. Plumer, "The Concept and and Application of Life Style Segmentation," *Journal of Marketing*, January 1974, pp. 33–37. Reprinted with permission.

Exhibit 17.10. What people do in their spare time is often a good indicator of their lifestyle. One consumer might like to engage in outdoor activities such as skiing, camping, and scuba diving, whereas another might prefer to stay at home, read, listen to music, or make a scrapbook. Consumers who have different activities, opinions, and interests may in fact represent distinct lifestyle segments.

For example, one study identified two lifestyle segments that were most likely to drink and drive: Good Timers, who are frequent partygoers, macho, and high on sensation seeking, and Problem Kids, who frequently display troublesome behaviors.[110] An affinity for nostalgia, or the desire for old things, also represents a lifestyle segment.[111] Obviously those high on this variable represent a key market for old movies, books, and antiques. Surfing on the Internet has created a new type of lifestyle.

Sometimes lifestyle research enables marketers to gain a better understanding of how their product fits into the consumers' general patterns of behavior. For example, a study of stomach remedies identified four main lifestyle segments: Severe Sufferers, Active Medicators, Hypochondriacs, and Practicalists.[112] Another study, this one of fashion consumers, found six major groups: Yester Years (older consumers), Power Purchasers (married households with college degree), Fashion Foregoers, Social Strivers, Dutifuls (highly practical), and Progressive Patrons (high-income/quality buyers).[113]

Finally, consumers in different countries may have characteristic lifestyles. One study found considerable lifestyle differences between Japanese and U.S. women. Japanese women were more home focused, less likely to visit restaurants, less price sensitive, and less likely to drive or go to the movies.[114] Given these preferences, we might surmise that Japanese women would be more likely than U.S. women to spend time preparing meals at home and would therefore pay a premium for products that enhance the quality of the meal. Popular lifestyle activities among Russian consumers include going to the movies and theater and participating in sports like soccer, ice hockey, and figure skating.[115] Another study found that watching sports on TV, going to movies, playing cards, reading a book, and listening to the stereo are the favorite activities of the Chinese.[116]

MARKETING IMPLICATIONS Like many of the other concepts in this book, consumer lifestyles can have important implications for market segmentation, communication, and new product ideas.

Market Segmentation.   Lifestyles can be used to identify consumer segments for various offerings. For example, microwavable dinners, fast food, day care centers, and housecleaning services will obviously appeal more to consumers whose lifestyle demands convenience and saving time, such as dual-career couples and working women.[117] These consumers are also a main reason that the percentage of take-out order requests at restaurants has been increasing dramatically and why Internet supermarket shopping services such as Peapod are increasing in popularity.[118] PowerGel was developed as a "fast fuel" for athletes who don't have time to chew; the product is simply swallowed.[119] This trend is also occurring in many countries around the world. As one example, the popularity of McDonald's, Burger King, Pizza Hut, and Dunkin' Donuts has been greatly increasing in Brazil.[120]

A line of Romantic Illusions fragrances was developed to appeal to lovers of romance novels. Five companies including Eastman Kodak and Fuji developed the Advanced Photo System of cameras and film for those who are "inept and impatient."[121] Wal-Mart is starting to build smaller stores because its giant stores require a lot of time and energy that consumers with fast-paced lifestyles don't have.[122]

Lifestyle segmentation also has important cross-cultural implications. For example, one study of 12 European countries used demographics, activities, behavior toward the media, political inclinations, and mood to identify six Eurotype lifestyle segments: Traditionalists (18 percent of the population), Homebodies (14 percent), Rationalists (23 percent), Pleasurists (17 percent), Strivers (15 percent), and Trendsetters (13 percent).[123] Lodging prospects for business travelers in Moscow used to be pretty dismal (a narrow bed in a dingy hotel with little service).[124] However, Western hotel chains now offer services that are more pleasing to and fulfill the needs of a typical traveler's lifestyle, such as dry cleaning, room service, and bistros. In Japan a strong market for recreational vehicles has developed among outdoorsy types—even though many never leave the city.[125] In Saudi Arabia alcohol is forbidden, but nonalcoholic beers have become very popular among young consumers with an active, hip lifestyle.[126]

Finally, marketers often monitor lifestyle changes to identify new product and service opportunities. For example, many companies now allow executives to dress more informally at work and have a casual day on Friday. In response, many clothiers and retailers are putting more emphasis on casual items. T.G.I. Friday's restaurant, which has a strong relaxed-lifestyle image, is now extending its name to menswear.[127] Also, the trend toward cocooning (a lifestyle of staying at home) has led to an increase in the market for home-related products and services. To illustrate, home entertainment centers are very popular with home-oriented consumers, as well as with videophiles who crave state-of-the-art technology.[128] ■

Communications   Ad messages and promotions are often designed to appeal to certain lifestyles, and ads often show products being used in the context of desired lifestyles.[129] The purpose of Nike's "Just Do It" campaign, for example, is to appeal to those with an active lifestyle. Likewise, because of the popularity of golf, a number of companies including Nike feature the sport in their ads.[130] Busch beer targets hunters with its "Official Busch Hunting Gear" catalog and store displays of giant inflatable Lab retrievers.[131]

Lifestyles also have implications for the specific media consumers use. For example, because many fathers have changed their lifestyle to become more involved in child rearing, parenting magazines, which were traditionally a women's forum, are starting to focus more on male readers and male-oriented advertising.[132] *Martha Stewart Living*, a magazine for women interested in home and style, now has a competitor in *B. Smith Style*, reflecting the increased size of this segment.[133] Philip Morris even created a lifestyle magazine, *Unlimited*, around the theme of "Action, Adventure, and Good Times" as a way to appeal to young adults in a time when tobacco marketing is under heavy fire.[134] The ABC network attempted to appeal to couch potatoes with lines like "The couch is your friend" and "Life is short. Watch TV."[135] Increased TV offerings have also created many couch potatoes in China.[136]

Clearly, the Internet with its huge variety of Web sites is a very targeted way to communicate with a wide variety of lifestyle segments, particularly among those who surf most often (teenagers and young adults). Teenagers are especially fickle surfers and a site must generate considerable interest before it will be visited or viewed for any length of time.[137] Music and clothing-related sites tend to be most successful with teens.

Finally, media usage patterns may be related to lifestyles.[138] For example, frequent TV watchers tend to be unemployed or have low-prestige occupations and to have little interest in cultural matters. Magazine and newspaper reading, on the other hand, is positively related to education and occupational prestige, as well as to community and political involvement. Interestingly, consumers who love to surf the Internet also tend to be heavy TV watchers.[139]

New Product Ideas   Often marketers can develop new product and service ideas by uncovering unfulfilled needs of certain lifestyle segments. For example, marketers discovered that many workers who bring their lunch to work were tired of having sandwiches. In response, companies such as Oscar Mayer, StarKist, and Libby's have developed "lunch kits" that are easy to carry and offer consumers more variety. To appeal to Web surfers and heavy computer users, many games such as Monopoly and Jeopardy are now offered in electronic versions. Trendy coffee houses and brew pubs (also growing in popularity in Japan) provide consumers with a place where they can separate themselves from work and engage in conversations.[140] The popularity of nights out on the town, drinking with colleagues, has created a huge market for hangover remedies in Japan.[141] In addition, an increasing number of Japanese consumers like to eat and drink without lifting a finger, and this trend has created a market for products like self-buttering bread, ready-mixed cocktails, and spoonless gelatin.[142]

PSYCHOGRAPHICS: COMBINING VALUES, PERSONALITY, AND LIFESTYLES

We began this chapter by noting that modern psychographic research tends to combine values, personality, and lifestyle variables. To illustrate this key point, this last section provides a brief description of several psychographic applications in marketing.

Values and Lifestyle Survey

Values and Life Style Survey (VALS)   A psychographic tool that measures demographic, value, attitude, and lifestyle variables.

One of the most widely known psychographic tools is the **Values and Lifestyle Survey (VALS)**, which is conducted by an organization called SRI. The original VALS study surveyed a broad section of U.S. consumers in the 1970s on several demographic, value, attitude, and lifestyle variables.[143] Although VALS was widely used to identify potential target markets and to understand better how they should communicate with consumers, researchers in the late 1980s were critical of the survey because it had become outdated and did not predict behavior well. Changes due to the aging of the baby boom generation, the greater diversity of ethnic groups, greater media choices (especially TV and interactive media), and changes in values and lifestyles made VALS an invalid tool for describing consumers in the 1990s.

In response to these criticisms, SRI developed VALS2. The newer survey includes only items that relate to consumer behavior and is therefore much more closely related to consumption than VALS was. The survey consists of four demographic and 42 attitudinal items. Examples of the latter include "My idea of fun at a national park would be to stay at an expensive lodge and dress up for dinner," "It is the luxuries in life which make life worth living," and "I often crave excitement."[144]

VALS2 identifies segments of U.S. consumers based on their consumption of 170 product categories. The segments are based on two factors: (1) consumers' resources, including income, education, self-confidence, health, eagerness to buy, intelligence, and energy level, and (2) their self-orientations, or what motivates them, including their activities and values. Three self-orientations are identified. Principle-oriented consumers are guided by intellectual aspects rather than by feelings or other people's opinions. Status-oriented individuals base their views on the actions and opinions of others and strive to win their approval. Action-oriented consumers desire social or physical action, variety, activity, and risk.

Based on the resource and self-oriented variables, we can identify the eight segments of consumers shown in Exhibit 17.11.[145] At the bottom end of the resource hierarchy are Strugglers (16 percent of the U.S. population), who have the lowest incomes of the VALS2 segments. Because their focus is on surviving, they are not described by any self-orientation. Believers (17 percent) are principle-oriented consumers with somewhat modest resources. They represent the largest of the VALS2 segments. Believers are poorly educated and have deeply held beliefs about moral codes of conduct and ethics. More than one-third of the consumers in this group are retired. The other principle-oriented group is the Fulfilleds (12 percent), who are mature, responsible, well educated, well informed, and older (more than half are over 50). They are also happy with their families, have high incomes, and are value oriented in their consumption practices.

Status-oriented segments include Strivers (14 percent), who have blue-collar backgrounds and strive to emulate people they find more successful than themselves. Achievers (10 percent) have higher resources, are focused on their work and families, and tend to be successful at their jobs. They are politically conservative, respect authority, and are not change oriented.

Those in the action-oriented group called Makers (12 percent) are relatively young and value self-sufficiency. They are not interested in material possessions or world events; instead, they are focused on family, work, and physical recreation. Experiencers (11 percent) are a young, energetic group who spend a great deal of time on physical exercise and social activities. They spend avidly in the clothing, fast food, and music categories. Fewer than 20 percent have completed college, but many are working toward their college degree. They love new products and are more risk oriented than consumers in other segments.

Finally, Actualizers (8 percent) represent the segment with the greatest resource base. They have a great deal of self-confidence, high incomes, and education and can therefore indulge themselves in any or all of the self-orientations. They use possessions to indicate their own personal style, taste, and character, and they have a wide range of interests.

 Note that although the VALS and VALS2 profiles were developed to describe U.S. consumers, profiles of European consumers are currently in the works. The

EXHIBIT 17.11
VALS2 American Segments

Based on the consumption of 170 products, VALS2 classifies consumers into eight major segments based on two dimensions: resources (education, income, intelligence, etc.) and self-orientation (principle, status, or action orientation). The general characteristics of each group are described in this exhibit. Into which group would you fall?

Source: VALS2, SRI International, Menlo Park, Calif.; cited in Judith Waldrop, "Markets with Attitude," *American Demographics,* July 1994, pp. 22–33. *American Demographics* © 1994. Reprinted with permission.

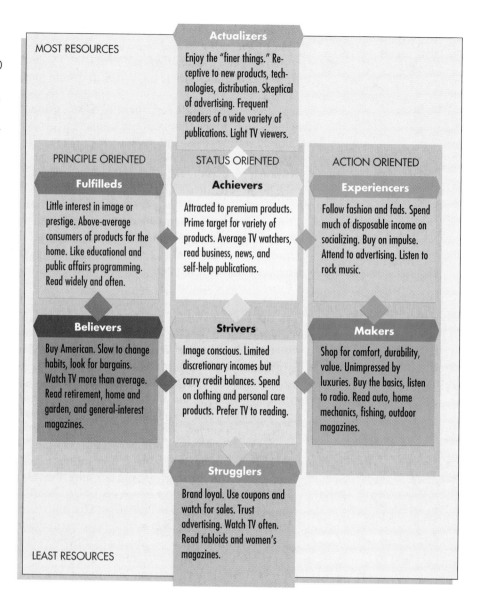

MOST RESOURCES

Actualizers

Enjoy the "finer things." Receptive to new products, technologies, distribution. Skeptical of advertising. Frequent readers of a wide variety of publications. Light TV viewers.

PRINCIPLE ORIENTED | STATUS ORIENTED | ACTION ORIENTED

Fulfilleds

Little interest in image or prestige. Above-average consumers of products for the home. Like educational and public affairs programming. Read widely and often.

Achievers

Attracted to premium products. Prime target for variety of products. Average TV watchers, read business, news, and self-help publications.

Experiencers

Follow fashion and fads. Spend much of disposable income on socializing. Buy on impulse. Attend to advertising. Listen to rock music.

Believers

Buy American. Slow to change habits, look for bargains. Watch TV more than average. Read retirement, home and garden, and general-interest magazines.

Strivers

Image conscious. Limited discretionary incomes but carry credit balances. Spend on clothing and personal care products. Prefer TV to reading.

Makers

Shop for comfort, durability, value. Unimpressed by luxuries. Buy the basics, listen to radio. Read auto, home mechanics, fishing, outdoor magazines.

Strugglers

Brand loyal. Use coupons and watch for sales. Trust advertising. Watch TV often. Read tabloids and women's magazines.

LEAST RESOURCES

 technique has also been applied in Japan, but with some modification. For example, instead of two orientations, the Japanese VALS has three: self-expression, achievement, and tradition. These orientations serve as the basis for identifying ten VALS segments.[146]

Reseachers have argued that other techniques such as the List of Values (described earlier in this chapter) may describe consumer segments more adequately. However, this issue is apparently still unresolved. One study found that the LOV was a better predictor of consumer behavior than VALS was, and another did not.[147] Also note that VALS2 works best with products and services that are related to the ego, such as clothes and cars, and for which felt involvement is likely to be high.

MARKETING IMPLICATIONS VALS2 can be a useful tool in market segmentation, new product ideas, and especially ad development. To illustrate, marketers can first identify heavy, medium, and light users of a product or service and then examine VALS2 profiles across these segments. For example, Exhibit 17.12 presents possible usage incidences for two major brands in the ibuprofen analgesic category. Nuprin is more likely to be used by Achievers, whereas Advil is favored most by Experiencers and then by Achievers.[148] Note also that Nuprin fares poorly with Actualizers, who tend to be heavy users of pain relievers. Thus, a strategy for Nuprin would be to continue to appeal to Achievers and try to improve its standing with Actualizers.

Pittsburgh's Iron City beer used VALS2 to improve its image and counteract lagging sales. From research Iron City discovered that it had two main markets: Makers and Believers, who were the dyed-in-the-wool consumers for many years. Strivers and Experiencers, a younger market of consumers, were rejecting the brand. To appeal to these important, yet diverse, segments, Iron City developed an advertising campaign that juxtaposed images of old Pittsburgh with live images of a new vibrant city. The ads showed Strivers and Experiencers working hard at having fun and were placed on television programs and radio stations that Strivers and Experiencers watched and listened to. The result of these efforts was an increase in sales of 26 percent. ▪

Other Applied Psychographic Research

Although VALS2 is probably the best known and most widely used psychographic tool, there are a variety of other ongoing surveys. One well-known lifestyle study, the Yankelovich Monitor, assesses key changes in values and lifestyle trends in the United States.[149] The Monitor measures and traces consumers' behavior and feelings toward a wide variety of issues, such as the family, money, institutions, change, stress, and the future. These items are then used to follow such major trends as female careers, beauty in the home, introspection, anti-bigness, liberal attitudes to sex, or self-improvement. Note that more than 80 corporations worldwide subscribe to the Monitor to keep up with changing consumer lifestyle trends.

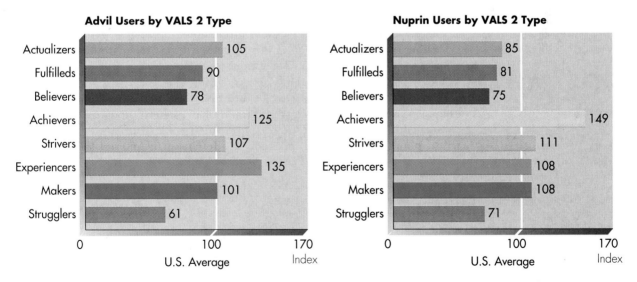

EXHIBIT 17.12
VALS2 Example

This exhibit shows how brand choice varies by VALS2 segment for the ibuprofen analgesic category. Nuprin is preferred by Achievers, and Advil is preferred by Experiencers and Achievers. A clear strategy for Nuprin, then, would be to appeal to Achievers.

Source: Rebecca Piirto, Beyond Mind Games (Ithaca, N.Y.: American Demographic Books, 1991), pp. 88–89. American Demographics, Inc. © 1991. Reprinted by permission.

Many advertising agencies engage in ongoing psychographic research as well. Common examples include Grey's New Grownups Study, which identifies four types of households based on their ideas about life and use of time; J. Walter Thompson's Life Stages (singles, married, married without children, and so on); Ogilvy & Mather's NEW WAVE, which identifies consumer trends; and DDB Needham's Life Style Study.[150] The psychographics of various demographic groups are also studied. As one example, the Hispanic Monitor identifies four main segments: Hopeful Loyalists, Recent Seekers (both foreign born), Young Strivers, and Established Adapters.

Some researchers use psychographics to identify global segments of consumers. GlobalScan, which is conducted by the ad agency Backer Spielvogel Bates Worldwide, surveys consumers in North America, Europe, Australia, Asia (Hong Kong and Japan), New Zealand, and Venezuela. GlobalScan measures a variety of attitudes, values, and behavior patterns including media use, product use, and buying patterns. Its research has thus far identified five consumer segments: Strivers (26 percent), Achievers (22 percent), Pressured (13 percent), Traditionals (16 percent), and Adapters (18 percent), with 5 percent unclassified.[151] Note, however, different countries may have different values.

The ad agency DMB&B has used personality traits, values, and products to divide the Russian market into key segments. The *kuptsi* are conservative, narrow-minded people who have roots in prerevolutionary Russia. They do not like foreign products and seek reliability and value in the products they buy. People known as Russian souls are passive and afraid of choice, need a lot of assurance from others that they are buying the right product, and are best persuaded by seeing others successfully buy and use a brand. The students have a broader, more cosmopolitan view of the world and are very open to Western products and ideas. However, although they covet Western products, they will often make do with a cheaper version.[152]

Finally, Young & Rubicam has a segmentation scheme called Cross-Cultural Consumer Characterizations or the 4Cs. Similar to VALS in design, the 4Cs focuses on goals, motivations, and values, as well as lifestyle and purchase patterns. It has identified seven key segments: Resigned Poor, Struggling Poor, Mainstreamers, Aspirers, Succeeders, Transitionals, and Reformers.[153]

Other researchers have questioned whether these psychographic techniques fully capture all the variation in consumers' lifestyles. Rather than relying on the traits measured in the research discussed above, one researcher identifies some consumption patterns that do not fit into the VALS framework. These include canonical aesthetics (which relates to traditional Western thought and tastes for art and culture such as Shakespeare), nurturing mother (consumption is centered on the home and caring for children), and Jeffersonian America (related to the styles and traditions of a pastoral United States).[154]

SUMMARY

Values are enduring beliefs about things that are important. They are learned through the processes of socialization and acculturation. Our values exist in an organized value system, where some are viewed as more important than others. Terminal values reflect desired end states that guide behavior in many situations. Domain-specific values are relevant within a given sphere of activity. Western cultures tend to place a relatively high value on material goods, youth, the home, the family, work and play, health, hedonism, and technology. Because groups of consumers may have different values, marketers use tools like value-based segmentation to identify consumer groups with different values. Three methods for identifying value-based segments are inferring values based on the cultural milieu of the group, the means-end chain analysis, and questionnaires like the Rokeach Value Survey and the List of Values.

Personality consists of the patterns of behaviors, tendencies, and personal dispositions that make people different from one another. Approaches to the study of personality include (1) the psychoanalytic approach, which sees personality as the result of unconscious struggles within individuals to complete key stages of development; (2) trait theories, which attempt to identify a set of personality characteristics that describe and differentiate individuals, such as introversion, extroversion, and stability; (3) phenomenological approaches, which propose that personality is shaped by an individual's interpretation of life events; (4) social-psychological theories, which focus on the way individuals act in social situations, such as compliant, detached, or aggressive; and (5) behavioral approaches, which view an individual's personality in terms of behavioral responses to past rewards and punishments.

Marketers also measure lifestyles, which are patterns of behavior or activities, interests, and opinions. Lifestyles can provide additional insight into consumers' consumption patterns.

Finally, some marketing researchers use psychographic techniques that involve all these factors—values, personality, and lifestyles—to predict consumer behavior. One of the best-known psychographic tools is the Values and Lifestyle Survey (VALS). The newer VALS2 identifies eight segments of consumers who are similar in their resources and value orientations.

EXERCISES

1. Conduct a content analysis of the advertisements that appear over four issues of a selected magazine. For each ad, record the type of product or service and whether and how each of the following values is reflected in the message: (a) materialism, (b) youthfulness, (c) the home, (d) work and play, (e) the family, (f) health, (g) hedonism, and (h) technology. Summarize this information and answer the following questions:

   a. Which values are most often reflected in the advertisements?

   b. Do certain types of values appear more often for certain types of products?

   c. Which themes appear in relationship to each value?

2. Develop a questionnaire to measure some of the key activities, interests, and opinions of college students. Also develop a series of items to measure the consumption of five product or service categories that may be related to college lifestyles. Administer this questionnaire to 20 fellow students (across different majors if possible). Summarize the results and answer the following questions:

   a. What are the key lifestyle segments of the college students you surveyed?

   b. For each segment, are there recognizable consumption patterns in terms of products or services?

   c. What general types of marketing strategies would you use to appeal to each group?

THE CONSUMER'S CULTURE

Age, Gender, and
Household Influences
(Ch. 15)

Social Class Influences
(Ch. 14)

Social Influences
(Ch. 16)

Regional, Ethnic and
Religious Influences
(Ch. 13)

THE PSYCHOLOGICAL CORE

- Motivation, Ability and
  Opportunity (Ch. 3)
- Exposure, Attention and
  Perception (Ch. 4)
- Knowing and
  Understanding (Ch. 5)
- Attitude Formation
  (Chs. 6 & 7)
- Memory and
  Retrieval (Ch. 8)

Psychographics:
Values, Personality
and Lifestyles
(Ch. 17)

THE PROCESS OF MAKING DECISIONS

- Problem Recognition and Information Search (Ch. 9)
- Judgment and Decision Making (Chs. 10-11)
- Post-Decision Processes (Ch. 12)

CONSUMER BEHAVIOR OUTCOMES

- Symbolic Consumer Behavior (Ch. 18)
- Adoption of, Resistance to, and Diffusion of
  Innovations (Ch. 19)

PART FIVE

Consumer Behavior Outcomes

CHAPTER 18 Symbolic Consumer Behavior
CHAPTER 19 Adoption of, Resistance to, and Diffusion of Innovations

Part Five examines the outcomes of the numerous influences and decision processes discussed in the previous sections. Chapter 18 discusses the interesting topic of symbolic consumer behavior. Products and services are often more than physical entities to consumers; they can reflect deep-felt and significant meanings. The chapter also highlights some interesting and important consumption rituals.

Chapter 19 builds on the topics of internal decision making and group processes by examining how consumers adopt new offerings and how their adoption decisions affect the spread or diffusion of an offering through a market. Thus this chapter focuses on how social factors influence decision making in a market over time.

CHAPTER 18

SYMBOLIC CONSUMER BEHAVIOR

INTRODUCTION

To many consumers the Harley-Davidson motorcycle and its accessory products, along with its symbol, the American eagle, *symbolize personal freedom, patriotism, and machismo*. Consider that the motorcycle itself is big, loud, heavy, and hence very macho. Some devotees paint eagles on their bikes; others tattoo the eagle on their bodies. Bikers sometimes adopt a Western motif, another symbol of freedom, U.S. heritage, and machismo. Like western folk heroes, they dress in black; wear leather chaps, boots, vests, and saddlebags; and "operate on both sides of the law." The wildest and most intimidating Harley riders are even called "outlaws."

The Harley motorcycle allows some consumers to stand out as unique and special and to break free of the traditional roles they occupy most of the time. As such, it helps them *symbolize their uniqueness*. Some bikers believe that riding a Harley is like a religious experience. Riding free and wild allows the rider to be close to nature; the throbbing of the machine is like a mantra; and riding makes bikers constantly aware of the risks they take and hence their vulnerabilities. Some bikers even use Harley paraphernalia as part of religious ceremonies like weddings and funerals.

Many riders view the Harley-Davidson motorcycle as a very special possession because it *symbolizes their connection* to others who are like themselves. Indeed, a number of specific Harley groups have formed across the country: Rich Urban Bikers (RUBS), the Fifth Chapter (a club that also is a support group for recovering alcoholics and addicts), Dykes on Bikes (a lesbian biker club), and Trinity Road Riders (a born-again Christian club). Each group has its own rituals that symbolize group membership. Membership is not automatic, and new group members, who often feel uncomfortable as novices, rely on images of the biker cultivated in magazines like *Biker*, *Easyriders*, *American Iron*, *Supercycle*, *Independent Biker*, and *HOG Tales*. Marketing and merchandise from Harley-Davidson also provide ideas about what it means to be a Harley rider (see Exhibit 18.1). Novices use such biker paraphernalia to demonstrate to others that they are true bikers. Once accepted into a biker group, a rider becomes a "brother," forever connected to the group's family. The Bros. Club is, in fact, a cooperative that gives roadside assistance to bikers.

Some owners view their Harley as so special, it is *sacred*. They build shrines like special sheds or garages for their bike and adorn the shrines with Harley posters, calendars, memorabilia, and paraphernalia. Taboos dictate that one biker is not to touch another's Harley—rather each bike should be revered. Bikers also

EXHIBIT 18.1
Marketers as Creators of Product Meaning

Marketers are one of the several sources that create meaning surrounding a product. This ad by Harley-Davidson clothes reinforces ideas about what it means to be a Harley-Davidson biker.

Source: Courtesy of Harley-Davidson, Inc.

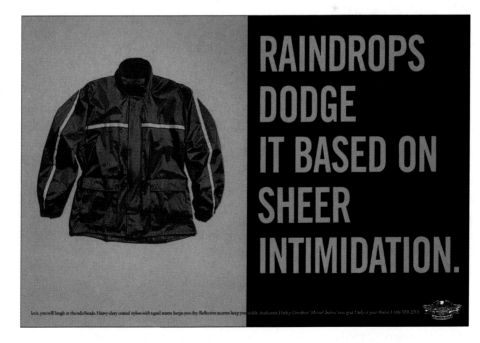

RAINDROPS DODGE IT BASED ON SHEER INTIMIDATION.

show respect for their bikes by performing cleaning rituals that enhance and retain their sacred status. Some outlaw bikers are also regarded with sacred status. New bikers feel humbled by their presence, and such outlaw bikers can evoke feelings of admiration and fear even among the most experienced biker enthusiasts.[1]

I n this chapter we describe several aspects of the broad topic of symbolic consumer behavior. We first consider how symbolic meaning is conferred on products or services (called "offerings" here for simplicity), what functions symbols serve, and how they affect our self-concept. We then explain why some offerings vary in their meaningfulness. Some symbols are special—even sacred—and require consumption practices to keep them so. Finally, we discuss how meaning is transferred from one individual to another through the process of gift giving.

SOURCES AND FUNCTIONS OF SYMBOLIC MEANING

To understand why some consumers are so crazy about Harley-Davidson motorcycles, consider where the meaning associated with products and consumption practices like those in the biker subculture comes from and what functions these products and practices fulfill. Exhibit 18.2 provides a framework that summarizes these sources and functions. It shows that the meaning associated with offerings and consumption practices can stem either from our culture or from ourselves as individuals.

Meaning Derived from Culture

cultural categories The natural grouping of objects that reflect our culture.

As Exhibit 18.3 shows, some of the meaning associated with products derives from our culture.[2] Anthropologists suggest that natural categories of objects reflect our culture. Examples of these **cultural categories** include categories for time, such as work time and leisure time; for space, such as home, office, and safe or unsafe places; and for occasions, such as festive versus somber events. We also

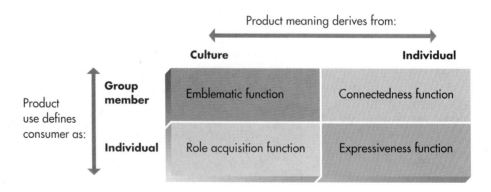

EXHIBIT 18.2
The Sources and Functions of Consumption Symbols

Consumers use products with various meanings to achieve a set of functions. Combined, these functions help define the consumer's self-concept.

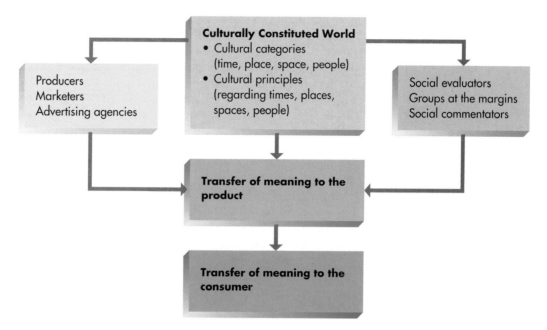

have cultural categories that reflect our perceptions of various groups of people based on their characteristics—for example, categories of gender, age, social class, and ethnicity.

Cultural categories are interesting because implicit in them are **cultural principles**—ideas or values that specify how aspects of our culture are organized and how they should be perceived or evaluated. For example, the cultural principles associated with the category known as work time dictate that it is more structured, organized, precise, and intense than leisure time. Cultural principles also give meaning to the products associated with categories. Thus clothing associated with work time is also more structured, organized, precise, and intense than clothing associated with leisure time. Our categories for occasions include festive and somber. The former are vibrant, active, and energetic, whereas the latter are dark, quiet, and inactive. Thus clothing associated with celebrations is generally bright, colorful, and comfortable. Clothing associated with somber activities is often dark, muted, and understated.

Of particular interest in this chapter are cultural categories of people, which identify consumers by characteristics such as social status, gender, age, and ethnicity. Various cultural principles are associated with these categories as well. For example, the category women has historically been associated with concepts like delicate, whimsical, expressive, and changeable. In contrast, the category men has historically been associated with concepts like disciplined, stable, and serious. Products are produced and used to be consistent with these principles. Thus

cultural principles Ideas or values that specify how aspects of our culture are organized and/or how they should be perceived or evaluated.

women's clothing is traditionally more delicate, whimsical, expressive, and change-able than clothing for men. Exhibit 18.3 shows that by associating and matching product characteristics with cultural principles and categories, we transfer to the product meaning that exists at the level of the culture. For example, we might classify certain clothing as feminine or as suitable for work because of its association with corresponding cultural principles and categories.

Exhibit 18.3 also shows that many agents can play a role in this association and matching process. First, producers and manufacturers introduce new products whose characteristics reflect cultural principles. For example, the Harley-Davidson motorcycle has characteristics that make it "macho." Producers and marketers may also give products meaning by associating them with certain cultural categories. Harley-Davidson develops clothing, accessories, and information that communicate what it means to be a biker.[3]

Meaning also comes from nonmarketing sources. Specific people in society may serve as opinion leaders (see Chapter 16) who shape, refine, or reshape cultural principles and the products and attributes with which they are associated. For example, Michael Jordan may define for boys the type of athletic shoe associated with status. In some cases groups on the margins of society can be agents of change. Punkers, who were associated with the principles of nonconformity and antiestablishment ideas, introduced new styles of clothing that reflected these principles.

Journalists who review goods as they come on the market also shape cultural principles and the products associated with them. For example, restaurant reviewers may determine whether a restaurant is associated with principles like status, and style editors may determine whether clothes are associated with young and hip categories or with others. Magazines like *Biker* and *Easyriders* communicate meaning associated with the biker category, for example, what bikers are like, who they hang around with, and what they like to do. Cultural heroes like Ricky Martin can also create meaning in products by their use of them. As Exhibit 18.3 shows, through all these sources, the meaning inherent in the product gets transferred to the consumer.

Meaning Derived from the Consumer

As Exhibit 18.2 indicates, culture is not the only thing that gives symbolic meaning to offerings; consumers can also develop their own individual meanings associated with products. Regardless of whether meaning stems from the culture or the consumer, however, consumption symbols can be used (1) to say something about the consumer as a member of a group or (2) to say something about the consumer as a unique individual. Combining these two dimensions produces the four functions for symbols noted in the boxes in Exhibit 18.2 and described in the following sections.

The Emblematic Function

emblematic function The use of products to symbolize membership in social groups.

Meaning derived from culture allows us to use products to symbolize our membership in various social groups. In this way products serve an **emblematic function**. Thus dresses are associated with women; surfboards are associated with young people from California, Australia, and Hawaii; and clerical collars are associated with priests. The music we listen to may symbolize our age, and the car we drive may symbolize our social status. Consciously or unconsciously, we constantly use products to symbolize the groups to which we belong. Similarly, people who observe us using these products may consciously or unconsciously categorize and make inferences about us and the groups we belong to. Thus just by looking at someone and his or her possessions, we might be able to tell whether that person is a member of the Mexican American, upper-middle class, or Catholic categories.[4] As we show next, emblematic products can symbolize a great deal about the social groups to which we belong.

Geographic Emblems Products can symbolize geographic identification. For example, the preppie clothing style symbolizes identification with New England. Brightly colored, loose-fitting clothing symbolizes identification with sunnier regions of the country, such as California, Arizona, Florida, and Hawaii. Products may also symbolize geographic identification with a region even if used by people who live elsewhere.

 Ethnic Emblems Products and consumption activities can also symbolize identification with a given culture or subculture. In the United States, African garb is sometimes worn to symbolize identification with this culture. In India males in the Sikh community wear five Ks as symbols of their ethnic and religious affiliation: *kesh* (hair), *kada* (bangle), *kangha* (comb), *kacha* (underpants), and *kirpan* (dagger). Consumers sometimes use ethnic emblems of other cultures or subcultures to differentiate themselves. In Japan teen rebels have adopted products symbolic of the Latino barrio: low riders; Latino music; and art, fashions, and tattoos with barrio images.[5] Clothing identified with African American urban culture has also become popular among Caucasian consumers in the United States.[6]

Food is commonly used to express ethnic identity. For example, grilled chicken, chicken mole, and steamed yellowfish reflect U.S., Mexican, and Chinese identities, respectively.[7] Cornmeal serves as an ethnic emblem for Haitians immigrating to the United States.[8] We can also express our ethnic identification by how and when we eat. Cultures differ in whether all elements of the meal are served at once or one item at a time.[9] Dinner is typically eaten at about 6:00 P.M. in the United States, but in Spain and Italy dinnertime is much later.

Social Class Emblems Products can also symbolize social class, such as the Schoeffel cultured pearls advertised in Exhibit 18.4. In Mexico the car symbolizes success and luxury because few people can afford to own one.[10] In China ownership of a color TV says much about one's status and self-worth.[11] Among the newly wealthy in Silicon Valley, symbols of social class include helicopters, backyard golf courses, private airplanes, and homes that resemble palaces.[12] Consider,

EXHIBIT 18.4
Social Class Emblems

Because only relatively wealthy people can afford cultured pearls, they symbolize the status and luxury that members of the upper class enjoy.

Source: Courtesy of Schoeffel Pearl Culture.

also, emblems of membership in the upper-upper class. The cultural principles of upper-upper-class membership include characteristics of refinement, understated restraint, and discipline. So too do the products and consumption activities of this class. One author notes that casual attire for the upper-class white Anglo-Saxon female is likely to consist of wool or cotton cuffed pants, embroidered wool or cashmere sweaters, flats, and a small leather handbag. Jewelry might include a small gold bracelet or necklace. Hair is pulled back off the face and worn up in a twist or chignon. Colors are subdued, and the fibers are generally natural (cotton, wool, silk). Clothing is loose fitting and unrevealing.[13]

The social classes also use different symbols in consumption rituals. For example, higher and lower social classes in the United States differ greatly in the types of clothing they wear at Thanksgiving, the importance placed on etiquette, the types of serving dishes used, and even the way an item like butter is served. Molded pieces of butter (perhaps embossed with the family crest) and individual butter knives and butter plates define the upper-upper-class dinner table. Middle-class families may serve butter on a crystal or china butter plate that is passed from person to person. At the lower end of the social spectrum, a tub of butter in its original container is passed around the table, and everyone uses the same knife.[14]

Interestingly, an increasing number of schools (both public and private) in the United States now require students to wear uniforms. Officials and some parents believe that uniforms help curb gang activity, remove social class emblems, and make students feel less anxious about keeping up with their peers.[15]

Gender Emblems Food, clothing, jewelry, and alcoholic beverages are only some of the product categories associated with membership in the male and female gender categories.[16] One study of consumers in France revealed that some foods are viewed as "man" foods, whereas others are viewed as "woman" foods. For example, celery is more clearly associated with women, and meat is more clearly associated with men.

In part, the designation of food to specific gender groups stems from culturally devised notions of fatness and thinness and the appropriateness of these attributes for men and women. The same research also revealed that the appropriateness of various foods for men and women is reflected in the way the food is eaten. Fish, for example, must be eaten slowly and delicately, with restraint, and chewed gently to avoid eating bones. According to this researcher, nibbling and picking is much more consistent with characteristics of women than of men. In contrast, steak, which may be cut roughly, is chewed intensively, and can be rather messy and bloody, is more consistent with culturally derived characteristics of men.[17] Other researchers have found gender differences in food preferences, with boys preferring chunky peanut butter, for instance, and girls preferring the smooth variety. These preferences may be related to culturally derived associations with boys (rough) and girls (not rough).[18]

Reference Group Emblems The Harley-Davidson example at the beginning of the chapter shows us that products can also serve as emblems of membership in a reference group. For example, one reason consumers become outlaw bikers is that they like being members of a reference group that adopts a counterculture ideology.

Private school uniforms; varsity jackets; and the special hats, colors, or jewelry that designate gangs may also symbolize reference group membership. One high school banned rosary beads because they were being worn as emblems of gang membership.[19]

In addition to products, rituals are sometimes important indicators and affirmations of group membership. For example, rituals like attending the Independence Day parade may reinforce our membership in the U.S. citizens group. Other rituals serve as public confirmation that we have become members of a group. Among the upper-upper class, the debutante ball is a ritual that formally introduces 16-year-old girls into the group of women eligible for dating.[20] In Jewish families the ceremony of male circumcision—called a Brith Milah—serves as a ritual inducting a newborn male child into the Jewish faith.

MARKETING IMPLICATIONS Marketers play three roles in establishing the emblematic function of products.

Symbol Development. The first role is symbol development, which identifies cultural principles associated with a category and confers on the product attributes believed to represent those characteristics. For example, Patek Philippe watches have characteristics associated with the upper class: timeless style, understated elegance, precision craftsmanship utilizing gold and precious stones, and exorbitant price tags that range from $7,000 to $25,000.[21] Sometimes marketers need to make sure that product attributes are appropriately linked with cultural principles. Miller, for example, found it necessary to position the *lite* in Lite beer as meaning less filling, not diet. The former was seen as appropriate for men, whereas the latter connotation made the beer appear more feminine. This masculine image was reinforced by associating the beer with macho sports figures.

Symbol Communication. The second role is symbol communication. Advertising can charge a product with meaning through the setting for the ad, whether fantasy or naturalistic, interior or exterior, or rural or urban, and through other details such as the time of day and types of people in the ad—their gender, age, ethnicity, occupation, clothing, body postures, and so on.[22] Each of these ad elements reinforces the meaning associated with the product.

Symbol Reinforcement. The third role of marketing in establishing emblematic functions is to design other elements of the marketing mix to reinforce the symbolic image.[23] Various pricing, distribution, and product strategies can be used to maintain a product's status image. The product may be given a premium price, distributed in outlets that have a status image, and made with certain features that are appropriate only for the targeted buyer. A clash among the elements of the marketing mix can hurt the symbolic image of a product.

Symbol Removal. Some marketers have made a business of helping consumers erase symbols associated with groups with whom they no longer identify. There is considerable growth, for example, in the tattoo removal market. Consumers often want tattoos removed because they are emblematic of an earlier time of life or an abandoned reference group and impede the development of new identifications.[24] ▪

The Role Acquisition Function

In addition to serving as emblems of group membership, products and services can also help us feel more comfortable in new roles. This function is called the **role acquisition function** (see Exhibit 18.2).

role acquisition function
The use of products as symbols to help us feel more comfortable in a new role.

Role Acquisition Phases We fill many roles in our lives, and these roles constantly change. You may currently occupy the role of student, son or daughter, brother or sister, and worker. At some point in your life (perhaps even now), you may occupy the role of husband or wife, uncle or aunt, parent, divorcee, grandparent, retiree, widow or widower, and so on.

Moving from one role to another typically involves three phases.[25] The first phase is separation from the old role. Separation often means disposing of products associated with the role we are leaving. Children may give up security blankets in their transition from baby to child. Consumers in the process of a divorce may symbolize the end of a marital relationship by giving away, throwing away, or destroying products that remind them of their former spouses.[26]

The second phase is the transition from one role to another. Often transition is marked by experimentation with new identities. Consumers may be willing to accept new possessions or styles they otherwise would have rejected. One study examined the use of techniques like plastic surgery, dieting, and new hairstyles as means to construct a new identity. Branding, body piercing, and tattooing may also be used in experimenting with new identities.

The final phase in acquiring a new role is incorporation, or the taking on of the new role and the identity associated with it.

Use of Symbols and Rituals in Role Transitions   Exhibit 18.5 illustrates how and why we use symbols and rituals when we acquire a new role. We often feel uncomfortable with a new role because we are inexperienced in occupying the role and have little knowledge about how to fulfill it. A common reaction is to use products stereotypically associated with that role. For example, researchers found that MBAs who were insecure about their job prospects were more likely than other MBAs to use symbols generally associated with the role of businessperson.[27] We often use a group of products to symbolize adoption of a new role. Having the appropriate combination of products is important because without it we may not elicit the appropriate response from others. Imagine, for example, the reaction we would get if we wore white socks or sneakers with a business suit.

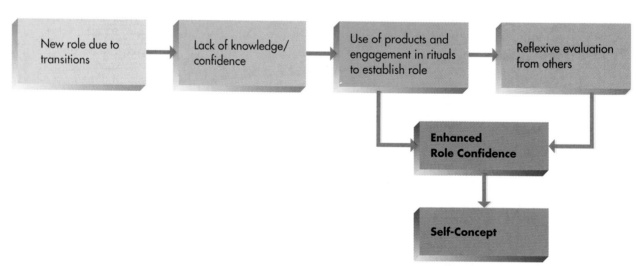

EXHIBIT 18.5
Model of Role Acquisition

When we are entering a new role (e.g., parenthood), we may lack some role confidence. As a result, we engage in activities (e.g., have baby showers) and buy groups of products (e.g., strollers) typically associated with that role. These activities and products, along with the way that others react to our behaviors, enhance our role confidence.

Source: Adapted from Michael Solomon, "The Role of Products as Social Stimuli: A Symbolic Interactionism Perspective," *Journal of Consumer Research,* December 1983, pp. 319–329. © 1983 University of Chicago. All rights reserved.

Rituals are also an important part of role transitions. Consider, for example, the transition from single to married status. A number of rituals mark this transition in the United States—wedding shower, stag party, rehearsal dinner, wedding, reception, and honeymoon. Each ritual uses relevant enabling products.[28] The wedding itself includes clothing for the attendants and flower girl, flowers, bridal veil, a bridal bouquet, pillow for the rings, organ music, wedding clothing for guests, and so on.

Rituals often involve others whose participation helps validate the role transition. As Exhibit 18.5 shows, by using symbols and engaging in rituals we hope to get feedback from participants who tell us whether we are fulfilling the role correctly. This feedback, called **reflexive evaluation**, helps us feel more confident in our role and thus validates our new status. We saw in the opening vignette that the novice Harley owner requires this evaluation from experienced owners before feeling confident in his or her "biker" role. The following discussion reviews types of role transitions and the importance of products as symbols of the transition process.

reflexive evaluation Feedback from others that tells us whether we are fulfilling the role correctly.

Marital Transitions Products are often an important component in the transition from single to married status. As part of this transition's separation phase, the couple must decide which of their possessions they wish to dispose of and which they will move to their new household. Thus presents from old boyfriends or girlfriends may be discarded, as well as products that symbolize one's former single status. As part of the incorporation phase, the couple acquires new products that are viewed as culturally appropriate for the role and that help them create a mutual history. The ad from Target's Club Wedd Gift Registry in Exhibit 18.6 shows some products that may symbolize the move from a single to a newly married state. Clearly, different cultures have different marital rituals. For example, the mother-in-law often gives the keys to the house to a Hindu bride following the wedding, symbolically handing over the charge of running the house.

A similar process operates in the transition from married to single status, as in the case of divorce. Here, too, dispositions are important in separating from the old role. Possessions are divested as each person takes back what was his or hers, and joint possessions are divided up. People may deliberately dispose of possessions that remind them of the other person. As one set of researchers notes, "Jettisoning symbols of the ex-spouse . . . may be psychologically necessary in the process of ending the relationship."[29] Some people destroy possessions, which perhaps serves several functions—symbolically representing the destruction of the marriage, punishing the ex-spouse, and getting rid of possessions that symbolize the marriage.

gotta have it!

Advertisement

dynamic design

1. Michael Graves Design™ two-slice toaster, $39.99 2. Mikasa Venetian Pearl Stemware—2-pc. set water goblet, wine or flute (not shown), $9.99 3. World View dinnerware by Furio® Home (Chalk, Onyx, Mineral, Jade), $1.99–$19.99 20-pc. World View flatware, $24.99 4. Wall clock, $19.99 5. Michael Graves Design™ teakettle, $34.99 6. Canon Elph LT camera, $96.99 7. Black & Decker Kitchentools coffeemaker, $99.99 8. KitchenAid stand mixer, $189.99 9. GE 900-megahertz headphone, $89.99

CLUB WEDD
GIFT REGISTRY
TARGET

EXHIBIT 18.6
Marital Role Transition Symbols

This ad identifies a set of products that are appropriate as gifts in the transition from single to married status.

Source: © 1999 Target Corporation. Club Wedd and Target are registered trademarks of Target Brands, Inc. Advertisement used with permission.

Ending a marriage can cause problems in fulfilling other symbolic functions. For example, the person may no longer have products that were conspicuous consumption items used to communicate social status. Thus someone who loses a house and a car (two important symbols of social prestige) may feel a loss of identity. Likewise, the acquisition of new products symbolic of the single status may also be observed in this role transition. Purchasing a sports car when returning to unmarried status is one example.

 Cultural Transitions   Consumers also engage in role changes when they move to a new culture. Often this transition process accompanies the abandonment or disposition of old customs and symbols and the adoption of new ones. One researcher reported that Mexican immigrants faced a number of different and in some cases difficult experiences in moving to the United States.[30] Among these were living in densely grouped apartments and condominiums, shopping in environments characterized by sometimes overwhelming choices, and dealing with unfamiliar currency. As evidence of acculturation, some of the young immigrants in the study were very brand conscious. Yet at the same time, immigrants held on to aspects of their culture including Mexican food and Spanish-language media.

Another study reported on the status symbols acquired by Indians moving to the United States. Interestingly, such symbols were not needed in India, where caste and family designate class membership.[31] One study found that Indians sometimes kept transitional items—things that reminded them of their home country and provided a sense of cultural identify. These included music and videos, photographs, heirloom furniture, saris, and jewelry. Whether one abandons or retains possessions that symbolize the old role may depend on the perceived permanence of the role. The Indians in this study, for example, still considered the possibility of returning to India someday.

Social Status Transitions   Individuals who have just come into money, the *nouveaux riches*, need possessions to demonstrate their newly acquired status. Very often their possessions are ostentatious. The notion that the *nouveaux riches* use possessions not only to demonstrate but also to validate their role is consistent with the model of symbols and role transitions in Exhibit 18.5. Reflexive evaluation from others that indicates one's successful role performance is very important. As one author notes, "Consumer satisfaction is derived from audience reactions to the wealth displayed by the purchaser in securing the product or service rather than to the positive attributes of the item in question."[32]

MARKETING IMPLICATIONS   Consumers' role transitions have many important implications for marketers.

Role Transitions and Target Consumers.   First, consumers in transition are an important target market for many marketers. Indeed, many of the 3,000-plus pages of ads in *Bride's* magazine explicitly target consumers in their transition to the stage of being married.[33]

Role Transitions as Means for Developing Inventory.   Second, because product disposition may represent an important aspect of role separation, marketers of secondhand products acquire inventory by marketing to people engaged in role transitions. For example, secondhand stores might target college students before graduation, knowing that in their role transitions many may wish to dispose of student-related paraphernalia such as furniture and clothing.

Role Transitions and Product Promotions.   Third, when consumers are anticipating role changes, marketers may find it useful to promote their products as instrumental in incorporating a new role. For example, marketers tout products from shower fixtures to contraceptives to home computers as acceptable wedding gifts. Furthermore, bridal registries are showing up in places as diverse as Ace Hardware, Tower Records, and the Metropolitan Museum of Art stores.[34] Products like wipe warmers, mobiles, and bouncing chairs are positioned as important to the new parent role.

Selling Product Constellations. Fourth, marketers might stress the importance of groups of products to consumers in the process of role acquisition.[35] For example, new parents shopping for baby paraphernalia may be attracted to a new crib sold complete with changing table, mattress, waterproof mattress pad, bumpers, quilt, and baby mobile. Bridal superstores that let brides purchase wedding dresses, bridesmaids gowns, and flower girl attire; shop for accessories; rent tuxedos; and interview photographers, florists, and limousine companies have opened across the country.[36] Advertising can suggest that the consumer will earn positive reflexive evaluation from others after using an appropriate constellation of products associated with a given role.

Managing Rituals. Marketers can also be instrumental in developing services that facilitate the planning and implementation of complex rituals that surround transitions. Funeral homes perform these services in the death ritual. The ad for WeddingChannel.com in Exhibit 18.7 indicates how the wedding channel can be a comprehensive source for helping brides-to-be manage the wedding ritual. ■

The Connectedness Function

We've noted that the meaning of offerings that serve the emblematic and role acquisition functions derives from the consumer's culture. However, an offering's meaning can also derive from the individual consumer in his or her role as a member of a group or as an individual (see Exhibit 18.2).[37]

Products and consumption activities that serve the **connectedness function** express our membership in a group and serve as symbols of our personal connections to significant people, events, or experiences in our lives. For example, we may

connectedness function
The use of products as symbols of our personal connections to significant people, events, or experiences.

EXHIBIT 18.7
Managing Rituals

Some marketers serve customers by providing products and services that help them manage complex transition rituals. WeddingChannel.com does this task for brides-to-be.

Source: WeddingChannel.com is a trademark of Wedcom Inc. All rights reserved. Photo © Geof Kern.

enjoy a special painting or an item of clothing because it was a gift from a close friend. Heirlooms and genealogy studies connect people with their ancestors. Family photos connect them to their descendants. Ticket stubs, programs from concerts, and souvenirs may also be valued as reminders of special people, events, and places.[38] Other products and acts can also symbolize connectedness. Mrs. Smith's pie is used in special occasion rituals to connect the celebrants to one another (see Exhibit 18.8). In the Chinese culture, for example, large round tables in restaurants symbolize wholeness and the connectedness of the group. Among Muslims food eaten at feasts is shared from a community plate; asking for a separate plate is considered a rude act.

Rituals may also symbolize connectedness. In the United States numerous symbols of connectedness predominate in the Thanksgiving ritual.[39] Family commitment may be indicated by attendance at these events. Those who travel long distances for the gathering are welcomed and celebrated. Those who do not attend despite living short distances away are often privately denigrated. Those with multiple family commitments are excused, although they are often pressured to meet several obligations. Significant others are also invited, although whether they are invited for the entire meal or just dessert may depend on the seriousness of the relationship. We also include people who have nowhere else to go as part of the Thanksgiving ritual. In cultures like the United States and England, connectedness at the Christmas ritual is focused on the family. In others cultures, for example, some Eskimo villages in Alaska, the Christmas ritual has more of a community focus.[40]

Connectedness is also illustrated by the maintenance of traditions peculiar to each family. Deviations from these traditions (such as a new stuffing recipe) are often met with considerable resistance. When we sit down at dinner, connectedness is also symbolized by the way in which we eat. We all eat together, serving ourselves from common bowls that are passed from person to person. Many families foster connectedness by taking out old photographs or slides of the family and telling stories about family members. This sense of connectedness may not only reaffirm social ties but also make us nostalgic about past times.[41]

The Expressiveness Function

expressiveness function The use of products as symbols to demonstrate our uniqueness—how we stand out as different from others.

A final use of products as symbols relates to their potential to say something about our uniqueness.[42] This **expressiveness function** reflects not how we relate to other groups of people, but how unique we are. Thus products can symbolize how we stand out from others. One study found that Eastern European youths liked Western products, because they allowed young consumers to create a new distinct appearance that set them apart.[43] Products like clothing, home decoration, art, music, leisure activities, and food consumption can be used to express our unique personalities. Consumers also use body piercing, branding, and tattooing because these practices symbolize their individuality and expressiveness.

MARKETING IMPLICATIONS Several marketing implications are associated with the connectedness and expressiveness functions. Primarily, marketers wish to invoke feelings of nostalgia by connecting their product with people, places, or events. Marketers of toys and games, movies, music, and shoes such as Keds have succeeded by getting consumers to connect their product to special times in consumers' lives.[44] In addition, marketers can suggest that their products help bring out consumers' unique quali-

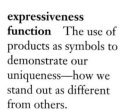

On this special occasion,
the silver is her grandmother's,
the china is her mother's,
and the pie is Mrs. Smith's.

Because you can taste the care in every bite, for special occasions Mrs. Thurber's pie is always *Mrs. Smith's.* Mrs. Thurber knows that making pies has been Mrs. Smith's specialty for over 75 years. Mrs. Thurber also knows that every Mrs. Smith's pie is made with high quality ingredients—like pumpkins grown especially for Mrs. Smith's. And this is precisely why Mrs. Smith's is a tradition Mrs. Thurber plans to keep in the family for generations. **Mrs. Smith's.® The taste that takes you home.™**

® Mrs. Smith's is a registered trademark of the J.M. Smucker Company ©1995 The J.M. Smucker Company.

EXHIBIT 18.8

Symbolizing Connectedness

This ad suggests that Mrs. Smith's pie, china, and silver are relevant parts of a "special occasion" celebration. The celebration itself is a ritual in which people connect with each other by acknowledging special life events.

Source: Courtesy of Mrs. Smith's.

self-concept Our mental conception of who we are.

actual identity schemas The set of multiple, salient identities that reflect our self-concept.

ideal identity schema A set of ideas about how the identity would be indicated in its ideal form.

ties. For example, one perfume manufacturer advertised that the brand smelled different on every woman and therefore helped to bring out each woman's unique qualities. ■

Multiple Functions

Although products and rituals can be used symbolically to serve many functions, a given product may serve several functions simultaneously. Consider, for example, a set of crystal wine goblets received as a wedding present from the bride's grandparents. These goblets could serve an emblematic function because their high price tag may communicate social status. They may also serve a role acquisition function, helping the newlyweds to internalize their new marital roles. Because they were a present from grandparents, the goblets may also serve a connectedness function—symbolizing the newlyweds' special relationship with their grandparents. Finally, if the goblets are personally appealing to the couple, they may symbolize the newlyweds' individual aesthetic tastes and, hence, serve an expressiveness function.

In some cases we deliberately use products because they fulfill one or more of the four functions noted in Exhibit 18.2. We may deliberately dress in a certain way to communicate the group to which we belong or the unique tastes we have, or we might deliberately pull out photos, artwork, or other items because we want to be reminded of people or times in our lives. However, we are not always aware that products serve a symbolic function, such as some of the clothing we wear that symbolizes our gender or our age. We may expect certain types of gifts when we go through role transitions like graduation and marriage, but we are probably not conscious that these products help us incorporate our new role. Finally, we may really like certain pieces of art in our homes but not realize that we like them so much because they remind us of the people who gave them to us.

Symbols and Self-Concept

The symbolic functions of products and consumption rituals are important because, combined, they help to define and maintain **our self-concept**, or our mental conception of who we are.[45] Social identity theory proposes that we evaluate brands in terms of their consistency with our individual identities.[46] According to the theory, our self-concept can be decomposed into many separate identities called **actual identity schemas**. For example, we may have various identities: student, worker, daughter, and so on. These identities may be driven, at least in part, by the roles we fulfill. Some identities may be especially salient or central to our self-concept. Our actual identity may be shaped by an **ideal identity schema**—that is, a set of ideas about how the identity we seek would be realized in its ideal form.

Our actual and ideal identity schemas influence which products we use and which consumption practices we engage in. The fact that possessions help shape our identity may explain why people who lose their possessions in natural disasters or wars and people who are in institutions like the military, nursing homes, or prisons often feel a loss of identity.[47] In fact, some consumers who have lost their possessions experience feelings of grief very similar to those experienced following the death of a loved one. Some institutions, such as the military and prisons, deliberately strip individuals of their possessions to erase their old identities.[48]

MARKETING IMPLICATIONS Several marketing implications stem from the preceding concepts.

Marketing and the Development of Consumer Self-Concepts. One implication is that marketers can play a role in both producing and maintaining an individual's self-concept. Although products may help define who we are, we also maintain our self-concept by selecting products whose image is consistent with it. For example, a consumer may purchase Guess? instead of Gap jeans because she views only Guess? as matching her self-image.

Product Fit with Self-Concepts. Another implication is that marketers should understand how their product fits with the various identities of their target consumers and try to create a fit between the image of the brand and the actual or ideal identity of the consumer. Research has found that the more similar a product's image is to a consumer's self-image, the more the consumer likes the product.[49]

Product Fit with Multiple Self-Concepts. Because self-images are multifaceted, marketers must also determine whether products consistent with one aspect of the target customers' identity may be inconsistent with another aspect. New parents may react negatively to disposable diapers because though the product is consistent with their new parent identity, it is inconsistent with their environmentally conscious identity. ■

SPECIAL POSSESSIONS

Some products come to hold a special, valued position in our minds, though they may or may not be relevant to our self-concepts.[50] For example, a consumer may regard his or her washing machine as a special possession because it is extremely functional. Another may view his or her skis as special because they give such enjoyment. Neither product may be viewed by these consumers as relevant to their self-concept, though.[51] Because there is a distinction between symbolic products and special possessions, marketers need to understand which products are special and why they become and remain so.

What Types of Possessions Are Special?

To help them understand special possessions, some researchers have identified the categories of possessions consumers tend to regard as special.[52] Although almost any possession can be special, for many consumers, pets, memory-evoking objects, achievement symbols, and collections take on special significance.

Pets We've mentioned that U.S. consumers tend to regard their pets as very special.[53] Consider that we give our pets names, buy them special food and clothes, talk to them, let them sleep on our beds, groom them, play with them, photograph them, buy them Christmas presents, take them on vacation, and even buy health insurance for them. Pets are often treated as family members or as extensions of ourselves. Some consumers buy animals whose personality or body type resembles their own. Furthermore, if someone mistreats our pet, we may react as if we are being mistreated. In China the government has recently passed a law prohibiting consumers from having dogs within city limits.[54] But pets are so special that many

Westerners living in China have moved outside the city limits and endure long commutes so they can keep their pets.

Notably, the treatment of pets as special is culturally specific. Pet owners in Korea rarely buy special dog food for a dog; instead, dogs eat leftovers. We are so attached to our pets that we may feel sad or guilty when we leave them to go to work or to travel. These feelings have created profitable opportunities for pet kennel operators, who offer doggie day care and comfortable boarding in temperature-controlled, noise-proof, and hygienic environments.[55]

Memory-Laden Objects   Some products acquire special meaning because they evoke memories or emotions of special people, places, or experiences.[56] Examples include heirlooms, antiques, souvenirs, mementos, and gifts from special people. A ticket stub, otherwise just a piece of paper, may be valued because it evokes memories of one's first date. A special song may evoke feelings of sentimentality or nostalgia. Such possessions can be therapeutic for elderly people because they evoke links to other people and happy times. Several researchers report the case of an individual who had to sell a favorite automobile because of a divorce but saved the license plates as a memento of this special possession. Photographs are often considered special because they remind us of special people. We often create shrines for our photographs, placing them prominently on TVs, mantles, and pianos.[57] Possessions that symbolize connectedness, therefore, clearly have the potential to become special. For example, the ad in Exhibit 18.9 suggests that the Lane cedar chest is a special product because it holds objects for which we have fond memories.

Achievement Symbols   Possessions that symbolize achievement are also regarded as special. One researcher who studied the Mormon migration to Utah in the 1800s found that people often moved possessions that demonstrated competence. For example, men brought tools, and women brought sewing machines and other objects that symbolized domestic achievement.[58] Modern-day symbols of achievement might include plaques, college diplomas, trophies, or even conspicuously consumed items like Rolex watches or expensive cars.

Collections   Collections can also be special. At least one in three U.S. consumers is a collector.[59] Examples of common collectible items are cars; seashells; stones; minerals; CDs; stamps; videos; and childhood objects like GI Joe, baseball cards, Barbie dolls, and cookie jars.[60] Uncommon collectibles include spark plugs, junk mail, drain tiles, and airsickness bags. Firms like the Bradford Exchange, the Franklin Mint, and the Danbury Mint produce collectible items for consumers. Rarity is what makes many an item within a collection special. For example, a Honus Wagner baseball card produced in 1910 is worth between $400,000 and $600,000. These cards are so expensive because only 50 of them exist today.[61]

Collectors often view their collections as extensions of themselves—sometimes symbolizing an aspect of their occupation, family heritage, or appearance. One research team focused on a grocery-store owner who collected antique product packages, an engineer who collected pocket watches, a woman

EXHIBIT 18.9
Memory-Laden Objects as Special Possessions

The Lane cedar chest may acquire special meaning because it serves as a repository for products that evoke memories of people, places, or experiences that are special to us.

Source: The Lane Company, Inc., Altavista, VA 24517.

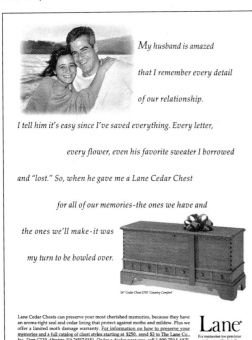

My husband is amazed

that I remember every detail

of our relationship.

I tell him it's easy since I've saved everything. Every letter,

every flower, even his favorite sweater I borrowed

and "lost." So, when he gave me a Lane Cedar Chest

for all of our memories-the ones we have and

the ones we'll make-it was

my turn to be bowled over.

54" Cedar Chest 2701 'Country Comfort'

Lane Cedar Chests can preserve your most cherished memories, because they have an aroma-tight seal and cedar lining that protect against moths and mildew. Plus we offer a limited moth damage warranty. For information on how to preserve your memories and a full catalog of chest styles starting at $250, send $3 to The Lane Co., Inc., Dept. C110, Altavista, VA 24517-0151. Or for a dealer near you, call 1-800-750-LANE.
©1995 The Lane Company, Inc.

Lane
For memories too precious to be erased by time.

61

named Bunny who collected rabbit replicas, and wealthy women who collected monogrammed silver spoons.[62] For some, collections represent a fantasy image of the self, as is sometimes the case with men who collect baseball cards—they are keeping alive the fantasy of themselves as ball players. As is often the case with people who have special possessions, collectors tend to believe that they take better care of their collections than anyone else would.[63]

What Characteristics Describe Special Possessions?

Special possessions have several distinct characteristics.[64] First, they will not be sold at market value, if at all. We could never, for example, sell our family pet or part with a piece of a special collection. If a painting was a gift from a special friend, we will be unlikely to sell it, even if someone offered more than its market value. Second, special possessions are often purchased with little regard for their price. Collectors, in particular, may pay exorbitant prices to acquire new pieces.

Third, special possessions have few or no substitutes. For example, when our family dog dies, we are unlikely to find or even want to find another like it. Insurance may pay to replace furniture that was damaged in a fire, but if the pieces were heirlooms passed down through generations, new furniture cannot possibly compensate for the old.

A fourth characteristic of special possessions is that they are not discarded, even after they lose their functional value. Children are often reluctant to part with security blankets and stuffed animals and will keep these favorite objects until they are mere threads of fabric. How many of your parents still keep your old report cards, bronzed baby shoes, and cards you or others have given to them?

Special possessions might not be used for their original purpose. Some consumers even believe that valued properties will be lost if their prized possessions are used to fulfill their original function. For example, a doll collector may not allow children to play with her collection. Indeed, collectibles such as Barbie dolls and Star Wars toys lose their collectible value if they have even been taken out of their packaging. One study described a woman who collected nutcrackers but would not consider using them to crack nuts.[65] Special possessions can also provide us with powerful emotions like achievement, affection, pride, or passion.[66] Depression, sadness, and pain may accompany their loss, destruction, or disposition.

Finally, special possessions are often personified. Some people give names to the individual items in their collections, name their houses, or use a feminine or masculine pronoun when referring to their cars or boats. Perhaps even more significant, we often treat these possessions as though they were our partners. We feel such commitment and are so attached to them that we would feel devastated by their loss.[67]

Why Are Some Products Special?

Possessions take on special meaning for several reasons, including their symbolic value, mood-altering properties, and instrumental importance. More specific reasons that underlie these three general categories are shown in Exhibit 18.10.

Symbolic Value   Possessions may be special, in part, because they fulfill the emblematic, role adoption, connectedness, and expressiveness functions noted earlier in the chapter. For example, art, heirlooms, and jewelry are often valued because they are expressions of our style or because they have been gifts and thus tie us to

EXHIBIT 18.10

Reasons Why Possessions Are Special

Take a possession you regard as special. Chances are, it is special to you because it has symbolic value, mood altering properties, and/or utilitarian value.

Take a possession you regard as special and answer the following questions using a 7 point scale (1 = not true of me; 7 = very true of me).

This possession is important to me because it . . .

SYMBOLIC VALUE	Symbolizes personal history	Reminds me of my childhood
		Reminds me of particular events or places
		Is a record of my personal history
	Represents achievement	Required a lot of effort to acquire or maintain
		Reminds me of my skills, achievements, or goals
	Represents interpersonal ties	Reminds me of my relationship with a particular person
		Reminds me of my family or a group of people I belong to
		Represents my family heritage or history
	Facilitates interpersonal ties	Allows me to spend time or share activities with other people
	Demonstrates status	Has social prestige value
		Gives me social status
		Makes others think well of me
	Is self-expressive	Allows me to express myself
		Expresses what is unique about me, different from others
MOOD-ALTERING PROPERTIES	Enjoyment	Provides enjoyment, entertainment, or relaxation
		Improves my mood
		Provides comfort or emotional security
	Spiritual	Provides a spiritual link to divine or higher forces
	Appearance related	Is beautiful or attractive in appearance
		Improves my appearance or the way I look
UTILITARIAN VALUE	Utilitarian	Allows me to be efficient in my daily life or work
		Has a lot of practical usefulness
		Provides me freedom or independence
	Financial aspects	Is valuable in terms of money

Source: Adapted from Marsha Richens, "Valuing Things: The Public and Private Meanings of Possessions," *Journal of Consumer Research,* 21 (December 1994), 504–521.

special people in our lives.[68] Objects like cars and houses may be valued for their reflection of social class. Still others, like wedding dresses, are valued because they reflect transitions we have gone through.

Mood-Altering Properties   Possessions may be special because they have mood-altering properties. For example, trophies, plaques, collections, and diplomas can evoke feelings of pride, happiness, and joy.[69] Pets can evoke feelings of comfort. A consumer in one study described her refrigerator as a special possession because making snacks always cheered her up. Others cited stereos and music as favorite possessions because of their capacity to put these consumers in a good mood.[70]

Instrumental Importance   Finally, possessions may be special because they are extremely useful. A consumer who describes her computer as special because she needs it to get through her day illustrates its instrumental value.

What Affects What We Regard as Special?

Our social class, gender, and age are among the background characteristics related to the types of things that become special to each of us.

Social Class   One study examined the meanings people of different social classes in England gave to their possessions. People in the business class were concerned about possessions that symbolized their personal history and self-development. Unemployed people were concerned about possessions that had utilitarian value.[71]

Gender   Gender has also been related to the type of product regarded as special. Men have been found to regard as special products that symbolize activity and physical achievement and that have instrumental and use-related features. On the other hand, women have been found to value symbols of identity and products that symbolize their attachment to other people.[72] Another set of researchers

found that in both Niger and the United States, women selected as special those possessions that symbolized their children's accomplishments and items indicative of connectedness. In the United States, these things included items such as heirlooms and pictures. In Niger they included tapestry, jewelry, and other items passed through generations. Men chose objects that showed material comfort, and possessions that indicated mastery over the environment.[73] Differences in the types of items men and women collect have been observed. Men are more likely to collect cars, books, and sports-related objects, and women are more likely to collect stuffed animals, jewelry, dishes, and silverware.[74] Exhibit 18.11 identifies the possessions that men and women regard as special at various stages of their lives.

Age   Age is also related to objects regarded as special. Although individuals at all ages may have special possessions, what is regarded as special changes with age.[75] As Exhibit 18.11 indicates, stuffed animals are very important possessions for children; music and motor vehicles are highly prized among adolescents; and photographs take on increasing importance as consumers enter adulthood and as they age.

Rituals Used with Special Possessions

Because possessions have special meaning, we often engage in rituals designed to create, energize, or enhance their meaning. We can identify these rituals as occurring at the acquisition, usage, or disposition stage of consumption.

   At the acquisition stage consumers may engage in **possession rituals**.[76] These rituals enable the consumer to claim personal possession of new goods. When we buy new clothes, for example, we may throw out the hangers that they came with and instead use our own hangers. We may adorn a new car with markers like per-

possession rituals   Rituals we engage in when we first acquire a product that help to make it "ours."

EXHIBIT 18.11

Frequently Named Special Possessions by Age and Gender

The possessions we regard as special may vary by cultural category (e.g., age and gender). Girls differ from boys and older consumers differ from younger ones in the possessions they regard as special. Can you think of other examples using other cultural categories (e.g., social class)?

Sources: Adapted with permission from N. Laura Kamptner, "Personal Possessions and Their Meanings: A Life-Span Perspective," in ed. Floyd W. Rudmin, To *Have Possessions: A Handbook on Ownership and Property,* Special Issue of the *Journal of Social Behavior and Personality,* 6(6), 1991, p. 215.

AGE	MALES	FEMALES
Middle childhood	Sports equipment* Stuffed animals Childhood toys Small appliances Pillows, blankets	Stuffed animals* Dolls Music Jewelry Books
Adolescence	Music Sports equipment Motor vehicles Small appliances Clothing	Jewelry Stuffed Animals Music Clothing Motor vehicles Small appliances
Early adulthood	Motor vehicles Music Photographs Jewelry Memorabilia Artwork	Jewelry Photographs Motor vehicles Pillows, blankets Stuffed animals
Middle adulthood	Photographs Jewelry Books Sports equipment Motor vehicles Small appliances	Dishes, silverware Jewelry Artwork Photographs Memorabilia Furniture
Late adulthood	Small appliances Photographs Motor vehicles Artwork Sports equipment	Jewelry Dishes, Silverware Photographs Religious Items Furniture

* Items are listed in order from most to least frequently cited.

sonalized license plates, tapes or CDs, a new radio–CD–tape player, special scent, seat covers, drink holders, and so on. When we move to a new house, we often rush to put pictures on the walls, to get the furniture in place, and to put the house in order.

With previously owned goods possession rituals include wiping away meaning conferred by the former owner.[77] For example, when we buy a new home, we thoroughly clean it, tear down old wallpaper, and take down personal markers like names on mailboxes. Interestingly, the wiping away of meaning may not always be possible. In China, for example, new houses are often built because occupants feel that the older structures are "contaminated" by the former occupants.

At the consumption stage consumers may engage in **grooming rituals** to bring out or maintain the best in special products.[78] Consider, for example, the consumer who spends hours washing, waxing, vacuuming, and cleaning the car or

grooming rituals   Rituals we engage in to bring out or maintain the best in special products.

scrubbing and dusting the house before visitors arrive. Sometimes the grooming ritual involves ourselves, as when we devote large amounts of time to making ourselves look good for a special event.

Finally, when the offering loses its symbolic meaning, we engage in **divestment rituals**—wiping away all traces of our personal meaning. For example, we will clean clothes that we are about to give to Goodwill. We remove all personal possessions when we sell our automobile. We might even get rid of a possession in stages—first moving it from the living room to the basement—before we finally decide to sell it or throw it away.

divestment rituals Rituals enacted at the disposition stage that are designed to wipe away all traces of our personal meaning in a product.

SACRED MEANING

Although many possessions are considered special, Exhibit 18.2 shows that some are so special they are regarded as sacred. **Sacred entities** are people, things, and places that are set apart, revered, worshiped, and treated with great respect. We may find such entities deeply moving, and we may feel anger and revulsion when they are not accorded their due honor. In contrast, **profane things** are those that are ordinary and hence have no special power. Profane objects are often distinguished from sacred ones by the fact that they are used for more mundane purposes.[79]

sacred entities People, things, and places that are set apart, revered, worshiped, and treated with great respect.

profane things Things that are ordinary and hence have no special power.

Sacred People

Movie stars, popular singers, historic figures like John F. Kennedy, and religious leaders such as the pope or Gandhi are regarded by many people as sacred. Artifacts from Gandhi's life, including his thongs, reading glasses, walking stick, and shawl, are preserved in the town of Ahmedabad as a mark of reverence. The sacred status we ascribe to famous people is exemplified by the popularity of visiting the graves of celebrities like Princess Diana; driving by or visiting homes of living or dead celebrities, for example, Graceland; and visiting Mann's Chinese Theater in Los Angeles to touch the famous handprints and footprints in the sidewalk. Japanese and Japanese American consumers regard Hideo Nomo, a Japanese pitcher for the Dodgers, as sacred. Nomo paraphernalia is popular, fans cheer Nomo on the Tornado Boy Web page, and they travel from afar to watch him play.[80]

One reason why heirlooms and photographs of ancestors take on sacred status is that we may view our ancestors as heroes. A similar phenomenon explains why we treat as sacred items associated with famous statesmen such as George Washington, Charles de Gaulle, and Winston Churchill. Although not part of our actual past, these heroes were instrumental in formulating national identities. Visits to the places that mark these historic figures illustrate our reverence for them.[81]

Sacred Objects and Places

Many consumers also regard as sacred such objects as national flags, patriotic songs, art, collections, family recipes, and the Bible and such places as museums, the Vietnam Memorial, the Taj Mahal, and the Great Wall of China. These sacred objects and places evoke powerful emotions. Many individuals, for example, have reported feeling overwhelmed with emotion when viewing them.

In addition to sacred people, objects, and places, we also identify certain times and events, religious holidays, weddings, births, deaths, and grace before meals, as sacred.

What Characteristics Describe Sacred Entities?

Sacred entities involve some mystery or myth that raises them above the ordinary.[82] The pope, for example, is viewed as being almost godlike. And legendary figures such as Jim Morrison, Elvis Presley, Marilyn Monroe, and John F. Kennedy are associated with mystery. Second, sacred entities have qualities that transcend time, place, or space. When we enter the Alamo, we almost feel as if we are back in the period when the historic fighting took place. Sacred objects also possess strong approach/avoidance characteristics and create an overwhelming feeling of power and fascination. For example, we may simultaneously desire to be close to but also watch from a distance people we regard as heroes and heroines. We may also experience certain special feelings when we encounter sacred entities—ecstasy and the sense that we are somehow smaller and more humble than the sacred entity. For example, we may feel that we have accomplished little in comparison to heroes like Gandhi or Abraham Lincoln. We may also feel humbled by the mass of humanity represented by the Vietnam Memorial.

Sacred objects can create strong feelings of attachment. We may also feel the need to take care of and nurture the sacred entity. Often sacred objects involve rituals that dictate how we should behave in the object's presence. For example, we know what is and what is not an appropriate way to treat the national flag.

Sacredness may be maintained by scarcity and exclusivity.[83] For example, the sacred status of special works of art derives from their uniqueness and the fact that their high price maintains their exclusivity. People like Greta Garbo and Jackie Kennedy Onassis became imbued with sacredness by their desire to be alone and away from the public view. Attempts to limit their public appearances only made them more interesting to their adoring public.

How Are Sacred Objects Profaned?

Entities that were once sacred can be made profane if they are not treated with due respect or if they are brought into the world of commerce and divested of their sacred status. In divorce, for example, some people profane things that were sacred in the marriage by throwing away, giving away, or selling their wedding ring, wedding dress, family furniture, special automobiles, or family jewelry.[84] We can feel considerable revulsion at the profaning of a sacred person or sacred object. Roseanne Arnold, for example, once generated social disapproval by delivering an off-key rendition of the U.S. national anthem. Finally, many consumers who were shocked to hear that Taco Bell had purchased the Liberty Bell were later relieved to discover that the news was an April Fool's Day joke.

MARKETING IMPLICATIONS Marketers need to be aware of the sacred meanings people attach to other people, objects, and events.

Creating and Maintaining Sacredness. Sometimes marketers create sacredness in objects or people. For example, the promoters of a famous movie star might heighten the sacred status of the star by creating or enhancing his or her mystery and myth, making the star exclusive, and promoting the powerful emotional effect that the celebrity has on people. Marketers may also be involved in maintaining sacredness—for example, by keeping the price of sacred objects like collections, precious works of art, and rare jewelry very high.

Avoiding the Profaning of Sacred Objects. Unsophisticated marketers sometimes profane sacred objects through commercialization. Some consumers believe that Elvis Presley is profaned in the hawking of Elvis paraphernalia. The sacred properties of certain religious sites, such as the Church of Jesus Christ of Latter-Day Saints and the Latter-Day Saint temples, may be profaned by the selling of religious trinkets outside the building. Bruce Springsteen, Paul Simon, and Led Zeplin are among a group of U.S. artists who have refused to turn their songs into ads. They believe that it is undignified and crass to turn their creative talents and hard work into a tool for selling products.[85]

Product Involvement in Sacred Activities and Rituals. In some cases marketers sell products regarded as instrumental to the continuation or conduct of sacred times and the rituals they involve. Marketers like Hallmark Cards profitably capitalize on sacred rituals such as Christmas celebrations by selling products (tree ornaments, ribbons, wrapping paper, cards) regarded as important components of this sacred event. ■

THE TRANSFER OF SYMBOLIC MEANING THROUGH GIFT GIVING

So far we've shown that consumers invest products, times, activities, places, and people with symbolic meaning. Some meanings enhance the special and/or sacred status of the product, and some are instrumental in developing or maintaining the consumer's self-concept. However, another aspect of symbolic consumption is the transfer of meaning from one individual to another. An important context in which the transfer of symbolic meaning occurs is gift giving.

When Do We Give Gifts?

Some gift-giving occasions are culturally determined and timed. In the United States these include Valentine's Day, Mother's Day, Father's Day, and Secretary's Day.[86] Koreans celebrate the 100th day of a baby's life, and in China families celebrate when a baby is 1 month old. Koreans also give gifts to elders and family members on New Year's Day. Religious gift-giving holidays such as Christmas, Hanukkah, and Kwanza are also celebrated in cultures around the world.[87]

We also have gift-giving occasions that are culturally prescribed but whose timing is specific to an individual.[88] These are often the transitions we discussed earlier: anniversaries, graduations, birthdays, weddings, bridal and baby showers, retirement parties, and transitions within one's religious community such as baptism, first communion, or bar mitzvah. Still other gift-giving occasions are ad hoc. For example, we may give gifts as part of a reconciliation attempt, in an attempt to form an alliance with another person, to cheer someone who is ill, or to thank someone for doing something for us.

gestation stage The first stage of gift giving, when we consider what to give someone.

presentation stage The second stage of gift giving, when we actually give the gift.

reformulation stage The final stage of gift giving, when we reevaluate the relationship based on the gift-giving experience.

Three Stages of Gift-Giving

The three stages of the gift-giving process are shown in Exhibit 18.12. In the **gestation stage** we consider what to give the recipient. The **presentation stage** occurs with the actual giving of the gift. Finally, in the **reformulation stage** we reevaluate the relationship based on the gift-giving experience.

The Gestation Stage The gestation stage occurs before a gift is given. It involves the motives for giving the gift, the nature and meaning of the gift, the value of the gift, and the amount of time spent searching for a gift.

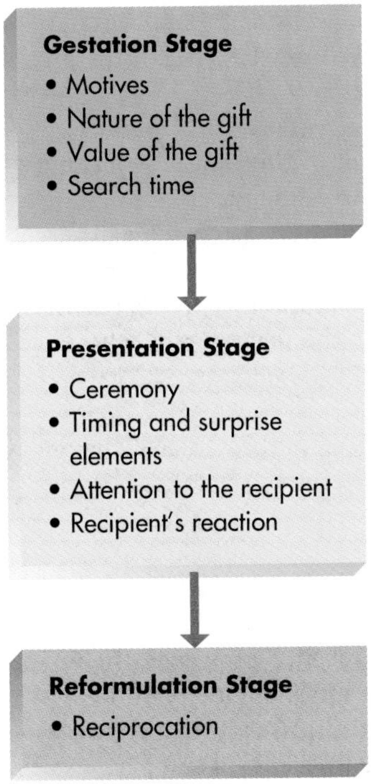

EXHIBIT 18.12
A Model of the Gift-Giving Process

The process of gift giving can be described in terms of three stages: (1) *the gestation stage*, at which we think about and buy the gift; (2) *the presentation stage*, at which we actually give the gift; and (3) *the reformulation stage*, at which we reevaluate our relationship based on the nature of the gift. At each stage we can identify several issues that affect the gift-giving process.

Gestation Stage
- Motives
- Nature of the gift
- Value of the gift
- Search time

Presentation Stage
- Ceremony
- Timing and surprise elements
- Attention to the recipient
- Recipient's reaction

Reformulation Stage
- Reciprocation

Motives for Giving   One aspect of the gestation stage is the development of our motives for gift giving.[89] On the one hand, people may give for altruistic reasons—to help the recipient. For example, an individual may give a young couple a large cash gift at their wedding to help them get a good start on their married life. We may also give for agnostic reasons because we derive positive emotional pleasure from the act of giving. Instrumental reasons indicate that we want the recipient to give us something in return. For example, a secretary may give a boss a nice gift in hopes of getting a raise.

Consumers may also give for purely obligatory reasons because they feel the situation or the relationship demands it. Indeed, sometimes we do not react positively to gifts given by others because we now feel the obligation to reciprocate.

Gifts may also serve to reduce guilt in the donor or alleviate hard feelings in the recipient. In divorce, for example, individuals who feel responsible for the breakup are more likely to give the partner more than a fair share, in what is called compensatory giving.[90] Finally, we might also have antagonistic motives for gift giving. For example, if you are invited to the wedding of someone you do not like, you might give the couple something you think is less than beautiful.

The Nature and Meaning of the Gift   Selection of the gift is important because several aspects of it signal our feelings toward the recipient. One is the nature of the gift. For example, a worker would not give his or her boss a gift of lingerie because such items are too personal. Likewise, you would not give good friends a token wedding gift because the relationship dictates something more substantial.

Notably, although token gifts may not be appropriate on a clearly defined gift-giving occasion, they can be highly significant when no gift is expected. Gifts given spontaneously, even small ones, can signify love and caring.[91] Thus you may feel quite touched when a significant other buys you "a little something." Likewise, token gifts are quite important for recipients with whom we do not have strong ties. For example, it is seen as appropriate and desirable to send holiday and birthday cards to those whom we do not see very often.[92]

The gift may also symbolize the meaning we wish to transfer to the donor.[93] For example, gifts can symbolize values we regard as appropriate for the recipient, such as domesticity for new brides and grooms, or a new set of expectations. Expectations regarding commitment and future fidelity are symbolized by the giving of an engagement ring. Expectations regarding future leisure are symbolized by gifts such as golf clubs at retirement. Gifts can also be symbolic of the self, as when an individual gives another a piece of art or something that the giver created.

The Value of the Gift   Another element of the gift-selection process is the value of the gift. For example, you might splurge on a Mother's Day gift because you want your mother to know how much she means to you. Decisions about the value of a gift are culturally determined. The Japanese, for example, lose face if the gift they receive exceeds the value of the gift they have given.[94]

The Amount of Time Spent Searching   The amount of time spent searching for a gift, another aspect of the gestation stage, symbolizes the nature and intensity of our relationship with the recipient. Interestingly, there are gender differences in how much time and effort men and women spend in searching for gifts. Women are reportedly more involved in holiday gift shopping than are men.[95] Women also appear to spend more time searching for the perfect gift, whereas men are more likely to settle for something that will do.[96]

The Presentation Stage   The presentation stage describes the actual exchange of the gift. Here, the ritual or ceremonial aspects of the giving process become very important.[97]

Ceremony   Are gifts wrapped, and if so how? The present may be nicely wrapped in paper appropriate for the occasion. Wrapping helps to *decommodify*, or make more personal, a gift that is otherwise mass-produced.[98] However, the importance of the gift packaging depends on the formality and spontaneity of the occasion. For example, unanticipated gifts, such as a boss's surprise gift to a secretary or a husband's surprise gift to his wife, may be less formally wrapped and may even be appropriate if left unwrapped.

Timing and Surprise   The timing of the gift giving and the surprise elements in the exchange process may also be important. For example, although we know that gifts will be given at Christmas and they are even prominently displayed under the tree—sometimes for days before the actual exchange—the surprise element of what they contain is often quite important. The excitement of unwrapping an item is heightened by having the individual guess what the package contains. It is sometimes appropriate to surprise a potential fiancée with a diamond. Although surprise is valued, it is not always realized. One study found that right before Christmas some men purchase items that have been chosen in advance by their wives. In these cases the gift is not a surprise, but an orchestrated event with the husband taking the role of "purchasing agent."[99]

Attention to the Recipient   Issues such as the attention devoted to the recipient may be important to the gift giver. For example, at wedding showers it is customary for all in attendance to pay full attention to the bride-to-be as she opens her gifts.

Recipient's Reaction   Another aspect of the presentation stage is the reaction the donor is hoping the gift will elicit from the recipient, the recipient's actual reaction, and the donor's response to the recipient's reaction. If we have spent a lot of time and effort looking for the perfect gift and the recipient opens the package quickly and goes on to the next gift without a word, we are bound to feel hurt. We may also feel anxiety at the presentation stage if we are uncertain about whether the recipient will like our gift.

The Reformulation Stage   The reformulation stage marks the third and final stage of the gift-giving process. At this stage the donor and recipient reevaluate their relationship based on the gift-giving process.

Relationship Bonding   An appropriate gift may maintain the strength of the tie between recipient and donor. A gift that is highly valued indicates considerable search costs, may strengthen the relationship between donor and recipient, as might a gift that is given as a surprise. A gift that is less than expected, one that indicates little prior thought, or no gift at all may weaken the relationship. One study found that gifts could strengthen a relationship by communicating feelings of connection, bonding, and commitment. Gifts can also affirm the relationship, validating existing feelings of commitment. On the negative side, inappropriate gifts or those showing limited search effort or interest in the recipient's desires can weaken a relationship, creating the perception that the relationship lacks bonding and connection.[100]

Reciprocation   The reformulation stage also has implications for how and whether the recipient will reciprocate on the next gift-giving occasion. If you gave someone a nice gift on one occasion, you would generally expect the recipient to reciprocate on the next occasion. If, on the other hand, you gave a gift that weakened the tie between you and the recipient, the latter may not give you a very nice gift or may give no gift at all on the next giving occasion.

However, some kinds of gift-giving situations or recipients are exempt from reciprocation.[101] For example, if we give someone a gift because she is ill or has experienced some tragedy (say, her house burned down), we do not expect her to reciprocate. If, on the other hand, someone unexpectedly gives us a gift for Christmas, we usually feel compelled to rush out and buy him a gift. People of limited financial means (children, students) or those of lower status (a secretary as opposed to a boss) may be seen as exempt from giving. Thus it is appropriate for parents to give their children gifts and not expect them to reciprocate. Women have also been reported to feel fewer obligations to reciprocate in dating-related gift giving, perhaps given culturally prescribed notions regarding the generally higher economic power of men.[102]

MARKETING IMPLICATIONS   Gift giving has many implications for marketers.
Promoting Products and Services as Gifts.   Many marketers promote their products for gift-giving occasions, and often gift-giving occasions are the primary focus of their business. Consider, for example that the greeting card industry earns an average of $6 billion a year in revenue in the United States, the majority of which is earned during the Christmas/Hanukkah/Kwanza season.[103] In some cases uncommon gifts are promoted as appropriate for various gift-giving occasions. For example, products from blenders and lingerie to stock certifications and power tools are touted as appropriate gifts on Mother's Day. Mortgage companies are now offering bridal registries. Rather than buying gifts, gift givers contribute money to the couple's down payment or mortgage. Some retail outlets are known exclusively as gift stores. Here the services the store provides to enhance the presentation of the gift and the salespeople's abilities to point out gifts with special meanings may be important.

Technology and Gift Shopping   Technology has created major changes in the gift-giving process. For example, *Bride's* magazine is developing Web pages that will soon allow gift givers to pull up an updated version of the couple's gift registry and buy gifts from retailers.[104] It is interesting to consider whether reduced search time afforded by these new technologies will alter receivers' feelings about the value of their relationship with the giver.

Ethnicity and Holiday Shopping.   Marketers have also become more sensitive to the ethnic and religious diversity within the United States. For example, because

Christmas, Hanukkah, and Kwanza are celebrated at about the same time of the year, Archway cookies decided to change its traditional holiday packaging from bells, wreaths, and candles to less culturally specific prints of snowy outdoor scenes.[105]

Alternatives to Traditional Gifts. Knowing that consumers are becoming weary of the commercialism, hassle, and materialism surrounding gift-giving occasions like Christmas, some charities are adopting the practice of asking consumers to give gifts to people from around the world who are truly in need. For example, the Global Gift Guide, a catalog produced by a nonprofit Christian organization called World Concern, allows consumers to purchase items such as chickens, fish, prenatal care, and business loans for needy families around the world.[106] For similar reasons, travel marketers are touting travel as a holiday gift. More two-income families have less time, more money, and more distance separating them from loved ones, creating a trend toward travel and family reunions at posh resorts around the world and away from holiday shopping.[107] ∎

SUMMARY

This chapter discussed the symbolic role that products can play. Some products are used as conscious or unconscious badges that designate the various social categories of which we are members. Products and rituals hold symbolic significance when we undergo role transitions; serve as symbols by connecting us to people, places, and times that have been important to us; and are symbols of our individuality and uniqueness. The combined symbolic uses of products and rituals affect our self-concept.

We regard some of our possessions as very special. They are nonsubstitutable, will not be sold at market value if at all, and will be purchased with little regard for price. They are rarely discarded, even if their functional value is gone, and they may not even be used for their original functional purpose. We personify these possessions, may feel powerful emotions in their presence, and may have feelings of fear or sadness over their potential or actual loss. In part, possessions are special because they serve as emblems, facilitate role transitions, connect us to others, or express our unique styles. They are special because they indicate personal mastery and achievements or are mood enhancing. Interestingly, background characteristics such as social class, gender, and age all seem to influence just what type of object is regarded as special.

Some entities are so special that they are worshiped, set apart, and treated with inordinate respect—that is, they are sacred. A number of things outside the realm of possessions—people, places, objects, times, and events—also take on sacred status. Sacred objects transcend time and space and have strong approach/avoidance powers and great fascination. They are cared for and nurtured. Often special rituals are devised to handle them. Sacred objects can be profaned or made ordinary by commercialization, inappropriate usage, or divestment patterns.

Gift giving is a process of transferring meaning in products from one person to another. Gift-giving occasions are often culturally prescribed but may vary in their timing. Gift giving is a complex process that entails three phases: gestation, presentation, and reformulation. The manner in which the first two phases are enacted can affect the long-term viability of the relationship between the donor and recipient.

EXERCISES

1. Consider the cultural category of occupational status and the typical clothing of doctors, farmers, waitresses, politicians, businesspeople, truck drivers, and pharmacists. Identify the cultural principles that reflect membership in each of these occupational groups and explain how the clothing worn by members of each group illustrates these characteristics.

2. Take two role transitions: graduation and new parenthood. For each, identify the rituals that mark these role transitions and the enabling products that mark their passage. (This task will be easier if you can actually attend a graduation or watch a new parent care for a baby.) Find several advertisements for the products or services that are relevant to these rituals. Identify a set of marketing implications regarding marketing to groups undergoing these transitions.

3. Interview someone you know about one or more possessions that they regard as special/sacred. Try to get them to indicate why these possessions are special and compare their answers to the reasons given in the chapter for why possessions are special. What marketing implications can you derive from their responses?

ADOPTION OF, RESISTANCE TO, AND DIFFUSION OF INNOVATIONS

INTRODUCTION

New products and services are fundamentally changing the way music is sold and played in the United States and around the world.[1] On-line music stores such as CDNow.com and Towerrecords.com allow consumers to find artists and songs, download samples of music using RealAudio software, and make purchases on-line (see Exhibit 19.1). Consumers can also acquire songs from the Internet by using an audio compression software called MP3. The company MP3.com allows consumers to download free songs by specific artists. Consumers can also order an artist's CD on-line. MP3.com is attractive to some artists because they can set the price of their own CDs and earn 50 percent of every sale (compared with the 10 percent royalty they typically earn from record companies).

Although MP3.com offers songs for free, consumers can also purchase songs on a per song basis and download them onto their PCs from sites like Good-Noise.com and Sony Music. Consumers can also transform songs from their CDs into MP3 files and store them on their computers. A software program from Real-Networks called RealJukebox also allows consumers to use information from the Internet to categorize songs on their PC by title, artist, and genre. Consumers can then sort songs in any order and play them back from their own special play lists.

EXHIBIT 19.1

Innovations at Tower Records

The Internet has fundamentally altered how consumers search for and buy music. At sites like Towerrecords.com, CDNow.com, and Amazon.com, consumers can listen to 30-second tracks of songs on recent albums and can make purchases on-line. Some sites allow consumers to purchase songs on-line and download them directly to their PCs.

Source: © 2000 CDNOW Online, Inc. All rights reserved.

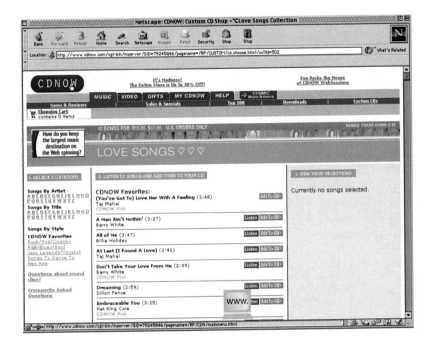

Realjukebox plays songs that are compressed in various formats such as MP3, WAV, and RealAudio. Songs in MP3 format can also be recorded onto a CD by using a CD burner and later played on a CD. These new technologies allow consumers to make their own compilations. In the fall of 1999, Diamond Multimedia Systems Rio player—the first portable machine for playing music files from the Internet—was introduced. So was the RCA Lyra, which can record and play music in MP3 format and store the audio on removable flash-memory cards.

These new products and services, which offer consumers a number of advantages, are also causing major problems for music producers and distributors. For example, MP3 not only enables aspiring musicians to distribute music samples to potential fans but also provides the potential for music piracy, as consumers trade songs electronically or purchase them from sites that do not pay the record companies royalties. In light of these problems, the major record companies—Sony Music, Warner Music, BMG Entertainment, EMI Recorded Music, and Universal Music Group—are rushing to develop standards for secure digital music. Companies like Microsoft are also developing their own format to MP3—which includes piracy protection. These developments leave uncertainty as to whether MP3 or some other format will be the standard format for compressed music.

EXHIBIT 19.2

Chapter Overview: Adoption of, Resistence to, and Diffusion of Innovations

Consumers may decide to adopt (e.g., purchase) or resist a new offering (an innovation). Diffusion reflects how fast an innovation spreads through a market. Several things affect adoption, resistance and diffusion: the type of innovation, its breadth, its characteristics and the social system in which it is introduced.

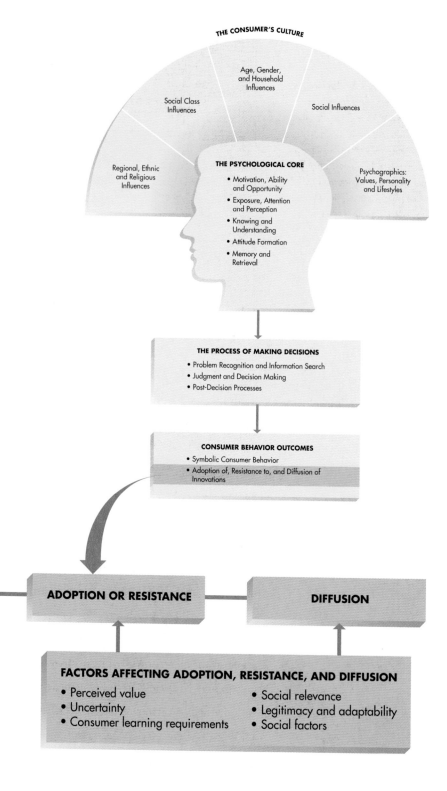

THE CONSUMER'S CULTURE

Age, Gender, and Household Influences

Social Class Influences

Social Influences

Regional, Ethnic and Religious Influences

Psychographics: Values, Personality and Lifestyles

THE PSYCHOLOGICAL CORE
- Motivation, Ability and Opportunity
- Exposure, Attention and Perception
- Knowing and Understanding
- Attitude Formation
- Memory and Retrieval

THE PROCESS OF MAKING DECISIONS
- Problem Recognition and Information Search
- Judgment and Decision Making
- Post-Decision Processes

CONSUMER BEHAVIOR OUTCOMES
- Symbolic Consumer Behavior
- Adoption of, Resistance to, and Diffusion of Innovations

INNOVATIONS

ADOPTION OR RESISTANCE

DIFFUSION

FACTORS AFFECTING ADOPTION, RESISTANCE, AND DIFFUSION
- Perceived value
- Uncertainty
- Consumer learning requirements
- Social relevance
- Legitimacy and adaptability
- Social factors

The changes in the music industry reflect some of the basic concepts we discuss in this chapter. Innovations in the music industry have provided consumers with a host of new products and services that offer considerable advantages over traditional forms of buying and playing music. These advantages include the functional benefits of convenient acquisition and choice in the selection and play order of specific songs, the hedonic benefits of good sound quality, and the symbolic benefits of owning cutting-edge products.

Using a computer to acquire and play music is compatible with the centrality of computers in consumers' lives and their attitudes toward music, Internet shopping, and technology. Moreover, the new music technologies are easy to try and simple to use. Consumers can learn by observing others download and upload files, create play lists, and burn CDs. Ease of use and the benefits of the new technology create favorable word of mouth, particularly among the largest and most cohesive group of MP3 users—high school students. Some of the software is free, making purchase costs irrelevant, and although CD burners and players are expensive, their prices will eventually drop as competition enters the market and consumer acceptance grows. These offerings, which were initially known to only a small group of technically inclined early adopters, are beginning to find acceptance in the mainstream consumer marketplace.

This chapter focuses on factors that affect consumers' choice of a new product. Following Exhibit 19.2, we define the concept of a new offering, also called an innovation. We describe several types of innovations, which can vary in the kind of novelty they offer and in the type of benefit they confer. We then discuss factors that affect an individual consumer's resistance to or adoption of a new product. Different groups of adopters are characterized by how soon they adopt a new product relative to other consumers, and we describe the types of consumers, including those who tend to buy new products first, the innovators. Finally, we examine factors that affect how quickly a new product spreads or diffuses through a market.

INNOVATIONS

The ability to develop successful new products is critical to a company's sales and future growth. Consider that as much as 49 percent of the total revenue of some of the world's leading companies has come from the new products they have developed.[2] Given the role that new products play in a company's sales and profitability, it becomes very important to understand new products and what drives their success.

What Is an Innovation?

innovation An offering that is perceived as new by consumers within a market segment and that has an effect on existing consumption patterns.

A new product, or an **innovation**, is an offering that is new to the marketplace. More formally, an innovation is a product, service, attribute, or idea that consumers within a market segment perceive as new and that has an effect on existing consumption patterns.[3]

Although we usually think of products as innovations, services can also be new to a market. For example, Telecom, a subsidiary of MCI WorldCom, lets users circumvent their usual long-distance telephone providers by dialing 10-10-321 before they make a call. Consumers simply use the service as desired. As another example, banks are currently offering electronic bill-paying as a new service to customers.

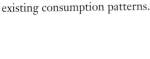

THE DARK AGE IS OVER.

Under the dash, in the crawl space, behind the stereo, in the closet, way back behind the
furnace, or under the eaves on the back porch. Now, when you need to tighten a loose screw
hiding in the shadows, you'll be happy we put a light on
the Craftsman rechargeable cordless power screwdriver.

CRAFTSMAN

MAKES ANYTHING POSSIBLE™

www.sears.com/craftsman

© 1998 Sears, Roebuck and Co.

EXHIBIT 19.3
Innovative Attributes

This Craftsman ad promotes an innovative attribute (a built-in flash-light) designed to make power screwdrivers easier to use in hard-to-see places.

Source: © Sears, Reobuck & Co.

Ideas can also be described as innovations. For example, social marketers have been active in persuading consumers to adopt such ideas as safe sex, smoke-free workplaces, and abstinence from drugs. In Third World countries social marketers have promoted ideas such as family planning, childhood immunization, and safer and more nutritious food-preparation practices.

Interestingly, in some cases new products are developed to help speed consumers' acceptance of ideas. For example, one new product called Baby Think It Over gives teenage girls a realistic glimpse at the responsibilities associated with having a child. The product is a cute, cuddly doll programmed to cry at random intervals throughout the day and night. The only way to stop the baby's crying is to hold and comfort it. Electronic monitors record whether the baby is abused or neglected.[4]

Finally, product attributes can be regarded as innovations. Frito-Lay is currently promoting a new potato chip made with Olean, Procter and Gamble's fat-free, calorie-free cooking oil. RC is promoting Diet RC with Splenda, a new alternative to aspartame.[5] Craftman's ad in Exhibit 19.3 is promoting an innovative product attribute—a power screwdriver with a built-in flashlight.

A second aspect of the definition of innovation is that products, services, attributes, packages, and ideas are innovations if they are *perceived as new by consumers*, whether they are actually new or not. Propecia, a new drug designed to reduce male baldness, is really the same drug that is sold as Proscar and used to treat prostate problems. However, consumers are not likely to know that the two drugs are the same.[6]

An innovation is also defined with respect to a market segment. To illustrate, although disco music has been around since the 1970s, it is currently popular in Poland and is perceived as innovative by Polish consumers.[7] Products like TVs and VCRs may be seen as new to consumers in Third World countries, even though we regard these items as near necessities.

Innovations bring about changes in consumption patterns. Some innovations change how, where, when, whether, or why we acquire products. For example, innovations like Internet shopping have altered the way we buy products. In the Netherlands, consumers can use a handheld scanning device to scan their own groceries while they shop.[8] This innovation changes the acquisition process.

Other innovations may change the way we use products or services. Microwave ovens have changed the way we cook, and e-mail has changed the way we communicate. Innovations like MP3s and Realjukebox affect where we listen to music (at our computers) and how much control we have over what we listen to and when. Disposable cameras have altered not only how often we buy a camera but also the way we process film.

Finally, some innovations influence disposition behavior. Ideas about recycling, for example, have brought about new product innovations in recyclable packaging materials and reusable containers. Can crushers, composters, and recycling centers were new products and services that affected consumers' disposition behaviors. Music recorded onto computers is likely to be disposed of quite differently from albums, CDs, and cassettes.

How Can Innovations Be Described?

We can classify innovations in several ways. One way is in terms of the type of innovation. The second is in terms of its breadth.

Types of Innovations   Innovations can be classified according to the degree of novelty, benefits offered, and the overall breadth of the innovation.

Types Based on Degree of Novelty   As Exhibit 19.3 indicates, one way to characterize innovations is to describe the degree of change they create in our consumption patterns.[9] A **continuous innovation** is one that has a limited effect on existing consumption patterns. We would use a continuous innovation in much the same way we used products that came before it. For example, Huggies has introduced new disposable swimming pants for toddlers who are not yet potty-trained. The product can be worn just like traditional diapers and plastic pants, but unlike traditional disposable diapers, the swimming pants won't "explode" when filled with water. The Braun ThermoScan EZ measures body temperature by placing an infrared scanning device inside the ear. Biore's Pore Perfect Cleansing Strips clean pores not with soap and water, but with strips that lift dirt from clogged pores. Perhaps not surprisingly, most of the new products on the market are continuous innovations.

A **dynamically continuous innovation** is one that has a pronounced effect on our consumption practices. Often these innovations incorporate a new technology (see Exhibit 19.4). Cellular phones are dynamically continuous innovations because they change the time and place in which we communicate with other people. The Realjukebox described in the opening vignette is a dynamically continuous innovation because it requires changes in the way we acquire, use, and dispose of music and may utilize other new technologies such as CD burners. Other examples of dynamically continuous innovations include electric cars, notebook computers, and digital cameras.

A **discontinuous innovation** is a product so new that we have never known anything like it before. For example, a former aeronautics professor has introduced a product called a "skycar"—a machine the flies through the air much like the cars on the TV cartoon *The Jetsons*. The skycar takes off and lands vertically and can fly at speeds up to 300 miles per hour.[10] Products like airplanes, automobiles, computers, televisions, and copy machines were all at one time discontinuous innovations. These innovations herald radical changes in consumer behavior.

Discontinuous and dynamically continuous innovations often spawn a host of peripheral products and associated innovations. For example, microwave ovens spawned the introduction of microwavable dishes and pans, as well as new recipes and new food products tailored to microwave cooking. They also fostered the development of products like probes and turntables. And they were responsible for renewed growth in categories whose products were compatible with microwave cooking practices, such as waxed paper and plastic wrap. Likewise, the computer

continuous innovation An innovation that has a limited effect on existing consumption patterns.

dynamically continuous innovation An innovation that that has a pronounced effect on consumption practices and often involves a new technology.

discontinuous innovation An offering that is so new that we have never known anything like it before.

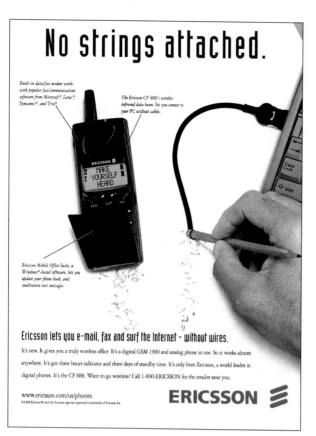

EXHIBIT 19.4

Example of Continuous Innovation and Dynamically Continuous Innovation

The new Ericsson cell phone is a continuous innovation because it does not require consumers to engage in behavior substantially different from that involved in using a regular cell phone. In contrast, the Canon PowerShot digital camera is a dynamically continuous innovation because it is used differently from a traditional camera. The PowerShot requires a television or personal computer and special software; a traditional camera does not.

Source: right: Courtesy of Ericsson; *left:* © 1999 Cannon U.S.A. Inc. "are you digital yet" and Power-Shot are trademarks of Cannon Inc.

has spawned innovations, including networked computers; computers with CD-ROM drives; notebook computers; multimedia PCs; and peripherals such as software, modems, acoustic speakers, sound cards, mouse pads, and tape backup devices.

Although we have identified three innovation types—continuous, dynamically continuous, and discontinuous, innovations are best characterized according to their *degree* of novelty on a continuum of newness. As Exhibit 19.5 indicates, the three types of innovations are best thought of as three of many possible points that characterize the continuum.

functional innovation
A new product, service, attribute or idea that proved utilitarian benefits different from or better than existing alternatives.

Types Based on Benefits Offered In addition to their degree of novelty, innovations can also be characterized by the benefits they offer. Some new products, services, attributes, or ideas are **functional innovations** because they offer functional performance benefits over existing alternatives. For example, portable fax machines offer functional performance benefits over stationary fax machines.

Often functional innovations rely on new technology that lets them perform better or do more than existing alternatives. For example, in Europe consumers can use advanced cellular phones to access flight arrival and departure schedules from the airlines, update bank balances, and even pay for a parking space or make a purchase from a vending machine. Consumers can even use the phone's speech recognition system to ask for the latest stock quotes or hear the latest weather report. Further technological advances have led industry insiders to predict that consumers will soon be able to download images from the Internet and conduct videoconferences via their cellular phones.[11] Exhibit 19.6 promotes GlaxcoWellcome's functional innovations in medicine.

aesthetic or hedonic innovation An innovation that appeals to our aesthetic, pleasure seeking, and/or sensory needs.

Aesthetic or hedonic innovations are new products, services, or ideas that appeal to our aesthetic, pleasure seeking, and/or sensory needs.[12] New forms of dance or exercise, new types of music, new clothing styles, and new types of food all qualify as aesthetic or hedonic innovations. Spinning classes, for example, are a novel way for consumers to exercise on stationary bicycles. New high-tech sleds are hedonic innovations designed to provide more thrilling yet safer rides to sled enthusiasts.

symbolic innovations A product, service, attribute or idea that has new social meaning.

Symbolic innovations are products, services, attributes, or ideas that have new social meaning. In some cases symbolic innovations include a new offering used exclusively by a particular group of consumers. Using the innovation, therefore, conveys meaning about group membership. For example, new styles of clothing that convey membership in a particular ethnic, age, or gender group may be regarded as symbolic innovations.

In some cases the product is not new, but rather the *meaning* associated with it is. For example, although condoms have been around for a long time, their meaning is now couched in terms of preventing the spread of AIDS as opposed

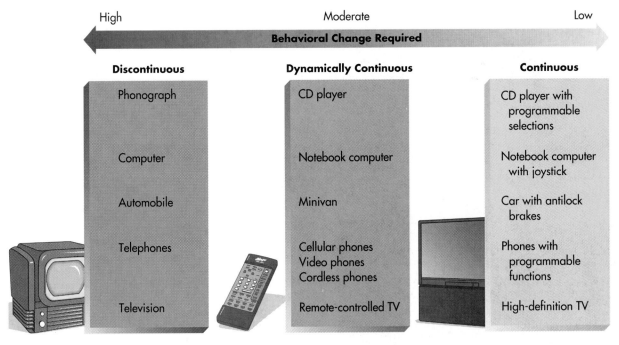

EXHIBIT 19.5
The Innovation Continuum

Innovations vary in how much behavioral change they require on the part of consumers. Discontinuous innovations (radically new products when they were first introduced) require considerable change in consumption patterns, whereas continuous innovations (often extensions of existing products) require very little change.

to controlling conception. Earrings, once worn by women, are fashionable with men as well. Beepers, once a functional innovation for doctors and other professionals, became a symbolic innovation for parents and teens. Finally, tattoos, once a symbol of machismo, have gained wide appeal and have different meaning among various consumer groups.

Many new products represent blends of innovation types. For example, nutrition bars are designed to offer functional benefits of protein and carbohydrates with good taste. A new product called the Pregnancy Survival Kit packages dresses, leggings, skirts, and tunics for the expectant mother. The benefits it offers in terms of comfort and style make it both a functional and a hedonic innovation.[13]

Breadth of Innovation   Breadth of innovation refers to the new and different uses to which a new product is put. Baking soda, for example, has enjoyed a long life in part because it has been used as a baking ingredient, a tooth polisher, a carpet deodorizer, and a refrigerator deodorizer. Teflon, a product originally designed to keep things from sticking to cookware, is now being used as an ingredient in men's suits. It helps to resist spills, and it retains its resistance through repeated washing and dry cleaning.[14]

ADOPTION OF INNOVATIONS AND RESISTANCE TO ADOPTION

Because the success of their new offerings is so important to companies, marketers are often interested in understanding consumers' decisions to adopt or buy an innovation. **Adoption** decisions therefore represent a continuation of the choice decisions we examined in Chapters 10 and 11. Initially, marketers are interested in whether consumers are even amenable to the idea of adopting an innovation. In some cases consumers resist adoption. If they do decide to adopt, marketers are interested in how they adopt products and how they decide whether to buy an innovation. Finally, marketers are interested in when, in relation to others, a consumer buys an innovation.

Are Consumers Willing to Adopt Innovations?

As much as marketers of new products may attempt to foster adoption, adoption will take place only if consumers do not resist the innovation. **Resistance** is consumers' desire *not* to buy the innovation, even in the face of pressure

adoption   A purchase of an innovation by an individual consumer or household.

resistance   A desire *not* to buy the innovation, even in the face of pressure to do so.

Allison lost the morning to a migraine. But a breakthrough medicine from Glaxo Wellcome gave her the afternoon with Christopher.

GlaxoWellcome
Breakthrough Medicines
For Everyday Living.

Asthma • Smoking Cessation • Allergy • Migraine • Depression • HIV • Cancer • Herpes • Epilepsy • Antibiotics

Talk to your doctor about Glaxo Wellcome products. www.glaxowellcome.com

EXHIBIT 19.6
A Functional Innovation

GlaxcoWellcome produces many innovative drugs designed to promote wellness.

Source: Reproduced with permission of Glaxo Wellcome Inc.

to do so.[15] Consumers sometimes resist adopting innovations because continuing to use a more familiar product or service seems simpler or preferable. For example, many consumers appear loathe to switch to Windows 2000 or adopt other high-tech replacement products for their PCs because they fear either that these new products will be too complicated and/or will offer little new that they can actually use.[16]

Resistance may also be high if consumers think that using the product involves some risk. For example, the practice of using ATMs was initially perceived to be risky, and many people resisted the idea of getting cash from them.[17] Similar concerns may underlie consumers' resistance to using credit cards to buy products over the Internet. Exhibit 19.7 shows that consumers often resist new technologies because, although they can create positive effects, they can also create negative effects. When consumers resist a technology, the perceived negative effects of the technology likely outweigh the positive effects.[18]

Note that resistance and adoption are separate concepts. First, an individual can experience resistance to purchasing an innovation without ever progressing to the point of adoption. Second, if an individual does adopt a product, he or she has presumably overcome any resistance that might have existed initially. Understanding whether, why, and when consumers resist innovations is important to marketers because if resistance is high, the product will not be successful. Marketers engage in a number of tactics designed to reduce consumers' resistance to an innovation. As you will see shortly, characteristics of the innovation, the social system in which consumers operate, and marketing tactics all influence consumers' resistance to innovations.

EXHIBIT 19.7

Eight Central Paradoxes of Technological Products

Consumers sometimes have mixed reactions to technologies because they create some of the paradoxes noted here. When the negative sides of these paradoxes are salient, consumers will likely resist an innovation.

Source: Mick, David Glen and Fournier, Susan, "Paradoxes of Technology: Consumer Cognizance, Emotions, and Coping Strategies," *Journal of Consumer Research*, 25, September 1998, p. 126. Used with permission from the University of Chicago Press.

PARADOX	DESCRIPTION
Control/chaos	Technology can facilitate regulation or order, and technology can lead to upheaval or disorder
Freedom/enslavement	Technology can facilitate independence or fewer restrictions, and technology can lead to dependence or more restrictions
New/obsolete	New technologies provide the user with the most recently developed benefits of scientific knowledge, and new technologies are already or soon to be outmoded as they reach the marketplace
Competence/incompetence	Technology can facilitate feelings of intelligence or efficacy, and technology can lead to feelings of ignorance or ineptitude
Efficiency/inefficiency	Technology can facilitate less effort or time spent in certain activities, and technology can lead to more effort or time in certain activities
Fulfills/creates needs	Technology can facilitate the fulfillment of needs or desires, and technology can lead to the development or awareness of needs or desires previously unrealized
Assimilation/isolation	Technology can facilitate human togetherness, and technology can lead to human separation
Engaging/disengaging	Technology can facilitate involvement, flow, or activity, and technology can lead to disconnection, disruption, or passivity

How Do Consumers Adopt Innovations?

If adoption does occur, it is sometimes useful to examine how it happens. Two models that characterize this process are the **high-effort hierarchy of effects** and the **low-effort hierarchy of effects**.

High-Effort Hierarchy of Effects   In some cases, after becoming aware of an innovation the consumer thinks carefully about the product, gathers as much information about it as possible, and forms an attitude based on this information. If his or her attitude is favorable, the consumer may try the product. If the trial experience is favorable, adoption may follow. This **high-effort hierarchy of effects** is illustrated in the top half of Exhibit 19.8 and corresponds to the high-effort attitude formation, search, and judgment and choice processes described in earlier chapters.

Consumers' motivation, ability, and opportunity determine whether a high-effort adoption process occurs. It often takes place when consumers think the innovation incurs psychological, social, economic, financial, or safety risk. For example, the consumer may think that wearing a new style of clothing is socially risky and will wait for others to make the first move. Or the consumer may consider carefully the benefits of buying a DVD player because of the high cost of changing one's entire collection of video tapes to DVDs.

Often a high-effort decision-making process is related to the type of innovation. Specifically, we might expect that a high-effort decision-making process is more likely when the innovation is discontinuous, as opposed to continuous, because consumers know less about the innovation and must learn about it. A high-effort adoption process also tends to be followed when many people make the adoption decision, as is the case in family or organizational decision-making contexts.[19]

Low-Effort Hierarchy of Effects   When the new product involves less risk (as might be the case with a continuous innovation) and when fewer people are involved in the buying process, decision making may follow the **low-effort hierarchy of effects** illustrated in the bottom half of Exhibit 19.8. Here consumers engage in trial after they become aware of the innovation. Less decision-making effort is given to the product before it is tried, and attitudes are based on this trial

high-effort hierarchy of effects   A purchase of an innovation based on considerable decision-making effort.

low-effort hierarchy of effects   A purchase of an innovation based on limited decision-making effort.

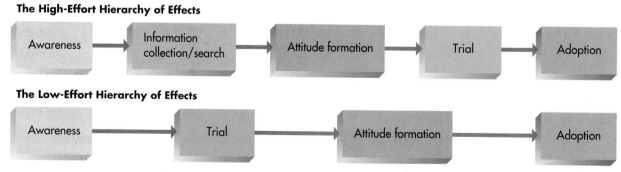

The High-Effort Hierarchy of Effects

Awareness → Information collection/search → Attitude formation → Trial → Adoption

The Low-Effort Hierarchy of Effects

Awareness → Trial → Attitude formation → Adoption

EXHIBIT 19.8
Adoption Decision Process

The amount of effort we engage in before we decide to adopt an innovation varies. In some cases we engage in considerable effort (e.g., extensive information search and evaluation of an offering). In other cases the adoption process involves limited effort. In such cases we first adopt the innovation and then decide whether we like it.

experience. Assuming attitudes are positive, adoption may follow. With a low-effort hierarchy of effects, the time between awareness of the innovation and its trial or adoption may be brief.

MARKETING IMPLICATIONS Understanding whether consumers' adoption decisions are based on a high- or low-effort adoption process has important implications for marketers. For example, if the adoption involves low effort, marketers need to do all they can to encourage trial because trial affects brand attitudes. To illustrate, when Procter & Gamble introduced Fat-Free Pringles, it distributed free samples of the product to lunchtime crowds in 20 major cities.[20]

If the adoption process is a high-effort one, marketers need to do all they can to reduce the perceived risk associated with the innovation. In the late 1970s, for example, one company developed a contact lens for chickens, designed to distort chickens' vision and reduce their tendencies to peck and cannibalize other chickens in the flock.[21] To chicken farmers, the use of this innovation entailed considerable economic risk—what if they paid for these lenses and the chickens cannibalized one another anyway?—as well as considerable social risk (what would other farmers think about someone who bought contact lenses for chickens?). If the economic risks associated with this product had been lowered (by means of a low price and money-back guarantees), if hard scientific data could have been presented on the efficacy of the product, and if opinion leaders could have advocated the product's use, the adoption rate might have been higher. ■

When Do Consumers Adopt Innovations?

A final issue about adoption is when a consumer decides to purchase an innovation relative to other consumers). Consumers differ in the timing of their adoption decisions. One scheme identifies five adopter groups, as indicated in Exhibit 19.9.[22] The first 2.5 percent of the market to adopt the innovation are described

EXHIBIT 19.9
Profile of Adopter Groups

Some researchers have identified five groups of consumers that differ in when they adopt an innovation relative to others. Innovators are the first in a market to adopt an innovation, and laggards are the last. Certain characteristics (e.g., venturesomeness) are associated with each adopter group.

Source: Adapted with the permission of The Free Press, a Division of Simon & Schuster, Inc., from *Diffusion of Innovations,* 3rd ed., by Everett M. Rogers. Copyright © 1962, 1971, 1983 by The Free Press.

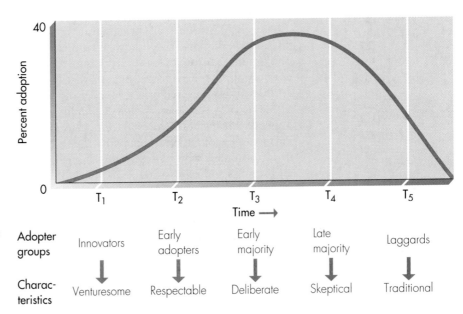

as *innovators*. The next 13.5 percent are called *early adopters*. The next 34 percent are called the *early majority*. The *late majority* represent the next 34 percent of adopters. The last 16 percent of the market to purchase the product are called *laggards*. Various characteristics have been linked to these adopter groups. For example, innovators have been characterized as venturesome, early adopters as respectable, early majority consumers as deliberate, late majority consumers as skeptical, and laggards as traditional.

Additional characteristics of these adopter groups have been found in studies of the adoption of high-tech products among organizations.[23] Innovators are technology enthusiasts. They appreciate technologically new products, they want to be the first to get them, and they are willing to live with bugs and deficiencies. Innovators represented the primary market for the WebTV developed and marketed in 1996. By the end of that year's holiday season, only 30,000 to 100,000 of the 97 million households with TVs had purchased WebTV.[24]

Early adopters are visionaries. They admire a technologically new product not so much for its features as for its abilities to create a revolutionary breakthrough in the way things are normally accomplished. Early adopters who are making buying decisions for the organization they work for want to see an order of magnitude return on their investment in this new technology. These individuals are not terribly concerned about price, and they are willing to serve as opinion leaders for products that do provide this revolutionary breakthrough.

As an example of early adopters, one research company has suggested that approximately 16 percent of U.S. households are TAFs—that is, technologically advanced families. These individuals want faster, newer, and more advanced products that help make home and work life more fun. Although they realize they are buying things that will be cheaper, faster, and easier to use in the future, they do not want to wait for these market changes. Technologically advanced families tend to be younger and better educated and to have more children than the average U.S. family.[25]

The early majority are pragmatists. They are looking for innovations that offer incremental, predictable improvements on an existing technology. They do not like risk, and hence they care deeply about who is making the innovation and the reputation of the company. They are interested in how well the innovation will fit into established technology systems, and they are concerned about the innovation's reliability. They are price sensitive, and they like to see competitors enter the market, because they can then compare features and be more assured about the product's ultimate feasibility. Competition also drives down the price of the innovation. Some evidence suggests that DVDs are catching on in the early majority market. Lowered prices, broader distribution of DVD players, wider acceptance by other consumers, and the ability to rent movies in DVD format from reputable mainstream stores like Blockbuster are partly responsible for their growing appeal among the early majority.[26]

Consumers who represent the late majority are conservatives. They are wary of progress and rely on tradition. They often fear high-tech products, and their goal in buying them is to not get stung. They like to buy preassembled products that include everything in a single, easy-to-use package. Consumers who are just now learning to use the Internet are late majority consumers. They are likely to place high value on bundled products that include everything they need (including connections with an Internet service provider) to connect to the Internet.

Laggards are skeptics. In the PC market consumers who have yet to buy a PC are likely to be regarded as laggards. In the area of office automation, laggards might point out that despite all the innovative products on the market, office productivity has not significantly increased over the years. Although laggards may resist innovations, much can be learned from understanding why they are skeptical of the innovation. Why, for example, has office automation *not* increased productivity? Is it because individuals now have more free time at work that they use as personal time? Or is it that the innovation is so advanced and complex that most users never learn to use it productively?

An important implication of this delineation of adopters into groups is that if an innovation is to spread through the market, it must appeal to every group. Unfortunately, many potentially useful innovations have never gained mass-market appeal because the marketing efforts for them did not acknowledge the characteristics of the adopter groups. For example, Prodigy, a software package for the IBM PC, was jointly developed by Sears and IBM. The product allowed users to connect to a nationwide computer network via modem and to perform a variety of activities such as shopping, consulting on-line encyclopedias, finding out about the weather and sports, and ordering airline tickets.

Although Prodigy featured a relatively new technology (hence it appealed to innovators) and promised a revolutionary way of getting information and ordering products (hence it appealed to early adopters), it did not gain widespread acceptance from the mass market because it did not fit with the early majority's mindset. First, few competitors were producing similar products, so the pragmatic early majority believed that the product was probably not going to make it. Because people rarely want to buy short-lived software, the early majority believed that buying the software was probably not a good idea. Moreover, the ads for Prodigy did not appeal to pragmatists. Rather than specifying how Prodigy would fit as an incremental improvement on current operations, the ads tried to create a vision of a new kind of world.[27] Such a strategy may encourage innovators, but not early adopters.

Some researchers have criticized the five-category scheme of adopter groups because it assumes these categories exist for all types of innovations. The critics say there may be more or fewer categories, depending on the innovation.[28] Also, the assumption that the number of consumers in the adopter categories forms a bell-shaped curve may not be true. For example, unlike the percentages that form the bell-shaped curve in Exhibit 19.9, for certain products it might be more accurate to define the first 1 percent of adopters as innovators, the next 60 percent as early adopters, the next 30 percent as the early majority, the following 5 percent as the late majority, and the last 4 percent as laggards.

Some researchers have rejected the definition of innovators as a certain percentage of people who have adopted a product just after it comes on the market. These researchers claim that innovators are instead those who make a decision to buy a new product at any time regardless of the decisions of others.[29] Often such consumers do buy the product soon after it comes to the marketplace, but they do so based on their own feelings, not on the opinions of others.

MARKETING IMPLICATIONS Regardless of whether we accept the five-category adopter scheme, we can recognize that those who are the first to buy a new product are important to marketers for several reasons. First, because innovators adopt innovations independently of the opinions of other people, they are more likely to be receptive to information about new products, including information provided by marketers. Second, by virtue of their experience with the innovation, they may also communicate information to others and thus influence the adoption decisions of others. Given these issues, a considerable amount of research has attempted to better understand who innovators are and how they can be reached. This knowledge helps marketers design their marketing communications and media selections.

Demographics. Several of the demographic variables described in Chapters 13 through 15 have been linked with the appeal of innovativeness.[30] For example, innovators tend to be younger and to have more income and education than other consumers. In contrast, laggards are older and have less income and education as well as lower occupational status. Religion has also been linked with innovativeness. The Amish, for example, avoid many forms of innovation, including cars, electricity, and telephones.

The fact that these demographic variables are linked with innovativeness makes sense. First, people who are highly educated tend to use the media more regularly and are therefore likely to learn about new products earlier than people who are less educated. Second, consumers with high incomes may have the discretionary income to purchase an innovation, and they may perceive less financial risk in association with its adoption. Demographic variables like culture of origin have also been linked with innovativeness. (Australians, for example, are regarded as innovators for new technology, and the Australian market has become a good one for launching new technologically oriented products and services, such as the cash card.[31]

Social Influence. Innovators have also been linked with the social influence factors discussed in Chapter 16.[32] They tend to have a great deal of social influence beyond their own immediate groups, and they tend to be opinion leaders. Although this finding has not been observed in all research, it makes sense that if innovators do influence non-adopters, it likely because their opinions are shared with and respected by non-adopters.

Personality. Several personality characteristics have also been linked with innovativeness.[33] For example, innovators are high in need for stimulation. They are inner directed and less dogmatic than other consumers. However, the relationships between personality traits and innovativeness are not very strong.[34] Innovators also differ from others in the way they make decisions; specifically, innovators do less planning and deliberate less than other consumers do.[35]

Some researchers have proposed that rather than measuring "innate innovativeness" (as a personality trait), a better approach is to examine how willing consumers are to be innovative in a specific consumption domain. For example, an innovator of rock music might respond positively to statements like "In general, I am among the first in my circle of friends to buy a new rock album when it appears" or "I know the names of new rock acts before other people do." Innovators in the area of fashion, however, might not respond similarly to these statements.[36]

 Cultural Values. Culture of origin and the values tied to culture have also been linked with innovativeness. One study of 11 European countries found that innovativeness was associated with cultures that value individualism over collectivism, those that value assertiveness over nurturing, and those that value openness to change over conservatism.[37]

Media Involvement. Other research has suggested that innovators are frequent users of the media and rely extensively on external information.[38] They tend to think of themselves as active seekers and disseminators of information.[39] This finding makes sense because to affect others' adoption decisions, innovators must not only get their information somewhere but also be willing to transmit it.

Usage. Finally, innovators may be heavy users within the product category.[40] Consumers who eat a lot of potato chips may be innovators of new fat-free chips because they are in the market often and hence are likely to notice these new products. In addition, innovators are usually experts in the product category, perhaps because of their usage and media involvement. ■

DIFFUSION

diffusion The percentage of the population that has adopted an innovation at a specific point in time.

As increasing numbers of consumers in a market adopt an innovation, we say that the innovation is spreading or diffusing through the market. Thus whereas adoption reflects the behavior of an individual, **diffusion** reflects the behavior of groups of consumers within a market. More specifically, diffusion reflects the percentage of the population that has adopted an innovation at a specific point in time. The diffusion of cell phones in various countries around the world for example, is quite varied. In the United States, for example, cell phones are used by 64 percent of the population; however, fewer than 1 percent use cell phones in Bangladesh (see Exhibit 19.10).[41]

Because marketers are interested in the success of their offering in a market, they want to know how quickly groups of consumers within the market adopt an innovation. Two important issues regarding diffusion are examined here. One is *how* an offering diffuses through the market; the other is *how fast* it does so.

How Do Offerings Diffuse Through a Market?

One way to examine how offerings spread through a market is to look at the pattern of adoption in the market over time. From the marketers' perspective, life would be easy if everyone adopted the new offering just as soon as it came out on the market. However, this situation does not always characterize the pattern of diffusion. In fact, several diffusion patterns have been identified.

S-shaped diffusion curve A diffusion curve characterized by slow initial growth followed by a rapid increase in diffusion.

The S-Shaped Diffusion Curve Some innovations exhibit an **S-shaped diffusion curve**, as illustrated in Exhibit 19.11a.[42] With this pattern, products at first spread through the market relatively slowly. For example, between time 1 and time 2, a relatively small percentage of the total market has adopted the product. After a certain period, however, the rate of adoption increases dramatically, with many consumers adopting the product within a relatively short period of time. Between times 2 and 3, a dramatic increase occurs in the number of consumers who have adopted the product. After that the rate of purchase increases at a decreasing rate, and the curve flattens out.

For example, the diffusion of microwave ovens was initially very slow. Then it increased dramatically as consumers became more aware of and knowledgeable about microwave technology and as more products compatible with microwave cooking (snacks, meals, cookware, and so forth) came on the market. Now there is general acceptance of the microwave,

EXHIBIT 19.10
Diffusion of Cell Phones

Cell phones have diffused widely through the U.S. market; however, their diffusion is just beginning in Third World countries like Bangladesh.

Source: AP/Wide World Photos.

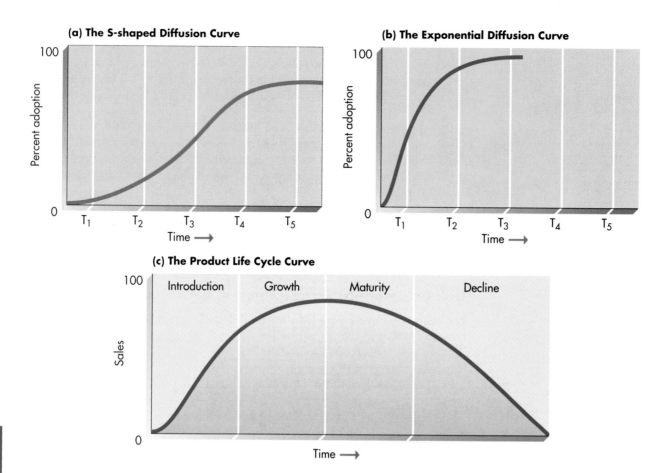

EXHIBIT 19.11
Diffusion and Product Life Cycle Curves

Several diffusion patterns have been identified. (a) With an *S-shaped diffusion curve*, diffusion starts out slowly, increases rapidly, and then flattens out again. (b) With an *exponential diffusion curve*, many people adopt the innovation quickly. (c) The product life cycle curve depicts *sales* (not cumulative diffusion) of an offering over time.

and many consumers have one in their house or workplace. Thus the diffusion rate has again slowed.

exponential diffusion curve
A diffusion curve characterized by rapid initial growth.

The Exponential Diffusion Curve   Another type of adoption curve is the **exponential diffusion curve**, illustrated in Exhibit 19.11b.[43] In contrast to the S-shaped curve, the exponential diffusion curve starts out much more quickly, with a large percentage of the market purchasing the product as soon as it is available. However, with each additional time period, the rate of adoption increases at a decreasing rate.

What Affects the Shape of the Diffusion Curve?

Many factors influence the ultimate shape of the diffusion curve. In general, we might expect an S-shaped diffusion curve under conditions in which there is some social, psychological, economic, performance, or physical risk is associated with the innovation. That is, before deciding to adopt the innovation, consumers might wait to see how other people use and react to it. Diffusion may also be slow initially if consumers are not sure whether the product will be on the market for a long period of time or whether its use carries high switching costs. The diffusion of computers and CD players followed this S-shaped curve. An S-shaped diffusion pattern might also occur when consumers are physically far apart, do not talk to one another about the innovation, or do not hold the same beliefs.

In contrast, when the innovation involves little risk, when switching costs are low, when consumers are similar in their beliefs and values, and when they talk often about the product and hence quickly disseminate knowledge throughout the social system, a rapid takeoff period may ensue, and an exponential curve may characterize the diffusion process. Note that these curves reflect only the *rate* at which consumers in the market adopt, not the *time period* under analysis. In other words, either an S-shaped or an exponential curve could reflect diffusion that has occurred over a 1-year or a 30-year period. Furthermore, the curves could reflect the diffusion of either a functional, symbolic, or hedonic innovation.

How Does Diffusion Relate to the Product Life Cycle?

product life cycle A concept that suggests that products go through an initial introductory period followed by periods of sales growth, maturity, and decline.

The **product life cycle** concept is illustrated in Exhibit 19.11c. This concept proposes that products initially go through a period of introduction, followed by relatively rapid growth as more competitors enter the market and consumer acceptance of the product increases. As competition increases, weaker competitors drop out of the market and product sales tend to stabilize. At some point, however, consumer acceptance of the product wanes, and product sales decline.

Product diffusion and the product life cycle are related but different concepts. First, diffusion focuses on the *percentage of the market* that has adopted the product. Complete diffusion is evidenced when 100 percent of the market has purchased the product. The product life cycle, on the other hand, deals with *sales* of the product over time. Second, diffusion curves are generally cumulative—that is, they continue to increase or at least level off over time. However, the product life cycle curve may decline as consumers decide not to purchase the product on future occasions. Thus although an innovation such as the rotary-dial telephone may have diffused through an entire market, it was replaced by another innovation, the touch-tone phone; thus sales of the old product eventually declined as the new innovation took hold.

MARKETING IMPLICATIONS Marketers who understand a product's life cycle can try to prevent that product's decline—perhaps by finding new uses for it. For example, nylon has enjoyed a long life cycle given the myriad uses to which it has been put since its introduction in the 1940s—as an ingredient in clothing, rope, fishing lines, and so on. Currently, marketers of products aimed at the defense industry are attempting to keep their products alive by finding applications in the consumer arena of virtual reality. To the extent that marketers develop new uses for a product or encourage **use innovativeness**, they can lengthen their product's life cycle.

use innovativeness The extent to which an old product is put to new uses.

fad A successful innovation that has a very short product life cycle.

Marketers can also try to diagnose the likely life cycle pattern of their offering. Just as diffusion curves differ, so too are there different product life cycle curves. A **fad** is a successful innovation that has a very short product life cycle. Beanie Babies, Pokemon cards, wide-leg pants, spinning, Tae-Bo, and certain diets are other examples of fads. Exhibit 19.12 shows another fad.

EXHIBIT 19.12
Fads

Examples of fads, including this one, abound. Can you think of other fads.
Source: Margaret Ross/Stock Boston.

A **fashion** or trend is a successful innovation with a lengthier and potentially cyclical life. For example, certain aesthetic styles like art deco run in fashion cycles, as do certain styles of clothing like cargo pants, twin sets, fur, and platform shoes. Some types of foods, like Thai or Mexican, run in fashion cycles, as do certain consumption practices (e.g., breast versus bottle-feeding infants).

Finally, a **classic** is a successful innovation that has a lengthy product life cycle. Jeans are a U.S. classic. Others include rock and roll music, Coke, and hamburgers.

Although the terms *fad*, *fashion*, and *classic* have most often been applied to aesthetic or hedonic innovations, they can also describe functional and symbolic innovations because the life cycle of these innovations can be similarly variable. ■

fashion   A successful innovation that has a moderately long and potentially cyclical product life cycle.

classic   A successful innovation that has a lengthy product life cycle.

WHAT INFLUENCES ADOPTION, RESISTANCE, AND DIFFUSION?

Because innovations may diffuse quickly or slowly through a market and because the success of a new product depends on how many people within the market adopt it, marketing managers need to understand what affects resistance, adoption, and diffusion. Exhibit 19.2 identified a number of factors, including aspects of the innovation itself and of the social system into which it is introduced. These factors have important marketing implications.

Characteristics of the Innovation

Several characteristics of the innovation affect resistance, adoption, and diffusion.

Perceived Value   An innovation is perceived to have value if it offers greater benefits or lower costs than existing alternatives.

relative advantage
Benefits in an innovation superior to those found in existing products.

Perceived Benefits   An innovation's value to consumers is affected by its perceived **relative advantage**—that is, the extent to which it offers benefits superior to those found in existing products. For example, digital phones like those in Europe that allow consumers to charge services to their cellular phone bill offer an advantage of convenience that traditional cellular phones lack.[44] New, "smart" cars have things like navigational systems that pinpoint your location and alarms that sound at the first sign of sleepiness, they also have cruise control that uses radar to gauge and automatically adjust your speed based on the speed of a slower vehicle ahead.[45] Advances on the horizon will allow ATM consumers to cash checks down to the penny; deposit checks without a deposit envelope; and buy travelers checks, plane tickets, and theater tickets—things that cannot be done with traditional ATM cards.[46]

A product or service offers a relative advantage if it can help consumers avoid risks, fulfill their needs, or achieve their goals and values. Thus the relative advantages of a product should serve as decision criteria that affect consumers' adoption decisions. Note that a relative advantage is something the product does for the consumer—not something that exists in the product. Thus smart cars' relative advantage lies not in their new product features, but in the safety they provide to the driver and passengers. The ad in Exhibit 19.13 emphasizes the advantage to shopping via landsend.com. As the ad states, "Shopping online beats standing in line." The idea is that catalog and on-line shopping is better, more direct, and more convenient than going to the mall and waiting to be served.

Note also that many new products have advantages over existing ones, but if consumers do not perceive the advantage or do not think it is important, the innovation will have little impact on their purchase.

Perceived Costs Another aspect of the value of the product is its perceived cost. The consumer may perceive two types of costs. One is the actual purchase cost. The higher the purchase cost, the greater the resistance and hence the slower the diffusion. Because smart cars offer a number of unique features, these vehicles are likely to cost more than other cars. If consumers perceive the cost to be significantly greater, adoption could lessen and diffusion could slow. In contrast, technological advances in light-sensor chips are allowing manufacturers to produce a cheaper digital camera—a phenomenon that will surely speed its diffusion. [47]

Another aspect of cost is switching costs—or the cost involved in changing from the current product to a new one. Switching costs for a new smart car would include the cost of selling your old car, for instance, placing ads, and any purchase costs beyond the sticker price, such as registration fees, higher insurance premiums, and so on.

MARKETING IMPLICATIONS If the innovation is not perceived to have a relative advantage, marketers may need to add one by physically redesigning or reengineering the innovation.

Communicate and Demonstrate the Relative Advantage. When consumers do not understand what a product is, or what its relative advantages are, education efforts are in order. The slow diffusion of WebTV was partly due to the fact that consumers didn't really understand the product, let alone why they should buy it.[48] Unfortunately, advertising failed to do a good job in this regard. In contrast, GM recently spent $25 million in California and Arizona alone to communicate and demonstrate the advantages of its EV1 electric car.[49] Union Carbide once demonstrated a new superinsulation product by using a dramatic advertisement. First, a baby chick was placed in a box lined with the material. Then the box with the chick in it was placed in a pot of boiling water for more than a minute. Given the product's high quality, the chick came out of the box completely unharmed. Marketers might also use a highly credible and visible opinion leader who can convincingly communicate the innovation's advantage.

EXHIBIT 19.13
Relative Advantage

Innovations are more likely to be adopted when their relative advantages are clear. This ad emphasizes the advantages of shopping at landsend.com.

Source: Reproduced with permission of Lands' End, Inc.

Shopping **online** beats standing **in line**.

From catalog to the web, the store is yours:
www.landsend.com/1-800-864-2896

Use Price Promotions to Reduce Perceived Costs. If the product is perceived to cost too much, special price-oriented sales promotions—price-offs, rebates, or refunds like the one in Exhibit 19.14—can reduce the product's perceived cost. Marketers can also provide guarantees or warranties that make the product seem less expensive. Alternatively, the marketer may find a cheaper way to manufacture the product and simply pass on the manufacturing savings as cost savings to the consumer. Marketers of digital watches adopted the latter strategy.

Provide Incentives for Switching. If innovations are not adopted because consumers think switching costs are high, marketers might provide incentives for switching. For example, companies like MCI offer incentives such as price discounts for consumers who switch from other long-distance carriers. Advertising might also inform consumers about the costs associated with not switching. For example, manufacturers of DVD players might describe the cost savings one can achieve by transforming one's current video collection into DVDs now, as compared with several years from now when one is likely to have a much larger inventory of videos to be replaced.

Finally, marketers might be able to force their product variant to become the industry standard, for instance, by having exceptionally high quality, great ease of use, or low price. In essence, Macintosh achieved this effect by forcing IBM machines to adopt a Macintosh-like operating system, Windows. ■

Uncertainty

A second general factor that affects adoption, resistance, and diffusion is the uncertainty of the innovation. Two aspects of uncertainty are important. One is doubt about what will become the standard product in the industry. For example, many consumers were reluctant to purchase VCRs because they were not sure whether the VHS or beta format would become the industry standard. The same is true regarding DVDs versus VCRs. MP3's popularity has currently made it an industry standard for compressing music.

A second aspect of uncertainty is the length of the product life cycle. If consumers think the product might be a fad, they are likely to feel more resistance than if they think it will become a fashion or a classic. For example, you may forgo spending $80 on platform shoes if you don't believe that they will be in style for a reasonable length of time. In clothing and high-tech markets where product improvements operate on a very short time frame, concern over life cycle length is often quite legitimate.

MARKETING IMPLICATIONS *Show Product Adaptability.* When consumers resist innovations because they are worried about a short life cycle, marketers might show how adaptable the product is and hence how likely it is to have a long life cycle. For example, marketers of computers can ease the fears of many consumers who do not really know what they will do with a computer or why they need one by demonstrating all the applications that can make their lives easier or more fun—using the Internet for shopping, booking airline tickets, and doing research, for example; playing games; and balancing their checkbooks. ■

Consumer Learning Requirements

A third characteristic affecting resistance, adoption, and diffusion is consumer learning requirements—or what consumers need to do to effectively use the innovation.

compatibility The extent to which the innovation or its usage is consistent with consumer values, norms, and behaviors.

Compatibility The more **compatible** the innovation is with consumers' values, norms, and behaviors, the less the resistance and the greater the diffusion. Products like the Clipfone 6300, a tiny cordless phone that clips onto a belt or lapel, and the tiny Elph Camera (that fits in a pocket) are compatible with consumers' desires to carry phones and cameras unencumbered. Motorola's two-way radio is easy to use and compatible with consumers' desires to stay in contact with family members and friends while on outings.[50]

We can evaluate other innovations according to how compatible they are with consumers' needs, values, goals, and behaviors. Yahoo!'s search engine and Amazon's search function, for example, are compatible with the way consumers search for information. In Russia the Polaroid camera has been quite successful, in part because the product's capability to make a picture without using a negative or requiring an outside source for developing the film is compatible with consumers' general suspicions about having more than one copy of a picture available.[51]

Some potentially serious consequences can arise when an innovation is not compatible with consumers' values, goals, and behaviors. One case in particular is marketers' attempts to encourage bottle-feeding by mothers in the Third World countries of Latin America, Africa, and Asia. Manufacturers' ads showed pictures of beautiful, fat, healthy babies with their mothers. The ad copy read, "Give your baby love and Lactogen." (Lactogen is an infant formula.) The ad, which had a modern flavor, was attractive to upper-income, well-educated consumers. It was also attractive to peasant families who aspired to be like the well educated. Unfortunately, most peasant families could not afford the expensive formula, so they diluted it with water, leaving their babies malnourished. Furthermore, they were unused to practices like sterilizing nipples and bottles, so the baby bottles became a haven for bacteria, which made the babies sick. The lack of compatibility between the innovation and the consumers' way of using it therefore caused problems in the ultimate success of the innovation.[52]

Lack of compatibility may also explain consumers' resistance to electric cars. Marketers who are testing such cars in Germany are finding that although the cars are compatible with German consumers' values promoting environmental friendliness, these vehicles are also slow, cannot climb hills quickly, and cannot travel for long distances before needing to be plugged in again. Thus they lack compatibility with consumers' needs for reliable, fast transportation.[53]

trialability The extent to which an innovation can be tried on a limited basis before it is adopted.

Trialability A second aspect of consumer learning requirements is the **trialability** of the innovation, or the extent to which the product can be tried on a limited basis before it is adopted. Products like the Palm Pilot are very trialable. The potential user can quickly learn the product's capabilities to make appointments, keep a phone book, and create to-do lists just by playing with it for a few minutes. Trial of other innovations, for example, new forms of breast implants, are virtually impossible. Because trial allows a consumer to see the product's relative advantages and assess the potential risks associated with purchase, products that are easy to try tend to diffuse through the market more quickly than those that do not lend themselves to trial.

Some research has found that the amount of importance placed on trialability depends on the type of adopter. For people who tend to adopt early, trialability may be very important because they have little else on which to base the value of the innovation. Trialability may be less important for later adopters, who are likely to know many people who have already adopted the innovation and who can therefore speak to its efficacy.[54]

Complexity A final product characteristic that affects how much consumers have to learn about an innovation is its complexity. The more difficult consumers think it is to understand or use the new product, the slower the diffusion. Some products, computers, for example, were perceived to be very complex, and hence they have had a slow diffusion rate. One man has developed an entirely new form of musical notation that eliminates traditional symbols such as treble clefs, flats, and sharps. Music is laid out on two stacked staffs, the top one of which has seven lines and six spaces and the bottom one of which has eight lines and seven spaces. Five new letters are added (Z, R, O, I and U). Although this system may be better than the one that has been around since the 13th century, existing musicians are likely to perceive it as complex. Adoption will be difficult and diffusion slow.[55] Other products, for example, Motorola's two-way radio, diffuse quickly, in part because they are so easy to use.

MARKETING IMPLICATIONS Marketers can use several tactics to reduce consumers' resistance to innovations.

Enhance Compatibility or Reduce Complexity. Consumers often resist innovations because they see them as incompatible with their needs, values, norms, or behaviors.[56] Sometimes compatibility can be enhanced simply by repositioning the innovation so that it appears to be more consistent with consumers' needs and values. Campbell's soup was able to enjoy new popularity when it was repositioned away from taste and toward nutrition and low calories.[57] Sometimes, however, product redesign is necessary to overcome compatibility and complexity. For example, because camcorders were initially too complex for the average user, companies like Sharp and Matsushita developed simpler, more user-friendly products.[58]

Educate About Compatibility. Advertising and promotion can also educate the market about how compatible the innovation really is with their needs, values, norms or behaviors. For example, in Third World countries consumers are not used to modern medicine and the techniques used to avoid many dreaded diseases. Organizations like the World Health Organization have dealt with this situation in part with educational programs that teach consumers the value of vaccinations and the procedures that can stop disorders like diarrhea.[59] Advertising can also show that although the offering calls for new behaviors, it is easier to use than current alternatives.

Use Change Agents.   Another marketing tactic aimed at enhancing perceived compatibility is to use change agents, such as opinion leaders (see Chapter 16). Marketers in such diverse fields as farming equipment, medicine, and computers have found it useful to target new products to influential and highly respected people who can be convinced of the product's merits and who can be counted on to spread positive word of mouth to others.[60]

Make the Product Fit with a System of Products.   Another way of avoiding incompatibility is to design the innovation to fit with a system of existing products. For example, the Palm Pilot has done well in part because users can transfer data between their Palm Pilot and their personal computer. They can also download programs and games from the Internet for use on the Palm Pilot.[61] Dishwashers did not fit into kitchens until builders built spaces and plumbing for them. Likewise, consumers are unlikely to adopt trash compactors because most kitchens do not have a ready-made space for them. By working with builders so that the products fit into the kitchen, makers of trash compactors can resolve this problem.

Force the Innovation to Be the Industry Standard.   Marketers can work with regulators to force the innovation to be used. For example, the use of smoke detectors, seat belts, and lead-free gasoline are all innovations that have been forced into usage by government mandate. A similar phenomenon may happen with electric cars. Car manufacturers' interest in electric cars has surged because clean-air mandates in several states require zero-emission vehicles.[62]

Use Promotions to Enhance Trialability.   Trialability problems can be overcome by advertising and promotion tactics. For example, free samples often encourage trial use by people who might otherwise be resistant to using the product. The makers of NutraSweet overcame potential trialability problems by sending millions of consumers free samples of gumballs that contained NutraSweet. This approach was important because NutraSweet is an ingredient in other products and by itself could not be tried.

Demonstrate Compatibility and Simplicity.   Demonstrations, either live or presented in advertising, can show how compatible the product is with existing needs, values, and behaviors and how simple it is to use. The Shower Massage, a product that does not lend itself well to prepurchase trial, uses extensive advertising that show consumers who seem to enjoy using the product.

Another way of enhancing trial is to use high-service outlets where salespeople can either provide demonstrations or discuss the benefits of using the product. Special promotions might also enhance trialability. Macintosh, for example, once held a special promotion called "Take a Mac for a Test Drive." The promotion encouraged consumers to take a Macintosh computer home with them over the weekend to try it out. Thus the marketers created a trial experience for a product that is generally not easily tried.

Simulate Trial.   A final way in which to enhance consumer's opportunities to try innovations is to simulate trial. For example, some hair salons offer computer systems that allow consumers to actually see what they will look like with different hair colors and styles. New innovations in virtual reality may also provide marketers with ways of simulating trial.

Reduce Complexity Through Product Redesign.   Sometimes the product can be changed to make it less complex. Universal remotes that allow for ready programming of VCRs, for example, are aimed at reducing product complexity. VCRs themselves have undergone fairly extensive changes to counter the popular view that they were too difficult to operate. Likewise, "dummy proof" 35mm cameras now allow novice consumers to take high-quality pictures once obtainable only by expert photographers. ■

Social Relevance

A fourth major factor that affects resistance, adoption, and diffusion is the innovation's **social relevance**. Social relevance has two dimensions: observability and social value.

Observability   Observability is the extent to which the innovation is observable to others. In general, the more consumers can observe others using the innovation, the more likely they are to adopt it.[63] Consumers are also more likely to learn about the existence of new products and their potential benefits when the products are visibly consumed by others. For example, a new shoulder strap designed to distribute the weight of a golf bag has gained some acceptance among caddies who can see others using this product.[64] On the other hand, a new scale that announces your body weight is unlikely to be very observable because few people are anxious to weigh themselves in public (or to want others to hear their weight!).[65] Thus diffusion should also be affected by the public or private nature of the product as we described in Chapter 16.

Social Value   Social value, the second aspect of social relevance, reflects the extent to which the product has *social cachet*, which means that it is seen as socially desirable and/or appropriate and therefore generates imitation. One study found that farmers adopted certain farming innovations because they were very expensive and thus had social prestige value. These studies also found that the earlier someone adopted the innovation, the more prestige was associated with it.[66] Aesthetic innovations like new fashions, new hairstyles, new cars, and so on are sometimes adopted solely on the basis of the social prestige their usage confers on the user. Thus the greater the innovation's social value, the faster its diffusion.

Observability and social value both help explain the growing popularity of knee-length socks for basketball players. It began because basketball stars like Seattle Supersonic Moochie Norris and Laker Michael Cooper started wearing them at basketball games. The products are very observable, and their use by sports stars gives them social cachet.[67]

Interestingly, although a product's social value may enhance its diffusion, the diffusion of a product based on a prestige image may actually shorten its life cycle because the adoption of the product by the masses reduces its prestige value. For example, designer jeans, once associated with prestige and exclusivity, lost prestige when everyone in the market started to wear them.[68]

MARKETING IMPLICATIONS   Extensive advertising, promotions, and distribution can be used to overcome problems associated with observability. Observability can also be enhanced by the use of distinctive packaging, styling, and color or unique promotions.[69] Thus many of the techniques discussed in Chapter 4 for enhancing attention and perception may enhance observability. Associating the product with a well-known person or developing ads to suggest that the consumer will be socially rewarded for using the product may also enhance observability. The social relevance of an innovation can be heightened by means of advertising, particularly advertising that ties product use with potential social approval. Finally, social value can be enhanced by associating the product with some social entity, cause, or value. Having a new beverage serve as the official drink of the Olympic team may enhance that beverage's social value. ■

Legitimacy and Adaptability

legitimacy The extent to which the innovation follows established guidelines for what seems appropriate in the category.

adaptability The extent to which the innovation can foster new styles.

Legitimacy and **adaptability** are two additional factors that influence resistance, adoption, and diffusion, particularly for symbolic and aesthetic innovations.[70] Legitimacy refers to the extent to which the innovation follows established guidelines for what seems appropriate in the category. An innovation that is too radical or that does not derive from a legitimate precursor lacks legitimacy. For example, it took the public a long time to accept modern art because it violated the traditions of classical art. Rock and roll and later rap music were seen as deviant forms of music when they were first introduced. Part of the success of artists like k. d. lang stemmed from their ability to blend two legitimate music styles (country and rock) into something that still was new.

The final factor affecting resistance, adoption, and diffusion is adaptability,[71] or the innovation's potential to fit in with existing products or styles. For example, certain forms of fashion or furniture may be seen as highly adaptable because they can be made to fit with a variety of other fashion or furniture trends. Some functional products, computers, for example, have high adaptability because they can perform various functions. Rock music has proven to be very adaptable as variants from soft rock to acid rock have emerged.

MARKETING IMPLICATIONS Legitimacy might be enhanced by demonstrating how the innovation came into being. For example, acupuncture may be legitimized by showing the history of the practice in China and its widespread use today. Finally, if the product is seen as lacking adaptability, marketers can show that it has uses extending beyond its original function. For example, the makers of cranberry sauce ask consumers to consider uses for their product other than simply as a condiment for Thanksgiving dinner.[72] ■

Characteristics of the Social System

Innovations diffuse rapidly or slowly in part because of their own characteristics and in part because of the characteristics of the social system into which they are introduced (see Exhibit 19.2). Both the kinds of people who represent the target market for the innovation and the nature of the relationships among the people in the social system affect the innovation's acceptance in a market.

modernity The extent to which consumers in the social system have positive attitudes toward change.

Modernity Resistance, adoption, and diffusion are affected by the **modernity** of the social system. Modern systems are those that have a positive attitude toward change. They value science, technology, and education and are technologically oriented in terms of both the products produced and the skill of the labor force.[73] The receptivity of consumers toward change, science, and technology is illustrated by the Du Pont ad in Exhibit 19.15. Consumers will easily believe that clothing made with the Du Pont fiber system will enable them to work, play, and relax in subzero temperatures. The more modern the social system, the more receptive consumers are to new products.

homophily The overall similarity among members in the social system.

Homophily A second general characteristic of the social system is **homophily**, or the overall similarity among members of the system. The more similar the

market is in terms of things like education, values, needs, and income, the faster the diffusion process.[74] Several factors explain this connection. First, the more similar peoples' backgrounds are, the more likely they are to have similar needs, values, and preferences. Second, similar people are more likely to interact with one another and transmit information. Third, similar people tend to model each other. In addition, normative influence is likely to be higher as homophily increases. Normative pressures toward adopting the innovation may speed adoption and diffusion.

Physical Distance   A third characteristic of the social system is the physical distance between its members. When members of the social system are spread apart, diffusion tends to be slower. Some marketers in Japan have found that high school girls excel at setting trends. No doubt this ability is due to the physical and emotional proximity of girls and their tendency to talk about new products they have seen.[75] Likewise, we might find slower diffusion of an innovation when consumers are in physically separated rather than physically contiguous cities, states, or countries.[76]

Opinion Leadership   A final characteristic of the social system that affects adoption and resistance is the key influencers in the diffusion process. Chapter 16 mentioned that certain people, for example, experts or opinion leaders, can have considerable influence on adoption and diffusion because they may spread credible positive or negative product information to a wide array of people.[77] For example, *US* magazine often features famous celebrity opinion leaders sporting new products juxtaposed with pictures of ordinary readers emulating them. One study that examined the diffusion of information about family-planning practices among women in a Korean village found that opinion leaders were very important sources of information. Not only was the information communicated by these women important, but the opinion leaders served as bridges connecting spatially related but separate cliques in the village.[78]

MARKETING IMPLICATIONS Marketing efforts can affect resistance, adoption, and diffusion by affecting the social system. For example, if the target market is heterogeneous, it may be necessary to use targeted marketing communications that show the product's relevance to consumers' unique needs, values, or norms and to use specialized (target-market-specific) media to reach them.

Marketers might also identify those who have not adopted the innovation. One researcher noted that nonadopters can be divided into several groups with very different characteristics. One group consists of passive consumers who have tried the product but are unlikely to provide much information to others about it. A second is active rejectors who have tried the product but are likely to provide unfavorable word of mouth to others. The third is potential adopters who have not yet tried the product but who may be influenced by active rejectors, active acceptors, or marketers.

Because even a small group can have a big impact on others' adoption decisions, it may be useful to specifically target some of these groups. Potential adopters may not be adopting the product because of lack of awareness. For them, advertising may enhance adoption. Product improvements may, however, be necessary for active rejectors. Thus different marketing strategies may be appropriate for different adopter groups.[79]

Marketing tactics may also affect the nature and extent of word-of-mouth communication. For example, targeting opinion leaders can facilitate word of mouth flows about the new product. Promotions that encourage consumers to "tell a friend about us" also aim at stimulating word of mouth. Promotions that target the network, rather than the consumer, might also be an effective way of speeding diffusion. Having the press describe the attributes and benefits of the innovation is generally regarded as providing more credibility than doing the same thing through advertising. Special events like trade shows are also ways of showcasing a product, demonstrating its features, and stimulating positive word of mouth.

If consumers are spreading negative word of mouth, marketing efforts must either (1) correct the problem so that word of mouth will become positive or (2) counteract negative information with advertising and personal selling. For example, advertising might use a two-sided message that not only recognizes the potentially bad outcomes associated with the product but also notes improvements that preclude the negative outcome.[80]

Because the elements of the marketing mix can influence diffusion by their effects on both the innovation and the social system, it is not surprising that the more intensive the marketing effort—the advertising, sales promotion, personal selling, and distribution—the faster the innovation spreads through a market.[81] ■

THE CONSEQUENCES OF INNOVATIONS

Although innovations often offer relative advantages that may not have previously existed, they are not always good from the standpoint of society. Several studies have suggested that negative social and economic consequences can arise from the diffusion of an innovation.

 One study examined the diffusion of the steel ax among a tribe of aborigines who lived in the Australian bush.[82] Before the innovation was introduced, the stone ax had served as the tribe's principal tool. It was used only by men and was awarded to them as a gift and as payment for work performed. It was generally regarded as a symbol of masculinity and respect. However, missionaries came into the social system with the steel ax and distributed it to men, women, and children. This distribution scheme disrupted the sex and age roles among tribal members and thus affected the social system.

Other innovations can have mixed consequences. For example, Monsanto has developed a new product derived from a natural pituitary hormone in cows that is designed to enhance their milk production. Although this product might yield more milk and make cow farmers richer, some consumers fear that it might be harmful to cows and even put small milk farmers out of business.[83]

Innovations can also have negative socioeconomic consequences. For example, one study examined the diffusion of the CAT scanner through the medical community. This innovation had two important sociological consequences. First, it tended to diffuse to markets that were generally wealthy, leaving the technology unavailable to families who lived in poorer rural areas. Second, the innovation was expensive and was viewed as driving up health care costs.[84]

Thus although innovations may often be advantageous to individuals, some unanticipated social and economic consequences may arise from their diffusion. We should therefore be careful to avoid adopting a universally pro-innovation bias.

SUMMARY

Innovations are products, services, ideas, or attributes that consumers in a market segment perceive to be new. Innovations can be characterized as functional, symbolic, or hedonic. They also vary in the degree of behavioral change their adoption requires. Innovativeness in products ranges along a continuum from continuous to discontinuous.

Innovations may represent fads, fashions, or classics and hence may exhibit a short, moderate, or long life cycle. Marketers can extend a product's life cycle by enhancing the breadth of the innovation and by encouraging consumers to find innovative uses for familiar products.

Strategies for marketers of innovations include breaking down consumers' resistance to innovations, facilitating consumers' adoption of the innovation, and affecting the diffusion of the innovation through the marketplace. A high-effort as opposed to low-effort hierarchy-of-effects adoption process occurs when the innovation is seen as economically, physically, socially, or psychologically risky. Some individuals, called innovators, adopt products independently of the decisions of others. Special marketing efforts may be geared toward innovators because their adoption directly or indirectly influences adoption by other consumers through word of mouth or social modeling. Characteristics of the innovation and the social system in which it is introduced affect resistance, adoption, and diffusion. Overcoming resistance is easiest when the innovation is perceived to provide value such as a relative advantage, low price, or low switching costs. Resistance is also more likely to be overcome when minimal versus extensive consumer learning is required, and when the product is highly compatible with existing needs, values, and behaviors; easy to try; easy to use; and low risk. Innovations viewed as high in social relevance, legitimacy, and adaptability also encounter less consumer resistance than those regarded as low in social relevance, legitimacy and/or adaptability. Marketers' actions can also affect consumers' perceptions of the characteristics of the innovation.

The characteristics of the social system in which the innovation operates also affect resistance, adoption, and diffusion. The more dense the social network and the more homophilous the social system, the more likely it is that information will be transmitted from adopters to nonadopters. This information transmission may directly affect the likelihood of adoption.

EXERCISES

1. Read several publications like *BusinessWeek*, *Fortune*, or the *Wall Street Journal* and identify two innovative products and/or services.
   a. Why are these offerings innovations? (Relate your answers to the chapter's definition of an innovation.)
   b. What type of innovations are they—continuous, dynamically continuous, discontinuous? functional, aesthetic, symbolic?
   c. Describe whether you think adoption of, resistance to, and diffusion of these offerings will be fast or slow by using concepts associated with the innovations, such as relative advantage, observability, and legitimacy.
   d. Indicate how marketers might overcome resistance and speed adoption and diffusion for those offerings whose diffusion is likely to be slow.

2. Consider a product that you think represents an innovation but that you have not yet purchased. Using the terms discussed in this chapter, indicate why your resistance to this product is high or low.

3. Identify a new product that you consider to be a fad. Why is it likely to be a fad? What can marketers do to enhance the length of the product's life cycle?

4. Think about a new product or service you have recently encountered. How did the social system of which you are a member influence your knowledge about, attitudes toward, and willingness to adopt this innovation?

5. Identify a set of offerings that you consider to be symbolic innovations. How has the meaning of each innovation changed? What cultural forces explain these changes?

THE CONSUMER'S CULTURE

Age, Gender, and Household Influences (Ch. 15)

Social Class Influences (Ch. 14)

Social Influences (Ch. 16)

Regional, Ethnic and Religious Influences (Ch. 13)

Psychographics: Values, Personality and Lifestyles (Ch. 17)

THE PSYCHOLOGICAL CORE

- Motivation, Ability and Opportunity (Ch. 3)
- Exposure, Attention and Perception (Ch. 4)
- Knowing and Understanding (Ch. 5)
- Attitude Formation (Chs. 6 & 7)
- Memory and Retrieval (Ch. 8)

THE PROCESS OF MAKING DECISIONS

- Problem Recognition and Information Search (Ch. 9)
- Judgment and Decision Making (Chs. 10-11)
- Post-Decision Processes (Ch. 12)

CONSUMER BEHAVIOR OUTCOMES

- Symbolic Consumer Behavior (Ch. 18)
- Adoption of, Resistance to, and Diffusion of Innovations (Ch. 19)

PART SIX

Consumer Welfare

The final section of the text covers two topics that focus on consumer welfare. Both topics have been of great interest to consumer researchers in recent years. Chapter 20 directs our attention to consumerism and public policy. This chapter examines how consumer behavior knowledge and research can be employed to protect consumers and design programs to improve the quality of life.

Chapter 21 recognizes that not all consumer behaviors are "good" and examines the dark side of consumer behavior. This chapter focuses on some negative outcomes of consumer-related behaviors as well as marketers' roles in these areas. The chapter also discusses the dark side of marketing, noting marketing practices that have been the focus of social commentary in recent years.

CHAPTER 20

CONSUMERISM AND PUBLIC POLICY ISSUES

INTRODUCTION

In recent years the tobacco industry has been under heavy fire for its advertising and promotional activities. Although there have long been some ethical concerns that these communications influence consumers to take up a habit harmful to their health, the issue really rose to the forefront with the Joe Camel controversy. The trouble began when a study published in the *Journal of the American Medical Association* in December 1991 reported that more than half of a sample of children ages 3 to 6 could match Joe Camel, a cartoon figure promoting the Camel brand, with a cigarette.[1] Furthermore, the study found that 6-year-old children were almost as familiar with Joe Camel as they were with a Mickey Mouse logo.

Since that time government agencies such as the Federal Trade Commission and the Food and Drug Administration have been closely scrutinizing the marketing activities of tobacco companies.[2] In particular, there is great concern that icons such as Joe Camel and the Marlboro Man greatly glamorize smoking, particularly to teenagers and children. As a result, Camel was forced to discontinue its Joe Camel advertising campaign. Further, the FTC recommended an outright ban on tobacco advertising, and the FDA has tried to assert jurisdiction over tobacco products as an addictive drug. More moderate solutions suggest banning outdoor

EXHIBIT 20.1

Concern Over Children and Smoking

Consumer and government groups have become concerned over how the use of cartoon characters in corporate ads may influence whether to smoke.

Source: David Young-Wolff/Photo Edit.

advertising and the use of people smoking in ads. In response, tobacco companies have been getting more creative in their ads, using cigarettes that act like people and a cigarette with two chili peppers that look like lips.

In addition, antismoking activist groups such as the Interfaith Center on Corporate Responsibility have put pressure on the various media to closely regulate cigarette advertising.[3] The American Lung Association and other activist groups have been concerned with the prevalence of smoking by main characters in movies (see Exhibit 20.1). A number of individual consumers have also filed suits holding tobacco companies responsible for marketing an addictive product that has caused them health problems.

The important point of this example is that sometimes marketing activities can cause consumers harm or lead them to make a decision that has negative consequences. When this situation occurs, government agencies as well as industry and consumer groups can take action to protect the rights of consumers. We refer to these activities as *consumerism*.

This chapter examines some key consumerism or public policy issues. First, we define consumerism and outline major consumer rights. A brief description of the government agencies, industry regulations, and consumer groups involved in various public policy aspects follows. In the remainder of the chapter, we explore issues relating to consumerism. Knowledge of consumer behavior is often useful in generating insights into these issues, and conversely, knowledge of these issues can contribute to a more thorough understanding of how consumers acquire, consume, and dispose of products and services.

WHAT IS CONSUMERISM?

consumerism Activities of government, business, independent organizations, and consumers designed to protect the rights of consumers.

consumer rights Protection and access to information in certain consumer-related areas that is guaranteed to consumers.

Formally defined, **consumerism** is "the set of activities of government, business, independent organizations, and concerned consumers that are designed to protect the rights of consumers."[4] Thus the key focus is on **consumer rights**.

In 1962 President John F. Kennedy sent Congress the Consumer Bill of Rights, the purpose of which was to guarantee consumers several basic rights fundamental to the effective functioning of our economic system.[5] These are the rights:

- *Right to Safety.* Protection from products or services that might be hazardous to health and safety.
- *Right to Be Informed.* Protection from fraudulent or misleading advertising and other forms of communications and access to the information needed to make an informed decision.
- *Right to Choose.* Access to a variety of products and services at competitive prices wherever possible. If choice is restricted, the government will ensure that consumers receive satisfactory quality and fair prices.
- *Right to Be Heard.* Full and sympathetic consideration of consumer interests in the formation of government policy.

Since 1962 several other rights have been added by various presidents. The rights include the following:

- *Right to Consumer Education.* Access to knowledge about the products or services acquired and consumed.
- *Right to Recourse and Redress.* Right to a fair settlement of problems encountered.
- *Right to an Environment That Enhances the Quality of Life.* Right to live in an environment that is not threatened by pollution and hazardous waste.

These basic consumer rights have formed the foundation for much public policy discussion and for research regarding consumer behavior over the last 40 years. Specifically, researchers have been interested in applying consumer behavior principles, theories, and research methods to better understand consumer issues and suggest ways for improving consumers' lives. Also, various government, industry, and advocacy groups and agencies can influence marketing practices and develop regulations that increase the likelihood that consumer rights will be protected.

GROUPS INVOLVED WITH PUBLIC POLICY AND CONSUMERISM

Before discussing some key public policy issues, we need to introduce some of the groups that play a major role in their formation. Protecting the rights and interests of consumers is the goal of various government agencies, self-regulating industry groups, and consumer groups.

Government Agencies

Many government agencies look after various consumer interests. Discussing all of them is beyond the scope of this chapter. The following agencies have the greatest impact on public policy issues at the national level:

- *Federal Trade Commission (FTC).* Established in 1914 to curtail unfair trade practices and limit monopolies, the FTC plays the most central role in protecting consumer interests, and its role has expanded to areas such as investigating advertising claims, selling practices, and price-fixing and issuing penalties for deceptive advertising and other illegal activities.

- *Food and Drug Administration (FDA).* The FDA protects consumers from drugs, food, cosmetics, and therapeutic devices that may be potentially harmful, and it is concerned with the amount and nature of information provided about these products on the package or in the advertising.
- *Federal Communications Commission (FCC).* The FCC regulates interstate television, radio, and wire broadcasts as well as advertisements that appear in these media.
- *Consumer Product Safety Commission (CPSC).* The CPSC was created to investigate product-related accidents and to recall products that are defective. In addition, the CPSC attempts to identify products that are unsafe and to ban those that have an unreasonably high level of risk.
- *Environmental Protection Agency (EPA).* The EPA is responsible for developing and enforcing standards to protect the environment from threats such as pollution, garbage, and hazardous waste.
- *National Highway Traffic Safety Administration (NHTSA).* The NHTSA regulates the safety of all motor vehicles (new and used), investigates dangerous motor vehicle defects, recalls products when necessary, and sets standards for fuel efficiency in new vehicles.

In addition, other agencies at the federal, state, and local levels play an important role, depending on the nature of the problem or situation. The common goal of all these organizations is protecting consumer interests and regulating fair trade.

Whether consumers should protect themselves from products and services or whether the government should intervene on their behalf is the subject of much debate.[6] Some argue that regulation threatens individual freedom of choice; however, government intervention is sometimes necessary because consumers do not or cannot take adequate measures to protect themselves. Consumers frequently do not accurately assess the risk inherent in the situation, either because they lack the necessary information or because such hazards occur infrequently. A good example is the issue of seat belts, which we discuss later in the chapter.

Industry Self-Regulation

Companies are not always "bad guys" who require constant monitoring to ensure that they are dealing with consumers fairly. For both ethical and business-related reasons, it is in companies' best interests to be concerned about consumer welfare because it is so closely tied to consumer satisfaction. As a result, numerous industries have set up mechanisms to regulate business activity themselves and to correct problems when necessary. One benefit of self-regulation is that it removes the government from an antagonistic role and reduces its caseload. In fear of government regulations, for example, which are typically more stringent than voluntary ones, ad agencies have considered setting their own limits on alcohol and tobacco advertising.[7] Likewise, the beer industry was in arms over drug imagery in Hemp Beer advertising because it violated a voluntary guideline against any activities that imply illegal activity of any kind.[8]

NAD/NARB system A system set up by the National Advertising Division to self-regulate advertising messages.

Another excellent example of self-regulation is the **NAD/NARB system**, which the ad industry set up to monitor advertising messages.[9] The National Advertising Division (NAD) monitors ad claims and investigates complaints from consumers, competitors, or local Better Business Bureaus. When an ad claim is found questionable, the NAD asks advertisers to substantiate it. If the claim cannot be substantiated, the NAD will ask the advertiser to alter the message. For example, in one ad Texaco claimed that its CleanSystem3 was a "breakthrough in technology," even though competitors had been offering the same product for years. All three major networks refused to run the ad, and the NAD got Texaco to alter its claim. An advertiser that disagrees with the NAD's assessment can appeal to the National Advertising Review Board (NARB), but appeals occur only in a very small percentage of cases.

TV networks often develop their own standards about what to allow on the air. For example, in 1991, ABC announced a new set of standards for advertising in controversial areas, such as ads making medical claims and children's ads.[10] One rule allows doctors to appear in ads, which was previously not permitted, as long as their claims can be substantiated. All four networks also rejected an animal rights campaign promoting vegetarianism because it was considered too controversial.[11] Until recently, the liquor industry followed a self-imposed trade regulation that prohibited hard-liquor advertising on television. Seagrams created an uproar over a decision to abandon this long-standing practice, which may create a flurry of formal regulations.[12] The FTC has also encouraged the cable TV industry to toughen its ad-screening procedures.[13]

Finally, many problems are resolved by individual companies or groups through litigation. That is, if a company is engaging in an illegal or unfair practice, competitors can take action and seek restitution through the legal system. As examples, Federal Express filed a complaint with the FTC that the U.S. Postal Service could not make good on some of its claims, such as priority Saturday delivery.[14] Polo Ralph Lauren, Inc., filed a suit against *Polo Magazine* for trademark infringement, and various groups of farmers and distributors brought a case before the U.S. Supreme Court concerning the fairness of making them pay for industry campaigns such as "Got Milk?"[15]

Consumer Groups

In addition to government and industry agencies, more than 100 national organizations and 600 local groups look out for various consumer interests. The most well-known groups include Ralph Nader's Public Citizen, National Consumer's League, Consumers Union, Consumer Federation of America, Better Business Bureaus, Action for Children's Television, National Wildlife Federation, and Environmental Defense Fund. These groups lobby various government agencies to influence the enactment of legislation and assist consumers in dealing with companies. The advertising division of the Council of Better Business Bureaus, for example, closely monitors infomercials for misleading claims.[16]

Groups such as the Politically Correct Squad monitor the media for offensive communications, attacking companies such as Calvin Klein for promoting an anorexic image of women and Coke for using reverse sexism in an ad that shows women ogling construction workers.[17] Animal rights groups have put pressure on the National Cattlemen's Beef Association by calling attention to poor treatment of calves and by calling for a veal boycott.[18] The American Cancer Society and American Heart Association challenged R.J. Reynolds Tobacco when its ads contained an apparent claim that Winston had fewer additives than other brands.[19]

Various local consumer groups and services such as consumer hot lines are responsive to consumer interests. In Austin, Texas, reporters for a local TV news show regularly investigated consumer fraud among local businesses. In one segment a reporter blew out a 60-cent fuse in his VCR and took it to several repair shops, where repair estimates ranged from $25 to more than $200. This alarming report was followed with advice on how to avoid being "taken."

HOW ADVERTISING AND SELLING PRACTICES VIOLATE CONSUMER RIGHTS

Regulators have long been interested in the types of information provided in marketing communications and the extent to which they violate consumer rights. This section discusses three areas of concern: (1) deceptive advertising and labeling, (2) deceptive selling practices, and (3) advertising to children.

Deceptive Advertising and Labeling

deception Marketing communications that leave consumers with information or beliefs that are incorrect or cannot be substantiated.

Sometimes marketing communications can leave consumers with information or beliefs that are incorrect or cannot be substantiated. In this case, **deception** has occurred. For example, when Continental Airlines once advertised low fares to Europe, the ad was misleading because the fares applied to only a very limited number of seats.[20]

As formally defined by the FDA, a *deceptive ad* is one that "either through (1) its verbal content, (2) its design, structure, and/or visual artwork, or (3) the context in which it appears causes at least *n* percent* of a representative group of consumers to have a common incorrect impression or belief."[21] According to the FTC, deception involves (1) a misrepresentation, omission, or practice that is likely to mislead the consumer, (2) consumers acting as they normally would in relation to a product or service or in a consumption situation, and (3) a material misrepresentation (one that will affect their choice).[22]

Just because consumers hold an incorrect belief, however, does not necessarily mean that deception is present. Remember from Chapter 5 that consumers can simply misunderstand the message.[23] In other words, because mass media is imperfect, every communication is naturally associated with some degree of miscomprehension. However, when a large proportion of consumers hold the same incorrect belief that can be traced to a specific message, then deception is considered to be a problem. In the eyes of the FTC, deception occurs when approximately 20 to 25 percent of consumers have an incorrect belief (this percentage may be lower for products or services that affect consumer safety).[24]

The severity of deception is determined by factors such as whether the claim influences behavior, what potentially harmful effects it has on consumers, and the extent to which it creates an unfair advantage in the marketplace.[25] In other words, action is taken only when the deception causes injury to consumers or unfair losses to competitors. Thus the consequences must be material. Some consumers, such as children or the elderly, may be more susceptible to deception than others and may need more protection.[26]

false objective claim A claim made by a company that has no validity.

Types of Deception Deception can occur in a variety of ways.[27] The most obvious type occurs when a company makes a **false objective claim** about a product or service (see Exhibit 20.1). For years Listerine claimed to be the mouthwash that "kills germs which cause colds." Research evidence subsequently demonstrated that this claim was not valid, and Listerine was found guilty by the FTC of deceptive

---

*The *n* percent (percentage of affected consumers) will vary and is determined by the nature of the situation and how severe the consequences of the incorrect belief are. The relevant government agency determines the *n* percent.

advertising. Retailers are often guilty of using "exaggerated reference prices" in ads to make consumers believe that a sale price is a really good deal.[28] Finally, Gerber was cited by the FTC for deceptive advertising for claiming that four out of five pediatricians recommend Gerber baby food when only 12 percent surveyed did so.[29]

As you saw in Chapter 5, the name of the product or service or the label can sometimes be misleading.[30] For example, the winemaker Canandaigua Brands was required to alter the labeling of its white zinfandel and chardonnay wines and to use the phrase *with natural flavors* because these brands add fruit flavors to do not conform to zealously guarded pedigrees.[31] Ragu Foods and Clorox were required to remove the word *fresh* from their product labels (spaghetti sauce and Hidden Valley microwavable dinners, respectively) because the products aren't really "fresh."[32] Various regional marketing groups have been actively monitoring produce labels that misrepresent the origin of a fruit or vegetable.[33]

Puffery Some false or unsubstantiated claims fall outside the realm of regulation. For example, companies may engage in **puffery**, a form of advertising that uses evaluative or subjective terms such as *best*, *excellent*, or *great* (see Exhibit 20.2). These claims cannot be proven, and most consumers do not believe them.[34] However, if "puff" claims are believed and have a significant effect on behavior, then some type of corrective action may be necessary.[35]

Missing Information Making a false claim about a product or service represents only one type of deception. Consumers can also be deceived by what is *not* said in an ad. In other words, everything that is stated in the ad can be true, but consumers can be left with a false impression because **information has been left out** or qualifications are presented in an inconspicuous place where consumers may not see them.[36] This type of deception is most likely to occur when motivation, ability, or opportunity to process are low.[37] Mazda was accused of deceptive advertising for its "zero down" car leases because information about the large fees was buried in fine print.[38] Labels on milk cartons that claim the product is free of growth hormone have been found misleading because consumers think these brands are healthier. Dairy companies have been required by the FDA to add a qualifier stating that there is "no significant difference between milk derived from cows that were given the hormone and those that were not."[39] Finally, weight-loss

puffery The exaggerated claims made by companies that are not generally believed by consumers.

information has been left out Deception created because of what is not said or is hidden in the message.

EXHIBIT 20.2
Example of Puffery

Advertisers often use terms like "world's biggest" and "greatest" even though this may be tough to prove.

Source: Eastcott/Momatiuk/ The Image Works.

plans have been the focus of regulatory activity because the ads do not provide information about how many consumers lose weight; nor do they mention that many times this loss is only temporary.[40]

In the past leaving out information has been particularly problematic in toy advertising. Dolls, for example, were advertised in settings that showed accessoriesthat must be purchased seperately, and children falsely concluded that the doll's price included everything in the ad. Hasbro was accused of showing items in its Batman toy ads (such as a collapsing pier) that were not for sale.[41] Also, Applause Toys was accused of creating deceptive ads showing its weird-looking Magic Trolls creating magical effects.

Allowing Incorrect Inferences to Be Made Finally, an ad can be deceptive simply because of the way it **interacts with consumers' beliefs**. In other words, everything said in the ad can be accurate, but it can still be deceptive because consumers develop an incorrect inference from it. This situation often occurs when consumers infer unrealistically high levels of attribute performance.[42] For example, the FDA required Clorox to change the name of Hidden Valley Ranch Take Heart Dressing to Low Fat Dressing to remove the false impression that the product would contribute to a healthy heart.[43] In the tobacco industry, advertising for low-tar and low-nicotine cigarettes has been attacked because consumers mistakenly believe these cigarettes are healthier for them.[44] In addition, health claims made by a particular food brand can incorrectly cause consumers to believe that all brands in the same category possess the same benefit; however, this problem can be corrected by providing easily understood nutrition information on the package.[45] Research on nutrition information found that consumers tend to draw misleading generalizations or inferences from one claim about an attribute to other nonmentioned attributes. Shoppers might, for instance, think a product advertised as low fat is also low in cholesterol.[46]

The key point is that what the ad actually says does not determine whether or not it is deceptive. What matters is what the consumer *believes* as a result of the ad. Therefore, consumer research studies that assess customers' reactions to advertising messages play a key role in assessing deceptive advertising.[47]

Regulation of Deceptive Advertising The FTC and FDA are the major agencies that regulate deceptive advertising. When companies, consumers, or other organizations complain about an advertising message and the case is considered severe enough to warrant attention, these agencies will investigate. If they find evidence of potential deception, the offending company can be required to engage in **substantiation** to prove the questionable claims. For example, a major condom maker was asked to verify the claim that its product was 30 percent stronger than the leading brand.[48] Wal-Mart and Winn-Dixie were forced to stop claiming that they had the lowest prices and to instead advertise "Everyday Low Prices". Neither chain was able to prove that it always had the lowest prices on every product.[49] The Home Shopping Network was asked to substantiate claims about the effectiveness of three vitamin sprays and an aerosol to help quit smoking,[50] and the FDA has become more active in seeking substantiation for nutritional claims made on food products, as well as health claims made by certain dietary supplements (that they prevent cancer, thwart hair loss, and so on).[51]

If claims cannot be substantiated, the FTC and FDA have several regulatory options. The most common one is to issue a **cease-and-desist order**, whereby the company must immediately discontinue all advertising that contains the offending claim. This order was given to Continental for its deceptive fare ads. The

interacts with consumers' beliefs A message is deceptive because consumers develop an incorrect inference from it.

substantiation Having to prove questionable claims.

cease-and-desist order An order whereby a company must immediately discontinue all advertising that contains an offending claim.

affirmative disclosure
Messages that must be altered to provide correct information.

makers of heartburn medicines Pepsid AC and Tagamet HB were both ordered to withdraw advertising that contained unsubstantiated or misleading claims.[52] Depending on the severity of the problem, the FTC can impose fines or punitive damages. Continental Airlines, for example, was fined $20,000. In other cases, **affirmative disclosure** requires ad claims to be altered to provide correct information. For example, the FTC now wants all weight-loss products to provide information about the chances of weight-loss success and to state that this loss may be only temporary.[53] A federal court required *Polo Magazine* to publish a disclaimer, saying that it has no association with the fashion design house Polo Ralph Lauren.[54] The FTC has required the company to include the following disclaimer in its ads: "No additives in our tobacco does NOT mean a safer cigarette."[55] Unfortunately, these affirmative disclosure statements, too, can sometimes be misunderstood or misleading.[56]

corrective advertising The formal statement a company must make to correct false beliefs.

Corrective advertising can be required when the infraction is considered very severe, and merely ceasing the misleading ad will not dissipate consumer beliefs. (Perhaps it has been shown so often that the incorrect belief will persist for a long period of time.) In these cases the company must make a formal statement to correct the false consumer belief. For example, for 2 years Listerine was required to spend more than $10 million on corrective ads to dispel the belief that Listerine prevents colds.[57] One TV ad stated, "While Listerine will not help prevent colds or sore throats or lessen their severity, breath tests prove Listerine fights onion breath better than Scope." The FTC ordered Doan's pills to conduct an $8 million corrective advertising campaign over the claim that Doan's is more effective than other pain relievers in combating back pain.[58] Research has generally supported the effectiveness of corrective ads in eradicating false beliefs.[59] However, one study found that brand evaluations were likely to be lower after exposure to corrective ads only when prior brand evaluations were negative.[60] Nevertheless, corrective ads did lead to lower evaluations of the *advertiser* when prior attitudes were positive.

Finally, other agencies and groups can also regulate deceptive advertising. The FCC is quite responsive to consumer complaints about broadcast ads. Various state and local organizations bear the responsibility for monitoring messages that are more regional or local in scope. Remember also that the advertising industry has a self-regulation procedure in the NAD/NARB system.

Deceptive Selling Tactics

Deceptive practices can also occur in the context of personal selling. There are more than 11 million consumer and 9 million industrial salespeople in the United States.[61] Naturally, so many interactions, both personal and telemarketing, are bound to lead to instances in which consumers are not treated fairly, and regulation is needed to protect their interests. In most cases companies attempt to prevent abuses because it is in their best interest to please consumers. Nevertheless, some practices have caused problems and required regulation, including (1) the bait-and-switch technique, (2) misrepresentation of the selling intent, and (3) incorrect statements or promises.

bait-and-switch technique
A technique whereby consumers are attracted by the advertising of a product or service at an attractive low price and then enticed to trade up to a higher product item.

The Bait-and-Switch Technique The **bait-and-switch** technique is one whereby a retailer draws a customer into the store by advertising a product or service at a very attractive low price. The retailer then tries to get the consumer to trade up to a higher priced item by not stocking the advertised item or by making it so unattractive upon close inspection that the consumer will not want it. Note that getting consumers to trade up to another model is not illegal in itself—it can be an honest attempt to better fulfill the consumer's needs. However, the procedure is illegal when the intent is to deceive the consumer.

As an example, Craftmatic-Contour Industries, Inc., which sells motorized adjustable beds, was accused of the bait-and-switch practice by the Pennsylvania Bureau of Consumer Protection.[62] Consumers were attracted by beds priced at $400, but salespeople put heavy pressure on them to buy a bed in the $2,000 to $6,000 range. Although the company strongly claimed that it was merely "up selling" and not engaging in the bait-and-switch technique, it paid a restitution fine of $300,000. In an investigation of the mail-order camcorder industry, 23 of 32 vendors misrepresented themselves as dealers of a particular brand, and four attempted a bait and switch.[63]

In instances in which infractions have occurred, the FTC can act as it does in the case of deceptive advertising, imposing fines and asking the company to engage in corrective advertising. Three carpet retailers in the Washington, D.C., area, for example, were ordered to include the following statement in a conspicuous place in their advertising and to surround the statement with a black border:

> The Federal Trade Commission has found that we engage in bait and switch advertising; that is, the salesman makes it difficult to buy the advertised product and he attempts to switch you to a higher priced item.[64]

Misrepresenting the Selling Intent   Often consumers do not like to interact with salespeople because consumers know they will be pressured into buying something they probably do not want. Salespeople realize this and sometimes devise strategies to "trick" consumers into entering a conversation. For example, consumers could be asked to answer a questionnaire or be told they have just won a valuable prize. Once these techniques get a "foot in the door," the salesperson attempts to sell a product or service. The elderly and poor are often victims of this type of fraud.

postcard scheme   A deceptive practice in which a consumer receives a postcard that claims he or she has won a valuable prize but is really a front for intensive selling pressure.

A common example is the **postcard scheme** in which consumers receive a postcard promising cash prizes, free vacations, or expensive cars, usually with the announcement: "Congratulations, you are a guaranteed winner!"[65] When consumers contact the company, they are subjected to an intense selling effort and pressured to buy worthless or unneeded items. In particular, certain land development projects have engaged in this type of activity.

In another instance, Encyclopaedia Britannica reportedly engaged in misrepresentation by contacting consumers and asking them to comment on the company's advertising in an interview that would "only take a few minutes."[66] Salespeople even presented a letter from the company president that verified the purpose of the visit. Upon gaining entry, they subjected consumers to a 1- to 2-hour sales presentation. The FTC investigated, found the company guilty of deceptive practices, and issued a legal order that required the salespeople to present themselves honestly to consumers with a business card containing the phrase *sales representative.*

When misrepresentations do occur, consumers are encouraged to report them. The National Consumer League sponsors a toll-free hot line to address this problem. Interestingly, in a study on the ethics of certain sales practices, misrepresentation was one of the most negatively viewed practices.[67]

Incorrect Statements or Promises   Another way in which salespeople can create legal problems for their company is to make statements, intentionally or not, that cannot be backed up or substantiated. Problem statements can (1) create un-intended warranties, (2) dilute the effectiveness of safety warnings, (3) disparage competitive offerings, (4) misrepresent one's own offerings, and (5) interfere with business relationships.[68] Sales managers must be careful to educate salespeople about what they can and cannot say and do. In addition, companies that promote "pyramid selling" schemes, such as Amway and Mary Kay, have been under attack because some recruited salespeople are sucked in with promises of big money that is unlikely to materialize.[69]

Some selling practices are outright deceptive or fraudulent, and elderly consumers are often victimized by them. For example, telemarketers contact elderly consumers and tell them they will win a million dollars if they will only send in a check for a certain amount of money. In another scheme salespeople claim to be bank employees and ask for the consumer's account number.[70] One consumer received more than 6,000 calls and pieces of mail for such scams. This situation has led organizations such as the American Association of Retired Persons to develop education programs to help consumers avoid being victims of fraud.[71]

Although the potential exists for many abuses and consumers need to be protected from fraudulent activities, government agencies have often had a difficult time regulating personal selling. The fact is that (1) these interactions are verbal and there is no written evidence, (2) the abuses usually occur at a local and individual level, making detection more difficult, and (3) it is hard to monitor compliance with the law. Thus protecting consumers from these selling activities is more difficult than protecting them from deceptive advertising.

Advertising to Children

Some of the efforts of government agencies and other groups are directed toward protecting certain types of consumers. Advertising to children has been the subject of considerable controversy and debate that focuses on the impact ads might have on these impressionable consumers. Such issues are especially important when we consider that the average child spends 3.5 hours a day watching TV, more time than in any other activity except sleeping and going to school, and is exposed to more than 30,000 ads a year.[72] Networks cluster children's programming in certain time periods, making it easy for marketers to target children, and they spend more than a billion dollars a year doing it.[73]

The Basic Problem   The basic problem for consumer advocacy is that young children, particularly those under 7 years of age, have not yet developed the cognitive abilities to distinguish between the ad and the program.[74] Even at an age when children can recognize this difference, they still may not understand that the purpose of the ad is to sell them something.[75] Thus young children do not possess the same skepticism as adults and are more likely to believe what they see in ads. Note, however, that children are better at understanding the informational intent ("ads tell you about things") than the persuasive intent.[76]

Children can also experience difficulties in both storing and retrieving information from long-term memory that can be used to evaluate ads.[77] Furthermore, the messages often prey on children's strong needs for sensual satisfaction, play, and affiliation and can influence them to select material objects over socially oriented options.[78] Critics argue that ads teach children to become materialistic, to be impulsive, and to seek immediate gratification.

Unfortunately, parents generally do not watch TV with their children and do not educate or teach them about advertising.[79] As a result, children may be particularly impressionable so that their attitudes are influenced and their behavior is suggested by ads.[80] For example, some younger children believe that little people inside the TV are speaking directly to them. One study found that children who viewed products advertised in school on Channel One liked these products better and had stronger consumption values than those who were not exposed.[81] Exposure to ads increases requests to parents to buy products, particularly toys, and this situation can lead to family conflict and disappointed children.[82] Children have also been especially vulnerable to ads encouraging them to call 900 numbers to order products or services, and they do not understand the costs involved.[83] In fact, mothers have reported that they perceived this practice more negatively than any other activity directed toward children.[84] Finally, children are exposed to numerous ads for products that shape, often negatively, their impressions of what it means to be an adult.[85]

Some companies have been cited by Consumers Union for directing unfair advertising toward children. Nike and Reebok were attacked for using emotional appeals with celebrities, and Hershey, Colgate-Palmolive, and Procter & Gamble were accused of developing ad messages that resembled editorial matter.[86]

host selling A technique that features a character in a TV show also in ads.

In a related problem a character in a TV program is featured in ads. For obvious reasons this technique, called **host selling**, can cause children to easily confuse the program with advertising. For example, PBS came under fire for featuring the popular children's character Barney in pledge drives during children's programming. These drives have tried to tantalize children with toys and tapes. As a result, many children asked their parents to "send money to Barney."[87] The NAD has therefore recommended that no program characters appear in ads within the program or even in adjacent programs. FCC rules now prohibit TV stations from engaging in host selling on children's programs.

Another controversy centers on the types of products advertised. Many ads directed at children are for foods that contain a lot of sugar, such as snacks, candy, and sugar-coated cereals, and some people believe that these ads will encourage bad eating habits. For example, children who watch candy or sugar-coated cereal ads are more likely to ask for these products than to ask for fruit as a snack.[88] Furthermore, children who have been exposed to these ads tend to consume more sugared products and be less well educated about nutrition.

Some Possible Solutions   In light of this problem, both the FTC and the FCC have recommended that television stations use a *separator* between the program and the ad whenever the program is directed toward younger children, particularly on Saturday morning. In both the video and audio portion of the broadcast, the following message is suggested for presentation prior to the ads, "We will return after these messages," followed by "We now return to [name of the program]" at the end of the break.[89] These types of separators have been successful in helping children recognize the difference between ads and programming.[90] The FCC has also ruled that TV stations and cable operators must keep records of their commitment to educational programming and that advertising to children must be limited to 12 minutes per hour on weekdays and 10.5 minutes per hour on weekends.[91] In 1999 the American Academy of Pediatricians recommended that children under age 2 watch *no* television at all.

In response to the problem of advertising sugary foods to children, the FTC has encouraged the use of public service announcements (PSAs) to teach children proper nutritional habits. Unfortunately, the success of this program has been limited because the PSAs tend to be shown infrequently and simply providing children with information about the four basic food groups is not sufficient to educate them on this issue. In addition, entertaining or emotional appeals tend to be more effective in reaching the stated goals.[92] An agreement has also been reached between the government and the four major U.S. TV networks to provide at least 3 hours of educational children's television per week.[93] Other programs have attempted to educate children about nutrition in schools, hoping that the children will influence their parents to be more conscious of nutrition. Companies such as Red Lobster provide schools with a package of nutrition information (in this case the material happens to mention how healthy seafood is).

The advertising industry has also developed guidelines for children's advertising that are enforced by the Children's Advertising Review Unit (CARU), a wing of the Council of Better Business Bureaus.[94] These guidelines encourage truthful and accurate advertising that recognizes children's cognitive limitations and does not create unrealistic expectations about what products can do. As one example, if an ad shows that a child can get a prize when buying the product, such as a toy with a McDonald's Happy Meal, attention should focus on the product, not the prize. A recent study found that most advertisers are following these guidelines. However, violations were more likely to occur on cable TV than on network TV, occur in the fast-food industry more than in others, and they be related to the amount of time a prize or premium was highlighted.

The issue of advertising to children has not been totally resolved. It has even been suggested that *all* advertising directed toward children be banned. However, this position is obviously very controversial and one that many companies would strongly oppose. Supporters of children's advertising maintain that ads deliver useful information to children; teach positive values such as achievement, success, individualism, and fairness; and provide entertainment.[95] Some supporters also believe that very young children are not old enough to buy or influence decisions.

PRODUCT INFORMATION AND SAFETY ISSUES

In addition to protecting consumers from unfair practices, government agencies and consumer groups also provide information to help consumers make better decisions and to use products and services safely.

Consumer Protection Through Information

The purpose of providing consumers with more and better product information is to help them make more informed decisions. For example, the FDA has paid a great deal of attention to the types of nutrition information provided on packages of food products, in the hope that consumers will purchase and consume in a more nutritionally sound manner.[96] As part of this effort, fast-food restaurants are now required to disclose nutrition information about their menu items, with the result that a number of fast-food chains have improved the nutritional content of their offerings. Other types of restaurants may have to provide this type of information in the future, especially to substantiate low-fat or low-salt claims.

Although such efforts to inform consumers have always been instituted with the most positive intentions, a number of problems have arisen. Much of the difficulty has occurred because regulators have not based their proposals on a solid understanding of consumer information processing and decision making. In particular, four areas of concern can be identified: (1) the comprehension of information, (2) consumer use of the information, (3) the amount of information, and (4) the format of information.

Can Consumers Comprehend the Information?   It is generally assumed that consumers can understand and correctly use detailed information when it is provided. Unfortunately, this assumption is not always valid. A summary of six studies concluded that the vast majority of consumers do not understand basic nutrition information, including common terms such as *calories*, *fat*, *carbohydrates*, and *protein*.[97] Also, older consumers (those over 60) are less accurate in their use of nutrition information than younger consumers.[98] Another study found that a large percentage of consumers do not understand the relationship between the contract interest rate and the annual percentage rate when acquiring a loan.[99]

Thus before information programs can be expected to help consumers make better decisions, regulators must be certain that consumers can understand the information they are given. One approach is through consumer education programs that use pamphlets or informal classes to instruct consumers on the meanings of useful types of information. However, these programs have generally been difficult to implement because of a lack of consumer interest, suggesting a low level of motivation, ability, and opportunity (MAO). So some regulators have attempted to develop simple formats that make it easier for consumers to understand the information, as we discuss later in the chapter.

Will Consumers Use the Information?   Another assumption of consumer information programs is that consumers will actually *use* this information. In one study fewer than 5 percent of consumers examined nutrition information when selecting breakfast cereals.[100] Another study found that the majority of consumers examined the front of the package only, especially when health claims are made.[101] Also, after an initial flare-up of public interest, fast-food fare is again becoming fattier because people have a craving for fatty foods and are not motivated to read nutrition information.[102] An attempt to provide consumers with health and nutrition information on the Health Club Television Network, which airs in health clubs, failed because consumers believed that it was an intrusion on their time and privacy.[103]

These disappointing findings have led some to question the validity and usefulness of consumer information programs. Others maintain, however, that even if only 5 percent of consumers use the information, it is still benefiting at least some segment of the population, and one that highly desires it. In support of this view, one study found that consumers who perceive that nutritional information can aid in preventing disease are more likely to read this information on the package.[104] Furthermore, some argue that even though consumers do not pay attention to this information when making a decision, they still might read it while the product is being consumed, such as at the breakfast table.

Can Consumers Be Given Too Much Information?   Another subject of controversy is how much information to provide consumers. Chapter 9 mentioned that providing consumers with too much information can result in information overload, consumer confusion, and poorer decisions (see Exhibit 20.3).[105] Some argue that consumers seldom acquire enough information to become confused—they will stop searching before they reach overload. Regardless, the key point is that more is not always necessarily better. Thus regulators should provide consumers with the most *useful* and *important* information, rather than with all that is available. The value of limited information is a key argument in the fight to shorten the lengthy disclosures required in direct-to-consumer pharmaceutical ads, where a short summary table might be easier to understand.[106]

EXHIBIT 20.3
Information Overload

Consumers now have more and better information available to them than ever before. However, some people believe that *too much* information will lead to confusion and less-than-optimal decisions (i.e., information overload). Here, Cathy is struggling with the many types of information and new attributes in the grocery store.

Source: CATHY copyright 1995 Cathy Guisewite. Reprinted with permission of Universal Press Syndicate. All rights reserved.

Can Information Be Made Easier to Use? In light of the problems just discussed, regulators have been vitally interested in developing formats that make information easier to understand and use. Research has shown that an impact on consumer decisions is more likely when the format makes it easier to process information, highlights information so it stands out, or provides a benchmark that allows easy comparisons.[107] The labeling format mandated by the Nutrition Labeling and Education Act of 1990 (NLEA) was enacted because it was supposed to permit easy comparisons of the nutritional content for different food items, as well as forcing manufacturers to adhere to stricter rules in labeling contents, thereby preventing deceptive claims (see Exhibit 20.4).[108] In support, one study found that the new label resulted in slightly more favorable attitudes and perceptions toward nutrition and an increase in the likelihood that a nutritious product would be purchased.[109] Another study found that the new label improved comprehension of nutrition information but had less impact on the purchase of healthier foods.[110]

It has been found that all education levels of the population were able to understand the information presented in this format, and consumers can evaluate the information even in the presence of a conflicting health claim on the package.[111]

Further, consumers are more likely to rely on information from the nutrition panel than to rely on claims made on the package, especially when the motivation to process is higher.[112] It has been suggested that verbal (instead of numerical) descriptors would improve performance further. However, when numerical descriptors are used, percentages of nutrient amounts appear to be the most effective.[113] Finally, one study found that using "average brand" values is more effective than using "daily values" as a reference point.[114]

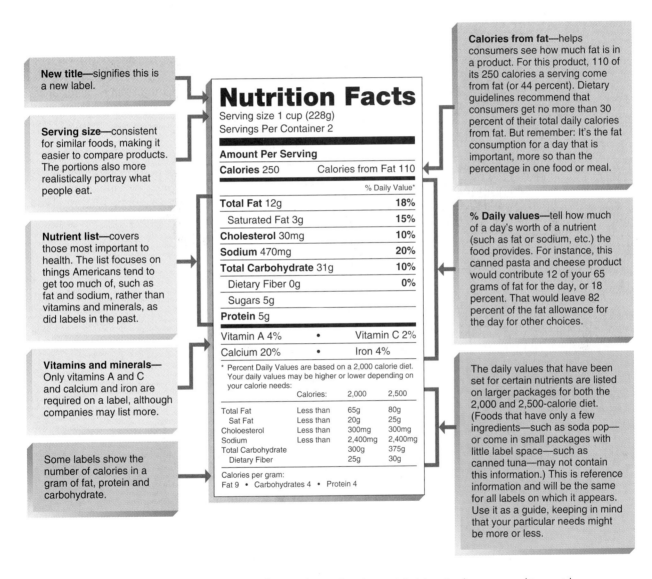

Calories from fat—helps consumers see how much fat is in a product. For this product, 110 of its 250 calories a serving come from fat (or 44 percent). Dietary guidelines recommend that consumers get no more than 30 percent of their total daily calories from fat. But remember: It's the fat consumption for a day that is important, more so than the percentage in one food or meal.

New title—signifies this is a new label.

Serving size—consistent for similar foods, making it easier to compare products. The portions also more realistically portray what people eat.

Nutrient list—covers those most important to health. The list focuses on things Americans tend to get too much of, such as fat and sodium, rather than vitamins and minerals, as did labels in the past.

% Daily values—tell how much of a day's worth of a nutrient (such as fat or sodium, etc.) the food provides. For instance, this canned pasta and cheese product would contribute 12 of your 65 grams of fat for the day, or 18 percent. That would leave 82 percent of the fat allowance for the day for other choices.

Vitamins and minerals—Only vitamins A and C and calcium and iron are required on a label, although companies may list more.

Some labels show the number of calories in a gram of fat, protein and carbohydrate.

The daily values that have been set for certain nutrients are listed on larger packages for both the 2,000 and 2,500-calorie diet. (Foods that have only a few ingredients—such as soda pop—or come in small packages with little label space—such as canned tuna—may not contain this information.) This is reference information and will be the same for all labels on which it appears. Use it as a guide, keeping in mind that your particular needs might be more or less.

Nutrition Facts
Serving size 1 cup (228g)
Servings Per Container 2

Amount Per Serving

Calories 250   Calories from Fat 110

% Daily Value*

Total Fat 12g	**18%**
Saturated Fat 3g	**15%**
Cholesterol 30mg	**10%**
Sodium 470mg	**20%**
Total Carbohydrate 31g	**10%**
Dietary Fiber 0g	**0%**
Sugars 5g	
Protein 5g	

Vitamin A 4%	•	Vitamin C 2%
Calcium 20%	•	Iron 4%

* Percent Daily Values are based on a 2,000 calorie diet. Your daily values may be higher or lower depending on your calorie needs.

	Calories:	2,000	2,500
Total Fat	Less than	65g	80g
Sat Fat	Less than	20g	25g
Choloesterol	Less than	300mg	300mg
Sodium	Less than	2,400mg	2,400mg
Total Carbohydrate		300g	375g
Dietary Fiber		25g	30g

Calories per gram:
Fat 9 • Carbohydrates 4 • Protein 4

EXHIBIT 20.4
FDA Food Labeling Format

For a number of years, the Food and Drug Administration has attempted to provide consumers with useful nutrition information by requiring every product to disclose this information on the label. Research studies have shown, however, that consumers have a hard time understanding and comparing this information across products. The Nutrition Labeling and Education Act of 1990 mandated a new format for food labeling, which is shown in this exhibit. Do you think consumers find this format easy to understand?

Source: Food and Drug Administration, as cited in "New Labels Give Consumers Breakdown in Nutrition," *Austin American Statesman,* May 7, 1994, p. A13.

Another example of making information easier for consumers to use is the U.S. government's efforts to standardize the energy-use information provided on various appliances. The goal is to help consumers conserve energy and save money by buying more energy-efficient appliances. As shown in Exhibit 20.5, this scale makes it easy to compare the product to all other appliances. The program has had a positive effect on consumer decisions.[115] The FDA has also proposed a makeover for labels for over-the-counter drugs to better inform consumers about the benefits and risks of these products.[116]

Consumer Protection Through Product Safety

Each year a great number of injuries, usually between 15 and 20 million, result from product-related accidents. Consumers have the right to be protected from products or services that may be hazardous to their health or safety. A product or service can be potentially harmful to consumers if (1) a problem exists with its quality or features, (2) it is used by the consumer in an unsafe manner, or (3) both.[117]

Product/Service Problems   The government, and in particular, the CPSC, sets safety standards for each industry. A product or service that fails to meet these standards can be recalled or altered. Procter & Gamble's Adult NyQuil Nighttime and Adult Formula 44M brands, for example, once contained high levels of alco-

EXHIBIT 20.5
Energy Guide

The Energy Guide provides consumers with information on energy use by appliances. The user-friendly guide shows consumers the yearly operating cost of the appliance and compares this model with others. It was hoped that this information would save consumers money and aid in conserving energy.

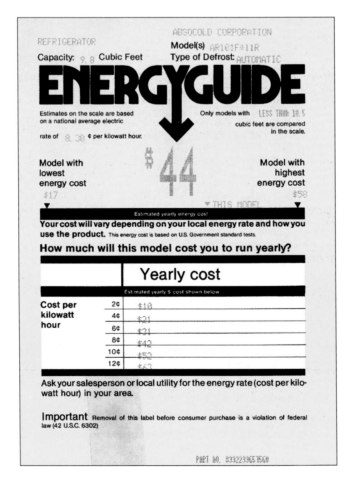

hol (25 percent and 24 percent, respectively), and the company was pressured to reduce these levels.[118] Highly publicized safety problems have plagued Dow Chemical's silicone breast implants and Procter & Gamble's fat substitute, Olestra, although the latter company strongly maintains that its product is safe.[119]

Toys for children raise perennial safety issues. Every year World against Toys Causing Harm releases a list of the ten most unsafe toys.[120] Note, however, that some companies have actively disputed the claims made by activists. Even auto airbags, which can save adult lives, have been seriously questioned for their potential to harm children.[121] The NHTSA also discovered that 50 percent of the time that children are in car seats, they are not buckled in safely. This discovery led to new safety rules for car seats.[122]

The activities of the CPSC have been more limited since 1980 because of funding cuts, and voluntary self-regulation has somewhat filled the gap.[123] In recent years, for example, car manufacturers such as Ford, General Motors and Chrysler have recalled various models to fix safety problems.[124] Nevertheless, when a significant infraction occurs, the CPSC can intercede and propose an appropriate remedial action. In addition, the FTC, FDA, EPA, and NHTSA undertake product-monitoring and recall actions.[125] For example, the FDA forced the withdrawal from the market of the diet drug Redux because of concerns that it may cause heart valves to leak and withdrew the antihistamine Seldane because of dangerous side effects.[126]

Individual consumers can also engage in litigation against companies in instances in which the company is liable for problems. In a highly publicized case against McDonald's, a woman was awarded $480,000 in damages because she received severe burns from hot coffee that spilled on her lap.

Incorrect Use of a Product   Failure to meet standards accounts for only about 20 percent of product-related injuries.[127] In other cases, injuries occur simply because consumers use products or services incorrectly. For example, a consumer might combine two combustible chemicals, such as different types of oven cleaners, and cause a fire); spray an insecticide near food preparation areas and poison someone; or use a plunger with a liquid drain opener and accidentally splash the acid on his or her skin.

To reduce these types of dangers, companies are expected to anticipate reasonable risks that may be inherent in the use of a product or service and take steps to avoid them. This expectation is known as the **doctrine of foreseeability**.[128] In other words, companies can be held responsible for misuses that might occur from normal consumption of a product or service and that could have been prevented or at least minimized. Research on consumer consumption patterns can be particularly useful in identifying common usage problems. For example, it is reasonable for a company to foresee the potential for a consumer to use a plunger with a liquid drain opener. Sometimes, however, consumer misuses are very hard to anticipate, and the company is not usually held responsible. Using a power mower to cut someone's hair would be unexpected, for example, and this abuse would not be the company's fault.

When potential dangers are identified, the company must attempt either to alter the product or to provide clear instructions to the consumer on how to avoid potential problems. Thus one of the key tools for protecting consumers from safety hazards is the warning label. Consumers are clearly warned about the danger of using a plunger with liquid drain opener, for instance. Pesticide labels warn consumers to keep the product away from their hands and face and that the product "should not be taken internally." Unfortunately, these warnings are not always as effective as they should be.[129]

doctrine of foreseeability
The expectation that companies should be able to anticipate normal risky uses of a product/service.

EXHIBIT 20.6

Effective Warning Label

Past warning labels have generally been ineffective in protecting consumers because the labels do not attract attention, are too difficult to understand, or the risks are not seen as very great. Here is a proposed labeling system that might capture consumers' attention, give them useful and easy-to-understand information, clearly identify the risks, and permit any easy comparisons with other products. Based on what you know about consumer behavior, do you think this label would be successful?

Source: James R. Bettman, John W. Payne, and Richard Staelin, "Cognitive Considerations in Designing Labels for Presenting Risk Information," *Journal of Public Policy on Marketing,* 5, 1986, pp. 1–28. Reprinted by permission.

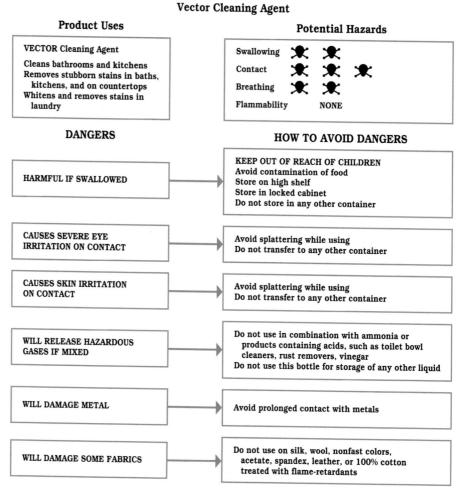

Vector Cleaning Agent

Product Uses

VECTOR Cleaning Agent

Cleans bathrooms and kitchens
Removes stubborn stains in baths, kitchens, and on countertops
Whitens and removes stains in laundry

Potential Hazards

Swallowing	☠	☠	
Contact	☠	☠	☠
Breathing	☠	☠	
Flammability	NONE		

DANGERS

HOW TO AVOID DANGERS

DANGERS	HOW TO AVOID DANGERS
HARMFUL IF SWALLOWED	KEEP OUT OF REACH OF CHILDREN Avoid contamination of food Store on high shelf Store in locked cabinet Do not store in any other container
CAUSES SEVERE EYE IRRITATION ON CONTACT	Avoid splattering while using Do not transfer to any other container
CAUSES SKIN IRRITATION ON CONTACT	Avoid splattering while using Do not transfer to any other container
WILL RELEASE HAZARDOUS GASES IF MIXED	Do not use in combination with ammonia or products containing acids, such as toilet bowl cleaners, rust removers, vinegar Do not use this bottle for storage of any other liquid
WILL DAMAGE METAL	Avoid prolonged contact with metals
WILL DAMAGE SOME FABRICS	Do not use on silk, wool, nonfast colors, acetate, spandex, leather, or 100% cotton treated with flame-retardants

DIRECTIONS FOR USE

How much Vector should you use?
To get the best laundering results use the proper amount of cleaning agent. See below for usage amounts.

- Large top-loading automatics – 1-1/2 cups
- Front-loading automatic – 1/2 cup
- Regular top-loading automatics – 1 cup
- Heavy soil – increase amount by 1/2 cup

What fabrics can you launder?
Cotton, linens, synthetics, permanent press, nylon, Dacron, Orlon, and rayon can be safely cleaned. You can test any article to determine if it is laundry-safe by applying one drop of Vector (1 teaspoon mixed with 1/4 cup water) to a hidden part of the fabric. Be sure to check all colors. If colors do not change, Vector can be safely used on the article.

What stains can be removed?
Fruit berry, wine, coffee, tea, grass, dye, and medicine stains can be removed.

EMERGENCY TREATMENT:
IF SWALLOWED: Induce vomiting. Feed milk for several days.
IN EYES: Flood with water. Call physician.
ON SKIN: Flood area with water. Call physican if irritation persists.

New label formats are being developed that should make it easier for consumers to notice and heed the warning when using the product. The label must be easy to locate, perhaps highlighted by different colors or sizes of type, and simple to understand.[130] One type of warning that shows some promise is illustrated in Exhibit 20.6. Companies can also design packaging and labels for poisonous products to make the items especially unattractive to children.[131] Consumer education programs might also be useful in reducing the number of product-related injuries.[132]

Some products or services are inherently risky. Riding a skateboard, bungee jumping, skydiving, driving a car, riding a bicycle, and using a tanning booth involve serious safety risks to the consumer. In these instances, however, consumers are made aware of these potential dangers and use the product at their own risk. Thus companies are not generally held liable for injuries associated with these products or services unless the injury was due to faulty manufacturing or negligence.

The Seat Belt Controversy   A controversial issue that involves consumer safety is the use of automobile seat belts. In the United States more than 30,000 people die every year from car accidents, and more than 500,000 are injured. Studies have consistently shown that wearing seat belts could cut in half the number of serious injuries. In fact, the positive effect of seat belts has been documented worldwide, especially in Europe and Japan.[133] Despite this evidence, many consumers are reluctant to "buckle up" on a consistent basis. Common excuses include "Seat belts are uncomfortable," "They restrict my movement," and "They wrinkle my clothes."

U.S. government efforts to regulate this problem began with requiring seat belts to be installed in all vehicles, followed by public service announcements that educated consumers about the importance of usage. Some of the early campaigns utilized fear appeals, depicting the negative and often grisly consequences of not wearing seat belts. Compliance, however, was dramatically lower than desired. A major part of the problem was that consumers simply were not in the habit of wearing the belts and often forgot, even though they would agree that buckling up could save their lives.[134]

As a result, many state governments now mandate the wearing of seat belts. Oregon was one of the first states to introduce a seat belt law, and it was effective in generating 70 percent compliance and reducing traffic fatalities by 14 percent within the first year.[135] Despite similar types of efforts across many states, however, compliance is still generally below 50 percent, illustrating how difficult it can be to force consumers to do anything, even when their personal safety is at stake.

Seat belt legislation is controversial because it attempts to restrict consumers' behavior. Opponents argue that consumers have the right to behave in any manner as long as it is not harmful to others, even if it is hazardous to themselves. This same point is also the basis for the controversy surrounding the wearing of helmets or head gear when riding a motorcycle or bicycle. It has been suggested that seat belt laws can actually increase fatalities because drivers feel safer when wearing a seat belt and therefore take more risks when driving.[136] In support of this view, studies in both the United States and New Zealand have found an increase in the number of deaths of pedestrians or people in other cars since the enactment of seat belt laws.

Some safety advocates also argue that public education is still the best way to promote seat belt use. Successful driver education programs must not only change consumer attitudes but also give drivers experience to get them in the habit of using a seat belt.[137] The NHTSA sponsored a series of public service announcements featuring Vince and Larry, the crash dummies who teach seat belt use in a powerful way by showing what happens when seat belts are not worn (see Exhibit 20.7).[138] The characters were even licensed to a toy company to develop figurines that could be used to educate children about seat belts in a more playful

EXHIBIT 20.7
Vince and Larry

Vince and Larry, the crash test dummies, have been used by the NHTSA to demonstrate what can happen when seat belts are not worn. It is hoped that these powerful visuals will convince consumers to wear their seat belts. These characters are also appealing to children and help in teaching them about highway safety.

Source: "Vince and Larry®" © 1985 U.S. DOT.

manner. In sum, government agencies still strongly feel that it is their duty to protect consumers, and seat belt laws are likely to stand.

ENVIRONMENTAL PROTECTION

One final area of consumer rights is the right to an environment that enhances the quality of life—one that is free of hazardous wastes, garbage, and pollutants and has adequate natural resources. Many efforts in this area have focused on developing laws and programs that attempt to improve air and water quality and protect individuals from waste disposal, especially hazardous waste.

Environmentally Conscious Behavior

One of the major causes of air pollution is automobile emissions. The U.S. government has required the use of unleaded gasoline and developed stricter emission control standards to reduce damage to the environment. Further attempts have been made to lower consumption of gasoline by increasing its price.[139] Aerosol spray cans have also been attacked for pumping volatile organic compounds into the environment, thereby damaging the earth's protective ozone layer. As a result, manufacturers have developed packaging and manufacturing methods that will limit these kinds of emissions. In the dry-cleaning industry, the chemical perc, a possible human carcinogen, is often used. Some "green" dry cleaners that do not use this chemical have opened up in response.[140]

Another major concern is the increasing amount of trash or garbage in our environment. Projections say that American consumers will generate 40 percent more trash by the year 2010 and that disposed packaging will account for 30 percent of it.[141] In response, many products (such as Lenor fabric softener in Germany; Jergen's lotion; and Lysol, Windex, and Resolve cleaners) are sold in refillable containers.[142] In some countries, such as Romania, consumers use refillable bottles for wine, beer, seltzer, oil, and milk. In addition, companies are being pressured to develop packaging materials that will reduce environmental pollution. For example, the Environmental Defense Fund urged McDonald's to use packaging that was more environmentally friendly, such as paper, instead of plastic foam, for hamburger containers and pump-style dispensers for ketchup.[143] Companies that use direct-mail advertising have been pressured to give consumers the option of refusing these materials because of the tremendous amount of wasted ink and paper associated with junk mail.[144] One study found that stressing societal benefits, self-efficacy, and behavioral control were the most effective ways to induce consumers to reduce household garbage.[145]

The trend toward the use of environmentally friendly products is growing. More consumers are abandoning caustic cleaning products in favor of those that are milder and less damaging to the environment[146] and are returning to natural cleansers such as baking soda, vinegar, and lemon juice, even if they are not as effective their regular cleansers.

One company awards a Green Seal to manufacturers of certain products that meet tough environmental standards (see Exhibit 20.8). This seal makes it easy for environmentally conscious consumers to identify so-called green, or environmentally friendly, products. Consumers who have a positive attitude toward ecologically conscious living, a negative attitude toward littering, and a perception that pollution is a problem are more likely to buy these ecologically packaged products than those without these attitudes.[147] Researchers have also found that a *general*

EXHIBIT 20.8
Labeling Products as Environmentally Friendly

The Green Seal organization awards the Green Seal to products that meet rigorous environmental standards. This seal helps consumers identify products that are environmentally safe.

Source: Green Seal PSA by D.D.B. Needham 1990.

BEFORE YOU BUY A PRODUCT MAKE SURE IT'S PROPERLY SEALED.

Most of the products that sit on the supermarket shelf look harmless. But how can you tell which ones are manufactured with the Earth in mind? ❂ It's simple. Just look for the Green Seal. ❂ We are a non-profit, environmental labeling organization that certifies products which meet rigorous environmental standards. ❂ For more information, write to:

Green Seal, P.O. Box 77438, Washington DC 20013

environmental concern has an indirect effect on intentions to purchase environmentally sensitive products.[148] Finally, environmentally conscious behaviors are most likely to occur when consumers perceive that their actions will make a difference—called *perceived consumer effectiveness.*[149]

There is still a long way to go in strengthening environmental concern. Although many consumers express concern for the environment, studies often show that these feelings still do not play a major role in the purchase of many products.[150] Other consumers believe the environmental movement is a fad and is already losing momentum.

Conservation Behavior

conservation Consumer preservation of natural resources.

One aspect of environmental protection that has been of great interest is **conservation behavior.** The need to conserve has become increasingly important in light of the rapidly escalating problems of garbage disposal and depletion of natural resources. Companies are now realizing that garbage has been a misused resource and are finding creative ways to reuse materials. For example, Wellman, Inc., has used old soda bottles to make carpeting, Marcal makes paper towels out of undelivered junk mail, and Prestone recycles old antifreeze rather than making it from scratch.[151] Ecofurniture, made of recycled wood, plastic, or paper, is also growing in popularity.[152] Finally, companies are attempting to make products more durable so they will last longer.

Programs have been developed to encourage consumers to conserve certain resources, especially energy. In particular, consumer researchers have been interested in three major aspects of conservation behavior: *when* are consumers likely to conserve, *who* is most likely to conserve, and *how* can consumers be motivated to conserve?

When Are Consumers Likely to Conserve? In general, consumers are most likely to conserve when they accept personal responsibility for the pollution problem.[153] For example, consumers who perceive that there is an energy short-age because every consumer (including themselves) is using too much are more likely to accept personal blame for this problem and do something about it. However, one of the major obstacles facing conservation programs is actually *getting* consumers to take personal responsibility. Consumers often do not feel account-able for many environmental problems and are therefore not motivated to act.

Thus for conservation programs to succeed, communications must make the problem personally relevant. For example, in trying to get consumers to conserve energy by turning down the thermostat, communications could focus on how much energy and money the household could save each year and over the long term, say, 10 years. Consumers are also most likely to conserve when there are not barriers to doing so such as the lack of of conservation information or salespeople who do not stress conservation.[154]

A study in the Netherlands points out the importance of bringing social norms to bear in influencing consumers to engage in environmental behaviors This study found that consumers in general perceive that they are more motivated to engage in pro-environmental behavior than other households but are lower in the ability to do so.[155] Further, they believe that ability is the greatest determinant and that their own behavior is influenced by others.

Who Is Most Likely to Conserve? A weak relationship exists between conser-vation behavior and some demographic characteristics. Younger consumers and in-dividuals with more education are slightly more likely to conserve than other groups.[156] However, researchers have not been able to identify a general profile of "the conserving consumer." Attitudes toward social responsibility and environ-mental consciousness generally do not relate to conservation behavior.[157] Instead, environmentally beneficial choices tend to be made on an activity-by-activity basis.

Physical or structural characteristics of the consumer's residence, such as the type of dwelling and number of appliances, tend to be strongly related to conser-vation behaviors.[158] Consumers who have fewer appliances and live in apartments and mobile homes are less likely to conserve. A study from the Netherlands found that characteristics of the house, such as the amount of insulation, and behavior of the household members, such as having curtains on the windows and lowering the thermostat when no one is home, were more likely to be related to energy use than were other factors such as demographics and attitudes.[159]

efficiency behaviors Activi-ties that result in more efficient energy usage.

curtailment behaviors Ac-tivities that result in using less energy.

demand-shift behaviors Ac-tivities that use more efficient energy sources.

Researchers have identified three major behaviors of energy conservers: (1) **efficiency behaviors**, which include driving fuel-efficient cars and insulating and weatherizing the home; (2) **curtailment behaviors**, which include lowering the thermostat setting, turning off lights when they are not needed, and reducing dri-ving by 10 percent; and (3) **demand-shift behaviors**, which include switching to solar heating units and converting from electric appliances to natural gas.[160] Con-servation programs are more likely to be effective when they emphasize efficiency behaviors rather than curtailment behaviors.

Can Consumers Be Motivated to Conserve? Many organizations and agen-cies, both government and private, are trying to motivate consumers to conserve. Ads sometimes encourage consumers to use products or packages that conserve resources (see Exhibit 20.9). Another approach focuses on providing consumers with detailed information about conservation through communications, home au-dits, and appliance labels. Unfortunately, these programs usually have only a lim-ited impact on conservation behavior.[161]

EXHIBIT 20.9
Emphasizing Conservation

Consumers can sometimes conserve resources by using certain products or packages. For example, this ad encourages the conservation of water by taking shorter showers.

Source: F. Pedrick/The Image Works.

A more promising approach is to provide consumers with incentives to conserve. Providing consumers with a free shower-water flow device, for instance, significantly increased participation in an energy conservation program.[162] Consumers have shown that they prefer incentives such as tax credits to those that focus on coercion, for example, higher taxes. Setting goals and providing feedback can be effective in curtailing energy use as well.

CONSUMERISM AROUND THE WORLD

 We have focused to a large extent on consumerism issues in the United States. Obviously, laws, regulatory agencies, and consumer movements abound in many other parts of the world. Countries with conservative governments usually impose fewer restrictions on activities.[163] Leftist or more liberal governments, on the other hand, usually produce a more restrictive regulatory environment. Clearly, companies must account for these forces when marketing internationally.

 As in the United States, many countries have regulatory agencies to monitor advertising. In the United Kingdom, advertising is controlled by two organizations: the Advertising Standards Authority (ASA) and the Independent Broadcasting Authority (IBA). The ASA is a self-regulatory agency that monitors nonbroadcast advertising to ensure its honesty and fairness and includes among its members individuals not connected with the advertising industry. The IBA is responsible for overseeing radio and television advertising. The British system tends to work more efficiently than similar organizations in the United States because there is better funding and staffing, substantial public participation, stronger remedies for infractions, better organization, and a stronger spirit of cooperation.[164]

 Germany has the strongest standards for truth. Deception is defined as occurring when 10 to 15 percent of reasonable consumers, even gullible ones, perceive a misleading message, as determined by research.[165] In Germany deception cases are tried in courts. The same is true in France and Belgium. In one highly publicized case in Germany, Philip Morris was ordered to discontinue an ad campaign claiming that passive exposure to cigarette smoke was no more dangerous than eating cookies.[166]

 In the Netherlands the Commercial Code Commission oversees ads and recently ruled that a mobile phone ad starring Leslie Nielsen and suggesting that phones drive people insane was distasteful and harmful to mental patients.[167] Industry self-regulation is also common in several European countries such as the United Kingdom, Italy, Belgium, Ireland, Switzerland, and the Netherlands. Germany and Austria permit private litigation against companies as well.

Product safety standards are becoming increasingly more stringent around the world, particularly in the European Community, which has adopted even tougher restrictions than the United States has.[168] Thus to minimize liability, companies need to maximize performance and safety. Countries also have widely varying laws regarding which marketing practices are legal and illegal. In Germany the words *best* or *better* are considered misleading.[169] Finland prohibits newspaper or TV advertising for political groups, religion, alcohol, weight-loss products, or "immoral literature," and the United Kingdom does not allow cigarette or liquor advertising on TV. In fact, most European Union countries are set to ban most kinds of tobacco advertising.[170] After the fall of communism, the Russian government banned cigarette and alcohol ads and then all advertising temporarily until a reasonable set of guidelines could be developed.[171] Regulations regarding advertising to children also vary widely in different countries, and companies must be very careful to account for local variations when marketing efforts cross national boundaries.[172] Finally, promotion techniques, such as premiums, sweepstakes, and free samples, are also often more heavily regulated in many other countries than in the United States.

For years advertisers in China have been making widely exaggerated false claims.[173] For example, one ad states that a brand of toothpaste cures cancer, and another claims a soap can wash 10 years off a woman's face. An ad for a Chinese drug maker shows an elderly woman with hepatitis swallowing a pill, jumping off the bed, and shouting, "My disease is cured!!" Interestingly, local advertisers, and not foreign companies, are the worst offenders. However, the Chinese government has now cracked down by passing its first comprehensive advertising law and backing it with stiff enforcement.

Finally, many consumer activist groups are at work around the world. For example, the environmental movement is strong in many European countries, and in Germany the Green Party has been increasing its representation in the government. International environmental groups such as Greenpeace monitor issues around the globe.

CONSUMERISM IN THE FUTURE

Most of the issues discussed in this chapter involve providing information in some way or another. Advances in information technology and electronic shopping will provide major improvements in these areas because consumers will have access to more and better information from independent sources. So much available information, however, brings with it the potential for abuse. Obviously, public policy regulations and protections are necessary to ensure the honesty of information providers and to guard against deceptive or fraudulent practices or conflicts of interest. The FTC has already begun regulating deceptive advertising on the Internet. As one example, iMall and the Home Shopping Network were recently required to pay fines of $750,000 and $1.1 million, respectively, for making deceptive claims in Internet ads.[174]

Serious potential for fraud exists on the Internet, and consumers have already been swindled, leading to a call for increased government regulation. Some observers worry, however, that too many regulations could crimp the very fast growth of Internet commerce.[175] In a related concern, many consumers still won't give out their credit card numbers on the Internet for fear that they can be intercepted by a third party. Thus manufacturers and programmers are currently working hard to increase security on the Internet.[176]

The Internet also offers companies the opportunity to collect a lot of detailed information about consumers. Therefore, another issue centers on privacy. Key issues are how much and which information should be made public and how it should be used. In one case the FTC found that Liberty Financial Company failed to protect the anonymity of children who participated in its Kids' Website survey.[177] Consumers are also increasingly worried about "identity theft," or the stealing of personal information over the Internet.[178]

A new set of consumer rights will likely emerge, and the following new Bill of Rights for Consumers in the Information Age has been suggested:

- The right to be educated about product strengths and weaknesses
- The right to trust sources of product information
- The right to a state-of-the-art information infrastructure that empowers consumers to efficiently use their time, money, and energy
- The right of all Americans, whether urban or rural, rich or poor, to access the information infrastructure
- The right to privacy, preventing sellers and others from abusing personal information gained in product transactions[179]

SUMMARY

Consumerism is "the set of activities of government, business, independent organizations, and concerned consumers that are designed to protect the rights of consumers" to (1) be safe, (2) be informed, (3) have choices, (4) be heard, (5) receive consumer education, (6) have recourse and redress, and (7) live in an environment that enhances the quality of life. The various means that influence consumerism and public policy issues are government agencies, industry self-regulation, and political consumer groups.

A key public policy issue is deceptive advertising and labeling. Ads can be deceptive when they provide false information, leave out relevant information, or interact with consumers' beliefs to mislead. Deceptive selling techniques include the bait-and-switch technique, misrepresentation of the selling intent, and incorrect statements. Several problems are associated with advertising to children. Young consumers do not have the cognitive capabilities to process ads and must sometimes be protected from certain practices.

The government has been interested in helping consumers become more informed. To be effective, however, information must be easy to understand, be reasonable in amount, be used by consumers, and appear in an easy-to-use format. The consumer's right to safety is ensured by protection from unsafe products and warnings of dangers or risks when present. Environmental protection and conservation behavior are key public policy issues.

Consumerism exists around the world. Countries have different rules and regulations as well as different agencies to handle these problems.

Finally, with advances in information technology and electronic shopping, consumers will have access to more and better information from independent sources. With so much available information, however, public policy regulations and protections are necessary to ensure the honesty of information providers and to guard against deceptive or fraudulent practices or conflicts of interest.

EXERCISES

1. Watch or tape 3 hours of television during Saturday morning children's programming. Code or analyze each ad in terms of the following: (a) type of product advertised, (b) message techniques used (fantasy, humor, music, etc.), (c) emotion evoked, (d) key message delivered, and (e) any aspects you think might confuse young children. Summarize this information and answer the following questions:

   a. What are the most frequently advertised types of products or services? Do you see any ethical problems?

   b. What are the main techniques used to influence children? Do you believe that these are reasonable marketing practices?

   c. Did you notice any efforts made to educate children and make them more aware of the advertising? Were these efforts effective?

   d. What types of messages are children being exposed to? Do you see any problems with them?

   e. Did any ads or messages seem to be unfair or unethical? If so, why?

2. Acquire and copy three nutrition labels from packages of food products. Ask ten consumers (as different from one another as possible) to describe what this information means. Alternatively, ask the ten consumers a series of multiple-choice questions about the terms contained on the label. Based on your observations, how well do you think the consumers understood the information? What types of consumers were most likely and least likely to understand the material? What could be done to make it more understandable and useful?

3. This chapter discussed several key public policy issues, but it only scratched the surface in each case. Select one of the key issues and do a thorough library search for information about it. Use this information to write a more detailed summary report of the key arguments and possible solutions for this issue.

4. We mentioned in the chapter that the regulation of public policy varies throughout the world. Select a particular country and research the nature of regulation for one of the key issues discussed in this chapter. How do the practices in that country differ from those in the United States? How are they similar?

CHAPTER 21

THE DARK SIDE OF CONSUMER BEHAVIOR AND MARKETING

INTRODUCTION

On-line companies collect a lot of personal information about you, and you may not even know it.[1] Tracking systems on Web sites enable companies to monitor the time of your visit, how long you stay, and what item you looked at. Such systems can also examine "cookies" placed on your Web browser that enable the company to track when you last visited the site and what you looked at then. Indeed, 24 percent of the 100 most frequently visited Web sites surreptitiously place these cookies on users' hard drives.

Some sites require visitors to provide information such as phone numbers, e-mail addresses, addresses, or even Social Security numbers before gaining access to the site. Consumers are rarely informed about what the company will do with this information or why it is required.

Other companies trade the information consumers provide for merchandise or services. One company allows consumers to print coupons from the Internet in exchange for demographic data and information about brand preferences and buying patterns. A number of sites even collect personal data from children. Some sites track your name even though the information they collect is billed as "anonymous."

In one instance, Liberty Financial tracked information from kids about their allowances, spending habits, and family finances on its younginvestor.com site.

Finally, the confidentiality of information can be violated, sometimes having severe and negative effects on consumers. One person resigned from the navy after America Online (AOL) confirmed to a navy investigator that the individual had identified himself as gay in an on-line profile depicted as anonymous. Consumers are reacting with increased resistance to these issues. For example, an enormous public outcry followed the announcement that AOL planned to make its members' phone numbers available to telemarketers. A number of consumer advocacy groups have also formed in an attempt to protect consumer privacy.

This example illustrates several issues discussed in this chapter. First, we examine whether marketing sometimes engages in practices that could be detrimental to consumers. We examine whether certain marketing practices invade consumer privacy, particularly the privacy of children. We also examine whether marketing targets children for unsafe products like cigarettes and alcohol, whether activities like advertising make people unhappy with their appearance or what and how much they own, and whether advertising unfairly depicts or represents key segments of our society. We also describe ways that consumers resist marketing efforts viewed as inappropriate. Both individual and group practices (e.g., boycotts) are discussed.

Although these issues represent the "dark side" of *marketing*, we also consider the dark side of *consumer behavior*. We discuss deviant consumer behaviors that stem from uncontrollable sources (compulsive buying, compulsive gambling, and smoking and alcohol additions). We also discuss consumer behaviors that are deviant because they are illegal (consumer theft, underage drinking and smoking, and black markets).

DEVIANT CONSUMER BEHAVIOR

Much of this book has focused on the behavior of the average consumer in an everyday consumption context, but sometimes consumer behavior is regarded as deviant. Behavior is deviant if it is either unexpected or not sanctioned by members of the society. Such behavior may be problematic to the consumer and/or to the society in which the consumer operates. As Exhibit 21.1 indicates, some forms of deviant consumer behavior occur with the purchase or acquisition of the product—before consumers even use it. Three types of deviant *acquisition* behaviors are discussed here: compulsive buying, consumer theft, and black markets. We then focus on deviant *consumption* behaviors, including addiction, compulsive consumption, and underage smoking and drinking.

Compulsive Buying

One problem faced by some individuals is that they buy compulsively. In other words, they tend to buy excessive numbers of objects they do not need and that

EXHIBIT 21.1

Framework for Deviant Consumer Behavior

Consumer behavior may be deviant because it involves a physical or psychological abnormality or involves a behavior regarded as illegal. Such deviant behaviors can be associated with the acquisition or usage of offerings.

Stage of the Consumer Behavior Process

	Deviant acquisition behavior	Deviant usage behavior
Why Deviant? Physical/ psychological abnormality	Compulsive buying	Addictive consumption • smoking • drugs • alcohol Compulsive consumption • compulsive gambling • binge eating
Illegal behavior	Consumer theft Black markets	Underage drinking Underage smoking Drug use

they sometimes cannot afford. The interesting thing about compulsive buying is that satisfaction comes from *buying*, not *owning* (see part a of Exhibit 21.2).[2]

What Is the Compulsive Buying Experience Like? Compulsive buying has a strong emotional component, and the emotions run the gamut from the most negative to the most positive.[3] Compulsive buyers feel anxious on days that they do not engage in buying. In fact, compulsive buying may be a response to tension or anxiety. As evidence, some research has found a relationship between compulsive buying and eating disorders like binge eating. While in the store, compulsive buyers may feel great emotional arousal at the stimulation evoked by the store's atmosphere. The act of buying, in turn, brings an immediate emotional high and often a feeling of loss of control (see part b of Exhibit 21.2). However, this emotional high is followed by feelings of remorse, guilt, shame, and depression. Compulsive buyers think that knowledge of their spending habits would horrify others. Some compulsive buyers even hide purchases in a closet or the trunk of a car.

What Causes Compulsive Buying? Buying products in excessive amounts seems antithetical to the buying processes described in earlier chapters. Why then do people buy compulsively? The answer to this question is not simple.[4]

Low Self-Esteem First, compulsive buyers tend to have low self-esteem. In fact, the emotional high consumers experience from compulsive buying comes in part from the attention and social approval they get when they buy. The salesperson can bring considerable satisfaction—being a doting helper, telling consumers how attractive they look in a particular outfit, and telling them how thoughtful they are to buy such a nice gift. Consumers can also feel that they are pleasing someone. They please the salesperson by buying the product. They please a company by making purchases. This attention and the feeling that they are pleasing others may temporarily raise compulsive buyers' self-esteem and act as a reinforcement for buying (see part c of Exhibit 21.2).

Fantasy Orientation Fantasy orientation is a personality trait associated with compulsive buying. Buying makes compulsive buyers feel more important and more grandiose than they actually are. These fantasy feelings may explain how compulsive buyers temporarily avoid or escape thoughts about the financial consequences of their shopping experience.

Alienation   Compulsive buyers tend to be somewhat alienated from society; they have fewer friends and social contacts than most people do. Compulsive buying therefore provides an opportunity for social gratification. Consumers may feel as if they are friends with a salesperson who has sold them items on repeated occasions. They may enjoy seeing the UPS driver arrive with a package. By buying, these consumers may feel more integrated and less alienated than they otherwise would.

EXHIBIT 21.2
Quotes from Compulsive Buyers

Compulsive buying can be an emotionally involving experience. Consumers who engage in compulsive buying often enjoy feelings of extra attention or feeling like they are pleasing someone else. But this emotional high may be followed by serious financial and negative emotional consequences.

EMOTIONAL ASPECTS OF COMPULSIVE BUYING

a. "I couldn't tell you what I bought or where I bought it. It was like I was on automatic."

"I really think it's the spending. It's not that I want it, because sometimes I'll just buy it and I'll think, Ugh, another sweatshirt."

b. "But it was like, it was almost like my heart was palpitating, I couldn't wait to get in to see what was there. It was such a sensation. In the store, the lights, the people; they were playing Christmas music. I was hyperventilating and my hands were starting to sweat, and all of a sudden I was touching sweaters and the whole feel of it was just beckoning to me. And if they had a SALE sign up, forget it; I was gone. You never know when you're going to need it. I bought ten shirts one time for $10.00 each."

"It's almost like you're drunk. You're so intoxicated;...I got this great high. It was like you couldn't have given me more of a rush."

FACTORS INFLUENCING COMPULSIVE BUYING

c. "The attention I got there was incredible. She waited on me very nicely, making sure it would fit and if it didn't they would do this and that. And I guess I enjoyed being on the other end of that. I had no idea how I was going to pay for it. I never do."

"I never bought one of anything. I always buy at least two. I still do. I can never even go into the Jewel and buy one quart of milk. I've always got to buy two...It's an act of pleasing. I had been brought up to please everybody and everyone around me because that was the way you got anything was to please. So I thought I was pleasing the store."

FINANCIAL AND EMOTIONAL CONSEQUENCES OF COMPULSIVE BUYING

d. "I would always have to borrow between paychecks. I could not make it between paychecks. Payday comes and I'd pay all my bills, but then I'd piss the rest away, and I'd need to borrow money to eat, and I would cry and cry and cry, and everyone would say, 'Well just make a budget.' Get serious. That's like telling an alcoholic not to go to the liquor store. It's not that simple."

e. "My husband said he couldn't deal with this and he said, 'I'm leaving you. We'll get a divorce. That's it. It's your problem. You did it. You fix it up.'"

"I didn't have one person in the world I could talk to. I don't drink. I don't smoke. I don't do dope. But I can't stop. I can't control it. I said I can't go on like this...My husband hates me. My kids hate me. I've destroyed everything. I was ashamed and just wanted to die."

Family History Finally, compulsive buyers are more likely to come from families whose members show compulsive or addictive behaviors or emotional disorders. For example, one study of Canadian consumers found that compulsive buyers were more likely to come from families showing problems of alcoholism, bulimia, extreme nervousness, or depression. Some evidence suggests that compulsive shopping may be hereditary.

What Are the Consequences of Compulsive Buying? Compulsive buying is more than an annoying habit. Its financial, emotional, and interpersonal consequences can be devastating. Some compulsive buyers spend roughly 50 percent of their income on purchases. To finance their buying habits, they rely extensively on credit cards. They have significantly more cards than the general population and are more likely to carry balances within $100 of their credit limit. Because their credit card debt is so great, they tend to pay the minimum monthly balance. They are also more likely to write checks for purchases, even though they know they do not have enough money to pay for them. And compulsive buyers are more likely to borrow money from others to make it from paycheck to paycheck (see part d of Exhibit 21.2).[5] A clinical screening test that incorporates many of these elements is shown in Exhibit 21.3.

1. Please indicate how much you agree or disagree with the statement below. Place an X on the line which best indicates how you feel.

	Strongly agree (1)	Somewhat agree (2)	Neither agree nor disagree (3)	Somewhat disagree (4)	Strongly disagree (5)
a. If I have any money left at the end of the pay period, I just have to spend it.	_____	_____	_____	_____	_____

2. Please indicate how often you have done each of the following things by placing an X on the appropriate line.

	Very often (1)	Often (2)	Sometimes (3)	Rarely (4)	Never (5)
a. Felt like others would be horrified if they knew of my spending habits.	_____	_____	_____	_____	_____
b. Bought things even though I couldn't afford them.	_____	_____	_____	_____	_____
c. Wrote a check when I knew I didn't have enough money in the bank to cover it.	_____	_____	_____	_____	_____
d. Bought myself something in order to make myself feel better.	_____	_____	_____	_____	_____
e. Felt anxious or nervous on days I didn't go shopping.	_____	_____	_____	_____	_____
e. Made only the minimum payments on my credit cards.	_____	_____	_____	_____	_____

Scoring equation = $-9.69 + (Q1a \times .33) + (Q2a \times .34) + (Q2b \times .50) + (Q2c \times .47) + (Q2d \times .33) + (Q2e \times .38) + (Q2f \times .31)$. If scoring is ≤ -1.34, subject is classified as a compulsive buyer.

EXHIBIT 21.3
A Clinical Screening Test for Compulsive Buying

Do you have compulsive buying tendencies? Take this screening test to find out.

Source: Thomas C. O'Guinn and Ronald J. Faber, "A Clinical Screener for Compulsive Buying," *Journal of Consumer Research*, December 1991, pp. 459–469. © 1991 University of Chicago. All rights reserved.

Compulsive buying can also wreak devastating emotional and interpersonal consequences. As part e of Exhibit 21.2 indicates, children, spouses, and friends can all be hurt by the spending habits of compulsive buyers.

MARKETING IMPLICATIONS   Several ethical implications can be raised about marketing and compulsive buying. However, little work has been done to clarify these difficult issues.

Do Marketing Practices Foster Compulsive Buying?   Although research on this issue is scarce, it seems quite likely that enticing sales, attractive displays, doting salespeople, and easy credit foster compulsive buying.

Are Marketers Ethically Bound to Help Compulsive Buyers?   Marketers might help compulsive buyers by direct actions such as liberal return policies, sales training in compulsive buying, denials for credit increases or in indirect actions such as contributions to self-help organizations like Spender Enders. ■

Consumer Theft

Whereas compulsive buying reflects uncontrollable desires to *purchase* things, consumer theft reflects an uncontrollable desire to *steal* things.

How Prevalent Is Consumer Theft?   When we think of consumer theft, perhaps the first thing that comes to mind is shoplifting. For retailers, shoplifting is indeed pervasive and significant, with yearly retail losses approximating $30 billion. Furthermore, theft seems to be on the rise as shoplifting reports to police stations have been increasing by 5 percent a year for the past decade.[6] Exhibit 21.4 shows the most commonly stolen items from various types of retailers.

However, theft is a problem for non-retailers as well.[7] For example, automobile insurance fraud has been estimated to exceed $10 billion per year, and phone service fraud is estimated to exceed $1 billion per year. Hotel theft is also pervasive, with losses exceeding $100 million per year. Officials at Holiday Inn estimate that a towel is stolen every 11 seconds. Clocks, hair dryers, bathroom items, and even artwork are among the items stolen from hotels. Credit card fraud, loan fraud, warranty fraud, theft of cable TV services, coupon fraud, fraudulent returns, and the practice of switching and altering price tags are other common forms of consumer theft. There is even an increasing incidence of financial-aid fraud as students and parents falsely state the amount of money they earn or submit false tax returns to college financial-aid offices. New forms of consumer theft occur whenever innovations in products or services are introduced. For example, theft of cable TV services, credit card fraud, software piracy, video piracy, and music piracy have grown along with these industries.

What Affects Consumer Theft?   Although you may think that consumer theft is driven by economic need, few demographic variables are associated with theft. Some *forms* of consumer theft are associated with certain demographic groups: shoplifting is most common among teens, and credit card fraud is usually associated with better-educated consumers. However, consumers from all walks of life engage in theft. Moreover, many consumers have engaged in some form of theft at one time. For example, roughly two-thirds of the public admits to having shoplifted.[8]

Instead, two psychological factors shown in Exhibit 21.5 seem to explain theft: (1) the temptation to steal and (2) the ability to rationalize theft behavior. As the exhibit also indicates, these factors are, in turn, affected by several other factors:

EXHIBIT 21.4
Consumer Theft

What are the most commonly stolen items? The list to the right breaks them down by type of retailer.

Source: Discount Merchandiser, March 1997, p. 3. Used with permission.

MOST FREQUENTLY STOLEN MERCHANDISE BY TYPE OF RETAILER.

TYPE OF RETAILER	MERCHANDISE
AUTO PARTS	AUTO ACCESSORIES
BOOKS	CASSETTE TAPES
CONSUMER ELECTRONICS	COMPACT DISCS
DEPARTMENT STORES	CLOTHING: SHIRTS
DISCOUNT STORES	CLOTHING, UNDERGARMENTS
DRUGSTORES	CIGARETTES, BATTERIES
FASHION MERCHANDISE	SNEAKERS
GENERAL MERCHANDISE	EARRINGS
GROCERY/SUPERMARKET	OVER-THE-COUNTER MEDICINES
HOME AND HARDWARE	ASSORTED HAND TOOLS
MUSIC	COMPACT DISCS
SHOES	SNEAKERS
SPECIALTY	BED SHEETS
SPECIALTY APPAREL	ASSORTED CLOTHES, SHOES
SPORTING GOODS	ATHLETIC SHOES
THEME PARKS	KEY CHAINS, JEWELRY
TOYS	ACTION FIGURES
VIDEO	VIDEO GAMES
WHOLESALE	PENS, PRERECORDED VIDEO TAPES

characteristics of the product, characteristics of the purchase environment, and characteristics of consumers.

Temptation to Steal   The *temptation* to steal arises when consumers want products that they simply cannot acquire through legitimate forms of acquisition. Some of these desires are derived by real needs, such as the mother who steals baby formula to feed her child. Others reflect greed, as in the case of upper-class consumers who steal jewelry. Some researchers suggest that desires for enticing products are stimulated by marketers who perpetuate materialistic tendencies and create insatiable desires for new goods and services.[9]

Consumers may also be tempted to steal because the offering is something they are too embarrassed to buy through conventional channels (e.g., condoms, pregnancy tests), or whose purchase is illegal (e.g., an underage consumer stealing alcohol).[10]

As Exhibit 21.5 shows, environmental factors also affect the temptation to steal. Temptation is greater when consumers perceive that they can get away with stealing and that it is worth doing. Thus consumers may assess the perceived risks associated with stealing and getting caught and may consider the benefits of having a product or using a service they did not pay for.[11] These factors might explain the rise in music piracy described in Chapter 19.

Many factors in the environment affect the perceived risks of shoplifting.[12] Merchandising arrangements may make it easy for consumers to simply pick products off the shelf. Stores may have little or no security, few salespeople, or nooks and crannies that make it easy for consumers to take items without being noticed.

Tags may be affixed by pins and easily switched. The store may have liberal return policies, making it easy for consumers to "return" items that they just picked up off the rack. Finally, noisy and crowded environments also reduce the perceived risks of shoplifting because they provide greater opportunity to shoplift without being noticed.

Sometimes theft is motivated by the thrill of doing something one is not supposed to do. This thrill-seeking tendency has been associated with many forms of consumer theft, including price-tag switching and shoplifting.[13]

Rationalizations for Stealing As Exhibit 21.5 shows, consumers also engage in theft because they can somehow *rationalize* their behavior as either being justified or driven by forces other than themselves. For example, consumers may justify stealing a low-ticket item such as grapes from a grocery store or candy from a checkout counter because the item's cost seems so negligible the word *stealing* hardly seems to apply.

Consumers may also believe that stealing is justified because the environment encourages it. Thus the consumer may believe that the marketer "asked for it" by keeping merchandise displays open, having no security guards, or having price tags that can be readily switched. Consumers in crowded environments may be-

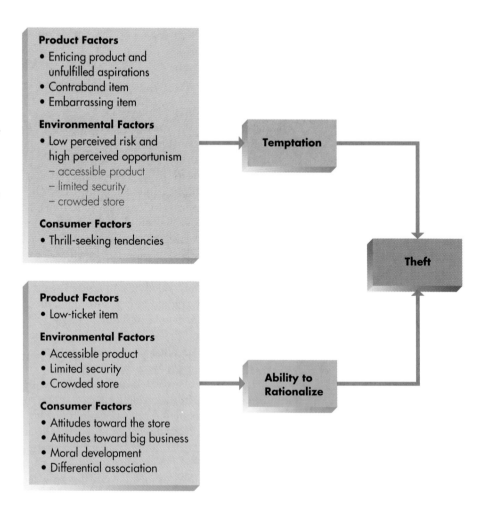

EXHIBIT 21.5
Motivations for Consumer Theft

Consumers may engage in theft because they (1) feel the temptation to steal and (2) they can somehow rationalize their behavior. Various factors associated with the product, the environment, and the consumer can influence temptation and the ability to rationalize.

PART SIX Consumer Welfare

542

come so frustrated from waiting for service that they finally give up and walk out with the item. They may justify their behavior by thinking that theft is compensation for the unpleasantness they suffered while waiting.[14]

Rationalization is also likely when social influences encourage theft, as is the case with someone who shoplifts as part of a dare.[15] The consumer can rationalize the behavior by indicating that "my friend made me do it." Interestingly, although teen shoplifting behavior is often attributed to dares, evidence that dares play a large role in shoplifting is quite limited.[16]

Consumers are also most likely to rationalize theft when stores have a negative public image. If the store is seen as unfriendly, intimidating, or somehow unfair, theft may be seen as a way of getting revenge against the retailer. Similarly, consumers may engage in theft because they have negative attitudes toward businesses and because they think that large businesses can readily absorb the cost of the theft. Consumers may also steal because they feel psychologically distanced from the retailer—they believe that they are dealing with a huge faceless conglomerate, not a shop owner. In sum, consumers are more likely to rationalize theft behavior when there is less personalization.[17]

Consumers whose moral development is weak may simply not see the act of stealing as wrong. One study found that shoplifters tend to be rule breakers in general. Some speculation suggests that the level of moral development of our society as a whole is changing, with fewer and fewer people viewing theft as wrong. In addition, some evidence suggests that adolescents' moral restraint is weakened simply by observing their peers shoplift. Thus socialization can affect moral development, which in turn can affect consumer theft.[18]

MARKETING IMPLICATIONS Theft is clearly a problem for marketers.

Increased Usage of Theft-Reducing Devices. Overall, U.S. businesses spent more than $82 billion on security systems in 1996.[19] A recent survey of supermarket retailers, showed that half planned to upgrade their existing security systems and 85 percent intended to install some kind of antitheft system.[20] New antitheft devices to be installed in minibars in European hotels can run anywhere from $200 to $1,000 each. Some 23,000 retail stores in Europe are using electromagnetic technology to deter shoplifting. A thin, invisible magnetic wire is implanted on a package. If someone tries to leave the store with the package, the wire triggers an alarm as it passes through a magnetic exit station. The wire is deactivated when the customer pays for the item at checkout. This system is also used to prevent theft of CDs. Some hotels use strips sewn into linen and towels that trip an alarm when consumers walk through sensitized exit doors. Another system combines closed circuit TVs with sophisticated computer software to track suspicious behavior. Marketers have also used some unusual tactics to reduce theft.[21] Some stores have piped classical and easy-listening music into stores to discourage teenage gangs. Others have used subliminal audio messages that say things like "Do not steal" and "Stealing is a crime."

Covering the Costs of Theft. Theft hurts consumers because retailers must find some way to pay for lost merchandise, cover theft insurance, and cover the costs of high-priced security systems; in the end, however, consumers pay higher prices.[22] In addition, theft adds to research and development costs as firms experiment with newer and better security systems, which also results in higher prices.

Reducing Ability to Serve Customers. Theft also hurts consumers because security systems may interfere with retailers' abilities to service customers. For example, retailers may be forced to secure their merchandise by putting it behind glass displays, locking it up, and so on.[23] This added security increases consumers' search costs, making it more difficult and more time-consuming for consumers to examine products and for salespeople to service customers. ■

Black Markets

While theft represents a situation in which consumers refuse to pay for available items, **black markets** represent situations in which consumers *pay* (often exorbitant amounts) for items *not* readily available. The markets are called black markets because the sellers are nonauthorized sellers. Hence the buying-selling process is typically illegal.

What Is Traded on Black Markets?   Many offerings are traded on black markets.

Legal Items in Short Supply   In some instances, items sold on the black market are legal items in short supply. In the United States entertainment is often sold on the black market. Consumers will buy blocks of tickets to popular sporting events, theaters, and concerts and then sell them at the last minute at exceptionally high prices. A vicious black market for soccer tickets was observed during the 1998 World Cup in France. Black markets for airbags in cars and Cuban cigars have also been prevalent in the United States in recent years.[24] Some black markets deal with the trade of very basic consumer goods. For example, prisoners will trade money and cigarettes for goods like food, books, and clothing.[25] The sale of basic consumer goods and services is also rampant in Third World and communist countries. For example, in rural Tanzania and Burma, basic items like soap, cooking oil, and matches are sold on the black market.

Brands   In some cases specific brands are sold on the black market. The black market for Levi jeans has long been strong in the former Soviet Union. Here in the United States, there is a growing black market for frequent-flyer tickets. Sellers, who sometimes work through brokers, can get $12 to $15 for each 1,000 miles accrued.[26]

Illegal Items   In some cases products and services that *cannot legally be sold* to consumers are sold through the black market. For example, a large black market deals in weapons and products used to build bombs.[27] Black markets for drugs are also common. For example, around the world a large black market exists for the male potency drug Viagra.[28]

What Affects Black Markets?   Black markets develop and continue for several reasons. First, they fulfill basic human needs. Black markets for goods like sugar, salt, blankets, matches, and batteries fulfill functional needs. Black markets for drugs, entertainment, and sexual services fulfill experiential needs. Black markets for Levi and Swatch watches may fulfill symbolic needs.

Addictive and Compulsive Consumption

Compulsive buying, consumer theft, and black markets are all forms of deviant *acquisition* behavior; however, in some cases it is not the acquisition process that is deviant but rather how or whether products are *used*. As Exhibit 21.1 shows, consumption behavior can also be deviant either because we lose control over consumption or because it is illegal.

addiction Excessive behavior typically brought on by a chemical dependence.

Addiction Addiction reflects excessive behaviors typically brought on by a chemical dependence. Addicted consumers feel a great attachment to and dependence on a product or activity and believe that they must use it simply to function.[29] Typically, an addiction involves a product that is used repetitively, even though it may be dangerous. Although in many cases addicted individuals want to stop consuming the product, they believe that stopping is beyond their control ("I can't help myself"). Individuals can become addicted to many consumer products and services, including cigarettes, drugs, alcohol, exercise, TV, video games, collecting, and so on.

Addictive behaviors can be harmful to addicts and to those around them.[30] For example, cigarette smoking has been labeled the most widespread form of drug dependence in our society. It is the number one preventable cause of death in the United States and is a leading cause of cancer, cardiovascular disease, and chronic obstructive lung disease. The social costs of cigarette smoking are also high. Smokers use more health benefits, take more sick leave, and have more occupation-related accidents and injuries than nonsmokers do. Although the number of people who smoke cigarettes is declining, smoking is still prevalent, and knowledge about its ill effects is weakest among those most vulnerable in our society. Furthermore, consumers seem to be switching from cigarettes to cigars and chewing tobacco, although these forms of tobacco are just as harmful as cigarettes are. Often individuals feel shame and guilt over their addiction and try to hide it. Strength is sometimes found in groups like Alcoholics Anonymous and Smoke Enders. The number of consumers who are recovering addicts is evidenced by the existence of a new television network called the Recovery Network.[31]

compulsive consumption An irresistible urge to perform an irrational consumption act.

Compulsive Consumption Compulsive consumption is an irresistible urge to perform an irrational consumption act. For example, betting twice one's weekly salary on a horse is not a rational act; however, compulsive gamblers might engage in such behaviors. Eating two dozen donuts is not rational, but compulsive (binge) eaters might consume food in such quantities. This discussion focuses on compulsive gambling because of its prevalence and the changes occurring in the gambling industry.

Compulsive Gambling: A Special Case of Compulsive Consumption An estimated 6 million to 9 million American consumers are compulsive gamblers. These individuals suffer from a chronic inability to resist impulses to gamble, and they engage in gambling behavior that is disruptive to both themselves and those around them.[32] Compulsive gambling typically evolves over a series of stages. In the first stage the individual experiences the pleasure of having a "big win." During the second stage gambling becomes more reckless, losses pile up, and gambling becomes a central force in the individual's life. Because legal loans are not feasible at this point, the individual takes loans from loan sharks. The compulsive gambler promises to stop gambling, but cannot. Faced with rising debt and compulsive gambling needs, many gamblers engage in crimes like forgery and embezzlement. The final stage occurs when the gambler realizes that he or she has hit rock bottom. The psychological and financial consequences of compulsive gambling can be disastrous. One study of 54 compulsive gamblers found that each had accumulated debts of nearly $28,000. Ninety-eight percent had turned to crime.[33]

Despite the popular stereotype of the compulsive gambler as a lower-income consumer, compulsive gamblers represent every ethnic and socioeconomic group in society. Even legendary figures such as baseball's Pete Rose can be affected. However, certain groups are particularly susceptible to compulsive gambling.

Teens, for example, are four times more likely to engage in compulsive gambling than adults are.[34] The typical compulsive gambler is 39 years old and married; nearly one-third have incomes between $25,000 and $50,000.

What Causes Addictive and Compulsive Consumption?   Why do some people become addicted to drugs or alcohol or eat or bet compulsively whereas others do not? The answers are neither clear nor simple, and many factors have been implicated in the development of addictive and compulsive tendencies.[35]

Inherited Tendencies   Some evidence suggests that addictive tendencies are inherited; for example, genetic markers of alcohol addiction have been the topic of much research. Personality has also been linked to compulsive and addictive behavior. For example, alcohol addiction has been linked with low self-esteem, anxiety, depression, sensation seeking, and antisocial personality disorders. Compared to nonaddicts, addicts are also more likely to exhibit an external locus of control, believing that control or responsibilities for events lie in factors outside of themselves. This belief may explain why addicts find it hard to stop their addictive behavior. Some of these personality factors (e.g., depression and low self-esteem) may be *outcomes* of being an addict rather than factors that predispose one to becoming an addict.

Family-Related Factors   Addictive behaviors may also have their roots in dysfunctional families. For example, children of alcoholics are more likely to become alcoholics, perhaps because they model the behavior of their parents. They may also have developed fewer coping mechanisms for dealing with their parents' addiction, thus making them more susceptible to using escapist means like drugs and alcohol. Clearly, addictive and compulsive behaviors are complex and multifaceted problems.

MARKETING IMPLICATIONS   *Do Marketing Activities Encourage Addictive and Compulsive Behaviors?*   Some might argue that marketing activities encourage addictive and compulsive behaviors. For example, cigarettes are heavily advertised in the United States, and the nicotine in cigarettes is addictive. Public policy makers clearly view marketers as entities that perpetuate this form of addictive consumption. Both Britain and Canada have enacted legislation to ban cigarette advertising.[36] The banning of cigarette ads from broadcast media and the practice of requiring warning labels on cigarette packages are other legislative acts that affect marketing practices. Among the most sweeping and significant marketing implications is discussion about whether the U.S. government should control the distribution of nicotine.[37]

Industry and marketing practices may also perpetuate behaviors like compulsive gambling.[38] Gambling is a fast-growing industry, as barriers against it are disappearing. Gambling is legal in places like Las Vegas, New Orleans, and Atlantic City, and it is prevalent on many Indian reservations. Some states (e.g., Texas) have passed bills to make gambling a legal state activity. In other states large contingents are lobbying for legalized gambling. Moreover, cash-strapped states and governments see casinos and lotteries as important revenue generators. Video Poker machines, available in some states at restaurants, gas stations, convenience stores, and bars, and Internet-based casinos are also creating opportunities for access to gambling sources 24 hours a day. Floating riverboat casinos have attracted thousands of Midwest consumers. British Airways even installed video gambling machines on its Boeing 747 jumbo jets.

EXHIBIT 21.6
Where Are Gambling Dollars Spent?

Casinos and lotteries represent common forms of gambling, but consumers gamble in a variety of ways.

Source: Reprinted from *American Demographics* magazine, May, 1997. Copyright 1997. Courtesy of Intertec Publishing Corp., Stamford, Connecticut. All rights reserved.

CONSUMER SPENDING IN BILLIONS OF DOLLARS ON LEGALIZED FORMS OF GAMBLING, AND MARKET SHARE, 1995; PERCENT CHANGE IN SPENDING, 1982-95.

	Spending (in billions)	Market-share	Percent change in spending 1982-95
TOTAL SPENDING	$44.4	100.0 %	326 %
CASINOS	$18.0	40.6 %	329 %
NV/NJ SLOT MACHINES	7.1	16.0	255
NV/NJ GAME TABLES	3.9	8.7	75
RIVERBOATS	4.7	10.5	N/A
NON-CASINO DEVICES	1.4	3.2	N/A
LOTTERIES	15.2	34.3	602
INDIAN RESERVATIONS	4.0	9.1	N/A
PARIMUTUELS	3.8	8.4	34
CHARITABLE GAMES*	2.5	3.4	111
CARD ROOMS	0.8	1.7	1,425

Note: does not sum to total due to rounding
*Includes charitable bingo.

Source: Christiansen/Cummings Associates, Inc.

Other practices encourage gambling as well. Advertising for gambling is increasing. For example, California and New York each spend roughly $30 million a year on state lottery advertising. Furthermore, some casinos have installed real-time monitoring systems that tell them how much a given consumer is winning or losing. Gambling cards enable casinos to track each gambler's gambling history. These activities cause concern that casinos can target people who are big spenders—including those who have gambling problems. Given these trends, it is perhaps not surprising that spending on gambling has increased dramatically over the past 20 years (see Exhibit 21.6).

Marketing Activities That Deal with Addictive and Compulsive Consumption. Notably, some marketing activities are aimed at reducing addictive and compulsive consumption. For example, compulsive gambling hot lines have been established by some states and casinos. These hot lines help suicidal and emotionally distraught compulsive gamblers. Such calls are especially frequent following the Super Bowl—perhaps because the hype surrounding the Super Bowl makes betting even more enticing to the compulsive gambler.[39] Some members of the public are concerned that the growth in the gambling industry will be followed by an increase in the number of consumers who become compulsive gamblers and/or an increase in the number of gambling opportunities for those already hooked. ∎

Underage Drinking and Smoking

As mentioned earlier, addictions to alcohol and tobacco represent one form of deviant consumer behavior. However, use of these products is associated with another deviant consumer behavior—their illegal use by minors (see Exhibit 21.1).

Although historically states have differed in their minimum drinking age, the passage of the National Minimum Drinking Age Act in 1984 mandated that all states wanting to receive federal highway funds raise the drinking age to 21.

How Prevalent Is Underage Drinking and Smoking? Although the use of alcohol and tobacco by minors is illegal, this practice is widespread.[40] High school and junior high school students drink 1.1 billion cans of beer and 35 percent of the wine coolers sold in the United States. Half of all junior and senior high school students have consumed alcohol. More than 8 million of the 207 million U.S. students in grades 7 to 12 drink weekly, and nearly 500,000 drink five or more drinks in a row at least once a week. Nearly one-third of high school students and nearly 45 percent of college students have engaged in "binge drinking" (drinking more than five drinks in one sitting). Binge drinking on college campuses is rising dramatically. Four million children are alcoholics or problem drinkers. One million young consumers begin smoking every year, and 90 percent of new smokers are teenagers. An estimated 3,000 children begin smoking each day. These figures are even more dramatic in Asian countries where there are few bans on cigarette adverting. In the Philippines half of those between the ages of 7 and 17 smoke.

What Are the Consequences of Underage Drinking and Smoking? It is not just the use of these products that is a problem. It is the consequences they bring to both the consumer and society at large.[41] Overuse of alcohol has been involved in 70 percent campus violence cases, 68 percent of campus property damage cases, and 40 percent of academic failures. Overuse of alcohol is regarded as the primary discipline, emotional, and physical problem on college campuses. Alcohol is also involved in roughly half of teen highway fatalities, half of all youth suicides, and 90 percent of campus hazing deaths. Almost half of all schools polled say that alcohol is the most serious problem they face. Alcohol is even implicated in the rising costs of college tuition. Now that colleges are liable for campus drinking incidents, the costs of insurance (and hence tuition) has skyrocketed. Accidents due to drinking also contribute to the high cost of automobile insurance for young consumers. Groups like Mothers Against Drunk Driving (MADD) and Students Against Drunk Driving (SADD) work to enact legislation to punish drinking and driving, use social disapproval to pressure students not to drink and drive, and institute programs that stress the importance of having a designated driver.

Cigarette smoking at an early age is also harmful, causing many health problems like lung cancer and heart disease. Moreover, these effects can even happen to nonsmokers through their exposure to secondhand smoke. Use of tobacco products also makes young consumers more vulnerable to the problems of addictive consumption previously noted. Furthermore, in any given year 75 percent of adolescent smokers have tried to quit smoking but cannot do so.[42] As with underage drinking, public interest groups and government organizations publicize the negative health consequences associated with smoking (see Exhibit 21.7).

MARKETING IMPLICATIONS A number of marketing issues are related to underage drinking and smoking.

Product Availability. First, some argue that it is all too easy for underage consumers to buy alcohol and tobacco.[43] They can easily get fake IDs, and store clerks are often lax in checking IDs. Indeed, most underage consumers who smoke buy their own cigarettes, usually at convenience stores and gas stations.

Exposure to Advertising. Second, questions arise as to whether kids are exposed to too much advertising for alcohol and tobacco and whether such exposure

EXHIBIT 21.7
Publicizing the Health Consequences of Smoking

Cigarette smoking at an early age can lead to serious health consequences, including lung cancer and heart disease. Public interest groups and government organizations sometimes call attention to these negative health consequences.

Source: AP/Wide World Photos.

increases their tendencies to buy these products. Arguments that disprove and support this notion have been advanced.

Some argue that alcohol and cigarette advertising has limited effects on underage consumers.[44] Traditionally, there has been a self-imposed ban by alcohol advertisers on advertising hard liquor (anything except beer and wine) on TV and a federally imposed ban on advertising cigarettes on TV. And in Canada, almost all cigarette advertising is banned. A recent survey also showed that only 8 percent of consumers name advertising as a cause of adolescent drinking. The major causes named were peer pressure and having parents who drink. Other studies show that peer influence, parental smoking, and self-esteem are the major factors affecting smoking.

Nevertheless, children are *exposed* to a lot of alcohol and tobacco advertising.[45] One study found that 15 alcohol commercials are broadcast for every hour of sports programs—and children are heavy viewers of sports. Furthermore, only 3 of 685 alcohol ads televised during 122 sporting events advertised drinking in moderation. Most ads depict alcohol as a positive and appropriate behavior of socially active and beautiful people. New media may further heighten children's exposure to alcohol ads. For example, Jim Beam has a "virtual bar" on the Internet.

Patrons enter a cartoon saloon that has ads for various alcohol brands. They can call up drink recipes and can even write graffiti on the bathroom walls. Although the system says consumers must be over 21 to access the bar, there are no checks on a user's age. Exposure is also likely to increase because the hard-liquor industry recently lifted its voluntary ban on showing alcohol ads on TV, arguing that the ban placed them at an unfair disadvantage relative to beer and wine alcohol advertisers—products with similar per drink alcohol content. Furthermore, increases in advertising expenditures have historically been associated with increased consumption of alcohol.[46]

Underage consumers are also exposed to a lot of cigarette advertising. Most magazines that youths read contain millions of dollars worth of ads by cigarette manufacturers. And most youthful smokers choose the most heavily advertised brands—further implicating advertising as a cause of smoking behavior. Exposure may be even greater as advertisers look for ways to get around advertising bans.[47] For example, in Canada and some parts of Asia, where tobacco advertising is banned, advertisers use sponsorships and licensed goods to stay in the public eye. These items do not need to carry the Surgeon General's warning label in foreign contries either. Thus consumers may not be warned of the dangers of smoking.

Not only is exposure to advertising for these products extensive, evidence suggests that the more young consumers view alcohol ads, the more they know about these products, and the more likely they are to use them.[48] One study found that almost 90 percent of 11- and 12-year-old children could identify Spuds MacKenzie as a character associated with Budweiser beer—a figure nine times the number who could identify a Coke slogan. Another found that the Budweiser frogs were among the most recognizable TV animals among 9- to 11-year-olds. Still another found that 10-year-old children had no trouble reeling off names of beers and their slogans. They could also recognize commercials based on photos in which the brand name was left out. Children who were the most aware of these ads were most likely to say that they intended to drink later in life.

A similar effect has been observed with cigarette advertising. Some research has found that teens who smoke are more likely to be aware of and recognize cigarette ads than teens who do not smoke. One study found that children were more likely than adults to associate Joe Camel with cigarettes. They were also more likely than adults to find Joe Camel appealing and to say he is "cool" and "someone they would like to be friends with." Moreover, compared with those who did not like the Joe Camel cartoon character, those who did like him were either ambivalent in their smoking intentions or expressed definite intentions to smoke. Several other studies have found that the popularity of the Camel brand has increased since the Joe Camel campaign and that today almost one-third of adolescents who buy their own cigarettes buy or prefer Camels. Furthermore, adolescents who have the greatest exposure to cigarette advertising in general tend to be the heaviest smokers, and the brands that do the most advertising tend to attract a significantly greater proportion of teenagers than adults. Thus teens appear to be particularly sensitive to advertising for cigarettes.

Targeting Youth.   Third, and perhaps of even more concern, is the suspicion that the cigarette and alcohol manufacturers explicitly *target* young consumers by portraying advertising images that youths find relevant.[49] The surgeon general, for example, has criticized the alcohol and tobacco industries for using lifestyle appeals that teens find desirable (associating the products with fun, beauty, social acceptance, sports, and sex). Many cigarette ads contain images of things like freedom from authority and independence—themes that clearly appeal to young consumers. Advertising content that shows individuals engaged in risky behavior while consuming alcohol has also been criticized.

Critics also charge that advertisers target youths by their use of fictional and cartoon characters. The most vehement criticism has been of the use of Joe Camel for Camel cigarettes, a campaign that was finally withdrawn in 1997.[50]

Advertisers claim that such characters have little effect on consumers' desires or purchasing behavior. As one advertiser said, children are not demanding Metropolitan Life insurance policies that are promoted by Snoopy and Charlie Brown.[51] Others argue that although children are aware of Joe Camel, their awareness is significantly lower than their awareness of other advertising characters. One study found that children who were most able to associate Joe Camel with cigarettes had the *least* favorable image of cigarettes.[52] The alcohol industry also argues that it does not target young consumers. And the industry argues that it has taken great strides to develop ads that promote responsible drinking. Anheuser-Busch alone has spent more than $100 million over the past decade promoting responsible drinking.[53]

Mainstream Companies Selling Smoking and Drinking.   Fourth, there is concern that mainstream advertisers may be sending inappropriate messages about cigarettes and alcohol even if they don't sell these products. For example, Aber-

EXHIBIT 21.8

Cigarette Warning Symbols

Cigarette ads and packages must carry one of the Surgeon General's warnings regarding the dangers of smoking. Are these warnings likely to be effective? Given what you know about customer behavior, think about how they could be made more effective.

Source: Michael Newman/ PhotoEdit.

crombie and Fitch recently came under public attack for producing a "back to school" issue of its catalog/magazine targeted to college students. Parents and organizations like MADD were upset over a feature titled "Drinking 101" that offered recipes for 10 hard-core cocktails.[54]

Warning Labels. Finally, marketers need to be concerned about the provision of warning labels on cigarette and alcohol packages and in ads.[55] Tobacco packages and ads are required to carry the Surgeon General's warning regarding the dangers of smoking (see Exhibit 21.8). Warning labels that reveal the dangers of drinking and driving and the risks of alcohol to pregnant women are also required. However, these warning labels have not been very effective in changing young consumers' behaviors. Perhaps one reason is that consumers' perceptual defenses make them tune out these messages. In response, the Surgeon General has called for more explicit health warnings on labels. For example, rather than saying that "alcohol *may* complicate pregnancy" or "smoking *may* cause cancer," the Surgeon General is recommending that the warnings say "alcohol *will* complicate pregnancy" and "smoking *will* cause cancer." Alcohol manufacturers also now list alcohol levels on their products so consumers clearly understand how strong the beverage is. Some researchers are also experimenting with more attention-getting warning labels. ■

NEGATIVE EFFECTS OF MARKETING

Marketing has also been implicated in creating other negative social outcomes—outcomes that are not necessarily related to deviant consumption. Several of these negative effects are examined here.

Does Advertising Affect Self-Image?

Advertising has long been accused of depicting idealized images of people and their lives. For example, few people have homes like those depicted in ads for household products, and few enjoy the holidays in the idealized manner depicted by Hallmark, Gallo, and Budweiser. Advertising may create an idealized image of what one's life *should* be like. If we do not measure up to this idealized image, we may feel dissatisfied. Here we consider two aspects of advertising and their impact on self-image:

- Does advertising make consumers dissatisfied with their appearance?
- Does advertising make consumers materialistic and hence dissatisfied with what they have achieved?

Idealized Body Images   The female models who most often appear in advertisements are young, very thin, and exceedingly beautiful. Because they represent society's conception of the ideal woman, they exemplify traits that many women will never achieve. A particularly salient issue to many women is how their body compares to that of thin models.

Obsessions with Thinness   American society places great value on thinness. As evidence, 70 percent of normal weight women want to be thinner, and 23 percent of underweight women want to be even thinner than they are.[56] A recent study of 9-year-old girls indicated that roughly 40 percent were dieting. Some children are dieting to such an extent that they are adversely affecting their growth.[57] A study in New Zealand found that thinness is popular and dieting is considered normal behavior. The same study found that from the 1950s through the 1980s, women depicted in ads got increasingly thinner.[58]

This focus on thinness is a relatively recent phenomenon. During the 15th through 18th centuries, being fat was considered fashionable and erotic.[59] Furthermore, being thin is clearly a Western value. In Third World countries, where food is lacking and disease is rampant, weight gain is associated with health and prosperity.[60]

Thinness, Advertising, and Self-Perceptions   Certainly, seeing ads with thin models does not make a woman become anorexic, but do such ads serve as an impetus to women with anorexic predispositions? Does identification with superthin models create dissatisfaction with one's own body and appearance?[61] Some evidence suggests the answer to these questions is yes.

social comparison theory A theory that proposes that individuals have a drive to compare themselves to other people.

Social comparison theory proposes that individuals have a drive to compare themselves to other people.[62] Consistent with this theory, some research has found that young adult females do compare themselves with models in advertisements and that such self-comparisons can affect self-esteem.[63] One outcome of this comparison process is that consumers feel inadequate if they do not live up to the comparison person. Exhibit 21.9 illustrates the statements female consumers in one study made when they looked at magazine ads that featured beautiful models. As one 16-year-old consumer put it, "Gosh, we thought we had to look like Cindy Crawford, and now we have to look like this!" Interestingly, some research has also found that consumers who are shown ads with beautiful models reduce their attractiveness ratings of average-looking women. A potentially strong conclusion, then, is that advertising can have a negative impact on satisfaction with one's appearance. Clearly, the ad for Chic Jeans in Exhibit 21.10 is trying to counter this effect with the following statements: "I'm not too short, I'm not too tall, I'm not too big, I'm not too small . . . I'm not too this, I'm not too that, I'm beautiful."

GENERAL COMPARISON	"God! I wish I looked like that." (written comment about a cosmetic ad before discussion began) "There's certain [ads] that I look at and say, 'Wow! I'd sure like to look like that.'" "In high school, you want to think that you could look like that if you try. Then in college, you realize, 'Oh, forget it.'"
ADS GENERATING SPECIFIC BODY COMPARISONS	"When I see ads, I always look at the chest. I like it when she has no chest. Because, you know, I don't either." "I have wide hips. I always look at the hips. I guess I'm just jealous." "When I look at a model I look at the arms, because my arms are awful."
NEGATIVE SELF-FEELINGS FROM VIEWING ADS	"You look at these ads and you feel inadequate, like you can't measure up." "It's frustrating when you start to realize you should look that way—I mean—I can't." "I used to go through these magazines every day and look at [models in the ads] and wish I looked like them. I used to go running every day, and really thought maybe I could look like them. I remember, I even picked one model in particular and cut out ads with her in them. I was pretty obsessed. And I finally realized this wasn't realistic. But I sometimes still look and think, 'Well, maybe.'" "Sometimes [ads with models] can make you feel a little depressed." "They make me feel self-critical." (participant viewing models in swimsuit ads)

EXHIBIT 21.9

Women's Reactions to Idealized Body Images in Ads

One study found that women exposed to ads with beautiful and thin models compared the models to themselves or specific parts of their bodies. In some cases, the ads made consumers feel bad about themselves.

Source: Marsha L. Richins, "Social Comparison and the Idealized Images of Advertising," *Journal of Consumer Research*, June 1991, pp. 71–83. © 1991 University of Chicago. All rights reserved.

MARKETING IMPLICATIONS Fortunately, some companies are becoming more sensitive to the effects of such messages. In the fashion industry demand for plus-size models is up—perhaps in response to consumers' demands for different types of women in fashion products and ads.[64] Furthermore, although some women may be unhappy about how they compare with models in ads, women in general are becoming more comfortable with themselves and are more hostile toward advertisers who perpetuate unrealistic images of women.[65]

Materialism In addition to affecting consumers' satisfaction with their appearance, advertising has also been criticized for perpetuating materialistic values and making consumers less satisfied with their lives. In support of this contention, social critics charge that advertising creates materialistic values.[66] For example, as advertising content has increasingly depicted materialistic themes, Americans have become more materialistic. Consumers in other countries have also become more materialistic, and the rise in materialism often coincides with the purchase of American products and exposure to American advertisements. Research has found that consumers who watch a lot of TV and who find that TV commercials are realistic tend to be more materialistic than consumers who do not watch as much TV.[67] Television shows may provide a biased or distorted view of reality by showing heroes who seem to have everything at their disposal.

Materialism, Advertising, and Perceptions of People Social comparison theory would predict that if advertising and the media show individuals with many material possessions, consumers might use advertising as a way of judging their personal accomplishments. Consumers who perceive that they are less well-off than the comparison population may be less satisfied with their lives

I'm not too short
I'm not too tall
I'm not too big
I'm not too small
I'm not too shy
I'm not too bold
I'm not too young
I'm not too old
I'm not too thin
I'm not too fat
I'm not too this
I'm not too that
I'm *beautiful*

chic
JEANS
www.chicjeans.com

EXHIBIT 21.10
Counteracting the Ideal Image

The ad for Chic jeans recognizes that women come in all shapes and sizes and that each one can be considered beautiful.

Source: Amodeo Petti Agency. John Amodeo Photograher.

and accomplishments. Some evidence supports this idea. Consumers who watch a lot of advertising tend to overestimate how well-off the average consumer is.[68] This misperception sets up a potentially false frame of reference regarding how much the average consumer owns.

Also, because the material "good life" often depicted in advertising is out of reach for many, consumers are set up for potential dissatisfaction. Governments in some countries have been reluctant to show U.S. ads, fearing that such ads will set off a wave of desires for products that the country cannot produce and/or the people cannot afford.[69] In Russia, children who were used to playing with stones and chalk are now encountering ads for toys such as Lego blocks, Barbie dolls, and My Pretty Pony and for foods such as Coke and chocolate bars. As one consumer put it, "Parents are now in the position of disappointing their children in ways that were once impossible."[70] We currently have little definitive evidence that advertising causes materialism and dissatisfaction, but what is available is provocative and deserving of more work.

Finally, materialistic consumers may place undue attention on the possessions of others and make inferences about them based on the possessions they own.[71]

Does Advertising Misrepresent Segments of Consumers?

Advertising has also been criticized for ignoring or inaccurately representing key segments in the marketplace.

Ignoring Key Segments   Although women represent 50 percent of the population, they have been conspicuously absent in ads for nondomestic products and large-ticket items like cars.[72] Even when women are represented, ads often contain male voice-overs. Advertisers have historically believed that male voices are more convincing, more credible, and better at conveying knowledge and expertise than female voices are. When women's voices are used, they are used primarily to speak to dogs, cats, babies, children, and women dieters rather than to the population at large.[73]

Likewise, although African Americans represent roughly 12 percent of the U.S. population and 11 percent of magazine readers, one study found that they appeared in less than 5 percent of all magazine ads and less than 8 percent of TV ads. Hispanics and Asians have been represented in even fewer TV commercials. Moreover, when these minorities are depicted in ads, they are often shown in primarily background roles.[74] Others charge that although marketers are more cognizant of the important Hispanic and African American markets, advertisers have tended to ignore consumers from countries such as Iran, Israel, Poland, Russia, Korea, and Vietnam.[75] Sometimes minorities are deliberately excluded from advertising. In Britain, Ford Motor Company was recently publicly railed for substituting white faces for black, Indian, and Pakistani workers who appeared in a company brochure.[76]

A similar situation describes advertising for mature consumers.[77] As with other groups, when they are represented, mature consumers tend to have minor roles in ads.

Stereotyping Key Segments   Unfortunately, groups are also sometimes represented in stereotypical ways.[78] For example, women have been represented in gender stereotyped ways—as the mother, wife, homemaker, and sex object. Interestingly, this pattern holds true whether the products are for men or for women. Women have historically been shown in ads for household cleaning products despite the fact that a relatively large number of households are headed by single or divorced men. Women are also more likely than men to be depicted without a paid occupation or are portrayed in lower status occupations than men—a portrayal that does not accurately represent the status of women in the workforce. Both in the United States and in other countries, women and girls have also been depicted as secondary, dependent, nurturant, receivers of help, and concerned about appearance. Men and boys have been portrayed as knowledgeable, achieving, independent, active, dynamic, masterful, and important. Brewing companies, notorious for portraying scantily clad women, have been criticized for being sexist and discriminating against women. Sex stereotypic portrayals are not restricted to ads in the United States.

Stereotypical images of minorities can also be identified.[79] For example, consistent with ethnic stereotypes regarding work ethic, Asian consumers are more likely to appear in work than in family or social roles.

The mature segment has also been stereotyped—sometimes in nonflattering ways.[80] Depictions of the mature consumer as blue-haired, weak, passive, unproductive, ailing, doddering, foolish, and sexless are not uncommon. Advertisers have also been known to alienate mature consumers by using terms such as *senior citizens*, *retirees*, and *golden years*. Mature consumers also react negatively to ads that show older people leading nonproductive lives. Because many mature consumers view themselves as being 10 to 15 years younger than their actual chronological age, they react more positively to ads whose models are somewhat younger than they are.

MARKETING IMPLICATIONS   Alienating consumers by excluding or failing to represent them accurately can negatively affect consumers' images of and attitudes toward brands and companies.[81] Offensive advertising can bring about even more severe reactions. Some Canadian women, for example, are boycotting clothing and cosmetic products that depict inaccurate and unrealistic images of women. Given the size of these markets, alienating comsumers can be very costly. Therefore, many marketers are taking steps to improve their depiction of these consumers.

Represent Key Segments.   Many advertisers have made efforts to represent key segments in their advertising (see Exhibit 21.11).[82] For example, a recent study found that 26 percent of all commercials shown by ABC, CBS, and NBC during one week of prime-time programming contained African American consumers. The representation of the elderly in print ads has also been on the rise. Some companies like Frito-Lay have dropped logos that represent minorities in stereotypical ways or have modified their logos to present more positive portrayals. For example, Quaker Oats changed Aunt Jemima from a black mammy to a black homemaker—someone akin to Betty Crocker.

Avoid Stereotypes.   Advertisers are also representing groups in more positive and less stereotypical ways. Several ads have done well by depicting the mature

"The rewards of a *good life insurance* plan can be seen generations after the paperwork is done."
~David Takagi

TRANSAMERICA LIFE COMPANIES

David and Verne Takagi and Joyce Takagi-Pavlis have the unique pleasure of seeing generations of people benefit from their family's counsel. In 1947, their father, Douglas J. Takagi, became a Transamerica agent. Today, his three children carry on a tradition of dedicated service to many of his original clients, their children and their grandchildren. As Transamerica sales professionals, the Takagis are people you can trust for life. To contact our representative nearest you, call 1-800-367-6842.

"If integrity, trust and genuine caring matter to you, you're not alone. They matter to us, too."

President, Life Insurance Division

EXHIBIT 21.11

Representing Under-represented Groups in Advertising

Advertisers are overcoming the criticism that they have (1) ignored key segments of consumers in their advertising or (2) represented them in stereotypical ways.

Source: Courtesy of Transamerica Life Companies.

consumer as wise, spunky, romantic, and simply as an individual. In general, ads that depict mature consumers as active, take-charge doers are more consistent with mature consumers' views of themselves.

Similarly, the portrayal of women in advertising is improving.[83] A recent Nike campaign focuses on female pride, and a recent Michelob ad portrays men and women as equals and professionals. Car companies have begun to depict women as decision makers. There is also a trend toward depicting men in activities historically assigned to women. Some ads, like the one in Exhibit 21.12, show poignant pictures of fathers engaged in gentle and nurturing activities with their children.

Tailor Communications to Key Targets. Companies are also recognizing that it is not sufficient simply to place a member of a minority group in an ad. Instead, advertisers need to understand more about these consumers.[84] Many companies are relying on specialty advertising agencies that have knowledge of these key target groups. Sosa and Associates in San Antonio, for example, is one of the leading Hispanic agencies in the country. Many other agencies have branches that specialize in advertising to Hispanic consumers. ■

Do Marketing Practices Invade Consumers' Privacy?

The opening vignette raised the question of whether companies that operate on-line invade consumers' privacy by collecting information about them—often without their knowledge. Consider the following scenario in a nonelectronic commerce context. You receive an application for a credit card in the mail. You fill in the necessary information (address, telephone number, banks where you do business, and income), and then use the card to buy kids' clothes, a jogging suit, and a high-definition color TV at a national retailer. You fill in and subsequently mail the product registration form for the TV. Some time later you get mail from an insurance company, indicating the importance of buying life insurance to protect your family. You also get mail from a real estate company, introducing you to an agent in your area and listing the area's more expensive and larger homes. Finally, you start getting specialty sports catalogs. Although these events may seem unrelated, they may be very much related, and all are based on information that you (wittingly or unwittingly) provided.

The retailer might own the credit card company and the real estate company. Thus between the information you provided to get your credit card and the information on your account about what you bought, the retailer and its subsidiaries now know a lot about you. They can use this information to target you for other products and services. The insurance company knows that you are a prime target for insurance because you have a young family (you bought clothes for the children). It also surmises that you are unlikely to make a life insurance claim (die) because you are young and because you exercise (you bought a jogging suit). Based on the address you provided and your income, the real estate agency knows roughly how much you paid for your house and what

There are a lot of good reasons for choosing the Quiet Company.

Some are more important than others.

Northwestern Mutual Life has always received the highest possible ratings from Moody's, Standard & Poor's, A.M. Best and Duff & Phelps. It has been voted "the most financially sound life insurance company" every year in a survey sponsored by FORTUNE® magazine. When you have a new reason for wanting the most secure life insurance, talk to the Quiet Company. Northwestern Mutual Life.

Northwestern Mutual Life®
The Quiet Company®

NORTHWESTERN MUTUAL LIFE IS AN ADVERTISING SPONSOR OF THE 1994 WINTER OLYMPICS BROADCAST ON CBS.
© 1994 The Northwestern Mutual Life Insurance Company, Milwaukee, Wisconsin.

EXHIBIT 21.12

Changing Images of Men in Advertising

Some advertisers have tried to depict less stereotypical images of men, showing them as prominent figures in sensitive and nurturing roles.

Source: Photographer: Victor Skrebneski.

types of houses are likely to be a step up from the one you own. Through your purchases, the credit card company also knows that you may be interested in catalogs or information related to the types of products you bought. Thus it may sell information about you to other marketers (e.g., catalog marketers) who think that you may also be interested in the products and services they sell. The product registration card you filled out may go a company that tracks other products you have bought. From your registration information, that company can determine what your lifestyle must be like and, therefore, what other products and services might appeal to you. In turn, the company can sell or rent your name to prospective marketers (including catalog marketers) who market to particular lifestyle segments. This scenario merely highlights the amount and type of information businesses are able to collect about consumers. Exhibit 21.13 provides more examples.

Where Does Information Come From? Interestingly, much of the information that companies have about consumers is information that consumers themselves provide. For example, marketers can keep track of a consumer's purchase decisions through scanner data at the supermarket. Many catalog companies know a great deal about consumers based on what neighborhood they live in. And there are ever-increasing attempts to get to know consumers through marketing research.

Considerable consumer information also exists in the public domain in the form of zip codes and census data. The government sells this information to marketers who use it to update their mailing lists, target people who have moved, determine consumers' likely income based on the type of neighborhood in which they live, and so on.[85]

Consumers' Responses Consumers are clearly uncomfortable with the amount of information marketers have about them.[86] A recent survey showed that 78 percent of consumers believe that businesses collect too much personal information, and 88 percent are concerned about threats to their personal privacy. Eighty-two percent perceive a lack of control over the use of their personal information by businesses, and 41 percent believe that businesses have already invaded their privacy.[87] In a survey of privacy and the Internet, 64 percent of respondents agreed that companies that use the Internet should not be allowed to track users for the purposes of sending them marketing messages.[88] Sixty percent of Americans believe that lack of privacy will be a serious issue in 25 to 50 years.[89] Consumers also complain that they do not receive any money from the sale of their name by credit card companies, publishers, and catalog companies (among others) to other companies. Furthermore, consumers must then spend time sifting through the mailings from companies that have bought their name.[90]

Moreover, consumers do not seem to trust marketers' use of personal information.[91] Consumers worry that information is collected about them for one pur-

BUSINESSES	WHAT THEY KNOW	WHAT THEY DO WITH IT	HOW YOU CAN STOP IT
Banks and thrifts	Your balances and transactions for all bank accounts, including loans and investments; how profitable your account is. Your age, children's ages, estimated income, value of your home, car; how long you've lived there; how many credit cards you have; how frequently you use them; estimate of your creditworthiness	Identify additional services and products they can sell you; provide loan-payment information to credit bureaus; share customer names with affiliated brokers insurance agents, or others who sell financial services.	Tell a customer service representative or bank officer to flag your file so you will no longer be solicited for bank and other financial products.
Mail order companies	What you buy, when you do it, and how much you spend; whether you buy by credit card; whether you order by phone or mail; whether you buy on sale; what sizes you order. Your age, occupation, whether you own a home, size of your home.	Identify other merchandise that they can sell to you; they rent or swap it with other catalogue companies, magazines, and nonprofit groups.	Write to the company's name-removal service or write to Direct Marketing Association Mail Preference Service (P.O. Box 9008, Farmingdale, NY 11735) and request that you be dropped from lists.
Telephone companies	What numbers you call and how often; whether you are a frequent caller of 800 or 900 lines; your payment history. Estimates of income, number and ages of children; interest in foreign travel; size of your home; marital status; occupation.	Sell you other services; some regional phone companies rent names, addresses, and phone numbers to local merchants and national marketers; long distance companies provide companies that buy 800 and 900 lines with the phone numbers of 800 and 900 callers.	Write your local phone company's customer service department saying that you do not want your name rented.

EXHIBIT 21.13
Big Businesses Have Your Number

Although consumers may not know it, many businesses collect a lot of information about them. As long as consumers do not object or take explicit action, businesses will use this information to help them market their products. Does the collection and use of this information represent "invasion of privacy"?

Source: Ruth Simon, "Stop Them From Selling Your Financial Secrets," *Money,* March 1992, pp. 99–110.

pose but is used by the company for another purpose or it is sold to another company without their knowledge. They also worry that personal data is handled by individuals who may not be properly authorized to handle it and who can therefore steal or abuse it. Finally, consumers worry that personal data such as credit histories may have errors and that protections against such errors are inadequate. Consumers and marketers also disagree on who should control information about consumers. For example, some businesses believe that they own whatever information they legitimately obtain about their customers. Businesses also justify their use of consumer information by saying that it helps them to provide better products and services to consumers.[92]

MARKETING IMPLICATIONS

Why are consumers so concerned about marketers' use of personal information?

Horror Stories Hurt All Marketers. One of the major reasons for concern is that a small number of unscrupulous marketers use marketing techniques to defraud consumers. For example, think of the stories you have heard about companies that have defrauded elderly consumers of their life savings.[93] These stories get considerable media attention and tarnish the image of all marketers. Consumers are also wary because information disclosures occurring on other fronts make them worry about the lack of privacy in general. For example, more and more workers are losing jobs or are being denied jobs because information about their current or past health history has been leaked to current or prospective employers.[94]

Communicating How Information Helps Consumers. Marketers believe that the biggest reason for privacy concerns is that consumers really do not understand how the information marketers collect is used and how it might benefit consumers. For example, the information collected by catalog companies on such things as consumers' household characteristics, clothing style, and sizes allows marketers to develop customized catalogs. This practice helps consumers in several ways. It eliminates waste because marketers can more accurately target consumers. Also, because they can offer specialized catalogs on a more targeted basis, marketers can keep down the costs involved in marketing the

product. These savings, in turn, may be passed on to the consumer. By tracking personal information on-line, companies can help consumers save time because they do not have to retype personal information; in addition, the companies can provide customized messages or services specific to the purchase needs of those consumers. Excite, for example, lets customers develop personalized Excite pages with local weather, news, movie listings, and so on. Customers who develop these personalized pages return to the site 20 times more often than those who do not.[95]

Laws and Self-Imposed Regulation. Recent trends are placing greater power in the hands of the consumer. In Canada a new privacy code requires direct marketers to give consumers the opportunity to opt out of mailing lists.[96] Consumers in the United States have the same option. They can write to the Direct Marketing Association and ask that their name not be sold to other companies. But many

consumers do not know that this option exists.[97] In Germany laws prohibit companies from exchanging customer lists. And in the European Union (EU), proposals are on the table to prohibit the transfer of personal information to companies outside the EU.[98]

The United States government is giving businesses a last chance to design self-imposed standards for consumer privacy protection. Two organizations, the Council of Better Bureaus and the Alliance for Privacy (a group of 50 top U.S. companies), are developing plans that require members to inform consumers about the personal information being collected on-line and how that information

will be shared. Members are also required to seek permission from parents before they collect personal information from children under the age of 13.[99] ■

How Can Consumers Resist Marketing Practices?

What can consumers do if they are upset about negative marketing practices like those just described? Can consumers change the nature of marketing activities? The answer is yes. Consumers can engage in several forms of consumer resistance.[100]

Individual Resistance Efforts   First, consumers who are upset or otherwise dissatisfied with marketing practices can demonstrate dissatisfaction by not patronizing the offending marketer in the future, by complaining to the offending marketer, and/or by spreading negative word of mouth. These individual consumer resistance strategies can be very effective. For example, Calvin Klein withdrew an ad campaign that showed very young girls in provocatively posed positions in response to public outcry and criticisms of child pornography.[101]

Advocacy Groups   Group strategies are potentially even more powerful than unorganized consumer efforts. Some formally organized advocacy groups engage in resistance by informing the public about marketing practices regarded as socially inappropriate. One advocacy group called the Center for the Study of Commercialism disseminates information via videos, pamphlets, books, and conferences and engages in lobbying efforts to stop forms of marketing like Channel One's advertising in schools. *Adbusters*, a magazine published by Canada's Media Foundation, publishes articles that make consumers aware of commercial excess, for example, "The McBraining of America," "American Excess," "Buy-ological Urge," and "The Casino Society."[102] The Media Foundation also produces TV campaigns on various consumer issues. Contributions from interested consumers help defray the cost of showing the campaigns in their hometowns.

boycott An organized activity in which consumers avoid purchasing products or services from a company whose policies or practices are seen as unfair or unjust.

Boycotts   Another type of group strategy is a boycott. A **boycott** is an organized activity in which consumers avoid purchasing products or services from a company whose policies or practices are seen as unfair or unjust. Products are not the only items that are boycotted. Sometimes boycotts are directed against a company's activities rather than against a product itself.[103] For example, a group called Neighbor to Neighbor boycotted Folgers coffee for buying coffee beans from El Salvador. The group argued that by buying beans from El Salvador, Procter & Gamble was indirectly financing the war taking place in that country. The National Hispanic Media Coalition recently boycotted Capital Cities/ABC because it had not included Latinos and Latin-themed roles in its programs. Other boycotts are listed in Exhibit 21.14. Finally, some consumers have chosen to boycott products made in sweatshops in foreign countries. Nike has come under attack for such practices. In Indonesia workers might make as little as $.15 per hour, though the shoes sell for $75.00 and up. Similarly, 80 percent of soccer balls sold in the United States are made with child labor in Pakistan.

Although only 20 national boycotts were recorded by the year 1981, more than 250 were recorded by the early 1990s.[104] This dramatic increase is partly due to government deregulation of businesses and the underfunding of agencies that monitor business practices.[105] Because the government was not regulating business practices, the people took on the action of doing so.

Clearly, boycotts can hurt companies financially. When Pizzeria Uno was besieged by protesters with leaflets decrying its use of coffee from El Salvador, sales dropped.[106] However, in some cases sales have risen because of boycotts (perhaps because the publicity made the company's brand name more familiar). For example, StarKist tuna sales rose during the tuna boycott, and when Shell Oil was targeted in the 1980s for its presence in South Africa, its sales also rose.[107] The primary indicators that a boycott has been successful are not its financial effects, but rather that it (1) changes the offending policies, (2) makes businesses more cautious and responsible in their future activities, and (3) forces changes in the behavior of nontargeted businesses that engage in similarly offensive practices.

EXHIBIT 21.14
Examples of Consumer Boycotts

Consumers sometimes engage in resistance strategies like boycotts to protest business activities.

GROUP ORGANIZING BOYCOTT	COMPANY BOYCOTTED	INFRACTION
American Family Association	Burger King	Advertising on programs that do not support "family values"
INFACT	General Electric	Operation of nuclear weapons plant
Gay and lesbian groups	Cracker Barrel	Firing of homosexual employees
In Defense of Animals	Anheuser-Busch	Sea World subsidiary keeps whales in captivity
Women and Guns	Estée Lauder	Supports gun control initiatives
Humane Society	Veal industry	Practice of raising calves in small crates
Rainforest Action Network	Mitsubishi	Logging operations are destroying tropical rainforests
Stop Teenage Addiction to Tobacco	Kraft General Foods and RJR Nabisco	Producing cigarettes through their Philip Morris and RJR subsidiaries
Irish National Caucus	Ford Motor Company	Says auto maker discriminates against Irish Catholics in Northern Ireland
Fierza Unida	Levi Strauss	Moved operations abroad displacing U.S. workers
Northwest Animal Rights Network	IAMS petfood	Sponsored Iditarod dogsled race in Alaska

Source: Todd Putnam, "Boycotts Are Busting Out All Over," *Business and Society Review,* Spring 1993, pp. 47–51. Reprinted by permission.

SUMMARY

Deviant consumer behavior includes both illegal and psychologically/physically abnormal behavior. Deviant acquisition behaviors include compulsive buying, consumer theft, and black markets, and deviant consumption behaviors include addictive and compulsive consumption and underage drinking and smoking. These behaviors are fairly pervasive in our consumer society, and although some of them (e.g., black markets) can offer consumer benefits, most others can have fairly negative effects on consumers and the social groups in which they operate.

Moreover, questions can be raised about whether and/or how much marketing practices influence these behaviors. Advertising has been accused of perpetuating idealized body images and creating materialistic values. It has also been accused of failing to represent key consumer segments in our society or representing them stereotypically. Whether marketers invade privacy, how they do so, and whether they can legitimately control the information they receive from consumers is currently under debate.

Because the socially redeeming benefits of advertising and some marketing practices are currently in question, many marketers are adopting strategies to both reduce the criticism and put marketing practices in a more favorable light. At the same time, sophisticated consumers are showing their disapproval of practices regarded as disreputable, objectionable, and/or unethical. Boycotts are one of the most pervasive and powerful consumer resistance strategies.

EXERCISES

1. Visit different types of retail establishments and different service organizations to learn about their yearly losses due to theft, insights about things that affect theft, whether theft has been increasing or decreasing over recent years, and the measures they are taking to reduce theft. Report your results to the class. Interview consumers about their theft behavior. Ask consumers whether they have ever engaged in theft and why. Discuss your findings with other members of the class. Do the findings support, enhance, or modify the findings shown in Exhibit 21.5?

2. Collect and share magazine advertisements that deal with cigarettes or alcohol. Do these ads suggest that such advertising (a) is excessive, (b) targets youths, or (c) represents images that are attractive to youths?

3. Collect and share magazine advertisements that use models. Use these advertisements and your own personal experience to argue for or against the idea that advertising perpetuates negative body images.

4. Collect and share magazine advertisements that portray women, minorities, and mature consumers. Based on your observations, evaluate whether advertisers misrepresent these key segments or represent them in stereotypical ways.

CHAPTER 1

1. Chad Rubel, "Young Firm Armed with Technology Fights an Old Giant," *Marketing News*, June 19, 1995, p. 2; "ETM to Provide BI-LO Ticketing," *Amusement Business*, August 31, 1998, p. 20.
2. Jacob Jacoby, "Consumer Psychology: An Octennium," in eds. Paul Mussen and Mark Rosenzweig, *Annual Review of Psychology*, 1976, Annual Reviews, Palo Alto, CA, pp. 331–358. With permission from the *Annual Review of Psychology*, Volume 27, © 1976, by Annual Reviews.
3. Morris B. Holbrook, "What Is Consumer Research?" *Journal of Consumer Research*, June 1987, pp. 128–132; Russell W. Belk, "Manifesto for a Consumer Behavior of Consumer Behavior," *Scientific Method in Marketing*, 1984, AMA Winter Educators' Conference.
4. Jonathan Arndt, "Role of Product-Related Conversations in the Diffusion of a New Product," *Journal of Marketing Research*, August 1967, pp. 291–295; Vijay Mahajan, Eitan Muller, and Frank M. Bass, "New Product Diffusion Models in Marketing: A Review and Directions," *Journal of Marketing*, January 1990, pp. 1–27.
5. Mark Robichaux, "Cable Industry Tries Guarantees of Better Service to Polish Image," *Wall Street Journal*, December 1, 1994, p. B1.
6. Jacob Jacoby, Carol K. Berning, and Thomas F. Dietworst, "What about Disposition?" *Journal of Marketing*, April 1977, pp. 22–28.
7. Tibbet L. Speer, "Growing the Green Market," *American Demographics*, August 1997, pp. 45–49.
8. John L. Mitchell, "Digging for Dollars," *Los Angeles Times*, October 30, 1995, pp. B1, B6.
9. John J. Keller, "Cellular Phones May Affect Use of Pacemakers," *Wall Street Journal*, April 28, 1995, pp. B1, B3; Julia Flynn and John Carey, "More Sound Fury Over Cell Phones: Do They Cause Brain Tumors? *Business Week*, January 26, 1998, p. 35.
10. Peter K. Francese, "Big Spenders," *American Demographics*, August 1997, pp. 51–58.
11. Mathis Chazanov, "Body Language," *Los Angeles Times: Westside News*, April 30, 1995, pp. 10–15.
12. Pichayaporn Utumporn, "For a Vacation That's a Real Blast, How about Launching a Grenade," *Wall Street Journal*, January 13, 1998, B1.
13. Yumiko Ono, "Buttering up Customers for Margarine," *Wall Street Journal*, June 7, 1994, pp. B1, B6.
14. Barry Newman, "Hungarians Have Cash to Buy Homes If There Were Any," *Wall Street Journal*, July 31, 1995, pp. A1, A4.
15. Craig S. Smith, "U.S. Bank Cards Fight to Win China's Millions," *Wall Street Journal*, July 17, 1995, pp. B1, B5.
16. Bob Ortega, "Swap the Sweat of Your Brow for a Suite Right on the Beach," *Wall Street Journal*, June 16, 1995, pp. B1, B7.
17. "At Clothiers, It's Many Unhappy Returns When Buyers Turn out to Be Borrowers," *Wall Street Journal*, June 2, 1992, pp. B1, B7.
18. Junda Woo, "Big Copyright Curbs Sought by Industry," *Wall Street Journal*, December 27, 1994, p. B5.
19. See, for example, Valerie S. Folkes, Ingrid M. Martin, and Kamal Gupta, "When to Say When: Effects of Supply on Usage," *Journal of Consumer Research*, December 1993, pp. 467–477.
20. Sara Kehaulani Goo, "Americans Shift Down and Out of Manual Transmissions," *Wall Street Journal*, August 19, 1998, pp. B1, B4.
21. Kevin Goldman, "Company Faces Challenge in Marketing Female Condom," *Wall Street Journal*, July 27, 1994, p. B4.
22. Mark A. Le Turck and Gerald M. Goldhaben, "Effectiveness of Product Warning Labels: Effects of Consumer Information Processing Objectives," *Journal of Public Affairs*, Summer 1989, pp. 111–125.
23. Jacoby, Berning, and Dietworst, "What about Disposition?"
24. Russell W. Belk, "Collecting as Luxury Consumption: Effects on Individuals and Households," *Journal of Economic Psychology*, September 1995, pp. 477–490.
25. G. Bruce Knecht and Eleena de Lisser, "Once and for All, Is the Cold Good or Bad for Business," *Wall Street Journal*, February 6, 1996, pp. B1, B9.
26. Sara McBride, "In Election Whitewash, Dentists Play a Covert but Cleansing Role," *Wall Street Journal*, November 6, 1996, p. B1.
27. Eileen Kinsella, "Eat Grits Sushi, Pitch Ears of Corn and Roll in a Big Bowl of Mush," *Wall Street Journal*, April 19, 1996, B1.
28. William M. Buckeley, "New On-Line Casinos May Thwart U.S. Laws," *Wall Street Journal*, May 10, 1995, p. B1.
29. Mary Beth Grover, "Christmas is Coming: Where's your Call Center", *Forbes*, December 13, 1999 pp. 86–90; Calmetta Y. Colman and Douglas A. Blackmon, "E-Business: Retailers Strive for Shopping Synergy," *Wall Street Journal*, December 20, 1999, p. B1; Abigail Goldman, "Who'll Be the Internet's Jolliest Holiday Merchants?; Customers", Los Angeles Times, December 12, 1999, p. 1.
30. Nancy Ann Jeffrey, "Attention Shoppers: Get a Loan While Picking up Groceries," *Wall Street Journal*, December 20, 1995, pp. C1, C18.
31. Lisa Gubernick, "Secondhand Chic", *Forbes*, April 26, 1993, p. 172; Louise Lee, "Secondhand Goods Make First-Rate Gifts, or So More Christmas Shoppers Believe," *Wall Street Journal*, December 19, 1995, p. B1.
32. "Click Here for Coverage," *Business Week*, June 1, 1998, pp. 162–163.
33. Morris B. Holbrook and Meryl P. Gardner, "How Motivation Moderates the Effects of Emotion on the

Duration of Consumption," *Journal of Business Research*, July 1998, pp. 241–252.

34. "Reading Tea Leaves in China: Start-up Sees Grounds for Coffee," *Los Angeles Times*, April 20, 1995, p. D4.

35. Matt Rees, "For Some, Frequent-Flier Miles a Passion," *Los Angeles Times*, April 6, 1995, p. D5.

36. Shannon Dorcht, "America Weighs In," *American Demographics*, June 1997, pp. 39–45.

37. Elyse Tanouye, "Researchers Report More Patients Ill with Bacterium Resistant to Antibiotics," *Wall Street Journal*, August 24, 1995, B9.

38. Philip Kotler and Gary Armstrong, *Principles of Marketing*, 8th ed. Copyright © 1999 by Prentice-Hall, Inc. Used with permission.

39. Albert R. Karr, "U.S. to Expand Reviews of Airlines to Halt Deceptive Marketing Practices," *Wall Street Journal*, January 24, 1995, p. B9.

40. Sam Loewenberg, "Western Advertisers Struggle to Conquer the Wild Romanian Frontier," *Los Angeles Times*, June 15, 1995, pp. D4, D9.

41. Eben Shapiro, "Ads Denounce Time Warner for Rap Music," *Wall Street Journal*, May 17, 1995, pp. B1, B6.

42. Robert Tomsho, "Costly Funerals Spur a Co-op Movement to Hold Down Bills," *Wall Street Journal*, November 12, 1996, pp. A1, A6.

43. Amy Harmon, "Fun and Games—and Gore," *Los Angeles Times*, May 12, 1995, pp. A1, A28–29.

44. Marilyn Chase, "The Vow to Eat More Fish Requires Knowing the Risks," *Wall Street Journal*, August 5, 1996, p. B1.

45. Kevin Goldman, "AIDS-Related Product Marketed in Mass Media, Drawing Critics," *Wall Street Journal*, December 2, 1994, p. B7.

46. Stephen Labaton, "Out of Work for a Year, R.J. Reynolds Tobacco's Cartoon Endorser Now Faces Government Charges," *New York Times*, November 9, 1998, p. 8.

47. Denise Gellene, "It's Good for You, But Don't Expect Labels to Say That," *Los Angeles Times*, May 8, 1995, pp. D1, D3.

48. James R. Bettman, *An Information Processing Theory of Consumer Choice* (Reading, Mass.: Addison-Wesley, 1979).

49. Amy Harmon, "FTC to Propose Laws to Protect Children On-line," *New York Times*, June 4, 1998, pp. C1, D1.

CHAPTER 2

1. Michelle Wirth Fellman, "Auto Researchers' Focus on Customers Can Help Drive Sales in Other Industries," *Marketing News*, January 4, 1999, pp. 1, 30–31; Anita Lienert, "These Are Not Your Father's Ads; Marketing Takes Risks: TV Characters and 'Toons Try to Attract Younger Women," *Detroit News*, October 20, 1998, p. B1.

2. Dick McCullough, "Web-Based Market Research Ushers in a New Age," *Marketing News*, September 14, 1998. pp. 27–28.

3. Simmons Market Research Bureau, 1994.

4. Tom McGee, "Getting inside Kids' Heads," *American Demographics*, January 1997, pp. 52–55.

5. Hillary Rosner, "Hocus Focus," *Village Voice*, December 15, 1998, p.43.

6. Chad Rubel, "Two Research Techniques Probe Shoppers' Minds," *Marketing News*, July 29, 1996, p. 16.

7. Ronald B. Lieber and Joyce E. Davis, "Storytelling: A New Way to Get Close to Your Customer", *Fortune*, February 3, 1997, pp. 102–108.

8. Deborah D. Heisley and Sidney J. Levy, "Autodriving: A Photoelicitation Technique," *Journal of Consumer Research*, December 1991, pp. 257–272.

9. www.hbs.edu/units/marketing/zmet, "The Zaltman Metaphor Elicitation Technique," January 5, 1999; Morris B. Holbrook, "Collective Stereographic Photo Essays: An Integrated Approach to Probing Consumption Experiences in Depth," *International Journal of Research in Marketing*, July 1998, pp. 201–221.

10. Lieber and Davis, "Storytelling: A New Way to Get Close to Your Customer."

11. McGee, "Getting inside Kids' Heads."

12. Mike Hofman, "Virtual Shopping," *Inc.*, October 1998, p. 88.

13. Geraldine Brooks, "It's Goo, Goo, Goo, Goo Vibrations at the Gerber Lab," *Wall Street Journal*, December 4, 1996, pp. A1, A6.

14. Lieber and Davis, "Storytelling: A New Way to Get Close to Your Customer."

15. Christina Brinkley, "Harrah's Builds Database about Patrons," *Wall Street Journal*, September 2, 1997, pp. B1, B10.

16. Direct Marketing Association, *Profitable Retailing Using Relationship and Database Marketing* (Ithaca N.Y.: American Demographics Books, 1999).

17. www.arfsite.org.

18. Jacob Jacoby and George J. Szybillo, "Consumer Research in FTC versus Kraft (1991): A Case of Heads We Win, Tails You Lose", *Journal of Public Policy and Marketing*, Spring 1995, pp. 1–14; David W. Stewart, "Deception Materiality, and Survey Research: Some Lessons from Kraft," *Journal of Public Policy and Marketing*, Spring 1995, pp.15–28.

19. Kelly Shermach, "Portrait of the World," *Marketing News*, August 28, 1995, pp. 20–21.

20. Eleena de Lisser, "More Marketers Leaving a (Prepaid) Calling Card," *Wall Street Journal*, July 25, 1994, p. B1.

21. Jennifer Lach, "Summer Overtures", *American Demographics*, June 1999, pp. 38–40.

22. Fara Warner, "Shake-Up in Light Trucks is Coming Down the Pike—New Marketing, Hybrids and Small, Specialized Runs May have a Big Impact," *Wall Street Journal*, August 23, 1999, p. B4.

23. Cliff Rothman, "Big Companies are Openly Courting Gay Consumers, *Los Angeles Times*, May 18, 1999, p. 1; Laura Koss Feder, "Out and About", *Marketing News*, May 25, 1998, p. 1, 20.

24. Allanna Sullivan, "Mobil Bets Drivers Pick Cappuccino over Low Prices," *Wall Street Journal*, January 30, 1995, pp. B1, B4.

25. Marj Carlier, "Chasing Buyers, Show Makers Back Races," *Wall Street Journal*, September 13, 1994, pp. B1, B9.

26. Sally D. Goll, "China's (Only) Children Get the Royal Treatment," *Wall Street Journal*, February 8, 1995, pp. B1, B2.

27. Fara Warner, "Condom Seller Lets Users Do the Talking," *Wall Street Journal*, March 22, 1995, pp. B3, B8.

28. Cyndee Miller, "Study Dispels '80s Stereotypes of Women," *Marketing News*, May 22, 1995, p. 3.

29. Shannon Stevens, "Return of the Red Lobster," *American Demographics*, October 1998, pp. 49–51.

30. Cacile Rohwedder, "Wella's Challenge: To Spice up Eau de Cologne's Fusty Image," *Wall Street Journal*, July 29, 1995, p. B5.

31. Dale Dauten, "Displaying Failures: A Help to Find Success?" *Chicago Tribune*, August 30, 1998, p. 7.

32. McGee, "Getting inside Kids' Heads."

33. Sullivan, "Mobil Bets Drivers Pick Cappuccino over Low Prices."

34. Elaine Erickson and Elaine Taylor-Gordon, "Finger on the Pulse," *Brandweek*, December 7, 1998, pp. 30–32.

35. Robert McNatt, "Hey, Its Green—It Must Be Healthy," *Business Week*, July 13, 1998, p. 6.

36. Benjamin Lipstein, "The Oppenheimer Fund Story: From 14 Million to 27 Billion," in ed. Larry Percy, *Marketing Research That Pays Off* (Birminghampton, N.Y.: Hayworth Press, 1997), pp. 209–248.

37. Mark Robichaux, "Cable Industry Tries Guarantees of Better Service to Polish Image," *Wall Street Journal*, December 1, 1994, p. B1.

38. Judith Langer, "Focus on Women: Three Decades of Qualitative Research," *Marketing News*, September 14, 1998, pp. 21–22.

39. Charlotte Clarke, "Language Classes," *Marketing Week*, July 24, 1997, pp. 35–39.

40. Erika Rasmusson, "This Database Is a Heavy Favorite," *Sales and Marketing Management*, June 1998, p. 73.

41. For example, see Sean Dwyer, Orlando Richard, and C. David Shepherd, "An Exploratory Study of Gender and Age Matching in the Salesperson-Prospective Customer Dyad: Testing Similarity-Performance Predictions," *Journal of Personal Selling and Sales Management*, Fall 1998, pp. 55–69.

42. Jennifer M. George, "Salesperson Mood at Work: Implications for Helping Customers," *Journal of Personal Selling and Sales Management*, Summer 1998, pp. 23–30.

43. Robert M. Schindler and Patrick N. Kirby, "Patterns of Rightmost Digits Used in Advertising Prices: Implications for Nine-Ending Effects," *Journal of Consumer Research*, September 1997, pp. 192–201.

44. Jacob Jacoby, Jerry Olson, and Rafael Haddock, "Price, Brand Name, and Product Composition Characteristics as Determinants of Perceived Quality," *Journal of Applied Psychology*, December 1971, pp. 470–479; Kent B. Monroe, "The Influence of Price Differences and Brand Familiarity on Brand Preferences," *Journal of Consumer Research*, June 1976, pp. 42–49.

45. Laura Bird, "Catalogs Cut Shipping, Handling Fees to Inspire Early Christmas Shopping," *Wall Street Journal*, October 24, 1995, pp. B1, B11.

46. Ronald E. Milliman, "The Influence of Background Music on the Behavior of Restaurant Patrons," *Journal of Consumer Research*, September 1986, pp. 286–289; Richard Yalch and Eric Spannenberg, "Effects of Store Music on Shopping Behavior," *Journal of Services Marketing*, Winter 1990, pp. 31–39; Joseph A. Bellizi, Ayn E. Crowley, and Ronald W. Hasty, "The Effects of Color in Store Design," *Journal of Retailing*, Spring 1983, pp. 21–45.

47. Naresh K. Malhotra, *Marketing Research* (Upper Saddle River, N.J.: Prentice-Hall, 1996).

48. Kenneth C. Schneider and Cynthia K. Holm, "Deceptive Practices in Marketing Research: The Consumer's Viewpoint," *California Management Review*, Spring 1982, pp. 89–97.

CHAPTER 3

1. Christine Blank, "Women Investing Wisely," *American Demographics*, August 1997, pp. 22–28.

2. C. Whan Park and Banwari Mittal, "A Theory of Involvement in Consumer Behavior: Problems and Issues," in ed. J. N. Sheth, *Research in Consumer Behavior* (Greenwich, Conn.: JAI Press, 1979), pp. 201–231; Deborah J. MacInnis, Christine Moorman, and Bernard J. Jaworski, "Enhancing and Measuring Consumers' Motivation, Opportunity, and Ability to Process Brand Information from Ads," *Journal of Marketing*, October 1991, pp. 32–53.

3. Deborah J. MacInnis and Bernard J. Jaworski, "Information Processing from Advertisements: Toward an Integrative Framework," *Journal of Marketing*, October 1989, pp. 1–23; Scott B. MacKenzie and Richard A. Spreng, "How Does Motivation Moderate the Impact of Central and Peripheral Processing on Brand Attitudes and Intentions?" *Journal of Consumer Research*, March 1992, pp. 519–529; Petty and Cacioppo, Communication and Persuasion; Anthony Greenwald and Leavitt, "Audience Involvement in Advertising"; Ronald C. Goodstein, "Category-Based Applications and Extensions in Advertising: Motivating More Extensive Ad Processing," *Journal of Consumer Research*, June 1993, pp. 87–99; Ellen Garbarino and Julie A. Edell, "Cognitive Effort, Affect, and Choice," *Journal of Consumer Research*, September 1997, pp. 147–158.

4. Wayne D. Hoyer, "An Examination of Consumer Decision Making for a Common Repeat Purchase Product," *Journal of Consumer Research*, December 1984, pp. 822–829.

5. Richard L. Celsi and Jerry C. Olson, "The Role of Involvement in Attention and Comprehension Processes," *Journal of Consumer Research*, September 1988, pp. 210–224.

6. Marsha L. Richins, Peter H. Bloch, and Edward F. McQuarrie, "How Enduring and Situational Involvement Combine to Create Involvement Responses," *Journal of Consumer Psychology*, September 1992, pp. 143–154; Peter H. Bloch and Marsha L. Richins, "A Theoretical Model for the Study of Product Importance Perceptions," *Journal of Marketing*, Summer 1983, pp. 69–81; Celsi and Olson, "The Role of Involvement in Attention and Comprehension Processes"; Andrew A. Mitchell, "The Dimensions of Advertising Involvement," in ed. Kent Monroe, *Advances in Consumer Research*, Vol. 8 (Ann Arbor, Mich.: Association for Consumer Research, 1981), pp. 25–30; Marsha L. Richins and Peter H. Bloch, "After the New Wears off: The Temporal Context of Product Involvement," *Journal of Consumer Research*, September 1986, pp. 280–285.

7. Michael J. Houston and Michael L. Rothschild, "Conceptual and Methodological Perspectives in Involvement," in ed. S. Jain, *Research Frontiers in Marketing: Dialogues and Directions* (Chicago: American

Marketing Association, 1978), pp. 184–187; Richins and Bloch, "After the New Wears off"; Gilles Laurent and Jean-Noel Kapferer, "Measuring Consumer Involvement Profiles," *Journal of Marketing Research*, February 1985, pp. 41–53.

8. C. Whan Park and S. Mark Young, "Consumer Response to Television Commercials: The Impact of Involvement and Background Music on Brand Attitude Formation," *Journal of Marketing Research*, February 1986, pp. 11–24.

9. Judith Lynne Zaichkowsky, "Measuring the Involvement Construct," *Journal of Consumer Research*, December 1985, pp. 341–352; Laurent and Kapferer, "Measuring Consumer Involvement Profiles."

10. Stefan Fatsis, "Futbol Invades the U.S.—Again," *Wall Street Journal*, April 5, 1996, p. B7.

11. J. Craig Andrews, Syed H. Akhter, Srinivas Durvasula, and Darrel D. Muehling, "The Effect of Advertising Distinctiveness and Message Content Involvement on Cognitive and Affective Responses to Advertising," *Journal of Current Issues and Research in Advertising*, Spring 1992, pp. 45–58; Laura M. Bucholz and Robert E. Smith, "The Role of Consumer Involvement in Determining Cognitive Response to Broadcast Advertising," *Journal of Advertising*, March 1991, pp. 4–17; Darrel D. Muehling, Russell N. Laczniak, and Jeffrey J. Stoltman, "The Moderating Effects of Ad Message Involvement: A Reassessment," *Journal of Advertising*, June 1991, pp. 29–38; Scott B. MacKenzie and Richard J. Lutz, "An Empirical Examination of the Structural Antecedents of Attitude Toward the Ad in an Advertising Pretesting Context," *Journal of Marketing*, April 1989, pp. 48–65.

12. Barbara Mueller, "Standardization vs. Specialization: An Examination of Westernization in Japanese Advertising," *Journal of Advertising Research*, January–February 1992, pp. 15–24.

13. Tammi S. Feltham and Stephen J. Arnold, "Program Involvement and Ad/Program Consistency as Moderators of Program Context Effects," *Journal of Consumer Psychology*, Vol. 3, issue 1, 1994, pp. 51–78; Nader Tavassoli, Clifford Schultz, and Gavan Fitzsimons, "Program Involvement: Are Moderate Levels Best for Ad Memory and Attitude toward the Ad," *Journal of Advertising Research*, Vol. 35, issue 5, 1995, pp. 61–72.

14. Houston and Rothschild, "Conceptual and Methodological Perspectives in Involvement"; Peter H. Bloch, Daniel Sherrell, and Nancy Ridgway, "Consumer Search: An Extended Framework," *Journal of Consumer Research*, June 1986, pp. 119–126; Peter H. Bloch, Nancy M. Ridgway, and Scott A. Dawson, "The Shopping Mall as Consumer Habitat," *Journal of Retailing*, Spring 1994, pp. 23–42; Richard L. Celsi, Randall L. Rose, and Thomas W. Leigh, "An Exploration of High-Risk Leisure Consumption through Skydiving," *Journal of Consumer Research*, June 1993, pp. 1–23; Eric J. Arnould and Linda L. Price, "River Magic: Extraordinary Experience and the Extended Service Encounter," *Journal of Consumer Research*, June 1993, pp. 24–45; Morris B. Holbrook and Elizabeth C. Hirschman, "The Experiential Aspects of Consumption: Consumer Fantasies, Feelings, and Fun," *Journal of Consumer Research*, September 1982, pp. 132–140; Elizabeth C.

Hirschman and Morris B. Holbrook, "Experience Seeking: Emerging Concepts, Methods, and Propositions," *Journal of Marketing*, Summer 1982, pp. 92–101; Morris B. Holbrook, Robert W. Chestnut, Terence A. Oliva, and Eric A. Greenleaf, "Play as a Consumption Experience: The Roles of Emotions, Performance, and Personality in the Enjoyment of Games," *Journal of Consumer Research*, September 1984, pp. 728–739.

15. Celsi and Olson, "The Role of Involvement in Attention and Comprehension Processes"; Greenwald and Leavitt, "Audience Involvement in Advertising"; Laurent and Kapferer, "Measuring Consumer Involvement Profiles"; Zaichkowsky, "Measuring the Involvement Construct"; Michael L. Rothschild, "Perspectives on Involvement: Current Problems and Future Directions," in ed. Tom Kinnear, *Advances in Consumer Research*, Vol. 11 (Ann Arbor, Mich.: Association for Consumer Research, 1984), pp. 216–217; Andrew A. Mitchell, "Involvement: A Potentially Important Mediator of Consumer Behavior" in ed. William L. Wilkie, *Advances in Consumer Research*, Vol. 6 (Ann Arbor, Mich.: Association for Consumer Research, 1979), pp. 191–196; Petty and Cacioppo, *Communication and Persuasion*.

16. Sharon Shavitt, Suzanne Swan, Tina M. Lowrey, and Michaela Wanke, "The Interaction of Endorser Attractiveness and Involvement in Persuasion Depends on the Goal That Guides Message Processing," *Journal of Consumer Psychology*, issue 2 1994, pp. 137–162; Robert Lawson, "Consumer Decision Making within a Goal-Driven Framework," *Psychology and Marketing*, August 1997, pp. 427–449.

17. Abraham H. Maslow, *Motivation and Personality*, 2nd ed. (New York: Harper & Row, 1970).

18. Judy Harris and Michael Lynn, "The Manifestations and Measurement of the Desire to Be a Unique Consumer," Proceedings of the 1994 AMA Winter Educators' Conference, Chicago, IL; Kelly Tepper, "Need for Uniqueness: An Individual Difference Factor Affecting Nonconformity in Consumer Responses," Proceedings of the 1994 AMA Winter Educators' Conference, Chicago, IL.

19. C. Whan Park, Bernard J. Jaworski, and Deborah J. MacInnis, "Strategic Brand Concept-Image Management," *Journal of Marketing*, October 1986, pp. 135–145.

20. John T. Cacioppo and Richard E. Petty, "The Need for Cognition," *Journal of Personality and Social Psychology*, February 1982, pp. 116–131; Douglas M. Stayman and Frank R. Kardes, "Spontaneous Inference Processes in Advertising: Effects of Need for Cognition and Self-Monitoring on Inference Generation and Utilization," *Journal of Consumer Psychology*, issue 2 1992, pp. 125–142; John T. Cacioppo, Richard Petty, and Katherine Morris, "Effects of Need for Cognition on Message Evaluation, Recall, and Persuasion," *Journal of Personality and Social Psychology*, October 1993, pp. 805–818.

21. P. S. Raju, "Optimum Stimulation Level: Its Relationship to Personality, Demographics, and Exploratory Behavior," *Journal of Consumer Research*, December 1980, pp. 272–282. Jan-Benedict E. M. Steenkamp, and Hans Baumgartner, "The Role of Optimum Stimulation Level in Exploratory Consumer

Behavior," *Journal of Consumer Research*, December 1992, pp. 434–448.

22. Patricia Bellew Gray, "Want to Search Your Soul at a Monastery? Get in Line," *Wall Street Journal*, December 19, 1997, pp. B1, B14.

23. Robert Roth, *International Marketing Communications* (Chicago: Crain Books, 1982), p. 5.

24. H. Murray, *Thematic Apperception Test Manual* (Cambridge, Mass.: Harvard University Press, 1943); Harold Kassarjian, "Projective Methods," in ed. Robert Ferber, *Handbook of Marketing Research* (New York: McGraw-Hill, 1974), pp. 85–100; Ernest Dichter, *Packaging the Sixth Sense: A Guide to Identifying Consumer Motivation* (Boston: Cahners Books, 1975); Dennis Rook, "Researching Consumer Fantasy," in ed. Elizabeth C. Hirschman, *Research in Consumer Behavior*, Vol. 3 (Greenwich, Conn.: JAI Press, 1990), pp. 247–270; David Mick, M. De Moss, and Ronald Faber, "A Projective Study of Motivations and Meanings of Self-Gifts: Implications for Retail Management," *Journal of Retailing*, Summer 1992, pp. 122–144; Mary Ann McGrath, John F. Sherry, and Sidney J. Levy, "Giving Voice to the Gift: The Use of Projective Techniques to Recover Lost Meanings," *Journal of Consumer Psychology*, issue 2 1993, pp. 171–191.

25. Harold H. Kassarjian and Joel B. Cohen, "Cognitive Dissonance and Consumer Behavior: Reaction to the Surgeon General's Report on Smoking and Health," *California Management Review*, Fall 1965, pp. 55–65; see also Kenneth E. Runyon and David W. Stewart, *Consumer Behavior*, 3rd ed. (Columbus, Ohio: Merrill, 1987).

26. G. H. Smith, *Motivation Research in Advertising and Marketing* (New York: McGraw-Hill, 1954).

27. Dom Del Prete, "Direct Mail Pays Big Dividends for Financial Services Marketers," *Marketing News*, September 29, 1997, pp. 1, 8.

28. Robert McMath, "Audio Books Make an Appearance on the Video Scene," *Brandweek*, November 16, 1992, p. 33.

29. Jule Kronholz, "It's Summertime and Kids are Bored. What Else is New," *Wall Street Journal*, July 23, 1997, pp. A1, A6.

30. Yumiko Ono, "Japan's Fast-Food Companies Cook Up Local Platter to Tempt Local Palates," *Wall Street Journal*, May 29, 1992, pp. B1, B5.

31. Ibid.

32. Joseph Pereira, "Guffaws Aside, New Scooter Makers Zip Ahead," *Wall Street Journal*, August 20, 1998, pp. B1, B2.

33. Robert Langreth, "Bulletins from the Battle of the Baldness Drug," *Wall Street Journal*, December 19, 1997, pp. B1, B12.

34. Park, Jaworski, and MacInnis, "Strategic Brand Concept-Image Management."

35. Raymond A. Bauer, "Consumer Behavior as Risk Taking," in ed. Robert S. Hancock, *Dynamic Marketing for a Changing World* (Chicago: American Marketing Association, 1960), pp. 389–398; Grahame R. Dowling, "Perceived Risk: The Concept and Its Measurement," *Psychology and Marketing*, Fall 1986, pp. 193–210; Lawrence X. Tarpey and J. Paul Peter, "A Comparative Analysis of Three Consumer Decision Strategies," *Journal of Consumer Research*, June 1975, pp. 29–37.

36. James R. Bettman, "Perceived Risk and Its Components: A Model and Empirical Test," *Journal of Marketing Research*, May 1973, pp. 184–190.

37. Dana L. Alden, Douglas M. Stayman, and Wayne D. Hoyer, "The Evaluation Strategies of American and Thai Consumers: A Cross Cultural Comparison," *Psychology and Marketing*, March–April 1994, pp. 145–161; Ugur Yavas, Bronislaw J. Verhage, and Robert T. Green, "Global Consumer Segmentation Versus Local Market Orientation: Empirical Findings," *Management International Review*, July 1992, pp. 265–272.

38. Vincent W. Mitchell and Michael Greatorex, "Consumer Purchasing in Foreign Countries: A Perceived Risk Analysis," *International Journal of Advertising*, issue 4 1990, pp. 295–307.

39. "Marketing Briefs," *Marketing News*, March 1995, p. 11.

40. Jacob Jacoby and Leon Kaplan, "The Components of Perceived Risk," in ed. M. Venkatesan, *Advances in Consumer Research*, Vol. 3 (Chicago: Association for Consumer Research, 1972), pp. 382–383; Tarpey and Peter, "A Comparative Analysis of Three Consumer Decision Strategies."

41. Joseph N. Boyce, "Landlords Turn to 'Commando' Patrols", *Wall Street Journal*, September 18, 1996, pp. B1, B2.

42. Paula Mergenhagen, "People Behaving Badly," *American Demographics*, August 1997, pp. 37–43.

43. Cyndee Miller, "Condom Sales Cool off: Carefree Attitudes of Youth, Poor Marketing Are Blamed," *Marketing News*, February 24, 1994, pp. 1, 9.

44. Miller, "Condom Sales Cool Off."

45. Priya Raghubir and Geeta Menon, "AIDS and Me, Never the Twain Shall Meet: The Effects of Information Accessibility on Judgments of Risk and Advertising Effectiveness," *Journal of Consumer Research*, June 1998, pp. 52–63.

46. Joan Meyers-Levy and Alice Tybout, "Schema-Congruity as a Basis for Product Evaluation," *Journal of Consumer Research*, June 1989, pp. 39–54.

47. MacInnis and Jaworski, "Information Processing from Advertisements."

48. Joseph W. Alba and J. Wesley Hutchinson, "Dimensions of Consumer Expertise," *Journal of Consumer Research*, March 1987, pp. 411–454; For an excellent overview of measures of consumer knowledge or expertise, see Andrew A. Mitchell and Peter A. Dacin, "The Assessment of Alternative Measures of Consumer Expertise," *Journal of Consumer Research*, December 1996, pp. 219–239.

49. Eric J. Johnson and J. Edward Russo, "Product Familiarity and Learning New Information," *Journal of Consumer Research*, June 1984, pp. 542–550; Merrie Brucks, "The Effects of Product Class Knowledge on Information Search Behavior," *Journal of Consumer Research*, June 1985, pp. 1–16; Alba and Hutchinson, "Dimensions of Consumer Expertise."

50. Oscar Suris, "New Data Help Car Lessees Shop Smarter," *Wall Street Journal*, July 11, 1995, pp. 1, B12.

51. Durairaj Maheswaran and Brian Sternthal, "The Effects of Knowledge, Motivation, and Type of Message on Ad Processing and Product Judgements," *Journal of Consumer Research*, June 1990, pp. 66–73.

52. Jennifer Gregan-Paxton and Deborah Roedder Jonn, "Consumer Learning by Analogy: A Model of Internal Knowledge Transfer," *Journal of Consumer Research*, December 1997, pp. 266–284.

53. Elizabeth C. Hirschman, "Cognitive Complexity, Intelligence, and Creativity: A Conceptual Overview with Implications for Consumer Research," *Research in Marketing*, 1981, pp. 59–99.

54. Jennifer Gregan-Paxton and Deborah Roedder John, "Are Young Children Adaptive Decision Makers? A Study of Age Differences in Information Search Behavior," *Journal of Consumer Research*, March 1995, pp. 567–580.

55. Catherine A. Cole and Gary J. Gaeth, "Cognitive and Age-Related Differences in the Ability to Use Nutrition Information in a Complex Environment," *Journal of Marketing Research*, May 1990, pp. 175–184.

56. Robin Frost, "Women On-Line: Cybergrrl Aims to Show the Way," *Wall Street Journal*, May 30, 1996, p. B8.

57. Elizabeth H. Weise, "On-Line Magazines: Will Readers Still Want Them after the Novelty Wears Off," *Marketing News*, January 29, 1996, pp. 1, 14.

58. Cynthia Crossen, "'Merry Christmas to Moi' Shoppers Say," *Wall Street Journal*, December 11, 1997, pp. B1, B14.

59. Peter Wright, "The Time Harassed Consumer: Time Pressures, Distraction, and the Use of Evidence," *Journal of Applied Psychology*, October 1974, pp. 555–561.

60. Danny L. Moore, Douglas Hausknecht, and Kanchana Thamodaran, "Time Compression, Response Opportunity, and Persuasion," *Journal of Consumer Research*, June 1986, pp. 85–99; Priscilla LaBarbera and James MacLaughlin, "Time Compressed Speech in Radio Advertising," *Journal of Marketing*, January 1979, pp. 30–36; Shelly Chaiken and Alice Eagly, "Communication Modality as a Determinant of Message Persuasiveness and Message Comprehensibility," *Journal of Personality and Social Psychology*, March 1976, pp. 605–614; Krugman, "The Impact of Television Advertising"; Patricia A. Stout and Benedicta Burda, "Zipped Commercials: Are They Effective?" *Journal of Advertising*, Fall 1989, pp. 23–32.

61. Park and Young, "Consumer Response to Television Commercials"; Deborah J. MacInnis and C. Whan Park, "The Differential Role of Characteristics of Music on High and Low Involvement Consumers' Processing of Ads," *Journal of Consumer Research*, September 1991, pp. 161–173; Shelly Chaiken and Alice Eagly, "Communication Modality as a Determinant of Persuasion: The Role of Communicator Salience," *Journal of Personality and Social Psychology*, August 1983, pp. 605–614.

62. Lord and Burnkrant, "Attention Versus Distraction"; Kenneth R. Lord and Robert E. Burnkrant, "Television Program Effects on Commercial Processing," in ed. Michael J. Houston, *Advances in Consumer Research*, Vol. 15 (Provo, Utah: Association for Consumer Research, 1988), pp. 213–218; Gary Soldow and Victor Principe, "Response to Commercials as a Function of Program Context," *Journal of Advertising Research*, February–March 1981, pp. 59–65.

63. Richard Yalch and Rebecca Elmore-Yalch, "The Effect of Numbers on the Route to Persuasion," *Journal of Consumer Research*, June 1984, pp. 522–527.

64. Capon and Davis, "Basic Cognitive Ability Measures as Predictors of Consumer Information Processing Strategies."

65. Rajeev Batra and Michael L. Ray, "Situational Effects of Advertising Repetitions: The Moderating Influence of Motivation, Ability, and Opportunity to Respond," *Journal of Consumer Research*, March 1986, pp. 432–435; Carl Obermiller, "Varieties of Mere Exposure: The Effects of Processing Style and Repetition on Affective Response," *Journal of Consumer Research*, June 1985, pp. 17–30; Arno Rethans, John L. Swazy, and Lawrence J. Marks, "The Effects of Television Commercial Repetition, Receiver Knowledge, and Commercial Length: A Test of the Two-Factor Model," *Journal of Marketing Research*, February 1986, pp. 50–61; Sharmistha Law and Scott A. Hawkins, "Advertising Repetition and Consumer Beliefs: The Role of Source Memory," in William Wells, ed., *Measuring Advertising Effectiveness* (Mahwah, N.J.: Lawrence Erlbaum Associates, 1997), pp. 67–75; Giles D'Sousa and Ram C. Rao, "Can Repeating an Advertisement More Frequently Than the Competition Affect Brand Preference in a Mature Market?" *Journal of Marketing*, 1995, pp. 32–43.

66. Matt Murray, "A Bit of Prosperity and Some Fast Food Fatten Zimbabweans," *Wall Street Journal*, August 8, 1997, pp. A1, A11.

CHAPTER 4

1. Allyson Stewart-Allen, "Product Placement Helps Sell Brand," *Marketing News*, February 15, 1999, p. 8.

2. Elizabeth Jensen, "Rosie and 'Friends' Make Drake's Cakes a Star," *Wall Street Journal*, February 10, 1997, pp. B1, B7.

3. Kelly Shermach, "Products Needed to Play Major Roles in Movies, TV Shows, *Marketing News*, July 31, 1995, pp. 1, 11.

4. Fara Warner, "Why It's Getting Harder to Tell the Shows from the Ads," *Wall Street Journal*, June 15, 1995, pp. B1, B10.

5. Ibid.

6. Stefan Fatsis, "Nike Kicks in Millions to Sponsor Soccer in U.S.," *Wall Street Journal*, October 22, 1997, pp. B1, B8.

7. Adam Finn, "Print Ad Recognition Readership Scores: An Information Processing Perspective," *Journal of Marketing Research*, May 1988, pp. 168–177.

8. John Battle, "Cashing in at the Register," *Aftermarket Business*, September 1, 1994, pp. 12–13.

9. Rebecca Blumenstein, "GM Takes Its Ads to New Heights, Depicting Buicks on Airline Snacks," *Wall Street Journal*, August 5, 1997, p. B1.

10. Robert W. Trott, "Shell Installs TV Sets at Some of Its Gas Stations," *Marketing News*, June 19, 1995, p. 8.

11. Douglas A. Blackmon, "New Ad Vehicles: Police Cars, School Bus, Garbage Trucks," *Wall Street Journal*, February 20, 1996, pp. B1, B6.

12. Amy Dockser Marcus, "Advertising Breezes Along the Nile River with Signs for Sails," *Wall Street Journal*, July 18, 1997, pp. A1, A11.

13. Paul Surgi Speck and Michael T. Elliott, "Predictors of Advertising Avoidance in Print and Broadcast Media," *Journal of Advertising*, Fall 1997, pp. 61–76.

14. Dean M. Krugman, Glen T. Cameron, and Candace McKearney White, "Visual Attention to Programming and Commercials: The Use of In-Home Observations," *Journal of Advertising*, Spring 1995, pp. 1–12; S. Siddarth and Amitava Chattopadhyay, "To Zap or Not to Zap: A Study of the Determinants of Channel Switching during Commercials," *Marketing Science*, issue 2 1998, pp. 124–138.

15. Sally Beatty, "Fashion Magazines Are Bulging with Ads," *Wall Street Journal*, September 2, 1998, p. B5.

16. Michelle Wirth Fellman, "Interception: Creative Firms Find Ways to Leverage Bowl," *Marketing News*, January 1, 1999, pp. 1, 12.

17. Andrea Petersen, "Plan Is Backed to Count Web-Ad Viewers," *Wall Street Journal*, March 2, 1999, p. B9.

18. Scott B. MacKenzie, "The Role of Attention in Mediating the Effect of Advertising on Attribute Importance," *Journal of Consumer Research*, September 1986, pp. 174–195; Richard E. Petty and Timothy C. Brock, "Thought Disruption and Persuasion: Assessing the Validity of Attitude Change Experiments," in eds. Richard E. Petty, Thomas Ostrom, and Timothy C. Brock, *Cognitive Responses in Persuasion* (Hillsdale, N. J.: Lawrence Erlbaum, 1981), pp. 55–79.

19. L. Hasher and R. T. Zacks, "Automatic and Effortful Processes in Memory," *Journal of Experimental Psychology: General*, September 1979, pp. 356–388; W. Schneider and R. M. Shiffrin, "Controlled and Automatic Human Information Processing: I. Detection, Search, and Attention," *Psychological Review*, January 1977, pp. 1–66; R. M. Shiffrin and W. Schneider, "Controlled and Automatic Human Information Processing: II. Perceptual Learning, Automatic Attending, and a General Theory," *Psychological Review*, March 1977, pp. 127–190.

20. Chris Janiszewski, "Preconscious Processing Effects: The Independence of Attitude Formation and Conscious Thought," *Journal of Consumer Research*, September 1988, pp. 199–209; Joan Meyers-Levy, "Priming Effects on Product Judgments: A Hemispheric Interpretation," *Journal of Consumer Research*, June 1989, pp. 76–87.

21. Chris Janiszewski, "Preconscious Processing Effects"; "The Influence of Print Advertisement Organization on Affect Toward a Brand Name," *Journal of Consumer Research*, June 1990, pp. 53–65.

22. Chris Janiszewski, "Preattentive Mere Exposure Effects," *Journal of Consumer Research*, December 1993, pp. 376–392; Chris Janiszewski, "Preconscious Processing Effects," Chris Janiszewski, "The Influence of Print Advertisement Organization on Affect Toward a Brand Name."

23. Janiszewski, "Preattentive Mere Exposure Effects"; Stewart Shapiro and Deborah J. MacInnis, "Mapping the Relationship between Preattentive Processing and Attitudes," in eds. John Sherry and Brian Sternthal, *Advances in Consumer Research*, Vol. 19 (Provo, Utah: Association for Consumer Research, 1992), pp. 505–513.

24. Stewart Shapiro, Deborah J. MacInnis and Susan E. Heckler, "The Effects of Incidental Ad Exposure on the Formation of Consideration Sets," Journal of Consumer Research, June 1997, pp. 94–104.

25. Celsi and Olson, "The Role of Involvement in Attention and Comprehension Processes."

26. Arch Woodside and J. William Davenport, Jr., "The Effect of Salesman Similarity and Expertise on Consumer Purchasing Behavior," *Journal of Marketing Research*, May 1974, pp. 198–202.

27. Robert E. Burnkrant and Daniel J. Howard, "Effects of the Use of Introductory Rhetorical Questions versus Statements on Information Processing," *Journal of Personality and Social Psychology*, December 1984, pp. 1218–1230.

28. Grant McCracken, "Who Is the Celebrity Endorser? Cultural Foundations of the Endorsement Process," *Journal of Consumer Research*, December 1989, pp. 310–321; Jeffrey Burroughs and Richard A. Feinberg, "Using Response Latency to Assess Spokesperson Effectiveness," *Journal of Consumer Research*, September 1987, pp. 295–299.

29. Rebecca Quick, "Victoria's Secret Causes a Stir with Web Blitz," *Wall Street Journal*, February 4, 1999, pp. B1, B12.

30. Deborah J. MacInnis and C. Whan Park, "The Differential Role of Characteristics of Music on High- and Low-Involvement Consumers' Processing of Ads," *Journal of Consumer Research*, September 1991, pp. 161–173; David W. Stewart and David H. Furse, *Effective Television Advertising: A Study of 1000 Commercials* (Lexington, Mass.: Lexington Books, 1986); James J. Kellaris and Robert J. Kent, "An Exploratory Investigation of Responses Elicited by Music Varying in Tempo, Tonality, and Texture," *Journal of Consumer Psychology*, March 1993, pp. 381–402.; James J. Kellaris, Anthony Cox, and Dena Cox, "The Effects of Background Music on Ad Processing Contingency Explanation," *Journal of Consumer Research*, October 1993, pp. 114–126.

31. Brian Sternthal and Samuel Craig, "Humor in Advertising," *Journal of Marketing*, October 1973, pp. 12–18; Thomas Madden and Marc G. Weinberger, "The Effect of Humor on Attention in Magazine Advertising," *Journal of Advertising*, September 1982, pp. 8–14.

32. Nikhil Deogun, "Pepsi Brings 'Good vs. Evil' to Soda War," *Wall Street Journal*, July 9, 1998, p. B7.

33. Yumiko Ono, "A Korean Car Maker's Strange Quest for Ads," *Wall Street Journal*, July 25, 1997, B1.

34. Eleena de Lisser, "Perfume Maker Stirs up Down-to-Earth Scents," *Wall Street Journal*, April 8, 1998, pp. B1, B2.

35. Bruce Stanley, "Redesigning Heinz Ketchup Label Is a Kid's Job," *Marketing News*, June 9, 1997, p. 5.

36. Sally Goll Beatty, "Knock, Knock! Who's There? Noisy New Internet Ads," *Wall Street Journal*, September 3, 1997, p. B1.

37. Celsi and Olson, "The Role of Involvement in Attention and Comprehension Processes."

38. Teri Agins, "Neiman Marcus Is Betting 'The Book' on Enhancing Its Mail-Order Sales," *Wall Street Journal*, February 1, 1996, p. B7.

39. Joan Meyers-Levy and Alice Tybout, "Schema Congruity as a Basis for Product Evaluation," *Journal of Consumer Research*, June 1989, pp. 39–54. Characteristics of music can also cause surprise; see Kellaris and Kent, "An Exploratory Investigation of Responses Elicited by Music Varying in Tempo, Tonality, and Texture."

ENDNOTES

40. Yumiko Ono, "Making 30 Chickens and Garlands of Post-Its Into an Ad," *Wall Street Journal*, August 20, 1997, pp. B1, B6.

41. Finn, "Print Ad Recognition Readership Scores."

42. W. F. Wagner, *Yellow Pages Report* (Scotts Valley, Calif.: Mark Publishing, 1988); Gerald Lohse, "Consumer Eye Movement Patterns on Yellow Pages Advertising," *Journal of Advertising*, Spring 1997, pp. 61–73.

43. Ibid.

44. Yukimo Ono, "'Wobblers' and 'Sidekicks' Clutter Stores, Irk Retailers," *Wall Street Journal*, September 8, 1998, pp. B1, B3.

45. Werner Krober-Riel, "Activation Research: Psychobiological Approaches in Consumer Research," *Journal of Consumer Research*, March 1979, pp. 240–250; Morris B. Holbrook and Donald R. Lehmann, "Form vs. Content in Predicting Starch Scores," *Journal of Advertising Research*, August 1980, pp. 53–62.

46. Mackenzie, "The Role of Attention in Mediating the Effect of Advertising on Attribute Importance."

47. Elizabeth Jensen, "Blue Bottles, Gimmicky Labels Sell Wine," *Wall Street Journal*, July 7, 1997, pp. B1, B6.

48. Gautam Naik, "Nokia Bets on Tarzan Yells and Whistles," *Wall Street Journal*, July 2, 1997, pp. B1, B7.

49. Chris Janiszewski, "The Influence of Display Characteristics on Visual Exploratory Search Behavior," *Journal of Consumer Research*, December 1998, pp. 290–301.

50. Edward Rosbergen, Rik Pieters, and Michel Wedel, "Visual Attention to Advertising: A Segment-Level Analysis," *Journal of Consumer Research*, December 1997, pp. 305–314.

51. Peter H. Lindsay and Donald A. Norman, *Human Information Processing: An Introduction to Psychology* (New York: Academic Press, 1973).

52. Ibid.

53. Ibid.

54. Gerald J. Gorn, Amitava Chattopadhyay, and Tracey Yi, "Effects of Color as an Executional Cue: They're in the Shade," *Management Science*, October 1997, pp. 1387–1401.

55. Marnell Jameson, "The Palette Patrol," *Los Angeles Times*, June 13, 1997, pp. E1, E8.

56. Tim Triplett, "Research Probes How Consumers Rely on Color for Their Purchases," *Marketing News*, August 28, 1995, pp. 1, 39.

57. Lindsay and Norman, *Human Information Processing.*

58. Ronald E. Millman, "Using Background Music to Affect the Behavior of Supermarket Shoppers," *Journal of Marketing*, Summer 1982, pp. 86–91.

59. Ronald E. Millman, "The Influence of Background Music on the Behavior of Restaurant Patrons," *Journal of Consumer Research*, September 1986, pp. 286–289.; Richard Yalch and Eric Spannenberg, "Effects of Store Music on Shopping Behavior," *Journal of Services Marketing*, Winter 1990, pp. 31–39.

60. Mark I. Alpert and Judy Alpert, "The Effects of Music in Advertising on Mood and Purchase Intentions," Working paper No. 85/86–5–4, Department of Marketing Administration, University of Texas, 1986.

61. Gerald J. Gorn, "The Effects of Music in Advertising on Choice Behavior," *Journal of Marketing*, Winter 1982, pp. 94–101; C. Whan Park and S. Mark Young, "Consumer Response to Television Commercials: The Impact of Involvement and Background Music on Brand Attitude Formation," *Journal of Marketing Research*, February 1986, pp. 11–24; MacInnis and Park, "The Differential Role of Characteristics of Music on High- and Low-Involvement Consumers' Processing of Ads."

62. Trygg Engen, *The Perception of Odors* (New York: Academic Press, 1982); Trygg Engen, "Remembering Odors and Their Names," *American Scientist*, September–October 1987, pp. 497–503.

63. T. Schemper, S. Voss, and W. S. Cain, "Odor Identification in Young and Elderly Persons," *Journal of Gerontology*, December 1981, pp. 446–452; J. C. Stevens and W. S. Cain, "Smelling via the Mouth: Effect of Aging," *Perception and Psychophysics*, September 1986, pp. 142–146.

64. W. S. Cain, "Odor Identification by Males and Females: Prediction vs. Performance," *Chemical Senses*, February 1982, pp. 129–142.

65. Beryl Leiff Benderly, "Aroma," *Health*, December 1988, pp. 62–77.

66. M. S. Kirk-Smith, C. Van Toller, and G. H. Dodd, "Unconscious Odour Conditioning in Human Subjects," *Biological Psychology*, 17, 1983, pp. 221–231.

67. Pamela Weentraug, "Sentimental Journeys: Smells Have the Power to Arouse Our Deepest Memories, Our Most Primitive Drives," *Omni*, August 1986, p. 815. Howard Erlichman and Jack N. Halpern, "Affect and Memory: Effects of Pleasant and Unpleasant Odors on Retrieval of Happy and Unhappy Memories," *Journal of Personality and Social Psychology*, May 1988, pp. 769–779; Frank R. Schab, "Odors and the Remembrance of Things Past," *Journal of Experimental Psychology: Learning, Memory and Cognition*, July 1990, pp. 648–655.

68. Roseanne Harper, "Super Kmart Alters Bakery Presentation," *Supermarket News*, August 15, 1994, pp. 25–26.

69. Susan Reda, "Dollars and Scents," *Stores*, August 1994, p. 38.

70. Tara Parker-Pope, "Body Spritzes Promise to Dispel Smokers' Odors," *Wall Street Journal*, March 31, 1998, pp. B1, B14.

71. Andrea Petersen, "Some Dog Owners Now Aspire to Smell as Good as Their Pets," *Wall Street Journal*, February 22, 1996, p. B1.

72. Tony Spleen, "Precut Future Debated: Convenience vs. Taste," *Supermarket News*, February 28, 1994, p. 29.

73. Maxine Wilkie, "Scent of a Market," *American Demographics*, August 1995, pp. 40–49.

74. Jacob Hornik, "Tactile Stimulation and Consumer Response," *Journal of Consumer Research*, December 1992, pp. 449–458.

75. Sak Onkvisit and John J. Shaw, *International Marketing: Analysis and Strategy* (Columbus, Ohio: Merrill, 1989).

76. Dean Takahashi, "New Mice Let You Shimmy and Shake across Your Screen," *Wall Street Journal*, November 20, 1997, p. B1.

77. Alison Fahey, "Party Hardly," *Brandweek*, October 26, 1992, pp. 24–25.

78. Richard Gibson, "Bigger Burger by McDonald's: A Two Ouncer," *Wall Street Journal*, April 18, 1996, p. B1.

79. Stuart Rogers, "How a Publicity Blitz Created the Myth of Subliminal Advertising," *Public Relations Quarterly*, Winter 1992, pp. 12–18.

80. Martha Rogers and Christine A. Seiler, "The Answer Is No," *Journal of Advertising Research*, March–April 1994, pp. 36–46; W. B. Key, *Subliminal Seduction* (Englewood Cliffs, N. J.: Prentice-Hall, 1973); W. B. Key, *Media Sexploitation* (Englewood Cliffs, N. J.: Prentice-Hall, 1976); W. B. Key, *The Clamplate Orgy* (Englewood Cliffs, N. J.: Prentice-Hall, 1980); Martha Rogers and Kirk H. Smith, "Public Perceptions of Subliminal Advertising: Why Practitioners Shouldn't Ignore This Issue," *Journal of Advertising Research*, March–April 1993, pp. 10–19; Michael Lev, "No Hidden Meaning Here: Survey Sees Subliminal Ads," *New York Times*, June 16, 1991, pp. 22, S12.

81. Sharon Beatty and Del I. Hawkins, "Subliminal Stimulation: Some New Data and Interpretation," *Journal of Advertising*, June 1989, pp. 4–9; Sharon Beatty and Del I. Hawkins, "Subliminal Stimulation: Some New Data and Interpretation," *Journal of Advertising*, June 1989, pp. 4–9; Myron Gable, Henry T. Wilkens, Lynn Harris, and Richard Feinberg, "An Evaluation of Subliminally Embedded Sexual Stimuli and Graphics," *Journal of Advertising*, March 1987, pp. 26–32; Dennis L. Rosen and Surendra N. Singh, "An Investigation of Subliminal Embed Effect on Multiple Measures of Advertising Effectiveness," *Psychology and Marketing*, March–April 1992, pp. 157–173; J. Steven Kelly, "Subliminal Embeds in Print Advertising: A Challenge to Advertising Ethics," *Journal of Advertising*, September 1979, pp. 20–24; Anthony R. Pratkanis and Anthony G. Greenwald, "Recent Perspectives on Unconscious Processing: Still No Marketing Applications," *Psychology and Marketing*, Winter 1988, pp. 337–353; Joel Saegert, "Why Marketing Should Quit Giving Subliminal Advertising the Benefit of the Doubt," *Psychology and Marketing*, March–April 1987, pp. 157–173.

82. A. J. Marcel, "Conscious and Unconscious Perception: Experiments on Visual Masking and Word Recognition," *Cognitive Psychology*, June 1983, pp. 197–237; A. J. Marcel, "Conscious and Unconscious Perception: An Approach to the Relations between Phenomenal Experience and Perceptual Processes," *Cognitive Psychology*, September 1983, pp. 238–300.

83. Ronald C. Goodstein and Ajay Kalra, "Incidental Exposure and Affective Reactions to Advertising," Working paper No. 239, School of Management, University of California at Los Angeles, January 1994.

84. Timothy E. Moore, "Subliminal Advertising: What You See Is What You Get," *Journal of Marketing*, Spring 1982, pp. 38–47.

85. Laura A. Peracchio and Joan Meyers-Levy, "How Ambiguous Cropped Objects in Ad Photos Can Affect Product Evaluations," *Journal of Consumer Research*, June 1994, pp. 190–204.

CHAPTER 5

1. Gerry Khermouch, "In Beer-Ad Wars, Some See Retreat to Conventional Weaponry," *Brandweek*, January 4, 1999, pp. 8; Sally Goll Beatty, "How the Beer Industry Uses TV Ads to Mollify Critics, Buff Its Image," *Wall Street Journal*, August 15, 1997, pp. A1, A6; Yumiko Ono, "Who Really Makes That Cute Little Beer? You'd Be Surprised," *Wall Street Journal*, April 15, 1996, pp. A1, A6; Evelyn Iritani, "Beer Battle Brewing in China," *Los Angeles Times*, July 25, 1995, pp. A1, A9.

2. Lawrence W. Barsalou, *Cognitive Psychology: An Overview for Cognitive Scientists* (Hillsdale, N. J.: Lawrence Erlbaum, 1992); James R. Bettman, "Memory Factors in Consumer Choice: A Review," *Journal of Marketing*, Spring 1979, pp. 37–53; Merrie Brucks and Andrew A. Mitchell, "Knowledge Structures, Production Systems and Decision Strategies," in ed. Kent B. Monroe, *Advances in Consumer Research*, Vol. 8 (Ann Arbor, Mich.: Association for Consumer Research, 1982), pp. 750–757.

3. Kevin L. Keller, "Conceptualizing, Measuring, and Managing Customer-Based Brand Equity," *Journal of Marketing*, January 1993, pp. 1–22; Deborah J. MacInnis, Kent Nakamoto, and Gayathri Mani, "Cognitive Associations and Product Category Comparisons: The Role of Knowledge Structure and Context," in eds. John F. Sherry and Brian Sternthal, *Advances in Consumer Research*, Vol. 19 (Provo, Utah: Association for Consumer Research, 1992), pp. 260–267.

4. Burleigh B. Gardner and Sidney Levy, "The Product and the Brand," *Harvard Business Review*, March–April 1955, pp. 33–39; also see David Ogilvy, *Confessions of an Advertising Man* (New York: Atheneum, 1964).

5. Marianne Wilson, "The Magic of Brand Identity," *Chain Store Age Executive with Shopping Center Age*, February 1994, p. 66.

6. Stewart Owen, "The Landor Image Power Survey: A Global Assessment of Brand Strength," in eds. David A. Aaker and Alexander L. Biel, *Brand Equity and Advertising* (Hillsdale, N. J.: Lawrence Erlbaum, 1993), pp. 11–30.

7. Joseph T. Plummer, "How Personality Makes a Difference," *Journal of Advertising Research*, December 1984–January 1985, pp. 27–31; William D. Wells, Frank J. Andriuli, Fedele J. Goi, and Stuart Seader, "An Adjective Check List for the Study of 'Product Personality,'" *Journal of Applied Psychology*, October 1957, pp. 317–319; Jennifer L. Aaker, "Dimensions of Brand Personality," *Journal of Marketing Research*, August 1997, pp. 347–356.

8. Tim Triplett, "Brand Personality Must Be Managed or It Will Assume a Life of Its Own," *Marketing News*, May 9, 1994, p. 9.

9. Elyette Roux and Frederic Lorange, "Brand Extension Research: A Review," in eds. Fred von Raaij and Gary Bamoussy, *European Advances in Consumer Research*, Vol. 1 (Provo, Utah: Association for Consumer Research, 1993), pp. 492–500; C. Whan Park, Bernard J. Jaworski, and Deborah J. MacInnis, "Strategic Brand Concept—Image Management," *Journal of Marketing*, October 1986, pp. 135–145; David A. Aaker and Kevin L. Keller, "Consumer Evaluations of Brand Extensions," *Journal of Marketing*, January 1990, pp. 27–41; Bernard Simonin and Julie A. Ruth, "Is a Company Known by the Company It Keeps: Assessing the Spillover Effects of Brand Alliances on Consumer Brand Attitudes, *Journal of Marketing Research*, February 1998, pp. 30–42; C. Whan Park, Sung Youl Jun and Allan D. Shocker, "Composite Branding Alliances: An Investigation of Extension and

Feedback Effects, *Journal of Marketing Research*, November 1996, pp. 453–466; MacInnis, Nakamoto, and Mani, "Cognitive Associations and Product Category Comparisons," pp. 260–267; David M. Bousch et al., "Affect Generalization to Similar and Dissimilar Brand Extensions," *Psychology and Marketing*, 1987, pp. 225–237; Susan M. Baroniarczyk and Joseph W. Alba, "The Importance of the Brand in Brand Extension," *Journal of Marketing Research*, May 1994, pp. 214–228.

10. Zeynep Burnah-Canli and Durairaj Maheswaran, "The Effects of Extensions on Brand Name Dilution and Enhancement," *Journal of Marketing Research*, November 1998, pp. 464–473. Sandra Milberg, C. Whan Park, and Michael S. McCarthy, "Managing Negative Feedback Effects Associated with Brand Extensions: The Impact of Alternative Branding Strategies," *Journal of Consumer Psychology*, Vol. 6, issue 2, 1997, pp. 119–140; Barbara Loken and Deborah Roedder-John, "Diluting Brand Beliefs: When Do Brand Extensions Have a Negative Impact," *Journal of Marketing*, July 1993, pp. 71–84; David A. Aaker, *Managing Brand Equity* (New York: The Free Press, 1991).

11. C. Whan Park, Bernard J. Jaworski, and Deborah J. MacInnis, "Strategic Brand Concept-Image Management," *Journal of Marketing*, October 1986, pp. 135–145.

12. Raju Narisetti, "Xerox Aims to Imprint High-Tech Image," *Wall Street Journal*, October 6, 1998, pp. B8.

13. Ian P. Miller, "RAMS Helps Best Western Tout Worldwide Positioning," *Marketing News*, January 6, 1997, p. 25.

14. Ernest Beck, "Häagen Dazs Alters European Market Strategy," *Wall Street Journal*, April 7, 1998, p. 6.

15. Ian P. Murphy, "All-American Icon Gets a New Look," *Marketing News*, August 18, 1997, pp. 6.

16. Lisa Bannon, "L. A. Hopes to Remake a Classic: Hollywood Boulevard," *Wall Street Journal*, March 11, 1997, pp. B1, B6.

17. "A New Denny's—Diner by Diner, *Business Week*, March 25, 1996, pp. 166+.

18. Chris Adams, "Steel Industry Tries to Fix Tarnished Image," *Wall Street Journal*, June 16, 1997, p. B5.

19. Sally Beatty, "Recasting the Gun as Sports Equipment, *Wall Street Journal*, April 5, 1999, pp. B1, B4.

20. Thomas W. Leigh and Arno J. Rethans, "Experiences in Script Elicitation within Consumer Decision-Making Contexts," in eds. Richard P. Bagozzi and Alice M. Tybout, *Advances in Consumer Research*, Vol. 10 (Ann Arbor, Mich.: Association for Consumer Research, 1983), pp. 667–672; Roger C. Shank and Robert P. Abelson, *Scripts, Plans, Goals, and Understanding: An Inquiry into Human Knowledge Structures* (Hillsdale, N. J.: Lawrence Erlbaum, 1977); Ruth Ann Smith and Michael J. Houston, "A Psychometric Assessment of Measures of Scripts in Consumer Memory," *Journal of Consumer Research*, September 1985, pp. 214–224; R. A. Lakshmi-Ratan and Easwar Iyer, "Similarity Analysis of Cognitive Scripts," *Journal of the Academy of Marketing Science*, Summer 1988, pp. 36–43; C. Whan Park, Easwar Iyer, and Daniel C. Smith, "The Effects of Situational Factors on In-Store Grocery Shopping Behavior: The Role of

Store Environment and Time Available for Shopping," *Journal of Consumer Research*, March 1989, pp. 422–432.

21. Eleanor Rosch, "Principles of Categorization," in eds. E. Rosch and B. Lloyd, *Cognition and Categorization* (Hillsdale, N. J.: Lawrence Erlbaum, 1978), pp. 119–160; Barsalou, *Cognitive Psychology*.

22. Rosch 1978; Barsalou 1985; Madhubalan Viswanathan and Terry L. Childers, "Understanding How Product Attributes Influence Product Categorization: Development and Validation of Fuzzy Set-Based Measures of Gradedness in Product Categories," *Journal of Marketing Research*, February 1999, pp. 75–94.

23. Lawrence Barsalou, "Ideals, Central Tendency, and Frequency of Instantiation as Determinants of Graded Structure in Categories," *Journal of Experimental Psychology: Learning, Memory and Cognition*, October 1985, pp. 629–649; Barbara Loken and James Ward, "Alternative Approaches to Understanding the Determinants of Typicality," *Journal of Consumer Research*, September 1990, pp. 111–126; James Ward and Barbara Loken, "The Quintessential Snack Food: Measurement of Product Prototypes," in ed. Richard J. Lutz, *Advances in Consumer Research*, Vol. 13 (Provo, Utah: Association for Consumer Research, 1986), pp. 126–131; Gregory S. Carpenter and Kent Nakamoto, "Consumer Preference Formation and Pioneering Advantage," *Journal of Marketing Research*, August 1989, pp. 285–298.

24. Gerald J. Gorn and Charles B. Weinberg, "The Impact of Comparative Advertising on Perception and Attitude: Some Positive Findings," *Journal of Consumer Research*, September 1984, pp. 719–727; Cornelia Pechmann and S. Ratneshwar, "The Use of Comparative Advertising for Brand Positioning: Association Versus Differentiation," *Journal of Consumer Research*, September 1991, pp. 145–160; Rita Snyder, "Comparative Advertising and Brand Evaluation: Toward Developing a Categorization Approach," *Journal of Consumer Psychology*, Vol. 1, issue 1, 1992, pp. 15–30.

25. Lisa Brownlee, "Out of Step: Infomercial Makers Spar over Fitness Flyer," *Wall Street Journal*, March 20, 1997, pp. B1, B6.

26. John Bissell, "How Do You Market an Image Brand When the Image Falls out of Favor?" *Brandweek*, July 6, 1994, p. 16.

27. Karen Schwartz and Ian P. Murphy, "Airline Food Is No Joke," *Marketing News*, October 13, 1997, pp. 1, 10.

28. "If You Don't Feel Like Fetching the Rental Car, It Fetches You," *Wall Street Journal*, June 10, 1995, pp. B1, B7.

29. Michael D. Johnson, "Consumer Choice Strategies for Comparing Noncomparable Alternatives," *Journal of Consumer Research*, December 1984, pp. 741–753; Michael D. Johnson, "Comparability and Hierarchical Processing in Multialternative Choice," *Journal of Consumer Research*, December 1988, pp. 303–314; James R. Bettman and Mita Sujan, "Effects of Framing of Comparable and Noncomparable Alternatives by Expert and Novice Consumers," *Journal of Consumer Research*, September 1987, pp. 141–154; C. Whan Park and Daniel C. Smith, "Product Level Choice: A Top Down or Bottom Up Process?" *Journal of Consumer Research*,

December 1989, pp. 151–162; Janet Whitman, "Nestle to Give Nescafe Coffees a New Image," *Wall Street Journal*, March 2, 1999, B10B.

30. Barsalou, *Cognitive Psychology*.

31. Eleanor Rosch, "Human Categorization," in ed. N. Warren, *Studies in Cross-Cultural Psychology* (New York: Academic Press, 1977), pp. 1–49; A. D. Pick, "Cognition: Psychological Perspectives," in eds. H. C. Triandis and W. Lonner, *Handbook of Cross-Cultural Psychology* (Boston: Allyn & Bacon, 1980), pp. 117–153; Bernd Schmitt and Shi Zhang, "Language Structure and Categorization: A Study of Classifiers in Consumer Cognition, Judgment and Choice," *Journal of Consumer Research*, September 1998, pp. 108–122.

32. Joseph W. Alba and J. Wesley Hutchinson, "Dimensions of Consumer Expertise," *Journal of Consumer Research*, March 1987, pp. 411–454; Deborah Roedder John and John Whitney Jr., "The Development of Consumer Knowledge in Children: A Cognitive Structure Approach," *Journal of Consumer Research*, March 1986, pp. 406–417; Merrie Brucks, "The Effects of Product Class Knowledge on Information Search Behavior," *Journal of Consumer Research*, June 1985, pp. 1–16; Deborah Roedder John and Mita Sujan, "Age Differences in Product Categorization," *Journal of Consumer Research*, March 1990, pp. 452–460. See also, Andrew A. Mitchell and Peter A. Dacin, "The Assessment of Alternative Measures of Consumer Expertise," *Journal of Consumer Research*, December 1996, pp. 219–239; C. Whan Park, David L. Mothersbaugh, and Lawrence Feick, "Consumer Knowledge Assessment," *Journal of Consumer Research*, June 1994, pp. 71–82.

33. Yumiko Ono, "Will Good Housekeeping Translate into Japanese?" *Wall Street Journal*, December 30, 1997, pp. B1, B6.

34. "Safety First in Sampling," *Advertising Age*, July 26, 1981.

35. Ronald C. Goodstein, "Category-Based Applications and Extensions in Advertising: Motivating More Extensive Ad Processing," *Journal of Consumer Research*, June 1993, pp. 87–99; Mita Sujan, "Consumer Knowledge: Effects on Evaluation Strategies Mediating Consumer Judgments," *Journal of Consumer Research*, June 1985, pp. 31–46.

36. Susan T. Fiske, "Schema Triggered Affect: Applications to Social Perception," in eds. Margaret S. Clark and Susan T. Fiske, *Affect and Cognition: The 17th Annual Carnegie Symposium on Cognition* (Hillsdale, N. J.: Lawrence Erlbaum, 1984), pp. 55–78; Susan T. Fiske and Mark A. Pavelchak, "Category-Based vs. Piecemeal-Based Affective Responses: Developments in Schema-Triggered Affect," in eds. Richard M. Sorrentino and E. Tory Higgins, *Handbook of Motivation and Cognition* (New York: Guilford, 1986), pp. 167–203; Joel B. Cohen, "The Role of Affect in Categorization: Toward a Reconsideration of the Concept of Attitude," in ed. Andrew A. Mitchell, *Advances in Consumer Research*, Vol. 9 (Ann Arbor, Mich.: Association for Consumer Research, 1982), pp. 94–100.

37. Douglas M. Stayman, Dana L. Alden, and Karen H. Smith, "Some Effects of Schematic Processing on Consumer Expectations and Disconfirmation Judgments," *Journal of Consumer Research*, September 1992, pp. 245–255.

38. David G. Mick, "Levels of Subjective Comprehension in Advertising Processing and Their Relations to Ad Perceptions, Attitudes, and Memory," *Journal of Consumer Research*, March 1992, pp. 411–424.

39. Jacob Jacoby, Wayne D. Hoyer, and David A. Sheluga, *Miscomprehension of Televised Communication* (New York: American Association of Advertising Agencies, 1980); Jacob Jacoby and Wayne D. Hoyer, *The Comprehension and Miscomprehension of Print Communications: An Investigation of Mass Media Magazines* (New York: Advertising Education Foundation, 1987); also see Jacob Jacoby and Wayne D. Hoyer, "The Miscomprehension of Mass-Media Advertising Claims: A Re-Analysis of Benchmark Data," *Journal of Advertising Research*, June–July 1990, pp. 9–17; Jacob Jacoby and Wayne D. Hoyer, "The Comprehension-Miscomprehension of Print Communication: Selected Findings," *Journal of Consumer Research*, March 1989, pp.434–444; Fliece R. Gates, "Further Comments on the Miscomprehension of Televised Advertisements," *Journal of Advertising*, Winter 1986, pp. 4–10.

40. Sak Onkvisit and John J. Shaw, *International Marketing: Analysis and Strategy*, (Columbus, Ohio: Merrill, 1989), pp. 223–224.

41. Richard L. Celsi and Jerry C. Olson, "The Role of Involvement in Attention and Comprehension Processes," *Journal of Consumer Research*, September 1988, pp. 210–224.

42. Jacob Jacoby, Robert W. Chestnut, and William Silberman, "Consumer Use and Comprehension of Nutrition Information," *Journal of Consumer Research*, September 1977, pp. 119–127.

43. Gary J. Gaeth and Timothy B. Heath, "The Cognitive Processing of Misleading Advertising in Young and Old Adults," *Journal of Consumer Research*, June 1987, pp. 43–54; Deborah Roedder John and Catherine A. Cole, "Age Differences in Information Processing: Understanding Deficits in Young and Elderly Consumers," *Journal of Consumer Research*, December 1986, pp. 297–315; Catherine A. Cole and Michael J. Houston, "Encoding and Media Effects on Consumer Learning Deficiencies in the Elderly," *Journal of Marketing Research*, February 1987, pp. 55–63.

44. Edward T. Hall, *Beyond Culture* (Garden City, N. Y.: Anchor Press/Doubleday, 1976); Onkvisit and Shaw, *International Marketing*, pp. 223–224.

45. Fara Warner, "Fahrvergnugen Takes a Back Seat," *Adweek's Marketing Week*, June 15, 1992, pp. 1, 6.

46. Onkvisit and Shaw, *International Marketing*.

47. Wayne D. Hoyer, Rajendra K. Srivastava, and Jacob Jacoby, "Examining Sources of Advertising Miscomprehension," *Journal of Advertising*, June 1984, pp. 17–26; Julie A. Edell and Richard Staelin, "The Information Processing of Pictures in Print Advertisements," *Journal of Consumer Research*, June 1983, pp. 45–61; Ann Beattie and Andrew A. Mitchell, "The Relationship Between Advertising Recall and Persuasion: An Experimental Investigation," in eds. Linda F. Alwitt and Andrew A. Mitchell, *Psychological Processes and Advertising Effects* (Hillsdale, N. J.: Lawrence Erlbaum, 1985), pp. 129–156.

48. Mick, "Levels of Subjective Comprehension in Advertising Processing and Their Relations to Perceptions, Attitudes, and Memory"; Deborah J. MacInnis and Bernard J. Jaworski, "Information Processing from Advertisements: Toward an Integrative Framework," *Journal of Marketing*, October 1989, pp. 1–23.

49. Katherine Ackley, "R.J. Reynolds to Settle Charges over Ads", *Wall Street Journal*, March 4, 1999, p. B4.

50. Mick, "Levels of Subjective Comprehension in Advertising Processing and Their Relations to Ad Perceptions, Attitudes, and Memory"; David G. Mick and Claus Buhl, "A Meaning-Based Model of Advertising Experiences," *Journal of Consumer Research*, December 1992, pp. 317–338.

51. Jennifer Gregan-Paxton and Deborah Roedder John, "Consumer Learning by Analogy: A Model of Internal Knowledge Transfer," *Journal of Consumer Research*, December 1997, pp. 266–284.

52. Richard D. Johnson and Irwin P. Levin, "More Than Meets the Eye: The Effect of Missing Information on Purchase Evaluations," *Journal of Consumer Research*, September 1985, pp. 169–177; Frank Kardes, "Spontaneous Inference Processes in Advertising: The Effects of Conclusion Omission and Involvement in Persuasion," *Journal of Consumer Research*, September 1988, pp. 225–233; Alba and Hutchinson, "Dimensions of Consumer Expertise."

53. Teresa Pavia and Janeen Arnold Costa, "The Winning Number: Consumer Perceptions of Alpha-Numeric Brand Names," *Journal of Marketing*, July 1993, pp. 85–99; France Leclerc, Bernd H. Schmitt, and Laurette Dube, "Foreign Branding and Its Effects on Product Perceptions and Attitudes," *Journal of Marketing Research*, May 1994, pp. 263–270; Mary Sullivan, "How Brand Names Affect the Demand for Twin Automobiles," *Journal of Marketing Research*, May 1998, pp. 154–165.

54. Bonnie B. Reece and Robert H. Ducoffe, "Deception in Brand Names," *Journal of Public Policy and Marketing*, 6, 1987, pp. 93–103.

55. Marilyn Chase, "Pretty Soon the Word 'Organic' on Foods Will Mean One Thing" *Wall Street Journal*, August 18, 1997, p. B1.

56. Benjamin A. Holden, "Utilities Pick New, Nonutilitarian Names," *Wall Street Journal*, April 7, 1997, pp. B1, B5.

57. Rodney Ho, "Was that Cybernet Inc. or Interweb Co.?", *Wall Street Journal*, January 8, 1997, pp. B1, B2.

58. Lisa Bronlee, "A Magazine Named Polo Angers a Firm Named Polo Ralph Loren," *Wall Street Journal*, October 21, 1997, p. B10.

59. Susan M. Broniarczyk and Joseph W. Alba, "The Role of Consumer' Intuitions in Inference Making," *Journal of Consumer Research*, December 1994, pp. 393–407.

60. Gary T. Ford and Ruth Ann Smith, "Inferential Beliefs in Consumer Evaluations: An Assessment of Alternative Processing Strategies," *Journal of Consumer Research*, December 1987, pp. 363–371.

61. Sung-Tai Hong and Robert S. Wyer Jr., "Determinants of Product Evaluation: Effects of Time Interval between Knowledge of a Product's Country of Origin and Information about Its Specific Attributes," *Journal of Consumer Research*, December 1990, pp. 277–288; Durairaj Maheswaran, "Country of Origin as a Stereotype: Effects of Consumer Expertise and Attribute Strength on Product Evaluations," *Journal of Consumer Research*, September 1994, pp. 354–365; Sung-Tai Hong and Robert S. Wyer Jr., "Effects of Country of Origin and Product-Attribute Information on Product Evaluation: An Information Processing Perspective," *Journal of Consumer Research*, September 1989, pp. 175–187; Johny K. Johansson, Susan P. Douglas, and Ikujiro Nonaka, "Assessing the Impact of Country of Origin on Product Evaluations," *Journal of Marketing Research*, November 1985, pp. 388–396; Maheswaran, "Country of Origin as a Stereotype"; Wai-Kwan Li and Robert S. Wyer Jr., "The Role of Country of Origin in Product Evaluations: Informational and Standard-of-Comparison Effects," *Journal of Consumer Psychology*, Month 1994, pp. 187–212.

62. Marieke K. De Mooij and Warren Keegan, *Advertising Worldwide* (Hertfordshire, U.K.: Prentice-Hall International, 1991), p. 97.

63. Lisa Miller, "For Some Jews, Chrysler Opens up a Delicate Debate," *Wall Street Journal*, May 13, 1998, pp. B1, B2.

64. Carl McDaniel and R. C. Baker, "Convenience Food Packaging and the Perception of Product Quality," *Journal of Marketing*, October 1977, pp. 57–58.

65. Ralph T. King Jr., "Grapes of Wrath: Kendall-Jackson Sues Gallo Winery in a Battle over a Bottle," *Wall Street Journal*, April 5, 1996, pp. B1, B11.

66. Maxine S. Lans, "Supreme Court to Rule on Colors as Trademarks," *Marketing News*, January 2, 1995, p. 28.

67. Ayn Crowley, "The Two-Dimensional Impact of Color on Shopping," *Marketing Letters*, Month 1993, pp. 59–69.

68. Donald Lichtenstein and Scott Burton, "The Relationship between Perceived and Objective Price-Quality," *Journal of Marketing Research*, November 1989, pp. 429–443; Etian Gerstner, "Do Higher Prices Signal Higher Quality?" *Journal of Marketing Research*, May 1985, pp. 209–215; Kent Monroe and R. Krishnan, "The Effects of Price on Subjective Product Evaluations," in eds. Jacob Jacoby and Jerry C. Olson, *Perceived Quality: How Consumers View Stores and Merchandise* (Lexington, Mass.: D. C. Heath, 1985), pp. 209–232; Susan M. Petroshius and Kent B. Monroe, "Effect of Product-Line Pricing Characteristics on Product Evaluations," *Journal of Consumer Research*, March 1987, pp. 511–519; Akshay R. Rao and Kent B. Monroe, "The Moderating Effect of Prior Knowledge on Cue Utilization in Product Evaluations," *Journal of Consumer Research*, September 1988, pp. 253–264; Cornelia Pechmann and S. Ratneshwar, "Consumer Covariation Judgments: Theory or Data Driven?" *Journal of Consumer Research*, December 1992, pp. 373–386.

69. Ruth Nicholas, "Comet in Music Retailing Move," *Marketing*, December 9, 1993, p. 9.

70. Tsune Shirai, "What Is an 'International' Mind?" *PHP*, June 1980, p. 25.

71. Barbara Mueller, "Standardization vs. Specialization: An Examination of Westernization in Japanese Advertising," *Journal of Advertising Research*, January–February 1992, pp. 15–22.

72. Onkvisit and Shaw, *International Marketing*.

73. Richard J. Harris, Julia C. Pounds, Melissa J. Maiorelle, and Maria Mermis, "The Effect of Type of Claim, Gender and Buying History on the Drawing of Pragmatic Inferences from Advertising Claims," *Journal of Consumer Psychology*, Vol. 2, issue 1, 1993, pp. 83–95; Richard J. Harris, R. E. Sturm, M. L. Kalssen, and J. I. Bechtold, "Language in Advertising: A Psycholinguistic Approach," *Current Issues and Research in Advertising*, Month 1986, pp. 1–26; Raymond R. Burke, Wayne S. DeSarbo, Richard L. Oliver, and Thomas S. Robertson, "Deception by Implication: An Experimental Investigation," *Journal of Consumer Research*, March 1988, pp. 483–494.

74. Terence Shimp, "Do Incomplete Comparisons Mislead?" *Journal of Advertising Research*, December 1978, pp. 21–27; Harris et al., "The Effect of Type of Claim, Gender, and Buying History on the Drawing of Pragmatic Inferences from Advertising Claims"; Gita Johar, "Consumer Involvement and Deception from Implied Advertising Claims," *Journal of Marketing Research*, August 1995, pp. 267–279.

75. Michael Barone and Paul W. Miniard, "How and When Factual Ad Claims Mislead Consumers: Examining the Deceptive Consequences of Copy x Copy Interactions for Partial Comparative Advertisements," *Journal of Marketing Research*, February 1999, pp. 58–74.

CHAPTER 6

1. Raju Narisetti, "Unisys Campaign Emphasizes Firm's Vigor," *Wall Street Journal*, September 24, 1998, p. B12.

2. Richard E. Petty, H. Rao Unnava, and Alan J. Strathman, "Theories of Attitude Change," in eds. Thomas S. Robertson and Harold H. Kassarjian, *Handbook of Consumer Behavior* (Englewood Cliffs, N. J.: Prentice-Hall, 1991), pp. 241–280.

3. Ida E. Berger and Andrew A. Mitchell, "The Effect of Advertising on Attitude Accessibility, Attitude Confidence, and the Attitude-Behavior Relationship," *Journal of Consumer Research*, December 1989, pp. 269–279.

4. Martin Fishbein and Icek Ajzen, *Belief, Attitude, Intention, and Behavior: An Introduction to Theory and Research* (Reading, Mass.: Addison-Wesley, 1975).

5. Petty, Unnava, and Strathman, "Theories of Attitude Change"; Richard Petty and John T. Cacioppo, *Communication and Persuasion* (New York: Springer, 1986).

6. Peter L. Wright, "Message Evoked Thoughts: Persuasion Research Using Thought Verbalizations," *Journal of Consumer Research*, September 1980, pp. 151–175.

7. Jerry C. Olson, Daniel R. Toy, and Philip A. Dover, "Do Cognitive Responses Mediate the Effects of Advertising Content on Cognitive Structure?" *Journal of Consumer Research*, December 1982, pp. 245–262.

8. Marian Friestad and Peter Wright, "The Persuasion Knowledge Model: How People Cope with Persuasion Attempts," *Journal of Consumer Research*, June 1994, pp. 1–31.

9. Daniel R. Toy, "Monitoring Communication Effects: Cognitive Structure/Cognitive Response Approach," *Journal of Consumer Research*, June 1982, pp. 66–76.

10. Petty, Unnava, and Strathman, "Theories of Attitude Change."

11. Punam Anand and Brian Sternthal, "The Effects of Program Involvement and Ease of Message Counterarguing on Advertising Persuasiveness," *Journal of Consumer Psychology*, 1(3), 1992, pp. 225–238; Kenneth R. Lord and Robert E. Burnkrant, "Attention versus Distraction: The Interactive Effect of Program Involvement and Attentional Devices on Commercial Processing," *Journal of Advertising*, March 1993, pp. 47–60.

12. Deborah J. MacInnis and C. Whan Park, "The Differential Role of Characteristics of Music on High- and Low-Involvement Consumers' Processing of Ads," *Journal of Consumer Research*, September 1991, pp. 161–173; Rajeev Batra and Douglas M. Stayman, "The Role of Mood in Advertising Effectiveness," *Journal of Consumer Research*, September 1990, pp. 203–214.

13. William L. Wilkie and Edgar A. Pessemier, "Issues in Marketing's Use of Multi-Attribute Models," *Journal of Marketing Research*, November 1973, pp. 428–441.

14. Icek Ajzen and Martin Fishbein, "Prediction of Goal-Directed Behavior: Attitudes, Intentions, and Perceived Behavioral Control," *Journal of Experimental Social Psychology*, September 1980, pp. 453–474; Blair H. Sheppard, Jon Hartwick, and Paul R. Warshaw, "The Theory of Reasoned Action: A Meta-Analysis of Past Research with Recommendations for Modifications and Future Research," *Journal of Consumer Research*, December 1988, pp. 325–342.

15. Calmetta Y. Coleman, "Hallmark to Spend $10 Million to Say Its Cards Aren't Expensive," *Wall Street Journal*, February 12, 1998, p. B6; Yumiko Ono, "SnackWell's Stresses Taste, Not Low Fat," *Wall Street Journal*, September 8, 1997, p. B12.

16. Stephen E. Frank, "Got a Bank? Industry Launches TV Ads," *Wall Street Journal*, September 23, 1997, pp. B1, B8.

17. Pichayaporn Utumporn, "McDonald's Proclaims Itself a Thai Patriot," *Wall Street Journal*, August 10, 1998, pp. B1, B6.

18. Wendy Bounds and Deborah Ball, "Italy Knits Support for Fashion Industry," *Wall Street Journal*, December 15, 1997, p. B8; Yumiko Ono, "A Korean Car Maker's Strange Quest for Ads," *Wall Street Journal*, July 24, 1997, pp. B1, B7; Fara Warner and Pichayaporn Utumporn, "Ads in Southeast Asia Capitalize on Slump There to Push Products," *Wall Street Journal*, December 10, 1997, p. B8.

19. Hugh Pope, "Plying Ex Soviet Asia with Pepsi, Barbie, and Barf," *Wall Street Journal*, June 6, 1998, pp. B1, B6.

20. Tara Parker-Pope, "P & G Dresses High-Tech Olestra in Down Home Image in New Ads," *Wall Street Journal*, February 11, 1998, p. B6.

21. Dana Milbank, "Made in America Becomes a Boast in Europe," *Wall Street Journal*, January 9, 1994, pp. B1, B5.

22. Fara Warner and Pichayaporn Utumporn, "Ads in Southeast Asia Capitalize on Slump There to Push Products."

23. Stephen M. Nowlis and Itamar Simonson, "The Effect of New Product Features on Brand Choice," *Journal of Marketing Research*, February 1996, pp. 36–46.

24. Andrea Petersen, "Cross, IBM Choose Low-Tech Imagery," *Wall Street Journal*, April 30, 1998, p. B5.

25. Gregory L. White, "Jeep's Challenge: Stay Rugged But Add Room for Gold Clubs," *Wall Street Journal*, September 29, 1998, pp. B1, B4.

26. Laura Bird, "Condom Campaign Fails to Increase Sales," *Wall Street Journal*, June 23, 1994, p. B7

27. Barbara Mueller, "Reflections of Culture: An Analysis of Japanese and American Advertising Appeals," *Journal of Advertising Research*, June–July 1987, pp. 51–59.

28. Brian Sternthal, Ruby R. Dholakia, and Clark Leavitt, "The Persuasive Effect of Source Credibility: A Situational Analysis," *Public Opinion Quarterly*, Fall 1978, pp. 285–314.

29. Martha Braningan, "Microsoft Wizard Moonlights as Gulfstream Pitchman," *Wall Street Journal*, October 2, 1998, pp. B1, B4.

30. Galceran and Berry, "A New World of Consumers."

31. Amna Kirmani and Baba Shiv, "Effects of Source Congruity on Brand Attitudes and Beliefs: The Moderating Role of Issue-Relevant Elaboration," *Journal of Consumer Psychology*, 7 (1) 1998, pp. 25–48.

32. Chenghuan Wu and David R. Schaffer, "Susceptibility to Persuasive Appeals as a Function of Source Credibility and Prior Experience with the Attitude Object," *Journal of Personality and Social Psychology*, April 1987, pp. 677–688.

33. Carolyn Tripp, Thomas D. Jensen, and Les Carlson, "The Effects of Multiple Endorsements by Celebrities on Consumers' Attitudes and Intentions," *Journal of Consumer Research*, March 1994, pp. 535–547.

34. William Power, "Some Brokers Promise that You Will Make Money; Not This One," *Wall Street Journal*, February 23, 1994, p. B1.

35. "More Firms Use Employees as Stars of Company Commercials," *Wall Street Journal*, February 22, 1993, pp. B1, B6.

36. Ignacio Galceran and Jon Berry, "A New World of Consumers," *American Demographics*, March 1995, pp. 26–33.

37. Yumiko Ono, "Trendy Japanese Cheer for U.S. Teams," *Wall Street Journal*, February 2, 1993, pp. B1, B12.

38. Kevin Goldman, "Women Endorsers More Credible than Men, a Survey Suggests," *Wall Street Journal*, October 22, 1995, p. B1.

39. Sternthal, Dholakia, and Leavitt, "The Persuasive Effect of Source Credibility."

40. Darlene B. Hannah and Brian Sternthal, "Detecting and Explaining the Sleeper Effect," *Journal of Consumer Research*, September 1984, pp. 632–642.

41. Goldberg and Hartwick, "The Effects of Advertiser Reputation and Extremity of Advertising Claim on Advertising Effectiveness."

42. Kevin Goldman, "Accounting Firm Goes for Super Bowl Play," *Wall Street Journal*, January 14, 1993, p. B5.

43. Petty, Unnava, and Strathman, "Theories of Attitude Change."; Charles S. Areni and Richard J. Lutz, "The Role of Argument Quality in the Elaboration Likelihood Model," in ed. Michael J. Houston, *Advances in Consumer Research*, Vol. 15 (Provo, Utah: Association for Consumer Research, 1987), pp. 197–203.

44. James S. Hirsch, "Fidelity Creates Ads Featuring the Day's News," *Wall Street Journal*, January 30, 1997, pp. B1, B12.

45. Darren McDermott, "All-American Infomercials Sizzle in Asia," *Wall Street Journal*, June 25, 1996, p. B5.

46. Sally Beatty, "Companies Push for Much Bigger, More Complicated On-Line Ads," *Wall Street Journal*, August 20, 1998 p. B1.

47. Timothy B. Heath, Michael S. McCarthy, and David L. Mothersbaugh, "Spokesperson Fame and Vividness Effects in the Context of Issue-Relevant Thinking: The Moderating Role of Competitive Setting," *Journal of Consumer Research*, March 1994, pp. 520–534.

48. Laura A. Peracchio, "Evaluating Persuasion-Enhancing Techniques from a Resource Matching Perspective," *Journal of Consumer Research*, September 1997, pp. 178–191.

49. Michael A. Kamins and Henry Assael, "Two-Sided versus One-Sided Appeals: A Cognitive Perspective on Argumentation, Source Derogation, and the Effect of Disconfirming Trial on Belief Change," *Journal of Marketing Research*, February 1984, pp. 29–39.

50. Cornelia Pechmann and David W. Stewart, "The Effects of Comparative Advertising on Attention, Memory, and Purchase Intentions," *Journal of Consumer Research*, September 1990, pp. 180–191.

51. Sally Beatty, "IBM Targets Sun with Guerilla Tactics," *Wall Street Journal*, September 11, 1998, p. B7.

52. Wendy Bounds, "Levi's Simply Says Its Rivals Wore Them," *Wall Street Journal*, May 5, 1998, p. B6.

53. Pechmann and Stewart, "The Effects of Comparative Advertising on Attention, Memory, and Purchase Intentions"; Rita Snyder, "Comparative Advertising and Brand Evaluation: Toward Developing a Categorization Approach," *Journal of Consumer Psychology*, 1 (1)1992, pp. 15–30.

54. Gene Koprowski, "Theories of Negativity," *Brandweek*, February 20, 1995, pp. 20–22.

55. Dhruv Grewal, Sukumar Kavanoor, Edward F. Fern, Carolyn Costley, and James Barnes, "Comparative versus Noncomparative Advertising: A Meta-Analysis," *Journal of Marketing*, October 1997, pp. 1–15.

56. Pechmann and Stewart, "The Effects of Comparative Advertising on Attention, Memory, and Purchase Intentions."

57. Jerry B. Gotlieb and Dan Sarel, "Comparative Advertising Effectiveness: The Role of Involvement and Source Credibility," *Journal of Advertising*, 20 (1), 1991, pp. 38–45; Koprowski, "Theories of Negativity."

58. Cornelia Pechmann and S. Ratneshwar, "The Use of Comparative Advertising for Brand Positioning: Association versus Differentiation," *Journal of Consumer Research*, September 1991, pp. 145–160.

59. Pechmann and Stewart, "The Effects of Comparative Advertising on Attention, Memory, and Purchase Intentions."

60. Barbara Mueller, "Reflections of Culture: An Analysis of Japanese and American Advertising Appeals," *Journal of Advertising Research*, June–July 1987, pp. 51–59.

61. Michel Tuan Pham, "Representativeness, Relevance, and the Use of Feelings in Decision Making," *Journal of Consumer Research*, September 1998, pp. 144–159.

62. MacInnis and Park, "The Differential Role of Characteristics of Music on High- and Low-Involvement Consumers' Processing of Ads."

63. Deborah J. MacInnis and Douglas M. Stayman, "Focal and Emotional Integration: Constructs, Measures and Preliminary Evidence," *Journal of Advertising*, December 1993, pp. 51–66; Chris T. Allen, Karen A. Machleit, and Susan Schultz Kleine, "A Comparison of Attitudes and Emotions as Predictors of Behavior at Diverse Levels of Behavioral Experience," *Journal of Consumer Research*, March 1992, pp. 493–504.

64. Deborah J. MacInnis and Bernard J. Jaworski, "Two Routes to Persuasion in Advertising: Review, Critique, and Research Directions," *Review of Marketing*, Vol. 10, 1990, pp. 1–25.

65. C. Whan Park and S. Mark Young, "Consumer Response to Television Commercials: The Impact of Involvement and Background Music on Brand Attitude Formation," *Journal of Marketing Research*, February 1986, pp. 11–24.

66. Rajeev Batra and Michael L. Ray, "Affective Responses Mediating Acceptance of Advertising," *Journal of Consumer Research*, September 1986, pp. 234–249.

67. Hans Baumgartner, Mita Sujan, and Dan Padgett, "Patterns of Affective Reactions to Advertisements: The Integration of Moment-to-Moment Responses into Overall Judgments," *Journal of Marketing Research*, May 1997, pp. 219–232.

68. Deborah J. MacInnis and Bernard J. Jaworski, "Information Processing from Advertisements: Toward an Integrative Framework," *Journal of Marketing*, October 1989, pp. 1–23.

69. Jennifer L. Aaker and Patti Williams, "Empathy versus Pride: The Influence of Emotional Appeals across Cultures,' *Journal of Consumer Research*, December 1998, pp. 241–261.

70. Richard P. Bagozzi and David J. Moore, "Public Service Announcements: Emotions and Empathy Guide Prosocial Behavior," *Journal of Marketing*, January 1994, pp. 56–57.

71. May Frances Luce, "Choosing to Avoid: Coping with Negatively Emotion-Laden Consumer Decisions," *Journal of Consumer Research*, March 1998, pp. 409–433.

72. Joel B. Cohen and Charles S. Areni, "Affect and Consumer Behavior," in eds. Thomas S. Robertson and Harold H. Kassarjian, *Handbook of Consumer Behavior* (Englewood Cliffs, N. J.: Prentice-Hall, 1991, pp. 188–240.

73. Petty, Unnava, and Strathman, "Theories of Attitude Change."

74. Harry C. Triandis, *Attitudes and Attitude Change* (New York: Wiley, 1971).

75. Stephen E. Frank, "Can Tiger Woods Sell Financial Services?" *Wall Street Journal*, May 20, 1997, pp. B1, B14.

76. Peter H. Reingen and Jerome B. Kernan, "Social Perception and Interpersonal Influence: Some Consequences of the Physical Attractiveness Stereotype in a Personal Selling Situation," *Journal of Consumer Psychology*, 2 (1), 1993, pp. 25–38.

77. Scott Ward and Frederick E. Webster Jr., "Organizational Buying Behavior," in eds. Thomas S. Robertson and Harold H. Kassarjian, *Handbook of Consumer Behavior* (Englewood Cliffs, N. J.: Prentice-Hall, 1991), pp. 419–458.

78. Herbert Simon, Nancy Berkowitz, and John Moyer, "Similarity, Credibility, and Attitude Change," *Psychological Bulletin*, January 1970, pp. 1–16.

79. "Goal: Nuprin," *Ad Week's Marketing Week*, June 15, 1992, p. 19.

80. Jonathan Karp, "A Toast to India's Independence Stirs a Tempest in a Soda Bottle," *Wall Street Journal*, August 15, 1997, p. B1.

81. Sally Goll Beatty, "Bad-Boy Nike Is Playing the Diplomat in China," *Wall Street Journal*, November 10, 1997, pp. B1, B10.

82. Sally Goll Beatty, "Just What Goes in a Viagra Ad? Dancing Couples," *Wall Street Journal*, June 17, 1998, pp. B1, B8.

83. Yumiko Ono, "Here's a Hot Job for the Nosy and Offbeat," *Wall Street Journal*, December 27, 1997, pp. B1, B8.

84. Batra and Stayman, "The Role of Mood in Advertising Effectiveness."

85. Kevin Goldman, "The Market for Pricey Sunglasses Heats Up," *Wall Street Journal*, March 22, 1993, pp. B1, B5.

86. Kevin Goldman, "Volvo Seeks to Soft-Pedal Safety Image," *Wall Street Journal*, March 16, 1993, p. B7.

87. Sally Goll Beatty, "Mercedes Hopes Duckie, Child Broaden Appeal," *Wall Street Journal*, May 21, 1997, pp. B1, B8; Lucette Lagnado, "Fuzzy Mascots Help Medicaid Put on a Happier Face," *Wall Street Journal*, September 24, 1998, pp. B1, B8.

88. Cacile Rohwedder, "Germany Drafts a Campaign for Recruits," *Wall Street Journal*, October 10, 1996, p. B6.

89. Lisa Shuchman, "How Does GM's Saturn Sell Cars in Japan? Very Slowly," *Wall Street Journal*, September 25, 1998, pp. B1, B4.

90. Valerie S. Folkes and Tina Kiesler, "Social Cognition: Consumers' Inferences about the Self and Others," in eds. Thomas S. Robertson and Harold H. Kassarjian, *Handbook of Consumer Behavior* (Englewood Cliffs, N. J.: Prentice-Hall, 1991), pp. 281–315.

91. John F. Tanner, James B. Hunt, and David R. Eppright, "The Protection Motivation Model: A Normative Model of Fear Appeals," *Journal of Marketing*, July 1991, pp. 36–45.

92. Sally Goll Beatty and Bruce Ingersoll, "Drug Marketers Try New Tactic: Fear," *Wall Street Journal*, June 12, 1997, pp. B1, B10.

93. Kathleen Deveny, "Marketers Exploit People's Fears of Everything," *Wall Street Journal*, November 15, 1993, pp. B1, B3.

94. Michael L. Ray and William L. Wilkie, "Fear: The Potential of an Appeal Neglected by Marketing," *Journal of Marketing*, January 1970, pp. 54–62.

95. Ibid.

96. Ibid. Herbert J. Rotfeld, "Fear Appeals and Persuasion: Assumptions and Errors in Advertising Research," in eds. James H. Leigh and Claude R. Martin, *Current Issues and Research in Advertising* (Ann Arbor, Mich.: Graduate School of Business Administration, University of Michigan, 1990), pp. 155–175.

97. John J. Wheatley, "Marketing and the Use of Fear- or Anxiety-Arousing Appeals," *Journal of Marketing*, April 1971, pp. 62–64; Peter L. Wright, "Concrete Action Plans in TV Messages to Increase Reading of Drug Warnings," *Journal of Consumer Research*, December 1979, pp. 256–269

ENDNOTES

98. John J. Burette and Richard L. Oliver, "Fear Appeal Effects in the Field: A Segmentation Approach," *Journal of Marketing Research*, May 1979, pp. 181–190.
99. MacInnis and Jaworski, "Two Routes to Persuasion in Advertising."
100. Thomas J. Olney, Morris B. Holbrook, and Rajeev Batra, "Consumer Responses to Advertising: The Effects of Ad Content, Emotions, and Attitude Toward the Ad on Viewing Time," *Journal of Consumer Research*, March 1991, pp. 440–453.
101. Paul W. Miniard, Sunil Bhatla, and Randall L. Rose, "On the Formation and Relationship of Ad and Brand Attitudes: An Experimental and Causal Analysis," *Journal of Marketing Research*, August 1990, pp. 290–303.
102. Beatty, "Companies Push for Much Bigger."
103. Sally Goll Beatty, "Executive Fears Effects of Political Ads," *Wall Street Journal*, April 29, 1996, p. B6.
104. Julie A. Edell and Richard E. Staelin, "The Information Processing of Pictures in Print Advertisements," *Journal of Consumer Research*, June 1983, pp. 45–60.
105. Scott B. MacKenzie, Richard J. Lutz, and George E. Belch, "The Role of Attitude toward the Ad as a Mediator of Advertising Effectiveness: A Test of Competing Explanations," *Journal of Marketing Research*, May 1986, pp. 130–143; Pamela M. Homer, "The Mediating Role of Attitude toward the Ad: Some Additional Evidence," *Journal of Marketing Research*, February 1990, pp. 78–86.
106. Andrea Petersen, "The Quest to Make URLs Look Cool in Ads," *Wall Street Journal*, February 26, 1997, pp. B1, B3.
107. Richard E. Petty, John T. Cacioppo, and David W. Schumann, "Central and Peripheral Routes to Advertising Persuasion," *Journal of Consumer Research*, September 1983, pp. 134–148.
108. Smith and Swinyard, "Attitude-Behavior Consistency"; Russell H. Fazio and Mark P. Zanna, "Direct Experience and Attitude-Behavior Consistency," in ed. Leonard Berkowitz, *Advances in Experimental Social Psychology* (New York: Academic Press, 1981), pp. 162–202.
109. Russell H. Fazio, Martha C. Powell, and Carol J. Williams, "The Role of Attitude Accessibility in the Attitude-to-Behavior Process," *Journal of Consumer Research*, December 1989, pp. 280–288; Ida E. Berger and Andrew A. Mitchell, "The Effect of Advertising on Attitude Accessibility, Attitude Confidence, and the Attitude-Behavior Relationship."
110. Smith and Swinyard, "Attitude-Behavior Consistency"; Alice A. Wright and John G. Lynch, "Communication Effects of Advertising vs. Direct Experience When Both Search and Experience Attributes Are Present," *Journal of Consumer Research*, March 1995, pp. 708–718.
111. Ida E. Berger, "The Nature of Attitude Accessibility and Attitude Confidence."
112. Fishbein and Ajzen, *Belief, Attitude, Intention, and Behavior.*
113. Ibid.
114. John T. Cacioppo, Richard E. Petty, Chuan Fang Kao, and Regina Rodriguez, "Central and Peripheral Routes to Persuasion: An Individual Difference Perspective," *Journal of Personality and Social Psychology*, 51, 1986, pp. 1032–1043.
115. Mark Snyder and William B. Swan Jr., "When Actions Reflect Attitudes: The Politics of Impression Management," *Journal of Personality and Social Psychology*, 34, 1976, pp. 1034–1042.

CHAPTER 7

1. Carol Bidwell, "Taco Bell Says, 'Ay, Chihuahua'" *Austin American Statesman*, March 6, 1998, p. E5.
2. Richard E. Petty and John T. Cacioppo, *Attitudes and Persuasion: Classic and Contemporary Approaches* (Dubuque, Iowa: William C. Brown, 1981); Richard E. Petty, John T. Cacioppo, and David Schumann, "Central and Peripheral Routes to Advertising Effectiveness: The Moderating Role of Involvement," *Journal of Consumer Research*, September 1983, pp. 135–146.
3. Jaideep Sengupta, Ronald C. Goodstein, and David S. Boninger, "All Cues Are Not Created Equal: Obtaining Attitude Persistence under Low Involvement Conditions," *Journal of Consumer Research*, March 1997, pp. 315–361.
4. Ronald C. Goodstein, "Category-Based Applications and Extensions in Advertising: Motivating More Extensive Ad Processing," *Journal of Consumer Research*, June 1993, pp. 87–99.
5. Valerie S. Folkes, "Recent Attribution Research in Consumer Behavior: A Review and New Directions," *Journal of Consumer Research*, March 1988, pp. 548–656.
6. Shelly Chaiken, "Heuristic versus Systematic Information Processing and the Use of Source Versus Message Cues in Persuasion," *Journal of Personality and Social Psychology*, 39, 1980, pp. 752–766; also, "The Heuristic Model of Persuasion," in eds. Mark P. Zanna, J. M. Olson, and C. P. Herman, *Social Influence: The Ontario Symposium*, Vol. 5 (Hillsdale, N. J.: Lawrence Erlbaum, 1987), pp. 3–49.
7. Amna Kirmani, "Advertising Repetition as a Signal of Quality: If It's Advertised So Much, Something Must Be Wrong," *Journal of Advertising*, Fall 1997, pp. 77–86.
8. Joseph W. Alba and Howard Marmorstein, "The Effects of Frequency Knowledge on Consumer Decision Making," *Journal of Consumer Research*, June 1987, pp. 14–25.
9. Scott A. Hawkins and Stephen J. Hoch, "Low-Involvement Learning: Memory without Evaluation," *Journal of Consumer Research*, September 1992, pp. 212–225; Lynn Hasher, David Goldstein, and Thomas Toppino, "Frequency and the Conference of Referential Validity," *Journal of Verbal Learning and Verbal Behavior*, February 1977, pp. 107–112.
10. S. Ratneshwar and Shelly Chaiken, "Comprehension's Role in Persuasion: The Case of Its Moderating Effect on the Persuasive Impact of Source Cues," *Journal of Consumer Research*, June 1991, pp. 52–62.
11. Richard Gibson and Sally Goll Beatty, "McDonald's Ad Barrage to Defend Fries," *Wall Street Journal*, January 13, 1997, p. B8.
12. Robert E. Burnkrant and H. Rao Unnava, Effects of Self-Referencing on Persuasion, *Journal of Consumer Research*, June 1995, pp. 17–26; Sharon Shavitt and Timothy C. Brock," Self-Relevant Responses in Commercial Persuasion," in eds. Jerry C. Olson and

Keith Sentis, *Advertising and Consumer Psychology* (New York: Praeger, 1986), pp. 149–171; Kathleen Debevec and Jean B. Romeo, "Self-Referent Processing in Perceptions of Verbal and Visual Commercial Information," *Journal of Consumer Psychology*, 1 (1), 1992, pp. 83–102; Joan Myers-Levy and Laura A. Peracchio, "Moderators of the Impact of Self-Reference on Persuasion," *Journal of Consumer Research*, March 1996, pp. 408–423.

13. Daniel J. Howard, Charles Gengler, and Ambuj Jain, "What's in a Name? A Complimentary Means of Persuasion," *Journal of Consumer Research*, September1 995, pp. 200–211.

14. Robert E. Burnkrant and Daniel J. Howard, "Effects of the Use of Introductory Rhetorical Questions versus Statements on Information Processing," *Journal of Personality and Social Psychology*, December 1984, pp. 1218–1230; James M. Munch, Gregory W. Boller, and John L. Swazy, "The Effects of Argument Structure and Affective Tagging on Product Attitude Formation," *Journal of Consumer Research*, September 1993, pp. 294–302.

15. Patrick M. Reilly, "Philips's Teaser" TV Ads Mystify Some," *Wall Street Journal*, November 4, 1992, p. B8.

16. Russell H. Fazio, Paul M. Herr, and Martha C. Powell, "On the Development and Strength of Category-Brand Associations in Memory: The Case of Mystery Ads," *Journal of Consumer Psychology*, 1 (1), 1992, pp. 1–14.

17. Lisa Marie Petersen, "Miller Plays Ball in NTN Bars," *Brandweek*, September 13, 1993, p. 14.

18. Joseph W. Alba, J. Wesley Hutchinson, and John G. Lynch, "Memory and Decision Making," in eds. Thomas S. Robertson and Harold H. Kassarjian, *Handbook of Consumer Behavior* (Englewood Cliffs, N. J.: Prentice-Hall, 1991).

19. H. Rao Unnava and Robert E. Burnkrant, "Effects of Repeating Varied Ad Executions on Brand Name Memory," *Journal of Marketing Research*, November 1991, pp. 406–416.

20. Ida E. Berger and Andrew A. Mitchell, "The Effect of Attitude Accessibility, Attitude Confidence, and the Attitude-Behavior Relationship," *Journal of Consumer Research*, December 1989, pp. 269–279.

21. "Effies," *Adweeks's Marketing Week*, June 15, 1992, p. 12.

22. Vanessa O'Connell, "Vlassic Posts Loss, Cites Insufficient Ads," *Wall Street Journal*, September 18, 1998, p. B6.

23. Prashant Malaviya and Brian Sternthal, "The Persuasive Impact of Message Spacing," *Journal of Consumer Psychology*, 6 (3), 1997, pp. 233–256.

24. Carl Obermiller, "Varieties of Mere Exposure: The Effects of Processing Style and Repetition in Affective Response," *Journal of Consumer Research*, June 1985, pp. 17–30.

25. Arno Rethans, John L. Swazy, and Lawrence J. Marks, "The Effects of Television Commercial Repetition, Receiver Knowledge, and Commercial Length: A Test of a Two Factor Model," *Journal of Marketing Research*, February 1986, pp. 50–61.

26. Leo Bogart, *Strategy in Advertising: Matching Media and Messages of Markets and Motivation* (Lincoln, Ill.: NTC Business, 1986), p. 208.

27. Norihiko Shirouzu, "Whoppers Face Entrenched Foes in Japan: Big Macs," *Wall Street Journal*, February 4, 1997, pp. B1, B5.

28. Herbert Krugman, "Why Three Exposures May Be Enough," *Journal of Advertising Research*, December 1972, pp. 11–14.

29. George E. Belch, "The Effects of Television Commercial Repetition on Cognitive Response and Message Acceptance," *Journal of Consumer Research*, June 1982, pp. 56–65.

30. Marian Burke and Julie A. Edell, "Ad Reactions over Time: Capturing Changes in the Real World," *Journal of Consumer Research*, June 1986, pp. 114–118; Curtis P. Haugtvedt, David W. Schumann, Wendy L. Schneier, and Wendy L. Warren, "Advertising Repetition and Variation Strategies: Implications for Understanding Attitude Strength," *Journal of Consumer Research*, June 1994, pp. 176–189.

31. Gerald J. Gorn, "The Effects of Music in Advertising on Choice Behavior: A Classical Conditioning Approach," *Journal of Marketing*, Winter 1982, pp. 94–101.

32. Calvin Bierley, Frances K. McSweeny, and Renee Vannieuwkerk, "Classical Conditioning of Preferences for Stimuli," *Journal of Consumer Research*, December 1985, pp. 316–323; James J. Kellaris and Anthony D. Cox, "The Effects of Background Music in Advertising: A Reassessment," *Journal of Consumer Research*, June 1989, pp. 113–118: Chris T. Allen and Thomas J. Madden, "A Closer Look at Classical Conditioning," *Journal of Consumer Research*, December 1985, pp. 301–315.

33. Bierley, McSweeny, and Vannieuwkerk, "Classical Conditioning of Preferences for Stimuli"; Elnora W. Stuart, Terence A. Shimp, and Randall W. Engle, "Classical Conditioning of Consumer Attitudes: Four Experiments in an Advertising Context," *Journal of Consumer Research*, December 1987, pp. 334–349; Terence A. Shimp, Elnora W. Stuart, and Randall W. Engle, "A Program of Classical Conditioning Experiments Testing Variations in the Conditioned Stimulus and Context," *Journal of Consumer Research*, June 1991, pp. 1–12; Chris T. Allen and Chris A. Janiszewski, "Assessing the Role of Contingency Awareness in Attitudinal Conditioning with Implications for Advertising Research," *Journal of Marketing Research*, February 1989, pp. 30–43.

34. Randi Priluck Grossman and Brian D. Till, "The Persistence of Classically Conditioned Brand Attitudes," *Journal of Advertising*, Spring 1998.

35. Terence A. Shimp, "Neo-Pavlovian Conditioning and Its Implications for Consumer Theory and Research," in eds. Thomas S. Robertson and Harold H. Kassarjian, *Handbook of Consumer Behavior* (Englewood Cliffs, N. J.: Prentice-Hall, 1991, pp. 162–187.

36. Steven P. Brown and Douglas M. Stayman, "Antecedents and Consequences of Attitude toward the Ad: A Meta-analysis," *Journal of Consumer Research*, June 1993, pp. 34–51; Andrew A. Mitchell and Jerry C. Olson, "Are Product Attributes Beliefs the Only Mediator of Advertising Effects on Brand Attitudes?" *Journal of Marketing Research*, August 1981, pp. 318–322; Terence A. Shimp, "Attitude toward the Ad as a Mediator of

Consumer Brand Choice," *Journal of Advertising*, 10 (2), 1981, pp. 9–15; Christian M. Derbaix, "The Impact of Affective Reactions on Attitudes toward the Advertisement and the Brand: A Step toward Ecological Validity," *Journal of Marketing Research*, November 1995, pp. 470–479.

37. Mitchell and Olson, "Are Product Attributes Beliefs the Only Mediator of Advertising Effects on Brand Attitudes?"

38. Srinivas Durvasula, J. Craig Andrews, Steven Lysonski, and Richard G. Netemeyer, "Assessing the Cross-National Applicability of Consumer Behavior Models: A Model of Attitude toward Advertising in General," *Journal of Consumer Research*, March 1993, pp. 626–636.

39. Russell I. Haley and Allan L. Baldinger, "The ARF Copy Research Validity Project," *Journal of Advertising Research*, April–May 1991, pp. 11–32.

40. Scott B. MacKenzie, Richard J. Lutz, and George E. Belch, "The Role of Attitude toward the Ad as a Mediator of Advertising Effectiveness: A Test of Competing Explanations," *Journal of Marketing Research*, May 1986, pp. 130–143; Pamela M. Homer, "The Mediating Role of Attitude toward the Ad: Some Additional Evidence," *Journal of Marketing Research*, February 1990, pp. 78–86; Brown and Stayman, "Antecedents and Consequences of Attitude toward the Ad."

41. Sally Beatty, "P & G Ad Agencies: Please Rewrite Our Old Formulas," *Wall Street Journal*, November 5, 1998, pp. B1, B10.

42. Brown and Stayman, "Antecedents and Consequences of Attitude toward the Ad."

43. Marian Chapman Burke and Julie A. Edell, "Ad Reactions over Time: Capturing Changes in the Real World," *Journal of Consumer Research*, June 1986, pp. 114–118; Amitava Chattopadhyay and Prakash Nedungadi, "Does Attitude toward the Ad Endure? The Moderating Effects of Attention and Delay," *Journal of Consumer Research*, June 1992, pp. 26–33.

44. Charles S. Areni and David Kim, "The Influence of In-store Lighting on Consumers' Examination of Merchandise in a Wine Store," *International Journal of Research in Marketing*, March 1994, pp. 117–125.

45. Ayn E. Crowley, "The Two-Dimension Impact of Color on Shopping," *Marketing Letters*, 4 (1), 1993, pp. 59–69.

46. Julie A. Edell and Marian Chapman Burke, "The Power of Feelings in Understanding Advertising Effects," *Journal of Consumer Research*, December 1987, pp. 421–433; Douglas M. Stayman and David A. Aaker, "Are All Effects of Ad-Induced Feelings Mediated by A_{ad}?" *Journal of Consumer Research*, December 1988, pp. 368–373; Morris B. Holbrook and Rajeev Batra, "Assessing the Role of Emotions as Mediators of Consumer Responses to Advertising," *Journal of Consumer Research*, December 1987, pp. 404–420.

47. Rajeev Batra and Michael L. Ray, "Affective Responses Mediating Acceptance of Advertising," *Journal of Consumer Research*, September 1986, pp. 234–249.

48. Laura Bird, "Heublein Sweetens the Pitch for Its Blossom Hill Wine," *Adweek's Marketing Week*, April 15, 1991, p. 6.

49. David A. Aaker, Douglas M. Stayman, and Michael R. Hagerty, "Warmth in Advertising: Measurement, Impact, and Sequence Effects," *Journal of Consumer Research*, March 1986, pp. 365–381.

50. Joseph A. Bellizzi, Ayn E. Crowley, and Ronald W. Hasty, "The Effects of Color in Store Design," *Journal of Retailing*, Spring 1983, pp. 21–45.

51. Tara Parker-Pope, "Tossing Tinted Manes, Stars Heat up Hair-Color Wars," *Wall Street Journal*, July 22, 1997, pp. B1, B6.

52. Curt Haugtvedt, Richard E. Petty, John T. Cacioppo, and T. Steidley, "Personality and Ad Effectiveness: Exploring the Utility of Need for Cognition," in eds. Michael J. Houston, *Advances in Consumer Research*, Vol. 15 (Provo, Utah: Association for Consumer Research, 1988), pp. 209–212.

53. Susan M. Petroshius and Kenneth E. Crocker, "An Empirical Analysis of Spokesperson Characteristics on Advertisement and Product Evaluations," *Journal of the Academy of Marketing Science*, Summer 1989, pp. 217–225; Lynn R. Kahle and Pamela M. Homer, "Physical Attractiveness of the Celebrity Endorser: A Social Adaptation Perspective," *Journal of Consumer Research*, March 1985, pp. 954–961.

54. Michael A. Kamins, "An Investigation into the 'Match-Up' Hypothesis in Celebrity Advertising: When Beauty May Be Only Skin Deep," *Journal of Advertising*, 19 (1), 1990, pp. 4–13: Marjorie J. Caballero and Paul J. Solomon, "Effects of Model Attractiveness on Sales Response," *Journal of Advertising*, 13 (1), 1984, pp. 17–23.

55. Kahle and Homer, "Physical Attractiveness of the Celebrity Endorser"; Kathleen Debevec and Jerome B. Kernan, "More Evidence on the Effects of a Presenter's Physical Attractiveness: Some Cognitive, Affective, and Behavioral Consequences," in ed. Thomas C. Kinnear, *Advances in Consumer Research*, Vol. 11 (Provo, Utah: Association for Consumer Research, 1984), pp. 127–132.; Caballero and Solomon, "Effects of Model Attractiveness on Sales Response"; Marjorie J. Caballero and William M. Pride, "Selected Effects of Salesperson Sex and Attractiveness in Direct Mail Advertising," *Journal of Marketing*, January 1984, pp. 94–100.Shelly Chaiken, "Communicator Physical Attractiveness and Persuasion," *Journal of Personality and Social Psychology*, August 1979, pp. 1387–1397; Peter H. Reingen and Jerome B. Kernan, "Social Perception and Interpersonal Influence: Some Consequences of the Physical Attractiveness Stereotype in a Personal Selling Situation," *Journal of Consumer Psychology*, 2 (1), 1993, pp. 25–38.

56. Richard E. Petty, H. Rao Unnava, and Alan J. Strathman, "Theories of Attitude Change," in eds. Thomas S. Robertson and Harold H. Kassarjian, *Handbook of Consumer Behavior* (Englewood Cliffs, N. J.: Prentice-Hall, 1991), pp. 241–280; Kahle and Homer, "Physical Attractiveness of the Celebrity Endorser".

57. Sally Goll Beatty, "Madison Avenue Picks an Average Joe as '90's Pitchman," *Wall Street Journal*, August 11, 1996, pp. B1, B4.

58. Yumiko Ono, "Japan Warms to Doting Dad Ads," *Wall Street Journal*, May 8, 1997, pp. B1, B12.

59. Joshua Harris Prager, "Disability Can Enable a Modeling Career," *Wall Street Journal*, October 17, 1997, pp. B1, B6.

60. Sengupta, Goodstein, and Boninger, "All Cues Are Not Created Equal."

61. Sally Goll Beatty, "Agencies Catch Rising Stars at the Olympics," *Wall Street Journal*, February 13, 1998, pp. B1, B7.

62. Kathleen Deveny, "Many Celebrity Foods Enjoy Only 15 Minutes of Fame," *Wall Street Journal*, July 18, 1994, p. B1.

63. "Effies," *Adweek's Marketing Week*, June 15, 1992, p. 14.

64. Carol Bidwell, "Taco Bell Says, 'Ay, Chihuahua,'" *Austin American Statesman*, March 6, 1998, p. E5; Michael J. McCarthy, "StarKist Still Has Charlie to Kick Around," *Wall Street Journal*, November 11, 1997, p. B8; Stephanie N. Metha, "Dog Teaches New Trick to AT & T," *Wall Street Journal*, October 7, 1998, pp. B1, B4.

65. Jonathan Friedland, "Under Siege in the U.S., Joe Camel Pops up Alive, Well in Argentina," *Wall Street Journal*, September 10, 1996, p. B1.

66. Bruce Orwall, "James Bond Gets a New License to Sell Everything from Credit to Watches," *Wall Street Journal*, June 12, 1997, p. B10.

67. Mitchell and Olson, "Are Product Attributes Beliefs the Only Mediator of Advertising Effects on Brand Attitudes?"; Andrew A. Mitchell, "The Effect of Verbal and Visual Components of Advertisements on Brand Attitudes and Attitude toward the Advertisement," *Journal of Consumer Research*, March 1986, pp. 12–24; Paul W. Miniard, Sunil Bhatla, Kenneth R. Lord, Peter R. Dickson, and H. Rao Unnava, "Picture-Based Persuasion Processes and the Moderating Role of Involvement," *Journal of Consumer Research*, June 1991, pp. 92–107.

68. Paul W. Miniard, Deepak Sirdeshmukh, and Daniel E. Innis, "Peripheral Persuasion and Brand Choice," *Journal of Consumer Research*, September 1992, pp. 226–239.

69. Yumiko Ono, "Making 30 Chickens and Garlands of Post-Its into an Ad, " *Wall Street Journal*, August 20, 1997, pp. B1, B5.

70. Andrea Petersen, "The Quest to Make URL's Look Cool in Ads," *Wall Street Journal*, February 26, 1997, pp. B1, B3.

71. Sally Beatty, "IBM HotMedia Aims to Speed Online Ads," *Wall Street Journal*, October 27, 1998, p. B8; Sally Goll Beatty, "Knock, Knock! Who's There/ Noisy New Internet Ads," *Wall Street Journal*, September 3, 1997, pp. B1, B6.

72. Gordon Fairclough, "Crabs Sing to Give ITT Industries a 'Name,'" *Wall Street Journal*, September 19, 1998, p. B8.

73. Kevin Goldman, "Count Me In: British Firm Enlists Rock n' Roll Artists to Do Jingles," *Wall Street Journal*, May 1, 1995, p. B6.

74. Patrick M. Reilly, "TV Commercials Turn Obscure Songs into Radio Hits," *Wall Street Journal*, October 9, 1998, pp. B1, B8.

75. Louise Lee, "To Sell Movies in Asia, Sing a Local Tune," *Wall Street Journal*, August 22, 1998, pp. B1, B4.

76. Janine Zuniga, "McDonald's Pipes in Bach to bug Thugs," *Austin American Statesman*, April 25, 1996, p. C1.

77. Gordon C. Bruner, "Music, Mood, and Marketing," *Journal of Marketing*, October 1990, pp. 94–104; Gorn, "The Effects of Music in Advertising on Choice Behavior"; Judy I. Alpert and Mark I. Alpert, "Background Music as an Influence in Consumer Mood and Advertising Responses," in ed. Thomas K. Srull, *Advances in Consumer Research*, Vol. 16 (Provo, Utah: Association for Consumer Research, 1989), pp. 485–491; Meryl Paula Gardner, "Mood States and Consumer Behavior: A Critical Review," *Journal of Consumer Research*, December 1985, pp. 281–300; C. Whan Park and S. Mark Young, "Consumer Response to Television Commercials: The Impact of Involvement and Background Music on Brand Attitude Formation," *Journal of Marketing Research*, February 1986, pp. 11–24.

78. Alpert and Alpert, "Background Music as an Influence in Consumer Mood and Advertising Responses"; Stout and Leckenby, "Let the Music Play."

79. Noel M. Murray and Sandra B. Murray, "Music and Lyrics in Commercials: A Cross-Cultural Comparison between Commercials Run in the Dominican Republic and the United States," *Journal of Advertising*, Summer 1996, pp. 51–64.

80. Marc G. Weinberger and Harlan E. Spotts, "Humor in U.S. vs. U.K. TV Advertising," *Journal of Advertising*, 18 (2), 1989, pp. 39–44; Paul Surgi Speck, "The Humorous Message Taxonomy: A Framework for the Study of Humorous Ads," in eds. James H. Leigh and Claude R. Martin, *Current Research and Issues in Advertising* (Ann Arbor, Mich.: University of Michigan, 1991), pp. 1–44.

81. Thomas J. Madden and Marc G. Weinberger, "Humor in Advertising: A Practitioner View," *Journal of Advertising Research*, August–September 1984, pp. 23–29; Stewart and Furse, *Effective Television Advertising*; Thomas J. Madden and Marc C. Weinberger, "The Effects of Humor on Attention in Magazine Advertising," *Journal of Advertising*, 1 (3), 1982, pp. 8–14; Marc C. Weinberger and Leland Campbell, "The Use and Impact of Humor in Radio Advertising," *Journal of Advertising Research*, December–January 1991, pp. 44–52.

82. George E. Belch and Michael A. Belch, "An Investigation of the Effects of Repetition on Cognitive and Affective Reactions to Humorous and Serious Television Commercials," in ed. Thomas C. Kinnear, *Advances in Consumer Research*, Vol. 11 (Provo, Utah: Association for Consumer Research, 1984), pp. 4–10; Calvin P. Duncan and James E. Nelson, "Effects of Humor in a Radio Advertising Experiment," *Journal of Advertising*, 14 (2), 1985, pp. 33–40, 64; Betsy D. Gelb and Charles M. Pickett, "Attitude-toward-the-Ad: Links to Humor and to Advertising Effectiveness," *Journal of Advertising*, 12 (2), 1983, pp. 34–42; Betsy D. Gelb and George M. Zinkhan, "The Effect of Repetition on Humor in a Radio Advertising Study," *Journal of Advertising*, 15 (2), 1986, pp. 15–20, 34.

83. Vanessa O'Connell, "Alliance Capital Tries to Spice up Funds with Offbeat TV Spots," *Wall Street Journal*, March 25, 1998, p. B8.

84. Northiko Shirouzu, "P & G's Joy Makes an Unlikely Splash in Japan," *Wall Street Journal*, December 10, 1997, pp. B1, B8.

85. Sally Goll Beatty, "Whose Ad Is It Anyway? Parodies Amuse, Bemuse," *Wall Street Journal*, April 4, 1997, pp. B1, B5,

86. Harlan E. Spotts, Marc. G. Weinberger, and Amy L. Parsons, "Assessing the Use and Impact of Humor on Advertising Effectiveness; A Contingency Approach," *Journal of Advertising*, Fall 1997, pp. 17–32.

87. Brian Sternthal and Samuel Craig, "Humor in Advertising," *Journal of Marketing*, 37 (4), 1973, pp. 12–18; Calvin P. Duncan, "Humor in Advertising: A Behavioral Perspective," *Journal of the Academy of Marketing Science*, 7 (4), 1979, pp. 285–306; Weinberger and Campbell, "The Use and Impact of Humor in Radio Advertising."

88. Madden and Weinberger, "Humor in Advertising"; Weinberger and Campbell, "The Use and Impact of Humor in Radio Advertising"; Weinberger and Spotts, "Humor in U.S. vs. U.K. TV Advertising."

89. Laura Bird, "Latest Infomercial: The Situation Comedy," *Wall Street Journal*, November 6, 1992, p. B7

90. Laurie Petersen, "And If You Think This Is Funny," *Adweek's Marketing Week*, September 9, 1991, p. 9.

91. Madden and Weinberger, "Humor in Advertising"; Thomas W. Whipple and Alice E. Courtney, "How Men and Women Judge Humor: Advertising Guidelines for Action and Research," in eds. James H. Leigh and Claude R. Martin, *Current Research and Issues in Advertising* (Ann Arbor, Mich.: University of Michigan, 1981), pp. 43–56.

92. Yong Zhang, "Responses to Humorous Advertising: The Moderating Effect of Need for Cognition," *Journal of Advertising*, Spring 1996: Amitava Chattopadhyay and Kunal Basu, "Prior Brand Evaluation as a Moderator of the Effects of Humor in Advertising," *Journal of Marketing Research*, November 1989, pp. 466–476.

93. Dana L. Alden, Wayne D. Hoyer, and Chol Lee, "Identifying Global and Culture-Specific Dimensions of Humor in Advertising: A Multi-National Analysis," *Journal of Marketing*, April 1993, pp. 64–75; Dana L. Alden, Wayne D. Hoyer, Chol Lee, and Guntalee Wechasara, "The Use of Humor in Asian and Western Advertising: A Four-Country Comparison," *Journal of Asian-Pacific Business*, 1 (2), 1995, pp. 3–23.

94. Weinberger and Spotts, "Humor in U.S. vs. U.K. TV Advertising."

95. Christopher Cooper, "Uncle Ben's New Ad Campaign Seeks to Steam up the TV Screen," *Wall Street Journal*, p. B6.

96. Sally Goll Beatty, "Mars Tries Sex to Bag Consumer into M&M's Arms," *Wall Street Journal*, p. B2.

97. Yumiko Ono, "Can Racy Ads Help Revitalize Old Fragrances?" *Wall Street Journal*, November 26, 1996, pp. B1, B10.

98. Rebecca Piirto, "The Romantic Sell," *American Demographics*, August 1989, pp. 38–41.

99. Lawrence Soley and Gary Kurzbard, "Sex in Advertising: A Comparison of 1964 and 1984 Magazine Advertisements," *Journal of Advertising*, 15 (3), 1986, pp. 46–54.

100. Cyndee Miller, "We've Been 'Cosbyized,'" *Marketing News*, April 16, 1990, pp. 1–2; Joshua Levine, "Marketing: Fantasy, Not Flesh," *Forbes*, January 22, 1990, pp. 118–120.

101. Eben Shapiro, "In the Safe-Sex Society, Advertisers Lose Inhibitions about How Much Sex Is Safe," *Wall Street Journal*, December 3, 1993, pp. B1, B6.

102. Lynn G. Coleman, "What Do People Really Lust After in Ads?" *Marketing News*, November 6, 1989, p. 12.

103. Robert S. Baron, "Sexual Content and Advertising Effectiveness: Comments on Belch et al. (1981) and Caccavale et al. (1981)," in ed. Andrew A. Mitchell, *Advances in Consumer Research*, Vol. 9 (Ann Arbor, Mich.: Association for Consumer Research, 1982), pp. 428–430.

104. Michael S. LaTour, Robert E. Pitts, and David C. Snook-Luther, "Female Nudity, Arousal, and Ad Response: An Experimental Investigation," *Journal of Advertising*, 19 (4), 1990, pp. 51–62.

105. Marilyn Y. Jones, Andrea J.S. Stanaland, and Betsy D. Gelb, "Beefcake and Cheesecake: Insights for Advertisers," *Journal of Advertising*, Summer 1998, pp. 33–52.

106. Kevin Goldman, "Sexy Sony Ad by Leo Burnett Has Electronic Bulletin Board Aflame," *Wall Street Journal*, August 23, 1993, p. B5.

107. Sally D. Goll, "Beer Ads in Hong Kong Criticized as Sexist," *Wall Street Journal*, June 29, 1995, p. B2.

108. Lisa Bannon and Margaret Studer, "For Two Revealing European Ads, Overexposure Can Have Benefits," *Wall Street Journal*, June 17, 1993, p. B8.

109. Miller, "We've Been 'Cosbyized.'"

110. "Poll on Ads: Too Sexy," *Wall Street Journal*, March 8, 1993, p. B5.

111. Robert A. Peterson and Roger A. Kerin, "The Female Role in Advertisements: Some Experimental Evidence," *Journal of Marketing*, October 1977, pp. 59–63.

112. Kathleen Deveny, "Lure of a Lovelier Smile Prompts a Rush to Buy Do-It-Yourself Teeth Whiteners," *Wall Street Journal*, July 6, 1992, pp. 11, 18.

113. Lisa Bannon and Margaret Studer, "For Two Revealing European Ads, Overexposure Can Have Benefits."

114. Sak Onkvisit and John J. Shaw, "A View of Marketing and Advertising Practices in Asia and Its Meaning for Marketing Managers," *Journal of Consumer Marketing*, Spring 1985, pp. 5–17.

115. M. Friestad and Esther Thorson, "Emotion-Eliciting Advertising: Effect on Long Term Memory and Judgment," in ed. R. J. Lutz, *Advances in Consumer Research*, Vol. 13 (Provo, Utah: Association for Consumer Research, 1986), pp. 111–116.

116. Nikhil Deogun and Sally Goll Beatty, "New Ads Aim to Make Diet Sodas Cool Again," *Wall Street Journal*, May 14, 1997, pp. B1, B8.

117. Barbara B. Stern, "Classical and Vignette Television Advertising Dramas: Structural Models, Formal Analysis, and Consumer Effects," *Journal of Consumer Research*, March 1994, pp. 601–615; William D. Wells, "Lectures and Dramas," in eds. Pat Cafferata and Alice M. Tybout, *Cognitive and Affective Responses to Advertising* (Lexington, Mass.: D.C. Heath, 1988); John Deighton, Daniel Romer, and Josh McQueen, "Using Dramas to Persuade," *Journal of Consumer Research*, December 1989, pp. 335–343.

118. Marvin E. Goldberg and Gerald J. Gorn, "Happy and Sad TV Programs: How They Affect Reactions to Commercials," *Journal of Consumer Research*, December 1987, pp. 387–403; John P. Murray Jr. and Peter A. Dacin, "Cognitive Moderators of Negative-Emotion

Effects: Implications for Understanding Media Context," *Journal of Consumer Research*, March 1996, pp. 439–447.

119. John P. Murray, John L. Lastovicka, and Surendra Singh, "Feeling and Liking Responses to Television Programs: An Examination of Two Explanations for Media-Context Effects," *Journal of Consumer Research*, March 1992, pp. 441–451.

120. S. N. Singh and Gilbert A. Churchill, "Arousal and Advertising Effectiveness," *Journal of Advertising*, 16 (1), 1987, pp. 4–10.

121. Mark A. Pavelchak, John H. Antil, and James M. Munch, "The Super Bowl: An Investigation into the Relationship among Program Context, Emotional Experience, and Ad Recall," *Journal of Consumer Research*, December 1988, pp. 360–367.

122. Sally Beatty, "Madison Avenue Should Rethink Television Violence, Study Finds," *Wall Street Journal*, December 1, 1998, p. B8.

CHAPTER 8

1. Keith Naughton and Bill Vlasic, "The Nostalgia Boom," *Business Week*, March 23, 1998, pp. 58–64; Sally Goll Beatty, "Staid Brands Put New Spin on Old Jingles," *Wall Street Journal*, January 19, 1996, p. B5.

2. G. Sperling, "The Information Available in Brief Visual Presentations," *Psychological Monographs*, Vol. 74, 1960, pp. 1–25; U. Neisser, *Cognitive Psychology* (New York: Appleton-Century-Crofts, 1967).

3. R. N. Haber, "The Impending Demise of the Icon: A Critique of the Concept of Iconic Storage in Visual Information Processing," *The Behavioral and Brain Sciences*, March 1983, pp. 1–54.

4. William James (1890) as described in Henry C. Ellis and R. Reed Hunt, *Fundamentals of Human Memory and Cognition* (Dubuque, Iowa: William C. Brown, 1989), pp. 65–66.

5. Deborah J. MacInnis and Linda L. Price, "The Role of Imagery in Information Processing: Review and Extensions," *Journal of Consumer Research*, March 1987, pp. 473–491.

6. Allan Paivio, "Perceptual Comparisons through the Mind's Eye," *Memory and Cognition*, November 1975, pp. 635–647; Stephen M. Kosslyn, "The Medium and the Message in Mental Imagery: A Theory," *Psychological Review*, January 1981, pp. 46–66; MacInnis and Price, "The Role of Imagery in Information Processing."

7. Morris B. Holbrook and Elizabeth C. Hirschman, "The Experiential Aspects of Consumption: Consumer Fantasies, Feelings, and Fun," *Journal of Consumer Research*, September 1982, pp. 132–140; MacInnis and Price, "The Role of Imagery in Information Processing"; Alan Richardson, "Imagery: Definitions and Types," in ed. Aness Sheikh, *Imagery: Current Theory, Research, and Applications* (New York: Wiley, 1983), pp. 3–42.

8. Martin S. Lindauer, "Imagery and the Arts," in ed. Aness Sheikh, *Imagery: Current Theory, Research, and Application* (New York: Wiley, 1983), pp. 468–506.

9. E. Tulving, "Episodic and Semantic Memory," in eds. E. Tulving and W. Donaldson, *Organization and Memory* (New York: Academic Press, 1972), pp. 381–403.

10. Hans Baumgartner, Mita Sujan, and James R. Bettman, "Autobiographical Memories, Affect, and Consumer Information Processing," *Journal of Consumer Psychology*, 1 (1), 1992, pp. 53–82.

11. Morris B. Holbrook, "Nostalgia and Consumer Preferences: Some Emerging Patterns of Consumer Tastes," *Journal of Consumer Research*, September 1993, pp. 245–256; Morris B. Holbrook and Robert M. Schindler, "Echoes of the Dear Departed Past: Some Work in Progress on Nostalgia," in eds. Rebecca H. Holman and Michael R. Solomon, *Advances in Consumer Research*, Vol. 18 (Provo, Utah: Association for Consumer Research, 1991), pp. 330–333.

12. Beth Burkstrand, "Scrapbook Mania: Pricey Labor of Love," *Wall Street Journal*, May 16, 1997, pp. B1, B6.

13. Annamma Joy and Ruby Roy Dholakia, "Remembrances of Things Past: The Meaning of Home and Possessions of Indian Professionals in Canada," in ed. Floyd W. Rudmin, *To Have Possessions: A Handbook on Ownership and Property, Journal of Social Behavior and Personality* [Special Issue], November 1991, pp. 385–402; Melanie Wallendorf and Eric J. Arnould, "My Favorite Things: A Cross-Cultural Inquiry into Object Attachment, Possessiveness, and Social Linkage," *Journal of Consumer Research*, March 1988, pp. 531–547.

14. Kathryn A. Braun, "Postexperience Advertising Effects on Consumer Memory," *Journal of Consumer Research*, March 1999, pp. 319–334.

15. R. C. Atkinson and R. M. Shiffrin, "Human Memory: A Proposed System and Its Control Processes," in eds. K. W. Spence and J. T. Spence, *The Psychology of Learning and Motivation: Advances in Theory and Research*, Vol. 2 (New York: Academic Press, 1968), pp. 89–195.

16. George A. Miller, "The Magical Number Seven, Plus or Minus Two: Some Limits on Our Capacity for Processing Information," *Psychological Review*, March 1956, pp. 81–97; James N. McGregor, "Short-Term Memory Capacity: Limitations or Optimization?" *Psychological Review*, January 1987, pp. 107–108.

17. Alan G. Sawyer, "The Effects of Repetition: Conclusions and Suggestions about Experimental Laboratory Research," in eds. G. David Hughes and Michael L. Ray, *Buyer/Consumer Information Processing* (Chapel Hill, N. C.: University of North Carolina Press, 1974), pp. 190–219; George E. Belch, "The Effects of Television Commercial Repetition on Cognitive Response and Message Acceptance," *Journal of Consumer Research*, June 1982, pp. 56–66; H. Rao Unnava and Robert E. Burnkrant, "Effects of Repeating Varied Ad Executions on Brand Name Memory," *Journal of Marketing Research*, November 1991, pp. 406–416; Murphy S. Sewall and Dan Sarel, "Characteristics of Radio Commercials and Their Recall Effectiveness," *Journal of Marketing*, January 1986, pp. 52–60.

18. F. I. M. Craik and R. S. Lockhart, "Levels of Processing: A Framework for Memory Research," *Verbal Learning and Verbal Behavior*, December 1972, pp. 671–684.

19. Susan E. Heckler and Terry L. Childers, "The Role of Expectancy and Relevancy in Memory for Verbal and Visual Information: What Is Incongruency?" *Journal of Consumer Research*, March 1992, pp. 475–492.

20. Kevin Goldman, "Robert Mitchum Adds Class to Trash Bags," *Wall Street Journal*, July 26, 1995, pp. B14.

21. Catherine A. Cole and Michael J. Houston, "Encoding and Media Effects on Consumer Learning Deficiencies

in the Elderly," *Journal of Marketing Research*, February 1987, pp. 55–64; Deborah Roedder John and John C. Whitney Jr., "The Development of Consumer Knowledge in Children: A Cognitive Structure Approach," *Journal of Consumer Research*, March 1986, pp. 406–418.

22. Gabriel Biehal and Dipankar Chakravarti, "Consumers' Use of Memory and External Information in Choice: Macro and Micro Perspectives," *Journal of Consumer Research*, March 1986, pp. 382–405; John G. Lynch, Howard Marmorstein, and Michael F. Weigold, "Choices from Sets Including Remembered Brands: Use of Recalled Attributes and Prior Overall Evaluations," *Journal of Consumer Research*, September 1988, pp. 225–233; Valerie S. Folkes, "The Availability Heuristic and Perceived Risk," *Journal of Consumer Research*, June 1988, pp. 13–23.

23. A. M. Collins and E. F. Loftus, "A Spreading Activation Theory of Semantic Processing," *Psychological Review*, November 1975, pp. 407–428; Lawrence W. Barsalou, *Cognitive Psychology: An Overview for Cognitive Scientists* (Hillsdale, N. J.: Lawrence Erlbaum, 1991); John R. Anderson, *Cognitive Psychology and Its Implications* (New York: W. H. Freeman, 1990); Michael Pham and Gita Venkataramani Johar, "Contingent Processes of Source Identification," *Journal of Consumer Research*, December 1997, pp. 249–265.

24. Frank S. Washington, "New Ads Represent Chrysler Brand Aid, *Automotive News*, November 26, 1996, p. 6.

25. Joseph W. Alba and J. Wesley Hutchinson, "Dimensions of Consumer Expertise," *Journal of Consumer Research*, March 1987, pp. 411–454.

26. David C. Riccio, Vita C. Rabinowitz, and Shari Axelrod, "Memory: When Less Is More," *American Psychologist*, November 1994, pp. 917–926.

27. Anthony Pratkanis, Anthony G. Greenwald, M. R. Leipe, and M. Hans Baumgartner, "In Search of Reliable Persuasion Effects: III. The Sleeper Effect Is Dead: Long Live the Sleeper Effect," *Journal of Personality and Social Psychology*, February 1988, pp. 203–218.

28. Raymond Burke and Thomas K. Srull, "Competitive Interference and Consumer Memory for Advertisements," *Journal of Consumer Research*, June 1988, pp. 55–68; Kevin Keller, "Memory and Evaluation Effects in Competitive Advertising Environments," *Journal of Consumer Research*, March 1991, pp. 463–476; Rik G. M. Pieters and Tammo H. A. Bijmolt, "Consumer Memory for Television Advertising: A Field Study of Duration, Serial Position and Competition Effects," *Journal of Consumer Research*, March 1997, pp. 362–372; Tom J. Brown and Michael L. Rothschild, "Reassessing the Impact of Television Advertising Clutter," *Journal of Consumer Research*, June 1993, pp. 138–147; Robert J. Kent and Chris T. Allen, "Competitive Interference Effects in Consumer Memory for Advertising: The Role of Brand Familiarity," *Journal of Marketing*, July 1994, pp. 97–105; H. Rao Unnava and Deepak Sirdeshmukh, "Reducing Competitive Ad Interference," *Journal of Marketing Research*, August 1994, pp. 403–411.

29. Joseph W. Alba and Amitava Chattopadhyay, "Effects of Context and Part-Category Cues on Recall of Competing Brands," *Journal of Marketing Research*,

August 1985, pp. 340–349; Joseph W. Alba and Amitava Chattopadhyay, "Salience Effects in Brand Recall," *Journal of Marketing Research*, November 1986, pp. 363–369; Manoj Hastak and Anusre Mitra, "Facilitating and Inhibiting Effects of Brand Cues on Recall, Consideration Set, and Choice," *Journal of Business Research*, October 1996, pp. 121–126.

30. Raymond Burke and Thomas K. Srull, "Competitive Interference and Consumer Memory for Advertising," *Journal of Consumer Research*, June 1988, pp. 55–68; Rik Pieters and Tammo H.A. Bijmolt, "Consumer Memory for Television Advertising: A Field Study of Duration, Serial Position, and Competition Effects," *Journal of Consumer Research*, March 1997, pp. 362–372.

31. Elizabeth F. Loftus, "When a Lie Becomes Memory's Truth: Memory and Distortion after Exposure to Misinformation," *Current Directions in Psychological Science*, August 1992, pp. 121–123.

32. Larry Percy and John R. Rossiter, "A Model of Brand Awareness and Brand Attitude in Advertising Strategies," *Psychology and Marketing*, July–August 1992, pp. 263–274.

33. Bradley Johnson, "Lucent to Study Consumer Reaction to Phone Brand," *Advertising Age*, June 2, 1997, p. 12; Andrea Petersen and Terzah Ewing, "iVillage Waits to See What It Takes to Make an IPO Success," *Wall Street Journal*, March 15, 1999, p. B1; Deborah Lohse, "E*Trade Bis to Be a Household Name," *Wall Street Journal*, September 5, 1997, pp. B4; Fara Warner, "Battle Looms for PC Buyers in Asian Homes," *Wall Street Journal*, September 29, 1995, p. A9. JoAnn Greco, "Kraft: The New Ubiquitous Brand Name," *Journal of Business Strategy*, September–October 1998, pp. 21–23.

34. John Furniss, "Rating American Banks in Japan: Survey Shows Importance of Image," *International Advertiser*, April 1986, pp. 22–23.

35. Catherine Cole and Michael J. Houston, " Encoding and Media Effects on Consumer Learning Deficiencies in the Elderly," *Journal of Marketing Research*, February 1987, pp. 55–63; Sharmistha Law, Scott A. Hawkins, and Fergus I. M. Craik, "Repetition-Induced Belief in the Elderly: Rehabilitating Age-Related Memory Deficits," *Journal of Consumer Research*, September 1998, pp. 91–107.

36. Susan T. Fiske and Shelley E. Taylor, *Social Cognition* (New York: McGraw-Hill, 1991).

37. Joseph W. Alba, J. Wesley Hutchinson, and John G. Lynch, Jr., "Memory and Decision Making," in eds. Thomas S. Robertson and Harold Kassarjian, *Handbook of Consumer Behavior* (Englewood Cliffs, N. J.: Prentice-Hall, 1991), pp. 1–49.

38. Rik G. M. Pieters and Tammo H. A. Bijmolt, "Consumer Memory for Television Advertising: A Field Study of Duration, Serial Position and Competition Effects," *Journal of Consumer Research*, March 1997, pp. 362–372; David W. Stewart and David H. Furse, *Effective Television Advertising: A Study of 1000 Commercials* (Cambridge, Mass.: Marketing Science Institute, 1986); Pamela Homer, "Ad Size as an Indicator of Perceived Advertising Costs and Effort: The Effects on Memory and Perceptions," *Journal of Advertising*, Winter 1995, pp. 1–12.

39. Frank R. Kardes and Gurumurthy Kalyanaram, "Order of Entry Effects on Consumer Memory and Judgment: An Information Integration Perspective," *Journal of Marketing Research*, August 1992, pp. 343–357; Frank Kardes, Murali Chandrashekaran, and Ronald Dornoff, "Brand Retrieval, Consideration Set Composition, Consumer Choice, and the Pioneering Advantage," *Journal of Consumer Research*, June 1993, pp. 62–75; Frank H. Alpert and Michael A. Kamins, "An Empirical Investigation of Consumer Memory, Attitude, and Perceptions Toward Pioneer and Follower Brands," *Journal of Marketing*, October 1995, pp. 34–44.

40. Janet Guyon, "Coke Wins Early Skirmishes in Its Drive to Take over Eastern Europe from Pepsi," *Wall Street Journal*, November 11, 1992, pp. B1, B10.

41. Sridar Samu, H. Shankar Krishnan, and Robert E. Smith, "Using Advertising Alliances for New Product Introduction: Interactions between Product Complementarity and Promotional Strategies," *Journal of Marketing*, January 1999, pp. 57–74.

42. Rex Briggs and Nigel Hollis, "Advertising on the Web: Is There Response before Click-Through," *Journal of Advertising Research*, March–April 1997, pp. 33–45.

43. Michael Pham and Gita Venkataramani Johar, "Contingent Processes of Source Identification," *Journal of Consumer Research*, December 1997, pp. 249–265.

44. Deborah D. Heisley and Sidney J. Levy, "Autodriving: A Photoelicitation Technique," *Journal of Consumer Research*, December 1991, pp. 257–272.

45. Joan Meyers-Levy, "The Influence of a Brand Name's Association Set Size and Word Frequency on Brand Memory," *Journal of Consumer Research*, September 1989, pp. 197–207; Alba and Hutchinson, "Dimensions of Consumer Expertise."

46. Cathy J. Cobb and Wayne D. Hoyer, "The Influence of Advertising at Moment of Brand Choice," *Journal of Advertising*, December 1986, pp. 5–27.

47. Keller, "Memory Factors in Advertising"; J. Wesley Hutchinson and Daniel L. Moore, "Issues Surrounding the Examination of Delay Effects of Advertising," in ed. Thomas C. Kinnear, *Advances in Consumer Research*, Vol. 11 (Provo, Utah: Association for Consumer Research, 1984), pp. 650–655.

48. Carolyn Costley, Samar Das, and Merrie Brucks, "Presentation Medium and Spontaneous Imaging Effects on Consumer Memory," *Journal of Consumer Psychology*, 6 (3) 1997, pp. 211–231; Daivd W. Sewart and Girish N. Punj, "Effects of Using a Nonverbal (Musical) Cue on Recall and Playback of Television Advertising: Implications for Advertising Tracking," *Journal of Business Research*, May 1998, pp. 39–51.

49. H. Rao Unnava and Robert E. Burnkrant, "An Imagery-Processing View of the Role of Pictures in Print Advertisements," *Journal of Marketing Research*, May 1991, pp. 226–231.

50. Alice M. Isen, "Some Ways in Which Affect Influences Cognitive Processes: Implications for Advertising and Consumer Behavior," in eds. Alice M. Tybout and P. Cafferata, *Advertising and Consumer Psychology* (Lexington, Mass.: Lexington Books, 1989), pp. 91–117; see also Patricia A. Knowles, Stephen J. Grove, and W. Jeffrey Burroughs, "An Experimental Examination of Mood Effects on Retrieval and Evaluation of Advertisement and Brand Information," *Journal of the Academy of Marketing Science*, Spring 1993, pp. 135–143; Gordon H. Bower, "Mood and Memory," *American Psychologist*, February 1981, pp. 129–148; Gordon H. Bower, Stephen Gilligan, and Kenneth Montiero, "Selectivity of Learning Caused by Affective States," *Journal of Experimental Psychology: General*, December 1981, pp. 451–473; Alice M. Isen, Thomas Shalker, Margaret Clark, and Lynn Karp, "Affect, Accessibility of Material in Memory and Behavior: A Cognitive Loop?" *Journal of Personality and Social Psychology*, January 1978, pp. 1–12.

51. Alice M. Isen, "Toward Understanding the Role of Affect in Cognition," in eds. Robert S. Wyer and Thomas K. Srull, *Handbook of Social Cognition* (Hillsdale, N. J.: Lawrence Erlbaum, 1984), pp. 179–236.

52. Alice M. Isen, "Some Ways in Which Affect Influences Cognitive Processes: Implications for Advertising and Consumer Behavior," in eds. Patricia Cafferata and Alice M. Tybout, *Cognitive and Affective Responses to Advertising* (Lexington, Mass.: Lexington Books, 1989), pp. 91–118.

53. Alba and Hutchinson, "Dimensions of Consumer Expertise."

CHAPTER 9

1. Norihiko Shirouzu, "P & G's Joy Makes an Unlikely Splash in Japan," *Wall Street Journal*, December 10, 1997, pp. B1, B8.

2. Jeffrey A. Trachtenberg, "Sony Launches Portable Products for Video CD Line," *Wall Street Journal*, June 4, 1996, p. B8.

3. Tara Parker-Pope, "Body Spritzes Promise to Dispel Smokers' Odors," *Wall Street Journal*, March 31, 1998, pp. B1, B9.

4. Norihiko Shirouzu, "Low-Smoke Cigarette Catches Fire in Japan," *Wall Street Journal*, September 8, 1997, pp. B1.

5. Quentin Hardy, "Mass Chinese PC Market Stymied by Massive Keyboard," *Wall Street Journal*, February 21, 1996, pp. B1, B6.

6. Joseph W. Alba, J. Wesley Hutchinson, and John G. Lynch, "Memory and Decision Making." In Thomas C. Roberton and Harold H. Kassarjian (eds.), Handbbook of Consumer Behavior (Englewood Cliffs, NJ: Prentice Hall, 1991).

7. John R. Hauser and Birger Wernerfelt, "An Evaluation Cost Model of Consideration Sets," *Journal of Consumer Research*, March 1990, pp. 393–408.

8. Susan Carey, "Even When It's Quicker to Travel by Train, Many Fly," *Wall Street Journal*, August 29, 1997, pp. B1, B5.

9. Prakash Nedungadi and J. Wesley Hutchinson, "The Prototypicality of Brands: Relationships with Brand Awareness, Preference, and Usage," in eds. Elizabeth C. Hirschman and Morris B. Holbrook, *Advances in Consumer Research*, Vol. 12 (Provo, Utah: Association for Consumer Research, 1985), pp. 498–503; Prakash Nedungadi, "Recall and Consumer Consideration Sets: Influencing Choice Without Altering Brand Evaluations," *Journal of Consumer Research*, December 1990, pp. 263–276.

10. Alba, Hutchinson, and Lynch, "Memory and Decision Making."

11. Nedungadi and Hutchinson, "The Prototypicality of Brands"; James Ward and Barbara Loken, "The Quintessential Snack Food: Measurement of Product Prototypes," in ed. Richard J. Lutz, *Advances in Consumer Research*, Vol. 13 (Provo, Utah: Association for Consumer Research, 1986), pp. 126–131.

12. "Armor All Wants to Clean Some Son of a Gun's Clock," *Brandweek*, October 18, 1993, pp. 32–33.

13. R. Whitaker Penteado, "Fast-Food Franchises Fight for Brazilian Aficionados," *Brandweek*, June 7, 1993, pp. 20–24.

14. Siew Meng Leong, Swee Hoon Ang, and Lai Leng Tham, "Increasing Brand Name Recall in Print Advertising among Asian Consumers," *Journal of Advertising*, Summer 1996, pp. 65–82.

15. Stewart Shapiro, Deborah J. MacInnis, and Susan E. Heckler, "The Effects of Incidental Ad Exposure on the Formation of Consideration Sets," *Journal of Consumer Research*, June 1997, pp. 94–104.

16. Robert Langreth, "Bulletins for the Battle of the Baldness Drugs," *Wall Street Journal*, December 19, 1997, pp. B1, B6; Yumiko Ono, "Sports Figures Tout Rogaine for Pharmacia," *Wall Street Journal*, December 19, 1997, pp. B1, B6.

17. Alba, Hutchinson, and Lynch, "Memory and Decision Making."

18. Norihiko Shirouzu, "How One Woman Is Shaking Up Shiseido," *Wall Street Journal*, May 19, 1997, pp. B1, B8.

19. S. Ratneshwar and Allan D. Shocker, "Substitution in Use and the Role of Usage Context in Product Category Structures," *Journal of Marketing Research*, August 1991, pp. 281–295.

20. Terry Lefton, "Kodak Teaming with NFL on Single-Use Cameras," *Brandweek*, December 14, 1992, p. 3.

21. Yumiko Ono, "Pizza in Japan Is Adapted to Local Tastes," *Wall Street Journal*, June 4, 1993, p. B1.

22. Nedungadi and Hutchinson, "The Prototypicality of Brands"; Ward and Loken, "The Quintessential Snack Food."

23. Yumiko Ono, "'King of Beers' Wants to Rule More of Japan," *Wall Street Journal*, October 28, 1993, pp. B1, B8.

24. Jonathan Friedland, "Under Siege in the US, Joe Camel Pops up Alive, Well in Argentina," *Wall Street Journal*, September 10, 1996, p. B1.

25. Gabriel Biehal and Dipankar Chakravarti, "Consumers' Use of Memory and External Information in Choice: Macro and Micro Perspectives," *Journal of Consumer Research*, March 1986, 382–405.

26. Gabriel Biehal and Dipankar Chakravarti, "Information Accessibility as a Moderator of Consumer Choice," *Journal of Consumer Research*, June 1983, pp. 1–14.

27. Michaela Waenke, Gerd Bohner, and Andreas Jurkowitsch, "There Are Many Reasons to Drive a BMW: Does Imagined Ease of Argument Generation Influence Attitudes," *Journal of Consumer Research*, September 1997, pp. 170–177.

28. Meryl Paula Gardner, "Advertising Effects on Attributes Recalled and Criteria Used for Brand Evaluations" *Journal of Consumer Research*, December 1983, pp. 310–318; Scott B. MacKenzie, "The Role of Attention in Mediating the Effect of Advertising on Attribute Importance," *Journal of Consumer Research*, September 1986, pp. 174–195; Priya Raghubir and Geeta Menon, "AIDS and Me, Never the Twain Shall Meet: The Effects of Information Accessibility on Judgments of Risk and Advertising Effectiveness," *Journal of Consumer Research*, June 1998, pp. 52–63.

29. Fellman and Lynch, "Self-Generated Validity and Other Effects of Measurement"; John G. Lynch, Howard Marmorstein, and Michael F. Weigold, "Choices from Sets Including Remembered Brands: Use of Recalled Attributes and Prior Overall Evaluations," *Journal of Consumer Research*, September 1988, pp. 169–184.

30. Carolyn L. Costley and Merrie Brucks, "Selective Recall and Information Use in Consumer Preferences," *Journal of Consumer Research*, March 1992, pp. 464–474; Geeta Menon, Priya Raghubit, and Norbert Schwarz, "Behavioral Frequency Judgments: An Accessbility-Diagnosticity Framework," *Journal of Consumer Research*, September 1995, pp. 212–228.

31. Paul M. Herr, Frank R. Kardes, and John Kim, "Effects of Word-of-Mouth and Product-Attribute Information on Persuasion: An Accessibility-Diagnosticity Perspective," *Journal of Consumer Research*, March 1991, pp. 454–462.

32. Richard Gibson, "Custom Burgers Get Speed Test at McDonald's," *Wall Street Journal*, June 30, 1997, pp. B1, B2.

33. Yumiko Ono, "Anheuser Plays on Tipsiness to Sell Japan Strong Brew," *Wall Street Journal*, November 17, 1998, pp. B1, B4.

34. Dana Milbank, "Made in America Becomes a Boast in Europe," *Wall Street Journal*, January 19, 1994, pp. B1, B5.

35. Walter Kintsch and Tuen A. Van Dyk, "Toward a Model of Text Comprehension and Production," *Psychological Review*, September 1978, pp. 363–394; S. Ratneshwar, David G. Mick, and Gail Reitinger, "Selective Attention in Consumer Information Processing: The Role of Chronically Accessible Attributes," in eds. Marvin E. Goldberg, Gerald Gorn, and Richard W. Pollay, *Advances in Consumer Research*, Vol. 17 (Provo, Utah: Association for Consumer Research, 1990), pp. 547–553.

36. Anne-Marie Chaker, "Antiacne Campaign Propels Birth-Control Pill," *Wall Street Journal*, September 28, 1998, pp. B1, B4.

37. "Drawing a Bead on Car Buyers for the Nineties," *Brandweek*, September 14, 1992, pp. 17, 20.

38. Leonidas C. Leonidou, "Understanding the Russian Consumer," *Marketing and Research Today*, March 1992, pp. 75–83.

39. Jacob Jacoby, Tracy Troutman, Alfred Kuss, and David Mazursky, "Experience and Expertise in Complex Decision Making," in ed. Richard J. Lutz, *Advances in Consumer Research*, Vol. 13 (Provo, Utah: Association for Consumer Research, 1986), pp. 469–475.

40. Gardner, "Advertising Effects on Attributes Recalled"; Mackenzie, "The Role of Attention in Mediating the Effect of Advertising."

41. Vanessa O'Connell, "Labels Suggesting the Benefits of Drinking Wine Look Likely," *Wall Street Journal*, October 26, 1998, pp. B1, B3.

42. Jennifer Cody, "Now Marketers in Japan Stress the Local Angle," *Wall Street Journal*, February 23, 1994, p. B1.

43. Mark I. Alpert, "Identification of Determinant Attributes: A Comparison of Methods," *Journal of Marketing Research*, May 1971, pp. 184–191.

44. Emily Nelson, "Camera Makers Focus on Tiny and Cute," *Wall Street Journal*, March 14, 1997, pp. B1, B2.

45. Jolita Kiselius and Brian Sternthal, "Examining the Vividness Controversy: An Availability-Valence Interpretation," *Journal of Consumer Research*, March 1986, pp. 418–431; Herr, Kardes, and Kim, "Effects of Word-of-Mouth and Product-Attribute Information."

46. Punam Anand Keller and Lauren G. Block, "Vividness Effects: A Resource-Matching Perspective," *Journal of Consumer Research*, December 1997, pp. 295–304.

47. Reid Hastie and Bernadette Park, "The Relationship between Memory and Judgment Depends on Whether the Judgment Task Is Memory-Based or On-Line," *Psychological Review*, June 1986, pp. 258–268; Barbara Loken and Ronald Hoverstad, "Relationships between Information Recall and Subsequent Attitudes: Some Exploratory Findings," *Journal of Consumer Research*, September 1985, pp. 155–168.

48. Biehal and Chakravarti, "Consumers' Use of Memory and External Information in Choice"; Jong-Won Park and Manoj Hastak, "Memory-Based Product Judgments: Effects of Involvement at Encoding and Retrieval," *Journal of Consumer Research*, December 1994, pp. 534–547.

49. Hans Baumgartner, Mita Sujan, and James R. Bettman, "Autobiographical Memories, Affect, and Consumer Information Processing," *Journal of Consumer Psychology*, 1 (1), 1992, pp. 53–82.

50. Rodney Ho, "Bowling for Dollars, Alleys Try Updating," *Wall Street Journal*, pp. B1, B2.

51. Dave Barrager, "Retro Power," *Brandweek*, March 15, 1993, pp. 14–17.

52. Fara Warner, "The Place to Be This Year," *Brandweek*, November 30, 1992, p. 24.

53. Michael J. Houston, Terry L. Childers, and Susan E. Heckler, "Picture-Word Consistency and the Elaborative Processing of Advertisements," *Journal of Marketing Research*, November 1987, pp. 359–369.

54. Joseph W. Alba and Amitava Chattopadhyay, "Salience Effects in Brand Recall," *Journal of Marketing Research*, November 1986, pp. 363–369; Kiselius and Sternthal, "Examining the Vividness Controversy."

55. Joseph W. Alba and Amitava Chattopadhyay, "Salience Effects in Brand Recall," *Journal of Marketing Research*, November 1986, pp. 363–369; Kiselius and Sternthal, "Examining the Vividness Controversy."

56. "Game Farmers Brand Deer Meat So It's Less Gamey," *Brandweek*, January 11, 1993, p. 7.

57. Gordon H. Bower, "Mood and Memory," *American Psychologist*, February 1981, pp. 129–148; Gordon H. Bower, Stephen Gilligan, and Kenneth Montiero, "Selectivity of Learning Caused by Affective States," *Journal of Experimental Psychology: General*, December 1981, pp. 451–473; Alice M. Isen, Thomas Shalker, Margaret Clark, and Lynn Karp, "Affect, Accessibility of Material in Memory and Behavior: A Cognitive Loop?"

Journal of Personality and Social Psychology, January 1978, pp. 1–12.

58. Peter H. Bloch, Daniel L. Sherrell, and Nancy M. Ridgway, "Consumer Search: An Extended Framework," *Journal of Consumer Research*, June 1986, pp. 119–126.

59. Sharon E. Beatty and Scott M. Smith, "External Search Effort: An Investigation across Several Product Categories," *Journal of Consumer Research*, June 1987, pp. 83–95.

60. Ibid.

61. David F. Midgley, "Patterns of Interpersonal Information Seeking for the Purchase of a Symbolic Product," *Journal of Marketing Research*, February 1983, pp. 74–83.

62. George Anders, Click and Buy," *Wall Street Journal*, December 7, 1998, p. R4; "Forrester Predicts WW eCommerce to Reach $3.2 Trillion by 2003," *eMarketer*, February 3, 2000.[On line reference].

63. Niranjan J. Raman, "A Qualitative Investigation of Web-Browsing Behavior," in Merrie Brucks and Deborah J. MacInnis, eds. *Advances in Consumer Research*, Vol. 24 (Provo, Utah: Association for Consumer Research, 1997), pp. 511–516.

64. Ken Shapiro, "Time Warner Builds an Internet Superstore," *Wall Street Journal*, August 14, 1998, pp. B1, B4.

65. "Cyber-Space Winners: How They Did It," *Business Week*, June 22, 1998, p. 154.

66. Kimberly A. Strassel, "Online Shopping Grows in Europe as Retailers Deal with Problems," *Wall Street Journal*, December 14, 1998, p. B5.

67. Ross Kerber, "Direct Hit Uses Popularity to Narrow Internet Searches," *Wall Street Journal*, July 2, 1998, p. B4.

68. Rebecca Quick, "Web's Robot Shoppers Don't Roam Free," *Wall Street Journal*, September 3, 1998, pp. B1, B8.

69. Sally Beatty, "IBM HotMedia Aims to Speed Online Ads," *Wall Street Journal*, October 27, 1998, p. B8.

70. Dean Takahashi, "Closer to Reality," *Wall Street Journal*, December 7, 1998, p. R8.

71. Burke, Raymond R. (1996), "Virtual Shopping: Breakthrough in Marketing Research," *Harvard Business Review*, 74 (March–April), 120–131; Feder, Barnaby (1997), "Test Marketers Use Virtual Shopping to Gauge Potential of Real Products," *New York Times* (December 22), p. C3.

72. Eileen Fischer, Julia Bristor, and Brenda Gainer, "Creating or Escaping Community?: An Exploratory Study of Internet Consumers' Behaviors," in Kim P. Corfman and John G. Lynch, eds. *Advances in Consumer Research*, Vol. 23 (Provo, Utah: Association for Consumer Research, 1996), pp. 178–182; John Buskin, "Tales from the Front," *Wall Street Journal*, December 7, 1998, p. R6.

73. Neil A. Granitz and James C. Ward, "Virtual Community: A Sociocognitive Analysis," in Kim P. Corfman and John G. Lynch, eds. *Advances in Consumer Research*, Vol. 23 (Provo, Utah: Association for Consumer Research, 1996), pp. 161–166.

74. Jim Sterne, *What Makes People Click: Advertising on the Web*, (Indianapolis, Ind.: Que, 1997).

75. Jacob Jacoby, Robert W. Chestnut, Karl Weigl, and William A. Fisher, "Prepurchase Information Acquisition: Description of a Process Methodology, Research Paradigm, and Pilot Investigation," in ed. Beverlee B. Anderson, *Advances in Consumer Research*, Vol. 3 (Cincinnati: Association for Consumer Research, 1976), pp. 306–314; Jacob Jacoby, Robert W. Chestnut, and William Silberman, "Consumer Use and Comprehension of Nutrition Information," *Journal of Consumer Research*, September 1977, pp. 119–128.

76. Geoffrey C. Kiel and Roger A. Layton, "Dimensions of Consumer Information Seeking," *Journal of Marketing Research*, May 1981, pp. 233–239.

77. Kiel and Layton, "Dimensions of Consumer Information Seeking."

78. John O. Claxton, Joseph N. Fry, and Bernard Portis, "A Taxonomy of Prepurchase Information Gathering Patterns," *Journal of Consumer Research*, December 1974, pp. 35–42.

79. Bloch, Sherrell, and Ridgway, "Consumer Search."

80. R. A. Bauer, "Consumer Behavior as Risk Taking," in ed. Robert S. Hancock, *Dynamic Marketing for a Changing World* (Chicago: American Marketing Association, 1960), pp. 389–398; Rohit Deshpande and Wayne D. Hoyer, "Consumer Decision Making: Strategies, Cognitive Effort, and Perceived Risk," in *1983 Educators' Conference Proceedings* (Chicago: American Marketing Association, 1983), pp. 88–91.

81. Keith B. Murray, "A Test of Services Marketing Theory: Consumer Information Acquisition Activities," *Journal of Marketing*, January 1991, pp. 10–25. Joel E. Urbany, Peter R. Dickson, and William L. Wilkie, "Buyer Uncertainty and Information Search," *Journal of Consumer Research*, September 1989, pp. 208–215;

82. David J. Furse, Girish N. Punj, and David W. Stewart, "A Typology of Individual Search Strategies among Purchasers of New Automobiles," *Journal of Consumer Research*, March 1984, pp. 417–431; Narasimhan Srinivasan and Brian T. Ratchford, "An Empirical Test of a Model of External Search for Automobiles," *Journal of Consumer Research*, September 1991, pp. 233–242; Jacob Jacoby, James J. Jaccard, Imran Currim, Alfred Kuss, Asim Ansari, and Tracy Troutman, "Tracing the Impact of Item-by-Item Information Accessing on Uncertainty Reduction," *Journal of Consumer Research*, September 1994, pp. 291–303.

83. Calmetta Y. Coleman, "Selling Jewelry, Dolls and TVs Next to Corn Flakes," *Wall Street Journal*, November 19, 1997, pp. B1, B8.

84. Sridhar Moorthy, Brian T. Ratchford, and Debabrata Talukdar, "Consumer Information Search Revisited: Theory and Empirical Analysis," *Journal of Consumer Research*, March 1997, pp. 263–277.

85. Calvin P. Duncan and Richard W. Olshavsky, "External Search: The Role of Consumer Beliefs," *Journal of Marketing Research*, February 1982, pp. 32–43; Girish N. Punj and Richard Staelin, "A Model of Information Search Behavior for New Automobiles," *Journal of Consumer Research*, September 1983, pp. 181–196.

86. Duncan and Olshavsky, "External Search."

87. Kathy Hammond, Gil McWilliam, and Andrea Narholz Diaz, "Fun and Work on the Web: Differences in Attitudes between Novices and Experienced Users," in Joseph W. Alba and J. Wesley Hutchinson, eds. *Advances in Consumer Research*, Vol. 25 (Provo, Utah: Association for Consumer Research, 1998), pp.372–378.

88. Joan E. Rigdon, "Advertisers Give Surfers Games to Play," *Wall Street Journal*, October 28, 1996, pp. B1, B6.

89. Laura A. Peracchio and Alice M. Tybout, "The Moderating Role of Prior Knowledge in Schema-Based Product Evaluation," *Journal of Consumer Research*, December 1996, pp. 177–192.

90. Joan Meyers-Levy and Alice Tybout, "Schema-Congruity as Basis for Product Evaluation," *Journal of Consumer Research*, June 1989, pp. 39–54.

91. Jonathan Welsh, "Vacuums Make Sweeping Health Claims," *Wall Street Journal*, September 9, 1996, pp. B1, B2.

92. Julie L. Ozanne, Merrie Brucks, and Dhruv Grewal, "A Study of Information Search Behavior during Categorization of New Products," *Journal of Consumer Research*, March 1992, pp. 452–463.

93. Punj and Staelin, "A Model of Consumer Information Search Behavior for New Automobiles"; Kiel and Layton, "Dimensions of Consumer Information Seeking."

94. Merrie Brucks, "The Effects of Product Class Knowledge on Information Search Behavior," *Journal of Consumer Research*, June 1985, pp. 1–16; James R. Bettman and C. Whan Park, "Effects of Prior Knowledge and Experience and Phase of the Choice Process on Consumer Decision Processes: A Protocol Analysis," *Journal of Consumer Research*, December 1980, pp. 234–248; Eric J. Johnson and J. Edward Russo, "Product Familiarity and Learning New Information," *Journal of Consumer Research*, June 1984, pp. 542–550; P. S. Raju, Subhas C. Lonial, and W. Glyn Mangold, "Differential Effects of Subjective Knowledge, Objective Knowledge, and Usage Experience on Decision Making; An Exploratory Investigation," *Journal of Consumer Psychology*, Month 1995, pp. 153–180; Joseph W. Alba and J. Wesley Hutchinson, "Dimensions of Consumer Expertise," *Journal of Consumer Research*, March 1987, pp. 411–454.

95. Noel Capon and Roger Davis, "Basic Cognitive Ability Measures as Predictors of Consumer Information Processing Strategies," *Journal of Consumer Research*, June 1984, pp. 551–563.

96. For a summary of a number of studies, see Joseph W. Newman, "Consumer External Search: Amount and Determinants," in eds. Arch Woodside, Jagdish Sheth, and Peter Bennett, *Consumer and Industrial Buying Behavior* (New York: North-Holland, 1977), pp. 79–94; Charles M. Schaninger and Donald Sciglimpaglia, "The Influences of Cognitive Personality Traits and Demographics on Consumer Information Acquisition," *Journal of Consumer Research*, September 1981, pp. 208–216.

97. "The eOverview Report," *Emarketer*, February 3, 2000. (on line report).

98. Scott Painton and James W. Gentry, "Another Look at the Impact of Information Presentation Format," *Journal of Consumer Research*, September 1985, pp. 240–244.

99. J. Edward Russo, Richard Staelin, Catherine A. Nolan, Gary J. Russell, and Barbara L. Metcalf, "Nutrition Information in the Supermarket," *Journal of Consumer Research*, June 1986, pp. 48–70.

100. Christine Moorman, "The Effects of Stimulus and Consumer Utilization of Nutrition Information," *Journal of Consumer Research*, December 1990, pp. 362–374.

101. Chris Janiszewski, "The Influence of Display Characteristics on Visual Exploratory Search Behavior," *Journal of Consumer Research*, December 1998, pp. 290–301.

102. William L. Moore and Donald L. Lehman, "Validity of Information Display Boards: An Assessment Using Longitudinal Data," *Journal of Marketing Research*, November 1980, pp. 296–307; C. Whan Park, Easwar S. Iyer, and Daniel C. Smith, "The Effects of Situational Factors on In-Store Grocery Shopping Behavior: The Role of Store Environment and Time Available for Shopping," *Journal of Consumer Research*, March 1989, pp. 422–433.

103. John R. Hauser, Glen L. Urban, and Bruce D. Weinberg, "How Consumers Allocate Their Time When Searching for Information," *Journal of Marketing Research*, November 1993, pp. 452–466.

104. Furse, Punj, and Stewart, "A Typology of Individual Search Strategies among Purchasers of New Automobiles."

105. Paul Manus, "Phone Marketer Sees Stroke of Brilliance in Retail Concept," *Marketing News*, October 27, 1997, p. 15; Pam Weisz, "Chesebrough, Bristol-Myers Healthtouch Shoppers In-Store," *Brandweek*, December 12, 1994, p. 14

106. Bruce Crumley, "Multipoints Adds up for Quick Burger," *Advertising Age*, November 29, 1993, p. 14.

107. Jacob Jacoby, Robert W. Chestnut, and William A. Fisher, "A Behavioral Process Approach to Information Acquisition in Nondurable Purchasing," *Journal of Marketing Research*, November 1978, pp. 532–544.

108. Kent B. Monroe, "The Influence of Price Differences and Brand Familiarity on Brand Preferences," *Journal of Consumer Research*, June 1976, pp. 42–49.

109. Dhruv Grewal and Howard Marmorstein, "Market Price Variation, Perceived Price Variation, and Consumers' Price Search Decision for Durable Goods," *Journal of Consumer Research*, December 1994, pp. 453–460.

110. P. H. Ferguson, "Shoppers Leave Ivory Towers for Bargain Basements in Japan," *Austin American Statesman*, December 26, 1993, p. A26.

111. Cynthia Huffman, "Goal Change, Information Acquisition, and Transfer," *Journal of Consumer Psychology*, 5 (1), 1996, pp. 1–26.

112. Deborah Roedder John, Carol A. Scott, and James R. Bettman, "Sampling Data for Covariation Assessment," *Journal of Consumer Research*, March 1986, pp. 406–417.

113. J. Edward Russo and France Leclerc, "An Eye-Fixation Analysis of Choice for Consumer Nondurables," *Journal of Consumer Research*, September 1994, pp. 274–290.

114. Jacoby et al., "Prepurchase Information Acquisition."

115. J. Edward Russo, Margaret G. Meloy, and Husted Medvec, "Predecisional Distortion of Product Information, *Journal of Marketing Research*, November 1998, pp. 438–452.

116. Carol A. Berning and Jacob Jacoby, "Patterns of Information Acquisition in New Product Purchases," *Journal of Consumer Research*, September 1974, pp. 18–22.

117. Itamar Simonson, Joel Huber, and John Payne, "The Relationship between Prior Brand Knowledge and Information Acquisition Order," *Journal of Consumer Research*, March 1988, pp. 566–578.

118. Jacoby et al., "Prepurchase Information Acquisition"; James R. Bettman, *An Information Processing Theory of Consumer Choice* (Reading, Mass.: Addison-Wesley, 1979).

119. Eric J. Johnson and J. Edward Russo, "Product Familiarity and Learning New Information," *Journal of Consumer Research*, June 1984, pp. 542–550; James R. Bettman and P. Kakkar, "Effects of Information Presentation Format on Consumer Information Acquisition Strategies," *Journal of Consumer Research*, March 1977, pp. 233–240.

120. Raj Sethuraman, Catherine Cole, and Dipak Jain, "Analyzing the Effect of Information Format and Task on Cutoff Search Strategies," *Journal of Consumer Psychology*, 3 (1994), pp. 103–136.

121. Jacoby et al., "Tracing the Impact of Item-by-Item Information Accessing on Uncertainty Reduction."

CHAPTER 10

1. This example was taken from an article by Evelyn Iritani, "Road Warriors," *Los Angeles Times*, July 9, 1995, pp. D1, D6.

2. Michael D. Johnson and Christopher P. Puto, "A Review of Consumer Judgment and Choice," in ed. Michael J. Houston, *Review of Marketing* (Chicago: American Marketing Association, 1987), pp. 236–292.

3. Itamar Simonson, Joel Huber, and John Payne, "The Relationship between Prior Brand Knowledge and Information Acquisition Order," *Journal of Consumer Research*, March 1988, pp. 566–578.

4. Eric J. Johnson and J. Edward Russo, "Product Familiarity and Learning New Information," *Journal of Consumer Research*, June 1984, pp. 528–541.

5. Eloise Coupey, Julie R. Irwin, and John W. Payne, "Product Category Familiarity and Preference Construction, *Journal of Consumer Research*, March 1998, pp. 459–468.

6. Daniel Kahneman and Amos Tversky, "On the Psychology of Prediction," *Psychology Review*, July 1973, pp. 251–275.

7. Joan Meyers-Levy and Alice M. Tybout, "Context Effects at Encoding and Judgment in Consumption Settings: The Role of Cognitive Resources," *Journal of Consumer Research*, June 1997, pp. 1–14.

8. Irwin Levin, "Associative Effects of Information Framing," *Bulletin of the Psychonomic Society*, March 1987, pp. 85–86.

9. Manjit S. Yadav, "How Buyers Evaluate Product Bundles: A Model of Anchoring and Adjustment," *Journal of Consumer Research*, September 1994, pp. 342–353.

10. Gita Venkataramani Johar, Kamel Jedidi, and Jacob Jacoby, "A Varying-Parameter Averaging Model of On-line Brand Evaluations," *Journal of Consumer Research*, September 1997, pp. 232–247.

11. John Carroll, "The Effect of Imagining an Event on Expectations for the Event," *Journal of Experimental Social Psychology*, January 1978, pp. 88–96.

12. Deborah J. MacInnis and Linda L. Price, "The Role of Imagery in Information Processing: Review and Extensions," *Journal of Consumer Research*, March 1987, pp. 473–491.

13. Calvin P. Duncan and Richard W. Olshavsky, "External Search: The Role of Consumer Beliefs," *Journal of Marketing Research*, February 1982, pp. 32–43.

14. Priya Raghubir and Geeta Menon, "AIDS and Me, Never the Twain Shall Meet: The Effects of Information Accessibility on Judgments of Risk and Advertising Effectiveness," *Journal of Consumer Research*, June 1998, pp. 52–63.

15. Meryl Paula Gardner, "Mood States and Consumer Behavior: A Critical Review," *Journal of Consumer Research*, December 1985, pp. 281–300.

16. Evan Ramstad, "Digital-TV Ads Aim to Shuffle Leadership," *Wall Street Journal*, November 3, 1998, p. B16.

17. Paul M. Herr, "Priming Price: Prior Knowledge and Context Effects," *Journal of Consumer Research*, June 1989, pp. 67–75.

18. Sung-Tai Hong and Robert S. Wyer Jr. "Effects of Country-of-Origin and Product-Attribute Information: An Information Processing Perspective," *Journal of Consumer Research*, September 1989, pp. 175–187.

19. Wendy Bounds and Deborah Ball, "Italy Knits Support for Fashion Industry," *Wall Street Journal*, December 15, 1997, p. B8.

20. Craig S. Smith, "Chinese Government Struggles to Rejuvenate National Brands," *Wall Street Journal*, June 24, 1996, pp. B1, B6.

21. James R. Bettman and Mita Sujan, "Effects of Framing on Evaluation of Comparable and Noncomparable Alternatives by Expert and Novice Consumers," *Journal of Consumer Research*, September 1987, pp. 141–151.

22. Ernest Beck, "Big Tobacco Uses Good Works to Woo Eastern Europe," *Wall Street Journal*, November 10, 1998, pp. B1, B8.

23. Valerie Reitman, "With Mercedes' New M-Class, Make That M for Mania," *Wall Street Journal*, October 9, 1997, pp. B1, B3.

24. Christina Duff, "Fruit's Loom Weaves Some New Threads in Effort to Shed Underwear-Only Image," *Wall Street Journal*, April 28, 1993, pp. B1, B10.

25. Hans Baumgartner, "On the Utility of Consumers' Theories in Judgments of Covariation," *Journal of Consumer Research*, March 1995, pp. 634–643; James R. Bettman, Deborah Roedder John, and Carol A. Scott, "Covariation Assessment by Consumers," *Journal of Consumer Research*, December 1986, pp. 316–326; Susan M. Broniarczyk and Joseph W. Alba, "Theory versus Data in Prediction and Correlation Tasks," *Organizational Behavior and Human Decision Processes*, January 1994, pp. 117–139.

26. Durairaj Maheswaran, "Country of Origin as a Stereotype: Effects of Consumer Expertise and Attribute Strength on Product Evaluations," *Journal of Consumer Research*, September 1994, pp. 354–365.

27. Amos Tversky and Daniel Kahneman, "Extensional versus Intuitive Reasoning: The Conjunction Fallacy," *Psychological Review*, October 1983, pp. 293–315.

28. David Kiley, "The End of the 'American' Car," *Adweek's Marketing Week*, March 4, 1991, pp. 18–20.

29. Suein Hwang, "Smokers May Mistake 'Clean' Cigarette for Safe," *Wall Street Journal*, September 30, 1995, pp. B1, B2.

30. "The Hyundai Syndrome," *Adweek's Marketing Week*, April 20, 1992, pp. 20–21.

31. F. May and R. Homans, "Evoked Set Size and the Level of Information Processing in Product Comprehension and Choice Criteria," in ed. William D. Perrault, *Advances in Consumer Research*, Vol. 4 (Chicago: Association for Consumer Research, 1977), pp. 172–175.

32. Ravi Dhar, "Consumer Preference for a No-Choice Option," *Journal of Consumer Research*, September 1997, pp. 215–231.

33. John W. Payne, James R. Bettman, and Eric J. Johnson, "The Adaptive Decision-Maker," in ed. Robin M. Hogarth, *Judgment and Decision Making Theory and Applications: A Tribute to Hillel Einhorn* (Chicago: University of Chicago Press, in press).

34. Mariele K. De Mooij and Warren Keegan, *Worldwide Advertising* (London: Prentice-Hall International, 1991).

35. Itamar Simonson, "Get Closer to Your Consumers by Understanding How They Make Choices," *California Management Review*, Summer 1993, pp. 68–84.

36. For a good review of multiattribute models, see William L. Wilkie and Edgar A. Pessemier, "Issues in Marketing's Use of Multiattribute Models," *Journal of Marketing Research*, November 1983, pp. 428–441; Blair H. Sheppard, Jon Hartwick, and Paul R. Warshaw, "The Theory of Reasoned Action: A Meta-analysis of Past Research with Recommendations for Modifications and Future Research," *Journal of Consumer Research*, December 1988, pp. 325–342.

37. Yumiko Ono, "Off-road Vehicles Leave Others in the Dust," *Wall Street Journal*, August 17, 1993, p. B1.

38. Cacile Rohwedder, "Germany Drafts a Campaign for Recruits," *Wall Street Journal*, October 10, 1996, p. B6.

39. Robert L. Simison, "Ford Aims to Resolve Brand Identity Crisis," *Wall Street Journal*, December 15, 1998, p. B6.

40. Valerie Reitman, "Strong Sales Rev up Ad Spending among Car Companies in Japan," *Wall Street Journal*, March 3, 1996, p. B3.

41. Amos Tversky, "Intransitivity of Preferences," *Psychological Review*, January 1969, pp. 31–48.

42. Nichole M. Christian, "Chrysler for the Masses: Plain and Plastic," *Wall Street Journal*, September 9, 1997, pp B1, B16.

43. Donna Bryson, "Traditional Fare Goes Fast-Food in S. Africa," *Austin American Statesman*, June 4, 1994, p. A16.

44. Peter Wright, "Consumer Choice Strategies: Simplifying vs. Optimizing," *Journal of Marketing Research*, February 1975, pp. 60–67. Noreen Klein and Stewart W. Bither, "An Investigation of Utility-Directed Cutoff Selection," *Journal of Consumer Research*, September 1987, pp. 240–256.

45. Christina Binkley, "Gamblers Prefer One-Armed Bandits That Have Arms," *Wall Street Journal*, February 3, 1997, pp. B1, B8.

46. David Grether and Louis Wilde, "An Analysis of Conjunctive Choice: Theory and Experiments," *Journal of Consumer Research*, March 1984, pp. 373–385.

47. Gautam Naik, "Prepaid Plans Open up Cellular-Phone Market," *Wall Street Journal*, September 16, 1998, pp. B1, B4.

48. Tara Parker-Pope, "Will the British Warm up to Iced Tea? Some Big Marketers Are Counting on It," *Wall Street Journal*, August 22, 1994, p. B1.

49. Simonson, "Get Closer to Your Consumers by Understanding How They Make Choices."

50. Itamar Simonson, Ziv Carmon, and Suzanne O'Curry, "Experimental Evidence on the Negative Effect of Product Features and Sales Promotions on Brand Choice," Winter 1994, *Marketing Science*, pp. 23–40.

51. Amos Tversky, "Elimination by Aspects: A Theory of Choice," *Psychological Review*, July 1972, pp. 281–299.

52. Lisa Shuchman, "How Does GM's Saturn Sell Cars in Japan? Very Slowly," *Wall Street Journal*, September 9, 1998, pp. B1, B4.

53. Kathleen Deveny, "Anatomy of a Fad: How Clear Products Were Hot and Then Suddenly Were Not," *Wall Street Journal*, March 15, 1994, pp. B1, B5.

54. Denis A. Lussier and Richard W. Olshavsky, "Task Complexity and Contingent Processing in Brand Choice," *Journal of Consumer Research*, September 1979, pp. 154–165; Eric J. Johnson and Robert J. Meyer, "Compensatory Choice Models of Noncompensatory Processes: The Effect of Varying Context," *Journal of Consumer Research*, June 1984, pp. 542–551.

55. James R. Bettman, Mary Frances Luce, and John W. Payne, "Constructive Consumer Choice Processes," *Journal of Consumer Research*, December 1998, pp.187–217.

56. Payne, Bettman, and Johnson, "The Adaptive Decision-Maker."

57. Joseph Pereira, "Nike's Rivals Hope Buyers Want Bargains," *Wall Street Journal*, June 2, 1997, pp. B1, B3.

58. Norihiko Shirouzu, "Flouting 'Rules' Sells GE Fridges in Japan," *Wall Street Journal*, October 31, 1995, pp. B1, B2.

59. Seymour Epstein, "Integration of the Cognitive and the Psychodynamic Unconscious," *American Psychologist*, August 1994, pp. 709–724.

60. Stephen J. Hoch and George F. Lowenstein, "Time-Inconsistent Preferences and Consumer Self-Control," *Journal of Consumer Research*, March 1991, pp. 492–507.

61. Michel Tuan Pham, "Representativeness, Relevance, and the Use of Feelings in Decision Making," *Journal of Consumer Research*, September 1998, pp. 144–159.

62. Epstein, "Integration of the Cognitive and the Psychodynamic Unconscious."

63. Pham, "Representativeness, Relevance, and the Use of Feelings in Decision Making; Morris B. Holbrook and Elizabeth C. Hirschman, "The Experiential Aspects of Consumption: Consumer Fantasies, Feelings, and Fun," *Journal of Consumer Research*, September 1982, pp. 132–140.

64. Kathleen T. Lacher and Richard W. Mizerski, "An Exploratory Study of the Responses and Relationships Involved in the Evaluation of, and in the Intention to Purchase New Rock Music," *Journal of Consumer Research*, September 1994, pp. 366–380.

65. Yumiko Ono, "Tiffany Glitters, Even in Gloomy Japan," *Wall Street Journal*, July 21, 1998, pp, B1, B8.

66. Morris B. Holbrook and Meryl P. Gardner, "An Approach to Investigating the Emotional Determinants of Consumption Durations: Why Do People Consume What They Consume for as Long as They Consume It?" *Journal of Consumer Psychology*, 2 (2), 1993, pp. 123–142.

67. Mary Frances Luce, "Choosing to Avoid: Coping with Negatively Emotion-Laden Consumer Decisions," *Journal of Consumer Research*, March 1998, pp. 409–433.

68. Ellen C. Garbarino and Julie A. Edell, "Cognitive Effort, Affect, and Choice," *Journal of Consumer Research*, September 1997, pp. 147–158.

69. Ann L. McGill and Punam Anand Keller, "Differences in the Relative Influence of Product Attributes under Alternative Processing Conditions: Attribute Importance versus Ease of Imaginability," *Journal of Consumer Psychology*, 3 (1), 1994, pp. 29–50; MacInnis and Price, "The Role of Imagery in Information Processing."

70. Joel B. Cohen, "The Role of Affect in Categorization: Toward a Reconceptualization of the Concept of Attitude," in ed. Andrew A. Mitchell, *Advances in Consumer Research*, Vol. 9 (Ann Arbor, Mich.: Association for Consumer Research, 1982), pp. 94–100; C. Whan Park and Banwari Mittal, "A Theory of Involvement in Consumer Behavior: Problems and Issues," in ed. Jagdish N. Sheth, *Research in Consumer Behavior* (Greenwich, Conn.: JAI Press, 1985), pp. 201–231.

71. Tamsin Carlisle, "Gamble by World's Biggest Mall Pays Off," *Wall Street Journal*, March 7, 1997, pp. B1, B14.

72. Deborah Lohse, "Insurers Facing Rivals, Try to Build Brands," *Wall Street Journal*, October 15, 1998, p. B12.

73. Michael D. Johnson, "Consumer Choice Strategies for Comparing Noncomparable Alternatives," *Journal of Consumer Research*, December 1984, pp. 741–753; Michael D. Johnson, "Comparability and Hierarchical Processing in Multialternative Choice," *Journal of Consumer Research*, December 1988, pp. 303–314.

74. Kim P. Corfman, "Comparability and Comparison Levels Used in Choices among Consumer Products," *Journal of Marketing Research*, August 1991, pp. 368–374.

75. C. Whan Park and Daniel Smith, "Product-Level Choice: A Top-Down or Bottom-Up Process?" *Journal of Consumer Research*, December 1989, pp. 289–299.

76. Girish N. Punj and David W. Stewart, "An Interaction Framework of Consumer Decision Making," *Journal of Consumer Research*, September 1983, pp. 181–196.

77. Payne, Bettman, and Johnson, "The Adaptive Decision-Maker."

78. Dennis H. Gensch and Rajshelhar G. Javalgi, "The Influence of Involvement on Disaggregate Attribute Choice Models," *Journal of Consumer Research*, June 1987, pp. 71–82.

79. Eric A. Greenleaf and Donald R. Lehmann, "Reasons for Substantial Delay in Consumer Decision Making," *Journal of Consumer Research*, September 1995, pp. 186–199.

80. Elaine Sherman and Ruth Belk Smith, "Mood States of Shoppers and Store Image: Promising Interactions and Possible Behavioral Effects," in eds. Paul Anderson and Melanie Wallendorf, *Advances in Consumer Research*, Vol. 14 (Provo, Utah: Association for Consumer Research, 1987), pp. 251–254.

81. Gerald J. Gorn, Marvin E. Goldberg, and Kunal Basu, "Mood, Awareness, and Product Evaluation," *Journal of Consumer Psychology*, 2 (3), 1993, pp. 237–256.

82. Patricia M. West, Christina L. Brown, and Stephen J. Hoch, "Consumption Vocabulary and Preference

Formation," *Journal of Consumer Research*, September 1996, pp. 120–135.

83. Johnson and Russo, "Product Familiarity and Learning New Information"; James R. Bettman and C. Whan Park, "Effects of Prior Knowledge and Experience and Phase of the Choice Process on Consumer Decision Processes, A Protocol Analysis," *Journal of Consumer Research*, December 1980, pp. 234–248.

84. Payne, Bettman, and Johnson, "The Adaptive Decision-Maker."

85. C. Whan Park, Easwar S. Iyer, and Daniel C. Smith, "The Effects of Situational Factors on In-store Grocery Shopping Behavior: The Role of Store Environment and Time Available for Shopping," *Journal of Consumer Research*, March 1989, pp. 422–433.

86. Greenleaf and Lehmann, "Reasons for Substantial Delay in Consumer Decision Making."

87. Michelle M. Bergadaa, "The Role of Time in the Action of the Consumer," *Journal of Consumer Research*, December 1990, pp. 289–302.

88. Lussier and Olshavsky, "Task Complexity and Contingent Processing in Brand Choice"; Johnson and Meyer, "Compensatory Choice Models of Noncompensatory Processes."

89. Noreen M. Klein and Manjit S. Yadav, "Context Effects on Effort and Accuracy: An Enquiry into Adaptive Decision Making," *Journal of Consumer Research*, March 1989, pp. 411–421; Payne, Bettman, and Johnson, "The Adaptive Decision-Maker."

90. Simonson, "Get Closer to Your Consumers by Understanding How They Make Choices."

91. Itamar Simonson and Amos Tversky, "Choice in Context: Tradeoff Contrast and Extremeness Aversion," *Journal of Marketing Research*, August 1992, pp. 281–295.

92. Joel Huber, John W. Payne, and Christopher Puto, "Adding Asymmetrically Dominated Alternatives: Violations of Regularity and the Similarity Hypothesis," *Journal of Consumer Research*, June 1982, pp. 90–98; Srinivasan Ratneshwar, Allan D. Shocker, and David W. Stewart, "Toward Understanding the Attraction Effect: The Implications of Product Stimulus Meaningfulness and Familiarity," *Journal of Consumer Research*, March 1987, pp. 520–533; Sanjay Mishra, U. N. Umesh, and Donald E. Stem, "Antecedents of the Attraction Effect: An Information Processing Approach," *Journal of Marketing Research*, August 1993, pp. 331–349; Yigang Pan, Sue O'Curry, and Robert Pitts, "The Attraction Effect and Political Choice in Two Elections," *Journal of Consumer Psychology*, 4 (1), 1995, pp. 85–101.

93. Sankar Sen, "Knowledge, Information Mode, and the Attraction Effect," *Journal of Consumer Research*, June 1998, 64–77.

94. Timothy B. Heath and Subimal Chatterjee, "Asymmetric Decoy Effects on Lower-Quality versus Higher-Quality Brands: Meta-analytic and Experimental Evidence," *Journal of Consumer Research*, December 1995, pp. 268–84.

95. Simonson, "Get Closer to Your Consumers by Understanding How They Make Choices."

96. Simonson and Tversky, "Choice in Context: Tradeoff Contrast and Extremeness Aversion."

97. Simonson, "Get Closer to Your Consumers by Understanding How They Make Choices."

98. Jacob Jacoby, "Perspectives on Information Overload," *Journal of Consumer Research*, March 1984, pp. 569–573; Kevin Lane Keller and Richard Staelin, "Effects of Quality and Quantity of Information on Decision Effectiveness," *Journal of Consumer Research*, September 1987, pp. 200–213.

99. Ger, "Problems of Marketization in Romania and Turkey."

100. Gabriella Stern, "Multiple Varieties of Established Brands Muddle Consumers, Make Retailers Mad," *Wall Street Journal*, 1992, pp. B1, B5.

101. Guliz Ger, Russell Belk, and Dana-Nicoleta Lascu, "The Development of Consumer Desire in Marketing and Developing Economies: The Cases of Romania and Turkey," in eds. Leigh McAlister and Michael L. Rothschild, *Advances in Consumer Research*, Vol. 20 (Provo, Utah: Association for Consumer Research, 1993), pp. 102–107.

102. Keller and Staelin, "Effects of Quality and Quantity of Information on Decision Effectiveness."

103. Ravi Dhar and Steven J. Sherman, "The Effect of Common and Unique Features in Consumer Choice," *Journal of Consumer Research*, December 1996, pp. 193–203.

104. A.V. Muthukrishnan, "Decision Ambiguity and Incumbent Brand Advantage," *Journal of Consumer Research*, June 1995, pp. 98–109.

105. Madhubalan Viswanathan and Sunder Narayanan, "Comparative Judgments of Numerical and Verbal Attribute Labels," *Journal of Consumer Psychology*, 3 (1), 1994, pp. 79–100.

106. Itamar Simonson, Stephen Nowlis, and Katherine Lemon, "The Effect of Local Consideration Sets on Global Choice Between Lower Price and Higher Quality," *Marketing Science*, Fall 1993.

107. Johnson and Russo, "Product Familiarity and Learning New Information"; J. Edward Russo, "The Value of Unit Price Information," *Journal of Marketing Research*, May 1977, pp. 193–201

108. Cyndee Miller, "Food Producers Appeal to Fat-Free Crowd," *Marketing News*, August 14, 1995, pp. 3, 15.

109. Itamar Simonson and Russell S. Winer, "The Influence of Purchase Quantity and Display Format on Consumer Preference for Variety," *Journal of Consumer Research*, June 1992, pp. 133–138.

110. Eloise Coupey, "Restructuring: Constructive Processing of Information Displays in Consumer Choice," *Journal of Consumer Research*, June 1994, pp. 83–99.

111. Barbara E. Kahn and Jonathan Baron, "An Exploratory Study of Choice Rules Favored for High-Stakes Decisions," *Journal of Consumer Psychology*, 4 (4), 1995, pp. 305–328.

112. Daniel Kahneman and Amos Tversky, "Prospect Theory: An Analysis of Decisions under Risk," *Econometrica*, March 1979, pp. 263–291.

113. William B. Diamond and Abhijit Sanyal, "The Effect of Framing on the Choice of Supermarket Coupons," in eds. Marvin E. Goldberg and Gerald Gorn, *Advances in Consumer Research*, Vol. 17 (Provo, Utah: Association for Consumer Research, 1990), pp. 488–493.

114. Christopher P. Puto, "The Framing of Buying Decisions," *Journal of Consumer Research*, December 1987, pp. 301–316.

115. Rajendra K. Srivastava, Allan D. Shocker, and George S. Day, "An Exploratory Study of the Influences of Usage Situations on Perceptions of Product Markets," in ed. H. Keith Hunt, *Advances in Consumer Research*, Vol. 5 (Ann Arbor, Mich.: Association for Consumer Research, 1978), pp. 32–38.

116. Kenneth E. Miller and James L. Ginter, "An Investigation of Situational Variation in Brand Choice Behavior and Attitude," *Journal of Marketing Research*, February 1979, pp. 111–123.

117. Kevin Goldman, "Computer Companies Try TV Ads' Mass Appeal," *Wall Street Journal*, September 20, 1994, pp. B1, B8.

118. Joseph Pereira, "Can Air Pockets Help Reebok Catch Nike in High Performance Sneaker Marathon?" *Wall Street Journal*, March 27, 1998, pp. B1, B8.

119. Sally D. Goll, "Odds and Ends," *Wall Street Journal*, May 27, 1994, p. B1.

120. Levin, "Associative Effects of Information Framing."

121. Christopher P. Puto, W. E. Patton, and Ronald H. King, "Risk Handling Strategies in Industrial Vendor Selection Decisions," *Journal of Marketing*, January 1987, pp. 89–98.

122. John T. Gourville, "Pennies-a-Day: The Effect of Temporal Reframing on Transaction Evaluation," *Journal of Consumer Research*, March 1998, pp. 395–408.

123. Yaacov Schul and Yoav Ganzach, "The Effects of Accessibility of Standards and Decision Framing on Product Evaluations," *Journal of Consumer Psychology*, 4 (1), 1995, pp. 61–83.

124. Baba Shiv, Julie A. Edell, and John W. Payne, "Factors Affecting the Impact of Negatively and Positively Framed Ad Messages," *Journal of Consumer Research*, December 1997, pp. 285–294.

125. Bettman and Sujan, "Effects of Framing on Evaluation of Comparable and Noncomparable Alternatives by Expert and Novice Consumers."

126. Cynthia Fraser, Robert E. Hite, and Paul L. Sauer, "Increasing Contributions in Solicitation Campaigns: The Use of Large and Small Anchor-Points," *Journal of Consumer Research*, September 1988, pp. 284–287.

127. Donald P. Green and Irene V. Blair, "Framing and Price Elasticity of Private and Public Goods," *Journal of Consumer Psychology*, 4 (1) 1995, pp. 1–32.

128. Kevin Goldman, "GM's Oldsmobile Lets Aurora Drive Solo," *Wall Street Journal*, August 19, 1994, p. B5.

129. Suein L. Hwang, "How Impotence Became a Weapon against Smoking," *Wall Street Journal*, November 9, 1998, pp. B1, B4.

CHAPTER 11

1. Samantha Marshall, "Soap Smugglers Cleaning up in Vietnam," *Wall Street Journal*, April 1, 1998, pp. B1, B15.

2. Rohit Deshpande, Wayne D. Hoyer, and Scott Jeffries, "Low Involvement Decision Processes: The Importance of Choice Tactics," in eds. R. F. Bush and S. D. Hunt, *Marketing Theory: Philosophy of Science Perspectives* (Chicago: American Marketing Association, 1982), pp. 155–158; Wayne D. Hoyer, "An Examination of Consumer Decision Making for a Common Repeat Purchase Product," *Journal of Consumer Research*, December 1984, pp. 822–829.

3. Alan Newell and Herbert A. Simon, *Human Problem Solving* (Englewood Cliffs, N. J.: Prentice-Hall, 1972); Daniel Kahneman and Amos Tversky, "On the Psychology of Prediction," *Psychological Review*, July 1973, pp. 237–251.

4. Daniel Kahneman and Amos Tversky, "Subjective Probability: A Judgment of Representativeness," *Cognitive Psychology*, July 1972, pp. 430–454.

5. Sally Beatty, "P & G's Comparisons Defend Toothpaste," *Wall Street Journal*, June 29, 1998, p. B4

6. Marshall, "Soap Smugglers Cleaning up in Vietnam."

7. Valerie S. Folkes, "The Availability Heuristic and Perceived Risk," *Journal of Consumer Research*, June 1988, pp. 13–23; Johnson and Puto, "A Review of Consumer Judgment and Choice," in ed. Michael J. Houston, *Review of Marketing* (Chicago: American Marketing Association, 1987), pp. 236–292.

8. Peter R. Dickson, "The Impact of Enriching Case and Statistical Information on Consumer Judgments," *Journal of Consumer Research*, March 1982, pp. 398–408.

9. Chezy Ofir and John G. Lynch Jr., "Context Effects on Judgment under Uncertainty," *Journal of Consumer Research*, September 1984, pp. 668–679.

10. Amos Tversky and Daniel Kahneman, "Belief in the Law of Small Numbers," *Psychological Bulletin*, August 1971, pp. 105–110; Amos Tversky and Daniel Kahneman, "Judgment under Uncertainty: Heuristics and Biases," *Science*, September 1974, pp. 1124–1131.

11. Vanessa O'Connell, "Bumble Bee Tuna Ads Claim a 2-to-1 Edge," *Wall Street Journal*, April 29, 1998, p. B2.

12. Hanjoon Lee, Acito Acito, and Ralph Day, "Evaluation and Use of Marketing Research by Decision Makers: A Behavioral Simulation," *Journal of Marketing Research*, May 1987, pp. 187–196.

13. Hoyer, "An Examination of Consumer Decision Making for a Common Repeat Purchase Product."

14. Herbert E. Krugman, "The Impact of Television Advertising: Learning without Involvement," *Public Opinion Quarterly*, Fall 1965, pp. 349–356.

15. Michael L. Ray, *Marketing Communications and the Hierarchy of Effects* (Cambridge, Mass.: Marketing Science Institute, 1973).

16. Robert B. Zajonc, "Feeling and Thinking: Preferences Need No Inferences," *American Psychologist*, February 1980, pp. 151–175; Robert B. Zajonc and Hazel B. Markus, "Affective and Cognitive Factors in Preferences," *Journal of Consumer Research*, September 1982, pp. 122–131.

17. Hoyer, "An Examination of Consumer Decision Making for a Common Repeat Purchase Product."

18. Cathy J. Cobb and Wayne D. Hoyer, "Direct Observation of Search Behavior in the Purchase of Two Nondurable Products," *Psychology and Marketing*, Fall 1983, pp. 161–179.

19. Alain d'Astous, Idriss Bensouda, and Jean Guindon, "A Reexamination of Consumer Decision Making for a Repeat Purchase Product: Variations in Product Importance and Purchase Frequency," in ed. Thomas K. Srull, *Advances in Consumer Research*, Vol. 16 (Provo, Utah: Association for Consumer Research, 1989), pp. 433–438.

20. Richard W. Olshavsky and Donald H. Granbois, "Consumer Decision Making: Fact or Fiction?" *Journal of Consumer Research*, September 1979, pp. 93–100.

21. Deshpande, Hoyer, and Jeffries, "Low Involvement Decision Processes."

22. Hoyer, "An Examination of Consumer Decision Making for a Common Repeat Purchase Product."

23. Siew Meng Leong, "Consumer Decision Making for Common, Repeat-Purchase Products: A Dual Replication," *Journal of Consumer Psychology*, 2 (2), 1993, pp. 193–208.

24. Dana L. Alden, Wayne D. Hoyer, and Guntalee Wechasara, "Choice Strategies and Involvement, A Cross-Cultural Analysis," in ed. Thomas K. Srull, *Advances in Consumer Research*, Vol. 16 (Provo, Utah: Association for Consumer Research, 1989), pp. 119–126.

25. Walter A. Nord and J. Paul Peter, "A Behavior Modification Perspective on Marketing," *Journal of Marketing*, Spring 1980, pp. 36–47; Michael Rothschild and William C. Gaidis, "Behavioral Learning Theory: Its Relevance to Marketing and Promotions," *Journal of Marketing*, Spring 1981, pp. 70–78.

26. Holly Heline, "Brand Loyalty Isn't Dead—But You're Not off the Hook," *Brandweek*, June 7, 1994, p. 14.

27. Robert E. Smith and William R. Swinyard, "Information Response Models: An Integrated Approach," *Journal of Marketing*, Winter 1982, pp. 81–93; Robert E. Smith and William R. Swinyard, "Attitude-Behavior Consistency: The Impact of Product Trial vs. Advertising," *Journal of Marketing Research*, August 1983, pp. 257–267.

28. Deanna S. Kempf and Robert E. Smith, "Consumer Processing of Product Trial and the Influence of Prior Advertising: A Structural Modeling Approach," *Journal of Marketing Research*, August 1998, pp. 325–38.

29. Michael L. Rothschild and Michael J. Houston, "The Consumer Involvement Matrix: Some Preliminary Findings," in eds. Barnett A. Greenberg and Danny N. Bellenger, *Proceedings of the American Marketing Association Educators' Conference*, Series. No. 41, 1977, pp. 95–98.

30. Wayne D. Hoyer, "Variations in Choice Strategies across Decision Contexts: An Examination of Contingent Factors," in ed. Richard J. Lutz, *Advances in Consumer Research*, Vol. 13 (Provo, Utah: Association for Consumer Research, 1986), pp. 32–36.

31. Wayne D. Hoyer and Cathy J. Cobb-Walgren, "Consumer Decision Making across Product Categories: The Influence of Task Environment," *Psychology and Marketing*, Spring 1988, pp. 45–69.

32. Leong, "Consumer Decision Making for Common, Repeat-Purchase Products."

33. Yumiko Ono, "Campbell's New Ads Heat up Soup Sales," *Wall Street Journal*, March 17, 1994, p. B5.

34. Robert E. Smith, "Integrating Information from Advertising and Trial: Processes and Effects on Consumer Response to Product Information," *Journal of Marketing Research*, May 1993, pp. 204–219.

35. Mark Maremont, "How Gillette Brought Its MACH3 to Market," *Wall Street Journal*, April 15, 1998, pp. B1, B8.

36. Norihiko Shirouzu, "Snapple in Japan: How a Splash Dried Up," *Wall Street Journal*, April 15, 1996, pp. B1, B3.

37. Jacob Jacoby and David B. Kyner, "Brand Loyalty vs. Repeat Purchasing Behavior," *Journal of Marketing Research*, February 1973, pp. 1–9.

38. Ted Roselius, "Consumer Rankings of Risk Reduction Methods," *Journal of Marketing*, January 1971, pp. 56–61.

39. Rothschild and Gaidis, "Behavioral Learning Theory."

40. Ernest Beck and Rekha Balu, "Europe is Deaf to Snap! Crackle! Pop!" *Wall Street Journal*, June 22, 1998, pp. B1, B8.

41. Raju Narisetti, "P & G Uses Packaging Savvy on Rx Drug," *Wall Street Journal*, January 30, 1997, pp. B1, B11.

42. Mark Maremont, "New Toothbrush Is Big Ticket Item," *Wall Street Journal*, October 27, 1998, pp.B1, B6; Raju Narisetti, "P & G's New Diaper Promises to Baby Skin," *Wall Street Journal*, July 21, 1997, p. B9; Vanessa O'Connell, "After Years of Trial and Error, a Pickle That Stays Put," *Wall Street Journal*, October 6, 1998, pp. B1, B4.

43. Ernest Beck, "New 3-D Tea Bag Rattles Cups in U.K." *Wall Street Journal*, March 24, 1997, pp. B1, B2.

44. Ronald Curhan, "The Relationship of Shelf Space to Unit Sales: A Review," Working Paper, Marketing Science Institute, 1972.

45. Gary F. McKinnon, J. Patrick Kelly, and E. Doyle Robinson, "Sales Effects of Point-of-Purchase In-store Signing," *Journal of Retailing*, Summer 1981, pp. 49–63.

46. Kathleen Deveny, "Displays Pay off for Grocery Marketers," *Wall Street Journal*, October 15, 1992, pp. B1, B5.

47. Ronald Grover, "Big Brother Is Grocery Shopping with You," *Business Week*, March 29, 1993, p. 60.

48. Janet Guyon, "Coke Wins Early Skirmishes in Its Drive to Take over Eastern Europe from Pepsi," *Wall Street Journal*, November 11, 1992, pp. B1, B10.

49. Norihiko Shirouzu, "For Coca-Cola in Japan, Things Go Better with Milk," *Wall Street Journal*, January 20, 1997, pp. B1, B2.

50. George S. Day, "A Two-Dimensional Concept of Brand Loyalty," *Journal of Advertising Research*, August-September 1969, pp. 29–36; Jacoby and Kyner, "Brand Loyalty vs. Repeat Purchasing Behavior"; Jacob Jacoby and Robert W. Chestnut, *Brand Loyalty: Measurement and Management* (New York: Wiley, 1978).

51. Jacob Jacoby, "A Model of Multi-Brand Loyalty," *Journal of Advertising Research*, June–July 1971, p. 26.

52. Ronald E. Frank, William F. Massy, and Thomas L. Lodahl, "Purchasing Behavior and Personal Attributes," *Journal of Advertising Research*, December 1969–January 1970, pp. 15–24.

53. R. M. Cunningham, "Brand Loyalty—What, Where, How Much," *Harvard Business Review*, January–February 1956, pp. 116–128; "Customer Loyalty to Store and Brand," *Harvard Business Review*, November–December 1961, pp. 127–137.

54. Day, "A Two-Dimensional Concept of Brand Loyalty."

55. Marnik G. Dekimpe, Martin Mellens, Jan-Benedict E.M. Steenkamp, and Piet Vanden Abeele, "Erosion and Variability in Brand Loyalty," Marketing Science Institute Report No. 96–114, August 1996, pp. 1–25.

56. Emily DeNitto, "Branding Fever Strikes among Prescription Drugs," *Advertising Age*, November 22, 1993, p. 12.

57. Norihiko Shirouzu, "Low Smoke Cigarette Catches Fire in Japan," *Wall Street Journal*, September 8, 1997, pp. B1.

58. Sally D. Goll, "U.S. Makers Aiming to Get China into the Habit," *Wall Street Journal*, May 27, 1994, p. B1.

59. Heline, "Brand Loyalty Isn't Dead."

60. Joanne Lee-Young, "In Hong Kong, Tobacco Promotes Away," *Wall Street Journal*, June 30, 1998, p. B8.

61. Bruce Crumley, "Multipoints Adds up for Quick Burger," *Advertising Age*, November 29, 1993, p. 14.

62. Louise Lee, "Hottest Topic in Fast Food Is the Insulated French Fry," *Wall Street Journal*, October 24, 1996, pp. B1, B6.

63. Laurie Petersen, "The Strategic Shopper,"*Adweek's Marketing Week*, March 30, 1992, pp. 18–20.

64. Peter D. Dickson and Alan G. Sawyer, "Methods to Research Shoppers' Knowledge of Supermarket Prices," in ed. Richard J. Lutz, *Advances in Consumer Research*, Vol. 12 (Provo, Utah: Association for Consumer Research, 1986), pp. 584–587.

65. Kent B. Monroe and Susan M. Petroshius, "Buyers' Perception of Price: An Update of the Evidence," in eds. Harold H. Kassarjian and Thomas S. Robertson, *Perspectives in Consumer Behavior*, 3rd ed. (Dallas, Tex.: Scott-Foresman, 1981), pp. 43–55.

66. Fred R. Bleakley, "Why Shoppers Think Food Is a Rip-Off," *Wall Street Journal*, March 6, 1997, pp. B1, B6.

67. Mark Stiving and Russell S. Winer, "An Empirical Analysis of Price Endings with Scanner Data," *Journal of Consumer Research*, June 1997, pp. 57–76; Zarrel V. Lambert, "Perceived Prices as Related to Odd and Even Price Endings," *Journal of Retailing*, Fall 1975, pp. 13–22.

68. Kent B. Monroe, "The Influence of Price Differences and Brand Familiarity on Brand Preferences," *Journal of Consumer Research*, June 1976, pp. 42–49.

69. J. Jeffrey Inman, Anil C. Peter, and Priya Raghubir, "Framing the Deal: The Role of Restrictions in Accentuating Deal Value," *Journal of Consumer Research*, June 1997, pp. 68–79.

70. Dhruv Grewal, Howard Marmorstein, and Arun Sharma, "Communicating Price Information through Semantic Cues: The Moderating Effects of Situation and Discount Size," *Journal of Consumer Research*, September 1996, pp. 148–155.

71. Richard Gibson, "McDonald's 'Campaign 55' Promotion to Be Clarified and Advertised More," *Wall Street Journal*, May 20, 1997, p. B14.

72. *Supermarket Shoppers in a Period of Economic Uncertainty*, (New York: Yankelovich, Skelly, & White, 1982), p. 53; Robert Blattberg, Thomas Buesing, Peter Peacock, and Subrata K. Sen, "Who Is the Deal Prone Consumer?" in ed. H. Keith Hunt, *Advances in Consumer Research*, Vol. 5 (Ann Arbor, Mich.: Association for Consumer Research, 1978), pp. 57–62.

73. Donald R. Lichtenstein, Richard G. Netemeyer, and Scot Burton, "Assessing the Domain Specificity of Deal Proneness: A Field Study," *Journal of Consumer Research*, December 1995, pp. 314–326.

74. Cliff Edwards, "Shoppers Counting Their Pennies, Show Less Brand Loyalty to Brands," *Austin American Statesman*, May 4, 1994, pp. E1, E2.

75. Eleena de Lisser and Kevin Helliker, "Private Labels Reign in British Groceries," *Wall Street Journal*, March 3, 1994, pp. B1, B9.

76. Suein L. Hwang, "Cigarette Makers in Discount War to Lock in Share," *Wall Street Journal*, September 23, 1998, pp. B1, B4; Elyse Tanouye, "Bayer's Ads Promote Drug for Low Cost," *Wall Street Journal*, May 7, 1996, p. B3; Robert Frank, "Pepsi and Coke Are Expected to Pour Ads for Low-Priced Tea over US," *Wall Street Journal*, June 17, 1996, p. B4

77. Norihiko Shirouzu, "Whoppers Face Entrenched Foes in Japan: Big Macs," *Wall Street Journal*, February 4, 1997, pp. B1, B5.

78. Betsy Spethmann, "Re-Engineering the Price-Value Equation," *Brandweek*, September 20, 1993, pp. 44–47.

79. Tara Parker-Pope, "Colgate Places a Huge Bet on a Germ-Fighter," *Wall Street Journal*, December 29, 1997, pp. B1, B2.

80. Rekha Balu, "Anheuser-Busch Plans to Increase Its Beer Prices by 2% to 4% a Case," *Wall Street Journal*, September 27, 1998, p. B11.

81. Yumiko Ono, "'King of Beers' Wants to Rule More of Japan," *Wall Street Journal*, October 28, 1993, pp. B1, B8.

82. Dianne Solis, "Cost No Object for Mexico's Makeup Junkies," *Wall Street Journal*, June 7, 1994, pp. B1, B6.

83. Kathleen Deveny, "How Country's Biggest Brands Are Faring at the Supermarket," *Wall Street Journal*, March 24, 1994, p. B1.

84. "International Coupon Trends," *Direct Marketing*, August 1993, pp. 47–49, 83.

85. John Bussey, "Japan's Wary Shoppers Worry Two Capitals," *Wall Street Journal*, April 26, 1993, p. A1.; Yumiko Ono, "Cosmetics Industry May Get Make-Over," *Wall Street Journal*, August 17, 1993, p. B1.

86. Susan T. Fiske, "Schema Triggered Affect: Applications to Social Perception," in eds. Margaret S. Clark and Susan T. Fiske, *Affect and Cognition: The 17th Annual Carnegie Symposium on Cognition* (Hillsdale, N. J.: Lawrence Erlbaum, 1982), pp. 55–77; Mita Sujan, James R. Bettman, and Harish Sujan, "Effects of Consumer Expectations on Information Processing and Selling Encounters," *Journal of Marketing Research*, November 1986, pp. 346–353.

87. Peter L. Wright, "An Adaptive Consumer's View of Attitudes and Choice Mechanisms as Viewed by an Equally Adaptive Advertiser," in ed. William D. Wells, *Attitude Research at Bay* (Chicago: American Marketing Association, 1976) pp. 113–131.

88. Susan T. Fiske and Mark A. Pavelchak, "Category-Based versus Piecemeal-Based Affective Responses: Developments in Schema-Triggered Affect," in eds. R. M. Sorrentino and E. T. Higgins, *The Handbook of Motivation and Cognition: Foundations of Social Behavior* (New York: Guilford, 1986) pp. 167–203; David M. Boush and Barbara Loken, "A Process-Tracing Study of Brand Extension Evaluation," *Journal of Marketing Research*, February 1991, pp. 16–28.

89. Fiske, "Schema Triggered Affect"; Mita Sujan, "Consumer Knowledge: Effects on Evaluation Strategies Mediating Consumer Judgments," *Journal of Consumer Research*, June 1985, pp. 31–46.

90. Ralph I. Allison and Kenneth P. Uhl, "Influence of Beer Brand Identification on Taste Perception," *Journal of Marketing Research*, August 1964, pp. 36–39.

91. Wayne D. Hoyer and Stephen P. Brown, "Effects of Brand Awareness on Choice for a Common, Repeat-Purchase Product," *Journal of Consumer Research*, September 1990, pp. 141–148.

92. M. Carole Macklin, "Preschoolers' Learning of Brand Names from Visual Cues," *Journal of Consumer Research*, December 1996, pp. 251–261.

93. Leong, "Consumer Decision Making for Common, Repeat-Purchase Products."

94. Durairaj Maheswaran, Diane M. Mackie, and Shelly Chaiken, "Brand Name as a Heuristic Cue: The Effects of Task Importance and Expectancy Confirmation on Consumer Judgments," *Journal of Consumer Psychology*, 1 (4), 1992, pp. 317–336.

95. Richard W. Stevenson, "The Brands with Billion Dollar Names," *New York Times*, October 28, 1988, p. A1.

96. Robert W. Veryzer and J. Wesley Hutchinson, "The Influence of Unity and Prototypicality on Aesthetic Responses to New Product Designs," *Journal of Consumer Research*, March 1998, pp. 374–394.

97. Guliz Ger, "Problems of Marketization in Romania and Turkey," in eds. Clifford Schultz, Russell Belk, and Guliz Ger, *Consumption in Marketizing Economies* (Greenwich, Conn.: JAI Press, 1995).

98. Pam Weisz, "Rx for Profitable Switch to OTC brand Before Others Join the Fray," *Brandweek*, September 12, 1994, pp. 30, 32; DeNitto, "Branding Fever Strikes among Prescription Drugs."

99. Pamela Sebastian, "Nonprofit Group's Name to Go on For-Profit Pills," *Wall Street Journal*, July 13, 1994, p. B1.

100. Rebecca Quick, "Vatican Library Will Allow Companies to Use Its Name," *Wall Street Journal*, October 26, 1996, p. B11.

101. Eric Yang, "Co-brand or Be Damned," *Brandweek*, November 21, 1994, pp. 21–24.

102. Laurie Snyder and Elizabeth Jensen, "Liquor Logos Pop up in Some Surprising Places," *Wall Street Journal*, August 26, 1997, pp. B1, B15.

103. Fara Warner, "Nathan's Takes Its Dogs Global," *Adweek's Marketing Week*, June 24, 1991, p. 10.

104. Janet Guyon, "Tobacco Companies Race for Advantage in Eastern Europe While Critics Fume," *Wall Street Journal*, December 28, 1992, pp. B1, B4.

105. Valerie Reitman, "Enticed by Visions of Enormous Numbers, More Western Marketers Move into China," *Wall Street Journal*, July 12, 1993, pp. B1, B6.

106. Karen Benezra, "Brock Party," *Brandweek*, March 27, 1995, pp. 25–30.

107. M. Venkatesan, "Cognitive Consistency and Novelty Seeking," in eds. Scott Ward and Thomas S. Robertson, *Consumer Behavior: Theoretical Sources* (Englewood Cliffs, N. J.: Prentice-Hall, 1973), pp. 354–384; Leigh McAlister, "A Dynamic Attribute Satiation Model of Variety Seeking Behavior," *Journal of Consumer Research*, September 1982, pp. 141–150.

108. Hans C.M. Van Trijp, Wayne D. Hoyer, and J. Jeffrey Inman, "Why Switch? Product Category-Level Explanaations for True Variety Seeking" *Journal of Marketing Research*, August 1996, pp. 281–292; Wayne D. Hoyer and Nancy M. Ridgway, "Variety Seeking as an Explanation for Exploratory Purchase Behavior: A Theoretical Model," in ed. Thomas C. Kinnear. *Advances in Consumer Research*, Vol. 11 (Ann Arbor, Mich.: Association for Consumer Research, 1984), pp. 114–119.

109. Saatya Menon and Barbara E. Kahn, "The Impact of Context on Variety Seeking in Product Choices," *Journal of Consumer Research*, December 1995, pp. 285–295.

110. Erich A. Joachimsthaler and John L. Lastovicka, "Optimal Stimulation Level-Exploratory Behavior Models," *Journal of Consumer Research*, December 1984, pp. 830–835.

111. Albert Mehrabian and James Russell, *An Approach to Environmental Psychology* (Cambridge, Mass.: MIT Press, 1974).

112. Linda L. Price and Nancy M. Ridgway, "Use Innovativeness, Vicarious Exploration and Purchase Exploration: Three Facets of Consumer Varied Behavior," in ed. Bruce Walker, *American Marketing Association Educators' Conference Proceedings* (Chicago: American Marketing Association, 1982), pp. 56–60.

113. Laurie M. Grossman, "Flavored Soda Growth Outpaces Colas as Thirst for Novelty Grows," *Wall Street Journal*, December 14, 1993, p. B8.

114. Michael Selz, "As Fast Food Menus Add Items, Dyspeptic Diners Cry, 'No More,' *Wall Street Journal*, July 25, 1995, pp. B1, B2.

115. Robert Frank, "Fruity Teas and Mystical Sodas Are Boring Consumers," *Wall Street Journal*, October 9, 1996, pp. B1, B2.

116. Dennis W. Rook, "The Buying Impulse," *Journal of Consumer Research*, September 1987, pp. 189–199; Craig J. Thompson, William B. Locander, and Howard R. Pollio, "The Lived Meaning of Free Choice: Existential-Phenomenological Description of Everyday Consumer Experiences of Contemporary Married Women," *Journal of Consumer Research*, December 1990, pp. 346–361.

117. Laura E. Keeton, "Travel Tempts Even the Thrifty to Splurge," *Wall Street Journal*, September 27, 1995, pp. B1, B8.

118. J. Jeffrey Inman and Russell S. Winer, "Where the Rubber Meets the Road: A Model of In-store Consumer Decision Making," *Marketing Science Institute Report Summary*, December 1998, pp. 98–122; "How We Shop . . . From Mass to Market," *Brandweek*, January 9, 1995, p. 17; Danny Bellenger, D. H. Robertson, and Elizabeth C. Hirschman, "Impulse Buying Varies by Product," *Journal of Advertising Research*, December 1978–January 1979, pp. 15–18.

119. Cathy J. Cobb and Wayne D. Hoyer, "Planned vs. Impulse Purchase Behavior," *Journal of Retailing*, Winter 1986, pp. 384–409.

120. Rook, "The Buying Impulse."

121. Russell W. Belk, "Materialism: Trait Aspects of Living in a Material World," *Journal of Consumer Research*, December 1985, pp. 265–280; P. S. Raju, "Optimum Stimulation Level: Its Relationship to Personality, Demographics, and Exploratory Behavior," *Journal of Consumer Research*, December 1980, pp. 272–282; Danny Bellenger and P. K. Korgaonkar, "Profiling the Recreational Shopper," *Journal of Retailing*, Fall 1980, pp. 77–92.

122. Dennis W. Rook and Robert J. Fisher, "Normative Influences on Impulsive Buying Behavior," *Journal of Consumer Research*, December 1995, pp. 305–313; Radhika Puri, "Measuring and Modifying Consumer Impulsiveness: A Cost-Benefit Accessibility Framework," *Journal of Consumer Psychology*, .5 (2), 1996, pp. 87–114.

123. Inman and Winer, "Where the Rubber Meets the Road"

124. Nancy Millman, "Horn of Plenty Has Its Price," *Austin American Statesman*, August 8, 1996, pp. D1, D2.

125. Pam Weisz, "Brach's, Tobler Slick up for Impulse Eyes," *Brandweek*, December 12, 1994, p. 8.
126. John Bussey, "Japan's Wary Shoppers Worry Two Capitals," *Wall Street Journal*, April 26, 1993, p. A1.

CHAPTER 12

1. Rachel Beck, "Online Shopping Horror Tales Begin to Emerge," *Austin American Statesman*, January 19, 1999, pp. D1, D2.
2. For a review, see William H. Cummings and M. Venkatesan, "Cognitive Dissonance and Consumer Behavior: A Review of the Evidence," *Journal of Marketing Research*, August 1976, pp. 303–308; also see Dieter Frey and Marita Rosch, "Information Seeking after Decisions: The Roles of Novelty of Information and Decision Reversibility," *Personality and Social Psychology Bulletin*, March 1984, pp. 91–98.
3. Stephen J. Hoch and John Deighton, "Managing What Consumers Learn from Experience," *Journal of Marketing*, April 1989, pp. 1–20.
4. Allan Pavio, *Imagery and Verbal Processes* (New York: Holt, Rinehart, & Winston, 1981).
5. Robert E. Smith and William R. Swinyard, "Information Response Models: An Integrated Approach," *Journal of Marketing*, Winter 1982, pp. 81–93; Deanna S. Kempf and Robert E. Smith, "Consumer Processing of Product Trial and the Influence of Prior Advertising: A Structural Modeling Approach," *Journal of Marketing Research*, August 1998, pp. 325–338.
6. Ida E. Berger and Andrew A. Mitchell, "The Effect of Advertising on Attitude Accessibility, Attitude Confidence, and the Attitude-Behavior Relationship," *Journal of Consumer Research*, December 1989, pp. 269–279. Alice A. Wright and John G. Lynch Jr., "Communication Effects of Advertising vs. Direct Experience When Both Search and Experience Attributes Are Present," *Journal of Consumer Research*, March 1995, pp. 708–718.
7. Patricia M. West, "Predicting Preferences: An Examination of Agent Learning," *Journal of Consumer Research*, June 1996, pp. 68–80.
8. Merrie Brucks, "The Effects of Product Class Knowledge on Information Search Behavior," *Journal of Consumer Research*, June 1985, pp. 1–16.
9. Joseph W. Alba and J. Wesley Hutchinson, "Dimensions of Consumer Expertise," *Journal of Consumer Research*, March 1987, pp. 411–454.
10. Eric J. Johnson and J. Edward Russo, "Product Familiarity and Learning New Information," *Journal of Consumer Research*, June 1984, pp. 542–551.
11. Stephen J. Hoch and Young-Won Ha, "Consumer Learning: Advertising and the Ambiguity of Product Experience," *Journal of Consumer Research*, October 1986, pp. 221–233.
12. Ibid; Paul Herr, Steven J. Sherman, and Russell H. Fazio, "On the Consequences of Priming: Assimilation and Contrast Effects," *Journal of Experimental Social Psychology*, July 1983, pp. 323–340.
13. Reid Hastie, "Causes and Effects of Causal Attributions," *Journal of Personality and Social Psychology*, July 1984, pp. 44–56; Thomas K. Srull, Meryl Lichtenstein, and Myron Rothbart, "Associative Storage and Retrieval Processes in Person Memory," *Journal of Experimental Psychology: General*, 11 (6), 1985, pp. 316–435.
14. Durairaj Maheswaran, "Country of Origin as a Stereotype: Effects of Consumer Expertise and Attribute Strength on Product Evaluations," *Journal of Consumer Research*, September 1994, pp. 354–365.
15. John Deighton, "The Interaction of Advertising and Evidence," *Journal of Consumer Research*, December 1984, pp. 763–770; Hoch and Ha, "Consumer Learning."
16. Bernard Weiner, "Spontaneous Causal Thinking," *Psychological Bulletin*, January 1985, pp. 74–84.
17. Hoch and Deighton, "Managing What Consumers Learn from Experience."
18. Rekha Balu, "Heinz Places Ketchup in Global Account," *Wall Street Journal*, September 9, 1998, pp. B8.
19. Kathry Chen, "KFC Rules Fast-Food Roost in Shanghai,' *Wall Street Journal*, December 2, 1997, pp. B1, B12.
20. Yumiko Ono, "Anheuser Plays on Tipsiness to Sell Japan Strong Brew," *Wall Street Journal*, November 17, 1998, pp. B1, B4.
21. Joseph Pereira, "Unknown Fruit Takes on Unfamiliar Markets," *Wall Street Journal*, November 9, 1995, pp. B1, B5.
22. Youjae Yi, "A Critical Review of Consumer Satisfaction," in *Review of Marketing* (Chicago: American Marketing Association, 1992), pp. 68–123.
23. Richard L. Oliver, "Processing of the Satisfaction Response in Consumption: A Suggested Framework and Research Propositions," *Journal of Consumer Satisfaction, Dissatisfaction, and Complaining Behavior*, 2 (1989), pp. 1–16; Mano and Oliver, "Assessing the Dimensionality and Structure of the Consumption Experience."
24. Haim Mano and Richard L. Oliver, "Assessing the Dimensionality and Structure of the Consumption Experience: Evaluation, Feeling, and Satisfaction," *Journal of Consumer Research*, December 1993, pp. 451–466.
25. Michael D. Johnson, Eugene W. Anderson, and Claes Fornell, "Rational and Adaptive Performance Expectations in a Customer Satisfaction Framework," *Journal of Consumer Research*, March 1995, pp. 695–707.
26. Richard L. Oliver, "Measurement and Evaluation of Satisfaction Processes in Retail Settings," *Journal of Retailing*, Fall 1981, pp. 25–48.
27. Sarah Fisher Gardial, D. Scott Clemons, Robert B. Woodruff, David W. Schumann, and Mary Jane Burns, "Comparing Consumers' Recall of Prepurchase and Postpurchase Evaluation Experiences," *Journal of Consumer Research*, March 1994, pp. 548–560.
28. Marsha L. Richins and Peter H. Bloch, "Post-purchase Satisfaction: Incorporating the Effects of Involvement and Time," *Journal of Business Research*, September 1991, pp. 145–158.
29. Mary C. Gilly and Betsy D. Gelb, "Post-purchase Consumer Processes and the Complaining Consumer," *Journal of Consumer Research*, December 1982, pp. 323–328.
30. Claes Fornell, "A National Customer Satisfaction Barometer: The Swedish Experience," *Journal of Marketing*, January 1992, pp. 6–21.

31. Roberto C. Goizueta, "The Business of Customer Satisfaction," *Quality Progress*, February 1989, pp. 42–43. © 1989 American Society for Quality. Reprinted with permission.

32. George Anders, "Amazon.com Sales More than Quadruple," *Wall Street Journal*, July 23, 1998, p. B5.

33. Terry Vavra, "Learning from Your Losses," *Brandweek*, December 7, 1992, pp. 20–22.

34. Tim Triplett, "Product Recall Spurs Company to Improve Customer Satisfaction," *Marketing News*, April 11, 1994, p. 6.

35. "American Customer Satisfaction Index (ACSI) Methodology Report," National Quality Research Center, University of Michigan, December 1995.

36. Chad Rubel, "Pizza Hut Explores Customer Satisfaction," Marketing News, March 25, 1996, p. 15.

37. Nick Wingfield, "A Marketer's Dream," *Wall Street Journal*, December 7, 1998, p. R20.

38. Randy Brandt, "Satisfaction Studies Must Measure What the Customer Wants and Expects," *Marketing News*, October 27, 1997, p. 17.

39. Robert A. Westbrook, "Product/Consumption-Based Affective Responses and Postpurchase Processes," *Journal of Marketing Research*, August 1987, pp. 258–270.

40. Charlotte Klopp and John Sterlickhi, "Customer Satisfaction Just Catching on in Europe," *Marketing News*, May 28, 1990, p. 5.

41. Fornell, "A National Customer Satisfaction Barometer."

42. F. G. Crane, "Consumer Satisfaction/Dissatisfaction with Professional Services," *Journal of Professional Services Marketing*, 7 (2), 1991, pp. 19–25.

43. Brad Gale, "Satisfaction Is Not Enough," *Marketing News*, October 27, 1997, p. 18.

44. Vavra, "Learning from Your Losses."

45. Klopp and Sterlickhi, "Customer Satisfaction Just Catching on in Europe."

46. Kathleen Deveney, "Blame It on Dashed Hopes (and Oprah): Disillusioned Dieters Shun Liquid Meals," *Wall Street Journal*, October 13, 1992, pp. B1, B10.

47. Richard Gibson, "Waiter, I'd Like Another Waiter," *Wall Street Journal*, July 14, 1993, p. B1.

48. "Dial 'A' for Aggravation," *Business Week*, March 11, 1996, p. 34.

49. Guliz Ger, Russell Belk, and Dana-Nicoleta Lascu, "The Development of Consumer Desire in Marketing and Developing Economies: The Cases of Romania and Turkey," in eds. Leigh McAlister and Michael L. Rothschild, *Advances in Consumer Research*, Vol. 20 (Provo, Utah: Association for Consumer Research, 1993), pp. 102–107.

50. Richard L. Oliver, "A Cognitive Model of the Antecedents and Consequences of Satisfaction Decisions," *Journal of Marketing Research*, November 1980, pp. 460–469; Yu, "A Critical Review of Consumer Satisfaction," p. 92; see also Douglas M. Stayman, Dana L. Alden, and Karen H. Smith, "Some Effects of Schematic Processing on Consumer Expectations and Disconfirmation Judgments," *Journal of Consumer Research*, September 1992, pp. 240–255.

51. Yi, "A Critical Review of Consumer Satisfaction," p. 92; see also Douglas M. Stayman, Dana L. Alden, and Karen H. Smith, "Some Effects of Schematic Processing on Consumer Expectations and Disconfirmation Judgments," *Journal of Consumer Research*, September 1992, pp. 240–255.

52. Praveen K. Kopalle and Donald R. Lehman, "The Effects of Advertised and Observed Quality on Expectations about New Product Quality," *Journal of Marketing Research*, August 1995, pp. 280–291; Stephen A. LaTour and Nancy C. Peat, "The Role of Situationally-Produced Expectations, Others' Experiences, and Prior Experiences in Determining Satisfaction," in ed. Jerry C. Olson, *Advances in Consumer Research* (Ann Arbor, Mich.: Association for Consumer Research, 1980), pp. 588–592; Ernest R. Cadotte, Robert B. Woodruff, and Roger L. Jenkins, "Expectations and Norms in Models of Consumer Satisfaction," *Journal of Marketing Research*, August 1987, pp. 305–314.

53. David K. Tse and Peter C. Wilson, "Models of Consumer Satisfaction Formation: An Extension," *Journal of Marketing Research*, May 1988, pp. 204–212.

54. Guliz Ger, "Problems of Marketization in Romania and Turkey," in eds. Clifford Shultz, Russell Belk, and Guliz Ger, *Consumption in Marketizing Economies* (Greenwich, Conn.: JAI Press, 1995).

55. Ruth N. Bolton and James H. Drew, "A Multistage Model of Customers' Assessments of Service Quality and Value," *Journal of Consumer Research*, March 1991, pp. 375–384; Michael D. Johnson, Eugene W. Anderson, and Claes Fornell, "Rational and Adaptive Performance Expectations in a Customer Satisfaction Framework," *Journal of Consumer Research*, March 1995, pp. 695–707.

56. Glenn B. Voss, A. Parasuraman, and Dhruv Grewal, "The Roles of Price, Performance, and Expectations in Determining Satisfaction in Service Exchanges," *Journal of Marketing*, October 1998, pp. 46–61; A. Parasuraman, Valerie A. Zeithaml, and Leonard L. Berry, "SERVQUAL: A Multiple-Item Scale for Measuring Consumer Perceptions of Service Quality," *Journal of Retailing*, Spring 1988, pp. 12–36.

57. Martha Slud, "Properly Packed Sacks Keep Customers Coming Back." *Marketing News*, May 20, 1996, p. 5.

58. Johnson, Anderson, and Fornell, "Rational and Adaptive Performance Expectations in a Customer Satisfaction Framework."

59. Tse and Wilson, "Models of Consumer Satisfaction Formation"; Richard L. Oliver, "Cognitive, Affective, and Attribute-Bases of the Satisfaction Response," *Journal of Consumer Research*, December 1993, pp. 418–430; Richard L. Oliver and Wayne S. DeSarbo, "Response Determinants in Satisfaction Judgments," *Journal of Consumer Research*, March 1988, pp. 495–507.

60. Gilbert A. Churchill and Carol Supranant, "An Investigation into the Determinants of Customer Satisfaction," *Journal of Marketing Research*, November 1982, pp. 491–504; Richard L. Oliver and William O. Bearden, "The Role of Involvement in Satisfaction Processes," in eds. Richard P. Bagozzi and Alice M. Tybout, *Advances in Consumer Research*, Vol. 10 (Ann Arbor, Mich.: Association for Consumer Research, 1983), pp. 250–255; Paul G. Patterson, "Expectations and Product Performance as Determinants of Satisfaction for a High Involvement Purchase," *Psychology and Marketing*, September–October 1993, pp. 449–465.

61. Robert A. Westbrook and Michael D. Reilly, "Value-Percept Disparity: An Alternative to the Disconfirmation of Expectations Theory of Consumer Satisfaction," in

eds. Richard P. Bagozzi and Alice M. Tybout, *Advances in Consumer Research*, Vol. 10 (Ann Arbor, Mich.: Association for Consumer Research, 1983), pp. 256–261.

62. William O. Bearden and Jesse E. Teel, "Selected Determinants of Consumer Satisfaction and Complaint Reports," *Journal of Marketing Research*, February 1983, pp. 21–28; John E. Swan and I. Frederick Trawick, "Disconfirmation of Expectations and Satisfaction with a Retail Service," *Journal of Retailing*, Fall 1981, pp. 49–67; Westbrook and Reilly, "Value-Percept Disparity."

63. Westbrook, "Product/Consumption-Based Affective Responses and Postpurchase Processes"; Robert A. Westbrook and Richard L. Oliver, "The Dimensionality of Consumption Emotion Patterns and Consumer Satisfaction," *Journal of Consumer Research*, June 1991, pp. 84–91; Mano and Oliver, "Assessing the Dimensionality and Structure of the Consumption Experience."

64. Westbrook and Oliver, "The Dimensionality of Consumption Emotion Patterns."

65. Paul W. Miniard, Sunil Bhatla, and Deepak Sirdeshmukh, "Mood as a Determinant of Postconsumption Product Evaluations: Mood Effects and Their Dependency on the Affective Intensity of the Consumption Experience," *Journal of Consumer Psychology*, 1992, pp. 173–195.

66. Scott McCartney, "Chaos in the Aisles: Airlines Try to Speed Up Boarding," *Wall Street Journal*, March 8, 1996, p. B1, B6.

67. Sally D. Goll, "Pizza Hut Tosses Its Pies into the Ring," *Wall Street Journal*, May 27, 1994, p. B1.

68. Richard W. Olshavsky and John A. Miller, "Consumer Expectations, Product Performance, and Perceived Product Quality," *Journal of Marketing Research*, February 1972, pp. 469–499.

69. Goll, "Pizza Hut Tosses Its Pies into the Ring."

70. Norihiko Shirouzu, "P & G's Joy Makes an Unlikely Splash in Japan," *Wall Street Journal*, December 10, 1997, pp. B1, B8.

71. Diane Halstead, Cornelia Droge, and M. Bixby Cooper, "Product Warranties and Post-purchase Service," *Journal of Services Marketing*, 7 (1), 1993, pp. 33–40; Joshua Lyle Wiener, "Are Warranties Accurate Signals of Product Reliability?" *Journal of Consumer Research*, September 1985, pp. 245–250.

72. Ger, "Problems of Marketization in Romania and Turkey."

73. Rebecca Quick, "Surging Volume of E-mail Brings Blackouts at AOL," *Wall Street Journal*, November 25, 1997, pp. B1, B7.

74. Rodney Ho, "Virtual Reality Games Aren't Scoring with Players," *Wall Street Journal*, September 16, 1997, pp. B1, B2.

75. Nichole M. Christain, "One Weekend, 52 Jeeps, a Chance to Bond," *Wall Street Journal*, May 23, 1997, pp. B1, B2.

76. Natalia A. Feduschak and Brian Coleman, "Air Ukraine Promises Friendly Skies, Too," *Wall Street Journal*, October 19, 1992, p. B3.

77. "Stretching to New Lengths," *Brandweek*, March 22, 1993, pp. 24–29.

78. Joanne Lee-Young, "In Hong Kond, Tobacco Promotes Away," *Wall Street Journal*, June 30, 1998, pp. B8.

79. Valerie S. Folkes, "Consumer Reactions to Product Failure: An Attributional Approach," *Journal of Consumer Research*, March 1984, pp. 398–409; Valerie S. Folkes, "Recent Attribution Research in Consumer Behavior: A Review and New Directions," *Journal of Consumer Research*, March 1988, pp. 548–565; Richard W. Mizerski, Linda L. Golden, and Jerome B. Kernan, "The Attribution Process in Consumer Decision Making," *Journal of Consumer Research*, September 1979, pp. 123–140.

80. Mary Jo Bitner, "Evaluating Service Encounters: The Effects of Physical Surrounding and Employee Responses," *Journal of Marketing*, April 1990, pp. 69–82.

81. Valerie S. Folkes, Susan Koletsky, and John L. Graham, "A Field Study of Causal Inferences and Consumer Reaction: The View from the Airport," *Journal of Consumer Research*, March 1987, pp. 534–539.

82. Elaine Underwood, "Up, Up, and Away," *Brandweek*, September 20, 1993, pp. 25–30.

83. Eleena de Lisser, "Banks Court Disenchanted Customers," *Wall Street Journal*, August 30, 1993, p. B1.

84. Eric Hollreiser, "Brand America Takes a Beating in Japan," *Adweek's Marketing Week*, January 13, 1992, p. 5.

85. Bitner, "Evaluating Service Encounters."

86. Richard L. Oliver and John E. Swan, "Equity and Disconfirmation Paradigms as Influences on Merchant and Product Satisfaction," *Journal of Consumer Research*, December 1989, pp. 372–383; Elaine G. Walster, G. William Walster, and Ellen Berscheid, *Equity: Theory and Research* (Boston: Allyn & Bacon, 1978).

87. Richard L. Oliver and John L. Swan, "Consumer Perceptions of Interpersonal Equity and Satisfaction in Transactions, A Field Survey Approach," *Journal of Marketing*, April 1989, pp. 21–35.

88. Ger, "Problems of Marketization in Romania and Turkey."

89. Day, "Modeling Choices among Alternative Responses to Dissatisfaction"; Marsha L. Richins, "Word-of-Mouth Communication as Negative Information," *Journal of Marketing*, Winter 1983, pp. 68–78.

90. Day, "Modeling Choices among Alternative Responses to Dissatisfaction"; Arthur Best and Alan R. Andreasen, "Consumer Response to Unsatisfactory Purchases," *Law and Society*, Spring 1977, pp. 701–742.

91. Gibson, "Waiter, I'd Like Another Waiter."

92. Lisa Miller, "Car Rental Industry Promises That Things Will Improve. Really," *Wall Street Journal*, July 17, 1997, pp. A1, A8.

93. Thomas Goetz, "Furious at Airlines, Travelers File Flurry of Complaints," *Wall Street Journal*, February 9, 1999, pp. B1, B4.

94. Kitty Crider, "Grocery Store Gripes," *Austin American Statesman*, October 23, 1991, pp. C1, C2.

95. Goizueta, "The Business of Customer Satisfaction."

96. Bearden and Teel, "Selected Determinants of Consumer Satisfaction and Complaint Reports."

97. Cathy Goodwin and Ivan Ross, "Consumer Evaluations of Responses to Complaints: What's Fair and Why," *Journal of Services Marketing*, Summer 1990, pp. 53–61.

98. Day, "Modeling Choices among Alternative Responses to Dissatisfaction"; Jagdip Singh and Roy D. Howell, "Consumer Complaining Behavior: A Review," in eds. H. Keith Hunt and Ralph L. Day, *Consumer Satisfaction, Dissatisfaction, and Complaining Behavior* (Bloomington, Ind.: Indiana University Press, 1985).

99. S. Krishnan and S. A. Valle, "Dissatisfaction Attributions and Consumer Complaint Behavior," in ed. William L. Wilkie, *Advances in Consumer Research* (Miami: Association for Consumer Research, 1979), pp. 445–449.

100. Folkes, "Consumer Reactions to Product Failure."

101. Kjell Gronhaug and Gerald R. Zaltman, "Complainers and Noncomplainers Revisited: Another Look at the Data," in ed. Kent B. Monroe, *Advances in Consumer Research* (Ann Arbor, Mich.: Association for Consumer Research, 1981), pp. 159–165.

102. Ger, "Problems of Marketization in Romania and Turkey."

103. Larry M. Robinson and Robert L. Berl, "What about Compliments? A Follow-up Study on Consumer Complaints and Compliments," in eds. H. Keith Hunt and Ralph L. Day, *Refining Concepts and Measures of Consumer Satisfaction and Complaining Behavior* (Bloomington, Ind.: Indiana University Press, 1980), pp. 144–148.

104. T. Bettina Cornwell, Alan David Bligh, and Emin Babakus, "Complaint Behaviors of Mexican-American Consumers to a Third Party Agency," *Journal of Consumer Affairs*, Summer 1991, pp. 1–18.

105. Sigfredo A. Hernandez, William Strahle, Hector Garcia, and Robert C. Sorenson, "A Cross-Cultural Study of Consumer Complaining Behavior: VCR Owners in the U.S. and Puerto Rico," *Journal of Consumer Policy*, June 1991, pp. 35–62.

106. Jagdip Singh, "A Typology of Consumer Dissatisfaction Response Styles," *Journal of Retailing*, Spring 1990, pp. 57–99.

107. Thomas Petzinger Jr., "Customer from Hell Can Be a Blessing in Disguise for Sales," *Wall Street Journal*, March 1, 1996, p. B1.

108. Denise T. Smart and Charles L. Martin, "Manufacturer Responsiveness to Consumer Correspondence: An Empirical Investigation of Consumer Perceptions," *Journal of Consumer Affairs*, Summer 1992, pp. 104–128; Mary Gilly and Betsy Gelb, "Post-purchase Consumer Processes and the Complaining Consumer Behavior," *Journal of Consumer Research*, December 1982, pp. 323–328.

109. Chow-Hou Wee and Celine Chong, "Determinants of Consumer Satisfaction/Dissatisfaction towards Dispute Settlements in Singapore," *European Journal of Marketing*, 25 (10), 1991, pp. 6–16.

110. Alan J. Resnick and Robert R. Harmon, "Consumer Complaints and Managerial Response: A Holistic Approach," *Journal of Marketing*, Winter 1983, pp. 86–97.

111. Emily Nelson, "Shower or Bath? It's a Hotel's Tough Call," *Wall Street Journal*, May 14, 1998, pp. B1, B11.

112. Stephanie Anderson Forest, "Customers Must Be Pleased, Not Just Satisfied," *Business Week*, August 3, 1992, p. 52.

113. Klopp and Sterlickhi, "Customer Satisfaction Just Catching on in Europe."

114. Halstead, Droge, and Cooper, "Product Warranties and Post-purchase Service."

115. Bill Spindle, "Tourists with Quake Discounts Might Ask: Is This Trip Necessary?" *Wall Street Journal*, May 6, 1998, p. B1.

116. Ger, "Problems of Marketization in Romania and Turkey."

117. Claes Fornell and Nicholas M. Didow, "Economic Constraints on Consumer Complaining Behavior," in ed. Jerry C. Olson, *Advances in Consumer Research*, Vol. 7 (Ann Arbor, Mich.: Association for Consumer Research, 1980), pp. 318–323; Claes Fornell and Birger Wernerfelt, "Defensive Marketing Strategy by Customer Complaint Management," *Journal of Marketing Research*, November 1987, pp. 337–346.

118. Claes Fornell and Robert A. Westbrook, "The Vicious Cycle of Consumer Complaints," *Journal of Marketing*, Summer 1984, pp. 68–78.

119. Richins, "Word-of-Mouth Communication as Negative Information."

120. Yi, "A Critical Review of Consumer Satisfaction"; Johan Arndt, "Word-of-Mouth Advertising and Perceived Risk," in eds. Harold H. Kassarjian and Thomas R. Robertson, *Perspectives in Consumer Behavior* (Glenview, Ill.: Scott-Foresman, 1968).

121. Rebecca Quick, "Cranky Consumers Devise Web Sites to Air Complaints," *Wall Street Journal*, December 26, 1997, pp. B1, B10.

122. Frederick F. Reichheld, *The Loyalty Effect: The Hidden Force behind Growth* (Boston: Harvard Business School Press, 1996).

123. Priscilla La Barbera and David W. Mazursky, "A Longitudinal Assessment of Consumer Satisfaction/ Dissatisfaction: The Dynamic Aspect of Cognitive Processes," *Journal of Marketing Research*, November 1983, pp. 393–404; Ruth Bolton, "A Dynamic Model of the Duration of the Customer's Relationship with a Continuous Service Provider," *Marketing Science*, 17 (1) 1998, pp. 45–65.

124. Thomas O. Jones and W. Earl Sasser, "Why Customers Defect," *Harvard Business Review*, November–December 1995, pp. 88–99.

125. Frederick F. Reichheld and W. Earl Sasser, "Zero Defections: Quality Comes to Services," *Harvard Business Review*, September 1990, pp. 105–111; Eugene Anderson, Claes Fornell, and Donald H. Lehman, "Customer Satisfaction, Market Share, and Profitablility: Findings from Sweden," *Journal of Marketing*, July 1994, pp. 53–66; Rajendra K. Srivastava, Tassadduq A. Shervani, and Liam Fahey, "Market-Based Assets and Shareholder Value: A Framework for Analysis," *Journal of Marketing*, 62 (1), 1998, pp. 2–18.

126. Reichheld, *The Loyalty Effect*.

127. Melissa Martin Young and Melanie Wallendorf, "Ashes to Ashes, Dust to Dust: Conceptualizing Consumer Disposition of Possessions," in *Proceedings, Marketing Educators' Conference* (Chicago: American Marketing Association, 1989), pp. 33–39.

128. Ibid; see also Jacob Jacoby, Carol K. Berning, and Thomas F. Dietvorst, "What about Disposition?" *Journal of Marketing*, April 1977, pp. 22–28; Gilbert D. Harrell and Diane M. McConocha, "Personal Factors Related to Consumer Product Disposal," *Journal of Consumer Affairs*, Winter 1992, pp. 397–417.

129. Jacoby, Berning, and Dietvorst, "What about Disposition?" Young and Wallendorf, "Ashes to Ashes, Dust to Dust."

130. Harrell and McConocha, "Personal Factors Related to Consumer Product Disposal Tendencies."

131. Jacoby, Berning, and Dietvorst, "What about Disposition?"

132. John B. Sherry, Mary Ann McGrath, and Sidney J. Levy, "The Disposition of the Gift and Many Unhappy Returns," *Journal of Retailing*, Spring 1992, pp. 40–65.

133. Young and Wallendorf, "Ashes to Ashes, Dust to Dust."

134. Russell W. Belk, "Possessions and the Extended Self," *Journal of Consumer Research*, September 1988, pp. 139–168.

135. Young and Wallendorf, "Ashes to Ashes, Dust to Dust."

136. Melissa Martin Young, "Disposition of Possessions during Role Transitions," in eds. Rebecca H. Holman and Michael R. Solomon, *Advances in Consumer Research*, Vol. 18 (Provo, Utah: Association for Consumer Research, 1991), pp. 33–39.

137. James H. Alexander, "Divorce, the Disposition of the Relationship, and Everything," in eds. Rebecca H. Holman and Michael R. Solomon, *Advances in Consumer Research*, Vol. 18 (Provo, Utah: Association for Consumer Research, 1991), pp. 43–48.

138. James H. Alexander, John W. Shouten, and Scott D. Roberts, "Consumer Behavior and Divorce," in eds. Janeen Costa and Russell W. Belk, *Research in Consumer Behavior*, Vol. 6 (Greenwich, Conn.: JAI Press, 1993), pp. 153–184.

139. For more information on this topic, see David J. Cheal, "Intergenerational Family Transfers," *Journal of Marriage and the Family*, November 1983, pp. 805–813; Jeffrey P. Rosenfeld, "Bequests from Resident to Resident: Inheritance in a Retirement Community," *The Gerontologist*, 19 (6), 1979, pp. 594–600.

140. John F. Sherry Jr., "A Sociocultural Analysis of a Midwestern Flea Market," *Journal of Consumer Research*, June 1990, pp. 13–30.

141. Ibid; Russell W. Belk, John F. Sherry, and Melanie Wallendorf, "A Naturalistic Inquiry into Buyer and Seller Behavior at a Swap Meet," *Journal of Consumer Research*, March 1988, pp. 449–470.

142. Michael D. Reilly and Melanie Wallendorf, "A Comparison of Group Differences in Food Consumption Using Household Refuse," *Journal of Consumer Research*, September 1987, pp. 289–294.

143. Jacoby, Berning, and Dietvorst, "What about Disposition?"

144. For a review, see L. J. Shrum, Tina M. Lowrey, and John A. McCarty, "Recycling as a Marketing Problem: A Framework for Strategy Development," *Psychology and Marketing*, July–August 1994, pp. 393–416.

145. J. M. Hines, H. R. Hungerford, and A. N. Tomera, "Analysis and Synthesis of Research on Responsible Environmental Behavior: A Meta-Analysis," *Journal of Environmental Education*, Winter 1987, pp. 1–8.

146. Rik G. M. Pieters, "Changing Garbage Disposal Patterns of Consumers: Motivation, Ability, and Performance," *Journal of Public Policy and Marketing*, Fall 1991, pp. 59–76.

147. Richard P. Bagozzi and Pratibha Dabholkar, "Consumer Recycling Goals and Their Effect on Decisions to Recycle," *Psychology and Marketing*, July–August 1994, pp. 313–340.

148. E. Howenstein, "Marketing Segmentation for Recycling," *Environment and Behavior*, March 1993, pp. 86–102.

149. Shrum, Lowrey, and McCarty, "Recycling as a Marketing Problem."

150. Susan E. Heckler, "The Role of Memory in Understanding and Encouraging Recycling Behavior," *Psychology and Marketing*, July–August 1994, pp. 375–392.

151. Rik G. M. Pieters, "Changing Garbage Disposal Patterns of Consumers."

152. Kenneth R. Lord, "Motivating Recycling Behavior: A Quasi-Experimental Investigation of Message and Source Strategies," *Psychology and Marketing*, July–August 1994, pp. 341–358.

153. S. M. Burn and Stuart Oskamp, "Increasing Community Recycling with Persuasive Communications and Public Commitment," *Journal of Applied Social Psychology*, Vol. 16, 1986, pp. 29–41.

154. Heckler, "The Role of Memory in Understanding and Encouraging Recycling Behavior."

CHAPTER 13

1. This example is taken from the article by Barbara Martinez, "Dog Food, Toothpaste and Oreos Star on Popular Hispanic Television Program," *Wall Street Journal*, March 25, 1997, pp. B1, B17.

2. Ignacio Vazquez, "Mexicans Are Buying 'Made in USA' Food," *Marketing News*, August 31, 1998, p. 14.

3. Melanie Wallendorf and Eric Arnould, "We Gather Together: Consumption Rituals of Thanksgiving Day," *Journal of Consumer Research*, June 1991, pp. 13–31.

4. Scott Kilman & Robert L. Rose, "Population of Rural America Is Swelling," *Wall Street Journal*, June 21, 1996, pp. B1, B2.

5. Thomas E. Weber, "Add Internet to List of Useful Farm Tools," *Wall Street Journal*, May 28, 1996, pp. A21, A26.

6. Joel Garreau, *The Nine Nations of North America* (Boston: Houghton-Mifflin, 1981).

7. Lynn R. Kahle, "The Nine Nations of North America and the Value Basis of Geographic Segmentation," *Journal of Marketing*, April 1986, pp. 37–47.

8. Susan Mitchell, "Birds of a Feather," *American Demographics*, February 1995, pp. 40–48.

9. Michael J. Weiss, *The Clustering of America* (New York: Harper & Row, 1988); Mitchell, "Birds of a Feather."

10. Kahle, "The Nine Nations of North America and the Value Basis of Geographic Segmentation."

11. J. Alex Targuino, "King of Grits Alters Menu to Reflect Northern Tastes," *Wall Street Journal*, August 22, 1997, pp. B1, B5.

12. Mitchell, "Birds of a Feather."

13. Yumiko Ono, "Kraft Foods, TCI to Target Cable-TV Ads," *Wall Street Journal*, February 5, 1998, p. B10.

14. Ricardo Sookdeo, "The New Global Consumer," *Fortune*, Autumn–Winter 1993, pp. 68–77.

15. Ignacio Galceran and Jon Berry, "A New World of Consumers," *American Demographics*, March 1995, pp. 27–33.

16. Sak Onkvisit and John J. Shaw, *International Marketing: Analysis and Strategy* (Columbus, Ohio: Merrill, 1989).

17. Ronald A. Fullerton, "Marketing and the Economic Redevelopment in East Germany: Field Observation and Theoretical Analysis," in ed. Luiz V. Dominguez,

Marketing and Economic Reconstruction in the Developing World: Proceedings of the Fourth International Conference on Marketing and Development (San Jose, Costa Rica: INCAE, 1993), pp. 145–151.

18. Galceran and Berry, "A New World of Consumers."
19. Valerie Reitman, "India Anticipates the Arrival of the Beefless Big Mac," *Wall Street Journal*, October 25, 1993, pp. B1, B5.
20. J.R. Whitaker Penteado, "Fast Food Franchises Fight for the Brazilian Aficiados," *Brandweek*, June 7, 1993, pp. 20–24.
21. Yumiko Ono, "Pizza in Japan Is Adapted to Local Tastes," *Wall Street Journal*, June 4, 1993, p. B1.
22. Suzanne Vranica, "Great Scot! Brogues, Kilts Become Madison Avenue's New Gimmick," *Wall Street Journal*, November 30, 1998, pp. B1.
23. Eric Hollreiser, "Brand America Takes a Beating in Japan," *Adweek's Marketing Week*, January 13, 1992, p. 5.
24. Onkvisit and Shaw, *International Marketing*.
25. Louise Lee, "In Asia, the Turn of the Century Doesn't Turn the Heads of Consumer," *Wall Street Journal*, January 8, 1999, p. B8.
26. George P. Moschis, *Consumer Socialization* (Lexington, Mass.: D.C. Heath, 1987); Lisa Penaloza, "Atravesando Fronteras/Border Crossings: A Critical Ethnographic Exploration of the Consumer Acculturation of Mexican Immigrants," *Journal of Consumer Research*, June 1994, pp. 32–54.
27. Geoffrey Paulin, "A Growing Market: Expenditures by Hispanics," *Monthly Labor Review*, March 1998, pp. 3–21; Jon Berry, "The Population Is Taking off Again; Here's What You Need to Know," *Brandweek*, December 7, 1992, p. 14; Jim Cooper, "Advertisers Rush into Growing Market," *Broadcasting and Cable*, November 15, 1993, p. 46.
28. Mayte Sera Weitzman, "Avoiding a Nova," *Marketing News*, July 20, 1998, p. 12
29. Cyndee Miller, "Researcher Says U.S. Is More of a Bowl Than a Pot," *Marketing News*, May 10, 1993, p. 6.
30. Paulin, "A Growing Market."
31. Carrie Goerne, "Go the Extra Mile to Catch up with Hispanics," *Marketing News*, December 24, 1990, p. 13; Marlene Rossman, *Multicultural Marketing* (New York: American Management Association, 1994).
32. Patricia Braus, "What Does Hispanic Mean?" *American Demographics*, June 1993, pp. 46–49.
33. Putterman, "Three Examples of What Marketing Can Do."
34. Van R. Wood and Roy Howell, "A Note on Hispanic Values and Subcultural Research: An Alternative View," *Journal of the Academy of Marketing Science*, Winter 1991, pp. 61–67.
35. Diane Crispell, "Materialism among Minorities," *American Demographics*, August 1993, pp. 14–16; Jacqueline Sanchez, "Some Approaches Better Than Others When Targeting Hispanics," *Marketing News*, May 25, 1992, pp. 8, 11
36. Paulin, "A Growing Market"; Rossman, *Multicultural Marketing*; Braus, "What Does Hispanic Mean?"
37. Joe Schwartz, "Rising Status," *American Demographics*, January 10, 1989, p. 10.
38. William H. Frey and William P. O'Hare, "Vivan Los Suburbios," *American Demographics*, April 1993, pp. 30–37.
39. Antonio Guernica, *U.S. Hispanics: A Market Profile* (New York: National Association of Spanish Broadcasters and Strategy Research Corporation, 1980); Christy Fisher, "Poll: Hispanics Stick to Brands—Asian-Americans Shop for Good Price, and African-Americans Look for Quality," *Advertising Age*, February 15, 1993, p. 6.
40. Benita Eisler, "Class Act: America's Last Dirty Secret," (New York:Franklin Watts, 1983).
41. Rodolfo M. Nayga and Oral Capps, "Determinants of Food away from Home Consumption: An Update," *Agribusiness*, November 1992, pp. 549–559; Rossman, *Multicultural Marketing*; Paulin, "A Growing Market".
42. Penaloza, "Atravesandro Fronteras/Border Crossings"; Rossman, *Multicultural Marketing*.
43. Kurt Topfer, "U.S. Spice Demand Grows as Ethnic Foods Take Hold," *Chemical Marketing Reporter*, September 14, 1992, p. 26; Molly O'Neil, "New Mainstream: Hot Dogs, Apple Pie, and Salsa," *Supermarket Business*, May 1992, pp. 92, 94.
44. Humberto Valencia, "Developing an Index to Measure Hispanicness," in eds. Elizabeth C. Hirschman and Morris B. Holbrook, *Advances in Consumer Research*, Vol. 12 (Provo, Utah: Association for Consumer Research, 1981), pp. 18–21; Rohit Deshpande, Wayne D. Hoyer, and Naveen Donthu, "The Intensity of Ethnic Affiliation: A Study of the Sociology of Hispanic Consumption," *Journal of Consumer Research*, September 1986, pp. 214–220.
45. Cynthia Webster, "Effects of Hispanic Ethnic Identification on Marital Roles in the Purchase Decision Process," *Journal of Consumer Research*, September 1994, pp. 319–331.
46. Cynthia Webster, "The Effects of Hispanic Subcultural Identification on Information Search Behavior," *Journal of Advertising Research*, September–October 1992, pp. 54–62; Naveen Donthu and Joseph Cherian, "Hispanic Coupon Usage: The Impact of Strong and Weak Ethnic Identification," *Psychology and Marketing*, November–December 1992, pp. 501–510.
47. "A Subculture with Very Different Needs," *Adweek*, May 11, 1992, p. 44.
48. Douglas M. Stayman and Rohit Deshpande, "Situational Ethnicity and Consumer Behavior," *Journal of Consumer Research*, December 1989, pp. 361–371.
49. David B. Wooten, "On-of-a-Kind in a Full House: Some Consequences of Ethnic and Gender Distinctiveness," *Journal of Consumer Psychology*, 1995, 4 (3), pp. 205–224.
50. Penaloza, "Atravesandro Fronteras/Border Crossings."
51. Melanie Wallendorf and Michael D. Reilly, "Ethnic Migration, Assimilation, and Consumption," *Journal of Consumer Research*, December 1983, pp. 292–302.
52. Penaloza, "Atravesandro Fronteras/Border Crossings."
53. Jeff Jensen, "Marketing to Hispanics,' *Advertising Age*, August 24, 1998, pp. S1–S2.
54. Cyndee Miller, "Cosmetics Firms Finally Discover the Ethnic Market," *Marketing News*, August 30, 1993, p. 2.
55. Julie Liesse, "General Mills Directly Targets Hispanic Market with New Cereal," *Advertising Age*, May 10, 1993, p. 12;Yumiko Ono, "Kraft Hopes Hispanic Market Says Cheese," *Wall Street Journal*, December 13, 1995, p. B7.
56. Thomas C. O'Guinn and Thomas P. Meyer, "Segmenting the Hispanic Market: The Use of Spanish

Language Radio," *Journal of Advertising Research*, December 1981, pp. 9–16; Steve Coe, "Hispanic Broadcasting and Cable," *Broadcasting and Cable*, November 15, 1993, pp. 39–43; Cyndee Miller, "Advertising in Hispanic Media Rises Sharply," *Marketing News*, January 19, 1993, p. 9; Laureen Miles, "Donde Este Senor Bart?" *Mediaweek*, September 13, 1993, p. 14.

57. Jeff Jensen, "Hispanics: Simpsons' No. 1," *Advertising Age*, September 20, 1993, p. 34.

58. Anne Marie Kerwin, "NY Times Plans Ad Supplement in Spanish," *Editor and Publisher*, February 27, 1993, pp. 24–25; Hanna Liebman, "Newspapers Hablon Espanol," *Mediaweek*, August 16, 1993, p. 10.

59. Christy Fisher, "Hispanic Networks Tap Nielsen Data to Show Ad Reach," *Advertising Age*, November 22, 1993, p. 28; Abbott Wool, "Measuring the Hispanic Buy," *Mediaweek*, August 9, 1993, p. 16.

60. Cooper, "Advertisers Rush into Growing Market"; Riccardo A. Davis, "Advertisers Boost Minority Efforts," *Advertising Age*, August 13, 1993, p. 12.

61. Frank S. Washington, "GM Will Aim Olds Alero at Hispanics and Blacks," *Advertising Age*, September 14, 1998, p. 65.

62. Suein L. Hwang, "Corona, of the Lime Wedge, Makes Unlikely Comeback," *Wall Street Journal*, November 20, 1997, pp. B1, B13.

63. Jacqueline Sanchez, "Some Approaches Better than Others When Targeting Hispanics," *Marketing News*, May 25, 1992, pp. 8, 11.

64. Rossman, *Multicultural Marketing*.

65. Rohit Deshpande and Douglas M. Stayman, "A Tale of Two Cities: Distinctiveness Theory and Advertising Effectiveness," *Journal of Marketing Research*, February 1994, pp. 57–64.

66. Robert E. Wilkes and Humberto Valencia, "Hispanics and Blacks in Television Commercials," *Journal of Advertising*, March 1989, pp. 19–25.

67. Joe Schwartz, "Hispanic Opportunities," *American Demographics*, May 1987, pp. 56–59; Rossman, *Multicultural Marketing*.

68. Scott Koslow, Prem N. Shamdasani, and Ellen E. Touchstone, "Exploring Language Effects in Ethnic Advertising: A Sociolinguistic Perspective," *Journal of Consumer Research*, March 1994, pp. 575–585.

69. Carol J. Kaufman, "Coupon Use in Ethnic Markets: Implications from a Retail Perspective," *Journal of Consumer Marketing*, Winter 1991, pp. 41–51; Christy Fisher, "Marketing to Hispanics: Delivery Systems Foil Couponing," *Advertising Age*, October 15, 1990, p. 47; Christy Fisher, "Marketing to Hispanics: Promotions Trickle Turns into Torrent," *Advertising Age*, October 15, 1990, p. 42.

70. Fisher, "Poll: Hispanics Stick to Brands—Asian-Americans Shop."

71. Rossman, *Multicultural Marketing*.

72. Gerry Khermouch, "All in the Coor's Family," *Brandweek*, August 24, 1998, pp. 18–20.

73. Alexia Vargas, "Harvard MBA's Chain Riles Chicago's Hispanic Grocers," *Wall Street Journal*, November 6, 1997, pp. B1, B2.; Mary Ann Linsen, "Store of the Month: Making It in Miami," *Progressive Grocer*, April 1991, pp. 128–136.

74. Laurie M. Grossman, "After Demographic Shift, Atlanta Mall Restyles Itself as Black Shopping Center," *Wall Street Journal*, February 26, 1992, pp. B1, B5.

75. "Black Consumers," *American Demographics*, Winter 1993, p. 4; Cyndee Miller, "Research on Black Consumers: Marketers with Much at Stake Step Up Their Efforts," *Marketing News*, September 13, 1993, pp. 1, 42.

76. Brigid Schulte, "Blacks Make Gains in Education, Lag in Income, Census Says," *Austin American Statesman*, February 23, 1995, p. A13.

77. William O'Hare, "Blacks and Whites: One Market or Two?" *American Demographics*, March 1987, pp. 44–48.

78. "Where Blacks, Whites Diverge," *Brandweek*, May 3, 1993, p. 22.

79. Howard Schlossberg, "Many Marketers Still Consider Blacks 'Dark-Skinned Whites,'" *Marketing News*, January 18, 1993, pp. 1, 13.

80. Roland L. Freeman, "Philadelphia's African-Americans: A Celebration of Life," cited in Rossman, *Multicultural Marketing*, p. 140.

81. Debra Goldman, "Black Like Me," *Adweek*, August 24, 1992, p. 25.

82. Miller, "Research on Black Consumers"; Cyndee Miller, "Shopping Patterns Vary Widely among Minorities," *Marketing News*, January 18, 1993, p. 11.

83. Rhonda Reynolds, "Courting Black Consumers," *Black Enterprise*, September 1993, p. 43.

84. Pepper Miller and Ronald Miller, "Trends Are Opportunities for Targeting African-Americans," *Marketing News*, January 20, 1992, p. 9.

85. "Blacks Get Wired," *Marketing News*, September 15, 1997, p. 1.

86. Martha T. Moore, "Marketers Take Note of Blacks," *USA Today*, August 20, 1993, p. 3B; Reynolds, "Courting Black Consumers"; Christy Fisher, "Retailers Target Ethnic Consumers," *Advertising Age*, September 30, 1991, p. 50.

87. Fitzgerald, "Increase in Blacks Buying Newspapers," *Editor and Publisher*, October 1993, p. 29; Eugene Morris, "The Difference in Black and White," *American Demographics*, January 1993, pp. 44–49.

88. Lisa L. Brownlee, "Motorola Gets Signal on Blacks' Pager Use," *Wall Street Journal*, June 24, 1996, p. B6.

89. Mike Freeman, "Producers Say Black Numbers Really Don't Add Up," *Broadcasting and Cable*, September 13, 1993, pp. 26–28; Davis, "Advertisers Boost Minority Efforts"; Moore, "Marketers Take Note of Blacks."

90. "L'eggs Joins New Approach in Marketing to African American Women," *Supermarket Business*, June 1998, p. 81; Miller, "Cosmetics Firms Finally Discover the Ethnic Market."

91. Robert McMath, "HBA Makers Pursue the Changing Face of America," *Brandweek*, January 25, 1993, p. 36.

92. John P. Cortez, "KFC Stores Boast Flavor of Neighborhood," *Advertising Age*, May 31, 1993, pp. 3, 46.

93. Cyndee Miller, "Toy Companies Release Ethnically Correct Dolls," *Marketing News*, September 30, 1991, pp. 1–2; Maria Mallory and Stephanie Anderson Forest, "Waking up to a Major Market," *BusinessWeek*, March 23, 1992, pp. 70–73.

94. Janice C. Simpson, "Buying Black," *Time*, August 31, 1992, pp. 52–53; James S. Hirsch, "New Credit Cards

Base Appeals on Sexual Orientation and Race," *Wall Street Journal*, November 6, 1995, pp. B1, B9.

95. Davis, "Advertisers Boost Minority Efforts."

96. Jake Holden, "The Ring of Truth, *American Demographics*, October 1998, p. 14.

97. Lisa Brownlee, "Magazines Win Black Readers Via Newspapers," *Wall Street Journal*, February 6, 1997, pp. B1, B9.

98. Angelo B. Henderson, "Chrysler Backs 'Hoop Dreams' to Court Blacks," *Wall Street Journal*, November 15, 1995, pp. B1, B8.

99. Matthew S. Scott, "Can Black Radio Stations Survive an Industry Shakedown?" *Black Enterprise*, June 1993, pp. 254–260.

100. Jim Kirk, "McDonald's Set to Run Infomercial," *Adweek*, July 12, 1993, p. 5.

101. "Black Consumers;" Jeff Jensen, "Blacks Favor Fox, NBC," *Advertising Age*, April 12, 1993, p. 28.

102. Alan Harman, "Advice to Canadian Papers," *Editor & Publisher*, June 5, 1993, pp. 18–19; Adrienne Ward, "What Roles Do Ads Play in Racial Tension?" *Advertising Age*, August 10, 1992, pp. 1, 35.

103. Reynolds, "Courting Black Consumers"; Russell H. Weigl, James W. Loomis, and Matthew J. Soja, "Race Relations on Prime-Time Television," *Journal of Personality and Social Psychology*, November 1980, pp. 884–893.

104. Thomas H. Stevenson, "How Are Blacks Portrayed in Business Ads?" *Industrial Marketing Management*, August 1991, pp. 193–199.

105. Judith Springer Riddle, "Mining the Non-White Market," *Brandweek*, April 12, 1993, pp. 29–32.

106. Alan Wolf, "Malt Liquors Gain Popularity, Notoriety," *Beverage World*, March 31, 1992, p. 8.

107. J. Clinton Brown, "Which Black Is Beautiful?" *Advertising Age*, February 1, 1993, p. 19.

108. Schlossberg, "Many Marketers Still Consider Blacks 'Dark-Skinned Whites'"; William J. Qualls and David J. Moore, "Stereotyping Effects on Consumers' Evaluation of Advertising: Impact of Racial Difference Between Actors and Viewers," *Psychology and Marketing*, Summer 1990, pp. 135–151.

109. Jamie M. Jamison, "Marketing to the African-American Segment," *Bank Marketing*, December 1993, pp. 21–23.

110. Gregg Cebrynski, "McDonald's Campaign Targets Denver Minorities," *Nation's Restaurant News*, February 9, 1998, pp. 8, 19.

111. Morris, "The Difference in Black and White."

112. Ann Cooper, "Cosmetics: Changing Looks for Changing Attitudes," *Adweek*, February 22, 1993, pp. 30–36.

113. Eric Hollreiser, "Caddy Tweaks Ad Mix to Woo Blacks," *Brandweek*, November 21, 1994, p. 10.

114. Barbara Lippert, "90's Icon Man," *Adweek*, November 30, 1992, p. 24.

115. Dan Fost, "Reaching the Hip-Hop Generation," *American Demographics*, May 1993, p. 15.

116. Tommy E. Whittler and Joan DiMeo, "Viewers' Reactions to Racial Cues in Advertising Stimuli," *Journal of Advertising Research*, December 1991, pp. 37–46.

117. Tommy E. Whittler, "Viewers' Processing of Source and Message Cues in Advertising Stimuli," *Psychology & Marketing*, July–August 1989, pp. 287–309.

118. Fisher, "Poll."

119. William Spain, "Baseball Makes a Pitch for Blacks," *Advertising Age*, August 24, 1992, pp. S1, S4.

120. Mallory and Forest, "Waking up to a Major Market."

121. Cortez, "KFC Stores Boast Flavor of Neighborhood."

122. Grossman, "After Demographic Shift, Atlanta Mall Restyles Itself as Black Shopping Center."

123. Fisher, "Retailers Target Ethnic Consumers"; Carrie Goerne, "Retailers Boost Efforts to Target African-American Consumers," *Marketing News*, June 22, 1992, p. 2.

124. Gregory Spencer and Frederick W. Hollman, "U.S. Census Bureau, the Official Statistics," September 21, 1998, pp. 8–9.

125. James Smart, "Diverse Markets Mean Big Business for Banks," *Bank Marketing*, October 1992, pp. 23–27.

126. Easy Klein, "The Asian-American Market: Climb aboard the Orient Express," *D & B Reports*, November–December 1990, pp. 38–40; Cyndee Miller, "Marketers Say Budgets Hinder Targeting of Asian-Americans," *Marketing News*, March 30, 1992, pp. 2, 15; Alice Z. Cuneo, "Companies Disoriented about Asians," *Advertising Age*, July 9, 1990, pp. S2, S8; Maria Shao, "Suddenly Asian-Americans Are a Marketer's Dream," *BusinessWeek*, June 17, 1991, pp. 54–55.

127. Jonathan Burton, "Advertising Targeting Asians," *Far Eastern Economic Review*, January 21, 1993, pp. 40–41.

128. Cuneo, "Companies Disoriented About Asians."

129. Dan Fost, "California's Asian Market," *American Demographics*, October 1990, pp. 34–37; Chui Li, "The Asian Market for Personal Products," *Drug & Cosmetic Industry*, November 1992, pp. 32–36; Klein, "The Asian-American Market."

130. Saul Gitlin, An Optional Data Base," *Brandweek*, January 5, 1998, p. 16.

131. Rossman, *Multicultural Marketing*; Fost, "California's Asian Market."

132. Li, "The Asian Market for Personal Products"; William Dunn, "The Move Toward Ethnic Marketing," *Nation's Business*, July 1992, pp. 39–41; Rossman, *Multicultural Marketing*.

133. Lisa Marie Petersen, "Advertisers Look to Asian Immigrants," *Mediaweek*, November 30, 1992, p. 2.

134. Banking on Asian-Americans," *Sales & Marketing Management*, September 1993, p. 88; Fost, "California's Asian Market;" Michelle Breyer, "East, West Meet in Magazine," *Austin American Statesman*, April 5, 1995, pp. C1, C8.

135. Cuneo, "Companies Disoriented about Asians."

136. Burton, "Advertising Targeting Asians; Shao, "Suddenly Asian-Americans Are a Marketer's Dream."

137. Charles R. Taylor and Barbara B. Stern, "Asian-Americans; Television Advertising and the 'Model Minority' Stereotype," *Journal of Advertising*, Summer 1997, pp. 47–62.

138. Ibid.

139. Judy Cohen, "White Consumer Response to Asian Models in Advertising," *Journal of Consumer Marketing*, Spring 1992, pp. 17–27.

140. Shao, "Suddenly Asian-Americans Are a Marketer's Dream."

141. Burton, "Advertising Targeting Asians."

142. Rossman, *Multicultural Marketing*.

143. "Banking on Asian-Americans."

144. Grossman, "After Demographic Shift, Atlanta Mall Restyles Itself as Black Shopping Center."

145. Marlene Rossman, "Inclusive Marketing Shows Sensitivity," *Marketing News*, October 10, 1994, p. 4.

146. Wynter, "Minorities Play the Hero in More TV Ads as Clients Discover Multicultural Sells."

147. Tara Parker Pope, "Ford Puts Blacks in Whiteface, Turns Red," *Wall Street Journal*, February 22, 1996, pp. B8.

148. Onkvisit and Shaw, *International Marketing*; Charles M. Schaninger, Jacques C. Bourgeois, and W. Christian Buss, "French-English Canadian Subcultural Consumption Differences," *Journal of Marketing*, Spring 1985, pp. 82–92.

149. Brian Dunn, "Nationalism in Advertising Dead or Alive?" *Adweek*, November 22, 1993.

150. Hans Hoefer, *Thailand* (Boston: Houghton Mifflin, 1993).

151. Elizabeth C. Hirschman, "American Jewish Ethnicity: Its Relationship to Some Selected Aspects of Consumer Behavior," *Journal of Marketing*, Summer 1981, pp. 102–110; Elizabeth C. Hirschman, "Religious Affiliation and Consumption Processes: An Initial Paradigm," *Research in Marketing* (Greenwich, Conn.: JAI Press, 1983), pp. 131–170.

152. Thomas C. O'Guinn and Russell W. Belk, "Heaven and Earth: Consumption at Heritage Village, USA," *Journal of Consumer Research*, September 1989, pp. 227–238.

153. Hirschman, "American Jewish Ethnicity."

154. Hirschman, "Religious Affiliation and Consumption Processes.

155. Priscilla L. Barbera, "Consumer Behavior and Born Again Christianity," in eds. Jagdish N. Sheth and Elizabeth C. Hirschman, *Research in Consumer Behavior* (Greenwich, Conn.: JAI Press, 1988), pp. 193–222.

156. Mark Robichaux, "Religious Cable Networks Fight Sin—and One Another," *Wall Street Journal*, August 12, 1996, p. B1.

157. O'Guinn and Belk, "Heaven and Earth."

158. Martha Brannigan, "Church-Run Tours Collide with Travel Agents," *Wall Street Journal*, August 9, 1996, pp. B1, B2.

159. Fara Warner, "Churches Develop Marketing Campaigns," *Wall Street Journal*, April 17, 1995, p. B4.

160. Lisa Miller, "Religious Ads Go through a Conversion," *Wall Street Journal*, February 24, 1998, p. B7.

161. Lisa Miller, "Trendy Taize Draws Kids with Soft Music and Prayers," *Wall Street Journal*, April 4, 1998, pp. B1, B7.

162. Anne Moore, "Silent Night, *Snowy* Night," *Marketing News*, December 8, 1997, pp. 1, 12.

CHAPTER 14

1. This example is based on an article by Ian Johnson, "China's Once-Admired Rich Now Viewed with Disdain," *New Orleans Times-Picayune*, April 9, 1995, p. A29.

2. Pierre Bourdieu, *Language and Symbolic Power* (Cambridge, Mass.: Harvard University Press, 1991).

3. Richard P. Coleman, "The Continuing Significance of Social Class to Marketing," *Journal of Consumer Research*, December 1983, pp. 265–280; Wendell Blanchard, *Thailand, Its People, Its Society, Its Culture* (New Haven, Conn.: HRAF Press, 1990) as cited in Sak Onkvisit and John J. Shaw, *International Marketing: Analysis and Strategy* (Columbus, Ohio: Merrill, 1989), p. 293.

4. Edward W. Cundiff and Marye T. Hilger, *Marketing in the International Environment* (New York: Prentice-Hall, 1988) as cited in Mariele K. DeMooij and Warren Keegan, *Advertising Worldwide* (New York: Prentice-Hall, 1991), p. 96.

5. Onkvisit and Shaw, *International Marketing*.

6. Russell W. Belk, "Daily Life in Romania," in *Studies in Consumption* (in press).

7. Ernest Dichter, "The World Consumer," *Harvard Business Review*, July–August 1962, pp. 113–123 as cited in Cundiff and Hilger, *Marketing in the International Environment*, p. 135.

8. Richard P. Coleman, "The Significance of Social Stratification in Selling," in ed. Martin L. Bell, *Marketing: A Maturing Discipline* (Chicago: American Marketing Association, 1960), pp. 171–184.

9. Douglas E. Allen and Paul F. Anderson, "Consumption and Social Stratification: Bourdieu's Distinction," in eds. Chris T. Allan and Deborah Roedder John, *Advances in Consumer Research*, Vol. 21 (Provo, Utah: Association for Consumer Research, 1994), pp. 70–73.

10. Pierre Bourdieu, *Distinction: A Social Critique of the Judgment of Taste* (Cambridge, Mass.: Harvard University Press, 1984).

11. Michael R. Solomon, "Deep Seated Materialism: The Case of Levi's 501 Jeans," in ed. Richard J. Lutz, *Advances in Consumer Research*, Vol. 13 (Provo, Utah: Association for Consumer Research, 1986), pp. 619–622.

12. Coleman, "The Continuing Significance of Social Class to Marketing."

13. Charles M. Schaninger, "Social Class Versus Income Revisited: An Empirical Investigation," *Journal of Marketing Research*, May 1981, pp. 192–208.

14. Gillian Stevens and Joo Hyun Cho, "Socioeconomic Indexes and the New 1980 Census Occupational Classification Scheme," *Social Science Research*, March 1985, pp. 142–168; Charles B. Nam and Mary G. Powers, *The Socioeconomic Approach to Status Measurement* (Houston, Tex.: Cap and Gown Press, 1983).

15. Diane Crispell, "The Real Middle Americans," *American Demographics*, October 1994, pp. 28–35; Michael Hout, "More Universalism, Less Structural Mobility: The American Occupational Structure in the 1980s," *American Journal of Sociology*, May 1988, pp. 1358–1400; Crispell, "The Real Middle Americans."

16. William L. Wilkie, *Consumer Behavior*, 2nd ed. (New York: Wiley, 1990).

17. Guliz Ger, Russell W. Belk, and Dana-Nicoleta Lascu, "The Development of Consumer Desire in Marketizing and Developing Economies: The Cases of Romania and Turkey," in eds. Leigh McAlister and Michael L. Rothschild, *Advances in Consumer Research*, Vol. 20 (Provo, Utah: Association for Consumer Research, 1992), pp. 102–107.

18. M. R. Haque, "Marketing Opportunities in the Middle East," in ed. V. H. Manek Kirpalani, *International Business Handbook* (New York: Haworth Press, 1990), pp. 375–416.

19. W. Lloyd Warner, Marchia Meeker, and Kenneth Eells, *Social Class in America* (Chicago: Science Research Associates, 1949); August B. Hollingshead and Fredrick C. Redlich, *Social Class and Mental Illness, A Community Study* (New York: Wiley, 1958).

20. Coleman, "The Continuing Significance of Social Class to Marketing."

21. Gerhard Lenski, "Status Crystallization: A Non-Vertical Dimension of Social Status," *American Sociological Review*, August 1956, pp. 458–464.

22. Benita Eisler, *Class Act: America's Last Dirty Secret* (New York: Franklin Watts, 1983); David L. Featherman and Robert M. Hauser, *Opportunity and Change* (New York: Academic Press, 1978).

23. Allen and Anderson, "Consumption and Social Stratification."

24. Jake Ryan and Charles Sackrey, *Strangers in Paradise: Academics from the Working Class* (Boston: South End Press, 1984).

25. Roger Burbach and Steve Painter, "Restoration in Czechoslovakia," *Monthly Review*, November 1990, pp. 36–49; Rahul Jacob, "The Big Rise," *Fortune*, May 30, 1994, pp. 74–80.

26. Haque, "Marketing Opportunities in the Middle East."

27. Jacob, "The Big Rise."

28. Greg J. Duncan, Martha Hill, and Willard Rogers, "The Changing Fortunes of Young and Old," *American Demographics*, August 1986, pp. 26–33; Katherine S. Newman, *Falling from Grace: The Experience of Downward Mobility in the American Middle Class* (New York: Free Press, 1988); Kenneth Labich, "Class in America," *Fortune*, February 7, 1994, pp. 114–126.

29. Joseph Spiers, "Upper-Middle-Class Woes," *Fortune*, December 27, 1993, pp. 80–86.

30. Newman, *Falling from Grace*; Eisler, *Class Act*.

31. "Japan's Consumer Boom: The Pricey Society," *The Economist*, September 9, 1989, pp. 21–24.

32. Scott D. Roberts, "Consumer Responses to Involuntary Job Loss," in eds. Rebecca H. Holman and Michael R. Solomon, *Advances in Consumer Research*, Vol. 18 (Provo, Utah: Association for Consumer Research, 1988), pp. 40–42.

33. Labich, "Class in America."

34. Ibid.

35. Brooks, *Showing Off in America*; for those interested in reading more about Veblen's theory, see Thorstein Veblen, *The Theory of the Leisure Class* (New York: Macmillan, 1899).

36. Christine Page, "A History of Conspicuous Consumption," in eds. Floyd Rudmin and Marsha Richins, *Meaning, Measure, and Morality of Materialism* (Provo, Utah: Association for Consumer Research, 1993), pp. 82–87.

37. Laura Bird, "Tired of T-Shirts and No-Name Watches, Shoppers Return to Tiffany and Chanel," *Wall Street Journal*, August 6, 1996, pp. B1, B2.

38. Ger, Belk, and Lascu, "The Development of Consumer Desire in Marketizing and Developing Economies."

39. Janeen Arnold Costa and Russell W. Belk, "Nouveaux Riches as Quintessential Americans: Case Studies of Consumption in the Extended Family," in ed. Russell W. Belk, *Advances in Nonprofit Marketing*, Vol. 3 (Greenwich, Conn.: JAI Press, 1990), pp. 83–140.

40. Christina Duff, "Indulging in Inconspicuous Consumption," *Wall Street Journal*, April 14, 1997, pp. B1, B4.

41. Rebecca H. Holman, "Product Use as Communication: A Fresh Appraisal of a Venerable Topic," in eds. Ben M. Enis and Kenneth J. Roering, *Review of Marketing* (Chicago: American Marketing Association, 1981), pp. 106–119.

42. Marlene Rossman, *Multicultural Marketing* (New York: American Management Association, 1994).

43. J. R. Whitaker Penteado, "Fast Food Franchises Fight for Brazilian Aficionados," *Brandweek*, June 7, 1993, pp. 20–24.

44. Ger, Belk, and Lascu, "The Development of Consumer Desire in Marketizing and Developing Economies."

45. Brooks, *Showing off in America*.

46. Sigmund Gronmo, "Compensatory Consumer Behavior: Theoretical Perspectives, Empirical Examples and Methodological Challenges," in eds. Paul F. Anderson and Michael J. Ryan, *1984 American Marketing Association Winter Educators' Conference* (Chicago: American Marketing Association, 1984), pp. 184–188.

47. Russell W. Belk, "Yuppies as Arbiters of the Emerging Consumption Style," in ed. Richard J. Lutz, *Advances in Consumer Research*, Vol. 13 (Provo, Utah: Association for Consumer Research, 1986), pp. 514–519.

48. Yumiko Ono, "Tiffany Glitters, Even in Gloomy Japan," *Wall Street Journal*, July 21, 1998, pp. B1, B8.; "Japan's Consumer Boom."

49. Russell W. Belk and Melanie Wallendorf, "The Sacred Meanings of Money," *Journal of Economic Psychology*, March 1990, pp. 35–67.

50. Nikhil Deogun, "The Smart Money Is on 'Smart Cards,' but Electronic Cash Seems Dumb to Some," *Wall Street Journal*, August 5, 1996, pp. B1, B2.

51. Thomas E. Weber, "On the Web, the Race for a Better Wallet," *Wall Street Journal*, December 18, 1998, pp. B1, B4.

52. C. Rubenstein, "Your Money or Your Life," *Psychology Today*, 12, 1980, pp. 47–58.

53. Adrian Furnham and Alan Lewis, *The Economic Mind, The Social Psychology of Economic Behavior* (Brighton, Sussex: Harvester Press, 1986); Belk and Wallendorf, "The Sacred Meanings of Money."

54. H. Goldberg and R. Lewis, *Money Madness: The Psychology of Saving, Spending, Loving, and Hating Money* (London: Springwood, 1979).

55. Thomas Wiseman, *The Money Motive* (New York: 1st American, 1974).

56. Rosalind H. Williams, *Dream Worlds: Mass Consumption in Late Nineteenth-Century France* (Berkeley, Calif.: University of California Press, 1982).

57. Elizabeth C. Hirschman, "Secular Immortality and the American Ideology of Affluence," *Journal of Consumer Research*, June 1990, pp. 31–42.

58. Notably not all research has found this to be true. One set of six case studies found that all were comfortable with their status. See Costa and Belk, "Nouveaux Riches as Quintessential Americans."

59. Bourdieu, *Distinction*.

60. Priscilla A. LaBarbera, "The Nouveau Riches, Conspicuous Consumption and the Issue of Self-Fulfillment," in eds. Elizabeth C. Hirschman and Jagdish

N. Sheth, *Research in Consumer Behavior* (Greenwich, Conn.: JAI Press, 1988), pp. 179–210; Brooks, *Showing off in America*; Leach and Rich, *Life Styles of the Rich and Famous*.

61. Brad Edmondson, "Wealth and Poverty," *American Demographics*, 20 (5), 1998, pp. 20–21.

62. C. W. Young, "Bijan Designs a Very Exclusive Image," *Advertising Age*, March 13, 1986, pp. 18, 19, 21 as cited in LaBarbera, "The Nouveaux Riches, Conspicuous Consumption and the Issue of Self-Fulfillment"; V. Kanti Prasad, "Socioeconomic Product Risk and Patronage Preferences of Retail Shoppers," *Journal of Marketing*, July 1975, pp. 42–47.

63. Elizabeth C. Hirschman, "Upper Class WASPS as Consumers: A Humanist Inquiry," in eds. Elizabeth C. Hirschman and Jagdish Sheth, *Research in Consumer Behavior*, Vol. 3 (Greenwich, Conn.: JAI Press, 1988), pp. 115–147.

64. Anita Sharpe, "The Rich Aren't So Different after All," *Wall Street Journal*, November 12, 1996, pp. B1, B12.

65. Coleman, "The Continuing Significance of Social Class to Marketing"; Crispell, "The Real Middle Americans."

66. Labich, "Class in America."

67. "Middle-Class on $10,000 a Year," *American Demographics*, September 1994, pp. 15–17.

68. Jacob, "The Big Rise."

69. Rebecca Piirto Heath, "The New Working Class," *American Demographics*, 20 (1), January 1998, pp. 51–55.

70. Coleman, "The Continuing Significance of Social Class to Marketing."

71. Michael Solomon and Henry Assael, "The Forest or the Trees: A Gestalt Approach to Symbolic Consumption," in ed. Jean Umiker-Sebek, *Semiotics: New Directions in the Study of Signs for Sale* (Berlin: Mouton de Gruyter, 1987), pp. 189–218; William O'Hare and Barbara O'Hare, "Upward Mobility," *American Demographics*, January 1993, pp. 26–34.

72. Prasad, "Socioeconomic Product Risk and Patronage Preferences of Retail Shoppers"; Stuart Rich and Subhish Jain, "Social Class and Life Cycle as Predictors of Shopping Behavior," *Journal of Marketing Research*, June–July 1987, pp. 51–59.

73. Frank Caro, *Estimating the Numbers of Homeless Families* (New York: Community Service Society of New York, 1981).

74. Richard B. Freeman and Brian Hall, "Permanent Homelessness in America?" *Population Research and Policy Review*, 6, 1987, pp. 3–27.

75. Ronald Paul Hill, "Homeless Women, Special Possessions, and the Meaning of 'Home': An Ethnographic Case Study," *Journal of Consumer Research*, December 1991, pp. 298–310.

76. David A. Snow and Leon Anderson, "Identity Work among the Homeless: The Verbal Construction and Avowal of Personal Identities," *American Journal of Sociology*, May 1987, pp. 1336–1371.

77. LaBarbera, "The Nouveaux Riches."

78. Robert Frank and Lisa Shuchman, "A British Foodie Tries to Tempt Manhattanites," *Wall Street Journal*, August 22, 1997, pp. B1, B2.

79. William M. Bulkeley, "Hold the Ketchup! Chic Restaurants Aim to Sell Haute Cuisine through Chains," *Wall Street Journal*, August 1, 1996, pp. B1, B7.

80. Ignacio Galceran and Jon Berry, "A New World of Consumers," *American Demographics*, March 1995, pp. 26–31.

81. Rahul Jacob, "India Is Open for Business," *Fortune*, November 16, 1992, pp. 128–130.

82. Kjell Gronhaug and Paul S. Trapp, "Perceived Social Class Appeals of Branded Goods and Services," *Journal of Consumer Marketing*, Winter 1989, pp. 13–18.

83. Allen and Anderson, "Consumption and Social Stratification."

84. Peter Pae, "Private Bankers Court Merely Affluent," *Wall Street Journal*, May 12, 1992, pp. B1, B7.

85. Jonathan Friedland and Michael J. McCarthy, "Pairing Bud with Sushi in South America," *Wall Street Journal*, February 20, 1997, pp. B1, B8.

86. LaBarbera, "The Nouveaux Riches."

87. Anita Sharpe, "Magazines for the Rich Rake in Readers," *Wall Street Journal*, February 16, 1996, pp. B1, B2.

88. G. Bruce Knecht, "New Magazine Pitches the Rich through Their Favorite Causes," *Wall Street Journal*, March 4, 1997, pp. B1, B7.

89. Kelly Shermach, "Study Identifies Types of Interactive Shoppers," *Marketing News*, September 25, 1995, p. 22. *eMarketer*, February 3, 2000 (on-line reference).

90. Rich and Jain, "Social Class and Life Cycle as Predictors of Shopping Behavior."

91. Page, "A History of Conspicuous Consumption."

92. James R. Hagerty, "Gilding the Drill Bit? Hardware Giants Go High End," *Wall Street Journal*, July 28, 1998, pp. B1, B7,

93. Wendy Bounds, "Discounters Dress up to Lure the Well Healed Shopper," *Wall Street Journal*, December 3, 1997, pp. B1, B13.

94. Matthew Rose, "Stodgy Savile Row Aims to Suit the Youth," *Wall Street Journal*. March 3, 1996, pp. B1, B5.

95. Carl Quintanilla, "Unsold Seats Sully Concorde's Snooty Image," *Wall Street Journal*, February 23, 1996, pp. B1, B6.

96. Labich, "Class in America."

97. Kevin Goldman, "Network Targets Drivers at Truck Stops," *Wall Street Journal*, November 11, 1992, pp. B1, B4.

CHAPTER 15

1. Joyce Barnathan, "China's Youth," *Business Week*, September 15, 1997, 62E2–62E10.

2. Michael M. Phillips, "Selling by Evoking What Defines a Generation," *Wall Street Journal*, August 13, 1996, pp. B1, B7.

3. Howard Schlossberg, "What Teenagers Find Hot Today Will Be Old News Tomorrow," *Marketing News*, December 6, 1993, p. 7.

4. Melinda Beck, "Maybe Rock 'N' Roll Really Is Here to Stay," *Wall Street Journal*, Febuary 5, 1997, pp. B1, B8.

5. Shawn Tully, "Teens, the Most Global Market of All," *Fortune*, May 16, 1994, pp. 90–96; Scott McCartney, "For Teens, Chatting on Internet Offers Comfort of Anonymity," *Wall Street Journal*, December 8, 1994, p. B1.

6. Elaine Underwood, "Jean-etics 101," *Brandweek*, August 17, 1992, pp. 14–15.

7. Deena Weinstein, *Heavy Metal, A Cultural Sociology* (New York: Lexington, 1991); Kathryn Joan Fox, "Real

Punks and Pretenders," *Journal of Contemporary Ethnography*, October 1987, pp. 344–370; Penelope Eckart, "Clothing and Geography in a Suburban High School," in ed. Conrad Phillip Kottak, *Researching American Culture* (Ann Arbor, Mich.: University of Michigan Press, 1982).

8. Laura Zinn, "Teens: Here Comes the Biggest Wave Yet," *BusinessWeek*, April 11, 1994, pp. 76–86; Lisa Marie Petersen, "I Bought What Was on Sale," *Brandweek*, February 22, 1993, pp. 12–13.

9. Dennis H. Tootelian and Ralph M. Gaedecke, "The Teen Market: An Exploratory Analysis of Income, Spending, and Shopping Patterns," *Journal of Consumer Marketing*, Fall 1994, pp. 35–44; George P. Moschis and Roy L. Moore, "Decision Making among the Young: A Socialization Perspective," *Journal of Consumer Research*, September 1979, pp. 101–112.

10. Ellen Graham, "When Terrible Twos Become Terrible Teens," *Wall Street Journal*, February 5, 1997, pp. B1, B8; Matthew Grimm, "Irvington, 10533," *Brandweek*, August 17, 1993, pp. 11–13.

11. "Those Precocious 13–Year Olds," *Brandweek*, January 25, 1993, p. 13; Tully, "Teens, the Most Global Market of All."

12. Paula Dwyer, "The Euroteens (and How to Sell to Them)," *BusinessWeek*, April 11, 1994, p. 84.

13. Roger Ricklefs, "Marketers Seek out Today's Coolest Kids to Plug into Tomorrow's Mall Trends," *Wall Street Journal*, July 11, 1996, pp. B1, B2; Michael J. McCarthy, "Stalking the Elusive Teenage Trendsetter," *Wall Street Journal*, November 19, 1998, pp. B1, B10.

14. Norihiko Shirouzu, "Japan's High-School Girls Excel in the Art of Setting Trends," *Wall Street Journal*, April 24, 1998, pp. B1, B7.

15. Judith S. Riddle, "Arrid's Teen Image Will Get $5.3M to Take on Teen Spirit," *Brandweek*, March 29, 1993, pp. 1, 6.

16. Rekha Balu, "Gatorade Targets Younger Fans in Bid to Best Sports-Drink Rivals," *Wall Street Journal*, January 28, 1998, pp. B7.

17. Fara Warner, "Booming Asia Lures Credit-Card Firms," *Wall Street Journal*, November 24, 1995, p. B10.

18. Louise Lee, "To Keep Teens Away, Malls Turn Snooty, "*Wall Street Journal*, October 17, 1996, pp. B1, B9.

19. Patrick M. Reilly and Stefan Fatsis, 'NFL Hands the Ball to Pop Stars, Trying to Score with Young Fans," *Wall Street Journal*, August 29, 1997, p. B1.

20. Grimm, "Irvington, 10533."

21. Helene Cooper, "Once Again, Ads Woo Teens with Slang," *Wall Street Journal*, March 29, 1993, pp. B1, B6; Adrienne Ward Fawcett, "When Using Slang in Advertising: BVC," *Advertising Age*, August 23, 1993, p. S-6.

22. Barbara Martinez, "Antismoking Ads Aim to Gross out Teens," *Wall Street Journal*, March 21, 1997, pp. B1, B8.

23. Wendy Bounds, "Teen-Magazine Boom: Beauty, Fashion, Stars, and Sex," *Wall Street Journal*, December 7, 1998, pp. B1, B10.

24. Calmetta Y. Coleman, "Target Aims at Younger Shoppers on MTV," *Wall Street Journal*, April 8, 1999.

25. Jeff Jensen, "A New Read on How to Reach Boys," *Advertising Age*, August 23, 1993, pp. S-10–11.

26. Yumiko Ono, "Fashion's New Queens: Heavy Teens," *Wall Street Journal*, July 31, 1998, pp. B1, 10.

27. Yumiko Ono, "Limited Too Plans a Preteen Catalog Blitz,' *Wall Street Journal*, August 25, 1998, p. B8.

28. Carrie Goerne, "Marketers Try to Get More Creative in Reaching Teens," *Marketing News*, August 5, 1991, pp. 2, 6.

29. Raju Narisetti, "Teenager Rates P & G's Virtual Makeover," *Wall Street Journal*, October 15, 1996, p. B12.

30. Thomas E. Weber, "Where the Boys and Girls Are: Teens Talk about the Web," *Wall Street Journal*, December 24, 1997, pp. B6, B7.

31. Jeff Giles, "Generalizations X," *Newsweek*, June 6, 1994, pp. 62–72.

32. Christina Duff, "It's Sad But True: Good Times Are Bad for Real Slackers," *Wall Street Journal*, August 6, 1998, pp. A1, A5.

33. Giles, "Generalizations X"; John Flinn, "'Generation X' Plugged in and Purchasing," *Austin American Statesman*, February 4, 1995, pp. A1, A9.

34. Bonnie Rochman, "American Twentysomethings Land in Vietnam," *Fortune*, June 24, 1996, pp. 114–126.

35. Kimberly Paterson, "Twentysomething Generation Is Tough to Target," *National Underwriter*, March 21, 1994, pp. 31–32; Randolph E. Schmid, "Young Adults Slow to Leave Home, Quick to Return," *Austin American Statesman*, April 8, 1994, p. A15.

36. Cyndee Miller, "X Marks the Lucrative Spot, But Some Advertisers Can't Hit Target," *Marketing News*, August 2, 1993, pp. 1, 14; Pat Sloan, "Xers Brush off Cosmetics Marketers," *Advertising Age*, September 27, 1993, p. 4.

37. Andrea Petersen, "Restaurants Bring in da Noise to Keep Out da Nerds," *Wall Street Journal*, December 30, 1997, pp. B1, B2.

38. Andrea Petersen, "Generation Xers Pick up a New Line at Bars: BINGO," *Wall Street Journal*, April 10, 1996, pp. V1, A8.

39. Judith Valente, "Scotch Makers Tell Youth It's Hip to Be Old-Fashioned," *Wall Street Journal*, December 29, 1993, pp. B1, B5; Eric Hollreiser, "Seagram Tries '7 & 7' Revisited, with a Slammin' GenX Twist," *Brandweek*, January 30, 1995, p. 14.

40. Alfred Schreiber, "Generation X the Next Big Event Target," *Advertising Age*, June 21, 1993, p. S-3; Robert Gustafson, "Marketing to Generation X? Better Practice Safe Sex," *Advertising Age*, March 7, 1994, p. 26.

41. Gerry Khermouch, "Would You Buy a Heineken from This Dude?" *Brandweek*, February 20, 1995, pp. 1, 6; Gerry Khermouch, "Zima Sets Alternative Course," *Brandweek*, April 24, 1995, p. 4.

42. Sally Goll Beatty, "If Barq's Has Bite, So Do the Spots Wieden Has Made for the Coke Brand," *Wall Street Journal*, June 30, 1997, p. B6.

43. Horst Stipp, "Xers Are Not Created Equal," *Mediaweek*, March 21, 1994, p. 20; Lisa Marie Petersen, "Previews of Coming Attractions," *Brandweek*, March 1993, pp. 22–23.

44. Laura Koss-Feder, "Want to Catch GenX? Try Looking on the Web," *Marketing News*, June 8, 1998, p. 20.

45. Joan E. Rigdon, "Hip Advertisers Bypass Madison Avenue When They Need Cutting-Edge Web Sites," *Wall Street Journal*, February 28, 1996, pp. B1, B2.

46. Sally Beatty, Alcohol Firms Boost Online Ads to Youth," *Wall Street Journal*, December 17, 1998, p. B8.

47. Andrea Petersen, "Charities Bet Young Will Come for the Music, Stay for the Pitch," *Wall Street Journal*, September 7, 1996, p. B1.

48. Tibbett L. Speer, "College Come-Ons," *American Demographics*, March 1998, pp. 41–45.

49. Cheryl Russell, "The Power of One," *Brandweek*, October 4, 1993, pp. 27–28, 30, 32.

50. Raymond Kotcher, "Gathering Moss," *Adweek*, November 23, 1992, p. 26; Campbell Gibson, "The Four Baby Booms," *American Demographics*, November 1993, pp. 36–40.

51. Heather Graulich, "Do You Fall into the Gap?" *Austin American Statesman*, July 28, 1997, pp. E1, E8.

52. Susan Mitchell, "How Boomers Save," *American Demographics*, September 1994, pp. 22–29; "Baby Boomers Are Top Dinner Consumers," *Frozen Food Age*, February 1994, p. 33; Fred Pampel, Dan Fost, and Sharon O'Malley, "Marketing the Movies," *American Demographics*, March 1994, pp. 48–54.

53. Jeffrey A. Trachtenberg, "Packaging Old Hits to Produce New Hits," *Wall Street Journal*, December 11, 1995, pp. B1, B4.

54. Fara Warner and Lisa Marie Petersen, "The Magic Bus Updated: Full-Sized Vans Are Back," *Brandweek*, September 30, 1993, pp. 34–35.

55. Penny Warneford and Pam Weisz, "Dial, Lever Eye Baby Boomlet," *Brandweek*, September 19, 1994, pp. 1, 6.

56. Cyndee Miller, "Jeans Marketers Loosen up, Adjust to Expanding Market," *Marketing News*, August 31, 1992, pp. 6–7.

57. Rick Bragg, "Aging Population Confounds Automakers," *Austin American Statesman*, March 1, 1999, p. A6.

58. Lisa Bannon, "Disney Decides World Isn't So Small, Creating Education Resort for Boomers," *Wall Street Journal*, March 1, 1996, pp. B1, B2.

59. Patricia Braus, "Boomers against Gravity," *American Demographics*, February 1995, pp. 50–57.

60. Judith Springer Riddle, "Fountain of Growth," *Brandweek*, August 16, 1993, pp. 19–21; Pam Weisz, "Marketers Discover the Fountain of Youth," *Brandweek*, January 30, 1995, p. 30; Raju Narisetti, "SmithKline's Whitener Toothpaste Shines," *Wall Street Journal*, February 18, 1997, p. B13.

61. Ernest Beck and Yumiko Ono, "Dewar's Profile Rises as Suitors Swirl Around," *Wall Street Journal*, March 11, 1998, p. B1.

62. Lisa Miller, "Water Toys at Resort Turn Sane Adults into Crazy Kids," *Wall Street Journal*, March 15, 1996, pp. B1, B6.

63. Yumiko Ono, "Kitty-Mania Grips Grown-Ups in Japan," *Wall Street Journal*, December 15, 1998, pp. B1, B4.

64. Kevin Goldman, "Advertisers Are at Last Treating Baby Boomers Like Grown-Ups," *Wall Street Journal*, December 29, 1993, p. B5.

65. Scott McCartney, "Vacations with Ringo, Elvis, and Cobain," *Wall Street Journal*, February 7, 1997, pp. B1, B7.

66. Patrick M. Reilly, "What a Long Strange Trip It's Been,' *Wall Street Journal*, April 7, 1999, pp. B1, B4.

67. Richard Gibson and Bruce Orwall, "New Mission for Mickey Mouse, Mickey D," *Wall Street Journal*, March 5, 1998, pp. B1, B5.

68. Vicki Thomas, "Which Media Reach Boomers Best," *Bank Marketing*, July 1993, pp. 68–72.

69. "Healthy, Wealthy, and Growing in Numbers," *Brandweek*, February 22, 1993, p. 32.

70. Christina Duff, "Profiling the Aged: Fat Cats or Hungry Victims?" *Wall Street Journal*, August 29, 1996, pp. B1, B8.

71. Carol M. Morgan, "The Psychographic Landscape of 50–Plus," *Brandweek*, July 19, 1993, pp. 28–32.

72. Stuart Van Auken and Thomas E. Barry, "An Assessment of the Trait Valdity of Cognitive Age Measures," *Journal of Consumer Psychology*, 4 (2), 1995, pp. 107–132; Robert E. Wilkes, "A Structural Modeling Approach to the Measurement and Meaning of Cognitive Age," *Journal of Consumer Research*, September 1992, pp. 292–301.

73. Morgan, "The Psychographic Landscape of 50-Plus"; Goodman, "Marketing to Age Groups Is All in the Mind Set."

74. Catherine A. Cole and Gary J. Gaeth, "Cognitive and Age-Related Differences in the Ability to Use Nutritional Information in a Complex Environment," *Journal of Marketing Research*, May 1990, pp. 175–184; Catherine A. Cole and Siva K. Balasubramanian, "Age Differences in Consumers' Search for Information: Public Policy Implications," *Journal of Consumer Research*, June 1993, pp. 157–169; Deborah Roedder John and Catherine A. Cole, "Age Differences in Information Processing: Understanding Deficits in Young and Elderly Consumers," *Journal of Consumer Research*, December 1986, pp. 297–315.

75. Carolyn Yoon, "Age Differences in Consumers' Processing Strategies: An Investigation of Moderating Differences," *Journal of Consumer Research*, December 1997, pp. 329–342.

76. Sharmistha Law, Scott A Hawkins, and Fergus I.M. Craik, "Repetition-Induced Belief in the Elderly: Rehabilitating Age-Related Memory Deficits," *Journal of Consumer Research*, September 1998, pp. 91–107.

77. Catherine A. Cole and Gary J. Gaeth, "Cognitive and Age-Related Differences in the Ability to Use Nutritional Information in a Complex Environment," *Journal of Marketing Research*, May 1990, pp. 175–184; Catherine A. Cole and Siva K. Balasubramanian, "Age Differences in Consumers' Search for Information: Public Policy Implications," *Journal of Consumer Research*, June 1993, pp. 157–169; Deborah Roedder John and Catherine A. Cole, "Age Differences in Information Processing: Understanding Deficits in Young and Elderly Consumers," *Journal of Consumer Research*, December 1986, pp. 297–315.

78. "America's Aging Consumers," *Discount Merchandiser*, September 1993, pp. 16–28; Mary C. Gilly and Valerie A. Zeithaml, "The Elderly Consumer and Adoption of Technologies," *Journal of Consumer Research*, December 1985, pp. 353–357.

79. Michael Moss, "Leon Black Bets Big on the Elderly," *Wall Street Journal*, July 24, 1998, pp. B1, B8.

80. Stephanie Mehta, "Retailer with Vision Aims to Make Fading Eyesight Chic," *Wall Street Journal*, October 23, 1996, pp. B1, B2.

81. Raju Narisetti, "Products to Aid the Incontinent are Growing Up," *Wall Street Journal*, November 13, 1995, pp. N1, B5.

82. Rhonda L. Rundle, "Alergan's Ads on Cataracts join health Debate at Awkward Time," *Wall Street Journal*, March 8, 1999, pp. B14.

83. Elyse Tanouye, "Pitching Wrinkles as Medical Malady, J&J Launches Rx Cream for Agin Skin," February 13, 1996, pp. B1, B9.

84. Xander Mellish, "Revivers of Burma-Shave Hope to Lure Stubble of a Certain Age," *Wall Street Journal*, December 22, 1995, pp. B12.

85. Vanessa O'Connell, "Alcohol Makers' New Target: Drinkers over 50," *Wall Street Journal*, August 5, 1998, pp, B1, B4.

86. Bonnie S. Guy, Terri L. Rittenburg, and Douglass K. Hawes, "Dimensions and Characteristics of Time Perceptions among Older Consumers," *Psychology and Marketing*, January–February 1994, pp. 35–56.

87. Dale A. Lunsford and Melissa S. Burnett, "Marketing Product Innovations to the Elderly: Understanding the Barriers to Adoption," *Journal of Consumer Marketing*, Fall 1992, pp. 53–63.

88. Ronald E. Milliman and Robert C. Erffmeyer, "Improving Advertising Aimed at Seniors," *Journal of Advertising Research*, December 1989–January 1990, pp. 31–36.

89. Robin T. Peterson, "The Depiction of Senior Citizens in Magazine Advertisements: A Content Analysis," *Journal of Business Ethics*, September 1992, pp. 701–706; Anthony C. Ursic, Michael L. Ursic, and Virginia L. Ursic, "A Longitudinal Study of the Use of the Elderly in Magazine Advertising," *Journal of Consumer Research*, June 1986, pp. 131–133; John J. Burnett, "Examining the Media Habits of the Affluent Elderly," *Journal of Advertising Research*, October–November 1991, pp. 33–41.

90. John and Cole, "Age Differences in Information Processing"; Burnett, "Examining the Media Habits of the Affluent Elderly."

91. Jim Carlton, "Web Sites, Other PC Wonders Draw Crowds of Retirees," *Wall Street Journal*, January 29, 1998, pp. B1, B11.

92. "America's Aging Consumers"; John and Cole, "Age Differences in Information Processing."

93. David C. Jones, "New Marketing Tool Targets Selling to Seniors," *National Underwriter*, December 20, 1993, p. 5.

94. John R. Emshwiller, "Having Lost Thousands to Con Artists, Elderly Widow Tells Cautionary Tale," *Wall Street Journal*, August 9, 1996, pp. B1, B5.

95. Lisa D. Spiller and Richard A. Hamilton, "Senior Citizen Discount Programs: Which Seniors to Target and Why," *Journal of Consumer Marketing*, Summer 1993, pp. 42–51; Kelly Tepper, "The Role of Labeling Processes in Elderly Consumers' Responses to Age Segmentation Cues," *Journal of Consumer Research*, March 1994, pp. 503–519.

96. Yumiko Ono, "Kraft Seeking Joint Marketing Arrangement,' *Wall Street Journal*, March 11, 1996, p. B6.

97. Joan Meyers-Levy, "The Influence of Sex Roles on Judgment," *Journal of Consumer Research*, March 1988, pp. 522–530.

98. Charles S. Areni and Pamela Kiecker, "Gender Differences in Motivation: Some Implications for Manipulating Task-Related Involvement," in ed. Janeen Arnold Costa, *Gender and Consumer Behavior* (Salt Lake City, Utah: University of Utah Printing Service, 1993), pp. 30–43; Brenda Giner and Eileen Fischer, "Women and Arts, Men and Sports: Two Phenomena or One?" in ed. Janeen Arnold Costa, *Gender and Consumer Behavior* (Salt Lake City, Utah: University of Utah Printing Service, 1993), p. 149.

99. "Women Are Slowly Approaching Majority of the U.S. Labor Force," *Wall Street Journal*, July 7, 1995, p. B3B.

100. Alladi Venkatesh, "Changing Roles of Women: A Life Style Analysis," *Journal of Consumer Research*, September 1980, pp. 189–197; Eleena de Lisser, "Women Shed Family Baggage on Trips," *Wall Street Journal*, February 9, 1996, pp. B1, B8.

101. Elia Kacapyr, "The Well-Being of American Women," *American Demographics*, August 1998, pp. 30, 32.

102. Beverly A. Browne and Sally K. Francis, "Skateboarders: Gender, Dress, and Social Comparison," in ed. Janeen Arnold Costa, *Gender and Consumer Behavior* (Salt Lake City, Utah: University of Utah Printing Service, 1993), pp. 46–52.

103. Alladi Venkatesh, "Gender Identity in the Indian Context, a Socio-Cultural Construction of the Female Consumer," in ed. Janeen Arnold Costa, *Gender and Consumer Behavior* (Salt Lake City, Utah: University of Utah Printing Service, 1993), pp. 119–129.

104. Teresa Watanabe, "Japanese Women Dancing up a Storm after Work Hours," *Austin American Statesman*, December 19, 1993, p. A24.

105. Matti Huuhtanen, "New Kits Help Dads Cope with Fatherhood," *Austin American Statesman*, December 17, 1994, p. A37.

106. Yumiko Ono, "Japan Warms to McDonald's Doting Dad Ads," *Wall Street Journal*, May 8, 1997, pp. B1, B12.

107. Lynn J. Jaffe and Paul D. Berger, "Impact on Purchase Intent of Sex-Role Identity and Product Positioning," *Psychology and Marketing*, Fall 1988, pp. 259–271.

108. Joan Meyers-Levy and Durairaj Maheswaran, "Exploring Differences in Males' and Females' Processing Strategies," *Journal of Consumer Research*, June 1991, pp. 63–70; William K. Darley and Robert E. Smith, "Gender Differences in Information Processing Strategies: An Empirical Test of the Selectivity Model in Advertising Response," *Journal of Advertising*, Spring 1995, pp. 41–56; Barbara B. Stern, "Feminist Literary Criticism and the Deconstruction of Ads: A Postmodern View of Advertising and Consumer Responses," *Journal of Consumer Research*, March 1993, pp. 556–566.

109. Meyers-Levy, "The Influence of Sex Roles on Judgment," Joan Meyers-Levy, "Priming Effects on Product Judgments: A Hemispheric Interpretation," *Journal of Consumer Research*, June 1989, pp. 76–86.

110. Laurette Dube and Michael S. Morgan, "Trend Effects and Gender Differences in Retrospective Judgments of Consumption Emotions," *Journal of Consumer Research*, September 1996, pp. 156–162.

111. Richard Elliot, "Gender and the Psychological Meaning of Fashion Brands," in ed. Janeen Arnold Costa, *Gender and Consumer Behavior* (Salt Lake City, Utah: University of Utah Printing Service, 1993), pp. 99–105.

112. Frederica Rudell, "Gender Differences in Consumer Decision Making for Personal Computers: A Test of Hypotheses," and Gary J. Bamossy and Paul Jansen, "Children's Apprehension and Comprehension: Gender Influences on Computer Literacy and Attitude Structures of Personal Computers," in ed. Janeen Arnold Costa, *Gender and Consumer Behavior* (Salt Lake City, Utah: University of Utah Printing Service, 1993), pp. 1–16 and 17–29.

113. Eileen Fischer and Stephen J. Arnold, "More Than a Labor of Love: Gender Roles and Christmas Gift Shopping," *Journal of Consumer Research*, December 1990, pp. 333–345; Gretchen M. Herrmann, "His and Hers: Gender and Garage Sales," in ed. Janeen Arnold Costa, *Gender and Consumer Behavior* (Salt Lake City, Utah: University of Utah Printing Service, 1993), pp. 88–98; Mehtap Kokturk and Yonca Karapaza, "A General Profile of Turkish Consumers Based on Gender Differences," in ed. Janeen Arnold Costa, *Gender and Consumer Behavior* (Salt Lake City, Utah: University of Utah Printing Service, 1993), pp. 107–118.

114. Suzanne C. Grunert, "On Gender Differences in Eating Behavior as Compensatory Consumption," in ed. Janeen Arnold Costa, *Gender and Consumer Behavior* (Salt Lake City, Utah: University of Utah Printing Service, 1993), pp. 74–86.

115. Nancy Ann Jeffrey, "Wall Street's Soft Sell Lures Women Investors," *Wall Street Journal*, July 28, 1995, pp. C1, C6.

116. James H. McAlexander, John H. Shouten, and Harold F. Koenig, "Born to Be Mild? Women in a Male Consumption Domain," in ed. Janeen Arnold Costa, *Gender and Consumer Behavior* (Salt Lake City, Utah: University of Utah Printing Service, 1993), p. 54.

117. Pam Weisz, "Glidden Makes Fashion Statement to Female Consumers," *Brandweek*, March 27, 1995, p. 14.

118. Mark Maremont, "Gillette's New Strategy Is to Sharpen Pitch to Women," *Wall Street Journal*, May 11, 1998, pp. B1, B16.

119. Fara Warner, "BMW, Martha Court Women," *Brandweek*, July 19, 1993, p. 4; Laurie Petersen, "What Makes a Winner in Europe," *Adweek's Marketing Week*, August 20, 1990, p. 35; Eben Shapiro, "Brewers Aim to Tap Younger Drinkers and Women by Rolling out Clear Beers," *Wall Street Journal*, February 11, 1993, pp. B1, B8.

120. Tara Parker-Pope, "All That Glitters Isn't Purchased by Men," *Wall Street Journal*, January 7, 1997, pp. B1, B10.

121. Pam Weisz, "Halston: $10M on Men's Scent," *Brandweek*, September 12, 1994, p. 14.

122. Pat Wechsler, "You're So Vain," *Business Week*, September 8, 1997. p. 6.

123. Yumiko Ono, "Beautifying the Japanese Male," *Wall Street Journal*, March 11, 1999, pp. B1, B8.

124. Cyndee Miller, "Perfume Maker Uses Mystery to Lure Assertive '90s Woman," *Marketing News*, August 31, 1992, p. 2.

125. John B. Ford, Patricia Kramer, and Voli, Earl D. Honeycutt Jr., and Susan L. Casey, "Gender Role Portrayals in Japanese Advertising: A Magazine Content Analysis," *Journal of Advertising*, Spring 1998, pp. 113–24.

126. Raju Narisetti, "She Gives a Whole New Meaning to the Phrase 'If Looks Could Kill,'" *Wall Street Journal*, May 16, 1994, p. B1; Sally D. Goll, "Beer Ads in Hong Kong Criticized as Sexist," *Wall Street Journal*, June 29, 1995, p. B2; Sally Goll Beatty, "Women's Views of Their Lives Aren't Reflected by Advertisers,' *Wall Street Journal*, December 19, 1995, p. B6.

127. Cyndee Miller, "Tapping into Women's Issues Is Potent Way to Reach Market," *Marketing News*, December 6, 1993, pp. 1, 13; Patrick M. Reilly, "Women's Music Tour Handpicks Backers," *Wall Street Journal*, June 9, 1997, pp. B1, B6; Leslie Cauley, "Lifetime's Breast-Cancer Shows Prove to Be Hit with Advertisers," Wall Street Journal, October 1, 1998, pp. B12.

128. Patrick M. Reilly, "Hard-Nosed Allure Wins Readers and Ads," *Wall Street Journal*, August 27, 1992, p. B8; Seema Nayyar, "Net TV Soap Ads: Lever Alone Hit Men," *Brandweek*, July 13, 1992, p. 10.

129. Mark Robichaux, "Lifetime Is Creating New Shows Aimed at Young Female Viewers," *Wall Street Journal*, June 6, 1996, pp. B1, B6.

130. Patrick M. Reilly, "Time out for Women's Sports Magazines," *Wall Street Journal*, January 19, 1998, p. B8.

131. Teri Agins, "'Real' Women Get a New Magazine Sized for Them," *Wall Street Journal*, December 3, 1996, pp. B8; Wendy Bounds, "Meredith Introduces 'More' for Women," *Wall Street Journal*, June 19, 1998, p. B4.

132. Maricris G. Briones, "On-line Retailers Seek Ways to Close Shopping Gender Gap," *Marketing News*, September 14, 1998, pp. 2, 10.

133. Rebecca Quick, "Victoria's Secret in Cyberspace," *Austin American Statesman*, January 14, 1999, p. E3.

134. Vanessa O'Connell, "Soap and Diaper Makers Pitch to Masses of Web Women," *Wall Street Journal*, July 20, 1998, pp. B1, B4.

135. Sak Onkvisit and John J. Shaw, *International Marketing: Analysis and Strategy* (Columbus, Ohio: Merrill, 1989).

136. "The Future of Households," *American Demographics*, December 1993, pp. 27–40.

137. Christina Diff, "Census Finds Striking Shift in Families," *Wall Street Journal*, May 28, 1998, pp. B1, B13.

138. Mary C. Gilly and Ben M. Enis, "Recycling the Family Life Cycle," in ed. Andrew A. Mitchell, *Advances in Consumer Research*, Vol. 9 (Ann Arbor, Mich.: Association for Consumer Research, 1982), pp. 271–276; William D. Danko and Charles M. Schaninger, "An Empirical Evaluation of the Gilly-Enis Updated Household Life Cycle Model," *Journal of Business Research*, August 1990, pp. 39–57.

139. Robert E. Wilkes, "Household Life-Cycle Stages, Transitions, and Product Expenditures," *Journal of Consumer Research*, June 1995, pp. 27–42.

140. Alan R. Andreasen, "Life Status Changes and Changes in Consumer Preferences and Satisfaction," *Journal of Consumer Research*, December 1984, pp. 784–794.

141. "The Mommies, in Numbers," *Brandweek*, November 13, 1993, p. 17; Lee Smith, "The New Wave of Illegitimacy," *Fortune*, April 18, 1994, pp. 81–94.

142. Elizabeth C. Hirschman, "Consumers and Their Animal Companions," *Journal of Consumer Research*, March 1994, pp. 616–632; Clinton R. Sanders, "The Animal 'Other': Self-Definition, Social Identity, and Companion Animals," in eds. Marvin E. Goldberg, Gerald Gorn, and Richard W. Pollay, *Advances in Consumer Research*, Vol. 17 (Provo, Utah: Association for Consumer Research, 1990), pp. 662–668; Alan Beck and Aaron Katcher, *Between Pets and People: The Importance of Animal Companionship* (New York: Putnam, 1983).

143. Ellen Graham, "Santa Has Lavish Plans for Cats, Dogs, Birds, Iguanas," *Wall Street Journal*, December 9, 1996, pp. B1, B2; Kathie Jenkins, "It's Dining Cats and Dogs," *Los Angeles Times*, June 22, 1995, pp. H14.

144. U.S. Bureau of the Census, Current Population Reports, Series P-20, No. 410, *Marital Status and Living Arrangements: March 1985* (Washington, D.C.: U.S. Government Printing Office, 1986); Judith Waldrop, "The Fashionable Family," *American Demographics*, March 1988, p. 22.

145. Patricia Braus, "Sex and the Single Spender," *American Demographics*, November 1993, pp. 28–34.

146. Barbara Carton, "It's a Niche! Twins, Triplets and Beyond," *Wall Street Journal*, February 2, 1999, pp. B1, B4.

147. "The Future of Households"; Karin Sandqvist, Bengt-Erik Andersson, and David Popenoe, "Thriving Families in the Swedish Welfare State; Family Decline: A Rejoinder," *Public Interest*, Fall 1992, pp. 114–122.

148. Clark D. Olson, "Materialism in the Home: The Impact of Artifacts on Dyadic Communication," in eds. Elizabeth C. Hirschman and Morris B. Holbrook, *Advances in Consumer Research*, Vol. 12 (Provo, Utah: Association for Consumer Research, 1985), pp. 388–393.

149. Jeanne L. Hafstrom and Marilyn M. Dunsing, "Socioeconomic and Social-Psychological Influences on Reasons Wives Work," *Journal of Consumer Research*, December 1978, pp. 169–175; Rena Bartos, *The Moving Target: What Every Marketer Should Know about Women* (New York: Free Press, 1982).

150. Rose M. Rubin, Bobye J. Riney, and David J. Molina, "Expenditure Pattern Differentials Between One-Earner and Dual-Earner Households: 1972–1973 and 1984," *Journal of Consumer Research*, June 1990, pp. 43–52; Horacio Soberon-Ferrer and Rachel Dardis, "Determinants of Household Expenditures for Services," *Journal of Consumer Research*, March 1991, pp. 385–397; Don Bellante and Ann C. Foster, "Working Wives and Expenditure on Services," *Journal of Consumer Research*, September 1984, pp. 700–707.

151. Michael D. Reilly, "Working Wives and Convenience Consumption," *Journal of Consumer Research*, March 1982, pp. 407–418; Ralph W. Jackson, Stephen W. McDaniel, and C. P. Rao, "Food Shopping and Preparation: Psychographic Differences of Working Wives and Housewives," *Journal of Consumer Research*, June 1985, pp. 110–113; Janet C. Hunt and B. F. Kiker, "The Effect of Fertility on the Time Use of Working Wives," *Journal of Consumer Research*, March 1981, pp. 380–387; Keith W. Bryant, "Durables and Wives' Employment Yet Again," *Journal of Consumer Research*, June 1988, pp. 37–47.

152. Sharon Y. Nickols and Karen D. Fox, "Buying Time and Saving Time: Strategies for Managing Household Production," *Journal of Consumer Research*, September 1983, pp. 197–208; R. S. Oropesa, "Female Labor Force Participation and Time-Saving Household Technology," *Journal of Consumer Research*, March 1993, pp. 567–579; Eugine H. Fram and Joel Axelrod, "The Distressed Shopper," *American Demographics*, October 1990, pp. 44–45.

153. Linda Thompson and Alexis Walker, "Gender in Families: Women and Men in Marriage, Work, and Parenthood," *Journal of Marriage and the Family*, November 1989, pp. 845–871.

154. James H. Alexander, John W. Shouten, and Scott D. Roberts, "Consumer Behavior and Divorce," in eds. Janeen Costa and Russell W. Belk, *Research in Consumer Behavior*, Vol. 6 (Greenwich, Conn.: JAI Press, 1993), pp. 153–184.

155. Kalpana Srinivasan, 'More Single Fathers Raising Kids, Though Moms Far More Common," *Austin American Statesman*, December 11, 1998, p. A23.

156. Barbara Rosewicz, "Here Comes the Bride . . . and for the Umpteenth Time," *Wall Street Journal*, September 10, 1996, pp. B1, B10.

157. Graham, "When Terrible Two's."

158. Jan Larson, "Understanding Stepfamilies," *American Demographics*, July 1992, pp. 36–40.

159. Hideo Takayama, "Spending More on Fewer Kids," *Journal of Japanese Trade and Industry*, May 1991, pp. 24–27.

160. Kathy Chen, "Chinese Babies Are Coveted Consumers," *Wall Street Journal*, May 15, 1998, pp. B1, B7.

161. "The Future of Households."

162. Norihiko Shirouzu, "Flouting 'Rules' Sells Fridges in Japan," *Wall Street Journal*, October 31, 1995, pp. B1, B2.

163. Lisa Gubernick, "Adoption in Ads: Trendy, but Touchy," *Wall Street Journal*, July 21, 1998, pp. B1, B8.

164. Louise Lee, "Your Chef Is Baking Sole in Your Oven," *Wall Street Journal*, May 21, 1998, pp. B1, B12.

165. Lyle V. Harris, "Shopping by Male," *Austin American Statesman*, April 27, 1999, pp. E1, E2.

166. Laura Koss-Feder, "Out and About," *Marketing News*, May 25, 1998, pp. 1, 20.

167. David D. Kirkpatrick, "Poz Magazine Sponsors Trade Fair Aimed at Consumers with HIV," *Wall Street Journal*, May 30, 1996, p. B12.

168. Harry L. Davis, "Dimensions of Marital Roles in Consumer Decision Making," *Journal of Marketing Research*, May 1970, pp. 168–177; Conway Lackman and John M. Lanasa, "Family Decision Making Theory: An Overview and Assessment," *Psychology and Marketing*, March–April 1993, pp. 81–93.

169. P. Doyle and P. Hutchinson, "Individual Differences in Family Decision Making," *Journal of the Market Research Society*, October 1973, pp. 193–206; Jagdish N. Sheth, "A Theory of Family Buying Decisions," in ed. J. N. Sheth, *Models of Buyer Behavior* (New York: Harper & Row, 1974), pp. 17–33; Daniel Seymour and Greg Lessne, "Spousal Conflict Arousal: Scale Development," *Journal of Consumer Research*, December 1984, pp. 810–821.

170. Neal Templin, "The PC Wars: Who Gets to Use the Family Computer?" *Wall Street Journal*, October 5, 1996, pp. B1, B2.

171. Sheth, "A Theory of Family Buying Decisions"; Michael A. Belch, George E. Belch, and Donald Sciglimpaglia, "Conflict in Family Decision Making: An Exploratory Investigation," in ed. Jerry C. Olson, *Advances in Consumer Research*, Vol. 7 (Chicago: Association for Consumer Research, 1980), pp. 475–479.

172. W. Christian Buss and Charles M. Schaninger, "The Influence of Family Decision Processes and Outcomes," in eds. Richard P. Bagozzi and Alice M. Tybout, *Advances in Consumer Research*, Vol. 10 (Ann Arbor, Mich.: Association for Consumer Research, 1983), pp. 439–444.

173. Terry L. Childers and Akshay R. Rao, "The Influence of Familial and Peer-Based Reference Groups on Consumer Decisions," *Journal of Consumer Research*, September 1992, pp. 198–211.

174. Harry L. Davis and Benny P. Rigaux, "Perception of Marital Roles in Decision Processes," *Journal of Consumer Research*, June 1974, pp. 5–14; Mandy Putnam and William R. Davidson, *Family Purchasing Behavior: 11 Family Roles by Product Category* (Columbus, Ohio: Management Horizons, Inc., a Division of Price Waterhouse, 1987).

175. Rosann Spiro, "Persuasion in Family Decision Making," *Journal of Consumer Research*, March 1983, pp. 393–402; Alvin Burns and Donald Granbois, "Factors Moderating the Resolution of Preference Conflict," *Journal of Marketing Research*, February 1977, pp. 68–77.

176. Pierre Filiarault and J. R. Brent Ritchie, "Joint Purchasing Decisions: A Comparison of Influence Structure in Family and Couple Decision Making Units," *Journal of Consumer Research*, September 1980, pp. 131–140; Dennis Rosen and Donald Granbois, "Determinants of Role Structure in Financial Management," *Journal of Consumer Research*, September 1983, pp. 253–258; Spiro, "Persuasion in Family Decision Making; Kim P. Corfman and Donald R. Lehmann, "Models of Cooperative Group Decision-Making and Relative Influence: An Experimental Investigation of Family Purchase Decisions," *Journal of Consumer Research*, June 1987, pp. 1–13.

177. William J. Qualls, "Household Decision Behavior: The Impact of Husbands' and Wives' Sex Role Orientation," *Journal of Consumer Research*, September 1987, pp. 264–279; Giovanna Imperia, Thomas O'Guinn, and Elizabeth MacAdams, "Family Decision Making Role Perceptions among Mexican-American and Anglo Wives: A Cross-Cultural Comparison," in eds. Elizabeth C. Hirschman and Morris B. Holbrook, *Advances in Consumer Research*, Vol. 12 (Provo, Utah: Association for Consumer Research, 1985), pp. 71–74.

178. Robert T. Green, Jean-Paul Leonardi, Jean-Louis Chandon, Isabella C. M. Cunningham, Bronis Verhage, and Alain Strazzieri, "Societal Development and Family Purchasing Roles: A Cross-National Study," *Journal of Consumer Research*, March 1983, pp. 436–442; Leonidas C. Leonidou, "Understanding the Russian Consumer," *Marketing and Research Today*, March 1992, pp. 75–83; Sak Onkvisit and John J. Shaw, *International Marketing: Analysis and Strategy* (Columbus, Ohio: Merrill, 1989).

179. Michael B. Menasco and David J. Curry, "Utility and Choice: An Empirical Study of Wife/Husband Decision Making," *Journal of Consumer Research*, June 1989, pp. 87–97; Qualls, "Household Decision Behavior."

180. C. Whan Park, "Joint Decisions in Home Purchasing: A Muddling-Through Process," *Journal of Consumer Research*, September 1982, pp. 151–162; Harry L. Davis, Stephen J. Hoch, and E. K. Easton Ragsdale, "An Anchoring and Adjustment Model of Spousal Predictions," *Journal of Consumer Research*, June 1986, pp. 25–37; Gary M. Munsinger, Jean E. Weber, and Richard W. Hansen, "Joint Home Purchasing by Husbands and Wives," *Journal of Consumer Research*, March 1975, pp. 60–66; Lakshman Krisnamurthi, "The Salience of Relevant Others and Its Effect on Individual and Joint Preferences: An Experimental Investigation," *Journal of Consumer Research*, June 1983, pp. 62–72; Robert F. Krampf, David J. Burns, and Dale M. Rayman, "Consumer Decision Making and the Nature of the Product: A Comparison of Husband and Wife Adoption Process Location," *Psychology and Marketing*, March–April 1993, pp. 95–109.

181. Tamara F. Mangleburg, "Children's Influence in Purchase Decisions: A Review and Critique," in eds. Marvin E. Goldberg, Gerald Gorn, and Richard W. Pollay, *Advances in Consumer Research*, Vol. 17 (Provo, Utah: Association for Consumer Research, 1990), pp. 813–825; Ellen R. Foxman, Patriya S. Tansuhaj, and Karin M. Ekstrom, "Family Members' Perceptions of Adolescents' Influence in Family Decision Making," *Journal of Consumer Research*, March 1989, pp. 481–490; George Belch, Michael A. Belch, and Gayle Ceresino, "Parental and Teenage Influences in Family Decision Making," *Journal of Business Research*, April 1985, pp. 163–176; Lackman and Lanasa, "Family Decision Making Theory."

182. Ernest Beck and Rekha Balu, "Europe Is Deaf to Snap! Crackle! Pop!" *Wall Street Journal*, June 22, 1998, pp. B1, B8.

183. Selina S. Guber and Jon Berry, "War Stories from the Sandbox: What Kids Say,"*Brandweek*, July 5, 1993, pp. 26–30; Andre Caron and Scott Ward, "Gift Decisions by Kids and Parents," *Journal of Advertising Research*, August–September 1975, pp. 15–20.

184. Mary Lou Roberts, Lawrence H. Wortzel, and Robert L. Berkeley, "Mothers' Attitudes and Perceptions of Children's Influence and Their Effect on Family Consumption," in ed. Jerry C. Olson, *Advances in Consumer Research*, Vol. 8 (Ann Arbor, Mich.: Association for Consumer Research, 1981), pp. 730–735; Ellen Foxman and Patriya Tansuhaj, "Adolescents' and Mothers' Perceptions of Relative Influence in Family Purchase Decisions: Patterns of Agreement and Disagreement," in ed. Michael J. Houston, *Advances in Consumer Research*, Vol. 15 (Provo, Utah: Association for Consumer Research, 1988), pp. 449–453.

185. Sharon E. Beatty and Salil Talpade, "Adolescent Influence in Family Decision Making: A Replication with Extension," *Journal of Consumer Research*, September 1994, pp. 332–341; Christopher Power, "Getting 'Em While They're Young," *BusinessWeek*, September 9, 1991, pp. 94–95; Scott Ward and Daniel B.

Wackman, "Children's Purchase Influence Attempts and Parental Yielding," *Journal of Marketing Research*, November 1972, pp. 316–319

186. William K. Darley and Jeen-Su Lim, "Family Decision Making in Leisure Time Activities: An Exploratory Analysis of the Impact of Locus of Control, Child Age Influence Factor and Parental Type on Perceived Child Influence," in ed. Richard J. Lutz, *Advances in Consumer Research*, Vol. 13 (Ann Arbor, Mich.: Association for Consumer Research, 1986), pp. 370–374; George P. Moschis and Linda G. Mitchell, "Television Advertising and Interpersonal Influences on Teenagers' Participation in Family Consumer Decisions," in ed. Richard J. Lutz, *Advances in Consumer Research*, Vol. 13 (Provo, Utah: Association for Consumer Research, 1986), pp. 181–186; James E. Nelson, "Children as Information Sources in Family Decisions to Eat Out," in ed. William L. Wilkie, *Advances in Consumer Research*, Vol. 6 (Ann Arbor, Mich.: Association for Consumer Research, 1978), pp. 419–423; Beatty and Talpade, "Adolescent Influence in Family Decision Making."

187. Kay M. Palan and Robert E. Wilkes, "Adolescent-Parent Interaction in Family Decision Making," *Journal of Consumer Research*, September 1997, pp. 159–169.

188. Les Carlson and Sanford Grossbart, "Parental Style and Consumer Socialization of Children," *Journal of Consumer Research*, June 1988, pp. 77–94.

189. Belch, Belch, and Ceresino, "Parental and Teenage Influences in Family Decision Making."

190. Calmetta Y. Coleman, "Supermarkets Build Sales by Beguiling Shoppers' Kids," *Wall Street Journal*, January 19, 1998, pp. B1, B8.

191. Petersen, "What Makes a Winner in Europe."

192. Rebecca Quick, "New Web Sites Let Kids Shop, Like, without Credit Cards," *Wall Street Journal*, June 14, 1999, pp. B1, B4.

193. Kevin Goldman, " Campbell Mithun Shows Its Stuff in a Kmart Makeover Campaign," *Wall Street Journal*, August 3, 1995, p. B3.

194. Betsy Spethmann, "Hilton Heads toward Tie-Ins," *Brandweek*, March 8, 1993, p. 4; Christina Binkley, "Marriott Outfits an Old Chain for New Market," *Wall Street Journal*, October 13, 1998, pp. B1, B4.

195. Pauline Yoshihashi, "Stars Fade as Las Vegas Bets on Families," *Wall Street Journal*, February 5, 1993, pp. B1, B2.

196. Terry Lefton, "Thomas Boards Amtrak Kidfare," *Brandweek*, September 19, 1994, p. 4.

197. Betsy Spethmann, "Chrysler Rolls in the Grass Roots," *Brandweek*, March 27, 1995.

198. Thomas C. O'Guinn and Timothy P. Meyer, "The Family VCR: Ordinary Family Life with a Common Textual Product," Working paper, University of Illinois, 1994.

CHAPTER 16

1. Lisa Bannon, "How a Rumor Spread about Subliminal Sex in Disney's *Aladdin*," *Wall Street Journal*, October 24, 1995, pp. A1, A13.

2. Frederick Koenig, *Rumor in the Marketplace: The Social Psychology of Commercial Hearsay* (Dover, Mass.: Auburn House, 1985); Paul M. Herr, Frank R. Kardes, and John Kim, "Effects of Word-of-Mouth and Product-Attribute Information on Persuasion: An Accessibility-Diagnosticity Perspective," *Journal of Consumer Research*, March 1991, pp. 454–462.

3. Paul F. Lazarsfeld, Bernard Berelson, and Hazel Gaudet, *The People's Choice; How the Voter Makes Up His Mind in a Presidential Campaign* (New York: Columbia University Press, 1948); see also Herr, Kardes, and Kim, "Effects of Word-of-Mouth and Product-Attribute Information on Persuasion: An Accessibility Diagnosticity Perspective."

4. Dale Duhan, Scott Johnson, James Wilcox, and Gilbert Harrell, "Influences on Consumer Use of Word-of-Mouth Recommendation Sources," *Journal of the Academy of Marketing Science*, 1997, 25 (Fall), pp. 283–295.

5. Vicki Clift, "Systematically Solicit Testimonial Letters," *Marketing News*, June 6, 1994, p. 7.

6. Wendy Bounds, "Keeping Teens from Smoking, with Style," *Wall Street Journal*, May 6, 1999, p. B6.

7. Fen Montaigne, "Name That Chintz! How Shelter Magazines Boost Brands," *Wall Street Journal*, March 14, 1997, pp. B1, B8.

8. Cyndee Miller, "Door-to-Door Selling Rings up Big Numbers for Phone Company," *Marketing News*, February 14, 1994, p. 2.

9. John W. Milligan, "Choosing Mediums for the Message," *US Banker*, February 1995, pp. 42–45.

10. Keiron Culligan, "Word-of-Mouth to Become True Measure of Ads," *Marketing*, February 9, 1995, p. 7.

11. "Wave of Internet Surfers Has Chinese Censors Nervous," *Los Angeles Times*, June 26, 1995, pp. D6; Jeffrey A. Trachtenberg, "Time Warner Unit Sets Joint Venture to Market TV Programming in China," *Wall Street Journal*, March 8, 1995, p. B2; Fred D. Reynolds and William R. Darden, "Mutually Adaptive Effects of Interpersonal Communication," *Journal of Marketing Research*, November 1971, pp. 449–454.

12. Kara Swisher, "The Gatekeeper," *Wall Street Journal*, Eastern Edition, December 8, 1997, pp. R18, R27.

13. Jacob Jacoby and Wayne D. Hoyer, "What If Opinion Leaders Didn't Really Know More: A Question of Nomological Validity," in ed. Kent B. Monroe, *Advances in Consumer Research*, Vol. 8 (Chicago, Ill.: Association for Consumer Research, 1980), pp. 299–302; Robin M. Higie, Lawrence F. Feick, and Linda L. Price, "Types and Amount of Word-of-Mouth Communications about Retailers," *Journal of Retailing*, Fall 1987, pp. 260–277; Related to innovativeness, Terry L. Childers ("Assessment of the Psychometric Properties of an Opinion Leadership Scale," *Journal of Marketing Research*, May 1986, pp. 184–187) found opinion leadership was related to consumer creativity/curiosity and to using products in multiple ways.

14. Marsha L. Richins and Teri Root-Shafer, "The Role of Involvement and Opinion Leadership in Consumer Word of Mouth: An Implicit Model Made Explicit," in ed. Michael J. Houston, *Advances in Consumer Research*, Vol. 15 (Provo, Utah: Association for Consumer Research, 1988), pp. 32–36.

15. Audrey Guskey-Federouch and Robert L. Heckman, "The Good Samaritan in the Marketplace: Motives for

Helpful Behavior," Paper presented at the Society for Consumer Psychology Conference, St. Petersburg, Fla., February 1994.

16. Lawrence F. Feick, Linda L. Price, and Robin Higie, "People Who Use People: The Opposite Side of Opinion Leadership," in ed. Richard J. Lutz, *Advances in Consumer Research*, Vol. 13 (Provo, Utah: Association for Consumer Research, 1986), pp. 301–305; see also Jagdish N. Sheth, "Word-of-Mouth in Low-Risk Innovations," *Journal of Advertising Research*, June–July 1971, pp. 15–18.

17. Lawrence F. Feick and Linda L. Price, "The Market Maven: A Diffuser of Marketplace Information," *Journal of Marketing*, January 1987, pp. 83–97.

18. See, for example, Dorothy Leonard-Barton, "Experts as Negative Opinion Leaders in the Diffusion of a Technological Innovation," *Journal of Consumer Research*, March 1985, pp. 914–926.

19. Everett M. Rogers, *Diffusion of Innovations*, New York: The Free Press, 1983.

20. Laura Bird, "Consumers Smile on Unilever's Mentadent," *Wall Street Journal*, May 31, 1994, p. B9; Joseph R. Mancuso, "Why Not Create Opinion Leaders for New Product Introduction?" *Journal of Marketing*, July 1969, pp. 20–25.

21. Gabriel Bar-Haim, "The Meaning of Western Commercial Artifacts for Eastern European Youth," *Journal of Contemporary Ethnography*, July 1987, pp. 205–226.

22. Stephan Fatsis, "In the NBA, Shoe Money is No Longer a Slam Dunk," *Wall Street Journal*, May 14, 1998, pp. B1, B5; Stefan Fatsis, "Grant Hill Signs New Fila Deal for $80 Million," *Wall Street Journal*, September 23, 1997, pp. B1, B8.

23. Basil G. Englis and Michael R. Solomon, "To Be and Not to Be: Lifestyle Imagery, Reference Groups, and the Clustering of America," *Journal of Advertising*, March 1995, pp. 13–28.

24. Stefan Fatsis, "'Rad' Sports Give Sponsors Cheap Thrills," *Wall Street Journal*, May 12, 1995, p. B8.

25. Todd Nissen, "McDonald's Sees Good Results in Middle East," *ClariNet Electronic News Service*, February 20, 1994.

26. Andrea Gerlin, "Scandals Imperil Products Tied to the Cowboys," *Wall Street Journal*, January 7, 1997, pp. B1, B9.

27. A. Benton Cocanougher and Grady D. Bruce, "Socially Distant Referent Groups and Consumer Aspiration," *Journal of Marketing Research*, August 1971, pp. 379–383.

28. Linda L. Price, Lawrence Feick, and Robin Higie, "Preference Heterogeneity and Coorientation as Determinants of Perceived Informational Influence," *Journal of Business Research*, November 1989, pp. 227–242; Jacqueline J. Brown and Peter Reingen, "Social Ties and Word-of-Mouth Referral Behavior," *Journal of Consumer Research*, December 1987, pp. 350–362; Mary C. Gilly, John L. Grahm, Mary Wolfinbarger, and Laura Yale, "A Dyadic Study of Interpersonal Information Search," *Journal of the Academy of Marketing Science*, 26 (2), pp. 83–100; George Moschis, "Social Comparison and Informal Group Influence," *Journal of Marketing Research*, August 1976, pp. 237–244.

29. Rohit Desphande, Wayne D. Hoyer, and Naveen Donthu, "The Intensity of Ethnic Affiliation: A Study of the Sociology of Hispanic Consumption," *Journal of Consumer Research*, September 1986, pp. 214–220; Douglas M. Stayman and Rohit Deshpande, "Situational Ethnicity and Consumer Behavior," *Journal of Consumer Research*, December 1989, pp. 361–371.

30. Jonathan K. Frenzen and Harry L. Davis, "Purchasing Behavior in Embedded Markets," *Journal of Consumer Research*, June 1990, pp. 1–12; see also Mark S. Granovetter, "The Strength of Weak Ties," *American Journal of Sociology*, May 1973, pp. 1360–1380; Brown and Reingen, "Social Ties and Word-of-Mouth Referral Behavior"; Jonathan K. Frenzen and Kent Nakamoto, "Structure, Cooperation, and the Flow of Market Information," *Journal of Consumer Research*, December 1993, pp. 360–375.

31. Reingen and Kernan, "Analysis of Referral Networks in Marketing"; Brown and Reingen, "Social Ties and Word-of-Mouth Referral Behavior"; see also Frenzen and Nakamoto, "Structure, Cooperation, and the Flow of Market Information."

32. Nicole Woolsey Biggart, *Charismatic Capitalism* (Chicago, Ill.: University of Chicago Press, 1989); see also Jonathan K. Frenzen and Harry L. Davis, "Purchasing Behavior in Embedded Markets," *Journal of Consumer Research*, June 1990, pp. 1–12.

33. Barbara Carton, "PCs Replace Lettuce Tubs at Sales Parties," *Wall Street Journal*, March 31, 1997, pp. B1, B10.

34. Frenzen and Davis, "Purchasing Behavior in Embedded Markets."

35. Scott Ward, "Consumer Socialization," *Journal of Consumer Research*, September 1974, pp. 1–16; George P. Moschis, "The Role of Family Communication in Consumer Socialization of Children and Adolescents," *Journal of Consumer Research*, March 1985, pp. 898–913; George P. Moschis, *Consumer Socialization: A Life Cycle Perspective* (Lexington Mass.: Lexington Books, 1987); Scott Ward, "Consumer Socialization," in eds. Harold H. Kassarjian and Thomas S. Robertson, *Perspectives in Consumer Behavior* (Glenview, Ill.: Scott-Foresman, 1980), pp. 380–396; Les Carlson and Sanford Grossbart, "Parental Style and Consumer Socialization of Children," *Journal of Consumer Research*, June 1988, pp. 77–92.

36. Moschis, "The Role of Family Communication in Consumer Socialization of Children and Adolescents."; Harriet L. Rheingold and Kaye V. Cook, "The Contents of Boys' and Girls' Rooms as an Index of Parents' Behavior," *Child Development*, June 1975, pp. 459–463; Scott Ward, Daniel B. Wackman, and Ellen Wartella, *How Children Learn to Buy: The Development of Consumer Information Processing Skills* (Beverly Hills, Calif.: Sage, 1979).

37. Ann Walsh, Russell Laczkiak, and Les Carlson, "Mothers' Preferences for Regulating Children's Television," *Journal of Advertising*, Fall 1998, pp. 23–36.

38. Dave Howland, "Ads Recruit Grandparents to Help Keep Kids from Drugs," *Marketing News*, January 18, 1999, p. 6.

39. Moschis, "The Role of Family Communication in Consumer Socialization of Children and Adolescents";

Conway Lackman and John M. Lanasa, "Family Decision Making Theory: An Overview and Assessment," *Psychology and Marketing*, March–April 1993, pp. 81–93; George P. Moschis, *Acquisition of the Consumer Role by Adolescents* (Atlanta: Georgia State University, 1978).

40. Beverly A. Browne, "Gender Stereotypes in Advertising on Children's Television in the 1990s: A Cross-National Analysis," *Journal of Advertising*, Spring 1998, pp. 83–96.

41. See, for example, Greta Fein, David Johnson, Nancy Kosson, Linda Stork, and Lisa Wasserman, "Sex Stereotypes and Preferences in the Toy Choices of 20-Month-Old Boys and Girls," *Developmental Psychology*, July 1975, pp. 527–528; Lenore A. DeLucia, "The Toy Preference Test: A Measure of Sex-Role Identification," *Child Development*, March 1963, pp. 107–117; Judith E. O. Blackmore and Asenath A. LaRue, "Sex-Appropriate Toy Preference and the Ability to Conceptualize Toys as Sex-Role Related," *Developmental Psychology*, May 1979, pp. 339–340; Nancy Eisenberg-Berg, Rita Boothby, and Tom Matson, "Correlates of Preschool Girls' Feminine and Masculine Toy Preferences," *Developmental Psychology*, May 1979, pp. 354–355.

42. Donna Rouner, "Rock Music Use as a Socializing Function," *Popular Music and Society*, Spring 1990, pp. 97–108; Thomas L. Eugene, "Clothing and Counterculture: An Empirical Study," *Adolescence*, Spring 1973, pp. 93–112.

43. Fein et al. "Sex Stereotypes and Preferences in the Toy Choices of 20-Month-Old Boys and Girls"; Eisenberg-Berg, Boothby, and Matson, "Correlates of Preschool Girls' Feminine and Masculine Toy Preferences"; Sheila Fling and Main Manosevitz, "Sex Typing in Nursery School Children's Play," *Developmental Psychology*, 7, 1972, pp. 146–152.

44. Tamara Mangleburg and Terry Bristol, "Socialization and Adolescents' Skepticism toward Advertising," *Journal of Advertising*, Fall 1998, pp. 11–21.

45. Robert E. Burnkrant and Alain Cousineau, "Informational and Normative Social Influence in Buyer Behavior," *Journal of Consumer Research*, December 1975, pp. 206–215; Morton Deutsch and Harold B. Gerard, "A Study of Normative and Informational Influence upon Individual Judgment," *Journal of Abnormal and Social Psychology*, November 1955, pp. 629–636.

46. Dennis Rook and Robert Fisher, "Normative Influences on Impulsive Buying Behavior," *Journal of Consumer Research*," December 1995, pp. 305–313.

47. Ernest Beck, "Let Labor Lean to Leisurewear: The Harrods Shopper Stays Proper," *Wall Street Journal*, May 27, 1997, p. B1.

48. Peter Reingen, Brian Foster, Jacqueline Brown, and Stephen B. Seidman, "Brand Congruence in Interpersonal Relations: A Social Network Analysis," *Journal of Consumer Research*, December 1984, pp. 771–783.

49. James E. Stafford, "Effects of Group Influence on Consumer Brand Preferences," *Journal of Marketing Research*, February 1966, pp. 68–75.

50. Randall L. Rose, William O. Bearden, and Jesse E. Teel, "An Attributional Analysis of Resistance to Group Pressure Regarding Illicit Drug and Alcohol

Consumption," *Journal of Consumer Research*, June 1992, pp. 1–13; see also Bobby J. Calder and Robert E. Burnkrant, "Interpersonal Influences on Consumer Behavior: An Attribution Theory Approach," *Journal of Consumer Research*, June 1977, pp. 29–38. 71; Solomon E. Asch, "Effects of Group Pressure upon the Modification and Distortion of Judgment," in ed. H. Guetzkow, *Groups, Leadership and Men* (Pittsburgh, Pa.: Carnegie Press, 1951); Sak Onkvisit and John J. Shaw, *International Marketing: Analysis and Strategy* (Columbus, Ohio: Merrill, 1989); see also Chin Tiong Tan and John U. Farley, "The Impact of Cultural Patterns on Cognition and Intention in Singapore," *Journal of Consumer Research*, March 1987, pp. 540–544.

51. For a general discussion of reactance behavior, see Mona A. Clee and Robert A. Wicklund, "Consumer Behavior and Psychological Reactance," *Journal of Consumer Research*, March 1980, pp. 389–405.

52. Bearden and Etzel, "Reference Group Influence on Product and Brand Purchase Decisions."

53. Robert E. Witt and Grady D. Bruce, "Group Influence and Brand Choice Congruence," *Journal of Marketing Research*, November 1972, pp. 440–443.

54. Bobby J. Calder and Robert E. Burnkrant, "Interpersonal Influences on Consumer Behavior: An Attribution Theory Approach," *Journal of Consumer Research*, June 1977, pp. 29–38; William O. Bearden, Richard G. Netemeyer, and Jesse E. Teel, "Measurement of Consumer Susceptibility to Interpersonal Influence," *Journal of Consumer Research*, March 1989, pp. 473–481; William O. Bearden and Randall L. Rose, "Attention to Social Comparison Information: An Individual Difference Factor Affecting Conformity," *Journal of Consumer Research*, March 1990, pp. 461–471.

55. C. Whan Park and Parker Lessig, "Students and Housewives: Differences in Susceptibility to Reference Group Influence," *Journal of Consumer Research*, September 1977, pp. 102–110.

56. Robert Fisher and Kirk Wakefield, "Factors Leading to Group Identification: A Field Study of Winners and Losers," *Psychology and Marketing*, January 1998, pp. 23–40.

57. John R. French and Bertram Raven, "The Bases of Social Power," in ed. D. Cartwright, *Studies in Social Power* (Ann Arbor, Mich.: Institute for Social Research, 1969), pp. 150–167.

58. Reingen et al., "Brand Congruence in Interpersonal Relations"; Witt, "Informal Social Group Influence on Brand Choice."; Park and Lessig, "Students and Housewives."

59. Dana-Nicoleta Lascu, William O. Bearden, and Randall L. Rose, "Norm Extremity and Interpersonal Influences on Consumer Conformity," *Journal of Business Research*, March 1995, pp. 200–212.

60. J. L. Freeman and S. Fraser, "Compliance without Pressure: The Foot-in-the-Door Technique," *Journal of Personality and Social Psychology*, August 1966, pp. 195–202.

61. Robert A. Hansen and Larry M. Robinson, "Testing the Effectiveness of Alternative Foot-in-the-Door Manipulations," *Journal of Marketing Research*, August 1980, pp. 359–364; Jacob Hornik, Tamar Zaig, and Diro

Shadmon, "Reducing Refusals in Telephone Surveys on Sensitive Topics," *Journal of Advertising Research*, June–July 1991, pp. 48–57; Michael Kamins, "The Enhancement of Response Rates to a Mail Survey through a Labeled Foot-in-the-Door Approach," *Journal of the Market Research Society*, April 1989, pp. 273–284.

62. Robert B. Cialdini, J. E. Vincent, S. K. Lewis, J. Caalan, D. Wheeler, and B. L. Darby, "Reciprocal Concessions Procedure for Inducing Compliance: The Door-in-the-Face Effect," *Journal of Personality and Social Psychology*, February 1975, pp. 200–215; John C. Mowen and Robert Cialdini, "On Implementing the Door-in-the-Face Compliance Strategy in a Marketing Context," *Journal of Marketing Research*, May 1980, pp. 253–258; see also Edward Fern, Kent Monroe, and Ramon Avila, "Effectiveness of Multiple Request Strategies: A Synthesis of Research Results," *Journal of Marketing Research*, May 1986, pp. 144–152.

63. Alice Tybout, Brian Sternthal, and Bobby J. Calder, "Information Availability as a Determinant of Multiple Request Effectiveness," *Journal of Marketing Research*, August 1983, pp. 279–290; John T. Gourville, "Pennies-a-Day: The Effect of Temporal Reframing on Transaction Evaluation," *Journal of Consumer Research*, March 1998, pp. 395–408.

64. Deutsch and Gerard, "A Study of Normative and Informational Influence upon Individual Judgment"; Park and Lessig, "Students and Housewives"; Dennis L. Rosen and Richard W. Olshavsky, "The Dual Role of Informational Social Influence: Implications for Marketing Management," *Journal of Business Research*, April 1987, pp. 123–144.

65. Ford and Ellis, "A Re-examination of Group Influence on Member Brand Preference"; Linda L. Price and Lawrence F. Feick, "The Role of Interpersonal Sources in External Search: An Informational Perspective," in ed. Thomas Kinnear, *Advances in Consumer Research*, Vol. 11 (Ann Arbor, Mich.: Association for Consumer Research, 1984), pp. 250–255.

66. Arch G. Woodside and M. Wayne DeLosier, "Effects of Word-of-Mouth Advertising on Consumer Risk Taking," *Journal of Advertising*, September 1976, pp. 17–26.

67. Henry Assael, *Consumer Behavior and Marketing Action*, 4th ed. (Boston, Mass.: PWS-Kent, 1992).

68. John R. French and Bertram Raven, "The Bases of Social Power," in ed. D. Cartwright, *Studies in Social Power* (Ann Arbor, Mich.: Institute for Social Research, 1959), pp. 150–167; Dana-Nicoleta Lascu, William Bearden, and Randall Rose, "Norm Extremity and Interpersonal Influences on Consumer Conformity," *Journal of Business Research*, March 1995, pp. 200–212; David B, Wooten and Americus Reed II, "Informational Influence and the Ambiguity of Product Experience: Order Effects on the Weighting of Evidence," *Journal of Consumer Psychology*, 1998, 7 (1), pp. 79–99.

69. Bearden, Netemeyer, and Teel, "Measurement of Consumer Susceptibility to Interpersonal Influence"; William O. Bearden and Randall L. Rose, "Attention to Social Comparison Information: An Individual Difference Factor Affecting Conformity," *Journal of Consumer Research*, March 1990, pp. 461–471.

70. Zaltman and Wallendorf, *Consumer Behavior*; Reingen et al., "Brand Congruence in Interpersonal Relations."

71. Charles R. Taylor, Gordon E. Miracle, and R. Dale Wilson, "The Impact of Information Level on the Effectiveness of U.S. and Korean Television Commercials," *Journal of Advertising*, Spring 1997, pp. 1–18.

72. Stephen A. LaTour and Ajay Manrai, "Interactive Impact of Informational and Normative Influence on Donations," *Journal of Marketing Research*, August 1989, pp. 327–335.

73. Johan Arndt, "Role of Product-Related Conversations in the Diffusion of a New Product," *Journal of Marketing Research*, August 1967, pp. 291–295.

74. Marsha L. Richins, "Negative Word of Mouth by Dissatisfied Consumers: A Pilot Study," *Journal of Marketing*, January 1983, pp. 68–78.

75. Laurence C. Harmon and Kathleen M. McKenna-Harmon, "The Hidden Costs of Resident Dissatisfaction," *Journal of Property Management*, May–June 1994, pp. 52–55.

76. Herr, Kardes, and Kim, "Effects of Word-of-Mouth and Product-Attribute Information on Persuasion"; Richard W. Mizerski, "An Attribution Explanation of the Disproportionate Influence of Unfavorable Information," *Journal of Consumer Research*, December 1982, pp. 301–310.

77. Brown and Reingen, "Social Ties and Word-of-Mouth Referral Behavior"; Arndt, "Role of Product-Related Conversations in the Diffusion of a New Product"; Laura Yale and Mary C. Gilly, "Dyadic Perceptions in Personal Source Information Search," *Journal of Business Research*, March 1995, pp. 225–238.

78. Chip Walker, "Word of Mouth," *American Demographics*, July 1995, pp. 39–46.

79. Herr, Kardes, and Kim, "Effects of Word-of-Mouth and Product-Attribute Information on Persuasion."

80. Elihu Katz and Paul F. Lazarsfeld, *Personal Influence* (Glencoe, Ill.: Free Press, 1955).

81. Bob Donath, "Shed Some Light: Handling On-line Threats to Firm's Image," *Marketing News*, February 16, 1998, p. 12.

82. Stephen Schurr, "Shawshank's Redemption: How A Movie Found an Afterlife," *Wall Street Journal*, April 39, 1999, pp. B1, B4.

83. A. Coskun and Cheryl J. Frohlich, "Service: The Competitive Edge in Banking," *Journal of Services Marketing*, Winter 1992, pp. 15–23; Jeffrey G. Blodgett, Donald H. Granbois, and Rockney Waters, "The Effects of Perceived Justice on Complainants' Negative Word-of-Mouth Behavior and Repatronage Intentions," *Journal of Retailing*, Winter 1993, pp. 399–429; Karen Maru File, Ben B. Judd, and Russ A. Prince, "Interactive Marketing: The Influence of Participation on Positive Word-of-Mouth Referrals," *Journal of Services Marketing*, Fall 1992, pp. 5–15; Gary L. Clark, Peter F. Kaminski, and David R. Rink, "Consumer Complaints: Advice on How Companies Should Respond Based on an Empirical Study," *Journal of Services Marketing*, Winter 1992, pp. 41–51.

84. Mara Adelman, "Social Support in the Service Sector: The Antecedents, Processes, and Outcomes of Social

Support in an Introductory Service," *Journal of Business Research*, March 1995, pp. 273–283; Jerry D. Rogers, Kenneth E. Clow, and Toby J. Kash, "Increasing Job Satisfaction of Service Personnel," *Journal of Services Marketing*, Winter 1994, pp. 14–27.

85. John Lippman, "Young Readers Get Hard Sell for Movie," *Wall Street Journal*, August 4, 1995, p. B1.

86. James Heckman, "Word-of-Mouth Advertising: Cheap, Credible, Created," *Marketing News*, February 1, 1999, p. 2.

87. Michael Kamins, Valerie Folkes, and Lars Perner, "Consumer Responses to Rumors: Good News, Bad News", *Journal of Consumer Psychology*, 1997, 6 (2), 165–187.

88. Frederick Koenig, *Rumor in the Marketplace: The Social Psychology of Commercial Hearsay* (Dover, Mass.: Auburn House, 1985); see also Alice M. Tybout, Bobby J. Calder, and Brian Sternthal, "Using Information Processing Theory to Design Marketing Strategies," *Journal of Marketing Research*, February 1981, pp. 73–79; Aliz M. Freedman, "Rumor Turns Fantasy into Bad Dream," *Wall Street Journal*, May 10, 1991, p. B1.

89. Koenig, Rumor in the Marketplace; see also Tybout, Calder, and Sternthal, "Using Information Processing Theory to Design Effective Marketing Strategies."

90. Susan Goggins as noted in Frederick Koenig, *Rumor in the Marketplace: The Social Psychology of Commercial Hearsay* (Dover, Mass.: Auburn House, 1985), pp. 163–164.

91. Samantha Marshall, "Labor Problems in Asia Hurt Nike's Image," *Wall Street Journal*, September 26, 1997, p. B18.

92. Jacqueline Mitchell, "Oldsmobile Launches Ads to Show It Has a Future in GM's Lineup," *Wall Street Journal*, November 16, 1992, p. B6.

93. Reingen and Kernan, "Analysis of Referral Networks in Marketing."

94. Vicki Clift, "Word-of-Mouth Can Be Easily Engineered," *Marketing News*, June 17, 1994, p. 11.

CHAPTER 17

1. Jim Sterne, *Advertising on the Web* (Indianapolis: Que, 1997).

2. Ann Carrns, "www.doctorsmedicines. *Wall Street Journal*, June 10, 1999, pp. B1, B4.

3. Gautam Naik, "In Digital Dorm, Click on Return for Soda," *Wall Street Journal*, January 23, 1997, pp. B1, B8.

4. Karen Benezra, "Don't Mislabel Gen X," *Brandweek*, May 15, 1995, pp. 32–34.

5. Milton Rokeach, *The Nature of Human Values* (New York: Free Press, 1973), p. 5.

6. Wagner A. Kamakura and Jose Alfonso Mazzon, "Value Segmentation: A Model for the Measurement of Values and Value Systems," *Journal of Consumer Research*, September 1991, pp. 208–218; see also Milton Rokeach and Sandra J. Ball-Rokeach, "Stability and Change in American Value Priorities, 1968–1981," *American Psychologist*, May 1989, pp. 775–784; Milton Rokeach, *Understanding Human Values* (New York: Free Press, 1979); Shalom H. Schwartz and Wolfgang Bilsky, "Toward a Universal Psychological Structure of Human Values," *Journal of Personality and Social Psychology*, September 1987, pp. 550–562.

7. Francesco M. Nicosia and Robert N. Mayer, "Toward a Sociology of Consumption," *Journal of Consumer Research*, September 1976, pp. 65–75; Hugh E. Kramer, "The Value of Higher Education and Its Impact on Value Formation," in eds. Robert E. Pitts and Arch G. Woodside, *Personal Values and Consumer Psychology* (Lexington Mass.: Lexington Books, 1984), pp. 239–251.

8. Mary Gilly and Lisa Penaloza, "Barriers and Incentives in Consumer Acculturation," in eds. W. Fred van Raaij and Gary J. Bamossy, *European Advances in Consumer Research*, Vol. 1 (Provo, Utah: Association for Consumer Research, 1993), pp. 278–286.

9. Rokeach, *The Nature of Human Values*; Schwartz and Bilsky, "Toward a Universal Psychological Structure of Human Values."

10. Russell W. Belk, "Materialism: Trait Aspects of Living in the Material World," *Journal of Consumer Research*, December 1985, pp. 265–280; Russell W. Belk, "Three Scales to Measure Constructs Related to Materialism: Reliability, Validity, and Relationships to Happiness," in ed. Thomas P. Kinnear, *Advances in Consumer Research*, Vol. 11 (Provo, Utah: Association for Consumer Research, 1984), pp. 291–297.

11. Marsha L. Richins, "Special Possessions and the Expression of Material Values," *Journal of Consumer Research*, December 1994, pp. 522–533.

12. Marsha L. Richins and Scott Dawson, "A Consumer Values Orientation for Materialism and Its Measurement: Scale Development and Validation," *Journal of Consumer Research*, December 1992, pp. 303–316.

13. Cheryl Russell, "The Power of One," *Brandweek*, October 4, 1993, pp. 27–32.

14. Mary Yoko Brannen, "Cross Cultural Materialism: Commodifying Culture in Japan," in eds. Floyd Rudmin and Marsha Richins, *Meaning, Measure, and Morality of Materialism* (Provo, Utah: The Association for Consumer Research, 1992), pp. 167–180; Dorothy E. Jones, Dorinda Elliott, Edith Terry, Carla A. Robbins, Charles Gaffney, and Bruce Nussbaum, "Capitalism in China," *BusinessWeek*, January 1985, pp. 53–59; see also David K. Tse, Russell W. Belk, and Nan Zhou, "Becoming a Consumer Society: A Longitudinal Analysis of Print Ads from Hong Kong, the People's Republic of China, and Taiwan," *Journal of Consumer Research*, March 1980, pp. 457–472.

15. Guliz Ger, "Problems of Marketization in Romania and Turkey," in eds. Clifford Schultz, Russell Belk, and Guliz Ger, *Consumption in Marketizing Economies* (Greenwich, Conn.: JAI Press, 1995); Guliz Ger, Russell Belk, and Dana–Nicoleta Lascu, "The Development of Consumer Desire in Marketizing and Developing Economies: The Cases of Romania and Turkey," in eds. Leigh McAlister and Michael L. Rothschild, *Advances in Consumer Research*, Vol. 20 (Provo, Utah: Association for Consumer Research, 1992), pp. 102–107.

16. P. H. Ferguson, "Shoppers Leave Ivory Towers for Bargain Basements in Japan," *Austin American Statesman*, December 26, 1993, p. A26.

17. Sally Goll Beatty, "Viacom's Blockbuster Rethinks Strategy," *Wall Street Journal*, November 20, 1995, p. B6.

18. Lisa Miller, "The New Dream Vacation Itinerary: Staying at Home," *Wall Street Journal*, October 20, 1996, pp. B1, B6.

19. Marleis Welms Floet, "Youth in Holland," *Industry Report.*

20. John P. Robinson, "Your Money or Your Time," *American Demographics*, November 1991, pp. 22–26.

21. Craig J. Thompson, "Caring Consumers: Gendered Consumption Meanings and the Juggling Lifestyle," *Journal of Consumer Research*, March 1996, pp. 388– 407.

22. Floet, "Youths in Holland."

23. Christopher T. Linen, "Marketing and the Global Economy," *Direct Marketing*, January 1991, pp. 54–56.

24. Joanne Lipman, "Marketers of Luxury Goods Are Turning from Self-Indulgence to Family Values," *Wall Street Journal*, October 22, 1992, pp. B1, B10.

25. Vanessa O'Connell, "Food Companies Plan New Pitches for Their Anticholesterol Products," *Wall Street Journal*, December 11, 1998; "Kellogg Unveils Line of Foods Designed to Improve Health," *Wall Street Journal*, November 6, 1998, p. B4.

26. Rekha Balu, "Forget 'Fat-Free'; Now It's Foods Packed with Protein," *Wall Street Journal*, September 9, 1998, pp. B1, B4.

27. Scott Kilman, "Monsanto Brings 'Genetic' Ads to Europe," *Wall Street Journal*, June 16, 1998, p. B8.

28. Sally Beatty, "Reader's Digest Targets Patients by Their Ailments," *Wall Street Journal*, April 17, 1998, pp. B1, B3.

29. Matt Murray, "GNC Makes Ginseng, Shark Pills Its Potion for Growth," *Wall Street Journal*, March 15, 1996, pp. B1, B3.

30. Tara Parker-Pope, "Antismoking Sentiment Flares in Europe's Smoke-Filled Cafes," *Wall Street Journal*, August 28, 1996, pp. B1, B8.

31. Carrns, www.doctorsmedicines.

32. Kathleen Deveny, "'Light' Foods Are Having Heavy Going," *Wall Street Journal*, March 4, 1993, pp. B1, B8.

33. Nikhil Deogun, "Fat-Free Snacks Aren't Wowing Frito Customers," *Wall Street Journal*, September 14, 1998, pp. B1, B4.

34. Kathleen Deveny, "Tempted by Taste, and Tiring of Tofu, Shoppers Are Bringing Home the Bacon," *Wall Street Journal*, March 18, 1993, pp. B1, B7; Laurie Grossman, "Steak Chains Sizzle as Healthier Eaters Splurge on T-Bones When They Dine Out," *Wall Street Journal*, December 14, 1992, pp. B1, B4; Scott Kilman, "Major Companies in the Food Industry Have Little Taste for Organic Products," *Wall Street Journal*, January 10, 1992, pp. B1, B8.

35. Sarah McBride, "Entrepreneurs Cater to a Growing Nation," *Wall Street Journal*, April 10, 1997, pp. B1, B15.

36. Fara Warner, "Cigarette Stores Offer Haven for Smokers Pressured by Smoking Laws, High Prices," *Wall Street Journal*, July 10, 1995, pp. B1, B7; Tara Parker-Pope, "Health Activists Light into Cigars' Glamorous Image," *Wall Street Journal*, July 8, 1997, pp. B1, B6.

37. Martha Brannigan and Frederic M. Biddle, "Fliers Favor a Jet with Space to Stretch," *Wall Street Journal*, December 12, 1997, pp. B1, B9; Anna Wilde Mathews, "Truck Stops Now Offer Massages, Movies, and Marriages," *Wall Street Journal*, July 22, 1997, pp. B1, B5.

38. Valerie Reitman, "For Frozen Yogurt, a Chill Wind Blows," *Wall Street Journal*, June 3, 1992, p. B1; Grossman, "Steak Chains Sizzle as Healthier Eaters Splurge on T-Bones When They Dine Out."

39. Eben Shapiro, "Portions and Packages Grow Bigger and BIGGER," *Wall Street Journal*, October 12, 1993, pp. B1, B10.

40. Diane Solis, "Cost No Object for Mexico's Makeup Junkies," *Wall Street Journal*, June 6, 1994, p. B1.

41. Paul Schweitzer, "The Third Millennium: Riding the Waves of Turbulence," *News Tribune*, December 1993, pp. 5–27.

42. Sak Onkvisit and John J. Shaw, *International Marketing: Analysis and Strategy* (Columbus, Ohio: Merrill, 1989), p. 243.

43. Robert Wilk, "INFOPLAN: The New Rich: A Psychographic Approach to Marketing to the Wealthy Japanese Consumer," ESOMAR Conference, Venice, Italy, June 1990, reported in Marieke K. de Mooij and Warren Keegan, *Advertising Worldwide*, pp. 122–129.

44. K. S. Yang, "Expressed Values of Chinese College Students, in eds. K. S. Yang and Y. Y. Li, *Symposium on the Character of the Chinese: An Interdisciplinary Approach* (Taipei, Taiwan: Institute of Ethnology Academic Sinica, 1972), pp. 257–312; see also Oliver H. M. Yau, *Consumer Behavior in China: Customer Satisfaction and Cultural Values* (New York: Rutledge, 1994).

45. Alfred S. Boote, cited in Piirto, *Beyond Mind Games*.

46. Geert Hofstede, "National Cultures in Four Dimensions," *International Studies of Management and Organization*, Spring–Summer 1983, pp. 46–74.

47. Michael Lynn, George M. Zinkhan, and Judy Harris, "Consumer Tipping: A Cross-Country Study," *Journal of Consumer Research*, December 1993, pp. 478–488.

48. Dana L. Alden, Wayne D. Hoyer, and Chol Lee, "Identifying Global and Culture-Specific Dimensions of Humor in Advertising: A Multinational Analysis," *Journal of Marketing*, April 1993, pp. 64–75.

49. Van R. Wood and Roy Howell, "A Note on Hispanic Values and Subcultural Research: An Alternative View," *Journal of the Academy of Marketing Science*, Winter 1991, pp. 61–67; see also Humberto Valencia, "Hispanic Values and Subcultural Research," *Journal of the Academy of Marketing Science*, Winter 1989, pp. 23–28.

50. Jonathan Burton, "Advertising Targeting Asians," *Far Eastern Economic Review*, January 21, 1993, pp. 40–41; see also Thomas E. Ness and Melvin T. Smith, "Middle-Class Values in Blacks and Whites," in eds. Robert E. Pitts and Arch G. Woodside, *Personal Values and Consumer Psychology* (Lexington Mass.: Lexington Books, 1984), pp. 231–237.

51. Richard P. Coleman, "The Continuing Significance of Social Class to Marketing," *Journal of Consumer Research*, December 1983, pp. 265–280.

52. William Strauss and Neil Howe, "The Cycle of Generations, *American Demographics*, April 1991, pp. 25–33, 52; see also William Strauss and Neil Howe, *Generations: The History of America's Future, 1584 to 2069* (New York: William Morrow, 1992); Lawrence A. Crosby, James D. Gill, and Robert E. Lee, "Life Status

and Age as Predictors of Value Orientation," in eds. Robert E. Pitts and Arch G. Woodside, *Personal Values and Consumer Psychology* (Lexington Mass.: Lexington Books, 1984), pp. 201–218.

53. Sharon Beatty, Lynn R. Kahle, Pamela Homer, and Shekhar Misra, "Alternative Measurement Approaches to Consumer Values: The List of Values and the Rokeach Value Survey," *Psychology and Marketing*, Fall 1985, pp. 181–200.

54. Lynn R. Kahle, *Social Values and Social Change: Adaptation to Life in America* (New York: Praeger, 1983).

55. Judith Valente, "Body Shop Has a Few Aches and Pains," *Wall Street Journal*, August 6, 1993, pp. B1, B12.

56. Yumiko Ono, "Will Good Housekeeping Translate into Japanese?" *Wall Street Journal*, December 30, 1997, pp. B1, B6.

57. Mark Van Roo, "Researching the Taiwan Market: A Very Different Consumer," *Marketing and Research Today*, February 1989, pp. 54–57.

58. Yoram Wind, "The Myth of Globalization," *Journal of Consumer Marketing*, Spring 1986, pp. 23–26.

59. Daniel Rosenberg, "Animal-Rights Ad, Toned Down, Still Hits a Wall at the Networks,' *Wall Street Journal*, December 29, 1998, p. B5.

60. David K. Tse, John K. Wong, and Chin Tiong Tan, "Towards Some Standardized Cross-Cultural Consumption Values," in ed. Michael J. Houston, *Advances in Consumer Research*, Vol. 15 (Provo, Utah: Association for Consumer Research, 1988), pp. 387–393; Ved Prakash, "Segmentation of Women's Market Based on Personal Values and the Means-End Chain Model: A Framework for Advertising Strategy," in ed. Richard J. Lutz, *Advances in Consumer Research*, Vol. 13 (Provo, Utah: Association for Consumer Research 1986), pp. 215–220.

61. Piirto, *Beyond Mind Games*.

62. Edward F. McWuarrie and Daniel Langmeyer, "Using Values to Measure Attitudes Toward Discontinuous Innovations," *Psychology and Marketing*, Winter 1985, pp. 239–252.

63. Patricia F. Kennedy, Roger J. Best, and Lynn R. Kahle, "An Alternative Method for Measuring Value-Based Segmentation and Advertisement Positioning," in eds. James H. Leigh and Claude R. Martin Jr., *Current Issues and Research in Advertising*, Vol. 11 (Ann Arbor, Mich.: Division of Research, School of Business Administration, University of Michigan, 1988), pp. 139–156; Daniel L. Sherrell, Joseph F. Hair, Jr., and Robert P. Bush, "The Influence of Personal Values on Measures of Advertising Effectiveness: Interactions with Audience Involvement," in eds. Robert E. Pitts and Arch G. Woodside, *Personal Values and Consumer Psychology* (Lexington, Mass.: Lexington Books, 1984), pp. 169–185.

64. Nikhil Deogun, "Seeking Rebound from Obscurity, RC Cola Wraps Itself in the Flag," *Wall Street Journal*, April 1, 1998, p. B8.

65. Pichayaporn Utumporn, "McDonald's Proclaims Itself a Thai Patriot," *Wall Street Journal*, August 10, 1998, p. B6.

66. Lisa Bannon and Margaret Studer, "For 2 Revealing European Ads, Overexposure Can Have Benefits," *Wall Street Journal*, June 17, 1993, p. B8.

67. "Calvin Klein Yanks Ads Showing Teen Skin," *Austin American Statesman*, August 29, 1995, p. C1.

68. Pichayaporn Utumporn, "Ad with Hitler Brings Outcry in Thailand," *Wall Street Journal*, June 5, 1995, p. C1.

69. Robert E. Pitts, John K. Wong, and D. Joel Whalen, "Consumers' Evaluative Structures in Two Ethical Situations: A Means-End Approach," *Journal of Business Research*, March 1991, pp. 119–130.

70. Elyse Tahouye, "Johnson & Johnson Tries to Shape Health-Care Debate with TV Ad," *Wall Street Journal*, May 11, 1993, p. B9.

71. Russell W. Belk and Richard W. Pollay, "Materialism and Status Appeals in Japanese and U.S. Print Advertising," *International Marketing Review*, Winter 1985, pp. 38–47; see also Russell W. Belk, Wendy J. Bryce, and Richard W. Pollay, "Advertising Themes and Cultural Values: A Comparison of U.S. and Japanese Advertising," in eds. K. C. Mun and T. S. Chan, *Proceedings of the Inaugural Meeting of the Southeast Asia Region Academy of International Business* (Hong Kong: The Chinese University of Hong Kong, 1985), pp. 11–20.

72. David K. Tse, Russell W. Belk, and Nan Zhou, "Becoming a Consumer Society: A Longitudinal and Cross-Cultural Content Analysis of Print Ads from Hong Kong, the People's Republic of China, and Taiwan," *Journal of Consumer Research*, March 1989, pp. 457–472.

73. Belk and Pollay, "Materialism and Status Appeals in Japanese and U.S. Print Advertising."

74. Tse, Belk, and Zhou, "Becoming a Consumer Society."

75. Russell W. Belk, "Material Values in the Comics: A Content Analysis of Comic Books Featuring Themes of Wealth," *Journal of Consumer Research*, June 1987, pp. 26–42.

76. For more information on means-end chain analysis, see Beth A. Walker and Jerry C. Olson, "Means-End Chains: Connecting Products with Self," *Journal of Business Research*, March 1991, pp. 111–118; Thomas J. Reynolds and John P. Richon, "Means-End Based Advertising Research: Copy Testing Is Not Strategy Assessment," *Journal of Business Research*, March 1991, pp. 131–142; Jonathan Gutman, "Exploring the Nature of Linkages between Consequences and Values," *Journal of Business Research*, March 1991, pp. 143–148; Thomas J. Reynolds and Jonathan Gutman, "Laddering Theory, Method, Analysis and Interpretation," *Journal of Advertising Research*, February/March 1988, pp. 11–31; Thomas J. Reynolds and Jonathan Gutman, "Laddering: Extending the Repertory Grid Methodology to Construct Attribute-Consequence-Value Hierarchies," in eds. Robert E. Pitts and Arch G. Woodside, *Personal Values and Consumer Psychology* (Lexington, Mass.: Lexington Books, 1984), pp. 155–167.

77. Thomas J. Reynolds and J. P. Jolly, "Measuring Personal Values: An Evaluation of Alternative Methods," *Journal of Marketing Research*, November 1980, pp. 531–536; Reynolds and Gutman, "Laddering;" Jonathan Gutman, "A Means-End Model Based on Consumer Categorization Processes," *Journal of Marketing*, Spring 1982, pp. 60–72.

78. T. L. Stanley, "Death of the Sports Car?" *Brandweek*, January 2, 1995, p. 38.

79. J. Michael Munson and Edward F. McQuarrie, "Shortening the Rokeach Value Survey for Use in Consumer Research," in ed. Michael J. Houston, *Advances in Consumer Research*, Vol. 15 (Provo, Utah: Association for Consumer Research, 1988), pp. 381–386.

80. Lynn R. Kahle, Sharon Beatty, and Pamela Homer, "Alternative Measurement Approaches to Consumer Values: The List of Values (LOV) and Values and Life Style (VALS)," *Journal of Consumer Research*, December 1986, pp. 405–409; Kahle, *Social Values and Social Change*.

81. Wagner Kamakura and Thomas P. Novak, "Value-System Segmentation: Exploring the Meaning of LOV," *Journal of Consumer Research*, June 1992, pp. 119–132.

82. Sigmund Freud, *Collected Papers*, Vols. I–V (New York: Basic Books, 1959); Erik Erickson, *Childhood and Society* (New York: Norton, 1963); Erik Erickson, *Identity: Youth and Crisis* (New York: Norton, 1968).

83. Yumiko Ono, "Marketers Seek the 'Naked' Truth," *Wall Street Journal*, May 30, 1997, pp. B1, B13.

84. Gordon Allport, *Personality: A Psychological Interpretation* (New York: Holt, Rinehart, & Winston, 1937); Raymond B. Cattell, *The Scientific Analysis of Personality* (Baltimore: Penguin, 1965).

85. Carl G. Jung, *Man and His Symbols* (Garden City, N.Y.: Doubleday, 1964); see also Hans J. Eysenck, "Personality, Stress and Disease: An Interactionistic Perspective," *Psychological Inquiry*, 2, 1991, pp. 221–232.

86. Carl R. Rogers, "Some Observations on the Organization of Personality," *American Psychologist*, September 1947, pp. 358–368; George A. Kelly, *The Psychology of Personal Constructs*, Vols. 1 and 2 (New York: Norton, 1955).

87. Bernard Weiner, "Attribution in Personality Psychology," in ed. Lawrence A. Pervin, *Handbook of Personality: Theory and Research* (New York: Guilford, 1990), pp. 465–484; Harold H. Kelly, "The Processes of Causal Attribution," *American Psychologist*, February 1973, pp. 107–128.

88. David Glen Mick and Claus Buhl, "A Meaning-Based Model of Advertising Experiences," *Journal of Consumer Research*, December 1992, pp. 317–338.

89. Karen B. Horney, *Our Inner Conflicts* (New York: Norton, 1945).

90. Joel B. Cohen, "An Interpersonal Orientation to the Study of Consumer Behavior," *Journal of Marketing Research*, August 1967, pp. 270–277; Jon P. Noerager, "An Assessment of CAD—A Personality Instrument Developed Specifically for Marketing Research," *Journal of Marketing Research*, February 1979, pp. 53–59.

91. Marsha L. Richins, "An Analysis of Consumer Interaction Styles in the Marketplace," *Journal of Consumer Research*, June 1983, pp. 73–82.

92. Richard P. Bagozzi, Hans Baumgartner, and Youjae Yi, "State versus Action Orientation and the Theory of Reasoned Action, An Application to Coupon Usage," *Journal of Consumer Research*, March 1992, pp. 505–518; William O. Bearden and Randall L. Rose, "Attention to Social Comparison Information: An Individual Difference Factor Affecting Consumer Conformity," *Journal of Consumer Research*, March 1990, pp. 461–471; Bobby J. Calder and Robert E. Burnkrant, "Interpersonal Influence on Consumer Behavior: An Attribution Theory Approach," *Journal of Consumer Research*, December 1979, pp. 29–38.

93. B. F. Skinner, *About Behaviorism* (New York: Knopf, 1974); B. F. Skinner, *Beyond Freedom and Dignity* (New York: Knopf, 1971).

94. Jacob Jacoby, "Multiple Indicant Approaches for Studying New Product Adopters," *Journal of Applied Psychology*, August 1971, pp. 384–388; Harold H. Kassarjian, "Personality and Consumer Behavior: A Review," *Journal of Marketing Research*, November 1971, pp. 409–418; see also Harold H. Kassarjian, "Personality: The Longest Fad," in ed. William L. Wilkie, *Advances in Consumer Research*, Vol. 6 (Ann Arbor, Mich.: Association for Consumer Research, 1979), pp. 122–124.

95. Franklin B. Evans, "Psychological and Objective Factors in the Prediction of Brand Choice," *Journal of Business*, October 1959, pp. 340–369.

96. John L. Lastovicka and Erich A. Joachimsthaler, "Improving the Detection of Personality-Behavior Relationships in Consumer Research," *Journal of Consumer Research*, March 1988, pp. 583–587; Kathryn E. A. Villani and Yoram Wind, "On the Usage of 'Modified' Personality Trait Measures in Consumer Research," *Journal of Consumer Research*, December 1975, pp. 223–228.

97. D. E. Berlyne, *Conflict, Arousal and Curiosity*, (New York: McGraw-Hill, 1960); D. E. Berlyne, "Novelty, Complexity, and Hedonic Value," *Perception and Psychophysics*, November 1970, pp. 279–286.

98. Marvin Zuckerman, *Sensation Seeking: Beyond the Optimal Level of Arousal* (Hillsdale, N.J.: Lawrence Erlbaum, 1979); Elizabeth C. Hirschman, "Innovativeness, Novelty Seeking, and Consumer Creativity," *Journal of Consumer Research*, December 1980, pp. 283–295.

99. R. A. Mittelstadt, S. L. Grossbart, W. W. Curtis, and S. P. DeVere, "Optimal Stimulation Level and the Adoption Decision Process," *Journal of Consumer Research*, September 1976, pp. 84–94; P. S. Raju, "Optimum Stimulation Level: Its Relationship to Personality, Demographics, and Exploratory Behavior," *Journal of Consumer Research*, December 1980, pp. 272–282; Jan-Benedict E. M. Steenkamp and Hans Baumgartner, "The Role of Optimum Stimulation Level in Exploratory Consumer Behavior," *Journal of Consumer Research*, December 1992, pp. 434–448; Erich A. Joachimsthaler and John Lastovicka, "Optimal Stimulation Level-Exploratory Behavior Models," *Journal of Consumer Research*, December 1984, pp. 830–835.

100. Leon G. Schiffman, William R. Dillon, and Festus E. Ngumah, "The Influence of Subcultural and Personality Factors on Consumer Acculturation," *Journal of International Business Studies*, Fall 1981, pp. 137–143.

101. John T. Cacioppo, Richard E. Petty, and Chuan F. Kao, "The Efficient Assessment of Need for Cognition," *Journal of Personality Assessment*, June 1984, pp. 306–307; Curtis R. Haugtvedt, Richard E. Petty, and John T. Cacioppo, "Need for Cognition and Advertising: Understanding the Role of Personality Variables in Consumer Behavior," *Journal of Consumer Psychology*, 1 (3), 1992, pp. 239–260; Rajeev Batra and Douglas M.

Stayman, "The Role of Mood in Advertising Effectiveness," *Journal of Consumer Research*, September 1990, pp. 203–214; John T. Cacioppo, Richard E. Petty, and K. Morris, "Effects of Need for Cognition on Message Evaluation, Recall and Persuasion," *Journal of Personality and Social Psychology*, October 1983, pp. 805–818.

102. William O. Bearden, Richard G. Netemeyer, and Jesse H. Teel, "Measurement of Consumer Susceptibility to Interpersonal Influence," *Journal of Consumer Research*, March 1989, pp. 472–480; Peter Wright, "Factors Affecting Cognitive Resistance to Ads," June 1975, pp. 1–9.

103. Richard C. Becherer and Lawrence C. Richard, "Self-Monitoring as a Moderating Variable in Consumer Behavior," *Journal of Consumer Research*, December 1978, pp. 159–162; Mark Snyder and Kenneth G. DeBono, "Appeals to Image and Claims about Quality: Understanding the Psychology of Advertising," *Journal of Personality and Social Psychology*, September 1985, pp. 586–597.

104. Dean Peabody, *National Characteristics* (Cambridge, England: Cambridge University Press, 1985); Allan B. Yates, "Americans, Canadians Similar but Vive La Difference," *Direct Marketing*, October 1985, p. 152

105. Terry Clark, "International Marketing and National Character: A Review and Proposal for an Integrative Theory," *Journal of Marketing*, October 1990, pp. 66–79.

106. Yates, "Americans, Canadians Similar but Vive La Difference,"

107. Robert Frank, "Moxie, Big Red, Other Cult Drinks Thrive on Being Hometown Heroes," *Wall Street Journal*, May 6, 1996, pp. B1, B5.

108. James P. Miller, "Hip and Irreverent, Alternative Papers Grab Readers," *Wall Street Journal*, July 29, 1997, pp. B1, B8.

109. Vanessa O'Connell, "Nabisco Ads Push Cookies for Self-Esteem," *Wall Street Journal*, July 10, 1998, p. B5.

110. John L. Lastovicka, John P. Murray, Erich A. Joachimsthaler, Gaurav Bhalla, and Jim Scheurich, "A Lifestyle Typology to Model Young Male Drinking and Driving," *Journal of Consumer Research*, September 1987, pp. 257–263.

111. Morris B. Holbrook, "Nostalgia and Consumption Preferences: Some Emerging Patterns of Consumer Tastes," *Journal of Consumer Research*, September 1993, pp. 245–256.

112. William D. Wells, "Psychographics: A Critical Review," *Journal of Marketing Research*, May 1975, pp. 196–213.

113. Rebecca Piirto, *Beyond Mind Games* (Ithaca, N.Y.: American Demographic Books, 1991).

114. Onkvisit and Shaw, *International Marketing*, p. 283.

115. Leonidas C. Leonidou, "Understanding the Russian Consumer," *Marketing and Research Today*, March 1992, pp. 75–83.

116. Sam Bradley, "Chinese Consumers Eyeing Hard Goods," *Brandweek*, June 12, 1995, p. 28.

117. Cyndee Miller, "Study Dispels '80s Stereotypes of Women," *Marketing News*, May 22, 1995, p. 3.

118. Kevin Helliker, "Forget Candlelight, Flowers, and Tips: More Restaurants Tout Takeout Service," *Wall Street Journal*, June 15, 1992, pp. B1, B5.

119. Ross Kerber, "Too Busy for Food, Athletes Go for Goo," *Wall Street Journal*, May 1, 1997, pp. B1, B9.

120. Pam Weisz, "Mead Johnson En Mass," *Wall Street Journal*, *Brandweek*, July 17, 1995, p. 8.

121. Wendy Bounds, "New Cameras and Film for the Inept and Impatient," *Wall Street Journal*, January 29, 1996, p. B1.

122. Louise Lee, "Facing Superstore Saturation, Wal-Mart Thinks Small," *Wall Street Journal*, March 25, 1998, pp. B1, B2.

123. ACE Brochure 1989; published by RISC, Paris, France; see also de Mooij and Keegan, *Advertising Worldwide*.

124. Elisabeth Rubinfien, "Travel Alert: Luxury Arrives in Moscow," *Wall Street Journal*, June 29, 1992, p. B7.

125. Yumiko Ono, "Off-Road Vehicles Leave Others in the Dust," *Wall Street Journal*, July 17, 1993, p. B1.

126. Tara Parker-Pope, "Nonalcoholic Beer Hits the Spot in Mideast," *Wall Street Journal*, December 6, 1996, pp. B1, B2.

127. Karen Benezra, "Friday's Puts Apparel on Expansion Menu," *Brandweek*, June 19, 1995, p. 5; Karen Benezra, "Landing the Casual Diner," *Brandweek*, May 22, 1995, pp. 26–32.

128. Steve Gelsi, "Pioneer Hits Videophiles with Audio," *Brandweek*, June 19, 1995, p. 16.

129. Basil G. Englis and Michael R. Solomon, "To Be and Not to Be: Life Style Imagery, Reference Groups, and The Clustering of America," *Journal of Advertising*, Spring 1995, pp. 13–28.

130. Kathryn Kranhold, "Golf's High Profile Drives Firms to Take Whack at Big Campaigns," *Wall Street Journal*, July 28, 1997, p. B8.

131. Sally Goll Beatty, "Busch Promotion Takes Aim at Hunters," *Wall Street Journal*, November 19, 1996, p. B1.

132. Chad Rubel, "Parents Magazines Make Room for Daddy," *Marketing News*, February 27, 1995, pp. 1, 5.

133. Wendy Bounds, "What Nerve! Rival Challenges Martha Stewart," *Wall Street Journal*. November 19, 1998, pp. B1, B16.

134. Sally Goll Beatty, "Philip Morris Starts Lifestyle Magazine," *Wall Street Journal*, September 16, 1996, pp. B1, B10.

135. Kyle Pope, "Reading the Paper Again, Loser? Chiat's Perverse ABC Campaign," *Wall Street Journal*, July 23, 1997, p. B6.

136. Fara Warner, "TV Study Tips, Lectures Win Chinese Viewers," *Wall Street Journal*, February 18, 1997, pp. B1, B9.

137. Thomas E. Weber, "Where the Boys and Girls Are: Teens Talk about the Web," *Wall Street Journal*, October 24, 1997, pp. B6, B7.

138. Jacob Hornik and Mary Jane Schlinger, "Allocation of Time to the Mass Media," *Journal of Consumer Research*, March 1981, pp. 343–355.

139. Eben Shapiro, "Web Lovers Love TV, Often Watch Both," *Wall Street Journal*, June 12, 1998, p. B9.

140. Deveny, "For Coffee's Big Three, A Gourmet-Brew Boom Proves Embarrassing Bust"; Gerry Khermouch, "Microbrews Come of Age in the Ways of Marketing," *Brandweek*, October 18, 1993, p. 30; Jennifer Cody, "Deregulation Opens Gate for Flood of Home Brews," *Wall Street Journal*, May 20, 1994, p. B1.

141. Yumiko Ono, "Hangover Drugs Keep Office Parties Going," *Wall Street Journal*, January 22, 1992, p. B1.

142. Yumiko Ono, "The Bread Can't Yet Put Itself in the Toaster," *Wall Street Journal*, July 21, 1993, p. B1.

143. Arnold Mitchell, *Consumer Values: A Typology*, (Menlo Park, Calif.: Stanford Research Institute, 1978).

144. Martha Fransworth Riche, "Psychographics for the 1990s," *American Demographics*, July 1989, pp. 24–54.

145. For descriptions of the VALS2 segments, see Riche, "Psychographics for the 1990s"; see also Judith Waldrop, "Markets with Attitude,'" *American Demographics*, July 1994, pp. 22–33.

146. For a description of these segments, see Piirto, *Beyond Mind Games*.

147. Kahle, Beatty, and Homer, "Alternative Measurement Approaches to Consumer Values"; Thomas P. Novak and Bruce MacEvoy, "On Comparing Alternative Segmentation Schemes: The List of Values (LOV) and Values and Life Styles (VALS)," *Journal of Consumer Research*, June 1990, pp. 105–109.

148. Piirto, *Beyond Mind Games*.

149. "The Yankelovich Monitor 1992," *Brandweek*, November 30, 1992, pp. 18–21.

150. Piirto, *Beyond Mind Games*.

151. Jacqueline Silver, "Turning Tables: America and Japan: The Market Opportunities for Companies of the EC," *ESOMAR Conference, America, Japan and the EC '92: The Prospects for Marketing, Advertising and Research* (Venice, Italy, June 18–20, 1990) in Marieke K. de Mooij and Warren Keegan, *Advertising Worldwide* (London: Prentice-Hall International, 1991), p. 122.

152. Cyndee Miller, "From Kuptsi to Cossacks: Ad Agency Divides Russia into Five Segments," *Marketing News*, June 8 1992, p. 18.

153. Piirto, *Beyond Mind Games*

154. Douglas B. Holt, "Poststructuralist Lifestyle Analysis: Conceptualizing the Social Patterning of Consumption in Postmodernity," *Journal of Consumer Research*, March 1997, pp. 326–350.

CHAPTER 18

1. From John W. Schouten and James H. McAlexander, "Subcultures of Consumption: An Ethnography of the New Bikers," *Journal of Consumer Research*, June 1995, pp. 43–61.

2. Grant McCracken, "Culture and Consumption: A Theoretical Account of the Structure and Movement of the Cultural Meaning of Consumer Goods," *Journal of Consumer Research*, June 1986, pp. 71–84; Grant McCracken, *Culture and Consumption* (Indianapolis: Indiana University Press, 1990).

3. McCracken, "Culture and Consumption"; McCracken, *Culture and Consumption*. See also Elizabeth C. Hirschman, Linda Scott, and William B. Wells, "A Model of Product Discourse: Linking Consumer Practice to Cultural Texts," *Journal of Advertising*, Spring 1998, pp. 33–50; Barbara A. Phillips, "Thinking into It: Consumer Interpretation of Complex Advertising Images," *Journal of Advertising*, Summer 1997, pp. 77–86; Cele Otnes and Linda Scott, "Something Old, Something New: Exploring the Interaction between Ritual and Advertising," *Journal of Advertising*, Spring 1996, pp. 33–50; Jonna Holland and James W. Gentry, "The Impact of Cultural Symbols on Advertising Effectiveness: A Theory of Intercultural Accommodation," in eds. Merrie Brucks and Debbie MacInnis, *Advances in Consumer Research*, Vol. 24 (Provo, Utah: Association for Consumer Research, 1997), pp. 483–489.

4. For an interesting discussion of the use of how consumers use fashion to both characterize their identity and infer aspects of others' identities, see Craig J. Thompson and Diana L. Haytko, "Speaking of Fashion: Consumers' Use of Fashion Discourses and the Appropriation of Countervailing Cultural Meanings," *Journal of Consumer Research*, June 1997, pp. 15–42.

5. Julie Laboy, "Clothiers Bring the Barrio to Japanese Teen Rebels," *Wall Street Journal*, April 8, 1998, pp. CA1, CA4.

6. Lauren Goldstein, "Urban Wear Goes Suburban," *Fortune*, December 21, 1998, pp. 169–172.

7. Douglas M. Stayman and Rohit Deshpande, "Situational Ethnicity and Consumer Behavior," *Journal of Consumer Research*, December 1989, pp. 361–371.

8. Laura R. Oswald, "Culture Swapping: Consumption and the Ethnogenesis of Middle-Class Haitian Immigrants," *Journal of Consumer Research*, March 1999, pp. 303–318.

9. Elisabeth Furst, "The Cultural Significance of Food," in ed. Per Otnes, *The Sociology of Consumption: An Anthology* (Oslo, Norway: Solum Forlag, 1988), pp. 89–100.

10. Lisa Penaloza, "Atravesando Fronteras/Border Crossings: A Critical Ethnographic Exploration of the Consumer Acculturation of Mexican Immigrants," *Journal of Consumer Research*, June 1994, pp. 32–54.

11. Kathleen, Brewer Doran, "Symbolic Consumption in China: The Color Television as a Life Statement," in eds. Merrie Brucks and Debbie MacInnis, *Advances in Consumer Research*, Vol. 24 (Provo, Utah: Association for Consumer Research, 1997), pp. 128–131.

12. Amy Cortese, "My Jet Is Bigger Than Your Jet," *BusinessWeek*, August 25, 1997, p. 126.

13. Elizabeth C. Hirschman, "Upper Class WASPs as Consumers: A Humanistic Inquiry," in eds. Elizabeth Hirschman and Jagdish N. Sheth, *Research in Consumer Behavior*, Vol. 3 (Greenwich, Conn.: JAI Press, 1988), pp. 115–147; see also Elizabeth C. Hirschman, "Primitive Aspects of Consumption in Modern American Society," *Journal of Consumer Research*, September 1985, pp. 142–154; for a study of the symbols of upper-middle class consumers, see Jeffrey F. Durgee, Morris B. Holbrook, and Melanie Wallendorf, "The Wives of Woodville," in ed. Russell W. Belk, *Highways and Buyways: Naturalistic Research from the Consumer Behavior Odyssey* (Provo, Utah: Association for Consumer Research, 1991), pp. 167–177.

14. Melanie Wallendorf and Eric Arnould, "We Gather Together: Consumption Rituals of Thanksgiving Day," *Journal of Consumer Research*, June 1991, pp. 13–31.

15. Stephanie Anderson Forest, "Dressed to Drill," *BusinessWeek*, September 7, 1997, p. 40.

16. For additional literature on the use of clothing as symbols, see Rebecca H. Holman, "Apparel as Communication," in eds. Elizabeth C. Hirschman and

Morris B. Holbrook, *Symbolic Consumer Behavior* (Ann Arbor, Mich.: Association for Consumer Research, 1981), pp. 7–15.

17. Bourdieu, Pierre, *Distinction: A Social Critique of the Judgment of Taste,* Cambridge MS: Harvard University Press, 1984; for other research on gender associations with food, see Deborah Heisley, "Gender Symbolism in Food," doctoral dissertation, Northwestern University, 1991.

18. Levy, "Interpreting Consumer Mythology."

19. Nancy Holt, "Glow-in-the-Dark Rosary: Badge of Faith or Forbidden Gang Garb," *Wall Street Journal*, July 22, 1997, p. B1.

20. Jennifer Edison Escalas, "The Consumption of Insignificant Rituals: A Look at Debutante Balls," in eds. Leigh McAlister and Michael L. Rothschild, *Advances in Consumer Research*, Vol. 20 (Provo, Utah: Association for Consumer Research, 1993), pp. 709–716.

21. Deborah Weisgall, "Buying Time," *Fortune*, September 8, 1997, p. 192.

22. Michael R. Solomon, "Building up and Breaking down: The Impact of Cultural Sorting on Symbolic Consumption," in eds. Elizabeth C. Hirschman and Jagdish N. Sheth, *Research in Consumer Behavior* (Greenwich Conn.: JAI Press, 1988), pp. 325–351; McCracken, "Culture and Consumption"; McCracken, *Culture and Consumption.*

23. Solomon, "Building up and Breaking down"; C. Whan Park, Bernard J. Jaworski, and Deborah J. MacInnis, "Strategic Brand Concept-Image Management," *Journal of Marketing*, October 1986, pp. 135–145; James H. Leigh and Terrace G. Gabel, "Symbolic Interactionism: Its Effects on Consumer Behavior and Implications for Marketing Strategy," *Journal of Consumer Marketing*, Winter 1992, pp. 27–39.

24. Myrna L. Armstrong and Donata C. Gabriel, "Motivation for Tattoo Removal," *Archives of Dermatology*, April 1996, pp. 412–416.

25. John W. Schouten, "Personal Rites of Passage and the Reconstruction of Self," in eds. Rebecca H. Holman and Michael R. Solomon, *Advances in Consumer Research*, Vol. 18 (Provo, Utah: Association for Consumer Research, 1991), pp. 49–51.

26. Melissa Martin Young, "Dispositions of Possessions During Role Transitions," in eds. Rebecca H. Holman and Michael R. Solomon, *Advances in Consumer Research*, Vol. 18 (Provo, Utah: Association for Consumer Research, 1991), pp. 33–39.

27. Robert A. Wicklund and Peter M. Gollwitzer, *Symbolic Self-Completion* (Hillsdale, N.J.: Lawrence Erlbaum, 1982).

28. Diane Ackerman, *A Natural History of Love* (New York: Random House, 1994).

29. James H. McAlexander, John W. Schouten, and Scott D. Roberts, "Consumer Behavior and Divorce," in eds. Janeen Arnold Costa and Russell W. Belk, *Research in Consumer Behavior*, Vol. 6 (Greenwich, Conn.: JAI Press, 1993), pp. 162; see also Rita Fullerman and Kathleen Debevec, "Till Death We Do Part: Family Dissolution, Transition, and Consumer Behavior," in eds. John F. Sherry and Brian Sternthal, *Advances in Consumer Research*, Vol. 19 (Provo, Utah: Association for Consumer Research, 1992), pp. 514–521.

30. Lisa Penaloza, "Atravesando Fronteras/Border Crossings"; Melanie Wallendorf and Michael D. Reilly, "Ethnic Migration, Assimilation, and Consumption," *Journal of Consumer Research*, December 1983, pp. 292–302; Rohit Deshpande, Wayne Hoyer, and Naveen Donthu, "The Intensity of Ethnic Affiliation: A Study of the Sociology of Hispanic Consumption," *Journal of Consumer Research*, September 1986, pp. 214–220. For a discussion of acculturation of Chinese Americans, see Wei-Na Lee, "Acculturation and Advertising Communication Strategies: A Cross-Cultural Study of Chinese Americans," *Psychology and Marketing*, September–October 1993, pp. 381–397. For an interesting study on the immigration of Haitian consumers see Laura R. Oswald, "Culture Swapping: Consumption and the Ethnogenesis of Middle-Class Haitian Immigrants," *Journal of Consumer Research*, March 1999, pp. 303–318. For a discussion of Turkish consumers immigrating to Denmark, see Guliz Gur and Per Ostergaard, "Constructing Immigrant Identities in Consumption: Appearance Among the Turko-Danes," in eds. Joseph W. Alba and Wesley Hutchinson, *Advances in Consumer Research*, Vol. 25, (Provo, Utah: Association for Consumer Research, 1998), pp. 48–52.

31. Annamma Joy and Ruby Roy Dholakia, "Remembrances of Things Past: The Meaning of Home and Possessions of Indian Professionals in Canada", in ed., Floyd W. Rudmin, *To Have Possessions: A Handbook of Ownership and Property, Journal of Social Behavior and Personality*, Special Issue, 6 (6), 1191, 385–402.; see also Raj Mehta and Russell W. Belk, "Artifacts, Identity, and Transition: Favorite Possessions of Indians and Indian Immigrants to the United States," *Journal of Consumer Research*, March 1991, pp. 398–411.

32. Priscilla A. LaBarbera, "The Nouveau Riches: Conspicuous Consumption and the Issue of Self-Fulfillment," in eds. Elizabeth C. Hirschman and Jagdish N. Sheth, *Research in Consumer Behavior* (Greenwich Conn.: JAI Press, 1988), pp. 181–182.

33. Cyndee Miller, "'Til Death Do They Part," *Marketing News*, March 27, 1995, pp. 1–2; for an extensive discussion of consumer life transitions and products relevant to these transitions, see Paula Mergenhagen, *Targeting Transitions* (Ithaca, N.Y.: *American Demographics* Books, 1995).

34. Miller, "'Til Death Do They Part."

35. Otnes and Scott, "Something Old, Something New."

36. Stephanie Mehta, "Bridal Superstores Woo Couples with Miles of Gowns and Tuxes," *Wall Street Journal*, February 14, 1995, pp. B1, B2.

37. In line with our notion that the meaning of the symbol may derive from the culture as opposed to the individual and that symbols may have public or private meaning, see Marsha L. Richins, "Valuing Things: The Public and Private Meaning of Possessions," *Journal of Consumer Research*, December 1994, pp. 504–521.

38. Mihaly Csikzentmihalyi and Eugene Rochberg-Halton, *The Meaning of Things: Domestic Symbols and the Self* (Cambridge, England: Cambridge University Press, 1981); N. Laura Kamptner, "Personal Possessions and Their Meanings: A Life Span Perspective," *Journal of Social Behavior and Personality*, 6, (6) 1991, pp. 209–228; see also Richins, "Valuing Things."

39. Wallendorf and Arnould, "We Gather Together."
40. Adam Kuper, "The English Christmas and the Family: Time out and Alternative Realities," in ed. Daniel Miller, *Unwrapping Christmas* (Oxford, England: Oxford University Press, 1993), pp. 157–175; Barbara Bodenhorn, "Christmas Present: Christmas Public," in ed. Daniel Miller, *Unwrapping Christmas* (Oxford, England: Oxford University Press, 1993), pp. 193–216.
41. See, for example, Russell W. Belk, "Possessions and the Sense of Past."
42. Howard L. Fromkin and C. R. Snyder, "The Search for Uniqueness and Valuation of Scarcity," in eds. Kenneth Gergen, Martin S. Greenberg, and Richard H. Willis, *Social Exchanges: Advances in Theory and Research* (New York: Plenum, 1980), pp. 57–75; Csikszenthmihalyi and Rochberg-Halton, *The Meaning of Things*; see also Richins, "Valuing Things."
43. Gabriel Bar-Haim, "The Meaning of Western Commercial Artifacts for Eastern European Youth.", Journal of Contemprary Ethnography, July 1987, pp. 205–226.
44. Baker and Kennedy, "Death by Nostalgia"; Holbrook and Schindler, "Echoes of the Dear Departed Past."
45. Russell W. Belk, "Possessions and the Extended Self," *Journal of Consumer Research*, September 1988, pp. 139–168; A. Dwayne Ball and Lori H. Tasaki, "The Role and Measurement of Attachment in Consumer Behavior," *Journal of Consumer Psychology*, 1 (2), 1992, pp. 155–172; M. Joseph Sirgy, "Self-Concept and Consumer Behavior: A Critical Review," *Journal of Consumer Research*, December 1982, pp. 287–300; Robert E. Kleine, Susan Schultz Kleine, and Jerome B. Kernan, "Mundane Consumption and the Self: A Social Identity Perspective," *Journal of Consumer Psychology*, 2 (3) 1993, pp. 209–235.
46. Kleine, Kleine, and Kernan, "Mundane Consumption and the Self"; see also M. Joseph Sirgy, "Self-Concept and Consumer Behavior"; M. Joseph Sirgy, *Social Cognition and Consumer Behavior* (New York: Praeger, 1983); George M. Zinkhan and J. W. Hong, "Self-Concept and Advertising Effectiveness: A Conceptual Model of Congruence, Conspicuousness, and Response Mode," in eds. Rebecca Holman and Michael Solomon, *Advances in Consumer Research*, Vol. 18 (Provo, Utah: Association for Consumer Research, 1991), pp. 348–354; Morris B. Holbrook, "Patterns, Personalities, and Complex Relationships in the Effects of Self on Mundane Everyday Consumption: These are 495 of My Most and Least Favorite Things," in eds. John F. Sherry and Brian Sternthal, *Advances in Consumer Research*, Vol. 19 (Provo, Utah: Association for Consumer Research, 1992), pp. 417–423.
47. Kleine, Kleine, and Kernan, "Mundane Consumption and the Self."
48. C. R. Snyder and Howard L. Fromkin, *Uniqueness: Human Pursuit of Difference* (New York: Plenum, 1981).
49. Sirgy, "Self-Concept and Consumer Behavior"; Sirgy, *Social Cognition and Consumer Behavior*.
50. Susan E. Schultz, Robert E. Kleine, and Jerome B. Kernan, "These Are a Few of My Favorite Things, Toward an Explication of Attachment as a Consumer Behavior Construct," in ed. Thomas K. Srull, *Advances in Consumer Research*, Vol. 16 (Provo, Utah: Association for Consumer Research, 1989), pp. 359–366; Richins, "Valuing Things"; Marsha L. Richins, "Special Possessions and the Expression of Material Values," *Journal of Consumer Research*, December 1994, pp. 522–533.
51. Richins, "Valuing Things."
52. Marsha Richins, "Valuing Things: The Public and Private Meanings of Possessions," *Journal of Consumer Research*, December 1994, pp. 504–521.
53. Belk, "Possessions and the Extended Self"; Elizabeth C. Hirschman, "Consumers and Their Animal Companions," *Journal of Consumer Research*, March 1994, pp. 616–632; Susan Alexander, "You and Your Dog Are Welcome to Stay a Week in Vermont," *Wall Street Journal*, June 30, 1992, pp. A1, A5; see also Clinton R. Sanders, "The Animal 'Other': Self Definition, Social Identity and Companion Animals," in eds. Marvin Goldberg, Jerry Gorn, and Richard Pollay, *Advances in Consumer Research*, Vol. 17 (Provo, Utah: Association for Consumer Research, 1990), pp. 662–668.
54. Kathy Chen, "Tough Rules for Dogs in Beijing Have Some Pet Owners Howling," *Wall Street Journal*, June 20, 1995, p. B1.
55. Stephen Mehta, "Executive's Pet Project: A Kennel Chain," *Wall Street Journal*, February 24, 1997, pp. B1, B2.
56. Belk, "Possessions and the Sense of Past"; Susan Schultz Kleine, Robert E. Kleine III, and Chris T. Allen, "How Is a Possession 'Me' or 'Not Me'? Characterizing Types and an Antecedent of Material Possession Attachment," *Journal of Consumer Research*, December 1995, pp. 327–343; McAlexander, Schouten, and Roberts, "Consumer Behavior and Divorce"; Lisa L. Love and Peter S. Sheldon, "Souvenirs: Messengers of Meaning," in eds. Joseph W. Alba and Wesley Hutchinson, *Advances in Consumer Research*, Vol. 25 (Provo, Utah: Association for Consumer Research, 1998), pp. 170–175.
57. Belk, "Possessions and the Sense of Past."
58. Russell W. Belk, "Moving Possessions: An Analysis Based on Personal Documents from the 1847–1869 Mormon Migration," *Journal of Consumer Research*, December 1992, pp. 339–361.
59. Temma Ehrenfeld, "Why Executives Collect," *Fortune*, January 11, 1993, pp. 94–97.
60. Russell W. Belk, Melanie Wallendorf, John F. Sherry Jr., and Morris B. Holbrook, "Collecting in a Consumer Culture," in ed. Belk, *Highways and Buyways*.
61. Alexandra Peers, "Baseball's Card of Cards Is up for Grabs," *Wall Street Journal*, September 20, 1996, pp. B1–B9.
62. Russell W. Belk, Melanie Wallendorf, John F. Sherry Jr., Morris Holbrook, and Scott Roberts, "Collectors and Collecting," in ed. Michael J. Houston, *Advances in Consumer Research*, Vol. 15 (Provo, Utah: Association for Consumer Research, 1988), pp. 548–553.
63. Ibid.
64. Russell W. Belk, "The Ineluctable Mysteries of Possessions," in ed. Floyd W. Rudmin, *To Have Possessions: A Handbook on Ownership and Property, Journal of Social Behavior and Personality*, special issue, 6 (6), 1991, pp. 17–55.
65. Belk et al., "Collecting in a Consumer Culture."

66. Susan Fournier, "The Development of Intense Consumer-Product Relationships," Paper presented at the AMA Winter Educator's Conference, St. Petersburg, Fla., February 20, 1994.

67. Ibid.

68. Csikszenthmihalyi and Rochberg-Halton, *The Meaning of Things*; Wallendorf and Arnould, "My Favorite Things"; Belk, "Moving Possessions"; Belk, "Moving Possessions."

69. Csikszenthmihalyi and Rochberg-Halton, *The Meaning of Things*.

70. Ibid.

71. Helga Dittmar, "Meaning of Material Possessions as Reflections of Identity: Gender and Social-Material Position in Society," in ed. Floyd W. Rudmin, *To Have Possessions: A Handbook on Ownership and Property, Journal of Social Behavior and Personality*, special issue, 6 (6), 1991, pp. 165–186; see also Helga Dittmar, *The Social Psychology of Material Possessions* (New York; St. Martin's, 1992).

72. Dittmar, "Meaning of Material Possessions as Reflections of Identity"; Kamptner, "Personal Possessions and Their Meanings."

73. Wallendorf and Arnould, "My Favorite Things."

74. Russell W. Belk and Melanie Wallendorf, "Of Mice and Men: Gender Identity in Collecting," in eds. K. Ames and K. Martinez, *The Gender of Material Culture* (Ann Arbor, Mich.: University of Michigan Press, in press), reprinted in ed. Susan M. Pearce, *Objects and Collections* (London: Routledge, 1994), pp. 240–253; Belk et al., "Collectors and Collecting."

75. Elizabeth Myers, "Phenomenological Analysis of the Importance of Special Possessions: An Exploratory Study," in eds. Elizabeth C. Hirschman and Morris B. Holbrook, *Advances in Consumer Research*, Vol. 12 (Provo, Utah: Association for Consumer Research, 1985), pp. 560–565.

76. McCracken, "Culture and Consumption"; McCracken, *Culture and Consumption*.

77. Ibid.

78. Ibid.

79. Russell W. Belk, Melanie Wallendorf, and John F. Sherry Jr., "The Sacred and the Profane in Consumer Behavior: Theodicy on the Odyssey," *Journal of Consumer Research*, June 1989, pp. 1–38.

80. Yumiko Ono, "Fans Cheer, 'Nomo': Foes Mutter, 'No More,'" *Wall Street Journal*, July 7, 1995, p. B11.

81. Belk, "Possessions and the Sense of Past."

82. Belk, Wallendorf, and Sherry, "The Sacred and the Profane in Consumer Behavior."

83. Amitai Etzioni, "The Socio-Economics of Property," in ed. Floyd W. Rudmin, *To Have Possessions: A Handbook on Ownership and Property, Journal of Social Behavior and Personality*, special issue, 6 (6), 1991, pp. 465–468.

84. McAlexander, Schouten, and Roberts, "Consumer Behavior and Divorce."

85. Kevin Goldman, "A Few Rockers Give Ad Makers No Satisfaction," *Wall Street Journal*, August 25, 1995, pp. B1, B4.

86. See, for example, Leigh Schmidt, "The Commercialization of the Calendar," *Journal of American History*, December 1991, pp. 887–916.

87. For fascinating historical and sociological accounts of Christmas, see Daniel Miller, "A Theory of Christmas," in ed. Daniel Miller, *Unwrapping Christmas* (Oxford, England: Oxford University Press, 1993), pp. 3–37; Claude Levi-Strauss, "Father Christmas Executed," in ed. Daniel Miller, *Unwrapping Christmas* (Oxford, England: Oxford University Press 1993), pp. 38–54; Belk, "Materialism and the Making of the Modern American Christmas"; Daniel Miller, "Christmas against Materialism in Trinidad," in ed. Daniel Miller, *Unwrapping Christmas* (Oxford, England: Oxford University Press 1993), pp. 134–153; Barbara Bodenhorn, "Christmas Present: Christmas Public," in ed. Daniel Miller, *Unwrapping Christmas* (Oxford, England: Oxford University Press, 1993), pp. 193–216; William B. Waits, *The Modern Christmas in America* (New York: New York University Press, 1993).

88. John F. Sherry Jr., "Gift Giving in Anthropological Perspective," *Journal of Consumer Research*, September 1983, pp. 157–168.

89. For a discussion of several of these motives, see Sherry, "Gift Giving in Anthropological Perspective"; for research on gender differences in motives, see Mary Ann McGrath, "Gender Differences in Gift Exchanges: New Directions from Projections," *Psychology and Marketing*, August 1995, pp. 229–234; Cele Otnes, Julie A. Ruth, and Constance Milbourne, "The Pleasure and Pain of Being Close: Men's Mixed Feelings about Participation in Valentine's Day Gift Exchange," in eds. Chris Allen and Debbie Roedder-John, *Advances in Consumer Research*, Vol. 21 (Provo, Utah: Association for Consumer Research, 1994), pp. 159–164; Cele Otnes, Kyle Zolner, and Tina M. Lowry, "In-Laws and Outlaws: The Impact of Divorce and Remarriage upon Christmas Gift Exchange," in eds. Chris Allen and Debbie Roedder-John, *Advances in Consumer Research*, Vol. 21 (Provo, Utah: Association for Consumer Research, 1994), pp. 25–29; for other gift-giving motives, see Russell W. Belk, "Gift Giving Behavior," in ed. Jagdish N. Sheth, *Research in Marketing* (Greenwich, Conn.: JAI Press, 1979), pp. 95–126; Russell W. Belk, "The Perfect Gift," in eds. Cele Otnes and Richard Beltrami, *Gift Giving Behavior: An Interdisciplinary Anthology* (Bowling Green, Ohio: Bowling Green University Popular Press, forthcoming); for a discussion of the roles played by gift givers (the pleaser, the provider, the compensator, the socializer, and the acknowledger), see Cele Otnes, Tina M. Lowrey, and Young Chan Kim, "Gift Selection for Easy and Difficult Recipients," *Journal of Consumer Research*, September 1993, pp. 229–244; Susan Schultz Kleine, Robert E. Kleine III, and Chris T. Allen, "How Is a Possession 'Me' or 'Not Me'?"

90. McAlexander, Schouten, and Roberts, "Consumer Behavior and Divorce."

91. Russell W. Belk and Gregory S. Coon, "Gift Giving as Agapic Love: An Alternative to the Exchange Paradigm Based on Dating Experiences," *Journal of Consumer Research*, December 1993, pp. 393–417.

92. Sherry, "Gift Giving in Anthropological Perspective"; Mary Searle-Chatterjee, "Christmas Cards and the Construction of Social Relations in Britain Today," in ed. Daniel Miller, *Unwrapping Christmas* (Oxford, England: Oxford University Press, 1993), pp. 176–192.

93. Belk and Coon, "Gift Giving as Agapic Love"; see also Sherry, "Gift Giving in Anthropological Perspective."

94. Sak Onkvisit and John J. Shaw, *International Marketing: Analysis and Strategy* (Columbus, Ohio: Merrill, 1989), pp. 241–242.

95. Eileen Fischer and Stephen J. Arnold, "More Than a Labor of Love: Gender Roles and Christmas Shopping," *Journal of Consumer Research*, December 1990, pp. 333–345.

96. John F. Sherry Jr. and Mary Ann McGrath, "Unpacking the Holiday Presence: A Comparative Ethnography of Two Gift Stores," in ed. Elizabeth C. Hirschman, *Interpretive Consumer Research* (Provo, Utah: Association for Consumer Research, 1989), pp. 148–167; see also David Cheal, "Showing Them You Love Them: Gift Giving and the Dialectic of Intimacy," *Sociological Review*, January 1987, pp. 151–169; Lewis Hyde, *The Gift* (New York: Vintage, 1979).

97. See, for example, Theodore Caplow, "Rule Enforcement without Visible Means: Christmas Gift Giving in Middletown," *American Journal of Sociology*, March 1984, pp. 1306–1323.

98. James G. Carrier, "The Rituals of Christmas Giving," in ed. Daniel Miller, *Unwrapping Christmas* (Oxford, England: Oxford University Press, 1993), pp. 55–74.

99. Mary Ann McGrath, "An Ethnography of a Gift Store: Trappings, Wrappings, and Rapture," *Journal of Retailing*, Winter 1989, p. 434.

100. Julie A. Ruth, Cele C. Tones, and Frederic F. Brunel, "Gift Receipt and the Reformulation of Interpersonal Relationships," *Journal of Consumer Research*, March 1999, pp. 385–402.

101. Belk, "Gift Giving Behavior"; see also Sherry, "Gift Giving in Anthropological Perspective." For research on this factor and others discussed above, see Rick G. M. Pieters, and Henry S. J. Robben, "Beyond the Horse's Mouth: Exploring Acquisition and Exchange Utility in Gift Evaluation," in eds. Joseph W. Alba and Wesley Hutchinson, *Advances in Consumer Research*, Vol. 25, (Provo, Utah: Association for Consumer Research 1998), pp. 160–163.

102. Belk and Coon, "Gift Giving as Agapic Love."

103. Kevin Helliker, "Sweet Sells Year after Year for Hallmark," *Wall Street Journal*, December 20, 1996, pp. B1, B7.

104. Wendy Bounds, "Here Comes the Bride, Clicking a Mouse," *Wall Street Journal*, January 14, 1999, pp. B1, B3.

105. More Marketers Wish You a Merry Winter, "*Wall Street Journal*, December 5, 1996, pp. B1, B12.

106. Joshua Harris Proger, "Out of Ideas? Give a Goat or a Seaweed Body Wrap," *Wall Street Journal*, December 23, 1997, pp. B1, B3.

107. Susan Carey, "Over the River, through the Woods, to a Posh Resort We Go," *Wall Street Journal*, November 21, 1997, pp. B1, B4.

CHAPTER 19

1. Evan Ramstad, "Device to Grab Music from Web", *Wall Street Journal*, May 3, 1999, p. B4; Eben Shapiro, "Sony Music Plans to Sell 'Virtual Songs,'" *Wall Street Journal*, May 12, 1999, pp B1, B4.; Lee Gomes, "Music: Free Tunes for Everyone—MP3 Moves into the High-School Mainstream," *Wall Street Journal*, June 15, 1999, p. B1; Walter S. Mossberg, "Music on the Web: At Last, It's Not Only for Hard-Core Techies," *Wall Street Journal*, May 27, 1999, p. B1; Jodi Mardesich, "How the Internet Hits Big Music," *Fortune*, May 10, 1999, pp. 96–102.

2. Gabriella Stern, "To Outpace Rivals, More Firms Step up Spending of New-Product Development," *Wall Street Journal*, October 28, 1992, pp. B1, B4.

3. Hubert Gatignon and Thomas S. Robertson, "Innovative Decision Processes," in eds. Thomas S. Robertson and Harold H. Kassarjian, *Handbook of Consumer Behavior* (New York: Prentice-Hall, 1991), pp. 316–317; see also Everett M. Rogers, *The Diffusion of Innovations* (New York: Free Press, 1983).

4. Wilton Woods, "1994 Products of the Year," *Fortune*, December 12, 1994, pp. 198–208.

5. Vanessa O'Connell, "Triarc's Diet RC Pushes 'No Aspartame,'" *Wall Street Journal*, June 18, 1998, p. B10.

6. Robert Langreth, "From a Prostate Drug Comes a Pill for Baldness," *Wall Street Journal*, March 20, 1997, pp. B1, B4.

7. Barry Newman, "'Disco Polo' Is Rocking the Pop Foundations of Polish Music Scene," *Wall Street Journal*, February 7, 1996, pp. A1, A8.

8. Tara Parker-Pope, "New Devices Add up Bill, Measure Shoppers' Honesty," "*Wall Street Journal*, June 6, 1995, pp. B1, B13.

9. Thomas S. Robertson, "The Process of Innovation and the Diffusion of Innovation," *Journal of Marketing*, January 1967, pp. 14–19; Thomas S. Robertson, *Innovative Behavior and Communication* (New York: Holt, Reinhart, & Winston, 1971).

10. Peter Waldman, "Great Idea...If It Flies," *Wall Street Journal*, June 24, 1999, pp. B1, B4.

11. Gautam Naik, "You Did *What* on a Cell Phone?," *Wall Street Journal*, June 3, 1999, pp. B1, B6.

12. Alfred R. Petrosky, "Extending Innovation Characteristic Perception to Diffusion Channel Intermediaries and Aesthetic Products," in eds. Rebecca Holman and Michael Solomon, *Advances in Consumer Research*, Vol. 18 (Provo, Utah: Association for Consumer Research, 1991), pp. 627–634.

13. Ricardo Sookdeo, "Growth Smocks," *Fortune*, October 31, 1994, p. 236.

14. Wilton Woods, "Dressed to Spill," *Fortune*, October 17, 1995, p. 209.

15. S. Ram, "A Model of Innovation Resistance," in eds. Melanie Wallendorf and Paul Anderson, *Advances in Consumer Research*, Vol. 14 (Provo, Utah: Association for Consumer Research, 1987), pp. 208–212; Jagdish N. Sheth, "Psychology of Innovation Resistance: The Less Developed Concept (LDC) in Diffusion Research," in *Research in Marketing* (Greenwich, Conn.: JAI Press, 1981), pp. 273–282.

16. Don Clark, "Upgrade Fatigue Threatens PC Profits," *Wall Street Journal*, May 14, 1998, pp. B1, B8.

17. Gene Murdock and Lori Franz, "Habit and Perceived Risk as Factors in the Resistance to the Use of ATMs," *Journal of Retail Banking*, February 1983, pp. 20–29.

18. David Glen Mick and Susan Fournier, "Paradoxes of Technology: Consumer Cognizance, Emotions, and

Coping Strategies, *Journal of Consumer Research*, September 1998, pp. 123–143.

19. Urban G. Ozanne and Gilbert A. Churchill, "Five Dimensions of the Industrial Adoption Process," *Journal of Marketing Research*, August 1971, pp. 322–327; Charles R. O'Neal, Hans B. Thorelli, and James M. Utterback, "Adoption of Innovation by Industrial Organizations," *Industrial Marketing Management*, March 1973, pp. 235–250; Zaltman, Duncan, and Holbek, *Innovations and Organizations*.

20. Tara Parker-Pope, "P&G Puts Lots of Chips on Plan to Give Away Fat-Free Pringles," *Wall Street Journal*, June 23, 1998, p. B8.

21. "Optical Distortion, Inc.," Case # 575–072, Boston, Mass.: Harvard Business School, HBS Case Series, 1975.

22. Rogers, *The Diffusion of Innovations*.

23. Geoffrey A. Moore, *Crossing the Chasm* (New York: HarperBusiness, 1991).

24. Thomas E. Weber, "Why WebTV Isn't Quite Ready for Prime Time," *Wall Street Journal*, January 2, 1997, pp. B1,B11.

25. Cristina Lourosa, "Understanding the User: Who Are the First Ones out There Buying the Latest Gadgets," *Wall Street Journal*, June 15, 1998, p. R18.

26. Bruce Orwall, "DVDs Catch on (but Don't Junk That VCR Yet)," *Wall Street Journal*, September 8, 1998, pp. B1, B4.

27. Geoffrey A. Moore, *Crossing the Chasm*.

28. Robert A. Peterson, "A Note on Optimal Adopter Category Determination," *Journal of Marketing Research*, August 1973, pp. 325–329; see also William R. Darden and Fred D. Reynolds, "Backward Profiling of Male Innovators," *Journal of Marketing Research*, February 1974, pp. 79–85; Steven A. Baumgarten, "The Innovative Communicator in the Diffusion Process," *Journal of Marketing Research*, February 1975, pp. 12–18. Schemes based on consumers' involvement in the new product development process, for example, might be utilized by managers (see Jerry Wind and Vijay Mahajan, "Issues and Opportunities in New Product Development: An Introduction to the Special Issue," *Journal of Marketing Research*, February 1997, pp.1–12.

29. David F. Midgley and Grahame R. Dowling, "Innovativeness: The Concept and Its Measurement," *Journal of Consumer Research*, March 1978, pp. 229–242; Mary Dee Dickerson and James W. Gentry, "Characteristics of Adopters and Non Adopters of Home Computers," *Journal of Consumer Research*, September 1983, pp. 225–235; see also Vijay Mahajan, Eitan Muller, and Rajendra Srivastava, "Determination of Adopter Categories by Using Innovation Diffusion Models," *Journal of Marketing Research*, February 1990, pp. 37–50; Kenneth C. Manning, William O. Bearden, and Thomas J. Madden," Consumer Innovativeness and the Adoption Process," *Journal of Consumer Psychology*, 4 (4, 1995), pp. 329–345.

30. See review in Thomas S. Robertson, Joan Zielinski, and Scott Ward, *Consumer Behavior* (Glenview, Ill.: Scott-Foresman, 1984); see also Dickerson and Gentry, "Characteristics of Adopters and Non Adopters of Home Computers"; Duncan G. Labay and Thomas C. Kinnear, "Exploring the Consumer Decision Process in the Adoption of Solar Energy Systems," *Journal of Consumer Research*, December 1981, pp. 271–277; Miller, "Interactive TV Finally Plugged In"; Kenneth Uhl, Roman Andrus, and Lance Poulsen, "How Are Laggards Different? An Empirical Inquiry," *Journal of Marketing Research*, February 1970, pp. 51–54; Rogers, *The Diffusion of Innovations*, pp. 383–384.

31. S. Karene Witcher, "Credit-Card Issuers Find Australia Fertile Ground for Launching Products," *Wall Street Journal*, March 31, 1995, p. B6.

32. Rogers, *The Diffusion of Innovations*; see also Mark S. Granovetter, "The Strength of Weak Ties," *American Journal of Sociology*, May 1973, pp. 1360–1380; John A. Czepiel, "Word-of-Mouth Processes in the Diffusion of a Major Technological Innovation," *Journal of Marketing Research*, May 1974, pp. 172–180.

33. Kenneth C. Manning, William O. Bearden, and Thomas J. Madden, "Consumer Innovativeness and the Adoption Process," *Journal of Consumer Psychology*, 4 (4, 1995), pp. 329–345.; Jan-Benedict Steenkamp and Hans Baumgartner, "The Role of Optimum Stimulation Level in Exploratory Consumer Behavior," *Journal of Consumer Research*, December 1992, pp. 434–448; P. S. Raju, "Optimum Stimulation Level: Its Relationship to Personality, Demographics, and Exploratory Behavior," *Journal of Consumer Research*, December 1980, pp. 272–282.

34. Ibid; Thomas S. Robertson and James H. Myers, "Personality Correlates of Opinion Leadership and Innovative Buying Behavior," *Journal of Marketing Research*, May 1969, pp. 164–167.

35. Gordon R. Foxall and Christopher G. Haskins, "Cognitive Style and Consumer Innovativeness," *Marketing Intelligence and Planning*, January 1986, pp. 26–46; Gordon R. Foxall, "Consumer Innovativeness: Novelty Seeking, Creativity and Cognitive Style," in eds. Elizabeth C. Hirschman and Jagdish N. Sheth, *Research in Consumer Behavior*, Vol. 3 (Greenwich, Conn.: JAI Press, 1988), pp. 79–114.

36. Ronald E. Goldsmith and Charles F. Hofacker, "Measuring Consumer Innovativeness," *Journal of the Academy of Marketing Science*, Summer 1991, pp. 209–221.

37. Jan-Benedict Steenkamp, Frenkel ter Hofstede and Michael Wedel, "A Cross-National Investigation into the Individual and National Cultural Antecedents of Consumer Innovativeness," *Journal of Marketing*, April 1999, pp. 55–69.

38. Hubert Gatignon and Thomas S. Robertson, "A Propositional Inventory for New Diffusion Research," *Journal of Consumer Research*, March 1985, pp. 849–867; see also John O. Summers, "Media Exposure Patterns of Consumer Innovators," *Journal of Marketing*, January 1972, pp. 43–49.

39. James J. Engel, Robert J. Kegerreis, and Roger D. Blackwell, "Word-of-Mouth Communication by the Innovator," *Journal of Marketing*, July 1969, pp. 15–19.

40. Dickerson and Gentry, "Characteristics of Adopters and Non Adopters of Home Computers"; Robertson, *Innovative Behavior and Communication*; James W. Taylor, "A Striking Characteristic of Innovators," *Journal of Marketing Research*, February 1977, pp. 104–107; see also Gatignon and Robertson, "A Propositional Inventory for New Diffusion Research"; Elizabeth C. Hirschman,

"Innovativeness, Novelty Seeking and Consumer Creativity," *Journal of Consumer Research*, December 1980, pp. 283–295; Engel, Kegerreis, and Blackwell, "Word-of-Mouth Communication by the Innovator."

41. Miriam Jordan, "It Takes a Cell Phone: A New Nokia Transforms a Village in Bangladesh," *Wall Street Journal*, June 25, 1999, pp. B1, B4.

42. Frank M. Bass, "New Product Growth Models for Consumer Durables," *Management Science*, September 1969, pp. 215–227; Wellesley Dodds, "An Application of the Bass Model in Long-Term New Product Forecasting," *Journal of Marketing Research*, August 1973, pp. 308–311; Roger M. Heeler and Thomas P. Hustad, "Problems in Predicting New Product Growth for Consumer Durables," *Management Science*, October 1980, pp. 1007–1020; Douglas Tigart and Behrooz Farivar, "The Bass New Product Growth Model: A Sensitivity Analysis for a High Technology Product," *Journal of Marketing*, Fall 1981, pp. 81–90.

43. William E. Cox Jr., "Product Life Cycles as Marketing Models," *Journal of Business*, October 1967, pp. 375–384; Rolando Polli and Victor Cook, "Validity of the Product Life Cycle," *Journal of Business*, October 1969, pp. 385–400; D. R. Rink and J. E. Swan, "Product Life Cycle Research: A Literature Review," *Journal of Business Research*, September 1979, pp. 219–242; Robertson, *Innovative Behavior and Communication*.

44. Gautam Naik, "You Did What on a Cell Phone?"

45. Otis Port and Larry Armstrong, "Your Car May Be Smarter Than You," *BusinessWeek*, June 29, 1998, pp. 85–86.

46. Nikhil Deogun, "Newest ATMs Dispense More Than Cash," *Wall Street Journal*, June 5, 1996, pp. B1, B10.

47. Laura Johannes, "A New Microchip Ushers in Cheaper Digital Cameras," *Wall Street Journal*, August 21, 1998, pp. B1, B4.

48. Thomas E. Weber, "Why WebTV Isn't Quite Ready for Prime Time," *Wall Street Journal*, January 2, 1997, pp. B1, B11.

49. Ian P. Murphy, "Electric Cars Get Jolt of Marketing," *Marketing News*, August 18, 1997, pp. 1, 7, 13.

50. Bruce Nussbaum, "Winners: The Best Product Designs of the Year," *BusinessWeek*, May 25, 1998, pp. 78–81.

51. "Polaroid Develops a Following in Russia," *Los Angeles Times*, March 17, 1995, p. D12.

52. Rogers, *Diffusion of Innovations*.

53. Audrey Choi and Gabriella Stern, "The Lessons of Ruegen: Electric Cars Are Slow, Temperamental and Exasperating," *Wall Street Journal*, March 30, 1995, pp. B1, B17.

54. Rogers, *The Diffusion of Innovations*, p. 231.

55. Louise Lee, "You Too, Can Play Sonatas in the Key of Z," *Wall Street Journal*, May 27, 1997, pp. B1, B11.

56. Gatignon and Robertson, "A Propositional Inventory for New Diffusion Research"; Vijay Mahajan, Eitan Muller, and Frank M. Bass, "New Product Diffusion Models in Marketing: A Review and Directions for Research," *Journal of Marketing*, April 1990, pp. 1–27.

57. Sheth and Ram, *Bringing Innovation to Market*.

58. David P. Hamilton, "Japanese Firms Focus on Simpler Camcorders," *Wall Street Journal*, May 5, 1993, p. B1.

59. Sheth and Ram, *Bringing Innovation to Market*.

60. Ibid.

61. Evan Ramstad, "The Pilot Is This Year's Digital Toy, And Those Who Love It Are Passionate," *Wall Street Journal*, April 1, 1997, pp. B1, B5.

62. Ian P. Murphy, "Electric Cars Get Jolt of Marketing."

63. Robert J. Fisher and Linda L. Price, "An Investigation into the Social Context of Early Adoption Behavior," *Journal of Consumer Research*, December 1992, pp. 477–486.

64. Sandra D. Atchison, "Lifting the Golf Bag Burden," *BusinessWeek*, July 25, 1994, p. 84.

65. June Fletcher, "New Machines Measure That Holiday Flab at Home," *Wall Street Journal*, December 26, 1997, p. B8.

66. Rogers, *The Diffusion of Innovations*, p. 99.

67. Steve McKee, "A Rally with Real Legs: Going Long in the Sock Market," *Wall Street Journal*, June 4, 1999, pp. B1, B3.

68. C. Whan Park, Bernard J. Jaworski, and Deborah J. MacInnis, "Strategic Brand Concept-Image Management," *Journal of Marketing*, October 1986, pp. 135–145.

69. Fisher and Price, "An Investigation into the Social Context of Early Adoption Behavior."

70. Petrosky, "Extending Innovation Characteristic Perception to Diffusion Channel Intermediaries and Aesthetic Products."

71. Alfred Petrosky labels this factor *genrefication* and discussed it in the context of aesthetic innovations. See Alfred Petrosky, "Extending Innovation Characteristic Perception to Diffusion Channel Intermediaries and Aesthetic Products."

72. Sheth and Ram, *Bringing Innovation to Market*.

73. Rogers and Pamela J. Shoemaker, *Communication of Innovations*; Elizabeth C. Hirschman, "Consumer Modernity, Cognitive Complexity, Creativity and Innovativeness," in ed. Richard P. Bagozzi, *Marketing in the 80s: Changes and Challenges* (Chicago: American Marketing Association, 1980), pp. 152–161.

74. Jaishankar Ganesh, V. Kumar, and Velavan Subramaniam, "Learning Effect in Multinational Diffusion of Consumer Durables: An Exploratory Investigation," *Journal of the Academy of Marketing Science*, 25 (Summer, 1997), pp. 214–228; Gatignon and Robertson, "A Propositional Inventory for New Diffusion Research."

75. Norihiko Shirouzu, "Japan's High-School Girls Excel in Art of Setting Trends, *Wall Street Journal*, April 24, 1998, pp. B1, B7.

76. Gatignon and Robertson, "A Propositional Inventory for New Diffusion Research"; Lawrence A. Brown, Edward J. Malecki, and Aron N. Spector, "Adopter Categories in a Spatial Context: Alternative Explanations for an Empirical Regularity," *Rural Sociology*, Spring 1976, pp. 99–118.

77. Dorothy Leonard-Barton, "Experts as Negative Opinion Leaders in the Diffusion of a Technological Innovation," *Journal of Consumer Research*, March 1985, pp. 914–926.

78. Everett Rogers and D. Lawrence Kincaid, *Communication Networks: Toward a New Paradigm for Research* (New York: Free Press, 1981).

79. Ibid.

80. Vijay Mahajan, Eitan Muller, and Roger Kerin, "Introduction Strategy for New Products with Positive

and Negative Word-of-Mouth," *Management Science*, December 1984, pp. 1389–1404.

81. Frank M. Bass, "The Relationship between Diffusion Curves, Experience Curves, and Demand Elasticities for Consumer Durable Technological Innovations," *Journal of Business*, July 1980, pp. s51–s57; Dan Horskey and Leonard S. Simon, "Advertising and the Diffusion of New Products," *Marketing Science*, Winter 1983, pp. 1–17; Vijay Mahajan and Eitan Muller, "Innovation Diffusion and New Product Growth Models in Marketing," *Journal of Marketing*, Fall 1979, pp. 55–68; Mahajan, Muller, and Bass, "New Product Diffusion Models in Marketing."

82. Lauriston Sharp, "Steel Axes for Stone Age Australians," in ed. Edward H. Spicer, *Human Problems in Technological Change* (New York: Russell Sage Foundation, 1952).

83. Melissa Levy, "FDA Gives Formal Approval to Drug That Boosts Milk Production in Cows," *Wall Street Journal*, November 8, 1993, pp. B6, B7.

84. H. David Banta, "The Diffusion of the Computer Tomography (CT) Scanner in the United States," *International Journal of Health Services*, 10, 1980, pp. 251–269 as reported in Rogers, *The Diffusion of Innovations*, pp. 231–237.

CHAPTER 20

1. Eben Shapiro, "FTC Staff Recommends Ban of Joe Camel Campaign," *Wall Street Journal*, August 11, 1993, pp. B1, B5.

2. Sally Goll Beatty, "Pact Could Send Marlboro Man into the Sunset," *Wall Street Journal*, April 17, 1997, pp. B1, B12; Yumiko Ono, "Tobacco Ads Seek Glamour without Camels, Cowboys," *Wall Street Journal*, February 20, 1998, pp. B1, B9; Tara Parker-Pope, "Push against Smoking Opens on Silver Screen," *Wall Street Journal*, May 19, 1997, pp. B1, B8.

3. Suein L. Hwang, "Antismokers Push Publishers to Censor Cigarette Ads," *Wall Street Journal*, November 14, 1995, pp. B1, B15.

4. Louis Harris and Associates, *Consumerism in the Eighties*, Study No. 822047, 1983 as referenced in John C. Mowen, *Consumer Behavior*, 3rd ed. (New York: Macmillan, 1993), p. 751.

5. Executive Office of the President, *Consumer Advisory Council*, First Report (Washington, D.C.: U.S. Government Printing Office, October 1963).

6. Rachel Dardis, "Risk Regulation and Consumer Welfare," *Journal of Consumer Affairs*, Summer 1988, pp. 303–317.

7. Sally Goll Beatty, "Agencies Weigh Regulating Ads for Alcohol, Tobacco Voluntarily," *Wall Street Journal*, December 9, 1996, p. B7.

8. Sally Beaty, "This Hemp Is Legal, but Its Ads Hint Otherwise," *Wall Street Journal*, July 15, 1997, pp. B1, B6.

9. Gary M. Armstrong and Julie L. Ozanne, "An Evaluation of the NAD/NARB Purpose and Performance," *Journal of Advertising*, 12 (3), 1983, pp. 15–26; Caleb Solomon, "Gasoline Ads Canceled: Lack of Truth Cited," *Wall Street Journal*, July 21, 1994, pp. B1, B5.

10. Rinler Buck, "ABC Amends the Rules for 'The Person in White,'" *Adweek's Marketing Week*, September 9, 1991, p. 11.

11. Daniel Rosenberg, "Animal-Rights Ad, Toned down, Still Hits a Wall at the Networks," *Wall Street Journal*, December 29, 1998, p. B5.

12. Sally Goll Beatty, "Seagram Flouts Ban on TV Ads Pitching Liquor," *Wall Street Journal*, June 11, 1996, pp. B1, B6; Sally Goll Beatty, "Seagram Baits the Ad Hook for Television," *Wall Street Journal*, August 15, 1997, p. B6.

13. Sally Goll Beatty, "Cable TV to Toughen Ad-Screening Policy," *Wall Street Journal*, March 19, 1996, p. B5.

14. Sally Goll Beatty, "Industry Panel Refers Fed Ex Case to FTC," *Wall Street Journal*, April 11, 1997, p. B7.

15. Edward Felsenthal, "Should the Government Market Pork and Peaches?" *Wall Street Journal*, November 26, 1996, pp. B1, B8.

16. Lisa Brownlee, "Ad Watchdogs Track Untruths, Sometimes Bite," *Wall Street Journal*, July 7, 1997, pp. B1, B9.

17. Kevin Goldman, "From Witches to Anorexics, Critical Eyes Scrutinize Ads for Political Correctness," *Wall Street Journal*, May 19, 1994, pp. B1, B10.

18. Daniel Rosenberg, "Veal Industry Focuses on Chefs in Countering Animal-Rights Ads," *Wall Street Journal*, March 18, 1998, p. B3.

19. Suein L. Hwang, "Health Groups Challenge Winston Ad Claims," *Wall Street Journal*, August 25, 1997, pp. B1, B12.

20. James H. Rubin, "Continental Airlines Is Fined for Misleading Ad Fare," *Austin American Statesman*, November 1, 1993, p. A8.

21. Jacob Jacoby and Constance Small, "The FDA Approach to Defining Misleading Advertising," *Journal of Marketing*, October 1975, pp. 65–68.

22. Federal Trade Commission, "Policy Statement on Deception," 45 ATRR 689, October 27, 1983, as cited in Gary T. Ford and John E. Calfee, "Recent Developments in FTC Policy on Deception," *Journal of Marketing*, July 1986, pp. 82–103; also see Jef I. Richards and Ivan L. Preston, "Proving and Disproving Materiality of Deceptive Advertising Claims," *Journal of Public Policy and Marketing*, Fall 1992, pp. 45–56.

23. Jacob Jacoby, Wayne D. Hoyer, and David A. Sheluga, *Miscomprehension of Televised Communication* (New York: American Association of Advertising Agencies, 1980); Jacob Jacoby and Wayne D. Hoyer, *The Comprehension and Miscomprehension of Print Communications: An Investigation of Mass Media Magazines* (New York: The Advertising Education Foundation, 1987).

24. Lee D. Dahringer and Denise R. Johnson, "The Federal Trade Commission Redefinition of Deception and Public Policy Implications: Let the Buyer Beware," *Journal of Consumer Affairs*, 18, 1984, pp. 326–342.

25. Gary Armstrong, Metin Gurol, and Frederick Russ, "Detecting and Correcting Deceptive Advertising," *Journal of Consumer Research*, December 1979, pp. 237–246; Dorothy Cohen, "Unfairness in Advertising Revisited," *Journal of Marketing*, Winter 1982, pp. 73–80; Michael R. Hyman, "Deception in Advertising: A Proposed Complex of Definitions for Researchers,

Lawyers, and Regulators," *International Journal of Advertising*, 9 (3), 1990, pp. 259–270; Richards and Preston, "Proving and Disproving Materiality of Deceptive Advertising Claims."

26. Gary J. Gaeth and Timothy B. Heath, "The Cognitive Processing of Misleading Advertising in Young and Old Adults: Assessment and Training," *Journal of Consumer Research*, June 1987, pp. 43–54.

27. David M. Gardner, "Deception in Advertising: A Conceptual Approach," *Journal of Marketing*, January 1975, pp. 40–46.

28. Joel E. Urbany, William O. Bearden, and Dan C. Weilbaker, "The Effect of Plausible and Exaggerated Reference Prices on Consumer Perceptions and Price Search," *Journal of Consumer Research*, June 1988, pp. 95–110; John Liefield and Louise A. Heslop, "Reference Prices and Deception in Newspaper Advertising," *Journal of Consumer Research*, March 1985, pp. 868–876.

29. Bruce Ingersoll, "Claim by Gerber for Baby Food Was Simply Mush, FTC Alleges," *Wall Street Journal*, March 13, 1997, p. B15.

30. Bonnie B. Reece and Robert H. Ducoffe, "Deception in Brand Names," *Journal of Public Policy and Marketing*, 6, 1987, pp. 93–103.

31. Vanessa O'Connell, "A Wine Label with a Bouquet of Controversy,' *Wall Street Journal*, December 8, 1998, pp. B1, B4.

32. David Kiley, "Rag Changes Label as 'Fresh' Talk Continues," *Adweek's Marketing Week*, May 6, 1991, p. 4; David Kiley, "Clorox Tests Meals from Hidden Valley," *Adweek's Marketing Week*, March 4, 1991, p. 6.

33. Aaron Lucchetti, "Produce Sleuths Search for Label Scams," *Wall Street Journal*, June 17, 1997, pp. B1, B6.

34. Ivan L. Preston, "The FTC's Handling of Puffery and Other Selling Claims Made 'By Implication,'" *Journal of Business Research*, June 1977, pp. 155–181.

35. Richard L. Oliver, "An Interpretation of the Attitudinal and Behavioral Effects of Puffery," *Journal of Consumer Affairs*, Summer 1979, pp. 8–27; Terence A. Shimp and Ivan L. Preston, "Deceptive and Nondeceptive Consequences of Evaluative Advertising," *Journal of Marketing*, Winter 1981, pp. 22–32.

36. Gardner, "Deception in Advertising."; Raymond R. Burke, Wayne S. De Sarbo, Richard L. Oliver, and Thomas S. Robertson, "Deception by Implication: An Empirical Investigation," *Journal of Consumer Research*, March 1988, pp. 483–494.

37. Gita Venkataramani Johar, "Consumer Involvement and Deception from Implied Advertising Claims," *Journal of Marketing Research*, August 1995, pp. 267–279.

38. Oscar Suris and Sally Goll Beatty, "'Zero Down' Car Leases Get Thumbs down in Law Suits," *Wall Street Journal*, Octoer 29, 1996, pp. B1, B7.

39. Keith Schneider, "Dairy Companies Warned against Misleading Labels," *Austin American Statesman*, February 8, 1994, p. A4.

40. John E. Calfee, "FTC's Hidden Weight Loss Ad Agenda," *Advertising Age*, October 25, 1993, p. 29.

41. Kevin Goldman, "Tis the Season for Bashing of Kiddie Ads," *Wall Street Journal*, December 18, 1992, p. B8.

42. Burke et al., "Deception by Implication."

43. "Buying the Ranch on Brand Equity," *Brandweek*, October 26, 1992, p. 9.

44. Carrie Goerne, "Court Ruling Lights Fire under Both Sides in Cigarette Dispute," *Marketing News*, August 17, 1992, p. 6.

45. Sandra J. Burke, Sandra J. Milberg, and Wendy W. Moe, "Displaying Common but Previously Neglected Health Claims on Product Labels: Understanding Competitive Advantages, Deception, and Education," *Journal of Public Policy and Marketing*, Fall 1997, pp. 242–255.

46. J. Craig Andrews, Richard G. Netemeyer, and Scot Burton, "Consumer Generalization of Nutrient Content Claims in Advertising," *Journal of Marketing*, October 1998, pp. 62–75.

47. J. Edward Russo, Barbara L. Metcalf, and Debra Stephens, "Identifying Misleading Advertising," *Journal of Consumer Research*, September 1981, pp. 119–131; Gardner, "Deception in Advertising"; Armstrong, Gurol, and Russ, "Detecting and Correcting Deceptive Advertising."

48. John R. Wilke, "Condom Maker Is Told to Back up Claims," *Wall Street Journal*, September 4, 1997, p. B8.

49. Nikhil Deogun, "Winn-Dixie's Lower Price Tactic Is Referred to FTC by Board," *Wall Street Journal*, December 23, 1996, p. B2.

50. "Feds Charge Shopping Network," *Austin American Statesman*, March 4, 1995, p. A7.

51. Laurie Mc Ginley, "FTC Probes Fat-Content Claims Made by Some Restaurant Chains," *Wall Street Journal*, April 30, 1996, p. B8; Lauran Neergaard, "FDA Requires That Health Claims on Dietary Supplements Be Verifiable," *Austin American Statesman*, December 30, 1993, p. A3.

52. Elyse Tanouye, "Heartburn Drug Makers Feel Judge's Heat," *Wall Street Journal*, October 16, 1995, p. B8.

53. Calfee, "FTC's Hidden Weight Loss Ad Agenda."

54. Wendy Bounds, "Polo Magazine Gets a Whipping from Lauren in Trademark Case," *Wall Street Journal*, July 7, 1997, p. B6.

55. Katherine Ackley, "R.J. Reynolds to Settle Charges over Ads," *Wall Street Journal*, March 4, 1999, p. B4.

56. Jacob Jacoby, Margaret C. Nelson, and Wayne D. Hoyer, "Corrective Advertising and Affirmative Disclosure Statements: Their Potential for Confusing and Misleading the Consumer," *Journal of Marketing*, Winter 1982, pp. 61–72; G. Ray Funkhouser, "An Empirical Study of Consumers' Sensitivity to the Wording of Affirmative Disclosure Messages," *Journal of Public Policy and Marketing*, 3, 1984, pp. 26–37; Ellen R. Foxman, Darrel D. Muehling, and Patrick A. Moore, "Disclaimer Footnotes in Ads: Discrepancies Between Purpose and Performance," *Journal of Public Policy and Marketing*, 7, 1988, pp. 127–137.

57. William L. Wilkie, Dennis L. McNeil, and Michael B. Mazis, "Marketing's 'Scarlet Letter': The Theory and Practice of Corrective Advertising," *Journal of Marketing*, Spring 1984, pp. 11–31; Gary M. Armstrong, Metin N. Gurol, and Frederick A. Russ, "A Longitudinal Evaluation of the Listerine Corrective Advertising Campaign," *Journal of Public Policy and Marketing*, 2, 1983, pp. 16–28.

58. Bruce Ingersoll, "FTC Orders Novartis Ads to Correct Claim," *Wall Street Journal*, May 28, 1999, p. B2.

59. Armstrong, Gurol, and Russ, "Detecting and Correcting Deceptive Advertising"; Richard W. Mizerski, Neil K. Allison, and Stephen Calvert, "A Controlled Field Study of Corrective Advertising Using Multiple Exposures and a Commercial Medium," *Journal of Marketing Research*, August 1979, pp. 341–348; Michael B. Mazis and Janice E. Atkinson, "An Experimental Evaluation of a Proposed Corrective Advertising Remedy," *Journal of Marketing Research*, May 1986, pp. 178–183; Tyzoon T. Tyebjee, "The Role of Publicity in FTC Corrective Advertising Remedies," *Journal of Public Policy and Marketing*, 1, 1982, pp. 111–121.

60. Gita Venkataramani Johar, "Intended and Unintended Effects of Corrective Advertising on Beliefs and Evaluations: An Exploratory Analysis," *Journal of Consumer Psychology*, 5, 3 (1996), pp. 209–230.

61. William L. Wilkie, *Consumer Behavior*, 2nd ed. (New York: Wiley, 1990).

62. Fleming Meeks, "Upselling," *Forbes*, January 8, 1990, pp. 70, 72.

63. Richard W. Easley, James A. Roberts, Mark G. Dunn, and Charles S. Madden, "Diagnosing Consumer Information Problems: An Investigation of Deception on the Mail-Order Video Camcorder Market," *Journal of Public Policy and Marketing*, Fall 1992, pp. 37–44.

64. Wilkie, *Consumer Behavior*.

65. Christopher Scanian, "Postcards Offering 'Free Prizes' Can Prove Costly, Experts Warn," *Austin American Statesman*, November 18, 1992, pp. A1, A17.

66. Wilkie, *Consumer Behavior*.

67. Pratibha A. Dabholkar and James J. Kellaris, "Toward Understanding Marketing Students' Ethical Judgment of Controversial Selling Practices," *Journal of Business Research*, June 1992, pp. 313–329.

68. Karl A. Boedecker, Fred W. Morgan, and Jeffrey J. Stoltman, "Legal Dimensions of Salespersons' Statements: A Review and Managerial Suggestions," *Journal of Marketing*, January 1991, pp. 70–80.

69. Stephanie N. Mehta, "Visions of Wealth and Independence Lead Professionals to Try Multilevel Marketing," *Wall Street Journal*, June 23, 1995, pp. B1, B2.

70. "Senior Citizens Warned about Fraud Schemes," *Austin American Statesman*, July 13, 1999, p. B2; John R. Emshwiller, "Having List Thousands to Con Artists, Elderly Widow Tells Cautionary Tale," *Wall Street Journal*, August 20, 1995, pp. B1, B5.

71. Samantha Levine, "AARP Educating Elderly on Telemarketing Dangers," *Austin American Statesman*, August 7, 1996, p. A3.

72. A. C. Nielsen Company, *1990 Nielsen Report on Television* (New York: Nielsen Media Research); J. Condry, P. Bence, and C. Scheibe, "Nonprogram Content of Children's Television," *Journal of Broadcasting and Electronic Media*, Summer 1988, pp. 255–270; Carol Lawson, "Guarding the Children's Hour on TV," *New York Times*, January 24, 1991, pp. C1, C13.

73. W. Melody, *Children's Television: The Economics of Exploitation* (New Haven, Conn.: Yale University Press, 1973); Ellen Notar, "Children and TV Commercials: Wave after Wave of Exploitation," *Childhood Education*, Winter 1989, pp. 66–67.

74. Scott Ward, "Consumer Socialization," *Journal of Consumer Research*, September 1974, pp. 1–13; Laurene Krasney Meringoff and Gerald S. Lesser, "Children's Ability to Distinguish Television Commercials from Program Material," in ed. R. P. Adler, *The Effect of Television Advertising on Children* (Lexington, Mass.: Lexington Books, 1980), pp. 29–42; S. Levin, T. Petros, and F. Petrella, "Preschoolers' Awareness of Television Advertising," *Child Development*, August 1982, pp. 933–937.

75. M. Carole Macklin, "Preschoolers' Understanding of the Informational Function of Advertising," *Journal of Consumer Research*, September 1987, pp. 229–239; Merrie Brucks, Gary M. Armstrong, and Marvin E. Goldberg, "Children's Use of Cognitive Defenses against Television Advertising: A Cognitive Response Approach," *Journal of Consumer Research*, March 1988, pp. 471–482.

76. Mary C. Martin, "Children's Understanding of the Intent of Advertising: A Meta-Analysis," *Journal of Public Policy and Marketing*, Fall 1997, pp. 205–216.

77. Deborah L. Roedder, "Age Differences in Children's Responses to Television Advertising: An Information Processing Approach," *Journal of Consumer Research*, September 1981, pp. 144–153.

78. Jon Berry, "The New Generation of Kids and Ads," *Adweek's Marketing Week*, April 15, 1991, pp. 25–28; Marvin E. Goldberg and Gerald J. Gorn, "Some Unintended Consequences of TV Advertising to Children," *Journal of Consumer Research*, June 1978, pp. 22–29; Gary M. Armstrong and Merrie Brucks, "Dealing with Children's Advertising: Public Policy Issues and Alternatives," *Journal of Public Policy and Marketing*, 7, 1988, pp. 98–113.

79. Bonnie B. Reece, "Children and Shopping: Some Public Policy Questions," *Journal of Public Policy and Marketing*, 5, 1986, pp. 185–194; Armstrong and Brucks, "Dealing with Children's Advertising."

80. Scott Ward and Daniel B. Wackman, "Children's Information Processing of Television Advertising," in ed. Peter Clarke, *New Models for Mass Communication Research* (Beverly Hills, Calif.: Sage, 1973), pp. 119–146; Thomas S. Robertson and John R. Rossiter, "Children and Commercial Persuasion: Testing the Defenses," *Journal of Consumer Research*, June 1974, pp. 13–20; Deborah L. Roedder, Brian B. Sternthal, and Bobby J. Calder, "Attitude-Behavior Consistency in Children's Responses to Television Advertising," *Journal of Marketing Research*, November 1983, pp. 337–349; Scott Ward, Daniel B. Wackman, and Ellen Wartella, *How Children Learn to Buy* (Beverly Hills, Calif.: Sage, 1977).

81. Jeffrey E. Brand and Bradley S. Greenberg, "Commercials in the Classroom: The Impact of Channel One Advertising," *Journal of Advertising Research*, January–February 1994, pp. 18–27.

82. Scott Ward and Daniel Wackman, "Children's Purchase Influence Attempts and Parental Yielding," *Journal of Marketing Research*, August 1972, pp. 316–319; Goldberg and Gorn, "Some Unintended Consequences of TV Advertising to Children"; Tamara F. Mangleburg, "Children's Influence in Purchase Decisions: A Review and Critique," in eds. Marvin E. Goldberg, Gerald

Gorn, and Richard W. Pollay, *Advances in Consumer Research*, Vol. 17 (Provo, Utah: Association for Consumer Research, 1990), pp. 813–825.

83. Joe Flint, "Proposed 900-Number and Rules Worry Advertisers," *Broadcasting and Cable*, April 5, 1993, p. 44.

84. Russell N. Laczniak, Darrel D. Muehling, and Les Carlson, "Mothers' Attitudes toward 900-Number Advertising Directed at Children," *Journal of Public Policy and Marketing*, Spring 1995, pp. 108–116.

85. Gerald J. Gorn and Renee Florsheim, "The Effects of Commercials for Adult Products on Children," *Journal of Consumer Research*, March 1985, pp. 962–967.

86. Judann Dagnoli, "Consumers Union Hits Kids Advertising," *Advertising Age*, July 23, 1990, p. 4.

87. Mary Lu Carnevale, "Parents Say PBS Stations Exploit Barney in Fund Drives," *Wall Street Journal*, March 19, 1993, pp. B1, B8; Maria Grubbs Hoy, Clifford Young, and John C. Mowen, "Animated Host-Selling Advertisements: Their Impact on Young Children's Recognition, Attitudes, and Behavior," *Journal of Public Policy and Marketing*, 5, 1986, pp. 171–184.

88. Marvin E. Goldberg, Gerald Gorn, and Wendy Gibson, "TV Messages for Snack and Breakfast Foods: Do They Influence Children's Preferences?" *Journal of Consumer Research*, September 1978, pp. 73–81; Debra L. Scammon and Carole L. Christopher, "Nutrition Education with Children via Television," *Journal of Advertising*, 10, 1981, pp. 26–36; Thomas S. Robertson and John R. Rossiter, "Children and Commercial Persuasion: An Attributional Approach," *Journal of Consumer Research*, June 1974, pp. 12–20.

89. Joan Blatt, Lyle Spencer, and Scott Ward, "A Cognitive-Developmental Study of Children's Reaction to Television Advertising," in eds. E. A. Rubenstein, G. A. Constock, and J. P. Murray, *Television and Social Behavior* (Washington, D.C.: U.S. Government Printing Office, 1972), pp. 452–467.

90. Meringoff and Lesser, "Children's Ability to Distinguish Television Commercials from Program Material."

91. Jon Berry, "Kids' Advocates to TV: 'We've Only Begun to Fight,'" *Adweek's Marketing Week*, April 15, 1991, p. 25.

92. Gerald J. Gorn and Marvin E. Goldberg, "Behavioral Evidence of the Effects of Televised Food Messages on Children," *Journal of Consumer Research*, September 1982, pp. 200–205; Cyndee Miller, "Marketers Find a Seat in the Classroom," *Marketing News*, June 20, 1994, p. 2.

93. Elizabeth Jensen and Albert R. Karr, "Summit on Kids' TV Yields Compromise," *Wall Street Journal*, July 30, 1996, p. B14.

94. Dale Kunkel and Walter Granz, "Assessing Compliance with Industry Self-Regulation of Television Advertising to Children," *Journal of Applied Communication Research*, May 1993, pp. 148–162.

95. Armstrong and Brucks, "Dealing with Children's Advertising."

96. Peter Barton Hutt, "FDA Regulation of Product Claims in Food Labeling," *Journal of Public Policy and Marketing*, Spring 1993, pp. 132–134; Gabriella Stern, "In a Turnabout, Fast-Food Fare Becomes Fattier," *Wall Street Journal*, August 23, 1993, pp. B1, B6; Richard Gibson, "Restaurant Menus' Health Claims May Be Regulated," *Wall Street Journal*, June 2, 1993, p. B1.

97. Jacob Jacoby, Robert W. Chestnut, and William Silberman, "Consumer Use and Comprehension of Nutrition Information," *Journal of Consumer Research*, March 1977, pp. 119–128.

98. Catherine A. Cole and Gary J. Gaeth, "Cognitive and Age-Related Differences in the Ability to Use Nutritional Information in a Complex Environment," *Journal of Marketing Research*, May 1990, pp. 175–184; Catherine A. Cole and Siva K. Balasubramanian, "Age Differences in Consumers' Search for Information: Public Policy Implications," *Journal of Consumer Research*, June 1993, pp. 157–169.

99. Jinkook Lee and Jeanne M. Hogarth, "The Price of Money: Consumers' Understanding of APRs and Contract Interest Rates," *Journal of Public Policy and Marketing*, Spring 1999, pp. 66–76.

100. Jacoby, Chestnut, and Silberman, "Consumer Use and Comprehension of Nutrition Information."

101. Brian Roe, Alan S. Levy, and Brenda M. Derby, "The Impact of Health Claims on Consumer Search and Product Evaluation Outcomes: Results from FDA Experimental Data," *Journal of Public Policy and Marketing*, Spring 1999, pp. 89–105.

102. Stern, "In a Turnabout, Fast-Food Fare Becomes Fattier."

103. Laura Bird, "Idea for TV Spots Plugging Soaps at Health Spas Goes down the Drain," *Wall Street Journal*, August 26, 1992, p. B7.

104. Lisa R. Szykman, Paul N. Bloom, and Alan S. Levy, "A Proposed Model of the Use of Package Claims and Nutrition Labels," *Journal of Public Policy and Marketing*, Fall 1997, pp. 228–241.

105. For example, see Jacob Jacoby, Donald E. Speller, and Carol A. Kohn, "Brand Choice Behavior as a Function of Information Load," *Journal of Marketing Research*, February 1974, pp. 63–69; Jacob Jacoby, "Perspectives on Information Overload," *Journal of Consumer Research*, March 1984, pp. 432–435; Naresh K. Malhotra, "Reflections on the Information Overload Paradigm in Consumer Decision Making," *Journal of Consumer Research*, March 1984, pp. 436–440; Kevin Lane Keller and Richard Staelin, "Effects of Quality and Quantity of Information on Decision Effectiveness," *Journal of Consumer Research*, September 1987, pp. 200–213.

106. Yumiko Ono, "Fine Print in Drug Ads Sparks a Debate," *Wall Street Journal*, April 1, 1997, pp. B1, B8.

107. J. Edward Russo, Richard Staelin, Catherine A. Nolan, Gary J. Russell, and Barbara L. Metcalf, "Nutrition Information in the Supermarket," *Journal of Consumer Research*, June 1986, pp. 48–70; James R. Bettman and Pradeep Kakkar, "Effects of Information Presentation Format on Consumer Information Acquisition Strategies," *Journal of Consumer Research*, March 1977, pp. 233–240; Cole and Gaeth, "Cognitive and Age–Related Differences in the Ability to Use Nutritional Information;" Christine Moorman, "The Effects of Stimulus and Consumer Characteristics on the Utilization of Nutrition Information," *Journal of Consumer Research*, December 1990, pp. 362–374.

108. Pauline M. Ippolito and Alan D. Mathios, "New Food Labeling Regulations and the Flow of Nutrition

Information to Consumers," *Journal of Public Policy and Marketing*, Fall 1993, pp. 118–205; John Sinisi, "New Rules Exact a Heavy Price as Labels Are Recast," *Brandweek*, December 7, 1992, p. 3; Nita Lelyveid, "What's in the Food You Eat," *Austin American Statesman*, May 3, 1994, pp. A7, A13.

109. Scot Burton and Abhijit Biswas, "Preliminary Assessment of Changes in Labels Required by the Nutrition Labeling and Education Act of 1990," *Journal of Consumer Affairs*, Summer 1993, pp. 127–144; Scot Burton, Abhijit Biswas, and Richard Netermeyer, "Effects of Alternative Nutrition Label Formats and Nutrition Reference Information on Consumer Perceptions, Comprehension, and Product Evaluations," *Journal of Public Policy and Marketing*, Spring 1994, pp. 36–47.

110. Christine Moorman, "A Quasi Experiment to Assess the Consumer and Information Determinants of Nutrition Information Processing Activities: The Case of the Nutrition Labeling and Education Act," *Journal of Public Policy and Marketing*, Spring 1996, pp. 28– 44.

111. Anu Mitra, Manoj Hastak, Gary T. Ford, and Debra Jones Ringold, "Can the Educationally Disadvantaged Interpret the FDA-Mandated Nutrition Facts Panel in the Presence of an Implied Health Claim?" *Journal of Public Policy and Marketing*, Spring 1999, pp. 106– 117; Gary T. Ford, Manoj Hastak, Anu Mitra, and Debra Jones Ringold, "Can Consumers Interpret Nutrition Information in the Presence of a Health Claim? A Laboratory Investigation," *Journal of Public Policy and Marketing*, Spring 1996, pp. 16– 27.

112. Scott B. Keller, Mike Landry, Jeanne Olson, Anne M. Velliquette, Scot Burton, and J. Craig Andrews, "The Effects of Nutrition Package Claims, Nutrition Facts Panels, and Motivation to Process Information on Consumer Product Evaluations," *Journal of Public Policy and Marketing*, Fall 1997, pp. 256–269.

113. Madhubalan Viswanathan, "The Influence of Summary Information on the Usage of Nutrition Information," *Journal of Public Policy and Marketing*, Spring 1994, pp. 48–60: Alan S. Levey, Sara B. Fein, and Raymond E. Schucker, "Performance Characteristics of Seven Nutrition Label Formats," *Journal of Public Policy and Marketing*, Spring 1996, pp. 1– 15.

114. Michael J. Barone, Randall L. Rose, Kenneth C. Manning, and Paul W. Miniard, "Another Look at the Impact of Reference Information on Consumer Impressions of Nutrition Information, *Journal of Public Policy and Marketing*, Spring 1996, pp. 55–62.

115. Dennis L. McNeill and William L. Wilkie, "Public Policy and Consumer Information: Impacts of the New Energy Labels," *Journal of Consumer Research*, June 1979, pp. 1–11; R. Bruce Hutton and William L. Wilkie, "Life Cycle Cost: A New Form of Consumer Information," *Journal of Consumer Research*, March 1980, pp. 349–360.

116. Bruce Ingersoll, "FDA Proposes Labels for Drugs Sold at Counter," *Wall Street Journal*, February 27, 1997, p. B8.

117. Fred W. Morgan and Dana I. Avrunin, "Consumer Conduct in Product Liability Litigation," *Journal of Consumer Research*, June 1982, pp. 47–55.

118. Judith S. Riddle, "New Alcohol-Reduced Remedies Put P & G in Re-Marketing Hotseat," *Brandweek*, April 12, 1993, pp. 1, 6.

119. Raju Narisetti, "P & G Ready to Fight Back over Olestra," *Wall Street Journal*, September 23, 1996, p. B6.

120. Joseph Pereira, "Toy Story: Industry Strikes Back against Safety Sleuth," *Wall Street Journal*, November 17, 1997, pp. B1, B15.

121. Rob Norton, "Why Airbags Are Killing Kids," *Fortune*, August 19, 1996, p. 40.

122. Asra Q. Nomani, "Regulators Plan Safety Rules for Child Seats," *Wall Street Journal*, February 13, 1997, pp. B1, B12.

123. Jennifer L. Gerner, "Product Safety: A Review," in ed. E. Scott Maynes, *The Frontiers of Research in the Consumer Interest* (Columbia, Mo.: American Council on Consumer Interests, 1988), pp. 19–36.

124. Oscar Suris, "General Motors Plans to Recall Million Vehicles," *Wall Street Journal*, February 5, 1996; Asra Q. Nomani, "Chrysler Effort to Fix Minivans Has Slow Start," *Wall Street Journal*, February 12, 1996, p. B2; Nichole M. Christain and Asra Q. Nomani, "Ford Recalls 8.7 Million Cars to Fix Ignitions," *Wall Street Journal*, April 26, 1996, pp. B1, B2.

125. George C. Jackson and Fred W. Morgan, "Responding to Recall Requests: A Strategy for Managing Goods Withdrawals," *Journal of Public Policy and Marketing*, 7, 1988, pp. 152–165.

126. Laura Johannes and Steve Stecklow, "Withdrawal of Redux Spotlights Predicament FDA Faces on Obesity," *Wall Street Journal*, September 16, 1997, pp. A1, A10; Bruce Ingersoll, "FDA Proposes to Force Seldane off the Market," *Wall Street Journal*, January 14, 1997, pp. B1, B8.

127. Walter Guzzardi, "The Mindless Pursuit of Safety," *Fortune*, April 9, 1979, pp. 54–64; Mowen, *Consumer Behavior*.

128. James F. Engel, Roger D. Blackwell, and Paul W. Miniard, *Consumer Behavior*, 8th ed. (Fort Worth, Tex.: Dryden Press, 1995).

129. Mark R. Lehto and James M. Miller, "The Effectiveness of Warning Labels," *Journal of Product Liability*, 11 (3), 1988, pp. 225–270.

130. James R. Bettman, John W. Payne, and Richard Staelin, "Cognitive Considerations in Designing Labels for Presenting Risk Information," *Journal of Public Policy and Marketing*, 5, 1986, pp. 1–28.

131. Kenneth C. Schneider, "Prevention of Accidental Poisoning through Package and Label Design," *Journal of Consumer Research*, September 1977, pp. 67–75.

132. Richard Staelin, "The Effects of Consumer Education on Consumer Product Safety Behavior," *Journal of Consumer Research*, June 1978, pp. 30–40.

133. Dennis C. McCornac, "The Efficacy of Government Safety Policies on Traffic-Related Fatalities: Empirical Estimates from Japan," *Applied Economics*, March 1993, pp. 409–412.

134. E. Scott Geller, "Seat Belt Psychology," *Psychology Today*, May 1985, pp. 12–13.

135. Walter Bussewitz, "Oregon's Seat Belt Law Blazes Trail," *National Underwriter*, September 23, 1991, pp. 4, 20.

136. Christopher Garbacz, "More Evidence on the Effectiveness of Seat Belt Laws," *Applied Economics*, March 1992, pp. 313–315; Christopher Garbacz, "Impact of the New Zealand Seat Belt Law," *Economic Inquiry*, April 1991, pp. 310–316.

137. Banwari Mittal, "Achieving Higher Seat Belt Usage: The Role of Habit in Bridging the Attitude-Behavior Gap," *Journal of Applied Social Psychology*, September 1988, pp. 993–1016; David L. Ryan and Guy A. Bridgeman, "Judging the Roles of Legislation, Education, and Offsetting Behavior in Seat Belt Use: A Survey and New Evidence from Alberta," *Canadian Public Policy*, March 1992, pp. 27–46.

138. Laura Bird, "U.S. Fears Success May Have Changed Crash Dummies," *Wall Street Journal*, June 8, 1992, pp. B1, B4

139. Robert E. Pitts, John F. Willenborg, and Daniel L. Sherrell, "Consumer Adaptation to Gasoline Price Increase," *Journal of Consumer Research*, December 1981, pp. 322–330.

140. Stacy Kravetz, "Dry Cleaners' New Wrinkle: Going Green," *Wall Street Journal*, June 3, 1998, pp. B1, B15.

141. Jacquelyn Ottman, "Use Less, Make It More Durable, and Then Take It Back," *Marketing News*, December 7, 1992, p. 13.

142. Seema Nayyar, "Refillable Pouch a Lotions First," *Brandweek*, October 26, 1992, p. 3; Seema Nayyar, "L & F Cleaner Refills Greener," *Brandweek*, September 14, 1992, p. 5; Russell Belk, "Daily Life in Romania."

143. Jaclyn Frierman, "The Big Muddle in Green Marketing," *Fortune*, June 3, 1991, pp. 92–102.

144. Howard Schlossberg, "'Project Clean Mail' Would Fine Tune Direct Marketing," *Marketing News*, September 14, 1992, pp. 18–19.

145. Shirley Taylor and Peter Todd, "Understanding Household Garbage Reduction: A Test of an Integrated Model," *Journal of Public Policy and Marketing*, Fall 1995, pp. 192–204.

146. Kathleen Deveny, "For Growing Band of Shoppers, Clean Means Green," *Wall Street Journal*, April 6, 1993, pp. B1, B7.

147. Charles H. Schwepker and T. Bettina Cornwell, "An Examination of Ecologically Concerned Consumers and Their Intention to Purchase Ecologically Packaged Products," *Journal of Public Policy and Marketing*, Fall 1991, pp. 77–101.

148. Linda F. Alwitt and Robert E. Pitts, "Predicting Purchase Intentions for an Environmentally Sensitive Product," *Journal of Consumer Psychology*, 5 (1- 1996), pp. 49– 64.

149. Pam Scholder Ellen, Joshua Lyle Wiener, and Cathy Cobb-Walgren, "The Role of Perceived Consumer Effectiveness in Motivating Environmentally Conscious Behaviors," *Journal of Public Policy and Marketing*, Fall 1991, pp. 102–117; Thomas C. Kinnear, James R. Taylor, and Sadrudin A. Ahmed, "Ecologically Concerned Consumers: Who Are They?" *Journal of Marketing*, April 1972, pp. 46–57.

150. Allan Glass, "Does a Green Message Still Belong on Your Package?" *Brandweek*, October 19, 1992, pp. 26, 28.

151. Jacquelyn Ottman, "Environmentalism Will Be the Trend of the 90s," *Marketing News*, December 7, 1992, p. 13.

152. Cheryl Powell, "The Green Movement Sows Demand for Ecofurniture," *Wall Street Journal*, August 2, 1994, pp. B1, B2.

153. Russell Belk, John Painter, and Richard Semenik, "Preferred Solutions to the Energy Crisis as a Function of Causal Attributions," *Journal of Consumer Research*, December 1981, pp. 306–312.

154. C. Dennis Anderson and John D. Claxton, "Barriers to Consumer Choice of Energy-Efficient Products," *Journal of Consumer Research*, September 1982, pp. 163–170.

155. Rik Peters, Tammo Bijmo, H. Fred van Raaij, and Mark de Kruijk, "Consumers'Attributions of Proenvironmental Behavior, Motivation, and Ability to Self and Others," *Journal of Public Policy and Marketing*, Fall 1998, pp. 215–225.

156. Dorothy Leonard-Barton, "Voluntary Simplicity Lifestyles and Energy Conservation," *Journal of Consumer Research*, December 1981, pp. 243–252.

157. Louise A. Helsop, Lori Moran, and Amy Cousineau, "'Consciousness' in Energy Conservation Behavior: An Exploratory Study," *Journal of Consumer Research*, December 1981, pp. 299–305; Gregory M. Pickett, Norman Kangun, and Stephen J. Grove, "Is There a General Conserving Consumer?" *Journal of Public Policy and Marketing*, Fall 1993, pp. 234–243.

158. Marta Tienda and Osei-Mensah Aborampah, "Energy-Related Adaptations in Low-Income Nonmetropolitan Wisconsin Counties," *Journal of Consumer Research*, December 1981, pp. 265–270.

159. Theo M. M. Verhallen and W. Fred van Raaij, "Household Behavior and the Use of Natural Gas for Heating," *Journal of Consumer Research*, December 1981, pp. 253–257.

160. Gordon H. G. McDougall, John D. Claxton, J. R. Brent Ritchie, and C. Dennis Anderson, "Consumer Energy Research: A Review," *Journal of Consumer Research*, December 1981, pp. 343–354.

161. Ibid; Dennis L. McNeill and William L. Wilkie, "Public Policy and Consumer Information: Impact of the New Energy Labels," *Journal of Consumer Research*, June 1979, pp. 1–11.

162. R. Bruce Hutton and Dennis L. McNeill, "The Value of Incentives in Stimulating Energy Conservation," *Journal of Consumer Research*, December 1981, pp. 291–298; Peter D. Bennett and Noreen Klein Moore, "Consumers' Preferences for Alternative Energy Conservation Policies: A Trade-off Analysis," *Journal of Consumer Research*, December 1981, pp. 313–321; Robert E. Pitts and James L. Wittenbach, "Tax Credits as a Means of Influencing Consumer Behavior," *Journal of Consumer Research*, December 1981, pp. 335–338; Bruce R. Hutton, Gary A. Mauser, Pierre Filiatrault, and Olli T. Ahtola, "Effects of Cost Related Feedback on Consumer Knowledge and Consumption Behavior: A Field Experiment," *Journal of Consumer Research*, December 1986, pp. 327–336; Jeannet H. van Houwelingen and W. Fred van Raaij, "The Effect of Goal-Setting and Daily Electronic Feedback on In-Home Energy Use," *Journal of Consumer Research*, June 1989, pp. 98–105.

163. Edward Cundiff and Marye Hilger Tharpe, *Marketing in the International Environment*, 2nd ed. (Englewood Cliffs, N.J.: Prentice-Hall, 1988).

164. Gary M. Armstrong and Merrie Brucks, "Dealing with Children's Advertising: Public Policy Issues and Alternatives," *Journal of Public Policy and Marketing*, 7, 1988, pp. 98–113.

165. Ross D. Petty, "Advertising Law in the United States and European Union," *Journal of Public Policy and Marketing*, Spring 1997,pp. 2–13.

166. Matthew Rose, "French Court Blocks Philip Morris Ads That Liken Passive Smoke to Cookies," *Wall Street Journal*, June 27, 1996, B1.

167. "Nielsen in Dutch over Ad," *Austin American Statesman*, April 3, 1999, p. B8.

168. Vern Terpstra and Ravi Sarathy, *International Marketing*, 5th ed. (Chicago, Ill.: Dryden Press, 1991).

169. Jean-Pierre Jeannet and Hubert D. Hennessey, *Global Marketing Strategies* (Boston: Houghton Mifflin, 1992); Terpstra and Sarathy, *International Marketing*.

170. Julie Wolf and Ernest Beck, "European Union Seems Set to Ban Most Kinds of Tobacco Advertising," *Wall Street Journal*, December 3, 1997, p. B13.

171. Marcia Kunstel and Joseph Albright, "Russia Mourns Assassination of Famous Television Journalist," *Austin American Statesman*, March 4, 1995, p. A16.

172. Laurel Wentz, "Playing by the Same Rules," *Advertising Age*, December 2, 1991, p. S2.

173. Sally D. Goll, "Chinese Officials Attempt to Ban False Ad Claims," *Wall Street Journal*, February 28, 1995, pp. B1, B9.

174. Bruce Ingersoll, "Home Shopping and iMall to Pay Millions in FTC Ad-Claim Cases," *Wall Street Journal*, April 16, 1999, p. B2.

175. Kara Swisher, "Seller Beware," *Wall Street Journal*, December 7, 1998, p. R22.

176. Don Clark, "Safety First," *Wall Street Journal*, December 7, 1998, p. R14.

177. Aaron Lucchetti, "FTC Tackles an 'Anonymous' Web Survey," *Wall Street Journal*, May 7, 1999, p. B2.

178. Neil Gross and Ira Sager, "Caution Signs Along the Road," *Wall Street Journal*, June 22, 1998, pp. B6, B8.

179. James H. Snider, "Consumers in the Information Age," *The Futurist*, January–February 1993, pp. 15–19.

CHAPTER 21

1. Rebecca Quick, "On-line Groups Are Offering up Privacy Plans," *Wall Street Journal*, June 22, 1998, pp. B1, B12; Paulette Thomas, "'Clicking' Coupons On-line Has a Cost; Privacy," *Wall Street Journal*, June 18, 1998, pp. B1, B8; Aaron Lucchetti, "FTC Tackles as 'Anonymous' Web Survey, *Wall Street Journal*, May 7, 1999, p. B2; Ann Reilly Dowd, "Protect Your Privacy," *Money*, August 1997, pp. 104–115.

2. Thomas C. O'Guinn and Ronald J. Faber, "Compulsive Buying: A Phenomenological Exploration," *Journal of Consumer Research*, September 1989, pp. 147–157.

3. Ronald Faber, Gary Christenson, Martina DeZwaan, and James Mitchell, "Two Forms of Compulsive Comsumption: Comorbidity of Compulsive Buying and Binge Eating," *Journal of Consumer Research*, December 1995, pp. 296–304; O'Guinn and Faber, "Compulsive Buying"; Ronald J. Faber and Thomas C. O'Guinn, "Compulsive Consumption and Credit Abuse," *Journal of Consumer Policy*, March 1988, pp. 97–109; Gilles Valence, Alain D'Astous, and Louis Fortier, "Compulsive Buying: Concept and Measurement," *Journal of Consumer Policy*, December 1988, pp. 419–433;

Rajan Nataraajan and Brent G. Goff, "Compulsive Buying: Toward a Reconceptualization," in ed. Floyd W. Rudman, *To Have Possessions: A Handbook on Ownership and Property* (Corte Madera, Calif.: Select Press, 1991), pp. 307–328; "Compulsive Shopping Could Be Hereditary," *Marketing News*, September 14, 1998, pp. 31; Wayne S. DeSarbo and Elizabeth A. Edwards, "Typologies of Compulsive Buying Behavior: A Constrained Clusterwise Regression Approach," *Journal of Consumer Psychology*, 5 (3, 1996), pp. 231–262.

4. Ibid.

5. Faber and O'Guinn, "Compulsive Consumption and Credit Abuse"; Ronald J. Faber and Thomas C. O'Guinn, "A Clinical Screener for Compulsive Buying," *Journal of Consumer Research*, December 1992, pp. 459–469; O'Guinn and Faber, "Compulsive Buying"; James A. Roberts, "Compulsive Buying among College Students: An Investigation of Its Antecedents, Consequences, and Implications for Public Policy," *Journal of Consumer Affairs*, Winter 1998, pp. 295–319.

6. Janine Latus Musick, "Keeping Would-Be Thieves at Bay," *Nation's Business*, October 1998, pp. 41–43; "Cops and Robbers," *Discount Merchandiser*, March 1997, p. 3.

7. Ronald A. Fullerton and Girish Punj, "Choosing to Misbehave: A Structural Model of Aberrant Consumer Behavior," in eds. Leigh McAlister and Michael Rothschild, *Advances in Consumer Research*, Vol. 20 (Provo, Utah: Association for Consumer Research, 1993), pp. 570–574; Ronald A. Fullerton and Girish Punj, "The Unintended Consequences of the Culture of Consumption: A Theory of Consumer Misbehavior," working paper, University of Hartford, Department of Marketing, 1994; John J. Keller, "Call-Sell Rings Steal Cellular Service," *Wall Street Journal*, March 13, 1992, pp. A5, B3; Jacqueline Simmons, "Hotels Snoop to Stop Guests' Thievery of Everything That Isn't Nailed Down," *Wall Street Journal*, March 17, 1995, pp. B1, B7; Musick, "Cops and Robbers"; Steven Stecklow, "Student Applications for Financial Aid Give Lots of False Answers," *Wall Street Journal*, March 11, 1997, pp. A1, A15; Ronald A. Fullerton and Girish Punj, "The Unintended Consequences of the Culture of Consumption: An Historical-Theoretical Analysis of Consumer Misbehavior," *Consumption, Markets and Culture*, 1 (4, 1998), pp. 393–423.

8. Dena Cox, Anthony P. Cox, and George P. Moschis, " When Consumer Behavior Goes Bad: An Investigation of Adolescent Shoplifting," *Journal of Consumer Research*, September 1990, pp. 149–159; Fullerton and Punj, "The Unintended Consequences of the Culture of Consumption"; Cox, Cox, and Moschis, " When Consumer Behavior Goes Bad"; George P. Moschis, Dena S. Cox, and James J. Kellaris, "An Exploratory Study of Adolescent Shoplifting Behavior," in eds. Melanie Wallendorf and Paul Anderson, *Advances in Consumer Research*, Vol. 14 (Provo, Utah: Association for Consumer Research, 1987), pp. 526–530.

9. Fullerton and Punj, "The Unintended Consequences of the Culture of Consumption."

10. Cox, Cox, and Moschis, " When Consumer Behavior Goes Bad."

11. Paul Bernstein, "Cheating—The New National Pastime?" *Business*, October–December 1985, pp. 24–33; Fullerton and Punj, "Some Unintended Consequences of the Culture of Consumption."

12. Fullerton and Punj, "Choosing to Misbehave"; Donald R. Katz, *The Big Store* (New York: Penguin, 1988).

13. Cox, Cox, and Moschis, " When Consumer Behavior Goes Bad"; Moschis, Cox, and Kellaris, "An Exploratory Study of Adolescent Shoplifting Behavior"; Fullerton and Punj, "Some Unintended Consequences of the Culture of Consumption."

14. Katz, *The Big Store*.

15. Cox, Cox, and Moschis, " When Consumer Behavior Goes Bad"; Moschis, Cox, and Kellaris, "An Exploratory Study of Adolescent Shoplifting Behavior."

16. Anthony D. Cox, Dena Cox, Ronald D. Anderson, and George P. Moschis, "Social Influences on Adolescent Shoplifting—Theory, Evidence, and Implications for the Retail Industry," *Journal of Retailing*, Summer 1993, p. 234.

17. Chok C. Hiew, "Prevention of Shoplifting: A Community Action Approach," *Canadian Journal of Criminology*, January 1981, pp. 57–68.

18. Cox, Cox, and Moschis, " When Consumer Behavior Goes Bad; Fullerton and Punj, "The Unintended Consequences of the Culture of Consumption"; Fullerton and Punj, "Choosing to Misbehave"; Cox, Cox, Anderson, and Moschis, "Social Influences on Adolescent Shoplifting."

19. Janine Latus Musick, "Keeping Would-Be Thieves at Bay."

20. Marc Millstein, "Cutting Losses," *Supermarket News*, March 20, 1995, pp. 13–16.

21. Junda Woo, "Retailers Use Bans, Guards and Ploys to Curb Teen Sport of 'Mall-Mauling,'" *Wall Street Journal*, August 7, 1990, p. B1; Mark McLaughlin, "Subliminal Tapes Urge Shoppers to Heed the Warning Sounds of Silence: 'Don't Steal,'" *New England Business*, February 1987, pp. 36–38.

22. "Retailers to Tighten up Security," *Retail World*, February 22–26, 1999; Charles Goldsmith, "Less Honor, More Case at Europe Mimibars," *Wall Street Journal*, March 22, 1996, pp. B6; Simmons, "Hotels Snoop to Stop Guests' Thievery of Everything That Isn't Nailed Down"; Steve Weinstein, "The Enemy Within," *Progressive Grocer*, May 1994, pp. 175–179.

23. Elizabeth Parks, "Let Fragrance Sales Break out of Their Glass Prison," *Drug Store News*, April 3, 1989, p. 28.

24. William Echikson, "Ticket Madness at the World Cup," *BusinessWeek*, July 13, 1998, pp. 126; Joel Engardio, "L.A. Air Bag Thieves May Be Popping up in East County," *Los Angeles Times*, July 1, 1998, p. 1; Ann Marie O'Connon, "Where There's Smoke," *Los Angeles Times*, September 7, 1997, p. A3R.

25. Lisa R. Szykman and Ronald P. Hill, "A Consumer-Behavior Investigation of a Prison Economy," in eds. Janeen Costa Arnold and Russell W. Belk, *Research in Consumer Behavior*, Vol. 6 (Greenwich, Conn.: JAI Press, 1993), pp. 231–260; David Bevan, Paul Collier, and Jan Willem Gunning, "Black Markets: Illegality, Information, and Rents," *World Development*, December 1989, pp. 1955–1963; "Black Market Holds Hope for Revival," *Far East Economic Review*, August 25, 1988, pp. 13–14.

26. Harvey D. Shapiro, "Buying Miles Is Thrifty—but Iffy," *Los Angeles Times*, March 9, 1995, p. D5.

27. "Hey, Anybody Want a Gun," *The Economist*, May 16, 1998, pp. 47–48; Mark Hosenball and Daniel Klaidman, "A Deadly Mix of Drugs and Firepower," *Newsweek*, April 19, 1999, p. 27.

28. Jonathan Karp, "Awaiting Knockoffs, Indians Buy Black-Market Viagra," *Wall Street Journal*, July 10, 1998, pp. B1, B2; M. B. Sheridan, "Men around the Globe Lust after Viagra," *Los Angeles Times*, May 26, 1998, p. 1.

29. Elizabeth C. Hirschman, "The Consciousness of Addiction: Toward a General Theory of Compulsive Consumption," *Journal of Consumer Research*, September, 1992, pp. 155–179.

30. Christine Gorman, Barbara Dolan, and Glenn Garelik, "Why It's So Hard to Quit Smoking," *Time*, May 30, 1988, p. 131; Gilbert J. Botvin, Catherine J. Goldberg, Elizabeth M. Botvin, and Linda Dusenbury, "Smoking Behavior of Adolescents Exposed to Cigarette Advertising," *Public Health Reports*, March–April 1993, pp. 217–223; James Ryan, Craig Zwerling, and Endel John Orav, "Occupational Risks Associated with Cigarette Smoking: A Prospective Study," *American Journal of Public Health*, January 1992, pp. 29–33; John R. Nelson and Jeanne E. Lukas, "Target: Minorities," *Marketing and Media Decisions*, October 1990, pp. 70–71; Clara Manfreid, Loretta Lacey, Richard Warnecke, and Marianne Buis, "Smoking-Related Behavior, Beliefs, and Social Environment of Young Black Women in Subsidized Public Housing in Chicago," *American Journal of Public Health*, February 1992, pp. 267–272; Tara Parker-Pope, "Health Activists Light into Cigars' Glamorous Image," *Wall Street Journal*, July 8, 1997, pp. B1, B6.

31. "Recovery Network Targets Substance Abusers," *Marketing News*, July 21, 1997, p. 9.

32. Ronald Gaudia, "Effects of Compulsive Gambling on the Family," *Social Work*, May–June 1987, pp. 254–256.

33. United Press International, "High Correlation Found between Gambling Addiction and Crime," *ClariNet Electronic News Service*, December 1, 1992.

34. Ibid; Ricardo Chavira, "The Rise of Teenage Gambling," *Time*, February 25, 1991, p. 78.

35. Patricia B. Sutker and Albert N. Allain Jr., "Issues in Personality Conceptualizations of Addictive Behavior," *Journal of Consulting and Clinical Psychology*, April 1988, pp. 172–182; Alex Blaszczynski, Neil McConaghy, and Anna Frankova, "Boredom Proneness in Pathological Gambling," *Psychological Reports*, August 1990, pp. 35–42; John R. Graham and Virginia E. Strenger, "MMPI Characteristics of Alcoholics: A Review," *Journal of Consulting and Clinical Psychology*, April 1988, pp. 197–205; Robert C. McMahon, David Gersh, and Robert S. Davidson, "Personality and Symptom Characteristics of Continuous vs. Episodic Drinkers," *Journal of Clinical Psychology*, January 1989, pp. 161–168; Robert K. Brooner, Chester W. Schmidt, Linda Felch, and George E. Bigelow, "Antisocial Behavior of Intravenous Drug Abusers: Implications for Diagnosis

of Antisocial Personality Disorder," *American Journal of Psychiatry*, April 1992, pp. 482–487; Ralph E. Tarter, "Are There Inherited Behavioral Traits That Predispose to Substance Abuse?" *Journal of Consulting and Clinical Psychology*, February 1988, pp. 189–196; Hirschman, "The Consciousness of Addiction."

36. "Fuming: Tobacco Adverts," *The Economist*, February 5, 1994, pp. 60–62.

37. Michael J. Goodman, "The Cigarette Papers," *Los Angeles Times Magazine*, September 18, 1994, pp. 34–39.

38. Kevin Heubusch, "Taking Chances on Casinos," *American Demographics*, May 1997, pp. 35–40; Tom Gorman, "Indian Casinos in Middle of Battle over Slots," *Los Angeles Times*, May 9, 1995, pp. A3, A24; Max Vanzi, "Gambling Industry Studies the Odds," *Los Angeles Times*, May 9, 1995, pp. A3, A24; James Popkin, "America's Gambling Craze," *US News and World Report*, March 14, 1994, pp. 42–45; Iris Cohen Selinger, "The Big Lottery Gamble," *Advertising Age*, May 10, 1993, pp. 22–26; Tony Horwitz, " In a Bible Belt State, Video Poker Mutates into an Unholy Mess," *Wall Street Journal*, December 2, 1997, pp. A1, A13; Bruce Orwall, "Place Your Bets," *Wall Street Journal*, March 28, 1996, p. R8; Rebecca Quick, "For Sports Fans, The Internet Is a Whole New Ball Game," *Wall Street Journal*, September 3, 1998, p. B9; Stephen Braun, "Lives Lost in a River of Debt," *Los Angeles Times*, June 22, 1997, pp. A1, A14, A15; Michael McCarthy, "In-Flight Gambling Is Ready to Take Off," *Wall Street Journal*, May 24, 1996, pp. B1, B6; Bruce Orwall, "Like Playing Slots? Casinos Know All about You," *Wall Street Journal*, December 20, 1995, pp. B1, B4.

39. Justin Supon, "Gambling Hotline Braces for Post-Super Bowl Calls,"*ClariNet Electronic News Service*, January 27, 1993; Donald Janson, "Two Casinos Post Compulsive Gambler Hot Line," *New York Times*, August 9, 1987, pp. 14, 36.

40. George A. Hacker, "Liquor Advertisements on Television: Just Say No," *Journal of Public Policy and Marketing*, Spring 1998, pp. 139–142; William K. Eaton, "College Binge Drinking Soars, Study Finds," *Los Angeles Times*, June 8, 1994, p. A21; Mike Fuer and Rita Walters, "Mixed Message Hurts Kids: Ban Tobacco, Alcohol Billboards: The Targeting of Children Is Indisputable and Intolerable," *Los Angeles Times*, June 8, 1997, p. M5; Joseph Coleman, "Big Tobacco Still Calls the Shots in Japan," *Marketing News*, August 4, 1997, p. 12.

41. Clark, "Underage Drinking"; Courtney Leatherman, "College Officials Are Split on Alcohol Policies: Some Seek to End Underage Drinking; Others Try to Encourage 'Responsible Use,'" *Chronicle of Higher Education*, January 31, 1990, pp. A33–A35.

42. Novello, "Alcohol and Tobacco Advertising."

43. Ibid; K. M.Cummings, E. Sciandra, T. F. Pechacek, J. P. Pierce, L. Wallack, S. L. Mills, W. R. Lynn, and S. E. Marcus, "Comparison of the Cigarette Brand Preferences of Adult and Teenaged Smokers—United States, 1989, and 10 U.S. Communities, 1988 and 1990," *Journal of the American Medical Association*, April 8, 1992, p. 1893.

44. Clark, "Underage Drinking"; Erica H. van Roosmalen and Susan A. McDaniel, "Peer Group Influence as a Factor in Smoking Behavior of Adolescents," *Adolescence*, Winter 1989, pp. 801–816; Nancy Twitchell Murphy and Cynthia J. Price, "The Influence of Self-Esteem, Parental Smoking, and Living in a Tobacco Production Region on Adolescent Smoking Behaviors," *Journal of School Health*, December 1988, pp. 401–450; Botvin et al., "Smoking Behavior of Adolescents Exposed to Cigarette Advertising"; Sarah A. McGraw, Kevin W. Smith, Jean J. Schensul, and J. Emilio Carrillo, "Sociocultural Factors Associated with Smoking Behavior by Puerto Rican Adolescents in Boston," *Social Science Medicine*, December 1991, pp. 1355–1364.

45. Associated Press, "Study: Kids Remember Beer Ads," *ClariNet Electronic News Service*, February 11, 1994; Fara Warner, "Cheers! It's Happy Hour in Cyberspace," *Wall Street Journal*, March 15, 1995, pp. B1, B4; Kirk Davidson, "Looking for Abundance of Opposition to TV Liquor Ads," *Marketing News*, January 6, 1997, pp. 4, 30; Rosanna Tamburri, "Dodging Bans on Cigarette Ads in Canada," *Wall Street Journal*, December 27, 1994, p. B5.

46. Arch G. Woodside, "Advertising and Consumption of Alcoholic Beverages," *Journal of Consumer Psychology*, 8, (2, 1999), pp. 167–186.

47. Fara Warner, "Tobacco Brands Outmaneuver Asian Ad Bans," *Wall Street Journal*, August 6, 1996, pp. B1, B3; Eben Shapiro, "Cigarette Makers Outfit Smokers in Icons Eluding Warning and Enraging Activists," *Wall Street Journal*, August 27, 1993, p. B1; Botvin et al., "Smoking Behavior of Adolescents Exposed to Cigarette Advertising"; Novello, "Alcohol and Tobacco Advertising"; Bruce Horovitz, "Most Advertised Cigarettes Are Teens' Choice, Study Says," *Los Angeles Times*, March 13, 1992, p. D4; K. M. Cummings, E. Sciandra, T. F. Pechacek, J. P. Pierce, L. Wallack, S. L. Mills, W. R. Lynn, and S. E. Marcus, "Comparison of the Cigarette Brand Preferences of Adult and Teenaged Smokers."

48. Elizabeth M. Botvin, Gilbert J. Botvin, John L. Michela, Eli Baker, and Anne D. Filazolla, "Adolescent Smoking Behavior and the Recognition of Cigarette Advertisements," *Journal of Applied Social Psychology*, November 1991, pp. 919–932. Botvin et al., "Smoking Behavior of Adolescents Exposed to Cigarette Advertising"; Richard W. Pollay, S. Siddarth, Michael Siegel, Anne Hadix, Robert K. Merritt, Gary A. Giovino, and Michael P. Eriksen, "The Last Straw? Cigarette Advertising and Realized Market Shares among Youths and Adults, 1979–1993," *Journal of Marketing*, April 1996, pp. 1–16; Joseph DiFranza, John W. Richards, Paul M. Paulman, Nancy Wolf-Gillespie, Christopher Fletcher, Robert D. Jaffe, and David Murray, "RJR Nabisco's Cartoon Camel Promotes Camel Cigarettes to Children," *Journal of the American Medical Association*, December 11, 1991, p. 3149; K. M. Cummings, E. Sciandra, T. F. Pechacek, J. P. Pierce, L. Wallack, S. L. Mills, W. R. Lynn, S. E. Marcus, "Comparison of the Cigarette Brand Preferences of Adult and Teenaged Smokers"; DiFranza et al., "RJR Nabisco's Cartoon Camel Promotes Camel Cigarettes to Children."

49. Richard W. Pollay and Ann M. Lavack, "The Targeting of Youths by Cigarette Marketers: Archival Evidence on

Trial," in eds. Leigh McAlister and Michael Rothschild, *Advances in Consumer Research*, Vol. 20 (Provo, Utah: Association for Consumer Research, 1993), pp. 266–271.

50. "RJR Denies Link to Teen Smoking; Tobacco: Executive Testifies at Minnesota Trial That Firm Doesn't Use Ads to Attract New Smokers," *Los Angeles Times*, April 21, 1998, p. 13.

51. Richard Morgan, "Is Old Joe Taking Too Much Heat?" *Adweek*, March 16, 1992, p. 44.

52. Reuters, "Joe Camel Doesn't Make Kids Smoke—RJR Funded Survey," *ClariNet Electronic News Service*, February 21, 1994.

53. Clark, "Underage Drinking."

54. Carl Quintanilla, "Du-ude! Clothier's Catalog Sells Students on Drinking." *Wall Street Journal*, July 24, 1998, p. B1.

55. Debra L. Scammon, Robert N. Mayer, and Ken R. Smith, "Alcohol Warnings: How Do You Know When You've Had One Too Many?" *Journal of Public Policy and Marketing*, Spring 1991, pp. 214–228; Michael B. Mazis, Louis A. Morris, and John L. Swasy, "An Evaluation of the Alcohol Warning Label: Initial Survey Results," *Journal of Public Policy and Marketing*, Spring 1991, pp. 229–241; Novello, "Alcohol and Tobacco Advertising"; Richard Gibson and Marj Charlier, "Anheuser Leads the Way in Listing Alcohol Levels," *Wall Street Journal*, March 11, 1993, pp. B1, B2; Richard J. Fox, Dean M. Krugman, James E. Fletcher, and Paul M. Fischer, "Adolescents' Attention to Beer and Cigarette Print Ads and Associated Product Warnings," *Journal of Advertising*, Fall 1998, pp. 57–68.

56. U.S. Department of Health and Human Services, as cited in Lague et al., "How Thin Is Too Thin?" *People*, September 20, 1993, pp. 74–80.

57. Hillel Schwartz, "Being Thin Isn't Always Being Happy," *US News and World Report*, February 9, 1987, p. 74.

58. Michael Fay and Christopher Price, "Female Body-Shape in Print Advertisements and the Increase in Anorexia Nervosa," *European Journal of Marketing*, December 1994, pp. 5–19.

59. R. Freedman, *Beauty Bound* (Lexington, Mass.: D.C. Heath, 1986).

60. P. S. Powers, *Obesity: The Regulation of Weight* (Baltimore, Md.: Williams and Wilkins, 1980). A. Furnham and N. Alibhai, "Cross-Cultural Differences in the Perception of Female Body Shapes," *Psychological Medicine*, November 1983, pp. 829–837.

61. See also Debra Lynn Stephens, Ronald P. Hill, and Cynthia Hanson, "The Beauty Myth and Female Consumers: The Controversial Role of Advertising," *Journal of Consumer Affairs*, Summer 1994, pp. 137–154.

62. Leon Festinger, "A Theory of Social Comparison Processes," *Human Relations*, May 1954, pp. 117–140.

63. Mary C. Martin and James W. Gentry, "Stuck in the Model Trap: The Effects of Beautiful Models in Ads on Female Pre-Adolescents and Adolescents," *Journal of Advertising*, Summer 1997, pp. 19–33. Marsha L. Richins, "Social Comparison and the Idealized Images of Advertising," *Journal of Consumer Research*, June 1991, pp. 71–83; Richard W. Pollay, "The Distorted Mirror: Reflections on the Unintended Consequences of Advertising," *Journal of Marketing*, April 1986, pp. 18–36; Lague et al., "How Thin Is Too Thin?"

64. Calmetta Y. Coleman, "Can't Be Too Thin, but Plus-Size Models Get More Work Now," *Wall Street Journal*, May 3, 1999, pp. A1, A10.

65. Sally Goll Beatty, "Women's View of Their Lives Aren't Reflected by Advertisers," *Wall Street Journal*, December 19, 1995, p. B2.

66. Richard W. Pollay, "The Distorted Mirror: Reflections on the Unintended Consequences of Advertising," *Journal of Marketing*, April 1986, pp. 18–36; Russell W. Belk and Richard W. Pollay, "Images of Ourselves: The Good Life in Twentieth Century Advertising," *Journal of Consumer Research*, March 1985, pp. 887–897; Russell W. Belk, "Materialism: Trait Aspects of Living in a Material World," *Journal of Consumer Research*, December 1985, pp. 265–280; Mary Yoko Brannen, "Cross-Cultural Materialism: Commodifying Culture in Japan," in eds. Floyd Rudmin and Marsha L. Richins, *Meaning, Measure, and Morality of Materialism* (Provo, Utah: Association for Consumer Research, 1992), pp. 167–180; Guliz Ger and Russell W. Belk, "Cross-Cultural Differences in Materialism," *Journal of Economic Psychology*, February 1996, pp. 55–77; Marsha L. Richins, "Media, Materialism, and Human Happiness," in eds. Melanie Wallendorf and Paul Anderson, *Advances in Consumer Research*, Vol. 14 (Provo, Utah: Association for Consumer Research, 1986), pp. 352–356; M. Joseph Sirgy, Dong-Jin Lee, Rustan Kosenko, H. Lee Meadow, Don Rahtz, et al., "Does Television Viewership Play a Role in the Perception of Quality of Life," *Journal of Advertising*, Spring 1998, pp. 125–143; Thomas C. O'Guinn and Ronald J. Faber, "Mass Mediated Consumer Socialization: Non-Utilitarian and Dysfunctional Outcomes," in eds. Melanie Wallendorf and Paul Anderson, *Advances in Consumer Research*, Vol. 14 (Provo, Utah; Association for Consumer Research, 1987), pp. 473–477; Ronald J. Faber and Thomas C. O'Guinn, "Expanding the View of Consumer Socialization: A Non-Utilitarian Mass Mediated Perspective" in eds. Elizabeth C. Hirschman and Jagdish N. Sheth, *Research in Consumer Behavior*, Vol. 3 (Greenwich, Conn.: JAI Press, 1988), pp. 49–78.

67. Marsha Richins, "Media, Materialism and Human Happiness".

68. Richins, "Media, Materialism, and Human Happiness."

69. Russell W. Belk, "The Third World Consumer Culture," in ed. Jagdish N. Sheth, *Research in Marketing* (Greenwich, Conn.: JAI Press, 1988), pp. 103–127.

70. Liesl Schillinger, "Barbski," *New Republic*, September 20 and 27, 1993, pp. 10–11.

71. See for example James M. Hunt, Jerome B. Kernan, and Deborah J. Mitchell, "Materialism as Social Cognition: People, Possessions, and Perception," *Journal of Consumer Psychology*, 5, (1, 1996), pp. 65–83.

72. Lynn T. Lovdal, "Sex Role Messages in Television Commercials: An Update," *Sex Roles*, November/December 1989, pp. 715–724; A. E. Courtney and T. Whipple, "Sex Stereotyping in Advertising: An Annotated Bibliography," Cambridge, Mass.: Marketing Science Institute, 1984.

73. Mary C. Gilly, "Sex Roles in Advertising: A Comparison of Television Advertisements in Australia, Mexico, and the United States," *Journal of Marketing*, April 1988, pp. 75–85.

74. Robert E. Wilkes and Humberto Valencia, "Hispanics and Blacks in Television Commercials," *Journal of Advertising*, December 1989, pp. 19–26; Helena Czepiec and J. Steven Kelly, "Analyzing Hispanic Roles in Advertising: A Portrait of an Emerging Subculture," in eds. James H. Leigh and Claude R. Martin, *Current Issues and Research in Advertising* (Ann Arbor, Mich.: University of Michigan Press, 1983), pp. 219–240.

75. Yuri Radzievsky, "Untapped Markets: Ethnics in the US," *Advertising Age*, June 21, 1993, p. 26.

76. Tara Parker-Pope, "Ford Puts Blacks in Whiteface, Turns Red," *Wall Street Journal*, February 22, 1996, p. B5.

77. Linda E. Swayne and Alan J. Greco, "The Portrayal of Older Americans in Television Commercials," *Journal of Advertising*, Winter 1987, pp. 47–56; Anthony C. Ursic, Michael L. Ursic, and Virginia L. Ursic, "A Longitudinal Study of the Use of the Elderly in Magazine Advertising," *Journal of Consumer Research*, June 1986, pp. 131–134; Walter Gantz, Howard M. Garenberg, and Cindy K. Rainbow, "Approaching Invisibility: The Portrayal of the Elderly in Magazine Advertisements," *Journal of Communication*, January 1980, pp. 56–60.

78. Michael L. Klassen, Cynthia R. Jasper, and Anne M. Schwartz, "Men and Women: Images of Their Relationships in Magazine Advertisements," *Journal of Advertising Research*, March–April 1993, pp. 30–39; Sall Goll Beatty, "Critics Rail at Racy TV Programs but Ads Are Often the Sexiest Fare," *Wall Street Journal*, May 28, 1996, p. A25; Courtney and Whipple, "Sex Stereotyping in Advertising: An Annotated Bibliography"; Beverly A. Browne, "Gender Stereotypes in Advertising on Children's Television in the 1990s: A Cross National Analysis, *Journal of Advertising*, Spring 1998, pp. 83–96; John B. Ford, Patricia Kramer Voli, Earl D. Honeycutt Jr., and Susan L. Casey, "Gender Role Portrayals in Japanese Advertising: A Magazine Content Analysis," *Journal of Advertising*, Spring 1998, pp. 113–124; Gilly, "Sex Roles in Advertising"; F. L. Geis, V. Brown, J. J. Walstedt, and N. Porter, "TV Commercials as Achievement Scripts for Women," *Sex Roles*, April 1984, pp. 513–525; Sally D. Goll, "Beer Ads in Hong Kong Criticized as Sexist," *Wall Street Journal*, June 19, 1995, p. B4; Cyndee Miller, "Babe-Based Beer Ads Likely to Flourish," *Marketing News*, January 6, 1992, p. 1; Jill Hicks Ferguson, Peggy J. Kreshel, and Spencer F. Tinkham, "In the Pages of *Ms:* Sex Role Portrayals of Women in Advertising," *Journal of Advertising*, December 1990, pp. 40–52; see also Michael Klassen, Cynthia R. Jasper, and Anne M. Schwartz, "Men and Women: Images of Their Relationships in Magazine Advertisements," *Journal of Advertising Research*, March–April 1993, pp. 30–40; Kathy Brown, "The Fine Line between Good Taste and Bad Taste Should Be Thicker Than a String Bikini," *Adweek*, April 27, 1992, p. 52.

79. Charles R. Taylor and Barbara B. Stern, "Asian-Americans: Television Advertising and the 'Model Minority' Stereotype," *Journal of Advertising*, Summer 1997, pp. 47–61.

80. Alan Greco, "The Elderly as Communicators," *Journal of Advertising Research*, June–July 1988, pp. 39–45; Kevin Goldman, "Seniors Get Little Respect on Madison Avenue," *Wall Street Journal*, September 20, 1993, p. B4; David B. Wolfe, "The Ageless Market," *American Demographics*, July 1987, pp. 26–29, 55–56; Warren A. French and Richard Fox, "Segmenting the Senior Citizen Market," *Journal of Consumer Marketing*, Winter 1985, pp. 61–74.

81. Thomas Stevenson, "How Are Blacks Portrayed in Business Ads?" *Industrial Marketing Management*, August 1991, pp. 193–200; Susan DeYoung, and F. G. Crane, "Females' Attitudes toward the Portrayal of Women in Advertising: A Canadian Study," *International Journal of Advertising*, Summer 1992, pp. 249–256; Leon Wynter, "Global Marketers Learn to Say No to Bad Ads," *Wall Street Journal*, April 1, 1998, p. B1.

82. Wilkes and Valencia, "Hispanics and Blacks in Television Commercials"; Ursic, Ursic, and Ursic, "A Longitudinal Study of the Use of the Elderly in Magazine Advertising"; Phyllis Furman, "The New Wrinkle in Casting," *Madison Avenue*, October 1985, pp. 66–70; Westerman, "Death of the Frito Bandito."

83. Nancy A. Reese, Thomas W. Whipple, and Alice E. Courtney, "Is Industrial Advertising Sexist?" *Industrial Marketing Management*, November 1987, pp. 231–241; Cyndee Miller, "Liberation for Women in Ads: Nymphettes, June Cleaver Are Out: Middle Ground Is In," *Marketing News*, August 17, 1992, pp. 1, 3; Cyndee Miller, "Michelob Ads Feature Women—And They're Not Wearing Bikinis," *Marketing News*, March 2, 1992, p. 2.

84. Gary Levin, "Shops Make the Most of Ethnic Niches," *Advertising Age*, September 17, 1990, p. 29.

85. Ruth Simon, "Stop Them from Selling Your Financial Secrets," *Money*, March 1992, pp. 99–110.

86. Ellen Foxman and Paula Kilcoyne, "Information Technology, Marketing Practice, and Consumer Privacy: Ethical Issues," *Journal of Public Policy and Marketing*, Spring 1993, p. 106.

87. Carol Krol, "Consumers Reach the Boiling Point Over Privacy Issues," *Advertising Age*, March 29, 1999, p. 22; "Survey Results Show Consumers Want Privacy," *Direct Marketing*, March 1999, p. 10.

88. Kevin Heubusch, "Big Brother and the Internet," *American Demographics*," February 1997, p. 22.

89. Dan Fost, "Inside the Information Industry: Privacy Concerns Threaten Database Marketing," *American Demographics*, May 1990, pp. 18–21; C. B. Rogers Jr., "Americans Could Grow More Negative about Research," *Marketing News*, August 16, 1993, p. A18.

90. G. Bruce Knecht, "Junk Mail Hater Seeks Profits from Sale of His Name," *Wall Street Journal*, October 13, 1995, pp. B1, B8.

91. Mag Gottleib, "If Trends Continue, Legislative Nightmare Will Become Reality," *Marketing News*, August 16, 1993, pp. A9–A16; H. Jeff Smith, Sandra J. Milberg, and Sandra J. Burke, "Information Privacy: Measuring Individuals' Concerns about Organizational Practices," *MIS Quarterly*, June 1996, pp. 167–196.

92. Foxman and Kilcoyne, " Information Technology, Marketing Practice, and Consumer Privacy."

93. Gottleib, "If Trends Continue, Legislative Nightmare Will Become Reality."

94. Simon, "Stop Them from Selling Your Financial Secrets."

95. Edward Baig, Marcia Stepanek, and Neil Gross, "Privacy," *BusinessWeek*, April 5, 1999, pp. 84–90.

96. Paula Nichols, "Canadian Privacy Code Shows U.S. the Way," *American Demographics*, September 1993, p. 15.

97. Ann Reilly Dowd, "Protect Your Privacy," *Money*, August 1997, pp. 104–115.

98. "Invasion of Privacy: When Is Access to Information Foul—or Fair?" *Harvard Business Review*, September–October 1993, pp. 154–155.

99. Rebecca Quick, "On-line Groups Are Offering up Privacy Plans."

100. N. Craig Smith and Elizabeth Cooper-Martin, "Ethics and Target Marketing: The Role of Product Harm and Consumer Vulnerability," *Journal of Marketing*, July 1997, pp. 1–20; Robert O. Hermann, "The Tactics of Consumer Resistance: Group Action and Marketplace Exit," in eds. Leigh McAlister and Michael Rothschild, *Advances in Consumer Research*, Vol. 20 (Provo, Utah: Association for Consumer Research, 1993), pp. 130–134; Lisa Penaloza and Linda L. Price, "Consumer Resistance: A Conceptual Overview," in eds. Leigh McAlister and Michael L. Rothschild, *Advances in Consumer Research*, Vol. 20 (Provo, Utah: Association for Consumer Research, 1993), pp. 123–128.

101. Cyndee Miller, "Sexy Sizzle Backfires," *Marketing News*, September 25, 1995, p. 1.

102. Richard W. Pollay, "Media Resistance to Consumer Resistance: On the Stonewalling of 'Adbusters' and Advocates," in eds. Leigh McAlister and Michael Rothschild, *Advances in Consumer Research*, Vol. 20 (Provo, Utah: Association for Consumer Research, 1993), p. 129.

103. Tony Spleen, "OJ Sales Off 6%, Limbaugh Effect?" *Supermarket News*, May 9, 1994, p. 3; Armando Duron, "Boycott Based on 30 Years of Waiting," *Los Angeles Times*, June 19, 1995, p. F3; Cyndee Miller, "Marketers Weigh Effects of Sweatshop Crackdown," *Marketing News*, May 12, 1997, pp. 1, 19.

104. Henry H. Rodkin, "Boycott Power"; see also Monroe Friedman, "Consumer Boycotts in the United States, 1970–1980: Contemporary Events in Historical Perspective," *Journal of Consumer Affairs*, Summer 1985, pp. 96–117.

105. Todd Putnam and Timothy Muck, " Wielding the Boycott Weapon for Social Change," *Business and Society Review*, Summer 1991, pp. 5–8.

106. Mabry and Sheniz, "Do Boycotts Work?"; Garrett, "The Effectiveness of Marketing Boycotts."

107. Henry H. Rodkin, "Boycott Power."

NAME INDEX

Numbers in italics indicate exhibits.

ORGANIZATON AND PRODUCT INDEX

SUBJECT INDEX